W9-CAP-794

CASES AND PROBLEMS ON
CONTRACTS

Sixth Edition

■ ■ ■

By
John D. Calamari
Late Agnes and Ignatius M. Wilkinson Professor of Law
Fordham University

Joseph M. Perillo
Distinguished Professor of Law, Emeritus
Fordham University

Helen Hadjiyannakis Bender
Associate Professor of Law
Fordham University

Caroline N. Brown
Professor of Law
University of North Carolina

AMERICAN CASEBOOK SERIES®

WEST®
A Thomson Reuters business

Mat #40794639

American Casebook Series is a trademark registered in the U.S. Patent and Trademark Office.

COPYRIGHT © 1978, 1989 WEST PUBLISHING CO.
© West, a Thomson business, 2000, 2004, 2007
2011 © Thomson Reuters

    610 Opperman Drive
    St. Paul, MN 55123
    1–800–313–9378

Printed in the United States of America

ISBN: 978–0–314–20285–7

PREFACE TO THE SIXTH EDITION

With this 6th edition, the Fordham Law School co-editors have been joined by Caroline Nicholson Brown of the University of North Carolina School of Law.

The methodology used in this casebook started as an experiment and we deem the experiment a success. The problem method in tandem with case dissection engenders students' interest, enlarges their store of knowledge, and most important, requires them to exercise analytic thinking not only in the classroom but also while preparing their assignments.

As before, the Appendices include Articles 1 and 2 of the UCC so that a supplement need not be purchased. There are sample examination questions interspersed throughout the book.

The scope of the material that a student should master in a basic contracts course has increased disproportionately to the amount of curricular time available for its mastery. Coverage of the entire book is not recommended even for professors who enjoy the luxury of a six-hour course. Because the casebook is keyed into the Calamari and Perillo hornbook, it is possible to cover some topics or subtopics by assigning the problems alone. On the other hand the professor may decide to omit discussion of some of the problems in class. In short, the casebook can be treated as a menu.

The principal cases have been edited, but less drastically than in many of the recent casebooks. String cites have been shortened to one or two cases, while encyclopedias and the sort have generally been omitted without indication. Numbered footnotes retain their original numbering, footnotes by the editors are indicated by asterisks, and other materials added by the editors are in brackets, sometimes indicated by the abbreviation, "Ed."

We are indebted to our able research assistants Matthew Silverman (Fordham), Joseph Kornbluh (Fordham) and Charles Kabugo–Musoke (North Carolina).

We lament the passing of our late co-editor, John D. Calamari, but his ideas continue to animate ours.

We welcome comments on the form and content of this casebook. Send them to jperillo@law.fordham.edu, hbender@law.fordham.edu, or cnbrown@email.unc.edu

JOSEPH M. PERILLO
HELEN HADJIYANNAKIS BENDER
CAROLINE N. BROWN

Copyright Acknowledgements

We are grateful to the following authors, law reviews and publishers for their gracious permission to reprint copyrighted materials: (1) The Harvard Law Record for Jorie Roberts, "Hawkins Case: A Hair–Raising Experience," Harvard Law Record, Vol. 66, No.6, March 17, 1978. (2) The Journal of Legal Studies and The University of Chicago for A.W.B. Simpson, "Quackery and Contract Law: The Case of the Carbolic Smoke Ball," 14 J. Leg. Stud. 345 (1985). ©1985 by The University of Chicago. All rights reserved. (3) Cardozo Law Review for A.W.B. Simpson, "Contracts for Cotton to Arrive: The Case of the Two Ships Peerless," 11 Cardozo L. Rev. 287 (1989). (4) The Journal of Legal Studies, The University of Chicago and Daniel Friedmann for Daniel Friedmann, "The Efficient Breach Fallacy," 18 J. Leg. Stud. 1 (1989). © 1989 by The University of Chicago. All rights reserved. (5) The Yale Law Journal and Alan Schwartz for "The Case for Specific Performance," 89 Yale L.J. 271 (1989). (6) Fordham Law Review for J.M. Perillo, "The Statute of Frauds in the Light of the Functions and Dysfunctions of Form," 43 Fordham L. Rev. 39 (1974).

Summary of Contents

TABLE OF CONTENTS

———————

TABLE OF CASES

References are to pages. Cases cited in principal cases and within other quoted materials are not included.

CASES AND PROBLEMS ON
CONTRACTS

Sixth Edition

CHAPTER 1

THE AGREEMENT PROCESS

■ ■ ■

SECTION 1. INTENT TO CONTRACT

(Calamari & Perillo on Contracts §§ 1.1—1.7, 2.1—2.4, 2.7 and 2.8)

LUCY v. ZEHMER

Supreme Court of Appeals of Virginia, 1954.
196 Va. 493, 84 S.E.2d 516.

BUCHANAN, JUSTICE. This suit was instituted by W.O. Lucy and J.C. Lucy, complainants, against A.H. Zehmer and Ida S. Zehmer, his wife, defendants, to have specific performance of a contract by which it was alleged the Zehmers had sold to W.O. Lucy a tract of land owned by A.H. Zehmer in Dinwiddie county containing 471.6 acres, more or less, known as the Ferguson farm, for $50,000. J.C. Lucy, the other complainant, is a brother of W.O. Lucy, to whom W.O. Lucy transferred a half interest in his alleged purchase.

The instrument sought to be enforced was written by A.H. Zehmer on December 20, 1952, in these words: "We hereby agree to sell to W.O. Lucy the Ferguson Farm complete for $50,000.00, title satisfactory to buyer," and signed by the defendants, A.H. Zehmer and Ida S. Zehmer.

The answer of A.H. Zehmer admitted that at the time mentioned W.O. Lucy offered him $50,000 cash for the farm, but that he, Zehmer, considered that the offer was made in jest; that so thinking, and both he and Lucy having had several drinks, he wrote out "the memorandum" quoted above and induced his wife to sign it; that he did not deliver the memorandum to Lucy, but that Lucy picked it up, read it, put it in his pocket, attempted to offer Zehmer $5 to bind the bargain, which Zehmer refused to accept, and realizing for the first time that Lucy was serious, Zehmer assured him that he had no intention of selling the farm and that the whole matter was a joke. Lucy left the premises insisting that he had purchased the farm.

1

Depositions were taken and the decree appealed from was entered holding that the complainants had failed to establish their right to specific performance, and dismissing their bill. The assignment of error is to this action of the court.

W.O. Lucy, a lumberman and farmer, thus testified in substance: . . . Seven or eight years ago he had offered Zehmer $20,000 for the farm which Zehmer had accepted, but the agreement was verbal and Zehmer backed out. On the night of December 20, 1952, around eight o'clock he took an employee to McKenney where Zehmer lived and operated a restaurant, filling station and motor court. While there he decided to see Zehmer and again try to buy the Ferguson farm. . . . He asked Zehmer if he had sold the Ferguson farm. Zehmer replied that he had not. Lucy said, "I bet you wouldn't take $50,000 for that place." Zehmer replied, "Yes, I would too; you wouldn't give fifty." Lucy said yes he would and told Zehmer to write up the agreement to that effect. . . .

The discussion leading to the signing of the agreement, said Lucy, lasted thirty or forty minutes, during which Zehmer seemed to doubt that Lucy could raise $50,000. Lucy suggested the provision for having the title examined and Zehmer made the suggestion that he would sell it "complete, everything there," and stated that all he had on the farm was three heifers. [The court then reviewed additional testimony of Lucy and testimony of Zehmer, his wife and a waitress. Ed.]

The defendants insist that the evidence was ample to support their contention that the writing sought to be enforced was prepared as a bluff or dare to force Lucy to admit that he did not have $50,000; that the whole matter was a joke; that the writing was not delivered to Lucy and no binding contract was ever made between the parties.

It is an unusual, if not bizarre defense. When made to the writing admittedly prepared by one of the defendants and signed by both, clear evidence is required to sustain it.

In his testimony Zehmer claimed that he "was high as a Georgia pine," and that the transaction "was just a bunch of two doggoned drunks bluffing to see who could talk the biggest and say the most." That claim is inconsistent with his attempt to testify in great detail as to what was said and what was done. It is contradicted by other evidence as to the condition of both parties, and rendered of no weight by the testimony of his wife that when Lucy left the restaurant she suggested that Zehmer drive him home. The record is convincing that Zehmer was not intoxicated to the extent of being unable to comprehend the nature and consequences of the instrument he executed, and hence that instrument is not to be invalidated on that ground. Taliaferro v. Emery, 124 Va. 674, 98 S.E. 627. It was in fact conceded by defendants' counsel in oral argument that under the evidence Zehmer was not too drunk to make a valid contract.

The evidence is convincing also that Zehmer wrote two agreements, the first one beginning "I hereby agree to sell." Zehmer first said he could not remember about that, then that "I don't think I wrote but one out."

Mrs. Zehmer said that what he wrote was "I hereby agree," but that the "I" was changed to "We" after that night. The agreement that was written and signed is in the record and indicates no such change. Neither are the mistakes in spelling that Zehmer sought to point out readily apparent. [Zehmer claimed that he had misspelled the name of the farm ("Firgerson") and the word "satisfactory." Ed.]

The appearance of the contract, the fact that it was under discussion for forty minutes or more before it was signed; Lucy's objection to the first draft because it was written in the singular, and he wanted Mrs. Zehmer to sign it also; the rewriting to meet that objection and the signing by Mrs. Zehmer; the discussion of what was to be included in the sale, the provision for the examination of the title, the completeness of the instrument that was executed, the taking possession of it by Lucy with no request or suggestion by either of the defendants that he give it back, are facts which furnish persuasive evidence that the execution of the contract was a serious business transaction rather than a casual, jesting matter as defendants now contend. . . .

If it be assumed, contrary to what we think the evidence shows, that Zehmer was jesting about selling his farm to Lucy and that the transaction was intended by him to be a joke, nevertheless the evidence shows that Lucy did not so understand it but considered it to be a serious business transaction and the contract to be binding on the Zehmers as well as on himself. The very next day he arranged with his brother to put up half the money and take a half interest in the land. The day after that he employed an attorney to examine the title. The next night, Tuesday, he was back at Zehmer's place and there Zehmer told him for the first time, Lucy said, that he wasn't going to sell and he told Zehmer, "You know you sold that place fair and square." After receiving the report from his attorney that the title was good he wrote to Zehmer that he was ready to close the deal.

Not only did Lucy actually believe, but the evidence shows he was warranted in believing, that the contract represented a serious business transaction and a good faith sale and purchase of the farm.

In the field of contracts, as generally elsewhere, "We must look to the outward expression of a person as manifesting his intention rather than to his secret and unexpressed intention. 'The law imputes to a person an intention corresponding to the reasonable meaning of his words and acts.'" First Nat. Exchange Bank of Roanoke v. Roanoke Oil Co., 169 Va. 99, 114, 192 S.E. 764, 770.

At no time prior to the execution of the contract had Zehmer indicated to Lucy by word or act that he was not in earnest about selling the farm. They had argued about it and discussed its terms, as Zehmer admitted, for a long time. Lucy testified that if there was any jesting it was about paying $50,000 that night. The contract and the evidence show that he was not expected to pay the money that night. Zehmer said that after the writing was signed he laid it down on the counter in front of

Lucy. Lucy said Zehmer handed it to him. In any event there had been what appeared to be a good faith offer and a good faith acceptance, followed by the execution and apparent delivery of a written contract. Both said that Lucy put the writing in his pocket and then offered Zehmer $5 to seal the bargain. Not until then, even under the defendants' evidence, was anything said or done to indicate that the matter was a joke. Both of the Zehmers testified that when Zehmer asked his wife to sign he whispered that it was a joke so Lucy wouldn't hear and that it was not intended that he should hear.

The mental assent of the parties is not requisite for the formation of a contract. If the words or other acts of one of the parties have but one reasonable meaning, his undisclosed intention is immaterial except when an unreasonable meaning which he attaches to his manifestations is known to the other party. *Restatement of the Law of Contracts*, Vol. I, § 71, p. 74. . . . So a person cannot set up that he was merely jesting when his conduct and words would warrant a reasonable person in believing that he intended a real agreement. *Clark on Contracts*, 4 ed., § 27, at p. 54.

Whether the writing signed by the defendants and now sought to be enforced by the complainants was the result of a serious offer by Lucy and a serious acceptance by the defendants, or was a serious offer by Lucy and an acceptance in secret jest by the defendants, in either event it constituted a binding contract of sale between the parties. . . .

The complainants are entitled to have specific performance of the contract sued on. The decree appealed from is therefore reversed and the cause is remanded for the entry of a proper decree requiring the defendants to perform the contract in accordance with the prayer of the bill.

Reversed and remanded.

———

The contract written on the back of the restaurant check:

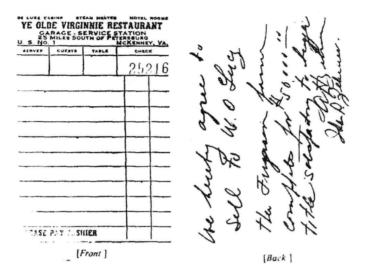

[Front]   [Back]

BALFOUR v. BALFOUR

Court of Appeal, 1919.
2 K.B. 571.

[The plaintiff and the defendant had been married in England in 1900. They were living in Ceylon (now known as Sri Lanka) where the husband was Director of Irrigation. In 1915 they returned to England to spend his leave. In 1916 when his leave was up he had to return to Ceylon. However, plaintiff, who was suffering from rheumatoid arthritis, decided, on doctor's advice, to spend a few more months in England. Before his departure, the husband promised to send her £30 per month for her support. Later, differences developed and they agreed to live apart. She sued and obtained an order for alimony. In the present suit, she sued him for money she claimed to be due under his agreement to send her £30 per month. Ed.]

ATKIN, L.J. [I]t is necessary to remember that there are agreements between parties which do not result in contracts within the meaning of that term in our law. The ordinary example is where two parties agree to take a walk together, or where there is an offer and an acceptance of hospitality. Nobody would suggest in ordinary circumstances that those agreements result in what we know as a contract, and one of the most usual forms of agreement which does not constitute a contract appears to me to be the arrangements which are made between husband and wife. It is quite common, and it is the natural and inevitable result of the relationship of husband and wife, that the two spouses should make arrangements between themselves—agreements such as are in dispute in this action—agreements for allowances, by which the husband agrees that he will pay to his wife a certain sum of money, per week, or per month, or per year, to cover either her own expenses or the necessary expenses of the household and of the children of the marriage, and in which the wife promises either expressly or impliedly to apply the allowance for the purpose for which it is given. To my mind those agreements, or many of them, do not result in contracts at all, . . . and they are not contracts because the parties did not intend that they should be attended by legal consequences. . . . All I can say is that the small Courts of this country would have to be multiplied one hundredfold if these arrangements were held to result in legal obligations. They are not sued upon, not because the parties are reluctant to enforce their legal rights when the agreement is broken, but because the parties, in the inception of the arrangement, never intended that they should be sued upon. Agreements such as these are outside the realm of contracts altogether. . . . In respect of these promises each house is a domain into which the King's writ does not seek to run, and to which his officers do not seek to be admitted. . . . [I]t appears to me to be plainly established that the promise here was not intended by either party to be attended by legal consequences. . . .

[Concurring opinions of DUKE, L.J. and WARRINGTON, L.J. are omitted.]

TEXACO, INC. v. PENNZOIL, CO.

Court of Appeals of Texas, Houston (1st Dist.), 1987.
729 S.W.2d 768.

WARREN, JUSTICE. This is an appeal from a judgment awarding Pennzoil damages for Texaco's tortious interference with a contract between Pennzoil and the "Getty entities" (Getty Oil Company, the Sarah C. Getty Trust, and the J. Paul Getty Museum).

The jury found, among other things, that:

(1) At the end of a board meeting on January 3, 1984, the Getty entities intended to bind themselves to an agreement providing for the purchase of Getty Oil stock, whereby the Sarah C. Getty Trust would own 4/7th of the stock and Pennzoil the remaining 3/7th; and providing for a division of Getty Oil's assets, according to their respective ownership if the Trust and Pennzoil were unable to agree on a restructuring of Getty Oil by December 31, 1984;

(2) Texaco knowingly interfered with the agreement between Pennzoil and the Getty entities;

(3) As a result of Texaco's interference, Pennzoil suffered damages of $7.53 billion;

(4) Texaco's actions were intentional, willful, and in wanton disregard of Pennzoil's rights; and,

(5) Pennzoil was entitled to punitive damages of $3 billion. . . .

Though many facts are disputed, the parties' main conflicts are over the inferences to be drawn from, and the legal significance of, these facts. There is evidence that for several months in late 1983, Pennzoil had followed with interest the well-publicized dissension between the board of directors of Getty Oil Company and Gordon Getty, who was a director of

Getty Oil and also the owner, as trustee, of approximately 40.2% of the outstanding shares of Getty Oil. On December 28, 1983, Pennzoil announced an unsolicited, public tender offer for 16 million shares of Getty Oil at $100 each.

Soon afterwards, Pennzoil contacted both Gordon Getty and a representative of the J. Paul Getty Museum, which held approximately 11.8% of the shares of Getty Oil, to discuss the tender offer and the possible purchase of Getty Oil. In the first two days of January 1984, a "Memorandum of Agreement" was drafted to reflect the terms that had been reached in conversations between representatives of Pennzoil, Gordon Getty, and the Museum. . . .

The Memorandum of Agreement stated that it was subject to approval of the board of Getty Oil, and it was to expire by its own terms if not approved at the board meeting that was to begin on January 2. Pennzoil's CEO, Liedtke, and Gordon Getty, for the Trust, signed the Memorandum of Agreement before the Getty Oil board meeting on January 2, and Harold Williams, the president of the Museum, signed it shortly after the board meeting began. Thus, before it was submitted to the Getty Oil board, the Memorandum of Agreement had been executed by parties who together controlled a majority of the outstanding shares of Getty Oil.

The Memorandum of Agreement was then presented to the Getty Oil board, which had previously held discussions on how the company should respond to Pennzoil's public tender offer. . . . The board voted to reject recommending Pennzoil's tender offer to Getty's shareholders, then later also rejected the Memorandum of Agreement price of $110 per share as too low. Before recessing at 3 a.m., the board decided to make a counter-proposal to Pennzoil of $110 per share plus a $10 debenture. . . . In the morning of January 3, Getty Oil's investment banker, Geoffrey Boisi, began calling other companies, seeking a higher bid than Pennzoil's for the Getty Oil shares.

When the board reconvened at 3 p.m. on January 3, a revised Pennzoil proposal was presented, offering $110 per share plus a $3 "stub" that was to be paid after the sale of a Getty Oil subsidiary ("ERC"), from the excess proceeds over $1 billion. Each shareholder was to receive a pro rata share of these excess proceeds, but in any case, a minimum of $3 per share at the end of five years. . . .

The Museum's lawyer told the board that, based on his discussions with Pennzoil, he believed that if the board went back "firm" with an offer of $110 plus a $5 stub, Pennzoil would accept it. After a recess, the Museum's president (also a director of Getty Oil) moved that the Getty board should accept Pennzoil's proposal provided that the stub be raised to $5, and the board voted 15 to 1 to approve this counter-proposal to Pennzoil. The board then voted themselves and Getty's officers and advisors indemnity for any liability arising from the events of the past few months. Additionally, the board authorized its executive compensation committee to give "golden parachutes" (generous termination benefits) to the top executives whose positions "were likely to be affected" by the change in management. There was evidence that during another brief recess of the board meeting, the counter-offer of $110 plus a $5 stub was presented to and accepted by Pennzoil. After Pennzoil's acceptance was conveyed to the Getty board, the meeting was adjourned, and most board members left town for their respective homes.

That evening, the lawyers and public relations staff of Getty Oil and the Museum drafted a press release describing the transaction between Pennzoil and the Getty entities. The press release, announcing an agreement in principle on the terms of the Memorandum of Agreement but with a price of $110 plus a $5 stub, was issued on Getty Oil letterhead the next morning, January 4, and later that day, Pennzoil issued an identical press release.

On January 4, Boisi continued to contact other companies, looking for a higher price than Pennzoil had offered. After talking briefly with Boisi, Texaco management called several meetings with its in-house financial planning group, which over the course of the day studied and reported to management on the value of Getty Oil, the Pennzoil offer terms, and a feasible price range at which Getty might be acquired. Later in the day, Texaco hired an investment banker, First Boston, to represent it with respect to a possible acquisition of Getty Oil. Meanwhile, also on January 4, Pennzoil's lawyers were working on a draft of a formal "transaction agreement" that described the transaction in more detail than the outline of terms contained in the Memorandum of Agreement and press release.

On January 5, the Wall Street Journal reported on an agreement reached between Pennzoil and the Getty entities, describing essentially the terms contained in the Memorandum of Agreement. The Pennzoil board met to ratify the actions of its officers in negotiating an agreement with the Getty entities, and Pennzoil's attorneys periodically attempted to contact the other parties' advisors and attorneys to continue work on the transaction agreement.

The board of Texaco also met on January 5, authorizing its officers to make an offer for 100% of Getty Oil and to take any necessary action in connection therewith. Texaco first contacted the Museum's lawyer, Lipton, and arranged a meeting to discuss the sale of the Museum's shares of Getty Oil to Texaco. Lipton instructed his associate, on her way to the meeting in progress of the lawyers drafting merger documents for the Pennzoil/Getty transaction, to not attend that meeting, because he needed her at his meeting with Texaco. At the meeting with Texaco, the Museum outlined various issues it wanted resolved in any transaction with Texaco, and then agreed to sell its 11.8% ownership in Getty Oil.

That evening, Texaco met with Gordon Getty to discuss the sale of the Trust's shares. He was informed that the Museum had agreed to sell its shares to Texaco. Gordon Getty's advisors had previously warned him that the Trust shares might be "locked out" in a minority position if Texaco bought, in addition to the Museum's shares, enough of the public shares to achieve over 50% ownership of the company. Gordon Getty accepted Texaco's offer of $125 per share and signed a letter of his intent to sell his stock to Texaco, as soon as a California temporary restraining order against his actions as trustee was lifted.

At noon on January 6, Getty Oil held a telephone board meeting to discuss the Texaco offer. The board voted to withdraw its previous counter-proposal to Pennzoil and unanimously voted to accept Texaco's offer. Texaco immediately issued a press release announcing that Getty Oil and Texaco would merge. Soon after the Texaco press release appeared, Pennzoil telexed the Getty entities, demanding that they honor their agreement with Pennzoil. ... The merger agreement between Texaco and Getty Oil was signed on January 6; the stock purchase agreement with the Museum was signed on January 6; and the stock exchange agreement with the Trust was signed on January 8, 1984. ...

SPECIAL ISSUE NO. 1

Texaco contends that under controlling principles of New York law, there was insufficient evidence to support the jury's finding that at the end of the Getty Oil board meeting on January 3, the Getty entities intended to bind themselves to an agreement with Pennzoil.*

Pennzoil responds that the question of the parties' intent is a fact question, and the jury was free to accept or reject Texaco's after-the-fact testimony of subjective intent. Pennzoil contends that the evidence showed that the parties intended to be bound to the terms in the Memorandum of Agreement plus a price term of $110 plus a $5 stub, even

---

* [The jury instructions on the issue of intent to be bound to an agreement with Pennzoil (Special Issue No. 1) are quoted below. In a later part of the opinion, the court found no reversible error with respect to the instructions. Ed.]

1. An agreement may be an oral, it may be written or it may be partly written and partly oral. Where an agreement is fully or partially in writing, the law provides that persons may bind themselves to that agreement even though they do not sign it, where their assent is otherwise indicated.

2. In answering Issue No. 1, you should look to the intent of Pennzoil and the Getty entities as outwardly or objectively demonstrated to each other by their words and deeds. The question is not determined by the parties' secret, inward, or subjective intentions.

3. Persons may intend to be bound to an agreement even though they plan to sign a more formal and detailed document at a later time. On the other hand, parties may intend not to be bound until such a document is signed.

4. There is no legal requirement that parties agree on all the matters incidental to their agreement before they can intend to be bound. Thus, even if certain matters were left for future negotiations, those matters may not have been regarded by Pennzoil and the Getty entities as essential to their agreement, if any, on January 3. On the other hand, you may find that the parties did not intend to be bound until each and every term of their transaction was resolved.

5. Every binding agreement carries with it a duty of good faith performance. If Pennzoil and the Getty entities intended to be bound at the end of the Getty Oil board meeting of January 3, they were obliged to negotiate in good faith the terms of the definitive merger agreement and to carry out the transaction.

6. Modification or discussions to modify an agreement do not defeat or nullify a prior intention to be bound. Parties may always, by mutual consent and understanding, add new provisions spelling out additional terms that were not included in their original agreement.

though the parties may have contemplated a later, more formal document to memorialize the agreement already reached. . . .

Under New York law, if parties do not intend to be bound to an agreement until it is reduced to writing and signed by both parties, then there is no contract until that event occurs. Scheck v. Francis, 26 N.Y.2d 466, 311 N.Y.S.2d 841, 260 N.E.2d 493 (1970). If there is no understanding that a signed writing is necessary before the parties will be bound, and the parties have agreed upon all substantial terms, then an informal agreement can be binding, even though the parties contemplate evidencing their agreement in a formal document later. Municipal Consultants & Publishers, Inc. v. Town of Ramapo, 47 N.Y.2d 144, 417 N.Y.S.2d 218, 220, 390 N.E.2d 1143.

If the parties do intend to contract orally, the mere intention to commit the agreement to writing does not prevent contract formation before execution of that writing, Winston v. Mediafare Entertainment Corp., 777 F.2d 78, 80 (2d Cir.1985), and even a failure to reduce their promises to writing is immaterial to whether they are bound. Schwartz v. Greenberg, 304 N.Y. 250, 107 N.E.2d 65 (1952). However, if either party communicates the intent not to be bound before a final formal document is executed, then no oral expression of agreement to specific terms will constitute a binding contract. Winston, 777 F.2d at 80. Thus, under New York law, the parties are given the power to obligate themselves informally or only by a formal signed writing, as they wish. R.G. Group[, Inc. v. Horn & Hardart Co., 751 F.2d 69, 74 (2d Cir.1984)]. The emphasis in deciding when a binding contract exists is on intent rather than on form. Reprosystem, B.V. v. SCM Corp., 727 F.2d 257, 261 (2d Cir.1984).

It is the parties' expressed intent that controls which rule of contract formation applies. To determine intent, a court must examine the words and deeds of the parties, because these constitute the objective signs of such intent. Winston, 777 F.2d at 80. Only the outward expressions of intent are considered—secret or subjective intent is immaterial to the question of whether the parties were bound. Porter v. Commercial Casualty Insurance Co., 292 N.Y. 176, 54 N.E.2d 353 (1944).

Several factors have been articulated to help determine whether the parties intended to be bound only by a formal, signed writing: (1) whether a party expressly reserved the right to be bound only when a written agreement is signed; (2) whether there was any partial performance by one party that the party disclaiming the contract accepted; (3) whether all essential terms of the alleged contract had been agreed upon; and (4) whether the complexity or magnitude of the transaction was such that a formal, executed writing would normally be expected. Winston, 777 F.2d at 80.

Evaluating the first factor, Texaco contends that the evidence of expressed intent not to be bound establishes conclusively that there was no contract at the time of Texaco's alleged inducement of breach. Texaco argues that this expressed intent is contained in (1) the press releases issued by the Getty entities and Pennzoil, which stated that "the transaction is subject to execution of a definitive merger agreement"; (2) the phrasing of drafts of the transaction agreement, which Texaco alleges "carefully stated that the parties' obligations would become binding only 'after the execution and delivery of this Agreement' "; and (3) the deliberate reference by the press releases to the parties' understanding as an "agreement in principle."

In its brief, Texaco asserts that, as a matter of black letter New York law, the "subject to" language in the press release established that the parties were not then bound and intended to be bound only after signing a definitive agreement, citing Banking & Trading Corp. v. Reconstruction Finance Corp., 147 F.Supp. 193, 204 (S.D.N.Y.1956), *aff'd*, 257 F.2d 765 (2d Cir.1958). The court in that case stated that "if the agreement is expressly subject to the execution of a formal contract, this intent must be respected and no contract found until then." However, the court went on to say that where intent is less sharply expressed, the trier of fact must determine it as best he can. *Id.* at 204–05. Although the intent to formalize an agreement is some evidence of an intent not to be bound before signing such a writing, it is not conclusive. *Id.* at 204. The issue of when the parties intended to be bound is a fact question to be decided from the parties' acts and communications. *Id.*

The press release issued first by Getty, then by Pennzoil, on January 4, 1984, stated:

> Getty Oil Company, The J. Paul Getty Museum and Gordon Getty, as Trustee of the Sarah C. Getty Trust, announced today that they have agreed in principle with Pennzoil Company to a merger of Getty Oil and a newly formed entity owned by Pennzoil and the Trustee.
>
> In connection with the transaction, the shareholders of Getty Oil ... *will* receive $110 per share cash plus the right to receive a deferred cash consideration in a formula amount. The deferred consideration *will* be equal to a pro rata share of the ... proceeds, in excess of $1 billion, ... of ERC Corporation, ... and *will* be paid upon the disposition. In any event, under the formula, each shareholder *will* receive at least $5 per share within five years.
>
> Prior to the merger, Pennzoil *will* contribute approximately $2.6 billion in cash and the Trustee and Pennzoil *will* contribute the Getty Oil shares owned by them to the new entity. Upon execution of a definitive merger agreement, the ... tender offer by a Pennzoil subsidiary for shares of Getty Oil stock *will* be withdrawn.
>
> The agreement in principle also provides that Getty Oil *will* grant to Pennzoil an option to purchase eight million treasury shares for $110 per share.
>
> The transaction is *subject to* execution of a definitive merger agreement, approval by the stockholders of Getty Oil and completion of various governmental filing and waiting period requirements.

Following consummation of the merger, the Trust *will* own 4/7ths of the ... stock of Getty Oil and Pennzoil *will* own 3/7ths. The Trust and Pennzoil have also agreed in principle that following consummation of the merger they *will* endeavor in good faith to agree upon a plan for restructuring Getty Oil (within a year) and that if they are unable to reach such an agreement then they *will* cause a division of assets of the company. (Emphasis added.)

Any intent of the parties not to be bound before signing a formal document is not so clearly expressed in the press release to establish, as a matter of law, that there was no contract at that time. The press release does refer to an agreement "in principle" and states that the "transaction" is subject to execution of a definitive merger agreement. But the release as a whole is worded in indicative terms, not in subjunctive or hypothetical ones. The press release describes what shareholders *will* receive, what Pennzoil *will* contribute, that Pennzoil *will* be granted an option, etc.

The description of the transaction as subject to a definitive merger agreement also includes the need for stockholder approval and the completion of various governmental filing and waiting requirements. There was evidence that this was a paragraph of routine details, that the referred to merger agreement was a standard formal document required in such a transaction under Delaware law, and that the parties considered these technical requirements of little consequence.

There is also an arguable difference between a "transaction" being subject to various requirements and the formation of the agreement itself being dependent upon completion of these matters. In F.W. Berk & Co. v. Derecktor, 301 N.Y. 110, 92 N.E.2d 914 (1950), cited in Texaco's brief, the defendant's very acceptance of the plaintiff's order was made subject to the occurrence of certain events. The court defined the phrase "subject to" as being the equivalent of "conditional upon or depending on" and held that making the acceptance of an offer subject to a condition was not the kind of assent required to make it a binding promise. However, making the acceptance of an offer conditional, or expressly making an agreement itself conditional, is a much clearer expression of an intent not to be bound than the use of the more ambiguous word "transaction."

Other cases cited by Texaco involved writings that specifically stated that no party would be committed until a written contract was executed. *See, e.g.,* Reprosystem, B.V., 727 F.2d at 260 (draft agreements clearly stated that formal execution was required before the contract would have any binding effect); Chromalloy American Corp.[v. Universal Housing Systems of America, Inc., 495 F.Supp. 544, 547–48 (S.D.N.Y.1980)] (letter of intent stated that neither party would be committed until a contract was executed). Yet, despite the clear language of reservation in those cases, the parties' intent to be bound was still evaluated as a question of fact to be determined from all the circumstances of the case. Reprosystem, B.V., 727 F.2d at 261–62; Chromalloy American Corp., 495 F.Supp. at 550.

So it is here. Regardless of what interpretation we give to the conditional language in the press release, we conclude that it did not so clearly express the intent of the parties not to be bound to conclusively resolve that issue, as Texaco asserts.

Texaco also contends that explicit language of reservation in drafts of Pennzoil's transaction agreement indicates the parties' expressed intent not to be bound without a signed writing. Texaco asserts that "Pennzoil's lawyers carefully stated that the parties' obligations would become binding only 'after the execution and delivery of this Agreement.' " That assertion is not accurate. In fact, "after the execution and delivery of this Agreement" was merely used as an introductory phrase before each party's obligations were described, *e.g.*, after the execution and delivery of this Agreement, Pennzoil shall terminate the tender offer; . . . Pennzoil and the Company shall terminate all legal proceedings; . . . the Company shall purchase all shares held by the Museum; etc. Other clauses in the transaction agreement did not contain that phrase, *e.g.*, the Company *hereby* grants to Pennzoil the option to purchase up to 8 million shares of treasury stock; *on or prior to the effective date,* Pennzoil and the Trustee shall form the merging company; etc. A reasonable conclusion from reading the entire drafts is that the phrase "after the execution and delivery of this Agreement" was used chiefly to indicate the timing of various acts that were to occur, and not to impose an express precondition to the formation of a contract. . . .

Next, Texaco states that the use of the term "agreement in principle" in the press release was a conscious and deliberate choice of words to convey that there was not yet any binding agreement. Texaco refers to defense testimony that lawyers for Getty Oil and the Museum changed the initial wording of the press release from "agreement" to "agreement in principle" because they understood and intended that phrase to mean that there was no binding contract with Pennzoil. . . . Pennzoil and Texaco presented conflicting evidence at trial on the common business usage and understanding of the term "agreement in principle." . . . There was sufficient evidence at trial on the common business usage of the expression "agreement in principle" and on its meaning in this case for the jury reasonably to decide that its use in the press release did not necessarily establish that the parties did not intend to be bound before signing a formal document.

A second factor that may indicate whether the parties intended to be bound only by a signed, formal writing is whether there was partial performance by one party that the party disclaiming the contract accepted. Winston, 777 F.2d at 80. Texaco asserts that there was no partial performance that would indicate an intent to be bound, but conversely, that the conduct of the parties here was inconsistent with the existence of a binding contract. . . . Other than the preliminary financial arrangements made by Pennzoil, we find little relevant partial performance in this case that might show that the parties believed that they were bound by a contract. However, the absence of relevant part performance in this short period of time does not compel the conclusion that no contract existed. Texaco has pointed out that there was some conduct inconsistent with the existence of an intent to be bound to a contract. But partial performance, and on the other hand, conduct that is inconsistent with an intent to be bound, are again merely circumstances that the finder of fact could consider in reaching a decision on whether the parties intended to be bound. The evidence on the parties' conduct was presented to the jury, which could either accept or reject the inferences the parties asked it to draw from these facts.

The next factor showing intent to be bound is whether there was agreement on all essential terms of the alleged agreement. Texaco contends that numerous items of "obvious importance" were still being negotiated at the time Pennzoil claims a contract had been formed. First, Texaco asserts that there was no agreement on which party would buy the Museum's stock [based on later discussions that since Getty Oil's purchase of the Museum's shares might trigger a tax penalty to Getty Oil, Pennzoil might purchase the Museum's shares instead, ed.]. Pennzoil contends that its contract was formed on January 3, and that intent to be bound must be determined as of that date. The jury specifically found, in response to Special Issue No. 6, that at the end of the January 3 board meeting, the Getty Oil Company, the Museum, the Trust, and Pennzoil each intended to be bound to an agreement that provided that Getty Oil would purchase the Museum's shares forthwith as provided in the Memorandum of Agreement. There is evidence in the record to support this finding. . . .

There was sufficient evidence for the jury to conclude that the parties had reached agreement on all essential terms of the transaction with only the mechanics and details left to be supplied by the parties' attorneys. Although there may have been many specific items relating to the transaction agreement draft that had yet to be put in final form, there is sufficient evidence to support a conclusion by the jury that the parties did not consider any of Texaco's asserted "open items" significant obstacles precluding an intent to be bound.

The fourth factor that Texaco discusses as showing that the parties did not intend to be bound before executing a formal contract is the magnitude and complexity of the transaction. There is little question that the transaction by which Getty Oil was to be taken private by the Trust and Pennzoil involved an extremely large amount of money. It is unlikely that parties to such a transaction would not have expected a detailed written document, specifically setting out the parties' obligations and the exact mechanics of the transaction, whether it was to be executed before the parties intended to be bound or only to memorialize an agreement already reached.

We agree with Texaco that this factor tends to support its position that the transaction was such that a signed contract would ordinarily be expected before the parties would consider themselves bound. However, we cannot say, as a matter of law, that this factor alone is determinative of the question of the parties' intent.

The trial of this case lasted many weeks, with witnesses for both sides testifying extensively about the events of those first days of January 1984. Eyewitnesses and expert witnesses interpreted and explained various aspects of the negotiations and the alleged agreement, and the jury was repeatedly made aware of the value of Getty Oil's assets and how much money would be involved in the company's sale. There was testimony on how the sale of the company could be structured and on the considerations involved in buying and restructuring, or later liquidating, the company. But there was also testimony that there were companies that in the past had bound themselves to short two-page acquisition agreements involving a lot of money, and Getty [Oil]'s [investment] banker testified that the Texaco transaction included "one page back-of-the-envelope kinds of agreements" that were formalized. The Memorandum of Agreement containing the essential terms of the Pennzoil/Getty agreement was only four pages long.

Although the magnitude of the transaction here was such that normally a signed writing would be expected, there was sufficient evidence to support an inference by the jury that that expectation was satisfied here initially by the Memorandum of Agreement, signed by a majority of shareholders of Getty Oil and approved by the board with a higher price, and by the transaction agreement in progress that had been intended to memorialize the agreement previously reached. . . .

[Other portions of the opinion are omitted. The judgment of the trial court was affirmed on condition that Pennzoil file a remittitur agreeing to the reduction of punitive damages from $3 billion to $1 billion. The judgment for $7.53 billion compensatory damages was unaffected by the remittitur. Ed.]

PROBLEMS

Students should read the following problems and propose an answer based upon the foregoing cases and the sections of *Calamari & Perillo on Contracts* cited at the beginning of this section.

1. Plaintiff was in the business of manufacturing automobile parts. Plaintiff's customers were the major auto manufacturers. Plaintiff wished to sell to other buyers, particularly to sellers of replacement auto parts (such as Midas Muffler), but it had reason to believe that its automobile manufacturer customers would be displeased and might cease doing business with plaintiff. To achieve secrecy, plaintiff set up a subsidiary to distribute its products. It then entered into a detailed formalized writing with defendant, a trusted employee, which stated that defendant agreed to purchase all shares of the subsidiary for $50,000 and plaintiff agreed to sell the shares at that price. At the same time, it was orally agreed between plaintiff and defendant that the agreement would not be carried out. For twenty years the parties proceeded without a transfer of the shares or of the money. As far as the business world knew, defendant was the sole owner of the distribution business. Between the parties, however, the defendant acted as a loyal employee of the plaintiff. Then the plaintiff decided to end its arrangement with the defendant and to let it be known to the trade that it was operating the distribution business.

Defendant tenders $50,000 and demands that plaintiff transfer the shares of stock pursuant to the written agreement. Plaintiff starts an action demanding a declaratory judgment to the effect that the written agreement is not binding. Will plaintiff succeed?

2. A written agreement regulating the commercial relations of the parties (B and S) contained the following clause: "This arrangement is not entered into, nor is the memorandum written as a formal or legal agreement and shall not be subject to legal jurisdiction in the law courts either of the United States or England but it is only a definite expression and record of the purpose and of the intention of the parties concerned to which they each honorably pledge themselves with the fullest confidence based on past business with each other, that it will be carried through by each of these parties with mutual loyalty and friendly cooperation." Before the parties' relationship had broken off, B had given and S had shipped some orders for goods pursuant to this agreement and S had accepted others which had not been shipped.

(a) Does B have a cause of action against S for refusal to ship goods pursuant to orders which S had accepted?

(b) Does S have a cause of action against B for refusing to pay for goods accepted by B?

3. Jim invited Amy to join him to see a play. She agreed, and it was further agreed that he would pick her up at her home at a specified date and time. He drove from San Francisco to San Jose to pick her up at the agreed time. She wasn't home. He sued, claiming $150—the cost of the ticket and the estimated cost of the wasted eighty-mile round trip. (a) Resolve the law suit. (b) Would the result be different if the parties had agreed that there would be a binding obligation?

4. Would your answer to Problem 3(a) be any different if Jim had flown cross-country at considerable expense, rented a car to pick her up and she wasn't home at the agreed time?

SECTION 2. THE OFFER

(a) OFFERS DISTINGUISHED FROM EXPRESSIONS OF OPINION, ADVERTISEMENTS, ETC.

———

(Calamari & Perillo on Contracts §§ 2.5 and 2.6)

HAWKINS v. McGEE

Supreme Court of New Hampshire, 1929.
146 A. 641, 84 N.H. 114.

[George Hawkins sued Dr. Edward McGee for $10,000 asserting negligence and breach of contract. The trial court directed a verdict for defendant on the negligence count. The jury's verdict awarded the plaintiff $3,000 for breach of contract. The court, concluding that the verdict was excessive, ordered that the verdict be set aside unless the plaintiff agreed to remit everything over $500. Upon the plaintiff's refusal, the verdict was set aside, and the plaintiff excepted. Ed.]

BRANCH, J. The operation in question consisted in the removal of a considerable quantity of scar tissue from the palm of the plaintiff's right hand and the grafting of skin taken from the plaintiff's chest in place thereof. The scar tissue was the result of a severe burn caused by contact with an electric wire, which the plaintiff received about nine years before the time of the transactions here involved.

There was evidence to the effect that before the operation was performed the plaintiff and his father went to the defendant's office, and that the defendant, in answer to the question, "How long will the boy be in the hospital?" replied, "Three or four days, not over four; then the boy can go home and it will be just a few days when he will go back to work with a good hand." Clearly this and other testimony to the same effect would not justify a finding that the doctor contracted to complete the hospital treatment in three or four days or that the plaintiff would be able to go back to work within a few days thereafter. The above statements could only be construed as expressions of opinion or predictions as to the probable duration of the treatment and plaintiff's resulting disability, and the fact that these estimates were exceeded would impose no contractual liability upon the defendant.

The only substantial basis for the plaintiff's claim is the testimony that the defendant also said before the operation was decided upon, "I will guarantee to make the hand a hundred per cent perfect hand or a hundred per cent good hand." The plaintiff was present when these words were alleged to have been spoken, and, if they are to be taken at their face value, it seems obvious that proof of their utterance would establish the giving of a warranty in accordance with his contention.

The defendant argues, however, that, even if these words were uttered by him, no reasonable man would understand that they were used with the intention of entering "into any contractual relation whatever," and that they could reasonably be understood only "as his expression in strong language that he believed and expected that as a result of the operation he would give the plaintiff a very good hand." It may be conceded, as the defendant contends, that, before the question of the making of a contract should be submitted to a jury, there is a preliminary question of law for the trial court to pass upon, *i.e.* "whether the words could possibly have the meaning imputed to them by the party who founds his case upon a certain interpretation," but it cannot be held that the trial court decided this question erroneously in the present case. It is unnecessary to determine at this time whether the argument of the defendant, based upon "common knowledge of the uncertainty which attends all surgical operations," and the improbability that a surgeon would ever contract to make a damaged part of the human body "one hundred per cent perfect," would, in the absence of countervailing considerations, be regarded as conclusive, for there were other factors in the present case which tended to support the contention of the plaintiff. There was evidence that the defendant repeatedly solicited from the plaintiff's father the opportunity to perform this operation, and the theory was advanced by plaintiff's counsel in cross-examination of defendant that he sought an opportunity to "experiment on skin grafting," in which he had had little previous experience. If the jury accepted this part of plaintiff's contention, there would be a reasonable basis for the further conclusion that, if defendant spoke the words attributed to him, he did so with the intention that they should be accepted at their face value, as an inducement for the granting of consent to the operation by the plaintiff and his father, and there was ample evidence that they were so accepted by them. The question of the making of the alleged contract was properly submitted to the jury.

The substance of the charge to the jury on the question of damages appears in the following quotation: "If you find the plaintiff entitled to anything, he is entitled to recover for what pain and suffering he has been made to endure and for what injury he has sustained over and above what injury he had before." To this instruction the defendant seasonably excepted. By it, the jury was permitted to consider two elements of damage: (1) Pain and suffering due to the operation; and (2) positive ill effects of the operation upon the plaintiff's hand. Authority for any specific rule of damages in cases of this kind seems to be lacking, but, when tested by general principle and by analogy, it appears that the foregoing instruction was erroneous.

"By 'damages,' as that term is used in the law of contracts, is intended compensation for a breach, measured in the terms of the contract." Davis v. New England Cotton Yarn Co., 77 N. H. 403, 404, 92 A. 732, 733. The purpose of the law is "to put the plaintiff in as good a position as he would have been in had the defendant kept his contract." 3 *Williston Cont.* § 1338; Hardie–Tynes Mfg. Co. v. Eastern Cotton Oil Co., 150 N. C. 150, 63 S. E. 676, 134 Am. St. Rep. 899. The measure of recovery "is based upon what the defendant should have given the plaintiff, not what the plaintiff has given the defendant or otherwise expended." 3 *Williston Cont.* § 1341. . . .

The present case is closely analogous to one in which a machine is built for a certain purpose and warranted to do certain work. In such cases, the usual rule of damages for breach of warranty in the sale of chattels is applied, and it is held that the measure of damages is the difference between the value of the machine, if it had corresponded with the warranty and its actual value, together with such incidental losses as the parties knew, or ought to have known, would probably result from a failure to comply with its terms. Hooper v. Story, 155 N.Y. 171, 175, 49 N.E. 773.

... We therefore conclude that the true measure of the plaintiff's damage in the present case is the difference between the value to him of a perfect hand or a good hand, such as the jury found the defendant promised him, and the value of his hand in its present condition, including any incidental consequences fairly within the contemplation of the parties when they made their contract. 1 Sutherland, *Damages* (4th Ed.) § 92. Damages not thus limited, although naturally resulting, are not to be given.

The extent of the plaintiff's suffering does not measure this difference in value. The pain necessarily incident to a serious surgical operation was a part of the contribution which the plaintiff was willing to make to his joint undertaking with the defendant to produce a good hand. ... It represented a part of the price which he was willing to pay for a good hand, but it furnished no test of the value of a good hand or the difference between the value of the hand which the defendant promised and the one which resulted from the operation.

It was also erroneous and misleading to submit to the jury as a separate element of damage any change for the worse in the condition of the plaintiff's hand resulting from the operation, although this error was probably more prejudicial to the plaintiff than to the defendant. Any such ill effect of the operation would be included under the true rule of damages set forth above, but damages might properly be assessed for the defendant's failure to improve the condition of the hand, even if there were no evidence that its condition was made worse as a result of the operation.

It must be assumed that the trial court, in setting aside the verdict, undertook to apply the same rule of damages which he had previously given to the jury, and, since this rule was erroneous, it is unnecessary for us to consider whether there was any evidence to justify his finding that all damages awarded by the jury above $500 were excessive. ...

New trial.

Editor's Note: After the decision in the principal case, Dr. McGee settled by paying Hawkins $1,400. He sued his malpractice insurance carrier which denied coverage on the ground that the verdict had been for breach of a contract to achieve a promised result and not for the tort of malpractice. The insurance company's defense was sustained. McGee v. United States Fidelity & Guaranty Co., 53 F.2d 953 (1st Cir. 1931).

Jorie Roberts, *Hawkins Case: A Hair–Raising Experience*, Harvard Law Record, March 17, 1978 at 1, 7, 13 (based on interviews and correspondence with plaintiff's brother and sister-in-law, Howard and Edith, plaintiff's sister, and a local lawyer):

... The case originated in 1922 in Berlin, New Hampshire, a small mill town near the Canadian border, when Dr. Edward McGee, a general practitioner, promised to restore George Hawkins' slightly scarred hand to "perfect condition" through surgery. ...

One morning in 1915, 11–year–old George burned his right hand while preparing breakfast for his father on the family's wood-burning stove. At the time, George was trying to turn on the kitchen light to illuminate the stove, but an electrical storm the night before had damaged the wiring so that George received a severe shock. One of George's younger brothers, Howard Hawkins ... described George's initial scar as a "small pencil-size scar" which was between his thumb and index finger and did not substantially affect his use of the hand. Nevertheless, Charles Hawkins took his son George to skin specialists in Montreal after the accident; but the doctors advised the Hawkinses against doing anything to restore the hand.

[T]he family physician, Edward McGee, ... after returning from several years of medical service in Europe during World War I, ... requested George and his parents to let him operate on the hand in order to restore it to "perfect" condition.

According to ... George's younger sister, McGee claimed to have done a number of similar skin grafts on soldiers in Germany during the war, although he later admitted that he had really only observed such operations.

... McGee encouraged the Hawkinses to allow him to operate on the hand for three years, until finally George agreed shortly after his 18th birthday. ...

McGee operated on George's hand ... in March of 1922. The skin graft operation was supposed to be quick, simple, and effective, and to require only a few days of hospitalization. Instead, ... George was, in the words of his brother Howard, "in the throes of death" for quite a while after the operation because of his extensive bleeding and the ensuing infection. Moreover, the post-operation scar covered his thumb and two fingers and was densely covered with hair. Howard Hawkins remembers that George's hand was partially closed up and continued to bleed periodically throughout his life. ...

... Charles Hawkins took the $1,400 [final settlement] and his injured son back to Montreal to see if any subsequent operations would alleviate George's deformity, but the doctors there said that the grafted skin was so tough that nothing more could be done. ...

Hawkins' crippled hand affected his employment and outlook throughout his lifetime. After the operation, George Hawkins never returned to high school ... because, in his siblings' view, he was embarrassed by his hand ... Because of his hand, George was unable to perform any heavy manual labor or learn to type. He worked for many years in the printing division of the Brown Company, a pulp and paper manufacturer in Berlin, and later in a tire store. ... According to his family members, George was always very sensitive about his hand and suffered lifelong emotional distress. His parents also grieved until their deaths because of the tragic and unnecessary crippling of their son's hand. ...

Howard Hawkins ... believes that George was somewhat aware of the case's importance before his 1958 death. Howard states: "I think he became aware of the importance of his case though a lawyer friend. ... I think it gave him a sense of importance, in that this was bringing the facts out in the public eye, but this was only temporary, as he really lived with this incapacity all his life, and he did suffer mentally as well as physically."

SULLIVAN v. O'CONNOR

Supreme Judicial Court of Massachusetts, 1973.
363 Mass. 579, 296 N.E.2d 183.

KAPLAN, JUSTICE. [Alice Sullivan, a professional entertainer, brought suit against her plastic surgeon, Dr. James O'Connor, for breach of promise to enhance her beauty and improve her appearance. She also sued for malpractice (negligence). The jury found the defendant was not negligent but awarded plaintiff $13,500 for defendant's breach of contract. The court's discussion of the damages issues is omitted. Ed.]

[T]he plaintiff's nose had been straight, but long and prominent. The defendant undertook by two operations to reduce its prominence and somewhat to shorten it, thus making it more pleasing in relation to the plaintiff's other features. Actually the plaintiff was obliged to undergo three operations, and her appearance was worsened. Her nose now had a concave line to about the midpoint, at which it became bulbous; viewed frontally, the nose from bridge to midpoint was flattened and broadened, and the two sides of the tip had lost symmetry. This configuration evidently could not be improved by further surgery. ...

It has been suggested on occasion that agreements between patients and physicians by which the physician undertakes to effect a cure or to bring about a given result should be declared unenforceable on grounds of public policy. See Guilmet v. Campbell, 385 Mich. 57, 76, 188 N.W.2d 601 (dissenting opinion). But there are many decisions recognizing and enforcing such contracts, and the law of Massachusetts has treated them as valid, although we have had no decision meeting head on the contention that they should be denied legal sanction. Small v. Howard, 128 Mass. 131. These causes of action are, however, considered a little suspect, and thus we find courts straining sometimes to read the pleadings as sounding only in tort for negligence, and not in contract for breach of promise, despite sedulous efforts by the pleaders to pursue the latter theory. *See* Gault v. Sideman, 42 Ill.App.2d 96, 191 N.E.2d 436.

It is not hard to see why the courts should be unenthusiastic or skeptical about the contract theory. Considering the uncertainties of medical science and the variations in the physical and psychological conditions of individual patients, doctors can seldom in good faith promise specific results. Therefore it is unlikely that physicians of even average integrity will in fact make such promises. Statements of opinion by the physician with some optimistic coloring are a different thing, and may indeed have therapeutic value. But patients may transform such statements into firm promises in their own minds, especially when they have been disappointed in the event, and testify in that sense to sympathetic juries.[2] If actions for breach of promise can be readily maintained, doctors, so it is said, will be frightened into practising "defensive medicine." On the other hand, if these actions were outlawed, leaving only the possibility of suits for malpractice, there is fear that the public might be exposed to the enticements of charlatans, and confidence in the profession might ultimately be shaken. *See* Miller, *The Contractual Liability of Physicians and Surgeons*, 1953 Wash.L.Q. 413, 416–423. The law has taken the middle of the road position of allowing actions based on alleged contract, but insisting on clear proof. Instructions to the jury may well stress this requirement and point to tests of truth, such as the complexity or difficulty of an operation as bearing on the probability that a given result was promised. . . .

Restatement (Second) Contracts § 344. Purposes of Remedies

Judicial remedies under the rules stated in this Restatement serve to protect one or more of the following interests of a promisee:

(a) his "expectation interest," which is his interest in having the benefit of his bargain by being put in as good a position as he would have been in had the contract been performed,

(b) his "reliance interest," which is his interest in being reimbursed for loss caused by reliance on the contract by being put in as good a position as he would have been in had the contract not been made, or

(c) his "restitution interest," which is his interest in having restored to him any benefit that he has conferred on the other party.

LEONARD v. PEPSICO, INC.

United States District Court, S.D. New York, 1999.
88 F.Supp.2d 116, *aff'd per curiam,* 210 F.3d 88 (2d Cir. 2000).

KIMBA M. WOOD, DISTRICT JUDGE. Plaintiff brought this action seeking, among other things, specific performance of an alleged offer of a Harrier

---

2. Judicial skepticism about whether a promise was in fact made derives also from the possibility that the truth has been tortured to give the plaintiff the advantage of the longer period of limitations sometimes available for actions on contract as distinguished from those in tort or for malpractice. *See* Lillich, *The Malpractice Statute of Limitations in New York and Other Jurisdictions*, 47 Cornell L.Q. 339.

Jet, featured in a television advertisement for defendant's "Pepsi Stuff" promotion. Defendant has moved for summary judgment pursuant to Federal Rule of Civil Procedure 56. For the reasons stated below, defendant's motion is granted.

I. Background

This case arises out of a promotional campaign conducted by defendant, the producer and distributor of the soft drinks Pepsi and Diet Pepsi. The promotion, entitled "Pepsi Stuff," encouraged consumers to collect "Pepsi Points" from specially marked packages of Pepsi or Diet Pepsi and redeem these points for merchandise featuring the Pepsi logo. Before introducing the promotion nationally, defendant conducted a test of the promotion in the Pacific Northwest from October 1995 to March 1996. A Pepsi Stuff catalog was distributed to consumers in the test market, including Washington State. Plaintiff is a resident of Seattle, Washington. While living in Seattle, plaintiff saw the Pepsi Stuff commercial that he contends constituted an offer of a Harrier Jet.

A. The Alleged Offer

Because whether the television commercial constituted an offer is the central question in this case, the Court will describe the commercial in detail. The commercial opens upon an idyllic, suburban morning, where the chirping of birds in sun-dappled trees welcomes a paperboy on his morning route. As the newspaper hits the stoop of a conventional two-story house, the tattoo of a military drum introduces the subtitle, "MONDAY 7:58 AM." The stirring strains of a martial air mark the appearance of a well-coiffed teenager preparing to leave for school, dressed in a shirt emblazoned with the Pepsi logo, a red-white-and-blue ball. While the teenager confidently preens, the military drumroll again sounds as the subtitle "T–SHIRT 75 PEPSI POINTS" scrolls across the screen. Bursting from his room, the teenager strides down the hallway wearing a leather jacket. The drumroll sounds again, as the subtitle "LEATHER JACKET 1450 PEPSI POINTS" appears. The teenager opens the door of his house and, unfazed by the glare of the early morning sunshine, puts on a pair of sunglasses. The drumroll then accompanies the subtitle "SHADES 175 PEPSI POINTS." A voiceover then intones, "Introducing the new Pepsi Stuff catalog," as the camera focuses on the cover of the catalog (the "Catalog").[1]

The scene then shifts to three young boys sitting in front of a high school building. The boy in the middle is intent on his Pepsi Stuff Catalog, while the boys on either side are each drinking Pepsi. The three boys gaze in awe at an object rushing overhead, as the military march builds to a

---

1. At this point, the following message appears at the bottom of the screen: "Offer not available in all areas. See details on specially marked packages."

crescendo. The Harrier Jet is not yet visible, but the observer senses the presence of a mighty plane as the extreme winds generated by its flight create a paper maelstrom in a classroom devoted to an otherwise dull physics lesson. Finally, the Harrier Jet swings into view and lands by the side of the school building, next to a bicycle rack. Several students run for cover, and the velocity of the wind strips one hapless faculty member down to his underwear. While the faculty member is being deprived of his dignity, the voiceover announces: "Now the more Pepsi you drink, the more great stuff you're gonna get."

The teenager opens the cockpit of the fighter and can be seen, helmetless, holding a Pepsi. "(L)ooking very pleased with himself," the teenager exclaims, "Sure beats the bus," and chortles. The military drumroll sounds a final time, as the following words appear: "HARRIER FIGHTER 7,000,000 PEPSI POINTS." A few seconds later, the following appears in more stylized script: "Drink Pepsi—Get Stuff." With that message, the music and the commercial end with a triumphant flourish.

Inspired by this commercial, plaintiff set out to obtain a Harrier Jet. Plaintiff explains that he is "typical of the 'Pepsi Generation' . . . he is young, has an adventurous spirit, and the notion of obtaining a Harrier Jet appealed to him enormously." Plaintiff consulted the Pepsi Stuff Catalog. The Catalog features youths dressed in Pepsi Stuff regalia or enjoying Pepsi Stuff accessories, such as "Blue Shades" ("As if you need another reason to look forward to sunny days."), "Pepsi Tees" ("Live in 'em. Laugh in 'em. Get in 'em."), "Bag of Balls" ("Three balls. One bag. No rules."), and "Pepsi Phone Card" ("Call your mom!"). The Catalog specifies the number of Pepsi Points required to obtain pro-motional merchandise. The Catalog includes an Order Form which lists, on one side, fifty-three items of Pepsi Stuff merchandise redeemable for Pepsi Points (the "Order Form"). Conspicuously absent from the Order Form is any entry or description of a Harrier Jet. The amount of Pepsi Points required to obtain the listed merchandise ranges from 15 (for a "Jacket Tattoo" ("Sew 'em on your jacket, not your arm.")) to 3300 (for a "Fila Mountain Bike" ("Rugged. All-terrain. Exclusively for Pepsi.")). It should be noted that plaintiff objects to the implication that because an item was not shown in the Catalog, it was unavailable.

The rear foldout pages of the Catalog contain directions for redeeming Pepsi Points for merchandise. These directions note that merchandise may be ordered "only" with the original Order Form. The Catalog notes that in the event that a consumer lacks enough Pepsi Points to obtain a desired item, additional Pepsi Points may be purchased for ten cents each; however, at least fifteen original Pepsi Points must accompany each order.

Although plaintiff initially set out to collect 7,000,000 Pepsi Points by consuming Pepsi products, it soon became clear to him that he "would not be able to buy (let alone drink) enough Pepsi to collect the necessary Pepsi Points fast enough." Reevaluating his strategy, plaintiff "focused for the first time on the packaging materials in the Pepsi Stuff promotion," and realized that buying Pepsi Points would be a more promising option. Through acquaintances, plaintiff ultimately raised about $700,000.

B. *Plaintiff's Efforts to Redeem the Alleged Offer*

On or about March 27, 1996, plaintiff submitted an Order Form, fifteen original Pepsi Points, and a check for $700,008.50. Plaintiff appears to have been represented by counsel at the time he mailed his check; the check is drawn on an account of plaintiff's first set of attorneys. At the bottom of the Order Form, plaintiff wrote in "1 Harrier Jet" in the "Item" column and "7,000,000" in the "Total Points" column. In a letter accompanying his submission, plaintiff stated that the check was to purchase additional Pepsi Points "expressly for obtaining a new Harrier jet as advertised in your Pepsi Stuff commercial."

On or about May 7, 1996, defendant's fulfillment house rejected plaintiff's submission and returned the check, explaining that:

> The item that you have requested is not part of the Pepsi Stuff collection. It is not included in the catalogue or on the order form, and only catalogue merchandise can be redeemed under this program.

> The Harrier jet in the Pepsi commercial is fanciful and is simply included to create a humorous and entertaining ad. We apologize for any misunderstanding or confusion that you may have experienced and are enclosing some free product coupons for your use.

Plaintiff's previous counsel responded on or about May 14, 1996, as follows:

> Your letter of May 7, 1996 is totally unacceptable. We have reviewed the video tape of the Pepsi Stuff commercial . . . and it clearly offers the new Harrier jet for 7,000,000 Pepsi Points. Our client followed your rules explicitly. . . .

> This is a formal demand that you honor your commitment and make immediate arrangements to transfer the new Harrier jet to our client. If we do not receive transfer instructions within ten (10) business days of the date of this letter you will leave us no choice but to file an appropriate action against Pepsi. . . .

This letter was apparently sent onward to the advertising company responsible for the actual commercial, BBDO New York ("BBDO"). In a letter dated May 30, 1996, BBDO Vice President Raymond E. McGovern, Jr., explained to plaintiff that:

> I find it hard to believe that you are of the opinion that the Pepsi Stuff commercial ("Commercial") really offers a new Harrier Jet. The use of the Jet was clearly a joke that was meant to make the Commercial more humorous and entertaining. In my opinion, no reasonable person would agree with your analysis of the Commercial.

On or about June 17, 1996, plaintiff mailed a similar demand letter to defendant. . . .

II. Discussion

A. *The Legal Framework*

On a motion for summary judgment, a court "cannot try issues of fact; it can only determine whether there are issues to be tried." Donahue v. Windsor Locks Bd. Of Fire Comm'rs, 834 F.2d 54, 58 (2d Cir. 1987). To prevail on a motion for summary judgment, the moving party therefore must show that there are no such genuine issues of material fact to be tried, and that he or she is entitled to judgment as a matter of law. *See* Fed.R.Civ.P. 56(c). . . .

B. *Defendant's Advertisement Was Not An Offer*

The general rule is that an advertisement does not constitute an offer. The *Restatement (Second) of Contracts* explains that:

> Advertisements of goods by display, sign, handbill, newspaper, radio or television are not ordinarily intended or understood as offers to sell. The same is true of catalogues, price lists and circulars, even though the terms of suggested bargains may be stated in some detail. It is of course possible to make an offer by an advertisement directed to the general public (*see* § 29), but there must ordinarily be some language of commitment or some invitation to take action without further communication.

Restatement (Second) of Contracts § 26 cmt. b (1979). Similarly, a leading treatise notes that:

> It is quite possible to make a definite and operative offer to buy or sell goods by advertisement, in a newspaper, by a handbill, a catalog or circular or on a placard in a store window. *It is not customary to do this, however; and the presumption is the other way.* . . . Such advertisements are understood to be mere requests to consider and examine and negotiate; and no one can reasonably regard them as otherwise unless the circumstances are exceptional and the words used are very plain and clear.

1 Arthur Linton Corbin & Joseph M. Perillo, *Corbin on Contracts* § 2.4, at 116–17 (rev. ed.1993) (emphasis added); *see also* 1 E. Allan Farnsworth, *Farnsworth on Contracts* § 3.10, at 239 (2d ed.1998); 1 Samuel Williston & Richard A. Lord, *A Treatise on the Law of Contracts* § 4:7, at 286–87 (4th ed.1990). . . .

An advertisement is not transformed into an enforceable offer merely by a potential offeree's expression of willingness to accept the offer through, among other means, completion of an order form. In Mesaros v. United States, 845 F.2d 1576 (Fed.Cir.1988), for example, the plaintiffs sued the United States Mint for failure to deliver a number of Statue of Liberty commemorative coins that they had ordered. When demand for the coins proved unexpectedly robust, a number of individuals who had sent in their orders in a timely fashion were left empty-handed. *See id.* at 1578–80. The court began by noting the "well-established" rule that advertisements and order forms are "mere notices and solicitations for offers which create no power of acceptance in the recipient." *Id.* at 1580; *Restatement (Second) of Contracts* § 26 ("A manifestation of willingness to enter a bargain is not an offer if the person to whom it is addressed knows or has reason to know that the person making it does not intend to conclude a bargain until he has made a further manifestation of assent."). The spurned coin collectors could not maintain a breach of contract action because no contract would be formed until the advertiser accepted the order form and processed payment. *See id.* at 1581.Under these principles, plaintiff's letter of March 27, 1996, with the Order Form and the appropriate number of Pepsi Points, constituted the offer. There would be no enforceable contract until defendant accepted the Order Form and cashed the check.

The exception to the rule that advertisements do not create any power of acceptance in potential offerees is where the advertisement is "clear, definite, and explicit, and leaves nothing open for negotiation," in that circumstance, "it constitutes an offer, acceptance of which will complete the contract." Lefkowitz v. Great Minneapolis Surplus Store, 251 Minn. 188, 86 N.W.2d 689, 691 (1957). In *Lefkowitz,* defendant had published a newspaper announcement stating: "Saturday 9 AM Sharp, 3 Brand New Fur Coats, Worth to $100.00, First Come First Served $1 Each." *Id.* at 690. Mr. Morris Lefkowitz arrived at the store, dollar in hand, but was informed that under defendant's "house rules," the offer was open to ladies, but not gentlemen. *See id.* The court ruled that because plaintiff had fulfilled all of the terms of the advertisement and the advertisement was specific and left nothing open for negotiation, a contract had been formed. . . .

The present case is distinguishable from *Lefkowitz.* First, the commercial cannot be regarded in itself as sufficiently definite, because it specifically reserved the details of the offer to a separate writing, the Catalog. The commercial itself made no mention of the steps a potential offeree would be required to take to accept the alleged offer of a Harrier Jet. The advertisement in *Lefkowitz,* in contrast, "identified the person who could accept." *Corbin, supra,* § 2.4, at 119. *See generally* United States v. Braunstein, 75 F.Supp. 137, 139 (S.D.N.Y.1947) ("Greater precision of expression may be required, and less help from the court given, when the parties are merely at the threshold of a contract."); *Farnsworth, supra,* at 239 ("The fact that a proposal is very detailed suggests that it is an offer, while omission of many terms suggests that it is not."). Second, even if the Catalog had included a Harrier Jet among the items that could be obtained by redemption of Pepsi Points, the advertisement of a Harrier Jet by both television commercial and catalog would still not constitute an offer. As the *Mesaros* court explained, the absence of any words of limitation such as "first come, first served," renders the alleged offer sufficiently indefinite that no contract could be formed. *See* Mesaros, 845 F.2d at 1581. "A customer would not usually have reason to believe that the shopkeeper intended exposure to the risk of a multitude of acceptances resulting in a number of contracts exceeding the shopkeeper's inventory." *Farnsworth, supra,* at 242. There was no such danger in *Lefkowitz,* owing to the limitation "first come, first served."

The Court finds, in sum, that the Harrier Jet commercial was merely an advertisement. . . . [The court continues with an analysis of rewards as offers. *See* p. 90, *infra.* Ed.]

C. *An Objective, Reasonable Person Would Not Have Considered the Commercial an Offer*

. . . An obvious joke, of course, would not give rise to a contract. *See, e.g.,* Graves v. Northern N.Y. Pub. Co., 260 A.D. 900, 22 N.Y.S.2d 537 (1940) (dismissing claim to offer of $1000, which appeared in the "joke column" of the newspaper, to any person who could provide a commonly available phone number). On the other hand, if there is no indication that the offer is "evidently in jest," and that an objective, reasonable person would find that the offer was serious, then there may be a valid offer. *See* Lucy v. Zehmer, 196 Va. 493, 84 S.E.2d 516, 518, 520 (1954) (ordering specific performance of a contract to purchase a farm despite defendant's protestation that the transaction was done in jest as "just a bunch of two doggoned drunks bluffing").

. . . The commercial is the embodiment of what defendant appropriately characterizes as "zany humor."

First, the . . . implication of the commercial is that Pepsi Stuff merchandise will inject drama and moment into hitherto unexceptional lives. . . . A reasonable viewer would understand such advertisements as mere puffery, not as statements of fact . . . and refrain from interpreting the promises of the commercial as being literally true.

Second, the callow youth featured in the commercial is a highly improbable pilot, one who could barely be trusted with the keys to his parents' car, much less the prize aircraft of the United States Marine Corps. . . .

Third, the notion of traveling to school in a Harrier Jet is an exaggerated adolescent fantasy. . . .

Fourth, . . . [i]n light of the Harrier Jet's well-documented function in attacking and destroying surface and air targets, armed reconnaissance and air interdiction, and offensive and defensive anti-aircraft warfare, depiction of such a jet as a way to get to school in the morning is clearly not serious even if, as plaintiff contends, the jet is capable of being acquired "in a form that eliminates (its) potential for military use."

Fifth, the . . . cost of a Harrier Jet is roughly $23 million dollars, a fact of which plaintiff was aware when he set out to gather the amount he believed necessary to accept the alleged offer. Even if an objective, reasonable person were not aware of this fact, he would conclude that purchasing a fighter plane for $700,000 is a deal too good to be true.

Plaintiff argues that a reasonable, objective person would have understood the commercial to make a serious offer of a Harrier Jet because there was "absolutely no distinction in the manner" in which the items in the commercial were presented. . . . [Plaintiff's argument suggests] merely that the humor of the promotional campaign was tongue in cheek. . . . In light of the obvious absurdity of the commercial, the Court rejects plaintiff's argument that the commercial was not clearly in jest. . . .

D. *The Alleged Contract Does Not Satisfy the Statute of Frauds*

The absence of any writing setting forth the alleged contract in this case provides an entirely separate reason for granting summary judgment. . . . The commercial is not a writing. . . .

III. *Conclusion*

In sum, there are three reasons why plaintiff's demand cannot prevail as a matter of law. First, the commercial was merely an advertisement. . . . Second, the tongue-in-cheek attitude of the commercial would not cause a reasonable person to conclude that a soft drink company would be giving away fighter planes as part of a promotion. Third, there is no writing between the parties sufficient to satisfy the Statute of Frauds.

For the reasons stated above, the Court grants defendant's motion for summary judgment. . . .

PROBLEMS

5. The Chicago Tribune, a daily newspaper, publishes a booklet called "General Advertising Rates" which lists its charges for advertisements and another booklet called "The Chicago Tribune Advertising Acceptability Guide" which indicates that the Tribune will refuse advertising which is dishonest, indecent or illegal. The plaintiff, a labor union, tendered to the Tribune an advertisement urging readers not to patronize a certain department store because of its policy of featuring imported clothing made by low wage foreign labor. The tendered advertisement was concededly not dishonest, indecent or illegal. The union also tendered sufficient funds to pay for the advertisement in accordance with the "General Advertising Rates." The Tribune refused to print the advertisement. Does plaintiff have a cause of action for breach of contract?

6. D inserted the following ad in a newspaper:

"OPPORTUNITY KNOCKS

We want enthusiastic, ambitious salespeople to represent us locally. Professional training program with $1950 monthly guarantee. Enthusiasm and ambition quickly rewarded with advancement."

P came to the office, applied for the position, and was hired. P started to work but did not receive the amount of pay specified in the ad. P was told that he had generated insufficient sales to merit the $1950 monthly amount. After two months P resigned. P brought an action for breach of contract. What result?

7. D, a medical school, distributed a catalog stating terms under which applications for admission would be evaluated. P received the catalog, applied for admission, paid a fee and was rejected. The catalog provided: "Students are selected on the basis of scholarship, character and motivation without regard to race, creed or sex. The student's potential for the study and practice of medicine will be evaluated on the basis of academic achievement, Medical College Admission Test results and personal appraisals by a pre-professional advisory committee or individual instructors."

P alleged that D evaluated such applications according to the ability of applicants or their families to make large monetary contributions to the school. Has P stated a cause of action for breach of contract?

(b) BIDS AND AUCTION SALES

(Calamari & Perillo on Contracts §§ 1.7 and 2.6)

HOFFMAN v. HORTON

Supreme Court of Virginia, 1972.
212 Va. 565, 186 S.E.2d 79.

CARRICO, JUSTICE. The question involved in this case is whether an auctioneer at a foreclosure sale may reopen the bidding when an overbid is made immediately prior to or simultaneously with the falling of the hammer in acceptance of a lower bid.

The question arises from an auction sale conducted to foreclose a deed of trust in the sum of $100,000 upon the "Field Tract" in Arlington County, owned by the defendants Howard P. Horton and wife and Ralph R. Kaul and wife. At the sale and after spirited bidding, a bid of $177,000 was made by Hubert N. Hoffman, the plaintiff, and received by the auctioneer. When no other bids appeared to be forthcoming, the auctioneer asked, "Are you all through bidding, gentlemen?" After a pause, he stated, "Going once for $177,000.00, going twice for $177,000.00, sold for $177,000.00." Whereupon, he struck the palm of his left hand with his right fist.

Immediately, one of the trustees, who had been standing nearby, rushed up to the auctioneer and told him that he had missed a bid of $178,000. The auctioneer, who had neither seen nor heard the bid, stated, "If I missed a bid, you people had better speak up. I am going ahead with the sale." The plaintiff then stepped forward and said, "Gentlemen, I have purchased this property for $177,000.00." The auctioneer and the trustee both disagreed with the plaintiff, and the auctioneer announced to the crowd that he had a bid of $178,000. The bidding proceeded, and the property was finally knocked down to the plaintiff for $194,000.

The plaintiff paid the $5,000 deposit required by the terms of the foreclosure but insisted that he had purchased the property for $177,000. Later, he paid the balance of the $194,000 under protest and brought an action against the former owners and the trustees to recover the $17,000 difference between the two bids in dispute. The trial court denied the plaintiff's claim, and we granted a writ of error to review the judgment. . . .

The trial court found as a matter of fact, and this finding is not questioned by the plaintiff, that the $178,000 bid was made "prior to or simultaneously with" the falling of the auctioneer's fist in acceptance of the plaintiff's bid of $177,000. Based upon its finding of fact, the court held that "the bid for $178,000.00 was made before the bid for $177,000.00 had been accepted" and that the auctioneer had "acted within the discretion permitted" him in reopening the bidding and continuing with the sale.

In holding that the auctioneer was vested with discretion to reopen the bidding, the trial court relied upon Code § 8.2–328(2), a part of the Uniform Commercial Code. The statutory language so relied upon reads as follows:

> A sale by auction is complete when the auctioneer so announces by the fall of the hammer or in other customary manner. Where a bid is made while the hammer is falling in acceptance of a prior bid the auctioneer may in his discretion reopen the bidding or declare the goods sold under the bid on which the hammer was falling.

We disagree with the trial court that the transaction in this case, involving the sale of land, is controlled by § 8.2–328(2) of the Uniform Commercial Code. Title 8.2 of the Commercial Code applies only to transactions relating to "goods." Code §§ 8.2–105,–107.

However, while the Uniform Commercial Code is not controlling here, we think it appropriate to borrow from it to establish the rule applicable to the transaction at hand. To vest the auctioneer crying a sale of land with the same discretion to reopen bidding that he has in the sale of goods is to achieve uniformity and, of more importance, to recognize a rule which is both necessary and fair.

We hold, therefore, that the auctioneer in this case was vested with discretion to reopen the bidding for the land which was being sold. And we agree with the trial court that the auctioneer "acted within" his discretion in reopening the bidding and continuing with the sale when it was made apparent to him that a higher bid had been submitted "prior to or simultaneously with" the falling of his fist in acceptance of the plaintiff's lower bid.

Accordingly, the judgment of the trial court will be affirmed.

Affirmed.

PROBLEMS

8. Defendant caused circulars to be distributed to dealers throughout the country announcing that an auction would be conducted without reserve of the famous Smith Collection of antiques. Plaintiff flew from California to New York, the announced site of the auction. On arrival plaintiff discovered that the auction had been canceled because of a recession in the antiques market. Does the plaintiff have a cause of action?

9. Elizabeth solicited bids from several contractors for her home remodeling project. She provided the contractors with plans and specifications. Three contractors, A, B, and C submitted bids of $50,000, $60,000 and $70,000 respectively. Elizabeth awarded the contract to B. Does A, as the low bidder, have a cause of action against Elizabeth for breach of contract?

(c) OFFERS DISTINGUISHED FROM PRELIMINARY NEGOTIATIONS AND PRICE QUOTATIONS

(Calamari & Perillo on Contracts § 2.6)

LONERGAN v. SCOLNICK

District Court of Appeal, Fourth District, California, 1954.
129 Cal.App.2d 179, 276 P.2d 8.

BARNARD, PRESIDING JUSTICE. . . .

The stipulated facts are as follows: During March, 1952, the defendant placed an ad in a Los Angeles paper reading, so far as material here, "Joshua Tree vic. 40 acres, . . . need cash, will sacrifice." In response to an inquiry resulting from this ad the defendant, who lived in New York, wrote a letter to the plaintiff dated March 26, briefly describing the property, giving directions as to how to get there, stating that his rock-bottom price was $2,500 cash, and further stating that "This is a form letter." On April 7, the plaintiff wrote a letter to the defendant saying that he was not sure he had found the property, asking for its legal description, asking whether the land was all level or whether it included certain jutting rock hills, and suggesting a certain bank as escrow agent "should I desire to purchase the land." On April 8, the defendant wrote to the plaintiff saying "From your description you have found the property"; that this bank "is O.K. for escrow agent"; that the land was fairly level; giving the legal description; and then saying, "If you are really interested, you will have to decide fast, as I expect to have a buyer in the next week or so." On April 12, the defendant sold the property to a third party for $2,500. The plaintiff received defendant's letter of April 8 on April 14. On April 15 he wrote to the defendant thanking him for his letter "confirming that I was on the right land," stating that he would immediately proceed to have the escrow opened and would deposit $2,500 therein "in conformity with your offer," and asking the defendant to forward a deed with his instructions to the escrow agent. On April 17, 1952, the plaintiff started an escrow and placed in the hands of the escrow agent $100, agreeing to furnish an additional $2,400 at an unspecified time, with the provision that if the escrow was not closed by May 15, 1952, it should be completed as soon thereafter as possible unless a written demand for a return of the money or instruments was made by either party after that date. It was further stipulated that the plaintiff was ready and willing at all times to deposit the $2,400. . . .

There can be no contract unless the minds of the parties have met and mutually agreed upon some specific thing. This is usually evidenced by one party making an offer which is accepted by the other party. Section 25 of the Restatement of the Law on Contracts reads:

> If from a promise, or manifestation of intention, or from the circumstances existing at the time, the person to whom the promise or manifestation is addressed knows or has reason to know that the person making it does not intend it as an expression of his fixed purpose until he has given a further expression of assent, he has not made an offer.

The language used in Niles v. Hancock, 140 Cal. 157, 73 P. 840, 842, "It is also clear from the correspondence that it was the intention of the defendant that the negotiations between him and the plaintiff were to be purely preliminary," is applicable here. The correspondence here indicates an intention on the part of the defendant to find out whether the plaintiff was interested, rather than an intention to make a definite offer to the plaintiff. The language used by the defendant in his letters of March 26 and April 8 rather clearly discloses that they were not intended as an expression of fixed purpose to make a definite offer, and was sufficient to advise the plaintiff that some further expression of assent on the part of the defendant was necessary.

The advertisement in the paper was a mere request for an offer. The letter of March 26 contains no definite offer, and clearly states that it is a form letter. It merely gives further particulars, in clarification of the advertisement, and tells the plaintiff how to locate the property if he was interested in looking into the matter. The letter of April 8 added nothing in the way of a definite offer. It merely answered some questions asked by the plaintiff, and stated that if the plaintiff was really interested he would have to act fast. The statement that he expected to have a buyer in the next week or so indicated that the defendant intended to sell to the first-comer, and was reserving the right to do so. From this statement, alone, the plaintiff knew or should have known that he was not being given time in which to accept an offer that was being made, but that some further assent on the part of the defendant was required. Under the language used the plaintiff was not being given a right to act within a reasonable time after receiving the letter; he was plainly told that the defendant intended to sell to another, if possible, and warned that he would have to act fast if he was interested in buying the land.

Regardless of any opinion previously expressed, the court found that no contract had been entered into between these parties, and we are in accord with the court's conclusion on that controlling issue. The court's construction of the letters involved was a reasonable one, and we think the most reasonable one, even if it be assumed that another construction was possible.

The judgment is affirmed.

FAIRMOUNT GLASS WORKS v. CRUNDEN–MARTIN WOODENWARE CO.

Court of Appeals of Kentucky, 1899.
106 Ky. 659, 51 S.W. 196.

HOBSON, J. On April 20, 1895, appellee [Crunden–Martin] wrote appellant [Fairmount Glass] the following letter:

St. Louis, Mo., April 20, 1895.
Gentlemen:
Please advise us the lowest price you can make us on our order for ten car loads of Mason green jars, complete, with caps, packed one dozen in a case, either delivered here, or f.o.b. cars your place, as you prefer. State terms and cash discount.
Very truly,
Crunden–Martin W.W. Co.*

To this letter Fairmount Glass answered as follows:

Fairmount, Ind., April 23, 1895.
Crunden–Martin Wooden Ware Co.,
St. Louis, Mo.
Gentlemen:
Replying to your favor of April 20, we quote you Mason fruit jars, complete, in one-dozen boxes, delivered in East St. Louis, Ill.: Pints $4.50, quarts $5.00, half gallons $6.50, per gross, for immediate acceptance, and shipment not later than May 15, 1895; sixty days' acceptance, or 2 off, cash in ten days.
Yours, truly,
Fairmount Glass Works.

Please note that we make all quotations and contracts subject to the contingencies of agencies or transportation, delays or accidents beyond our control.

For reply thereto, Crunden–Martin sent the following telegram on April 24, 1895:

* The name of the appellee in the title of the case is correctly given as "Crunden–Martin" but in the body of the opinion, as "Grunden–Martin." The spelling has been corrected here to correspond with the title. Ed.

Fairmount Glass Works, Fairmount, Ind.:
Your letter twenty-third received. Enter order ten car loads as per your quotation. Specifications mailed.
Crunden–Martin W.W. Co.

In response to this telegram, Fairmount Glass sent the following:

Fairmount, Ind., April 24, 1895.
Crunden–Martin W.W. Co.,
St. Louis, Mo.:
Impossible to book your order. Output all sold. See letter.
Fairmount Glass Works.

Crunden–Martin insists that, by its telegram sent in answer to the letter of April 23d, the contract was closed for the purchase of 10 car loads of Mason fruit jars. Fairmount Glass insists that the contract was not closed by this telegram, and that it had the right to decline to fill the order at the time it sent its telegram of April 24. This is the chief question in the case. The court below gave judgment in favor of Crunden–Martin, and Fairmount Glass has appealed, earnestly insisting that the judgment is erroneous.

We are referred to a number of authorities holding that a quotation of prices is not an offer to sell, in the sense that a completed contract will arise out of the giving of an order for merchandise in accordance with the proposed terms. There are a number of cases holding that the transaction is not completed until the order so made is accepted. Smith v. Gowdy, 8 Allen 566; Beaupre v. Telegraph Co., 21 Minn. 155. But each case must turn largely upon the language there used. In this case we think there was more than a quotation of prices, although Fairmount Glass's letter uses the word "quote" in stating the prices given. The true meaning of the correspondence must be determined by reading it as a whole. Crunden–Martin's letter of April 20th, which began the transaction, did not ask for a quotation of prices. It reads: "Please advise us the lowest price you can make us on our order for ten car loads of Mason green jars. . . . State terms and cash discount." From this Fairmount Glass could not fail to understand that Crunden–Martin wanted to know at what price it would sell it ten car loads of these jars; so when, in answer, it wrote: "We quote you Mason fruit jars . . . pints $4.50, quarts $5.00, half gallons $6.50, per gross, for immediate acceptance; . . . 2 off, cash in ten days,"—it must be deemed as intending to give Crunden–Martin the information it had asked for. We can hardly understand what was meant by the words "for immediate acceptance," unless the latter was intended as a proposition to sell at these prices if accepted immediately. In construing every contract, the aim of the court is to arrive at the intention of the parties. In none of the cases to which we have been referred on behalf of Fairmount Glass was there on the face of the correspondence any such expression of intention to make an offer to sell on the terms indicated. . . .

It will be observed that the telegram of acceptance refers to the specifications mailed. These specifications were contained in the following letter:

St. Louis, Mo., April 24, 1895.
Fairmount Glass–Works Co., Fairmount, Ind.
Gentlemen:
We received your letter of 23rd this morning, and telegraphed you in reply as follows: "Your letter 23rd received. Enter order ten car loads as per your quotation. Specifications mailed,"—which we now confirm. We have accordingly entered this contract on our books for the ten cars Mason green jars, complete, with caps and rubbers, one dozen in case, delivered to us in East St. Louis at $4.50 per gross for pint, $5.00 for quart, $6.50 for one-half gallon. Terms, 60 days' acceptance, or 2 per cent. for cash in ten days, to be shipped not later than May 15, 1895. The jars and caps to be strictly first-quality goods. You may ship the first car to us here assorted: Five gross pint, fifty-five gross quart, forty gross one-half gallon. Specifications for the remaining 9 cars we will send later.
Crunden–Martin W.W. Co.

It is insisted for Fairmount Glass that this was not an acceptance of the offer as made; that the stipulation, "The jars and caps to be strictly first-quality goods," was not in their offer; and that, it not having been accepted as made, Fairmount Glass is not bound. But it will be observed that Fairmount Glass declined to furnish the goods before it got this letter, and in the correspondence with Crunden–Martin it nowhere complained of these words as an addition to the contract. Quite a number of other letters passed, in which the refusal to deliver the goods was placed on other grounds, none of which have been sustained by the evidence. Crunden–Martin offers proof tending to show that these words, in the trade in which parties were engaged, conveyed the same meaning as the words used in Fairmount Glass's letter, and were only a different form of expressing the same idea. Fairmount Glass's conduct would seem to confirm this evidence.

Fairmount Glass also insists that the contract was indefinite, because the quantity of each size of the jars was not fixed, that 10 car loads is too indefinite a specification of the quantity sold, and that Crunden–Martin had no right to accept the goods to be delivered on different days. The proof shows that "10 car loads" is an expression used in the trade as equivalent to 1,000 gross, 100 gross being regarded a car load. The offer to sell the different sizes at different prices gave the purchaser the right to name the quantity of each size, and, the offer being to ship not later than May 15th, the buyer had the right to fix the time of delivery at any time before that. ... Judgment affirmed.

PROBLEMS

10. A states to B that he would like certain work done and asks B for an estimate. B says that he estimates he could do the work for $5,000. A says "I accept." Is there a contract?

11. A states to B that he would like certain plumbing work done and asks B for an estimate. B gives an estimate of $31,000. A says "Go ahead" and B does the work. Upon completion of the work B presents a bill for $42,000, which is in fact the reasonable price. May B collect $42,000?

12. Would the result be different in Problem 10 if A had said "Go ahead and do it at that price" and B did the work?

13. A writes to B: "I am eager to sell my house. I would consider $200,000 for it." B promptly replies: "I will buy your house for $200,000." Is there a contract?

14. On December 9 plaintiff asked defendant if he would consider selling certain property. Defendant stated that if plaintiff made an offer defendant would consider it. Plaintiff named a sum and defendant refused. Plaintiff then stated, "Will you accept $49,000?" Defendant answered, "I will not sell it for less than $56,000." Plaintiff said, "I accept." Was there a contract?

15. Defendant wrote to plaintiff: "In consequence of a rupture in the salt trade we are authorized to offer Michigan fine salt in full carload lots of 80 to 95 bbls. delivered at your city at 85per bbl. At this price it is a bargain as the price in general remains unchanged. Shall be pleased to receive your order." Plaintiff answered: "You may ship me 2,000 barrels Michigan fine salt, as offered in your letter." Was there a contract?

16. Defendant, a farmer who raises millet seed, wrote the following letter to a number of seed dealers including plaintiff: "I have 1800 bu. of millet seed of which I am mailing you a sample. This millet is recleaned and was grown on sod and is good seed. I want $2.25 per hundredweight for this seed f.o.b. Lowell." Plaintiff answered, "I accept your offer." Is there a contract?

17. Defendant knew that plaintiff was planning to bid as general contractor on a State construction project. Defendant sent an unsolicited letter to plaintiff, stating: "In connection with the above job we are pleased to quote a job price of $14,450 covering items 4, 11, 11a, 12, 13, 14, 16, 17, and 23." Plaintiff used defendant's quote in calculating its bid. Plaintiff was awarded the State contract and accepted defendant's "offer." Defendant argues that the quote was not an offer. Resolve the issue.

18. G, a general contractor, requested a bid from S, a subcontractor, to be used by G in connection with a particular project. S replied, "I can't give no bid, because I don't trust those specifications. But it should be about $1.25 per yard. It is O.K. if you want to use this quote and O.K. if you don't want to use it." G used it and was awarded the contract in connection with the project and now claims that S is bound to perform at $1.25 per yard. What result? Is S's quote an offer?

SECTION 3.   INDEFINITENESS

(Calamari & Perillo on Contracts §§ 1.7, 1.8, and 2.9)

HAINES v. CITY OF NEW YORK
Court of Appeals of New York, 1977.
41 N.Y.2d 769, 396 N.Y.S.2d 155, 364 N.E.2d 820.

GABRIELLI, JUDGE. In the early 1920's, respondent City of New York and intervenors Town of Hunter and Village of Tannersville embarked upon negotiations for the construction of a sewage system to serve the village and a portion of the town. These negotiations were prompted by the city's need and desire to prevent the discharge of untreated sewage by residents of the area into Gooseberry Creek, a stream which fed a reservoir of the city's water supply system in the Schoharie watershed.

In 1923, the Legislature enacted enabling legislation authorizing the city to enter into contracts with municipalities in the watershed area "for the purpose of providing, maintaining (and) operating systems and plants for the collection and disposal of sewage" (L.1923, ch. 630, § 1). The statute further provided that any such contracts would be subject to the approval of the New York City Board of Estimate and Apportionment.

The negotiations culminated in an agreement in 1924 between the city and intervenors. By this agreement, the city assumed the obligation of constructing a sewage system consisting of a sewage disposal plant and sewer mains and laterals, and agreed that "all costs of construction and subsequent operation, maintenance and repair of said sewerage system with the house connections thereof and said disposal works shall be at the expense" of the city. The agreement also required the city to extend the sewer lines when "necessitated by future growth and building constructions of the respective communities." The village and town were obligated to and did obtain the necessary easements for the construction of the system and sewage lines.

The Board of Estimate, on December 9, 1926, approved the agreement and authorized the issuance of $500,000 of "corporate stock" of the City of New York for construction of the system by appropriate resolution. It is interesting to here note that a modification of the original agreement occurred in 1925 wherein the village agreed to reimburse the city for a specified amount representing the expense of changing the location of certain sewer lines. The plant was completed and commenced operation in 1928. The city has continued to maintain the plant through the ensuing years and in 1958 expended $193,000 to rehabilitate and expand the treatment plant and facilities.

Presently, the average flow of the plant has increased from an initial figure of 118,000 gallons per day to over 600,000 gallons daily and the trial court found that the plant "was operating substantially in excess of design capacity." The city asserts, and it is not disputed by any of the parties in this action, that the system cannot bear any significant additional "loadings" because this would result in inadequate treatment of all the sewage and consequently harm the city's water supply. The instant controversy arose when plaintiff, who is the owner of a tract of unimproved land which he seeks to develop into 50 residential lots, applied to the city for permission to connect houses, which he intends to construct on the lots, to existing sewer lines. The city refused permission on the ground that it had no obligation to further expand the plant, which is presently operating at full capacity, to accommodate this new construction.

Plaintiff then commenced this action for declaratory and injunctive relief, in which intervenors town and village joined as plaintiffs, maintaining that the 1924 agreement is perpetual in duration and obligates the city to expend additional capital funds to enlarge the existing plant or build a new one to accommodate the present and future needs of the municipalities. Both the trial court and the Appellate Division, by a divided court, held in favor of plaintiff and intervenors concluding, that, while the contract did not call for perpetual performance, the city was bound to construct additional facilities to meet increased demand until such time as the village or town is legally obligated to maintain a sewage disposal system. Two members of the court dissented in part stating that the agreement should not be construed as requiring the city to construct new or additional facilities.

We conclude that the city is presently obligated to maintain the existing plant but is not required to expand that plant or construct any new facilities to accommodate plaintiff's substantial, or any other increased demands on the sewage system. The initial problem encountered in ascertaining the nature and extent of the city's obligation pursuant to the 1924 agreement, is its duration. We reject, as did the courts below, the plaintiff's contention that the city is perpetually bound under the agreement. The contract did not expressly provide for perpetual performance and both the trial court and the Appellate Division found that the parties did not so intend. Under these circumstances, the law will not imply that a contract calling for continuing performance is perpetual in duration (Mitler v. Freideberg, 32 Misc.2d 78, 85, 222 N.Y.S.2d 480, 488; Town of Readsboro v. Hoosac Tunnel & Wilmington R.R. Co., 2 Cir., 6 F.2d 733 (L. Hand, J.); 1 Williston, *Contracts* (3d ed.), § 38, p. 113).

On the other hand, the city's contention that the contract is terminable at will because it provides for no express duration should also be rejected. In the absence of an express term fixing the duration of a contract, the courts may inquire into the intent of the parties and supply the missing term if a duration may be fairly and reasonably fixed by the surrounding circumstances and the parties' intent (Warner–Lambert Pharm. Co. v. John J. Reynolds, Inc., [178 F.Supp. 655, 661, *aff'd*, 2 Cir., 280 F.2d 197]). It is generally agreed that where a duration may be fairly and reasonably supplied by implication, a contract is not terminable at will (1 *Williston, op.cit.*, p. 112; *see, also, Restatement, Contracts 2d* (Tent.Draft No. 7), § 230 [now § 204, ed.]).

While we have not previously had occasion to apply it, the weight of authority supports the related rule that where the parties have not clearly expressed the duration of a contract, the courts will imply that they intended performance to continue for a reasonable time (Colony Liq. Distrs. v. Daniel Distillery–Lem Motlow Prop., 22 A.D.2d 247, 249–250, 254 N.Y.S.2d 547, 549, 550 (Aulisi, J.); Simpson, *Contracts*, § 48, p. 74; 1 *Williston, op.cit.*, pp. 116–117). . . . Thus, we hold that it is reasonable to infer from the circumstances of the 1924 agreement that the parties intended the city to maintain the sewage disposal facility until such time as the city no longer needed or desired the water, the purity of which the plant was designed to insure. . . .

Having determined the duration of the city's obligation, the scope of its duty remains to be defined. By the agreement, the city obligated itself to build a specifically described disposal facility and to extend the lines of that facility to meet future increased demand. At the present time, the extension of those lines would result in the overloading of the system. Plaintiff claims that the city is required to build a new plant or expand the existing facility to overcome the problem. We disagree. The city should not be required to extend the lines to plaintiffs' property if to do so would overload the system and result in its inability to properly treat sewage. In providing for the extension of sewer lines, the contract does not obligate the city to provide sewage disposal services for properties in areas of the municipalities not presently served or even to new properties in areas which are presently served where to do so could reasonably be expected to significantly increase the demand on present plant facilities.

Thus, those paragraphs of the judgment which provide that the city is obligated to construct any additional facilities required to meet increased demand and that plaintiff is entitled to full use of the sewer lines should be stricken.

Accordingly, the order of the Appellate Division should be modified and the case remitted to Supreme Court, Greene County, for the entry of judgment in accordance with the opinion herein and, as so modified, affirmed, with costs to appellants against plaintiffs-respondents only.

WAGENSELLER v. SCOTTSDALE MEMORIAL HOSPITAL

Supreme Court of Arizona, En Banc, 1985.
147 Ariz. 370, 710 P.2d 1025.

FELDMAN, JUSTICE. Catherine Sue Wagenseller petitioned this court to review a decision of the court of appeals affirming in part the trial court's judgment in favor of Scottsdale Memorial Hospital and certain Hospital employees (defendants). The trial court had dismissed all causes of action on defendants' motion for summary judgment. The court of appeals affirmed in part and remanded, ruling that the only cause of action available to plaintiff was the claim against her supervisor, Kay Smith. . . . We granted review to consider the law of this state with regard to the employment-at-will doctrine. The issues we address are:

1. Is an employer's right to terminate an at-will employee limited by any rules which, if breached, give rise to a cause of action for wrongful termination?

2. If "public policy" or some other doctrine does form the basis for such an action, how is it determined?

3. Did the trial court err, in view of Leikvold v. Valley View Community Hospital, 141 Ariz. 544, 688 P.2d 170 (1984), when it determined as a matter of law that the terms of Scottsdale Memorial Hospital's personnel policy manual were not part of the employment contract?

4. Do employment contracts contain an implied covenant of "good faith and fair dealing," and, if so, what is the nature of the covenant? . . .

FACTUAL BACKGROUND

Catherine Wagenseller began her employment at Scottsdale Memorial Hospital as a staff nurse in March 1975, having been personally recruited by the manager of the emergency department, Kay Smith. Wagenseller was an "at-will" employee—one hired without specific contractual term. Smith was her supervisor. In August 1978, Wagenseller was assigned to the position of ambulance charge nurse, and approximately one year later was promoted to the position of paramedic coordinator, a newly approved management position in the emergency department. Three months later, on November 1, 1979, Wagenseller was terminated.

Most of the events surrounding Wagenseller's work at the Hospital and her subsequent termination are not disputed, although the parties differ in their interpretation of the inferences to be drawn from and the significance of these events. For more than four years, Smith and Wagenseller maintained a friendly, professional, working relationship. In May 1979, they joined a group consisting largely of personnel from other hospitals for an eight-day camping and rafting trip down the Colorado River. According to Wagenseller, "an uncomfortable feeling" developed between her and Smith as the trip progressed—a feeling that Wagenseller ascribed to "the behavior that Kay Smith was displaying." Wagenseller states that this included public urination, defecation and bathing, heavy drinking, and "grouping up" with other rafters. Wagenseller did not participate in any of these activities. She also refused to join in the group's staging of a parody of the song "Moon River," which allegedly concluded with members of the group "mooning" the audience. Smith and others allegedly performed the "Moon River" skit twice at the Hospital following the group's return from the river, but Wagenseller declined to participate there as well.

Wagenseller contends that her refusal to engage in these activities caused her relationship with Smith to deteriorate and was the proximate cause of her termination. She claims that following the river trip Smith began harassing her, using abusive language and embarrassing her in the company of other staff. Other emergency department staff reported a similar marked change in Smith's behavior toward Wagenseller after the trip, although Smith denied it.

Up to the time of the river trip, Wagenseller had received consistently favorable job performance evaluations. Two months before the trip, Smith completed an annual evaluation report in which she rated Wagenseller's performance as "exceed(ing) results expected," the second highest of five possible ratings. In August and October 1979, Wagenseller met first with Smith and then with Smith's successor, Jeannie Steindorff, to discuss some problems regarding her duties as paramedic coordinator and her attitude toward the job. On November 1, 1979, following an exit interview at which Wagenseller was asked to resign and refused, she was terminated.

She appealed her dismissal in letters to her supervisor and to the Hospital administrative and personnel department, answering the Hospital's stated reasons for her termination, claiming violations of the disciplinary procedure contained in the Hospital's personnel policy manual, and requesting reinstatement and other remedies. When this appeal was denied, Wagenseller brought suit against the Hospital, its personnel administrators, and her supervisor, Kay Smith.

Wagenseller, an "at-will" employee, contends that she was fired for reasons which contravene public policy and without legitimate cause related to job performance. She claims that her termination was wrongful, and that damages are recoverable under both tort and contract theories. The Hospital argues that an "at-will" employee may be fired for cause, without cause, or for "bad" cause. We hold that in the absence of contractual provision such an employee may be fired for good cause or for no cause, but not for "bad" cause.

THE EMPLOYMENT-AT-WILL DOCTRINE

History

As early as 1562, the English common law presumed that an employment contract containing an annual salary provision or computation was for a one-year term. Murg & Scharman, *Employment at Will: Do the Exceptions Overwhelm the Rule?* 23 B.C.L.Rev. 329, 332 (1982). . . .

. . . The late nineteenth century, however, brought the Industrial Revolution; with it came the decline of the master-servant relationship and the rise of the more impersonal employer-employee relationship. In apparent response to the economic changes sweeping the country, American courts abandoned the English rule and adopted the employment-at-will doctrine. *Murg & Scharman, supra,* at 334. This new doctrine gave the employer freedom to terminate an at-will employee for any reason, good or bad.

The at-will rule has been traced to an 1877 treatise by H.G. Wood, in which he wrote:

> With us the rule is inflexible, that a general or indefinite hiring is *prima facie* a hiring at will, and if the servant seeks to make it out a yearly hiring, the burden is upon him to establish it by proof.... (I)t is an indefinite hiring and is determinable at the will of either party....

H.G. Wood, *Law of Master and Servant* § 134 at 273 (1877). As commentators and courts later would point out, none of the four cases cited by Wood actually supported the rule. ...

However unsound its foundation, Wood's at-will doctrine was adopted by the New York courts in Martin v. New York Life Insurance Co., 148 N.Y. 117, 42 N.E. 416 (1895), and soon became the generally accepted American rule. In 1932, this court first adopted the rule for Arizona: "The general rule in regard to contracts for personal services, ... where no time limit is provided, is that they are terminable at pleasure by either party, or at most upon reasonable notice." Dover Copper Mining Co. v. Doenges, 40 Ariz. 349, 357, 12 P.2d 288, 291–92 (1932). Thus, an employer was free to fire an employee hired for an indefinite term "for good cause, for no cause, or even for cause morally wrong, without being thereby guilty of legal wrong." Blades, *Employment at Will v. Individual Freedom: On Limiting the Abusive Exercise of Employer Power,* 67 Colum.L.Rev. 1404, 1405 (1967).

Present–Day Status of the At–Will Rule

In recent years there has been apparent dissatisfaction with the absolutist formulation of the common law at-will rule. The Illinois Supreme Court is representative of courts that have acknowledged a need for a less mechanical application of the rule:

> With the rise of large corporations conducting specialized operations and employing relatively immobile workers who often have no other place to market their skills, recognition that the employer and employee do not stand on equal footing is realistic. In addition, unchecked employer power, like unchecked employee power, has been seen to present a distinct threat to the public policy carefully considered and adopted by society as a whole. As a result, it is now recognized that a proper balance must be maintained among the employer's interest in operating a business efficiently and profitably, the employee's interest in earning a livelihood, and society's interest in seeing its public policies carried out.

Palmateer v. International Harvester Co., 85 Ill.2d 124, 129, 52 Ill.Dec. 13, 15, 421 N.E.2d 876, 878 (1981). Today, courts in three-fifths of the states have recognized some form of a cause of action for wrongful discharge. Lopatka, *The Emerging Law of Wrongful Discharge—A Quadrennial Assessment of the Labor Law Issue of the 80s,* 40 Bus.Law. 1 (1984).

The trend has been to modify the at-will rule by creating exceptions
to its operation. Three general exceptions have developed. The most
widely accepted approach is the "public policy" exception, which permits
recovery upon a finding that the employer's conduct undermined some
important public policy. The second exception, based on contract, requires
proof of an implied-in-fact promise of employment for a specific duration,
as found in the circumstances surrounding the employment relationship,
including assurances of job security in company personnel manuals or
memoranda. Under the third approach, courts have found in the employment contract an implied-in-law covenant of "good faith and fair dealing"
and have held employers liable in both contract and tort for breach of that
covenant. Wagenseller raises all three doctrines.

THE PUBLIC POLICY EXCEPTION

The public policy exception to the at-will doctrine began with a
narrow rule permitting employees to sue their employers when a statute
expressly prohibited their discharge. *See* Kouff v. Bethlehem–Alameda
Shipyard, 90 Cal.App.2d 322, 202 P.2d 1059 (1949) (statute prohibiting
discharge for serving as an election officer). This formulation was then
expanded to include any discharge in violation of a statutory expression of
public policy. *See* Petermann v. Teamsters Local 396, 174 Cal.App.2d 184,
344 P.2d 25 (1959) (discharge for refusal to commit perjury). Courts later
allowed a cause of action for violation of public policy, even in the absence
of a specific statutory prohibition. *See* Nees v. Hocks, 272 Or. 210, 536
P.2d 512 (1975) (discharge for being absent from work to serve on jury
duty). The New Hampshire Supreme Court announced perhaps the most
expansive rule when it held an employer liable for discharging an employee who refused to go out with her foreman. The court concluded that
termination "motivated by bad faith or malice or based on retaliation is
not (in) the best interest of the economic system or the public good and
constitutes a breach of the employment contract." Monge v. Beebe Rubber
Co., 114 N.H. 130, 133, 316 A.2d 549, 551 (1974).[3] Although no other
court has gone this far, a majority of the states have now either recognized
a cause of action based on the public policy exception or have indicated
their willingness to consider it, given appropriate facts.[4] The key to an
employee's claim in all of these cases is the proper definition of a public
policy that has been violated by the employer's actions. . . .

It is difficult to justify this court's further adherence to a rule which
permits an employer to fire someone for "cause morally wrong." So far as
we can tell, no court faced with a termination that violated a "clear

3. Although *Monge* held that the aggrieved employee had a cause of action for breach of her
employment contract based on the employer's "bad faith," the New Hampshire Supreme Court
later restricted the reach of *Monge*, construing it to apply "only to a situation where an employee
is discharged because he performed an act that public policy would encourage, or refused to do
that which public policy condemned." Howard v. Dorr Woolen Co., 120 N.H. 295, 297, 414 A.2d
1273, 1274 (1980).

4. Twelve states have recognized a wrongful discharge cause of action for violation of public
policy; fifteen additional states have acknowledged a willingness to consider it, if presented with
appropriate facts. . . .

mandate of public policy'' has refused to adopt the public policy exception. Certainly, a court would be hard-pressed to find a rationale to hold that an employer could with impunity fire an employee who refused to commit perjury. Why should the law imply an agreement which would give the employer such power? It may be argued, of course, that our economic system functions best if employers are given wide latitude in dealing with employees. We assume that it is in the public interest that employers continue to have that freedom. We also believe, however, that the interests of the economic system will be fully served if employers may fire for good cause or without cause. The interests of society as a whole will be promoted if employers are forbidden to fire for cause which is "morally wrong."

We therefore adopt the public policy exception to the at-will termination rule. We hold that an employer may fire for good cause or for no cause. He may not fire for bad cause—that which violates public policy. To the extent that it is contrary to the foregoing, we overrule Dover Copper Mining Co. v. Doenges, *supra*.

We turn then to the questions of where "public policy" may be found and how it may be recognized and articulated. As the expressions of our founders and those we have elected to our legislature, our state's constitution and statutes embody the public conscience of the people of this state. It is thus in furtherance of their interests to hold that an employer may not with impunity violate the dictates of public policy found in the provisions of our statutory and constitutional law.

We do not believe, however, that expressions of public policy are contained only in the statutory and constitutional law, nor do we believe that all statements made in either a statute or the constitution are expressions of public policy. Turning first to the identification of other sources, we note our agreement with the following:

> Public policy is usually defined by the political branches of government. Something "against public policy" is something that the Legislature has forbidden. But the Legislature is not the only source of such policy. In common-law jurisdictions the courts too have been sources of law, always subject to legislative correction, and with progressively less freedom as legislation occupies a given field. It is the courts, to give one example, that originated the whole doctrine that certain kinds of businesses—common carriers and innkeepers—must serve the public without discrimination or preference. In this sense, then, courts make law, and they have done so for years.

Lucas v. Brown & Root, 736 F.2d 1202, 1205 (8th Cir.1984). ... Thus, we believe that reliance on prior judicial decisions, as part of the body of applicable common law, is appropriate, although we agree with the Hawaii Supreme Court that "courts should proceed cautiously if called upon to declare public policy absent some prior legislative or judicial expression on the subject." Parnar v. Americana Hotels, 65 Hawaii at 380, 652 P.2d at

631. Thus, we will look to the pronouncements of our founders, our legislature, and our courts to discern the public policy of this state.

All such pronouncements, however, will not provide the basis for a claim of wrongful discharge. Only those which have a singularly *public* purpose will have such force. . . . Where the interest involved is merely private or proprietary, the exception does not apply. In Pierce v. Ortho Pharmaceutical Corp., [84 N.J. 58, 417 A.2d 505 (1980)], for instance, the court held that the plaintiff did not have a cause of action for wrongful discharge based on her refusal to do certain research, where she had failed to articulate a clear public policy that had been violated. Citing the personal nature of Dr. Pierce's opposition, the court stated:

> Chaos would result if a single doctor engaged in research were allowed to determine, according to his or her individual conscience, whether a project should continue. An employee does not have a right to continued employment when he or she refuses to conduct research simply because it would contravene his or her personal morals. An employee at will who refuses to work in answer to a call of conscience should recognize that other employees and their employer might heed a different call.

84 N.J. at 75, 417 A.2d at 514. Although an employee facing such a quandary may refuse to do the work believed to violate her moral philosophy, she may not also claim a right to continued employment. *Id.*
. . .

However, some legal principles, whether statutory or decisional, have a discernible, comprehensive public purpose. A state's criminal code provides clear examples of such statutes. Thus, courts in other jurisdictions have consistently recognized a cause of action for a discharge in violation of a criminal statute. . . .

Although we do not limit our recognition of the public policy exception to cases involving a violation of a criminal statute, we do believe that our duty will seldom be clearer than when such a violation is involved. . . .

In the case before us, Wagenseller refused to participate in activities which arguably would have violated our indecent exposure statute, A.R.S. § 13–1402. She claims that she was fired because of this refusal. The statute provides:

§ 13–1402. Indecent exposure; classifications

A. A person commits indecent exposure if he or she exposes his or her genitals or anus or she exposes the areola or nipple of her breast or breasts and another person is present, and the defendant is reckless about whether such other person, as a reasonable person, would be offended or alarmed by the act.

B. Indecent exposure is a class 1 misdemeanor. Indecent exposure to a person under the age of fifteen years is a class 6 felony.

While this statute may not embody a policy which "strikes at the heart of a citizen's social right, duties and responsibilities" (*Palmateer, supra*) as clearly and forcefully as a statute prohibiting perjury, we believe that it was enacted to preserve and protect the commonly recognized sense of public privacy and decency. The statute does, therefore, recognize bodily privacy as a "citizen's social right." We disagree with the court of appeals' conclusion that a minor violation of the statute would not violate public policy. The nature of the act, and not its magnitude, is the issue. The legislature has already concluded that acts fitting the statutory description contravene the public policy of this state. We thus uphold this state's public policy by holding that termination for refusal to commit an act which might violate A.R.S. § 13–1402 may provide the basis of a claim for wrongful discharge. The relevant inquiry here is not whether the alleged "mooning" incidents were either felonies or misdemeanors or constituted purely technical violations of the statute, but whether they contravened the important public policy interests embodied in the law. The law enacted by the legislature establishes a clear policy that public exposure of one's anus or genitals is contrary to public standards of morality. We are compelled to conclude that termination of employment for refusal to participate in public exposure of one's buttocks[5] is a termination contrary to the policy of this state, even if, for instance, the employer might have grounds to believe that all of the onlookers were voyeurs and would not be offended. In this situation, there might be no crime, but there would be a violation of public policy to compel the employee to do an act ordinarily proscribed by the law.

From a theoretical standpoint, we emphasize that the "public policy exception" which we adopt does not require the court to make a new contract for the parties. In an at-will situation, the parties have made no express agreement regarding the duration of employment or the grounds for discharge. The common law has presumed that in so doing the parties have intended to allow termination at any time, with or without good cause. It might be more properly argued that the law has recognized an implied covenant to that effect. Whether it be presumption or implied contractual covenant, we do not disturb it. We simply do not raise a presumption or imply a covenant that would require an employee to do that which public policy forbids or refrain from doing that which it commands.

Thus, in an at-will hiring we continue to recognize the presumption or to imply the covenant of termination at the pleasure of either party, whether with or without cause. Firing for bad cause—one against public policy articulated by constitutional, statutory, or decisional law—is not a

---

5. We have little expertise in the techniques of mooning. We cannot say as a matter of law, therefore, whether mooning would always violate the statute by revealing the mooner's anus or genitalia. That question could only be determined, we suppose, by an examination of the facts of each case. We deem such an inquiry unseemly and unnecessary in a civil case. Compelled exposure of the bare buttocks, on pain of termination of employment, is a sufficient violation of the *policy* embodied in the statute to support the action, even if there would have been no technical violation of the statute.

right inherent in the at-will contract, or in any other contract, even if expressly provided. *See 1 A. Corbin, Contracts* § 7; 6A *A. Corbin, Contracts* §§ 1373–75 (1962). Such a termination violates rights guaranteed to the employee by law and is tortious. *See Prosser & Keeton on Torts* § 92 at 655 (5th ed. 1984).

THE "PERSONNEL POLICY MANUAL" EXCEPTION

Although an employment contract for an indefinite term is presumed to be terminable at will, that presumption, like any other presumption, is rebuttable by contrary evidence. . . .

An implied-in-fact contract term . . . is inferred from the statements or conduct of the parties. It is not a promise defined by the law, but one made by the parties, though not expressly. Courts have found such terms in an employer's policy statements regarding such things as job security and employee disciplinary procedures, holding that by the conduct of the parties these statements may become part of the contract, supplementing the verbalized at-will agreement, and thus limiting the employer's absolute right to discharge an at-will employee. Toussaint v. Blue Cross & Blue Shield, [408 Mich. 579, 292 N.W.2d 880 (1980)]. Arizona is among the jurisdictions that have recognized the implied-in-fact contract term as an exception to the at-will rule. In Leikvold v. Valley View Community Hospital, *supra*, this court held that a personnel manual can become part of an employment contract and remanded the cause for a jury determination as to whether the particular manual given to Leikvold had become part of her employment contract with Valley View. 141 Ariz. at 548, 688 P.2d at 174.

The relevant facts in the case before us are not dissimilar to those in *Leikvold*. In October 1978, Scottsdale Memorial Hospital established a four-step disciplinary procedure to achieve the Hospital's stated policy of "provid(ing) fair and consistent discipline as required to assist with the improvement of employees' behavior or performance." Subject to 32 listed exceptions, prior to being terminated a Hospital employee must be given a verbal warning, a written performance warning, a letter of formal reprimand, and a notice of dismissal. The manual further qualifies the mandatory procedure by providing that the 32 exceptions "are not inclusive and are only guidelines." In appealing her dismissal, Wagenseller cited violations of this procedure, but the trial court ruled as a matter of law that the manual had not become part of the employment contract between Wagenseller and the Hospital. The court of appeals held that the Hospital's failure to follow the four-step disciplinary procedure did not violate Wagenseller's contract rights because she failed to prove her reliance on the procedure as a part of her employment contract. We disagree with both of these rulings.

First, we need look only to *Leikvold* for the rule governing the determination of whether a particular statement by an employer becomes a part of an employment contract:

> Whether any particular personnel manual modifies any particular employment-at-will relationship and becomes part of the particular employment contract is a *question of fact*. Evidence relevant to this factual decision includes the language used in the personnel manual as well as the employer's course of conduct and oral representations regarding it.

141 Ariz. at 548, 688 P.2d at 174 (emphasis added). Thus, we held in *Leikvold* that entry of summary judgment was inappropriate "(b)ecause a material question—whether the policies manual was incorporated into and became part of the terms of the employment contract—remain(ed) in dispute." *Id.* The court may determine as a matter of law the proper construction of contract terms which are "clear and unambiguous." *Id.* Here, the court of appeals ruled, in effect, that the Hospital had adequately disclaimed any liability for failing to follow the procedure it had established. It found this disclaimer in the final item in the Hospital's list of exceptions to its disciplinary procedure: "20. These major and minor infractions are not inclusive and are only guidelines." The court concluded that the effect of this "clear" and "conspicuous" provision was "to create, by its terms, no rights at all."

We do not believe this document, read in its entirety, has the clarity that the court of appeals attributed to its individual portions. One reading the document might well infer that the Hospital had established a procedure that would generally apply in disciplinary actions taken against employees. Although such a person would also note the long list of exceptions, he might not conclude from reading the list that an exception would apply in every case so as to swallow the general rule completely. We do not believe that the provision for unarticulated exceptions destroys the entire articulated general policy as a matter of law. Not only does such a result defy common sense, it runs afoul of our reasoning in *Leikvold,* where we addressed this problem directly:

> Employers are certainly free to issue no personnel manual at all or to issue a personnel manual that clearly and conspicuously tells their employees that the manual is not part of the employment contract and that their jobs are terminable at the will of the employer with or without reason. Such actions, either not issuing a personnel manual or issuing one with clear language of limitation, instill no reasonable expectations of job security and do not give employees any reason to rely on representations in the manual. However, if an employer does choose to issue a policy statement, in a manual or otherwise, and, by its language or by the employer's actions, encourages reliance thereon, the employer cannot be free to only selectively abide by it. Having announced a policy, the employer may not treat it as illusory.

141 Ariz. at 548, 688 P.2d at 174. . . .

The general rule is that the determination whether in a particular case a promise should be implied in fact is a question of fact. 1 A. *Corbin, supra,* § 17 at 38; *see also* Leikvold, 141 Ariz. at 548, 688 P.2d at 174. . . .

We believe that reasonable persons could differ in the inferences and conclusions they would draw from the Hospital's published manual regarding disciplinary policy and procedure. Thus, there are questions of fact as to whether this policy and procedure became a part of Wagenseller's employment contract. *See* Leikvold, 141 Ariz. at 548, 688 P.2d at 174. The trial court therefore erred in granting summary judgment on this issue.

The court of appeals' resolution of the reliance issue also was incorrect. A party may enforce a contractual provision without showing reliance. *Leikvold* does not require a plaintiff employee to show reliance in fact. The employee's reliance on an announced policy is only one of several factors that are relevant in determining whether a particular policy was intended by the parties to modify an at-will agreement. The employer's course of conduct and oral representations regarding the policy, as well as the words of the policy itself, also may provide evidence of such a modification. Leikvold, 141 Ariz. at 548, 688 P.2d at 174.

The "Good Faith and Fair Dealing" Exception

We turn next to a consideration of implied-in-law contract terms which may limit an employer's right to discharge an at-will employee. Wagenseller claims that discharge without good cause breaches the implied-in-law covenant of good faith and fair dealing contained in every contract. *See Restatement (Second) of Contracts § 205*, Savoca Masonry Co. v. Homes & Son Construction Co., 112 Ariz. 392, 396, 542 P.2d 817, 821 (1975). *See also* 3A. Corbin, *supra*, § 541 at 97, 5 S. Williston, *The Law of Contracts* § 670 at 159 (3d ed. 1961). In the context of this case, she argues that discharge without good cause violates the covenant of good faith and is, therefore, wrongful. The covenant requires that neither party do anything that will injure the right of the other to receive the benefits of their agreement. Comunale v. Traders & General Insurance Co., 50 Cal.2d 654, 658, 328 P.2d 198, 200 (1958). The duty not to act in bad faith or deal unfairly thus becomes a part of the contract, and, as with any other element of the contract, the remedy for its breach generally is on the contract itself. Zancanaro v. Cross, 85 Ariz. 394, 339 P.2d 746 (1959). In certain circumstances, breach of contract, including breach of the covenant of good faith and fair dealing, may provide the basis for a tort claim. Noble v. National American Life Insurance Co., 128 Ariz. 188, 190, 624 P.2d 866, 868 (1981); Seamen's Direct Buying Service v. Standard Oil Co., 36 Cal.3d 752, 206 Cal.Rptr. 354, 686 P.2d 1158 (1984).

The question whether a duty to terminate only for good cause should be implied into all employment-at-will contracts has received much attention in the case law and other literature. *See, e.g.*, Pugh v. See's Candies, 116 Cal.App.3d 311, 171 Cal.Rptr. 917 (1981); Diamond, *The Tort of Bad Faith Breach of Contract: When, If at All, Should It Be Extended Beyond Insurance Transactions?* 64 Marq.L.Rev. 425 (1981); *Murg & Scharman, supra*, at 361–67. Courts have generally rejected the invitation to imply such a duty in employment contracts, voicing the concern that to do so would place undue restrictions on management and would infringe the employer's "legitimate exercise of management discretion." Pugh v. See's Candies, 116 Cal.App.3d at 330, 171 Cal.Rptr. at 928. We think this concern is appropriate.

California has come closer than any other jurisdiction to implying a good cause duty in all employment-at-will contracts. The case most often cited for this rule is Cleary v. American Airlines, 111 Cal.App.3d 443, 168 Cal.Rptr. 722 (1980). In *Cleary,* the plaintiff was discharged after eighteen years of employment with the defendant. He alleged that the discharge violated both an express policy of the company regarding employee grievances and the implied covenant of good faith and fair dealing. *Id.* at 448, 168 Cal.Rptr. at 725. The court agreed:

> Termination of employment without legal cause after such a period of time offends the implied-in-law covenant of good faith and fair dealing contained in all contracts, including employment contracts. As a result of this covenant, a duty arose on the part of the employer ... to do nothing which would deprive plaintiff, the employee, of the benefits of the employment bargain—benefits described in the complaint as having accrued during plaintiff's 18 years of employment.

Id. at 455, 168 Cal.Rptr. at 729. Thus, the court held that the employer could not discharge this employee without good cause, based on both the longevity of the employee's service and the express policy of the employer. *Id.* If the plaintiff could sustain his burden of proving that he had been terminated unjustly, the court held further that his cause of action would sound in tort as well as contract. *Id.* Only one other court has allowed a tort recovery for breach of the implied covenant of good faith in an employment contract, and, in that case as well as in *Cleary,* the court relied in part upon the existence of an employee handbook on which plaintiff had relied. Gates v. Life of Montana Insurance Co., [638 P.2d 1063 (Mont. 1982)].....

We find neither the logic of the California cases nor their factual circumstances compelling for recognition of so broad a rule in the case before us. Were we to adopt such a rule, we fear that we would tread perilously close to abolishing completely the at-will doctrine and establishing by judicial fiat the benefits which employees can and should get *only* through collective bargaining agreements or tenure provisions. ...

In reaching this conclusion, however, we do not feel that we should treat employment contracts as a special type of agreement in which the law refuses to imply the covenant of good faith and fair dealing that it implies in all other contracts. As we noted above, the implied-in-law covenant of good faith and fair dealing protects the right of the parties to an agreement to receive the benefits of the agreement that they have entered into. The denial of a party's right to those benefits, whatever they are, will breach the duty of good faith implicit in the contract. Thus, the relevant inquiry always will focus on the contract itself, to determine what the parties did agree to. In the case of an employment-at-will contract, it may be said that the parties have agreed, for example, that the employee will do the work required by the employer and that the employer will provide the necessary working conditions and pay the employee for work done. What cannot be said is that one of the agreed benefits to the at-will employee is a guarantee of continued employment or tenure. The very nature of the at-will agreement precludes any claim for a prospective benefit. Either employer or employee may terminate the contract at any time.

We do, however, recognize an implied covenant of good faith and fair dealing in the employment-at-will contract, although that covenant does not create a duty for the employer to terminate the employee only for good cause. The covenant does not protect the employee from a "no cause" termination because tenure was never a benefit inherent in the at-will agreement. The covenant does protect an employee from a discharge based on an employer's desire to avoid the payment of benefits already earned by the employee, such as the sales commissions in Fortune [v. National Cash Register, 364 N.E.2d 1251 (Mass. 1977)], but not the tenure required to earn the pension and retirement benefits in *Cleary, supra*. Thus, plaintiff here has a right to receive the benefits that were a part of her employment agreement with defendant Hospital. To the extent, however, that the benefits represent a claim for prospective employment, her claim must fail. The terminable-at-will contract between her and the Hospital made no promise of continued employment. To the contrary, it was, by its nature, subject to termination by either party at any time, subject only to the legal prohibition that she could not be fired for reasons which contravene public policy.

Thus, because we are concerned not to place undue restrictions on the employer's discretion in managing his workforce and because tenure is contrary to the bargain in an at-will contract, we reject the argument that a no cause termination breaches the implied covenant of good faith and fair dealing in an employment-at-will relationship. . . .

SUMMARY AND CONCLUSIONS

The trial court granted summary judgment against Wagenseller on the count alleging the tort of wrongful discharge in violation of public policy. We adopt the "public policy" exception to the at-will termination rule and hold that the trial court erred in granting judgment against plaintiff on this theory. On remand plaintiff will be entitled to a jury trial if she can make a *prima facie* showing that her termination was caused by her refusal to perform some act contrary to public policy, or her performance of some act which, as a matter of public policy, she had a right to do. The obverse, however, is that mere dispute over an issue involving a question of public policy is not equivalent to establishing causation as a matter of law and will not automatically entitle plaintiff to judgment. In the face of conflicting evidence or inferences as to the actual reason for termination, the question of causation will be a question of fact.

The trial court granted summary judgment against Wagenseller on the count alleging breach of implied-in-fact provisions of the contract. We hold that this was error. On this record, there is a jury question as to whether the provisions of the employment manual were part of the contract of employment.

We affirm the grant of summary judgment on the count seeking recovery for breach of the implied covenant of good faith and fair dealing. We recognize that covenant as part of this and other contracts, but do not construe it to give either party to the contract rights—such as tenure— different from those for which they contracted. . . .

For the foregoing reasons, we affirm in part and reverse in part. The decision of the court of appeals is vacated and the case remanded to the trial court for proceedings not inconsistent with this opinion.

[The dissenting and specially concurring opinion of HOLOHAN, C.J., and the supplemental opinion of FELDMAN, J., are omitted. Ed.]

Editor's note: *Wagenseller* was superceded by statute, A.R.S. § 23–1501, effective 20, 1996, which limited the grounds under which an employee could claim wrongful discharge.

JOSEPH MARTIN, JR., DELICATESSEN
v. SCHUMACHER

Court of Appeals of New York, 1981.
52 N.Y.2d 105, 436 N.Y.S.2d 247, 417 N.E.2d 541.

FUCHSBERG, JUDGE. This case raises an issue fundamental to the law of contracts. It calls upon us to review a decision of the Appellate Division, 70 A.D.2d 1, 419 N.Y.S.2d 558, which held that a realty lease's provision that the rent for a renewal period was "to be agreed upon" may be enforceable.

The pertinent factual and procedural contexts in which the case reaches this court are uncomplicated. In 1973, the appellant, as landlord, leased a retail store to the respondent for a five-year term at a rent graduated upwards from $500 per month for the first year to $650 for the fifth. The renewal clause stated that

> (t)he Tenant may renew this lease for an additional period of five years at annual rentals to be agreed upon; Tenant shall give Landlord thirty (30) days written notice, to be mailed certified mail, return receipt requested, of the intention to exercise such right.

It is not disputed that the tenant gave timely notice of its desire to renew or that, once the landlord made it clear that he would do so only at a rental starting at $900 a month, the tenant engaged an appraiser who opined that a fair market rental value would be $545.41.

The tenant thereupon commenced an action for specific performance in Supreme Court, Suffolk County, to compel the landlord to extend the lease for the additional term at the appraiser's figure or such other sum as the court would decide was reasonable. For his part, the landlord in due course brought a holdover proceeding in the local District Court to evict the tenant. On the landlord's motion for summary judgment, the Supreme Court, holding that a bald agreement to agree on a future rental was unenforceable for uncertainty as a matter of law, dismissed the tenant's complaint. Concordantly, it denied as moot the tenant's motion to remove the District Court case to the Supreme Court and to consolidate the two suits.

It was on appeal by the tenant from these orders that the Appellate Division, expressly overruling an established line of cases in the process, reinstated the tenant's complaint and granted consolidation. In so doing, it reasoned that "a renewal clause in a lease providing for future agreement on the rent to be paid during the renewal term is enforceable if it is established that the parties' intent was not to terminate in the event of a failure to agree." It went on to provide that, if the tenant met that burden, the trial court could proceed to set a "reasonable rent." One of the Justices, concurring, would have eliminated the first step and required the trial court to proceed directly to the fixation of the rent. Each party now appeals by leave of the Appellate Division. . . . The tenant seeks only a modification adopting the concurrer's position. The question formally certified to us by the Appellate Division is simply whether its order was properly made. Since we conclude that the disposition at the Supreme Court was the correct one, our answer must be in the negative.

We begin our analysis with the basic observation that, unless otherwise mandated by law (*e.g.*, residential emergency rent control statutes), a contract is a private "ordering" in which a party binds himself to do, or not to do, a particular thing (Fletcher v. Peck, 6 Cranch (10 U.S.) 87, 136, 3 L.Ed. 162. Hart and Sachs, *Legal Process*, 147–148 (1958)). This liberty is no right at all if it is not accompanied by freedom not to contract. The corollary is that, before one may secure redress in our courts because another has failed to honor a promise, it must appear that the promisee assented to the obligation in question.

It also follows that, before the power of law can be invoked to enforce a promise, it must be sufficiently certain and specific so that what was promised can be ascertained. Otherwise, a court, in intervening, would be imposing its own conception of what the parties should or might have undertaken, rather than confining itself to the implementation of a bargain to which they have mutually committed themselves. Thus, definiteness as to material matters is of the very essence in contract law. Impenetrable vagueness and uncertainty will not do (1 Corbin, *Contracts*, § 95, p 394; *Restatement, Contracts 2d*, § 32, Comment a).

Dictated by these principles, it is rightfully well settled in the common law of contracts in this State that a mere agreement to agree, in which a material term is left for future negotiations, is unenforceable (Willmott v. Giarraputo, 5 N.Y.2d 250, 253, 184 N.Y.S.2d 97). This is especially true of the amount to be paid for the sale or lease of real property (*see* Forma v.

Moran, 273 App.Div. 818, 76 N.Y.S.2d 232). The rule applies all the more, and not the less, when, as here, the extraordinary remedy of specific performance is sought (11 Williston, *Contracts* (Jaeger 3d ed.), § 1424; Pomeroy, *Equity Jurisprudence*, § 1405).

This is not to say that the requirement for definiteness in the case before us now could only have been met by explicit expression of the rent to be paid. The concern is with substance, not form. It certainly would have sufficed, for instance, if a methodology for determining the rent was to be found within the four corners of the lease, for a rent so arrived at would have been the end product of agreement between the parties themselves. Nor would the agreement have failed for indefiniteness because it invited recourse to an objective extrinsic event, condition or standard on which the amount was made to depend. All of these, *inter alia*, would have come within the embrace of the maxim that what can be made certain is certain (9 Coke 47a). (*Cf.* Backer Mgt. Corp. v. Acme Quilting Co., 46 N.Y.2d 211, 219, 413 N.Y.S.2d 135, 385 N.E.2d 1062 (escalation of rent keyed to building employees' future wage increases); City of Hope v. Fisk Bldg. Assoc., 63 A.D.2d 946, 406 N.Y.S.2d 472 (rental increase to be adjusted for upward movement in US Consumer Price Index).)

But the renewal clause here in fact contains no such ingredients. Its unrevealing, unamplified language speaks to no more than "annual rentals to be agreed upon." Its simple words leave no room for legal construction or resolution of ambiguity. Neither tenant nor landlord is bound to any formula. There is not so much as a hint at a commitment to be bound by the "fair market rental value" which the tenant's expert reported or the "reasonable rent" the Appellate Division would impose, much less any definition of either. Nowhere is there an inkling that either of the parties directly or indirectly assented, upon accepting the clause, to subordinate the figure on which it ultimately would insist, to one fixed judicially, as the Appellate Division decreed be done, or, for that matter, by an arbitrator or other third party.

Finally, in this context, we note that the tenant's reliance on May Metropolitan Corp. v. May Oil Burner Corp., 290 N.Y. 260, 49 N.E.2d 13 is misplaced. There the parties had executed a franchise agreement for the sale of oil burners. The contract provided for annual renewal, at which time each year's sales quota was "to be mutually agreed upon." In holding that the defendant's motion for summary judgment should have been denied, the court indicated that the plaintiff should be given an opportunity to establish that a series of annual renewals had ripened into a course of dealing from which it might be possible to give meaning to an otherwise uncertain term. This decision, in the more fluid sales setting in which it occurred, may be seen as a precursor to the subsequently enacted Uniform Commercial Code's treatment of open terms in contracts for the sale of goods (*see* Uniform Commercial Code, § 1–205, subd. (1) [Rev. § 1–303(b), ed.]; § 2–204, subd. (3); *see, also, Restatement, Contracts 2d*, § 249). As the tenant candidly concedes, the code, by its very terms, is limited to the sale of goods. The *May* case is therefore not applicable to real estate contracts. Stability is a hallmark of the law controlling such transactions (*see* Heyert v. Orange & Rockland Utilities, 17 N.Y.2d 352, 362, 271 N.Y.S.2d 201).

For all these reasons, the order of the Appellate Division should be reversed, with costs, and the orders of the Supreme Court, Suffolk County, reinstated. The certified question, therefore, should be answered in the negative. As to the plaintiff's appeal, since that party was not aggrieved by the order of the Appellate Division, the appeal should be dismissed (CPLR 5511), without costs.

MEYER, JUDGE (concurring). While I concur in the result because the facts of this case do not fit the rule of May Metropolitan Corp. v. May Oil Burner Corp., 290 N.Y. 260, 49 N.E.2d 13, I cannot concur in the majority's rejection of that case as necessarily inapplicable to litigation concerning leases. That the setting of that case was commercial and that its principle is now incorporated in a statute (the Uniform Commercial Code) which by its terms is not applicable to real estate is irrelevant to the question whether the principle can be applied in real estate cases.

As we recognized in Farrell Lines v. City of New York, 30 N.Y.2d 76, 82, 330 N.Y.S.2d 358, quoting from A.Z.A. Realty Corp. v. Harrigan's Cafe, 113 Misc 141, 147, 185 N.Y.S. 212: "An agreement of lease possesses no peculiar sanctity requiring the application of rules of construction different from those applicable to an ordinary contract." To the extent that the majority opinion can be read as holding that no course of dealing between the parties to a lease could make a clause providing for renewal at a rental "to be agreed upon" enforceable I do not concur.

JASEN, JUDGE (dissenting in part). While I recognize that the traditional rule is that a provision for renewal of a lease must be "certain" in order to render it binding and enforceable, in my view the better rule would be that if the tenant can establish its entitlement to renewal under the lease, the mere presence of a provision calling for renewal at "rentals to be agreed upon" should not prevent judicial intervention to fix rent at a reasonable rate in order to avoid a forfeiture. Therefore, I would affirm the order of the Appellate Division. . . .

BMC INDUSTRIES, INC. v. BARTH INDUSTRIES, INC.

United States Court of Appeals, Eleventh Circuit, 1998.
160 F.3d 1322.

TJOFLAT, CIRCUIT JUDGE: This appeal arises from a contract entered into between BMC Industries, Inc., and Barth Industries, Inc., for the design, manufacture, and installation of equipment to automate BMC's production line for unfinished eyeglass lenses. Eighteen months after the delivery date set out in the contract had passed, BMC filed suit against Barth for breach of contract. Barth, in turn, counterclaimed for breach of contract. . . .

A jury resolved the . . . issues in favor of BMC, and returned a verdict of $3 million against Barth. . . . After denying Barth's . . . alternative motions for judgment as a matter of law and for a new trial, the district court rendered judgment in accordance with the jury's [verdict], and Barth . . . appealed. We affirm the district court's decision denying Barth judgment as a matter of law. We conclude, however, that the court erroneously instructed the jury on the contract issues, and therefore vacate the judgment against Barth and remand the case for a new trial on these issues. . . .

BMC, through its Vision–Ease division, manufactures semi-finished polymer opthalmic [*sic*] lenses that are used in the production of eyeglasses. . . . In order to decrease labor costs, and thereby remain competitive with other lens manufacturers who were utilizing cheaper foreign labor, BMC decided to become the first company to automate portions of its lens manufacturing process. . . . Barth and BMC entered into a contract (the "Contract") which provided that Barth would "design, fabricate, debug/test and supervise field installation and start up of equipment to automate the operations of mold assembly declipping, clip transport, mold assembly clipping, and mold filling." The Contract, which stated that it was governed by Florida law, listed a price of $515,200 and provided for delivery of four automated production lines by June 1987. . . .

On appeal, Barth contends that the district court erred when it concluded that the UCC did not apply to the Contract. . . .

The district court held that the Contract was predominantly for services rather than goods, and that the UCC was therefore inapplicable. We disagree.

The UCC's Article 2 only applies to "transactions in goods." Fla. Stat. ch. 672–102 [UCC § 2–102] (1997). Goods are defined as "all things (including specially manufactured goods) which are movable at the time of identification to the contract for sale other than the money in which the price is to be paid, investment securities (chapter 678) and things in action." Fla. Stat. ch. 672.105(1) [UCC § 2–105] (1997).[12] A contract that is exclusively for services, therefore, is not governed by Article 2. Courts are frequently faced, however, with contracts involving both goods and services—so-called "hybrid" contracts. Most courts follow the "predominant factor" test to determine whether such hybrid contracts are transactions in goods, and therefore covered by the UCC, or transactions in services, and therefore excluded.[13] *See* Bonebrake v. Cox, 499 F.2d 951,

---

12. "Identification to the contract" occurs "when goods are shipped, marked or otherwise designated by the seller as goods to which the contract refers." Fla. Stat. ch. 672.501(1)(b) [UCC § 2–501(1)(b)] (1997). . . . [In footnote 15, the court continues (Ed.): Mobility is measured as of the time the goods are identified to the contract rather than after the contract is completed. Consequently, equipment or materials that were movable, but were installed and became immobile fixtures as part of the contract, are still "movable" within the UCC's meaning. *See* Bonebrake, 499 F.2d at 959 n. 12. . . .]

13. A few courts do not categorize hybrid contracts as either transactions in goods or services, but rather apply the UCC only to the sale of goods elements of the contract. *See, e.g.,* Foster v. Colorado Radio Corp., 381 F.2d 222, 226 (10th Cir.1967).

960 (8th Cir.1974). Under this test, the court determines "whether their predominant factor, their thrust, their purpose, reasonably stated, is the rendition of service, with goods incidentally involved (*e.g.*, contract with artist for painting) or is a transaction of sale, with labor incidentally involved (*e.g.*, installation of a water heater in a bathroom)."[14] *Id.* At least one Florida court has implicitly adopted the predominant factor test. *See* United States Fidelity & Guar. Co. v. North Am. Steel Corp., 335 So.2d 18, 21 (Fla. 2d DCA 1976) ("Since the predominate nature of the transaction was the furnishing of a product rather than services, we believe that the fabricated pipe could properly be characterized as goods.").

Although courts generally have not found any single factor determinative in classifying a hybrid contract as one for goods or services, courts find several aspects of a contract particularly significant. First, the language of the contract itself provides insight into whether the parties believed the goods or services were the more important element of their agreement. Contractual language that refers to the transaction as a "purchase," for example, or identifies the parties as the "buyer" and "seller," indicates that the transaction is for goods rather than services. *See* Bonebrake, 499 F.2d at 958 (stating that language referring to "equipment" is peculiar to goods rather than services); Bailey v. Montgomery Ward & Co., 690 P.2d 1280, 1282 (Colo.Ct.App.1984) (holding that a contract that identifies the transaction as a "purchase" and one of the parties as the "customer" signals a transaction in goods); Meeker v. Hamilton Grain Elevator Co., 442 N.E.2d 921, 923 (Ill.App.Ct.1982) (stating that a contract that calls the parties "seller" and "purchaser" indicates a contract for goods).

Courts also examine the manner in which the transaction was billed; when the contract price does not include the cost of services, or the charge for goods exceeds that for services, the contract is more likely to be for goods. *See* Triangle Underwriters Inc. v. Honeywell, 604 F.2d 737, 743 (2d Cir.1979) (stating that a bill that does not include services indicates a contract for goods); Lincoln Pulp & Paper Co. v. Dravo Corp., 436 F.Supp. 262, 275 & n. 15 (D.Me.1977) (holding that the contract at issue was for services after noting that the bill did not allocate costs between services and goods, and the evidence showed that the cost of the goods was less than half of the contract price). . . .

In this case, the district court relied primarily on *Lincoln Pulp & Paper* for its conclusion that the contract was for services rather than goods. The contract at issue in *Lincoln Pulp & Paper* involved the design and construction of a heat and chemical recovery unit in a pulp mill. The district court noted that, similar to *Lincoln Pulp & Paper,* the Contract obligated Barth to design, manufacture, test, and construct equipment, and also that the Contract's price did not allocate expenses between

14. We note that at least some courts believe the trend is to apply Article 2 to hybrid contracts. *See* Cambridge Plating Co. v. Napco, Inc., 991 F.2d 21, 24 (1st Cir.1993); United States ex rel. Union Bldg. Materials Corp. v. Haas & Haynie Corp., 577 F.2d 568, 572 n. 2 (9th Cir.1978).

services and materials. The district court concluded that this case was sufficiently analogous to *Lincoln Pulp & Paper* to warrant the same result: a determination that the Contract was for services rather than goods.

The question whether a contract is predominantly for goods or services is generally one of fact. *See* Allmand Assocs., Inc. v. Hercules, Inc., 960 F.Supp. 1216, 1223 (E.D.Mich.1997). When there is no genuine issue of material fact concerning the contract's provisions, however, a court may determine the issue as a matter of law. *See id.* Concluding that there are no material issues of fact as to the terms of the contract, the district court decided as a matter of law that the contract was for services. We review questions of law *de novo*. *See* Preserve Endangered Areas of Cobb's History, Inc. v. United States Army Corps of Eng'rs, 87 F.3d 1242, 1246 (11th Cir.1996).

Applying the "predominant factor" test to the Contract, we conclude that it was predominantly a transaction in goods. We reach this conclusion based on the contractual language, the circumstances surrounding the Contract, and the nature of the goods at issue.

Our starting point is the language of the Contract itself, which provides a number of indicia that the parties intended a contract for goods rather than services. First, the Contract is titled "PURCHASE ORDER," a reference that is used repeatedly throughout the document. This title is most instructive, as the parties have chosen to identify their agreement with a name that is almost exclusively used for transactions in goods. Second, the parties refer to themselves in the Contract as the "Buyer" and "Seller." Third, the Contract states that it is a purchase order "for the fabrication and installation of automated *equipment*." (emphasis added). All of this contractual language is "peculiar to goods, not services," Bonebrake, 499 F.2d at 958, and indicates that the parties had a contract for goods in mind.

[In footnote 16 of the opinion, the court found it a significant, though not dispositive, factor that the goods at issue were movable when completed and delivered to Barth, "unlike some contracts that only involve movable materials, which are subsequently used to construct an immovable fixture (such as a house or swimming pool)." Ed.]

Lincoln Pulp & Paper is distinguishable from this case. The district court stated that the Contract price, similar to *Lincoln Pulp & Paper*, does not allocate costs between services and goods. The district court failed to note, however, that the Contract allocates payments according to delivery of automated equipment; the Contract's payment schedule calls for the delivery and acceptance of each automated equipment line to be met by a $70,050 payment from BMC. If the Contract price were being paid predominantly for Barth's design and engineering services as BMC claims, then the parties would have pegged payments to completion of the engineering and design services, not to the delivery of equipment. Furthermore, while the cost of services made up over half of the contract price in *Lincoln Pulp & Paper,* the opposite appears to be true in this case. A total of $280,200, which is over half of the contract price, is pegged to the delivery of equipment.

Finally, we note that the court in *Lincoln Pulp & Paper* stated that "(a) sale of equipment is not removed from the scope of Article 2 merely because the equipment was specially designed and manufactured before delivery or installed by the supplier." 436 F.Supp. at 276 n. 16. In fact, it is not surprising that the Barth–BMC Contract included such a significant services element (i.e., design and manufacturing). Because no other company had successfully automated its eyeglass lens production, Barth had to spend considerable time designing this first-of-its-kind machinery. This necessary services element, however, does not remove the Contract from the category of agreements for specially designed and manufactured equipment to which Article 2 applies.

The other two cases on which BMC relies are also inapposite. Both cases involved parties that clearly contemplated a contract for services. The first case, Wells v. 10–X Mfg. Co., 609 F.2d 248 (6th Cir.1979), involved the production of cloth hunting shirts. In that case, however, the buyer provided all of the materials (except thread) that the manufacturer used to produce the clothing. *Id.* at 225. Consequently, the manufacturer did not sell goods, only the service of turning the materials into a finished product.

The other case BMC cites, Inhabitants of the City of Saco v. General Elec. Co., 779 F.Supp. 186 (D.Me.1991), involved a contract for the design and construction of a solid waste disposal facility. That case is also distinguishable because it involved a typical construction contract for a non-movable product—the disposal facility. The only movable goods were the materials that were used to construct the immobile structure. Even more significantly, the contractual language in that case clearly identified the contract as a transaction in services. The contract stated that its purpose was "for the furnishing of *services* in Phase I of the project, and 'to establish the conditions on which *Contractor* (GE) will propose to furnish *services* under Phase II'." *Id.* at 197 (first and second emphases added). Not only did the language state that the contract was for services, it also referred to one of the parties as the "Contractor," a term typically used in services transactions. . . .

For the foregoing reasons, we hold that the district court erred in concluding that the UCC did not apply to the Contract. . . . We therefore VACATE the district court's judgment against Barth and REMAND the case to the district court for retrial of BMC's claims against Barth as well as Barth's counterclaims in accordance with the UCC. . . .

SOUTHWEST ENGINEERING CO. v. MARTIN TRACTOR CO., INC.

Supreme Court of Kansas, 1970.
205 Kan. 684, 473 P.2d 18.

FONTRON, JUSTICE. This is an action to recover damages for breach of contract. Trial was had to the court which entered judgment in favor of the plaintiff. The defendant has appealed.

Southwest Engineering Company, Inc., the plaintiff, is a Missouri corporation engaged in general contracting work, while the defendant, Martin Tractor Company, Inc., is a Kansas corporation. The two parties will be referred to hereafter either as plaintiff, or Southwest, on the one hand and defendant, or Martin, on the other.

We glean from the record that in April, 1966, the plaintiff was interested in submitting a bid to the United States Corps of Engineers for the construction of certain runway lighting facilities at McConnell Air Force Base at Wichita. However, before submitting a bid, and on April 11, 1966, the plaintiff's construction superintendent, Mr. R.E. Cloepfil, called the manager of Martin's engine department, Mr. Ken Hurt, who at the time was at Colby, asking for a price on a standby generator and accessory equipment. Mr. Hurt replied that he would phone him back from Topeka, which he did the next day, quoting a price of $18,500. This quotation was re-confirmed by Hurt over the phone on April 13.

Southwest submitted its bid on April 14, 1966, using Hurt's figure of $18,500 for the generator equipment, and its bid was accepted. On April 20, Southwest notified Martin that its bid had been accepted. Hurt and Cloepfil thereafter agreed over the phone to meet in Springfield on April 28. On that date Hurt flew to Springfield, where the two men conferred at the airfield restaurant for about an hour. Hurt took to the meeting a copy of the job specifications which the government had supplied Martin prior to the letting.

At the Springfield meeting it developed that Martin had upped its price for the generator and accessory equipment from $18,500 to $21,500. Despite this change of position by Martin, concerning which Cloepfil was understandably amazed, the two men continued their conversation and, according to Cloepfil, they arrived at an agreement for the sale of a D353 generator and accessories for the sum of $21,500. . . .

On May 2, 1966, Cloepfil addressed a letter to the Martin Tractor Company, directing Martin to proceed with shop drawings and submittal documents for the McConnell lighting job and calling attention to the fact that applicable government regulations were required to be followed. Further reference to this communication will be made when necessary.

Some three weeks thereafter, on May 24, 1966, Hurt wrote Cloepfil the following letter:

MARTIN TRACTOR COMPANY, INC.
Topeka Chanute Concordia Colby
CATERPILLAR*

P.O. Box 1698
Topeka, Kansas
May 24, 1966

Mr. R.E. Cloepfil
Southwest Engineering Co., Inc.
P.O. Box 3314, Glenstone Station
Springfield, Missouri 65804

Dear Sir:

Due to restrictions placed on Caterpillar products, accessory suppliers, and other stipulations by the district governing agency, we cannot accept your letter to proceed dated May 2, 1966, and hereby withdraw all verbal quotations.

Regretfully,

/s/ Ken Hurt
Ken Hurt, Manager Engine Division

. . .

It is quite true, as the trial court found, that terms of payment were not agreed upon at the Springfield meeting. Hurt testified that as the memorandum was being made out, he said they wanted 10 per cent with the order, 50 per cent on delivery and the balance on acceptance, but he did not recall Cloepfil's response. Cloepfil's version was somewhat different. He stated that after the two had shaken hands in the lobby preparing to leave, Hurt said their terms usually were 20 per cent down and the balance on delivery; while he (Cloepfil) said the way they generally paid was 90 per cent on the tenth of the month following delivery and the balance on final acceptance. It is obvious the parties reached no agreement on this point.

However, a failure on the part of Messrs. Hurt and Cloepfil to agree on terms of payment would not, of itself, defeat an otherwise valid agreement reached by them. K.S.A. 84–2–204(3) [UCC § 2–204(3)] reads:

Even though one or more terms are left open a contract for sale does not fail for indefiniteness if the parties have intended to make a contract and there is a reasonably certain basis for giving an appropriate remedy.

The official U.C.C. Comment is enlightening:

Subsection (3) states the principle as to "open terms" underlying later sections of the Article. If the parties intend to enter into a binding agreement, this subsection recognizes that agreement as valid in law despite missing terms, if there is any reasonably certain basis for granting a remedy. The test is not certainty as to what the parties were to do nor as to the exact amount of damages due the plaintiff.

Nor is the fact that one or more terms are left to be agreed upon enough of itself to defeat an otherwise adequate agreement. Rather, commercial standards on the point of "indefiniteness" are intended to be applied, this Act making provision elsewhere for missing terms needed for performance, open price, remedies and the like.

The more terms the parties leave open, the less likely it is that they have intended to conclude a binding agreement, but their actions may be frequently conclusive on the matter despite the omissions.

The above Code provision and accompanying Comment were quoted in Pennsylvania Co. v. Wilmington Trust Co., 39 Del.Ch. 453, 166 A.2d 726, where the court made this observation:

There appears to be no pertinent court authority interpreting this rather recent but controlling statute. In an article entitled *The Law of Sales In the Proposed Uniform Commercial Code*, 63 Harv.Law Rev. 561, 576, Mr. Williston wanted to limit omissions to "minor" terms. He wanted "business honor" to be the only compulsion where "important terms" are left open. Nevertheless, his recommendation was rejected (*see* note on p. 561). This shows that those drafting the statute intended that the omission of even an important term does not prevent the finding under the statute that the parties intended to make a contract." (pp. 731, 732.)

So far as the present case is concerned, K.S.A. 84–2–310 [UCC § 2–310] supplies the omitted term. This statute provides in pertinent part:

Unless otherwise agreed

(*a*) payment is due at the time and place at which the buyer is to receive the goods even though the place of shipment is the place of delivery;

In our view, the language of the two Code provisions is clear and positive. Considered together, we take the two sections to mean that where parties have reached an enforceable agreement for the sale of goods, but omit therefrom the terms of payment, the law will imply, as part of the agreement, that payment is to be made at time of delivery. In this respect the law does not greatly differ from the rule this court laid down years ago. . . .

We do not mean to infer that terms of payment are not of importance under many circumstances, or that parties may not condition an agreement on their being included. However, the facts before us hardly indicate that Hurt and Cloepfil considered the terms of payment to be significant, or of more than passing interest. Hurt testified that while he stated his terms he did not recall Cloepfil's response, while Cloepfil stated that as the two were on the point of leaving, each stated their usual terms and that was as far as it went. The trial court found that only a brief and casual conversation ensued as to payment, and we think that is a valid summation of what took place.

Moreover, it is worthy of note that Martin first mentioned the omission of the terms of payment, as justifying its breach, in a letter written by counsel on September 15, 1966, more than four months after the memorandum was prepared by Hurt. On prior occasions Martin attributed its cancellation of the Springfield understanding to other causes. In its May 24 letter, Martin ascribed its withdrawal of "all verbal quotations" to "restrictions placed on Caterpillar products, accessory suppliers, and other stipulations by the district governing agency." In explaining the meaning of the letter to Cloepfil, Hurt said that Martin was doing work for the Corps of Engineers in the Kansas City and Tulsa districts and did not want to take on additional work with them at this time.

The entire circumstances may well give rise to a suspicion that Martin's present insistence that future negotiations were contemplated concerning terms of payment, is primarily an afterthought, for use as an escape hatch. Doubtless the trial court so considered the excuse in arriving at its findings.

We are aware of Martin's argument that Southwest's letter of May 2, 1966, referring to the sale is evidence that no firm contract had been concluded. Granted that some of the language employed might be subject to that interpretation, the trial court found, on what we deem to be substantial, competent evidence, that an agreement of sale *was* concluded at Springfield. Under our invariable rule those findings are binding upon this court on appeal even though there may have been evidence to the contrary. (*See* cases in 1 *Hatcher's Kansas Digest* (Rev.Ed.) Appeal & Error, §§ 507, 508.)

The defendant points particularly to the following portion of the May 2 letter, as interjecting a new and unacceptable term in the agreement made at Springfield.

> . . . We are not prepared to make a partial payment at the time of placing of this order. However, we will be able to include 100% of the engine-generator price in our first payment estimate after it is delivered, and only 10% will have to be withheld pending acceptance. Ordinarily this means that suppliers can expect payment of 90% within about thirty days after delivery.

It must be conceded that the terms of payment proposed in Southwest's letter had not been agreed to by Martin. However, we view the proposal as irrelevant. Although terms of payment had not been mutually agreed upon, K.S.A. 84–2–310 [UCC § 2–310] supplied the missing terms, *i.e.*, payment on delivery, which thus became part of the agreement already concluded. In legal effect the proposal was no more than one to change the terms of payment implied by law. Since Martin did not accept the change, the proposal had no effect, either as altering or terminating the agreement reached at Springfield. . . .

We find no error in this case and the judgment of the trial court is affirmed.

COPELAND v. BASKIN ROBBINS U.S.A.

Court of Appeal, Second District, 2002.
96 Cal.App.4th 1251, 117 Cal.Rptr.2d 875.

JOHNSON, ACTING P.J. We address an unsettled question in California: may a party sue for breach of a contract to negotiate an agreement or is such a "contract" merely an unenforceable "agreement to agree?" We hold a contract to negotiate an agreement is distinguishable from a so-called "agreement to agree" and can be formed and breached just like any other contract. We further hold, however, even if the plaintiff in this case could establish the defendant's liability for breach of contract he is limited to reliance damages—a form of recovery he has disavowed and defendant has shown he cannot prove. For this reason we affirm the trial court's judgment for defendant.

Facts and Proceedings Below

The following facts are undisputed.

Baskin Robbins operated an ice cream manufacturing plant in the city of Vernon. When the company announced its intention to close the plant, Copeland expressed an interest in acquiring it. The parties commenced negotiations. Copeland made clear from the outset his agreement to purchase the plant was contingent on Baskin Robbins' agreeing to purchase the ice cream he manufactured there. Copeland testified at his deposition the ice cream purchase arrangement, known as "co-packing," was "critical" and "a key to the deal." Without co-packing, Copeland testified, "this deal doesn't work." Baskin Robbins does not deny the co-packing arrangement was an indispensable part of the contract to purchase the plant.

After several months of negotiations an agreement took shape under which Copeland would purchase the plant's manufacturing assets and sublease the plant property. Baskin Robbins would purchase seven million gallons of ice cream from Copeland over a three year period.

In May 1999 Baskin Robbins sent Copeland a letter, which stated in relevant part:

> This letter details the terms which our Supply Chain executives have approved for subletting and sale of our Vernon manufacturing facility/equipment and a product supply agreement.... (1) Baskin Robbins will sell (Copeland) Vernon's ice cream manufacturing equipment ... for $1,300,000 cash.... (2) Baskin Robbins would agree, subject to a separate co-packing agreement and negotiated pricing, to provide (Copeland) a three year co-packing agreement for 3,000,000 gallons in year 1, 2,000,000 gallons in year 2 and 2,000,000 in year 3.... If the above is acceptable please acknowledge by returning a copy of this letter with a non-refundable check for three thousand dollars.... We should be able to coordinate a closing (within) thirty days thereafter.

Copeland signed a statement at the bottom of the letter agreeing "(t)he above terms are acceptable" and returned the letter to Baskin Robbins along with the $3000 deposit.

After Copeland accepted the terms in the May 1999 letter, the parties continued negotiating over the terms of the co-packing agreement. Among the issues to be settled were the price Baskin Robbins would pay for the ice cream, the flavors Copeland would produce, quality standards and controls, who would bear the loss from spoilage, and trademark protection. Copeland testified he believed in June 1999 he reached an oral agreement with Baskin Robbins on a price for the ice cream of his cost plus 85 cents per tub. He conceded, however, the parties had not agreed on how the cost component was to be determined and so far as he knew there was no written memorandum of this pricing agreement. None of the other issues were settled before Baskin Robbins allegedly breached the contract.

In July 1999, Baskin Robbins wrote to Copeland breaking off negotiations over the co-packing arrangement and returning his $3000 deposit. The letter explained Baskin Robbins' parent company had "recently ... made strategic decisions around the Baskin Robbins business" and "the proposed co-packing arrangement (is) out of alignment with our strategy." Therefore, Baskin Robbins informed Copeland, "we will not be engaging in any further negotiations of a co-packing arrangement." Although Baskin Robbins offered to proceed with the agreement for the sale and lease of the Vernon plant assets it did not insist on doing so, apparently accepting Copeland's view the lack of a co-packing agreement was a "deal-breaker."

In his suit for breach of contract, Copeland alleged he and Baskin Robbins entered into a contract which provided Baskin Robbins would enter into a co-packing agreement with Copeland under the terms set out in the May 1999 letter and additional terms to be negotiated. Baskin Robbins breached this contract by "unreasonably and wrongfully refusing to enter into any co-packing agreement with (Copeland)." As a result of this breach of contract Copeland suffered expectation damages "in the form of lost profits ... as well as lost employment opportunities and injury to his reputation." In response to a discovery request, Copeland stated his damages consisted of "lost profits from (the) three year co-packing agreement with defendants" as well as lost profits from other sales he could have made had he acquired the plant and the profit he could have earned from selling the plant equipment. Copeland's discovery responses did not provide or allege he could provide evidence of damages he suffered as a result of his relying on Baskin Robbins' promise to negotiate a co-packing agreement.

The trial court granted Baskin Robbins' motion for summary judgment based on the undisputed facts described above. The court concluded the May 1999 letter was susceptible to several interpretations but no matter how it was interpreted it failed as a contract because the essential terms of the co-packing deal were never agreed to and there was no reasonable basis upon which to determine them. Copeland filed a timely appeal from the subsequent judgment.

For the reasons discussed below we affirm the judgment albeit on a ground different from those relied upon by the trial court.

Discussion

When Baskin Robbins refused to continue negotiating the terms of the co-packing agreement Copeland faced a dilemma. "Many millions of dollars" in anticipated profits had melted away like so much banana ripple ice cream on a hot summer day. True enough, he could proceed with the contract for the purchase and lease of the Vernon plant's assets and use those assets to produce ice cream for other retailers. But, as he explained in his deposition, without the Baskin Robbins co-packing agreement he could not afford to purchase the assets and pay the on-going costs of operating the plant while he searched for other business. Alternatively he could attempt to sue Baskin Robbins for breach of the co-packing agreement on the theory the terms of the agreement set out in the May 1999 letter plus additional terms supplied by the court constituted an enforceable contract. Such a suit, however, had a slim prospect of success. While courts have been increasingly liberal in supplying missing terms in order to find an enforceable contract they do so only where the "reasonable intentions of the parties" can be ascertained. It is still the general rule that where any of the essential elements of a promise are reserved for the future agreement of both parties, no legal obligation arises "until such future agreement is made." Here, the parties agreed in the May 1999 letter as to the amount of ice cream Baskin Robbins would purchase over a three year period but, as Copeland candidly admitted, "a variety of complex terms" remained for agreement before the co-packing contract could be completed. These included price, the flavors to be manufactured, quality control standards, and responsibility for waste.

Copeland chose a third course. Rather than insist the parties had formed a co-packing contract and Baskin Robbins had breached it, he claimed the May 1999 letter constituted a contract to negotiate the remaining terms of the co-packing agreement and Baskin Robbins breached this contract by refusing without excuse to continue negotiations or, alternatively, by failing to negotiate in good faith. This path too has its difficulties. No reported California case has held breach of a contract to negotiate an agreement gives rise to a cause of action for damages. On the other hand numerous California cases have expressed the view the law provides no remedy for breach of an "agreement to agree" in the future. We believe, however, these difficulties could be overcome in an appropriate case.

Initially, we see no reason why in principle the parties could not enter into a valid, enforceable contract to negotiate the terms of a co-packing agreement. . . . Persons are free to contract to do just about anything that is not illegal or immoral.[7] Conducting negotiations to buy and sell ice cream is neither.

Furthermore, as we will demonstrate below, purported contracts which the courts have dismissed as mere "agreements to agree" are distinguishable from contracts to negotiate in at least two respects.

A contract to negotiate the terms of an agreement is not, in form or substance, an "agreement to agree." If, despite their good faith efforts, the parties fail to reach ultimate agreement on the terms in issue the contract to negotiate is deemed performed and the parties are discharged from their obligations. Failure to agree is not, itself, a breach of the contract to negotiate.[8] A party will be liable only if a failure to reach ultimate agreement resulted from a breach of that party's obligation to negotiate or to negotiate in good faith.[9] For these reasons, criticisms of an "agreement to agree" as "absurd" and a "contradiction in terms" do not apply to a contract to negotiate an agreement.

In addition, it is important to note courts which have found purported contracts to be unenforceable "agreements to agree" have focused on the enforceability of the underlying substantive contract, not on whether the agreement to negotiate the terms of that contract is enforceable in its own right. In Autry v. Republic Productions, [30 Cal.2d 144, 180 P.2d 888 (1947)], for example, after stating the law "provides (no) remedy for breach of an agreement to agree" the court explained this was so because "(t)he court may not imply what the parties will agree upon." ...

Most jurisdictions which have considered the question have concluded a cause of action will lie for breach of a contract to negotiate the terms of an agreement.[15]

The *Channel Home Centers* case is illustrative. There the parties executed a letter of intent to enter into the lease of a store in a shopping center. The letter stated, inter alia, Grossman the lessor "will withdraw the store from the rental market, and only negotiate the above described leasing transaction to completion." After Channel Home Centers expended approximately $25,000 in activities associated with the negotiations, Grossman unilaterally terminated negotiations. The following day Grossman leased the store to one of Channel Home Centers' competitors, Mr. Good Buys. Channel Home Centers sued Grossman for breach of contract based on the letter of intent. After a court trial, the court awarded judgment to Grossman. The Third Circuit Court of Appeals reversed.

---

7. Under Civil Code section 1667 persons are not permitted to enter into contracts which are: "1. Contrary to an express provision of law; 2. Contrary to the policy of express law, though not expressly prohibited; or, 3. Otherwise contrary to good morals."

8. Itek Corporation v. Chicago Aerial Industries, Inc. (Del.1968) 248 A.2d 625, 629.

9. Itek Corporation v. Chicago Aerial Industries, Inc., 248 A.2d at p. 629; *and see* Farnsworth, *Precontractual Liability and Preliminary Agreements: Fair Dealing and Failed Negotiations* (1987) 87 Colum. L. Rev. 217, 251. (Hereafter Farnsworth.)

15. Channel Home Centers, Grace Retail v. Grossman (3d Cir.1986) 795 F.2d 291, 293–294, 299 (applying Pennsylvania law); *see also* Venture Associates v. Zenith Data Systems (7th Cir.1993) 987 F.2d 429, 433 (applying Illinois law).

Distinguishing this case from one alleging merely the breach of an agreement to agree the court pointed out: "(I)t is Channel's position that (the letter of intent) is enforceable as a mutually binding obligation *to negotiate in good faith.* By unilaterally terminating negotiations with Channel and precipitously entering into a lease agreement with Mr. Good Buys, Channel argues, Grossman acted in bad faith and breached his promise to 'withdraw the Store from the rental market and only negotiate the above-described leasing transaction to completion.'" The court concluded under Pennsylvania law an agreement to negotiate in good faith is an enforceable contract.

Baskin Robbins maintains there are sound public policy reasons for not enforcing a contract to negotiate an agreement. In doing so, we would be injecting a covenant of good faith and fair dealing into the negotiation process whether or not the parties specifically agreed to such a term.[18] Citing Professor Farnsworth,[19] Baskin Robbins argues that instead of having a salutary effect on contract negotiations, imposing a regime of good faith and fair dealing would actually discourage parties from entering into negotiations, especially where the chances of success were slight. Alternatively, such an obligation might increase the pressure on the parties to bring the negotiations to a hasty, even if unsatisfactory conclusion, rather than risk being charged with the ill-defined wrong of bad faith negotiation. Most parties, Baskin Robbins suggests, would prefer to risk losing their out-of-pocket costs if the negotiation fails rather than risk losing perhaps millions of dollars in expectation damages if their disappointed negotiating partner can prove bad faith. Finally, Baskin Robbins argues, any precontractual wrong-doing can be adequately remedied by existing causes of action for unjust enrichment, promissory fraud and promissory estoppel.

We find Baskin Robbins' policy arguments unpersuasive.

Allowing a party to sue for breach of a contract to negotiate an agreement would not inject a covenant of good faith and fair dealing into the negotiation process in violation of the parties' intent. When two parties, under no compulsion to do so, engage in negotiations to form or modify a contract neither party has any obligation to continue negotiating or to negotiate in good faith. Only when the parties are under a contractual compulsion to negotiate does the covenant of good faith and fair dealing attach, as it does in every contract. In the latter situation the implied covenant of good faith and fair dealing has the salutary effect of creating a disincentive for acting in bad faith in contract negotiations.

Professor Farnsworth's criticisms were not directed toward a cause of action for breach of a contract to negotiate the terms of an agreement. On the contrary, Farnsworth supports such a cause of action.[22] Rather, his

---

18. In California, a covenant of good faith and fair dealing is implied in every contract. (Foley v. Interactive Data Corp. (1988) 47 Cal.3d 654, 684, 254 Cal.Rptr. 211, 765 P.2d 373.)

19. *See* fn. 9, above.

22. *Farnsworth,* 87 Colum. L.Rev. at pp. 251, 263–269.

criticisms were directed at the theory propounded by some European courts and legal scholars that, even absent a contractual agreement to negotiate, a general obligation of fair dealing arises out of the negotiations themselves.[23] . . .

Arguing bad faith is an uncertain concept which could cost the defendant millions of dollars in expectation damages is also without merit. For the reasons we explain below, the appropriate remedy for breach of a contract to negotiate is not damages for the injured party's lost expectations under the prospective contract but damages caused by the injured party's reliance on the agreement to negotiate.[26] Furthermore, we disagree with those who say the courts, unlike the National Labor Relations Board or labor arbitrators, are ill equipped to determine whether people are negotiating with each other in good faith.[27] While few of us will ever negotiate a multi-million dollar contract, each of us participates in some form of negotiation nearly every day. In most cases the question whether the defendant negotiated in good faith will be a question of fact for the jury. In our view ordinary citizens applying their experience and common sense are very well equipped to determine whether the parties negotiated with each other in good faith.

Recovery for unjust enrichment in the context of contract negotiations is usually based on ideas disclosed or services rendered during the negotiations.[28] Where, as here, the negotiations are over the sale of goods, the subject matter of the contract is not an idea nor does the potential seller typically confer a precontractual service on the potential buyer.

A cause of action for promissory fraud is based on "(a) promise made without any intention of performing it."[29] In many cases the defendant may have intended to negotiate in good faith when it contracted to do so but changed its mind later when, for example, a more attractive contracting partner came along.

Thus, we conclude neither unjust enrichment nor promissory fraud provide a party an adequate vehicle for relief when its negotiating partner breaks off negotiations or negotiates in bad faith.

The doctrine of promissory estoppel is generally used to enforce the defendant's clear and unambiguous promise when the plaintiff has reasonably and foreseeably relied on it. We agree a cause of action for promissory estoppel might lie if the defendant made a clear, unambiguous promise to negotiate in good faith and the plaintiff reasonably and foreseeably relied

---

23. *Farnsworth*, 87 Colum. L.Rev. at pp. 239–243.

26. *See Farnsworth*, 87 Colum. L.Rev. at p. 267.

27. *See e.g.*, Venture Associates v. Zenith Data Systems (7th Cir.1996) 96 F.3d 275, 277. (Venture Associates II.)

28. *See e.g.*, Blaustein v. Burton (1970) 9 Cal.App.3d 161, 184, 88 Cal.Rptr. 319 (idea for motion picture disclosed to defendants in discussing production contract); *Hill v. Waxberg* (9th Cir.1956) 237 F.2d 936, 938–939 (services of architect rendered to contractor during negotiation for building contract).

29. Civ.Code, § 1572 subdivision 4. Muraoka v. Budget Rent–A–Car Inc. (1984) 160 Cal. App.3d 107, 119, 206 Cal.Rptr. 476.

on that promise in incurring expenditures connected with the negotiation.[32] We may also assume for the sake of argument such a cause of action could be based on an implied promise to negotiate in good faith.[33] If these propositions are correct, then promissory estoppel is just a different rubric for determining the enforceability of a contract to negotiate an agreement.

Finally, we believe there are sound public policy reasons for protecting parties to a business negotiation from bad faith practices by their negotiating partners. Gone are the days when our ancestors sat around a fire and bargained for the exchange of stone axes for bear hides. Today the stakes are much higher and negotiations are much more complex. Deals are rarely made in a single negotiating session. Rather, they are the product of a gradual process in which agreements are reached piecemeal on a variety of issues in a series of face-to-face meetings, telephone calls, e-mails and letters involving corporate officers, lawyers, bankers, accountants, architects, engineers and others. As Professor Farnsworth observes, contracts today are not formed by discrete offers, counter-offers and acceptances. Instead they result from a gradual flow of information between the parties followed by a series of compromises and tentative agreements on major points which are finally refined into contract terms.[36] These slow contracts are not only time-consuming but costly. For these reasons, the parties should have some assurance "their investments in time and money and effort will not be wiped out by the other party's footdragging or change of heart or taking advantage of a vulnerable position created by the negotiation."[37] . . .

For obvious reasons, damages for breach of a contract to negotiate an agreement are measured by the injury the plaintiff suffered in relying on the defendant to negotiate in good faith. This measure encompasses the plaintiff's out-of-pocket costs in conducting the negotiations and may or may not include lost opportunity costs.[40] The plaintiff cannot recover for lost expectations (profits) because there is no way of knowing what the ultimate terms of the agreement would have been or even if there would have been an ultimate agreement. . . .

[The court concluded that Baskin Robbins is entitled to summary judgment because it showed that Copeland could not establish reliance damages. Ed.]

Disposition

The judgment is affirmed.

---

32. *See* Arcadian Phosphates, Inc. v. Arcadian Corp. (2d Cir.1989) 884 F.2d 69, 74.

33. *See* Drennan v. Star Paving Co. (1958) 51 Cal.2d 409, 333 P.2d 757. . . .

36. *Farnsworth*, 87 Colum. L.Rev. at p. 219.

37. Venture Associates II, 96 F.3d at p. 278. . . .

40. *Farnsworth*, 87 Colum. L.Rev. at pp. 225–229. Because Copeland cannot establish lost opportunity costs in this case we need not decide whether, in principle, such damages are recoverable for breach of a contract to negotiate. . . .

We concur: WOODS AND PERLUSS, JJ.

OGLEBAY NORTON CO. v. ARMCO, INC.

Supreme Court of Ohio, 1990.
52 Ohio St.3d 232, 556 N.E.2d 515.

On January 9, 1957, Armco Steel Corporation, n.k.a. Armco, Inc., appellant, entered into a long-term contract with Columbia Transportation Company, which later became a division of Oglebay Norton Company, appellee. The principal term of this contract required Oglebay to have adequate shipping capacity available and Armco to utilize such shipping capacity if Armco wished to transport iron ore on the Great Lakes from mines in the Lake Superior district to Armco's plants in the lower Great Lakes region.

In the 1957 contract, Armco and Oglebay established a primary and a secondary price rate mechanism which stated:

> Armco agrees to pay ... for all iron ore transported hereunder *the regular net contract rates for the season* in which the ore is transported, *as recognized by the leading iron ore shippers* in such season for the transportation of iron ore.... *If*, in any season of navigation hereunder, *there is no regular net contract rate recognized by the leading iron ore shippers* for such transportation, *the parties shall mutually agree upon a rate* for such transportation, *taking into consideration the contract rate being charged for similar transportation* by the leading independent vessel operators engaged in transportation of iron ore from The Lake Superior District. (Emphasis added.)

During the next twenty-three years, Armco and Oglebay modified the 1957 contract four times. With each modification Armco agreed to extend the time span of the contracts beyond the original date. Both parties acknowledged that the ever-increasing requirements capacity Armco sought from Oglebay would require a substantial capital investment from Oglebay to maintain, upgrade, and purchase iron ore carrier vessels.

The fourth amendment, signed in 1980, required Oglebay to modify and upgrade its fleet to give each Oglebay vessel that Armco utilized a self-unloading capability. It is undisputed that Oglebay began a $95 million capital improvement program at least in part to accommodate Armco's new shipping needs. For its part, Armco agreed to pay an additional twenty-five cents per ton for ore shipped in Oglebay's self-unloading vessels and agreed to extend the running of the contract until December 31, 2010.

During trial, the court recognized Armco's and Oglebay's close and long-standing business relationship, which included a seat for Armco on Oglebay's Board of Directors, Armco's owning Oglebay Norton stock, and a partnership in another venture. In fact, one of Oglebay's vessels was named "The Armco."

This relationship is perhaps best characterized by the language contained in the 1962 amendment, wherein the parties provided:

> ... Armco has a vital and unique interest in the continued dedication of ... (Oglebay's) bulk vessel fleet ... since such service is a necessary prerequisite to Armco's operation as a major steel producer. ... Armco's right to require the dedication of ... (Oglebay's) bulk vessels to Armco's service ... is the essence of this Agreement(.) ...

The amendment also granted to Armco the right to seek a court order for specific performance of the terms of the contract.

From 1957 through 1983 the parties established the contract shipping rate that Oglebay charged Armco by referring to a specified rate published in "Skillings Mining Review," in accordance with the 1957 contract's primary price mechanism. The published rate usually represented the price that Innerlake Steamship Company, a leading independent iron ore shipper, charged its customers for a similar service. Oglebay would quote this rate to Armco, which would then pay it to Oglebay.

Unfortunately, in 1983 the iron and steel industry suffered a serious downturn in business. Thus, in late 1983, when Oglebay quoted Armco the shipping rate for the 1984 season, Armco challenged that rate. Due to its weakened economic position, Armco requested that Oglebay reduce the rate Oglebay was going to charge Armco. The parties then negotiated a mutually satisfactory rate for the 1984 season.

In late 1984 the parties were unable to establish a mutually satisfactory shipping rate for the 1985 season. Oglebay billed Armco $7.66 ($.25 self-unloading vessel surcharge included) per gross ton, and Armco reduced the invoice amount to $5 per gross ton. Armco then paid the $5 per ton figure, indicating payment in full language on the check to Oglebay, and explaining its position in an accompanying letter. In late 1985, the parties again attempted to negotiate a rate, this time for the 1986 season. Again they failed to reach a mutually satisfactory rate.

On April 11, 1986, Oglebay filed a declaratory judgment action requesting the court to declare the rate set forth in the contract to be the correct rate, or in the absence of such a rate, to declare a reasonable rate for Oglebay's services. Armco's answer denied that the $7.41 rate sought by Oglebay was the "contract rate," and denied that the trial court had jurisdiction to declare this rate of its own accord, as a "reasonable rate" or otherwise.

During the 1986 season, Oglebay continued to ship iron ore for Armco. Armco paid Oglebay $4.22 per gross ton for ore shipped prior to August 1, 1986 and $3.85 per gross ton for ore shipped after August 1, 1986.

On August 12, 1987, Armco filed a supplemental counterclaim seeking a declaration that the contract was no longer enforceable, because the contract had failed of its purpose due to the complete breakdown of the rate pricing mechanisms.

After a lengthy bench trial, the trial court on November 20, 1987 issued its declaratory judgment, which made four basic findings of fact and law. First, the court held that it was apparent from the evidence presented that Oglebay and Armco intended to be bound by the 1957 contract, even though the rate or price provisions in the contract were not settled.

Second, the court held that where the parties intended to be bound, but where a service contract pricing mechanism based upon the mutual agreement of the parties fails, ". . . then the price shall be the price that is 'reasonable' under all the circumstances at the time the service is rendered."

Third, the trial court held that the parties must continue to comply with the alternative pricing provision contained within paragraph two of the 1957 contract. That alternative pricing provision mandates that the parties consider rates charged for similar services by leading independent iron ore vessel operators.

Fourth, the trial court held that if the parties were unable to agree upon a rate for the upcoming seasons, then the parties must notify the court immediately. Upon such notification, the court, through its equitable jurisdiction, would appoint a mediator and require the parties' chief executive officers ". . . to meet for the purpose of mediating and determining the rate for such season, *i.e.*, that they 'mutually agree upon a rate.' "

The court of appeals affirmed the judgment of the trial court. . . .

Per Curiam. This case presents three mixed questions of fact and law. First, did the parties intend to be bound by the terms of this contract despite the failure of its primary and secondary pricing mechanisms? Second, if the parties did intend to be bound, may the trial court establish $6.25 per gross ton as a reasonable rate for Armco to pay Oglebay for shipping Armco ore during the 1986 shipping season? Third, may the trial court continue to exercise its equitable jurisdiction over the parties, and may it order the parties to utilize a mediator if they are unable to mutually agree on a shipping rate for each annual shipping season? We answer each of these questions in the affirmative and for the reasons set forth below affirm the decision of the court of appeals.

I

Appellant Armco argues that the complete breakdown of the primary and secondary contract pricing mechanisms renders the 1957 contract unenforceable, because the parties never manifested an intent to be bound in the event of the breakdown of the primary and secondary pricing mechanisms. Armco asserts that it became impossible after 1985 to utilize the first pricing mechanism in the 1957 contract, *i.e.*, examining the published rate for a leading shipper in the "Skillings Mining Review," because after 1985 a new rate was no longer published. Armco asserts as well that it also became impossible to obtain the information necessary to determine and take into consideration the rates charged by leading independent vessel operators in accordance with the secondary pricing mechanism. This is because that information was no longer publicly available after 1985 and because the trial court granted the motions to quash of non-parties, who were subpoenaed to obtain this specific information. Armco argues that since the parties never consented to be bound by a contract whose specific pricing mechanisms had failed, the trial court should have declared the contract to be void and unenforceable.

The trial court recognized the failure of the 1957 contract pricing mechanisms. Yet the trial court had competent, credible evidence before it to conclude that the parties intended to be bound despite the failure of the pricing mechanisms. The evidence demonstrated the long-standing and close business relationship of the parties, including joint ventures, interlocking directorates and Armco's ownership of Oglebay stock. As the trial court pointed out, the parties themselves contractually recognized Armco's vital and unique interest in the combined dedication of Oglebay's bulk vessel fleet, and the parties recognized that Oglebay could be required to ship up to 7.1 million gross tons of Armco iron ore per year.

Whether the parties intended to be bound, even upon the failure of the pricing mechanisms, is a question of fact properly resolved by the trier of fact. Normandy Place Assoc. v. Beyer (1982), 2 Ohio St.3d 102, 106, 2 OBR 653, 656, 443 N.E.2d 161, 164. Since the trial court had ample evidence before it to conclude that the parties did so intend, the court of appeals correctly affirmed the trial court regarding the parties' intent. We thus affirm the court of appeals on this question.

II

Armco also argues that the trial court lacked jurisdiction to impose a shipping rate of $6.25 per gross ton when that rate did not conform to the 1957 contract pricing mechanisms. The trial court held that it had the authority to determine a reasonable rate for Oglebay's services, even though the price mechanism of the contract had failed, since the parties intended to be bound by the contract. The court cited 1 *Restatement of the Law 2d, Contracts* (1981) 92, Section 33, and its relevant comments to support this proposition. Comment *e* to Section 33 explains in part:

> ... Where ... (the parties) ... intend to conclude a contract for the sale of goods ... and the price is not settled, the price is a reasonable price at the time of delivery if ... (c) the price is to be fixed in terms of some agreed market or other standard as set or recorded by a third person or agency and it is not so set or recorded. Uniform Commercial Code § 2–305(1).

Id. at 94–95.

As the trial court noted, Section 33 was cited with approval by the Court of Appeals for Cuyahoga County [citations]. *Restatement* Section 33, Comment *e* follows virtually identical language contained in Section 2–305(1) of the Uniform Commercial Code, which was adopted in Ohio as R.C. 1302.18(A). Moreover the Court of Appeals for Cuyahoga County applied R.C. 1302.18 by analogy to a contract for services involving an open price term in Winning Sheet Metal Mfg. Co. v. Heat Sealing Equip. Mfg. Co. (Sept. 30, 1982), Cuyahoga App. No. 44365, unreported, at 3–4, 1982 WL 5944.

The court therefore determined that a reasonable rate for Armco to pay to Oglebay for transporting Armco's iron ore during the 1986 shipping season was $6.00 per gross ton with an additional rate of twenty-five cents per gross ton when self-unloading vessels were used. The court based this determination upon the parties' extensive course of dealing, "... the detriment to the parties respectively, and valid comparisons of market price which reflect (the) economic reality of current depressed conditions in the American steel industry."

The court of appeals concluded that the trial court was justified in setting $6.25 per gross ton as a "reasonable rate" for Armco to pay Oglebay for the 1986 season, given the evidence presented to the trial court concerning various rates charged in the industry and given the intent of the parties to be bound by the agreement.

The court of appeals also held that an open price term could be filled by a trial court, which has the authority to review evidence and establish a "reasonable price," when the parties clearly intended to be bound by the contract. To support this holding, the court cited *Restatement of the Law 2d, Contracts, supra,* at 92, Section 33, and its comments, and 179, Section 362, and its comments.

Section 33, Comment *a* provides in part:

> ... (T)he actions of the parties may show conclusively that they have intended to conclude a binding agreement, even though one or more terms are missing or are left to be agreed upon. In such cases courts endeavor, if possible, to attach a sufficiently definite meaning to the bargain.
>
> An offer which appears to be indefinite may be given precision by usage of trade or by course of dealing between the parties. Terms may be supplied by factual implication, and in recurring situations the law often supplies a term in the absence of agreement to the contrary. ..." *Id.* at 92.

As the court of appeals noted, we have held that "agreements to agree," such as the pricing mechanisms in the 1957 contract, are enforceable when the parties have manifested an intention to be bound by their terms and when these intentions are sufficiently definite to be specifically enforced. Normandy Place Assoc., *supra,* 2 Ohio St.3d at 105–106, 2 OBR at 656, 443 N.E.2d at 164. We have also held that "(i)f it is found that the parties intended to be bound, the court should not frustrate this intention, if it is reasonably possible to fill in some gaps that the parties have left, and reach a fair and just result." Litsinger Sign Co. v. American Sign Co. (1967), 11 Ohio St.2d 1, 14, 40 O.O.2d 30, 37, 227 N.E.2d 609, 619.

The court of appeals conducted an extensive review of the evidence presented to the trial court and concluded that the $6.25 per gross ton figure was a "reasonable rate" in this situation. The court of appeals noted that Oglebay presented evidence from Jesse J. Friedman, an economic and financial expert, who testified that $7.44 per gross ton was a reasonable rate for such services. Further evidence showed that Armco paid $5.00 per gross ton to Oglebay for the 1985 season, even though the published rate for that season was $7.41 per gross ton.

There was also testimony that Oglebay quoted Armco $5.66 per gross ton as the rate for the 1987 season. The evidence also showed that LTV Steel, prior to its bankruptcy renegotiations with Oglebay, had paid Oglebay the published rate of $7.41 per gross ton. Evidence also indicated that American Steamship Co. had quoted Armco a $5.90 per gross ton rate for the 1986 season.

The court of appeals concluded that the $6.25 per gross ton figure fell acceptably between the rate range extremes proven at trial. The court found this to be a reasonable figure. We find there was competent, credible evidence in the record to support this holding and affirm the court of appeals on this question.

III

Armco also argues that the trial court lacks equitable jurisdiction to order the parties to negotiate or in the failure of negotiations, to mediate, during each annual shipping season through the year 2010. The court of appeals ruled that the trial court did not exceed its jurisdiction in issuing such an order.

3 *Restatement of the Law 2d, Contracts* (1981) 179, Section 362, entitled "Effect of Uncertainty of Terms," is similar in effect to Section 33 and states:

> Specific performance or an injunction will not be granted unless the terms of the contract are sufficiently certain to provide a basis for an appropriate order.

Comment *b* to Section 362 explains:

> ... Before concluding that the required certainty is lacking, however, a court will avail itself of all of the usual aids in determining the scope of the agreement. ... Expressions that at first appear incomplete may not appear so after resort to usage ... or the addition of a term supplied by law....

Id. at 179.

Ordering specific performance of this contract was necessary, since, as the court of appeals pointed out, "... the undisputed dramatic changes in the market prices of great lakes shipping rates and the length of the contract would make it impossible for a court to award Oglebay accurate damages due to Armco's breach of the contract." We agree with the court of appeals that the appointment of a mediator upon the breakdown of court-ordered contract negotiations neither added to nor detracted from the parties' significant obligations under the contract.

It is well-settled that a trial court may exercise its equitable jurisdiction and order specific performance if the parties intend to be bound by a contract, where determination of long-term damages would be too speculative. *See* 3 *Restatement of the Law 2d, Contracts, supra,* at 171–172, Section 360(a), Cmt. *b*; Columbus Packing Co. v. State, ex rel. Schlesinger (1919), 100 Ohio St. 285, 294, 126 N.E. 291, 293–294. Indeed, the court of appeals pointed out that under the 1962 amendment, Armco itself had the contractual right to seek a court order compelling Oglebay to specifically perform its contractual duties.

The court of appeals was correct in concluding that ordering the parties to negotiate and mediate during each shipping season for the duration of the contract was proper, given the unique and long-lasting business relationship between the parties, and given their intent to be bound and the difficulty of properly ascertaining damages in this case. The court of appeals was also correct in concluding that ordering the parties to negotiate and mediate with each shipping season would neither add to nor detract from the parties' significant contractual obligations. This is because the order would merely facilitate in the most practical manner the parties' own ability to interact under the contract. Thus we affirm the court of appeals on this question.

The court of appeals had before it competent, credible evidence from which to conclude that the parties intended to be bound by the terms of the contract, to conclude that the $6.25 per gross ton figure was a "reasonable rate" under the circumstances, and to conclude that the trial court's exercise of continuing equitable jurisdiction was proper in this situation. Accordingly, we affirm the decision of the court of appeals.

Judgment affirmed. MOYER, C.J. and SWEENEY, HOLMES, DOUGLAS, WRIGHT, HERBERT R. BROWN and RESNICK, JJ., concur.

ECKLES v. SHARMAN

United States Court of Appeals, Tenth Circuit, 1977.
548 F.2d 905.

BREITENSTEIN, CIRCUIT JUDGE. This is an action by the owner of a professional basketball team for breach of contract by a former coach and for the inducement of that breach by the owner of another professional basketball team. Judgment was entered on a jury verdict for $250,000 against the coach and for $175,000 against the inducing owner. We reverse and remand with directions.

After these appeals were filed, the plaintiff-appellee Mountain States Sports, Inc., became bankrupt and R.T. Eckles, trustee in bankruptcy, was substituted as the appellee in each case. References herein will be to Mountain States rather than to the trustee.

Defendant-appellant Sharman was the coach of the San Francisco Warriors, a professional basketball team of the National Basketball Association, NBA. In 1968 he was persuaded to leave the San Francisco team and to coach the Los Angeles Stars of the newly formed American Basketball Association, ABA. The contract between Sharman and the Los Angeles team was for seven years and called for a starting salary of $55,000 with yearly increases of 5%. Provisions of the contract pertinent to these cases are:

(1)—Sharman was given an "option to purchase 5% ownership of the Club" at a price to be agreed upon between him and the owner.

(2)—Sharman was to participate in a "pension plan" of an undefined nature.

(3)—The parties agreed that: "In the event any one paragraph of this Agreement is invalid, this Agreement will not fail by reason thereof but will be interpreted as if the invalid portion were omitted."

(4)—California law governs the agreement.

In 1970 the Los Angeles Stars were sold for $345,000 to plaintiff Mountain States Sports, Inc., a Colorado corporation, of which Bill Daniels was the president and principal stockholder. An addendum to the sale agreement provided:

Buyer shall not be obligated to assume the Sharman contract unless he shall have confirmed his willingness to transfer to the city selected by Buyer for operation of the team. Seller states that Sharman has orally expressed his willingness to do so.

The team was moved to Salt Lake City, Utah, and became the Utah Stars. Without anything in writing pertaining to his participation in the move, Sharman went to Salt Lake City with the team. Sharman coached the Utah Stars during the 1970–1971 season and the team won the ABA championship.

During the two years that the team was in Los Angeles with Sharman as coach nothing was done with regard to the option and pension provisions of the contract. Boryla, the general manager of the Utah Stars, told Sharman that the pension provision would be worked out. Later Sharman and Daniels, the president of Mountain States, had numerous communications, both oral and written, concerning Sharman's pension rights. No final agreement was reached. In June, 1971, Sharman resigned as coach of the Utah Stars and, in July, signed a contract to coach the Los Angeles Lakers of the NBA.

Mountain States brought suit in Utah state court charging Sharman with breach of contract. The complaint was amended to assert a claim against defendant-appellant California Sports, Inc., the owner of the Los Angeles Lakers, and two individuals for the tortious inducement of Sharman's breach of contract. . . .

. . . At the conclusion of the plaintiff's case, Judge Ritter denied a defense motion to dismiss saying that the claim of contract invalidity because of the option and pension clauses presented nothing but a "red herring" and that Sharman and the owners of the Utah Stars had made a "good faith" effort to "clear up those terms." At the conclusion of all of the evidence, Judge Ritter directed a verdict against Sharman on the question of liability.

The case went to the jury on the questions of damages recoverable from Sharman, liability of the other defendants charged with inducement of contract breach and, if there was inducement, the damages resulting therefrom. The jury returned verdicts (1) in favor of the individuals sued for inducement, (2) against Sharman in the amount of $250,000, and (3) against California Sports in the amount of $175,000.

Implicit in the direction of a verdict against Sharman on the question of liability is a ruling that as a matter of law (1) the contract between Sharman and the Los Angeles Stars was valid and enforceable, (2) the contract was validly assigned to Mountain States Sports, and (3) the option and pension provisions of the contract were severable from the remainder thereof.

The option clause was unenforceable because it was nothing more than an agreement to agree. The pension clause did not state (1) the amount of pension, (2) the manner in which it would be funded, and (3) the age at which the pension would begin. The plaintiff does not seriously contest the defense claim that the pension clause is ambiguous.

Plaintiff relies on the severance clause which says that "(i)n the event any one paragraph of this Agreement is invalid," the agreement will not fail but will be interpreted as if the invalid portion was omitted. We have a failure of two paragraphs. Sharman and representatives of the plaintiff negotiated for about 15 months over the two mentioned clauses, principally that pertaining to the pension.

Good faith negotiations over various terms of an agreement do not make a fatally ambiguous contract valid and enforceable. The controlling California law is that for there to be an enforceable contract the parties must agree on the essential and material terms. *See e.g.* Coleman Engineering Co. v. North America Aviation, 65 Cal.2d 396, 55 Cal.Rptr. 1, 420 P.2d 713, and Ablett v. Clauson, 43 Cal.2d 280, 272 P.2d 753. If a contract has been agreed upon and all that remains is good faith negotiations or elaboration of non-essential terms, the contract will be held legally cognizable despite the uncertainties. *See* White Point Co. v. Herrington, 268 Cal.App.2d 458, 73 Cal.Rptr 885, 889. The question is not whether good faith negotiations had taken place but whether the option and pension were so essential to the contract that failure to agree on the pertinent terms made the contract unenforceable.

Moffat Tunnel Improvement Dist. v. Denver & S.L. Ry. Co., 10 Cir., 45 F.2d 715, 731, says that a severability clause "is but an aid to construction, and will not justify a court in declaring a clause as divisible when, considering the entire contract, it obviously is not." The crucial question is whether the clauses to be severed are essential to the contract. Essentiality depends on the intent of the parties. . . .

The intent evidence is not all one way. Sharman testified that without the option and pension provisions he would not have left the well-established NBA for the newly-established ABA. His testimony was corroborated by other witnesses. On the other hand, the record reveals that Sharman never made any serious efforts to clarify or enforce the option clause. Nothing was done about the pension clause during the two years that Sharman and the team were in Los Angeles. During the fifteen months that Sharman was with the Utah Stars many communications, both written and verbal, passed between Sharman and representatives of the team owners. Nothing was accomplished. From the evidence in the record a reasonable man could have drawn an inference one way or the other on the question of intent.

We have repeatedly held that a verdict may not be directed unless the evidence all points one way and is susceptible of no reasonable inferences which sustain the position of the party against whom the motion is made. ... On the record presented it may not be said, as a matter of law, that the option and pension clauses were unessential and hence severable. Neither can it be said, as a matter of law, that without the resolution of the controversy over those clauses Sharman agreed to the assignment of the contract to the owners of the Utah Stars. The pertinent intent questions required factual determination by the jury under proper instructions. The court erred in directing a verdict against Sharman and in favor of Mountain States on the liability issue.

The liability of California Sports depends on whether the contract between Sharman and the owner of the Los Angeles Stars was valid and whether the contract was enforceable by the owner of the Utah Stars against Sharman. If the contract was not valid, and if the contract was not enforceable by the Utah Stars, California Sports is not liable under the claim of tortious inducement of breach. The error of the court in directing a verdict on the question of Sharman's liability requires the reversal of the judgment against California Sports. ...

[Retrial ordered. Ed.]

PROBLEMS

19. O owned a resort hotel. O was approached by the defendant railroad company which asked for a right-of-way across O's land adjacent to the hotel. O granted the right-of-way in exchange for the railroad's promise to build "a neat and tasteful railway station" at a specified spot near O's hotel. The railroad was built on the right-of-way but no station was built at or near the specified spot. Does O have a contractual right to have a station built?

20. Is an agreement to remodel in accordance with blueprints for $27,000 void where the blueprints do not specify the materials to be used?

21. Landlord leased a commercial building to Tenant for a 10–year term. The lease permitted Tenant to make improvements to the premises. The lease also provided that "lessee at his option shall be entitled to the privilege of

purchasing the aforesaid building." Tenant made substantial improvements and then notified Landlord in writing that he exercised the option to purchase. Landlord refused to sell on the grounds that the option had no price term. Tenant sues for specific performance. What result?

22. A offers to hire B at $52,000 per year payable $1,000 per week and B agrees to take the job. Are the parties bound for a year?

23. A agrees to sell and B agrees to buy 1000 widgets. All of the terms are set out except that the parties "agree to agree" on the price at a later date. Is there a contract? If so, what are the legal consequences if they fail to agree?

24. A agrees to sell and B agrees to buy widgets, "the quantity to be agreed upon from time to time." Is there a contract?

25. "A and B shall make every reasonable effort to agree upon and have prepared as quickly as possible a contract providing for the foregoing purchase by B and sale by A, subject to the approval of B's stockholders, embodying the above terms and such other terms and conditions as the parties shall agree upon. If the parties fail to agree upon and execute such a contract they shall be under no further obligation to one another." What are the obligations, if any, of the parties under this provision?

26. V gave P a six month option to buy real property which P accepted within the six month period. The option agreement described the property, the price and the amount of the purchase money mortgage. The agreement also provided with respect to the mortgage: "The payment of interest and amortization of principal shall be mutually agreed upon at the time of entering into a more formal contract." (a) Was there a contract? (b) Would the result be different if the subject matter was a tractor?

SECTION 4. THE ACCEPTANCE

(a) PRELIMINARY PROBLEMS WITH RESPECT TO ACCEPTANCE

———

(Calamari & Perillo on Contracts §§ 2.10(a), 2.11, 2.13—2.17)

———

BROADNAX v. LEDBETTER

Supreme Court of Texas, 1907.
100 Tex. 375, 99 S.W. 1111.

[A Texas sheriff, the appellee, had published a $500 reward for the capture and return of an escaped prisoner. Plaintiff captured and returned the prisoner and claimed the reward which the sheriff refused to pay. The Court of Civil Appeals of the Third Supreme Judicial District certified the following question to the Supreme Court. Ed.]

"In the trial court the appellee interposed demurrers on the ground that the petition stated no cause of action, because it was not alleged that the plaintiff had knowledge or notice of the reward when the escaped prisoner was captured and returned to jail by the plaintiff. These demurrers were by the court sustained, and, plaintiff declining to amend, judgment was entered dismissing plaintiff's case, with a judgment against him for all costs, etc. In view of the above statement, we propound the following question: Was notice or knowledge to plaintiff of the existence of the reward when the recapture was made essential to his right to recover?"

Upon the question stated there is a conflict among the authorities in other states. All that have been cited or found by us have received due consideration, and our conclusion is that those holding the affirmative are correct. The liability for a reward of this kind must be created, if at all, by contract. There is no rule of law which imposes it except that which enforces contracts voluntarily entered into. A mere offer or promise to pay does not give rise to a contract. That requires the assent or meeting of two minds, and therefore is not complete until the offer is accepted. Such an offer as that alleged may be accepted by any one who performs the service called for when the acceptor knows that it has been made and acts in performance of it, but not otherwise. He may do such things as are specified in the offer, but, in so doing, does not act in performance of it, and therefore does not accept it, when he is ignorant of its having been made. There is no such mutual agreement of minds as is essential to a contract. ... The mere doing of the specified things without reference to the offer is not the consideration for which it calls. This is the theory of the authorities which we regard as sound. *Pollock on Contracts*, 20; *Anson on Contracts*, 41; *Wharton on Contracts* §§ 24, 507; *Story on Contracts* (5th Ed.) 493; *Page on Contracts*, § 32. ...

Some of the authorities taking the opposite view seem to think that the principles of contracts do not control the question, and in one of them, at least, it is said that "the sum offered is but a boon, gratuity, or bounty, generally offered in a spirit of liberality, and not as a mere price...." Eagle v. Smith, 4 Houst. (Del.) 293. But the law does not force persons to bestow boons, gratuities or bounties merely because they have promised to do so. ...

Other authorities say that it is immaterial to the offerer that the person doing that which the offer calls for did not know of its existence; that the services are as valuable to him when rendered without as when rendered with knowledge. Dawkins v. Sappington, 26 Ind. 199. But the value to the offerer of the acts done by the other party is not the test. ... He is responsible, if at all, because, by his promise, he has induced another to do the specified things. ... The acting upon this inducement is what supplies, at once, the mutual assent and the contemplated consideration. Without the legal obligation thus arising from contract there is nothing which the law enforces.

Reasons have also been put forward of a supposed public policy, assuming that persons will be stimulated by the enforcement of offers of rewards in such cases to aid in the detection of crime and the arrest and punishment of criminals. But, aside from the fact that the principles of law to be laid down cannot on any sound system of reasoning be restricted to offers made for such purposes, it is difficult to see how the activities of people can be excited by offers of rewards of which they know nothing. . . . [I]t may well be supposed that a person might become legally entitled to a reward for arresting a criminal, although he knew nothing of its having been offered, where it is or was offered in accordance with law by the government. A legal right might in such a case be given by law without the aid of contract. But the liability of the individual citizen must arise from a contract binding him to pay.

The question is answered in the affirmative.

MCC–MARBLE CERAMIC CENTER, INC. v. CERAMICA NUOVA D'AGOSTINO

United States Court of Appeals, Eleventh Circuit, 1998.
144 F.3d 1384.

[Plaintiff (MCC) claimed not to be bound by certain terms written on the reverse side of a printed contract for a variety of reasons, including the fact that the agreement signed in Italy was in the Italian language. Part of footnote 9 of the opinion is reproduced here. Ed.]

MCC makes much of the fact that the written order form is entirely in Italian and that Monzon, who signed the contract on MCC's behalf directly below this provision incorporating the terms on the reverse of the form, neither spoke nor read Italian. This fact is of no assistance to MCC's position. We find it nothing short of astounding that an individual purportedly experienced in commercial matters, would sign a contract in a foreign language and expect not to be bound simply because he could not comprehend its terms. We find nothing in the CISG [Convention on International Sale of Goods] that might counsel this type of reckless behavior and nothing that signals any retreat from the proposition that parties who sign contracts will be bound by them regardless of whether they have read them or understood them. . . .

CARLILL v. CARBOLIC SMOKE BALL CO.

Court of Appeal, 1893.
1 Q.B. 256.

Appeal from a decision of HAWKINS, J., (1892) 2 Q.B. 484.

The defendants, who were the proprietors and vendors of a medical preparation called "The Carbolic Smoke Ball," inserted in the *Pall Mall Gazette* of November 13, 1891, and in other newspapers, the following advertisement:

£100 reward will be paid by the Carbolic Smoke Ball Company to any person who contracts the increasing epidemic influenza, colds or any disease caused by taking cold, after having used the ball three times daily for two weeks according to the printed directions supplied with each ball. £1000 is deposited with the Alliance Bank, Regent Street shewing our sincerity in the matter.

During the last epidemic of influenza many thousand carbolic smoke balls were sold as preventives against the disease, and in no ascertained case was the disease contracted by those using the carbolic smoke ball.

One carbolic smoke ball will last a family several months, making it the cheapest remedy in the world at the price, 10s., post free. The ball can be refilled at a cost of 5s. Address, Carbolic Smoke Ball Company, 27, Princes Street, Hanover Square, London.

The plaintiff, a lady, on the faith of this advertisement, bought one of the balls at a chemist's and used it as directed, three times a day, from November 20, 1891, to January 17, 1892, when she was attacked by influenza. Hawkins, J., held that she was entitled to recover the £100. The defendants appealed.

LINDLEY, L.J. . . . We are dealing with an express promise to pay £100 in certain events. Read the advertisement how you will, and twist it about as you will, here is a distinct promise expressed in language which is perfectly unmistakable: "£100 reward will be paid by the Carbolic Smoke Ball Company to any person who contracts the influenza after having used the ball three times daily for two weeks according to the printed directions supplied with each ball."

We must first consider whether this was intended to be a promise at all, or whether it was a mere puff which meant nothing. Was it a mere puff? My answer to that question is "No," and I base my answer upon this passage: "£1000 is deposited with the Alliance Bank, shewing our sincerity in the matter." Now, for what was that money deposited or that statement made except to negative the suggestion that this was a mere puff and meant nothing at all? The deposit is called in aid by the advertiser as proof of his sincerity in the matter, that is, the sincerity of his promise to pay this £100 in the event which he has specified. I say this for the purpose of giving point to the observation that we are not inferring a promise; there is the promise, as plain as words can make it.

Then it is contended that it is not binding. In the first place, it is said that it is not made with anybody in particular. Now that point is common to the words of this advertisement and to the words of all other advertisements offering rewards. They are offers to anybody who performs the conditions named in the advertisement, and anybody who does perform the conditions accepts the offer. In point of law this advertisement is an offer to pay £100 to anybody who will perform these conditions, and the performance of the conditions, is the acceptance of the offer. That rests upon a string of authorities, the earliest of which is Williams v. Carwardine, 4 Barn. & Adol. 621, which has been followed by many other decisions upon advertisements offering rewards. . . .

It appears to me, therefore, that the defendants must perform their promise, and, if they have been so unwary as to expose themselves to a great many actions, so much the worse for them.

BOWEN, L.J. I am of the same opinion. . . .

Then it was said that there was no notification of the acceptance of the contract. One cannot doubt that, as an ordinary rule of law, an acceptance of an offer made ought to be notified to the person who makes the offer, in order that the two minds may come together. Unless this is done the two minds may be apart, and there is not that consensus which is necessary according to the English law—I say nothing about the laws of other countries—to make a contract. But there is this clear gloss to be made upon that doctrine, that is notification of acceptance is required for the benefit of the person who makes the offer, the person who makes the offer may dispense with notice to himself if he thinks it desirable to do so, and I suppose there can be no doubt that where a person in an offer made by him to another person, expressly or impliedly intimates a particular mode of acceptance as sufficient to make the bargain binding, it is only necessary for the other person to whom such offer is made to follow the indicated method of acceptance; and if the person making the offer, expressly or impliedly intimates in his offer that it will be sufficient to act on the proposal without communicating acceptance of it to himself, performance of the condition is a sufficient acceptance without notification. . . .

Now, if that is the law, how are we to find out whether the person who makes the offer does intimate that notification of acceptance will not be necessary in order to constitute a binding bargain? In many cases you look to the offer itself. In many cases you extract from the character of the transaction that notification is not required, and in the advertisement cases it seems to me to follow as an inference to be drawn from the transaction itself that a person is not to notify his acceptance of the offer before he performs the condition, but that if he performs the condition notification is dispensed with. It seems to me that from the point of view of common sense no other idea could be entertained. If I advertise to the world that my dog is lost, and that anybody who brings the dog to a particular place will be paid some money, are all the police or other persons whose business it is to find lost dogs to be expected to sit down and write a note saying that they have accepted my proposal? Why, of course, they at once look after the dog, and as soon as they find the dog they have performed the condition. The essence of the transaction is that the dog should be found, and it is not necessary under such circumstances, as it seems to me, that in order to make the contract binding there should be any notification of acceptance. It follows from the nature of the thing that the performance of the condition is sufficient acceptance without the notification of it, and a person who makes an offer in an advertisement of that kind makes an offer which must be read by the light of that common sense reflection. He does, therefore, in his offer impliedly indicate that he does not require notification of the acceptance of the offer. . . .

Appeal dismissed.

———

A. W. Brian Simpson, *Quackery and Contract Law: The Case of the Carbolic Smoke Ball*, 14 J. Leg. Stud. 345 (1985): ...

On October 30, 1889, one Frederick Augustus Roe, "of 202 Regent St. in the County of Middlesex, Gentleman," submitted an application to patent what he described as "An Improved Device for Facilitating the Distribution, Inhalation and Application of Medicated and Other Powder." ... As described in the specification, the improved device "comprises a compressible hollow ball or receptacle of India Rubber or other suitable elastic material, having an orifice or nozzle provided with a porous or perforated disc or diaphragm consisting of muslin, silk, wire or gauze, perforated sheet metal or the like, through which, when the ball or receptacle is compressed, the powder will be forced *in a cloud of infinitesimally small particles resembling smoke.*" ... By a fortunate chance the directions for use of the ball as marketed [have survived] ...:

> Hold the ball by the loose end below the silk floss, with the thumb and forefinger in front of the mouth. Snap or flip rapidly on the side of the ball, on the place marked "S" and a fine powder resembling smoke will arise. Inhale this smoke or powder as it arises, as shown in the above illustration. This will cause sneezing, and for a few moments you will feel as if you were taking cold. This feeling will soon pass away and the cure has commenced. If you do not feel the effects at the first inhalation by it making you sneeze, take a second in the same manner. ...

Patent records also show that Roe was from New York; ... though in 1885 he was living [in] London.... The American origin of the smoke ball is confirmed by an advertising leaflet ... which describes it as the "New American Remedy" and the "Standard Remedy of America."

Whether the ball was in fact marketed in America, perhaps as "the Pulverator," is unknown, but late in 1889 or early in 1890 Roe began to market his Carbolic Smoke Ball in England, moving his premises to 27 Princes Street, Hanover Square, at about this time. The influenza epidemic which had begun ... in December of 1889, must have come as a godsend to his new enterprise, but the utility of the ball was by no means restricted to this single ailment. The earliest of his advertisements that I have located appeared in the *Illustrated London News* on January 11, 1890. He claimed that the ball, to be had from the Carbolic Smoke Ball Company at their new premises for a price of ten shillings, "Will positively cure Influenza, Catarrh, Asthma, Bronchitis, Hay Fever, Neuralgia, Throat Deafness, Hoarseness, Loss of Voice, Whooping Cough, Croup, Coughs, Colds, and all other ailments caused by Taking Cold." Behind this optimism lay a theory, more fully articulated in some of his later advertisements. It was that all these ailments arose from a single cause, taking cold, and were therefore all amenable to the same single remedy, the Carbolic Smoke Ball. . . .

Influenza again became established in London during 1891, first in June and July and again during the winter of 1891–92. . . .

The advertisement that gave rise to the litigation first appeared . . . in the *Pall Mall Gazette* on November 13, 1891, and again on November 24 and December 8; apparently it also appeared in substantially the same form in other newspapers. . . .

To the lasting benefit of the law of contract, Mrs. Carlill saw this advertisement on the evening of November 13, 1891. . . .

Mrs. Carlill saw the advertisement, and on November 20 she purchased a smoke ball from Messrs. Wilcox and Company, who operated a druggist's shop at 239 Oxford Street. . . . According to her account of the matter, which was given in evidence at the trial and not disputed, she assiduously used the ball three times daily for two weeks, in accordance with the already quoted printed instructions supplied with it: "In the morning before breakfast, at about 2 o'clock, and again when I went to bed." Whether she continued to use the ball thereafter does not appear. On January 17, that is, at the height of the epidemic, she contracted influenza. She remained ill under the care of a Dr. Robertson for some two weeks.

On January 20 her husband, James Briggs Carlill, wrote to the Carbolic Smoke Ball Company informing them of what had occurred; possibly her letter was only one of many received at this time:

Dear Sir,

Seeing your offer of a reward, dated July 20, in the "Pall Mall Gazette" of November 13, my wife purchased one of your smoke balls, and has used it three times a day since the beginning of December. She was, however, attacked by influenza. Dr. Robertson, of West Dulwich, attended, and will no doubt be able to certify in the matter. I think it right to give you notice of this, and shall be prepared to answer any inquiry or furnish any evidence you require. I am, yours obediently,

J. B. Carlill.

This was ignored. He wrote again, threatening to place the matter in the hands of his solicitors, and received in reply a post card saying the matter would receive attention. He wrote a third time, and received in reply a printed circular, undated, endorsed "In answer to your letter of January 20." This remarkable document read:

Re reward of £100—The Carbolic Smoke Ball Company, seeing that claims for the above reward have been made by persons who have either not purchased the smoke ball at all, or else have failed to use it as directed, consider it necessary that they should state the conditions in which alone such reward would be paid. They have such confidence in the efficacy of the carbolic smoke ball, if used according to the printed directions supplied to each person, that they made the aforesaid offer in entire good faith, believing it impossible for the influenza to be taken during the daily inhalation of the smoke ball as prescribed. In order to protect themselves against all fraudulent claims, the Carbolic Smoke Ball Company require that the smoke ball be administered, free of charge, at their office, to those who have already purchased it. Intending claimants must attend three times daily for three weeks, and inhale the smoke ball under the directions of the Smoke Ball Company. These visits will be specially recorded by the secretary in a book. 27 Princes St., Hanover Square, London.

Why this gem was not quoted in the law reports must forever remain a mystery, for it goes a long way toward explaining the hostile judicial attitude to the company. It certainly irritated James Briggs Carlill, who replied, insisting his claim was perfectly honest. To this Roe replied that "the company considered his letter impertinent and gave him the names of his solicitors." And so it was that on February 15 an action was commenced to claim the £100 promised. . . .

[The case] came on for trial on June 16, 1892. . . . Neither side appears to have been parsimonious in securing the very best legal representation. Indeed the plaintiff's expenditure on counsel supports the suggestion that principle, not money, was at issue. . . . The defense was led by no less than Herbert Henry Asquith, Q.C., future prime minister. . . .

The litigation with Mrs. Carlill took from February 15 to December 7, 1892, to wend its way through the courts. . . .

. . . On February 25 we find [the Carbolic Smoke Ball Company] boldly publishing in the *Illustrated London News* a new advertisement, cunningly framed in order to turn the whole affair to his advantage. In it he pointed out that a reward of £100 pounds had recently been promised to anyone who contracted influenza, or eleven other diseases "caused by taking cold," after using the ball according to the instructions. The text continues: "Many thousand Carbolic Smoke Balls were sold on these advertisements, but only three persons claimed the reward of £100, thus proving conclusively that this invaluable remedy will prevent and cure the above mentioned diseases. THE CARBOLIC SMOKE BALL COMPANY LTD. now offer £200 REWARD to the person who purchases a Carbolic Smoke Ball and afterwards contracts any of the following diseases. . . ." There followed a list of nineteen ailments: influenza, coughs, cold in the head, cold in the chest, catarrh, asthma, bronchitis, sore throat, hoarseness, throat deafness, loss of voice, laryngitis, snoring, sore eyes, diphtheria, croup, whooping cough, neuralgia, headache. . . . It will be noted that this offer appears to envisage only a single prize, and the small print went on to restrict the scope of the offer still further in a way which suggests legal advice: "This offer is made to those who have purchased a Carbolic Smoke Ball since Jan. 1, 1893, and is subject to conditions to be obtained on application, a duplicate of which must be signed and deposited with the Company in London by the applicant before commencing the treatment specified in the conditions. This offer will remain open only till March 31, 1893." ...

LEONARD v. PEPSICO, INC.

United States District Court, S.D. New York, 1999.
88 F.Supp.2d 116, *aff'd per curiam*, 210 F.3d 88 (2nd Cir. 2000).

[The following excerpt continues the discussion in part II B of the opinion entitled, "Defendant's Advertisement Was Not An Offer." *See* p. 26. *supra.* In this excerpt the Court addresses plaintiff's contention, relying on the *Carbolic Smoke Ball* case, that Pepsi offered to give him a Harrier Jet as a reward for collecting 7,000,000 Pepsi Points. Ed.]

... The Court now turns to the line of cases upon which plaintiff rests much of his argument.

Rewards as Offers

In opposing the present motion, plaintiff largely relies on a different species of unilateral offer, involving public offers of a reward for performance of a specified act. Because these cases generally involve public declarations regarding the efficacy or trustworthiness of specific products, one court has aptly characterized these authorities as "prove me wrong" cases. *See* Rosenthal v. Al Packer Ford, 36 Md.App. 349, 374 A.2d 377, 380 (1977). The most venerable of these precedents is the case of Carlill v. Carbolic Smoke Ball Co., 1 Q.B. 256 (Court of Appeal, 1892), a quote from which heads plaintiff's memorandum of law: "(I)f a person chooses to make extravagant promises ... he probably does so because it pays him to make them, and, if he has made them, the extravagance of the promises is no reason in law why he should not be bound by them." Carbolic Smoke Ball, 1 Q.B. at 268 (Bowen, L.J.).

Long a staple of law school curricula, *Carbolic Smoke Ball* owes its fame not merely to "the comic and slightly mysterious object involved," A.W. Brian Simpson, *Quackery and Contract Law: Carlill v. Carbolic Smoke Ball Company (1893)*, in *Leading Cases in the Common Law* 259, 281 (1995), but also to its role in developing the law of unilateral offers. The case arose during the London influenza epidemic of the 1890s. Among other advertisements of the time, for Clarke's World Famous Blood Mixture, Towle's Pennyroyal and Steel Pills for Females, Sequah's Prairie Flower, and Epp's Glycerine Jube–Jubes, *see Simpson, supra,* at 267, appeared solicitations for the Carbolic Smoke Ball. The specific advertisement that Mrs. Carlill saw, and relied upon, read as follows:

100 £ reward will be paid by the Carbolic Smoke Ball Company to any person who contracts the increasing epidemic influenza, colds, or any diseases caused by taking cold, after having used the ball three times daily for two weeks according to the printed directions supplied with

each ball. 1000 £ is deposited with the Alliance Bank, Regent Street, shewing our sincerity in the matter.

During the last epidemic of influenza many thousand carbolic smoke balls were sold as preventives against this disease, and in no ascertained case was the disease contracted by those using the carbolic smoke ball.

Carbolic Smoke Ball, 1 Q.B. at 256–57. "On the faith of this advertisement," *id.* at 257, Mrs. Carlill purchased the smoke ball and used it as directed, but contracted influenza nevertheless. The lower court held that she was entitled to recover the promised reward.

Affirming the lower court's decision, Lord Justice Lindley began by noting that the advertisement was an express promise to pay £ 100 in the event that a consumer of the Carbolic Smoke Ball was stricken with influenza. *See id.* at 261. The advertisement was construed as offering a reward because it sought to induce performance, unlike an invitation to negotiate, which seeks a reciprocal promise. As Lord Justice Lindley explained, "advertisements offering rewards ... are offers to anybody who performs the conditions named in the advertisement, and anybody who does perform the condition accepts the offer." *Id.* at 262; *see also id.* at 268 (Bowen, L.J.). Because Mrs. Carlill had complied with the terms of the offer, yet contracted influenza, she was entitled to £100.

Like *Carbolic Smoke Ball*, the decisions relied upon by plaintiff involve offers of reward. In Barnes v. Treece, 15 Wash.App. 437, 549 P.2d 1152 (1976), for example, the vice-president of a punchboard distributor, in the course of hearings before the Washington State Gambling Commission, asserted that, " 'I'll put a hundred thousand dollars to anyone to find a crooked board. If they find it, I'll pay it.' " *Id.* at 1154. Plaintiff, a former bartender, heard of the offer and located two crooked punchboards. Defendant, after reiterating that the offer was serious, providing plaintiff with a receipt for the punchboard on company stationery, and assuring plaintiff that the reward was being held in escrow, nevertheless repudiated the offer. *See id.* at 1154. The court ruled that the offer was valid and that plaintiff was entitled to his reward. *See id.* at 1155. The plaintiff in this case also cites cases involving prizes for skill (or luck) in the game of golf. *See* Las Vegas Hacienda v. Gibson, 77 Nev. 25, 359 P.2d 85 (1961) (awarding $5,000 to plaintiff, who successfully shot a hole-in-one); *see also* Grove v. Charbonneau Buick–Pontiac, Inc., 240 N.W.2d 853 (N.D.1976) (awarding automobile to plaintiff, who successfully shot a hole-in-one).

Other "reward" cases underscore the distinction between typical advertisements, in which the alleged offer is merely an invitation to negotiate for purchase of commercial goods, and promises of reward, in which the alleged offer is intended to induce a potential offeree to perform a specific action, often for noncommercial reasons. In Newman v. Schiff, 778 F.2d 460 (8th Cir.1985), for example, the Fifth Circuit held that a tax protestor's assertion that, "If anybody calls this show ... and cites any section of the code that says an individual is required to file a tax return,

I'll pay them $100,000," would have been an enforceable offer had the plaintiff called the television show to claim the reward while the tax protestor was appearing. *See id.* at 466–67. The court noted that, like *Carbolic Smoke Ball*, the case "concerns a special type of offer: an offer for a reward." *Id.* at 465. James v. Turilli, 473 S.W.2d 757 (Mo.Ct.App.1971), arose from a boast by defendant that the "notorious Missouri desperado" Jesse James had not been killed in 1882, as portrayed in song and legend, but had lived under the alias "J. Frank Dalton" at the "Jesse James Museum" operated by none other than defendant. Defendant offered $10,000 "to anyone who could prove me wrong." *See id.* at 758–59. The widow of the outlaw's son demonstrated, at trial, that the outlaw had in fact been killed in 1882. On appeal, the court held that defendant should be liable to pay the amount offered. *See id.* at 762; *see also* Mears v. Nationwide Mutual Ins. Co., 91 F.3d 1118, 1122–23 (8th Cir.1996) (plaintiff entitled to cost of two Mercedes as reward for coining slogan for insurance company).

In the present case, the Harrier Jet commercial did not direct that anyone who appeared at Pepsi headquarters with 7,000,000 Pepsi Points on the Fourth of July would receive a Harrier Jet. Instead, the commercial urged consumers to accumulate Pepsi Points and to refer to the Catalog to determine how they could redeem their Pepsi Points. The commercial sought a reciprocal promise, expressed through acceptance of, and compliance with, the terms of the Order Form. As noted previously, the Catalog contains no mention of the Harrier Jet. Plaintiff states that he "noted that the Harrier Jet was not among the items described in the catalog, but this did not affect (his) understanding of the offer." . . . It should have.

Carbolic Smoke Ball itself draws a distinction between the offer of reward in that case, and typical advertisements, which are merely offers to negotiate. As Lord Justice Bowen explains:

> It is an offer to become liable to any one who, before it is retracted, performs the condition. . . . It is not like cases in which you offer to negotiate, or you issue advertisements that you have got a stock of books to sell, or houses to let, in which case there is no offer to be bound by any contract. Such advertisements are offers to negotiate— offers to receive offers—offers to chaffer, as, I think, some learned judge in one of the cases has said.

Carbolic Smoke Ball, 1 Q.B. at 268. . . . Because the alleged offer in this case was, at most, an advertisement to receive offers rather than an offer of reward, plaintiff cannot show that there was an offer made in the circumstances of this case.

PROBLEMS

27. Grandfather says to granddaughter, if you make Phi Beta Kappa, I will pay you $20,000. Granddaughter promises to attain membership. Is there a contract?

28. On June 10, the defendants executed an instrument for the purpose of having the plaintiff reroof their residence. The document contained all of the material terms and in addition, the following provision: "This agreement shall become binding only upon written acceptance hereof or upon performance of the work." Is this an offer to a unilateral contract, bilateral contract or some variation thereof?

29. A says to B, "If you promise to rake my lawn I promise to pay you $25." B starts to rake in A's presence. Is there a contract?

30. On January 2, A promises B to pay $7,500 if B paints the outside of A's summer house at Point Lookout within two weeks from January 2. A further states that this offer is open for three days. B makes no promise but begins the job on January 4 and completes it on January 9. Is there a contract?

31. S has been B's regular supplier of various component parts for machinery manufactured by B. Lately S has been unwilling to sell to B on credit terms. B sends an e-mail to S, reading, "Will you ship 15, catalog No. 337K, at $5,000 each? Urgent. Need to have your reply today. We have deposited $75,000 to your account in Geneva." Is B's order an offer to a unilateral contract, bilateral contract or some variation thereof?

32. A found a lost article and, knowing the owner, decided to return it. A went to the owner's house for that purpose but before arriving A learned that a reward had been offered for the return of the article and returned the article without mentioning the reward. Later A claimed it. Is A entitled to the reward?

33. D, Harry Eaton's brother, in Nova Scotia, wrote P, in Illinois: "If Harry needs money, let him have it, or assist him in getting it, and I will see that it is paid." The following month P helped Harry borrow money by signing Harry's note as guarantor. After signing, P so notified D by letter which D never received. Harry did not pay the debt at maturity. P paid and sued D. What result?

34. On March 15, P signed an agreement to purchase specific residential property from D Corp. The agreement was not signed by anyone for D Corp. The agreement provided as follows: "This Agreement has been obtained by Seller's salesman or agent who has no authority to bind Seller to this Agreement. *This Agreement becomes a contract when accepted by Buyer and signed by Seller at its executive office within thirty (30) calendar days from the date below*."

    (a) D Corp. never signed the agreement. Is there a contract?

    (b) What result if D Corp. signed within 30 days but did not notify P and later attempted to withdraw?

    (c) What result on the facts of (b) if the italicized language were changed to: "This Agreement shall not be binding upon Seller unless signed by Seller within 30 days"?

35. G called E about re-roofing G's residence. E's salesman and G signed a document which set out the details of the work and the price. The document contained a provision that, "this agreement shall become binding only upon

written acceptance hereof by the home office or upon commencing performance of the work." Is this an offer to a unilateral contract, bilateral contract or some variation thereof?

(b) ACCEPTANCE BY SILENCE AND CONDUCT

(Calamari & Perillo on Contracts §§ 1.8, 2.18 and 2.19)

DAY v. CATON

Supreme Judicial Court of Massachusetts, 1876.
119 Mass. 513, 20 Am Rep. 347.

CONTRACT to recover the value of one half of a brick party wall built by the plaintiff upon and between the adjoining estates, 27 and 29 Greenwich Park, Boston.

At the trial in the Superior Court, before Allen, J., it appeared that, in 1871, the plaintiff, having an equitable interest in lot 29, built the wall in question, placing one half of it on the vacant lot 27, in which the defendant then had an equitable interest. The plaintiff testified that there was an express agreement on the defendant's part to pay him one half the value of the wall when the defendant should use it in building upon lot 27. The defendant denied this, and testified that he never had any conversation with the plaintiff about the wall; and there was no other direct testimony on this point.

The defendant requested the judge to rule that,

1. The plaintiff can recover in this case only upon an express agreement.

2. If the jury find there was no express agreement about the wall, but the defendant knew that the plaintiff was building upon land in which the defendant had an equitable interest, the defendant's rights would not be affected by such knowledge, and his silence and subsequent use of the wall would raise no implied promise to pay anything for the wall.

The judge refused so to rule, but instructed the jury as follows:

A promise would not be implied from the fact that the plaintiff, with the defendant's knowledge, built the wall and the defendant used it, but it might be implied from the conduct of the parties. If the jury find that the plaintiff undertook and completed the building of the wall with the expectation that the defendant would pay him for it, and the defendant had reason to know that the plaintiff was so acting with that expectation and allowed him so to act without objection, then the jury might infer a promise on the part of the defendant to pay the plaintiff.

The jury found for the plaintiff; and the defendant alleged exceptions.

DEVENS, J. The ruling that a promise to pay for the wall would not be implied from the fact that the plaintiff, with the defendant's knowledge, built the wall, and that the defendant used it, was substantially in accordance with the request of the defendant, and is conceded to have been correct. *Chit. Con.* (11th Am. ed.) 86; Wells v. Banister, 4 Mass. 514.

The defendant, however, contends that the presiding judge incorrectly ruled that such promise might be inferred from the fact that the plaintiff undertook and completed the building of the wall with the expectation that the defendant would pay him for it, the defendant having reason to know that the plaintiff was acting with that expectation, and allowed him thus to act without objection.

The fact that the plaintiff expected to be paid for the work would certainly not be sufficient of itself to establish the existence of a contract, when the question between the parties was whether one was made. Taft v. Dickinson, 6 Allen, 553. It must be shown that, in some manner, the party sought to be charged assented to it. If a party, however, voluntarily accepts and avails himself of valuable services rendered for his benefit, when he has the option whether to accept or reject them, even if there is no distinct proof that they were rendered by his authority or request, a promise to pay for them may be inferred. His knowledge that they were valuable, and his exercise of the option to avail himself of them, justify this inference. Abbot v. Hermon, 7 Greenl. 118. And when one stands by in silence and sees valuable services rendered upon his real estate by the erection of a structure, (of which he must necessarily avail himself afterwards in his proper use thereof,) such silence, accompanied with the knowledge on his part that the party rendering the services expects payment therefor, may fairly be treated as evidence of an acceptance of it, and as tending to show an agreement to pay for it. . . .

If a person saw day after day a laborer at work in his field doing services, which must of necessity enure to his benefit, knowing that the laborer expected pay for his work, when it was perfectly easy to notify him if his services were not wanted, even if a request were not expressly proved, such a request, either previous to or contemporaneous with the performance of the services, might fairly be inferred. But if the fact was merely brought to his attention upon a single occasion and casually, if he had little opportunity to notify the other that he did not desire the work and should not pay for it, or could only do so at the expense of much time and trouble, the same inference might not be made. The circumstances of each case would necessarily determine whether silence with a knowledge that another was doing valuable work for his benefit, and with the expectation of payment, indicated that consent which would give rise to the inference of a contract. The question would be one for the jury, and to them it was properly submitted in the case before us by the presiding judge.

Exceptions overruled.

WILHOITE v. BECK

Appellate Court of Indiana, Division No. 1, 1967.
141 Ind.App. 543, 230 N.E.2d 616.

FAULCONER, JUDGE. Appellant's decedent, Flossie B. Lawrence, arrived at the home of appellee Ruth Beck in 1939 or 1940, apparently uninvited, unannounced and unexpected, and stayed until her death on July 12, 1963. After decedent's death appellee [Beck] filed a claim against the estate of decedent for room, board and care and companionship allegedly furnished decedent from January 15, 1942 until July 12, 1963, all of the total value of $27,837, for which Beck prayed judgment. The claim was tried by the court, without a jury, and the court found for Beck and entered judgment in the sum of $11,368. Appellant's motion for new trial was overruled and such action is the only error assigned on this appeal.

The specifications of appellant's motion for new trial argued on this appeal are ... 2) the decision of the court is not sustained by sufficient evidence; 3) the decision of the court is contrary to law; and 4)....

Appellant groups, for the purpose of argument, specifications 2 and 3 of her motion for new trial, that the evidence is insufficient and the decision of the court is contrary to law.

> Where one accepts valuable services from another the law implies a promise to pay for them and the contract implied by law may support a claim against his estate. To warrant a finding of an implied contract of decedent to pay for services rendered by claimant, the elements of intention to pay and expectation of payment must be found to exist. The intention of decedent to pay for services rendered and claimant's expectation of compensation may be inferred from conduct, where equity and justice require compensation, as well as from direct communications between the parties ..., or such inference of compensation may arise from the relation and situation of the parties, the nature and character of the services rendered, and any other facts and circumstances shedding light on the question at issue.

C.J.S. Executors and Administrators § 784, pp. 853–854;....

Appellant argues that the evidence shows that Beck and decedent were second cousins and, therefore, there is a presumption that such services and accommodations were rendered gratuitously.

The evidence clearly establishes that Beck and decedent were distant cousins, second or third. To our knowledge our courts have not ruled upon such a relationship in this type of action.

We are of the opinion, after a review of the text writers and decisions of those jurisdictions having passed upon the issue, that the relationship of second or third cousins in and of itself is insufficient to raise the presumption of gratuity.

However, the presumption that such services were rendered gratuitously may also arise where the parties live together as a family which alone, or in conjunction with blood relationship, may raise the presumption.

> This presumption affecting members of a household applies to all who actually live together as a family, however related, or whether related, or not, by blood or affinity, though the presumption may be strengthened or weakened by the closeness or remoteness of the relation and intimacy of the parties as a circumstance of the case.

Crampton v. Logan (1902), 28 Ind.App. 405, 407, 408, 63 N.E. 51, 52.

Such presumption is rebuttable by proof of a contract, express or implied. The presumption of gratuity indulged as to persons living as members of the same family may be rebutted by an express contract to pay and a recovery may be had upon the contract, or it may be rebutted by facts and circumstances which exclude the intention on the part of such persons that the thing furnished or services rendered were gratuitous, and raise an inference that compensation was intended and in justice and fairness under the circumstances they ought to have made a contract to pay; under such circumstances the law will imply a contract and require payment. Hill v. Hill (1889), 121 Ind. 255, 260, 23 N.E. 87. . . .

> (T)he term "family" means a collection of persons who form one household, under one head and one domestic government, and who have reciprocal, natural or moral duties to support and care for each other.

58 Am.Jur., Work and Labor, § 11, p. 520.

Although decedent lived in claimant's home for more than 20 years, we are of the opinion that the evidence in the record is not such that we could say, as a matter of law, that reasonable minds could reach only the conclusion that there existed a family relationship between them. There is evidence that the decedent was an independent person in the extreme, came and went when and as she pleased; and most of the time she took her meals alone, cooked for herself and entertained her own guests alone. Although she did some chores around the house they were evidently voluntary on her part as she was never asked to do anything.

Since there was no contention that there existed an express contract between decedent and Beck, the trial court was concerned with whether an implied contract was proven. We are unable to determine, from its general finding for claimant-Beck, whether the trial court, in arriving at its finding, found there were facts or reasonable inferences therefrom establishing an implied contract sufficient to rebut the presumption of gratuity having first determined either a blood relationship or family relationship or both, existed, or whether it first determined that no such relationship existed and, therefore, claimant had the benefit of the general presumption of intention to pay and expectation of payment.

We will on appeal however adopt that theory, within the pleadings and proof, which will uphold the action of the trial court as all presumptions are indulged in favor of the trial court's findings.

(A)n implied contract or promise is inferred from the conduct, situation or mutual relations of the parties, and is enforced by the law on the ground of justice. Hays v. McConnell (1873), 42 Ind. 285, 286–287.

. . .

Although during the time decedent lived at Beck's home there is no evidence of any conversation between them concerning the matter of payment, we are of the opinion that the facts and reasonable inferences therefrom meet the requirement that the finding of an implied contract be supported by substantial evidence of probative value. Nor can we say that reasonable minds could not so conclude.

There was evidence that decedent first occupied a basement room; that she later shared a room on the second floor with claimant's mother, and when the latter was taken to a nursing home decedent occupied said room alone until her death. Although decedent could go anywhere in the house she was not treated, nor did she expect to be treated, as one of the family. Decedent was employed most of the time she lived in the house. One definite strain runs throughout the record of the evidence in this cause as related by several witnesses, and that is the fact that decedent was an independent woman in the extreme, that she did not want charity and in fact, when her meals were brought to her room it was necessary to tell her someone brought them to her or that they were "left-overs." There was further evidence that claimant instructed her hired girl to keep an eye on decedent, but not to allow decedent to suspect it as she would be resentful. Claimant–Beck testified that she never intended to give the services and accommodations gratuitously. There was evidence that at one time Beck decided to move but cancelled the move because decedent resented the fact that no room would be available for her. One reading this record can hardly conceive that decedent did not intend to pay for these accommodations. She was an intelligent woman, "well read," and employed in a responsible position most of the time. One is impressed by the apparent attitude taken by all parties of giving decedent "a wide berth," so to speak, due to her independence and pride in "taking care of herself."

Appellant further argues that decedent named Beck as beneficiary in her will, thus carrying out a statement of decedent to a third party that claimant "would be taken care of." This does not, however, necessarily preclude recovery by a beneficiary of a legitimate claim for services rendered decedent against decedent's estate. Witt v. Witt, Executrix (1938), 105 Ind.App. 415, 421, 12 N.E.2d 1013. It is only an element to be considered in determining whether there was an express or implied contract to pay and be paid.

An examination of the will discloses that decedent left $500 to each of four persons, unrelated to her, and the residue of her estate to six cousins, including Beck, to share equally. There is no evidence of the value of decedent's estate or of what it consisted.

The trial court, in our opinion, could reasonably conclude from the facts and circumstances of this cause, and from the fact that decedent directed her executrix to pay "all of my (her) just debts," that she did not intend such bequest to Beck to compensate for such accommodations and services provided her by claimant. At least we could not hold otherwise as a matter of law. It is further evident from the record that none of the other beneficiaries offered or performed more than perfunctory and infrequent services for the decedent during this time although at least some of them were aware of her needs and failure to pay claimant.

No general rule can be set forth as to what facts are necessary to prove the existence of an implied contract. We are of the opinion, on reviewing the evidence in the record before us, the circumstances, and the inferences the court could have drawn therefrom, that the finding of the trial court and the judgment entered thereon is just and fair and should be affirmed.

Judgment affirmed.

MILLER v. NBD BANK, N.A.

Court of Appeals of Indiana, 1998.
701 N.E.2d 282.

[Some students wax indignant at the decision in *Wilhoite v. Beck*, wondering why Beck and decedent had not discussed compensation. Maybe such discussions had taken place but could not be placed in the record. This excerpt may explain. Ed.]

[The statute] commonly known as the "Dead Man's Statute," provided in relevant part:

In suits or proceedings in which an executor or administrator is a party, involving matters which occurred during a lifetime of the decedent, where a judgment or allowance may be made or rendered for or against the estate represented by such executor or administrator; any person who is a necessary party to the issue or record, whose interest is adverse to such estate, shall not be a competent witness as to such matters against such estate. . . .

One purpose of the statute is to prevent persons from testifying against the estate as to transactions, acts or conversations of the decedent when the decedent's "lips are sealed by death." *In re* Sutherland's Estate, 246 Ind. 234, 240–41, 204 N.E.2d 520, 523 (1965). "It is, in fact, a statute for the prevention of fraud." *Id.* at 241, 204 N.E.2d at 523. Rather than excluding evidence, the statute prevents a particular class of witnesses from testifying regarding claims against an estate. Fisher v. Estate of Haley, 695 N.E.2d 1022, 1027 (Ind.Ct.App.1998). . . .

HOBBS v. MASSASOIT WHIP CO.

Supreme Judicial Court of Massachusetts, 1893.
158 Mass. 194, 33 N.E. 495.

HOLMES, J. This is an action for the price of eel skins sent by the plaintiff to the defendant, and kept by the defendant some months, until they were destroyed. It must be taken that the plaintiff received no notice that the defendants declined to accept the skins. The case comes before us on exceptions to an instruction to the jury that, whether there was any prior contract or not, if skins are sent to the defendant, and it sees fit, whether it has agreed to take them or not, to lie back, and to say nothing, having reason to suppose that the man who has sent them believes that it is taking them, since it says nothing about it, then, if it fails to notify, the jury would be warranted in finding for the plaintiff.

Standing alone, and unexplained, this proposition might seem to imply that one stranger may impose a duty upon another, and make him a purchaser, in spite of himself, by sending goods to him, unless he will take the trouble, and bear the expense, of notifying the sender that he will not buy. The case was argued for the defendant on that interpretation. But, in view of the evidence, we do not understand that to have been the meaning of the judge, and we do not think that the jury can have understood that to have been his meaning. The plaintiff was not a stranger to the defendant, even if there was no contract between them. He had sent eel skins in the same way four or five times before, and they had been accepted and paid for. On the defendant's testimony, it was fair to assume that if it had admitted the eel skins to be over twenty-two inches in length, and fit for its business, as the plaintiff testified and the jury found that they were, it would have accepted them; that this was understood by the plaintiff; and, indeed, that there was a standing offer to him for such skins.

In such a condition of things, the plaintiff was warranted in sending the defendant skins conforming to the requirements, and even if the offer was not such that the contract was made as soon as skins corresponding to its terms were sent, sending them did impose on the defendant a duty to act about them; and silence on its part, coupled with a retention of the skins for an unreasonable time, might be found by the jury to warrant the plaintiff in assuming that they were accepted, and thus to amount to an acceptance. *See* Bushel v. Wheeler, 15 Q.B. 442; Benj. Sales, (6th Amer. Ed.) §§ 162–164; Taylor v. Dexter Engine Co., 146 Mass. 613, 615, 16 N.E.Rep. 462. The proposition stands on the general principle that conduct which imports acceptance or assent is acceptance or assent, in the view of the law, whatever may have been the actual state of mind of the party,—a principle sometimes lost sight of in the cases. O'Donnell v. Clinton, 145 Mass. 461, 463, 14 N.E.Rep. 747.

Exceptions overruled.

39 UNITED STATES CODE

39 U.S.C. § 3009. Mailing of unordered merchandise

(a) Except for (1) free samples clearly and conspicuously marked as such, and (2) merchandise mailed by a charitable organization soliciting contributions, the mailing of unordered merchandise or of communications prohibited by subsection (c) of this section constitutes an unfair method of competition and an unfair trade practice in violation of section 45(a)(1) of title 15.

(b) Any merchandise mailed in violation of subsection (a) of this section, or within the exceptions contained therein, may be treated as a gift by the recipient, who shall have the right to retain, use, discard, or dispose of it in any manner he sees fit without any obligation whatsoever to the sender. All such merchandise shall have attached to it a clear and conspicuous statement informing the recipient that he may treat the merchandise as a gift to him and has the right to retain, use, discard, or dispose of it in any manner he sees fit without any obligation whatsoever to the sender.

(c) No mailer of any merchandise mailed in violation of subsection (a) of this section, or within the exceptions contained therein, shall mail to any recipient of such merchandise a bill for such merchandise or any dunning communications.

(d) For the purposes of this section, "unordered merchandise" means merchandise mailed without the prior expressed request or consent of the recipient.

[Many state statutes adopt the same principle, but go beyond mailing to any sending, *e.g.*, McKinney's New York General Business Law § 396. Ed.]

PROBLEMS

36. A makes an unsolicited offer to B by mail and states: "If I do not hear from you by next Tuesday I shall assume you accept." B does not reply. Is there a contract?

37. P and D, an unmarried couple, had been living together. When the relationship ended, P claimed D was contractually obligated to pay for her services in preparing his meals, doing his laundry, etc. Is she right?

38. On August 23, P ordered for prompt shipment 942 cases of shortening at 70½ cents per pound through Tweedy, D's traveling salesman. This order was sent to D by Tweedy, who had no authority to accept. On September 4, P called to ascertain what happened to his order and he was told that the order had been declined. Tweedy had represented D in the area for eight months, and during that time he had taken several orders from P, which orders in every case had been accepted and shipped, without any communication from D. In an action by P against D, what result?

Answer problems 39 through 41 as a common law proposition without reference to the statute quoted above.

39. A sends a one-volume edition of Shakespeare with a letter saying "If you wish to buy this book send me $36.50 within one week after receipt hereof, otherwise notify me and I will forward postage for return." B examines the book and without replying makes a gift of it to his wife. What result?

40. The facts being otherwise as stated in problem 39, B examines the book and without replying carefully lays it on a shelf to await A's messenger. What result?

41. The facts being otherwise as stated in problem 39, B examines the book and uses it or gives it to his wife, writing A at the same time that he has taken the book, but that it is worth only $25 and that he will pay no more. What result?

42. Under a claim of right made in error but in good faith, B digs a well on A's unused land and takes water therefrom which has no market value and no value to A, doing no injury to the value of the land. A notifies B that B will have to pay $500 a day for every day on which B takes water from this source. Does B accept A's offer by taking water?

43. B was the owner of an unimproved piece of realty. B spent the summer in Europe and upon returning found a beautiful house where the empty lot had been. As B was about to enter, A came up to B and informed B that A had caused the structure to be built and that, if B used it, B would be *contractually* obligated to pay. Is A correct?

44. P and D, the City of Shady Grove, entered into an agreement by which P gave D an option to acquire a perpetual right of way for sewer lines across P's property. In exchange, P was to be allowed a specified number of sewer connections. (The option is an irrevocable offer by which P agrees to give D the right of way to install the sewer lines if D agrees to give P the sewer connections.) By the terms of the agreement, D was to exercise the option (accept P's irrevocable offer) by giving written notice in a specified way. D never gave such notice but it did proceed to install sewer lines across P's property. When P discovered this, P asked for the promised sewer connections and D refused. In a breach of contract action by P against D, what result?

Bank and Credit Card Problems

Bank cards are issued to depositors to provide them with identification for cashing checks at branches of the bank and to allow them electronic access to their bank accounts at automatic teller machines. *Credit* cards are issued to customers of banks and other financial services institutions to allow them to make purchases on credit at cooperating retailers and to borrow directly against their credit card accounts with no red tape.

Consider the following two paragraphs. Under what common law theories did the attorneys for the banks draft the quoted provisions?

   (a) A form agreement pursuant to which bank cards were issued to depositors contains a provision with respect to changes in the agreement which provides as follows: "We can change this Agreement at any time. We will mail you a copy of any changes by ordinary mail.

You must notify us within ten days of your nonacceptance of the changes. If you do not, you will have agreed to the changes."

(b) A notice to holders of Visa credit cards issued by a bank informed them of an increase both in annual fees and in the interest rate. The notice contained the following provision: "This change will not apply to your account unless you accept it. If you incur any further indebtedness for purchases under your Visa account after March 1, that will constitute your acceptance of the change."

SECTION 5. WHEN MAY AN OFFER TO A UNILATERAL CONTRACT NO LONGER BE REVOKED?

————

(Calamari & Perillo on Contracts § 2.22)

PETTERSON v. PATTBERG

New York Court of Appeals, 1928.
248 N.Y. 86, 161 N.E. 428.

KELLOGG, J. The evidence given upon the trial sanctions the following statement of facts: John Petterson, of whose last will and testament the plaintiff is the executrix, was the owner of a parcel of real estate in Brooklyn, known as 5301 Sixth avenue. The defendant was the owner of a bond executed by Petterson, which was secured by a third mortgage upon the parcel. On April 4, 1924, there remained unpaid upon the principal the sum of $5,450. This amount was payable in installments of $250 on April 25, 1924, and upon a like monthly date every three months thereafter. Thus the bond and mortgage had more than five years to run before the entire sum became due. Under date of the 4th of April, 1924, the defendant wrote Petterson as follows:

> I hereby agree to accept cash for the mortgage which I hold against premises 5301 6th Ave., Brooklyn, N.Y. It is understood and agreed as a consideration I will allow you $780 providing said mortgage is paid on or before May 31, 1924, and the regular quarterly payment due April 25, 1924, is paid when due.

On April 25, 1924, Petterson paid the defendant the installment of principal due on that date. Subsequently, on a day in the latter part of May, 1924, Petterson presented himself at the defendant's home, and knocked at the door. The defendant demanded the name of his caller. Petterson replied: "It is Mr. Petterson. I have come to pay off the mortgage." The defendant answered that he had sold the mortgage. Petterson stated that he would like to talk with the defendant, so the defendant partly opened the door. Thereupon Petterson exhibited the cash and said he was ready to pay off the mortgage according to the agreement.

The defendant refused to take the money. Prior to this conversation Petterson had made a contract to sell the land to a third person free and clear of the mortgage to the defendant. Meanwhile, also, the defendant had sold the bond and mortgage to a third party. It, therefore, became necessary for Petterson to pay to such person the full amount of the bond and mortgage. It is claimed that he thereby sustained a loss of $780, the sum which the defendant agreed to allow upon the bond and mortgage if payment in full of principal, less that sum, was made on or before May 31, 1924. The plaintiff has had a recovery for the sum thus claimed, with interest.

Clearly the defendant's letter proposed to Petterson the making of a unilateral contract, the gift of a promise in exchange for the performance of an act. The thing conditionally promised by the defendant was the reduction of the mortgage debt. The act requested to be done, in consideration of the offered promise, was payment in full of the reduced principal of the debt prior to the due date thereof. "If an act is requested, that very act and no other must be given." *Williston on Contracts*, § 73. "In case of offers for a consideration, the performance of the consideration is always deemed a condition." *Langdell's Summary of the Law of Contracts*, § 4. It is elementary that any offer to enter into a unilateral contract may be withdrawn before the act requested to be done has been performed. *Williston on Contracts*, § 60; *Langdell's Summary*, § 4; Offord v. Davies, 12 C.B.(N.S.) 748. A bidder at a sheriff's sale may revoke his bid at any time before the property is struck down to him. Fisher v. Seltzer, 23 Penn.St. 308. The offer of a reward in consideration of an act to be performed is revocable before the very act requested has been done. Shuey v. United States, 92 U.S. 73; Biggers v. Owen, 79 Ga. 658; Fitch v. Snedaker, 38 N.Y. 248. So, also, an offer to pay a broker commissions, upon a sale of land for the offeror, is revocable at any time before the land is sold, although prior to revocation the broker performs services in an effort to effectuate a sale. Stensgaard v. Smith, 43 Minn. 11; Smith v. Cauthen, 98 Miss. 746.

An interesting question arises when, as here, the offeree approaches the offeror with the intention of proffering performance and, before actual tender is made, the offer is withdrawn. Of such a case Williston says:

> The offeror may see the approach of the offeree and know that an acceptance is contemplated. If the offeror can say 'I revoke' before the offeree accepts, however brief the interval of time between the two acts, there is no escape from the conclusion that the offer is terminated.

Williston on Contracts, § 60–b.

In this instance Petterson, standing at the door of the defendant's house, stated to the defendant that he had come to pay off the mortgage. Before a tender of the necessary moneys had been made the defendant informed Petterson that he had sold the mortgage. That was a definite notice to Petterson that the defendant could not perform his offered promise and that a tender to the defendant, who was no longer the creditor, would be ineffective to satisfy the debt. "An offer to sell property may be withdrawn before acceptance without any formal notice to the person to whom the offer is made. It is sufficient if that person has actual knowledge that the person who made the offer has done some act inconsistent with the continuance of the offer, such as selling the property to a third person." Dickinson v. Dodds, 2 Ch.Div. 463, headnote. To the same effect is Coleman v. Applegarth, 68 Md. 21, 11 A. 284. Thus, it clearly appears that the defendant's offer was withdrawn before its acceptance had been tendered. It is unnecessary to determine, therefore, what the legal situation might have been had tender been made before withdrawal. It is the individual view of the writer that the same result would follow. This would be so, for the act requested to be performed was the completed act of payment, a thing incapable of performance unless assented to by the person to be paid. *Williston on Contracts*, § 60–b. Clearly an offering party has the right to name the precise act performance of which would convert his offer into a binding promise. Whatever the act may be until it is performed the offer must be revocable. However, the supposed case is not before us for decision. We think that in this particular instance the offer of the defendant was withdrawn before it became a binding promise, and, therefore, that no contract was ever made for the breach of which the plaintiff may claim damages.

The judgment of the Appellate Division and that of the Trial Term should be reversed and the complaint dismissed, with costs in all courts.

LEHMAN, J. (dissenting). The defendant's letter to Petterson constituted a promise on his part to accept payment at a discount of the mortgage he held, provided the mortgage is paid on or before May 31, 1924. Doubtless by the terms of the promise itself, the defendant made payment of the mortgage by the plaintiff, before the stipulated time, a condition precedent to performance by the defendant of his promise to accept payment at a discount. If the condition precedent has not been performed, it is because the defendant made performance impossible by refusing to accept payment, when the plaintiff came with an offer of immediate performance. "It is a principle of fundamental justice that if a promisor is himself the cause of the failure of performance either of an obligation due him or of a condition upon which his own liability depends, he cannot take advantage of the failure." *Williston on Contracts*, § 677. The question in this case is not whether payment of the mortgage is a condition precedent to the performance of a promise made by the defendant, but, rather, whether at the time the defendant refused the offer of payment, he had assumed any binding obligation, even though subject to condition.

The promise made by the defendant lacked consideration at the time it was made. Nevertheless the promise was not made as a gift or mere gratuity to the plaintiff. It was made for the purpose of obtaining from the defendant something which the plaintiff desired. It constituted an offer which was to become binding whenever the plaintiff should give, in return for the defendant's promise, exactly the consideration which the defendant requested.

Here the defendant requested no counter promise from the plaintiff. The consideration requested by the defendant for his promise to accept payment was, I agree, some act to be performed by the plaintiff. Until the act requested was performed, the defendant might undoubtedly revoke his offer. Our problem is to determine from the words of the letter read in the light of surrounding circumstances what act the defendant requested as consideration for his promise.

The defendant undoubtedly made his offer as an inducement to the plaintiff to "pay" the mortgage before it was due. Therefore, it is said, that "the act requested to be performed was the completed act of payment, a thing incapable of performance unless assented to by the person to be paid." In unmistakable terms the defendant agreed to accept payment, yet we are told that the defendant intended, and the plaintiff should have understood, that the act requested by the defendant, as consideration for his promise to accept payment, included performance by the defendant himself of the very promise for which the act was to be consideration. The defendant's promise was to become binding only when fully performed; and part of the consideration to be furnished by the plaintiff for the defendant's promise was to be the performance of that promise by the defendant. So construed, the defendant's promise or offer, though intended to induce action by the plaintiff, is but a snare and delusion. The plaintiff could not reasonably suppose that the defendant was asking him to procure the performance by the defendant of the very act which the defendant promised to do, yet we are told that even after the plaintiff had done all else which the defendant requested, the defendant's promise was still not binding because the defendant chose not to perform.

I cannot believe that a result so extraordinary could have been intended when the defendant wrote the letter. "The thought behind the phrase proclaims itself misread when the outcome of the reading is injustice or absurdity." *See* opinion of Cardozo, C. J., in Surace v. Danna, 248 N.Y. 18, 161 N.E. 315. If the defendant intended to induce payment by the plaintiff and yet reserve the right to refuse payment when offered he should have used a phrase better calculated to express his meaning than the words: "I agree to accept." A promise to accept payment, by its very terms, must necessarily become binding, if at all, not later than when a present offer to pay is made.

I recognize that in this case only an offer of payment, and not a formal tender of payment, was made before the defendant withdrew his offer to accept payment. Even the plaintiff's part in the act of payment was then not technically complete. Even so, under a fair construction of the words of the letter I think the plaintiff had done the act which the defendant requested as consideration for his promise. The plaintiff offered to pay with present intention and ability to make that payment. A formal tender is seldom made in business transactions, except to lay the foundation for subsequent assertion in a court of justice of rights which spring from refusal of the tender. If the defendant acted in good faith in making his offer to accept payment, he could not well have intended to draw a distinction in the act requested of the plaintiff in return, between an offer which unless refused would ripen into completed payment, and a formal tender. Certainly the defendant could not have expected or intended that the plaintiff would make a formal tender of payment without first stating that he had come to make payment. We should not read into the language of the defendant's offer a meaning which would prevent enforcement of the defendant's promise after it had been accepted by the plaintiff in the very way which the defendant must have intended it should be accepted, if he acted in good faith.

The judgment should be affirmed.

BRACKENBURY v. HODGKIN

Supreme Judicial Court of Maine, 1917.
116 Me. 399, 102 A. 106.

CORNISH, C.J. The defendant Mrs. Sarah D.P. Hodgkin on the 8th day of February, 1915, was the owner of certain real estate—her home farm, situated in the outskirts of Lewiston. She was a widow and was living alone. She was the mother of six adult children, five sons, one of whom, Walter, is the codefendant, and one daughter, who is the coplaintiff. The plaintiffs were then residing in Independence, Mo. Many letters had passed between mother and daughter concerning the daughter and her husband returning to the old home and taking care of the mother, and finally on February 8, 1915, the mother sent a letter to the daughter and her husband which is the foundation of this bill in equity. In this letter she made a definite proposal, the substance of which was that if the Brackenburys would move to Lewiston, and maintain and care for Mrs. Hodgkin on the home place during her life, and pay the moving expenses, they were to have the use and income of the premises, together with the use of the household goods, with certain exceptions, Mrs. Hodgkin to have what rooms she might need. The letter closed, by way of postscript, with the words, "you to have the place when I have passed away."

Relying upon this offer, which was neither withdrawn nor modified, and in acceptance thereof, the plaintiffs moved from Missouri to Maine late in April, 1915, went upon the premises described and entered upon the performance of the contract. Trouble developed after a few weeks, and the relations between the parties grew most disagreeable. The mother brought two suits against her son-in-law on trifling matters, and finally ordered the plaintiffs from the place, but they refused to leave. Then on November 7, 1916, she executed and delivered to her son, Walter C. Hodgkin, a deed of the premises, reserving a life estate in herself. Walter, however, was not a bona fide purchaser for value without notice, but took the deed with full knowledge of the agreement between the parties and for the sole purpose of evicting the plaintiffs. On the very day the deed was executed he served a notice to quit upon Mr. Brackenbury, as preliminary to an action of forcible entry and detainer which was brought on November 13, 1916. This bill in equity was brought by the plaintiffs to secure a reconveyance of the farm from Walter to his mother, to restrain and enjoin Walter from further prosecuting his action of forcible entry and detainer, and to obtain an adjudication that the mother holds the legal title impressed with a trust in favor of the plaintiffs in accordance with their contract.

The sitting justice made an elaborate and carefully considered finding of facts and signed a decree, sustaining the bill with costs against Walter C. Hodgkin, and granting the relief prayed for. The case is before the law court on the defendants' appeal from this decree.

Four main issues are raised.

1.   As to the completion and existence of a valid contract.

A legal and binding contract is clearly proven. The offer on the part of the mother was in writing, and its terms cannot successfully be disputed. There was no need that it be accepted in words, nor that a counter promise on the part of the plaintiffs be made. The offer was the basis, not of a bilateral contract, requiring a reciprocal promise, a promise for a promise, but of a unilateral contract requiring an act for a promise. "In the latter case the only acceptance of the offer that is necessary is the performance of the act. In other words, the promise becomes binding when the act is performed." 6 R.C.L. 607. This is elementary law.

The plaintiffs here accepted the offer by moving from Missouri to the mother's farm in Lewiston and entering upon the performance of the specified acts, and they have continued performance since that time so far as they have been permitted by the mother to do so. The existence of a completed and valid contract is clear. . . .

Appeal dismissed. . . .

MOTEL SERVICES, INC. v. CENTRAL MAINE POWER CO.

Supreme Judicial Court of Maine, 1978.
394 A.2d 786.

POMEROY, JUSTICE. This is an appeal from a final judgment entered in favor of Central Maine Power Company (CMP), the defendant and third party plaintiff. The third party action against Waterville Housing Authority (WHA) was dismissed. No cross-appeal was taken. The case was heard by a single Justice, sitting without a jury.

On August 5, 1971 Motel Services, Inc. entered into an agreement with WHA whereby Motel Services would build two housing projects for WHA on a "*turnkey*" basis. After the agreement became effective, appellant sought to change the construction specifications to provide for an electrical rather than an oil heating system. Appellant sought this change in order to qualify for a promotional allowance given by CMP to the

> *owner of a home either new or existing which is initially built for or converted to the use of electricity as the primary method of heating ...,* *provided that the installation of such electric heating equipment complies with the Company's* "Standard Requirement Electric Service and Meter Installation" And "Standards of Insulation For Use with Electric House Heating."

Appellant took the initiative in persuading WHA and the Federal Department of Housing and Urban Development (HUD) to consent to the modifications. Appellant, with CMP's assistance, demonstrated that electric heating was ultimately more economical; appellant also promised to reduce its contract price by $16,000 if the change was approved. Both WHA and HUD agreed to the modification. Appellant never informed either agency of the existence of the promotional allowance, however, despite the fact that approximately $8,000 of the $16,000 reduction was due to appellant's expectation of receiving the allowance.

After the electrical system had been completely installed, but before all the *"Standards"* required by CMP had been complied with, appellant conveyed both premises to WHA. This conveyance prior to final completion was designed primarily to avoid the imposition upon appellant of the tax to be exacted on April 1. The projects, however, were completed after closing to the full satisfaction of WHA and in compliance with the CMP standards.

After inspection of the premises by a CMP employee, the appropriate forms for receipt of the allowance were prepared. Unaware that appellant expected the allowance, the employee sent the forms and eventually the allowance to WHA, the owner on the date of completion of the projects. Appellant brought this action against CMP, claiming it was entitled to the allowance. CMP sued WHA in a third party action seeking return of the allowance in the event of a judgment in appellant's favor.

The Justice below made findings of fact and conclusions of law. Most significantly, these included a finding that appellant had not fully complied with the requirements of the allowance policy prior to conveyance of the property. Having concluded that CMP's policy was a standing offer to enter into a unilateral contract, the presiding Justice ruled that appellant did not fully perform prior to relinquishing ownership, and no enforceable contract was therefore produced.

I.

Our first conclusion, which we have little difficulty in reaching, is that WHA is not entitled to the allowance. Not having known of it prior to completion of the construction, WHA provided no consideration, and did not bargain for it. The completion of the claim forms does not constitute performance of the acts requested by the offer....

II.

The Court below correctly characterized CMP's marketing policy as an offer to enter into a unilateral contract. Despite the general rule that contracts are presumed to be bilateral, Restatement of Contracts, § 31, the presumption is rebutted by the clear import of the offer, which requested not a promise to perform, but complete performance in accordance with its terms. Such is the essential hallmark of a unilateral contract.

We find error, however, in the presiding Justice's interpretation of the law of unilateral contracts. Specifically, the Court erred in ruling as a matter of law that *"(i)f an act is required in return for a promise, that act and only that act and the whole of that act must be performed or there is no contract."* Brackenbury v. Hodgkin, 116 Me. 399, 401, 102 A. 106 (1917). . . . Professor Corbin discusses *Brackenbury* in some detail, as illustrative of the rule that part performance by the promisee renders an offer of a unilateral contract irrevocable. *See Corbin on Contracts*, § 49 [(1963)]. [This last sentence was in a footnote. Ed.] . . .

In the instant case, it is clear that when appellant undertook to install the heating system in accordance with CMP's policy, it was not only entitled as owner of the homes to accept the offer, but in fact did so. Appellant's failure to notify CMP of its acceptance, in the context of an offer of a unilateral contract, does not undermine the validity of the acceptance. *See* 1 *Williston on Contracts*, § 68 (3rd ed. 1957).

However, while CMP's offer was rendered irrevocable by appellant's acceptance, payment of the allowance remained contingent upon appellant's completion of the required performance.

III.

Appellees set forth two grounds by which they contend that appellant failed completely to perform. First, appellant did not complete the final steps necessary to claim the allowance, namely, the submission of the forms to CMP. Second, appellant was no longer the owner of the buildings at the time it fully complied with CMP's construction standards.

The first contention is unpersuasive. Appellant failed to fill out the requisite forms because CMP sent them to WHA, and instructed WHA on how to complete them to claim the allowance. It is undisputed that, had CMP provided the forms, appellant would have completed this final requirement.

Where the offeree of a unilateral contract is prevented from completing performance by the actions of the offeror, such failure will not be a defense to an action by the offeree on the contract. Brackenbury v. Hodgkin, *supra*, at 402, 102 A. 106; 1 *Williston*, § 74A, p. 246.

Appellee's second argument presents a more substantial issue, but is likewise unpersuasive, in the last analysis. The failure of appellant to maintain his *"owner"* status through the period of completion of work does not, we think, preclude recovery.

CMP extended its offer

> *to the owner of a home . . . which is initially built for or converted to the use of electricity as the primary method of heating. . . . An allowance will be paid at the above stated rate (also) to owners of homes, which use electricity . . . who install additional electric heating. . . .*

Appellant was the owner of the buildings under construction until April 1, when it persuaded WHA to accept an early conveyance of the property in order to protect themselves from an imminent property tax imposition. Appellees contend that such transfer, occurring prior to full compliance with CMP's standards, precluded appellant from entitlement to the allowance.

We do not agree.

The offeror is the master of his offer, and is entitled to establish such standards of acceptance, notice, and the like as he sees fit. Among such powers is the right to designate the person, persons, or class of persons entitled to accept the offer. 1 *Williston,* § 80; 1 *Corbin,* § 64. In this case, CMP's offer was explicitly limited to acceptance by *"owners"*. Appellant, at the time it undertook to perform the requested acts, was owner of the buildings and entitled to, and did, accept the offer.

CMP contends that a major purpose of its policy of requiring adequate insulation as a prerequisite to payment of the allowance was to insure that the customer would obtain satisfactory results from his heating system. Therefore, it urges, the emphasis in the quoted passage should be upon the word *"use"*; The allowance was intended to go to the *"user"* of the system, who was in most cases also the owner. Thus the crucial determinant respecting entitlement to the allowance was the identity of the user, rather than the owner.

CMP's management aims in developing its policy, however, are less important than its outward manifestations. We believe that a plain reading of the offer leads to the conclusion that the class of offerees consisted of owners of homes who undertook to install electrical heating equipment. No conditions are attached to the offer plainly indicating a requirement that the owner occupy the home and use the system after installation. Indeed CMP admitted that no such requirement had ever been imposed. Any emphasis CMP chose to place on who the *"ultimate user"* was is absent from the terms of the offer. It is to those terms that we must look in determining the class of persons empowered by CMP to accept its offer. . . .

Here, CMP received what it had bargained for by the terms of its offer. The owner of a home undertook to install an electric heating system; 90% of the work was completed before the property was conveyed, the remaining details shortly thereafter. Had appellant retained title to the property until it received the allowance, and conveyed it immediately thereafter, there is no doubt but that the case would not be before us. We are not convinced that the conveyance should change the result. . . .

Appeal sustained. Remanded with instructions to enter judgment for appellant on its claim.

PROBLEMS

45. A, a property owner, says to B, the CEO of a railroad, "if you extend your lines to my property (up to a spot that A designated on a map), I will pay your company" a specified amount. When the railroad company had extended its rails halfway to the designated spot, A sent B a notice of revocation. Should the railroad continue to extend its rails? Does the railroad have an action for breach of contract against A?

46. A promises B to rake her lawn in return for $25 paid in advance. B tenders $25 within a reasonable time. A refuses to accept the tender. What result?

47. Mortgagee agreed to accept a smaller amount than the total mortgage debt in satisfaction, if mortgagor would pay it within 90 days. In reliance on the promise, mortgagor completed a bank loan. Mortgagee revoked. Advise mortgagor.

SECTION 6. ACCEPTANCE OF INDIFFERENT OFFERS

———

(Calamari & Perillo on Contracts §§ 2.10(b) & (c))

HORTON v. DAIMLERCHRYSLER FINANCIAL SERVICES AMERICAS, L.L.C.

Court of Appeals of Texas–Texarkana, 2008.
262 S.W.3d 1.

MORRISS, CHIEF JUSTICE. All seem to concede that the debt Larry D. Horton owed to DaimlerChrysler Financial Services Americas, L.L.C. . . . had been settled in 2003 through Daimler's agent, Commercial Recovery Systems, Inc. Horton believed that settlement included an obligation of Daimler and Commercial to remove from his credit report any adverse information about the Daimler debt. When Horton applied in 2005 to purchase a house and a commercial truck, he discovered his credit report still contained adverse information concerning the account. Horton sued Daimler and Commercial for breach of contract. Horton appeals from a summary judgment that held he was not entitled to removal of the adverse credit information. For the reasons set out below, we reverse the summary judgment and remand this matter to the trial court for further proceedings.

The settlement in question resulted from negotiations during 2003 and rests on the meaning of two letters: one from Commercial and one to

Commercial. In a letter dated June 5, 2003, Commercial offered Horton a settlement:

> As an authorized representative of DaimlerChrysler/Mercedes, Commercial Recovery Systems, Inc. will accept $1,000 as full and final settlement of the $25,038.85 owed on the above referenced account. No further funds will be due. This offer will be extended through June 30, 2003, after which time the full balance will be due.
>
> In addition, all derogatory credit information regarding this account will reflect the account to be settled. Please allow ninety (90) days for credit information to be updated.
>
> This settlement is being made with the mutual understanding that the debt is not currently secured.
>
> Terms: $500.00 due 6/15/03 & $500.00 due 6/30/03.

On June 18, 2003, Commercial received a check from Horton in the amount of $500.00. This check was dated June 14, 2003. A second check, dated June 27, 2003, was received by Commercial July 2, 2003. The second check was accompanied by a letter dated July 1, 2003, that indicated it had been mailed "(v)ia Express Mail" and provided some terms of its own:

> Enclosed please find Mr. Horton's final payment in the amount of $500.00 payment with regard to the above-referenced account. This check is tendered with the understanding that it is to be accepted in full and complete satisfaction of all sums due and owing, and in complete release with regard to these matters. This check is tendered in trust and is not to be negotiated otherwise.

Commercial accepted both checks.

In response to Horton's suit, Daimler and Commercial sought summary judgment by denying that a contract had been formed pursuant to the June 5 offer. Daimler and Commercial contended that Horton failed to accept the June 5 offer by tendering $1,000.00 by the date specified. Instead, Daimler and Commercial argued the July 1 letter constituted a counter-offer. Daimler and Commercial claimed that, by accepting the check, they formed a new contract that did not contain the contractual duty to correct derogatory credit information on Horton's credit report.

On appeal, Horton argues it was error to grant the summary judgment because there are genuine issues of material fact concerning whether the acceptance of the checks was a waiver or modification of the time limitations contained in the June 5 offer. ... We conclude that ... genuine issues of material fact preclude the summary judgment....

The dispute in this case concerns the parties' differing interpretations of the negotiations. When interpreting a contract, our primary objective is to ascertain and give effect to the intent of the parties as expressed in the contract. Seagull Energy E & P, Inc. v. Eland Energy, Inc., 207 S.W.3d 342, 345 (Tex.2006). ... If a written instrument's text can be given a definite legal meaning, it is not ambiguous and must be construed as a matter of law. Coker v. Coker, 650 S.W.2d 391, 393 (Tex.1983).

Daimler and Commercial argue that, as a matter of law, the June 5 offer was never accepted. According to Daimler and Commercial, the offer could be accepted only by timely payment of the full $1,000.00. Since that amount was not paid by the due dates stated in the June 5 letter, Daimler and Commercial claim no contract was formed pursuant to the original offer.[3] Horton argues that the [offer] was accepted when he tendered the first installment and that there are fact issues concerning whether Daimler and Commercial waived any breach caused by not tendering payment in a timely manner. Our analysis leads us to three conclusions: (a) the offer did not require a specific manner of acceptance, (b) Horton accepted the offer by tendering the first payment, and (c) there are issues of fact concerning waiver.

The Offer Did Not Require a Specific Manner of Acceptance

Daimler and Commercial argue the June 5, 2003, offer provided specific means by which Horton could accept the offer—making full payment by a date certain. "Where an offer prescribes the time and manner of acceptance, those terms must ordinarily be complied with to create a contract." Padilla v. LaFrance, 907 S.W.2d 454, 460 (Tex.1995); *see Restatement (Second) of Contracts* § 58 (1981). The question in this case is whether the offer provided that it could be accepted only by tendering the full payment on or before June 30, 2003.

An offeror may specify a particular mode of acceptance. Franklin Life Ins. Co. v. Winney, 469 S.W.2d 21, 23 (Tex.Civ.App.–San Antonio 1971, writ ref'd n.r.e.). While the June 5 offer specifies terms of payment, it does not specify a particular manner of acceptance of the offer. Daimler and Commercial claim the only method available to accept the offer was a timely full payment. They fail to direct this Court to the language of the contract dictating such a conclusion—nor have we been able to locate any.

None of the language of the offer specifies a manner of acceptance. The offer provides "(t)his offer will be extended through June 30, 2003, after which time the full balance will be due." This language refers to the length of time the offer will remain open for acceptance, not the manner by which the offer could be accepted. The language that Daimler and Commercial "will accept $1,000 as full and final settlement of the $25,038.85" refers to the terms of the settlement, not the manner of acceptance. Finally, the payment due dates imposed by the contract— "Terms: $500.00 due 6/15/03 & $500.00 due 6/30/03"—are terms of the contract, not a manner of acceptance.

---

3. Daimler and Commercial claim a contract was formed based on Horton's counteroffer in the July 1 letter. If a contract had not been formed at this point, such an argument might prove successful. An "acceptance" must be identical to the offer. Long Trusts v. Griffin, 144 S.W.3d 99, 111–12 (Tex.App.–Texarkana 2004), *rev'd in part & remanded in part on other grounds,* 222 S.W.3d 412 (Tex.2006). We conclude, however, that a contract was formed when Horton tendered the first payment.

We note that, in *Padilla,* the Texas Supreme Court held a Rule 11 agreement, which specified payment must be made by a certain date and time, was "clear that the offer could only be accepted by *payment of the money* by a specific deadline." 907 S.W.2d at 460. We believe this conclusion of *Padilla* is distinguishable from this case. The letter in *Padilla* stated, "I look forward to *receipt* of the checks on or before date specified, failing which this offer to settle will be withdrawn...." *Id.* at 456. While the letter in this case clearly specifies the time for acceptance of the offer, the letter in this case does not describe the manner of acceptance in any manner similar to the offer in *Padilla.*

While Daimler and Commercial could have included a specific manner of acceptance in the offer, the plain language of the offer does not contain any such requirement. "The parties' intent must be taken from the agreement itself, not from the parties' present interpretation, and the agreement must be enforced as it is written." Nicol v. Gonzales, 127 S.W.3d 390, 394 (Tex.App.–Dallas 2004, no pet.). The offer, as written, does not provide for a specific manner of acceptance.

Horton Accepted the Offer By Tendering The First Payment

Unless otherwise indicated, an offer may be accepted in any manner reasonable under the circumstances. *Restatement (Second) of Contracts* § 30 (1981). Generally, "(t)he mode of expressing assent is inconsequential so long as it effectively makes known to the offeror that his offer has been accepted." Fujimoto v. Rio Grande Pickle Co., 414 F.2d 648, 652 (5th Cir.1969). It is well established that acceptance may be shown by conduct. Patrick v. Smith, 90 Tex. 267, 38 S.W. 17, 19 (1896); *see Restatement (Second) of Contracts* § 50 (1981). Horton's act in tendering the first installment of $500.00 was a clear, unequivocal act indicating acceptance. The act effectively informed Daimler and Commercial that the offer had been accepted and was within the time specified for acceptance of the offer. The contract was formed when Horton tendered the first installment.

There Are Issues of Fact Concerning Waiver

Although Horton clearly breached the contract by not tendering payment by the due dates contained in the contract, there are genuine issues of material fact concerning ... whether Daimler and Commercial waived the payment due date requirements. Because there are genuine issues of material fact, the trial court erred in granting the joint motion for summary judgment. ...

We reverse the judgment of the trial court and remand this case to that court for further proceedings consistent with this opinion.

PROBLEMS

48. A writes to B, "If you will paint my fence next week, I will pay you $200." B paints but not in A's presence. Is there a contract?

49. A writes to B, "If you paint my fence next week, I promise to pay you $200." B replies, "I'll do it." Is there a contract?

50. P sent a purchase order to D requesting the prompt shipment of certain items. D sent a written promise to ship the goods that were ordered. Is there a contract?

51. B sent S a purchase order for 200,000 blue medical bottles at $1 each. S responded by shipping 200,000 clear medical bottles the market price of which was 90 cents per bottle. B accepted the bottles, promptly notified S of breach and sued S for breach of contract. What result?

52. B sent a purchase order to S which amounted to an offer to buy goods. S began to execute B's order. B knew that S was beginning performance. (a) Was B entitled to cancel the order? (b) Would B be entitled to cancel the order if B was unaware of the beginning of performance?

SECTION 7.   PRESCRIBED MEDIUM OF ACCEPTANCE AND MAILBOX RULE

———

(Calamari & Perillo on Contracts § 2.23)

FUJIMOTO v. RIO GRANDE PICKLE CO.

United States Court of Appeals, Fifth Circuit, 1969.
414 F.2d 648.

GOLDBERG, CIRCUIT JUDGE: This appeal involves claims by George Fujimoto and Jose Bravo against the Rio Grande Pickle Company upon written contracts of employment. The questions before us are of contract formation and construction.

Rio Grande Pickle Company, a Colorado corporation engaged in the business of raising and selling cucumbers for the pickling industry, hired Fujimoto in the Spring of 1965 and Bravo in the following Fall. Both of these employees were given important jobs. Fujimoto was employed as the supervisor of the planting and growing operations, while Bravo functioned as the labor recruiter.

In order to encourage them to work with zeal and not to leave the company's employ, Rio Grande offered contracts with profit sharing bonus provisions to both Fujimoto and Bravo. Prior to the offer of the written contracts, the company had responded to the offerees' demands for more compensation by orally agreeing to pay them a salary plus a bonus of ten per cent of the company's annual profits. Bravo told the president of Rio Grande that he wanted the agreement in writing, and the president replied "I will prepare one and send you a contract in writing." The contractual documents sent to Fujimoto and Bravo did not specify how the offers could be accepted or how the acceptances should be communicated to the company. Under these circumstances Fujimoto and Bravo signed their respective contracts but did not return them to the company. Believing that they had accepted the company's offers and that they were working under the proffered bonus contracts, the two employees remained in the employ of Rio Grande until November 30, 1966.

The written contracts called for the employees to devote their best efforts to Rio Grande and promised in return that the company would pay each offeree a bonus amounting to ten per cent of the company's net profits for each fiscal year. Each employee was to agree to return half of his bonus to the company as an investment in company stock. ...

In answer to special interrogatories the jury found that Fujimoto and Bravo each had entered into a written contract in October, 1965. ...

On appeal Rio Grande argues that there is insufficient evidence in the record to support the jury's finding that Fujimoto and Bravo had accepted the offered bonus contracts. ...

Rio Grande argues that there were no contracts because Fujimoto and Bravo did not accept the written bonus offers by signing and returning the written instruments to the company. Each contract was signed by the respective employee, but neither was returned. Thus the first issue is whether the offers, which by their terms did not specify the means by which they could be accepted, could be accepted by a mode other than the return of the signed instruments.

Professor Corbin has summarized the law on this issue as follows:

> In the first place, there is no question that the offeror can require notice of acceptance in any form that he pleases. He can require that it shall be in any language and transmitted in any manner. He may require notice to be given by a nod of the head, by flags, by wig-wag, by a smoke signal on a high hill. He may require that it be by letter, telegraph or radio, and that there shall be no contract unless and until he is himself made conscious of it.
>
> Secondly, the offeror can specify a mode of making an acceptance of his offer, without making that method exclusive of all others. If the mode that he specifies is one that may not bring home to him the knowledge that his offer has been accepted, then such knowledge by him is not a requisite. The offeror can specify a mode of acceptance without any knowledge of the law of contract and without thinking in terms of offer and acceptance at all. This will be considered below.
>
> Thirdly, if the offeror specifies no mode of acceptance, the law requires no more than that the mode adopted shall be in accord with the usage and custom of men in similar cases. If proof of such usage and custom is wanting or is uncertain, the court must consider probable convenience and results and then help by its decision to establish a custom for the future and a rule of law.

Corbin on Contracts § 67, p. 109 (Student Ed. 1952).

This case falls within the third of Professor Corbin's rules. Neither written offer specified a particular mode of acceptance, and there is no evidence that Rio Grande ever manifested any intent that the offers could be accepted only by the return of the signed instruments. Moreover, there is substantial and convincing evidence to the contrary. The record is replete with evidence that the company conditioned the bonus offers primarily upon the offerees remaining in the company's employment and that the employees understood that they did not have to return the signed contracts in order to have contracts under which they would each get a ten per cent bonus.

Since we have found that the return of the signed documents was not the exclusive means by which the offerees could convey their acceptances, we must now determine whether Fujimoto and Bravo in fact adequately communicated such acceptances to the company. Where, as here, the offer and surrounding circumstances are silent as to permissible modes of acceptance, the law requires only that there be some clear and unmistakable expression of the offeree's intention to accept. In the words of Professor Corbin:

> Whenever the case is such as to require a notice of acceptance, it is not enough for the offeree to express mental assent, or even to do some overt act that is not known to the offeror and is not one that constitutes a customary method of giving notice. *If the overt act is one that clearly expresses an intention* to accept the specific offer and is in fact known by the offeror, there is an effective acceptance. This is because the offeror has actual knowledge. (Emphasis added.) *Corbin on Contracts, supra,* § 67 at p. 111.

As Professor Corbin indicates, the mode of expressing assent is inconsequential so long as it effectively makes known to the offeror that his offer has been accepted. One usually thinks of acceptance in terms of oral or written incantations, but in many situations acts or symbols may be equally effective communicative media. *See Restatement of Contracts* § 21. In the words of Chief Judge Brown in Aetna Casualty & Surety Co. v. Berry, 5 Cir.1965, 350 F.2d 49, 54:

> That the communication from the Berry Companies to Aetna was not in words express goes only to the weight and clarity of the message, but it does not mean that no contract came into existence. Of necessity, the law has long recognized the efficacy of nonverbal communications. From the formation of contracts by an offeree's silence, nod, hand signal "√" or "x" on an order blank to the doctrine of admission by silence, the law has legally realized that to offer guidance and comment meaningfully on the full range of human conduct, cognizance must be taken of communications other than by words. Symbols for words often suffice. Lawyers and Judges live by them, as the citation to this very case may sometime demonstrate.

See also McCarty v. Langdeau, Tex.Civ.App.1960, 337 S.W.2d 407, 412 (writ ref'd n.r.e.).

In the case at bar there is substantial evidence to support the jury's finding that the company knew that the offerees had agreed to the terms of the proffered bonus contracts. Of particular importance is the fact that Fujimoto and Bravo, who had threatened to quit unless their remuneration was substantially increased, continued to work for the company for fourteen months after receiving the offers. Moreover, during this fourteen-month period they did not again express dissatisfaction with their compensation. There is also evidence that Fujimoto and Bravo discussed the bonus contracts with the company president in such circumstances and in such a manner that their assent and acceptance should have been unmistakable to him. In view of these circumstances, Rio Grande could not have been besieged with any Hamlet-like doubts regarding the existence of a contract. Since Rio Grande knew that Fujimoto and Bravo had accepted its offer, there was a valid and binding contract. *See Williston on Contracts* § 90 (1957). . . .

Affirmed in part and reversed and remanded in part.

CANTU v. CENTRAL EDUCATION AGENCY

Court of Appeals of Texas, Austin, 1994.
884 S.W.2d 565.

BEA ANNE SMITH, JUSTICE. Appellant Maria Diosel Cantu sued for judicial review of a final order of the State Commissioner of Education, Lionel Meno. The district court affirmed the Commissioner's decision. We will affirm the trial-court judgment.

Background

The facts in this cause are undisputed. Cantu was hired as a special-education teacher by the San Benito Consolidated Independent School District under a one-year contract for the 1990–91 school year. On Saturday, August 18, 1990, shortly before the start of the school year, Cantu hand-delivered to her supervisor a letter of resignation, effective August 17, 1990. In this letter, Cantu requested that her final paycheck be forwarded to an address in McAllen, Texas, some fifty miles from the San Benito office where she tendered the resignation. The San Benito superintendent of schools, the only official authorized to accept resignations on behalf of the school district, received Cantu's resignation on Monday, August 20. The superintendent wrote a letter accepting Cantu's resignation the same day and deposited the letter, properly stamped and addressed, in the mail at approximately 5:15 p.m. that afternoon. At about 8:00 a.m. the next morning, August 21, Cantu hand-delivered to the superintendent's office a letter withdrawing her resignation. This letter contained a San Benito return address. In response, the superintendent hand-delivered that same day a copy of his letter mailed the previous day to inform Cantu that her resignation had been accepted and could not be withdrawn.

The State Commissioner of Education concluded that, because the school district's acceptance of Cantu's resignation was effective when mailed, an agreement to rescind Cantu's employment contract was in force when she attempted to withdraw her offer of resignation and the school district's refusal to honor her contract was not unlawful.

Discussion

The sole legal question presented for our review is the proper scope of the "mailbox rule"[4] under Texas law and whether the rule was correctly applied by the Commissioner and district court. None of the parties to this appeal disputes that an agreement to rescind Cantu's employment contract requires the elements of an offer, acceptance, and consideration. *See* Texas Gas Util. Co. v. Barrett, 460 S.W.2d 409, 414 (Tex.1970). Rather, Cantu contends in a single point of error that the trial court erred in ruling that the agreement to rescind her contract of employment became effective when the superintendent deposited his letter accepting Cantu's resignation in the mail. Cantu argues that, under Texas law, an acceptance binds the parties in contract on mailing only if the offeror has sent the offer by mail or has expressly authorized acceptance by mail. There was no express authorization for the school district to accept Cantu's offer by mail. The question presented is whether authorization to accept by mail may be implied only when the offer is delivered by mail or also when the existing circumstances make it reasonable for the offeree to so accept.

The aphorism "the offeror is the master of his offer" reflects the power of the offeror to impose conditions on acceptance of an offer, specify the manner of acceptance, or withdraw the offer before the offeree has effectively exercised the power of acceptance. However, more often than not, an offeror does not expressly authorize a particular mode, medium, or manner of acceptance. Consequently, particularly with parties communicating at a distance, a rule of law is needed to establish the point of contract formation and allocate the risk of loss and inconvenience that inevitably falls to one of the parties between the time that the offeree exercises, and the offeror receives, the acceptance. *See* 1 Arthur L. Corbin, *Contracts* § 78 (1963).

As Professor Corbin notes, courts could adopt a rule that no acceptance is effective until received, absent express authorization by the offeror; however, the mailbox rule, which makes acceptance effective on dispatch, closes the deal and enables performance more promptly, and places the risk of inconvenience on the party who originally has power to control the manner of acceptance. *Id.* Moreover, "the mailing of a letter has long been a customary and expected way of accepting (an) offer." *Id.* Therefore, "(e)ven though the offer was not made by mail and there was no (express) authorization, the existing circumstances may be such as to make it reasonable for the offeree to accept by mail and to give the offeror

---

4. The mailbox rule provides that the properly addressed acceptance of an offer is effective when deposited in the mail, unless otherwise agreed or provided by law. Black's Law Dictionary 952 (6th ed. 1990).

reason to know that the acceptance will be so made." *Id.* In short, acceptance by mail is impliedly authorized if reasonable under the circumstances.

The Restatement approves and adopts this approach: an acceptance by any medium reasonable under the circumstances is effective on dispatch, absent a contrary indication in the offer. *Restatement (Second) of Contracts* §§ 30(2), 63(a), 65, 66 (1979). In addition, the Restatement specifically recognizes that acceptance by mail is ordinarily reasonable if the parties are negotiating at a distance or *even if a written offer is delivered in person to an offeree in the same city. Id.* § 65 cmt. c (emphasis added). The same standard, *viz.*, whether the manner of acceptance is reasonable under the circumstances, governs offer and acceptance in commercial transactions under the Texas Business and Commerce Code. *See* Tex.Bus. & Com.Code Ann. § 2.206 (West 1968) [UCC § 2–206]. . . .

. . . We hold that it is proper to consider whether acceptance by mail is reasonably implied under the circumstances, whether or not the offer was delivered by mail.

Looking at the circumstances presented for our review, we agree with the Commissioner and the trial court that it was reasonable for the superintendent to accept Cantu's offer of resignation by mail. Cantu tendered her resignation shortly before the start of the school year—at a time when both parties could not fail to appreciate the need for immediate action by the district to locate a replacement. In fact, she delivered the letter on a Saturday, when the Superintendent could neither receive nor respond to her offer, further delaying matters by two days. Finally, Cantu's request that her final paycheck be forwarded to an address some fifty miles away indicated that she could no longer be reached in San Benito and that she did not intend to return to the school premises or school-district offices. The Commissioner of Education and district court properly concluded that it was reasonable for the school district to accept Cantu's offer by mail. We overrule appellant's point of error.

Conclusion

We affirm the trial-court judgment that the Commission correctly determined that the school district accepted Cantu's resignation, rescinding her employment contract, before Cantu attempted to withdraw her offer of resignation.

PROBLEMS

53. B sends an offer to Y stating, "You can accept this offer only by signing your name on the line provided below my signature." Y sends a letter of acceptance. Is there a contract?

54. Seller mailed Buyer a letter offering to sell specified goods which Seller was prepared to purchase from a third party. The letter contained the sentence, "Please reply by fax at once so I can make a deposit and close the deal." Buyer called Seller and "accepted" on the phone. Is there a contract?

55. A made an offer to B stating, "This offer shall be accepted by signing in the appropriate place and by returning it to me." B called A and stated that the offer was accepted. Is there a contract?

56. A makes an offer by mail to sell her used car to B. B immediately sends an acceptance by mail, changes his mind, and then sends a rejection by fax. The fax is received before the acceptance is received. a) In a suit by A against B for breach of contract, what result? b) Suppose A had sold her car to C after she had received the message of rejection but before she had received the letter of acceptance. In an action by B against A for breach of contract, what result?

57. A calls B on the telephone. A is in New York and B is in New Jersey. A makes an offer. B speaks words of acceptance into the phone which A does not hear because of the fault of the Telephone Company. Is there a contract?

58. A made an offer to B by mail. B promptly sent a letter of acceptance which was lost and never received. a) If A's offer had stated, "Your acceptance is effective when sent provided that it is received," was there a contract?

b) What result if A's offer had stated, "As soon as the acceptance is received we shall send amongst the farmers and secure the first lots"?

59. A makes B an offer to be accepted by mail or messenger, and B promptly sends an acceptance by his own employee. When does the contract arise? Would the result be different if the acceptance were given to a private messenger service?

SECTION 8. MISTAKE IN TRANSMISSION

(Calamari & Perillo on Contracts § 2.24)

PROBLEMS

60. S made an offer to sell a certain quantity of oranges to B at $2.60 per box. When transmitted by the telegraph company the offer read $1.60 per box. B accepted this offer when the market price was $2.30 per box. B had reason to know that at the time and place of the offer the oranges were worth at least $2.30 per box. In an action by B against S for refusal to deliver for $1.60 per box, what result?

61. A writes an offer to B which he encloses in an envelope and addresses and stamps. Shortly afterwards A decides not to send the offer but by mistake deposits it in the mail. It is delivered to B who "accepts" the offer. What result?

Would the result be different if A sent the offer while sleepwalking?

SECTION 9. TERMINATION OF A REVOCABLE OFFER

(Calamari & Perillo on Contracts § 2.20)

SWIFT & CO. v. SMIGEL

Superior Court of New Jersey, Appellate Division, 1971.
115 N.J.Super. 391, 279 A.2d 895, aff'd 60 N.J. 348, 289 A.2d 793.

CONFORD, P.J.A.D. Plaintiff Swift & Company instituted an action in the Superior Court against Erwin Smigel, executor of the estate of Joseph O. Smigel, for $8,509.60, the amount of merchandise it supplied the Pine Haven Nursing Home & Sanitarium, Inc. ("Pine Haven") upon credit. Plaintiff held continuing guaranties by decedent Smigel and third-party defendant Abe Kraig for payment of the indebtedness. The trial court granted defendant Erwin Smigel's motion for summary judgment, and entered judgment dismissing Swift's complaint and Smigel's third-party complaint against Kraig. Swift appeals from that judgment.

The action of the trial court was predicated upon Joseph Smigel's adjudication as an incompetent prior to the delivery of any of the merchandise for which claim is here made, and upon the authority of the supposed rule that mental incompetency of an offeror prior to acceptance by the offeree terminates the offer whether or not the offeree had notice of the incompetency at the time of the acceptance. *Restatement, Contracts*, § 48 at 56 (1932). The justification for any such rule, which has not heretofore been passed upon in any reported New Jersey case, is the main question before us for resolution.

The undisputed facts which emerge from the pleadings, motion papers, briefs and oral argument are these. To induce plaintiff to sell provisions to Pine Haven, the two equal owners of its stock, decedent Smigel and one Abe Kraig, on November 11, 1962 each entered into a written agreement of "continuing guaranty" with plaintiff undertaking to pay at maturity all indebtedness of Pine Haven for goods to be sold and delivered to it by plaintiff. Among other provisions, the agreement signed by Smigel purported to cover all liabilities the buyer might incur until ten days after receipt of notice from the guarantor or his legal representatives of withdrawal of the guaranty. No notice of withdrawal was ever given by Smigel or his representatives. Plaintiff asserts, and for the purpose of this appeal it must be accepted as a fact, that it never had knowledge of Smigel's incompetency during the period of delivery of the merchandise giving rise to the present claims, or previously.

We are without information on the basis of which it could be determined whether plaintiff reasonably should have known or been put on inquiry of facts which would have disclosed Smigel's incompetence. Smigel was adjudicated incompetent January 16, 1966, and letters of guardianship were issued to his son, the present defendant, on February 1, 1966.

The unpaid-for merchandise was delivered during the period from January 4, 1967 to October 12, 1967. What the course of deliveries and payments therefor previously may have been is not disclosed by the record. . . .

Neither of the parties to this appeal disputes that the agreement upon which this action was brought was a continuing guaranty of the kind "which is not limited to a particular transaction . . . but which is intended to cover future transactions." *See* Fidelity Union Trust Co. v. Galm, 109 N.J.L. 111, 116, 160 A. 645 (E. & A.1932). A continuing guaranty is at its inception an offer from the guarantor and is accepted by the creditor each time the latter does a specified act (*e.g.*, extending credit to the debtor). Typically, as here, such a guaranty reserves in the guarantor the power to revoke it unilaterally prior to action by way of acceptance by the creditor.

The specific question which concerns us here—whether an adjudication of mental incompetency of a guarantor operates automatically to revoke a continuing guaranty—has not been decided in any American case disclosed by research of the parties or our own. An English trial court decided that the continuing efficacy of the guaranty ceased only when the creditor became aware of the guarantor's insanity. The issue, however, was not involved in the reported appeal. Bradford Old Bank v. Sutcliffe, 2 K.B. 833 (Ct.App.1918).

The treatment of the question in the texts has been subsumed under the assumed analogy of death of the guarantor. Most of the few decided cases on the latter point have held that death terminates the guaranty without regard to knowledge by the creditor, on the purported general principle that the death of an offeror destroys one of the two essential assenting entities to a contract. *See* 10 *Williston, Contracts* (Jaeger–3d ed. 1967) § 1253 at 809–810; 1 *id.* § 62 at 206–207 (1957); *Restatement, Contracts*, § 48 at 56 (1932); *Restatement, Security*, § 87 at 250–252 (1941). A New Jersey trial court followed the general rule. Teplitz Thrown Silk Co. v. Rich, 13 N.J.Misc. 494, 179 A. 305 (Cir.Ct.1935). Other typical such cases are Jordan v. Dobbins, 122 Mass. 168 (Sup.Jud.Ct.1877); Aitken v. Lang, 106 Ky. 652, 51 S.W. 154 (Ct.App.1899). The leading case to the contrary is Gay v. Ward, 67 Conn. 147, 34 A. 1025 (Sup.Ct.Err. 1895), which stressed the diminished business utility of continuing guaranties if terminable without notice on death. Professor Corbin treats that case as representative of the preferred rule. 1 *Corbin, Contracts* (1963) § 54 at 229. *See infra.*

The conceptual underpinning of the notion that an offer should be deemed automatically revoked upon death or insanity of the offeror despite good-faith action by way of acceptance thereof by an unknowing offeree has been criticized by the leading writers on the subject.

Corbin comments:

> It is very generally said that the death of the offeror terminates the offeree's power of acceptance even though the offeree has no knowledge of such death. Such general statements arose out of the earlier notion that a contract cannot be made without an actual

meeting of minds at a single moment of time, a notion that has long been abandoned. The rule has also been supposed to follow by some logical necessity from the dictum that it takes two persons to make a contract. It is not contrary to that dictum to deny that death terminates power to accept; the offer was made by a living man and is accepted by another living man. . . .

It has even been held, *and justly,* that the doing of the requested acts after the death of the offeror, but in ignorance thereof, consummates a contract. Thus, where through an agent an offeror orders the shipment of goods to the agent, and the offeree ships the goods in ignorance that the offeror has died, the offeree can collect the price from the offeror's estate. So, also, where one has given his promise to guarantee payment for goods to be sold, money to be lent, or service to be rendered to another, the sale or loan or service in ignorance of the promisor's death has been held to enable the promisee to enforce the promise of guaranty against the guarantor's estate. Some cases have held the contrary, however; and also it has been held that the offeree can not accept after he has knowledge that the offeror is dead. (1 *Corbin, op. cit.,* § 54 at 227–228, 229; emphasis added.)

The case for terminating the offer on subsequent insanity of the offeror without knowledge of the offeree is found by Corbin "even more doubtful than the rule as to the offeror's death" as "(i)nsanity is far less easily determinable as a fact than is death, either by the contracting parties themselves or by a court." *Id.* at 231. . . .

It is noteworthy, in the same vein, that the American Law Institute, although retaining in proposed *Restatement, Contracts 2d* (Tent.Dr. No. 1, 1964) the substance of section 48 of the *Restatement,* terminating an offeree's power of acceptance when the offeror (or offeree) dies or is deprived of legal capacity to enter into the proposed contract, apparently does so reluctantly and critically. Comment (a) to section 48 in *Restatement 2d,* reads:

> *Death of offeror.* The offeror's death terminates the power of the offeree without notice to him. *This rule seems to be a relic of the obsolete view* that a contract requires a "meeting of minds," and it is out of harmony with the modern doctrine that a manifestation of assent is effective without regard to actual mental assent. *See* § 21. Some inroads have been made on the rule by statutes and decisions with respect to bank deposits and collections, and by legislation with respect to powers of attorney given by servicemen. *See* Uniform Commercial Code § 4–405; *Restatement of Agency Second* § 120 and cmt. a. In the absence of legislation, the rule remains in effect. (Emphasis added.)

See the comparable criticism of the rationale of the principle of automatic revocation of offers on death or insanity of the offeror in Oliphant, *Duration and Termination of an Offer,* 18 Mich.L.Rev. 201, 209–211 (1919), and in *Note,* 24 Colum.L.Rev. 294 (1924), in both of which that rule is found to violate the reasonable expectations of an offeree without knowledge of the offeror's death or other disability. In the latter the observation is made:

> Contract and tort liabilities pass to personal representatives. Why not liability under an offer? If we adopt a test objective as to the offeror and ask, "What is the scope of the offeree's reasonable expectation?," it would seem that notice of the death should be required to terminate the offer. (at 295)

In view of the foregoing criticisms of the conventional approach, which strike us as persuasive, we are not disposed, in determination of this first-instance litigation on the point, routinely to follow existing standard formulations on the subject. The search should be for the rule which will accord with the reasonable expectations of persons in the business community involved in transactions of this kind. In that regard, moreover, we bear no responsibility in this case for determining the rule in the case of death of the guarantor but only in that of his adjudication of incompetency. There may be material differences in the respective situations, as noted in the excerpt quoted from *Corbin, supra*. Furthermore, our New Jersey cases on the effect of insanity on contract liability, as will be seen *infra*, also call for a special approach to the guaranty question in the insanity context.

In broad terms, the law of contracts has been said to "attempt the realization of reasonable expectations that have been induced by the making of a promise." 1 *Corbin, op. cit.*, § 1 at 2. In the present instance decedent promised plaintiff to make good any bills for provisions incurred by a corporate business enterprise in which he had a one-half stock interest. Had he not done so plaintiff presumably would not have taken on the business risk of selling to the corporation. It would seem to us that if plaintiff neither knew nor had any reason to know of decedent's later adjudication as an incompetent during any portion of the time it was making the deliveries which gave rise to the debts here sued on, plaintiff's reasonable expectations based on decedent's original continuing promise would be unjustifiably defeated by denial of recovery.

If the situation is judged in terms of relative convenience, it would seem easier and more expectable for the guardian of the incompetent to notify at least those people with whom the incompetent had been doing business of the fact of adjudication than for the holder of a guaranty such as here to have to make a specific inquiry as to competency of the guarantor on each occasion of an advance of credit to the principal debtor.

We have thus far been considering the problem presented on the theory that decedent's accountability should soundly be appraised on the basis of reasonable expectations and reliance of others stemming from his act of execution of the guaranty. On that approach his subsequent incompetency would be irrelevant, for he was competent when he acted. The theoretical basis for the conventional view of automatic termination of the continuing guaranty on insanity, however, is that there is a renewal of the offer on each occasion of acceptance thereof by the offeree, and that renewal cannot be effected by one without legal capacity at the time. *See Note*, 24 Colum.Law Rev., *op. cit.*, at p. 295. But even if we adhered to that concept of the jural conduct of the guarantor in a continuing guaranty, immunity of defendant in the present situation as a matter of law would not square with existing New Jersey cases as to the liability of persons who, lacking mental capacity, contract with others having no knowledge of that fact and parting with valuable consideration.

In Manufacturers Trust Co. v. Podvin, 10 N.J. 199, 207–208, 89 A.2d 672 (1952), the court approved the rule declared in the early case of Drake v. Crowell, 40 N.J.L. 58, 59 (Sup.Ct.1878), to the effect that

> The law in this state is settled, that contracts with lunatics and insane persons are invalid, subject to the qualification that a contract made in good faith with a lunatic, for a full consideration, which has been executed without knowledge of the insanity, or such information as would lead a prudent person to the belief of the incapacity, will be sustained.

The qualification stated was applied by the court in the *Drake* case in favor of an unknowing party dealing with the alleged incompetent. . . .

It is thus clear that whatever view is taken as to the appropriate theoretical basis for determining the decedent's liability in this fact pattern, the decisive consideration should be the presence or absence of knowledge by plaintiff, actual or reasonably to be imputed, of decedent's incompetency at the time of each advance of credit pursuant to the guaranty.

Moreover, if at the trial plaintiff's knowledge is established by defendant, the issue of decedent's incompetency would not necessarily be concluded by proof of the fact of adjudication of incompetency. The decisions in this State leave no doubt that that fact is not conclusive but only *prima facie* evidence of legal incompetency. Eckman v. Wood, 108 N.J.L. 105, 108, 154 A. 862 (E. & A.1931).

The entire judgment, including the dismissal of the third-party complaint, is reversed and the cause is remanded to the Law Division for further proceedings consonant with this opinion.

PROBLEMS

Lapse

62.   On January 29, D sent a letter dated January 29, which stated, "Will give you eight days to accept or reject." P received the offer on February 2. On February 8, P sent an acceptance which was received by D on February 9th. (a) Was the acceptance timely? (b) Would the result be different if there was a delay in transmission of the offer and without the delay the offer would have arrived on January 30th?

63.   A sends a telegraphic offer to sell oil at a fixed price which at the time is subject to rapid fluctuations in price. The offer is received near the

close of business hours, and a telegraphic acceptance is sent the next day, after the offeree has learned of a sharp price rise. Is there a contract?

64. On May 27, 1837 the City of Boston caused the following reward offer to be published: "The frequent and successful repetition of incendiary attempts renders it necessary that the most vigorous efforts should be made to prevent their recurrence. One thousand dollars will be paid by the City for information leading to the apprehension and conviction of any person engaged in these nefarious practices." The offer was published for one week. No attempt was ever made to withdraw it. From the time of the reward notice until early 1841 there were very few fires in Boston. The fire in question was set in January of 1841 and the conviction occurred in March of 1841. Is the plaintiff entitled to the reward if he supplied information leading to the apprehension and conviction of an arsonist?

65. The defendant offered a reward of $200 for information leading to the conviction of the person who set a specific fire. Three years and 2 months later the culprit was convicted as a result of information supplied by the plaintiff three months before the trial. Is the plaintiff entitled to the reward?

66. D was interviewed live for a late-night TV news show in which viewers were encouraged to call in. The name of the show and the telephone number were flashed periodically on the screen. During the interview, D stated that "If anybody calls this show and cites any section of the Internal Revenue Code that says an individual is required to file a tax return, I'll pay them $100,000." A few hours later a taped segment of this interview was rebroadcast on the morning news. P saw the rebroadcast, researched income tax law and the following day called the morning news show (at a different number than had been flashed on the screen during the original broadcast) and cited the appropriate Code sections. D refused to pay. P sues D. What result?

67. On June 15 B mailed S an offer to buy at a specified price certain hay. On June 20, within what could plausibly be considered to be a reasonable time, S sent a card of acceptance. B didn't reply. Later, after circumstances had changed, B claimed there was no contract because S's acceptance was late. Could the trier of fact conclude there was a contract?

68. O, the owner of Greenacre sent offers to sell the property on specified terms to a number of prospective buyers. Each offer contained the phrase, "subject to prior sale." Within a reasonable time, A accepted the offer. Thereafter, but still within a reasonable time, B sent an acceptance to O. Is O liable to both A and B?

Supervening illegality

69. B offered to buy from S a specified quantity of a certain pesticide. While the offer was still open the Environmental Protection Agency promulgated a rule banning the sale or use of the pesticide. S immediately dispatched an acceptance of the offer. Is there a contract?

Revocation

70. Hoover offered to buy certain real property from Clements. Soon thereafter they talked on the telephone. Clements expressed a strong interest

in accepting and suggested that they meet to discuss certain details. Hoover then said: "We have not decided, we might not want to go through with it." Clements immediately responded, "I accept your offer." Was there a contract?

71. A, a newspaper, publishes an offer of prizes to the persons who procure the largest number of subscriptions as evidenced by cash or checks received by a specified time. B completes and mails an entry blank giving B's name and address, that is received by A. Thereafter during the contest, A publishes a notice that personal checks will not be counted; B does not see the notice. Is B bound by the notice?

72. S makes an offer to sell a piece of real property to A and then makes the same offer to B; A accepts; B learns of A's acceptance. May B accept?

73. (a) A offers to work as a full-time typist in B's office during the next year, the offer to remain open for 10 days. B then hears reliable information that A has agreed to work full-time for C during the same year. May B accept A's offer?

(b) B offers to hire A as a typist and A hears reliable information that B hired another typist for his office for the same period. May A accept B's offer?

SECTION 10. COUNTER–OFFERS AND THE BATTLE OF THE FORMS

(a) MIRROR IMAGE RULE, LAST SHOT PRINCIPLE AND UCC § 2–207

(Calamari & Perillo on Contracts § 2.21)

ARDENTE v. HORAN

Supreme Court of Rhode Island, 1976.
117 R.I. 254, 366 A.2d 162.

DORIS, JUSTICE. Ernest P. Ardente, the plaintiff, brought this civil action in Superior Court to specifically enforce an agreement between himself and William A. and Katherine L. Horan, the defendants, to sell certain real property. The defendants filed an answer together with a motion for summary judgment.... [Summary] judgment was entered by a Superior Court justice for the defendants. The plaintiff now appeals.

In August 1975, certain residential property in the city of Newport was offered for sale by defendants. The plaintiff made a bid of $250,000 for the property which was communicated to defendants by their attorney. After defendants' attorney advised plaintiff that the bid was acceptable to defendants, he prepared a purchase and sale agreement at the direction of defendants and forwarded it to plaintiff's attorney for plaintiff's signature. After investigating certain title conditions, plaintiff executed the agreement. Thereafter plaintiff's attorney returned the document to defendants along with a check in the amount of $20,000 and a letter dated September 8, 1975, which read in relevant part as follows:

My clients are concerned that the following items remain with the real estate: a) dining room set and tapestry wall covering in dining room; b) fireplace fixtures throughout; c) the sun parlor furniture. I would appreciate your confirming that these items are a part of the transaction, as they would be difficult to replace.

The defendants refused to agree to sell the enumerated items and did not sign the purchase and sale agreement. They directed their attorney to return the agreement and the deposit check to plaintiff and subsequently refused to sell the property to plaintiff. This action for specific performance followed.

In Superior Court, defendants moved for summary judgment on the ground that the facts were not in dispute and no contract had been formed as a matter of law. The trial justice ruled that the letter quoted above constituted a conditional acceptance of defendants' offer to sell the property and consequently must be construed as a counteroffer. Since defendants never accepted the counteroffer, it followed that no contract was formed, and summary judgment was granted. . . .

The plaintiff's . . . contention is that the trial justice incorrectly applied the principles of contract law in deciding that the facts did not disclose a valid acceptance of defendants' offer. [W]e cannot agree.

The trial justice proceeded on the theory that the delivery of the purchase and sale agreement to plaintiff constituted an offer by defendants to sell the property. Because we must view the evidence in the light most favorable to the party against whom summary judgment was entered, in this case plaintiff, we assume as the trial justice did that the delivery of the agreement was in fact an offer.[3]

The question we must answer next is whether there was an acceptance of that offer. . . . A review of the record shows that the only expression of acceptance which was communicated to defendants was the delivery of the executed purchase and sale agreement accompanied by the letter of September 8. Therefore it is solely on the basis of the language used in these two documents that we must determine whether there was a valid acceptance. Whatever plaintiff's unexpressed intention may have been in sending the documents is irrelevant. We must be concerned only with the language actually used, not the language plaintiff thought he was using or intended to use.

There is no doubt that the execution and delivery of the purchase and sale agreement by plaintiff, without more, would have operated as an

---

3. The conclusion that the delivery of the agreement was an offer is not unassailable in view of the fact that defendants did not sign the agreement before sending it to plaintiff, and the fact that plaintiff told defendants' attorney *after* the agreement was received that he would have to investigate certain conditions of title before signing the agreement. If it was not an offer, plaintiff's execution of the agreement could itself be no more than an offer, which defendants never accepted.

acceptance. The terms of the accompanying letter, however, apparently conditioned the acceptance upon the inclusion of various items of personalty. In assessing the effect of the terms of that letter we must keep in mind certain generally accepted rules. To be effective, an acceptance must be definite and unequivocal. "An offeror is entitled to know in clear terms whether the offeree accepts his proposal. It is not enough that the words of a reply justify a probable inference of assent." 1 *Restatement Contracts* § 58, cmt. a (1932). The acceptance may not impose additional conditions on the offer, nor may it add limitations. "An acceptance which is equivocal or upon condition or with a limitation is a counteroffer and requires acceptance by the original offeror before a contractual relationship can exist." John Hancock Mut. Life Ins. Co. v. Dietlin, 97 R.I. 515, 518, 199 A.2d 311, 313 (1964).

However, an acceptance may be valid despite conditional language if the acceptance is clearly independent of the condition. Many cases have so held. Williston states the rule as follows:

> Frequently an offeree, while making a positive acceptance of the offer, also makes a request or suggestion that some addition or modification be made. So long as it is clear that the meaning of the acceptance is positively and unequivocally to accept the offer whether such request is granted or not, a contract is formed. 1 Williston, *Contracts* § 79 at 261–62 (3d ed. 1957).

Corbin is in agreement with the above view. 1 Corbin, [*Contracts*] § 84 [1963] at 363–65. Thus our task is to decide whether plaintiff's letter is more reasonably interpreted as a qualified acceptance or as an absolute acceptance together with a mere inquiry concerning a collateral matter.

In making our decision we recognize that, as one text states, "The question whether a communication by an offeree is a conditional acceptance or counter-offer is not always easy to answer. It must be determined by the same common-sense process of interpretation that must be applied in so many other cases." 1 *Corbin*, *supra* § 82 at 353. In our opinion the language used in plaintiff's letter of September 8 is not consistent with an absolute acceptance accompanied by a request for a gratuitous benefit. We interpret the letter to impose a condition on plaintiff's acceptance of defendants' offer. The letter does not unequivocally state that even without the enumerated items plaintiff is willing to complete the contract. In fact, the letter seeks "confirmation" that the listed items "are a part of the transaction." Thus, far from being an independent, collateral request, the sale of the items in question is explicitly referred to as a part of the real estate transaction. Moreover, the letter goes on to stress the difficulty of finding replacements for these items. This is a further indication that plaintiff did not view the inclusion of the listed items as merely collateral or incidental to the real estate transaction. . . .

Accordingly, we hold that since the plaintiff's letter of acceptance dated September 8 was conditional, it operated as a rejection of the defendants' offer and no contractual obligation was created.

The plaintiff's appeal is denied and dismissed, the judgment appealed from is affirmed and the case is remanded to the Superior Court.

DORTON v. COLLINS & AIKMAN CORP.

United States Court of Appeals, Sixth Circuit, 1972.
453 F.2d 1161.

CELEBREZZE, CIRCUIT JUDGE. . . .

The primary question before us on appeal is whether the District Court, in denying Collins & Aikman's motion for a stay pending arbitration, erred in holding that The Carpet Mart was not bound by the arbitration agreement appearing on the back of Collins & Aikman's acknowledgment forms. . . .

In each of the more than 55 transactions, one of the partners in The Carpet Mart, or, on some occasions, Collins & Aikman's visiting salesman, telephoned Collins & Aikman's order department in Dalton, Georgia, and ordered certain quantities of carpets listed in Collins & Aikman's catalogue. There is some dispute as to what, if any, agreements were reached through the telephone calls and through the visits by Collins & Aikman's salesman. After each oral order was placed, the price, if any, quoted by the buyer was checked against Collins & Aikman's price list, and the credit department was consulted to determine if The Carpet Mart had paid for all previous shipments. After it was found that everything was in order, Collins & Aikman's order department typed the information concerning the particular order on one of its printed acknowledgment forms. Each acknowledgment form bore one of three legends: "Acknowledgment," "Customer Acknowledgment," or "Sales Contract." The following provision was printed on the face of the forms bearing the "Acknowledgment" legend:

> The acceptance of your order is subject to all of the terms and conditions on the face and reverse side hereof, including arbitration, all of which are accepted by buyer; it supersedes buyer's order form, if any. It shall become a contract either (a) when signed and delivered by buyer to seller and accepted in writing by seller, or (b) at Seller's option, when buyer shall have given to seller specification of assortments, delivery dates, shipping instructions, or instructions to bill and hold as to all or any part of the merchandise herein described, or when buyer has received delivery of the whole or any part thereof, or when buyer has otherwise assented to the terms and conditions hereof. . . .

The small print on the reverse side of the forms provided, among other things, that all claims arising out of the contract would be submitted to arbitration in New York City. Each acknowledgment form was signed by an employee of Collins & Aikman's order department and mailed to The Carpet Mart on the day the telephone order was received or, at the latest, on the following day. The carpets were thereafter shipped to The Carpet Mart, with the interval between the mailing of the acknowledgment form and shipment of the carpets varying from a brief interval to a period of several weeks or months. Absent a delay in the mails, however, The Carpet Mart always received the acknowledgment forms prior to receiving the carpets. In all cases The Carpet Mart took delivery of and paid for the carpets without objecting to any terms contained in the acknowledgment form.

In holding that no binding arbitration agreement was created between the parties through the transactions above, the District Court relied on T.C.A. 47 2–207 [UCC § 2–207]*, which provides:

> (1) A definite and seasonable expression of acceptance or a written confirmation which is sent within a reasonable time operates as an acceptance even though it states terms additional to or different from those offered or agreed upon, unless acceptance is expressly made conditional on assent to the additional or different terms.

> (2) The additional terms are to be construed as proposals for addition to the contract. Between merchants such terms become part of the contract unless: (a) the offer expressly limits acceptance to the terms of the offer; (b) they materially alter it; or (c) notification of objection to them has already been given or is given within a reasonable time after notice of them is received.

> (3) Conduct by both parties which recognizes the existence of a contract is sufficient to establish a contract for sale although the writings of the parties do not otherwise establish a contract. In such case the terms of the particular contract consist of those terms on which the writings of the parties agree, together with any supplementary terms incorporated under any other provisions of chapters 1 through 9 of this title.

The District Court found that Subsection 2–207(3) controlled the instant case, quoting the following passage from 1 W. Hawkland, *A Transactional Guide to the Uniform Commercial Code* 1.090303, at 19–20 (1964):

> If the seller ... ships the goods and the buyer accepts them, a contract is formed under subsection (3). The terms of this contract are those on which the purchase order and acknowledgment agree, and the additional terms needed for a contract are to be found throughout the U.C.C. ... (T)he U.C.C. does not impose an arbitration term on the parties where their contract is silent on the matter. Hence, a conflict between an arbitration and an no-arbitration clause would result in the no-arbitration clause becoming effective.

Under this authority alone the District Court concluded that the arbitration clause on the back of Collins & Aikman's sales acknowledgment had not become a binding term in the 50 odd transactions with The Carpet Mart. . . .

---

* Tennessee Code Annotated citations are replaced by UCC citations for the balance of the opinion. Ed.

[I]t is clear that ... Subsection 2–207(1), was intended to alter the "ribbon matching" or "mirror" rule of common law, under which the terms of an acceptance ... were required to be identical to the terms of the offer.... 1 *W. Hawkland, supra,* at 16; R. Nordstrom, *Handbook of the Law of Sales,* Sec. 37, at 99 100 (1970). Under the common law, an acceptance ... which contained terms additional to or different from those of the offer ... constituted a rejection of the offer ... and thus became a counter-offer. The terms of the counter-offer were said to have been accepted by the original offeror when he proceeded to perform under the contract without objecting to the counter-offer. Thus, a buyer was deemed to have accepted the seller's counter-offer if he took receipt of the goods and paid for them without objection.

Under Section 2–207 the result is different. This section of the Code recognizes that in current commercial transactions, the terms of the offer and those of the acceptance will seldom be identical. Rather, under the current "battle of the forms," each party typically has a printed form drafted by his attorney and containing as many terms as could be envisioned to favor that party in his sales transactions. Whereas under common law the disparity between the fine-print terms in the parties' forms would have prevented the consummation of a contract when these forms are exchanged, Section 2–207 recognizes that in many, but not all, cases the parties do not impart such significance to the terms on the printed forms. *See* 1 *W. Hawkland, supra*; 1.0903, at 14, 1.090301, at 16. ... Thus, under Subsection (1), a contract is recognized notwithstanding the fact that an acceptance ... contains terms additional to or different from those of the offer ..., provided that the offeree's intent to accept the offer is definitely expressed, *see* Sections 2–204 and 2–206, and provided that the offeree's acceptance is not expressly conditioned on the offeror's assent to the additional or different terms. When a contract is recognized under Subsection (1), the additional terms are treated as "proposals for addition to the contract" under Subsection (2), which contains special provisions under which such additional terms are deemed to have been accepted when the transaction is between merchants. Conversely, when no contract is recognized under Subsection 2–207(1)—either because no definite expression of acceptance exists or, more specifically, because the offeree's acceptance is expressly conditioned on the offeror's assent to the additional or different terms—the entire transaction aborts at this point. If, however, the subsequent conduct of the parties—particularly, performance by both parties under what they apparently believe to be a contract—recognizes the existence of a contract, under Subsection 2–207(3) such conduct by both parties is sufficient to establish a contract, notwithstanding the fact that no contract would have been recognized on the basis of their writings alone. Subsection 2–207(3) further provides how the terms of contracts recognized thereunder shall be determined.

With the above analysis and purposes of Section 2–207 in mind, we turn to their application in the present case. We initially observe that the affidavits and the acknowledgment forms themselves raise the question of whether Collins & Aikman's forms constituted acceptances or confirmations under Section 2–207. The language of some of the acknowledgment forms ("The acceptance of your order is subject to . . .") and the affidavit of Mr. William T. Hester, Collins & Aikman's marketing operations manager, suggest that the forms were the only acceptances issued in response to The Carpet Mart's oral offers. However, in his affidavit Mr. J.A. Castle, a partner in The Carpet Mart, asserted that when he personally called Collins & Aikman to order carpets, someone from the latter's order department would agree to sell the requested carpets, or, alternatively, when Collins & Aikman's visiting salesman took the order, he would agree to the sale, on some occasions after he had used The Carpet Mart's telephone to call Collins & Aikman's order department. Absent the District Court's determination of whether Collins & Aikman's acknowledgment forms were acceptances or, alternatively, confirmations of prior oral agreements, we will consider the application of Section 2–207 to both situations for the guidance of the District Court on remand.

Viewing Collins & Aikman's acknowledgment forms as acceptances under Subsection 2–207(1), we are initially faced with the question of whether the arbitration provision in Collins & Aikman's acknowledgment forms were in fact "additional to or different from" the terms of The Carpet Mart's oral offers. In the typical case under Section 2–207, there exist both a written purchase order and a written acknowledgment, and this determination can be readily made by comparing the two forms. In the present case, where the only written forms were Collins & Aikman's sales acknowledgments, we believe that such a comparison must be made between the oral offers and the written acceptances. Although the District Court apparently assumed that The Carpet Mart's oral orders did not include in their terms the arbitration provision which appeared in Collins & Aikman's acknowledgment forms, we believe that a specific finding on this point will be required on remand.

Assuming, for purposes of analysis, that the arbitration provision was an addition to the terms of The Carpet Mart's oral offers, we must next determine whether or not Collins & Aikman's acceptances were "expressly made conditional on assent to the additional . . . terms" therein, within the proviso of Subsection 2–207(1). As set forth in full above, the provision appearing on the face of Collins & Aikman's acknowledgment forms stated that the acceptances . . . were "subject to all of the terms and conditions on the face and reverse side hereof, including arbitration, all of which are accepted by buyer." The provision on the "Acknowledgment" forms further stated that Collins & Aikman's terms would become the basis of the contract between the parties

> either (a) when signed and delivered by buyer to seller and accepted in writing by seller, or (b) at Seller's option, when buyer shall have given to seller specification of assortments, delivery dates, shipping instructions, or instructions to bill and hold as to all or any part of the merchandise herein described, or when buyer has received deliv-

ery of the whole or any part thereof, or when buyer has otherwise assented to the terms and conditions hereof. . . .

Although Collins & Aikman's use of the words "subject to" suggests that the acceptances were conditional to some extent, we do not believe the acceptances were "expressly made conditional on (the buyer's) assent to the additional or different terms," as specifically required under the Subsection 2–207(1) proviso. In order to fall within this proviso, it is not enough that an acceptance is expressly conditional on additional or different terms; rather, an acceptance must be *expressly* conditional on the offeror's *assent* to those terms. Viewing the Subsection (1) proviso within the context of the rest of that Subsection and within the policies of Section 2–207 itself, we believe that it was intended to apply only to an acceptance which clearly reveals that the offeree is unwilling to proceed with the transaction unless he is assured of the offeror's assent to the additional or different terms therein. *See* 1 *W. Hawkland, supra*, 1.090303, at 21. That the acceptance is predicated on the offeror's assent must be "directly and distinctly stated or expressed rather than implied or left to inference." Webster's Third International Dictionary (defining "express").

Although the UCC does not provide a definition of "assent," it is significant that Collins & Aikman's printed acknowledgment forms specified at least seven types of action or inaction on the part of the buyer which—sometimes at Collins & Aikman's option—would be deemed to bind the buyer to the terms therein. These ranged from the buyer's signing and delivering the acknowledgment to the seller—which indeed could have been recognized as the buyer's assent to Collins & Aikman's terms—to the buyer's retention of the acknowledgment for ten days without objection—which could never have been recognized as the buyer's assent to the additional or different terms where acceptance is expressly conditional on that assent.

To recognize Collins & Aikman's acceptances as "expressly conditional on (the buyer's) assent to the additional . . . terms" therein, within the proviso of Subsection 2–207(1), would thus require us to ignore the specific language of that provision. Such an interpretation is not justified in view of the fact that Subsection 2–207(1) is clearly designed to give legal recognition to many contracts where the variance between the offer and acceptance would have precluded such recognition at common law.

Because Collins & Aikman's acceptances were not expressly conditional on the buyer's assent to the additional terms within the proviso of Subsection 2–207(1), a contract is recognized under Subsection (1), and the additional terms are treated as "proposals" for addition to the contract under Subsection 2–207(2). Since both Collins & Aikman and The Carpet Mart are clearly "merchants" as that term is defined in Subsection 2–104(1), the arbitration provision will be deemed to have been accepted by The Carpet Mart under Subsection 2–207(2) unless it materially altered the terms of The Carpet Mart's oral offers. UCC § 2–207(2)(b). We believe that the question of whether the arbitration provision materially altered the oral offer under Subsection 2–207(2)(b) is one which can be resolved only by the District Court on further findings of fact in the present case. If the arbitration provision did in fact materially alter The Carpet Mart's offer, it could not become a part of the contract "unless expressly agreed to" by The Carpet Mart. UCC § 2–207, Official Comment No. 3.

We therefore conclude that if on remand the District Court finds that Collins & Aikman's acknowledgments were in fact acceptances and that the arbitration provision was additional to the terms of The Carpet Mart's oral orders, contracts will be recognized under Subsection 2–207(1). The arbitration clause will then be viewed as a "proposal" under Subsection 2–207(2) which will be deemed to have been accepted by The Carpet Mart unless it materially altered the oral offers.

If the District Court finds that Collins & Aikman's acknowledgment forms were not acceptances but rather were confirmations of prior oral agreements between the parties, an application of Section 2–207 similar to that above will be required. Subsection 2–207(1) will require an initial determination of whether the arbitration provision in the confirmations was "additional to or different from" the terms orally agreed upon. Assuming that the District Court finds that the arbitration provision was not a term of the oral agreements between the parties, the arbitration clause will be treated as a "proposal" for addition to the contract under Subsection 2–207(2), as was the case when Collins & Aikman's acknowledgments were viewed as acceptances above. The provision for arbitration will be deemed to have been accepted by The Carpet Mart unless the District Court finds that it materially altered the prior oral agreements, in which case The Carpet Mart could not become bound thereby absent an express agreement to that effect.

As a result of the above application of Section 2–207 to the limited facts before us in the present case, we find it necessary to remand the case to the District Court for the following findings: (1) whether oral agreements were reached between the parties prior to the sending of Collins & Aikman's acknowledgment forms; if there were no such oral agreements, (2) whether the arbitration provision appearing in Collins & Aikman's "acceptances" was additional to the terms of The Carpet Mart's oral offers; and, if so, (3) whether the arbitration provision materially altered the terms of The Carpet Mart's oral offers. Alternatively, if the District Court does find that oral agreements were reached between the parties before Collins & Aikman's acknowledgment forms were sent in each instance, it will be necessary for the District Court to make the following findings: (1) whether the prior oral agreements embodied the arbitration provision appearing in Collins & Aikman's "confirmations"; and, if not, (2) whether the arbitration provision materially altered the prior oral agreements. Regardless of whether the District Court finds Collins & Aikman's acknowledgment forms to have been acceptances or confirmations, if the arbitration provision was additional to, and a material alteration of, the offers or prior oral agreements, The Carpet Mart will not be bound to that provision absent a finding that it expressly agreed to be bound thereby. . . .

[Remanded for further findings.]

DIAMOND FRUIT GROWERS, INC. v. KRACK CORP.

United States Court of Appeals, Ninth Circuit, 1986.
794 F.2d 1440.

WIGGINS, CIRCUIT JUDGE: Metal–Matic, Inc. (Metal–Matic) appeals from judgment entered after a jury verdict in favor of Krack Corporation (Krack) on Krack's third-party complaint against Metal–Matic. Metal–Matic also appeals from the district court's denial of its motion for judgment n.o.v. We have jurisdiction under 28 U.S.C. § 1291 (1982) and affirm.

FACTS AND PROCEEDINGS BELOW

Krack is a manufacturer of cooling units that contain steel tubing it purchases from outside suppliers. Metal–Matic is one of Krack's tubing suppliers. At the time this dispute arose, Metal–Matic had been supplying tubing to Krack for about ten years. The parties followed the same course of dealing during the entire ten years. At the beginning of each year, Krack sent a blanket purchase order to Metal–Matic stating how much tubing Krack would need for the year. Then, throughout the year as Krack needed tubing, it sent release purchase orders to Metal–Matic requesting that tubing be shipped. Metal–Matic responded to Krack's release purchase orders by sending Krack an acknowledgment form and then shipping the tubing.[1]

Metal–Matic's acknowledgment form disclaimed all liability for consequential damages and limited Metal–Matic's liability for defects in the tubing to refund of the purchase price or replacement or repair of the tubing. As one would expect, these terms were not contained in Krack's purchase order. The following statement was printed on Metal–Matic's form:

> Metal–Matic, Inc.'s acceptance of purchaser's offer or its offer to purchaser is hereby expressly made conditional to purchaser's acceptance of the terms and provisions of the acknowledgment form.

This statement and the disclaimer of liability were on the back of the acknowledgment form. However, printed at the bottom of the front of the form in bold-face capitals was the following statement: "SEE REVERSE SIDE FOR TERMS AND CONDITIONS OF SALE."

On at least one occasion during the ten-year relationship between Metal–Matic and Krack, Allen Zver, Krack's purchasing manager, dis-

---

1. The blanket purchase order apparently did no more than establish Krack's willingness to purchase an amount of tubing during the year. The parties' conduct indicates that they intended to establish their contract based on Krack's release purchase orders and Metal–Matic's acknowledgments sent in response to those purchase orders.

cussed the limitation of warranty and disclaimer of liability terms contained in Metal–Matic's acknowledgment form with Robert Van Krevelen, Executive Vice President of Metal–Matic. Zver told Van Krevelen that Krack objected to the terms and tried to convince him to change them, but Van Krevelen refused to do so. After the discussions, Krack continued to accept and pay for tubing from Metal–Matic.

In February 1981, Krack sold one of its cooling units to Diamond Fruit Growers, Inc. (Diamond) in Oregon, and in September 1981, Diamond installed the unit in a controlled-atmosphere warehouse. In January 1982, the unit began leaking ammonia from a cooling coil made of steel tubing.

After Diamond discovered that ammonia was leaking into the warehouse, Joseph Smith, the engineer who had been responsible for building Diamond's controlled-atmosphere warehouses, was called in to find the source of the leak. Smith testified that he found a pinhole leak in the cooling coil of the Krack cooling unit. Smith inspected the coil while it was still inside the unit. He last inspected the coil on April 23, 1982. The coil then sat in a hall at Diamond's warehouse until May, 1984, when John Myers inspected the coil for Metal–Matic.

Myers cut the defective tubing out of the unit and took it to his office. At his office, he did more cutting on the tubing. After Myers inspected the tubing, it was also inspected by Bruce Wong for Diamond and Paul Irish for Krack.

Diamond sued Krack to recover the loss in value of fruit that it was forced to remove from the storage room as a result of the leak. Krack in turn brought a third-party complaint against Metal–Matic and Van Huffel Tube Corporation (Van Huffel), another of its tubing suppliers, seeking contribution or indemnity in the event it was held liable to Diamond. At the close of the evidence, both Metal–Matic and Van Huffel moved for a directed verdict on the third party complaint. The court granted Van Huffel's motion based on evidence that the failed tubing was not manufactured by Van Huffel. The court denied Metal–Matic's motion.

The jury returned a verdict in favor of Diamond against Krack. It then found that Krack was entitled to contribution from Metal–Matic for thirty percent of Diamond's damages. Metal–Matic moved for judgment n.o.v. The court denied that motion and entered judgment on the jury verdict.

Metal–Matic raises two grounds for reversal. First, Metal–Matic contends that as part of its contract with Krack, it disclaimed all liability for consequential damages and specifically limited its liability for defects in the tubing to refund of the purchase price or replacement or repair of the tubing. Second, Metal–Matic asserts that the evidence does not support a finding that it manufactured the tubing in which the leak developed or that it caused the leak. We address each of these contentions in turn. . . .

DISCUSSION

A. Metal–Matic's Disclaimer of Liability for Consequential Damages

If the contract between Metal–Matic and Krack contains Metal–Matic's disclaimer of liability, Metal–Matic is not liable to indemnify Krack for part of Diamond's damages. Therefore, the principal issue before us on this appeal is whether Metal–Matic's disclaimer of liability became part of the contract between these parties.

Relying on Uniform Commercial Code (U.C.C.) § 2–207, Or.Rev.Stat. § 72.2070 (1985), Krack argues that Metal–Matic's disclaimer did not become part of the contract. Metal–Matic, on the other hand, argues that section 2–207 is inapplicable to this case because the parties discussed the disclaimer, and Krack assented to it.

Krack is correct in its assertion that section 2–207 applies to this case. One intended application of section 2–207 is to commercial transactions in which the parties exchange printed purchase order and acknowledgment forms. *See* U.C.C. § 2–207 comment 1. The drafters of the U.C.C. recognized that "(b)ecause the (purchase order and acknowledgment) forms are oriented to the thinking of the respective drafting parties, the terms contained in them often do not correspond." *Id.* Section 2–207 is an attempt to provide rules of contract formation in such cases. In this case, Krack and Metal–Matic exchanged purchase order and acknowledgment forms that contained different or additional terms. This, then, is a typical section 2–207 situation. The fact that the parties discussed the terms of their contract after they exchanged their forms does not put this case outside section 2–207. *See* 3 R. Duesenburg & L. King, *Sales and Bulk Transfers under the Uniform Commercial Code* (Bender's U.C.C. Service) § 3.05(2) (1986). Section 2–207 provides rules of contract formation in cases such as this one in which the parties exchange forms but do not agree on all the terms of their contract.

A brief summary of section 2–207 is necessary to an understanding of its application to this case. Section 2–207 changes the common law's mirror-image rule for transactions that fall within article 2 of the U.C.C. At common law, an acceptance that varies the terms of the offer is a counteroffer and operates as a rejection of the original offer. *See* Idaho Power Co. v. Westinghouse Electric Corp., 596 F.2d 924, 926 (9th Cir. 1979). If the offeror goes ahead with the contract after receiving the counteroffer, his performance is an acceptance of the terms of the counteroffer. *See* C. Itoh & Co. v. Jordan International Co., 552 F.2d 1228, 1236 (7th Cir.1977); J. White & R. Summers, *Handbook of the Law Under the Uniform Commercial Code,* § 1–2 at 34 (2d ed. 1980).

Generally, section 2–207(1) "converts a common law counteroffer into an acceptance even though it states additional or different terms." *Idaho Power,* 596 F.2d at 926; *see* U.C.C. § 2–207(1). The only requirement under section 2–207(1) is that the responding form contain a definite and seasonable expression of acceptance. The terms of the responding form that correspond to the offer constitute the contract. Under section 2–

207(2), the additional terms of the responding form become proposals for additions to the contract. Between merchants the additional terms become part of the contract unless the offer is specifically limited to its terms, the offeror objects to the additional terms, or the additional terms materially alter the terms of the offer. U.C.C. § 2–207(2); *see J. White & R. Summers*, § 1–2 at 32.

However, section 2–207(1) is subject to a proviso. If a definite and seasonable expression of acceptance expressly conditions acceptance on the offeror's assent to additional or different terms contained therein, the parties' differing forms do not result in a contract unless the offeror assents to the additional terms. *See J. White & R. Summers*, § 1–2 at 32–33. If the offeror assents, the parties have a contract and the additional terms are a part of that contract. If, however, the offeror does not assent, but the parties proceed with the transaction as if they have a contract, their performance results in formation of a contract. U.C.C. § 2–207(3). In that case, the terms of the contract are those on which the parties' forms agree plus any terms supplied by the U.C.C. *Id.; see* Boise Cascade Corp. v. Etsco, Ltd., 39 U.C.C.Rep.Serv. (Callaghan) 410, 414 (D.Or.1984); *J. White & R. Summers*, § 1–2 at 34.

In this case, Metal–Matic expressly conditioned its acceptance on Krack's assent to the additional terms contained in Metal–Matic's acknowledgment form. That form tracks the language of the section 2–207(1) proviso, stating that "Metal–Matic, Inc.'s acceptance . . . is hereby *expressly made conditional* to purchaser's acceptance of the terms and provisions of the acknowledgment form." (emphasis added). *See C. Itoh & Co.*, 552 F.2d at 1235. Therefore, we must determine whether Krack assented to Metal–Matic's limitation of liability term.

Metal–Matic argues that Krack did assent to the limitation of liability term. This argument is based on the discussions between Zver for Krack and Van Krevelen for Metal–Matic. Some time during the ten-year relationship between the companies, these two men discussed Krack's objections to the warranty and liability limitation terms in Metal–Matic's acknowledgment form. Krack attempted to persuade Metal–Matic to change its form, but Metal–Matic refused to do so. After the discussions, the companies continued to do business as in the past. Metal–Matic contends that Krack assented to the limitation of liability term when it continued to accept and pay for tubing after Metal–Matic insisted that the contract contain its terms.

To address Metal–Matic's argument, we must determine what constitutes assent to additional or different terms for purposes of section 2–207(1). The parties have not directed us to any cases that analyze this question and our research has revealed none.[6] We therefore look to the

---

6. The United States District Court for the District of Columbia has decided a case on this issue. However, the case is of little precedential value because the court provided no analysis to support its decision. In *McKenzie v. Alla–Ohio Coals, Inc.*, 29 U.C.C.Rep.Serv. (Callaghan) 852, 855 (D.D.C.1979), the offeror objected to a term in the offeree's form. The offeree reaffirmed that term, and the offeror made no further objection. The court held that the term was part of the

language and structure of section 2–207 and to the purposes behind that section to determine the correct standard.

One of the principles underlying section 2–207 is neutrality. If possible, the section should be interpreted so as to give neither party to a contract an advantage simply because it happened to send the first or in some cases the last form. *See J. White & R. Summers*, § 1–2 at 26–27. Section 2–207 accomplishes this result in part by doing away with the common law's "last shot" rule. *See 3 R. Duesenberg & L. King*, § 3.05(1)(a)(iii) at 3–73. At common law, the offeree/counterofferor gets all of its terms simply because it fired the last shot in the exchange of forms. Section 2–207(3) does away with this result by giving neither party the terms it attempted to impose unilaterally on the other. *See id.* at 3–71. Instead, all of the terms on which the parties' forms do not agree drop out, and the U.C.C. supplies the missing terms.

Generally, this result is fair because both parties are responsible for the ambiguity in their contract. The parties could have negotiated a contract and agreed on its terms, but for whatever reason, they failed to do so. Therefore, neither party should get its terms. *See 3 R. Duesenberg & L. King*, § 3.05(2) at 3–88. However, as White and Summers point out, resort to section 2–207(3) will often work to the disadvantage of the seller because he will "wish to undertake less responsibility for the quality of his goods than the Code imposes or else wish to limit his damages liability more narrowly than would the Code." *J. White & R. Summers*, § 1–2 at 34. Nevertheless, White and Summers recommend that section 2–207(3) be applied in such cases. *Id.* We agree. Application of section 2–207(3) is more equitable than giving one party its terms simply because it sent the last form. Further, the terms imposed by the code are presumably equitable and consistent with public policy because they are statutorily imposed. *See 3 R. Duesenberg & L. King*, § 3.05(2) at 3–88.

With these general principles in mind, we turn now to Metal–Matic's argument that Krack assented to the disclaimer when it continued to accept and pay for tubing once Metal–Matic indicated that it was willing to sell tubing only if its warranty and liability terms were part of the contract. Metal–Matic's argument is appealing. Sound policy supports permitting a seller to control the terms on which it will sell its products, especially in a case in which the seller has indicated both in writing and orally that those are the only terms on which it is willing to sell the product. Nevertheless, we reject Metal–Matic's argument because we find that these considerations are outweighed by the public policy reflected by Oregon's enactment of the U.C.C.

If we were to accept Metal–Matic's argument, we would reinstate to some extent the common law's last shot rule. To illustrate, assume that the parties in this case had sent the same forms but in the reverse order and that Krack's form contained terms stating that Metal–Matic is liable

---

contract because the parties continued to behave as if they had a contract after the offeree reaffirmed the term.

for all consequential damages and conditioning acceptance on Metal–Matic's assent to Krack's terms. Assume also that Metal–Matic objected to Krack's terms but Krack refused to change them and that the parties continued with their transaction anyway. If we applied Metal–Matic's argument in that case, we would find that Krack's term was part of the contract because Metal–Matic continued to ship tubing to Krack after Krack reaffirmed that it would purchase tubing only if Metal–Matic were fully liable for consequential damages. Thus, the result would turn on which party sent the last form, and would therefore be inconsistent with section 2–207's purpose of doing away with the last shot rule.

That result is avoided by requiring a specific and unequivocal expression of assent on the part of the offeror when the offeree conditions its acceptance on assent to additional or different terms. If the offeror does not give specific and unequivocal assent but the parties act as if they have a contract, the provisions of section 2–207(3) apply to fill in the terms of the contract. Application of section 2–207(3) is appropriate in that situation because by going ahead with the transaction without resolving their dispute, both parties are responsible for introducing ambiguity into the contract. Further, in a case such as this one, requiring the seller to assume more liability than it intends is not altogether inappropriate. The seller is most responsible for the ambiguity because it inserts a term in its form that requires assent to additional terms and then does not enforce that requirement. If the seller truly does not want to be bound unless the buyer assents to its terms, it can protect itself by not shipping until it obtains that assent. *See* C. Itoh & Co., 552 F.2d at 1238.

We hold that because Krack's conduct did not indicate unequivocally that Krack intended to assent to Metal–Matic's terms, that conduct did not amount to the assent contemplated by section 2–207(1). *See* 3 *R. Duesenberg & L. King*, § 3.05(1)(a)(iii) at 3–74. . . .

The jury verdict is supported by the evidence and consistent with the U.C.C. Therefore, the district court did not err in denying Metal–Matic's motion for a directed verdict.

Affirmed.

PROBLEMS

74. A offers to sell B Blackacre for $5,000, the offer to be open for 30 days.

    (a) B replies immediately, "I'll pay $4,800." A refuses; B accepts within 30 days. Is there a contract?

    (b) B replies immediately, "I'll pay $4,800." A replies, "Cannot reduce price." B accepts within 30 days. Is there a contract?

    (c) B says, "Won't you take $4,800?" A refuses. B accepts within 30 days. Is there a contract?

    (d) B says "I am keeping your offer under advisement but if you wish to close the deal now I'll give you $4,800." A refuses. B accepts within 30 days. Is there a contract?

(e) B replies immediately, "I accept but I still insist that you are driving a hard bargain." Is there a contract?

75.   A makes a written offer to B to sell him Blackacre. B replies: "I accept your offer if you can convey me a good title." Is there a contract?

76.   After negotiations, the State Department of Transportation ("DOT") offered to renew Express Industries' expired lease for the use of a state-owned pier for a four-year period for $3,500,000. The offeree's president signified acceptance of the offer by signing and returning it. An environmental group, HRC, had been a party to the negotiations. The offeree's cover letter returning the offer stated that "certain parts of the deal are still under discussion with the HRC and when Mr. McGowan of that group returns from vacation we can resolve an outstanding issue: the exclusion of 70,000 square feet of the truck yard from the lease." Upon receipt of the letter and signed offer, the DOT received an offer of $4,500,000 from another party and proceeded to accept the higher offer. Express Industries sues the State for breach of contract. What result?

77.   A makes an offer for the sale of goods to B and B accepts but adds: "Prompt acknowledgment must be made of receipt of this letter." Is there a contract? If so, what are its terms?

78.   B made an offer to buy goods, S sent a letter to B accepting the offer but made its acceptance expressly conditional on assent to its limited warranty terms and to certain payment terms. B then, by letter, requested a change in the payment terms and S agreed. S then delivered the goods which B accepted. Do S's limited warranty terms form part of the contract, or do the implied warranty terms of the Code form part of the contract?

79.   X and Y exchanged correspondence and entered into a contract for the sale of goods containing terms A, B and C.

(a) If X sent a written confirmation listing terms A, B, C and D what would be the result?

(b) Suppose that both parties send memos. X's memo lists terms A, B, C and D and Y's memo sets forth terms A, B, C and "not D." What result?

80.   B and S entered into a verbal agreement for the sale of certain restaurant equipment at which time they discussed an approximate price. An invoice was delivered with the equipment. B accepted the goods without reading the invoice and did not contest the invoice price, which was several thousand dollars higher than the approximate price discussed, until 90 days later. S sues to recover the invoice price. Does the invoice operate as a confirmation? If so, what is the result?

(b) TERMS IN THE BOX

(Calamari & Perillo on Contracts § 2.12)

PROCD, INC. v. ZEIDENBERG
United States Court of Appeals, Seventh Circuit, 1996.
86 F.3d 1447.

EASTERBROOK, CIRCUIT JUDGE. Must buyers of computer software obey the terms of shrinkwrap licenses? The district court held not, for two reasons: first, they are not contracts because the licenses are inside the box rather than printed on the outside; second, federal law forbids enforcement even if the licenses are contracts. 908 F.Supp. 640 (W.D.Wis. 1996). The parties and numerous *amici curiae* have briefed many other issues, but these are the only two that matter—and we disagree with the district judge's conclusion on each. Shrinkwrap licenses are enforceable unless their terms are objectionable on grounds applicable to contracts in general (for example, if they violate a rule of positive law, or if they are unconscionable). Because no one argues that the terms of the license at issue here are troublesome, we remand with instructions to enter judgment for the plaintiff.

I

ProCD, the plaintiff, has compiled information from more than 3,000 telephone directories into a computer database. We may assume that this database cannot be copyrighted, although it is more complex, contains more information (nine-digit zip codes and census industrial codes), is organized differently, and therefore is more original than the single alphabetical directory at issue in Feist Publications, Inc. v. Rural Telephone Service Co., 499 U.S. 340, 111 S.Ct. 1282, 113 L.Ed.2d 358 (1991). *See* Paul J. Heald, *The Vices of Originality*, 1991 Sup.Ct. Rev. 143, 160–68. ProCD sells a version of the database, called SelectPhone (trademark), on CD–ROM discs. (CD–ROM means "compact disc—read only memory." The "shrinkwrap license" gets its name from the fact that retail software packages are covered in plastic or cellophane "shrinkwrap," and some vendors, though not ProCD, have written licenses that become effective as soon as the customer tears the wrapping from the package. Vendors prefer "end user license," but we use the more common term.) A proprietary method of compressing the data serves as effective encryption too. Customers decrypt and use the data with the aid of an application program that ProCD has written. This program, which is copyrighted, searches the database in response to users' criteria (such as "find all people named Tatum in Tennessee, plus all firms with 'Door Systems' in the corporate name"). The resulting lists (or, as ProCD prefers, "listings") can be read and manipulated by other software, such as word processing programs.

The database in SelectPhone (trademark) cost more than $10 million to compile and is expensive to keep current. It is much more valuable to some users than to others. The combination of names, addresses, and SIC*

---

* Standard Industrial Codes. Ed.

codes enables manufacturers to compile lists of potential customers. Manufacturers and retailers pay high prices to specialized information intermediaries for such mailing lists; ProCD offers a potentially cheaper alternative. People with nothing to sell could use the database as a substitute for calling long distance information, or as a way to look up old friends who have moved to unknown towns, or just as an electronic substitute for the local phone book. ProCD decided to engage in price discrimination, selling its database to the general public for personal use at a low price (approximately $150 for the set of five discs) while selling information to the trade for a higher price. It has adopted some intermediate strategies too: access to the SelectPhone (trademark) database is available via the America Online service for the price America Online charges to its clients (approximately $3 per hour), but this service has been tailored to be useful only to the general public.

If ProCD had to recover all of its costs and make a profit by charging a single price—that is, if it could not charge more to commercial users than to the general public—it would have to raise the price substantially over $150. The ensuing reduction in sales would harm consumers who value the information at, say, $200. They get consumer surplus of $50 under the current arrangement but would cease to buy if the price rose substantially. If because of high elasticity of demand in the consumer segment of the market the only way to make a profit turned out to be a price attractive to commercial users alone, then all consumers would lose out—and so would the commercial clients, who would have to pay more for the listings because ProCD could not obtain any contribution toward costs from the consumer market.

To make price discrimination work, however, the seller must be able to control arbitrage. An air carrier sells tickets for less to vacationers than to business travelers, using advance purchase and Saturday-night-stay requirements to distinguish the categories. A producer of movies segments the market by time, releasing first to theaters, then to pay-per-view services, next to the videotape and laserdisc market, and finally to cable and commercial tv. Vendors of computer software have a harder task. Anyone can walk into a retail store and buy a box. Customers do not wear tags saying "commercial user" or "consumer user." Anyway, even a commercial-user-detector at the door would not work, because a consumer could buy the software and resell to a commercial user. That arbitrage would break down the price discrimination and drive up the minimum price at which ProCD would sell to anyone.

Instead of tinkering with the product and letting users sort themselves—for example, furnishing current data at a high price that would be attractive only to commercial customers, and two-year-old data at a low price—ProCD turned to the institution of contract. Every box containing its consumer product declares that the software comes with restrictions stated in an enclosed license. This license, which is encoded on the CD-ROM disks as well as printed in the manual, and which appears on a user's screen every time the software runs, limits use of the application program and listings to non-commercial purposes.

Matthew Zeidenberg bought a consumer package of SelectPhone (trademark) in 1994 from a retail outlet in Madison, Wisconsin, but decided to ignore the license. He formed Silken Mountain Web Services, Inc., to resell the information in the SelectPhone (trademark) database. The corporation makes the database available on the Internet to anyone willing to pay its price—which, needless to say, is less than ProCD charges its commercial customers. Zeidenberg has purchased two additional Select-Phone (trademark) packages, each with an updated version of the database, and made the latest information available over the World Wide Web, for a price, through his corporation. ProCD filed this suit seeking an injunction against further dissemination that exceeds the rights specified in the licenses (identical in each of the three packages Zeidenberg purchased). The district court held the licenses ineffectual because their terms do not appear on the outside of the packages. The court added that the second and third licenses stand no different from the first, even though they are identical, because they *might* have been different, and a purchaser does not agree to—and cannot be bound by—terms that were secret at the time of purchase. 908 F.Supp. at 654.

II

Following the district court, we treat the licenses as ordinary contracts accompanying the sale of products, and therefore as governed by the common law of contracts and the Uniform Commercial Code. Whether there are legal differences between "contracts" and "licenses" (which may matter under the copyright doctrine of first sale) is a subject for another day. *See* Microsoft Corp. v. Harmony Computers & Electronics, Inc., 846 F.Supp. 208 (E.D.N.Y.1994). Zeidenberg does not argue that Silken Mountain Web Services is free of any restrictions that apply to Zeidenberg himself, because any effort to treat the two parties as distinct would put Silken Mountain behind the eight ball on ProCD's argument that copying the application program onto its hard disk violates the copyright laws. Zeidenberg does argue, and the district court held, that placing the package of software on the shelf is an "offer," which the customer "accepts" by paying the asking price and leaving the store with the goods. Peeters v. State, 154 Wis. 111, 142 N.W. 181 (1913). In Wisconsin, as elsewhere, a contract includes only the terms on which the parties have agreed. One cannot agree to hidden terms, the judge concluded. So far, so good—but one of the terms to which Zeidenberg agreed by purchasing the software is that the transaction was subject to a license. Zeidenberg's position therefore must be that the printed terms on the outside of a box are the parties' contract—except for printed terms that refer to or incorporate other terms. But why would Wisconsin fetter the parties' choice in this way? Vendors can put the entire terms of a contract on the outside of a box only by using microscopic type, removing other information that buyers might find more useful (such as what the software does, and on which computers it works), or both. The "Read Me" file included with most software, describing system requirements and potential incompatibilities, may be equivalent to ten pages of type; warranties and license restrictions take still more space. Notice on the outside, terms on the inside, and a right to return the software for a refund if the terms are unacceptable (a right that the license expressly extends), may be a means of doing business valuable to buyers and sellers alike. *See* E. Allan Farnsworth, 1 *Farnsworth on Contracts* § 4.26 (1990); *Restatement (2d) of Contracts* § 211 comment a (1981) ("Standardization of agreements serves many of the same functions as standardization of goods and services; both are essential to a system of mass production and distribution. Scarce and costly time and skill can be devoted to a class of transactions rather than the details of individual transactions."). Doubtless a state could forbid the use of standard contracts in the software business, but we do not think that Wisconsin has done so.

Transactions in which the exchange of money precedes the communication of detailed terms are common. Consider the purchase of insurance. The buyer goes to an agent, who explains the essentials (amount of coverage, number of years) and remits the premium to the home office, which sends back a policy. On the district judge's understanding, the terms of the policy are irrelevant because the insured paid before receiving them. Yet the device of payment, often with a "binder" (so that the insurance takes effect immediately even though the home office reserves the right to withdraw coverage later), in advance of the policy, serves buyers' interests by accelerating effectiveness and reducing transactions costs. Or consider the purchase of an airline ticket. The traveler calls the carrier or an agent, is quoted a price, reserves a seat, pays, and gets a ticket, in that order. The ticket contains elaborate terms, which the traveler can reject by canceling the reservation. To use the ticket is to accept the terms, even terms that in retrospect are disadvantageous. *See* Carnival Cruise Lines, Inc. v. Shute, 499 U.S. 585, 111 S.Ct. 1522, 113 L.Ed.2d 622 (1991). Just so with a ticket to a concert. The back of the ticket states that the patron promises not to record the concert; to attend is to agree. A theater that detects a violation will confiscate the tape and escort the violator to the exit. One *could* arrange things so that every concertgoer signs this promise before forking over the money, but that cumbersome way of doing things not only would lengthen queues and raise prices but also would scotch the sale of tickets by phone or electronic data service.

Consumer goods work the same way. Someone who wants to buy a radio set visits a store, pays, and walks out with a box. Inside the box is a leaflet containing some terms, the most important of which usually is the warranty, read for the first time in the comfort of home. By Zeidenberg's lights, the warranty in the box is irrelevant; every consumer gets the standard warranty implied by the UCC in the event the contract is silent; yet so far as we are aware no state disregards warranties furnished with consumer products. Drugs come with a list of ingredients on the outside and an elaborate package insert on the inside. The package insert describes drug interactions, contraindications, and other vital information—but, if Zeidenberg is right, the purchaser need not read the package insert, because it is not part of the contract.

Next consider the software industry itself. Only a minority of sales take place over the counter, where there are boxes to peruse. A customer may place an order by phone in response to a line item in a catalog or a review in a magazine. Much software is ordered over the Internet by purchasers who have never seen a box. Increasingly software arrives by wire. There is no box; there is only a stream of electrons, a collection of information that includes data, an application program, instructions, many limitations ("MegaPixel 3.14159 cannot be used with BytePusher 2.718"), and the terms of sale. The user purchases a serial number, which activates the software's features. On Zeidenberg's arguments, these unboxed sales are unfettered by terms—so the seller has made a broad warranty and must pay consequential damages for any shortfalls in performance, two "promises" that if taken seriously would drive prices through the ceiling or return transactions to the horse-and-buggy age.

According to the district court, the UCC does not countenance the sequence of money now, terms later. (Wisconsin's version of the UCC does not differ from the Official Version in any material respect, so we use the regular numbering system. Wis. Stat. § 402.201 corresponds to UCC § 2–201, and other citations are easy to derive.) One of the court's reasons—that by proposing as part of the draft Article 2B a new UCC § 2–2203 that would explicitly validate standard-form user licenses, the American Law Institute and the National Conference of Commissioners on Uniform Laws have conceded the invalidity of shrinkwrap licenses under current law, *see* 908 F.Supp. at 655–56—depends on a faulty inference. To propose a change in a law's *text* is not necessarily to propose a change in the law's *effect*. New words may be designed to fortify the current rule with a more precise text that curtails uncertainty. To judge by the flux of law review articles discussing shrinkwrap licenses, uncertainty is much in need of reduction—although businesses seem to feel less uncertainty than do scholars, for only three cases (other than ours) touch on the subject, and none directly addresses it. *See* Step–Saver Data Systems, Inc. v. Wyse Technology, 939 F.2d 91 (3d Cir.1991); Vault Corp. v. Quaid Software Ltd., 847 F.2d 255, 268–70 (5th Cir.1988); Arizona Retail Systems, Inc. v. Software Link, Inc., 831 F.Supp. 759 (D.Ariz.1993). As their titles suggest, these are not consumer transactions. *Step–Saver* is a battle-of-the-forms case, in which the parties exchange incompatible forms and a court must decide which prevails. *See* Northrop Corp. v. Litronic Industries, 29 F.3d 1173 (7th Cir.1994) (Illinois law); Douglas G. Baird & Robert Weisberg, *Rules, Standards, and the Battle of the Forms: A Reassessment of § 2–207*, 68 Va. L.Rev. 1217, 1227–31 (1982). Our case has only one form; UCC § 2–207 is irrelevant. *Vault* holds that Louisiana's special shrinkwrap-license statute is preempted by federal law, a question to which we return. And *Arizona Retail Systems* did not reach the question, because the court found that the buyer knew the terms of the license before purchasing the software.

What then does the current version of the UCC have to say? We think that the place to start is § 2–204(1): "A contract for sale of goods may be made in any manner sufficient to show agreement, including conduct by both parties which recognizes the existence of such a contract." A vendor, as master of the offer, may invite acceptance by conduct, and may propose limitations on the kind of conduct that constitutes acceptance. A buyer may accept by performing the acts the vendor proposes to treat as acceptance. And that is what happened. ProCD proposed a contract that a buyer would accept by *using* the software after having an opportunity to read the license at leisure. This Zeidenberg did. He had no choice, because the software splashed the license on the screen and would not let him proceed without indicating acceptance. So although the district judge was right to say that a contract can be, and often is, formed simply by paying the price and walking out of the store, the UCC permits contracts to be formed in other ways. ProCD proposed such a different way, and without protest Zeidenberg agreed. Ours is not a case in which a consumer opens a package to find an insert saying "you owe us an extra $10,000" and the seller files suit to collect. Any buyer finding such a demand can prevent formation of the contract by returning the package, as can any consumer who concludes that the terms of the license make the software worth less than the purchase price. Nothing in the UCC requires a seller to maximize the buyer's net gains.

Section 2–606, which defines "acceptance of goods," reinforces this understanding. A buyer accepts goods under § 2–606(1)(b) when, after an opportunity to inspect, he fails to make an effective rejection under § 2–602(1). ProCD extended an opportunity to reject if a buyer should find the license terms unsatisfactory; Zeidenberg inspected the package, tried out the software, learned of the license, and did not reject the goods. We refer to § 2–606 only to show that the opportunity to return goods can be important; acceptance of an offer differs from acceptance of goods after delivery, *see* Gillen v. Atalanta Systems, Inc., 997 F.2d 280, 284 n. 1 (7th Cir.1993); but the UCC consistently permits the parties to structure their relations so that the buyer has a chance to make a final decision after a detailed review.

Some portions of the UCC impose additional requirements on the way parties agree on terms. A disclaimer of the implied warranty of merchantability must be "conspicuous." UCC § 2–316(2), incorporating UCC § 1–201(10). Promises to make firm offers, or to negate oral modifications, must be "separately signed." UCC §§ 2–205, 2–209(2). These special provisos reinforce the impression that, so far as the UCC is concerned, other terms may be as inconspicuous as the forum-selection clause on the back of the cruise ship ticket in *Carnival Lines*. Zeidenberg has not located any Wisconsin case—for that matter, any case in any state—holding that under the UCC the ordinary terms found in shrinkwrap licenses require any special prominence, or otherwise are to be undercut rather than enforced. In the end, the terms of the license are conceptually identical to the contents of the package. Just as no court would dream of saying that SelectPhone (trademark) must contain 3,100 phone books rather than 3,000, or must have data no more than 30 days old, or must sell for $100 rather than $150—although any of these changes would be welcomed by the customer, if all other things were held constant—so, we believe, Wisconsin would not let the buyer pick and choose among terms. Terms of use are no less a part of "the product" than are the size of the database and the speed with which the software compiles listings. Competition among vendors, not judicial revision of a package's contents, is how consumers are protected in a market economy. Digital Equipment Corp. v. Uniq Digital Technologies, Inc., 73 F.3d 756 (7th Cir.1996). ProCD has rivals, which may elect to compete by offering superior software, monthly updates, improved terms of use, lower price, or a better compromise among these elements. As we stressed above, adjusting terms in buyers' favor might help Matthew Zeidenberg today (he already has the software) but would lead to a response, such as a higher price, that might make consumers as a whole worse off. . . .

Reversed and remanded.

HILL v. GATEWAY 2000, INC.

United States Court of Appeals, Seventh Circuit, 1997.
105 F.3d 1147.

EASTERBROOK, CIRCUIT JUDGE. A customer picks up the phone, orders a computer, and gives a credit card number. Presently a box arrives, containing the computer and a list of terms, said to govern unless the customer returns the computer within 30 days. Are these terms effective as the parties' contract, or is the contract term-free because the order-taker did not read any terms over the phone and elicit the customer's assent?

One of the terms in the box containing a Gateway 2000 system was an arbitration clause. Rich and Enza Hill, the customers, kept the computer more than 30 days before complaining about its components and performance. They filed suit in federal court arguing, among other things, that the product's shortcomings make Gateway a racketeer (mail and wire fraud are said to be the predicate offenses), leading to treble damages under RICO for the Hills and a class of all other purchasers. Gateway asked the district court to enforce the arbitration clause; the judge refused, writing that "(t)he present record is insufficient to support a finding of a valid arbitration agreement between the parties or that the plaintiffs were given adequate notice of the arbitration clause." Gateway took an immediate appeal, as is its right. 9 U.S.C. § 16(a)(1)(A).

The Hills say that the arbitration clause did not stand out: they concede noticing the statement of terms but deny reading it closely enough to discover the agreement to arbitrate, and they ask us to conclude that they therefore may go to court. Yet an agreement to arbitrate must be enforced "save upon such grounds as exist at law or in equity for the revocation of any contract." 9 U.S.C. § 2. Doctor's Associates, Inc. v. Casarotto, 517 U.S. 681, 116 S.Ct. 1652, 134 L.Ed.2d 902 (1996), holds that this provision of the Federal Arbitration Act is inconsistent with any requirement that an arbitration clause be prominent. A contract need not be read to be effective; people who accept take the risk that the unread terms may in retrospect prove unwelcome. Carr v. CIGNA Securities, Inc., 95 F.3d 544, 547 (7th Cir.1996). Terms inside Gateway's box stand or fall together. If they constitute the parties' contract because the Hills had an opportunity to return the computer after reading them, then all must be enforced.

ProCD, Inc. v. Zeidenberg, 86 F.3d 1447 (7th Cir.1996), holds that terms inside a box of software bind consumers who use the software after an opportunity to read the terms and to reject them by returning the product. Likewise, Carnival Cruise Lines, Inc. v. Shute, 499 U.S. 585, 111 S.Ct. 1522, 113 L.Ed.2d 622 (1991), enforces a forum-selection clause that was included among three pages of terms attached to a cruise ship ticket. *ProCD* and *Carnival Cruise Lines* exemplify the many commercial transactions in which people pay for products with terms to follow; *ProCD* discusses others. 86 F.3d at 1451–52. The district court concluded in *ProCD* that the contract is formed when the consumer pays for the software; as a result, the court held, only terms known to the consumer at that moment are part of the contract, and provisos inside the box do not count. Although this is one way a contract could be formed, it is not the only way: "A vendor, as master of the offer, may invite acceptance by conduct, and may propose limitations on the kind of conduct that constitutes acceptance. A buyer may accept by performing the acts the vendor proposes to treat as acceptance." *Id.* at 1452. Gateway shipped computers with the same sort of accept-or-return offer ProCD made to users of its software. *ProCD* relied on the Uniform Commercial Code rather than any peculiarities of Wisconsin law; both Illinois and South Dakota, the two states whose law might govern relations between Gateway and the Hills, have adopted the UCC; neither side has pointed us to any atypical doctrines in those states that might be pertinent; *ProCD* therefore applies to this dispute.

Plaintiffs ask us to limit *ProCD* to software, but where's the sense in that? *ProCD* is about the law of contract, not the law of software. Payment preceding the revelation of full terms is common for air transportation, insurance, and many other endeavors. Practical considerations support allowing vendors to enclose the full legal terms with their products. Cashiers cannot be expected to read legal documents to customers before ringing up sales. If the staff at the other end of the phone for direct-sales operations such as Gateway's had to read the four-page statement of terms before taking the buyer's credit card number, the droning voice would anesthetize rather than enlighten many potential buyers. Others would hang up in a rage over the waste of their time. And oral recitation would not avoid customers' assertions (whether true or feigned) that the clerk did not read term X to them, or that they did not remember or understand it. Writing provides benefits for both sides of commercial transactions. Customers as a group are better off when vendors skip costly and ineffectual steps such as telephonic recitation, and use instead a simple approve-or-return device. Competent adults are bound by such documents, read or unread. For what little it is worth, we add that the box from Gateway was crammed with software. The computer came with an operating system, without which it was useful only as a boat anchor. *See* Digital Equipment Corp. v. Uniq Digital Technologies, Inc., 73 F.3d 756, 761 (7th Cir.1996). Gateway also included many application programs. So the Hills' effort to limit *ProCD* to software would not avail them factually, even if it were sound legally—which it is not.

For their second sally, the Hills contend that *ProCD* should be limited to executory contracts (to licenses in particular), and therefore does not apply because both parties' performance of this contract was complete when the box arrived at their home. This is legally and factually wrong: legally because the question at hand concerns the formation of the contract rather than its performance, and factually because both contracts were incompletely performed. *ProCD* did not depend on the fact that the seller characterized the transaction as a license rather than as a contract; we treated it as a contract for the sale of goods and reserved the question whether for other purposes a "license" characterization might be preferable. 86 F.3d at 1450. All debates about characterization to one side, the transaction in *ProCD* was no more executory than the one here: Zeidenberg paid for the software and walked out of the store with a box under his arm, so if arrival of the box with the product ends the time for revelation of contractual terms, then the time ended in *ProCD* before Zeidenberg opened the box. But of course ProCD had not completed performance with delivery of the box, and neither had Gateway. One element of the transaction was the warranty, which obliges sellers to fix defects in their products. The Hills have invoked Gateway's warranty and are not satisfied with its response, so they are not well positioned to say that Gateway's obligations were fulfilled when the motor carrier unloaded the box. What is more, both ProCD and Gateway promised to help customers to use their products. Long-term service and information obligations are common in the computer business, on both hardware and software sides. Gateway offers "lifetime service" and has a round-the-clock telephone hotline to fulfil this promise. Some vendors spend more money helping customers use their products than on developing and manufacturing them. The document in Gateway's box includes promises of future performance that some consumers value highly; these promises bind Gateway just as the arbitration clause binds the Hills.

Next the Hills insist that *ProCD* is irrelevant because Zeidenberg was a "merchant" and they are not. Section 2–207(2) of the UCC, the infamous battle-of-the-forms section, states that "additional terms (following acceptance of an offer) are to be construed as proposals for addition to a contract. Between merchants such terms become part of the contract unless. . . ." Plaintiffs tell us that *ProCD* came out as it did only because Zeidenberg was a "merchant" and the terms inside ProCD's box were not excluded by the "unless" clause. This argument pays scant attention to the opinion in *ProCD*, which concluded that, when there is only one form, "sec. 2–207 is irrelevant." 86 F.3d at 1452. The question in *ProCD* was not whether terms were added to a contract after its formation, but how and when the contract was formed—in particular, whether a vendor may propose that a contract of sale be formed, not in the store (or over the phone) with the payment of money or a general "send me the product," but after the customer has had a chance to inspect both the item and the terms. *ProCD* answers "yes," for merchants and consumers alike. Yet again, for what little it is worth we observe that the Hills misunderstand the setting of *ProCD*. A "merchant" under the UCC "means a person who deals in goods of the kind or otherwise by his occupation holds himself out as having knowledge or skill peculiar to the practices or goods involved in the transaction," § 2–104(1). Zeidenberg bought the product at a retail store, an uncommon place for merchants to acquire inventory. His corporation put ProCD's database on the Internet for anyone to browse, which led to the litigation but did not make Zeidenberg a software merchant.

At oral argument the Hills propounded still another distinction: the box containing ProCD's software displayed a notice that additional terms were within, while the box containing Gateway's computer did not. The difference is functional, not legal. Consumers browsing the aisles of a store can look at the box, and if they are unwilling to deal with the prospect of additional terms can leave the box alone, avoiding the transactions costs of returning the package after reviewing its contents. Gateway's box, by contrast, is just a shipping carton; it is not on display anywhere. Its function is to protect the product during transit, and the information on its sides is for the use of handlers . . . rather than would-be purchasers.

Perhaps the Hills would have had a better argument if they were first alerted to the bundling of hardware and legal-ware after opening the box and wanted to return the computer in order to avoid disagreeable terms, but were dissuaded by the expense of shipping. What the remedy would be in such a case—could it exceed the shipping charges?—is an interesting question, but one that need not detain us because the Hills knew before they ordered the computer that the carton would include some important terms, and they did not seek to discover these in advance. Gateway's ads state that their products come with limited warranties and lifetime support. How limited was the warranty—30 days, with service contingent on shipping the computer back, or five years, with free onsite service? What sort of support was offered? Shoppers have three principal ways to discover these things. First, they can ask the vendor to send a copy before deciding whether to buy. The Magnuson–Moss Warranty Act requires firms to distribute their warranty terms on request, 15 U.S.C. § 2302(b)(1)(A); the Hills do not contend that Gateway would have refused to enclose the remaining terms too. Concealment would be bad for business, scaring some customers away and leading to excess returns from others. Second, shoppers can consult public sources (computer magazines, the Web sites of vendors) that may contain this information. Third, they may inspect the documents after the product's delivery. Like Zeidenberg, the Hills took the third option. By keeping the computer beyond 30 days, the Hills accepted Gateway's offer, including the arbitration clause.

. . . The decision of the district court is vacated, and this case is remanded with instructions to compel the Hills to submit the dispute to arbitration.

KLOCEK v. GATEWAY, INC.

United States District Court, District of Kansas, 2000.
104 F.Supp.2d 1332.

Memorandum and Order

VRATIL, DISTRICT JUDGE. William S. Klocek brings suit against Gateway, Inc. . . . on claims arising from purchases of a Gateway computer. . . . For reasons stated below, the Court overrules Gateway's motion to dismiss. . . .

A. *Gateway's Motion to Dismiss*

Plaintiff brings individual and class action claims against Gateway, alleging that it induced him and other consumers to purchase computers and special support packages by making false promises of technical support. Individually, plaintiff also claims breach of contract and breach of warranty, in that Gateway breached certain warranties that its computer would be compatible with standard peripherals and standard internet services.

Gateway asserts that plaintiff must arbitrate his claims under Gateway's Standard Terms and Conditions Agreement ("Standard Terms"). Whenever it sells a computer, Gateway includes a copy of the Standard Terms in the box which contains the computer battery power cables and instruction manuals. At the top of the first page, the Standard Terms include the following notice:

NOTE TO THE CUSTOMER:

This document contains Gateway 2000's Standard Terms and Conditions. By keeping your Gateway 2000 computer system beyond five (5) days after the date of delivery, you accept these Terms and Conditions.

The notice is in emphasized type and is located inside a printed box which sets it apart from other provisions of the document. The Standard Terms are four pages long and contain 16 numbered paragraphs. Paragraph 10 provides the following arbitration clause:

DISPUTE RESOLUTION. Any dispute or controversy arising out of or relating to this Agreement or its interpretation shall be settled exclusively and finally by arbitration. The arbitration shall be conducted in accordance with the Rules of Conciliation and Arbitration of the International Chamber of Commerce. The arbitration shall be conducted in Chicago, Illinois, U.S.A. before a sole arbitrator. Any award rendered in any such arbitration proceeding shall be final and binding on each of the parties, and judgment may be entered thereon in a court of competent jurisdiction.[1]

Gateway urges the Court to dismiss plaintiff's claims under the Federal Arbitration Act ("FAA"), 9 U.S.C. § 1 et seq. The FAA ensures that written arbitration agreements . . . involving interstate commerce are "valid, irrevocable, and enforceable." 9 U.S.C. § 2.[2] . . .

Gateway bears an initial summary-judgment-like burden of establishing that it is entitled to arbitration. . . . Thus, Gateway must present evidence sufficient to demonstrate the existence of an enforceable agreement to arbitrate. . . . If Gateway makes such a showing, the burden shifts to plaintiff to submit evidence demonstrating a genuine issue for trial. . . . In this case, Gateway fails to present evidence establishing the most basic facts regarding the transaction. The gaping holes in the evidentiary record preclude the Court from determining what state law controls the formation of the contract in this case and, consequently, prevent the Court from agreeing that Gateway's motion is well taken.

Before granting a stay or dismissing a case pending arbitration, the Court must determine that the parties have a written agreement to arbitrate. . . . The existence of an arbitration agreement "is simply a matter of contract between the parties; (arbitration) is a way to resolve those disputes—but only those disputes—that the parties have agreed to submit to arbitration." . . .

Before evaluating whether the parties agreed to arbitrate, the Court must determine what state law controls the formation of the contract in this case. . . . Kansas courts apply the doctrine of *lex loci contractus*, which requires that the Court interpret the contract according to the law of the state in which the parties performed the last act necessary to form the contract. . . .

The parties do not address the choice of law issue, and the record is unclear where they performed the last act necessary to complete the contract. Gateway . . . provides no details regarding the transaction. . . . [I]t appears that the parties may have performed the last act necessary to form the contract in Kansas (with plaintiff purchasing the computer in

---

1. Gateway states that after it sold plaintiff's computer, it mailed all existing customers in the United States a copy of its quarterly magazine, which contained notice of a change in the arbitration policy set forth in the Standard Terms. The new arbitration policy afforded customers the option of arbitrating before the International Chamber of Commerce ("ICC"), the American Arbitration Association ("AAA"), or the National Arbitration Forum ("NAF") in Chicago, Illinois, or any other location agreed upon by the parties. Plaintiff denies receiving notice of the amended arbitration policy. Neither party explains why—if the arbitration agreement was an enforceable contract—Gateway was entitled to unilaterally amend it by sending a magazine to computer customers.

2. The FAA does not create independent federal-question jurisdiction; rather, "there must be diversity of citizenship or some other independent basis for federal jurisdiction" before the Court may act. Moses H. Cone Memorial Hosp. v. Mercury Const. Corp., 460 U.S. 1, 25 n. 32, 103 S.Ct. 927, 74 L.Ed.2d 765 (1983). In this case, plaintiff asserts diversity jurisdiction.

Kansas), Missouri (with Gateway shipping the computer to plaintiff in Missouri), or some unidentified other states (with Gateway agreeing to ship plaintiff's catalog order and/or Gateway actually shipping the order).

The Court discerns no material difference between the applicable substantive law in Kansas and Missouri and—as to those two states—it perhaps would not need to resolve the choice of law issue at this time. . . .

The Uniform Commercial Code ("UCC") governs the parties' transaction under both Kansas and Missouri law. . . . [T]he issue is whether the contract of sale includes the Standard Terms as part of the agreement.

State courts in Kansas and Missouri apparently have not decided whether terms received with a product become part of the parties' agreement. Authority from other courts is split. *Compare* Step–Saver, 939 F.2d 91 (printed terms on computer software package not part of agreement); Arizona Retail Sys., Inc. v. Software Link, Inc., 831 F.Supp. 759 (D.Ariz.1993) (license agreement shipped with computer software not part of agreement); *and* U.S. Surgical Corp. v. Orris, Inc., 5 F.Supp.2d 1201 (D.Kan.1998) (single use restriction on product package not binding agreement); *with* Hill v. Gateway 2000, Inc., 105 F.3d 1147 (7th Cir. 1997) (arbitration provision shipped with computer binding on buyer); ProCD, Inc. v. Zeidenberg, 86 F.3d 1447 (7th Cir.1996) (shrinkwrap license binding on buyer);[6] *and* M.A. Mortenson Co., Inc. v. Timberline Software Corp., 140 Wash.2d 568, 998 P.2d 305 (2000) (following Hill and ProCD on license agreement supplied with software).[7] It appears that at least in part, the cases turn on whether the court finds that the parties formed their contract *before* or *after* the vendor communicated its terms to the purchaser. *Compare* Step–Saver, 939 F.2d at 98 (parties' conduct in shipping, receiving and paying for product demonstrates existence of contract; box top license constitutes proposal for additional terms under § 2–207 which requires express agreement by purchaser); Arizona Retail, 831 F.Supp. at 765 (vendor entered into contract by agreeing to ship goods, or at latest by shipping goods to buyer; license agreement constitutes proposal to modify agreement under § 2–209 which requires express assent by buyer); *and* Orris, 5 F.Supp.2d at 1206 (sales contract concluded when vendor received consumer orders; single-use language on product's label was proposed modification under § 2–209 which requires express assent by purchaser); *with* ProCD, 86 F.3d at 1452 (under § 2–204 vendor,

---

6. The term "shrinkwrap license" gets its name from retail software packages that are covered in plastic or cellophane "shrinkwrap" and contain licenses that purport to become effective as soon as the customer tears the wrapping from the package. *See* ProCD, 86 F.3d at 1449.

7. The *Mortenson* court also found support for its holding in the proposed Uniform Computer Information Transactions Act ("UCITA") (formerly known as proposed UCC Article 2B) (text located at www.law.upenn.edu/library/ulc/ucita/UCITA _ 99.htm), which the National Conference of Commissioners on Uniform State Laws approved and recommended for enactment by the states in July 1999. *See* Mortenson, 998 P.2d at 310 n. 6, 313 n. 10. The proposed UCITA, however, would not apply to the Court's analysis in this case. The UCITA applies to computer information transactions, which are defined as agreements "to create, modify, transfer, or license computer information or informational rights in computer information." UCITA, §§ 102(11) and 103. In transactions involving the sale of computers, such as our case, the UCITA applies only to the computer programs and copies, not to the sale of the computer itself. *See* UCITA § 103(c)(2).

as master of offer, may propose limitations on kind of conduct that constitutes acceptance; § 2–207 does not apply in case with only one form); Hill, 105 F.3d at 1148–49 (same); *and* Mortenson, 998 P.2d at 311–314 (where vendor and purchaser utilized license agreement in prior course of dealing, shrinkwrap license agreement constituted issue of contract formation under § 2–204, not contract alteration under § 2–207).

Gateway urges the Court to follow the Seventh Circuit decision in *Hill*. That case involved the shipment of a Gateway computer with terms similar to the Standard Terms in this case, except that Gateway gave the customer 30 days—instead of 5 days—to return the computer. In enforcing the arbitration clause, the Seventh Circuit relied on its decision in *ProCD*, where it enforced a software license which was contained inside a product box. *See* Hill, 105 F.3d at 1148–50. In *ProCD*, the Seventh Circuit noted that the exchange of money frequently precedes the communication of detailed terms in a commercial transaction. *See* ProCD, 86 F.3d at 1451. Citing UCC § 2–204, the court reasoned that by including the license with the software, the vendor proposed a contract that the buyer could accept by using the software after having an opportunity to read the license.[8] ProCD, 86 F.3d at 1452. Specifically, the court stated:

> A vendor, as master of the offer, may invite acceptance by conduct, and may propose limitations on the kind of conduct that constitutes acceptance. A buyer may accept by performing the acts the vendor proposes to treat as acceptance.

ProCD, 86 F.3d at 1452. The *Hill* court followed the *ProCD* analysis, noting that "(p)ractical considerations support allowing vendors to enclose the full legal terms with their products." Hill, 105 F.3d at 1149.[9]

The Court is not persuaded that Kansas or Missouri courts would follow the Seventh Circuit reasoning in *Hill* and *ProCD*. In each case the

---

8. Section 2–204 provides: "A contract for sale of goods may be made in any manner sufficient to show agreement, including conduct by both parties which recognizes the existence of such contract." . . .

9. Legal commentators have criticized the reasoning of the Seventh Circuit in this regard. *See, e.g.,* Jean R. Sternlight, *Gateway Widens Doorway to Imposing Unfair Binding Arbitration on Consumers*, Fla. Bar J., Nov. 1997, at 8, 10–12 (outcome in *Gateway* is questionable on federal statutory, common law and constitutional grounds and as a matter of contract law and is unwise as a matter of policy because it unreasonably shifts to consumers search cost of ascertaining existence of arbitration clause and return cost to avoid such clause); Thomas J. McCarthy *et al., Survey: Uniform Commercial Code*, 53 Bus. Law. 1461, 1465–66 (Seventh Circuit finding that UCC § 2–207 did not apply is inconsistent with official comment); Batya Goodman, *Honey, I Shrink–Wrapped the Consumer: the Shrink–Wrap Agreement as an Adhesion Contract*, 21 Cardozo L.Rev. 319, 344–352 (Seventh Circuit failed to consider principles of adhesion contracts); Jeremy Senderowicz, *Consumer Arbitration and Freedom of Contract: A Proposal to Facilitate Consumers' Informed Consent to Arbitration Clauses in Form Contracts*, 32 Colum. J.L. & Soc. Probs. 275, 296–299 (judiciary (in multiple decisions, including *Hill*) has ignored issue of consumer consent to an arbitration clause). Nonetheless, several courts have followed the Seventh Circuit decisions in *Hill* and *ProCD. See, e.g.,* M.A. Mortenson Co., Inc. v. Timberline Software Corp., 140 Wash.2d 568, 998 P.2d 305 (license agreement supplied with software); Rinaldi v. Iomega Corp., 1999 WL 1442014, Case No. 98C–09–064–RRC (Del.Super. Sept. 3, 1999) (warranty disclaimer included inside computer Zip drive packaging); Westendorf v. Gateway 2000, Inc., 2000 WL 307369, Case No. 16913 (Del. Ch. March 16, 2000) (arbitration provision shipped with computer); Brower v. Gateway 2000, Inc., 246 A.D.2d 246, 676 N.Y.S.2d 569 (N.Y.App.Div.1998) (same); Levy v. Gateway 2000, Inc., 1997 WL 823611, 33 UCC Rep. Serv.2d 1060 (N.Y.Sup. Oct. 31, 1997) (same).

Seventh Circuit concluded without support that UCC § 2–207 was irrelevant because the cases involved only one written form. *See* ProCD, 86 F.3d at 1452 (citing no authority); Hill, 105 F.3d at 1150 (citing *ProCD*). This conclusion is not supported by the statute or by Kansas or Missouri law. Disputes under § 2–207 often arise in the context of a "battle of forms," *see, e.g.,* Daitom, Inc. v. Pennwalt Corp., 741 F.2d 1569, 1574 (10th Cir.1984), but nothing in its language precludes application in a case which involves only one form. ... By its terms, § 2–207 applies to an acceptance or written confirmation. It states nothing which requires another form before the provision becomes effective. In fact, the official comment to the section specifically provides that §§ 2–207(1) and (2) apply "where an agreement has been reached orally ... and is followed by one or both of the parties sending formal memoranda embodying the terms so far agreed and adding terms not discussed." Official Comment 1 of UCC § 2–207. Kansas and Missouri courts have followed this analysis. ... Thus, the Court concludes that Kansas and Missouri courts would apply § 2–207 to the facts in this case. ...

In addition, the Seventh Circuit provided no explanation for its conclusion that "the vendor is the master of the offer." *See* ProCD, 86 F.3d at 1452 (citing nothing in support of proposition); Hill, 105 F.3d at 1149 (citing *ProCD*). In typical consumer transactions, the purchaser is the offeror, and the vendor is the offeree. *See* Brown Mach., Div. of John Brown, Inc. v. Hercules, Inc., 770 S.W.2d 416, 419 (Mo.App.1989) (as general rule orders are considered offers to purchase); Rich Prods. Corp. v. Kemutec Inc., 66 F.Supp.2d 937, 956 (E.D.Wis.1999) (generally price quotation is invitation to make offer and purchase order is offer). While it is possible for the vendor to be the offeror, *see* Brown Machine, 770 S.W.2d at 419 (price quote can amount to offer if it reasonably appears from quote that assent to quote is all that is needed to ripen offer into contract), Gateway provides no factual evidence which would support such a finding in this case. The Court therefore assumes for purposes of the motion to dismiss that plaintiff offered to purchase the computer (either in person or through catalog order) and that Gateway accepted plaintiff's offer (either by completing the sales transaction in person or by agreeing to ship and/or shipping the computer to plaintiff).[11] *Accord* Arizona Retail, 831 F.Supp. at 765 (vendor entered into contract by agreeing to ship goods, or at latest, by shipping goods).

Under § 2–207, the Standard Terms constitute either an expression of acceptance or written confirmation. As an expression of acceptance, the Standard Terms would constitute a counter-offer only if Gateway expressly made its acceptance conditional on plaintiff's assent to the additional or different terms. ... "(T)he conditional nature of the acceptance must be clearly expressed in a manner sufficient to notify the offeror that the

---

11. UCC § 2–206(b) provides that "an order or other offer to buy goods for prompt or current shipment shall be construed as inviting acceptance either by a prompt promise to ship or by the prompt or current shipment...." The official comment states that "(e)ither shipment or a prompt promise to ship is made a proper means of acceptance of an offer looking to current shipment." UCC § 2–206, Official Comment 2.

offeree is unwilling to proceed with the transaction unless the additional or different terms are included in the contract." Brown Machine, 770 S.W.2d at 420.[12] Gateway provides no evidence that at the time of the sales transaction, it informed plaintiff that the transaction was conditioned on plaintiff's acceptance of the Standard Terms. Moreover, the mere fact that Gateway shipped the goods with the terms attached did not communicate to plaintiff any unwillingness to proceed without plaintiff's agreement to the Standard Terms. *See, e.g.,* Arizona Retail, 831 F.Supp. at 765 (conditional acceptance analysis rarely appropriate where contract formed by performance but goods arrive with conditions attached); Leighton Indus., Inc. v. Callier Steel Pipe & Tube, Inc., 1991 WL 18413, *6, Case No. 89–C–8235 (N.D.Ill. Feb. 6, 1991) (applying Missouri law) (pre-printed forms insufficient to notify offeror of conditional nature of acceptance, particularly where form arrives after delivery of goods).

Because plaintiff is not a merchant, additional or different terms contained in the Standard Terms did not become part of the parties' agreement unless plaintiff expressly agreed to them. . . . Gateway argues that plaintiff demonstrated acceptance of the arbitration provision by keeping the computer more than five days after the date of delivery. Although the Standard Terms purport to work that result, Gateway has not presented evidence that plaintiff expressly agreed to those Standard Terms. Gateway states only that it enclosed the Standard Terms inside the computer box for plaintiff to read afterwards. It provides no evidence that it informed plaintiff of the five-day review-and-return period as a condition of the sales transaction, or that the parties contemplated additional terms to the agreement.[14] *See* Step–Saver, 939 F.2d at 99 (during negotiations leading to purchase, vendor never mentioned box-top license or obtained buyer's express assent thereto). The Court finds that the act

---

12. Courts are split on the standard for a conditional acceptance under § 2–207. *See* Daitom, 741 F.2d at 1576 (finding that Pennsylvania would most likely adopt "better" view that offeree must explicitly communicate unwillingness to proceed with transaction unless additional terms in response are accepted by offeror). On one extreme of the spectrum, courts hold that the offeree's response stating a materially different term solely to the disadvantage of the offeror constitutes a conditional acceptance. *See* Daitom, 741 F.2d at 1569 (citing Roto–Lith, Ltd. v. F.P. Bartlett & Co., 297 F.2d 497 (1st Cir.1962)). At the other end of the spectrum, courts hold that the conditional nature of the acceptance should be so clearly expressed in a manner sufficient to notify the offeror that the offeree is unwilling to proceed without the additional or different terms. *See* Daitom, 741 F.2d at 1569 (citing Dorton v. Collins & Aikman Corp., 453 F.2d 1161 (6th Cir.1972)). The middle approach requires that the response predicate acceptance on clarification, addition or modification. *See* Daitom, 741 F.2d at 1569 (citing Construction Aggregates Corp. v. Hewitt–Robins, Inc., 404 F.2d 505 (7th Cir.1968)). The First Circuit has since overruled its decision in *Roto–Lith, see* Ionics, Inc. v. Elmwood Sensors, Inc., 110 F.3d 184, and the Court finds that neither Kansas nor Missouri would apply the standard set forth therein. *See* Boese–Hilburn Co. v. Dean Machinery Co., 616 S.W.2d 520, (Mo.App.1981) (rejecting *Roto–Lith* standard); Owens–Corning Fiberglas Corp. v. Sonic Dev. Corp., 546 F.Supp. 533, 538 (D.Kan.1982) (acceptance is not counteroffer under Kansas law unless it is made conditional on assent to additional or different terms (citing *Roto–Lith* as comparison)); Daitom, 741 F.2d at 1569 (finding that *Dorton* is "better" view). Because Gateway does not satisfy the standard for conditional acceptance under either of the remaining standards (*Dorton* or *Construction Aggregates*), the Court does not decide which of the remaining two standards would apply in Kansas and/or Missouri.

14. The Court is mindful of the practical considerations which are involved in commercial transactions, but it is not unreasonable for a vendor to clearly communicate to a buyer—at the time of sale—either the complete terms of the sale or the fact that the vendor will propose additional terms as a condition of sale, if that be the case.

of keeping the computer past five days was not sufficient to demonstrate that plaintiff expressly agreed to the Standard Terms. *Accord* Brown Machine, 770 S.W.2d at 421 (express assent cannot be presumed by silence or mere failure to object). Thus, because Gateway has not provided evidence sufficient to support a finding under Kansas or Missouri law that plaintiff agreed to the arbitration provision contained in Gateway's Standard Terms, the Court overrules Gateway's motion to dismiss.

The motion also must be overruled because Kansas and Missouri law may not apply. ... If Gateway contends that the issue of contract formation is governed by some law other than that of Kansas or Missouri, it shall file a supplemental motion which cites the factual and legal basis for its position. The Court will review that submission and decide whether to order a jury trial on the existence of an agreement to arbitrate. ...

SECTION 11. E–COMMERCE

SPECHT v. NETSCAPE COMMUNICATIONS CORP.

United States Court of Appeals, Second Circuit, 2002.
306 F.3d 17.

SOTOMAYOR, CIRCUIT JUDGE. This is an appeal from a judgment of the Southern District of New York denying a motion by defendants-appellants Netscape Communications Corporation and its corporate parent, America Online, Inc. (collectively, "defendants" or "Netscape"), to compel arbitration and to stay court proceedings. In order to resolve the central question of arbitrability presented here, we must address issues of contract formation in cyberspace. ...

We ... affirm the district court's denial of defendants' motion to compel arbitration and to stay court proceedings.

Background

I. Facts

... [P]laintiffs alleged that when they first used Netscape's Communicator—a software program that permits Internet browsing—the program created and stored on each of their computer hard drives a small text file known as a "cookie" that functioned "as a kind of electronic identification tag for future communications" between their computers and Netscape. Plaintiffs further alleged that when they installed Smart-Download—a separate software "plug-in"[2] that served to enhance Communicator's browsing capabilities—SmartDownload created and stored on their computer hard drives another string of characters, known as a

---

2. Netscape's website defines "plug-ins" as "software programs that extend the capabilities of the Netscape Browser in a specific way—giving you, for example, the ability to play audio samples or view video movies from within your browser." (http://wp.netscape.com/plugins/) SmartDownload purportedly made it easier for users of browser programs like Communicator to download files from the Internet without losing their progress when they paused to engage in some other task, or if their Internet connection was severed. *See* Specht [v. Netscape Communications Corp., 150 F.Supp.2d 585, 587 (S.D.N.Y.2001)].

"Key," which similarly functioned as an identification tag in future communications with Netscape. According to the complaints in this case, each time a computer user employed Communicator to download a file from the Internet, SmartDownload "assume(d) from Communicator the task of downloading" the file and transmitted to Netscape the address of the file being downloaded together with the cookie created by Communicator and the Key created by SmartDownload. These processes, plaintiffs claim, constituted unlawful "eavesdropping" on users of Netscape's software products as well as on Internet websites from which users employing SmartDownload downloaded files [in violation of two federal statutes, the Electronic Communications Privacy Act, 18 U.S.C. §§ 2510 *et seq*, and the Computer Fraud and Abuse Act, 18 U.S.C. § 1030].

In the time period relevant to this litigation, Netscape offered on its website various software programs, including Communicator and Smart-Download, which visitors to the site were invited to obtain free of charge. It is undisputed that ... plaintiffs ... downloaded Communicator from the Netscape website. [P]laintiffs acknowledge that when they proceeded to initiate installation[3] of Communicator, they were automatically shown a scrollable text of that program's license agreement and were not permitted to complete the installation until they had clicked on a "Yes" button to indicate that they accepted all the license terms.[4] If a user attempted to install Communicator without clicking "Yes," the installation would be aborted. All five named user plaintiffs expressly agreed to Communicator's license terms by clicking "Yes." The Communicator license agreement that these plaintiffs saw made no mention of SmartDownload or other plug-in programs, and stated that "(t)hese terms apply to Netscape Communicator and Netscape Navigator"[6] and that "all disputes relating to this Agreement (excepting any dispute relating to intellectual property rights)" are subject to "binding arbitration in Santa Clara County, California."

---

3. There is a difference between downloading and installing a software program. When a user downloads a program from the Internet to his or her computer, the program file is stored on the user's hard drive but typically is not operable until the user installs or executes it, usually by double-clicking on the file and causing the program to run.

4. This kind of online software license agreement has come to be known as "clickwrap" (by analogy to "shrinkwrap," used in the licensing of tangible forms of software sold in packages) because it "presents the user with a message on his or her computer screen, requiring that the user manifest his or her assent to the terms of the license agreement by clicking on an icon. The product cannot be obtained or used unless and until the icon is clicked." *Specht*, 150 F.Supp.2d at 593–94 (footnote omitted). Just as breaking the shrinkwrap seal and using the enclosed computer program after encountering notice of the existence of governing license terms has been deemed by some courts to constitute assent to those terms in the context of tangible software, *see, e.g.,* ProCD, Inc. v. Zeidenberg, 86 F.3d 1447, 1451 (7th Cir.1996), so clicking on a webpage's clickwrap button after receiving notice of the existence of license terms has been held by some courts to manifest an Internet user's assent to terms governing the use of downloadable intangible software, *see, e.g.,* Hotmail Corp. v. Van$Money Pie Inc., 47 U.S.P.Q.2d 1020, 1025 (N.D.Cal.1998).

6. While Navigator was Netscape's "stand-alone" Internet browser program during the period in question, Communicator was a "software suite" that comprised Navigator and other software products. ...

Although Communicator could be obtained independently of Smart-Download, ... plaintiffs ... downloaded and installed Communicator in connection with downloading SmartDownload. [P]laintiffs allegedly arrived at a Netscape webpage[8] captioned "SmartDownload Communicator" that urged them to "Download With Confidence Using SmartDownload!" At or near the bottom of the screen facing plaintiffs was the prompt "Start Download" and a tinted button labeled "Download." By clicking on the button, plaintiffs initiated the download of SmartDownload. Once that process was complete, SmartDownload, as its first plug-in task, permitted plaintiffs to proceed with downloading and installing Communicator, an operation that was accompanied by the clickwrap display of Communicator's license terms described above.

The signal difference between downloading Communicator and downloading SmartDownload was that no clickwrap presentation accompanied the latter operation. Instead, once plaintiffs ... had clicked on the "Download" button located at or near the bottom of their screen, and the downloading of SmartDownload was complete, ... plaintiffs encountered no further information about the plug-in program or the existence of license terms governing its use.[9] The sole reference to SmartDownload's license terms on the "SmartDownload Communicator" webpage was located in text that would have become visible to plaintiffs only if they had scrolled down to the next screen. [SmartDownload's license terms included an identical arbitration clause. Ed.]

Had plaintiffs scrolled down instead of acting on defendants' invitation to click on the "Download" button, they would have encountered the following invitation: "Please review and agree to the terms of the *Netscape SmartDownload software license agreement* before downloading and using the software." Plaintiffs ... averred in their affidavits that they never saw this reference to the SmartDownload license agreement when they clicked on the "Download" button. ...

In sum, plaintiffs ... allege that the process of obtaining SmartDownload contrasted sharply with that of obtaining Communicator. Having selected SmartDownload, they were required neither to express unambiguous assent to that program's license agreement nor even to view the license terms or become aware of their existence before proceeding with the invited download of the free plug-in program. Moreover, once ... plaintiffs had initiated the download, the existence of SmartDownload's license terms was not mentioned while the software was running or at any later point in plaintiffs' experience of the product. ...

---

8. For purposes of this opinion, the term "webpage" or "page" is used to designate a document that resides, usually with other webpages, on a single Internet website and that contains information that is viewed on a computer monitor by scrolling through the document. To view a webpage in its entirety, a user typically must scroll through multiple screens.

9. Plaintiff Kelly, a relatively sophisticated Internet user, testified that when he clicked to download SmartDownload, he did not think that he was downloading a software program at all, but rather that SmartDownload "was merely a piece of download technology." He later became aware that SmartDownload was residing as software on his hard drive when he attempted to download electronic files from the Internet.

II. Proceedings Below

In the district court, defendants moved to compel arbitration and to stay court proceedings pursuant to the Federal Arbitration Act ("FAA"), 9 U.S.C. § 4.... Finding that Netscape's webpage, unlike typical examples of clickwrap, neither adequately alerted users to the existence of Smart-Download's license terms nor required users unambiguously to manifest assent to those terms as a condition of downloading the product, the court held that the ... plaintiffs had not entered into the SmartDownload license agreement. Specht, 150 F.Supp.2d at 595–96.

The district court also ruled that the separate license agreement governing use of Communicator, even though the ... plaintiffs had assented to its terms, involved an independent transaction that made no mention of SmartDownload and so did not bind plaintiffs to arbitrate their claims relating to SmartDownload. *Id.* at 596. ...

Discussion

I. Standard of Review and Applicable Law

... The FAA provides that a "written provision in any ... contract evidencing a transaction involving commerce to settle by arbitration a controversy thereafter arising out of such contract or transaction ... shall be valid, irrevocable, and enforceable, save upon such grounds as exist at law or in equity for the revocation of any contract."[11] 9 U.S.C. § 2. ...

II. Whether This Court Should Remand for a Trial on Contract Formation

... [W]e conclude that the district court properly decided the question of reasonable notice and objective manifestation of assent as a matter of law on the record before it, and we decline defendants' request to remand for a full trial on that question.

III. Whether the User Plaintiffs Had Reasonable Notice of and Manifested Assent to the SmartDownload License Agreement

Whether governed by the common law or by Article 2 of the Uniform Commercial Code ("UCC"), a transaction, in order to be a contract, requires a manifestation of agreement between the parties. *See* Windsor Mills, Inc. v. Collins & Aikman Corp., 25 Cal.App.3d 987, 991, 101 Cal.Rptr. 347, 350 (1972) ("'(C)onsent to, or acceptance of, the arbitration provision (is) necessary to create an agreement to arbitrate."); *see also* Cal. Com.Code § 2204(1) [U.C.C. § 2–204(1), Ed.] ("A contract for sale of

---

11. The parties do not dispute ... that the agreement is a "written provision" despite being provided to users in a downloadable electronic form. The ... point has been settled by the Electronic Signatures in Global and National Commerce Act ("E–Sign Act"), Pub.L. No. 106–229, 114 Stat. 464 (2000) (codified at 15 U.S.C. §§ 7001 *et seq.*), which provides that "a signature, contract, or other record relating to such transaction may not be denied legal effect, validity, or enforceability solely because it is in electronic form." *Id.* § 7001(a)(1); *see also* Cal. Civ.Code § 1633.7(b) ("A contract may not be denied legal effect or enforceability solely because an electronic record was used in its formation.").

goods may be made in any manner sufficient to show agreement, including conduct by both parties which recognizes the existence of such a contract.").[13] Mutual manifestation of assent, whether by written or spoken word or by conduct, is the touchstone of contract. Binder v. Aetna Life Ins. Co., 75 Cal.App.4th 832, 848, 89 Cal.Rptr.2d 540, 551 (1999); *cf. Restatement (Second) of Contracts* § 19(2) (1981) ("The conduct of a party is not effective as a manifestation of his assent unless he intends to engage in the conduct and knows or has reason to know that the other party may infer from his conduct that he assents."). Although an onlooker observing the disputed transactions in this case would have seen each of the user plaintiffs click on the SmartDownload "Download" button ... a consumer's clicking on a download button does not communicate assent to contractual terms if the offer did not make clear to the consumer that clicking on the download button would signify assent to those terms.... California's common law is clear that "an offeree, regardless of apparent manifestation of his consent, is not bound by inconspicuous contractual provisions of which he is unaware, contained in a document whose contractual nature is not obvious." [Cedars Sinai Med. Ctr. v. Mid–West Nat'l Life Ins. Co., 118 F.Supp.2d 1002, 1008 (C.D. Cal. 2000)]....

Arbitration agreements are no exception to the requirement of manifestation of assent. ...

A. *The Reasonably Prudent Offeree of Downloadable Software*

Defendants argue that plaintiffs must be held to a standard of reasonable prudence and that, because notice of the existence of Smart-Download license terms was on the next scrollable screen, plaintiffs were on "inquiry notice" of those terms.[14] We disagree with the proposition that a reasonably prudent offeree in plaintiffs' position would necessarily have known or learned of the existence of the SmartDownload license agreement prior to acting, so that plaintiffs may be held to have assented to that agreement with constructive notice of its terms. ... It is true that "(a) party cannot avoid the terms of a contract on the ground that he or she failed to read it before signing." Marin Storage & Trucking [Inc. v. Benco Contracting & Eng'g, 89 Cal.App.4th 1042, 1049, 107 Cal.Rptr.2d 645, 651 (2001)]. But courts are quick to add: "An exception to this general rule exists when the writing does not appear to be a contract and the terms are not called to the attention of the recipient. In such a case, no contract is formed with respect to the undisclosed term." *Id.* ....

Most of the cases cited by defendants in support of their inquiry-notice argument are drawn from the world of paper contracting. ...

[R]eceipt of a physical document containing contract terms or notice thereof is frequently deemed, in the world of paper transactions, a sufficient circumstance to place the offeree on inquiry notice of those

---

13. [Footnote 13 is reproduced as an Editors' note at the conclusion of the opinion.]

14. "Inquiry notice" is "actual notice of circumstances sufficient to put a prudent man upon inquiry." Cal. State Auto. Ass'n Inter–Ins. Bureau v. Barrett Garages, Inc., 257 Cal.App.2d 71, 64 Cal.Rptr. 699, 703 (Cal.Ct.App.1967) (internal quotation marks omitted).

terms. . . . These principles apply equally to the emergent world of online product delivery, pop-up screens, hyperlinked pages, clickwrap licensing, scrollable documents, and urgent admonitions to "Download Now!." What plaintiffs saw when they were being invited by defendants to download this fast, free plug-in called SmartDownload was a screen containing praise for the product and, at the very bottom of the screen, a "Download" button. Defendants argue that under the principles set forth in the cases cited above, a "fair and prudent person using ordinary care" would have been on inquiry notice of SmartDownload's license terms. Shacket, 651 F.Supp. at 690.

We are not persuaded that a reasonably prudent offeree in these circumstances would have known of the existence of license terms. Plaintiffs were responding to an offer that did not carry an immediately visible notice of the existence of license terms or require unambiguous manifestation of assent to those terms. Thus, plaintiffs' "apparent manifestation of . . . consent" was to terms "contained in a document whose contractual nature (was) not obvious." Windsor Mills, 25 Cal.App.3d at 992, 101 Cal.Rptr. at 351. Moreover, the fact that, given the position of the scroll bar on their computer screens, plaintiffs may have been aware that an unexplored portion of the Netscape webpage remained below the download button does not mean that they reasonably should have concluded that this portion contained a notice of license terms. In their deposition testimony, plaintiffs variously stated that they used the scroll bar "(o)nly if there is something that I feel I need to see that is on—that is off the page," or that the elevated position of the scroll bar suggested the presence of "mere . . . formalities, standard lower banner links" or "that the page is bigger than what I can see." Plaintiffs testified, and defendants did not refute, that plaintiffs were in fact unaware that defendants intended to attach license terms to the use of SmartDownload.

. . . Internet users may have, as defendants put it, "as much time as they need" to scroll through multiple screens on a webpage, but there is no reason to assume that viewers will scroll down to subsequent screens simply because screens are there. When products are "free" and users are invited to download them in the absence of reasonably conspicuous notice that they are about to bind themselves to contract terms, the transactional circumstances cannot be fully analogized to those in the paper world of arm's-length bargaining. . . .

B. Shrinkwrap Licensing and Related Practices

Defendants cite certain well-known cases involving shrinkwrap licensing and related commercial practices in support of their contention that plaintiffs became bound by the SmartDownload license terms by virtue of inquiry notice. For example, in Hill v. Gateway 2000, Inc., 105 F.3d 1147 (7th Cir.1997), the Seventh Circuit held that where a purchaser had ordered a computer over the telephone, received the order in a shipped box containing the computer along with printed contract terms, and did not return the computer within the thirty days required by the terms, the purchaser was bound by the contract. *Id.* at 1148–49. In ProCD, Inc. v. Zeidenberg, the same court held that where an individual purchased software in a box containing license terms which were displayed on the computer screen every time the user executed the software program, the user had sufficient opportunity to review the terms and to return the software, and so was contractually bound after retaining the product. ProCD, 86 F.3d at 1452; *cf.* Moore v. Microsoft Corp., 293 A.D.2d 587, 587, 741 N.Y.S.2d 91, 92 (2d Dep't 2002) (software user was bound by license agreement where terms were prominently displayed on computer screen before software could be installed and where user was required to indicate assent by clicking "I agree"); Brower v. Gateway 2000, Inc., 246 A.D.2d 246, 251, 676 N.Y.S.2d 569, 572 (1st Dep't 1998) (buyer assented to arbitration clause shipped inside box with computer and software by retaining items beyond date specified by license terms); M.A. Mortenson Co. v. Timberline Software Corp., 93 Wash.App. 819, 970 P.2d 803, 809 (1999) (buyer manifested assent to software license terms by installing and using software), *aff'd,* 140 Wash.2d 568, 998 P.2d 305 (2000).

These cases do not help defendants. To the extent that they hold that the purchaser of a computer or tangible software is contractually bound after failing to object to printed license terms provided with the product, *Hill* and *Brower* do not differ markedly from the cases involving traditional paper contracting discussed in the previous section. Insofar as the purchaser in *ProCD* was confronted with conspicuous, mandatory license terms every time he ran the software on his computer, that case actually undermines defendants' contention that downloading in the absence of conspicuous terms is an act that binds plaintiffs to those terms. In *Mortenson,* the full text of license terms was printed on each sealed diskette envelope inside the software box, printed again on the inside cover of the user manual, and notice of the terms appeared on the computer screen every time the purchaser executed the program. Mortenson, 970 P.2d at 806. In sum, the foregoing cases are clearly distinguishable from the facts of the present action.

C. Online Transactions

Cases in which courts have found contracts arising from Internet use do not assist defendants, because in those circumstances there was much clearer notice than in the present case that a user's act would manifest assent to contract terms. *See, e.g.,* . . . Caspi v. Microsoft Network, L.L.C., 323 N.J.Super. 118, 732 A.2d 528, 530, 532–33 (N.J.Super.Ct.App.Div.1999) (upholding forum selection clause where subscribers to online software were required to review license terms in scrollable window and to click "I Agree" or "I Don't Agree"); Barnett v. Network Solutions, Inc., 38 S.W.3d 200, 203–04 (Tex.App.2001) (upholding forum selection clause in online contract for registering Internet domain names that required users to scroll through terms before accepting or rejecting them).[17]

---

17. Although the parties here do not refer to it, California's consumer fraud statute, Cal. Bus. & Prof.Code § 17538, is one of the few state statutes to regulate online transactions in goods or

After reviewing the California common law and other relevant legal authority, we conclude that under the circumstances here, plaintiffs' downloading of SmartDownload did not constitute acceptance of defendants' license terms. Reasonably conspicuous notice of the existence of contract terms and unambiguous manifestation of assent to those terms by consumers are essential if electronic bargaining is to have integrity and credibility. We hold that a reasonably prudent offeree in plaintiffs' position would not have known or learned, prior to acting on the invitation to download, of the reference to SmartDownload's license terms hidden below the "Download" button on the next screen. We affirm the district court's conclusion that the ... plaintiffs ... are not bound by the arbitration clause contained in those terms.

IV. Whether Plaintiffs' Assent to Communicator's License Agreement Requires Them To Arbitrate Their Claims Regarding SmartDownload

Plaintiffs do not dispute that they assented to the license terms governing Netscape's Communicator. The parties disagree, however, over the scope of that license's arbitration clause. Defendants contend that the scope is broad enough to encompass plaintiffs' claims regarding Smart-Download, even if plaintiffs did not separately assent to SmartDownload's license terms and even though Communicator's license terms did not expressly mention SmartDownload. Thus, defendants argue, plaintiffs must arbitrate. . . .

To begin with, we find that the underlying dispute in this case—whether defendants violated plaintiff's rights under the Electronic Com-

---

services. The statute provides that in disclosing information regarding return and refund policies and other vital consumer information, online vendors must legibly display the information either:

(i) (on) the first screen displayed when the vendor's electronic site is accessed, (ii) on the screen on which goods or services are first offered, (iii) on the screen on which a buyer may place the order for goods or services, (iv) on the screen on which the buyer may enter payment information, such as a credit card account number, or (v) for nonbrowser-based technologies, in a manner that gives the user a reasonable opportunity to review that information. *Id.* § 17538(d)(2)(A).

The statute's clear purpose is to ensure that consumers engaging in online transactions have relevant information before they can be bound. Although consumer fraud as such is not alleged in the present action, and § 17538 protects only California residents, we note that the statute is consistent with the principle of conspicuous notice of the existence of contract terms that is also found in California's common law of contracts.

In addition, the model code, UCITA, discussed [in note 13] generally recognizes the importance of conspicuous notice and unambiguous manifestation of assent in online sales and licensing of computer information. For example, § 112, which addresses manifestation of assent, provides that a user's opportunity to review online contract terms exists if a "record" (or electronic writing) of the contract terms is "made available in a manner that ought to call it to the attention of a reasonable person and permit review." UCITA, § 112(e)(1) (rev. ed. Aug.23, 2001) (available at *www.ucitaonline.com/ucita.html*). . . .

We hasten to point out that UCITA, which has been enacted into law only in Maryland and Virginia, does not govern the parties' transactions in the present case, but we nevertheless find that UCITA's provisions offer insight into the evolving online "circumstances" that defendants argue placed plaintiffs on inquiry notice of the existence of the SmartDownload license terms. UCITA has been controversial as a result of the perceived breadth of some of its provisions. . . . Nonetheless, UCITA's notice and assent provisions seem to be consistent with well-established principles governing contract formation and enforcement. . . .

munications Privacy Act and the Computer Fraud and Abuse Act—involves matters that are clearly collateral to the Communicator license agreement. . . .

Having determined this much, we next . . . must determine whether plaintiffs by their particular allegations have brought the dispute within the license terms. Defendants argue that plaintiffs' complaints "literally bristled with allegations that Communicator and Smart Download operated in conjunction with one another to eavesdrop on Plaintiffs' Internet communications." We disagree. . . .

In the course of their description of the installation and downloading process, plaintiffs keep SmartDownload separate from Communicator and clearly indicate that it is SmartDownload that performed the allegedly unlawful eavesdropping and made use of the otherwise innocuous Communicator cookie as well as its own "Key" and "UserID" to transmit plaintiffs' information to Netscape. . . .

After careful review of these allegations, we conclude that . . . the claims of the . . . plaintiffs are beyond the scope of the arbitration clause contained in the Communicator license agreement. Because those claims are not arbitrable under that agreement or under the SmartDownload license agreement, to which plaintiffs never assented, we affirm the district court's holding that the . . . plaintiffs may not be compelled to arbitrate their claims. . . .

Conclusion

For the foregoing reasons, we affirm the district court's denial of defendants' motion to compel arbitration and to stay court proceedings.

Editors' note on Software and Information under the UCC: In footnote 13 of the *Specht* opinion, the court reviewed the question of whether the UCC governed the transaction. It found it unnecessary to decide the question. That footnote is reproduced here:

The district court concluded that the SmartDownload transactions here should be governed by "California law as it relates to the sale of goods, including the Uniform Commercial Code in effect in California." Specht, 150 F.Supp.2d at 591. It is not obvious, however, that UCC Article 2 ("sales of goods") applies to the licensing of software that is downloadable from the Internet. . . . There is no doubt that a sale of tangible goods over the Internet is governed by Article 2 of the UCC. *See, e.g.,* Butler v. Beer Across Am., 83 F.Supp.2d 1261, 1263–64 & n. 6 (N.D.Ala.2000) (applying Article 2 to an Internet sale of bottles of beer). Some courts have also applied Article 2, occasionally with misgivings, to sales of off-the-shelf software in tangible, packaged formats. *See, e.g.,* ProCD, 86 F.3d at 1450. . . . Downloadable software, however, is scarcely a "tangible" good, and, in part because software may be obtained, copied, or transferred effortlessly at the stroke of a computer key, licensing of such Internet products has assumed a vast importance in recent years. Recognizing that "a body of law based on images of the sale of manufactured goods ill fits licenses and other transactions in computer information," the National Conference of Commissioners on Uniform State Laws has promulgated the Uniform Computer Information Transactions Act ("UCITA"), a code resembling UCC Article 2 in many respects but drafted to reflect emergent practices in the sale and licensing of computer information. UCITA, prefatory note (rev. ed. Aug.23, 2001) (available at www.ucitaonline.com/ucita.html). UCITA—originally intended as a new Article 2B to supplement Articles 2 and 2A of the UCC but later proposed as an independent code—has been adopted by two states, Maryland and Virginia. *See* Md.Code Ann. Com. Law §§ 22–101 *et seq.;* Va.Code Ann. §§ 59.1–501.1 *et seq.*

We need not decide today whether UCC Article 2 applies to Internet transactions in downloadable products. The district court's analysis and the parties' arguments on appeal show that, for present purposes, there is no essential difference between UCC Article 2 and the common law of contracts. We therefore apply the common law, with exceptions as noted.

Editor's note on the law applicable to software licenses: Efforts to enact legislation covering software have so far been unsuccessful. In the mid 1990's the original drafting committee to revise UCC Article 2, under the leadership of the late Professor Dick Speidel, attempted to include software in a "hub-and-spoke" approach that was eventually abandoned. Ultimately, the watered-down revision of Article 2 (2003), which has failed to be enacted by a single state, expressly excluded "information" from its scope. NCCUSL (National Conference of Commissioners on Uniform State Laws, now titled Uniform Law Commission) sought to address software licenses separately in a new UCC Article 2B, but its proposal was rejected by its UCC co-sponsor, ALI (American Law Institute). A subsequent NCCUSL proposal, UCITA (Uniform Computer Information Transactions Act), likewise failed, having achieved only two state adoptions. The currently-enacted version of Article 2 makes no express provision including or excluding software, leaving courts divided as to the wisdom of applying the common law or Article 2 to software and related issues.

SECTION 12. OPTION CONTRACTS

(Calamari & Perillo on Contracts § 2.25 and 2.26)

BEALL v. BEALL

Court of Special Appeals of Maryland, 1980.
45 Md.App. 489, 413 A.2d 1365.

MOORE, JUDGE. This appeal concerns an alleged option agreement and a suit by Carlton G. Beall for the specific performance thereof. The Circuit Court for Prince George's County (Melbourne, J.) found the agreement unsupported by consideration and dismissed plaintiff's bill of complaint. . . . From that order, he appeals to this Court.

I

In 1968, the plaintiff, Carlton G. Beall, purchased a farm in Prince George's County from Pearl Beall. At that time, the property was farmed by Pearl's son, Calvin Beall. The record discloses that Carlton, the plaintiff, and Calvin were second cousins. Calvin was married to Cecelia M. Beall, the defendant herein. Carlton agreed that Calvin could continue to farm the property if he would pay the annual property taxes. Calvin and Cecelia owned and resided on a parcel of about one-half acre that was bordered on three sides by the farm bought by the plaintiff; and it is that parcel that is the subject of this dispute.

On the day that plaintiff contracted to buy Pearl's farm, he obtained a three-year option to purchase Calvin's and Cecelia's parcel for $28,000.00. The option recited a consideration of $100.00 which was paid by check. In 1971, the parties executed a new option, for five years, but on the same terms and reciting an additional $100.00 consideration.

This 1971 option was never exercised by the plaintiff, but prior to its expiration the following language was appended at the bottom of the page:

> As of October 6, 1975, we, Calvin E. Beall and Cecelia M. Beall, agree to continue this option agreement three more years Feb. 1, 1976 to Feb. 1, 1979.

> /s/ Calvin E. Beall

> /s/ Cecelia M. Beall.

It is this purported extension that forms the basis for plaintiff's bill of complaint seeking specific performance of the agreement. Calvin died in August 1977, and Cecelia now holds the fee simple title by right of survivorship. In letters dated May 24, 1978 and September 14, 1978, the plaintiff advised Cecelia that he was electing to exercise the option. He scheduled settlement for October 5, 1978. As the chancellor found:

> It is undisputed in this case that Mr. Carlton Beall did eventually hire attorneys to search the title, set a settlement date, attend the settlement, and was ready, willing and able to perform the contract.

Cecelia refused to attend settlement, and this suit for specific performance ensued. At trial, after plaintiff presented his evidence, Cecelia moved to dismiss the bill of complaint. The chancellor granted the motion because she felt that the option agreements were not supported by consideration in that "no benefit . . . flowed to Cecelia Beall." In addition, as to the 1975 alleged option, the chancellor ruled:

> (T)here is no consideration recited in that extension or purported extension of the original option contract. . . . It is clear that consideration must pass for the extension each time, in some form of consideration. None is stated within the written four lines.

On appeal, the plaintiff contends that the chancellor erred in dismissing the bill of complaint and in excluding certain testimony relative to oral transactions with Calvin, the deceased husband of the defendant.

II

Under Maryland law it is clear that "an option is not a mere offer to sell, which can be withdrawn by the optionor at any time before acceptance, but a binding agreement if supported by consideration." Blondell v. Turover, 195 Md. 251, 256, 72 A.2d 697, 699 (1950). In other words, an option is an agreement to keep an offer open that requires consideration to give it its irrevocable character. Goldman v. Connecticut General Life Insurance Co., 251 Md. 575, 581, 248 A.2d 154, 158 (1968). Once the option is exercised by the optionee a binding contract is created that may be enforced through a decree commanding specific performance. *Diggs* v. *Siomporas*, 248 Md. 677, 681, 237 A.2d 725, 727 (1968). It is apparent, then, that an option must be supported by consideration in order to be irrevocable for the period provided in the option.

When, however, the consideration allegedly supporting an option fails or is nonexistent, the option is no longer irrevocable but rather it becomes "a mere offer to sell, which can be withdrawn by the optionor at any time before acceptance...." Blondell v. Turover, *supra*, 195 Md. at 256, 72 A.2d at 699. The failure of consideration destroys the irrevocability of the option; it nonetheless retains its essential characteristic as an offer to buy or sell for the period stated in the option or until revoked. It has been recognized that equity will enforce a resulting contract despite lack of consideration for the option....

Assuming, arguendo, that the 1975 option was unsupported by consideration, it remained as an offer to sell the parcel for $28,000. The offer was open until February 1, 1979, but it was revocable at any time by action of Calvin and Cecelia Beall. As stated in the case of Holifield v. Veterans' Farm & Home Board, 218 Miss. 446, 450, 67 So.2d 456, 457 (1953):

> It is well settled that an option is not binding as a contract where there is no consideration, unless it is accepted within the time limit and before the offer is withdrawn. Since there was no consideration paid by the Veterans' Farm and Home Board and Mauldin for the option, it could have been revoked by the Holifields at any time before the Veterans' Farm and Home Board and Mauldin notified them that

they intended to buy the land; *but since the offer was accepted within the time limit and before withdrawal, the contract became binding upon all parties as it was thereafter supported by the consideration of the mutual promises.* (Emphasis added.)

This statement is generally in accord with the Maryland cases, *supra.*

The chancellor should, therefore, have determined whether or not there was a valid, unrevoked offer to sell the property in dispute and whether or not there was a proper acceptance of that offer sufficient to create a contract specifically enforceable in equity. These issues of offer and acceptance primarily involve factual determinations that initially must be evaluated by the chancellor. As an appellate court, we are limited to a review of the chancellor's findings under the "clearly erroneous" standard. . . . But our review is dependent upon the existence of factual findings on the issues material to the case. Such findings were not made below.

It was error for the chancellor to dismiss plaintiff's bill of complaint at the close of his case. A new trial, in accordance with this opinion, is necessitated.

Order reversed; cause remanded for a new trial in accordance with this opinion; costs to abide the final result.

Editor's Note. This case was reversed on other grounds. 291 Md. 224, 434 A.2d 1015 (1981). Reread the facts of the case. Can you determine why the appellate court held that the power of acceptance had terminated before Carlton tried to accept the offer in 1978?

PROBLEMS

81. A makes an offer to B by mail which states that the offer will be open for thirty days. Before B accepts, A calls and revokes the offer. Is the revocation effective? Would the result be different if the offer had read: "This offer is irrevocable for 30 days"; "This is a firm offer for 30 days"; "I must have your answer within 30 days"?

82. A, in a signed writing, sent B an offer that stated: "This offer is not subject to revocation for thirty days." B immediately rejected the offer and A then purported to revoke the offer. Was the offer still open so that it could be accepted?

83. In June 1980 L agreed to lease certain commercial premises to T for a term of 10 years. A clause of the lease gave T a right of first refusal to purchase the property during the term of the lease. This clause provided that if L decided to sell the property and found a bona fide purchaser ready to buy it, L would give T immediate notification of the terms of the proposed sale. T then had the right for 30 days to purchase the property on the same terms as those negotiated with the third party purchaser. On June 24, T received a letter from L notifying T of the proposed sale to C, enclosing a copy of the contract signed by L and C and giving T 30 days to exercise its right of first

refusal. On July 22, T sent a notice of exercise to L which was received on August 6. Is T entitled to purchase the property?

EXAMINATION QUESTIONS AND MULTIPLE CHOICE QUESTION

First Examination Question

Case owned a tractor located in the woods near Oswego, New York. On February 16, Thompson called Case about buying the tractor. Case said: "I will sell the tractor to you, or to anybody else for that matter, for $450. Upon an agreement you may take possession of the tractor." On March 1st Thompson picked up the tractor and brought it to his place and so informed Case on March 15. On March 1st Peterson, who had learned of the offer from Thompson, sent in a notice of acceptance.

(a) Discuss the rights of the parties.

(b) Would the result be different if Case had not said "Upon an agreement you may take possession of the Tractor?"

(c) What would be the result if instead of picking up the tractor on March 1, Thompson had sent a letter stating: "This letter is sent to confirm that I am purchasing the tractor of which we spoke on the terms indicated. Naturally, I expect that an arbitration clause is part of our deal."

Second Examination Question

Proctor & Gamble (P & G) manufactures Pampers, a brand of disposable diapers. For some years each package of Pampers bore a Teddy Bear symbol and this legend:

> Save these Teddy Bear points and use them to save money on toys, clothes, furniture and lots of other baby things when you shop the Pampers Baby Catalog. For your free copy of the Catalog send your name, complete address and youngest baby's date of birth to: Pampers Baby Catalog, P.O. Box 8634, Clinton Iowa 52736.

In April 1989, P & G sent out its final catalog. On the front cover was a statement that the offer would expire on February 28, 1990.

Plaintiffs are a class of individuals who had faithfully collected Teddy Bear symbols, and had not seen the April 1989 catalog, were unaware of the February 28, 1990 expiration statement, and who have sued P & G.

Discuss the rights of the parties including theories available, probable defenses, and your estimate of the likely result of the lawsuit.

Multiple Choice Question

John and his 9–year–old daughter visited Tony, a breeder of golden retrievers, in response to Tony's newspaper ad for sale of puppies. During the visit, John offered to buy a specific 8–week–old puppy selected by his daughter for $450, payment to be made when the puppy is picked up at 10 weeks of age. Tony indicated that another customer had expressed an interest in this particular puppy and that he would check with that customer and get back to John. In fact, though he gave Tony no reason to know this, John had no intention of buying the puppy but had made the offer just to please his daughter. Two days later Tony sent John a fax stating that he accepted John's offer.

a) John is not contractually bound to buy the puppy because he did not intend to make an offer.

b) John is not contractually bound to buy the puppy because his offer, made in a face-to face conversation, lapsed before acceptance.

c) John is not contractually bound to buy the puppy because the fax was an unreasonable medium to transmit the acceptance.

d) John is contractually bound to buy the puppy.

CHAPTER 2

CONSIDERATION

■ ■ ■

SECTION 1. WHAT IS CONSIDERATION?

(Calamari & Perillo on Contracts §§ 4.1–4.8, 4.14–4.15)

KIM v. SON

Court of Appeal, Fourth District, Division 3, California, 2009.
Unpublished Opinion.

2009 WL 597232.

O'LEARY, J. Jinsoo Kim begins his opening brief by stating, "Blood may be thicker than water, but here it's far weightier than a peppercorn."[1] Kim appeals from the trial court's refusal to enforce a gratuitous promise, handwritten in his friend's own blood, to repay money Kim loaned and lost in two failed business ventures. ... We conclude the trial court's statement of decision sufficiently set forth the facts and law supporting its ultimate conclusion [that] Son's promise to repay the money was entirely gratuitous and unenforceable, even when reduced to blood. ... In the context of this contract dispute, Son's blood was not weightier than a peppercorn.

Son was the majority shareholder (70 percent owner) and operated a South Korean company, MJ, Inc. (MJ). He was also the sole owner of a California corporation, Netouch International Inc. (Netouch). After several months of investigation, Kim loaned money and invested in these companies. It was undisputed he wired the money directly to the corporate bank accounts. Son did not personally receive any of the funds. Kim invested 100 million won,[2] and later loaned 30 million won to MJ. He

---

1. The obscure peppercorn reference can be found in *Hobbs v. Duff* (1863) 23 Cal. 596, 602–603 ("What is a valuable consideration? A peppercorn; and for aught that appears by the pleadings in this case, there was no greater consideration than that for the supposed assignment" ...).

2. The won ... is the currency of South Korea.

loaned $40,000 to Netouch. There was no evidence these investments or loans were personally guaranteed by Son.

Unfortunately, these businesses failed and Kim lost his money. In October 2004, Son and Kim met in a sushi bar where they consumed a great deal of alcohol. When they were at the bar, Son asked the waiter for a safety pin, used it to prick his finger, and then wrote a "promissory note" with his blood. The document, translated from Korean to English, reads, "Sir, please forgive me. Because of my deeds you have suffered financially. I will repay you to the best of my ability." At some point that same day, Son also wrote in ink "I hereby swear (promise) that I will pay back, to the best of my ability, the estimated amount of 170,000,000 (w)ons to (Kim)."

Well over a year later, in June 2006, this blood-written note became the basis for Kim's lawsuit against Son alleging: (1) default of promissory note.... He claimed Son agreed in the "promissory note" to pay Kim 170 million won, which is approximately equivalent to $170,000.

After holding a bench trial, the court ruled in Son's favor. In its statement of decision, the court determined the "blood agreement" was not an enforceable contract. The court made the following findings: There was no evidence Son agreed to personally guarantee the loan or investment money. Son wrote the note in his own blood "while extremely intoxicated and feeling sorry for (Kim's) losses." The blood agreement lacked sufficient consideration because it "was not a result of a bargained-for-exchange, but rather a gratuitous promise by (Son) who took personally that (Kim), his good friend, had a failure in his investments that (Son) had initially brought him into." ... The (c)ourt refuses to enforce a gratuitous promise even when it is reduced to blood." ...

The judgment is affirmed. ...

HAMER v. SIDWAY

Court of Appeals of New York, 1891.
124 N.Y. 538, 27 N.E. 256.

Appeal from an order of the General Term of the Supreme Court in the fourth judicial department, made July 1, 1890, which reversed a judgment in favor of the plaintiff entered upon a decision of the court on trial at Special Term and granted a new trial.

This action was brought upon an alleged contract.

The plaintiff presented a claim to the executor of William E. Story, Sr., for $5,000 and interest from the 6th day of February, 1875. She acquired it through several mesne assignments* from William E. Story, 2d. The claim being rejected by the executor, this action was brought. It

---

* Later in the opinion the court, quoting the trial court, states that on March 1, 1877, "with the knowledge and consent of his said uncle, he duly sold, transferred, and assigned all his right, title, and interest in and to said sum of $5,000 to his wife, Libbie H. Story, who thereafter duly sold, transferred, and assigned the same to the plaintiff in this action." Ed.

appears that William E. Story, Sr., was the uncle of William E. Story, 2d; that at the celebration of the golden wedding of Samuel Story and wife, father and mother of William E. Story, Sr., on the 20th day of March, 1869, in the presence of the family and invited guests, he promised his nephew that if he would refrain from drinking, using tobacco, swearing, and playing cards or billiards for money until he became 21 years of age, he would pay him the sum of $5,000. The nephew assented thereto, and fully performed the conditions inducing the promise. When the nephew arrived at the age of 21 years, and on the 31st day of January, 1875, he wrote to his uncle, informing him that he had performed his part of the agreement, and had thereby become entitled to the sum of $5,000. The uncle received the letter, and a few days later, and on the 6th day of February, he wrote and mailed to his nephew the following letter:

Buffalo, Feb. 6, 1875.

W.E. Story, Jr.:

Dear Nephew—Your letter of the 31st ult. came to hand all right, saying that you had lived up to the promise made to me several years ago. I have no doubt but you have, for which you shall have five thousand dollars as I promised you. I had the money in the bank the day you was twenty-one years old that I intend for you, and you shall have the money certain. . . .

P.S.—You can consider this money on interest.

The nephew received the letter, and thereafter consented that the money should remain with his uncle in accordance with the terms and conditions of the letter. The uncle died on the 29th day of January, 1887, without having paid over to his nephew any portion of the said $5,000 and interest.

PARKER, J. . . . The question which provoked the most discussion by counsel on this appeal, and which lies at the foundation of plaintiff's asserted right of recovery, is whether by virtue of a contract defendant's testator, William E. Story, became indebted to his nephew, William E. Story, 2d, on his twenty-first birthday in the sum of $5,000. The trial court found as a fact that "on the 20th day of March, 1869, . . . William E. Story agreed to and with William E. Story, 2d, that if he would refrain from drinking liquor, using tobacco, swearing, and playing cards or billiards for money until he should become twenty-one years of age, then he, the said William E. Story, would at that time pay him, the said William E. Story, 2d, the sum of $5,000 for such refraining, to which the said William E. Story, 2d, agreed," and that he "in all things fully performed his part of said agreement."

The defendant contends that the contract was without consideration to support it, and therefore invalid. He asserts that the promisee, by refraining from the use of liquor and tobacco, was not harmed, but benefited; that that which he did was best for him to do, independently of his uncle's promise,—and insists that it follows that, unless the promisor was benefited, the contract was without consideration,—a contention which, if well founded, would seem to leave open for controversy in many cases whether that which the promisee did or omitted to do was in fact of such benefit to him as to leave no consideration to support the enforcement of the promisor's agreement. Such a rule could not be tolerated, and is without foundation in the law.

The exchequer chamber in 1875 defined "consideration" as follows: "A valuable consideration, in the sense of the law, may consist either in some right, interest, profit, or benefit accruing to the one party, or some forbearance, detriment, loss, or responsibility given, suffered, or undertaken by the other." Courts "will not ask whether the thing which forms the consideration does in fact benefit the promisee or a third party, or is of any substantial value to any one. It is enough that something is promised, done, forborne, or suffered by the party to whom the promise is made as consideration for the promise made to him." (*Anson's Prin. of Con.* 63.)

"In general a waiver of any legal right at the request of another party is a sufficient consideration for a promise." (*Parsons on Contracts*, 444.) "Any damage, or suspension, or forbearance of a right will be sufficient to sustain a promise." (*Kent,* vol 2, 465, 12th ed.)

Pollock in his work on Contracts, page 166, after citing the definition given by the exchequer chamber, already quoted, says:

> The second branch of this judicial description is really the most important one. Consideration means not so much that one party is profiting as that the other abandons some legal right in the present, or limits his legal freedom of action in the future, as an inducement for the promise of the first.

Now, applying this rule to the facts before us, the promisee used tobacco, occasionally drank liquor, and he had a legal right to do so. That right he abandoned for a period of years upon the strength of the promise of the testator that for such forbearance he would give him $5,000. We need not speculate on the effort which may have been required to give up the use of those stimulants. It is sufficient that he restricted his lawful freedom of action within certain prescribed limits upon the faith of his uncle's agreement, and now, having fully performed the conditions imposed, it is of no moment whether such performance actually proved a benefit to the promisor, and the court will not inquire into it; but, were it a proper subject of inquiry, we see nothing in this record that would permit a determination that the uncle was not benefited in a legal sense. Few cases have been found which may be said to be precisely in point, but such as have been, support the position we have taken. . . .

In Lakota v. Newton, (an unreported case in the superior court of Worcester, Mass.,) the complaint averred defendant's promise that "if you (meaning the plaintiff) will leave off drinking for a year I will give you $100," plaintiff's assent thereto, performance of the condition by him, and demanded judgment therefor. Defendant demurred, on the ground, among others, that the plaintiff's declaration did not allege a valid and sufficient consideration for the agreement of the defendant. The demurrer was overruled.

In Talbott v. Stemmons, [12 S.W.Rep. 297], the step-grandmother of the plaintiff made with him the following agreement: "I do promise and bind myself to give my grandson Albert R. Talbott $500 at my death if he will never take another chew of tobacco or smoke another cigar during my life, from this date up to my death; and if he breaks this pledge he is to refund double the amount to his mother." The executor of Mrs. Stemmons demurred to the complaint on the ground that the agreement was not based on a sufficient consideration. The demurrer was sustained, and an appeal taken therefrom to the court of appeals, where the decision of the court below was reversed. In the opinion of the court it is said that "the right to use and enjoy the use of tobacco was a right that belonged to the plaintiff, and not forbidden by law. The abandonment of its use may have saved him money, or contributed to his health; nevertheless, the surrender of that right caused the promise, and, having the right to contract with reference to the subject-matter, the abandonment of the use was a sufficient consideration to uphold the promise." Abstinence from the use of intoxicating liquors was held to furnish a good consideration for a promissory note in Lindell v. Rokes, (60 Mo. 249).

The cases cited by the defendant on this question are not in point. . . .

The order appealed from should be reversed and the judgment of the Special Term affirmed, with costs payable out of the estate.

All concur.

KIRKSEY v. KIRKSEY

Supreme Court of Alabama, 1845.
8 Ala. 131.

Error to the Circuit Court of Talladega.

Assumpsit by the defendant, against the Plaintiff in error. The question is presented in this Court, upon a case agreed, which shows the following facts:

The plaintiff was the wife of defendant's brother, but had for some time been a widow, and had several children. In 1840, the plaintiff resided on public land, under a contract of lease, she had held over and was comfortably settled, and would have attempted to secure the land she lived on. The defendant resided in Talladega county, some sixty, or seventy miles off. On the 10th October, 1840, he wrote to her the following letter:

> Dear sister Antillico—Much to my mortification, I heard, that brother Henry was dead, and one of his children. I know that your situation is one of grief, and difficulty. You had a bad chance before, but a great deal worse now. I should like to come and see you, but cannot with convenience at present. . . . I do not know whether you have a preference on the place you live on, or not. If you had, I would advise you to obtain your preference, and sell the land and quit the

country, as I understand it is very unhealthy, and I know society is very bad. If you will come down and see me, I will let you have a place to raise your family, and I have more open land than I can tend; and on the account of your situation, and that of your family, I feel like I want you and the children to do well.

Within a month or two after the receipt of this letter, the plaintiff abandoned her possession, without disposing of it, and removed with her family, to the residence of the defendant, who put her in comfortable houses, and gave her land to cultivate for two years, at the end of which time he notified her to remove, and put her in a house, not comfortable, in the woods, which he afterwards required her to leave.

A verdict being found for the plaintiff, for two hundred dollars, the above facts were agreed, and if they will sustain the action, the judgment is to be affirmed, otherwise it is to be reversed. . . .

ORMOND, J. The inclination of my mind, is, that the loss and inconvenience, which the plaintiff sustained in breaking up, and moving to the defendant's, a distance of sixty miles, is a sufficient consideration to support the promise, to furnish her with a house, and land to cultivate, until she could raise her family. My brothers, however think, that the promise on the part of the defendant, was a mere gratuity, and that an action will not lie for its breach. The judgment of the Court below must therefore be reversed, pursuant to the agreement of the parties.

PENNSY SUPPLY, INC. v. AMERICAN ASH RECYCLING CORP.

Superior Court of Pennsylvania, 2006.
895 A.2d 595.

ORIE MELVIN, J. Appellant, Pennsy Supply, Inc. ("Pennsy"), appeals from the grant of preliminary objections in the nature of a demurrer in favor of Appellee, American Ash Recycling Corp. of Pennsylvania ("American Ash"). We reverse and remand for further proceedings.

The trial court summarized the allegations of the complaint as follows:

The instant case arises out of a construction project for Northern York High School (Project) owned by Northern York County School District (District) in York County, Pennsylvania. The District entered into a construction contract for the Project with a general contractor, Lobar, Inc. (Lobar). Lobar, in turn, subcontracted the paving of driveways and a parking lot to (Pennsy). The contract between Lobar and the District included Project Specifications for paving work which required Lobar, through its subcontractor Pennsy, to use certain base aggregates. The Project Specifications permitted substitution of the aggregates with an alternate material known as Treated Ash Aggregate (TAA) or AggRite.

The Project Specifications included a "notice to bidders" of the availability of AggRite at no cost from (American Ash), a supplier of

AggRite. The Project Specifications also included a letter to the Project architect from American Ash confirming the availability of a certain amount of free AggRite on a first come, first served basis.

Pennsy contacted American Ash and informed American Ash that it would require approximately 11,000 tons of AggRite for the Project. Pennsy subsequently picked up the AggRite from American Ash and used it for the paving work, in accordance with the Project Specifications.

Pennsy completed the paving work in December 2001. The pavement ultimately developed extensive cracking in February 2002. The District notified ... Lobar ... as to the defects and Lobar in turn directed Pennsy to remedy the defective work. Pennsy performed the remedial work during summer 2003 at no cost to the District.

The scope and cost of the remedial work included the removal and appropriate disposal of the AggRite, which is classified as a hazardous waste material by the Pennsylvania Department of Environmental Protection. Pennsy requested American Ash to arrange for the removal and disposal of the AggRite; however, American Ash did not do so. Pennsy provided notice to American Ash of its intention to recover costs.

Pennsy also alleged that the remedial work cost it $251,940.20 to perform and that it expended an additional $133,777.48 to dispose of the AggRite it removed.

On November 18, 2004, Pennsy filed a five-count complaint against American Ash alleging [among other counts] breach of contract (Count I).... American Ash filed demurrers to all five counts. ... The trial court sustained the demurrers by order and opinion dated May 25, 2005 and dismissed the complaint. This appeal followed.

Pennsy raises three questions for our review: [Discussion of two of these questions is omitted. Ed.]

(1) Whether the trial court erred in not accepting as true ... (the) Complaint allegations that (a) (American Ash) promotes the use of its AggRite material, which is classified as hazardous waste, in order to avoid the high cost of disposing (of) the material itself; and (b) (American Ash) incurred a benefit from Pennsy's use of the material in the form of avoidance of the costs of said disposal sufficient to ground contract and warranty claims. ...

Instantly, the trial court determined that "any alleged agreement between the parties is unenforceable for lack of consideration." The trial court also stated "the facts as pleaded do not support an inference that disposal costs were part of any bargaining process *or* that American Ash offered the AggRite with an intent to avoid disposal costs." (emphasis added). Thus, we understand the trial court to have dismissed Count I for two reasons related to the necessary element of consideration: one, the allegations of the Complaint established that Pennsy had received a conditional gift from American Ash and, two, there were no allegations in the Complaint to show that American Ash's avoidance of disposal costs was part of any bargaining process between the parties.

It is axiomatic that consideration is "an essential element of an enforceable contract." Stelmack v. Glen Alden Coal Co., 339 Pa. 410, 414–415, 14 A.2d 127, 128 (1940). *See also* .. "Consideration consists of a benefit to the promisor or a detriment to the promisee." Weavertown [Transport Leasing, Inc. v. Moran, 834 A.2d 1169, 1172 (Pa.Super. 2003)](citing *Stelmack*). . . .

> It is not enough, however, that the promisee has suffered a legal detriment at the request of the promisor. The detriment incurred must be the "quid pro quo," or the "price" of the promise, and the inducement for which it was made.... If the promisor merely intends to make a gift to the promisee upon the performance of a condition, the promise is gratuitous and the satisfaction of the condition is not consideration for a contract. The distinction between such a conditional gift and a contract is well illustrated in *Williston on Contracts*, Rev.Ed., Vol. 1, Section 112, where it is said: "If a benevolent man says to a tramp,-'If you go around the corner to the clothing shop there, you may purchase an overcoat on my credit,' no reasonable person would understand that the short walk was requested as the consideration for the promise, but that in the event of the tramp going to the shop the promisor would make him a gift."

Weavertown, 834 A.2d at 1172 (quoting Stelmack, 339 Pa. at 414, 14 A.2d at 128–29). Whether a contract is supported by consideration presents a question of law. Davis & Warde, Inc. v. Tripodi, 420 Pa.Super. 450, 616 A.2d 1384 (1992).

The classic formula for the difficult concept of consideration was stated by Justice Oliver Wendell Holmes, Jr. as "the promise must induce the detriment and the detriment must induce the promise." John Edward Murray, Jr., *Murray on Contracts* § 60 (3d ed.1990), at 227 (citing Wisconsin & Michigan Ry. v. Powers, 191 U.S. 379, 24 S.Ct. 107, 48 L.Ed. 229 (1903)). As explained by Professor Murray:

> If the promisor made the promise for the purpose of inducing the detriment, the detriment induced the promise. *If, however, the promisor made the promise with no particular interest in the detriment that the promisee had to suffer to take advantage of the promised gift or other benefit, the detriment was incidental or conditional to the promisee's receipt of the benefit.* Even though the promisee suffered a detriment induced by the promise, the purpose of the promisor was not to have the promisee suffer the detriment because she did not seek that detriment in exchange for her promise.

Id. § 60.C, at 230 (emphasis added). This concept is also well summarized in American Jurisprudence:

As to the distinction between consideration and a condition, it is often difficult to determine whether words of condition in a promise indicate a request for consideration or state a mere condition in a gratuitous promise. An aid, though not a conclusive test, in determining which construction of the promise is more reasonable is an inquiry into *whether the occurrence of the condition would benefit the promisor. If so, it is a fair inference that the occurrence was requested as consideration.* On the other hand, if the occurrence of the condition is no benefit to the promisor but is merely to enable the promisee to receive a gift, the occurrence of the event on which the promise is conditional, though brought about by the promisee in reliance on the promise, is not properly construed as consideration.

17A AM. JUR.2d § 104 (2004 & 2005 Supp.) (emphasis added). *See also Restatement (Second) of Contracts* § 71 comment c (noting "the distinction between bargain and gift may be a fine one, depending on the motives manifested by the parties"); Carlisle v. T & R Excavating, Inc., 123 Ohio App.3d 277, 704 N.E.2d 39 (1997) (discussing the difference between consideration and a conditional gift and finding no consideration where promisor who promised to do excavating work for preschool being built by ex-wife would receive no benefit from wife's reimbursement of his material costs).

Upon review, we disagree with the trial court that the allegations of the Complaint show only that American Ash made a conditional gift of the AggRite to Pennsy. In paragraphs 8 and 9 of the Complaint, Pennsy alleged:

American Ash actively promotes the use of AggRite as a building material to be used in base course of paved structures, and provides the material free of charge, in an effort to have others dispose of the material and thereby avoid incurring the disposal costs itself ... American Ash provided the AggRite to Pennsy for use on the Project, which saved American Ash thousands of dollars in disposal costs it otherwise would have incurred.

Accepting these allegations as true and using the Holmesian formula for consideration, it is a fair interpretation of the Complaint that American Ash's promise to supply AggRite free of charge induced Pennsy to assume the detriment of collecting and taking title to the material, and critically, that it was this very detriment, whether assumed by Pennsy or some other successful bidder to the paving subcontract, which induced American Ash to make the promise to provide free AggRite for the project. Paragraphs 8–9 of the Complaint simply belie the notion that American Ash offered AggRite as a conditional gift to the successful bidder on the paving subcontract for which American Ash desired and expected nothing in return.

We turn now to whether consideration is lacking because Pennsy did not allege that American Ash's avoidance of disposal costs was part of any bargaining process between the parties. The Complaint does not allege that the parties discussed or even that Pennsy understood at the time it requested or accepted the AggRite that Pennsy's use of the AggRite would allow American Ash to avoid disposal costs. However, we do not believe such is necessary.

> The bargain theory of consideration does not actually require that the parties bargain over the terms of the agreement.... According to Holmes, an influential advocate of the bargain theory, what is required (for consideration to exist) is that the promise and the consideration be in "the relation of reciprocal conventional inducement, each for the other."

E. Allen Farnsworth, *Farnsworth on Contracts* § 2.6 (1990) (citing O. Holmes, *The Common Law* 293–94 (1881)); *see also Restatement (Second) of Contracts* § 71 (defining "bargained for" in terms of the Holmesian formula). Here, as explained above, the Complaint alleges facts which, if proven, would show the promise induced the detriment and the detriment induced the promise. This would be consideration. Accordingly, we reverse the dismissal of Count I. ...

For all of the foregoing reasons, we reverse the trial court's order granting the demurrers and dismissing the Complaint and remand for further proceedings. Jurisdiction relinquished.

GOTTLIEB v. TROPICANA HOTEL AND CASINO

United States District Court, E.D. Pennsylvania, 2000.
109 F.Supp.2d 324.

BARTLE, DISTRICT JUDGE. ... Tropicana, a New Jersey corporation that operates a gambling casino in Atlantic City, offers people membership in its "Diamond Club." In order to become a Diamond Club member, an individual must visit a promotional booth in the casino, obtain and fill out an application form, and show identification. There is no charge. The application form lists the individual's name, address, telephone number, and e-mail address, and the information provided is entered into the casino's computer database. Each member receives a Diamond Club card bearing a unique identification number. The member then presents or "swipes" the card in a machine each time he or she plays a game at the casino, and the casino obtains information about the member's gambling habits. The casino's marketing department then uses that information to tailor its promotions.

Ms. Gottlieb was, and had been for a number of years, a member of Tropicana's Diamond Club. Upon entering the casino on July 24, 1999, she immediately went to the Fun House Million Dollar Wheel Promotion ("Million Dollar Wheel") and waited in line for approximately five minutes before it was her turn to play. Diamond Club members were entitled to one free spin of the Million Dollar Wheel each day. As its name suggests, the promotion offered participants the chance to win a grand prize of $1 million. Ms. Gottlieb had played the game several times before. In both New Jersey and Pennsylvania, Tropicana had advertised the

Million Dollar Wheel in newspapers, magazines, and with direct mailings, although there is no evidence that the Gottliebs saw any of the advertisements.

Not surprisingly, the parties do not agree as to everything that happened once Ms. Gottlieb started play. However, they do agree that she presented her Diamond Club card, a casino operator swiped it through the card reader, she pressed a button to activate the wheel, and the Million Dollar Wheel began spinning. Ms. Gottlieb contends that the wheel landed on the $1 million grand prize, but that when it did so, the casino attendant immediately swiped another card through the machine, reactivated the wheel, and then the wheel landed on a prize of two show tickets. Tropicana avers that the wheel simply landed on the lesser prize. The casino says the wheel never landed on $1 million, and the attendant never intervened and reactivated the wheel. . . .

Under both Pennsylvania and New Jersey law, adequate consideration is necessary in order to form an enforceable contract. *See* Continental Bank of Pennsylvania v. Barclay Riding Academy, Inc., 93 N.J. 153, 459 A.2d 1163, 1171 (1983). Consideration is a bargained for exchange, and it may take the form of either a detriment to the promisee or a benefit to the promisor. *See Continental Bank*, 459 A.2d at 1172. In support of its contention that New Jersey law holds that no valid consideration exists when a person participates in a promotion, Tropicana cites only one case, a 1985 unpublished transcript of a ruling of the Superior Court of New Jersey. There, the Resorts International Hotel, Inc., a licensed casino operator in New Jersey, sued the New Jersey Division of Gaming Enforcement seeking a declaratory judgment that three promotions it was conducting, a gin rummy tournament and two stock market games, did not violate New Jersey law. *See* Resorts Int'l Hotel, Inc. v. New Jersey Div. of Gaming Enforcement, No. L39436–85, slip op. (N.J.Super. Ct. Law Div., Atlantic Co. Oct. 25, 1985). The question before the court was whether "something of value" passed from the player to the casino, making the promotions illegal gambling in violation of New Jersey law.[3] The court did not determine whether a contract had been formed. It did observe, however, that in the past the presence of only "minute consideration" made a promotion illegal gambling under New Jersey law. *Id.* at 11. Over time, though, the scope of "something of value" had been restricted and "strictly defined." *Id.* at 12. In other words, "something of value" requires more than the minimum consideration that would support the formation of a contract. The court concluded that nothing "of value" had passed from player to casino in the course of the three promotions. *Id.* at 13. It did not decide, as Tropicana contends, that participation in a promotion cannot constitute adequate consideration for a contract.

---

3. According to the court, New Jersey law defined "something of value" as "any money or property, any token, object or article exchangeable for money or property or any form of credit or promise directly or indirectly contemplating transfer of money or property or of any interest therein or involving extension of a service, entertainment or a privilege of playing at a game or scheme without charge." *Id.* at 12 (citing N.J. Stat. Ann. § 2C:37–1(d)).

We find the decision of the New Jersey Supreme Court in Lucky Calendar Co. v. Cohen, 19 N.J. 399, 117 A.2d 487 (1955), *op. adhered to on reh'g*, 20 N.J. 451, 120 A.2d 107 (1956), to be on point. There, an advertising company brought a declaratory judgment action against the Camden County prosecutor, seeking a determination that its promotional advertisement campaign for Acme Super Markets did not violate New Jersey's Lottery Act. The centerpiece of the campaign was a calendar that had Acme coupons bordering it, which was distributed by mass mailings. *See* Lucky Calendar, 117 A.2d at 489–90. The calendar contained an explanation of the "Lucky Calendar Prize Contest." Entrants had the opportunity to win prizes in monthly drawings. All they had to do to enter was tear the entry form off of the calendar, enter a name, address, and phone number, and have the form deposited in a box at any Acme store. There was no charge, and they were not required to be present for the drawing. *See id.* at 490.

The question in *Lucky Calendar* was whether there had been consideration for participation in the drawings. The Supreme Court of New Jersey noted that, assuming consideration was required in order for something to qualify as an illegal lottery under the Lottery Act, it need only be the minimum consideration that is necessary to form a contract. *See id.* at 495. It explained:

> (T)he consideration in a lottery, as in any form of simple contract, need not be money or the promise of money. Nor need it be of intrinsic value; "a rose, a hawk or a peppercorn" will suffice, provided it is what is asked for by the promisor and is not illegal.... Whether a "peppercorn" or the filling in and delivering of a coupon is sufficient consideration for a promise depends only on whether it was the requested detriment to the promisee induced by the promise. That is consideration which is regarded as such by the parties.

Id. (citing *Williston on Contracts* (rev. ed.1936), §§ 100 n.8 and 115).[4]

The court determined that consideration was present "both in the form of a detriment or inconvenience to the promisee at the request of the promisor and of a benefit to the promisor." *Id.* "Completing the coupon and arranging for the deposit of it in the box" at the store was the detriment to the promisee, and the "increase in volume of business" was the benefit to the promisor and its customer, the owner of the Acme stores. *Id.* at 496. As the court pointed out, "The motives of the plaintiff and its customer (in offering the Lucky Calendar Prize Contest) ... are in nowise altruistic." *Id.*

In Cobaugh v. Klick–Lewis, Inc., 385 Pa.Super. 587, 561 A.2d 1248, (1989), the Superior Court of Pennsylvania decided that there was adequate consideration to form a binding contract where a golfer, who was participating in a tournament, shot a hole-in-one after seeing a contest announcement offering a new car to anyone who could ace the particular

---

4. The legislature of New Jersey has repealed the Lottery Act that was in effect at the time of this case.

hole. *See* Cobaugh, 561 A.2d at 1249–50. The court noted that the promisor benefitted from the publicity of the promotional advertising, and the golfer performed an act that he was under no legal obligation to perform. *See id.* at 1250.

The laws of New Jersey and Pennsylvania similarly hold that the minimal detriment to a participant in a promotional contest is sufficient consideration for a valid contract. As there is no conflict between the laws of the two states, we need not engage in any conflict of laws analysis. It simply does not matter which law we apply.

Ms. Gottlieb had to go to the casino to participate in the promotion. She had to wait in line to spin the wheel. By presenting her Diamond Club card to the casino attendant and allowing it to be swiped into the casino's machine, she was permitting the casino to gather information about her gambling habits. Additionally, by participating in the game, she was a part of the entertainment that casinos, by their very nature, are designed to offer to all of those present. All of these detriments to Ms. Gottlieb were "the requested detriment(s) to the promisee induced by the promise" of Tropicana to offer her a chance to win $1 million. Lucky Calendar, 117 A.2d at 495. Tropicana's motives in offering the promotion were "in nowise altruistic." *Id.* at 496. It offered the promotion in order to generate patronage of and excitement within the casino. In short, Ms. Gottlieb provided adequate consideration to form a contract with Tropicana. ...

Tropicana's motion for summary judgment against Ms. Gottlieb on Count I of the complaint will be denied.

FIEGE v. BOEHM

Court of Appeals of Maryland, 1956.
210 Md. 352, 123 A.2d 316.

DELAPLAINE, JUDGE. This suit was brought in the Superior Court of Baltimore City by Hilda Louise Boehm against Louis Gail Fiege to recover for breach of a contract to pay the expenses incident to the birth of his bastard child and to provide for its support upon condition that she would refrain from prosecuting him for bastardy.

Plaintiff alleged in her declaration substantially as follows: (1) that early in 1951 defendant had sexual intercourse with her although she was unmarried, and as a result thereof she became pregnant, and defendant acknowledged that he was responsible for her pregnancy; (2) that on September 29, 1951, she gave birth to a female child; that defendant is the father of the child; and that he acknowledged on many occasions that he is its father; (3) that before the child was born, defendant agreed to pay all her medical and miscellaneous expenses and to compensate her for the loss of her salary caused by the child's birth, and also to pay her ten dollars per week for its support until it reached the age of 21, upon condition that she would not institute bastardy proceedings against him as long as he made the payments in accordance with the agreement; (4) that she placed the child for adoption on July 13, 1954, and she claimed the following sums: Union Memorial Hospital, $110; Florence Crittenton Home, $100; Dr. George Merrill, her physician, $50; medicines, $70.35; miscellaneous expenses, $20.45; loss of earnings for 26 weeks, $1,105; support of the child, $1,440; total, $2,895.80; and (5) that defendant paid her only $480, and she demanded that he pay her the further sum of $2,415.80, the balance due under the agreement, but he failed and refused to pay the same.

Defendant demurred to the declaration on the ground that it failed to allege that in September, 1953, plaintiff instituted bastardy proceedings against him in the Criminal Court of Baltimore, but since it had been found from blood tests that he could not have been the father of the child, he was acquitted of bastardy. The Court sustained the demurrer with leave to amend.

Plaintiff then filed an amended declaration, which contained the additional allegation that, after the breach of the agreement by defendant, she filed a charge with the State's Attorney that defendant was the father of her bastard child; and that on October 8, 1953, the Criminal Court found defendant not guilty solely on a physician's testimony that "on the basis of certain blood tests made, the defendant can be excluded as the father of the said child, which testimony is not conclusive upon a jury in a trial court."

Defendant also demurred to the amended declaration, but the Court overruled that demurrer.

Plaintiff, a typist, now over 35 years old, who has been employed by the Government in Washington and Baltimore for over thirteen years, testified in the Court below that she had never been married, but that at about midnight on January 21, 1951, defendant, after taking her to a moving picture theater on York Road and then to a restaurant, had sexual intercourse with her in his automobile. She further testified that he agreed to pay all her medical and hospital expenses, to compensate her for loss of salary caused by the pregnancy and birth, and to pay her ten dollars per week for the support of the child upon condition that she would refrain from instituting bastardy proceedings against him. She further testified that between September 17, 1951, and May, 1953, defendant paid her a total of $480.

Defendant admitted that he had taken plaintiff to restaurants, had danced with her several times, had taken her to Washington, and had brought her home in the country; but he asserted that he had never had sexual intercourse with her. He also claimed that he did not enter into any agreement with her. He admitted, however, that he had paid her a total of $480. His father also testified that he stated "that he did not want his mother to know, and if it were just kept quiet, kept principally away from his mother and the public and the courts, that he would take care of it."

Defendant further testified that in May, 1953, he went to see plaintiff's physician to make inquiry about blood tests to show the paternity of the child; and that those tests were made and they indicated that it was not possible that he could have been the child's father. He then stopped making payments. Plaintiff thereupon filed a charge of bastardy with the State's Attorney.

The testimony which was given in the Criminal Court by Dr. Milton Sachs, hematologist at the University Hospital, was read to the jury in the Superior Court. ... Dr. Sachs reported that Fiege's blood group was Type O, Miss Boehm's was Type B, and the infant's was Type A. He further testified that on the basis of these tests, Fiege could not have been the father of the child, as it is impossible for a mating of Type O and Type B to result in a child of Type A.

Although defendant was acquitted by the Criminal Court, the Superior Court overruled his motion for a directed verdict. In the charge to the jury the Court instructed them that defendant's acquittal in the Criminal Court was not binding upon them. The jury found a verdict in favor of plaintiff for $2,415.80, the full amount of her claim.

Defendant filed a motion for judgment n.o.v. or a new trial. The Court overruled that motion also, and entered judgment on the verdict of the jury. Defendant appealed from that judgment.

Defendant contends that, even if he did enter into the contract as alleged, it was not enforceable, because plaintiff's forbearance to prosecute was not based on a valid claim, and hence the contract was without consideration. He, therefore, asserts that the Court erred in overruling (1) his demurrer to the amended declaration, (2) his motion for a directed verdict, and (3) his motion for judgment n.o.v. or a new trial.

It was originally held at common law that a child born out of wedlock is *filius nullius,* and a putative father is not under any legal liability to contribute to the support of his illegitimate child, and his promise to do so is unenforceable because it is based on purely a moral obligation. ...

However, where statutes are in force to compel the father of a bastard to contribute to its support, the courts have invariably held that a contract by the putative father with the mother of his bastard child to provide for the support of the child upon the agreement of the mother to refrain from invoking the bastardy statute against the father, or to abandon proceedings already commenced, is supported by sufficient consideration. Jangraw v. Perkins, 77 Vt. 375, 60 A. 385.

In Maryland it is now provided by statute that whenever a person is found guilty of bastardy, the court shall issue an order directing such person (1) to pay for the maintenance and support of the child until it reaches the age of eighteen years, such sum as may be agreed upon, if consent proceedings be had, or in the absence of agreement, such sum as the court may fix, with due regard to the circumstances of the accused person; and (2) to give bond to the State of Maryland in such penalty as the court may fix, with good and sufficient securities, conditioned on making the payments required by the court's order, or any amendments thereof. Failure to give such bond shall be punished by commitment to the jail or the House of Correction until bond is given but not exceeding two years. Code Supp.1955, art. 12, § 8.

Prosecutions for bastardy are treated in Maryland as criminal proceedings, but they are actually civil in purpose. Kennard v. State, 177 Md. 549, 10 A.2d 710. While the prime object of the Maryland Bastardy Act is to protect the public from the burden of maintaining illegitimate children, it is so distinctly in the interest of the mother that she becomes the beneficiary of it. Accordingly a contract by the putative father of an illegitimate child to provide for its support upon condition that bastardy proceedings will not be instituted is a compromise of civil injuries resulting from a criminal act, and not a contract to compound a criminal prosecution, and if it is fair and reasonable, it is in accord with the Bastardy Act and the public policy of the State.

Of course, a contract of a putative father to provide for the support of his illegitimate child must be based, like any other contract, upon sufficient consideration. . . .

In 1867 the Maryland Court of Appeals, in the opinion delivered by Judge Bartol in Hartle v. Stahl, 27 Md. 157, 172, held: (1) that forbearance to assert a claim before institution of suit, if not in fact a legal claim, is not of itself sufficient consideration to support a promise; but (2) that a compromise of a doubtful claim or a relinquishment of a pending suit is good consideration for a promise; and (3) that in order to support a compromise, it is sufficient that the parties entering into it thought at the time that there was a *bona fide* question between them, although it may eventually be found that there was in fact no such question.

We have thus adopted the rule that the surrender of, or forbearance to assert, an invalid claim by one who has not an honest and reasonable belief in its possible validity is not sufficient consideration for a contract. 1 *Restatement, Contracts*, sec. 76(b). We combine the subjective requisite that the claim be *bona fide* with the objective requisite that it must have a reasonable basis of support. Accordingly a promise not to prosecute a claim which is not founded in good faith does not of itself give a right of action on an agreement to pay for refraining from so acting, because a release from mere annoyance and unfounded litigation does not furnish valuable consideration.

Professor Williston was not entirely certain whether the test of reasonableness is based upon the intelligence of the claimant himself, who may be an ignorant person with no knowledge of law and little sense as to facts; but he seemed inclined to favor the view that "the claim forborne must be neither absurd in fact from the standpoint of a reasonable man in the position of the claimant, nor, obviously unfounded in law to one who has an elementary knowledge of legal principles." 1 *Williston on Contracts*, Rev.Ed., sec. 135. We agree that while stress is placed upon the honesty and good faith of the claimant, forbearance to prosecute a claim is insufficient consideration if the claim forborne is so lacking in foundation as to make its assertion incompatible with honesty and a reasonable degree of intelligence. Thus, if the mother of a bastard knows that there is no foundation, either in law or fact, for a charge against a certain man that he is the father of the child, but that man promises to pay her in order to prevent bastardy proceedings against him, the forbearance to institute proceedings is not sufficient consideration.

On the other hand, forbearance to sue for a lawful claim or demand is sufficient consideration for a promise to pay for the forbearance if the party forbearing had an honest intention to prosecute litigation which is not frivolous, vexatious, or unlawful, and which he believed to be well founded. Snyder v. Cearfoss, 187 Md. 635, 643, 51 A.2d. Thus the promise of a woman who is expecting an illegitimate child that she will not institute bastardy proceedings against a certain man is sufficient consideration for his promise to pay for the child's support, even though it may not be certain whether the man is the father or whether the prosecution would be successful, if she makes the charge in good faith. . . .

Another analogous case is Thompson v. Nelson, 28 Ind. 431. There the plaintiff sought to recover back money which he had paid to compromise a prosecution for bastardy. He claimed that the prosecuting witness was not pregnant and therefore the prosecution was fraudulent. It was held by the Supreme Court of Indiana, however, that the settlement of the prosecution was a good consideration for the payment of the money and it could not be recovered back, inasmuch as it appeared from the evidence that the prosecution was instituted in good faith, and at that time there was reason to believe that the prosecuting witness was pregnant, although it was found out afterwards that she was not pregnant. . . .

In the case at bar there was no proof of fraud or unfairness. Assuming that the hematologists were accurate in their laboratory tests and findings, nevertheless plaintiff gave testimony which indicated that she made the charge of bastardy against defendant in good faith. For these reasons the Court acted properly in overruling the demurrer to the amended declaration and the motion for a directed verdict. . . .

Judgment affirmed, with costs.

PROBLEMS

1. A promises B that A will sell and deliver a set of books to B if B's father, C, pays $150 for the set. C pays, but A fails to deliver the books. May B enforce A's promise?

2. A and B entered into a contract under which A would do specified work and B would pay $10,000 when the work was done. After the work was completed, B said to A, "You have done such a good job that I'll pay you $5,000 extra." B paid A $15,000. May B recover $5,000?

3. H and W were living in a house owned by H's father (F). H made valuable improvements upon the property. Upon H's death F wrote to W and stated: "In view of the fact that my son has made improvements upon the

property for which I feel that you should receive adequate compensation, I give you the privilege of purchasing said property for the sum of $230,000 at my death." F signed and mailed the letter which was received by W. F is now deceased and W wishes to purchase the property. Does she have an enforceable right to purchase it for $230,000?

4. D promised P that, if P continued to deliver specified kinds of merchandise to D's brother, D would pay for the items already delivered and for the items to be delivered. P duly performed. Does P have a cause of action against D?

5. Rising water levels in an abandoned gravel pit near Maureen's property threatened her property with flooding. She appealed to the county for help. Though the gravel pit was not the responsibility of the county, it agreed to furnish a pump to lower the water level by two feet. The county did not want to have to operate the pump or worry about being sued as a result of the pumping, so it required Maureen to agree to operate the pump and to release the county from any liability for damages or injury caused by the pumping. The county did provide the pump, but after several months of heavy rainfall, it removed the pump though the water level had not been reduced because other landowners complained that the pump caused flooding on their property. Maureen brings a suit against the county alleging breach of promise to provide the pump until the water level in the gravel pit was reduced by two feet. Was there consideration for the county's alleged promise?

6. D, a father, conveyed property to his daughter, P, and stated that it was a Christmas present. As part of the same transaction D agreed to continue to pay off two mortgages that encumbered the property. At the same time one of P's brothers gave P a dollar which in turn she gave to her father. Is there consideration to support D's promise?

7. R Corp. owns a restaurant. S is a supplier of restaurant equipment. D is R Corp.'s principal shareholder. D gave S the following guaranty signed by D: "For and in consideration of $1 paid by S (receipt of which is hereby acknowledged) I hereby guaranty to S any indebtedness of R Corp. to the extent of $10,000." The $1 mentioned was not in fact paid.

a) At the time D gave S the guaranty, R Corp. was not indebted to S but did become indebted to S in the amount of $5,000 for restaurant equipment delivered on credit. Is the guaranty enforceable?

b) What result if the $5,000 debt had been incurred before the guarantee was given?

SECTION 2. PRE–EXISTING DUTY RULE

(Calamari & Perillo on Contracts §§ 4.9—4.11)

SCHWARTZREICH v. BAUMAN–BASCH, INC.

New York Court of Appeals, 1921.
231 N.Y. 196, 131 N.E. 887.

CRANE, J. On the 31st day of August, 1917, the plaintiff entered into the following employment agreement with the defendant:

Bauman–Basch, Inc.,
Coats & Wraps
31–33 East 32nd Street
New York

Agreement entered into this 31st day of August, 1917, by and between Bauman–Basch, Inc., a domestic corporation, party of the first part, and Louis Schwartzreich, of the Borough of Bronx, City of New York, party of the second part, witnesseth:

The party of the first part does hereby employ the party of the second part, and the party of the second part agrees to enter the services of the party of the first part as a designer of coats and wraps.

The employment herein shall commence on the 22nd day of November, 1917, and shall continue for twelve months thereafter. The party of the second part shall receive a salary of Ninety ($90.00) per week, payable weekly.

The party of the second part shall devote his entire time and attention to the business of the party of the first part, and shall use his best energies and endeavors in the furtherance of its business.

In witness whereof, the party of the first part has caused its seal to be affixed hereto and these presents to be signed, and the party of the second part has hereunto set his hand and seal the day and year first above written.

BAUMAN–BASCH, INC.

S. Bauman

LOUIS SCHWARTZREICH

In the presence of:

In October the plaintiff was offered more money by another concern. Mr. Bauman, an officer of the Bauman–Basch, Inc., says that in that month he heard that the plaintiff was going to leave and thereupon had with him the following conversation:

A. I called him in the office, and I asked him, "Is that true that you want to leave us?" and he said "Yes," and I said, "Mr. Schwartzreich, how can you do that; you are under contract with us?" He said, "Somebody offered me more money." ... I said, "How much do they offer you?" He said, "They offered him $115 a week." ... I said, "I cannot get a designer now, and, in view of the fact that I have to send my sample line out on the road, I will give you a hundred dollars a week rather than to let you go." He said, "if you will give me $100, I will stay."

Thereupon Mr. Bauman dictated to his stenographer a new contract, dated October 17, 1917, in the exact words of the first contract and running for the same period, the salary being $100 a week, which contract was duly executed by the parties and witnessed. Duplicate originals were kept by the plaintiff and defendant.

Simultaneously with the signing of this new contract, the plaintiff's copy of the old contract was either given to or left with Mr. Bauman. He testifies that the plaintiff gave him the paper but that he did not take it from him. The signatures to the old contract plaintiff tore off at the time according to Mr. Bauman.

The plaintiff's version as to the execution of the new contract is as follows:

> A. I told Mr. Bauman that I have an offer from Scheer & Mayer of $110 a week, and I said to him, "Do you advise me as a friendly matter—will you advise me as a friendly matter what to do; you see I have a contract with you, and I should not accept the offer of $110 a week, and I ask you, as a matter of friendship, do you advise me to take it or not." At the minute he did not say anything, but the day afterwards he came to me in and he said, "I will give you $100 a week, and I want you to stay with me." I said, "All right, I will accept it; it is very nice of you that you do that, and I appreciate it very much."

The plaintiff says that on the 17th of October when the new contract was signed, he gave his copy of the old contract back to Mr. Bauman, who said: "You do not want this contract any more because the new one takes its place."

The plaintiff remained in the defendant's employ until the following December when he was discharged. He brought this action under the contract of October 17th for his damages.

The defense, insisted upon through all the courts, is that there was no consideration for the new contract as the plaintiff was already bound under his agreement of August 31, 1917, to do the same work for the same period at $90 a week.

The trial justice submitted to the jury the question whether there was a cancellation of the old contract and charged as follows:

> If you find that the $90 contract was prior to or at the time of the execution of the $100 contract cancelled and revoked by the parties by their mutual consent, then it is your duty to find that there was a consideration for the making of the contract in suit, viz., the $100 contract and, in that event, the plaintiff would be entitled to your verdict for such damages as you may find resulted proximately,

naturally and necessarily in consequence of the plaintiff's discharge prior to the termination of the contract period of which I shall speak later on.

Defendant's counsel thereupon excepted to that portion of the charge in which the court permitted the jury to find that the prior contract may have been canceled simultaneously with the execution of the other agreement. Again the court said:

> The test question is whether by word or by act, either prior to or at the time of the signing of the $100 contract, these parties mutually agreed that the old contract from that instant should be null and void.

The jury having rendered a verdict for the plaintiff the trial justice set it aside and dismissed the complaint on the ground that there was not sufficient evidence that the first contract was canceled to warrant the jury's findings.

The above quotations from the record show that a question of fact was presented and that the evidence most favorable for the plaintiff would sustain a finding that the first contract was destroyed, canceled or abrogated by the consent of both parties.

The Appellate Term was right in reversing this ruling. Instead of granting a new trial, however, it reinstated the verdict of the jury and the judgment for the plaintiff. The question remains, therefore, whether the charge of the court as above given, was a correct statement of the law or whether on all the evidence in the plaintiff's favor a cause of action was made out.

Can a contract of employment be set aside or terminated by the parties to it and a new one made or substituted in its place? If so, is it competent to end the one and make the other at the same time?

It has been repeatedly held that a promise made to induce a party to do that which he is already bound by contract to perform is without consideration. But the cases in this state, while enforcing this rule, also recognize that a contract may be canceled by mutual consent and a new one made. Thus Vanderbilt v. Schreyer (91 N.Y. 392, 402) held that it was no consideration for a guaranty that a party promise to do only that which he was before legally bound to perform. This court stated, however:

> It would doubtless be competent for parties to cancel an existing contract and make a new one to complete the same work at a different rate of compensation, but it seems that it would be essential to its validity that there should be a valid cancellation of the original contract. Such was the case of Lattimore v. Harsen (14 Johns. 330).

In Cosgray v. New England Piano Co. (10 App.Div. 351, 353) it was decided that where the plaintiff had bound himself to work for a year at $30 a week, there was no consideration for a promise thereafter made by the defendant that he should notwithstanding receive $1,800 a year. Here it will be noticed there was no termination of the first agreement which gave occasion for Bartlett, J., to say in the opinion:

The case might be different if the parties had, by word of mouth, agreed wholly to abrogate and do away with a pre-existing written contract in regard to service and compensation, and had substituted for it another agreement.

Any change in an existing contract, such as a modification of the rate of compensation, or a supplemental agreement, must have a new consideration to support it. In such a case the contract is continued, not ended. Where, however, an existing contract is terminated by consent of both parties and a new one executed in its place and stead, we have a different situation and the mutual promises are again a consideration. Very little difference may appear in a mere change of compensation in an existing and continuing contract and a termination of one contract and the making of a new one for the same time and work, but at an increased compensation. There is, however, a marked difference in principle. Where the new contract gives any new privilege or advantage to the promisor, a consideration has been recognized, though in the main it is the same contract. (Triangle Waist Co., Inc. v. Todd, 223 N.Y. 27.)

If this which we are now holding were not the rule, parties having once made a contract would be prevented from changing it no matter how willing and desirous they might be to do so, unless the terms conferred an additional benefit to the promisor.

All concede that an agreement may be rescinded by mutual consent and a new agreement made thereafter on any terms to which the parties may assent. Prof. Williston in his work on *Contracts* says (Vol. I, § 130a): "A rescission followed shortly afterwards by a new agreement in regard to the same subject-matter would create the legal obligations provided in the subsequent agreement."

The same effect follows in our judgment from a new contract entered into at the same time the old one is destroyed and rescinded by mutual consent. The determining factor is the rescission by consent. Provided this is the expressed and acted upon intention, the time of the rescission, whether a moment before or at the same time as the making of the new contract, is unimportant. . . .

For the reasons here stated, the charge of the trial court was correct, and the judgments of the Appellate Division and the Appellate Term should be affirmed, with costs.

Judgments affirmed.

ANGEL v. MURRAY

Supreme Court of Rhode Island, 1974.
113 R.I. 482, 322 A.2d 630.

ROBERTS, CHIEF JUSTICE. This is a civil action brought by Alfred L. Angel and others against John E. Murray, Jr., Director of Finance of the City of Newport, the city of Newport, and James L. Maher, alleging that Maher had illegally been paid the sum of $20,000 by the Director of

Finance and praying that the defendant Maher be ordered to repay the city such sum. The case was heard by a justice of the Superior Court, sitting without a jury, who entered a judgment ordering Maher to repay the sum of $20,000 to the city of Newport. Maher is now before this court prosecuting an appeal.

The record discloses that Maher has provided the city of Newport with a refuse-collection service under a series of five-year contracts beginning in 1946. On March 12, 1964, Maher and the city entered into another such contract for a period of five years commencing on July 1, 1964, and terminating on June 30, 1969. The contract provided, among other things, that Maher would receive $137,000 per year in return for collecting and removing all combustible and noncombustible waste materials generated within the city.

In June of 1967 Maher requested an additional $10,000 per year from the city council because there had been a substantial increase in the cost of collection due to an unexpected and unanticipated increase of 400 new dwelling units. Maher's testimony, which is uncontradicted, indicates the 1964 contract had been predicated on the fact that since 1946 there had been an average increase of 20 to 25 new dwelling units per year. After a public meeting of the city council where Maher explained in detail the reasons for his request and was questioned by members of the city council, the city council agreed to pay him an additional $10,000 for the year ending on June 30, 1968. Maher made a similar request again in June of 1968 for the same reasons, and the city council again agreed to pay an additional $10,000 for the year ending on June 30, 1969.

The trial justice found that each such $10,000 payment was made in violation of law. ... [H]e found that Maher was not entitled to extra compensation because the original contract already required him to collect all refuse generated within the city and, therefore, included the 400 additional units. The trial justice further found that these 400 additional units were within the contemplation of the parties when they entered into the contract. It appears that he based this portion of the decision upon the rule that Maher had a preexisting duty to collect the refuse generated by the 400 additional units, and thus there was no consideration for the two additional payments.

[The court points out that it is illegal for a municipality to pay out money as a gift; if there is no consideration the payments were illegal gifts. Ed.] ...

It is generally held that a modification of a contract is itself a contract, which is unenforceable unless supported by consideration. *See* Simpson, [*Contracts*] § 93 [(2d ed. 1965)]. In Rose v. Daniels, 8 R.I. 381 (1866), this court held that an agreement by a debtor with a creditor to discharge a debt for a sum of money less than the amount due is unenforceable because it was not supported by consideration.

Rose is a perfect example of the preexisting duty rule. Under this rule an agreement modifying a contract is not supported by consideration if one of the parties to the agreement does or promises to do something that he is legally obligated to do or refrains or promises to refrain from doing something he is not legally privileged to do. *See* Calamari & Perillo, *Contracts* § 60 (1970); 1A Corbin, *Contracts* §§ 171–72 (1963); 1 Williston, [*Contracts*] § 130 [(Jaeger 3d ed. 1957)]. In *Rose* there was no consideration for the new agreement because the debtor was already legally obligated to repay the full amount of the debt.

Although the preexisting duty rule is followed by most jurisdictions, a small minority of jurisdictions, Massachusetts, for example, find that there is consideration for a promise to perform what one is already legally obligated to do because the new promise is given in place of an action for damages to secure performance. *See* Swartz v. Lieberman, 323 Mass. 109, 80 N.E.2d 5 (1948). *Swartz* is premised on the theory that a promisor's forbearance of the power to breach his original agreement and be sued in an action for damages is consideration for a subsequent agreement by the promisee to pay extra compensation. This rule, however, has been widely criticized as an anomaly. *See Calamari & Perillo, supra,* § 61.

The primary purpose of the preexisting duty rule is to prevent what has been referred to as the "hold-up game." *See* 1A *Corbin, supra,* § 171. A classic example of the "hold-up game" is found in Alaska Packers' Ass'n v. Domenico, 117 F. 99 (9th Cir.1902). There 21 seamen entered into a written contract with Domenico to sail from San Francisco to Pyramid Harbor, Alaska. They were to work as sailors and fishermen out of Pyramid Harbor during the fishing season of 1900. The contract specified that each man would be paid $50 plus two cents for each red salmon he caught. Subsequent to their arrival at Pyramid Harbor, the men stopped work and demanded an additional $50. They threatened to return to San Francisco if Domenico did not agree to their demand. Since it was impossible for Domenico to find other men, he agreed to pay the men an additional $50. After they returned to San Francisco, Domenico refused to pay the men an additional $50. The court found that the subsequent agreement to pay the men an additional $50 was not supported by consideration because the men had a preexisting duty to work on the ship under the original contract, and thus the subsequent agreement was unenforceable.

Another example of the "hold-up game" is found in the area of construction contracts. Frequently, a contractor will refuse to complete work under an unprofitable contract unless he is awarded additional compensation. The courts have generally held that a subsequent agreement to award additional compensation is unenforceable if the contractor is only performing work which would have been required of him under the original contract. . . .

These examples clearly illustrate that the courts will not enforce an agreement that has been procured by coercion or duress and will hold the parties to their original contract regardless of whether it is profitable or unprofitable. However, the courts have been reluctant to apply the preexisting duty rule when a party to a contract encounters unanticipated difficulties and the other party, not influenced by coercion or duress, voluntarily agrees to pay additional compensation for work already required to be performed under the contract. For example, the courts have found that the original contract was rescinded, Linz v. Schuck, 106 Md. 220, 67 A. 286 (1907); abandoned, Connelly v. Devoe, 37 Conn. 570 (1871), or waived, Michaud v. McGregor, 61 Minn. 198, 63 N.W. 479 (1895).

Although the preexisting duty rule has served a useful purpose insofar as it deters parties from using coercion and duress to obtain additional compensation, it has been widely criticized as a general rule of law. With regard to the preexisting duty rule, one legal scholar has stated:

> There has been a growing doubt as to the soundness of this doctrine as a matter of social policy. . . . In certain classes of cases, this doubt has influenced courts to refuse to apply the rule, or to ignore it, in their actual decisions. Like other legal rules, this rule is in process of growth and change, the process being more active here than in most instances. The result of this is that a court should no longer accept this rule as fully established. It should never use it as the major premise of a decision, at least without giving careful thought to the circumstances of the particular case, to the moral deserts of the parties, and to the social feelings and interests that are involved. It is certain that the rule, stated in general and all-inclusive terms, is no longer so well-settled that a court must apply it though the heavens fall.

1A *Corbin, supra,* § 171; *see also Calamari & Perillo, supra,* § 61.

The modern trend appears to recognize the necessity that courts should enforce agreements modifying contracts when unexpected or unanticipated difficulties arise during the course of the performance of a contract, even though there is no consideration for the modification, as long as the parties agree voluntarily.

Under the Uniform Commercial Code, § 2–209(1), which has been adopted by 49 states, "(a)n agreement modifying a contract (for the sale of goods) needs no consideration to be binding." *See* G.L.1956 (1969 Reenactment) § 6A–2–209(1). Although at first blush this section appears to validate modifications obtained by coercion and duress, the comments to this section indicate that a modification under this section must meet the test of good faith imposed by the Code, and a modification obtained by extortion without a legitimate commercial reason is unenforceable.

The modern trend away from a rigid application of the preexisting duty rule is reflected by § 89D(a) [now 89(a), ed.] of the American Law Institute's Restatement Second of the Law of Contracts, which provides: "A promise modifying a duty under a contract not fully performed on either side is binding (a) if the modification is fair and equitable in view of circumstances not anticipated by the parties when the contract was made. . . ."

We believe that § 89D(a) is the proper rule of law and find it applicable to the facts of this case. It not only prohibits modifications obtained by coercion, duress, or extortion but also fulfills society's expectation that agreements entered into voluntarily will be enforced by the courts. *See generally* Horwitz, *The Historical Foundations of Modern Contract Law*, 87 Harv.L.Rev. 917 (1974). Section 89D(a), of course, does not compel a modification of an unprofitable or unfair contract; it only enforces a modification if the parties voluntarily agree and if (1) the promise modifying the original contract was made before the contract was fully performed on either side, (2) the underlying circumstances which prompted the modification were unanticipated by the parties, and (3) the modification is fair and equitable.

The evidence, which is uncontradicted, reveals that in June of 1968 Maher requested the city council to pay him an additional $10,000 for the year beginning on July 1, 1968, and ending on June 30, 1969. This request was made at a public meeting of the city council, where Maher explained in detail his reasons for making the request. Thereafter, the city council voted to authorize the Mayor to sign an amendment to the 1964 contract which provided that Maher would receive an additional $10,000 per year for the duration of the contract. Under such circumstances we have no doubt that the city voluntarily agreed to modify the 1964 contract.

Having determined the voluntariness of this agreement, we turn our attention to the three criteria delineated above. First, the modification was made in June of 1968 at a time when the five-year contract which was made in 1964 had not been fully performed by either party. Second, although the 1964 contract provided that Maher collect all refuse generated within the city, it appears this contract was premised on Maher's past experience that the number of refuse-generating units would increase at a rate of 20 to 25 per year. Furthermore, the evidence is uncontradicted that the 1967–1968 increase of 400 units "went beyond any previous expectation." Clearly, the circumstances which prompted the city council to modify the 1964 contract were unanticipated. Third, although the evidence does not indicate what proportion of the total this increase comprised, the evidence does indicate that it was a "substantial" increase. In light of this, we cannot say that the council's agreement to pay Maher the $10,000 increase was not fair and equitable in the circumstances.

The judgment appealed from is reversed, and the cause is remanded to the Superior Court for entry of judgment for the defendants.

KIBLER v. FRANK L. GARRETT & SONS, INC.

Supreme Court of Washington, En Banc, 1968.
73 Wash.2d 523, 439 P.2d 416.

ROSELLINI, JUDGE. This action on a contract was dismissed at the close of the plaintiff's evidence, the trial court finding, although it had not been pleaded, that there had been an accord and satisfaction. The plaintiff has appealed.

The facts are these: The plaintiff was hired by the defendant to harvest his wheat crop. There was no agreement on the price to be paid. According to the plaintiff's evidence, he told the defendant that, if the wheat crop proved to be more than 50 bushels per acre, the price would be 18 cents per bushel and perhaps more, depending on the circumstances. He testified that the crop was in excess of 50 bushels per acre and there were harvesting difficulties which had not been anticipated due to the presence of guy wires, roads, and risers. He sent the defendant a bill based upon a charge of 25 cents per bushel, but later sent a corrected bill for $876.20 based on 20 cents per bushel. The response which he eventually received to this billing was the following letter and a check for $444:

> This check is for $10.00 an acre, and 37 acres is $370.00. This is what you offered to harvest our wheat for. Seeing that the wheat was fairly heavy, we are paying you $2.00 an acre more, which makes a total of $444.00. Your total pay is 50% more than we paid last year for harvesting the same acres, and 20% more than you agreed to do it for. Billing on this acreage for approximately $30.00 an acre is ridiculous.

Upon receipt of these items, the plaintiff called his attorney and asked if he could safely deposit the check. The attorney asked him to read the notations on it. He read the typewritten notation: "Harvesting Wheat Washington Ranch" and the printed words "Frank L. Garrett & Sons, Inc.," but he did not see a line of fine print on the check which read: "By endorsement this check when paid is accepted in full payment of the following account." The attorney told him he could deposit the check. He did not communicate further with the defendant but proceeded to bring this action.

As we have said, accord and satisfaction was not pleaded as a defense. However, the trial court, observing the fine print on the check and drawing it to the attention of the parties, concluded that, taken in conjunction with the letter, this notation established as a matter of law that there had been an accord and satisfaction.

The rules governing the question of accord and satisfaction are set forth in the leading case of Graham v. New York Life Ins. Co., 182 Wash. 612, 47 P.2d 1029 (1935). They are as follows:

(1) Whether there has been an accord and satisfaction in any given case is generally a mixed question of law and fact.

(2) But where the facts are not in controversy, it is purely a question of law for the court.

(3) To create an accord and satisfaction in law, there must be a meeting of minds of the parties upon the subject and an intention on the part of both to make such an agreement.

(4) An accord and satisfaction is founded on contract, and a consideration therefor is as necessary as for any other contract. . . .

(9) Where the amount of a debt or obligation is unliquidated or in dispute, then the tender by the debtor of a certain sum in full payment of

the debt, followed by acceptance and retention of the amount tendered, establishes an accord and satisfaction; but if the amount be liquidated or undisputed, then such tender and acceptance do not establish an accord and satisfaction.

The facts are not in dispute in this case, therefore the question is one of law. Did the letter and the check and the cashing of the latter constitute an accord and satisfaction? The claim was unliquidated; therefore, if the check was intended as full payment and that fact was communicated to the plaintiff, his cashing of the check completed the accord.

The important question to determine is whether there was a meeting of the minds. In order for this to have occurred, the defendant must have made his intention clear to the plaintiff. The trial court was of the opinion that the letter, when read in conjunction with the fine print on the check, manifested that intention.

The letter itself does not state that the check is sent in full payment. Such an intent might be gleaned from the language that he considers it all that is reasonably owing to the plaintiff. Yet the last sentence equivocates. The amount asked by the plaintiff is ridiculous, the defendant says, but he does not say, "I will pay no more than the amount enclosed." We think the letter leaves the question of the amount owed open to further negotiation. The fact that the plaintiff did not attempt further negotiation does not alter the import of the language of the letter. . . .

Since there were no conditions attached to the acceptance of the check in this case, the letter was not an offer of an accord.

Was the condition sufficiently expressed on the check itself? It is unquestioned that the plaintiff did not see the fine print, and his attorney did not see it. The defendant's attorney did not notice it, apparently, until it was called to his attention at the trial. This was a form check, presumably used in the payment of all of the defendant's accounts, whether the payments made were payments in full or partial payments. There was nothing on the check to indicate that the language was particularly applicable to the plaintiff's claim. The trial court felt that the tone of the letter cast upon the plaintiff the duty to examine the check minutely or cash it at his peril. We do not agree. The burden is upon the party alleging an accord and satisfaction to show that there was indeed a meeting of the minds. *See* Brear v. Klinker Sand & Gravel Co., 60 Wash.2d 443, 374 P.2d 370 (1962). If the language contained in the fine print on the check was of significance in forming an accord, it must appear that the fact of its significance was brought to the plaintiff's attention. The evidence is to the contrary. . . .

We hold that the proof in this case did not show an accord and satisfaction, since while the claim was disputed, there was no showing that the defendant manifested to the plaintiff his intention to pay no more than the amount which he remitted. . . .

The judgment is reversed and the cause remanded for a new trial. . . .

HALE, J. (dissenting). The facts of this case, in my judgment, present a classic example of accord and satisfaction, and I would, therefore, affirm the trial court. After all, the question of whether the parties have resolved their differences by an accord and satisfaction is largely a question of fact to be determined by the jury, or, as in this case, by the court as trier of the fact.

I agree that the printed notation on the check was insufficient to engender an accord and satisfaction, but the events leading up to the delivery of the check and the circumstance of its cashing provided more than adequate evidence, in my view, to support the trial court's factual finding that Mr. Kibler knowingly cashed the check in full payment and satisfaction of the debt for which it had been tendered. Here are the circumstances as I see them which led inexorably to an accord and satisfaction. . . .

The instant case began with an unliquidated claim, an agreement to harvest the wheat for an unspecified sum running from $10 per acre to a greater amount, depending vaguely on unspecified contingencies. Then the creditor sent a bill demanding 25 cents per bushel for a total demand of $1,095.25. A few days later he sent his debtor a corrected or new billing at 20 cents per bushel in the total sum of $876.20, thus conclusively establishing the unliquidated and uncertain nature of the obligation. The debt at the outset was unliquidated and for an uncertain amount; it remained so through the first erroneous billing for $1,095.25 and the second billing at $876.20.

It was still unliquidated and uncertain when defendant sent plaintiff a check for $444 on November 3, 1965, and stated specifically that the check was for the agreed price of $10 per acre, with an added $2 per acre because the wheat was very heavy. The assertions in the letter of transmittal that the enclosed check was 50 per cent more than plaintiff agreed to do the work for, and that the billing sent by plaintiff at nearly $30 an acre was ridiculous, all unmistakably convey the notion that the check was tendered in full payment. Under these circumstances, it should have been clear to a person of ordinary understanding that cashing the check constituted an acceptance of the $444 in full payment and discharge of plaintiff's claim for harvesting defendant's 37 acres.

I would, therefore, affirm. . . .

PROBLEMS

Analyze these problems from a common law perspective. Ignore any statutory changes.

8. A bank in Kentucky was robbed. A bankers' association offered a reward of $5,000 to anyone who apprehended the robber. Within a week, P, who was a police officer in the jurisdiction in which the bank was located, apprehended the robber who was convicted. P sues the association. What result?

9. Plaintiffs were sailors on defendant's vessel and agreed to work for a certain sum for a particular voyage. Midway through the voyage the plaintiffs demanded an increase in wages and defendant promised to pay $X more. Plaintiffs completed the voyage. Was the defendant's promise enforceable?

10. Plaintiff and defendant entered into a contract for the sale and delivery (in installments) of 4,000 wooden display stands at a price of 65 cents each. After 2,000 stands had been delivered and paid for, the plaintiff told defendant that due to increased costs he would have to charge 75 cents for each stand and defendant agreed to pay the higher rate. Plaintiff delivered the stands. At what rate is plaintiff entitled to be paid?

11. Angela applied to the Village of Homewood to become a firefighter. Under State law, the Village was required to process her application; the processing included a physical agility test. Prior to administering the test, the Village required Angela to sign a release of liability for all injuries she might suffer as a result of the test. During the test, she fell and was injured. She claims that the injuries were the result of the Village's negligence. The Village raises the release as a defense. Will the defense succeed?

12. P was employed by D under a contract for the year. D got into financial difficulties and during the contract year, P agreed with other key personnel that they all would accept a lesser salary for the balance of the year. Is there consideration for P's promise to take less?

13. D bought a tractor-trailer and financed the purchase through C, a bank. D missed a number of payments. C declared D in default on the loan agreement and threatened to exercise its right of repossession. D and C reached an agreement whereby D promised to have the broker, for whom D worked, subtract the money D owed C from D's paycheck and give it directly to C in exchange for C's promise not to exercise its right of repossession. The next day the tractor-trailer was repossessed on C's order. D sued C. Was there a binding agreement?

14. A, a subcontractor, contracts with B, a general contractor, to install heating units in houses being built by B for C. A discontinues work without justification. C promises to pay A an additional amount if A completes the installation in accordance with A's contract with B. A performs. Is there consideration for C's promise?

15. Plaintiff, as landlord, entered into a lease with defendant as tenant. The lease was for a five-year period at the agreed rental of $500 per month. Two years later, the parties entered into an oral agreement whereby rentals were reduced to $450. The reduced rent was paid and plaintiff now seeks to recover the $50 per month that was not paid.

16. Tenant terminated its lease as it was empowered to do by a clause in the lease providing that Tenant could terminate the lease by paying a termination fee of $380,000. It delivered a check in that amount clearly marked that it was tendered in full satisfaction of all claims Landlord had against Tenant. Landlord protested the language on the check but deposited it into its account. Landlord now sues Tenant, claiming damages for Tenant's breach of an obligation to restore the premises to their pre-rental condition.

Tenant pleads the affirmative defense of accord and satisfaction. How can Landlord meet this defense?

17. The plaintiff sold and delivered to defendant at various times bricks for which defendant was billed for the total of $820. On May 12th plaintiff sent bricks which would have been worth $448 if they had conformed to the contract. The defendant rejected them as non-conforming and asked plaintiff what to do with the bricks. On August 3 the defendant wrote the plaintiff as follows:

> Enclosed find check for $820 which pays our account up to July 1st. We have deducted the $448 for non-conforming bricks.

> Please advise us what disposition we shall make of these bricks for you.

Plaintiff received and cashed the check and now sues for the $448, alleging that the bricks are conforming. (a) If you were representing the defendant what would you set forth in your answer? (b) What issues will arise as to the validity of this defense?

SECTION 3. STATUTORY CHANGES

(Calamari & Perillo on Contracts §§ 5.12—5.17)

U.C.C. § 1–201. General Definitions*

(a) Unless the context otherwise requires....

(b) Subject to definitions contained in other articles of [the Uniform Commercial Code] that apply to particular articles or parts thereof: ...

(20) "Good faith," except as otherwise provided in Article 5, means honesty in fact and the observance of reasonable commercial standards of fair dealing.

U.C.C. § 1–302. Variation by Agreement**

(a) Except as otherwise provided in subsection (b) or elsewhere in [the Uniform Commercial Code], the effect of provisions of [the Uniform Commercial Code] may be varied by agreement.

(b) The obligations of good faith, diligence, reasonableness, and care prescribed by [the Uniform Commercial Code] may not be disclaimed by agreement. The parties, by agreement, may determine the standards by which the performance of those obligations is to be measured if those standards are not manifestly unreasonable. Whenever [the Uniform Commercial Code] requires an action to be taken within a reasonable time, a time that is not manifestly unreasonable may be fixed by agreement.

(c) The presence in certain provisions of [the Uniform Commercial Code] of the phrase "unless otherwise agreed", or words of similar import,

---

* Revised § 1–201(b)(20) combines former § 1–201 (19) (*see* Appendix B) and § 2–103 (1)(b) ("good faith" in the case of a merchant) (*see* Appendix A).

** Former § 1–102(3) & (4) (*see* Appendix B).

does not imply that the effect of other provisions may not be varied by agreement under this section.

U.C.C. § 1–304. Obligation of Good Faith***

Every contract or duty within [the Uniform Commercial Code] imposes an obligation of good faith in its performance and enforcement.

ROTH STEEL PRODUCTS v. SHARON STEEL CORP.

United States Court of Appeals, Sixth Circuit, 1983.
705 F.2d 134.

CELEBREZZE, SENIOR CIRCUIT JUDGE. This diversity action for breach of contract involves issues which require us to explore some relatively uncharted areas of Article Two of the Uniform Commercial Code....

The plaintiffs-appellees ..., Roth Steel Products Company and Toledo Steel Tube Company, are subsidiaries of Roth Industries, Inc. Roth Steel produces welded straight tubing for a variety of uses; Toledo Steel Tube produces fabricated steel tubing for use in automobile exhaust systems. ...

... In 1973, Sharon [Steel Corporation, defendant-appellant] was an integrated steel producer which accounted for approximately one percent of the steel produced in this country. It produced hot rolled and cold rolled sheet steel in carbon and alloy grades, as well as pickled and oiled sheet steel. ...

In 1972, the steel industry operated at approximately 70% of its capacity. Steel prices were highly competitive and discounts from published prices were given customers in an effort to increase the productive use of steel making capacity. ... [In November 1972, in response to defendant's letter of November 17, plaintiffs agreed to purchase certain fixed quantities of hot and cold rolled steel from Sharon Steel at discounted prices through December 31, 1973. Ed.]

In early 1973, several factors influenced the market for steel. Federal price controls discouraged foreign producers from importing steel; conversely, domestic producers exported a substantial portion of the steel produced domestically, in an effort to avoid federal price controls. Thus, the domestic steel supply was sharply reduced. In addition, the industry experienced substantial increases in demand as well as increases in labor, raw material, and energy costs. These increased labor, raw material, and energy costs compelled steel producers to increase prices. The increased demand and the attractive export market caused the entire industry to operate at full capacity in 1973 and 1974. Consequently, nearly every domestic producer experienced substantial delays in delivery.

As a result of the changed market conditions, Sharon decided to withdraw all price concessions, including those it had given the plaintiffs. The plaintiffs were notified of this decision on March 23, 1973 and they

---

*** Former § 1–203 (see Appendix B).

immediately protested, asserting that the price increase was a breach of the November, 1972 agreement. . . . As a result of this protest, discussions ensued and Sharon agreed to continue to sell steel to the plaintiffs at the discount prices of November, 1972 until June 30, 1973. For the remainder of 1973, Sharon proposed to sell rolled steel to plaintiffs at modified prices; these prices were higher than the prices [agreed to], but were lower than the published prices which Sharon charged its other customers. Sharon clearly indicated to plaintiffs that Sharon would sell no steel to plaintiffs after June 30, 1973 except at modified prices. Although plaintiffs initially were reluctant to accept Sharon's compromise, they finally agreed to Sharon's compromise proposal primarily because they were unable to purchase sufficient steel elsewhere to meet their production requirements. . . .

. . . Following a five day trial, the district court issued a lengthy and exhaustive memorandum of opinion. In the opinion, the district court concluded . . . that Sharon's attempt, in June, [1973], to modify the contract was ineffective; and that Sharon had breached the contract by charging prices higher than agreed upon in the November, 1972 contract. . . .

Before the district court, Sharon asserted that it properly increased prices because the parties had modified the November, 1973 contract to reflect changed market conditions. The district court, however, made several findings which, it believed, indicated that Sharon did not seek a modification to avoid a loss on the contract. The district court also found that the plaintiffs' inventories of rolled steel were "alarmingly deficient" at the time modification was sought and that Sharon had threatened to cease selling steel to the plaintiffs in the second-half of 1973 unless the plaintiffs agreed to the modification. Because Sharon had used its position as the plaintiffs' chief supplier to extract the price modification, the district court concluded that Sharon had acted in bad faith by seeking to modify the contract. In the alternative, the court concluded that the modification agreement was voidable because it was extracted by means of economic duress; the tight steel market prevented the plaintiffs from obtaining steel elsewhere at an affordable price and, consequently, the plaintiffs were forced to agree to the modification in order to assure a continued supply of steel. *See e.g.* Oskey Gasoline & Oil Co. v. Continental Oil Co., 534 F.2d 1281 (8th Cir.1976). Sharon challenges these conclusions on appeal.

The ability of a party to modify a contract which is subject to Article Two of the Uniform Commercial Code is broader than common law, primarily because the modification needs no consideration to be binding. O.R.C. Sec. 1302.12 (U.C.C. Sec. 2–209(1)). A party's ability to modify an agreement is limited only by Article Two's general obligation of good faith. Ralston Purina Co. v. McNabb, 381 F.Supp. 181, 183 (W.D.Tenn.1974); Official Comment 2, UCC § 2–209. *See* UCC § 2–103 [UCC Revised § 1–201(b)(20), ed.] In determining whether a particular modification was obtained in good faith, a court must make two distinct inquiries: whether the party's conduct is consistent with "reasonable commercial standards of fair dealing in the trade," U.S. for Use and Benefit of Crane Co. v. Progressive Enterprises, 418 F.Supp. 662, 664 n. 1 (E.D.Va.1976), and whether the parties were in fact motivated to seek modification by an honest desire to compensate for commercial exigencies. *See* Ralston Purina Co. v. McNabb, 381 F.Supp. at 183 (subjective purpose (to maximize damages) of extending time of performance under contract indicates bad faith and renders modification invalid); UCC § 2–103 [UCC Revised § 1–201(b)(20), ed.]. The first inquiry is relatively straightforward; the party asserting the modification must demonstrate that his decision to seek modification was the result of a factor, such as increased costs, which would cause an ordinary merchant to seek a modification of the contract. *See* Official Comment 2, UCC § 2–209 (reasonable commercial standards may require objective reason); J. White & R. Summers, *Handbook of Law under the U.C.C.* at 41. The second inquiry, regarding the subjective honesty of the parties, is less clearly defined. Essentially, this inquiry requires the party asserting the modification to demonstrate that he was, in fact, motivated by a legitimate commercial reason and that such a reason is not offered merely as a pretext. Ralston Purina Co. v. McNabb, 381 F.Supp. at 183–84. Moreover, the trier of fact must determine whether the means used to obtain the modification are an impermissible attempt to obtain a modification by extortion or overreaching. Erie County Water Authority v. Hen–Gar Construction [Corp., 473 F.Supp.1310, 1313 (W.D.N.Y.1979)]; Official Comment 2, UCC § 2–209. *See* J.White and R. Summers, *Handbook of the Law under the Uniform Commercial Code*, at 40–41 (1972).

Sharon argues that its decision to seek a modification was consistent with reasonable commercial standards of fair dealing because market exigencies made further performance entail a substantial loss. The district court, however, made three findings which caused it to conclude that economic circumstances were not the reason that Sharon sought a modification: it found that Sharon was partially insulated from raw material price increases, that Sharon bargained for a contract with a slim profit margin and thus implicitly assumed the risk that performance might come to involve a loss, and that Sharon's overall profit in 1973 and its profit on the contract in the first quarter of 1973 were inconsistent with Sharon's position that the modification was sought to avoid a loss. Although all of these findings are marginally related to the question whether Sharon's conduct was consistent with reasonable commercial standards of fair dealing, we do not believe that they are sufficient to support a finding that Sharon did not observe reasonable commercial standards by seeking a modification. In our view, these findings do not support a conclusion that a reasonable merchant, in light of the circumstances, would not have sought a modification in order to avoid a loss. For example, the district court's finding that Sharon's steel slab contract insulated it from industry wide cost increases is correct, so far as it goes. Although Sharon was able to purchase steel slabs at pre–1973 prices, the district court's findings also indicate that it was not able to purchase, at those prices, a sufficient tonnage of steel slabs to meet its production requirements. The district court also found that Sharon experienced substantial cost increases for other raw materials, ranging from 4% to nearly 20%. In light of these facts, the finding regarding the fixed-price contract for slab steel, without more, cannot support an inference that Sharon was unaffected by the market shifts that occurred in 1973. Similarly, the district court's finding that Sharon entered a contract in November, 1972 which would yield only a slim profit does not support a conclusion that Sharon was willing to risk a loss on the contract. Absent a finding that the market shifts and the raw material price increases were foreseeable at the time the contract was formed—a finding which was not made—Sharon's willingness to absorb a loss cannot be inferred from the fact that it contracted for a smaller profit than usual. Finally, the findings regarding Sharon's profits are not sufficient, by themselves, to warrant a conclusion that Sharon was not justified in seeking a modification. Clearly, Sharon's initial profit on the contract is an important consideration; the district court's findings indicate, however, that at the time modification was sought substantial future losses were foreseeable. A party who has not actually suffered a loss on the contract may still seek a modification if a future loss on the agreement was reasonably foreseeable. Similarly, the overall profit earned by the party seeking modification is an important factor; this finding, however, does not support a conclusion that the decision to seek a modification was unwarranted. The more relevant inquiry is into the profit obtained through sales of the product line in question. This conclusion is reinforced by the fact that only a few product lines may be affected by market exigencies; the opportunity to seek modification of a contract for the sale of goods of a product line should not be limited solely because some other product line produced a substantial profit.

In the final analysis, the single most important consideration in determining whether the decision to seek a modification is justified in this context is whether, because of changes in the market or other unforeseeable conditions, performance of the contract has come to involve a loss. In this case, the district court found that Sharon suffered substantial losses by performing the contract as *modified*. We are convinced that unforeseen economic exigencies existed which would prompt an ordinary merchant to seek a modification to avoid a loss on the contract; thus, we believe that the district court's findings to the contrary are clearly erroneous. . . .

The second part of the analysis, honesty in fact, is pivotal. The district court found that Sharon "threatened not to sell Roth and Toledo any steel if they refused to pay increased prices after July 1, 1973" and, consequently, that Sharon acted wrongfully. Sharon does not dispute the finding that it threatened to stop selling steel to the plaintiffs. Instead, it asserts that such a finding is merely evidence of bad faith and that it has rebutted any inference of bad faith based on that finding. We agree with this analysis; although coercive conduct is evidence that a modification of a contract is sought in bad faith, that prima facie showing may be effectively rebutted by the party seeking to enforce the modification. *E.g.,* Business Incentives Co., Inc. v. Sony Corp. of America, 397 F.Supp. 63, 69 (S.D.N.Y.1975) (in context of economic duress, coercive conduct permissible in light of contractual right to terminate). *See* Jamestown Farmers Elevator, Inc. v. General Mills, 552 F.2d 1285, 1290 (8th Cir.1977) ("good faith insistence upon a legal right (with coercive effect) which one believes he has usually is not duress, even if it turns out that that party is mistaken and, in fact, has no such right"); *White & Summers, supra,* at 41 (good faith exists if a party believes that contract permits party seeking modification to refuse to perform if modification not effected). Although we agree with Sharon's statement of principles, we do not agree that Sharon has rebutted the inference of bad faith that rises from its coercive conduct. Sharon asserts that its decision to unilaterally raise prices was based on language in the November 17, 1972 letter which allowed it to raise prices to the extent of any general industry-wide price increase. Because prices in the steel industry had increased, Sharon concludes that it was justified in raising its prices. Because it was justified in raising the contract price, the plaintiffs were bound by the terms of the contract to pay the increased prices. Consequently, any refusal by the plaintiffs to pay the price increase sought by Sharon must be viewed as a material breach of the November, 1972 contract which would excuse Sharon from any further performance. Thus, Sharon reasons that its refusal to perform absent a price increase was justified under the contract and consistent with good faith.

This argument fails in two respects. First, the contractual language on which Sharon relies only permits, at most, a price increase for cold rolled steel; thus, even if Sharon's position were supported by the evidence, Sharon would not have been justified in refusing to sell the plaintiffs hot rolled steel because of the plaintiffs' refusal to pay higher prices for the product. More importantly, however, the evidence does not indicate that Sharon ever offered this theory as a justification until this matter was tried. Sharon's representatives, in their testimony, did not attempt to justify Sharon's refusal to ship steel at 1972 prices in this fashion. Furthermore, none of the contemporaneous communications contain this justification for Sharon's action. In short, we can find no evidence in the record which indicates that Sharon offered this theory as a justification at the time the modification was sought. Consequently, we believe that the district court's conclusion that Sharon acted in bad faith by using coercive conduct to extract the price modification is not clearly erroneous. Therefore, we hold that Sharon's attempt to modify the November, 1972 contract, in order to compensate for increased costs which made performance come to involve a loss, is ineffective because Sharon did not act in a manner consistent with Article Two's requirement of honesty in fact when it refused to perform its remaining obligations under the contract at 1972 prices.[31] . . .

---

31. The district court also found, as an alternative ground, that the modification was voidable because the plaintiffs agreed to the modification due to economic duress. *See, e.g.,* Oskey Gasoline & Oil Co. v. Continental Oil, 534 F.2d 1281 (8th Cir.1976). Because we conclude that the

We have exhaustively reviewed the record, and have considered nearly every facet of the district court's decision. We believe, for the most part, that the district court has correctly resolved the factual and legal questions which the parties have so bitterly contested for the past eight years. . . . [The court remanded for findings of fact unrelated to the modification issue. Ed.]

PROBLEMS

18. Assume you bought a used truck. The bill of sale says "AS IS, WITHOUT WARRANTY." Soon after you had inspected the truck and accepted delivery, defects showed up. The seller, a dealer, agrees to repair the truck at no cost to you. The dealer makes major engine repairs and bills you $19,000. Is the dealer bound by the promise to repair without charging anything?

19. Seller agreed to manufacture and deliver an automated production line for eyeglass lenses. The agreed-upon delivery date was October 30, 2004. The contract contained a clause forbidding non-written modifications. Various delays ensued and delivery was not made in October. Buyer thereafter cooperated with Seller in trying to get a finished product, and agreed to pay for cost overruns and urged completion, but complained about the delay. This combination of cooperation and complaints continued during the Spring of 2005. Near the end of May 2005, Seller tendered delivery; Buyer rejected the goods on the grounds that "it was too late" and sued for breach. Seller claims that the delivery date was waived; Buyer relies on the clause forbidding non-written modifications. Both parties rely on UCC § 2–209. Resolve the dispute.

SECTION 4. CONSIDERATION IN BILATERAL CONTRACTS AND MUTUALITY OF OBLIGATION

———

(Calamari & Perillo on Contracts §§ 4.12—4.16)

RIDGE RUNNER FORESTRY v. ANN M. VENEMAN, SECRETARY OF AGRICULTURE

United States Court of Appeals, Federal Circuit, 2002.
287 F.3d 1058.

MAYER, CHIEF JUDGE. Ridge Runner Forestry appeals from the decision of the Department of Agriculture Board of Contract Appeals dismissing its

---

modification was ineffective as a result of Sharon's bad faith, we do not reach the issue whether the contract modification was also voidable because of economic duress. We note, however, that proof that coercive means were used is necessary to establish that a contract is voidable because of economic duress. *Id.* at 1286. Normally, it cannot be used to void a contract modification which has been sought in good faith; if a contract modification has been found to be in good faith, then presumably no wrongful coercive means have been used to extract the modification.

cause of action for lack of jurisdiction pursuant to 41 U.S.C. §§ 601–613. . . . Because no contract had been formed, we affirm the board's decision.

Background

Ridge Runner Forestry is a fire protection company located in the Pacific Northwest. In response to a request for quotations ("RFQ") issued by the Forestry Service, Ridge Runner submitted a proposal and ultimately signed a document entitled Pacific Northwest Interagency Engine Tender Agreement ("Tender Agreement"). The Tender Agreement incorporated the RFQ in its entirety, including the following two provisions in bold faced lettering:

> (1) Award of an Interagency Equipment Rental Agreement based on response to this Request for Quotations (RFQ) does not preclude the Government from using any agency or cooperator or local EERA resources;

and

> (2) Award of an Interagency Equipment Rental Agreement does not guarantee there will be a need for the equipment offered nor does it guarantee orders will be placed against the awarded agreements.

Additionally, because the government could not foresee its actual equipment needs, the RFQ contained language that allowed the contractor to decline the government's request for equipment for any reason:

> Because the equipment needs of the government and availability of contractor's equipment during an emergency cannot be determined in advance, it is mutually agreed that, upon request of the government, the contractor shall furnish the equipment offered herein *to the extent the contractor is willing and able at the time of order.*

Id. (emphasis added). The RFQ also included a clause informing bidders that they would not be reimbursed for any costs incurred in submitting a quotation. Ridge Runner signed Tender Agreements in 1996, 1997, 1998, and 1999. In 1999, it presented a claim for $180,000 to the contracting officer alleging that the Forestry Service had violated an "implied duty of good faith and fair dealing" because Ridge Runner had been "systematically excluded for the past several years from providing services to the Government." In response, the contracting officer told Ridge Runner that she lacked the proper authority to decide the claim. Ridge Runner timely appealed the decision to the Department of Agriculture Board of Contract Appeals. The board granted the government's motion to dismiss concluding that because no contract had been entered into, it lacked jurisdiction under the Contract Disputes Act ("CDA"), 41 U.S.C. §§ 601–613.

Discussion

We have jurisdiction over an appeal from a decision of an agency board of contract appeals by virtue of 28 U.S.C. § 1295(a)(10). The board's jurisdiction under the CDA requires, at a minimum, a contract between an agency and another party. 41 U.S.C. § 607(d) (1994, amended in 2000).

Therefore, the threshold matter is whether the Tender Agreements constituted contracts between the parties, which is a question of law that we review *de novo*. *See* Oman–Fischbach Int'l v. Pirie, 276 F.3d 1380, 1383 (Fed.Cir.2002). . . .

Ridge Runner argues that the Tender Agreement was a binding contract that placed specific obligations upon the government; namely, the government was obligated to call upon Ridge Runner, and the other winning vendors, for its fire fighting needs, and in return, the vendors were to remain ready with acceptable equipment and trained staff to answer the government's call. This, Ridge Runner argues, places the alleged contract squarely within our holding in Ace–Federal [Reporters, Inc. v. Barram, 226 F.3d 1329 (Fed.Cir.2000)]. . . .

The contract in *Ace–Federal* is quite distinct from the Tender Agreements at issue in this case. That contract obligated the government to fulfill all of its requirements for transcription services from enumerated vendors or obtain a [General Services Administration] waiver. The Tender Agreements here are nothing but illusory promises. By the phrase illusory promise is meant words in promissory form that promise nothing; they do not purport to put any limitation on the freedom of the alleged promisor, but leave his future action subject to his own future will, just as it would have been had he said no words at all. Torncello v. United States, 231 Ct.Cl. 20, 681 F.2d 756, 769 (1982) (quoting 1 *Corbin on Contracts* § 145 (1963)). The government had the option of attempting to obtain firefighting services from Ridge Runner or any other source, regardless of whether that source had signed a tender agreement. The Agreements contained no clause limiting the government's options for firefighting services; the government merely "promised" to consider using Ridge Runner for firefighting services. Also, the Tender Agreement placed no obligation upon Ridge Runner. If the government came calling, Ridge Runner "promised" to provide the requested equipment only if it was "willing and able." It is axiomatic that a valid contract cannot be based upon the illusory promise of one party, much less illusory promises of both parties. *See Restatement (Second) of Contracts* § 71(1).

Conclusion

Accordingly, the decision of the Department of Agriculture Board of Contract Appeals is affirmed.

WOOD v. LUCY, LADY DUFF–GORDON
New York Court of Appeals, 1917.
222 N.Y. 88, 118 N.E. 214.

CARDOZO, J. The defendant styles herself "a creator of fashions." Her favor helps a sale. Manufacturers of dresses, millinery and like articles are glad to pay for a certificate of her approval. The things which she designs, fabrics, parasols and what not, have a new value in the public mind when issued in her name. She employed the plaintiff to help her to turn this vogue into money. He was to have the exclusive right, subject always to her approval, to place her indorsements on the designs of others. He was also to have the exclusive right to place her own designs on sale, or to license others to market them. In return, she was to have one-half of "all profits and revenues" derived from any contracts he might make. The exclusive right was to last at least one year from April 1, 1915, and thereafter from year to year unless terminated by notice of ninety days. The plaintiff says that he kept the contract on his part, and that the defendant broke it. She placed her indorsement on fabrics, dresses and millinery without his knowledge, and withheld the profits. He sues her for the damages, and the case comes here on demurrer.

The agreement of employment is signed by both parties. It has a wealth of recitals. The defendant insists, however, that it lacks the elements of a contract. She says that the plaintiff does not bind himself to anything. It is true that he does not promise in so many words that he will use reasonable efforts to place the defendant's indorsements and market her designs. We think, however, that such a promise is fairly to be implied. The law has outgrown its primitive stage of formalism when the precise word was the sovereign talisman, and every slip was fatal. It takes a broader view to-day. A promise may be lacking, and yet the whole writing may be "instinct with an obligation," imperfectly expressed (SCOTT, J., in McCall Co. v. Wright, 133 App.Div. 62. If that is so, there is a contract.

The implication of a promise here finds support in many circumstances. The defendant gave an exclusive privilege. She was to have no right for at least a year to place her own indorsements or market her own designs except through the agency of the plaintiff. The acceptance of the exclusive agency was an assumption of its duties (Phoenix Hermetic Co. v. Filtrine Mfg. Co., 164 App.Div. 424). We are not to suppose that one party was to be placed at the mercy of the other (Hearn v. Stevens & Bro., 111 App.Div. 101). Many other terms of the agreement point the same way. We are told at the outset by way of recital that "the said Otis F. Wood possesses a business organization adapted to the placing of such indorsements as the said Lucy, Lady Duff–Gordon has approved." The implication is that the plaintiff's business organization will be used for the purpose for which it is adapted. But the terms of the defendant's compensation are even more significant. Her sole compensation for the grant of an exclusive agency is to be one-half of all the profits resulting from the plaintiff's efforts. Unless he gave his efforts, she could never get anything. Without an implied promise, the transaction cannot have such business "efficacy as both parties must have intended that at all events it should have" (BOWEN, L.J., in The Moorcock, 14 P.D. 64, 68). But the contract does not stop there. The plaintiff goes on to promise that he will account monthly for all moneys received by him, and that he will take out all such patents and copyrights and trademarks as may in his judgment be necessary to protect the rights and articles affected by the agreement. It is true, of course, as the Appellate Division has said, that if he was under no duty to try to market designs or to place certificates of indorsement, his promise to account for profits or take out copyrights would be valueless. But in determining the intention of the parties, the promise *has* a value. It helps to enforce the conclusion that the plaintiff *had* some duties. His promise to pay the defendant one-half of the profits and revenues resulting from the exclusive agency and to render accounts monthly, was a promise to use reasonable efforts to bring profits and revenues into existence. For this conclusion, the authorities are ample (Wilson v. Mechanical Orguinette Co., 170 N.Y. 542).

The judgment of the Appellate Division should be reversed, and the order of the Special Term affirmed, with costs in the Appellate Division and in this court. . . .

MEZZANOTTE v. FREELAND

Court of Appeals of North Carolina, 1973.
20 N.C.App. 11, 200 S.E.2d 410.

This is an action seeking specific performance of a contract of sale and damages for breach of contract.

On 2 May 1972 plaintiffs and defendants executed a contract under the terms of which plaintiffs agreed to buy and defendants agreed to sell a tract of land in Orange County, together with improvements and facilities, known as the Daniel Boone Complex. The contract set out the sales price and terms of payment which included a good faith deposit by plaintiffs of $5,000.00. . . .

Among the other provisions of the 2 May 1972 agreement [was] the following:

> 2. This agreement is contingent upon parties of the second part (plaintiffs) being able to secure a second mortgage from North Carolina National Bank on such terms and conditions as are satisfactory to them in order to finance the closing and to secure additional working capital. . . .

> . . .

[Plaintiffs] were unable to obtain a loan from the North Carolina National Bank but raised the necessary funds through other sources and on 5 September tendered the required down payment of $200,000.00 together with note and deed of trust for the balance of the purchase price in accordance with the terms of the contract. Defendants rejected plaintiffs' tender and refused to complete the sale. Plaintiffs then brought this action. . . .

The court made findings of fact and determined as a matter of law that the [agreement] executed by plaintiffs and defendants on 2 May 1972 . . . constituted a valid contract of sale. He further found that plaintiffs' tender of performance on 5 September 1972 was a substantial compliance with their contract obligations and that defendants' refusal to convey the property constituted a breach of their contract entitling plaintiffs to specific performance and damages. . . .

[T]he defendants have appealed. . . .

BALEY, JUDGE. . . . [Defendants] contend that there is no enforceable contract of sale because . . . [t]here was no consideration on the part of plaintiffs since the liability of plaintiffs was contingent upon their ability to obtain financing satisfactory to themselves. . . .

The [defendants' contention] . . . is dependent upon the interpretation to be placed upon the promise of plaintiffs to purchase the properties in accordance with the terms of the contract. Defendants assert that since the agreement was contingent upon the plaintiffs' obtaining "satisfactory" financing from North Carolina National Bank the promise to buy was illusory and cannot constitute consideration.

It seems clear that the parties in signing the contract of sale intended to be mutually bound to comply with its terms. They understood that plaintiffs would make an honest good faith effort to acquire financing satisfactory to themselves from NCNB. The contract implies that plaintiffs would in good faith seek proper financing from NCNB and that such financing in keeping with reasonable business standards could not be rejected at the personal whim of plaintiffs but only for a satisfactory cause. Where a contract confers on one party a discretionary power affecting the rights of the other, this discretion must be exercised in a reasonable manner based upon good faith and fair play. The record here indicates that the parties so understood their obligation and that plaintiffs applied for a loan from NCNB and obtained a verbal commitment but were not able to secure the loan and arranged other financing in order to meet their obligations under the contract. A promise conditioned upon an event within the promisor's control is not illusory if the promisor also "impliedly promises to make reasonable effort to bring the event about or to use good faith and honest judgment in determining whether or not it has in fact occurred." 1 *Corbin on Contracts*, § 149, at 659. The implied promise . . . furnishes sufficient consideration to support a return promise. . . .

Although there are no North Carolina cases specifically in point, courts in other jurisdictions have recognized that a conditional promise may be accompanied by an implied promise of good faith and reasonable effort, and that it need not be illusory.

For example, in Jay Dreher Corp. v. Delco Appliance Corp., 93 F.2d 275 (2d Cir.1937), defendant granted plaintiff a franchise to sell its products in a certain territory. Plaintiff agreed to sell these products and build up defendant's business in the specified territory. Defendant reserved the right to reject any order sent in by plaintiff, and plaintiff contended that this made defendant's promise illusory. In an opinion by Judge Learned Hand, the court held that the contract was supported by consideration, finding an implied promise "that the defendant will use an honest judgment in passing upon orders submitted." *Id.* at 277.

In Commercial Credit Co. v. Insular Motor Corp., 17 F.2d 896 (1st Cir.1927), defendant, an automobile dealer, agreed to sell plaintiff all the time sales obligations of its customers for two years, and plaintiff agreed to purchase these obligations. The contract provided that plaintiff would purchase only "acceptable" time sales obligations. The court rejected defendant's contention that the contract lacked consideration. It held that the contract did not allow plaintiff to refuse arbitrarily to purchase defendant's obligations. "Acceptable does not mean acceptable by whim; it means acceptable within the usual business meaning of the word as applied to this kind of business dealings." *Id.* at 899–900.

In Richard Bruce & Co. v. J. Simpson & Co., 40 Misc.2d 501, 243 N.Y.S.2d 503 (Sup.Ct.1963), plaintiff agreed to underwrite a public offering of defendant's stock, and defendant agreed to pay plaintiff a commission. Defendant violated the agreement, and plaintiff sued for breach of contract. Defendant asserted that the contract was void for lack of consideration, pointing to a provision allowing plaintiff to terminate the contract if it "in its absolute discretion, shall determine that market conditions or the prospects of the public offering are such as to make it undesirable or inadvisable." The court held the contract enforceable, stating that plaintiff's discretion was only "a discretion based upon fair dealing and good faith—a reasonable discretion." *Id.* at 504, 243 N.Y.S.2d at 506.

Several cases have upheld the validity of contracts quite similar to the one involved in the present case. In Mattei v. Hopper, 51 Cal.2d 119, 330 P.2d 625 (1958), plaintiff agreed to buy a tract of land from defendant. The contract provided that it was "(s)ubject to Coldwell Banker & Company obtaining leases satisfactory to the purchaser." The court held that plaintiff was bound by an implied promise to use good faith in determining whether Coldwell Banker's leases were "satisfactory." Therefore, his promise was not illusory and the contract was enforceable. . . .

Most closely in point is Sheldon Simms Co. v. Wilder, 108 Ga.App. 4, 131 S.E.2d 854 (1963). Here plaintiff entered into a contract to purchase real property from defendant. The contract provided: "This contract is contingent upon the purchaser's ability to obtain a loan on said property of $24,000.00 with maximum interest of 6¼ percent per annum, for a maximum period of twenty years." The court held that the contract was valid and supported by consideration. Plaintiff was required to make "a diligent effort" to obtain a loan. *Id.* at 5, 131 S.E.2d at 855. He could not frustrate the contract by deciding at whim not to get a loan.

All of these cases tend to indicate that the agreement signed on 2 May 1972 by the Mezzanottes and the Freelands was a valid and enforceable contract, supported by consideration. The contract included an implied promise by the Mezzanottes to use reasonable effort to procure a loan and to exercise good faith in deciding whether the terms of the loan were satisfactory. . . .

Affirmed.

MIAMI COCA–COLA BOTTLING CO.
v. ORANGE CRUSH CO.

Circuit Court of Appeals, Fifth Circuit, 1924.
296 F. 693.

BRYAN, CIRCUIT JUDGE. This is an appeal from an order dismissing appellant's [Miami Coca–Cola's] bill, which seeks to enjoin the cancellation by the appellee [Orange Crush] of a contract and to compel its specific performance. The contract is in the form of a license, whereby Orange Crush grants to Miami Coca–Cola the exclusive right, within a designated territory, to manufacture a certain drink called "orange crush," and to bottle and distribute it in bottles under Orange Crush's trade-mark. Orange Crush agreed, among other things, to supply its concentrate to be used in the manufacture of orange crush at stated prices, and to do certain advertising. Miami Coca–Cola agreed to purchase a specified quantity of the concentrate, to maintain a bottling plant, to solicit orders, and generally to undertake to promote the sale of orange crush, and to develop an increase in the volume of sales. The license granted was perpetual, but contained a proviso to the effect that Miami Coca–Cola might at any time cancel the contract.

The bill avers that Miami Coca–Cola bought a quantity of the concentrate, manufactured orange crush, and was engaged in the performance of its obligations, when, about a year after the contract was entered into, Orange Crush gave written notice that it would no longer be bound.

We agree with the District Judge that the contract was void for lack of mutuality. It may be conceded that Orange Crush is liable to Miami Coca–Cola for damages for the period during which the contract was performed; but for such damages Miami Coca–Cola has an adequate remedy at law. So far, however, as the contract remains executory, it is not binding, since it can be terminated at the will of one of the parties to it. The consideration was a promise for a promise. But Miami Coca–Cola did not promise to do anything, and could at any time cancel the contract. According to the great weight of authority such a contract is unenforceable. Marble Co. v. Ripley, 10 Wall. 339, 359, 19 L.Ed. 955; 1 *Williston*, pp. 219, 222. The contract cannot be upheld upon the theory that Miami Coca–Cola had a continuing option, because an option to be valid must be supported by a consideration. . . .

The decree is affirmed.

TEXAS GAS UTILITIES COMPANY v. S.A. BARRETT

Supreme Court of Texas, 1970.
460 S.W.2d 409.

STEAKLEY, JUSTICE. This is a suit for minimum payments under a contract for natural gas service. It was instituted by petitioner, Texas Gas Utilities Company, sometimes called the gas company, against respondents S.A. Barrett, John Barrett and James Beavers. After trial to a jury, the trial court ruled in response to respondents' motion for judgment that they were entitled to judgment on the jury verdict and as a matter of law. A take nothing judgment was accordingly rendered against petitioner. The court of civil appeals affirmed upon the holding that the contract is unenforceable for lack of mutuality of obligation. 452 S.W.2d 508. Our views are otherwise which, in turn, calls for consideration of points not discussed by the intermediate court.

The contract upon which suit was brought was dated April 21, 1964 and was for a term of five years with an option to renew for an additional five years. The signatories were Associated Oil and Gas Company, petitioner's predecessor-assignor (the assignment being dated January 1, 1965) and respondents. The purpose of the contract was the supplying of natural gas for use by respondents in fueling irrigation water well pumps on farm properties which they held under a five year agricultural lease dated January 17, 1964. The contract required an annual minimum payment during the life of the contract of $7.50 per 1400 h.p. for each engine installed. A five mile pipe line to the properties was constructed by petitioner's predecessor in March, 1964, at an expense in excess of $100,000 and deliveries of natural gas were commenced on April 6, 1964. ... It does not appear to be disputed that natural gas was available at all times; that the gas company furnished gas as ordered by respondents; and that the gas company delivered gas to the successors of respondents, billed them therefor, and will credit respondents with the sums paid by such successors.

The basic obligation assumed by Associated Oil and Gas Company, and by petitioner as assignee of the contract in question, was the delivery of natural gas to respondents as set forth in Article I:

> Subject to the terms and conditions herein stated Company will from April 21, 1964 to April 21st, 1969 until the expiration or other termination of this agreement (unless prevented by one or more of the causes mentioned in Article VI hereof) deliver to Customer at a meter installed by Company on the service line owned by Customer downstream of Billing Meter, set at various water well locations on a 4100.33 Acre Farm, ... natural gas for use by Customer for the following purposes only: Fuel for irrigation purposes for approximately twenty (20) water wells.

The obligation to furnish gas was subject, however, to these provisions in Article VI of the contract:

> Company will make reasonable provision to insure a continuous supply of natural gas but does not guarantee a continuous supply of natural gas, and shall not be liable for damages occasioned by interruptions to service or failure to commence delivery, caused by conditions beyond its reasonable control, by an Act of God or the public enemy, inevitable accident, floods, fire, explosions, strikes, riots, war, delay in receiving shipments of required material, order of court or judge granted in any bonafide adverse legal proceedings or actions, or

any order of any commission or tribunal having jurisdiction in the premises or without limitation by the preceding enumeration any other act or thing reasonably beyond its control or interruptions necessary for repairs or changes in Company's distributing system. No payment, however, shall be required from Customer for service which Company herein agrees but fails to furnish.

It is further and distinctly understood and agreed that the Company assumes no obligation whatever regarding the quantity or quality of gas delivered hereunder, or the continuity of service, and shall not be liable therefor, but Company will endeavor to supply the requirements of Customer for the above class of service to the extent of the amount of gas available for such service and to the extent permitted under any agreement between Company and any producer of gas available to Company for the supply of natural gas to Company, and subject to such limitations in the sale of gas for this class of service as in Company's opinion may be necessary for the continued maintenance of the supply of gas for domestic use, it being recognized that Company is dependent for gas to be supplied hereunder upon gas produced by (*sic*) Company by other producers." (Italics are added.)

It was the view of the court of civil appeals that under Article VI, particularly the italicized portion, the gas company was not obligated to furnish gas and for this reason the contract was unenforceable as lacking in mutuality of obligation. This, in respondents' words, is their "first and foremost" position in asserting non-liability for the minimum payments which petitioner seeks to recover.

As has been noted by recognized legal scholars, a commonly repeated statement by the courts is that mutuality of obligation is a requisite in the formation of a contract, and that both parties to a contract must be bound or neither is bound. *See* 1 *Williston on Contracts* § 105A, at 420 (1957); 1A *Corbin on Contracts* § 152, at 2 (1963); 1 *Page on Contracts* § 565, at 949 (1920). The Williston treatise suggests that however limited, this is but a way of stating that there must be valid consideration. Professor Corbin urges the view that mutuality of obligations should be used solely to express the idea that each party is under a legal duty to the other; each has made a promise and each is an obligor. This is said to be the meaning with which the term is commonly used and that it is more correct to say that it is consideration that is necessary, not mutuality of obligation. But it has also been concluded "that logic is as powerless to disprove the existence of the mutuality rule as it has been shown to be powerless to establish its existence ... that no logic is able to connect the supposed mutuality rule with any formulation of the doctrine of consideration and no other logical justification for it has ever been suggested." Oliphant, *Mutuality of Obligation in Bilateral Contracts at Law*, 25 Colum.L.Rev. 705 (1925); 28 Colum.L.Rev. 997 (1928). . . .

It is clear to us that the agreement here in question is a binding and enforceable contract. The writing embodies an exchange of obligations of value to each contracting party, reciprocally or mutually induced. The gas company was bound to deliver natural gas to the various water well delivery points specified in the contract; to make reasonable provisions to insure a continuous supply of natural gas; to endeavor to supply the requirements of respondents; and to install the necessary metering equipment at its own expense. Respondents were in turn bound to pay for the gas delivered to their wells upon their order and to pay the minimum charges provided in the contract. These mutually imposed obligations are not negated by the language used. *See* Portland Gasoline Co. v. Superior Marketing Co., Inc., [150 Tex. 533, 243 S.W.2d 823 (1951)]. The gas company explicitly bound itself in Article I to deliver natural gas to respondents "unless prevented by one or more of the causes mentioned in Article VI hereof." The exculpatory clause in Article VI did not relieve the gas company of this obligation. It would have been subject to liability for breach of contract if it had failed upon order to furnish gas to respondents for causes other than those specified in Article VI. The extent of the exculpatory clause is that the gas company assumed no obligation—made no guarantee—either that gas would always be available or that gas of a particular quality would always be available. It was bound, however, to supply *available* natural gas to respondents. . . .

We accordingly hold that the contract upon which petitioner sued is enforceable against respondents. . . .

. . . The judgments below will therefore be reversed and the cause remanded to the trial court for entry of judgment consistent with this opinion.

It is so ordered.

WISECO, INC. v. JOHNSON CONTROLS, INC.

United States Court of Appeals, Sixth Circuit, 2005.
2005 WL 2931896, 59 UCC Rep.Serv.2d 884. Unpublished Opinion

SUTTON, CIRCUIT JUDGE. Wiseco, Inc., a Kentucky-based tool-and-die company, seeks review of a ruling summarily rejecting its claim that Johnson Controls, Inc. (JCI) breached a requirements contract between the two companies. Because Wiseco has failed to establish a material fact dispute that JCI acted in bad faith in reducing its requirements under the contract, we affirm.

In 1998, JCI produced metal headrest stays for several DaimlerChrysler vehicles. In December of that year, an employee at JCI's Foamech plant in Georgetown, Kentucky sought to out-source two aspects of the stay-manufacturing operation to Wiseco: bending the metal rods into a staple shape and chamfering (rounding) the ends. The parties agreed orally that Wiseco would prepare the necessary tooling for the job at its own expense and that it would receive 50¢ per part with a manufacturing capacity of approximately 4000 parts per day (with actual requirements to be set by DaimlerChrysler's needs). JCI also informed Wiseco that the life of the part was at least four years, which Wiseco took to be the expected term of the contract. Using manufacturing plans for the part provided by JCI, Wiseco "tooled-up" for the production, which is to say it bought and prepared equipment to handle the manufacturing work, and for six months produced approximately 4000 parts per day, which were then sent to the Foamech plant for finishing (notching and applying protective coating) before being shipped to JCI's Tillsonberg, Canada plant for assembly into finished headrests.

About six months after beginning production, JCI told Wiseco that it soon would be terminating orders of part 684F, as the part Wiseco had been producing was called—and indeed over the next six months JCI's requirements for the part decreased substantially. At the same time, however, JCI asked Wiseco to take over the finishing functions for part 684F, formerly performed by JCI at its Foamech plant, so that not only would Wiseco bend and chamfer the rods, it also would notch and finish them, creating a finished part referred to as 684B. While JCI's orders to Wiseco for part 684B were well under 4000 parts per day, the company paid Wiseco more for its additional work.

According to JCI, the decline in its requirements for parts 684F and 684B stemmed from changes at DaimlerChrysler. Originally part 684F was used in DaimlerChrysler's 1999 Cherokee and 1999 Grand Cherokee models. The part was not used in the 2000 Grand Cherokee and subsequent models, but part 684B was used in the 2000 and 2001Cherokee. DaimlerChrysler retired the Cherokee after the 2001 model year. The newer Grand Cherokee's headrest used part 611, a metal rod that is 40 millimeters longer than part 684, has two additional notches and is chamfered to pointed rather than rounded ends. Part 611 was made by Guelph Tool and Die, a company located near the Tillsonberg, Canada plant where the headrests were finally assembled.

On May 14, 2001, Wiseco sued JCI in Kentucky state court for breach of the 684 contract. . . . JCI removed the case to federal court based on diversity jurisdiction. . . . On Aug 31, 2004, the District Court granted summary judgment to JCI. In doing so, it concluded that "JCI purchased all of its requirements for part 684 from Wiseco and did not breach the contract in this regard" and that because there was no proof that any replacement part was ever used in "any headrest assembled in the Foamech plant," the undisputed evidence showed that JCI had reduced its requirements in good faith.

. . . Did JCI's significant reduction in its requirements for part 684 six months after production began breach this requirements contract? Under the U.C.C., as adopted in Kentucky and as adopted in almost every jurisdiction, a requirements contract demands that the buyer order from the seller "such actual output or requirements as may occur in good faith, except that no quantity unreasonably disproportionate to any stated estimate . . . may be tendered or demanded." KRS § 355.2–306(1)*. With

---

* Further references are to UCC 2–306. Ed.

just one exception, courts addressing this provision have concluded that it applies differently to increased and decreased requirements. "(T)he majority of authorities have construed U.C.C. § 2–306(1) as permitting good faith reductions in requirements, as opposed to increases, even though the reductions may be highly disproportionate to stated estimates." Godchaux–Henderson Sugar Co., Inc. v. Dr. Pepper–Pepsi Cola Bottling Co., No. 83–5730, 1985 WL 13561, at *6, 1985 U.S.App. LEXIS 14121, at *18 (6th Cir. August 29, 1985); *see also* Empire Gas Corp. v. Am. Bakeries Co., 840 F.2d 1333, 1337 (7th Cir.1988). In view of this distinction, courts generally have concluded that "the seller assumes the risk of all good faith variations in the buyer's requirements even to the extent of a determination to liquidate or discontinue the business." Empire Gas, 840 F.2d at 1337–38; Brewster, 33 F.3d at 365.

Whether a breach occurred in this case, then, depends in part on Kentucky's understanding of the good faith required by UCC § 2–306. While no Kentucky or Sixth Circuit case evaluates the meaning of good faith under Kentucky's U.C.C. law, Judge Posner's decision in Empire Gas Corporation v. American Bakeries Co., 840 F.2d 1333 (7th Cir.1988), appears to be the most frequently consulted case in analyzing the good faith component of a requirements contract under the U.C.C. ... In *Empire Gas*, the court explained that a requirements contract is not an option contract and thus the decision to forgo purchasing goods under the contract cannot be made for any reason or for no reason at all. 840 F.2d at 1339–40. The "good faith" requirement, the court reasoned, places several constraints on the buyer: The buyer may not purchase the good in question from another seller; the buyer may not "merely have had second thoughts about the terms of the contract"; and the "buyer assumes the risk of (small) change(s) in his circumstances." *Id.* at 1340–41. At the same time, the buyer does not act in bad faith if it reduced its requirements for "business reasons ... independent of the terms of the contract or any other aspect of its relationship with the (seller)." *Id.* at 1339.

In applying this good-faith rule, several court decisions have helped to clarify its contours. ... The First Circuit had found no bad faith when a buyer chose to shut down an unprofitable manufacturing plant and ended its requirements under a supply contract as a result. Brewster, 33 F.3d at 366. To like effect, several other cases have found no bad faith for reducing and eliminating orders where the buyer wanted to reduce existing inventory, where an existing operation had become more efficient, where the buyer's customers no longer required the product or where a part was needed less than expected. [citations]

The seller bears the burden of demonstrating bad faith. *See* Technical [Assistance Int'l, Inc. v. United States, 150 F.3d 1369, 1373 (Fed.Cir. 1998)] ("In the absence of such a showing (of bad faith), the buyer will be presumed to have varied its requirements for valid business reasons, *i.e.*, to have acted in good faith, and will not be liable for the change in requirements.")

When it comes to the application of these cases here, JCI argues that Wiseco met all of its requirements for part 684F and part 684B and that no other company ever sold that part to JCI. Wiseco initially supplied the headrest stay for the Jeep Cherokee contract as well as for the Jeep Grand Cherokee contract—using part 684F and part 684B. But DaimlerChrysler asked JCI to produce longer metal rods to allow for an additional notch in the headrest stay for the Jeep Grand Cherokee. And JCI's engineering department requested that the ends of the Jeep Grand Cherokee headrest stay be chamfered differently, with pointed ends instead of rounded ones, for ease of assembly. As JCI sees the matter, once DaimlerChrysler "ceased to have requirements" for the part in question, that became "a good faith" reason for shrinking orders, and the change in orders accordingly did not amount to "a breach of contract." *See* Tri–State Generation, 874 F.2d at 1360. Likewise, the decision of JCI's engineering department to alter the specifications for the parts was a legitimate business reason for reducing requirements because it would be "unreasonable" to make JCI continue to manufacture with inefficient parts simply to honor a requirements contract. *See* Empire Gas, 840 F.2d at 1340. Under these circumstances, without some evidence that it had continuing needs for part 684, JCI contends that its circumstances changed in a material way and that it accordingly did not breach the requirements contract. *Cf.* Empire Gas, 840 F.2d at 1339.

Wiseco responds that the allegedly different part is substantially the same part. To substantiate this claim, Wiseco introduced an expert report [of David Smith] concluding that the 684 parts were substantially similar to part 610. But part 610 is used in European production of the Chrysler Grand Cherokee. The part was made from November 1999 to August 2000 by Guelph Tool and shipped directly to Austria by the supplier. There is no indication that Wiseco ever supplied part 684 for use in the European Chrysler Grand Cherokee. All evidence suggests that each of the parts made by Wiseco was used only in the North American versions of the Jeep Cherokee and Jeep Grand Cherokee.

Wiseco next claims that part 684 mirrors part 611, the part that replaced the 684 in the 2000 Jeep Grand Cherokee and the later models of this Jeep. But . . . Wiseco . . . has presented no evidence that the two parts are essentially one and the same. JCI, by contrast, introduced evidence about the differences between the parts, namely that the rods used to make part 611 were 40 millimeters longer and that the two rods were chamfered differently. JCI also introduced evidence that it would take substantial retooling to produce the 611 instead of the 684. And to produce the two parts interchangeably on the same equipment, JCI showed, would cost over $20,000, and the transition would take eight weeks. On this record, we cannot conclude Wiseco has met its burden of establishing a triable issue of fact that JCI reduced requirements under the 684 contract in bad faith simply by identifying the existence of a part that succeeded 684 in the construction of the Grand Cherokee headrest.

Doubtless, the law would not permit JCI to change the number of the part that Wiseco was manufacturing to avoid the demands of a requirements contract. But Wiseco has not supported its burden of proof in bringing this claim. And lacking sufficient evidence to prove such a claim, Wiseco began expanding its premise, from a contract to produce a particular part, to a contract to produce similar parts, to a contract to produce all headrest stays, regardless of the part involved, for all Jeep vehicles. Because the requirements contract recognized by the district court made no such promise and because the good-faith restrictions imposed on the buyer by the U.C.C. impose no such requirement, the district court correctly rejected this claim.

On top of the difference between the parts—whether between the 684 and the 610 or between the 684 and the 611—JCI offered another reason for the change: the shift in production and finishing of the headrest stays from the Foamech plant in Kentucky to a plant in Tillsonberg, Canada. When Wiseco and JCI together produced the final part 684 at the Foamech plant, JCI shipped the finished stays to Tillsonberg for assembly into the final headrest. JCI based its decision to manufacture part 611 at the Canada plant on business efficiencies (shipping costs, time delay, etc.) and on its conclusion that the Foamech plant had repeatedly failed to produce parts effectively, both of which constitute legitimate business reasons independent of the terms of the contract with Wiseco. Wiseco never offered any evidence to rebut these legitimate business reasons, and in fact acknowledged that it did not know why JCI had shifted manufacture of the headrest stays to Canada. This additional explanation for the decline in part 684 orders also supports the district court's decision to reject this claim as a matter of law. . . .

For these reasons, we affirm.

SUMMITS 7, INC. v. KELLY

Supreme Court of Vermont, 2005.
178 Vt. 396, 886 A.2d 365.

ALLEN, C.J. (Ret.), Specially Assigned. Defendant Staci Lasker[1] appeals the superior court's order enjoining her from working for a competitor of her former employer, plaintiff Summits 7, Inc., based on the terms of a noncompetition agreement entered into by the parties during Lasker's at-will employment with Summits 7. The principal issue in dispute is whether there was sufficient consideration to support the agreement. The superior court ruled that either Lasker's continued employment or the promotions and increased pay she received during her employment with Summits 7 was sufficient consideration to support the agreement. We agree with the superior court that Lasker's continued employment constituted sufficient consideration. . . .

The primary issue that Lasker raises in this case is whether the . . . noncompetition agreement she signed was supported by adequate consid-

---

1. Defendant's maiden name is Staci Kelly, but by the time of trial she was using her married name, Staci Lasker.

eration. We emphasize that Lasker has not challenged the agreement on the basis that it is unreasonable with respect to the type of restrictions imposed on her or whether those restrictions are narrowly tailored to address Summits 7's legitimate interests. Nor has Lasker contended that the agreement is unreasonable with respect to the length of time that it imposes restrictions on competition. Lasker does argue that the superior court erred by not addressing whether the geographic scope of the agreement was unreasonably broad, but ... we need not consider this issue because Lasker plainly sought and obtained employment within a reasonably restricted geographic area, and the court may enforce the agreement to the extent that it is reasonable. Hence, if we conclude that the agreement was supported by adequate consideration, we will affirm the superior court's judgment in favor of Summits 7.

As noted, the trial court ruled that continued employment would be sufficient consideration to support the covenant not to compete, but that it was unnecessary to even reach that conclusion because the increased compensation and promotions that Lasker received during her employment with Summits 7 were adequate consideration to support the covenant. We disagree with the latter determination. There is no evidence that Lasker's promotions and raises were connected in any way with the noncompetition agreements she signed. *See* [Sanborn Mfg. Co. v. Currie, 500 N.W.2d 161, 164 (Minn.Ct. App.1993)] (no evidence that employee's promotions and salary increases were attributable to anything other than performance that was expected of him under initial employment agreement). We can only assume that she received these promotions and raises because she performed her job well and was rewarded for that performance.

We also decline to give controlling weight to the fact that, by its terms, the noncompetition agreement could be enforced only if Lasker were fired for cause or left her employment voluntarily. One might argue that the agreement provided some incentive for Summits 7 not to fire Lasker without cause, but any such incentive did not constitute a tangible benefit beyond continued employment in exchange for signing the agreement. Indeed, the agreement explicitly states that it neither creates a contract of employment nor alters in any way Lasker's status as an at-will employee.

Nevertheless, we agree with the superior court, the majority of other courts, and the recent Restatement [of Employment Law] draft that continued employment alone is sufficient consideration to support a covenant not to compete entered into during an at-will employment relationship. *See* Mattison [v. Johnston], 730 P.2d [286] at 288 [1986] (although there is authority to contrary, most jurisdictions have found that continued employment is sufficient consideration to support restrictive covenant executed after at-will employment has begun); *Restatement (Third) of Employment Law*, Preliminary Draft No. 2, *supra*, § 6.05 cmt. d....

Moreover, because an at-will employee can be fired without cause at any time after the initial hire, the consideration is the same regardless of what point during the employment relationship the employee signs the covenant not to compete. *See* [Copeco, Inc. v. Caley, 91 Ohio App.3d 474, 632 N.E.2d 1299, 1301 (1992)] (there is no substantive difference between promise of employment upon initial hire and promise of continued employment during employment relationship). . . .

In either case, the employee is, in effect, agreeing not to compete for a given period following employment in exchange for either initial or continued employment. Looked at another way, in either case the consideration is the employer's forbearance from terminating the at-will employment relationship. . . . Regardless of what point during the employment relationship the parties agree to a covenant not to compete, legitimate consideration for the covenant exists as long as the employer does not act in bad faith by terminating the employee shortly after the employee signs the covenant. *See* [Zellner v. Conrad, 183 A.D.2d 250, 589 N.Y.S.2d 903, 907 (1992)] (forbearance of right to terminate at-will employee is legal detriment that can stand as consideration for restrictive covenant; where employment relationship continues for substantial period after covenant is signed, that forbearance is real, and not illusory). . . .

Affirmed.

JOHNSON, J., dissenting. . . . Long after Staci Lasker began working for Summits 7, the company required her to sign an extremely broad noncompetition agreement forbidding her from directly or indirectly participating in any enterprise providing services related to those offered by Summits 7. The restriction on her employment was for one year following her termination for cause or voluntary resignation and covered all of Vermont and New Hampshire and part of New York. For signing this highly restrictive agreement, Lasker received nothing other than the right to continue the job that she already had. . . .

A brief examination of the facts demonstrates that Lasker's continued employment is illusory consideration for her signing the noncompetition agreement. The day before Summits 7 presented the agreement to Lasker, she was an at-will employee who could be fired at any time with or without cause, but who was free to leave her employ at any time and seek any other job. The day after she signed the agreement, she was still an at-will employee who could be fired at any time for any or no reason, but she had lost her right to seek any other job after leaving her employ. . . .

The majority obscures the illusory nature of the consideration it finds here by suggesting that continued employment is sufficient consideration as long as the employer does not terminate the employment relationship in bad faith shortly after the agreement is reached. I find this reasoning illogical and unpersuasive. Whether there is adequate consideration should be judged based on the expectations of the parties at the time they enter into the agreement. Applying a retrospective analysis to determine whether there was consideration gets us away from traditional notions of consideration and instead transforms an illusory promise into enforceable consideration through performance. T. Staidl, *The Enforceability of Noncompetition Agreements when Employment is At–Will: Reformulating the Analysis*, 2 Employee Rts. & Emp. Pol'y J. 95, 106 (1998). . . .

[H]istorically courts have closely scrutinized post-employment covenants not to compete. 1 H. Specter & M. Finkin, *Individual Employment Law and Litigation* § 8.01, at 443 (1989). Judicial scrutiny is necessary because such covenants are often the result of unequal bargaining power between the parties. *Id.* Employers may take advantage of that unequal bargaining power by imposing restrictions intended to ensure that their employees will not compete with them after they leave their employ. On the other side, employees interested in obtaining or keeping their jobs are likely to give scant attention to the hardship that they may suffer later through the loss of their livelihood as the result of the restriction on their future employment. *Id.* § 8.08, at 485. In the interests of free commerce and freedom to choose one's employment, courts have felt obligated to assure that restrictive covenants are aimed at protecting legitimate employer interests rather than restricting trade or competition.

Although these public policy concerns are ultimately addressed by determining whether the covenant in dispute is reasonably related to a legitimate employer interest and has reasonable geographic and temporal restrictions, the issue of whether adequate consideration exists for such covenants has become a flashpoint for those same concerns. In light of the increasing criticism of and restrictions upon at-will employment relationships, and the lack of any real bargaining between employer and employee when continued at-will employment is exchanged for restrictions on future employment, the "better view" is to require additional consideration beyond continued employment to support a restrictive covenant entered into during the employment relationship. *Id.* § 8.02, at 450. . . .

In this case, Staci Lasker began working for Summits 7 in 2000 as a ten-dollar-an-hour employee and gradually progressed in the company. More than a year after she commenced her employment with Summits 7, the company required her to sign a noncompetition agreement severely restricting her post-employment rights. The trial court suggested in its decision that Lasker's general development as an employee—her learning how to handle increased responsibilities concerning the business—was adequate consideration for signing the noncompetition agreement. I concur with the majority's rejection of this position. . . .

The trial court also rejected Lasker's argument that requiring her to sign the noncompetition agreement upon threat of dismissal amounted to coercion. . . . Lasker had argued that she did not really have a choice as to whether to sign the agreement because her marriage was breaking up at the time and she had to stay financially solvent to support her two children. Her situation illustrates the unequal bargaining power that typically exists between employer and employee, particularly when the employer requires the employee to sign a noncompetition agreement upon

threat of dismissal after the employee has become established in the job.
. . .

In sum, I believe that requiring an employee to sign a post-employment covenant not to compete upon threat of dismissal, without conferring any benefit upon the employee other than continued at-will employment, which can be terminated at any time after the agreement is reached, is coercive in nature and unsupported by any real consideration. I would strike the agreement in this case for lack of consideration.

PROBLEMS

20.   On April 30, B and S signed a contract which provided that B agreed to buy and S to sell special pre-mixed barbecue sauce, at a designated price per gallon, to be used in toasted buns in B's restaurant. S also agreed to give B an exclusive right to use this sauce in the State of Oregon. The agreement was for a period of 10 years. Beginning in May, B began purchasing several gallons of sauce per month. In October, B decided it could make a similar sauce for less money. Thus, B did not place an order for sauce that month and informed S that it did not expect to buy any additional sauce. Does S have a cause of action against B?

21.   D, an oil company, agreed to supply P, a public utility, and P agreed to buy, its requirements for fuel oil at one of its generators. The contract was for a five-year period at a fixed rate per barrel and contained estimates of the amounts of oil which P would require per year. These estimates were made based upon the assumption that P would primarily burn gas. At the time the agreement was signed, gas was less expensive than oil and, in the agreement, P explicitly reserved the right to burn as much gas as it chose.

Within five months of the signing of the agreement, the market price of oil increased sharply. P revised its requirements for oil, demanding a 63 percent increase over the contract estimate. D refused to meet the increased demand but supplied P with the amount of the contract estimate plus ten percent.

The increase in P's demand was occasioned by a sixfold increase in sales of electricity by P to other utilities. In addition, P proposed to sell to a supplier of gas a large quantity of gas that it could have used to produce electricity. P sued D for failure to deliver its increased demands of oil. What result?

22.   Kemp owned and operated a gasoline station. He entered into a contract with plaintiff, a petroleum company, agreeing to purchase all his supplies of gasoline from plaintiff for a period of 7 years. In the second year of performance, Kemp formed a corporation wholly owned by himself and transferred the gasoline station and all its assets to this corporation. He then informed plaintiff that he had no further requirements for gasoline. Kemp's corporation then began purchasing gasoline from one of plaintiff's competitors. Plaintiff sues. What result?

23.   A, a jockey, enters into a bilateral contract with B in which A promises to ride B's horse in the Derby in return for B's promise to pay

$1,000. A threatens not to ride. C, the owner of horses related to B's horse, promises A an additional $1,000 paid in advance if A will promise to ride. A makes the promise to C and C pays $1,000. However, A fails to ride without justification. C sues A for breach. Under the traditional view, the bilateral contract between A and C is void. Does the doctrine of forging a good unilateral contract out of a bad bilateral contract apply to this case?

24. A promises to work for B for one year in return for B's promise to pay her a fair share of the profits. A performs. Does the doctrine of forging a good unilateral contract out of a bad bilateral contract apply to this case?

25. Husband and Wife had marital problems that in large part stemmed from his off again, on again addiction to cocaine. At a time when he was free of his addiction, the parties entered into an agreement as follows: Wife agreed not to leave him as long as he refrained from using illicit drugs and Husband promised to refrain from using illicit drugs. The agreement further provided that if Husband breached, he would forfeit to her his interest in certain community property. He did not keep his promise. She sued for divorce and asked for a declaration that the community property be forfeited to her. Put aside any ideas you may have about matrimonial law; is the contract enforceable under principles of contract law?

26. P and D, who were brothers, owned adjacent parcels of land. There was a dock on D's parcel. They entered into an agreement which permitted P to use the dock for 10 years in exchange for P's promise to pay one half of the maintenance expenses each year. By the terms of the agreement, P was permitted to terminate the agreement at will. After five years D refused to allow P to continue to use the dock. P brings an action against D for breach of contract and D sets up a defense of mutuality of obligation. During the five years prior to the commencement of the suit P had paid one half of the maintenance expenses of the dock. Make one or more arguments for P.

27. S and B entered into an agreement by the terms of which S agreed to sell and B agreed to buy 12 carloads of Ko–Hi flasks at a stipulated price. There was a clause in the agreement which read as follows: "It is agreed that Buyer may have the privilege of increasing quantity by an additional 13 carloads at price shown herein during the period covered by this agreement." An additional 13 carloads were ordered but not delivered. What are the rights of the parties?

28. The defendant, acting under its power of eminent domain, took title to the plaintiff's building. The defendant promised plaintiff to pay plaintiff's moving expenses if the plaintiff promised (1) to depart the premises peacefully and expeditiously without requiring the defendant to resort to legal action; (2) to relocate its business elsewhere in the same community and not liquidate. Plaintiff so promised. Was defendant's promise supported by consideration?

CHAPTER 3

MORAL OBLIGATION AND CONSIDERATION

■ ■ ■

(Calamari & Perillo on Contracts §§ 5.1—5.11 and 5.18)

SHELDON v. BLACKMAN

Supreme Court of Wisconsin, 1925.
188 Wis. 4, 205 N.W. 486.

This is an appeal from the judgment of the county court of Walworth county in probate, rendered in favor of the respondent for a claim against the estate of Henry J. Wilkinson, deceased. The claim, the allowance of which is the subject of this appeal, is based upon a written promise of the deceased to compensate the respondent in the sum of $30,000 for services rendered, and to pay reasonable value for services rendered him subsequently to the date of the written instrument. The instrument in question reads as follows:

$30,000.00.

Whitewater, Wisconsin, May 10, 1919.

At the date of my death, for value received, I promise to pay to Julia H. Sheldon, of Whitewater, Wisconsin, the sum of thirty thousand ($30,000) dollars, without interest.

The consideration for this note is the services rendered by the said Julia H. Sheldon for me, at my request, in the care of my home and the care of myself and wife during the thirty years next preceding the date hereof, for which services so rendered to date I am indebted to her in the above amount, no part of which has been paid.

And it is hereby understood and agreed that for future services rendered by her she shall be paid their reasonable value from my estate, at the time of my decease, the amount to be paid for future services however, not to cause the abatement of any general legacies provided for by my last will and testament now made or that hereafter may be made.

($6.00 Rev. Stamps.)

H.J. Wilkinson. (Seal.)

The respondent, a niece of the wife of the deceased, came to live with Mr. Wilkinson and his wife in 1889, at the request of Mr. Wilkinson and upon the understanding that she would receive his property upon the death of himself and his wife, if she cared for them until the death of both of them. The respondent performed the services required for 34 years, giving up a dress making establishment which she was operating in Woodstock, Ill., at the time the request for her services was made. In May, 1919, the written instrument set out above and a will were made; the latter, after providing for certain small legacies, leaving the residue of the property of the deceased to the respondent. The will has been lost or destroyed, and upon filing a claim against the estate of the deceased, based upon the written instrument, it was opposed by the next of kin and the administrator, upon the grounds that it was not properly delivered, that there was not sufficient consideration for it, and that it was testamentary in character, but not properly attested to take effect as a will.

Mr. Wilkinson was a banker, and, so far as appears from the record, of good business ability. The nearest other relatives were cousins. Mrs. Wilkinson was quite deaf and dim of vision. Her health for many years was poor, and she required much personal physical care before she died. The claimant always assisted her to dress, and when she went upon the street attended her. Mr. Wilkinson had serious bladder trouble, and was cared for by the claimant, acting as a trained nurse, who catheterized him for about 10 years. In other respects she performed delicate and disagreeable services for him. The claimant lived in and was treated as a member of the family, but performed all kinds of domestic service. During the period she bought a house, for which she paid $1,500, but title was taken in the name of the deceased. When she commenced rendering service, she was 42 years old. Mrs. Wilkinson died at the age of 84 and Mr. Wilkinson died at the age of 94.

When the writing in question and the last will of the deceased were executed, they were prepared by the attorney of Mr. Wilkinson at his home, and although the claimant was in the house, she was not present when the note was signed, and did not know the contents of the will, but saw it in a box thereafter, and had access to the box and its contents. The first time she saw the note, or knew of its existence, was August 5, 1920, about 15 months after its execution, when Mr. Wilkinson had it in his hand. She took the note to Mr. Ferris, attorney for the deceased, for safekeeping on August 6, 1920, and took a receipt. Mr. Ferris held the note thereafter, and produced it at the trial. On the 28th of June, 1917, both Mr. and Mrs. Wilkinson executed wills, in which each devised all of his or her estate to the other in case of survival, but in the event that the other did not survive certain small legacies were given to various people, and all the rest and residue was bequeathed to the claimant, and she was named executrix without bond.

It is admitted that the respondent has a claim for services upon a *quantum meruit* basis. The probate court found that the instrument in question was a nonnegotiable promissory note for good and sufficient consideration, and allowed the sum of $30,000 and the reasonable value of the services of the respondent from the date of the instrument until the date of the death of the deceased, at $30 a week, in all $35,925, with interest. From this judgment this appeal is brought.

JONES, J. (after stating the facts as above). It is the first broad contention of the appellant's counsel that there was no consideration for the writing in question; that, since it appeared that Wilkinson's property included real estate when the original parol agreement was made, it was void under the statute of frauds. It is further argued that the relations between the parties were such that no compensation could be recovered without an express contract; that under the arrangement then made the deceased would owe the claimant nothing at any particular time, as she could recover only on complete performance. . . .

It is conceded, however, that . . . although a parol agreement of this nature is void, it may be resorted to, to rebut the presumption that the services rendered were gratuitous, and it is claimed that the cause of action accrues only after the services have been rendered, and unless there is an open mutual account, or partial payments, the claim for services for more than 6 years is barred by the statute of limitations. It is argued that at best the deceased owed the claimant merely the reasonable value of her services for the 6 years next preceding the execution of the written instrument. The complaint was in two counts. One claimed compensation for the reasonable value of the services during the 34 years, and the other was based upon the written instrument. The defendant's counsel offered proof of the reasonable value of the services, which was ruled out on objection, and the question is thus raised whether this ruling was correct.

Mr. and Mrs. Wilkinson, when 60 and 54 years of age, respectively, seemed to realize since they had no children or near relatives, that they might need, as old age approached, faithful and competent care, and they were willing that the bulk of their property should be devoted to that object. They selected the claimant as the person best fitted to comply with their wishes, and Mr. Wilkinson made with her the arrangement that, if she should faithfully serve them during their lives, she should have the residue of their estate. Although this parol agreement was invalid, it showed the intention that she should be paid and well paid. This intention was again manifested by the two wills executed in 1917. The failing health they had anticipated came in due time. Their later years were clouded by such physical ailments as called for the most devoted service, and they were not favored with an "old age serene and bright."

No question is raised that the claimant did not perform in full measure the arduous task she had assumed. In 1919, after the aged couple had enjoyed and had the benefit of this service for 30 years, Mr. Wilkinson, after advice of its legal effect, made the note in question. If the last will had been proven, the claimant would have received more than the sum stipulated in the note, since probably no valid objection could have been made to it; and yet Mr. Wilkinson may have shared the fear and dread of many laymen, lest a will may be contested. With all this background he deliberately executed the note now relied on by the claimant. . . .

In this case the services had been rendered under such conditions and were of so intimate and delicate a character that their value could be estimated with no degree of mathematical certainty. No one knew their value so well as Mr. and Mrs. Wilkinson, and if he had not appreciated their value he would have been guilty of gross ingratitude. Evidently he did realize their worth, and desired to make liberal compensation, which he had the perfect right to do. If he deliberately chose to pay more than the services were really worth, he had the right to do so. To receive the consideration and respect of others, and to be able to be generous in later life, are among the motives which prompt men to practice economy and self-denial. There had been a consideration of inestimable value for the execution of the note, and it was in no sense a gift. The utmost that can be fairly claimed is that the consideration for the note was inadequate. But under such facts as here exist mere inadequacy does not amount to a failure or partial failure of consideration. Of course, that may be a circumstance relevant to the issue, where fraud or duress or undue influence is claimed; but in this case there is no suggestion of such a claim. There might be circumstances under which the inadequacy of consideration might be so grossly disproportionate to the value of the benefit received or the services rendered that a court might feel justified in refusing to enforce the contract.

In this case, where there was no element of fraud or misrepresentation, the value of the services may be measured by the wants of the persons benefited. To hold that this agreement, deliberately made, should be set aside or impaired, would be a denial of the right of parties to make their own contracts. There is abundant authority for the rule that, when the value of services is indefinite or indeterminate, or largely a matter of opinion, the courts will not substitute their judgments for that of the contracting parties. . . .

It does not follow that, because the note was not to take effect until after the maker's death, it was testamentary. As often happens, the title was vested in the payee on delivery and acceptance, although the enjoyment was postponed. "The mere fact that a writing is to become effective only on the death of the maker is not sufficient to give it a testamentary character." *Schouler on Wills*, § 356. . . .

In this connection there is some argument by counsel for the appellants that the plan of the execution of the note and the will at the same time was adopted with the purpose of evading in part, at least, the inheritance tax. We are aware that there are some persons who regard the inheritance taxes as a new and added terror to death, and that they sometimes adopt ingenious devices to shield their survivors from its burdens. But the argument in this respect rests in sheer speculation, and there is not a scintilla of evidence to support it.

It is our conclusion that the findings and judgment of the trial court should be sustained.

Judgment affirmed.

BANCO DO BRASIL S.A v. STATE OF ANTIGUA AND BARBUDA

N.Y. Appellate Division, First Department, 2000.
268 A.D.2d 75, 707 N.Y.S.2d 151.

LERNER, J. In this action for breach of a loan agreement and associated promissory notes and guarantees, we are called upon to determine whether defendants' 1997 letter regarding their loan agreement, sent to plaintiffs after the Statute of Limitations had run, constituted an acknowledgment or promise within the meaning of General Obligations Law § 17–101 and was sufficient to revive plaintiffs' time-barred claims.

On or about November 12, 1981, plaintiff Banco do Brasil, a Brazilian banking corporation with its principal place of business in Brasilia, Brazil, entered into a loan agreement with defendant, the State of Antigua and Barbuda ("the State"), wherein Banco do Brasil agreed to grant the State a loan in the principal amount of $3,000,000 plus interest. In connection with the loan agreement, the State executed certain promissory notes providing for the repayment of the loan with interest. Under the terms of the loan agreement, defendant, the Ministry of Finance of the State of Antigua and Barbuda ("the Ministry"), agreed to act as guarantor of the loan and the promissory notes on behalf of the State. As guarantor, the Ministry agreed to pay the amount due under the loan agreement and the promissory notes in the event of the State's default.

The State failed to pay the amount due within the time period provided in the promissory notes. The last payment was due on January 21, 1985. By letter dated October 5, 1989, the Ministry wrote to Banco do Brasil, confirming its obligation to pay the amount due under the loan agreement. However, the Ministry advised that due to the damages which the State sustained from Hurricane Hugo, it needed to reschedule its loan payments and requested six months to devise a plan for repayment.

In a second letter signed by its financial secretary and dated February 24, 1997, the Ministry confirmed the then-current balances (principal plus interest) due under the original loan agreement. The letter set forth the original loan amount, accrued interest, past-due interest and the total of $11,400,810.96 due and owing on that date.

Despite repeated demands, defendants failed to pay the amount due and owing under the loan agreement. Plaintiffs commenced the instant action for breach of the loan agreement, breach of promissory notes and breach of the guarantee agreement.

Defendants moved to dismiss plaintiffs' complaint upon the ground that plaintiffs' claims were barred under CPLR 213(2), the applicable six-year Statute of Limitations. Defendants argued that neither their October

5, 1989 letter, nor their February 24, 1997 letter satisfied the requirements of General Obligations Law § 17–101 that these writings indicate an absolute and unqualified intention to repay the debt owed to the plaintiffs.

The IAS court denied defendants' motion to dismiss and concluded that the six-year Statute of Limitations was revived under General Obligations Law § 17–101, because the 1997 letter constituted a plain admission of indebtedness and nothing in the letter was inconsistent with a clear intent to repay the loan.

General Obligations Law § 17–101 states, in pertinent part, as follows:

> An acknowledgment or promise contained in a writing signed by the party to be charged thereby is the only competent evidence of a new or continuing contract whereby to take an action out of the operation of the provisions of limitations of time for commencing actions under the civil practice law and rules.

"This section restates the rule that a written acknowledgment or promise will toll the Statute of Limitations.... The writing, in order to constitute an acknowledgment, must recognize an existing debt and must contain nothing inconsistent with an intention on the part of the debtor to pay it" (Morris Demolition Co. v. Board of Educ., 40 N.Y.2d 516, 520–521, 387 N.Y.S.2d 409, 355 N.E.2d 369).

The motion court correctly held that defendants' 1997 letter to plaintiffs constituted an "acknowledgment or promise" within the meaning of General Obligations Law § 17–101 that revived plaintiffs' otherwise time-barred claims. In its entirety, such letter refers to the parties' 1981 loan agreement and then "confirms" four "balances," namely, the original loan amount, accrued interest, past-due interest, and, adding up the first three balances, the "total amount." Even if this recital of a repayment obligation that is current and increasing with time is something less than a new promise to pay a past-due debt, it clearly conveys and is consistent with an intention to pay, which is all that need be shown in order to satisfy section 17–101.

Further, there is no merit to defendants' contention that their motion to dismiss should have been held in abeyance for disclosure on the issue of whether their letter imported an intention to repay. Defendants do not need to discover their own intention.

Accordingly, the order of the Supreme Court, New York County (Charles Ramos, J.), entered February 17, 1999, which denied defendants' motion to dismiss the complaint as time barred, should be affirmed, with costs. . . .

HARRINGTON v. TAYLOR

Supreme Court of North Carolina, 1945.
225 N.C. 690, 36 S.E.2d 227.

PER CURIAM. The plaintiff in this case sought to recover of the defendant upon a promise made by him under the following peculiar circumstances:

The defendant had assaulted his wife, who took refuge in plaintiff's house. The next day the defendant gained access to the house and began another assault upon his wife. The defendant's wife knocked him down with an axe, and was on the point of cutting his head open or decapitating him while he was laying on the floor, and the plaintiff intervened, caught the axe as it was descending and the blow intended for defendant fell upon her hand, mutilating it badly, but saving defendant's life.

Subsequently, defendant orally promised to pay the plaintiff her damages; but, after paying a small sum, failed to pay anything more. So, substantially, states the complaint.

The defendant demurred to the complaint as not stating a cause of action, and the demurrer was sustained. Plaintiff appealed.

The question presented is whether there was a consideration recognized by our law as sufficient to support the promise. The Court is of the opinion that, however much the defendant should be impelled by common gratitude to alleviate the plaintiff's misfortune, a humanitarian act of this kind, voluntarily performed, is not such consideration as would entitle her to recover at law.

The judgment sustaining the demurrer is

Affirmed.

WEBB v. McGOWIN

Court of Appeals of Alabama, 1935.
27 Ala.App. 82, 168 So. 196.

BRICKEN, PRESIDING JUDGE. This action is in assumpsit. . . . The demurrers to the complaint as amended were sustained, and because of this adverse ruling by the court the plaintiff took a nonsuit, and the assignment of errors on this appeal are predicated upon said action or ruling of the court.

A fair statement of the case presenting the questions for decision is set out in appellant's brief, which we adopt.

On the 3d day of August, 1925, appellant [plaintiff Webb] while in the employ of the W.T. Smith Lumber Company, a corporation, and acting within the scope of his employment, was engaged in clearing the upper floor of mill No. 2 of the company. While so engaged he was in the act of dropping a pine block from the upper floor of the mill to the ground below; this being the usual and ordinary way of clearing the floor, and it being the duty of the plaintiff in the course of his employment to so drop it. The block weighed about 75 pounds.

As appellant was in the act of dropping the block to the ground below, he was on the edge of the upper floor of the mill. As he started to turn the block loose so that it would drop to the ground, he saw J. Greeley McGowin, testator of the defendants, on the ground below and directly under where the block would have fallen had appellant turned it loose. Had he turned it loose it would have struck McGowin with such force as to have caused him serious bodily harm or death. Appellant could have remained safely on the upper floor of the mill by turning the block loose and allowing it to drop, but had he done this the block would have fallen on McGowin and caused him serious injuries or death. The only safe and reasonable way to prevent this was for appellant to hold to the block and divert its direction in falling from the place where McGowin was standing and the only safe way to divert it so as to prevent its coming into contact with McGowin was for appellant to fall with it to the ground below. Appellant did this, and by holding to the block and falling with it to the ground below, he diverted the course of its fall in such way that McGowin was not injured. In thus preventing the injuries to McGowin appellant himself received serious bodily injuries, resulting in his right leg being broken, the heel of his right foot torn off and his right arm broken. He was badly crippled for life and rendered unable to do physical or mental labor.

On September 1, 1925, in consideration of appellant having prevented him from sustaining death or serious bodily harm and in consideration of the injuries appellant had received, McGowin agreed with him to care for and maintain him for the remainder of appellant's life at the rate of $15 every two weeks from the time he sustained his injuries to and during the remainder of appellant's life; it being agreed that McGowin would pay this sum to appellant for his maintenance. Under the agreement McGowin paid or caused to be paid to appellant the sum so agreed on up until McGowin's death on January 1, 1934. After his death the payments were continued to and including January 27, 1934, at which time they were discontinued. Thereupon plaintiff brought suit to recover the unpaid installments accruing up to the time of the bringing of the suit.

The material averments of the different counts of the original complaint and the amended complaint are predicated upon the foregoing statement of facts.

. . .

1. The averments of the complaint show that appellant saved McGowin from death or grievous bodily harm. This was a material benefit to him of infinitely more value than any financial aid he could have received. Receiving this benefit, McGowin became morally bound to compensate appellant for the services rendered. Recognizing his moral obli-

gation, he expressly agreed to pay appellant as alleged in the complaint and complied with this agreement up to the time of his death; a period of more than 8 years.

Had McGowin been accidentally poisoned and a physician, without his knowledge or request, had administered an antidote, thus saving his life, a subsequent promise by McGowin to pay the physician would have been valid. Likewise, McGowin's agreement as disclosed by the complaint to compensate appellant for saving him from death or grievous bodily injury is valid and enforceable.

Where the promisee cares for, improves, and preserves the property of the promisor, though done without his request, it is sufficient consideration for the promisor's subsequent agreement to pay for the service, because of the material benefit received. Pittsburg Vitrified Paving & Building Brick Co. v. Cerebus Oil Co., 79 Kan. 603, 100 P. 631.

In Boothe v. Fitzpatrick, 36 Vt. 681, the court held that a promise by defendant to pay for the past keeping of a bull which had escaped from defendant's premises and been cared for by plaintiff was valid, although there was no previous request, because the subsequent promise obviated that objection; it being equivalent to a previous request. On the same principle, had the promisee saved the promisor's life or his body from grievous harm, [the promisor's] subsequent promise to pay for the services rendered would have been valid. Such service would have been far more material than caring for his bull. Any holding that saving a man from death or grievous bodily harm is not a material benefit sufficient to uphold a subsequent promise to pay for the service, necessarily rests on the assumption that saving life and preservation of the body from harm have only a sentimental value. The converse of this is true. Life and preservation of the body have material, pecuniary values, measurable in dollars and cents. Because of this, physicians practice their profession charging for services rendered in saving life and curing the body of its ills, and surgeons perform operations. The same is true as to the law of negligence, authorizing the assessment of damages in personal injury cases based upon the extent of the injuries, earnings, and life expectancies of those injured.

In the business of life insurance, the value of a man's life is measured in dollars and cents according to his expectancy, the soundness of his body, and his ability to pay premiums. The same is true as to health and accident insurance.

It follows that if, as alleged in the complaint, appellant saved J. Greeley McGowin from death or grievous bodily harm, and McGowin subsequently agreed to pay him for the service rendered, it became a valid and enforceable contract.

2. It is well settled that a moral obligation is a sufficient consideration to support a subsequent promise to pay where the promisor has received a material benefit, although there was no original duty or liability resting on the promisor. . . .

The case at bar is clearly distinguishable from that class of cases where the consideration is a mere moral obligation or conscientious duty unconnected with receipt by promisor of benefits of a material or pecuniary nature. Park Falls State Bank v. Fordyce, [206 Wis. 628, 238 N.W. 516]. Here the promisor received a material benefit constituting a valid consideration for his promise.

3.   Some authorities hold that, for a moral obligation to support a subsequent promise to pay, there must have existed a prior legal or equitable obligation, which for some reason had become unenforceable, but for which the promisor was still morally bound. This rule, however, is subject to qualification in those cases where the promisor, having received a material benefit from the promisee, is morally bound to compensate him for the services rendered and in consideration of this obligation promises to pay. In such cases the subsequent promise to pay is an affirmance or ratification of the services rendered carrying with it the presumption that a previous request for the service was made. McMorris v. Herndon, 2 Bailey (S.C.) 56, 21 Am.Dec. 515.

Under the decisions above cited, McGowin's express promise to pay appellant for the services rendered was an affirmance or ratification of what appellant had done raising the presumption that the services had been rendered at McGowin's request.

4.   The averments of the complaint show that in saving McGowin from death or grievous bodily harm, appellant was crippled for life. This was part of the consideration of the contract declared on. McGowin was benefited. Appellant was injured. Benefit to the promisor or injury to the promisee is a sufficient legal consideration for the promisor's agreement to pay. Fisher v. Bartlett, 8 Greenl. (Me.) 122, 22 Am Dec. 225.

5.   Under the averments of the complaint the services rendered by appellant were not gratuitous. The agreement of McGowin to pay and the acceptance of payment by appellant conclusively shows the contrary. . . .

The cases of Shaw v. Boyd, 1 Stew. & P. 83, and Duncan v. Hall, 9 Ala. 128, are not in conflict with the principles here announced. In those cases the lands were owned by the United States at the time the alleged improvements were made, for which subsequent purchasers from the government agreed to pay. These subsequent purchasers were not the owners of the lands at the time the improvements were made. Consequently, they could not have been made for their benefit.

From what has been said, we are of the opinion that the court below erred in the ruling complained of; that is to say, in sustaining the demurrer, and for this error the case is reversed and remanded.

Reversed and remanded.

SAMFORD, JUDGE (concurring). The questions involved in this case are not free from doubt, and perhaps the strict letter of the rule, as stated by judges, though not always in accord, would bar a recovery by plaintiff, but following the principle announced by Chief Justice Marshall in Hoffman v.

Porter, Fed.Cas. No. 6,577, 2 Brock. 156, 159, where he says, "I do not think that law ought to be separated from justice, where it is at most doubtful," I concur in the conclusions reached by the court.

PROBLEMS

1. Mrs. V. owed $13,500 to each of her two adult sons. She died without having paid any part of these debts. Mr. V., the stepfather of Mrs. V.'s sons, gave each of these stepsons a promissory note signed by him in the amount of $13,500. He died without having made any payments on these notes. The stepsons filed claims against his estate. Should the executor honor the claims?

2. A is employed by B to repair a vacant house. By mistake A repairs the house next door which belongs to C. C subsequently promises to pay A the value of the repairs. Is C's promise binding?

3. Father's coal company was near bankruptcy, owing $18,000 to creditors. Son contracted with Father to enter the business and assume all of the company's prior debts. Two years later, Father told Son that by assuming the debts he had saved the company and that he could have an option to purchase Father's stock. Father then wrote a memorandum to Son stating: "Upon my death my son has an irrevocable option to buy all of my stock in Black's Coal Company." Father died and Son brought suit to enforce the writing. What result at common law? What result in New York? See *Calamari & Perillo on Contracts* § 5–18.

CHAPTER 4

PROMISSORY ESTOPPEL

■ ■ ■

(Calamari & Perillo on Contracts §§ 6.1—6.4)

FEINBERG v. PFEIFFER CO.

Court of Appeals of Missouri, 1959.
322 S.W.2d 163.

DOERNER, COMMISSIONER. This is a suit brought in the Circuit Court of the City of St. Louis by plaintiff, a former employee of the defendant corporation, on an alleged contract whereby defendant agreed to pay plaintiff the sum of $200 per month for life upon her retirement. A jury being waived, the case was tried by the court alone. Judgment below was for plaintiff for $5,100, the amount of the pension claimed to be due as of the date of the trial, together with interest thereon, and defendant duly appealed.

The parties are in substantial agreement on the essential facts. Plaintiff began working for the defendant, a manufacturer of pharmaceuticals, in 1910, when she was but 17 years of age. By 1947 she had attained the position of bookkeeper, office manager, and assistant treasurer of the defendant, and owned 70 shares of its stock out of a total of 6,503 shares issued and outstanding. ... Over the years she received substantial dividends on the stock she owned, as did all of the other stockholders. Also, in addition to her salary, plaintiff from 1937 to 1949, inclusive, received each year a bonus varying in amount from $300 in the beginning to $2,000 in the later years.

On December 27, 1947, the annual meeting of the defendant's Board of Directors was held at the Company's offices in St. Louis, presided over by Max Lippman, its then president and largest individual stockholder. ... At that meeting the Board of Directors adopted the following resolution, which, because it is the crux of the case, we quote in full:

> The Chairman thereupon pointed out that the Assistant Treasurer, Mrs. Anna Sacks Feinberg, has given the corporation many years of long and faithful service. Not only has she served the corporation devotedly, but with exceptional ability and skill. The President point-

243

ed out that although all of the officers and directors sincerely hoped and desired that Mrs. Feinberg would continue in her present position for as long as she felt able, nevertheless, in view of the length of service which she has contributed provision should be made to afford her retirement privileges and benefits which should become a firm obligation of the corporation to be available to her whenever she should see fit to retire from active duty, however many years in the future such retirement may become effective. It was, accordingly, proposed that Mrs. Feinberg's salary which is presently $350.00 per month, be increased to $400.00 per month, and that Mrs. Feinberg would be given the privilege of retiring from active duty at any time she may elect to see fit so to do upon a retirement pay of $200.00 per month for life, with the distinct understanding that the retirement plan is merely being adopted at the present time in order to afford Mrs. Feinberg security for the future and in the hope that her active services will continue with the corporation for many years to come. After due discussion and consideration, and upon motion duly made and seconded, it was—

Resolved, that the salary of Anna Sacks Feinberg be increased from $350.00 to $400.00 per month and that she be afforded the privilege of retiring from active duty in the corporation at any time she may elect to see fit so to do upon retirement pay of $200.00 per month, for the remainder of her life.

At the request of Mr. Lippman his sons-in-law, Messrs. Harris and Flammer, called upon the plaintiff at her apartment on the same day to advise her of the passage of the resolution. Plaintiff testified on cross-examination that she had no prior information that such a pension plan was contemplated, that it came as a surprise to her, and that she would have continued in her employment whether or not such a resolution had been adopted. It is clear from the evidence that there was no contract, oral or written, as to plaintiff's length of employment, and that she was free to quit, and the defendant to discharge her, at any time.

Plaintiff did continue to work for the defendant through June 30, 1949, on which date she retired. In accordance with the foregoing resolution, the defendant began paying her the sum of $200 on the first of each month. Mr. Lippman died on November 18, 1949, and was succeeded as president of the company by his widow. Because of an illness, she retired from that office and was succeeded in October, 1953, by her son-in-law, Sidney M. Harris. Mr. Harris testified that while Mrs. Lippman had been president she signed the monthly pension check paid plaintiff, but fussed about doing so, and considered the payments as gifts. After his election, he stated, a new accounting firm employed by the defendant questioned the validity of the payments to plaintiff on several occasions, and in the Spring of 1956, upon its recommendation, he consulted the Company's then attorney, Mr. Ralph Kalish. Harris testified that both Ernst and Ernst, the accounting firm, and Kalish told him there was no need of giving plaintiff the money. He also stated that he had concurred in the

view that the payments to plaintiff were mere gratuities rather than amounts due under a contractual obligation, and that following his discussion with the Company's attorney plaintiff was sent a check for $100 on April 1, 1956. Plaintiff declined to accept the reduced amount, and this action followed. Additional facts will be referred to later in this opinion.
. . .

Appellant's next complaint is that there was insufficient evidence to support the court's finding that plaintiff would not have quit defendant's employ had she not known and relied upon the promise of defendant to pay her $200 a month for life, and the finding that, from her voluntary retirement until April 1, 1956, plaintiff relied upon the continued receipt of the pension installments. The trial court so found, and, in our opinion, justifiably so. Plaintiff testified, and was corroborated by Harris, defendant's witness, that knowledge of the passage of the resolution was communicated to her on December 27, 1947, the very day it was adopted. She was told at that time by Harris and Flammer, she stated, that she could take the pension as of that day, if she wished. She testified further that she continued to work for another year and a half, through June 30, 1949; that at that time her health was good and she could have continued to work, but that after working for almost forty years she thought she would take a rest. Her testimony continued:

Q. Now, what was the reason—I'm sorry. Did you then quit the employment of the company after you—after this year and a half? A. Yes.

Q. What was the reason that you left? A. Well, I thought almost forty years, it was a long time and I thought I would take a little rest.

Q. Yes. A. And with the pension and what earnings my husband had, we figured we could get along.

Q. Did you rely upon this pension? A. We certainly did.

Q. Being paid? A. Very much so. We relied upon it because I was positive that I was going to get it as long as I lived.

Q. Would you have . . . quit the employment of the company at that time had you not relied upon this pension plan? A. No, I wouldn't.

Q. You would not have. Did you ever seek employment while this pension was being paid to you—A. (interrupting): No.

Q. Wait a minute, at any time prior—at any other place? A. No sir.

Q. Were you able to hold any other employment during that time? A. Yes, I think so.

Q. Was your health good? A. My health was good.

It is obvious from the foregoing that there was ample evidence to support the findings of fact made by the court below. . . .

It is defendant's contention, in essence, that the resolution adopted by its Board of Directors was a mere promise to make a gift, and that no contract resulted either thereby, or when plaintiff retired, because there was no consideration given or paid by the plaintiff. It urges that a promise to make a gift is not binding unless supported by a legal consideration; that the only apparent consideration for the adoption of the foregoing resolution was the "many years of long and faithful service" expressed therein; and that past services are not a valid consideration for a promise. Defendant argues further that there is nothing in the resolution which made its effectiveness conditional upon plaintiff's continued employment, that she was not under contract to work for any length of time but was free to quit whenever she wished, and that she had no contractual right to her position and could have been discharged at any time.

Plaintiff concedes that a promise based upon past services would be without consideration, but contends that there were two other elements which supplied the required element: First, the continuation by plaintiff in the employ of the defendant for the period from December 27, 1947, the date when the resolution was adopted, until the date of her retirement on June 30, 1949. And second, her change of position, *i.e.*, her retirement, and the abandonment by her of her opportunity to continue in gainful employment, made in reliance on defendant's promise to pay her $200 per month for life.

We must agree with the defendant that the evidence does not support the first of these contentions. There is no language in the resolution predicating plaintiff's right to a pension upon her continued employment. She was not required to work for the defendant for any period of time as a condition to gaining such retirement benefits. She was told that she could quit the day upon which the resolution was adopted, as she herself testified, and it is clear from her own testimony that she made no promise or agreement to continue in the employ of the defendant in return for its promise to pay her a pension. Hence there was lacking that mutuality of obligation which is essential to the validity of a contract. Middleton v. Holecroft, Mo.App., 270 S.W.2d 90.

But as to the second of these contentions we must agree with plaintiff. By the terms of the resolution defendant promised to pay plaintiff the sum of $200 a month upon her retirement. . . .

Section 90 of the *Restatement of the Law of Contracts* states that:

A promise which the promisor should reasonably expect to induce action or forbearance of a definite and substantial character on the part of the promisee and which does induce such action or forbearance is binding if injustice can be avoided only by enforcement of the promise.

. . .

Was there such an act on the part of plaintiff, in reliance upon the promise contained in the resolution, as will estop the defendant, and therefore create an enforceable contract under the doctrine of promissory estoppel? We think there was. One of the illustrations cited under Section 90 of the *Restatement* is:

> 2. A promises B to pay him an annuity during B's life. B thereupon resigns a profitable employment, as A expected that he might. B receives the annuity for some years, in the meantime becoming disqualified from again obtaining good employment. A's promise is binding.

This illustration is objected to by defendant as not being applicable to the case at hand. The reason advanced by it is that in the illustration B became "disqualified" from obtaining other employment *before* A discontinued the payments, whereas in this case the plaintiff did not discover that she had cancer and thereby became unemployable until *after* the defendant had discontinued the payments of $200 per month. We think the distinction is immaterial. The only reason for the reference in the illustration to the disqualification of A is in connection with that part of Section 90 regarding the prevention of injustice. The injustice would occur regardless of when the disability occurred. Would defendant contend that the contract would be enforceable if the plaintiff's illness had been discovered on March 31, 1956, the day before it discontinued the payment of the $200 a month, but not if it occurred on April 2nd, the day after? Furthermore, there are more ways to become disqualified for work, or unemployable, than as the result of illness. At the time she retired plaintiff was 57 years of age. At the time the payments were discontinued she was over 63 years of age. It is a matter of common knowledge that it is virtually impossible for a woman of that age to find satisfactory employment, much less a position comparable to that which plaintiff enjoyed at the time of her retirement.

The fact of the matter is that plaintiff's subsequent illness was not the "action or forbearance" which was induced by the promise contained in the resolution. As the trial court correctly decided, such action on plaintiff's part was her retirement from a lucrative position in reliance upon defendant's promise to pay her an annuity or pension. . . .

The Commissioner therefore recommends, for the reasons stated, that the judgment be affirmed.

Per Curiam. The foregoing opinion by Doerner, C., is adopted as the opinion of the court. The judgment is, accordingly, affirmed. . . .

CONRAD v. FIELDS

Court of Appeals of Minnesota, 2007.
Unpublished Opinion.
2007 WL 2106302.

Peterson, Judge. This appeal is from a judgment and an order denying posttrial motions. The judgment awarded respondent damages in the amount of the cost of her law-school tuition and books based on a determination that the elements of promissory estoppel were proved with respect to appellant's promise to pay for the tuition and books. We affirm the judgment. . . .

FACTS

Appellant Walter R. Fields and respondent Marjorie Conrad met and became friends when they were neighbors in an apartment complex in the early 1990's. Appellant [Fields] started his own business and became a financially successful businessman. Fields built a $1.2 million house in the Kenwood neighborhood in Minneapolis and leased a Bentley automobile for more than $50,000 a year. Fields is a philanthropic individual who has sometimes paid education costs for others.

In the fall of 2000, Fields suggested that respondent [Conrad] attend law school, and he offered to pay for her education. Conrad, who had recently paid off an $11,000 medical bill and still owed about $5,000 for undergraduate student loans, did not feel capable of paying for law school on her own. Fields promised that he would pay tuition and other expenses associated with law school as they became due. Fields quit her job at Qwest, where she had been earning $45,000 per year, to attend law school. Fields admitted at trial that before Conrad enrolled in law school, he agreed to pay her tuition.

Conrad testified that she enrolled in law school in the summer of 2001 as a result of Fields's "inducement and assurance to pay for (her) education." Fields made two tuition payments, each in the amount of $1,949.75, in August and October 2001, but he stopped payment on the check for the second payment. At some point, Fields told Conrad that his assets had been frozen due to an Internal Revenue Service audit and that payment of her education expenses would be delayed until he got the matter straightened out. In May 2004, Fields and Conrad exchanged e-mail messages about Conrad's difficulties in managing the debts that she had incurred for law school. In response to one of Conrad's messages, Fields wrote, "to be clear and in writing, when you graduate law school and pas(s) your bar exam, I will pay your tuition." Later, Fields told Conrad that he would not pay her expenses, and he threatened to get a restraining order against her if she continued attempting to communicate with him.

Conrad brought suit against Fields, alleging that in reliance on Fields's promise to pay her education expenses, she gave up the opportunity to earn income through full-time employment and enrolled in law school. The case was tried to the court, which awarded Conrad damages in the amount of $87,314.63 under the doctrine of promissory estoppel. The district court denied Fields's motion for a new trial or amended findings. This appeal followed.

DECISION

. . . "Promissory estoppel implies a contract in law where no contract exists in fact." Deli v. Univ. of Minn., 578 N.W.2d 779, 781 (Minn.App.

1998). "A promise which the promisor should reasonably expect to induce action or forbearance on the part of the promisee or a third person and which does induce such action or forbearance is binding if injustice can be avoided only by enforcement of the promise." *Restatement (Second) of Contracts* § 90(1) (1981).

The elements of a promissory estoppel claim are (1) a clear and definite promise, (2) the promisor intended to induce reliance by the promisee, and the promisee relied to the promisee's detriment, and (3) the promise must be enforced to prevent injustice. Cohen v. Cowles Media Co., 479 N.W.2d 387, 391 (Minn.1992). Judicial determinations of injustice involve a number of considerations, "including the reasonableness of a promisee's reliance." Faimon v. Winona State Univ., 540 N.W.2d 879, 883 (Minn.App.1995).

"Granting equitable relief is within the sound discretion of the trial court. Only a clear abuse of that discretion will result in reversal." Nadeau v. County of Ramsey, 277 N.W.2d 520, 524 (Minn.1979). But

> (t)he court considers the injustice factor as a matter of law, looking to the reasonableness of the promisee's reliance and weighing public policies (in favor of both enforcing bargains and preventing unjust enrichment). When the facts are taken as true, it is a question of law as to whether they rise to the level of promissory estoppel.

Greuling v. Wells Fargo Home Mortgage, Inc., 690 N.W.2d 757, 761 (Minn.App.2005).

I.

Fields argues that Conrad did not plead or prove the elements of promissory estoppel. . . .

Paragraph 12 of Conrad's complaint states, "That as a direct and approximate result of the negligent conduct and breach of contract conduct of [Fields], [Conrad] has been damaged. . . ." But the complaint also states:

> 4. That in 2000, based on the assurance and inducement of [Fields] to pay for [Conrad's] legal education, [Conrad] made the decision to enroll in law school at Hamline University School of Law (Hamline) in St. Paul, Minnesota which she did in 2001.

> 5. That but for the inducement and assurance of [Fields] to pay for [Conrad's] legal education, [Conrad] would not have enrolled in law school. [Fields] was aware of this fact.

Paragraphs four and five of the complaint are sufficient to put Fields on notice of the promissory-estoppel claim.

At a pretrial deposition, Conrad testified that negligence and breach of contract were the only two causes of action that she was pleading. Because promissory estoppel is described as a contract implied at law,

Conrad's deposition testimony can be interpreted to include a promissory-estoppel claim.

In its legal analysis, the district court stated:

The Court finds credible [Conrad's] testimony that [Fields] encouraged her to go to law school, knowing that she would not be able to pay for it on her own. He knew that she was short on money, having helped her pay for food and other necessities. He knew that she was working at Qwest and would need to quit her job to go to law school. He offered to pay for the cost of her going to law school, knowing that she had debts from her undergraduate tuition. He made a payment on her law school tuition after she enrolled. [Conrad] knew that [Fields] was a wealthy philanthropist, and that he had offered to pay for the education of strangers he had met in chance encounters. She knew that he had the wealth to pay for her law school education. She knew that ( ) he was established in society, older than she, not married, without children, an owner of a successful company, an owner of an expensive home, and a lessor of an expensive car. Moreover, [Fields] was a friend who had performed many kindnesses for her already, and she trusted him. [Fields's] promise in fact induced [Conrad] to quit her job at Qwest and enroll in law school, which she had not otherwise planned to do. . . .

. . . (T)he circumstances support a finding that it would be unjust not to enforce the promise. Upon reliance on [Fields's] promise, [Conrad] quit her job. She attended law school despite a serious health condition that might otherwise have deterred her from going.

These findings are sufficient to show that Conrad proved the elements of promissory estoppel.

Fields argues that because he advised Conrad shortly after she enrolled in law school that he would not be paying her law-school expenses as they came due, Conrad could not have reasonably relied on his promise to pay her expenses to her detriment after he repudiated the promise. Fields contends that the only injustice that resulted from his promise involved the original $5,000 in expenses that Conrad incurred to enter law school. But Fields's statement that he would not pay the expenses as they came due did not make Conrad's reliance unreasonable because Fields also told Conrad that his financial problems were temporary and that he would pay her tuition when she graduated and passed the bar exam. This statement made it reasonable for Conrad to continue to rely on Fields's promise that he would pay her expenses.

II.

[The court emphasizes the equitable nature of promissory estoppel in Minnesota, with remedies limited to the extent necessary to prevent injustice. Ed.]

III.

[The court addresses the statute of frauds defense, applying reliance theory under *Restatement (Second) of Contracts* § 139(1) (1981). It concludes that the promise is not barred by the statute of frauds.]

Because Fields's expensive home and car and position as a successful business owner made it appear as if he was fully capable of keeping his promise to pay Conrad's law-school expenses and because Fields had bestowed his generosity on Conrad several times before he promised to pay her law-school expenses, Fields reasonably should have expected his promise to induce action by Conrad. The promise did induce action by Conrad and left her with a substantial debt when Fields failed to keep his promise. Conrad quit her job and attended law school with the expectation that Fields would pay her law-school expenses and she would not be in debt for these expenses when she graduated. . . . .

IV.

In actions based on promissory estoppel, "(r)elief may be limited to damages measured by the promisee's reliance." Dallum v. Farmers Union Cent. Exchange, Inc., 462 N.W.2d 608, 613 (Minn.App.1990). "In other words, relief may be limited to the party's out-of-pocket expenses made in reliance on the promise." *Id.*

. . . [T]he district court awarded Conrad damages . . . for the cost of tuition and books. . . . [A]n exhibit prepared by Conrad and admitted into evidence shows that tuition totaled $86,462.21 and books cost $2,802.17. The district court awarded Conrad $87,314.63 (tuition plus books minus payment made by Fields).

Fields argues that Conrad was obligated to mitigate her damages and she could have avoided all of her damages by dropping out of law school immediately after Fields refused to pay her tuition as it was incurred. But as we explained when addressing the reasonableness of Conrad's reliance, Fields told Conrad that his financial difficulties were temporary and that he would pay her expenses after graduation. Under these circumstances, Conrad was not aware until after she graduated that she would suffer damages, and by the time she graduated, she had already paid for her tuition and books and had no opportunity to mitigate damages.

V.

Fields argues that because Conrad received a valuable law degree, she did not suffer any real detriment by relying on his promise. But receiving a law degree was the expected and intended consequence of Fields's promise, and the essence of Fields's promise was that Conrad would receive the law degree without the debt associated with attending law school. Although Conrad benefited from attending law school, the debt that she incurred in reliance on Fields's promise is a detriment to her. . . .

Affirmed. . . .

SALSBURY v. NORTHWESTERN BELL TELEPHONE CO.

Supreme Court of Iowa, 1974.
221 N.W.2d 609.

HARRIS, JUSTICE. . . . John Salsbury (plaintiff) participated in the efforts to establish Charles City College (the college). He was the first and only chairman of the college's board of trustees. . . . As part of the funding drive Peter Bruno, a professional fund raiser, solicited a subscription from Northwestern Bell Telephone Company (defendant) . . . [whose representative] wrote a letter to Bruno as follows:

> This is to advise you that the contribution from Northwestern Bell Telephone Co. to the Charles City College has been approved by Mr. E.A. McDaniel, District Manager, Mason City.

> The $15,000 contribution will be made over a three year period, in three equal payments. Our first $5000 payment will be made in 1968.

> We are very pleased to add our name to the list of contributors to this fine community undertaking.

> If I can be of further assistance, please feel free to contact me.

. . . In this appeal we are faced with the question of whether defendant is bound to pay his subscription by reason of the letter. . . .

Cases throughout the country clearly reflect a conflict between the desired goal of enforcing charitable subscriptions and the realities of contract law. The result has been strained reasoning which has been the subject of considerable criticism. This criticism is directed toward efforts by the courts to secure a substitute for consideration in charitable subscriptions. These efforts were thought necessary to bind the subscriber on a contract theory. Yet, in the nature of charitable subscriptions, it is presupposed the promise is made as a gift and not in return for consideration. 1 *Williston on Contracts*, Third Ed., § 116, page 473.

Consideration sufficient for a binding contract has been found under various criticized theories. *Id.* at 476–479. We have found consideration in the promises of other subscribers. Brokaw v. McElroy, 162 Iowa 288, 143 N.W. 1087. This theory is also criticized:

> . . . The difficulty with this view is its lack of conformity to the facts. It is doubtless possible for two or more persons to make mutual promises that each will give a specified amount to a charity or other object, but in the case of ordinary charitable subscriptions, the promise of each subscriber is made directly to the charity or its trustees, and it is frequently made without any reference to the subscription of others. If induced at all by previous or expected subscriptions, this inducement only affects the motive of the subscriber; it cannot be said that the previous subscriptions were given in exchange for the later one. Indeed the earlier subscriptions would be open to the objection of

being past consideration so far as a later subscription was concerned. . . .

1 *Williston on Contracts, supra*, pages 476–477.

In reaction to this widespread criticism a number of courts have turned to promissory estoppel as an alternative for the consideration requirement. 1 *Williston on Contracts*, Third Ed., § 140, pages 607–619.

If promissory estoppel were to be the standard or criterion for enforcement this defendant probably could not be bound on the pledge. Estoppel can never arise unless there has been reliance. McKeon v. City of Council Bluffs, 206 Iowa 556, 221 N.W. 351, 62 A.L.R. 1006. . . . Plaintiff conceded he had not even seen the letter until shortly before trial. . . .

We acknowledge as valid the criticism of cases which enforce charitable subscriptions only on a fictional finding of consideration. But we are reluctant to adopt promissory estoppel as the sole alternative basis for such enforcement.

> . . . (W)ide variation in reasoning indicates the difficulty of enforcing a charitable subscription on grounds of consideration. Yet, the courts have generally striven to find grounds for enforcement, indicating the depth of feeling in this country that private philanthropy serves a highly important function in our society.
>
> Of late, courts have tended to abandon the attempt to utilize traditional contract doctrines to sustain subscriptions and have placed their decision on grounds of promissory estoppel. Surprisingly, however, if promissory estoppel, in its traditional form, is widely adopted as the grounds upon which such subscriptions are to be tested, fewer subscriptions are likely to be enforced than previously. Under previous holdings, despite the conceptual inadequacy of the reasoning, promises were frequently enforced without regard to detrimental reliance on the promise. It was enough that the promisor had subscribed. If enforcement of charitable subscriptions is a desirable goal, it would seem sounder to view the preponderance of the cases as supporting the proposition that a charitable subscription is enforceable without consideration and without detrimental reliance. This seems to be the position taken in *Restatement Second*. Recognition of such a rule would also put an end to the flood of needless litigation created by the caution of executors and administrators who, for self-protection against surcharging, will not pay out on a subscription without a court decree.

Calamari & Perillo, *Law of Contracts*, § 103, pages 177–178.

The tentative draft of *Restatement of Contracts, Second*, includes a new subparagraph 2. *Section 90* now reads as follows:

> (1) A promise which the promisor should reasonably expect to induce action or forbearance on the part of the promisee or a third person and which does induce such action or forbearance is binding if

injustice can be avoided only by enforcement of the promise. The remedy granted for breach may be limited as justice requires.

(2) A charitable subscription or a marriage settlement is binding under Subsection (1) without proof that the promise induced action or forbearance.

We believe public policy supports this view. It is more logical to bind charitable subscriptions without requiring a showing of consideration or detrimental reliance.

Charitable subscriptions often serve the public interest by making possible projects which otherwise could never come about. It is true some fund raising campaigns are not conducted on a plan which calls for subscriptions to be binding. In such cases we do not hesitate to hold them not binding. Pappas v. Bever, [219 N.W.2d 720 (Iowa 1974)]. However where a subscription is unequivocal the pledgor should be made to keep his word.

Affirmed.

All Justices concur except LeGrand and Reynoldson, J.J., who dissent.

DRENNAN v. STAR PAVING CO.

Supreme Court of California, In Bank, 1958.
51 Cal.2d 409, 333 P.2d 757.

Traynor, Justice. Defendant appeals from a judgment for plaintiff in an action to recover damages caused by defendant's refusal to perform certain paving work according to a bid it submitted to plaintiff.

On July 28, 1955, plaintiff, a licensed general contractor, was preparing a bid on the "Monte Vista School Job" in the Lancaster school district. Bids had to be submitted before 8:00 p.m. Plaintiff testified that it was customary in that area for general contractors to receive the bids of subcontractors by telephone on the day set for bidding and to rely on them in computing their own bids. Thus on that day plaintiff's secretary, Mrs. Johnson, received by telephone between fifty and seventy-five subcontractors' bids for various parts of the school job. As each bid came in, she wrote it on a special form, which she brought into plaintiff's office. He then posted it on a master cost sheet setting forth the names and bids of all subcontractors. His own bid had to include the names of subcontractors who were to perform one-half of one per cent or more of the construction work, and he had also to provide a bidder's bond of ten per cent of his total bid of $317,385 as a guarantee that he would enter the contract if awarded the work.

Late in the afternoon, Mrs. Johnson had a telephone conversation with Kenneth R. Hoon, an estimator for defendant. He gave his name and telephone number and stated that he was bidding for defendant for the paving work at the Monte Vista School according to plans and specifications and that his bid was $7,131.60. At Mrs. Johnson's request he repeated his bid. Plaintiff listened to the bid over an extension telephone in his office and posted it on the master sheet after receiving the bid form from Mrs. Johnson. Defendant's was the lowest bid for the paving. Plaintiff computed his own bid accordingly and submitted it with the name of defendant as the subcontractor for the paving. When the bids were opened on July 28th, plaintiff's proved to be the lowest, and he was awarded the contract.

On his way to Los Angeles the next morning plaintiff stopped at defendant's office. The first person he met was defendant's construction engineer, Mr. Oppenheimer. Plaintiff testified:

> I introduced myself and he immediately told me that they had made a mistake in their bid to me the night before, they couldn't do it for the price they had bid, and I told him I would expect him to carry through with their original bid because I had used it in compiling my bid and the job was being awarded them. And I would have to go and do the job according to my bid and I would expect them to do the same.

Defendant refused to do the paving work for less than $15,000. Plaintiff testified that he "got figures from other people" and after trying for several months to get as low a bid as possible engaged L & H Paving Company, a firm in Lancaster, to do the work for $10,948.60.

The trial court found on substantial evidence that defendant made a definite offer to do the paving on the Monte Vista job according to the plans and specifications for $7,131.60, and that plaintiff relied on defendant's bid in computing his own bid for the school job and naming defendant therein as the subcontractor for the paving work. Accordingly, it entered judgment for plaintiff in the amount of $3,817.00 (the difference between defendant's bid and the cost of the paving to plaintiff) plus costs.

Defendant contends that there was no enforceable contract between the parties on the ground that it made a revocable offer and revoked it before plaintiff communicated his acceptance to defendant.

There is no evidence that defendant offered to make its bid irrevocable in exchange for plaintiff's use of its figures in computing his bid. Nor is there evidence that would warrant interpreting plaintiff's use of defendant's bid as the acceptance thereof, binding plaintiff, on condition he received the main contract, to award the subcontract to defendant. In sum, there was neither an option supported by consideration nor a bilateral contract binding on both parties.

Plaintiff contends, however, that he relied to his detriment on defendant's offer and that defendant must therefore answer in damages for its refusal to perform. Thus the question is squarely presented: Did plaintiff's reliance make defendant's offer irrevocable?

Section 90 of the *Restatement of Contracts* states:

> A promise which the promisor should reasonably expect to induce action or forbearance of a definite and substantial character on the part of the promisee and which does induce such action or forbear-

ance is binding if injustice can be avoided only by enforcement of the promise.

This rule applies in this state. [citations]

Defendant's offer constituted a promise to perform on such conditions as were stated expressly or by implication therein or annexed thereto by operation of law. (*See* 1 Williston, *Contracts* (3rd. ed.), § 24A, p. 56, § 61, p. 196.) Defendant had reason to expect that if its bid proved the lowest it would be used by plaintiff. It induced "action ... of a definite and substantial character on the part of the promisee."

Had defendant's bid expressly stated or clearly implied that it was revocable at any time before acceptance we would treat it accordingly. It was silent on revocation, however, and we must therefore determine whether there are conditions to the right of revocation imposed by law or reasonably inferable in fact. In the analogous problem of an offer for a unilateral contract, the theory is now obsolete that the offer is revocable at any time before complete performance. Thus section 45 of the *Restatement of Contracts* provides:

> If an offer for a unilateral contract is made, and part of the consideration requested in the offer is given or tendered by the offeree in response thereto, the offeror is bound by a contract, the duty of immediate performance of which is conditional on the full consideration being given or tendered within the time stated in the offer, or, if no time is stated therein, within a reasonable time.

In explanation, comment b states that the

> main offer includes as a subsidiary promise, necessarily implied, that if part of the requested performance is given, the offeror will not revoke his offer, and that if tender is made it will be accepted. Part performance or tender may thus furnish consideration for the subsidiary promise. Moreover, merely acting in justifiable reliance on an offer may in some cases serve as sufficient reason for making a promise binding (*see § 90*).

Whether implied in fact or law, the subsidiary promise serves to preclude the injustice that would result if the offer could be revoked after the offeree had acted in detrimental reliance thereon. Reasonable reliance resulting in a foreseeable prejudicial change in position affords a compelling basis also for implying a subsidiary promise not to revoke an offer for a bilateral contract.

The absence of consideration is not fatal to the enforcement of such a promise. It is true that in the case of unilateral contracts the *Restatement* finds consideration for the implied subsidiary promise in the part performance of the bargained-for exchange, but its reference to *section 90* makes clear that consideration for such a promise is not always necessary. The very purpose of *section 90* is to make a promise binding even though there was no consideration "in the sense of something that is bargained for and given in exchange." (*See* 1 Corbin, *Contracts*, § 634 *et seq.*) Reasonable reliance serves to hold the offeror in lieu of the consideration ordinarily required to make the offer binding. In a case involving similar facts the Supreme Court of South Dakota stated that

> we believe that reason and justice demand that the doctrine (of *section 90*) be applied to the present facts. We cannot believe that by accepting this doctrine as controlling in the state of facts before us we will abolish the requirement of a consideration in contract cases, in any different sense than an ordinary estoppel abolishes some legal requirement in its application. We are of the opinion, therefore, that the defendants in executing the agreement (which was not supported by consideration) made a promise which they should have reasonably expected would induce the plaintiff to submit a bid based thereon to the Government, that such promise did induce this action, and that injustice can be avoided only by enforcement of the promise.

Northwestern Engineering Co. v. Ellerman, 69 S.D. 397, 408, 10 N.W.2d 879, 884; *cf.* James Baird Co. v. Gimbel Bros., 2 Cir., 64 F.2d 344.

When plaintiff used defendant's offer in computing his own bid, he bound himself to perform in reliance on defendant's terms. Though defendant did not bargain for this use of its bid neither did defendant make it idly, indifferent to whether it would be used or not. On the contrary it is reasonable to suppose that defendant submitted its bid to obtain the subcontract. It was bound to realize the substantial possibility that its bid would be the lowest, and that it would be included by plaintiff in his bid. It was to its own interest that the contractor be awarded the general contract; the lower the subcontract bid, the lower the general contractor's bid was likely to be and the greater its chance of acceptance and hence the greater defendant's chance of getting the paving subcontract. Defendant had reason not only to expect plaintiff to rely on its bid but to want him to. Clearly defendant had a stake in plaintiff's reliance on its bid. Given this interest and the fact that plaintiff is bound by his own bid, it is only fair that plaintiff should have at least an opportunity to accept defendant's bid after the general contract has been awarded to him.

It bears noting that a general contractor is not free to delay acceptance after he has been awarded the general contract in the hope of getting a better price. Nor can he reopen bargaining with the subcontractor and at the same time claim a continuing right to accept the original offer. *See* R.J. Daum Const. Co. v. Child, Utah, 247 P.2d 817, 823. In the present case plaintiff promptly informed defendant that plaintiff was being awarded the job and that the subcontract was being awarded to defendant.

Defendant contends, however, that its bid was the result of mistake and that it was therefore entitled to revoke it. It relies on ... rescission cases ... [in which] the bidder's mistake was known or should have been known to the offeree, and the offeree could be placed in status quo. Of course, if plaintiff had reason to believe that defendant's bid was in error, he could not justifiably rely on it, and *section 90* would afford no basis for enforcing it. Robert Gordon, Inc. v. Ingersoll–Rand, Co., 7 Cir., 117 F.2d 654, 660. Plaintiff, however, had no reason to know that defendant had made a mistake in submitting its bid, since there was usually a variance of 160 per cent between the highest and lowest bids for paving in the desert around Lancaster. He committed himself to performing the main contract in reliance on defendant's figures. Under these circumstances defendant's mistake, far from relieving it of its obligation, constitutes an additional reason for enforcing it, for it misled plaintiff as to the cost of doing the paving. Even had it been clearly understood that defendant's offer was revocable until accepted, it would not necessarily follow that defendant had no duty to exercise reasonable care in preparing its bid. It presented its bid with knowledge of the substantial possibility that it would be used by plaintiff; it could foresee the harm that would ensue from an erroneous underestimate of the cost. Moreover, it was motivated by its own business interest. Whether or not these considerations alone would justify recovery for negligence had the case been tried on that theory, they are persuasive that defendant's mistake should not defeat recovery under the rule of section 90 of the *Restatement of Contracts*. As between the subcontractor who made the bid and the general contractor who reasonably relied on it, the loss resulting from the mistake should fall on the party who caused it.

Leo F. Piazza Paving Co. v. Bebek & Brkich, 141 Cal.App.2d 226, 296 P.2d 368, 371, and Bard v. Kent, 19 Cal.2d 449, 122 P.2d 8, 139 A.L.R. 1032, are not to the contrary. In the *Piazza* case the court sustained a finding that defendants intended, not to make a firm bid, but only to give the plaintiff "some kind of an idea to use" in making its bid; there was evidence that the defendants had told plaintiff they were unsure of the significance of the specifications. There was thus no offer, promise, or representation on which the defendants should reasonably have expected the plaintiff to rely. The *Bard* case held that an option not supported by consideration was revoked by the death of the optionor. The issue of recovery under the rule of *section 90* was not pleaded at the trial, and it does not appear that the offeree's reliance was "of a definite and substantial character" so that injustice could be avoided "only by the enforcement of the promise."

There is no merit in defendant's contention that plaintiff failed to state a cause of action, on the ground that the complaint failed to allege that plaintiff attempted to mitigate the damages or that they could not have been mitigated. Plaintiff alleged that after defendant's default, "plaintiff had to procure the services of the L & H Co. to perform said asphaltic paving for the sum of $10,948.60." Plaintiff's uncontradicted evidence showed that he spent several months trying to get bids from other subcontractors and that he took the lowest bid. Clearly he acted reasonably to mitigate damages. . . .

The judgment is affirmed. . . .

COSGROVE v. BARTOLOTTA

United States Court of Appeals, Seventh Circuit, 1998.
150 F.3d 729.

POSNER, CHIEF JUDGE. A jury awarded the plaintiff damages of $135,000 in a diversity suit governed by Wisconsin law. The damages were broken down as follows: $117,000 for promissory estoppel, $1,000 for misrepresentation, and $17,000 for unjust enrichment. In response to the defendants' motion under Fed.R.Civ.P. 59(e) to alter or amend the judgment [which this court treats as a Rule 50(b) motion for judgment notwithstanding the verdict, ed.], the judge rendered judgment for the defendants on the promissory estoppel claim on the ground that the plaintiff had failed to prove reliance; but he let the jury's verdict stand with respect to the other claims. . . . Both sides appeal. . . .

This brings us to the merits of the appeals. Bartolotta wanted to open a new restaurant in Milwaukee. He asked a family friend—Barry Cosgrove—for help. The help sought was a $100,000 loan from Cosgrove plus Cosgrove's business and legal advice, Cosgrove being an experienced corporate lawyer. Bartolotta promised Cosgrove not only to repay the loan with interest within three years but also to give him a 19 percent ownership interest in the restaurant. Armed with Cosgrove's pledge of the $100,000 loan, Bartolotta was able to obtain the bank financing that he needed for the venture. In reliance on the promise of a share in the ownership of the restaurant, Cosgrove assisted Bartolotta in negotiating the lease of the restaurant premises and the loan from the bank, and it was on Cosgrove's advice that the venture was organized in the form of an LLC. But Cosgrove never actually made the loan and was never given an ownership interest in the restaurant. For after all the arrangements were complete, and though Cosgrove was willing and able to make the loan, Bartolotta obtained alternative financing and cut Cosgrove out of the deal. The restaurant opened and was a success, so the ownership interest that Cosgrove would have gotten had Bartolotta not reneged on his [promise] has turned out to be worth something; hence this lawsuit.

We have stated the facts as favorably to Cosgrove as the record permits, as we must do in deciding whether it was error for the district judge to take the promissory estoppel case away from the jury. Cosgrove's evidence was vigorously contested, but there was enough to enable a reasonable jury to find the facts that we have summarized. It is true that the jury found against Cosgrove on his breach of contract claim, but this was not inconsistent with its finding promissory estoppel. Cosgrove and Bartolotta never worked out the exact terms under which Cosgrove would receive a share in the restaurant, so the jury could reasonably find that there was no contract even if it believed his testimony about the promise made to him and the services that he performed in reliance on the promise. Promissory estoppel is an alternative basis to breach of contract for seeking damages from the breakdown of a relation. If there is a promise of a kind likely to induce a costly change in position by the promisee in reliance on the promise being carried out, and it does induce such a change, he can enforce the promise even though there was no contract. U.S. Oil Co. v. Midwest Auto Care Services, Inc., 150 Wis.2d 80, 440 N.W.2d 825, 828 (1989).

Buried in our capsule summary of the law of promissory estoppel is an important qualification: the reliance that makes the promise legally enforceable must be induced by a reasonable expectation that the promise will be carried out. A promise that is vague and hedged about with conditions may nevertheless have a sufficient expected value to induce a reasonable person to invest time and effort in trying to maximize the likelihood that the promise will be carried out. But if he does so knowing that he is investing for a chance, rather than relying on a firm promise that a reasonable person would expect to be carried out, he cannot plead promissory estoppel. *See* Major Mat Co. v. Monsanto Co., 969 F.2d 579, 583 (7th Cir.1992). Suppose a father tells his son that he is thinking of promising the son on his next birthday that if he gives up smoking the father will restore him as a beneficiary under his will. In an effort to make sure that he will be able to comply with this condition, the son enrolls in an expensive program for cigarette addicts. His birthday arrives, and the father does not make the promise that the son was hoping for. The son relied, and relied reasonably, on his father's statement, in enrolling in the anti-smoking program; but he was not relying on the carrying out of the promise (not yet made) of being restored as a beneficiary of his father's will, and therefore he has no claim of promissory estoppel. Or suppose a contractor told a subcontractor that it was thinking of hiring him for a job but wouldn't consider him unless the subcontractor had more minority workers in his employ, and the subcontractor goes out and hires some, and, as before, the contractor does not hire him. Again there would be no basis for a claim of promissory estoppel.

The defendants argue that this was such a case. But the jury was entitled to conclude differently. Bartolotta was quite definite in promising Cosgrove an ownership interest in the restaurant, though at first the size of the interest was uncertain. Bartolotta specified no contingencies that might defeat the promise. A reasonable jury could find that Cosgrove invested time and effort in the venture, and pledged to make a $100,000 loan, not because he hoped that this would induce Bartolotta to give him a share in the new company but because he thought he had already been firmly promised a share, contingent only on his honoring his pledge (if called on to do so) and providing business and legal advice as needed—all of which he did or was prepared to do.

A more difficult question is whether Cosgrove actually relied on the promise. It is dangerous to take a legal term in its lay sense. To "rely," in the law of promissory estoppel, is not merely to do something in response to the inducement offered by the promise. There must be a cost to the promisee of doing it. Hoffman v. Red Owl Stores, Inc., 26 Wis.2d 683, 133 N.W.2d 267, 275 (1965). The pledge of $100,000 was not shown to be a cost to Cosgrove. He never actually made the loan, and there is no evidence that the making of the pledge imposed an out-of-pocket cost, as it would have done if, for example, he had had to pay a capital-gains tax in order to obtain cash needed to make the loan if asked to do so. One could not even be certain that the personal services which Cosgrove rendered to Bartolotta cost him something without knowing what the alternative uses of his time were. If he performed these services in his spare time—time for which he had no valuable professional or even leisure use—the cost to him of performing the services for Bartolotta may have been so slight as not to count as reliance for purposes of promissory estoppel doctrine. But this is hardly plausible; Cosgrove was a professional rendering professional services. And, if nothing else, the pledge put Cosgrove at risk, since he would have been bound—by the very doctrine of promissory estoppel that he invokes—had Bartolotta relied, and since, as the subsequent course of events proved, Bartolotta was likely to enforce the pledge only if he couldn't get better terms elsewhere, which would be a sign that the venture might be riskier than it had appeared to be originally. ...

The defendants appeal from the part of the judgment that awarded damages for misrepresentation and unjust enrichment. The evidence that Bartolotta misrepresented a present fact—his state of mind when he made the promise—was sufficient to support the jury's verdict. So was the evidence that Cosgrove conferred on Bartolotta a benefit (the pledge of the loan, which was instrumental in enabling Bartolotta to line up bank financing, along with Cosgrove's business and legal advice) for which Cosgrove was entitled to be compensated. When one person confers a benefit on another in circumstances in which the benefactor reasonably believes that he will be paid—that is, when the benefit is not rendered gratuitously, as by an officious intermeddler, or donatively, as by an altruist or friend or relative—then he is entitled to demand the restitution of the market value of the benefit if the recipient refuses to pay. Ramsey v. Ellis, 168 Wis.2d 779, 484 N.W.2d 331, 333–34 (1992). That describes the present case. The jury could and did find that Cosgrove conferred benefits on Bartolotta in reliance on being compensated by the receipt of an ownership interest in the restaurant.

Where, however, the plaintiff has a good claim for either breach of contract or, as in this case, promissory estoppel, restitution is not really an alternative theory of liability, but an alternative method of computing damages. Should it turn out to be too difficult to value the restaurant business or to determine just how large an ownership interest in it Cosgrove had been promised or even to determine what it cost him in opportunities forgone to render these services, the value of the services that he rendered was available as an alternative measure of damages— alternative to either the opportunity or other costs to Cosgrove of the services that he rendered (the reliance measure of damages) or the value of Bartolotta's promise to him (the expectation measure of damages).

This assumes that you can get an award of expectation damages on a claim of promissory estoppel in Wisconsin, and apparently you can, *see*

Kramer v. Alpine Valley Resort, Inc., 108 Wis.2d 417, 321 N.W.2d 293, 294 (1982), although we said you couldn't in Werner v. Xerox Corp., 732 F.2d 580, 585 (7th Cir.1984). That is of no importance here; what is important is that alternative and cumulative are not synonyms and that it was triple counting for the jury to give Cosgrove the value of the promised interest in the restaurant and the loss that he suffered as a result of Bartolotta's misrepresentation and the value of the services that he rendered to Bartolotta. All that Cosgrove sought was an award of compensatory damages, which is to say an award that would put him in the position that he would have occupied had the defendant not committed wrongful acts. Where Cosgrove would be had Bartolotta carried out his promise would be owning a chunk of Bartolotta's business, a chunk the jury valued at $117,000, presumably taking into account the risk of Cosgrove's losing his $100,000 loan should the business sour (the restaurant business is highly risky). He would not also have been paid $17,000 for services rendered or $1,000 as a kind of "kill fee" (we don't know what other sense to make of this part of the jury's award), for the ownership share was to be the full compensation for his services. So the damages awarded by the jury were excessive, but as the defendants do not object to the verdict on this ground, the point is waived.

To summarize, the judgment is affirmed in part and reversed in part with directions to reinstate the original judgment. . . .

PROBLEMS

1. The Coors Brewing Company decided to market its product in Missouri where it had previously refrained from marketing. It publicly solicited applicants for distributorships, dividing the state into districts. Plaintiff was one of thirty-five applicants for District No. 10. He was the only such applicant selected for an in-house interview. Coors determined that none of the applicants was satisfactory and took over distribution in District No. 10 through a subsidiary. About a year later Coors awarded the distributorship to a company that was not one of the original thirty-five applicants. Plaintiff seeks to prove that he relied on obtaining the distributorship at a heavy cost to himself. Has Plaintiff stated a case?

2. Father (F) promised to give his daughter (D) $17,000 so she could buy a two-family house. She would live in one apartment and he in the other. In reliance on the promise, D paid $2,000 of her own money for an option on a suitable house. F died and his executor refuses to pay the $17,000 promised. What result?

3. Plaintiff (P) is the father of H. P had placed his son (H) and his daughter-in-law (W) in possession of a lot of land and told them that it was theirs as long as they lived. Thereupon H and W kept possession of the land, cleared the property and made some other improvements upon it. P brought an action in ejectment. The answer set up a claim for specific performance. What result?

4. Would the result in Kirksey v. Kirksey on p. 180 be different if the doctrine of promissory estoppel had been applied by the court?

5. At the request of B, a bank, D gave the bank a note in the sum of $350,000. At the same time B gave D a written statement to the effect that D would not be held liable on the note. The note, however, was treated on B's books as an asset of the bank and was shown to bank examiners. The bank became bankrupt. Can the bank's liquidators enforce the note against D?

6. Employer delivered to employee a certificate which stated that, if the employee died while still an employee, his beneficiary would receive a lump sum payment of $10,000. The certificate further provided that it was purely voluntary and gratuitous and could be withdrawn or discontinued by employer at any time. Employee worked for employer for 20 years and died while he was still an employee. Must employer pay the death benefit?

7. B, a Bank, lent O $25,000, secured by a mortgage on O's home. Although the loan agreement required O to carry insurance, O eventually let her home-owners' policy expire. O then received a letter suggesting that in case of O's failure to obtain a new policy, B might be "forced" to acquire insurance, adding the premium to O's balance. O alleges a follow-up phone call asserting that B would obtain the insurance if O did not, and would add its cost to the balance of the mortgage; O responded, "Go ahead." B acquired insurance and added the premiums to O's balance, but later elected to let the new policy lapse. O denies receiving notice from B that the policy had lapsed, claiming to have relied upon B's promise. When the home was destroyed by fire, O sued B for breach of a promise to obtain insurance. Can O make out a case for promissory estoppel?

EXAMINATION PROBLEMS

In solving these problems consider relevant material in the Offer and Acceptance, Consideration, and Promissory Estoppel chapters.

I.

The Deadbeat (hereafter "Group") is a rock music group. Hot Sound, Inc., is a nationally known recording company (hereafter "Company"). The parties signed a written agreement under which Group agreed to record exclusively for Company for a five-year period and to record a specified minimum number of records. Company agreed to pay specified royalties on the sale of records and on the sale of sheet music for any songs composed by Group. The instrument also contained the following provision:

> Company is not obligated to make or sell records manufactured from any master recordings made hereunder or to have Group record any minimum number of record sides. The decision to publish sheet music or other printed editions of any musical composition shall be entirely within the discretion of Company.

Pursuant to the terms of the agreement, at the time of signing Company's president handed Group a check for $1,000 with the notation "non-refundable advance against royalties."

During the 21 months that followed, Group made 4 single recordings and two albums, one of which eventually received a gold record for one million dollars in sales. But during those 21 months, Group was in need of money to pay for recording sessions, traveling expenses, back income taxes and to settle a litigation against them. Company, without obligation to do so, gave Group a total of $80,000 advances against royalties to cover these expenses.

At the end of 24 months, Group signed a contract with a rival recording company.

What issues will arise in Company's action against Group?

II.

On July 1, Ben E. Factor sent a letter to O. Byer, that read as follows:

Dear Mr. Byer:

I hereby offer to sell you Greenacre for $600,000, closing on or prior to December 31. The price includes a few of my fine thoroughbred horses that are pasturing there. We can work out which ones at the time of closing. Indicate your acceptance by signing and returning a copy of this letter.

Sincerely,

/s/ Ben E. Factor

On November 10, Factor, after being told about the great charitable work the Plutonian Church was doing and having been advised by his tax lawyer that he should make some charitable donations prior to the end of the year, wrote to Reverend F. Tuck, the head of the Church, the following:

Dear Reverend Tuck:

In consideration of the tremendous work the Plutonian Church has done with the poor and to enable the Church to continue to do its great work with the poor, I promise to convey Greenacre to the Church on or prior to December 31.

Sincerely,

/s/ Ben E. Factor

On November 13, an article about Factor's donation appeared in the *National Enquiry*, offered for sale in supermarkets, and Byer read it. While he had not intended to accept the July 1 offer anyway, (the property was not worth the asking price), Byer was infuriated that Factor had not conferred with him prior to the donation. His only thought was that of showing Factor that he couldn't kick Byer around and get away with it. Accordingly, he quickly faxed the following:

I HEREBY ACCEPT YOUR OFFER OF JULY 1 AND EXPECT STRICT ADHERENCE TO THE TERMS OF OUR DEAL. PUT YOUR LAWYERS IN TOUCH WITH ME TO PUT TOGETHER A WRITTEN CONTRACT.

/s/ O. Byer

Byer's intent in sending the fax was simply to scare Factor into paying money to extricate himself from a so-called agreement that Byer believed Factor couldn't perform. He planned to settle his claim against Factor for a modest sum, in the neighborhood of $1,000.

Factor had, in fact, forgotten about the July 1 offer made to Byer and, when he received Byer's fax, felt morally bound to go through with the sale to Byer. Accordingly, on November 14, he telephoned Reverend Tuck at the monastery to tell Tuck about the problem, and suggested a cash gift of $400,000 instead of a gift of Greenacre. Tuck was disappointed, but was not about to express disappointment to Factor. Instead, he agreed to the change, feigned gratitude, and thanked Factor for his kindness. The next day, (November 15), Factor wrote Tuck as follows:

Dear Reverend Tuck:

> In accordance with my letter of November 10 and our discussion yesterday, I hereby promise to pay the Plutonian Church $400,000 on or prior to December 31.

Sincerely,

/s/ Ben E. Factor

On receiving the November 15 letter, Tuck immediately purchased on credit a new stereo system for the monastery ($3,000) and a new Mercedes Benz ($50,000) so that the clergy of the Church could finally travel in style.

After Factor had written to Tuck on November 15, he called his lawyer on November 17, and told her to contact Byer and get moving on the sale of the property. She immediately called Byer and said:

> I'm glad to hear that my client has a deal with you. Let's get the draft of a formal agreement together so we can iron out the bumps before the end of the year.

Byer was startled by the call and told Factor's lawyer that the November 13 "acceptance" was a joke which anyone would have known because news of the donation of the property was "public." He concluded by saying that under no circumstances was he going through with the sale.

Factor's lawyer reported the conversation to her client. Factor was furious because he was going to make the $400,000 gift out of the proceeds of the sale of the property. He immediately telephoned Reverend Tuck to advise him that he could not make the gift by the end of the year because some other pressures had come up. Pleading for reconsideration, Tuck referred to purchases already made by the Church. Responding to Factor's questions, Tuck explained the nature of the purchases. Factor expressed his displeasure with the Church and, before hanging up, Factor said, "You'll have to sue to get a cent out of me."

What are the rights of the parties? Discuss all the contracts issues raised by this statement of facts although some may be resolved by subsequent events.

III.

A MODEL ANSWER TO THIS QUESTION IS IN APPENDIX C, ENTITLED "THE PLUMBER AND HIS SUPPLIERS"

B, a plumbing contractor, received a spring catalog from S, a plumbing supplier. S distributed a new catalog quarterly. B wrote to S as follows:

I see from your catalog that prices have gone up again. You know that we have always bought a lot from you. Right now I am preparing a number of bids, and I would like a favor. Will you promise me that I can buy what I want for the rest of this year at the prices in this spring catalog?

S wrote in reply:

"You are a most valued customer. We will give you the price protection you seek for the rest of the year. Naturally, however, we insist that you agree to buy all your plumbing supplies from us during this period."

B wrote in reply:

Thanks for your cooperation. I agree with what you insist on. Of course we have to be flexible though. Sometimes contract specifications call for brand names you don't handle and sometimes when we're in a rush we've got to buy from a local guy. Other special situations sometimes pop up. Like a plumber named Jones is going to jail and I'm trying to buy his stuff at a good price.

This letter was not delivered for three months as the airplane carrying it crashed into Lake Ontario. It has only recently been dredged up.

Soon after this letter was mailed, B bought Jones' inventory of supplies for $20,000 which was paid on the spot. On the same day B was approached by C, another plumbing supplier, who told B that because of a cash shortage, he would supply B at a discount of 30% off his list prices. B, delighted at this, bid for three major plumbing subcontracts using C's list prices less 30% in calculating his costs. He was awarded all three contracts. When he placed his first order with C, C informed him that because of a change in his cash position all supplies would be sold at list price. B then placed the same order with S who informed him that the price he must pay is 10% above the spring catalog price.

Meanwhile, from his jail cell, Jones wrote to B stating:

I think I was robbed. $20,000 was much too low a price. You took advantage of me. I had to sell in a hurry and I wasn't thinking straight. The materials were worth $60,000, but if you send me another $10,000, I won't pester you none.

B wrote back that he would pay the $10,000.

Discuss all the contract problems raised by this set of facts.

CHAPTER 5

PAROL EVIDENCE AND INTERPRETATION

■ ■ ■

SECTION 1. THE PAROL EVIDENCE RULE

(Calamari & Perillo on Contracts §§ 3.1—3.8)

MITCHILL v. LATH

Court of Appeals of New York, 1928.
247 N.Y. 377, 160 N.E. 646.

ANDREWS, J. In the fall of 1923 the Laths owned a farm. This they wished to sell. Across the road, on land belonging to Lieutenant Governor Lunn, they had an ice house which they might remove. Mrs. Mitchill looked over the land with a view to its purchase. She found the ice house objectionable. Thereupon "the defendants orally promised and agreed, for and in consideration of the purchase of their farm by the plaintiff, to remove the said ice house in the spring of 1924." Relying upon this promise, she made a written contract to buy the property for $8,400, for cash and a mortgage and containing various provisions usual in such papers. Later receiving a deed, she entered into possession and has spent considerable sums in improving the property for use as a summer residence. The defendants have not fulfilled their promise as to the ice house and do not intend to do so. We are not dealing, however, with their moral delinquencies. The question before us is whether their oral agreement may be enforced in a court of equity.

This requires a discussion of the parol evidence rule—a rule of law which defines the limits of the contract to be construed. (Glackin v. Bennett, 226 Mass. 316.) It is more than a rule of evidence and oral testimony even if admitted will not control the written contract (O'Malley v. Grady, 222 Mass. 202), unless admitted without objection. (Brady v. Nally, 151 N.Y. 258.) It applies, however, to attempts to modify such a contract by parol. It does not affect a parol collateral contract distinct from and independent of the written agreement. It is, at times, troublesome to draw the line. Williston, in his work on *Contracts* (sec. 637) points out the difficulty. "Two entirely distinct contracts," he says, "each for a separate consideration may be made at the same time and will be distinct legally. Where, however, one agreement is entered into wholly or partly in consideration of the simultaneous agreement to enter into another, the transactions are necessarily bound together ... Then if one of the agreements is oral and the other is written, the problem arises whether the bond is sufficiently close to prevent proof of the oral agreement." That is the situation here. It is claimed that the defendants are called upon to do more than is required by their written contract in connection with the sale as to which it deals.

The principle may be clear, but it can be given effect by no mechanical rule. As so often happens, it is a matter of degree, for as Professor Williston also says where a contract contains several promises on each side it is not difficult to put any one of them in the form of a collateral agreement. If this were enough written contracts might always be modified by parol. Not form, but substance is the test.

In applying this test the policy of our courts is to be considered. We have believed that the purpose behind the rule was a wise one not easily to be abandoned. Notwithstanding injustice here and there, on the whole it works for good. Old precedents and principles are not to be lightly cast aside unless it is certain that they are an obstruction under present conditions. New York has been less open to arguments that would modify this particular rule, than some jurisdictions elsewhere. Thus in Eighmie v. Taylor (98 N.Y. 288) it was held that a parol warranty might not be shown although no warranties were contained in the writing.

Under our decisions before such an oral agreement as the present is received to vary the written contract at least three conditions must exist, (1) the agreement must in form be a collateral one; (2) it must not contradict express or implied provisions of the written contract; (3) it must be one that parties would not ordinarily be expected to embody in the writing; or put in another way, an inspection of the written contract, read in the light of surrounding circumstances must not indicate that the writing appears "to contain the engagements of the parties, and to define the object and measure the extent of such engagement." Or again, it must not be so clearly connected with the principal transaction as to be part and parcel of it.

The respondent does not satisfy the third of these requirements. It may be, not the second. We have a written contract for the purchase and sale of land. The buyer is to pay $8,400 in the way described. She is also to pay her portion of any rents, interest on mortgages, insurance premiums and water meter charges. She may have a survey made of the premises. On their part the sellers are to give a full covenant deed of the premises as described, or as they may be described by the surveyor if the survey is had, executed and acknowledged at their own expense; they sell the personal property on the farm and represent they own it; they agree that all amounts paid them on the contract and the expense of examining the title shall be a lien on the property; they assume the risk of loss or damage by fire until the deed is delivered; and they agree to pay the broker his commissions. Are they to do more? Or is such a claim inconsistent with these precise provisions? It could not be shown that the plaintiff was to pay $500 additional. Is it also implied that the defendants are not to do anything unexpressed in the writing?

That we need not decide. At least, however, an inspection of this contract shows a full and complete agreement, setting forth in detail the obligations of each party. On reading it one would conclude that the reciprocal obligations of the parties were fully detailed. Nor would his opinion alter if he knew the surrounding circumstances. The presence of the ice house, even the knowledge that Mrs. Mitchill thought it objectionable would not lead to the belief that a separate agreement existed with regard to it. Were such an agreement made it would seem most natural that the inquirer should find it in the contract. Collateral in form it is found to be, but it is closely related to the subject dealt with in the written agreement—so closely that we hold it may not be proved.

Where the line between the competent and the incompetent is narrow the citation of authorities is of slight use. Each represents the judgment of the court on the precise facts before it. How closely bound to the contract is the supposed collateral agreement is the decisive factor in each case. . . .

A line of cases in Massachusetts, of which Durkin v. Cobleigh (156 Mass. 108) is an example, have to do with collateral contracts made before a deed is given. But the fixed form of a deed makes it inappropriate to insert collateral agreements, however closely connected with the sale. This may be cause for an exception. Here we deal with the contract on the basis of which the deed to Mrs. Mitchill was given subsequently, and we confine ourselves to the question whether its terms may be modified. . . .

Our conclusion is that the judgment of the Appellate Division and that of the Special Term should be reversed and the complaint dismissed, with costs in all courts.

LEHMAN, J. (dissenting). I accept the general rule as formulated by Judge Andrews. I differ with him only as to its application to the facts shown in the record. The plaintiff contracted to purchase land from the defendants for an agreed price. [The] formal written agreement . . . is on its face a complete contract for the conveyance of the land. It describes the property to be conveyed. It sets forth the purchase price to be paid. All the conditions and terms of the conveyance to be made are clearly stated. I concede at the outset that parol evidence to show additional conditions and terms of the conveyance would be inadmissible. . . .

The parol agreement which the court below found the parties had made was collateral to, yet connected with, the agreement of purchase and sale. It has been found that the defendants induced the plaintiff to agree to purchase the land by a promise to remove an ice house from land not covered by the agreement of purchase and sale. No independent consideration passed to the defendants for the parol promise. To that extent the written contract and the alleged oral contract are bound together. The same bond usually exists wherever attempt is made to prove a parol agreement which is collateral to a written agreement. Hence "the problem arises whether the bond is sufficiently close to prevent proof of the oral agreement." *See* Judge Andrews' citation from *Williston on Contracts*, section 637.

Judge Andrews has formulated a standard to measure the closeness of the bond. Three conditions, at least, must exist before an oral agreement may be proven to increase the obligation imposed by the written agreement. I think we agree that the first condition that the agreement "must in form be a collateral one" is met by the evidence. I concede that this condition is met in most cases where the courts have nevertheless excluded evidence of the collateral oral agreement. The difficulty here, as in most cases, arises in connection with the two other conditions.

The second condition is that the "parol agreement must not contradict express or implied provisions of the written contract." Judge Andrews voices doubt whether this condition is satisfied. The written contract has been carried out. The purchase price has been paid; conveyance has been made, title has passed in accordance with the terms of the written contract. The mutual obligations expressed in the written contract are left unchanged by the alleged oral contract. When performance was required of the written contract, the obligations of the parties were measured solely by its terms. By the oral agreement the plaintiff seeks to hold the defendants to other obligations to be performed by them thereafter upon land which was not conveyed to the plaintiff. The assertion of such further obligation is not inconsistent with the written contract unless the written contract contains a provision, express or implied, that the defendants are not to do anything not expressed in the writing. Concededly there is no such express provision in the contract, and such a provision may be implied, if at all, only if the asserted additional obligation is "so clearly connected with the principal transaction as to be part and parcel of it," and is not "one that the parties would not ordinarily be expected to embody in the writing." The hypothesis so formulated for a conclusion that the asserted additional obligation is inconsistent with an implied term of the contract is that the alleged oral agreement does not comply with the third condition as formulated by Judge Andrews. In this case, therefore, the problem reduces itself to the one question whether or not the oral agreement meets the third condition.

I have conceded that upon inspection the contract is complete. "It appears to contain the engagements of the parties, and to define the object and measure the extent of such engagement;" it constitutes the contract between them and is presumed to contain the whole of that contract. (Eighmie v. Taylor, 98 N.Y. 288.) That engagement was on the one side to convey land; on the other to pay the price. The plaintiff asserts further agreement based on the same consideration to be performed by the defendants after the conveyance was complete, and directly affecting only other land. It is true, as Judge Andrews points out, that "the presence of the ice house, even the knowledge that Mrs. Mitchill thought it objectionable, would not lead to the belief that a separate agreement existed with regard to it;" but the question we must decide is whether or not, *assuming* an agreement was made for the removal of an unsightly ice house from one parcel of land as an inducement for the purchase of another parcel, the parties would ordinarily or naturally be expected to embody the agreement for the removal of the ice house from one parcel in the written agreement to convey the other parcel. Exclusion of proof of the oral agreement on the ground that it varies the contract embodied in the writing may be based only upon a finding or presumption that the written contract was intended to cover the oral negotiations for the removal of the ice house which lead up to the contract of purchase and sale. To determine what the writing was intended to cover "the document alone will not suffice. What it was intended to cover cannot be known till we know what there was to cover. The question being whether certain subjects of negotiation were intended to be covered, we must compare the writing and the negotiations before we can determine whether they were in fact covered." (*Wigmore on Evidence* (2d ed.), section 2430.)

The subject-matter of the written contract was the conveyance of land. The contract was so complete on its face that the conclusion is inevitable that the parties intended to embody in the writing all the negotiations covering at least the conveyance. The promise by the defendants to remove the ice house from other land was not connected with their obligation to convey, except that one agreement would not have been made unless the other was also made. The plaintiff's assertion of a parol agreement by the defendants to remove the ice house was completely established by the great weight of evidence. It must prevail unless that agreement was part of the agreement to convey and the entire agreement was embodied in the writing.

The fact that in this case the parol agreement is established by the overwhelming weight of evidence is, of course, not a factor which may be considered in determining the competency or legal effect of the evidence. Hardship in the particular case would not justify the court in disregarding or emasculating the general rule. It merely accentuates the outlines of our problem. The assumption that the parol agreement was made is no longer obscured by any doubts. The problem then is clearly whether the parties are presumed to have intended to render that parol agreement legally ineffective and non-existent by failure to embody it in the writing. Though we are driven to say that nothing in the written contract which fixed the terms and conditions of the stipulated conveyance suggests the existence of any further parol agreement, an inspection of the contract, though it is complete on its face in regard to the subject of the conveyance, does not, I think, show that it was intended to embody negotiations or agreements, if any, in regard to a matter so loosely bound to the conveyance as the removal of an ice house from land not conveyed.

The rule of integration undoubtedly frequently prevents the assertion of fraudulent claims. Parties who take the precaution of embodying their oral agreements in a writing should be protected against the assertion that other terms of the same agreement were not integrated in the writing. The limits of the integration are determined by the writing, read in the light of the surrounding circumstances. A written contract, however complete, yet covers only a limited field. I do not think that in the written contract for the conveyance of land here under consideration we can find an intention to cover a field so broad as to include prior agreements, if any such were made, to do other acts on other property after the stipulated conveyance was made.

In each case where such a problem is presented, varying factors enter into its solution. Citation of authority in this or other jurisdictions is useless, at least without minute analysis of the facts. The analysis I have made of the decisions in this State leads me to the view that the decision of the courts below is in accordance with our own authorities and should be affirmed.

CARDOZO, CH. J., POUND, KELLOGG and O'BRIEN, JJ., concur with ANDREWS, J.; LEHMAN, J., dissents in opinion in which CRANE, J., concurs.

Judgment accordingly.

LEE v. JOSEPH E. SEAGRAM & SONS, INC.

United States Court of Appeals, Second Circuit, 1977.
552 F.2d 447.

GURFEIN, CIRCUIT JUDGE: This is an appeal by defendant Joseph E. Seagram & Sons, Inc. ("Seagram") from a judgment entered by the District Court, Hon. Charles H. Tenney, upon the verdict of a jury in the amount of $407,850 in favor of the plaintiffs on a claim asserting common law breach of an oral contract. The court also denied Seagram's motion under Rule 50(b), Fed.R.Civ.P., for judgment notwithstanding the verdict. Harold S. Lee, et al. v. Joseph E. Seagram and Sons, 413 F.Supp. 693 (S.D.N.Y.1976). It had earlier denied Seagram's motion for summary judgment. The plaintiffs are Harold S. Lee (now deceased) and his two sons, Lester and Eric ("the Lees"). Jurisdiction is based on diversity of citizenship. We affirm.

The jury could have found the following. The Lees owned a 50% interest in Capitol City Liquor Company, Inc. ("Capitol City"), a wholesale liquor distributorship located in Washington, D.C. The other 50% was owned by Harold's brother, Henry D. Lee, and his nephew, Arthur Lee. Seagram is a distiller of alcoholic beverages. Capitol City carried numerous Seagram brands and a large portion of its sales were generated by Seagram lines.

The Lees and the other owners of Capitol City wanted to sell their respective interests in the business and, in May 1970, Harold Lee, the father, discussed the possible sale of Capitol City with Jack Yogman ("Yogman"), then Executive Vice President of Seagram (and now President), whom he had known for many years. Lee offered to sell Capitol City to Seagram but conditioned the offer on Seagram's agreement to relocate

Harold and his sons, the 50% owners of Capitol City, in a new distributorship of their own in a different city.

About a month later, another officer of Seagram, John Barth, an assistant to Yogman, visited the Lees and their co-owners in Washington and began negotiations for the purchase of the assets of Capitol City by Seagram on behalf of a new distributor, one Carter, who would take it over after the purchase. The purchase of the assets of Capitol City was consummated on September 30, 1970 pursuant to a written agreement. The promise to relocate the father and sons thereafter was not reduced to writing.

Harold Lee had served the Seagram organization for thirty-six years in positions of responsibility before he acquired the half interest in the Capitol City distributorship. From 1958 to 1962, he was chief executive officer of Calvert Distillers Company, a wholly-owned subsidiary. During this long period he enjoyed the friendship and confidence of the principals of Seagram.

In 1958, Harold Lee had purchased from Seagram its holdings of Capitol City stock in order to introduce his sons into the liquor distribution business, and also to satisfy Seagram's desire to have a strong and friendly distributor for Seagram products in Washington, D.C. Harold Lee and Yogman had known each other for 13 years.

The plaintiffs claimed a breach of the oral agreement to relocate Harold Lee's sons, alleging that Seagram had had opportunities to procure another distributorship for the Lees but had refused to do so. The Lees brought this action on January 18, 1972, fifteen months after the sale of the Capitol City distributorship to Seagram. They contended that they had performed their obligation by agreeing to the sale by Capitol City of its assets to Seagram, but that Seagram had failed to perform its obligation under the separate oral contract between the Lees and Seagram. The agreement which the trial court permitted the jury to find was "an oral agreement with defendant which provided that if they agreed to sell their interest in Capitol City, defendant in return, within a reasonable time, would provide the plaintiffs a Seagram distributorship whose price would require roughly an amount equal to the capital obtained by the plaintiffs for the sale of their interest in Capitol City, and which distributorship would be in a location acceptable to plaintiffs." No specific exception was taken to this portion of the charge. By its verdict for the plaintiffs, we must assume—as Seagram notes in its brief—that this is the agreement which the jury found was made before the sale of Capitol City was agreed upon. . . .

I

Judge Tenney, in a careful analysis of the application of the parol evidence rule, decided that the rule did not bar proof of the oral agreement. We agree.

The District Court, in its denial of the defendant's motion for summary judgment, treated the issue as whether the written agreement for the sale of assets was an "integrated" agreement not only of all the mutual agreements concerning the sale of Capitol City assets, but also of *all* the mutual agreements of the parties. Finding the language of the sales agreement "somewhat ambiguous," the court decided that the determination of whether the parol evidence rule applies must await the taking of evidence on the issue of whether the sales agreement was intended to be a complete and accurate integration of all of the mutual promises of the parties.

Seagram did not avail itself of this invitation. It failed to call as witnesses any of the three persons who negotiated the sales agreement on behalf of Seagram regarding the intention of the parties to integrate all mutual promises or regarding the failure of the written agreement to contain an integration clause.

Appellant contends that, as a matter of law, the oral agreement was "part and parcel" of the subject-matter of the sales contract and that failure to include it in the written contract barred proof of its existence. Mitchill v. Lath, 247 N.Y. 377, 380, 160 N.E. 646 (1928). The position of appellant, fairly stated, is that the oral agreement was either an inducing cause for the sale or was a part of the consideration for the sale, and in either case, should have been contained in the written contract. In either case, it argues that the parol evidence rule bars its admission.

Appellees maintain, on the other hand, that the oral agreement was a collateral agreement and that, since it is not contradictory of any of the terms of the sales agreement, proof of it is not barred by the parol evidence rule. Because the case comes to us after a jury verdict we must assume that there actually was an oral contract, such as the court instructed the jury it could find. The question is whether the strong policy for avoiding fraudulent claims through application of the parol evidence rule nevertheless mandates reversal on the ground that the jury should not have been permitted to hear the evidence.

The District Court stated the cardinal issue to be whether the parties "intended" the written agreement for the sale of assets to be the complete and accurate integration of all the mutual promises of the parties. If the written contract was not a complete integration, the court held, then the parol evidence rule has no application. We assume that the District Court determined intention by objective standards. *See* 3 *Corbin on Contracts* §§ 573–574. The parol evidence rule is a rule of substantive law. ...

The law of New York is not rigid or categorical, but is in harmony with this approach. As Judge Fuld said in *Fogelson*: "Decision in each case must, of course, turn upon the type of transaction involved, the scope of the written contract and the content of the oral agreement asserted. 300 N.Y. at 338, 90 N.E.2d at 883. And the Court of Appeals wrote in Ball v. Grady, 267 N.Y. 470, 472, 196 N.E. 402, 403 (1935): "In the end, the court must find the limits of the integration as best it may by reading the writing in the light of surrounding circumstances." Thus, certain oral collateral agreements, even though made contemporaneously, are not within the prohibition of the parol evidence rule "because (if) they are separate, independent, and complete contracts, although relating to the same subject ... (t)hey are allowed to be proved by parol, because they were made by parol, and no part thereof committed to writing." Thomas v. Scutt, 127 N.Y. 133, 140–41, 27 N.E. 961, 963 (1891).

Although there is New York authority which in general terms supports defendant's thesis that an oral contract inducing a written one or varying the consideration may be barred, the overarching question is whether, in the context of the particular setting, the oral agreement was one which the parties would ordinarily be expected to embody in the writing. Ball v. Grady, *supra*, 267 N.Y. at 470, 196 N.E. 402; *accord,* Fogelson v. Rackfay Constr. Co., *supra*, 300 N.Y. at 338, 90 N.E.2d 881. *See Restatement on Contracts* § 240. For example, integration is most easily inferred in the case of real estate contracts for the sale of land, *e.g.,* Mitchill v. Lath, *supra*, 247 N.Y. 377, 160 N.E. 646, or leases, *Fogelson, supra*. In more complex situations, in which customary business practice may be more varied, an oral agreement can be treated as separate and independent of the written agreement even though the written contract contains a strong integration clause. *See* Gem Corrugated Box Corp. v. National Kraft Container Corp., 427 F.2d 499, 503 (2d Cir.1970).

Thus, as we see it, the issue is whether the oral promise to the plaintiffs, as individuals, would be an expectable term of the contract for the sale of assets by a corporation in which plaintiffs have only a 50% interest, considering as well the history of their relationship to Seagram.

Here, there are several reasons why it would *not* be expected that the oral agreement to give Harold Lee's sons another distributorship would be integrated into the sales contract. In the usual case, there is an identity of parties in both the claimed integrated instrument and in the oral agreement asserted. Here, although it would have been physically possible to insert a provision dealing with only the shareholders of a 50% interest, the transaction itself was a *corporate* sale of assets. Collateral agreements which survive the closing of a corporate deal, such as employment agreements for particular shareholders of the seller or consulting agreements, are often set forth in separate agreements. *See* Gem Corrugated Box Corp. v. National Kraft Container Corp., *supra*, 427 F.2d at 503 ("it is ... plain that the parties ordinarily would not embody the stock purchase agreement in a writing concerned only with box materials purchase terms"). It was expectable that such an agreement as one to obtain a new distributorship for certain persons, some of whom were not even parties to the contract, would not necessarily be integrated into an instrument for the sale of *corporate* assets. As with an oral condition precedent to the legal effectiveness of an otherwise integrated written contract, which is not barred by the parol evidence rule if it is not directly contradictory of its terms, Hicks v. Bush, 10 N.Y.2d 488, 225 N.Y.S.2d 34, 180 N.E.2d 425 (1962); *cf.* 3 *Corbin on Contracts* § 589, "it is certainly not improbable that parties contracting in these circumstances would make the asserted oral agreement. . . ." 10 N.Y.2d at 493, 225 N.Y.S.2d at 39, 180 N.E.2d at 428.

Similarly, it is significant that there was a close relationship of confidence and friendship over many years between two old men, Harold Lee and Yogman, whose authority to bind Seagram has not been questioned. It would not be surprising that a handshake for the benefit of Harold's sons would have been thought sufficient. In point, as well, is the circumstance that the negotiations concerning the provisions of the sales agreement were not conducted by Yogman but by three other Seagram representatives, headed by John Barth. The two transactions may not have been integrated in their minds when the contract was drafted.[4]

Finally, the written agreement does not contain the customary integration clause, even though a good part of it (relating to warranties and negative covenants) is boilerplate. The omission may, of course, have been caused by mutual trust and confidence, but in any event, there is not such strong presumption of exclusion because of the existence of a detailed integration clause, as was relied upon by the Court of Appeals in Fogelson, *supra*, 300 N.Y. at 340, 90 N.E.2d 881.

Nor do we see any contradiction of the terms of the sales agreement. Mitchill v. Lath, *supra*, 247 N.Y. at 381, 160 N.E. 646; 3 *Corbin on Contracts* § 573, at 357. The written agreement dealt with the sale of corporate assets, the oral agreement with the relocation of the Lees. Thus, the oral agreement does not vary or contradict the money consideration recited in the contract as flowing to the selling corporation. That is the only consideration recited, and it is still the only consideration to the corporation.

We affirm Judge Tenney's reception in evidence of the oral agreement and his denial of the motion under Rule 50(b) with respect to the parol evidence rule. . . .

Affirmed.

GEORGE v. DAVOLI
City Court, City of Geneva, N.Y., 1977.
91 Misc.2d 296, 397 N.Y.S.2d 895.

DAVID H. BRIND, JUDGE. At the trial of this matter the Defendant was called by the Plaintiff as his only witness. The Plaintiff's attendance was waived by his attorney and he did not testify. The gravamen of this action revolves about a sale of certain jewelry on approval. A memorandum of sale was submitted to the Court which was signed by both the Plaintiff and the Defendant. The Memorandum stated that the Plaintiff was

---

4. Barth in a confidential memorandum dated June 12, 1970 to Yogman and Edgar Bronfman stated that "he (Harold Lee) would very much like to have another distributorship in another area for his two sons." Apparently Barth, who was not present at Harold Lee's meeting with Yogman, assumed that this was a desire on the part of Lee rather than a promise made by Yogman for Seagram.

purchasing certain Indian jewelry for the sum of $500.00, but if the jewelry were not acceptable, the seller would accept its return and refund $440.00 of the purchase price to the buyer. The memorandum in question is silent as to the time within which such jewelry had to be returned by the buyer to the seller.

The court allowed the Defendant, over the objection of Plaintiff's counsel, to testify to a contemporaneous oral agreement between the buyer and seller to the effect that the jewelry had to be returned by the following Monday evening, or the sale would be deemed completed. The Plaintiff did not contact the Defendant until the following Wednesday of the same week, two days after the orally agreed upon deadline. The Plaintiff at that time tendered the return of the jewelry stating that they were not acceptable and demanded the return of $440.00 of his purchase price. The Defendant refused to accept the jewelry or to return the money, stating the sale had been completed in accordance with the agreement.

The law of this case is governed by the Uniform Commercial Code of the State of New York. ...

There is no question that under the Uniform Commercial Code that *unless [otherwise] agreed upon*, the goods must be returned "seasonably" (UCC 2–326 and 2–327). Returning the merchandise within one week as is the situation in the present case would ordinarily be seasonable or within a reasonable time. However, where there is an agreement setting forth a specific time limit, the Court is bound to enforce such limit.

Section 2–202 of UCC compels a court to allow oral testimony supplementing the written agreement where not inconsistent and where the writing is not intended as a complete and exclusive statement of the terms of the agreement. The court finds the absence of an agreed upon time limit, that type of omission which comes within the area provided for in this statute. There is nothing inconsistent with the Defendant's testimony inasmuch as the written memorandum makes no reference to the time of return of the merchandise. Likewise it cannot be said that the written memorandum is a complete and exclusive statement of the terms of the agreement since the time of return is an important part of the arrangement between the parties. Is it therefore such an additional term that the parties would certainly have included it in the written document if it had been agreed upon and consequently one not to be admitted on trial? The Appellate Division in Hunt Foods & Ind. v. Doliner, 26 A.D.2d 41, 270 N.Y.S.2d 937; interpreting UCC 2–202 held that under like circumstances the oral testimony must be admitted. The Court held:

> So the first question presented is whether that term is "consistent" with the instrument. In a sense any oral provision which would prevent the ripening of the obligations of a writing is inconsistent with the writing. But that obviously is not the sense in which the word is used (Hicks v. Bush, 10 N.Y.2d 488, 491, 225 N.Y.S.2d 34, 180 N.E.2d 425). To be inconsistent the term must contradict or negate a

term of the writing. *A term or condition which has a lesser effect is provable.*

The Official Comment prepared by the drafters of the code contains this statement: "If the additional terms are such that, if agreed upon, they would certainly have been included in the document in the view of the court, then evidence of their alleged making must be kept from the trier of fact." (UCC § 2–202, (cmt. 3).)

Special Term interpreted this language as not only calling for an adjudication by the court in all instances where proof of an "additional oral term" is offered, but making that determination exclusively the function of the court. We believe the proffered evidence to be *inadmissible only* where the writing contradicts the existence of the claimed additional term (Meadow Brook Nat. Bank v. Bzura, 20 A.D.2d 287, 290, 246 N.Y.S.2d 787, 790). The conversations in this case, some of which are not disputed, and the expectation of all the parties for further negotiations, suggest that the alleged oral condition precedent cannot be precluded as a matter of law or as factually impossible. It is not sufficient that the existence of the condition is implausible. *It must be impossible.* (emphasis supplied.)

Therefore, the Court finds that parol evidence as to the agreement setting forth the time within which the merchandise was to be returned if not acceptable, is admissable [*sic*] to supplement the written memorandum and further finds that Mitchill v. Lath, 247 N.Y. 377, 160 N.E. 646 decided by the Court of Appeals in 1928, cited by the Plaintiff, does not apply herein as its application to the instant case has been changed by legislative enactment (UCC § 2–202(b)) which took effect in 1964.

Since the parol evidence as to such agreement stands unrebutted, the Court must find that the Plaintiff failed to comply with the parties' agreement to the return of the goods by Monday evening, the consequence of which is that title therein passed to the Plaintiff, and the Defendant is under no legal obligation to accept the return thereof.

The complaint of the Plaintiff is hereby dismissed without costs.

VAL–FORD REALTY CORP. v. J.Z.'S TOY WORLD, INC.

N.Y. Supreme Court, Appellate Division, 1996.
231 A.D.2d 434, 647 N.Y.S.2d 488.

MEMORANDUM DECISION: Order, Supreme Court, New York County (Herman Cahn, J.), entered on or about October 26, 1995, which, insofar as appealed from, denied plaintiff's motion for summary judgment, unanimously affirmed, without costs.

Plaintiff seeks to recover rent due under a written lease executed by the corporate defendant and guaranteed by the individual defendant. Defendants admit executing these documents, but assert that their purpose was to defraud plaintiff's construction lender into advancing additional funds and were never intended by the parties to be enforceable, and that the parties are not strangers in that, among other things, the individual defendant is one of the plaintiff corporation's three directors. We agree with the motion court that this parol evidence offered by defendants raises issues of credibility inappropriate for summary judgment treatment. While parol evidence is generally inadmissible to contradict, vary, add to, or subtract from the terms of an integrated agreement such as the instant lease and guarantee, it is admissible to show that a " 'writing, although purporting to be a contract, is, in fact, no contract at all' " (Greenleaf v. Lachman, 216 A.D.2d 65, 66, 628 N.Y.S.2d 268, *lv denied* 88 N.Y.2d 802, 645 N.Y.S.2d 445, 668 N.E.2d 416, quoting *Richardson on Evidence* § 606 (Prince, 10th ed.). We have considered plaintiff's other arguments and find them to be without merit. . . .

PROBLEMS

1. A and B made an oral agreement and signed a writing that incorporated its terms. However, they were not fully satisfied with the writing and they agreed to have it redrafted. Does this writing constitute an integration?

2. P opened a T-shirt store in D's mall pursuant to a written commercial lease with D as landlord. Subsequently, D leased space in the same mall to X for another T-shirt store. P sued D for breach of P's lease. At trial P offered evidence that it had been orally agreed at the time the lease was signed that P would have the only store of its kind in the mall. The written lease had no such provision. Is P's proffered evidence admissible?

3. P applied for and received a construction loan from D in order to build a house on land owned by P. The house was built by G, a general contractor selected on the advice of D. The construction contract contained an estimated, rather than a fixed, price. P sues D for negligence with the allegation that additional costs were caused by G's incompetence. P offers evidence at trial that D orally agreed to help select the contractor, guarantee the contractor's competence and supervise construction to assure that the house would be built for the estimated price. The loan agreement contained a merger clause and also a provision that selection of a contractor was the exclusive responsibility of the borrower. Should P's evidence be excluded?

4. B entered into a written contract by which S agreed to sell B its requirements of raw material for a stated consideration. There was a merger clause in this agreement. B sues S for breach of a contemporaneous oral agreement that S would sell 7000 shares of its stock to B for an agreed price. Is evidence of this agreement admissible?

5. Defendant agreed to create customized software for plaintiff trucking company. A written contract described what the software should be designed to accomplish in terms of tracking the location of individual trucks, planning service intervals, etc. The writing contained the following provision: "There are no promises, verbal understandings or agreements of any kind pertaining to this contract other than specified herein." The instrument was dated Sept. 6. At the trial, plaintiff offered evidence that either on Sept. 5, or 7, S's general manager agreed that B might try out the software for a month and if

it did not prove satisfactory, B might delete the software from its computer and have its money back. Is plaintiff's evidence admissible?

6. X and Y exchanged correspondence and entered into a contract for the sale of goods containing terms A (subject matter), B (quantity) and C (warranty).

(a) If X sent a written confirmation within a reasonable time stating that the terms are A and B, could Y prove the existence of term C?

(b) If X's memo states that the terms are A, B and "not C (disclaimer of warranty)," could Y prove term C?

(c) If X and Y both sent memos containing terms A and B (omitting term C), could Y prove term C?

7. P had been working for D for about a year as an employee at an agreed fixed salary. Subsequently the parties signed a document which stated that P was an independent contractor. According to this writing, P was to be paid according to the work done and was to carry the necessary Workers' Compensation Insurance. P sues on the initial contract for unpaid salary and offers to testify that the second agreement was not intended to be binding. It's purpose was to enable D to avoid the Compensation Law. Is the evidence admissible?

8. H & W, a young married couple, purchased a home. W's parents made a $70,000 payment toward the purchase price. H & W signed a promissory note in this amount payable to W's parents in which they jointly and severally agreed to be liable for payment on demand. After 12 years, W brought divorce proceedings against H. W's parents demanded payment of the note from H. When he refused to pay, they sued. In defense, he offered testimony to the effect that W's parents had represented that the $70,000 was a gift, specifically, an advance on W's inheritance. Is this testimony admissible?

9. B made an offer to buy S's stock for $5.50 per share. The negotiations at this point were recessed. Since B was afraid that S would use B's offer to obtain a higher price from a third party, B requested and received from S a written option (supported by consideration) to purchase the stock at $5.50 per share. After the negotiations collapsed, B attempted to exercise the option. At the trial S offered evidence that it was orally agreed simultaneously with the granting of the option that the option was not to be exercised unless S sought outside bids for the stock. Is the evidence admissible?

SECTION 2. INTERPRETATION

(Calamari & Perillo on Contracts §§ 3.9—3.17)

PACIFIC GAS AND ELEC. CO. v. G. W. THOMAS DRAYAGE & RIGGING CO.

Supreme Court of California, In Bank, 1968.
69 Cal.2d 33, 69 Cal.Rptr. 561, 442 P.2d 641.

TRAYNOR, CHIEF JUSTICE. Defendant appeals from a judgment for plaintiff in an action for damages for injury to property under an indemnity clause of a contract.

In 1960 defendant entered into a contract with plaintiff to furnish the labor and equipment necessary to remove and replace the upper metal cover of plaintiff's steam turbine. Defendant agreed to perform the work "at (its) own risk and expense" and to "indemnify" plaintiff "against all loss, damage, expense and liability resulting from . . . injury to property, arising out of or in any way connected with the performance of this contract." Defendant also agreed to procure not less than $50,000 insurance to cover liability for injury to property. . . .

During the work the cover fell and injured the exposed rotor of the turbine. Plaintiff brought this action to recover $25,144.51, the amount it subsequently spent on repairs. During the trial it dismissed a count based on negligence and thereafter secured judgment on the theory that the indemnity provision covered injury to all property regardless of ownership.

Defendant offered to prove by admissions of plaintiff's agents, by defendant's conduct under similar contracts entered into with plaintiff, and by other proof that in the indemnity clause the parties meant to cover injury to property of third parties only and not to plaintiff's property. Although the trial court observed that the language used was "the classic language for a third party indemnity provision" and that "one could very easily conclude that . . . its whole intendment is to indemnify third parties," it nevertheless held that the "plain language" of the agreement also required defendant to indemnify plaintiff for injuries to plaintiff's property. Having determined that the contract had a plain meaning, the court refused to admit any extrinsic evidence that would contradict its interpretation.

When a court interprets a contract on this basis, it determines the meaning of the instrument in accordance with the ". . . extrinsic evidence of the judge's own linguistic education and experience." (3 *Corbin on Contracts* (1960 ed.) (1964 Supp. § 579, p. 225, fn. 56).) The exclusion of testimony that might contradict the linguistic background of the judge reflects a judicial belief in the possibility of perfect verbal expression. (9 *Wigmore on Evidence* (3d ed. 1940) § 2461, p. 187.) This belief is a remnant of a primitive faith in the inherent potency[2] and inherent meaning of words.[3]

The test of admissibility of extrinsic evidence to explain the meaning of a written instrument is not whether it appears to the court to be plain and unambiguous on its face, but whether the offered evidence is relevant

---

2. *E.g.*, "The elaborate system of taboo and verbal prohibitions in primitive groups; the ancient Egyptian myth of Khern, the apotheosis of the word, and of Thoth, the Scribe of Truth, the Giver of Words and Script, the Master of Incantations; the avoidance of the name of God in Brahmanism, Judaism and Islam; totemistic and protective names in mediaeval Turkish and Finno–Ugrian languages; the misplaced verbal scruples of the 'Précieuses'; the Swedish peasant custom of curing sick cattle smitten by witchcraft, by making them swallow a page torn out of the psalter and put in dough. . . ." from Ullman, *The Principles of Semantics* (1963 ed.) 43. (*See also* Ogden and Richards, *The Meaning of Meaning* (rev. ed. 1956) pp. 24–47.)

3. " '*Rerum enim vocabula immutabilia sunt, homines mutabilia,*' " (Words are unchangeable, men changeable) from Dig. XXXIII, 10, 7, § 2, *de sup. leg.* as quoted in 9 *Wigmore on Evidence, op. cit. supra*, § 2461, p. 187.

to prove a meaning to which the language of the instrument is reasonably susceptible. . . .

A rule that would limit the determination of the meaning of a written instrument to its four-corners merely because it seems to the court to be clear and unambiguous, would either deny the relevance of the intention of the parties or presuppose a degree of verbal precision and stability our language has not attained.

Some courts have expressed the opinion that contractual obligations are created by the mere use of certain words, whether or not there was any intention to incur such obligations.[4] Under this view, contractual obligations flow, not from the intention of the parties but from the fact that they used certain magic words. Evidence of the parties' intention therefore becomes irrelevant.

In this state, however, the intention of the parties as expressed in the contract is the source of contractual rights and duties.[5] A court must ascertain and give effect to this intention by determining what the parties meant by the words they used. Accordingly, the exclusion of relevant, extrinsic evidence to explain the meaning of a written instrument could be justified only if it were feasible to determine the meaning the parties gave to the words from the instrument alone.

If words had absolute and constant referents, it might be possible to discover contractual intention in the words themselves and in the manner in which they were arranged. Words, however, do not have absolute and constant referents. "A word is a symbol of thought but has no arbitrary and fixed meaning like a symbol of algebra or chemistry. . . ." (Pearson v. State Social Welfare Board (1960) 54 Cal.2d 184, 195, 5 Cal.Rptr. 553, 559, 353 P.2d 33, 39.) The meaning of particular words or groups of words varies with the ". . . verbal context and surrounding circumstances and purposes in view of the linguistic education and experience of their users and their hearers or readers (not excluding judges). . . . A word has no meaning apart from these factors; much less does it have an objective meaning, one true meaning." (Corbin, *The Interpretation of Words and the Parol Evidence Rule* (1965) 50 Cornell L.Q. 161, 187.) Accordingly, the meaning of a writing ". . . can only be found by interpretation in the light of all the circumstances that reveal the sense in which the writer used the words. The exclusion of parol evidence regarding such circumstances merely because the words do not appear ambiguous to the reader can easily lead to the attribution to a written instrument of a meaning that was never intended." (Universal Sales Corp. v. California Press Mfg. Co.,

---

4. "A contract has, strictly speaking, nothing to do with the personal, or individual, intent of the parties. A contract is an obligation attached by the mere force of law to certain acts of the parties, usually words, which ordinarily accompany and represent a known intent." (Hotchkiss v. National City Bank of New York (S.D.N.Y.1911) 200 F. 287, 293. *See also* C.H. Pope & Co. v. Bibb Mfg. Co. (2d Cir.1923) 290 F. 586, 587; *see* 4 *Williston on Contracts* (3d ed. 1961) § 612, pp. 577–578, § 613, p. 583.)

5. "A contract must be so interpreted as to give effect to the mutual intention of the parties as it existed at the time of contracting, so far as the same is ascertainable and lawful." (Civ.Code, § 1636; *see also* Code Civ.Proc. § 1859. . . .)

... 20 Cal.2d 751, 776, 128 P.2d 665, 679 (concurring opinion) ... 3 *Corbin on Contracts* (1960 ed.) § 579, pp. 412–431; Ogden and Richards, *The Meaning of Meaning, op. cit.* 15; Ullmann, *The Principles of Semantics, supra*, 61; McBaine, *The Rule Against Disturbing Plain Meaning of Writings* (1943) 31 Cal.L.Rev. 145.)

Although extrinsic evidence is not admissible to add to, detract from, or vary the terms of a written contract, these terms must first be determined before it can be decided whether or not extrinsic evidence is being offered for a prohibited purpose. The fact that the terms of an instrument appear clear to a judge does not preclude the possibility that the parties chose the language of the instrument to express different terms. That possibility is not limited to contracts whose terms have acquired a particular meaning by trade usage,[6] but exists whenever the parties' understanding of the words used may have differed from the judge's understanding.

Accordingly, rational interpretation requires at least a preliminary consideration of all credible evidence offered to prove the intention of the parties.[7] ... Such evidence includes testimony as to the "circumstances surrounding the making of the agreement ... including the object, nature and subject matter of the writing ..." so that the court can "place itself in the same situation in which the parties found themselves at the time of contracting." (Universal Sales Corp. v. Cal. Press Mfg. Co., *supra*, 20 Cal.2d 751, 761, 128 P.2d 665, 671.) If the court decides, after considering this evidence, that the language of a contract, in the light of all the circumstances, is "fairly susceptible of either one of the two interpretations contended for...." (Balfour v. Fresno C. & I. Co. (1895) 109 Cal. 221, 225, 41 P. 876, 877.), extrinsic evidence relevant to prove either of such meanings is admissible.[8]

In the present case the court erroneously refused to consider extrinsic evidence offered to show that the indemnity clause in the contract was not

---

6. Extrinsic evidence of trade usage or custom has been admitted to show that the term "United Kingdom" in a motion picture distribution contract included Ireland (Ermolieff v. R.K.O. Radio Pictures, Inc. (1942) 19 Cal.2d 543, 549–552, 122 P.2d 3); that the word "ton" in a lease meant a long ton or 2,240 pounds and not the statutory ton of 2,000 pounds (Higgins v. Cal. Petroleum, etc., Co. (1898) 120 Cal. 629, 630–632, 52 P. 1080); that the word "stubble" in a lease included not only stumps left in the ground but everything "left on the ground after the harvest time" (Callahan v. Stanley (1881) 57 Cal. 476, 477–479); that the term "north" in a contract dividing mining claims indicated a boundary line running along the "magnetic and not the true meridian" (Jenny Lind Co. v. Bower & Co. (1858) 11 Cal. 194, 197–199) and that a form contract for purchase and sale was actually an agency contract (Body–Steffner Co. v. Flotill Products (1944) 63 Cal.App.2d 555, 558–562, 147 P.2d 84). ...

7. When objection is made to any particular item of evidence offered to prove the intention of the parties, the trial court may not yet be in a position to determine whether in the light of all of the offered evidence, the item objected to will turn out to be admissible as tending to prove a meaning of which the language of the instrument is reasonably susceptible or inadmissible as tending to prove a meaning of which the language is not reasonably susceptible. In such case the court may admit the evidence conditionally by either reserving its ruling on the objection or by admitting the evidence subject to a motion to strike. ...

8. Extrinsic evidence has often been admitted in such cases on the stated ground that the contract was ambiguous.... This statement of the rule is harmless if it is kept in mind that the ambiguity may be exposed by extrinsic evidence that reveals more than one possible meaning.

intended to cover injuries to plaintiff's property. Although that evidence was not necessary to show that the indemnity clause was reasonably susceptible of the meaning contended for by defendant, it was nevertheless relevant and admissible on that issue. Moreover, since that clause was reasonably susceptible of that meaning, the offered evidence was also admissible to prove that the clause had that meaning and did not cover injuries to plaintiff's property.[9] Accordingly, the judgment must be reversed. . . .

TRIDENT CENTER v. CONNECTICUT GENERAL LIFE INSURANCE CO.

United States Court of Appeals, Ninth Circuit, 1988.
847 F.2d 564.

KOZINSKI, CIRCUIT JUDGE: The parties to this transaction are, by any standard, highly sophisticated business people: Plaintiff is a partnership consisting of an insurance company and two of Los Angeles' largest and most prestigious law firms; defendant is another insurance company. Dealing at arm's length and from positions of roughly equal bargaining strength, they negotiated a commercial loan amounting to more than $56 million. The contract documents are lengthy and detailed; they squarely address the precise issue that is the subject of this dispute; to all who read English, they appear to resolve the issue fully and conclusively.

Plaintiff nevertheless argues here, as it did below, that it is entitled to introduce extrinsic evidence that the contract means something other than what it says. This case therefore presents the question whether parties in California can ever draft a contract that is proof to parol evidence. Somewhat surprisingly, the answer is no.

Facts

The facts are rather simple. Sometime in 1983 Security First Life Insurance Company and the law firms of Mitchell, Silberberg & Knupp

---

9. The court's exclusion of extrinsic evidence in this case would be error even under a rule that excluded such evidence when the instrument appeared to the court to be clear and unambiguous on its face. The controversy centers on the meaning of the word "indemnify" and the phrase "all loss, damage, expense and liability." The trial court's recognition of the language as typical of a third party indemnity clause and the double sense in which the word "indemnify" is used in statutes and defined in dictionaries demonstrate the existence of an ambiguity. . . .

Plaintiff's assertion that the use of the word "all" to modify "loss, damage, expense and liability" dictates an all inclusive interpretation is not persuasive. If the word "indemnify" encompasses only third-party claims, the word "all" simply refers to all such claims. The use of the words "loss," "damage," and "expense" in addition to the word "liability" is likewise inconclusive. These words do not imply an agreement to reimburse for injury to an indemnitee's property since they are commonly inserted in third-party indemnity clauses, to enable an indemnitee who settles a claim to recover from his indemnitor without proving his liability. . . .

The provision that defendant perform the work "at his own risk and expense" and the provisions relating to insurance are equally inconclusive. By agreeing to work at its own risk defendant may have released plaintiff from liability for any injuries to defendant's property arising out of the contract's performance, but this provision did not necessarily make defendant an insurer against injuries to plaintiff's property. Defendant's agreement to procure liability insurance to cover damages to plaintiff's property does not indicate whether the insurance was to cover all injuries or only injuries caused by defendant's negligence.

and Manatt, Phelps, Rothenberg & Tunney formed a limited partnership for the purpose of constructing an office building complex on Olympic Boulevard in West Los Angeles. The partnership, Trident Center, the plaintiff herein, sought and obtained financing for the project from defendant, Connecticut General Life Insurance Company. The loan documents provide for a loan of $56,500,000 at 12¼ percent interest for a term of 15 years, secured by a deed of trust on the project. The promissory note provides that "(m)aker shall not have the right to prepay the principal amount hereof in whole or in part" for the first 12 years. . . . In years 13–15, the loan may be prepaid, subject to a sliding prepayment fee. The note also provides that in case of a default during years 1–12, Connecticut General has the option of accelerating the note and adding a 10 percent prepayment fee.

Everything was copacetic for a few years until interest rates began to drop. The 12¼ percent rate that had seemed reasonable in 1983 compared unfavorably with 1987 market rates and Trident started looking for ways of refinancing the loan to take advantage of the lower rates. Connecticut General was unwilling to oblige, insisting that the loan could not be prepaid for the first 12 years of its life, that is, until January 1996.

Trident then brought suit in state court seeking a declaration that it was entitled to prepay the loan now, subject only to a 10 percent prepayment fee. Connecticut General promptly removed to federal court and brought a motion to dismiss, claiming that the loan documents clearly and unambiguously precluded prepayment during the first 12 years. The district court agreed and dismissed Trident's complaint. The court also "*sua sponte,* sanction(ed) the plaintiff for the filing of a frivolous lawsuit." Order of Dismissal, No. CV 87–2712 JMI (Kx), at 3 (C.D.Cal. June 8, 1987). Trident appeals both aspects of the district court's ruling.

Discussion

I

Trident makes two arguments as to why the district court's ruling is wrong. First, it contends that the language of the contract is ambiguous and proffers a construction that it believes supports its position. Second, Trident argues that, under California law, even seemingly unambiguous contracts are subject to modification by parol or extrinsic evidence. Trident faults the district court for denying it the opportunity to present evidence that the contract language did not accurately reflect the parties' intentions.

A. The Contract

As noted earlier, the promissory note provides that Trident "shall not have the right to prepay the principal amount hereof in whole or in part before January 1996." . . . It is difficult to imagine language that more clearly or unambiguously expresses the idea that Trident may not unilaterally prepay the loan during its first 12 years. Trident, however, argues that there is an ambiguity because another clause of the note provides that "(i)n the event of a prepayment resulting from a default hereunder or the Deed of Trust prior to January 10, 1996 the prepayment fee will be ten percent (10%)." ... Trident interprets this clause as giving it the option of prepaying the loan if only it is willing to incur the prepayment fee.

We reject Trident's argument out of hand. In the first place, its proffered interpretation would result in a contradiction between two clauses of the contract; the default clause would swallow up the clause prohibiting Trident from prepaying during the first 12 years of the contract. The normal rule of construction, of course, is that courts must interpret contracts, if possible, so as to avoid internal conflict. *See* ... 4 S. Williston, *A Treatise on the Law of Contracts* § 618, at 714–15 (3d ed. 1961); *id.* § 624, at 825.

In any event, the clause on which Trident relies is not on its face reasonably susceptible to Trident's proffered interpretation. Whether to accelerate repayment of the loan in the event of default is entirely Connecticut General's decision. The contract makes this clear at several points. ...("in each such event (of default), the entire principal indebtedness, or so much thereof as may remain unpaid at the time, shall, *at the option of Holder,* become due and payable immediately" (emphasis added)); ... ("(i)n the event Holder exercises its *option to accelerate* the maturity hereof ..." (emphasis added)); ... ("in each such event (of default), Beneficiary *may* declare all sums secured hereby immediately due and payable ..." (emphasis added)). Even if Connecticut General decides to declare a default and accelerate, it "may rescind any notice of breach or default." ... Finally, Connecticut General has the option of doing nothing at all: "Beneficiary reserves the right at its sole option to waive noncompliance by Trustor with any of the conditions or covenants to be performed by Trustor hereunder." ...

Once again, it is difficult to imagine language that could more clearly assign to Connecticut General the exclusive right to decide whether to declare a default, whether and when to accelerate, and whether, having chosen to take advantage of any of its remedies, to rescind the process before its completion.

Trident nevertheless argues that it is entitled to precipitate a default and insist on acceleration by tendering the balance due on the note plus the 10 percent prepayment fee. The contract language, cited above, leaves no room for this construction. It is true, of course, that Trident is free to stop making payments, which may then cause Connecticut General to declare a default and accelerate. But that is not to say that Connecticut General would be required to so respond.[2] The contract quite clearly gives

---

2. *See* 1 H. Miller & M. Starr, *Current Law of California Real Estate* § 3:62, at 428 ("(w)hen there is a default, acceleration does not occur automatically. It is merely a contractual *option* given to beneficiary for his benefit, and acceleration only occurs when the beneficiary *affirmatively* elects to declare the balance of the principal and interest due" (emphasis original)); *id.* § 3:69, at 449.

Connecticut General other options: It may choose to waive the default, or to take advantage of some other remedy such as the right to collect "all the income, rents, royalties, revenue, issues, profits, and proceeds of the Property." ... By interpreting the contract as Trident suggests, we would ignore those provisions giving Connecticut General, not Trident, the exclusive right to decide how, when and whether the contract will be terminated upon default during the first 12 years.

In effect, Trident is attempting to obtain judicial sterilization of its intended default. But defaults are messy things; they are supposed to be. Once the maker of a note secured by a deed of trust defaults, its credit rating may deteriorate; attempts at favorable refinancing may be thwarted by the need to meet the trustee's sale schedule; its cash flow may be impaired if the beneficiary takes advantage of the assignment of rents remedy; default provisions in its loan agreements with other lenders may be triggered. Fear of these repercussions is strong medicine that keeps debtors from shirking their obligations when interest rates go down and they become disenchanted with their loans.[4] That Trident is willing to suffer the cost and delay of a lawsuit, rather than simply defaulting, shows far better than anything we might say that these provisions are having their intended effect. We decline Trident's invitation to truncate the lender's remedies and deprive Connecticut General of its bargained-for protection.

B. *Extrinsic Evidence*

Trident argues in the alternative that, even if the language of the contract appears to be unambiguous, the deal the parties actually struck is in fact quite different. It wishes to offer extrinsic evidence that the parties had agreed Trident could prepay at any time within the first 12 years by tendering the full amount plus a 10 percent prepayment fee. As discussed above, this is an interpretation to which the contract, as written, is not reasonably susceptible. Under traditional contract principles, extrinsic evidence is inadmissible to interpret, vary or add to the terms of an unambiguous integrated written instrument. *See 4 S. Williston, supra* p. 5, § 631, at 948–49....

Trident points out, however, that California does not follow the traditional rule. Two decades ago the California Supreme Court in Pacific Gas & Electric Co. v. G.W. Thomas Drayage & Rigging Co., 69 Cal.2d 33, 442 P.2d 641, 69 Cal.Rptr. 561 (1968), turned its back on the notion that a contract can ever have a plain meaning discernible by a court without resort to extrinsic evidence. The court reasoned that contractual obligations flow not from the words of the contract, but from the intention of the parties. "Accordingly," the court stated, "the exclusion of relevant, extrinsic, evidence to explain the meaning of a written instrument could

---

4. This provides a symmetry with the situation where interest rates go up and it is the lender who is stuck with a loan it would prefer to turn over at market rates. In an economy where interest rates fluctuate, it is all but certain that one side or the other will be dissatisfied with a long-term loan at some time. Mutuality calls for enforcing the contract as written no matter whose ox is being gored.

be justified only if it were feasible to determine the meaning the parties gave to the words from the instrument alone." 69 Cal.2d at 38, 442 P.2d 641, 69 Cal.Rptr. 561. This, the California Supreme Court concluded, is impossible: "If words had absolute and constant referents, it might be possible to discover contractual intention in the words themselves and in the manner in which they were arranged. Words, however, do not have absolute and constant referents." *Id.* In the same vein, the court noted that "(t)he exclusion of testimony that might contradict the linguistic background of the judge reflects a judicial belief in the possibility of perfect verbal expression. This belief is a remnant of a primitive faith in the inherent potency and inherent meaning of words." *Id.* at 37, 442 P.2d 641, 69 Cal.Rptr. 561.[5]

Under *Pacific Gas,* it matters not how clearly a contract is written, nor how completely it is integrated, nor how carefully it is negotiated, nor how squarely it addresses the issue before the court: the contract cannot be rendered impervious to attack by parol evidence. If one side is willing to claim that the parties intended one thing but the agreement provides for another, the court must consider extrinsic evidence of possible ambiguity. If that evidence raises the specter of ambiguity where there was none before, the contract language is displaced and the intention of the parties must be divined from self-serving testimony offered by partisan witnesses whose recollection is hazy from passage of time and colored by their conflicting interests. We question whether this approach is more likely to divulge the original intention of the parties than reliance on the seemingly clear words they agreed upon at the time.

Pacific Gas casts a long shadow of uncertainty over all transactions negotiated and executed under the law of California. As this case illustrates, even when the transaction is very sizeable, even if it involves only sophisticated parties, even if it was negotiated with the aid of counsel, even if it results in contract language that is devoid of ambiguity, costly and protracted litigation cannot be avoided if one party has a strong enough motive for challenging the contract. While this rule creates much business for lawyers and an occasional windfall to some clients, it leads only to frustration and delay for most litigants and clogs already overburdened courts.

It also chips away at the foundation of our legal system. By giving credence to the idea that words are inadequate to express concepts, *Pacific Gas* undermines the basic principle that language provides a meaningful constraint on public and private conduct. If we are unwilling to say that parties, dealing face to face, can come up with language that binds them, how can we send anyone to jail for violating statutes consisting of mere words lacking "absolute and constant referents"? How can courts ever

---

5. In an unusual footnote, the court compared the belief in the immutable meaning of words with " '(t)he elaborate system of taboo and verbal prohibitions in primitive groups ... (such as) the Swedish peasant custom of curing sick cattle smitten by witchcraft, by making them swallow a page torn out of a psalter and put in dough....' " *Id.* n. 2 (quoting Ullman, *The Principles of Semantics* 43 (1963)).

enforce decrees, not written in language understandable to all, but encoded in a dialect reflecting only the "linguistic background of the judge"? Can lower courts ever be faulted for failing to carry out the mandate of higher courts when "perfect verbal expression" is impossible? Are all attempts to develop the law in a reasoned and principled fashion doomed to failure as "remnant(s) of a primitive faith in the inherent potency and inherent meaning of words"?

Be that as it may. While we have our doubts about the wisdom of *Pacific Gas,* we have no difficulty understanding its meaning, even without extrinsic evidence to guide us. As we read the rule in California, we must reverse and remand to the district court in order to give plaintiff an opportunity to present extrinsic evidence as to the intention of the parties in drafting the contract. It may not be a wise rule we are applying, but it is a rule that binds us. Erie R.R. Co. v. Tompkins, 304 U.S. 64, 78, 58 S.Ct. 817, 822, 82 L.Ed. 1188 (1938).

II

In imposing sanctions on plaintiff, the district court stated:

> Pursuant to Fed.R.Civ.P. 11, the Court, *sua sponte,* sanctions the plaintiff for the filing of a frivolous lawsuit. The Court concludes that the language in the note and deed of trust is plain and clear. No reasonable person, much less firms of able attorneys, could possibly misunderstand this crystal-clear language. Therefore, this action was brought in bad faith.

Order of Dismissal at 3. Having reversed the district court on its substantive ruling, we must, of course, also reverse it as to the award of sanctions. While we share the district judge's impatience with this litigation, we would suggest that his irritation may have been misdirected. It is difficult to blame plaintiff and its lawyers for bringing this lawsuit. With this much money at stake, they would have been foolish not to pursue all remedies available to them under the applicable law. At fault, it seems to us, are not the parties and their lawyers but the legal system that encourages this kind of lawsuit. By holding that language has no objective meaning, and that contracts mean only what courts ultimately say they do, *Pacific Gas* invites precisely this type of lawsuit. With the benefit of 20 years of hindsight, the California Supreme Court may wish to revisit the issue. If it does so, we commend to it the facts of this case as a paradigmatic example of why the traditional rule, based on centuries of experience, reflects the far wiser approach.

Conclusion

The judgment of the district court is reversed. . . .

RAFFLES v. WICHELHAUS

Court of Exchequer, 1864.
2 H. & C. 906, 159 Eng.Rep. 375.

Declaration. For that it was agreed between the plaintiff and the defendants, to wit, at Liverpool, that the plaintiff should sell to the defendants, and the defendants buy of the plaintiff, certain goods, to wit, 125 bales of Surat cotton, guaranteed middling fair merchant's Dhollorah, to arrive ex Peerless from Bombay; and that the cotton should be taken from the quay, and that the defendants would pay the plaintiff for the same at a certain rate, to wit, at the rate of 17¼ d. per pound, within a certain time then agreed upon after the arrival of the said goods in England. Averments: that the said goods did arrive by the said ship from Bombay in England, to wit, at Liverpool, and the plaintiff was then and there ready and willing and offered to deliver the said goods to the defendants, etc. Breach: that the defendants refused to accept the said goods or pay the plaintiff for them.

Plea. That the said ship mentioned in the said agreement was meant and intended by the defendants to be the ship called the Peerless, which sailed from Bombay, to wit, in October; and that the plaintiff was not ready and willing, and did not offer, to deliver to the defendants any bales of cotton which arrived by the last-mentioned ship, but instead thereof was only ready and willing, and offered to deliver to the defendants 125 bales of Surat cotton which arrived by another and different ship, which was also called the Peerless, and which sailed from Bombay, to wit, in December.

Demurrer, and joinder therein.

Milward in support of the demurrer. The contract was for the sale of a number of bales of cotton of a particular description, which the plaintiff was ready to deliver. It is immaterial by what ship the cotton was to arrive, so that it was a ship called the Peerless. The words "to arrive ex Peerless," only meant that if the vessel is lost on the voyage, the contract is to be at an end. (Pollock, C.B. It would be a question for the jury whether both parties meant the same ship called the Peerless.) That would be so if the contract was for the sale of a ship called the Peerless; but it is for the sale of cotton on board a ship of that name. (Pollock, C.B. The defendant only bought that cotton which was to arrive by a particular ship. It may as well be said, that if there is a contract for the purchase of certain goods in warehouse A that is satisfied by the delivery of goods of the same description in warehouse B.) In that case there would be goods in both warehouses; here it does not appear that the plaintiff had any goods on board the other Peerless. (Martin, B. It is imposing on the defendant a contract different from that which he entered into. Pollock, C.B. It is like a contract for the purchase of wine coming from a particular estate in France or Spain, where there are two estates of that name.) The defendant has no right to contradict by parol evidence a written contract good upon the face of it. He does not impute misrepresentation or fraud, but only says that he fancied the ship was a different one. Intention is of no avail, unless stated at the time of the contract. (Pollock, C.B. One vessel sailed in October and the other in December.) The time of sailing is no part of the contract.

MELLISH (Cohen with him) in support of the plea. There is nothing on the face of the contract to show that any particular ship called the Peerless was meant; but the moment it appears that two ships called the Peerless were about to sail from Bombay there is a latent ambiguity, and parol evidence may be given for the purpose of showing that the defendant meant one Peerless and the plaintiff another. That being so, there was no consensus ad idem, and therefore no binding contract. He was then stopped by the court.

PER CURIAM. There must be judgment for the defendants.

———

Note on *Raffles*: Was the identity of the ship important? Why? If the case had gone to the jury what would have been the result? Was there a genuine misunderstanding? Can we attribute fault for the misunderstanding? The case has been thoroughly researched by the noted historian, A.W. Brian Simpson, in *Contracts for Cotton to Arrive: The Case of the Two Ships* Peerless, 11 Cardozo L.Rev. 287 (1989). Some of the background relevant to these questions is summarized below:

Raffles was a Liverpool cotton broker. Wichelhaus and Busch were not cotton brokers but "general commission merchants," also from Liverpool. The market price for cotton was very volatile due to the Civil War in America and particularly the North's naval blockade of the South which kept American cotton from the marketplace. American cotton was superior to Indian cotton and the market price for Indian cotton rose and fell depending on news from America regarding the likely duration of the war. (It was erroneously thought that lifting of the blockade would result in flooding the market with large amounts of stored American cotton.) Speculation in cotton was rampant. The contract involved in the *Raffles* case was an example of this speculation. Buyers were not buying for use but in the hopes of a profitable resale (or possibly assignment of their rights to purchase).

Why was the identity of the vessel important? Sellers couldn't promise a delivery date since it was uncertain when, or even if, the sailing vessel would arrive, or when it would be able to unload its cargo. Generally, sellers identified the cotton by the name of the vessel on which it was carried and contracts were made for sale of the cotton while the ship was en route to the destination or even on its arrival. Reliable reports of the movements of ships were available at the time. Thus, the identity of the ship was critical as it enabled the buyers to estimate the approximate date of delivery of the cotton. In a volatile market this date would determine the success or failure of the speculation.

There were no fewer than eleven ships *Peerless* sailing at the time, two registered at Liverpool—the two involved in the litigation. Vessels of the same name were usually differentiated by the name of their captain. Thus, had the parties been aware of two vessels named *Peerless* loading cotton in Bombay, they would have been expected to have identified the vessel not just by name but also by captain, *e.g.*, "*Peerless* (Major)" for the October *Peerless*, whose master was Roger Major, or "*Peerless* (Flavin)" for the December *Peerless*, whose master was Thomas Flavin.

Buyers' claim that they intended the October *Peerless* finds some support in the fact that the October *Peerless* had made a trip to India the year before, whereas the December *Peerless* was newly registered in Liverpool and its previous voyages under Captain Flavin had been to Australia and North America, not to India.

The date of contracting could also shed some light on the plausibility of the parties' conflicting claims. News of the departure of the October *Peerless* from Bombay for Liverpool was published in England on November 21, 1862; but news of the departure of the December *Peerless* did not reach England until January 21, 1863. Buyers' claim that they intended the October *Peerless* is more plausible if the contract was entered into before January 21, 1863. On the other hand, if the contract was entered into after January 21, 1863, Raffles' claim that he intended the December ship becomes more plausible, or at least there could have been reason to know that two ships by the same name were en route from Bombay to Liverpool.

The date of the contract is not known, but the fluctuation in the market price of cotton helps determine the date of contracting. (It is likely that the contract date was no earlier than November 21, 1862, the date that it was known in England that the October *Peerless* had sailed from Bombay.) After a sharp decline in the market, prices were rising due to news from America that indicated prolongation of the Civil War. The contract would probably have been made when the relevant market price for cotton was at or slightly below the contract price (17 1/4d. per pound) with the expectation that the market price would rise by the time of delivery. During the week of January 10, 1863 there was a great deal of speculation in cotton, the relevant market price was between 17 and 17 3/8d., and there is evidence that sales of the October shipment from Bombay were being made as well as sales for December shipment. Thus, it appears that the contract was entered into during the week of January 10, 1863, before the departure of the December *Peerless* was known in England. (It is also interesting to note that published reports in England of the *arrival* of the two ships *Peerless* in Bombay were dated September 22 and November 5, 1862, respectively.)

Subsequently prices started to fall. The October *Peerless* arrived in Liverpool on February 18 and was unloading at a time when the relevant market price was between 15 and 15 1/4d. Raffles' counsel stated that his client had no cotton on board that vessel. If he had, he would have surely tendered it to the buyers. The buyers did not complain.

The December *Peerless* arrived in Liverpool on April 19 and was unloading when the relevant market price was at approximately 16 3/4d. Had the buyers accepted delivery they would have suffered a loss, but less of a loss than they would have suffered had the seller tendered delivery from the October *Peerless* in February. "The misunderstanding had in a sense worked in their favor...." *Id.* at 323.

Had the dispute been submitted to arbitration, which would have been the customary way to proceed, what would have been the result?

> [The] arbitrators might well have decided that the sensible and decent way to handle the problem, the equitable solution, would be to require them to take delivery from Raffles,[168] or even, though this would be less favorable to them, to do something which courts are always reluctant to do—split the difference. Furthermore, if Wichelhaus and Busch deliberately kept quiet when no cotton was tendered by Raffles from *Peerless* (Major), hoping that when the second ship arrived, the price would have moved in their favor, it would hardly seem fair to allow them both to have their cake and eat it by now refusing to accept the cotton when they discovered that their hopes had been in vain.

Id. at 323–24.

NANAKULI PAVING AND ROCK CO. v. SHELL OIL CO.

United States Court of Appeals, Ninth Circuit, 1981.
664 F.2d 772.

HOFFMAN, DISTRICT JUDGE: Appellant Nanakuli Paving and Rock Company (Nanakuli) initially filed this breach of contract action against appellee Shell Oil Company (Shell) in Hawaiian State Court in February, 1976. Nanakuli, the second largest asphaltic paving contractor in Hawaii, had bought all its asphalt requirements from 1963 to 1974 from Shell under two long-term supply contracts; its suit charged Shell with breach of the later 1969 contract. The jury returned a verdict of $220,800 for Nanakuli on its first claim, which is that Shell breached the 1969 contract in January, 1974, by failing to price protect Nanakuli on 7200 tons of asphalt at the time Shell raised the price for asphalt from $44 to $76. Nanakuli's theory is that price-protection, as a usage of the asphaltic paving trade in Hawaii, was incorporated into the 1969 agreement between the parties, as demonstrated by the routine use of price protection by suppliers to that trade, and reinforced by the way in which Shell actually performed the 1969 contract up until 1974. Price protection, appellant claims, required that Shell hold the price on the tonnage

---

168. In terms of a money award, compensate Raffles by paying the difference between the contract price and market price.

Nanakuli had already committed because Nanakuli had incorporated that price into bids put out to or contracts awarded by general contractors and government agencies. The District Judge set aside the verdict and granted Shell's motion for judgment n. o. v., which decision we vacate. We reinstate the jury verdict....

Nanakuli ... argues, all material suppliers to the asphaltic paving trade in Hawaii followed the trade usage of price protection and thus it should be assumed, under the U.C.C., that the parties intended to incorporate price protection into their 1969 agreement. This is so, Nanakuli continues, even though the written contract provided for price to be "Shell's Posted Price at time of delivery," F.O.B. Honolulu. Its proof of a usage that was incorporated into the contract is reinforced by evidence of the commercial context, which under the U.C.C. should form the background for viewing a particular contract. The full agreement must be examined in light of the close, almost symbiotic relations between Shell and Nanakuli on the island of Oahu, whereby the expansion of Shell on the island was intimately connected to the business growth of Nanakuli. The U.C.C. looks to the actual performance of a contract as the best indication of what the parties intended those terms to mean. Nanakuli points out that Shell had price protected it on the two occasions of price increases under the 1969 contract other than the 1974 increase. In 1970 and 1971 Shell extended the old price for four and three months, respectively, after an announced increase. This was done, in the words of Shell's agent in Hawaii, in order to permit Nanakuli's to "chew up" tonnage already committed at Shell's old price. ...

Shell presents three arguments for upholding the judgment n.o.v. or, on cross appeal, urging that the District Judge erred in admitting certain evidence. First, it says, the District Court should not have denied Shell's motion *in limine* to define trade, for purposes of trade usage evidence, as the sale and purchase of asphalt in Hawaii, rather than expanding the definition of trade to include other suppliers of materials to the asphaltic paving trade. Asphalt, its argument runs, was the subject matter of the disputed contract and the only product Shell supplied to the asphaltic paving trade. Shell protests that the judge, by expanding the definition of trade to include the other major suppliers to the asphaltic paving trade, allowed the admission of highly prejudicial evidence of routine price protection by all suppliers of aggregate. Asphaltic concrete paving is formed by mixing paving asphalt with crushed rock, or aggregate, in a "hot-mix" plant and then pouring the mixture onto the surface to be paved. Shell's second complaint is that the two prior occasions on which it price protected Nanakuli, although representing the only other instances of price increases under the 1969 contract, constituted mere waivers of the contract's price term, not a course of performance of the contract. A course of performance of the contract, in contrast to a waiver, demonstrates how the parties understand the terms of their agreement. Shell cites two U.C.C. Comments in support of that argument: (1) that, when the meaning of acts is ambiguous, the preference is for the waiver interpretation, and (2) that one act alone does not constitute a relevant course of performance. Shell's final argument is that, even assuming its prior price protection constituted a course of performance and that the broad trade definition was correct and evidence of trade usages by aggregate suppliers was admissible, price protection could not be construed as reasonably consistent with the express price term in the contract, in which case the Code provides that the express term controls.

We hold that the judge did not abuse his discretion in defining the applicable trade, for purposes of trade usages, as the asphaltic paving trade in Hawaii, rather than the purchase and sale of asphalt alone, given the unusual, not to say unique, circumstances: the smallness of the marketplace on Oahu; the existence of only two suppliers on the island; the long and intimate connection between the two companies on Oahu, including the background of how the development of Shell's asphalt sales on Oahu was inextricably linked to Nanakuli's own expansion on the island; the knowledge of the aggregate business on the part of Shell's Hawaiian representative, Bohner; his awareness of the economics of Nanakuli's bid estimates, which included only two major materials, asphalt and aggregate; his familiarity with realities of the Hawaiian marketplace in which all government agencies refused to include escalation clauses in contract awards and thus pavers would face tremendous losses on price increases if all their material suppliers did not routinely offer them price protection; and Shell's determination to build Nanakuli up to compete for those lucrative government contracts with the largest paver on the island, Hawaiian Bitumuls (H.B.), which was supplied by the only other asphalt company on the islands, Chevron, and which was routinely price protected on materials. We base our holding on the reading of the Code Comments as defining trade more broadly than transaction and as binding parties not only to usages of their particular trade but also to usages of trade in general in a given locality. This latter seems an equitable application of usage evidence where the usage is almost universally practiced in a small market such as was Oahu in the 1960's before Shell signed its 1969 contract with Nanakuli. Additionally, we hold that, under the facts of this case, a jury could reasonably have found that Shell's acts on two occasions to price protect Nanakuli were not ambiguous and therefore indicated Shell's understanding of the terms of the agreement with Nanakuli rather than being a waiver by Shell of those terms.[8]

Lastly we hold that, although the express price terms of Shell's posted price of delivery may seem, at first glance, inconsistent with a trade usage of price protection at time of increases in price, a closer reading shows that the jury could have reasonably construed price protection as consistent with the express term. We reach this holding for several reasons.

---

8. In addition, Shell's Bohner volunteered on direct for Shell that Shell price protected Nanakuli again after 1974 on the only two occasions of later price increases in 1977 and 1978. Although not constituting a course of performance, since the occasions took place under different contracts, these two additional instances of price protection could have reinforced the jury's impression that Shell's earlier actions were a carrying out of the price term.

First, we are persuaded by a careful reading of the U.C.C., one of whose underlying purposes is to promote flexibility in the expansion of commercial practices and which rather drastically overhauls this particular area of the law. The Code would have us look beyond the printed pages of the contract to usages and the entire commercial context of the agreement in order to reach the "true understanding" of the parties. Second, decisions of other courts in similar situations have managed to reconcile such trade usages with seemingly contradictory express terms where the prior course of dealings between the parties, trade usages, and the actual performance of the contract by the parties showed a clear intent by the parties to incorporate those usages into the agreement or to give to the express term the particular meaning provided by those usages, even at times varying the apparent meaning of the express terms. Third, the delineation by thoughtful commentators of the degree of consistency demanded between express terms and usage is that a usage should be allowed to modify the apparent agreement, as seen in the written terms, as long as it does not totally negate it. We believe the usage here falls within the limits set forth by commentators and generally followed in the better reasoned decisions. The manner in which price protection was actually practiced in Hawaii was that it only came into play at times of price increases and only for work committed prior to those increases on non-escalating contracts. Thus, it formed an exception to, rather than a total negation of, the express price term of "Shell's Posted Price at time of delivery." Our decision is reinforced by the overwhelming nature of the evidence that price protection was routinely practiced by all suppliers in the small Oahu market of the asphaltic paving trade and therefore was known to Shell; that it was a realistic necessity to operate in that market and thus vital to Nanakuli's ability to get large government contracts and to Shell's continued business growth on Oahu; and that it therefore constituted an intended part of the agreement, as that term is broadly defined by the Code, between Shell and Nanakuli. . . .

Perhaps one of the most fundamental departures of the Code from prior contract law is found in the parol evidence rule and the definition of an agreement between two parties. Under the U.C.C., an agreement goes beyond the written words on a piece of paper. " 'Agreement' means the bargain of the parties in fact as found in their language or by implication from other circumstances including course of dealing or usage of trade or course of performance as provided in this chapter (sections 490:1–205 and 490:2–208) [Revised UCC 1–303, ed.]." *Id.* § 490:1–201(3). Express terms, then, do not constitute the entire agreement, which must be sought also in evidence of usages, dealings, and performance of the contract itself. The purpose of evidence of usages, which are defined in the previous section, is to help to understand the entire agreement. . . .

A commercial agreement, then, is broader than the written paper and its meaning is to be determined not just by the language used by them in the written contract but "by their action, read and interpreted in the light of commercial practices and other surrounding circumstances. The measure and background for interpretation are set by the commercial context, which may explain and supplement even the language of a formal or final writing." *Id.*, Cmt. 1. Performance, usages, and prior dealings are important enough to be admitted always, even for a final and complete agreement; only if they cannot be reasonably reconciled with the express terms of the contract are they not binding on the parties. "The express terms of an agreement and an applicable course of dealing or usage of trade shall be construed wherever reasonable as consistent with each other; but when such construction is unreasonable express terms control both course of dealing and usage of trade and course of dealing controls usage of trade." *Id.* § 490:1–205(4) [Revised UCC 1–303(e), ed.].

Of these three, then, the most important evidence of the agreement of the parties is their actual performance of the contract. *Id.* The operative definition of course of performance is as follows: "Where the contract for sale involves repeated occasions for performance by either party with knowledge of the nature of the performance and opportunity for objection to it by the other, any course of performance accepted or acquiesced in without objection shall be relevant to determine the meaning of the agreement." *Id.* § 490:2–208(1) [Revised UCC 1–303(a)*, ed.]. "Course of dealing . . . is restricted, literally, to a sequence of conduct between the parties previous to the agreement. However, the provisions of the Act on course of performance make it clear that a sequence of conduct after or under the agreement may have equivalent meaning (Section 2–208)." *Id.* 490:1–205, Cmt. 2. The importance of evidence of course of performance is explained: "The parties themselves know best what they have meant by their words of agreement and their action under that agreement is the best indication of what that meaning was. This section thus rounds out the set of factors which determines the meaning of the 'agreement' . . ." *Id.* § 490:2–208, Cmt. 1. "Under this section a course of performance is always relevant to determine the meaning of the agreement." *Id.*, Cmt. 2.

Our study of the Code provisions and Comments, then, form the first basis of our holding that a trade usage to price protect pavers at times of price increases for work committed on nonescalating contracts could reasonably be construed as consistent with an express term of seller's posted price at delivery. Since the agreement of the parties is broader than the express terms and includes usages, which may even add terms to the agreement, and since the commercial background provided by those usages is vital to an understanding of the agreement, we follow the Code's mandate to proceed on the assumption that the parties have included

---

* Revised UCC 1–303(a) reads:

(a) A "course of performance" is a sequence of conduct between the parties to a particular transaction that exists if:

(1) the agreement of the parties with respect to the transaction involves repeated occasions for performance by a party; and

(2) the other party, with knowledge of the nature of the performance and opportunity for objection to it, accepts the performance or acquiesces in it without objection.

those usages unless they cannot reasonably be construed as consistent with the express terms. . . .

. . . Here the evidence was overwhelming that all suppliers to the asphaltic paving trade price protected customers under the same types of circumstances. Chevron's contract with H.B. was a similar long-term supply contract between a buyer and seller with very close relations, on a form supplied by the seller, covering sales of asphalt, and setting the price at seller's posted price, with no mention of price protection. . . . Here, the express price term was "Shell's Posted Price at time of delivery." A total negation of that term would be that the buyer was to set the price. It is a less than complete negation of the term that an unstated exception exists at times of price increases, at which times the old price is to be charged, for a certain period or for a specified tonnage, on work already committed at the lower price on nonescalating contracts. Such a usage forms a broad and important exception to the express term, but does not swallow it entirely. Therefore, we hold that, under these particular facts, a reasonable jury could have found that price protection was incorporated into the 1969 agreement between Nanakuli and Shell and that price protection was reasonably consistent with the express term of seller's posted price at delivery. . . .

Nanakuli offers an alternative theory why Shell should have offered price protection at the time of the price increases of 1974. Even if price protection was not a term of the agreement, Shell could not have exercised good faith in carrying out its 1969 contract with Nanakuli when it raised its price by $32 effective January 1 in a letter written December 31st and only received on January 4, given the universal practice of advance notice of such an increase in the asphaltic paving trade. The Code provides, "A price to be fixed by the seller or by the buyer means a price for him to fix in good faith," Haw.Rev.Stat. s 490:2–305(2). For a merchant good faith means "the observance of reasonable commercial standards of fair dealing in the trade." *Id.* 490:2–103(1)(b). The comment to Section 2–305 explains, "(I)n the normal case a 'posted price' . . . satisfies the good faith requirement." *Id.*, Cmt. 3. However, the words "in the normal case" mean that, although a posted price will usually be satisfactory, it will not be so under all circumstances. In addition, the dispute here was not over the amount of the increase—that is, the price that the seller fixed—but over the manner in which that increase was put into effect. . . . Nanakuli presented evidence that Chevron, in raising its price to $76, gave at least six weeks' advance notice, in accord with the long-time usage of the asphaltic paving trade. Shell, on the other hand, gave absolutely no notice, from which the jury could have concluded that Shell's manner of carrying out the price increase of 1974 did not conform to commercially reasonable standards. In both the timing of the announcement and its refusal to protect work already bid at the old price, Shell could be found to have breached the obligation of good faith imposed by the Code. . . . "Every contract or duty within this chapter imposes an obligation of good faith in its performance or enforcement," *id.* s 490:1–203 [Revised UCC § 1–304, ed.], which for merchants entails the observance of commercially reasonable standards of fair dealing in the trade.** The Comment to 1–203 [Revised UCC § 1–304, ed.] reads:

> This section sets forth a basic principle running throughout this Act. The principle involved is that in commercial transactions good faith is required in the performance and enforcement of all agreements or duties. Particular applications of this general principle appear in specific provisions of the Act. . . . It is further implemented by Section 1–205 [Revised UCC § 1–303, ed.] on course of dealing and usage of trade. . . .

Because the jury could have found for Nanakuli on its price protection claim under either theory, we reverse the judgment of the District Court and reinstate the jury verdict for Nanakuli in the amount of $220,800, plus interest according to law. . . .

KENNEDY, CIRCUIT JUDGE, concurring specially: The case involves specific pricing practices, not an allegation of unfair dealing generally. Our opinion should not be interpreted to permit juries to import price protection or a similarly specific contract term from a concept of good faith that is not based on well-established custom and usage or other objective standards of which the parties had clear notice. . . .

PROBLEMS

10. The parties entered into an agreement for the sale and purchase of coal in which the quantity term was expressed in "metric tons" rather than "dry metric tons." One of the parties sought to introduce evidence that there was a course of dealing which showed that there was a common basis between the parties for interpreting "metric tons" to be the equivalent of "dry metric tons." Is the evidence admissible?

11. S, a manufacturer, sues B, an authorized dealer, for the price of electronic equipment supplied and delivered. B counterclaims based on S's refusal to accept conforming goods returned for credit. The agreement stated that B had no right to return conforming goods and obtain a credit. B now asserts that the parties continually ignored the agreement and that over a period of time 210 units were returned for credit. May this evidence be introduced as a relevant course of performance? May it be introduced as the basis of a modification?

12. Defendant asked Young, one of his employees, to shop for a surge protector. Young's initial search found surge protectors in the range of $50 to $200. For various reasons, he found that none of them fully met his employer's needs until he found the plaintiff's product. Young asked plaintiff's salesperson the price of the protector. The salesperson replied "fifty-six

---

** Revised UCC Article 1, defines "good faith" to require both "honesty in fact and the observance of reasonable commercial standards of fair dealing." UCC § 1–201(b)(20). Former UCC § 1–201(19) defined "good faith" as "honesty in fact in the conduct or transaction concerned," and UCC § 2–103(1)(b) applied the additional requirement of "the observance of reasonable commercial standards of good faith and fair dealing in the trade," only to a merchant. Ed.

twenty" which Young took to mean $56.20. The salesperson meant $5,620. When the protector was delivered, Defendant immediately realized that it had to cost much more than $56.20 and asked the plaintiff to take it back. Plaintiff refused and sued for the price. What result?

13. Plaintiff subscribed to DIRECTV. The subscription agreement contained this clause: "DIRECTV reserves the right to change these terms and conditions. . . . If any changes are made DIRECTV will send you a written notice describing the change and its effective date. If a change is not acceptable to you, you may cancel your service. If you do not cancel your service, your continued receipt of any service is considered to be your acceptance of that change." Soon thereafter, in an envelope containing the monthly bill, DIRECTV included a new agreement that differed from the old by a clause that stated that any claim "arising out of, or relating to this agreement . . . shall be resolved in according to binding arbitration." Plaintiff, who had not read the enclosure, did not cancel the service and continued to receive DIRECTV's signal. Plaintiff has brought a court case based on an alleged breach of the agreement. DIRECTV argues that the case should be dismissed and that Plaintiff is bound by the arbitration clause. Think of a successful argument on behalf of Plaintiff based on interpretation.

EXAMINATION PROBLEM

A MODEL ANSWER TO THIS QUESTION IS IN APPENDIX C, ENTITLED "FLOOD AND THE WELL"

Lessor leased to Lessee a lot for use as a gasoline station for a term of 10 years at a monthly rental of $1,000. All material terms were included in a written signed lease. The lease recited that in consideration of $1 B had the privilege of buying the lot at any time during the term of the lease for the price of $50,000. The lease also provided that: "Lessor agrees to furnish Lessee with water for the station insofar as Lessor is able to do so with Lessor's present water supply. In case Lessor's well fails to supply sufficient water, Lessor is not responsible and Lessee is required to make his own arrangements for securing water."

Some months into the lease, the parties had a dispute as to whether the water supply was adequate. The parties entered into a written, signed agreement under which an additional well would be drilled on the premises and each would pay one-half of the cost.

The parties hired Flood, a well-driller, to drill a well to a depth of 200 feet. The agreed price was $3,000. Flood encountered difficulties because there was more rock than anticipated. When Flood threatened to quit, Lessor and Lessee agreed to pay Flood an additional $1,000. Flood finished the work but neither Lessor nor Lessee made any payment. Eventually, Flood stated in a signed writing that he would take $3,000 in full payment and Lessor and Lessee sent a check in that amount which Flood cashed.

Subsequently, Lessee decided to exercise the option to purchase and tendered the $50,000 called for in the lease. Lessor refused to accept the tender claiming that when the agreement with respect to the new well was made, the parties had agreed that Lessee was to bear the entire cost of the well if Lessee exercised the option to purchase.

Discuss all of the contract problems involved in this set of facts.

CHAPTER 6

CAPACITY OF PARTIES

■ ■ ■

(Calamari & Perillo on Contracts §§ 8.1—8.17)

PETTIT v. LISTON

Supreme Court of Oregon, 1920.
97 Or. 464, 191 P. 660.

Plaintiff, a minor, brings this action by his guardian to recover $125 paid by him upon the purchase price of a certain motorcycle purchased from the defendants.

The case involves the question of whether or not a minor who has purchased an article of this kind, and taken and used the same, after paying part or all of the purchase price, can return the article and recover the money paid without making good to the vendors the wear and tear and depreciation of the same while in his hands.

The defendants in the case were engaged in the selling of motorcycles and attachments. The plaintiff purchased from them a motorcycle at the agreed price of $325. He paid $125 down, and was to pay $25 per month upon the purchase price until the payments were completed. He took and used the motorcycle for a little over a month and finally returned the same to the defendants and demanded the return of his money. The defendants answer and allege that plaintiff used the machine, and in so doing damaged it to the amount of $156.65. There was a demurrer to the answer, which was overruled by the court, and the plaintiff refusing to reply or plead further and standing upon his demurrer, a judgment and order were entered dismissing the cause, from which the plaintiff appeals.

BENNETT, J. (after stating the facts as above). The amount involved in this proceeding is not large, but the question of law presented is a very important one, and one which has been much disputed in the courts, and about which there is a great and irreconcilable conflict in the authorities, and we have therefore given the matter careful attention.

The courts, in an attempt to protect the minor upon the one hand, and to prevent wrong or injustice to persons who have dealt fairly and reasonably with such minor upon the other, have indulged in many fine distinctions and recognized various slight shades of difference.

In dealing with the right of the minor to rescind his contract and the conditions under which he may do so, the decisions of the courts in the different states have not only conflicted upon the main questions involved, but many of the decisions of the same court in the same state seem to be inconsistent with each other; and oftentimes one court has made its decision turn upon a distinction or difference not recognized by the courts of other states as a distinguishing feature. The result has been that there are not only two general lines of decisions directly upon the question involved, but there are many others, which diverge more or less from the main line, and make particular cases turn upon real or fancied differences and distinctions, depending upon whether the contract was executory or partly or wholly executed, whether it was for necessaries, whether it was beneficial to the minor, whether it was fair and reasonable, whether the minor still had the property purchased in his possession, whether he had received any beneficial use of the same, etc.

Many courts have held broadly that a minor may so purchase property and keep it for an indefinite time, if he chooses, until it is worn out and destroyed, and then recover the payments made on the purchase price, without allowing the seller anything whatever for the use and depreciation of the property.

Many other authorities hold that where the transaction is fair and reasonable, and the minor was not overcharged or taken advantage of in any way, and he takes and keeps the property and uses or destroys it, he cannot recover the payments made on the purchase price, without allowing the seller for the wear and tear and depreciation of the article while in his hands.

The plaintiff contends for the former rule, and supports his contention with citations from the courts of last resort of Maine, Connecticut, Indiana, Massachusetts, Vermont, Nebraska, Virginia, Iowa, Mississippi, and West Virginia, most of which (although not all) support his contention. On the contrary, the courts of New York, Maryland, Montana, Illinois, Kentucky, New Hampshire, and Minnesota, with some others, support the latter rule, which seems to be also the English rule. Some of the cyclopedias and some of the different series of selected cases state the rule contended for by plaintiff, as supported by the strong weight of authority; but we find the decisions rather equally balanced, both in number and respectability.

In Rice v. Butler, 160 N.Y. 578, 55 N.E. 275, 47 L.R.A. 303, 73 Am.St.Rep. 703, in an opinion by Mr. Justice Haight, concurred in by the entire court, it is said:

> There are numerous authorities bearing upon the question, but they are not in entire harmony. We have examined them with some care, but have found none in this court which appears to settle the question now presented. We, consequently, are left free to adopt such

a rule as in our judgment will best promote justice and equity. The contract in this case in its entirety must be held to be executory; for, under its terms, payments were to mature in the future and the title was only to pass to the minor upon making all of the payments stipulated; but in so far as the payments made were concerned the contract was in a sense executed, for nothing further remained to be done with reference to those payments. Kent, in his *Commentaries* (volume 2, p. 240), says: "If an infant pays money on his contract and enjoys the benefit of it and then avoids it when he comes of age he cannot recover back the consideration paid. On the other hand, if he avoids an executed contract when he comes of age on the ground of infancy, he must restore the consideration which he had received. The privilege of infancy is to be used as a shield and not as a sword. He cannot have the benefit of the contract on one side without returning the equivalent on the other."

. . .

Our attention has not been called to any Oregon case bearing upon the question, and as far as our investigation has disclosed, there is none. In this condition of the authorities, we feel that we are in a position to pass upon the question as one of first impression, and announce the rule which seems to us to be the better one, upon considerations of principle and public policy.

We think, where the minor has not been overreached in any way, and there has been no undue influence, and the contract is a fair and reasonable one, and the minor has actually paid money on the purchase price, and taken and used the article, that he ought not to be permitted to recover the amount actually paid, without allowing the vendor of the goods the reasonable compensation for the use and depreciation of the article, while in his hands.

Of course, if there has been any fraud or imposition on the part of the seller, or if the contract is unfair, or any unfair advantage has been taken of the minor in inducing him to make the purchase, then a different rule would apply. And whether there had been such an overreaching on the part of the seller would always, in case of a jury trial, be a question for the jury.

We think this rule will fully and fairly protect the minor against injustice or imposition, and at the same time it will be fair to the business man who has dealt with such minor in good faith. This rule is best adapted to modern conditions, and especially to the conditions in our Far Western states. Here, minors are permitted to and do in fact transact a great deal of business for themselves, long before they have reached the age of legal majority. Most young men have their own time long before reaching that age. They work and earn money and collect it and spend it oftentimes without any oversight or restriction. No business man questions their right to buy, if they have the money to pay for their purchases. They not only buy for themselves, but they often are intrusted with the making of purchases for their parents and guardians. It would be intolerably burdensome for every one concerned if merchants and other business men could not deal with them safely, in a fair and reasonable way, in cash transactions of this kind.

Again, it will not exert any good moral influence upon boys and young men, and will not tend to encourage honesty and integrity, or lend them to a good and useful business future, if they are taught that they can make purchases with their own money, for their own benefit, and after paying for them in this way, and using them until they are worn out and destroyed, go back and compel the business man to return to them what they have paid upon the purchase price. Such a doctrine, as it seems to us, can only lead to the corruption of young men's principles and encourage them in habits of trickery and dishonesty.

In view of all these considerations, we think that the rule we have indicated, and which is substantially the rule adopted in New York, is the better rule, and we adopt the same in this state.

We must not be understood as deciding at this time what would be the rule where the vendor is seeking to enforce an executory contract against the minor, which is a different question not necessarily involved in this case.

It follows that the judgment of the court below should be affirmed.
. . .

ORTELERE v. TEACHERS' RETIREMENT BOARD

Court of Appeals of New York, 1969.
25 N.Y.2d 196, 303 N.Y.S.2d 362, 250 N.E.2d 460.

BREITEL, JUDGE. This appeal involves the revocability of an election of benefits under a public employees' retirement system and suggests the need for a renewed examination of the kinds of mental incompetency which may render voidable the exercise of contractual rights. The particular issue arises on the evidently unwise and foolhardy selection of benefits by a 60–year–old teacher, on leave for mental illness and suffering from cerebral arteriosclerosis, after service as a public schoolteacher and participation in a public retirement system for over 40 years. The teacher died a little less than two months after making her election of maximum benefits, payable to her during her life, thus causing the entire reserve to fall in. She left surviving her husband of 38 years of marriage and two grown children.

There is no doubt that any retirement system depends for its soundness on an actuarial experience based on the purely prospective selections of benefits and mortality rates among the covered group, and that retrospective or adverse selection after the fact would be destructive of a sound system. It is also true that members of retirement systems are free to make choices which to others may seem unwise or foolhardy. The issue here is narrower than any suggested by these basic principles. It is whether an otherwise irrevocable election may be avoided for incapacity because of known mental illness which resulted in the election when, except in the barest actuarial sense, the system would sustain no unfavorable consequences.

The husband and executor of Grace W. Ortelere, the deceased New York City schoolteacher, sues to set aside her application for retirement without option, in the event of her death. It is alleged that Mrs. Ortelere, on February 11, 1965, two months before her death from natural causes, was not mentally competent to execute a retirement application. By this application, effective the next day, she elected the maximum retirement allowance (Administrative Code of City of New York, § B20–46.0). She thus revoked her earlier election of benefits under which she named her husband a beneficiary of the unexhausted reserve upon her death. Selection of the maximum allowance extinguished all interests upon her death.

Following a nonjury trial in Supreme Court, it was held that Grace Ortelere had been mentally incompetent at the time of her February 11 application, thus rendering it "null and void and of no legal effect." The Appellate Division, by a divided court, reversed the judgment of the Supreme Court and held that, as a matter of law, there was insufficient proof of mental incompetency as to this transaction.

Mrs. Ortelere's mental illness, indeed, psychosis, is undisputed. It is not seriously disputable, however, that she had complete cognitive judgment or awareness when she made her selection. A modern understanding of mental illness, however, suggests that incapacity to contract or exercise contractual rights may exist, because of volitional and affective impediments or disruptions in the personality, despite the intellectual or cognitive ability to understand. It will be recognized as the civil law parallel to the question of criminal responsibility which has been the recent concern of so many and has resulted in statutory and decisional changes in the criminal law (*e.g.*, A.L.I. Model Penal Code, § 4.01; Penal Law, § 30.05; Durham v. United States, 214 F.2d 862).

Mrs. Ortelere, an elementary schoolteacher since 1924, suffered a "nervous breakdown" in March, 1964 and went on a leave of absence expiring February 5, 1965. She was then 60 years old and had been happily married for 38 years. On July 1, 1964 she came under the care of Dr. D'Angelo, a psychiatrist, who diagnosed her breakdown as involutional psychosis, melancholia type. Dr. D'Angelo prescribed, and for about six weeks decedent underwent, tranquilizer and shock therapy. Although moderately successful, the therapy was not continued since it was suspected that she also suffered from cerebral arteriosclerosis, an ailment later confirmed. However, the psychiatrist continued to see her at monthly intervals until March, 1965. On March 28, 1965 she was hospitalized after collapsing at home from an aneurysm. She died 10 days later; the cause of death was "Cerebral thrombosis due to H(ypertensive) H(eart) D(isease)."

As a teacher she had been a member of the Teachers' Retirement System of the City of New York (Administrative Code, § B20–3.0). This entitled her to certain annuity and pension rights, preretirement death benefits, and empowered her to exercise various options concerning the payment of her retirement allowance.

Some years before, on June 28, 1958, she had executed a "Selection of Benefits under Option One" naming her husband as beneficiary of the unexhausted reserve. Under this option upon retirement her allowance would be less by way of periodic retirement allowances, but if she died before receipt of her full reserve the balance of the reserve would be payable to her husband. On June 16, 1960, two years later, she had designated her husband as beneficiary of her service death benefits in the event of her death prior to retirement.

Then on February 11, 1965, when her leave of absence had just expired and she was still under treatment, she executed a retirement application, the one here involved, selecting the maximum retirement allowance payable during her lifetime with nothing payable on or after death. She also, at this time, borrowed from the system the maximum cash withdrawal permitted, namely, $8,760. Three days earlier she had written the board, stating that she intended to retire on February 12 or 15 or as soon as she received "the information I need in order to decide whether to take an option or maximum allowance." She then listed eight specific questions, reflecting great understanding of the retirement system, concerning the various alternatives available. An extremely detailed reply was sent, by letter of February 15, 1965, although by that date it was technically impossible for her to change her selection. However, the board's chief clerk, before whom Mrs. Ortelere executed the application, testified that the questions were "answered verbally by me on February 11th." Her retirement reserve totalled $62,165 (after deducting the $8,760 withdrawal), and the difference between electing the maximum retirement allowance (no option) and the allowance under "option one" was $901 per year or $75 per month. That is, had the teacher selected "option one" she would have received an annual allowance of $4,494 or $375 per month, while if no option had been selected she would have received an annual allowance of $5,395 or $450 per month. Had she not withdrawn the cash the annual figures would be $5,247 and $6,148 respectively.

Following her taking a leave of absence for her condition, Mrs. Ortelere had become very depressed and was unable to care for herself. As a result her husband gave up his electrician's job, in which he earned $222 per week, to stay home and take care of her on a full-time basis. She left their home only when he accompanied her. Although he took her to the Retirement Board on February 11, 1965, he did not know why she went, and did not question her for fear "she'd start crying hysterically that I was scolding her. That's the way she was. And I wouldn't upset her."

The Orteleres were in quite modest circumstances. They owned their own home, valued at $20,000, and had $8,000 in a savings account. They also owned some farm land worth about $5,000. Under these circumstances, as revealed in this record, retirement for both of the Orteleres or the survivor of them had to be provided, as a practical matter, largely out of Mrs. Ortelere's retirement benefits.

According to Dr. D'Angelo, the psychiatrist who treated her, Mrs. Ortelere never improved enough to "warrant my sending her back (to teaching)." A physician for the Board of Education examined her on February 2, 1965 to determine her fitness to return to teaching. Although not a psychiatrist but rather a specialist in internal medicine, this physician "judged that she had apparently recovered from the depression" and that she appeared rational. However, before allowing her to return to teaching, a report was requested from Dr. D'Angelo concerning her condition. It is notable that the Medical Division of the Board of Education on February 24, 1965 requested that Mrs. Ortelere report to the board's "panel psychiatrist" on March 11, 1965.

Dr. D'Angelo stated "(a)t no time since she was under my care was she ever mentally competent"; that "(m)entally she couldn't make a decision of any kind, actually, of any kind, small or large." He also described how involutional melancholia affects the judgment process:

> They can't think rationally, no matter what the situation is. They will even tell you, "I used to be able to think of anything and make any decision. Now," they say, "even getting up, I don't know whether I should get up or whether I should stay in bed." Or, "I don't even know how to make a slice of toast any more." Everything is impossible to decide, and everything is too great an effort to even think of doing. They just don't have the effort, actually, because their nervous breakdown drains them of all their physical energies.

While the psychiatrist used terms referring to "rationality," it is quite evident that Mrs. Ortelere's psychopathology did not lend itself to a classification under the legal test of irrationality. It is undoubtedly, for this reason, that the Appellate Division was unable to accept his testimony and the trial court's finding of irrationality in the light of the prevailing rules as they have been formulated.

The well-established rule is that contracts of a mentally incompetent person who has not been adjudicated insane are voidable. Even where the contract has been partly or fully performed it will still be avoided upon restoration of the *status quo*. (Verstandig v. Schlaffer, 296 N. Y. 62, 64.)

Traditionally, in this State and elsewhere, contractual mental capacity has been measured by what is largely a cognitive test (Aldrich v. Bailey, 132 N.Y. 85, 30 N.E. 264; 2 Williston, *Contracts* (3d ed.), § 256). Under this standard the "inquiry" is whether the mind was "so affected as to render him wholly and absolutely incompetent to comprehend and understand the nature of the transaction" (Aldrich v. Bailey, *supra*, at p. 89, 30 N.E. at p. 265). A requirement that the party also be able to make a rational judgment concerning the particular transaction qualified the cognitive test (Paine v. Aldrich, 133 N.Y. 544, 546, 30 N.E. 725, 726, Note, *"Civil Insanity": The New York Treatment of the Issue of Mental Incompetency in Non–Criminal Cases*, 44 Cornell L.Q. 76). Conversely, it is also well recognized that contractual ability would be affected by insane delusions intimately related to the particular transaction (Moritz v. Moritz, 153 App.Div. 147, 138 N.Y.S. 124, *affd,* 211 N.Y. 580, 105 N.E. 1090, see Green, *Judicial Tests of Mental Incompetency,* 6 Mo.L.Rev. 141, 151).

These traditional standards governing competency to contract were formulated when psychiatric knowledge was quite primitive. They fail to account for one who by reason of mental illness is unable to control his conduct even though his cognitive ability seems unimpaired. When these standards were evolving it was thought that all the mental faculties were simultaneously affected by mental illness. (Green, *Mental Incompetency,* 38 Mich.L.Rev. 1189, 1197–1202.) This is no longer the prevailing view (Note, *Mental Illness and the Law of Contracts,* 57 Mich.L.Rev. 1020, 1033–1036).

Of course, the greatest movement in revamping legal notions of mental responsibility has occurred in the criminal law. The nineteenth century cognitive test embraced in the *M'Naghten* rules has long been criticized and changed by statute and decision in many jurisdictions (*see* M'Naghten's Case, 10 Clark & Fin. 200; 8 Eng.Rep. 718 (House of Lords, 1843); Weihofen, *Mental Disorder as a Criminal Defense* (1954), pp. 65–68; British Royal Comm. on Capital Punishment (1953), ch. 4; A.L.I. Model Penal Code, § 4.01, *supra; cf.* Penal Law, § 30.05).

While the policy considerations for the criminal law and the civil law are different, both share in common the premise that policy considerations must be based on a sound understanding of the human mind and, therefore, its illnesses. Hence, because the cognitive rules are, for the most part, too restrictive and rest on a false factual basis they must be re-examined. Once it is understood that, accepting plaintiff's proof, Mrs. Ortelere was psychotic and because of that psychosis could have been incapable of making a voluntary selection of her retirement system benefits, there is an issue that a modern jurisprudence should not exclude, merely because her mind could pass a "cognition" test based on nineteenth century psychology.

There has also been some movement on the civil law side to achieve a modern posture. For the most part, the movement has been glacial and has been disguised under traditional formulations. Various devices have been used to avoid unacceptable results under the old rules by finding unfairness or overreaching in order to avoid transactions (*see, e.g.,* Green, *Proof of Mental Incompetency and the Unexpressed Major Premise,* 53 Yale L.J. 271, 298–305).

In this State there has been at least one candid approach. In Faber v. Sweet Style Mfg. Corp., 40 Misc.2d 212, at p. 216, 242 N.Y.S.2d 763, at p. 768, Mr. Justice Meyer wrote: "(i)ncompetence to contract also exists when a contract is entered into under the compulsion of a mental disease or disorder but for which the contract would not have been made" (noted in 39 N.Y.U.L.Rev. 356). This is the first known time a court has recognized that the traditional standards of incompetency for contractual capacity are inadequate in light of contemporary psychiatric learning and applied modern standards. Prior to this, courts applied the cognitive standard giving great weight to objective evidence of rationality (*e.g.*, Beisman v. New York City Employees' Retirement System, 81 N. Y. S. 2d 373, *revd.*, 275 App. Div. 836, *affd*, 300 N. Y. 580).

It is quite significant that *Restatement, 2d, Contracts,* states the modern rule on competency to contract. This is in evident recognition, and the Reporter's Notes support this inference, that, regardless of how the cases formulated their reasoning, the old cognitive test no longer explains the results. Thus, the new *Restatement* section reads: "(1) A person incurs only voidable contractual duties by entering into a transaction if by reason of mental illness or defect ... (b) he is unable to act in a reasonable manner in relation to the transaction and the other party has reason to know of his condition." (*Restatement, 2d, Contracts* (T.D. No. 1, April 13, 1964), § 18C [now § 15, ed.].) *(See, also,* Allen, Ferster, Weihofen, *Mental Impairment and Legal Incompetency*, p. 253 (Recommendation b) and pp. 260–282; and *Note,* 57 Mich.L.Rev. 1020, *supra,* where it is recommended "that a complete test for contractual incapacity should provide protection to those persons whose contracts are merely uncontrolled reactions to their mental illness, as well as for those who could not understand the nature and consequences of their actions" (at p. 1036)).

The avoidance of duties under an agreement entered into by those who have done so by reason of mental illness, but who have understanding, depends on balancing competing policy considerations. There must be stability in contractual relations and protection of the expectations of parties who bargain in good faith. On the other hand, it is also desirable to protect persons who may understand the nature of the transaction but who, due to mental illness, cannot control their conduct. Hence, there should be relief only if the other party knew or was put on notice as to the contractor's mental illness. Thus, the *Restatement* provision for avoidance contemplates that "the other party has reason to know" of the mental illness (*id.*).

When, however, the other party is without knowledge of the contractor's mental illness and the agreement is made on fair terms, the proposed *Restatement* rule is: "The power of avoidance under subsection (1) terminates to the extent that the contract has been so performed in whole or in part or the circumstances have so changed that avoidance would be inequitable. In such a case a court may grant relief on such equitable terms as the situation requires." (*Restatement, 2d, Contracts, supra,* § 18C, subd. (2) [now § 15, ed.].)

The system was, or should have been, fully aware of Mrs. Ortelere's condition. They, or the Board of Education, knew of her leave of absence for medical reasons and the resort to staff psychiatrists by the Board of Education. Hence, the other of the conditions for avoidance is satisfied.

Lastly, there are no significant changes of position by the system other than those that flow from the barest actuarial consequences of benefit selection.

Nor should one ignore that in the relationship between retirement system and member, and especially in a public system, there is not involved a commercial, let alone an ordinary commercial, transaction. Instead the nature of the system and its announced goal is the protection of its members and those in whom its members have an interest. It is not a sound scheme which would permit 40 years of contribution and participation in the system to be nullified by a one-instant act committed by one known to be mentally ill. This is especially true if there would be no substantial harm to the system if the act were avoided. On the record none may gainsay that her selection of a "no option" retirement while under psychiatric care, ill with cerebral arteriosclerosis, aged 60, and with a family in which she had always manifested concern, was so unwise and foolhardy that a factfinder might conclude that it was explainable only as a product of psychosis.

On this analysis it is not difficult to see that plaintiff's evidence was sufficient to sustain a finding that, when she acted as she did on February 11, 1965, she did so solely as a result of serious mental illness, namely, psychosis. Of course, nothing less serious than medically classified psychosis should suffice or else few contracts would be invulnerable to some kind of psychological attack. Mrs. Ortelere's psychiatrist testified quite flatly that as an involutional melancholiac in depression she was incapable of making a voluntary "rational" decision. Of course, as noted earlier, the trial court's finding and perhaps some of the testimony attempted to fit into the rubrics of the traditional rules. For that reason rather than reinstatement of the judgment at Trial Term there should be a new trial under the proper standards frankly considered and applied.

Accordingly, the order of the Appellate Division should be reversed, without costs, and the action remanded to Special Term for a new trial.

JASEN, JUDGE (dissenting). . . .

The evidence conclusively establishes that the decedent, at the time she made her application to retire, understood not only that she was retiring, but also that she had selected the maximum payment during her lifetime. Indeed, the letter written by the deceased to the Teachers' Retirement System prior to her retirement demonstrates her full mental capacity to understand and to decide whether to take an option or the maximum allowance. The full text of the letter reads as follows:

February 8, 1965

Gentlemen:

I would like to retire on Feb. 12 or Feb. 15. In other words, just as soon as possible after I receive the information I need in order to decide whether to take an option or maximum allowance. Following are the questions I would like to have answered:

1. What is my "average" five-year salary?

2. What is my maximum allowance?

3. I am 60 years old. If I select option four-a with a beneficiary (female) 27 years younger, what is my allowance?

4. If I select four-a on the pension part only, and take the maximum annuity, what is my allowance?

5. If I take a loan of 89% of my year's salary before retirement, what would my maximum allowance be?

6. If I take a loan of $5,000 before retiring, and select option four—a on both the pension and annuity, what would my allowance be?

7. What is my total service credit? I have been on a leave without pay since Oct. 26, 1964.

8. What is the "factor" used for calculating option four—a with the above beneficiary?

Thank you for your promptness in making the necessary calculations. I will come to your office on Thursday afternoon of this week.

It seems clear that this detailed, explicit and extremely pertinent list of queries reveals a mind fully in command of the salient features of the Teachers' Retirement System. Certainly, it cannot be said that the decedent could possess sufficient capacity to compose a letter indicating such a comprehensive understanding of the retirement system, and yet lack the capacity to understand the answers.

As I read the record, the evidence establishes that the decedent's election to receive maximum payments was predicated on the need for a higher income to support two retired persons—her husband and herself. Since the only source of income available to decedent and her husband was decedent's retirement pay, the additional payment of $75 per month which she would receive by electing the maximal payment was a necessity. Indeed, the additional payments represented an increase of 20% over the benefits payable under option 1. Under these circumstances, an election of maximal income during decedent's lifetime was not only a rational, but a necessary decision.

Further indication of decedent's knowledge of the financial needs of her family is evidenced by the fact that she took a loan for the maximum amount ($8,760) permitted by the retirement system at the time she made application for retirement. . . .

Decedent's election of the maximum retirement benefits, therefore, was not so contrary to her best interests so as to create an inference of her mental incompetence. . . .

Nor can I agree with the majority's view that the traditional rules governing competency to contract "are, for the most part, too restrictive and rest on a false factual basis."

The issue confronting the courts concerning mental capacity to contract is under what circumstances and conditions should a party be relieved of contractual obligations freely entered. This is peculiarly a legal decision, although, of course, available medical knowledge forms a datum which influences the legal choice. . . .

As in every situation where the law must draw a line between liability and nonliability, between responsibility and nonresponsibility, there will be borderline cases, and injustices may occur by deciding erroneously that an individual belongs on one side of the line or the other. To minimize the chances of such injustices occurring, the line should be drawn as clearly as possible. . . .

Accordingly, I would affirm the order appealed from. . . .

Order reversed, without costs, and a new trial granted.

PROBLEMS

1. P, a fifteen-year-old employee of a Toyota dealership, injured his back in the course of his employment. An adjuster for the dealer's insurer negotiated a settlement of P's worker's compensation claim with P and with P's mother. The final agreed settlement was for $6,136.40. P signed the settlement agreement; P's mother did not. She, however, was aware of its terms and had advised P to accept the offered settlement. P has now declared that he disaffirms the agreement and has filed a petition to reopen his claim. Should it be granted?

2. Plaintiff's parents bought cruise tickets for themselves and for Plaintiff, their four-year-old daughter. Plaintiff was injured on the cruise ship when a ladder she was climbing detached and fell backwards. Upon completion of the cruise, her parents brought suit for damages in the U. S. District Court for the E.D. of Pennsylvania on her behalf. The cruise tickets provided that all lawsuits for injuries that occurred while on the cruise were to be brought in Dade County, Florida. Defendant moves for a change of venue to the U. S. District Court for the Southern District of Florida, located in Dade County. Plaintiff argues that, as a minor, she is not bound by the choice of forum clause. What result?

3. A 17–year–old high school senior in N.Y. has been accepted by Berkeley. Ace Airlines offers a discount flight for persons under 18 for $150, one-half of the adult fare. To attend the school the student, who cannot afford $150, misrepresents his age in order to obtain a full-fare ticket (costing $300) from the airline on its "fly now, pay later" plan. (This plan is only available to adults.) Upon arrival in San Francisco the student's grandmother gives the student $200, as she has previously promised to reimburse him for the cost of the flight. The student then disaffirms the contract and the airline brings suit. What result?

4. On March 1, Icarus went to a Rolls Royce dealer and bought a Silver Cloud with cash. The deal went smoothly and was fair. Icarus immediately attempted flight and the car was destroyed. Icarus' executor brought suit to recover the purchase price. During the trial it was established that Icarus had

been incompetent since February 1, although no adjudication of incompetence had been made. (a) What result? (b) What result if Icarus had been adjudicated incompetent and a guardian of his property appointed on February 1? (c) Would the result be different, assuming no prior adjudication of incompetence, if, when paying, Icarus had made paper planes of the money and, with each plane that landed successfully in the dealer's cash register, jumped up and down shouting, "Not even the sun will stop me now"?

5.   On February 1, A purchased a car on credit. Though normal by all appearances, A was suffering from a mental affliction which deprived A of knowledge of the transaction. By March 1, A had fully recovered, but had no recollection of how the car had been acquired, and continued driving the car for nine months. Could A now successfully disaffirm the contract?

6.   Jill had long sought Pete's Stradivarius to no avail. One night she plied Pete with a pint of Vodka and convinced Pete to part with the instrument for a fair price. When once again sober, could Pete disaffirm the contract?

CHAPTER 7

AVOIDANCE FOR MISCONDUCT OR MISTAKE

■ ■ ■

SECTION 1. DURESS

(Calamari & Perillo on Contracts §§ 9.1—9.8)

GALLON v. LLOYD–THOMAS CO.
United States Court of Appeals, Eighth Circuit, 1959.
264 F.2d 821.

MATTHES, CIRCUIT JUDGE. For the second time we are asked to review the action of the trial court in rendering judgment for defendant notwithstanding the verdict favorable to appellant (plaintiff) on Counts I and IX of plaintiff's amended complaint. . . .

As reference to our former opinion will reveal, in Count I plaintiff alleged that on October 13, 1954, as the result of defendant's duress, threats and coercion, he was compelled to sign an agreement with respect to his employment. In this count plaintiff prayed for rescission and cancellation of the contract, and for $25,000 actual damages. The jury awarded him $100 as damages. Count IX sought punitive damages and thereon plaintiff received a verdict for $20,000.

The court's judgment n.o.v. on Counts I and IX, was predicated on the conclusion that if the contract of October 13, 1954, was entered into by plaintiff under duress, it was nevertheless ratified in all respects by him as a matter of law. . . .

Plaintiff was employed by defendant in November, 1949. In March, 1950, he was appointed district manager in St. Louis, Missouri. For his services in selling appraisal service to business concerns, plaintiff received 15 per cent commission of the initial appraisal charge as well as the annual service charge. In 1952, for reasons not here material, plaintiff was transferred by defendant to New York with a drawing account of $225, with the oral understanding that defendant would not charge any overdrafts which plaintiff might incur in New York against his commissions earned in St. Louis. Plaintiff's operations in New York proved unsuccessful. His draw or advancement of $225 a week exceeded his earnings of 15 per cent of the defendant's fee on all contracts closed by plaintiff, and in September, 1954, defendant reduced plaintiff's drawing account to $175 a week. Pursuant to a telephone call from Ernest E. Goran, president of defendant company, plaintiff met Mr. Goran at the Sheraton Park Plaza Hotel in New York on or about October 12, 1954. Plaintiff testified that in the telephone conversation Goran said, "... that I had stuck my neck out too far and that a few days or weeks earlier he had received a call from an officer of the Department of Justice in Chicago; that they were investigating my character; that the investigator asked Goran if he knew that I was a bigamist; that he, Goran, didn't want to be implicated so he turned the investigator over to Mr. Gatenbey (vice-president of defendant) to deal with." Getting down to the events in the hotel, it appears that plaintiff's wife was with him, but Goran would not permit her to accompany plaintiff and Goran to the latter's room in the hotel. Plaintiff stated that he was very upset; that he and Goran found Gatenbey in the room and the latter began reading from a paper "... and telling me that I was a bad man, a bigamist, promiscuous or maybe worse and went on for nearly an hour and a half or two *until I was completely broken down.*" Continuing, plaintiff testified that Gatenbey "said that if he had had his way he would have fired me long ago; that I would have to get out of the country in twelve hours or else take the consequences." From other testimony we learn that plaintiff came to the United States from England in November, 1949; that he first married Ethel Charle, apparently in England; he then married one Margaret Duffin in Gretna Green, Scotland; he again married in East St. Louis, Illinois, to a woman whom he had met in Toronto, Canada. This marriage was annulled in New York in September, 1953, and on August 10, 1954, plaintiff married his fourth and present wife. At the time of the Sheraton Plaza Hotel incident on October 12, 1954, plaintiff had not been naturalized, and it is apparent that the statements made by Gatenbey in the hotel room caused plaintiff great anxiety and fear that he would be deported from the United States. Following the encounter with Gatenbey, above related, and after Gatenbey had gone into the washroom, Goran informed plaintiff that he had told Gatenbey "not to be so hard on me"; that Gatenbey's friend (a prominent citizen of New York, then an official of that state) would be contacted in an effort to delay the investigation. According to plaintiff's testimony, when he left the hotel room he was so sick that Mr. Goran had to walk him around in the hall before he was in a condition to be taken downstairs.

Mrs. Gallon testified that when she and her husband met Goran in the hotel lobby he stated to plaintiff: "John, you've gone too far this time. We're going to have a terrible time to keep the investigators from bothering you and I am afraid you will be deported, but we will see (what) Mr. Gatenbey and I can figure out about it." Mrs. Gallon stated she waited in the hotel lobby from two until four o'clock p.m. while her husband was with Goran and Gatenbey. That when Mr. Gallon appeared "he was very, very sick. I do not know what he went through, but he really went through something with those people, believe me. My husband was very, very upset. He had been crying you could see." While in the cocktail lounge later in the day, Goran again stated that he and Gatenbey would try to figure out what could be done to prevent the investigation, and plaintiff would be advised. Out of the foregoing came the contract which materially changed plaintiff's remuneration. From further testimony, it seems that following the events above set forth, and within a day or two thereafter, Goran and Gatenbey presented the contract to plaintiff who expressed some reluctance on signing it. Thereupon, Gatenbey lost his temper and stated he was in favor of firing plaintiff right then. In this setting, and with plaintiff still laboring under the fear of deportation, he signed the October 13, 1954, contract. The inference is clear from his testimony that he was then assured by Goran and Gatenbey that the investigation relating to deportation of plaintiff would be stopped and everything would be all right.

The salient features and terms of the October 13, 1954, contract were: Plaintiff acknowledged his services had not been performed satisfactorily; defendant was to retain plaintiff in its employ as long as his services were satisfactory, and his compensation was to be in an amount agreed upon between the parties; plaintiff acknowledged that he was overdrawn in his account with defendant in an amount in excess of $15,000, and authorized defendant to apply any and all credits and moneys due plaintiff from defendant toward payment of the overdraft (this terminated plaintiff's right to continue drawing commission on St. Louis business); plaintiff authorized defendant to pay out of moneys due him the sum of $200 to Mrs. Georgina Bird Gallon, one of his former wives, being the amount of a note held by her.

It is clear to us that the genuine trial issue revolved around and was focused upon the circumstances under which plaintiff entered into the October 13, 1954, contract. Was it the result of duress? That was the question. Plaintiff's testimony was sufficient to warrant a jury in finding that the contract came into existence as the direct result of the threats of Goran and Gatenbey, and that such threats caused plaintiff to be bereft of the quality of mind essential to the making of a contract.[2] . . .

Did plaintiff ratify the contract as a matter of law? Appellee insists that in view of plaintiff's actions and conduct, and his attitude toward the contract following its execution, the question must be answered in the affirmative. We agree. In resolving this crucial issue, we are mindful of the well-established principle of law that a contract entered into as the result of duress is not void, but merely voidable, and is capable of being ratified after the duress is removed. Ratification results if the party who executed

---

2. "Under the modern doctrine there is no legal standard of resistance with which the victim must comply at the peril of being remediless for duress imposed, and no general rule respecting the sufficiency of facts to produce duress; the question in each case is whether or not the victim was so acted on by threats of the person claiming the benefit of the contract, as to be bereft of the quality of mind essential to the making of a contract, and whether or not the contract was thereby so obtained." 17 C.J.S. *Contracts* § 175. [citations]

the contract under duress accepts the benefits flowing from it or remains silent or acquiesces in the contract for any considerable length of time after opportunity is afforded to annul or void it. [citations] An essential element in the doctrine of ratification is intention: indeed, it has authoritatively been said that it is "... at the foundation of the doctrine of waiver or ratification." 17A Am.Jur., *Duress and Undue Influence* § 26 at page 594.

Measured by the foregoing standard, the conclusion is inevitable that plaintiff ratified the contract in question. It appears without dispute that at the time the contract was signed, plaintiff was represented by an attorney, and in November or December, 1954, plaintiff informed his attorney of the conference in the hotel room preceding the execution of the contract, and also asked his attorney whether he could in fact be deported. From the time plaintiff signed the contract until he left defendant's employ in July, 1955, he never on a single occasion voiced any objection to the circumstances leading up to the contract nor did he at any time, after the alleged duress was removed, protest to Goran, Gatenbey or any other official of defendant that he had been pressured into signing the contract. To the contrary, he recognized the contract in all of its terms and provisions. He made weekly reports to defendant, in which he requested payment of his draw allowance of $175, which had been agreed upon. The commissions on the St. Louis, Missouri, business, which accrued after the contract was executed, were retained by defendant; the $200 due plaintiff's former wife was sent to her by defendant in accordance with one of the contract provisions, and in plaintiff's own words: "I never asked them (Goran and Gatenbey) to set the contract aside at anytime until after I resigned from the company. I never made such a claim to Goran, and I never made such a claim to Gatenbey until after I left the company." ...

In June or the early part of July, 1955, defendant reduced plaintiff's drawing account from $175 to $125 a week. This brought two letters from plaintiff, both written July 21, 1955. In one plaintiff proposed that his headquarters be transferred to Syracuse with a territory in out-state New York, and that he be permitted to draw $175 a week against his earnings. The other letter constituted his resignation to take effect within thirty days in the event his proposal was rejected. In neither letter did plaintiff question the validity of the contract. When defendant remained firm in its prior decision to reduce the weekly draw to $125, the parties parted company—and it was not until September, 1955, that plaintiff decided to take legal action to rescind or cancel the contract on the ground of duress in its procurement.

Without further discussion of undisputed testimony, bearing on ratification, we are of the opinion and so hold that when all of the facts and circumstances, viewed collectively, are fairly considered, only one conclusion can be reached and that is that plaintiff ratified the contract as a matter of law. Having done so, it necessarily follows that under no theory is plaintiff entitled to actual damages (awarded in Count I) or punitive damages (awarded in Count IX), and that the Court properly entered judgment for defendant on both of said counts.

Affirmed.

AUSTIN INSTRUMENT, INC. v. LORAL CORP.

Court of Appeals of New York, 1971.
29 N.Y.2d 124, 324 N.Y.S.2d 22, 272 N.E.2d 533.

FULD, CHIEF JUDGE. The defendant, Loral Corporation, seeks to recover payment for goods delivered under a contract which it had with the plaintiff Austin Instrument, Inc., on the ground that the evidence establishes, as a matter of law, that it was forced to agree to an increase in price on the items in question under circumstances amounting to economic duress.

In July of 1965, Loral was awarded a $6,000,000 contract by the Navy for the production of radar sets. The contract contained a schedule of deliveries, a liquidated damages clause applying to late deliveries and a cancellation clause in case of default by Loral. The latter thereupon solicited bids for some 40 precision gear components needed to produce the radar sets, and awarded Austin a subcontract to supply 23 such parts. That party commenced delivery in early 1966.

In May, 1966, Loral was awarded a second Navy contract for the production of more radar sets and again went about soliciting bids. Austin bid on all 40 gear components but, on July 15, a representative from Loral informed Austin's president, Mr. Krauss, that his company would be awarded the subcontract only for those items on which it was low bidder. The Austin officer refused to accept an order for less than all 40 of the gear parts and on the next day he told Loral that Austin would cease deliveries of the parts due under the existing subcontract unless Loral consented to substantial increases in the prices provided for by that agreement—both retroactively for parts already delivered and prospectively on those not yet shipped—and placed with Austin the order for all 40 parts needed under Loral's second Navy contract. Shortly thereafter, Austin did, indeed, stop delivery. After contacting 10 manufacturers of precision gears and finding none who could produce the parts in time to meet its commitments to the Navy,[1] Loral acceded to Austin's demands; in a letter dated July 22, Loral wrote to Austin that

> We have feverishly surveyed other sources of supply and find that because of the prevailing military exigencies, were they to start from scratch as would have to be the case, they could not even remotely begin to deliver on time to meet the delivery requirements established by the Government. ... Accordingly, we are left with no choice or alternative but to meet your conditions.

---

1. The best reply Loral received was from a vendor who stated he could commence deliveries sometime in October.

Loral thereupon consented to the price increases insisted upon by Austin under the first subcontract and the latter was awarded a second subcontract making it the supplier of all 40 gear parts for Loral's second contract with the Navy.[2] Although Austin was granted until September to resume deliveries, Loral did, in fact, receive parts in August and was able to produce the radar sets in time to meet its commitments to the Navy on both contracts. After Austin's last delivery under the second subcontract in July, 1967, Loral notified it of its intention to seek recovery of the price increases.

On September 15, 1967, Austin instituted this action against Loral to recover an amount in excess of $17,750 which was still due on the second subcontract. On the same day, Loral commenced an action against Austin claiming damages of some $22,250—the aggregate of the price increases under the first subcontract—on the ground of economic duress. The two actions were consolidated and, following a trial, Austin was awarded the sum it requested and Loral's complaint against Austin was dismissed on the ground that it was not shown that "it could not have obtained the items in question from other sources in time to meet its commitment to the Navy under the first contract." A closely divided Appellate Division affirmed. There was no material disagreement concerning the facts; as Justice Steuer stated in the course of his dissent below, "(t)he facts are virtually undisputed, nor is there any serious question of law. The difficulty lies in the application of the law to these facts."

The applicable law is clear and, indeed, is not disputed by the parties. A contract is voidable on the ground of duress when it is established that the party making the claim was forced to agree to it by means of a wrongful threat precluding the exercise of his free will. (*See* Allstate Med. Labs., Inc. v. Blaivas, 20 N.Y.2d 654, 282 N.Y.S.2d 268, 229 N.E.2d 50; *see, also,* 13 Williston, *Contracts* (3d ed., 1970), § 1603, p. 658.) The existence of economic duress or business compulsion is demonstrated by proof that "immediate possession of needful goods is threatened" (Mercury Mach. Importing Corp. v. City of New York, 3 N.Y.2d 418, 425, 165 N.Y.S.2d 517, 520, 144 N.E.2d 400) or, more particularly, in cases such as the one before us, by proof that one party to a contract has threatened to breach the agreement by withholding goods unless the other party agrees to some further demand. However, a mere threat by one party to breach the contract by not delivering the required items, though wrongful, does not in itself constitute economic duress. It must also appear that the threatened party could not obtain the goods from another source of supply and that the ordinary remedy of an action for breach of contract would not be adequate.

We find without any support in the record the conclusion reached by the courts below that Loral failed to establish that it was the victim of economic duress. On the contrary, the evidence makes out a classic case, as a matter of law, of such duress.

---

2. Loral makes no claim in this action on the second subcontract.

It is manifest that Austin's threat—to stop deliveries unless the prices were increased—deprived Loral of its free will. As bearing on this, Loral's relationship with the Government is most significant. As mentioned above, its contract called for staggered monthly deliveries of the radar sets, with clauses calling for liquidated damages and possible cancellation on default. Because of its production schedule, Loral was, in July, 1966, concerned with meeting its delivery requirements in September, October and November, and it was for the sets to be delivered in those months that the withheld gears were needed. Loral had to plan ahead, and the substantial liquidated damages for which it would be liable, plus the threat of default, were genuine possibilities. Moreover, Loral did a substantial portion of its business with the Government, and it feared that a failure to deliver as agreed upon would jeopardize its chances for future contracts. These genuine concerns do not merit the label " 'self-imposed, undisclosed and subjective' " which the Appellate Division majority placed upon them. It was perfectly reasonable for Loral, or any other party similarly placed, to consider itself in an emergency, duress situation.

Austin, however, claims that the fact that Loral extended its time to resume deliveries until September negates its alleged dire need for the parts. A Loral official testified on this point that Austin's president told him he could deliver some parts in August and that the extension of deliveries was a formality. In any event, the parts necessary for production of the radar sets to be delivered in September were delivered to Loral on September 1, and the parts needed for the October schedule were delivered in late August and early September. Even so, Loral had to "work . . . around the clock" to meet its commitments. Considering that the best offer Loral received from the other vendors it contacted was commencement of delivery sometime in October, which, as the record shows, would have made it late in its deliveries to the Navy in both September and October, Loral's claim that it had no choice but to accede to Austin's demands is conclusively demonstrated.

We find unconvincing Austin's contention that Loral, in order to meet its burden, should have contacted the Government and asked for an extension of its delivery dates so as to enable it to purchase the parts from another vendor. Aside from the consideration that Loral was anxious to perform well in the Government's eyes, it could not be sure when it would obtain enough parts from a substitute vendor to meet its commitments. The only promise which it received from the companies it contacted was for *commencement* of deliveries, not full supply, and, with vendor delay common in this field, it would have been nearly impossible to know the length of the extension it should request. It must be remembered that Loral was producing a needed item of military hardware. Moreover, there is authority for Loral's position that nonperformance by a subcontractor is not an excuse for default in the main contract. (*See, e.g.*, McBride & Wachtel, *Government Contracts*, § 35.10, (11).) In light of all this, Loral's claim should not be held insufficiently supported because it did not request an extension from the Government.

Loral, as indicated above, also had the burden of demonstrating that it could not obtain the parts elsewhere within a reasonable time, and there can be no doubt that it met this burden. The 10 manufacturers whom Loral contacted comprised its entire list of "approved vendors" for precision gears, and none was able to commence delivery soon enough. As Loral was producing a highly sophisticated item of military machinery requiring parts made to the strictest engineering standards, it would be unreasonable to hold that Loral should have gone to other vendors, with whom it was either unfamiliar or dissatisfied, to procure the needed parts. As Justice Steuer noted in his dissent, Loral "contacted all the manufacturers whom it believed capable of making these parts," and this was all the law requires.

It is hardly necessary to add that Loral's normal legal remedy of accepting Austin's breach of the contract and then suing for damages would have been inadequate under the circumstances, as Loral would still have had to obtain the gears elsewhere with all the concomitant consequences mentioned above. In other words, Loral actually had no choice, when the prices were raised by Austin, except to take the gears at the "coerced" prices and then sue to get the excess back.

Austin's final argument is that Loral, even if it did enter into the contract under duress, lost any rights it had to a refund of money by waiting until July, 1967, long after the termination date of the contract, to disaffirm it. It is true that one who would recover moneys allegedly paid under duress must act promptly to make his claim known. (*See* Oregon Pacific R.R. Co. v. Forrest, 128 N.Y. 83, 93, 28 N.E. 137, 139.) In this case, Loral delayed making its demand for a refund until three days after Austin's last delivery on the second subcontract. Loral's reason—for waiting until that time—is that it feared another stoppage of deliveries which would again put it in an untenable situation. Considering Austin's conduct in the past, this was perfectly reasonable, as the possibility of an application by Austin of further business compulsion still existed until all of the parts were delivered.

In sum, the record before us demonstrates that Loral agreed to the price increases in consequence of the economic duress employed by Austin. Accordingly, the matter should be remanded to the trial court for a computation of its damages.

The order appealed from should be modified, with costs, by reversing so much thereof as affirms the dismissal of defendant Loral Corporation's claim and, except as so modified, affirmed.

BERGAN, JUDGE (dissenting). Whether acts charged as constituting economic duress produce or do not produce the damaging effect attributed to them is normally a routine type of factual issue. Here the fact question was resolved against Loral both by the Special Term and by the affirmance at the Appellate Division. It should not be open for different resolution here.

In summarizing the Special Term's decision and its own, the Appellate Division decided that "the conclusion that Loral acted deliberately and voluntarily, without being under immediate pressure of incurring severe business reverses, precludes a recovery on the theory of economic duress."

When the testimony of the witnesses who actually took part in the negotiations for the two disputing parties is examined, sharp conflicts of fact emerge. Under Austin's version the request for a renegotiation of the existing contract was based on Austin's contention that Loral had failed to carry out an understanding as to the items to be furnished under that contract and this was the source of dissatisfaction which led both to a revision of the existing agreement and to entering into a new one.

This is not necessarily and as a matter of law to be held economic duress. On this appeal it is needful to look at the facts resolved in favor of Austin most favorably to that party. Austin's version of events was that a threat was not made but rather a request to accommodate the closing of its plant for a customary vacation period in accordance with the general understanding of the parties.

Moreover, critical to the issue of economic duress was the availability of alternative suppliers to the purchaser Loral. The demonstration is replete in the direct testimony of Austin's witnesses and on cross-examination of Loral's principal and purchasing agent that the availability of practical alternatives was a highly controverted issue of fact. On that issue of fact the explicit findings made by the Special Referee were affirmed by the Appellate Division. Nor is the issue of fact made the less so by assertion that the facts are undisputed and that only the application of equally undisputed rules of law is involved.

Austin asserted and Loral admitted on cross-examination that there were many suppliers listed in a trade registry but that Loral chose to rely only on those who had in the past come to them for orders and with whom they were familiar. It was, therefore, at least a fair issue of fact whether under the circumstances such conduct was reasonable and made what might otherwise have been a commercially understandable renegotiation an exercise of duress.

The order should be affirmed. . . .

PROBLEMS

1. Loral entered into a number of negotiated fixed-price contracts with the Navy for the manufacture of electronic equipment. The contract prices were based on the Navy's calculation of production costs. The Navy, however, did not adequately calculate rental value of Loral's factory. Despite Loral's protestations on this point, Loral entered into the contracts. Loral is now in court, seeking additional compensation by alleging duress. It argues that since it dealt almost exclusively with the government, it would have committed financial suicide by refusing to enter into the contracts at the Navy's price. What result?

2. Plaintiff's father had made a will in which he treated each of his three children, including Plaintiff, equally. Subsequently, Plaintiff informed her father that she was pregnant and had no intention to marry. He told her that unless she had the pregnancy terminated he would disinherit her. She refused and within a few days he changed his will. Shortly thereafter, he agreed that if she would terminate the pregnancy he would execute a will that was the same as the will he had just revoked. She complied, but he died before carrying out his end of the bargain. In her action against the estate and her siblings, they raise the defense that she had been coerced into making the agreement with the decedent and therefore it is voidable for duress. How viable is the defense?

3. P operated a large department store. Its fur department was operated by T, a concessionaire. Customers of the store, however, assumed they were dealing with P. Some 400 furs were left by their owners with T for cleaning and storage. T, in turn, delivered these to D for cleaning and storage. D was aware that T was an independent contractor. T went bankrupt and P cancelled the concession. In November, P requested D to return the furs, offering to pay for the cleaning and storage. D refused unless P paid $700 due for cleaning and storing the furs plus $3,300 which T owed D on past due accounts. The temperature dropped to 15° F and P's customers were clamoring for the return of their furs. After several days of vehement protests, P paid D $4,000. Two weeks later, it brought this action for restitution of $3,300. What result?

SECTION 2.   UNDUE INFLUENCE

(Calamari & Perillo on Contracts §§ 9.9—9.12)

FRANCOIS v. FRANCOIS

United States Court of Appeals, Third Circuit, 1979.
599 F.2d 1286.

ROSENN, CIRCUIT JUDGE. We are asked in this appeal to assess whether the district court properly relieved a husband from the disastrous financial consequences of a "Property Settlement and Separation Agreement" (agreement) entered into with his wife. The plaintiff, Victor H. Francois, instituted an action in the district court against his wife, A. Jane Francois, seeking rescission of the agreement and various real and personal property transfers made pursuant to that agreement. The district court declared the agreement and the conveyances to be null and void on the grounds, *inter alia,* that Jane Francois had exerted undue influence over her husband. The district court restored title to one parcel of real property and various securities to Victor Francois in his name alone. From the final order of the district court, Jane Francois appeals alleging that the district court improperly invalidated the agreement and reconveyed properties to her husband. We affirm.

I.

The controversy before us arises out of the troubled and relatively brief marriage of the parties. Victor H. Francois (Victor) and A. Jane Francois (Jane) were married on May 13, 1971 after a brief courtship of several months. At the time of the wedding, Victor was fifty years old, a bachelor residing with his elderly mother. Jane was thirty years old, twice divorced and the mother of two minor children, one approximately sixteen years old, and the other thirteen. Victor was relatively secure financially, possessing an acre lot, Lilliendal and Marienhoj, St. Thomas, V.I. (Lilliendal), with a two story, five bedroom building containing two apartments, a one-fourth interest in his family's hardware business, thirty shares of a family close corporation (Francois Realty), four shares of stock in a multi-family close corporation (21 Queen's Quarter), a portfolio of publicly held stock valued at between $18,000 and $19,000, and two bank accounts. Victor also received income from his job as manager of the family hardware business. Jane was gainfully employed at the time of the marriage but ceased working shortly thereafter. She apparently brought no money or property to the marriage.

The couple began to experience difficulties not long after the marriage. A series of events over the next four years centering on financial disputes led to the deterioration and eventual collapse of the marital relation. Within months of the wedding, Jane began to express anxiety over her financial security in the event that Victor died. To allay his wife's fears, Victor opened a joint savings account into which he deposited $5,000 for her use.

Jane also expressed a continuing desire for a marital homestead. In response, in March of 1972, Victor purchased a fairly large house with a swimming pool (Misgunst) for a sum of $107,000. Victor supplied a $37,000 downpayment from his assets and undertook the responsibility for the monthly mortgage payments in excess of $860 per month. Title was taken by the entireties. The same year, Victor filed a petition seeking adoption of Jane's two children. The court granted the petition after Victor acknowledged under oath that he voluntarily assumed responsibility for the children.

In the fall of 1973, the couple's finances became further consolidated. Victor conveyed all of his interest in his Lilliendal property to Jane and assigned to her a half interest in both his thirty shares of Francois Realty stock and four shares of 21 Queen's Quarter stock. He also gave Jane a power of attorney over his portfolio of publicly held stock. Jane also insisted on having a boat. Victor sold $18,000 of his stock in order to purchase a boat for Jane in her name at the cost of $17,000. Jane sold this boat approximately a year later for $16,000 and personally invested the proceeds for herself. The couple also executed reciprocal wills leaving the entirety of the marital estate to the surviving spouse or, if no spouse survived, to the children.

In September of 1974 a domestic quarrel precipitated the demise of the marriage. The dispute centered on an incident in which Victor allegedly embarrassed Jane by his behavior in front of one of Jane's friends. As a result of the incident, Jane determined to divorce Victor and on October 8, 1974, contacted an attorney, Harold Monoson, to draw up divorce papers. Victor was unaware of his wife's decision to terminate the marriage. Two days later, Jane, without any explanation, invited Victor to accompany her to Monoson's office where Victor, to his complete surprise, was presented for his signature a "Property Settlement and Separation Agreement." Monoson advised Victor that he would need an attorney, but Victor's choice was vetoed by his wife's insistence that this attorney was unacceptable. Monoson then asked a lawyer with an office in the same building, Gregory Ball, to come into the office. Ball read the agreement, which interestingly already had his name on it as Victor's counsel. Ball strenuously advised Victor not to sign the agreement because it would commit him to "financial suicide." When Victor persisted in his determination to sign, Ball informed him that he could not represent him in the matter, and left the office.

Victor, relying on representations made to him by Monoson and Jane, was persuaded that only by signing the agreement could he preserve his marriage. Victor signed the agreement and several related documents apparently in hope of saving his marriage. He conveyed to Jane his one-half interest in the marital home, Misgunst, and assigned to her his stock portfolio and his remaining stock interest in both close corporations. In addition, the agreement required Victor to pay $300 per month in alimony to his wife.

After signing the agreement, however, the parties resumed cohabitation for approximately one year. But early in 1975, Jane informed Victor that she had sold the entire portfolio of publicly held stock for around $20,000. In October of 1975, Jane informed Victor that she had sold the Misgunst and Lilliendal properties in exchange for properties owned in California by AD'M Enterprises, a limited partnership. In mid-October Jane also summarily informed Victor that she was leaving him permanently and promptly left the Virgin Islands. AD'M took title to the properties by a single deed dated October 15, 1975 but before it could record the deed, Victor instituted these proceedings. Apparently when AD'M learned of this litigation, it never recorded the deed but instead sued Jane for rescission of the conveyance.

Victor's suit against Jane and AD'M sought rescission of the agreement and reconveyance of all properties transferred to Jane. AD'M was duly served but never appeared and a default judgment was entered against them from which no appeal has been taken. The case was tried to the court without a jury.

Chief Judge Christian, the trial judge, declared the Property Settlement and Separation Agreement to be null and void as the result of: 1) the cohabitation of the parties subsequent to the signing of the agreement; 2) the undue influence exerted by Jane over Victor in connection with the signing of the agreement; 3) fraud and misrepresentation on the part of Jane; and 4) the unconscionable terms of the agreement. Judge Christian also declared the deed of October 10, 1974 transferring sole title in the Misgunst property to Jane to be null and void and awarded title to the property solely in Victor's name. The court held the attempted transfer of Misgunst and Lilliendal properties by Jane to AD'M to be null and void. The court likewise voided the assignment made to Jane, pursuant to the agreement of Victor's stock in the two close corporations, Francois Realty and 21 Queen's Quarters, and restored sole title to the stock to Victor. The court decreed that title to the Lilliendal property remain in Jane's name because "the circumstances of that transfer were not explicated before the court in the testimony." The court, however, placed a lien against the Lilliendal property to secure Victor's reimbursement for the value of the stock and monies converted by Jane in early 1975. Finally, the district court awarded costs and attorneys fees to Victor.

II.

Jane's first contention on appeal is that the district court erred in setting aside the Property Settlement and Separation Agreement. She challenges each of the four theories underpinning the district court's order of nullification. Because we agree that the district court properly voided the agreement on the grounds of undue influence exerted by Jane over her husband, we need not examine Jane's contentions relating to the three other theories supporting the district court's judgment. . . .

The key inquiry in the case before us is whether Jane and Victor Francois, as husband and wife, also enjoyed a confidential relationship. The marital relation does not automatically give rise to a confidential relation, but it "arises when one party places confidence in the other with a resulting superiority and influence on the other side." Yohe [v. Yohe, 353 A.2d 417, 421 (1976)]. Thus, each marriage must be examined on its own facts to determine if a confidential relation exists.

The district court unequivocally found that a confidential relationship existed between Jane and Victor Francois and that Jane was clearly the dominant partner. The district court found the evidence to be "replete with instances" in which Jane was able to secure her wishes simply by badgering Victor into submission. The record reveals that Victor, very early in the marriage, began to turn over the management of his finances to Jane who subsequently used her position to gain control incrementally over most of Victor's assets. The evidence supports the district court's findings that the relationship between the parties was one in which Victor reposed total trust and confidence in Jane who used her superior position in the marriage to Victor's financial detriment.

. . . The trial court, after determining the existence of a confidential relation quite properly allocated the burden of proof to Jane [to demonstrate the fairness of the agreement].

We must now consider whether Jane met her burden of proof to rebut the charge of undue influence. If she failed, a constructive trust may be imposed on the couple's properties in order to prevent Jane's unjust enrichment.

Undue influence is not a concept susceptible of unitary definition. The essence of the idea is the subversion of another person's free will in order to obtain assent to an agreement.

> If a party in whom another reposes confidence misuses that confidence to gain his own advantage while the other has been made to feel that the party in question will not act against his welfare, the transaction is the result of undue influence. The influence must be such that the victim acts in a way contrary to his own best interest and thus in a fashion in which he would not have operated but for the undue influence.

Williston on Contracts, § 1625 at 776–77 (3d ed. 1970).

The degree of persuasion that is necessary to constitute undue influence varies from case to case. The proper inquiry is not just whether persuasion induced the transaction but whether the result was produced by the domination of the will of the victim by the person exerting undue influence. *Restatement of Contracts* § 497, cmt. c. Hence, the particular transaction must be scrutinized to determine if the agreement was truly the product of a free and independent mind. In this respect, the fairness of the agreement must be shown by clear and convincing evidence. [*Williston, supra*] § 1627B at 823, Buchanan [v. Brentwood Fed'l Sav. & L. Ass'n, 320 A.2d 117, 127 (1974)]. . . .

The district court found that Jane alone caused the agreement to be made and that she alone benefited from it. The district court described the circumstances under which Victor was urged to obtain legal advice as a charade. There is no evidence that the independent advice received by Victor was from an attorney of his choosing. In fact, the meeting with Attorney Ball was arranged spontaneously and without an opportunity for a full and private consultation. Ball's name was already on the agreement as Victor's counsel. (For importance of independent counseling, *see Williston, supra* § 1625 at 778.) Victor was apparently surprised by his wife's decision to terminate the marriage and there is evidence that Monoson and/or Jane misled him into believing that by signing the agreement, the marriage could be salvaged. The district court also found that Jane, at the time the agreement was signed, had no real intent to save the marriage.

The terms of the agreement were hardly fair. Attorney Ball's assessment that the agreement was financial suicide for Victor was accurate. On this record, we conclude that the district court was correct in its finding that Jane had failed to rebut the presumption of undue influence.

We thus have a classic situation in which a constructive trust should be imposed over all the assets acquired by Jane. The district court properly used its equitable power to declare the agreement to be null and void. Equity should fully protect one spouse from exploitation through the exercise of undue influence by the other in whom confidence and trust has been innocently reposed. . . .

Appellant raises other contentions on appeal, all of which are without merit. Accordingly the judgment of the district court will be affirmed. Costs taxed against appellant.

METHODIST MISSION HOME OF TEXAS
v. N_____ A_____ B_____

Court of Civil Appeals of Texas, 1970.
451 S.W.2d 539.

CADENA, JUSTICE. Defendant, Methodist Mission Home of Texas, a licensed adoption agency, appeals from a judgment declaring that certain instruments executed by plaintiff, surrendering parental custody and control of her infant illegitimate child to, and permitting placement of the child for adoption by, defendant are void. The judgment is based on a jury finding that the execution of the instruments by plaintiff was the result of undue influence exerted on her by defendant's agents and employees.

Defendant seeks a reversal of the judgment and a remand of the case on the ground that there is insufficient evidence to support the jury finding of undue influence.

The parties agree that, since plaintiff consented to the placement of her child for adoption by an agency licensed by the State of Texas, the consent is revocable only on proof of "fraud, mistake, misrepresentation, overreaching and the like." Catholic Charities of Diocese of Galveston, Inc. v. Harper, 161 Tex. 21, 337 S.W.2d 111, 114–115 (1960). The case was tried below on the theory, not questioned here by either party, that a consent executed as the result of the exertion of undue influence on the consenting natural parent is subject to revocation under the *Harper Rule*.

The Methodist Mission Home in San Antonio is operated by the United Methodist Church as a maternity home to provide "proper care for the girl or woman who finds herself faced with an out-of-wedlock pregnancy." The United Methodist Church is the principal source of financial support for the Home. Additional sources of revenue include fees paid by girls who are admitted to the Home, contributions made by other religious organizations, and donations made by individuals, including gifts made by persons who adopt the children surrendered to the Home.

In addition to board, lodging and medical care, girls admitted to the Home receive the benefit of counselling by trained social workers who are members of the Home's counselling staff. This counselling concerns the girls' personal problems and vocational plans as well as "plans for the unborn child." Once each week, the residents participate in group counselling sessions, conducted by Rev. Don Lilljedahl, Director of Counselling, assisted by Mrs. Sharon Burrows. In addition, each resident meets privately with her individual counsellor about once a week. Plaintiff's individual counsellor was Mrs. Jo Ann Burns. Plaintiff's claim of undue influence concerns the conduct and statements of Rev. Lilljedahl, Mrs. Burrows and, particularly, Mrs. Burns.

When the question before us concerns the "sufficiency" of the evidence to support a jury finding, we must consider and weigh all of the evidence in the case, not merely that which supports the verdict. We may set aside the verdict and remand the cause for a new trial if we conclude that, in view of all the evidence, the verdict is manifestly unjust, even though the record contains some evidence of probative force in support of the jury finding.

An examination of the entire statement of facts reveals that there is sufficient evidence to support the following conclusions:

1. It is the policy of the Home to encourage unwed mothers to release their children to the Home for placement for adoption.

2. The Home's counselling staff attempted to persuade the residents to release their children for adoption.

3. During the time, prior to the birth of plaintiff's son, that the Home's staff believed plaintiff intended to give up her child no effort was made by the counsellors to induce plaintiff to reconsider her decision.

4. After plaintiff, subsequent to the birth of her son, announced her decision to keep the child, Mrs. Burns initiated a series of interviews with plaintiff, extending over a period of about five days, as the result of which plaintiff consented to the placement of the baby for adoption.

5. Although Mrs. Burns testified that she initiated the interviews for the purpose of discussing with plaintiff the "pros and cons" of the problem, the counsellor's contributions to the discussions consisted solely of a recital of the reasons why plaintiff should give up her baby.

6. Mrs. Burns implanted in plaintiff's mind the belief that plaintiff's parents, who had announced they would support plaintiff in her decision to keep the child, were attempting to take advantage of plaintiff. As a result, plaintiff successfully insisted that her step-father and sister, who had started the journey to Texas for the purpose of driving plaintiff and the child to California, "turn around and go back" to California.

During the period between Tuesday, November 26, and Tuesday, December 3, when plaintiff signed the instruments consenting to the adoption, plaintiff was very weak and Mrs. Burns, according to plaintiff, repeatedly and "emphatically stressed" that if plaintiff "was any sort of person" she would give up the child. Plaintiff described this period as a "nightmare" during which she was able to sleep only about three hours a day. She testified that, as a result of her discussions with Mrs. Burns, she felt "trapped," and that on Monday, December 2, after Mrs. Burns had repeated everything that the counsellor had said before, she consented to the adoption of her child in order to avoid "harassment."

What constitutes "undue influence" depends on the particular facts and circumstances of each case, viewed in the light of applicable principles of law. It is said that a finding of undue influence is justified only where the actor's free agency and will have been destroyed and subverted to the extent that his act, instead of expressing his own will, expresses the will of the person exerting the influence. Rothermel v. Duncan, 369 S.W.2d 917 (Tex.Sup.1963). Such statements of principles of law, since they involve inquiry into the metaphysical concept of will, furnish no concrete guidelines which are helpful in the decisional process. Since each case is more or less *sui generis,* any attempt to formulate a precise definition will be futile.

It is true that exerted influence cannot be branded as "undue" merely because it is persuasive and effective, and that the law does not condemn all persuasion, entreaty, cajolery, importunity, intercession, argument and solicitation. Robinson v. Stuart, 73 Tex. 267, 11 S.W. 275 (1889). It may be conceded that calling to the attention of an unwed mother the considerations which tend to show that her best interest, and that of her child would best be served by placement of the child for adoption cannot be branded as undue influence, even though she is thereby induced to give up her child.

But in this case we have testimony which amply supports the conclusion that plaintiff was subjected to excessive persuasion. All of the witnesses agreed that plaintiff was shy and reluctant to discuss her personal problems. Plaintiff's testimony concerning her emotional distress during the critical period following the birth of her child is rendered credible by the fact that an unwed mother who has just given birth is usually emotionally distraught and peculiarly vulnerable to efforts, well-meaning or unscrupulous, to persuade her to give up her child. Immediately following plaintiff's announcement that, contrary to the expectations of Mrs. Burns, she intended to keep her son, she was subjected to an intensive campaign, extending over a five-day period, designed to convince her to give up her baby, rather than to insure that her decision, whatever it might be, would be based on a consideration of all relevant factors. Plaintiff was told, falsely, that she had no right to keep her child. She was accused of being selfish and told that if she "was any kind of person" she would consent to the adoption of her baby. Her parents, the only persons who were willing to accept plaintiff's decision to keep her child, were accused by Mrs. Burns, with no factual support, of acting out of improper motives and with the intention of "putting something over" on plaintiff. What Mrs. Burns described as a discussion of the "pros and cons" consisted entirely of an endless recital only of the "cons"—a repetitive monologue of the reasons why plaintiff should not keep her child. The polemic by Mrs. Burns was in keeping with the policy of the Home to encourage the residents to surrender their children to the Home's placement agency. Further, this concentrated assault on plaintiff's will came from a person to whom plaintiff was encouraged to look for guidance, a member of an organization to which plaintiff was undoubtedly indebted and on which, according to all the testimony, she was dependent for help in finding her employment and a place to live.

Viewing the totality of the situation, we cannot say that, under the evidence, the jury acted unreasonably in concluding that the influence exerted on plaintiff was such as to constrain her to execute a consent which she would not otherwise have executed. Nor can we say that, considering all of the evidence, the finding is such as to "shock the conscience," or that it is "clearly unjust," or that it "clearly indicates bias" so that a court would "have to go blind" in order to accept it. Garwood, *The Question of Insufficient Evidence on Appeal*, 30 Tex.L.Rev. 803, 811 (1952).

The judgment of the trial court is affirmed.

PROBLEMS

4.   Decedent, an enfeebled woman over the age of 80, made a gift of almost all her assets to D, a physician. In addition to being her physician, D was her business adviser, agent and friend. Decedent in her lifetime had spoken of D with much affection and, on one occasion, stated that she regarded him as a son. She left, as surviving relatives, two sisters and their children. There was a conflict of evidence as to whether she had stated her intention to leave her estate to her relatives. Has a *prima facie* case for undue influence been presented?

5.   P, a woman factory worker, was seriously injured by the negligence of D. An adjuster for D's insurer made numerous visits to P while she was hospitalized. On the last visit, P was still in a cast from multiple fractures received in the accident. For two hours the adjuster repeatedly importuned her to sign a release in return for one-half of the estimated medical expenses. P testified that she became highly nervous and hysterical and signed the release in order to get the adjuster out of the room. The jury returned a verdict on P's negligence claim for damages substantially greater than the amount stated in the release and the trial court entered judgment for P for the amount of the verdict. On appeal, what result?

SECTION 3. MISREPRESENTATION, NONDISCLOSURE AND WARRANTY

(Calamari & Perillo on Contracts §§ 9.13—9.24)

COUSINEAU v. WALKER

Supreme Court of Alaska, 1980.
613 P.2d 608.

BOOCHEVER, JUSTICE. The question in this case is whether the appellants are entitled to rescission of a land sale contract because of false statements made by the sellers. The superior court concluded that the buyers did not rely on any misrepresentations made by the sellers, that the misrepresentations were not material to the transaction, and that reliance by the buyers was not justified. Restitution of money paid under the contract was denied. We reverse and remand the case to the superior court to determine the amount of damages owed the appellants.

In 1975, Devon Walker and his wife purchased 9.1 acres of land in Eagle River, Alaska, known as Lot 1, Cross Estates. They paid $140,000.00 for it. A little over a year later, in October, 1976, they signed a multiple listing agreement with Pat Davis, an Anchorage realtor. The listing stated that the property had 580 feet of highway frontage on the Old Glenn Highway and that "ENGINEER REPORT SAYS OVER 1 MILLION IN GRAVEL ON PROP." The asking price was $245,000.00.

When the multiple listing expired, Walker signed a new agreement to retain Davis as an exclusive agent. In the broker's contract, the property was again described as having 580 feet of highway frontage, but the gravel content was listed as "minimum 80,000 cubic yds of gravel." The agreement also stated that 2.6 acres on the front of the parcel had been proposed for B–3 zoning (a commercial use), and the asking price was raised to $470,000.00.

An appraisal was prepared to determine the property's value as of December 31, 1976. Walker specifically instructed the appraiser not to include the value of gravel in the appraisal. A rough draft of the appraisal and the appraiser's notes were introduced at trial. Under the heading, "Assumptions and Limiting Conditions," the report stated the appraisal "does not take into account any gravel...." But later in the report the ground was described as "all good gravel base ... covered with birch and spruce trees." The report did not mention the highway frontage of the lot.

Wayne Cousineau, a contractor who was also in the gravel extraction business, became aware of the property when he saw the multiple listing. He consulted Camille Davis, another Anchorage realtor, to see if the property was available. In January, Cousineau and Camille Davis visited the property and discussed gravel extraction with Walker, although according to Walker's testimony commercial extraction was not considered. About this time Cousineau offered Walker $360,000.00 for the property.

Cousineau tendered a proposed sales agreement which stated that all gravel rights would be granted to the purchaser at closing.

Sometime after his first offer, Cousineau attempted to determine the lot's road frontage. The property was covered with snow, and he found only one boundary marker. At trial the appraiser testified he could not find any markers. Cousineau testified that he went to the borough office to determine if any regulations prevented gravel extraction.

Despite Walker's reference to an "Engineer Report" allegedly showing "over 1 million in gravel," Walker admitted at trial that he had never seen a copy of the report. According to Walker's agent, Pat Davis, Camille Davis was told that if either she or Cousineau wanted the report they would have to pay for it themselves. It was undisputed that Cousineau never obtained the report.

In February, 1977, the parties agreed on a purchase price of $385,000.00 and signed an earnest money agreement. The sale was contingent upon approval of the zoning change of the front portion of the lot to commercial use. The amount of highway frontage was not included in the agreement. Paragraph 4(e) of the agreement conditionally granted gravel rights to Cousineau.[1] According to the agreement, Cousineau would be entitled to remove only so much gravel as was necessary to establish a construction grade on the commercial portion of the property. To remove additional gravel, Cousineau would be required to pay releases on those portions of ground where gravel was removed. This language was used to prevent Walker's security interest in the property from being impaired before he was fully paid.

Soon after the earnest money agreement was signed, the front portion of the property was rezoned and a month later the parties closed the sale.

There is no reference to the amount of highway frontage in the final purchase agreement. An addendum to a third deed of trust incorporates essentially the same language as the earnest money agreement with regard to the release of gravel rights.

After closing, Cousineau and his partners began developing the commercial portion of the property. They bought a gravel scale for $12,000.00 and used two of Cousineau's trucks and a loader. The partners contracted with South Construction to remove the gravel. According to Cousineau's testimony, he first learned of discrepancies in the real estate listing which described the lot when a neighbor threatened to sue Cousineau because he was removing gravel from the neighbor's adjacent lot. A recent survey shows that there is 415 feet of highway frontage on the property—not 580 feet, as advertised.

At the same time Cousineau discovered the shortage in highway frontage, South Construction ran out of gravel. They had removed 6,000 cubic yards. To determine if there was any more gravel on the property, a South Construction employee bulldozed a trench about fifty feet long and

---

1. Paragraph IX of the judge's factual findings states that there was no mention of the amount of gravel or road frontage in the purchase agreement. This statement is correct insofar as the agreement did not mention specific amounts of gravel or frontage, but the agreement plainly does provide for the transfer of gravel rights.

twenty feet deep. There was no gravel. A soils report prepared in 1978 confirmed that there were no gravel deposits on the property.

After December, 1977, Cousineau and his partners stopped making monthly payments. At that time they had paid a total of $99,000.00 for the property, including a down payment and monthly installments. In March, 1978, they informed Walker of their intention to rescind the contract. A deed of trust foreclosure sale was held in the fall of 1978, and Walker reacquired the property. At a bench trial in December, Cousineau and his partners were denied rescission and restitution.

Among his written findings of fact, the trial judge found:

> At some point in time, between October 24, 1976, and January 11, 1977, there existed a multiple listing advertisement which included information relating to gravel as well as road frontage, said information subsequently determined to be incorrect.

He further found:

> The plaintiffs did not rely on any misinformation or misrepresentations of defendants. The claimed misinformation about gravel on the property and the road frontage was not a material element of the parties' negotiations, and these pieces of information did not appear in the February 16, 1977 purchase agreement document prepared by attorney Harland Davis, attorney for the plaintiffs and signed by the parties.

In part, based on these findings, the court adopted the following conclusions of law:

> The plaintiffs are not entitled to rescission of the contract of sale or restitution as they were not entitled to rely on the alleged misrepresentation.

> The information which allegedly formed the basis of the misrepresentation was not material in the instant transaction, the agreement reached by the parties was valid and does not suffer any taint or defect of misrepresentation.

I. RESCISSION OF THE CONTRACT

Numerous cases hold and the *Restatement* provides that an innocent misrepresentation may be the basis for rescinding a contract. There is no question, as the trial judge's findings of fact state, that the statements made by Walker and his real estate agent in the multiple listing were false.[4] Three questions must be resolved, however, to determine whether Cousineau is entitled to rescission and restitution of the amount paid for

---

4. The statements made regarding highway frontage and gravel content in the two listing agreements cannot be characterized as "puffing." They were positive statements "susceptible of exact knowledge" at the time they were made. Young & Cooper, Inc. v. Vestring, 214 Kan. 311, 521 P.2d 281, 290 (1974). Although not applicable to real property sales, it is revealing that under the Uniform Commercial Code, where it is frequently necessary to distinguish "sales talk" from those statements which create express warranties, such definite statements as those made in the listing agreements would most probably be construed as creating an express warranty.

the property on the basis of the misrepresentations. First, it must be determined whether Cousineau in fact relied on the statements. Second, it must be determined whether the statements were material to the transaction—that is, objectively, whether a reasonable person would have considered the statements important in deciding whether to purchase the property. Finally, assuming that Cousineau relied on the statements and that they were material, it must be determined whether his reliance was justified.

A. *Reliance on the False Statements*

As quoted above, in his findings of fact, the trial judge stated, "The plaintiffs did not rely on any misinformation or misrepresentations of defendants." ... In our opinion, the trial judge's finding that Cousineau and his partners did not rely on the statements made by Walker is clearly erroneous.

Regardless of the credibility of some witnesses, the uncontroverted facts are that Wayne Cousineau was in the gravel extraction business. He first became aware of the property through a multiple listing that said "1 MILLION IN GRAVEL." The subsequent listing stated that there were 80,000 cubic yards of gravel. Even if Walker might have taken the position that the sale was based on the appraisal, rather than the listings, the appraisal does not disclaim the earlier statements regarding the amount of highway frontage and the existence of gravel. In fact, the appraisal might well reaffirm a buyer's belief that gravel existed, since it stated there was a good gravel base. All the documents prepared regarding the sale from the first offer through the final deed of trust make provisions for the transfer of gravel rights. Cousineau's first act upon acquiring the property was to contract with South Construction for gravel removal, and to purchase gravel scales for $12,000.00. We conclude that the court erred in finding that Cousineau did not rely on Walker's statement that there was gravel on the property.

We are also convinced that the trial court's finding that Cousineau did not rely on Walker's statement regarding the amount of highway frontage was clearly erroneous. The Cousineaus were experienced and knowledgeable in real estate matters. In determining whether to purchase the property, they would certainly have considered the amount of highway frontage to be of importance. Despite Walker's insistence that Cousineau knew the location of the boundary markers, neither Cousineau nor the appraiser ever found them. It is improbable that Cousineau would have started removing gravel from a neighbor's property had he known the correct location of his boundary line.

B. *Materiality of the Statements*

Materiality is a mixed question of law and fact. A material fact is one "to which a reasonable man might be expected to attach importance in making his choice of action." W. Prosser, *Law of Torts* § 108, at 719 (4th ed. 1971). It is a fact which could reasonably be expected to influence someone's judgment or conduct concerning a transaction. Under § 306 of the tentative draft of the *Restatement (Second) of Contracts* [now § 164, ed.], a misrepresentation may be grounds for voiding a contract if it is either fraudulent or material. The reason behind the rule requiring proof of materiality is to encourage stability in contractual relations. The rule prevents parties who later become disappointed at the outcome of their bargain from capitalizing on any insignificant discrepancy to void the contract.

We conclude as a matter of law that the statements regarding highway frontage and gravel content were material. A reasonable person would be likely to consider the existence of gravel deposits an important consideration in developing a piece of property. Even if not valuable for commercial extraction, a gravel base would save the cost of obtaining suitable fill from other sources. Walker's real estate agent testified that the statements regarding gravel were placed in the listings because gravel would be among the property's "best points" and a "selling point." It seems obvious that the sellers themselves thought a buyer would consider gravel content important.

The buyers received less than three-fourths of the highway frontage described in the listings. Certainly the amount of highway frontage on a commercial tract would be considered important. . . .

C. Justifiable Reliance

The trial judge concluded as a matter of law that the plaintiffs "were not entitled to rely on the alleged misrepresentation."

The bulk of the appellee's brief is devoted to the argument that Cousineau's unquestioning reliance on Walker and his real estate agent was imprudent and unreasonable. Cousineau failed to obtain and review the engineer's report. He failed to obtain a survey or examine the plat available at the recorder's office. He failed to make calculations that would have revealed the true frontage of the lot. Although the property was covered with snow, the plaintiffs, according to Walker, had ample time to inspect it. The plaintiffs were experienced businessmen who frequently bought and sold real estate. Discrepancies existed in the various property descriptions which should have alerted Cousineau and his partners to potential problems. In short, the appellees urge that the doctrine of *caveat emptor* precludes recovery.

In fashioning an appropriate rule for land sale contracts, we note initially that, in the area of commercial and consumer goods, the doctrine of *caveat emptor* has been nearly abolished by the Uniform Commercial Code and imposition of strict products liability. In real property transactions, the doctrine is also rapidly receding. Alaska has passed the Uniform Land Sales Practices Act, AS 34.55.004–.046, which imposes numerous restrictions on vendors of subdivided property. Criminal penalties may be imposed for violations. The Uniform Residential Landlord and Tenant Act, AS 34.03.010–.380, has greatly altered the common law of landlord and tenant in favor of tenants. Many states now imply warranties of merchantability in new home sales. Wyoming has recently extended this warranty beyond the initial purchaser to subsequent buyers. Moxley v. Laramie Builders, Inc., 600 P.2d 733, 735–36 (Wyo.1979).

There is a split of authority regarding a buyer's duty to investigate a vendor's fraudulent statements, but the prevailing trend is toward placing a minimal duty on a buyer. Recently, a Florida appellate court reversed long-standing precedent which held that a buyer must use due diligence to protect his interest, regardless of fraud, if the means for acquiring knowledge concerning the transaction were open and available. In the context of a building sale the court concluded: "A person guilty of fraudulent misrepresentation should not be permitted to hide behind the doctrine of *caveat emptor.*" Upledger v. Vilanor, Inc., 369 So.2d 427, 430 (Fla.App.).

The Supreme Court of Maine has also recently reversed a line of its prior cases, concluding that a defense based upon lack of due care should not be allowed in land sales contracts where a reckless or knowing misrepresentation has been made. Letellier v. Small, 400 A.2d 371, 375 (Me.1979). This is also the prevailing view in California, Idaho, Kansas, Massachusetts, and Oregon. On the other hand, some jurisdictions have reaffirmed the doctrine of *caveat emptor*, but as noted in *Williston on Contracts*, "(t)he growing trend and tendency of the courts will continue to move toward the doctrine that negligence in trusting in a misrepresentation will not excuse positive willful fraud or deprive the defrauded person of his remedy." W. Jaeger, *Williston on Contracts* § 1515B at 487 (3d ed. 1970).

There is also authority for not applying the doctrine of *caveat emptor* even though the misrepresentation is innocent. The *Restatements*, case law, and a ready analogy to express warranties in the sale of goods support this view.

The recent draft of the *Restatement of Contracts* allows rescission for an innocent material misrepresentation unless a buyer's fault was so negligent as to amount to "a failure to act in good faith and in accordance with reasonable standards of fair dealing." *Restatement (Second) of Contracts* § 314, cmt. b (Tent. Draft. no. 11, 1976) [now § 172, ed.].

In Van Meter v. Bent Construction Co., 46 Cal.2d 588, 297 P.2d 644 (1956), the city of San Diego failed to properly mark the area of a reservoir that needed to be cleared of brush. A lower court concluded that the city's failure to mark the area properly was an innocent mistake, and that a bidder's actions in failing to discover the true area to be cleared was negligent. Recovery was denied because the city's misrepresentation was not willful. The California Supreme Court reversed, first noting that a party's negligence does not bar rescission for mutual mistake, and then concluding:

> There is even more reason for not barring a plaintiff from equitable relief where his negligence is due in part to his reliance in

good faith upon the false representations of a defendant, although the statements were not made with intent to deceive. A defendant who misrepresents the facts and induces the plaintiff to rely on his statements should not be heard in an equitable action to assert that the reliance was negligent unless plaintiff's conduct, in the light of his intelligence and information, is preposterous or irrational.

Id. 297 P.2d at 648. The Massachusetts Supreme Judicial Court has expressed a similar view in Yorke v. Taylor, 332 Mass. 368, 124 N.E.2d 912, 916 (1955).

We do not contend that real property transactions are the same as those involving sales of goods. Nevertheless, an analogy to the applicability of the doctrine of *caveat emptor* under the Uniform Commercial Code is helpful. Under the Code, factual statements regarding the sale of goods constitute an express warranty. AS 45.05.094. The official comment to section 2–316 of the Code (codified as AS 45.05.100), dealing with disclaimers of warranties, states:

> Application of the doctrine of *"caveat emptor"* in all cases where the buyer examines the goods regardless of statements made by the seller is, however, rejected by this Article. Thus, if the offer of examination is accompanied by words as to their merchantability or specific attributes and the buyer indicates clearly that he is relying on those words rather than on his examination, they give rise to an "express" warranty.

Numerous cases have concluded that a buyer is entitled to rely on an express warranty, regardless of an inadequate examination of the goods.

Furthermore, the protections of the Code extend to highly sophisticated buyers in arms length transactions as well as to household consumers. Other than tradition, no reason exists for treating land sales differently from the sale of commercial goods insofar as application of the doctrine of *caveat emptor* is involved. We conclude that a purchaser of land may rely on material representations made by the seller and is not obligated to ascertain whether such representations are truthful.

A buyer of land, relying on an innocent misrepresentation, is barred from recovery only if the buyer's acts in failing to discover defects were wholly irrational, preposterous, or in bad faith.

Although Cousineau's actions may well have exhibited poor judgment for an experienced businessman, they were not so unreasonable or preposterous in view of Walker's description of the property that recovery should be denied. Consequently, we reverse the judgment of the superior court.

II. RESTITUTION

Walker received a total of $99,000.00 from Cousineau and his partners, but the appellants are not entitled to restitution of this amount. Cousineau apparently caused extensive damage to one building on the property, and he removed 6,000 cubic yards of gravel. Walker should be allowed some recoupment for these items, plus an amount for the fair rental value of the property less reasonable costs of rental.

It is necessary to remand this case to the trial court to determine the correct amount of damages.

Reversed and remanded.

VOKES v. ARTHUR MURRAY, INC.

District Court of Appeal of Florida, 1968.
212 So.2d 906.

PIERCE, JUDGE. This is an appeal by Audrey E. Vokes, plaintiff below, from a final order dismissing with prejudice, for failure to state a cause of action, her fourth amended complaint, hereinafter referred to as plaintiff's complaint.

Defendant Arthur Murray, Inc., a corporation, authorizes the operation throughout the nation of dancing schools under the name of "Arthur Murray School of Dancing" through local franchised operators, one of whom was defendant J.P. Davenport whose dancing establishment was in Clearwater.

Plaintiff Mrs. Audrey E. Vokes, a widow of 51 years and without family, had a yen to be "an accomplished dancer" with the hopes of finding "new interest in life." So, on February 10, 1961, a dubious fate, with the assist of a motivated acquaintance, procured her to attend a "dance party" at Davenport's "School of Dancing" where she whiled away the pleasant hours, sometimes in a private room, absorbing his accomplished sales technique, during which her grace and poise were elaborated upon and her rosy future as "an excellent dancer" was painted for her in vivid and glowing colors. As an incident to this interlude, he sold her eight ½–hour dance lessons to be utilized within one calendar month therefrom, for the sum of $14.50 cash in hand paid, obviously a baited "come-on."

Thus she embarked upon an almost endless pursuit of the terpsichorean art during which, over a period of less than sixteen months, she was sold fourteen "dance courses" totalling in the aggregate 2302 hours of dancing lessons for a total cash outlay of $31,090.45, all at Davenport's dance emporium. All of these fourteen courses were evidenced by execution of a written "Enrollment Agreement—Arthur Murray's School of Dancing" with the addendum in heavy black print, "No one will be informed that you are taking dancing lessons. Your relations with us are held in strict confidence," setting forth the number of "dancing lessons" and the "lessons in rhythm sessions" currently sold to her from time to time, and always of course accompanied by payment of cash of the realm.

These dance lesson contracts and the monetary consideration therefor of over $31,000 were procured from her by means and methods of Davenport and his associates which went beyond the unsavory, yet legally permissible, perimeter of "sales puffing" and intruded well into the forbidden area of undue influence, the suggestion of falsehood, the suppression of truth, and the free exercise of rational judgment, if what plaintiff alleged in her complaint was true. From the time of her first contact with the dancing school in February, 1961, she was influenced unwittingly by a constant and continuous barrage of flattery, false praise, excessive compliments, and panegyric encomiums, to such extent that it would be not only inequitable, but unconscionable, for a Court exercising inherent chancery power to allow such contracts to stand.

She was incessantly subjected to overreaching blandishment and cajolery. She was assured she had "grace and poise"; that she was "rapidly improving and developing in her dancing skill"; that the additional lessons would "make her a beautiful dancer, capable of dancing with the most accomplished dancers"; that she was "rapidly progressing in the development of her dancing skill and gracefulness," etc., etc. She was given "dance aptitude tests" for the ostensible purpose of "determining" the number of remaining hours [of instruction] needed by her from time to time.

At one point she was sold 545 additional hours of dancing lessons to be entitled to award of the "Bronze Medal" signifying that she had reached "the Bronze Standard," a supposed designation of dance achievement by students of Arthur Murray, Inc. Later she was sold an additional 926 hours in order to gain the "Silver Medal," indicating she had reached "the Silver Standard," at a cost of $12,501.35. At one point, while she still had to her credit about 900 unused hours of instructions, she was induced to purchase an additional 24 hours of lessons to participate in a trip to Miami at her own expense, where she would be "given the opportunity to dance with members of the Miami Studio." She was induced at another point to purchase an additional 126 hours of lessons in order to be not only eligible for the Miami trip but also to become "a life member of the Arthur Murray Studio," carrying with it certain dubious emoluments, at a further cost of $1,752.30. At another point, while she still had over 1,000 unused hours of instruction she was induced to buy 151 additional hours at a cost of $2,049.00 to be eligible for a "Student Trip to Trinidad," at her own expense as she later learned. Also, when she still had 1100 unused hours to her credit, she was prevailed upon to purchase an additional 347 hours at a cost of $4,235.74, to qualify her to receive a "Gold Medal" for achievement, indicating she had advanced to "the Gold Standard." On another occasion, while she still had over 1200 unused hours, she was induced to buy an additional 175 hours of instruction at a cost of $2,472.75 to be eligible "to take a trip to Mexico." Finally, sandwiched in between other lesser sales promotions, she was influenced to buy an additional 481 hours of instruction at a cost of $6,523.81 in order to "be classified as a Gold Bar Member, the ultimate achievement of the dancing studio."

All the foregoing sales promotions, illustrative of the entire fourteen separate contracts, were procured by defendant Davenport and Arthur Murray, Inc., by false representations to her that she was improving in her dancing ability, that she had excellent potential, that she was responding to instructions in dancing grace, and that they were developing her into a beautiful dancer, whereas in truth and in fact she did not develop in her dancing ability, she had no "dance aptitude," and in fact had difficulty in "hearing the musical beat." The complaint alleged that such representations to her "were in fact false and known by the defendant to be false and contrary to the plaintiff's true ability, the truth of plaintiff's ability being fully known to the defendants, but withheld from the plaintiff for the sole and specific intent to deceive and defraud the plaintiff and to induce her in the purchasing of additional hours of dance lessons." It was averred that the lessons were sold to her "in total disregard to the true physical, rhythm, and mental ability of the plaintiff." In other words, while she first exulted that she was entering the "spring of her life," she finally was awakened to the fact there was "spring" neither in her life nor in her feet.

The complaint prayed that the Court decree the dance contracts to be null and void and to be cancelled, that an accounting be had, and judgment entered against the defendants "for that portion of the $31,090.45 not charged against specific hours of instruction given to the plaintiff." The Court held the complaint not to state a cause of action and dismissed it with prejudice. We disagree and reverse.

The material allegations of the complaint must of course be accepted as true for the purpose of testing its legal sufficiency. Defendants contend that contracts can only be rescinded for fraud or misrepresentation when the alleged misrepresentation is as to a material fact, rather than an opinion, prediction or expectation, and that the statements and representations set forth at length in the complaint were in the category of "trade puffing". . . .

It is true that "generally a misrepresentation, to be actionable, must be one of fact rather than of opinion." Tonkovich v. South Florida Citrus Industries, Inc., Fla.App.1966, 185 So.2d 710. But this rule has significant qualifications, applicable here. It does not apply where there is a fiduciary relationship between the parties, or where there has been some artifice or trick employed by the representor, or where the parties do not in general deal at "arm's length" as we understand the phrase, or where the representee does not have equal opportunity to become apprised of the truth or falsity of the fact represented. Kitchen v. Long, 1914, 67 Fla. 72, 64 So. 429. As stated by Judge Allen of this Court in Ramel v. Chasebrook Construction Company, Fla.App.1961, 135 So.2d 876: ". . . A statement of a party having . . . superior knowledge may be regarded as a statement of fact although it would be considered as opinion if the parties were dealing on equal terms."

It could be reasonably supposed here that defendants had "superior knowledge" as to whether plaintiff had "dance potential" and as to whether she was noticeably improving in the art of terpsichore. And it would be a reasonable inference from the undenied averments of the complaint that the flowery eulogiums heaped upon her by defendants as a prelude to her contracting for 1944 additional hours of instruction in order to attain the rank of the Bronze Standard, thence to the bracket of the Silver Standard, thence to the class of the Gold Bar Standard, and finally to the crowning plateau of a Life Member of the Studio, proceeded as much or more from the urge to "ring the cash register" as from any honest or realistic appraisal of her dancing prowess or a factual representation of her progress.

Even in contractual situations where a party to a transaction owes no duty to disclose facts within his knowledge or to answer inquiries respecting such facts, the law is if he undertakes to do so he must disclose the *whole truth*. Ramel v. Chasebrook Construction Company, *supra*. From the face of the complaint, it should have been reasonably apparent to defendants that her vast outlay of cash for the many hundreds of additional hours of instruction was not justified by her slow and awkward progress, which she would have been made well aware of if they had spoken the "whole truth."

In Hirschman v. Hodges, etc., 1910, 59 Fla. 517, 51 So. 550, it was said that "what is plainly injurious to good faith ought to be considered as a fraud sufficient to impeach a contract," and that an improvident agreement may be avoided "because of surprise, or mistake, *want of freedom, undue influence, the suggestion of falsehood, or the suppression of truth.*" (Emphasis supplied.)

We repeat that where parties are dealing on a contractual basis at arm's length with no inequities or inherently unfair practices employed, the Courts will in general "leave the parties where they find themselves." But in the case *sub judice*, from the allegations of the unanswered complaint, we cannot say that enough of the accompanying ingredients, as mentioned in the foregoing authorities, were not present which otherwise would have barred the equitable arm of the Court to her. In our view, from the showing made in her complaint, plaintiff is entitled to her day in Court.

It accordingly follows that the order dismissing plaintiff's last amended complaint with prejudice should be and is reversed.

Reversed.

SMITH v. ZIMBALIST

Court of Appeal, Second District, Division 1, California, 1934.
2 Cal.App.2d 324, 38 P.2d 170.

HOUSER, JUSTICE. From the "findings of fact" made pursuant to the trial of the action, it appears that plaintiff [henceforth, Smith], who was of the age of 86 years, although not a dealer in violins, had been a collector of rare violins for many years; "that defendant [henceforth, Zimbalist] was a violinist of great prominence, internationally known, and himself the owner and collector of rare and old violins made by the old masters"; that at the suggestion of a third person, and without the knowledge by Smith of Zimbalist's intention in the matter, Zimbalist visited Smith at the home of the latter and there asked Smith if he might see Smith's collection of old violins; that in the course of such visit and inspection, "Smith showed a part of his collection to Zimbalist; that Zimbalist picked up one violin and asked Smith what he would take for the violin, calling it a 'Stradivarius'; that Smith did not offer his violins, or any of them, for sale, but on account of his age, after he had been asked what he would take for them, said he would not charge as much as a regular dealer, but that he would sell it for $5,000; that thereafter Zimbalist picked up another violin, calling it a 'Guarnerius', and asked Smith what he would take for that violin, and Smith said if Zimbalist took both violins, he could have them for $8,000; that the Zimbalist said 'all right,' thereupon stating his financial condition and asking if he could pay $2,000 cash and the balance in monthly payments of $1,000." Thereupon a memorandum was signed by Zimbalist as follows:

> I hereby acknowledge receipt of one violin by Joseph Guarnerius and one violin by Stradivarius dated 1717 purchased by me from George Smith for the total sum of Eight Thousand Dollars toward which purchase price I have paid Two Thousand Dollars the balance I agree to pay at the rate of one thousand dollars on the fifteenth day of each month until paid in full.

In addition thereto, a "bill of sale" in the following language was signed by Smith:

> This certifies that I have on this date sold to Mr. Efrem Zimbalist one Joseph Guarnerius violin and one Stradivarius violin dated 1717, for the full price of $8,000.00 on which has been paid $2,000.00. The balance of $6,000.00 to be paid $1,000.00 fifteenth of each month until paid in full, I agree that Mr. Zimbalist shall have the right to exchange these for any others in my collection should he so desire.

That at the time said transaction was consummated each of the parties thereto "fully believed that said violins were made one by Antonius Stradivarius and one by Josef Guarnerius ... in the early part of the eighteenth century; that Smith did not fraudulently make any representations or warranties to Zimbalist at the time of said purchase"; that there was "a preponderance of evidence to the effect that said violins are not Stradivarius or Guarnerius violins, nor made by either Antonius Stradivarius or Josef Guarnerius, but were in fact made as imitations thereof, and were not worth more than $300.00."

The action which is the foundation of the instant appeal was brought by Smith against Zimbalist to recover judgment for the unpaid balance of the purchase price of the two violins. As is shown by the conclusions of law reached by the trial court from such facts, the theory upon which the case was decided was that the transaction in question was the result of "a mutual mistake on the part of Smith and Zimbalist," and consequently that Smith was not entitled to recover judgment. From a judgment rendered in favor of Zimbalist, Smith has appealed to this court. In urging a reversal of the judgment, it is the contention of Smith that the doctrine of *caveat emptor* should have been applied to the facts in the case; that is to say, that in the circumstances shown by the evidence and reflected in the findings of fact, the trial court should have held that Zimbalist bought the violins at his own risk and peril. . . .

In the case of Chandelor v. Lopus (1603) 2 Cr. Rep. 4, 79 English Rep. 3 (Full Reprint), which in the state of New York for many years was relied upon as the leading authority in situations similar to that present herein, it was held that where one sold a jewel as a bezoar stone which in truth it was not, no action would lie, unless in the complaint or declaration it was alleged that the seller knew that it was not a bezoar stone, or that he warranted the stone to be such. . . .

[However, in] Hawkins v. Pemberton (1872) 51 N. Y. 198, 10 Am. Rep. 595, . . . in referring to the case of Chandelor v. Lopus, (1603) [*supra*] . . . the court said: "The doctrine (there) laid down is that a mere affirmation or representation as to the character or quality of goods sold will not constitute a warranty; and that doctrine has long since been exploded, and the case itself is no longer regarded as good law in this country or England." . . .

The governing principle of law to the effect that an article described in a "bill of parcels," or, as in the instant case, in a "bill of sale," amounts to a warranty that such article in fact conforms to such description and that the seller is bound by such description, has been applied in this state in the case of Flint v. Lyon, 4 Cal. 17. . . .

Although it may be that by some authorities a different rule may be indicated, it is the opinion of this court that, in accord with the weight of the later authorities . . ., the strict rule of *caveat emptor* may not be applied to the facts of the instant case, but that such rule is subject to the exception thereto to the effect that on the purported sale of personal property the parties to the proposed contract are not bound where it appears that in its essence each of them is honestly mistaken or in error with reference to the identity of the subject-matter of such contract. In other words, in such circumstances, no enforceable sale has taken place. [Furthermore,] . . . from a consideration of the language employed by the parties in each of the documents that was exchanged between them (to which reference hereinbefore has been had), together with the general conduct of the parties, and particularly the acquiescence by Smith in the declaration made by Zimbalist regarding each of the violins and by whom it was made, it becomes apparent that, in law, a warranty was given by Smith that one of the violins was a Guarnerius and that the other was a Stradivarius.

The findings of fact unquestionably show that each of the parties believed and assumed that one of said violins was a genuine Guarnerius and that the other was a genuine Stradivarius; the receipt given by Zimbalist to Smith for said violins so described them, and the "bill of sale" given by Smith to Zimbalist certifies that Smith "sold to Mr. Efrem

Zimbalist (defendant) one Joseph Guarnerius violin and one Stradivarius violin dated 1717 for the full price of $8,000.00 on which has been paid $2,000.00.''

[I]t may suffice to state that, although the very early decisions may hold to a different rule, all the more modern authorities, including many of those in California to which attention has been directed (besides the provision now contained in section 1734, Civ. Code), are agreed that the description in a bill of parcels or sale note of the thing sold amounts to a warranty on the part of the seller that the subject-matter of the sale conforms to such description.

It is ordered that the judgment be and it is affirmed.

BENTLEY v. SLAVIK

United States District Court, S.D. Illinois, 1987.
663 F.Supp. 736.

STIEHL, DISTRICT JUDGE. This cause was tried before the Court, without a jury. . . . Having heard and considered the evidence and arguments of all parties, the Court makes the following findings of fact and conclusions of law. . . .

FINDINGS OF FACT

. . . During January, 1984, plaintiff [Karen Bentley] observed, on a bulletin board located at Indiana University, a notice which the defendant, Charles Slavik, asked to be placed there. In the notice, Slavik represented that he had for sale an Auguste Sebastien Philippe Bernardel violin made in 1835 with an appraised value ranging from $15,000 to $20,000. In response to the notice, plaintiff contacted Slavik by telephone to inquire about the violin. During the telephone conversation, Slavik again represented that he had an authentic 1835 Bernardel violin with an appraised value ranging from $15,000 to $20,000, and invited the plaintiff to visit the defendants at their home in Edwardsville, Illinois, to see the violin.

On January 28, 1984, plaintiff travelled to defendants' home, saw the violin, played and inspected it for at least two hours. During the plaintiff's visit, Charles Slavik again represented to the plaintiff that the violin was an authentic 1835 Auguste Sebastien Philippe Bernardel violin, and further showed her Certificate No. 5500 from one Robert Bernard Tipple dated September 21, 1980, which certificate estimated that the violin was an authentic Auguste Sebastien Philippe Bernardel violin, which had a value of $15,000 to $20,000. Tipple, since deceased, was a violin maker, authenticator, and appraiser in Mount Vernon, Illinois.

In reliance upon the representations of Slavik, and the certificate presented by him, plaintiff purchased the violin from defendant, Charles Slavik, for $17,500. At that time, plaintiff paid Charles Slavik $15,000 by check, and agreed to pay the balance of $2,500 by February 15, 1984. The bill of sale signed by Slavik referred to the sale of "One Bernardel A.S.P.

Violin." The second payment was made by check dated February 13, 1984, mailed from Indiana. A letter which accompanied the $2,500 check expressed the plaintiff's pleasure with the violin. From the date of purchase until the end of 1985, the plaintiff played the violin for an average of eight hours a day.

Sometime in April of 1985, plaintiff became aware that the violin might not be a genuine work of Auguste Sebastien Philippe Bernardel made in 1835. Shortly after the plaintiff became aware the violin might not be a genuine Bernardel, plaintiff made demand upon Charles Slavik to return the purchase price and offered to return the violin, but Slavik refused to do so. Despite this, the plaintiff continued to play the violin until December of 1985.

During the plaintiff's use of the violin it required serious repair. . . . The repair was poorly done. . . . The Court finds that the violin is in poorer condition now than it was when purchased by the plaintiff. Although the defendants presented this evidence of the changed condition of the violin with fervor, they presented a theme without a resolution. No evidence was introduced to establish the extent to which the damage and repairs decreased the value of the violin. By failing to complete the theme, the defendants, in effect, leave the Court to speculate as to the measure of the diminution in the value of the violin and thereby improvise the final passage. The Court must, however, decline this offer.

On the crucial question of authenticity, the plaintiff presented the testimony of [two] experts in the authentication and appraisal of violins. . . . [Both are] member[s] of the International Society of Violin and Bow Makers, of which there are fewer than 25 members in this country. . . . These men examined the violin in question, and both asserted unequivocally that the instrument is not a Bernardel. They placed its value at between $750 and $2,000. As counterpoint, defendants offered the testimony of . . . Professor Perry. . . . [I]t is clear that he is not an expert in the field of authenticating violins. Additional evidence as to the authenticity of the violin as a Bernardel came in the form of the certificate of authenticity issued by Tipple and introduced as a joint exhibit of the parties. Tipple's certificate was less than compelling; it merely stated that it was his "estimation" the violin was a Bernardel. . . .

The Court finds the evidence presented by plaintiff on the determinative question of authenticity to be the more credible, and finds from a preponderance of the evidence that the violin is not the work of Auguste Sebastien Phillipe Bernardel, and that its value at the time of sale was $2,000. Despite this, the Court finds that Charles Slavik neither purposefully nor willfully misrepresented the maker or value of the violin, though he referred to the instrument as a Bernardel both orally and on the Bill of Sale. Slavik is neither an expert on the masters of violins, nor is he in the business, occupation or vocation of selling violins. . . .

CONCLUSIONS OF LAW

... In a diversity action, the choice of law rules of the state in which the district court sits are applied. Klaxon Co. v. Stentor Electric Mfg. Co., 313 U.S. 487, 61 S.Ct. 1020, 85 L.Ed. 1477 (1941). In contract cases, the Illinois rule is that the law of the place of execution applies when the contract is to be performed in more than one state. Because the second payment from Bentley was made from Indiana, the "place of execution" rule will be followed in this case, and Illinois law will be applied by the Court. ...

The plaintiff alleges ... that defendants breached the contract by not delivering a Bernardel. The defendants deny this, and assert that Charles Slavik delivered the violin bargained for and that the contract was ratified through a letter written by the plaintiff on February 13, 1984. Under the Illinois Uniform Commercial Code, Ill.Rev.Stat. ch. 26, para. 2–313(1)(b) (1983), an express warranty is created at time of sale that the goods sold by a seller will conform to any description of the goods that is a part of the basis of the bargain. The plaintiff, in effect, asserts that the certificate of authentication issued by Tipple and the sellers' reference to the violin as a Bernardel, both orally and in the bill of sale, as well as in the announcement letter posted on the bulletin board, was an express warranty by Charles Slavik to plaintiff.

In a similar dispute arising more than 50 years ago, a California Court of Appeals found that a bill of sale reciting the sale of two violins, a "Stradivarius" and a "Guarnerius," served as a warranty from the seller to the buyer that the violins sold were, in fact, Stradivarius and Guarnerius violins. Smith v. Zimbalist, 2 Cal.App.2d 324, 38 P.2d 170 (1934). To determine whether a warranty was created under Illinois law, the Court must examine the intent of the parties as expressed in the bill of sale and in the circumstances surrounding the sale itself. Alan Wood Steel Co. v. Capital Equipment Enterprises, Inc., 39 Ill.App.3d 48, 349 N.E.2d 627 (1976). This determination is generally considered a question of fact. Redmac, Inc. v. Computerland of Peoria, 140 Ill.App.3d 741, 95 Ill.Dec. 159, 489 N.E.2d 380 (1986). When examining ¶ 2–313(1)(b) of the Illinois Uniform Commercial Code, courts have used a "basis of the bargain" test which looks to the descriptions or affirmations forming the basic assumption of the bargain between the parties. *Alan Wood*, [*supra*] at 632.

From the evidence presented to the Court, it is clear that the description of the violin as a Bernardel, the affirmation created by the seller's repeated use of the term "Bernardel," and the presentation of a certificate of authentication support the conclusion that there existed a basic assumption that the transaction concerned a 1835 Auguste Sebastien Philippe Bernardel violin. The Court finds that ¶ 2–313(1)(b) applies to this dispute, and that a warranty under the statute was created by Charles Slavik. Consistent with the findings of fact, the Court concludes that an Auguste Sebastien Philippe Bernardel violin was not delivered by Charles Slavik to Bentley, and therefore Slavik breached the contract with plaintiff. . . . There has been no evidence that at the time of the February 13, 1984, letter Bentley knew or had reason to know the violin was not a Bernardel. Therefore, no ratification occurred when plaintiff expressed pleasure with the "Bernardel" in February, 1984. [Slavik also] asserted that Bentley should be estopped from rescinding the contract because of her 16 month delay in having the violin inspected. . . . However, there has been no evidence of any reliance or changed position on the part of Slavik. For this reason, estoppel has not been shown.

The plaintiff claims $20,000 in damages for the breach of contract. . . . The Court has concluded there was a breach of contract resulting from the warranty created by Slavik. Under Ill.Rev.Stat. ch. 26 ¶ 2–714(2) (1983), "the measure of damages for breach of warranty is the difference at the time and place of acceptance between the value of the goods accepted and the value they would have had if they had been as warranted. . . ." *Id.* The Court has found the violin had a value of $2,000 when sold, and that it was sold for $17,500, a value it would have had were it a Bernardel as warranted. In this case, the sale may be over, but the warranty lingers on. The plaintiff's measure of damages . . . therefore, is $15,500.

[Plaintiff's complaint] was amended at the close of plaintiff's evidence to allege mutual mistake on the part of buyer and seller. Mutual mistake, as defined in *Restatement (Second) of Contracts* § 152 (1981), has been recognized in Illinois courts. . . . If a mistake by both parties as to "a basic assumption on which the contract was made has a material effect on the agreed exchange of performance, the contract is voidable by the adversely affected party. . . ." *Restatement (Second) of Contracts* § 152 (1981). . . . [T]he adversely affected party [has] the remedy of the return of the excess purchase price. It is this relief the plaintiff appears to request.

From the facts already discussed, it appears there did exist a mistake by both parties as to the maker of the violin sold to plaintiff by defendant Charles Slavik. Moreover, it is clear the basic assumption that the violin was a Bernardel materially affected the agreed price, the exchange of performance. Yet it must be determined whether either party assumed the risk of mistake referred to in § 152(1) and explained in § 154, comment c of the *Restatement (Second) of Contracts* (1981). This Court concludes that neither party assumed the risk.

While the conclusion that Slavik did not assume the risk of mistake is apparent from the facts, a similar conclusion as to plaintiff merits further discussion. Thorough examination of § 154(b) and comment c therein reveals that plaintiff did not bear the risk the violin was not a Bernardel. "Conscious ignorance" is defined in comment c as an awareness of a contracting party prior to agreement that it is unknowledgeable about certain facts that later become the basis for the mutual mistake claim. The party that was aware of the uncertainty prior to the contract may not assert mutual mistake of fact, according to comment c.

The Illinois Supreme Court has long recognized that mutual mistakes of fact may make contracts voidable. Harley v. Magnolia Petroleum Co.,

378 Ill. 19, 37 N.E.2d 760 (1941). It is further stated that mutual mistakes must have been unknown at the time the contract is made, and that neither party may have borne the risk of any unknown facts. [*Id.*] at 765. It is this voluntary bearing of the risk of unknown facts that the *Restatement* refers to as "conscious ignorance." The court describes this as a "conscious present want of knowledge of facts" which a party has manifestly concluded will not influence the decision to contract. [*Id.*] Another court has referred to it as an "attitude of indifference." Southern National Bank of Houston v. Crateo, Inc., 458 F.2d 688, 698 (5th Cir. 1972). Regardless of the terms used, the Fifth Circuit and the Illinois Supreme Court require a showing that the ignorant party is willing to bear the risk of the unknown facts before that party will be barred from asserting mutual mistake of fact. *Harley*, at 765; *Southern National Bank*, at 693. The evidence presented before the Court gives no reason for finding that plaintiff exhibited a willingness to bear the risk that the violin was not a Bernardel. The evidence shows she would not have purchased the violin for the price paid had she not been convinced the violin was a Bernardel. She was not consciously ignorant of, nor did she exhibit an attitude of indifference about, the authenticity of the violin when she purchased the instrument. For these reasons, the Court concludes plaintiff did not bear the risk of mistake under § 154 or § 152 of the *Restatement (Second) of Contracts* (1981).

The Court therefore concludes that there existed a mutual mistake of fact between defendant, Charles Slavik, and plaintiff, Karen Bentley, and that plaintiff is entitled to return of the excess purchase price paid due to the mutual mistake. The excess price is $15,500, the difference between the $17,500 purchase price, and the value of the violin at the time it was sold, $2,000.

CADENZA

This case gave the Court an insight into the relationship classical musicians develop with their instruments. The plaintiff referred to violins as "living," "breathing" and possessing "souls." Mr. Slavik spoke of his care of the violin over 33 years of ownership with pride and intensity. It is clear that this dispute concerned more than a simple commercial transaction. The defendant felt his integrity attacked; the plaintiff felt victimized.

While sympathetic, the law is ill-equipped to soothe such emotions. The Court must examine the matter with detachment. Yet, it is this detachment that gives the law a timeless quality similar to that of the music the litigants so love. The law's disinterest gives it consistency, and its consistency, in turn, gives it endurance. It is this enduring quality that the law and great music share. Just as many classic works of music are based on a simple melody, the law of this case is based on a consistent rule: that a seller's description of an item amounts to a warranty that the object sold is as described. Returning to an earlier refrain: the sale may be over, but the warranty lingers on. . . .

It is so ordered.

PROBLEMS

6.   D, an electric power company, formulated a plan to acquire land for a large hydro-electric project. P owned 138 acres of timberland in the area. A, who was D's undisclosed agent, contacted P and offered to purchase P's tract. When P asked him why he wanted the land, A falsely replied that he had come into a large sum of money which he wanted to invest in timber. D agreed to sell the tract for $4,100 and the contract was performed. P sues in equity to rescind the deed, alleging that had he known A's and D's true motive, he could have demanded and received $27,000 for the tract. What result?

7.   D operated a small but highly successful chicken processing plant. A key reason for this success was that D had developed machines for stripping meat from chicken necks and emulsifying the meat for use in baby food. These machines were adaptations of existing vegetable pulpers bought from FMC on which FMC held patents. D's application for a patent on the adaptations was pending. P had negotiations with D to purchase D's business. After investigating D's application and discovering that it was an adaptation of FMC's patent, P's patent attorney asked D what was new and novel about D's adaptation. D replied that the key innovation was the precise setting of the gap between the vanes and the blades. P offered to purchase on the condition that the patent application be granted. D refused to accept the condition. P then agreed to purchase after P's patent attorney gave an opinion that the adaptation was patentable. P made the purchase of the business along with rights in the patent application. The application was denied. P sued to rescind. The trial judge found that D's statement as to the importance of the gap was innocent but incorrect and granted rescission and restitution. On appeal, what are the issues and how should they be resolved?

8.   P contracted to purchase from D a tract of land which was used as a vacation resort. The land was irrigated from Grouse Creek. P inquired about water rights and D replied that the tract had water rights to Grouse Creek. D did not inform P that a neighboring landowner had questioned the water rights and on several occasions had by words and actions asserted rights to the water inconsistent with those of D. Upon discovery of this adverse claim, P seeks to rescind. What result?

9.   A and B reach an agreement and agree to reduce it to writing. A prepares a writing, which B reads, that accurately reflects their understanding. Prior to signing the writing, A substitutes a writing that is similar in appearance, but which contains terms that are radically different. B signs this second writing. What is the legal effect of the signed writing?

10.   At the request of her husband, W signed a document whereby she personally guaranteed to the plaintiff bank the obligations of a corporation controlled by her husband. Her husband told her that her signature was required by the bank but that she would not be under any liability to the bank. Although literate, she did not read the document. When the corporation defaulted on its obligation to the bank, the latter brought suit against W. Can she rescind?

11.   Who ought to bear the risk of the violins' provenance in Smith v. Zimbalist? in Bentley v. Slavik? Why? How do remedies differ for mutual mistake and breach of warranty? Is the court in *Bentley* correct in finding both breach of warranty and mutual mistake?

SECTION 4.   MISTAKE

(Calamari & Perillo on Contracts §§ 9.25—9.30)

NELSON v. RICE

Court of Appeals of Arizona, Division 2, Department B, 2000.
198 Ariz. 563, 12 P.3d 238.

ESPINOSA, CHIEF JUDGE. ¶ 1 Plaintiff/appellant the Estate of Martha Nelson, through its copersonal representatives Edward Franz and Kenneth Newman, appeals from a summary judgment in favor of defendants/appellees Carl and Anne Rice in the Estate's action seeking rescission or reformation of the sale of two paintings to the Rices. The Estate argues that these remedies are required because the sale was based upon a mutual mistake. The Estate also contends that enforcing the sale "contract" would be unconscionable. We affirm.

Facts and Procedural History

¶ 2 We view the evidence and all reasonable inferences therefrom in the light most favorable to the party opposing the summary judgment. After Martha Nelson died in February 1996, Newman and Franz, the copersonal representatives of her estate, employed Judith McKenzie–Larson to appraise the Estate's personal property in preparation for an estate sale. McKenzie–Larson told them that she did not appraise fine art and that, if she saw any, they would need to hire an additional appraiser. McKenzie–Larson did not report finding any fine art, and relying on her silence and her appraisal, Newman and Franz priced and sold the Estate's personal property.

¶ 3 Responding to a newspaper advertisement, Carl Rice attended the public estate sale and paid the asking price of $60 for two oil paintings. Although Carl had bought and sold some art, he was not an educated purchaser, had never made more than $55 on any single piece, and had bought many pieces that had "turned out to be frauds, forgeries or . . . to have been (created) by less popular artists." He assumed the paintings were not originals given their price and the fact that the Estate was managed by professionals, but was attracted to the subject matter of one of the paintings and the frame of the other. At home, he compared the signatures on the paintings to those in a book of artists' signatures, noticing they "appeared to be similar" to that of Martin Johnson Heade. As they had done in the past, the Rices sent pictures of the paintings to

Christie's in New York, hoping they might be Heade's work. Christie's authenticated the paintings, Magnolia Blossoms on Blue Velvet and Cherokee Roses, as paintings by Heade and offered to sell them on consignment. Christie's subsequently sold the paintings at auction for $1,072,000. After subtracting the buyer's premium and the commission, the Rices realized $911,780 from the sale.

¶ 4 Newman and Franz learned about the sale in February 1997 and thereafter sued McKenzie–Larson on behalf of the Estate, believing she was entirely responsible for the Estate's loss. The following November, they settled the lawsuit because McKenzie–Larson had no assets with which to pay damages. During 1997, the Rices paid income taxes of $337,000 on the profit from the sale of the paintings, purchased a home, created a family trust, and spent some of the funds on living expenses.

¶ 5 The Estate sued the Rices in late January 1998, alleging the sale contract should be rescinded or reformed on grounds of mutual mistake and unconscionability. In its subsequent motion for summary judgment, the Estate argued the parties were not aware the transaction had involved fine art, believing instead that the items exchanged were "relatively valueless, wall decorations." In their opposition and cross-motion, the Rices argued the Estate bore the risk of mistake, the doctrine of laches precluded reformation of the contract, and unconscionability was not a basis for rescission. The trial court concluded that, although the parties had been mistaken about the value of the paintings, the Estate bore the risk of that mistake. The court ruled the contract was not unconscionable, finding the parties had not negotiated Carl's paying the prices the Estate had set. Accordingly, the court denied the Estate's motion for summary judgment and granted the Rices' cross-motion. The Estate's motion for new trial was denied, and this appeal followed. . . .

Mutual Mistake

¶ 7 The Estate first argues that it established a mutual mistake sufficient to permit the reformation or rescission of the sale of the paintings to the Rices.[5] A party seeking to rescind a contract on the basis of mutual mistake must show by clear and convincing evidence that the agreement should be set aside. Emmons v. Superior Court, 192 Ariz. 509, 968 P.2d 582 (App.1998). A contract may be rescinded on the ground of a mutual mistake as to a " 'basic assumption on which both parties made the contract.' " Renner v. Kehl, 150 Ariz. 94, 97, 722 P.2d 262, 265 (1986), *quoting Restatement (Second) of Contracts* § 152 cmt. b (1979). Furthermore, the parties' mutual mistake must have had " 'such a material effect on the agreed exchange of performances as to upset the very bases of the contract.' " *Id., quoting Restatement* § 152 cmt. a. However, the mistake

---

5. Reformation is not an available remedy under these facts. It is a remedy to correct a written instrument that fails to express the terms agreed upon by the parties and "is not intended to enforce the terms of an agreement the parties never made." Isaak v. Massachusetts Indem. Life Ins. Co., 127 Ariz. 581, 584, 623 P.2d 11, 14 (1981); *see also* Ashton Co., Inc., Contractors & Engineers v. State, 9 Ariz.App. 564, 454 P.2d 1004 (1969) (contractor not entitled to reform contract in absence of showing it did not express parties' real agreement).

must not be one on which the party seeking relief bears the risk under the rules stated in § 154(b) of the *Restatement. Emmons; Restatement* § 152.

¶ 8 In concluding that the Estate was not entitled to rescind the sale, the trial court found that, although a mistake had existed as to the value of the paintings, the Estate bore the risk of that mistake under § 154(b) of the *Restatement*, citing the example in comment a. Section 154(b) states that a party bears the risk of mistake when "he is aware, at the time the contract is made, that he has only limited knowledge with respect to the facts to which the mistake relates but treats his limited knowledge as sufficient." In explaining that provision, the Washington Supreme Court stated, "In such a situation there is no mistake. Instead, there is an awareness of uncertainty or conscious ignorance of the future." Bennett v. Shinoda Floral, Inc., 108 Wash.2d 386, 739 P.2d 648, 653–54 (1987).

¶ 9 The Estate contends neither party bore the risk of mistake, arguing that § 154 and comment a are not applicable to these facts. In the example in comment a, the risk of mistake is allocated to the seller when the buyer discovers valuable mineral deposits on property priced and purchased as farmland. Even were we to accept the Estate's argument that this example is not analogous, comment c clearly applies here and states:

> *Conscious ignorance.* Even though the mistaken party did not agree to bear the risk, he may have been aware when he made the contract that his knowledge with respect to the facts to which the mistake relates was limited. If he was not only so aware that his knowledge was limited but undertook to perform in the face of that awareness, he bears the risk of the mistake. It is sometimes said in such a situation that, in a sense, there was not mistake but "conscious ignorance."

¶ 10 Through its personal representatives, the Estate hired two appraisers, McKenzie–Larson and an Indian art expert, to evaluate the Estate's collection of Indian art and artifacts. McKenzie–Larson specifically told Newman that she did not appraise fine art. In his deposition, Newman testified that he had not been concerned that McKenzie–Larson had no expertise in fine art, believing the Estate contained nothing of "significant value" except the house and the Indian art collection. Despite the knowledge that the Estate contained framed art other than the Indian art, and that McKenzie–Larson was not qualified to appraise fine art, the personal representatives relied on her to notify them of any fine art or whether a fine arts appraiser was needed. Because McKenzie–Larson did not say they needed an additional appraiser, Newman and Franz did not hire anyone qualified to appraise fine art. By relying on the opinion of someone who was admittedly unqualified to appraise fine art to determine its existence, the personal representatives consciously ignored the possibility that the Estate's assets might include fine art, thus assuming that risk. *See* Klas v. Van Wagoner, 829 P.2d 135, 141 n. 8 (Utah App.1992) (real estate buyers not entitled to rescind sale contract because they bore risk of mistake as to property's value; by hiring architects, decorators, and electricians to examine realty, but failing to have it appraised, purchasers executed sale contract knowing they "had only 'limited knowledge' with respect to the value of the home"). Accordingly, the trial court correctly found that the Estate bore the risk of mistake as to the paintings' value.

¶ 11 The Estate asserts that the facts here are similar to those in *Renner*, in which real estate buyers sued to rescind a contract for acreage upon which they wished to commercially grow jojoba after discovering the water supply was inadequate for that purpose. The supreme court concluded that the buyers could rescind the contract based upon mutual mistake because both the buyers and the sellers had believed there was an adequate water supply, a basic assumption underlying formation of the contract. The parties' failure to thoroughly investigate the water supply did not preclude rescission when "the risk of mistake was not allocated among the parties." 150 Ariz. at 97 n. 2, 722 P.2d at 265 n. 2. The Estate's reliance on *Renner* is unavailing because, as stated above, the Estate bore the risk of mistake based on its own conscious ignorance.

¶ 12 Furthermore, under *Restatement* § 154(c), the court may allocate the risk of mistake to one party "on the ground that it is reasonable in the circumstances to do so." In making this determination, "the court will consider the purposes of the parties and will have recourse to its own general knowledge of human behavior in bargain transactions." *Restatement* § 154 cmt. d. Here, the Estate had had ample opportunity to discover what it was selling and failed to do so; instead, it ignored the possibility that the paintings were valuable and attempted to take action only after learning of their worth as a result of the efforts of the Rices. Under these circumstances, the Estate was a victim of its own folly and it was reasonable for the court to allocate to it the burden of its mistake.

Unconscionability

¶ 13 The Estate also argues that enforcement of the "contract" to sell the paintings is unconscionable. The determination of a contract's unconscionability is for the trial court as a matter of law. Maxwell v. Fidelity Financial Services, Inc., 184 Ariz. 82, 907 P.2d 51 (1995). We review that ruling *de novo*. Samaritan Health Sys. v. Superior Court, 194 Ariz. 284, 981 P.2d 584 (App.1998). " 'Unconscionability includes both procedural unconscionability, *i.e.*, something wrong in the bargaining process, and substantive unconscionability, *i.e.*, the contract terms per se.' " Phoenix Baptist Hosp. & Medical Ctr., Inc. v. Aiken, 179 Ariz. 289, 293, 877 P.2d 1345, 1349 (App.1994), *quoting* Pacific Am. Leasing Corp. v. S.P.E. Bldg. Sys., 152 Ariz. 96, 103, 730 P.2d 273, 280 (App.1986).

¶ 14 Citing *Maxwell*, the Estate contends this is a case of substantive unconscionability, which concerns the actual terms of the contract and the relative fairness of the parties' obligations. Indicia of substantive unconscionability include one-sided terms that oppress or unfairly surprise an innocent party, an overall imbalance in the obligations and rights imposed by the bargain, and significant cost-price disparity. *Maxwell*. Unconscionability is determined as of the time the parties entered into the contract. *See id.*; *cf.* A.R.S. § 47–2302 [UCC § 2–302].

¶ 15 In refusing to rescind the sale on the basis of unconscionability, the trial court stated that, "(w)hile the results of the transaction may seem unconscionable to the (Estate) in hindsight, the terms of the contract certainly were not." We agree. The transaction involved no negotiation, the Estate dictated the terms of the contract by naming a price for each painting, and Carl paid the asking prices. " 'Courts should not assume an overly paternalistic attitude toward the parties to a contract by relieving one or another of them of the consequences of what is at worst a bad bargain ... and in declaring the [contract] at issue here unconscionable, we would be doing exactly that.' " Pacific Am. Leasing, 152 Ariz. at 103, 730 P.2d at 280, *quoting* Dillman and Assocs., Inc. v. Capitol Leasing Co., 110 Ill.App.3d 335, 66 Ill.Dec. 39, 442 N.E.2d 311, 317 (1982).

¶ 16 Affirmed. In our discretion, we deny the Rices' request for attorney's fees on appeal. ...

SHERWOOD v. WALKER

Supreme Court of Michigan, 1887.
66 Mich. 568, 33 N.W. 919.

MORSE, J. Replevin for a cow. Suit commenced in justice's court; judgment for plaintiff; appealed to circuit court of Wayne county, and verdict and judgment for plaintiff in that court. The defendants bring error, and set out 25 assignments of the same.

The main controversy depends upon the construction of a contract for the sale of the cow. The plaintiff claims that the title passed, and bases his action upon such claim. The defendants contend that the contract was executory, and by its terms no title to the animal was acquired by plaintiff. The defendants reside at Detroit, but are in business at Walkerville, Ontario, and have a farm at Greenfield, in Wayne county, upon which were some blooded cattle supposed to be barren as breeders. The Walkers are importers and breeders of polled Angus cattle. The plaintiff is a banker living at Plymouth, in Wayne county. He called upon the defendants at Walkerville for the purchase of some of their stock, but found none there that suited him. Meeting one of the defendants afterwards, he was informed that they had a few head upon their Greenfield farm. He was asked to go out and look at them, with the statement at the time that they were probably barren, and would not breed. May 5, 1886, plaintiff went out to Greenfield, and saw the cattle. A few days thereafter, he called upon one of the defendants with the view of purchasing a cow, known as "Rose 2d of Aberlone." After considerable talk, it was agreed that defendants would telephone Sherwood at his home in Plymouth in reference to the price. The second morning after this talk he was called up by telephone, and the terms of the sale were finally agreed upon. He was to pay five and one-half cents per pound, live weight, fifty pounds shrinkage. He was asked how he intended to take the cow home, and replied that he might ship her from King's cattle-yard. He requested defendants to confirm the sale in writing, which they did by sending him the following letter:

WALKERVILLE, May 15, 1886.

T.C. Sherwood, President, etc.—

DEAR SIR:

We confirm sale to you of the cow Rose 2d of Aberlone, lot 56 of our catalogue, at five and half cents per pound, less fifty pounds shrink. We inclose herewith order on Mr. Graham for the cow. You might leave check with him, or mail to us here, as you prefer.

Yours, truly,
HIRAM WALKER & SONS.

The order upon Graham inclosed in the letter read as follows:

WALKERVILLE, May 15, 1886.

George Graham:

You will please deliver at King's cattle-yard to Mr. T.C. Sherwood, Plymouth, the cow Rose 2d of Aberlone, lot 56 of our catalogue. Send halter with the cow, and have her weighed.

Yours truly,
HIRAM WALKER & SONS.

On the twenty-first of the same month the plaintiff went to defendants' farm at Greenfield, and presented the order and letter to Graham, who informed him that the defendants had instructed him not to deliver the cow. Soon after, the plaintiff tendered to Hiram Walker, one of the defendants, $80, and demanded the cow. Walker refused to take the money or deliver the cow. The plaintiff then instituted this suit. After he had secured possession of the cow under the writ of replevin, the plaintiff caused her to be weighed by the constable who served the writ, at a place other than King's cattle-yard. She weighed 1,420 pounds.

When the plaintiff, upon the trial in the circuit court, had submitted his proofs showing the above transaction, defendants moved to strike out and exclude the testimony from the case, for the reason that it was irrelevant and did not tend to show that the title to the cow passed, and that it showed that the contract of sale was merely executory. The court refused the motion, and an exception was taken. The defendants then introduced evidence tending to show that at the time of the alleged sale it was believed by both the plaintiff and themselves that the cow was barren and would not breed; that she cost $850, and if not barren would be worth from $750 to $1,000; that after the date of the letter, and the order to Graham, the defendants were informed by said Graham that in his judgment the cow was with calf, and therefore they instructed him not to deliver her to plaintiff, and on the twentieth of May, 1886, telegraphed plaintiff what Graham thought about the cow being with calf, and that consequently they could not sell her. The cow had a calf in the month of October following. On the nineteenth of May, the plaintiff wrote Graham as follows:

PLYMOUTH, May 19, 1886.

Mr. George Graham, Greenfield—
DEAR SIR:

I have bought Rose or Lucy from Mr. Walker, and will be there for her Friday morning, nine or ten o'clock. Do not water her in the morning.

Yours, etc., T.C. SHERWOOD.

Plaintiff explained the mention of the two cows in this letter by testifying that, when he wrote this letter, the order and letter of defendants was at his home, and, writing in a hurry, and being uncertain as to the name of the cow, and not wishing his cow watered, he thought it would do no harm to name them both, as his bill of sale would show which one he had purchased. Plaintiff also testified that he asked defendants to give him a price on the balance of their herd at Greenfield, as a friend thought of buying some, and received a letter dated May 17, 1886, in which they named the price of five cattle, including Lucy, at $90, and Rose 2d at $80. When he received the letter he called defendants up by telephone, and asked them why they put Rose 2d in the list, as he had already purchased her. They replied that they knew he had, but thought it would make no difference if plaintiff and his friend concluded to take the whole herd.

The foregoing is the substance of all the testimony in the case.

. . . [We omit an extended discussion of title. Although passage of title to buyer once controlled many risks, it now bears less significance. *See, e.g.,* UCC § 2–401. Ed.]

The refusal to deliver the cow grew entirely out of the fact that, before the plaintiff called upon Graham for her, they discovered she was not barren, and therefore of greater value than they had sold her for. . . . It appears from the record that both parties supposed this cow was barren and would not breed, and she was sold by the pound for an insignificant sum as compared with her real value if a breeder. She was evidently sold and purchased on the relation of her value for beef, unless the plaintiff had learned of her true condition, and concealed such knowledge from the defendants. Before the plaintiff secured the possession of the animal, the defendants learned that she was with calf, and therefore of great value, and undertook to rescind the sale by refusing to deliver her. The question arises whether they had a right to do so. The circuit judge ruled that this fact did not avoid the sale and it made no difference whether she was barren or not. I am of the opinion that the court erred in this holding. I know that this is a close question, and the dividing line between the adjudicated cases is not easily discerned. But it must be considered as well settled that a party who has given an apparent consent to a contract of sale may refuse to execute it, or he may avoid it after it has been completed, if the assent was founded, or the contract made, upon the mistake of a material fact,—such as the subject-matter of the sale, the price, or some collateral fact materially inducing the agreement; and this can be done when the mistake is mutual. 1 Benj. *Sales*, §§ 605, 606.

If there is a difference or misapprehension as to the substance of the thing bargained for; if the thing actually delivered or received is different in substance from the thing bargained for, and intended to be sold,—then there is no contract; but if it be only a difference in some quality or accident, even though the mistake may have been the actuating motive to the purchaser or seller, or both of them, yet the contract remains binding.

> The difficulty in every case is to determine whether the mistake or misapprehension is as to the substance of the whole contract, going, as it were, to the root of the matter, or only to some point, even though a material point, an error as to which does not affect the substance of the whole consideration.

Kennedy v. Panama, etc., Mail Co., L.R. 2 Q.B. 580, 587. It has been held, in accordance with the principles above stated, that where a horse is bought under the belief that he is sound, and both vendor and vendee honestly believe him to be sound, the purchaser must stand by his bargain, and pay the full price, unless there was a warranty.

It seems to me, however, in the case made by this record, that the mistake or misapprehension of the parties went to the whole substance of the agreement. If the cow was a breeder, she was worth at least $750; if barren, she was worth not over $80. The parties would not have made the contract of sale except upon the understanding and belief that she was incapable of breeding, and of no use as a cow. It is true she is now the identical animal that they thought her to be when the contract was made; there is no mistake as to the identity of the creature. Yet the mistake was not of the mere quality of the animal, but went to the very nature of the thing. A barren cow is substantially a different creature than a breeding one. There is as much difference between them for all purposes of use as there is between an ox and a cow that is capable of breeding and giving milk. If the mutual mistake had simply related to the fact whether she was with calf or not for one season, then it might have been a good sale, but the mistake affected the character of the animal for all time, and for its present and ultimate use. She was not in fact the animal, or the kind of animal, the defendants intended to sell or the plaintiff to buy. She was not a barren cow, and, if this fact had been known, there would have been no contract. The mistake affected the substance of the whole consideration, and it must be considered that there was no contract to sell or sale of the cow as she actually was. The thing sold and bought had in fact no existence. She was sold as a beef creature would be sold; she is in fact a breeding cow, and a valuable one.

The court should have instructed the jury that if they found that the cow was sold, or contracted to be sold, upon the understanding of both parties that she was barren, and useless for the purpose of breeding, and that in fact she was not barren, but capable of breeding, then the defendants had a right to rescind, and to refuse to deliver, and the verdict should be in their favor.

The judgment of the court below must be reversed, and a new trial granted, with costs of this court to defendants. . . .

SHERWOOD, J., (Dissenting.) I do not concur in the opinion given by my brethren in this case. . . . [T]he plaintiff was entitled to a delivery of the property to him when the suit was brought, unless there was a mistake made which would invalidate the contract, and I can find no such mistake. There is no pretense there was any fraud or concealment in the case, and an intimation or insinuation that such a thing might have existed on the part of either of the parties would undoubtedly be a greater surprise to them than anything else that has occurred in their dealings or in the case.

[T]he record shows that the plaintiff is a banker and farmer as well, carrying on a farm, and raising the best breeds of stock, and lived in Plymouth, in the county of Wayne, 23 miles from Detroit; that the defendants lived in Detroit, and were also dealers in stock of the higher grades; that they had a farm at Walkerville, in Canada, and also one in Greenfield in said county of Wayne, and upon these farms the defendants kept their stock. The Greenfield farm was about 15 miles from the plaintiff's. In the spring of 1886 the plaintiff, learning that the defendants had some "polled Angus cattle" for sale, was desirous of purchasing some of that breed, and meeting the defendants, or some of them, at Walkerville, inquired about them, and was informed that they had none at Walkerville, "but had a few head left on their farm in Greenfield, and asked the plaintiff to go and see them, stating that in all probability they were sterile and would not breed." In accordance with said request, the plaintiff, on the fifth day of May, went out and looked at the defendants' cattle at Greenfield, and found one called "Rose, Second," which he wished to purchase, and the terms were finally agreed upon at five and a half cents per pound, live weight, 50 pounds to be deducted for shrinkage. The sale was in writing, and the defendants gave an order to the plaintiff directing the man in charge of the Greenfield farm to deliver the cow to plaintiff. This was done on the fifteenth of May. On the twenty-first of May plaintiff went to get his cow, and the defendants refused to let him have her; claiming at the time that the man in charge at the farm thought the cow was with calf, and, if such was the case, they would not sell her for the price agreed upon. The record further shows that the defendants, when they sold the cow, believed the cow was not with calf, and barren; that from what the plaintiff had been told by defendants (for it does not appear he had any other knowledge or facts from which he could form an opinion) he believed the cow was farrow, but still thought she could be made to breed. The foregoing shows the entire interview and treaty between the parties as to the sterility and qualities of the cow sold to the plaintiff. The cow had a calf in the month of October.

There is no question but that the defendants sold the cow representing her of the breed and quality they believed the cow to be, and that the purchaser so understood it. And the buyer purchased her believing her to be of the breed represented by the sellers, and possessing all the qualities stated, and even more. He believed she would breed. There is no pretense that the plaintiff bought the cow for beef, and there is nothing in the record indicating that he would have bought her at all only that he thought she might be made to breed. Under the foregoing facts,—and these are all that are contained in the record material to the contract,—it is held that because it turned out that the plaintiff was more correct in his judgment as to one quality of the cow than the defendants, and a quality, too, which could not by any possibility be positively known at the time by either party to exist, the contract may be annulled by the defendants at their pleasure. I know of no law, and have not been referred to any, which will justify any such holding, and I think the circuit judge was right in his construction of the contract between the parties.

It is claimed that a mutual mistake of a material fact was made by the parties when the contract of sale was made. There was no warranty in the case of the quality of the animal. When a mistaken fact is relied upon as ground for rescinding, such fact must not only exist at the time the contract is made, but must have been known to one or both of the parties. Where there is no warranty, there can be no mistake of fact when no such fact exists, or, if in existence, neither party knew of it, or could know of it; and that is precisely this case. If the owner of a Hambletonian horse had speeded him, and was only able to make him go a mile in three minutes, and should sell him to another, believing that was his greatest speed, for $300, when the purchaser believed he could go much faster, and made the purchase for that sum, and a few days thereafter, under more favorable circumstances, the horse was driven a mile in 2 min. 16 sec., and was found to be worth $20,000, I hardly think it would be held, either at law or in equity, by any one, that the seller in such case could rescind the contract. The same legal principles apply in each case.

In this case neither party knew the actual quality and condition of this cow at the time of the sale. The defendants say, or rather said, to the plaintiff, "they had a few head left on their farm in Greenfield, and asked plaintiff to go and see them, stating to plaintiff that in all probability they were sterile and would not breed." Plaintiff did go as requested, and found there these cows, including the one purchased, with a bull. The cow had been exposed, but neither knew she was with calf or whether she would breed. The defendants thought she would not, but the plaintiff says that he thought she could be made to breed, but believed she was not with calf. The defendants sold the cow for what they believed her to be, and the plaintiff bought her as he believed she was, after the statements made by the defendants. No conditions whatever were attached to the terms of sale by either party. It was in fact as absolute as it could well be made, and I know of no precedent as authority by which this court can alter the contract thus made by these parties in writing,—interpolate in it a condition by which, if the defendants should be mistaken in their belief that the cow was barren, she could be returned to them and their contract should be annulled. It is not the duty of courts to destroy contracts when called upon to enforce them, after they have been legally made. There was no mistake of any material fact by either of the parties in the case as would license the vendors to rescind. There was no difference between the parties, nor misapprehension, as to the substance of the thing bargained for, which was a cow supposed to be barren by one party, and believed not to be by the other. As to the quality of the animal, subsequently developed, both parties were equally ignorant, and as to this each party took his chances. If this were not the law, there would be no safety in purchasing this kind of stock.

I entirely agree with my brethren that the right to rescind occurs whenever "the thing actually delivered or received is different in substance from the thing bargained for, and intended to be sold; but if it be only a difference in some quality or accident, even though the misapprehension may have been the actuating motive" of the parties in making the contract, yet it will remain binding. In this case the cow sold was the one delivered. What might or might not happen to her after the sale formed no element in the contract. . . .

According to this record, whatever the mistake was, if any, in this case, it was upon the part of the defendants, and while acting upon their own judgment. It is, however, elementary law, and very elementary, too, "that the mistaken party, without any common understanding with the other party in the premises as to the quality of an animal, is remediless if he is injured through his own mistake." Leake, *Cont.* 338.

. . . In this case, if either party had superior knowledge as to the qualities of this animal to the other, certainly the defendants had such advantage. I understand the law to be well settled that "there is no breach of any implied confidence that one party will not profit by his superior knowledge as to facts and circumstances" actually within the knowledge of both, because neither party reposes in any such confidence unless it be specially tendered or required, and that a general sale does not imply warranty of any quality, or the absence of any; and if the seller represents to the purchaser what he himself believes as to the qualities of an animal, and the purchaser buys relying upon his own judgment as to such qualities, there is no warranty in the case, and neither has a cause of action against the other if he finds himself to have been mistaken in judgment.

The only pretense for avoiding this contract by the defendants is that they erred in judgment as to the qualities and value of the animal. . . . The judgment should be affirmed.

WHITE v. BERENDA MESA WATER DIST.

Court of Appeal, Fifth District, 1970.
7 Cal.App.3d 894, 87 Cal.Rptr. 338.

COAKLEY, ASSOCIATE JUSTICE. The plaintiffs shall be referred to herein as "White" and "Aetna"; the defendant as "The District."

This is an action for declaratory relief in which White and Aetna seek rescission of a construction contract and the return of a bid bond posted by Aetna on behalf of White, the low bidder. The District filed a cross-complaint for damages. Following a trial to the court, judgment was entered in favor of The District on the complaint and on the cross-complaint, and against White and Aetna. The District's damages were fixed at $42,789. . . .

The controversy arose in this way: The District invited bids on a construction project which was divided into four separate entities for bidding purposes. White was low bidder on one segment of the project, i.e., a regulating reservoir. With his bid, White filed a surety bond by Aetna in the sum of $42,789. [A number of jurisdictions require that a bidder on a public contract post a bond that will be forfeited if the bid is withdrawn. Ed.]

Eight other bids were received for the work on which White was the low bidder. When the bids were opened, they ran from White's low bid of $427,890 to a high bid of $721,851. The bid next lowest to White's was by Einer Brothers, et al., for $494,320, or $66,430 above White's bid. The estimate of Boyle Engineering, the consulting engineers for The District, was $512,250, or $84,360 above White's bid. Concerned that he had made an error in his bid, White reviewed it in detail and concluded that he had made a mistake in computing item 13, i.e., the cost of excavating 230,000 cubic yards of material. On discovery of his mistake, and prior to acceptance or rejection of any of the bids by The District, White notified The District, in writing, that because of an error in computation, "We hereby withdraw our bid . . . and request the return of the deposit submitted therewith." . . .

Counsel for the board advised the board that if White's error was due to a mistake of fact the bid could not be accepted, but if it was due to a mistake of judgment the bid was binding upon White. The board then voted to accept the bid which White had asked permission to withdraw. Shortly thereafter, White advised the board, in writing, that he rescinded his bid. The District, thereupon, awarded the contract to Einer Brothers, the next lowest bidder. This action by White followed. . . .

Before preparing his bid, White studied the plans and specifications, visited the site, and made a visual examination of the terrain. While White visited the site, his son, Kelly, called at the office of Boyle Engineering for the purpose of examining a soil report relating to the material to be excavated. There, he examined plates 3 and 4, which were part of the soil report and available for examination by all bidders. Prior to looking at the soil report, he had also examined sheet 10, which was part of the plans and specifications. Plates 3 and 4 show the location of various test holes drilled by the soil engineers. One such hole is marked B–51. Plate 3 also shows a broken line terminating about 100 feet east of point B–51. The broken line represents a proposed penstock alignment, which was not part of the work included in the regulating reservoir phase of the total project. Plate 4 shows "decomposed shale and sandstone" as comprising all but a small portion of the terrain lying west of B–51. Kelly White testified that, on the basis of his examination of plates 3 and 4, he concluded and reported to his father that only a small quantity of hard rock was involved in the work of excavating. His estimate of hard rock was seven percent. White then called Boyle Engineering, and Mr. Thomas of that firm told him that very little hard rock would be encountered. Thereupon, White submitted his bid and surety bond. It is a fact that decomposed shale and sandstone comprised 90 percent or more of the terrain west of point B–51, with hard rock comprising the balance of the terrain. Thus, Kelly White's estimate of only seven percent hard rock was reasonably close for the area west of point B–51.

However, sheet 10 and the plans and specifications, as distinguished from plates 3 and 4 of the soil report, clearly show the penstock alignment terminating at a point 400 feet or more east of point B–51, and not 100 feet as indicated in plate 3. A hill, composed almost exclusively of hard rock, lay between point B–51 and the western terminus of the penstock alignment. Excavation of this hill and the hard rock material was part of item 13 of the bid and, therefore, the responsibility of the excavating contractor.

With reference to the entire area to be excavated as called for by item 13, i.e., 230,000 cubic yards of material, the evidence established that, instead of 10,000 cubic yards of hard rock to be removed, there was 110,000 cubic yards; instead of hard rock constituting only seven percent of the total excavation, as Kelly White had estimated, it constituted approximately 50 percent thereof, with the remaining 50 percent being made up of decomposed shale and sandstone. It was established that hard rock is substantially more costly to excavate than decomposed shale and sandstone.

White had a copy of the specifications which he examined before preparing his bid. Section 108 thereof provided that The District did not warrant the accuracy of the soil report. White was an experienced contractor. As such, he knew that soil reports are prepared in advance of the detailed specifications for a project, and that the specifications, not the soil report, control. There was, therefore, an element of negligence in the preparation of White's bid, more particularly, in White's failure to correlate plates 3 and 4 of the soil report, which White knew from experience were not warranted as accurate, with sheet 10 and the other specifications.

The findings recite only that White made a mistake in estimating the amount of hard rock material to be excavated; that the mistake was material to the contract; and that the mistake was one of judgment. . . .

Where, as here, the facts are not in dispute, the issue is one of law, and this court is free to draw its own conclusions of law from such undisputed facts. Doing so, we conclude that White's mistake was a mixed mistake of fact and of judgment. White's estimate or calculation of the amount of hard rock to be excavated was judgmental, and in that sense his mistake was one of judgment. On the other hand, his estimate or calculation was predicated on a misunderstanding of the true facts, occasioned in part, at least, by reliance on the soil report (plates 3 and 4) and Mr. Thomas' statement. It is in this posture that we now examine the law on the subject.

The Law

We commence our discussion of the law by pointing out that counsel has not cited any case, from California or elsewhere, and our independent research has failed to find such a case, where the mistake, whether of fact or of judgment, so called, was occasioned by circumstances similar to those present in this case.

M.F. Kemper Const. Co. v. City of L.A., 37 Cal.2d 696, 235 P.2d 7, is a leading case on the subject of rescission of bids on a public project. It enumerates the elements essential to rescission for a mistake of fact. They are summarized in headnote 4 of the official report in these words:

> Recission may be had for mistake of fact if the mistake is material to the contract and is not the result of neglect of a legal duty, if enforcement of the contract as made would be unconscionable, if the other party can be placed *in statu quo*, if the party seeking relief gives prompt notice of his election to rescind, and if he restores or offers to restore to the other party everything of value which he has received under the contract. (Civ.Code, §§ 1577, 1689, 1691, 3406, 3407.)

The District's brief acknowledges that all of the elements required for rescission as set forth in *Kemper* are present in our case, except that the mistake was one of judgment, not fact, and the mistake resulted from the neglect of a legal duty. We have held, *supra*, that White's mistake was not solely one of judgment, but was a mixed mistake of fact and of judgment. We shall return to that subject after we first examine the meaning of the term "neglect of a legal duty." (*Kemper, supra.*)

That term appears in Civil Code, section 1577, which reads in part as follows: "Mistake of fact is a mistake, not caused by the neglect of a legal duty on the part of the person making the mistake, and consisting in: . . . ." In construing Civil Code, section 1577, the court said in *Kemper, supra*, 37 Cal.2d 696, 702, 235 P.2d 7, 10, that: "It has been recognized numerous times that not all carelessness constitutes a 'neglect of legal duty' within the meaning of the section." . . .

The soil report on which White relied in part, while not warranted as accurate, was a report used by The District's engineers in preparing the specifications; it was available for study by all prospective bidders; Kelly White examined it, and, in a mistaken reliance on plates 3 and 4 of the report, informed his father that hard rock constituted seven percent of the excavation. *After* receiving this information from his son, White spoke with Mr. Thomas of Boyle Engineering and was told by him that very little hard rock would be encountered. The undisputed fact is that almost 50 percent of the material to be excavated was hard rock. We hold, therefore, that White's negligence was ordinary and not gross; that his error "is one which will sometimes occur in the conduct of reasonable and cautious businessmen," and did not constitute neglect of a legal duty. (M.F. Kemper Const. Co. v. City of L.A., *supra*, 37 Cal.2d 696, 702, 235 P.2d 7, 11.)

We next consider the meaning of mistake of fact "versus" mistake of judgment. Where the mistake in preparing a bid is due to clerical error, *e.g.*, in mathematical computation or in the transposition of figures from work sheets to final bid forms, and where all the other elements calling for rescission are present, the cases uniformly hold the mistake to be one of fact and release the bidder from any obligation under his bid.

Statements appear in some of the cases to the effect that courts of equity will grant relief where the mistake is one of fact, but not where the mistake is one of judgment. Such a statement appears in *Kemper, supra,* [at 703, 235 P.2d at 11]. . . .

We first observe that in *Kemper* the Supreme Court said, "*Generally,* relief is refused for error in judgment." (Emphasis added.) It was careful not to lay down a hard and fast rule to the effect that relief may never be granted for a mistake in judgment. . . .

In *Kemper, supra,* the contractor brought an action against the city to cancel a bid it had submitted on public construction work and to obtain discharge of its bid bond. The city cross-complained for forfeiture of the bond and damages. The trial court canceled the bid, discharged the bond, and allowed the city nothing on its cross-complaint. In affirming, the Supreme Court said: "The sole issue is whether the company is entitled to relief on the ground of unilateral mistake." (37 Cal.2d p. 699, 235 P.2d p. 9.) The unilateral mistake found by the court in *Kemper* was the typical mistake of fact, *i.e.*, an error in the transposition of figures arrived at by the contractor's estimators, to a final accumulation sheet from which the total amount of the bid was taken. An item of over $300,000 was inadvertently omitted in transposition from the work sheet to the accumulation sheet, and, accordingly, omitted from the final bid. From that point on that case and our case are identical. Thus, there, as here, (1) the contractor was the low bidder; (2) it discovered its mistake shortly after the bids were opened; (3) it immediately explained its mistake to the city's board of public works, and withdrew its bid; (4) a few days later, the bidder again appeared before the board and submitted evidence of its

mistake; (5) notwithstanding, the board thereafter passed a resolution accepting the bid; (6) the company refused to enter into a contract at its bid figure; (7) without readvertising, the board awarded the contract to the next lowest bidder; (8) the city then demanded forfeiture of the bond; (9) the company's suit followed to cancel its bid and to discharge the bond.
. . .

The sole distinction between the *Kemper* case and our case is in the nature of the mistake made by the bidder. There the error was in transposing figures and the inadvertent omission of a substantial amount from an accumulation sheet and bid, the classic "mistake of fact." In our case, White's error was his negligence in failing to properly correlate plates 3 and 4 with the plans and specifications, and as a consequence he underestimated or miscalculated the amount of hard rock to be removed.
. . .

In our opinion, the judgment below draws too fine a line between so called mistakes of fact and mistakes of judgment, producing a result which finds no support in equity.

To deny White and Aetna the relief they seek would be grossly unjust and would set a harsh and unnecessary precedent. In our opinion, the fact that White said he made a mistake of judgment and that the court "took him at his word," should not change the result. It is the facts surrounding the mistake, not the label, *i.e.*, "mistake of fact" or "mistake of judgment," which should control.

In holding that White is entitled to withdraw his bid and to a return of the bond, we are not unmindful that the system of public bidding, developed by experience and usual in public contracts, should not be broken down by lightly permitting bidders to withdraw because of a change of mind. Such a course would be unfair to other straightforward bidders, as well as disruptive of public business. But we are confident that our public agencies and our courts are capable of preventing, and will prevent, abuses where, unlike our case, the facts do not justify relieving the low bidder from his bid.

The judgment is reversed, and the court below is directed to enter judgment permitting White to withdraw his bid and to return to White and Aetna the bid bond posted by them.

PROBLEMS

12. P found a pretty stone and someone told her it was probably a topaz. While at a jewelry store, she showed it to the proprietor who agreed it was pretty but was uncertain as to what it was. (The trial court found that both parties were truthful.) The storekeeper told P that if she would want to sell it he would pay $1. Later, she brought it back to the store and exchanged it for $1. Still later, P discovered that it was an uncut diamond worth about $700. She tendered $1 plus interest to the storekeeper and asked for restitution of the stone. What result?

13. S contracted to sell to B a parcel of hilly land on the waterfront. S was aware that B planned to build a residence on the parcel. After contracting, geological reports as well as the practical experience of the local building inspector revealed that a house constructed on the site would have a significant chance of being carried into the water by a landslide. In fact, after contracting, several neighboring houses were totally destroyed by landslides. B notified S that he rescinded the contract and sues for restitution. What result?

14. P, a tennis and swim club, contracted to purchase a 50–acre estate from D, revealing its intention to relocate its facilities to the estate. Neither party knew that, after P had checked the zoning ordinances and 4 days prior to signing the contract, a new zoning ordinance had been enacted limiting the premises to residential uses. P sues for restitution. What result?

15. A State official notified S and B, two landowners of adjacent acreage, that the boundary lines described in their deeds were ambiguous and appeared to overlap. The parties met and agreed that S would convey a parcel of land to B for $1,400. A State employee had prepared the description. When asked how much acreage was included in the description, he had said that 15 acres was a "ball park figure." Three years later, a survey commissioned by B showed that 68 acres had been conveyed. B then conveyed the parcel to his wife, without consideration. What remedies, if any, are available to S?

16. D, a municipality, conducted an auction on March 25th to sell surplus real property which it owned. A brochure described the various properties. On page 73 of the brochure, parcel #212 was carelessly described as "unimproved." In fact, it contained a two-family house. The parcel was knocked down to P, the high bidder, for $6,500. Title was to close on or before May 27th. On April 29th, D learned of its mistake and notified P that it was avoiding the contract. What result?

17. McDonald's Corporation, as tenant, leased for 30 years a parcel of land in South Carolina for a fast food establishment. The monthly rental was $375. Because of a delay in the first month's payment, a check for $750 was sent for two months' rent. Negligently, in the belief that $750 was the monthly rent, McDonald's clerk in Chicago prepared checks for $750 each month thereafter for three years. Each month an officer of McDonald's signed the check prepared by the clerk. The checks were sent to the Landlord in South Carolina who cashed them on receipt. McDonald's sues for recovery of the overpayments. What result?

SECTION 5. REFORMATION

(Calamari & Perillo on Contracts §§ 9.31—9.36)

HOFFMAN v. CHAPMAN

Court of Appeals of Maryland, 1943.
182 Md. 208, 34 A.2d 438.

DELAPLAINE, JUDGE. This appeal was brought by Joseph Stanley Hoffman and wife from a decree of the Circuit Court for Montgomery County reforming their deed for a house and lot in a suburban real estate development at Kensington.

On August 18, 1941, William A. Chapman and wife, of Gaithersburg, through a real estate agent, agreed to sell to appellants part of lot 4 in the section known as Homewood on Edgewood Road, the size to be 96 by 150 feet. The purchase price of this part, improved by a bungalow, was $3,600. Before the parcel was surveyed, appellants were given immediate possession. After the survey was made, the real estate agent sent the plat to the Suburban Title and Investment Corporation with instructions to examine the title and arrange for settlement. On October 20, 1941, when appellants made final payment in the office of the title company, they clearly understood that they were receiving only a part of lot 4 containing one dwelling; but the deed actually conveyed the entire lot, which was improved by other dwelling property. When the mistake was discovered some time afterwards, they were requested to deed back the unsold part, but they refused to reconvey. The grantors thereupon entered suit in equity to reform the deed on the ground of mistake.

It is a settled principle that a court of equity will reform a written instrument to make it conform to the real intention of the parties, when the evidence is so clear, strong and convincing as to leave no reasonable doubt that a mutual mistake was made in the instrument contrary to their agreement. Gaver v. Gaver, 119 Md. 634, 639, 87 A. 396. It is a general rule of the common law that parol evidence is inadmissible to vary or contradict the terms of a written instrument. Markoff v. Kreiner, 180 Md. 150, 23 A.2d 19. But equity refuses to enforce this rule whenever it is alleged that fraud, accident or mistake occurred in the making of the instrument, and will admit parol evidence to reform the instrument, even though it is within the Statute of Frauds. [citations] "A court of equity would be of little value," Justice Story said, "if it could suppress only positive frauds, and leave mutual mistakes, innocently made, to work intolerable mischiefs contrary to the intention of parties. It would be to allow an act, originating in innocence, to operate ultimately as a fraud by enabling the party, who receives the benefit of the mistake, to resist the claims of justice under the shelter of a rule framed to promote it. ... We must, therefore, treat the cases in which equity affords relief, and allows parol evidence to vary and reform written contracts and instruments, upon the ground of accident and mistake, as properly forming, like cases of fraud, exceptions to the general rule which excludes parol evidence, and as standing upon the same policy as the rule itself." 1 Story, *Equity Jurisprudence*, 12th Ed., secs. 155, 156. . . .

Equity reforms an instrument not for the purpose of relieving against a hard or oppressive bargain, but simply to enforce the actual agreement of the parties to prevent an injustice which would ensue if this were not done. Chief Judge Alvey warned: "The court will never, by assuming to rectify an instrument, add to it a term or provision which had not been agreed upon, though it may afterwards appear very expedient or proper that it should have been incorporated." Stiles v. Willis, 66 Md. 552, 556, 8 A. 353, 354. Nevertheless, where the description in a deed is not complete, but the contract of sale specified the amount of land to be conveyed, and thereafter a plat was prepared from a survey, extrinsic evidence may be admitted to show the real intention of the parties, and thereupon the court has power to make the description more definite under the maxim, "*Id certum est, quod certum reddi potest.*" [That is certain which may be made certain.] Nolen v. Henry, 190 Ala. 540, 67 So. 500, 501, Ann.Cas. 1917B, 792. In the present case there could not be any doubt about the identity of the dwelling which appellants agreed to buy, because they lived in it about two months before they made their final payment on the purchase price. It was understood and agreed by the parties that the parcel should have a frontage of 96 feet on the north side of Edgewood Road, and its depth should be 150 feet. Shortly thereafter the surveyor found that a part of the road ran across the southwest corner of the lot, and he suggested that the County Engineer might be induced to shift the road slightly so as to enable the owners to convey a parcel exactly 150 feet in depth. But when the real estate agent gave assurance that the owners would be willing to convey a few more feet on account of the curve in the road, the surveyor made a revised plat allowing a depth of 150 feet on the east side and 161.24 feet on the west side. Therefore, since the decree of the chancellor, based upon the revised survey, allows dimensions slightly larger than those stipulated in the contract, appellants certainly have no reason to complain.

Appellants insisted that the mistake in the deed was not due to their fault, but to culpable negligence of the grantors and their agents, and that no relief can be granted because the mistake was unilateral. It is axiomatic that equity aids the vigilant, and will not grant relief to a litigant who has failed to exercise reasonable diligence. In Boyle v. Rider, 136 Md. 286, 191, 100 A. 524, it was stated that people cannot sign papers carelessly and then expect a court to excuse them from their negligence, especially when their action has misled others. But mere inadvertence, or negligence not amounting to a violation of a positive legal duty, does not bar a complainant from relief, especially if the defendant has not been prejudiced thereby. Benesh v. Travelers' Insurance Co., 14 N.D. 39, 103 N.W. 405. Hence, it is not necessary for the complainant in a suit for reformation to prove that he exercised diligence to ascertain what the instrument contained at the time he signed it. The term "mistake" conveys the idea of fault, and the mere fact that a mistake was made in the phraseology of an instrument does not establish such negligence as to preclude the right of reformation; for if it did, a court of equity could never grant relief in such a case. Wilkins v. Dagle, Tex.Civ.App., 265 S.W. 918, 924.

The general rule is accepted in Maryland that a mistake of law in the making of an agreement is not a ground for reformation, and where a mistake, either of law or of fact, is unilateral, equity will not afford relief except by rescinding the agreement on the ground of fraud, duress or other inequitable conduct. Boyle v. Maryland State Fair, 150 Md. 333, 340, 134 A. 124. The mistake in this case was not unilateral. Here the draftsman of the deed was acting as the agent of the parties. His mistake in the description of the real estate became the mistake of all the parties. The Court of Appeals recognized in Boulden v. Wood, 96 Md. 332, 337, 53 A. 911, that a court of equity may correct an instrument wherein a provision was inserted by mistake of an attorney. Where a deed is intended to carry into execution a written or oral agreement, but fails to express the manifest intention of the parties on account of a mistake of the draftsman, whether from carelessness, forgetfulness or lack of skill, equity will rectify the mistake to make the deed express the real intention of the parties. Archer v. McClure, 166 N.C. 140, 81 S.E. 1081, Ann.Cas. 1916C, 180.

As it is beyond doubt that a mutual mistake was made in the description of the property in this case, the decree of the chancellor reforming the deed will be affirmed.

Decree affirmed, with costs.

PROBLEMS

18. S sold to B a large tract of land. It was orally agreed that S could remove mill machinery and the rails of a light railroad that ran through the tract. The deed, however, provided that "all improvements" were conveyed along with the land. S removed the machinery and the rails and B sues for damages. S counterclaims for reformation, alleging that the parties were unaware that the legal effect of the term "all improvements" was to transfer the machinery and the rails. Does the counterclaim state a claim for relief?

19. Joan was suing her husband, Tim, for divorce. They agreed that they would split their property evenly. They and their attorneys had protracted negotiations about the value of certain of their holdings. Tim thought that a parcel of realty was worth $450,000 while Joan valued it at $550,000. Joan made an offer of settlement based on the $550,000 value. The offer contained an arithmetical error in Tim's favor of $100,000. Tim, noting the error, accepted the offer, explaining to his accountant that the arithmetical error canceled out his disagreement about the value she had placed upon the realty. Anxious to have the last word, after Joan had obtained her divorce decree, Tim sent her a copy of the calculations with this message: "PLEASE NOTE $100,000 MISTAKE IN YOUR FIGURES." Joan responded with an action for reformation. What result?

20. Hand, an attorney employed by D Corp., lost his job when D restructured its operations. D offered to pay Hand $38,000 in severance pay if he would sign a general release. He refused, contending that he was entitled to this sum under his existing contract. Nonetheless D caused a release document to be drafted and typed and tendered it to Hand renewing its previous offer of $38,000. Hand caused the document to be retyped in identical form and in identical language with the exception of the insertion of a clause stating "except as to claims of age discrimination and breach of contract." He brought this new document to a meeting with an officer of D where both parties signed the document. Thereafter Hand brought this action for age discrimination and breach of contract. D raised the affirmative defense of release, requesting reformation of the release to conform to its original offer. Should the release be reformed?

SECTION 6. UNCONSCIONABILITY AND DUTY TO READ

(Calamari & Perillo on Contracts §§ 9.37—9.45)

WILLIAMS v. WALKER–THOMAS FURNITURE CO.

United States Court of Appeals, District of Columbia Circuit, 1965.
350 F.2d 445, 18 A.L.R.3d 1297.

J. Skelly Wright, Circuit Judge: Appellee, Walker–Thomas Furniture Company, operates a retail furniture store in the District of Columbia. During the period from 1957 to 1962 each appellant in these cases purchased a number of household items from Walker–Thomas, for which payment was to be made in installments. The terms of each purchase were contained in a printed form contract which set forth the value of the purchased item and purported to lease the item to appellant for a stipulated monthly rent payment. The contract then provided, in substance, that title would remain in Walker–Thomas until the total of all the monthly payments made equaled the stated value of the item, at which time appellants could take title. In the event of a default in the payment of any monthly installment, Walker–Thomas could repossess the item.

The contract further provided that "the amount of each periodical installment payment to be made by (purchaser) to the Company under this present lease shall be inclusive of and not in addition to the amount of each installment payment to be made by (purchaser) under such prior leases, bills or accounts; *and all payments now and hereafter made by (purchaser) shall be credited pro rata on all outstanding leases, bills and accounts* due the Company by (purchaser) at the time each such payment is made." The effect of this rather obscure provision was to keep a balance due on every item purchased until the balance due on all items, whenever purchased, was liquidated. As a result, the debt incurred at the time of purchase of each item was secured by the right to repossess all the items previously purchased by the same purchaser, and each new item purchased automatically became subject to a security interest arising out of the previous dealings.

On May 12, 1962, appellant Thorne purchased an item described as a Daveno, three tables, and two lamps, having total stated value of $391.10. Shortly thereafter, he defaulted on his monthly payments and appellee sought to replevy all the items purchased since the first transaction in 1958. Similarly, on April 17, 1962, appellant Williams bought a stereo set of stated value of $514.95.[1] She too defaulted shortly thereafter, and appellee sought to replevy all the items purchased since December, 1957. The Court of General Sessions granted judgment for appellee. The District of Columbia Court of Appeals affirmed, and we granted appellants' motion for leave to appeal to this court.

Appellants' principal contention, rejected by both the trial and the appellate courts below, is that these contracts, or at least some of them, are unconscionable and, hence, not enforceable. In its opinion in Williams v. Walker–Thomas Furniture Company, 198 A.2d 914, 916 (1964), the District of Columbia Court of Appeals explained its rejection of this contention as follows:

> Appellant's second argument presents a more serious question. The record reveals that prior to the last purchase appellant had reduced the balance in her account to $164. The last purchase, a stereo set, raised the balance due to $678. Significantly, at the time of this and the preceding purchases, appellee was aware of appellant's financial position. The reverse side of the stereo contract listed the name of appellant's social worker and her $218 monthly stipend from the government. Nevertheless, with full knowledge that appellant had to feed, clothe and support both herself and seven children on this amount, appellee sold her a $514 stereo set.

> We cannot condemn too strongly appellee's conduct. It raises serious questions of sharp practice and irresponsible business dealings. A review of the legislation in the District of Columbia affecting retail sales and the pertinent decisions of the highest court in this jurisdiction disclose, however, no ground upon which this court can declare the contracts in question contrary to public policy. We note that were the Maryland Retail Installment Sales Act, Art. 83 §§ 128–153, or its equivalent, in force in the District of Columbia, we could grant appellant appropriate relief. We think Congress should consider corrective legislation to protect the public from such exploitive contracts as were utilized in the case at bar.

We do not agree that the court lacked the power to refuse enforcement to contracts found to be unconscionable. In other jurisdictions, it has been held as a matter of common law that unconscionable contracts are

---

1. At the time of this purchase her account showed a balance of $164 still owing from her prior purchases. The total of all the purchases made over the years in question came to $1,800. The total payments amounted to $1,400.

not enforceable. While no decision of this court so holding has been found, the notion that an unconscionable bargain should not be given full enforcement is by no means novel. In Scott v. United States, 79 U.S. (12 Wall.) 443, 445, 20 L.Ed. 438 (1870), the Supreme Court stated:

> ... If a contract be unreasonable and unconscionable, but not void for fraud, a court of law will give to the party who sues for its breach damages, not according to its letter, but only such as he is equitably entitled to. ...

Since we have never adopted or rejected such a rule, the question here presented is actually one of first impression.

Congress has recently enacted the Uniform Commercial Code, which specifically provides that the court may refuse to enforce a contract which it finds to be unconscionable at the time it was made. 28 D.C. Code § 2–302 (Supp. IV 1965). The enactment of this section, which occurred subsequent to the contracts here in suit, does not mean that the common law of the District of Columbia was otherwise at the time of enactment, nor does it preclude the court from adopting a similar rule in the exercise of its powers to develop the common law for the District of Columbia. In fact, in view of the absence of prior authority on the point, we consider the congressional adoption of § 2–302 persuasive authority for following the rationale of the cases from which the section is explicitly derived.[5] Accordingly, we hold that where the element of unconscionability is present at the time a contract is made, the contract should not be enforced.

Unconscionability has generally been recognized to include an absence of meaningful choice on the part of one of the parties together with contract terms which are unreasonably favorable to the other party. Whether a meaningful choice is present in a particular case can only be determined by consideration of all the circumstances surrounding the transaction. In many cases the meaningfulness of the choice is negated by a gross inequality of bargaining power.[7] The manner in which the contract was entered is also relevant to this consideration. Did each party to the contract, considering his obvious education or lack of it, have a reasonable

---

5. *See* Comment, § 2–302, Uniform Commercial Code (1962). *Compare* Note, 45 Va.L.Rev. 583, 590 (1959), where it is predicted that the rule of § 2–302 will be followed by analogy in cases which involve contracts not specifically covered by the section. *Cf.* 1 State of New York Law Revision Commission, Report and Record of Hearings on the Uniform Commercial Code 108–110 (1954) (remarks of Professor Llewellyn).

7. *See* Henningsen v. Bloomfield Motors, Inc., [32 N.J. 358], 161 A.2d at 86, and authorities there cited. Inquiry into the relative bargaining power of the two parties is not an inquiry wholly divorced from the general question of unconscionability, since a one-sided bargain is itself evidence of the inequality of the bargaining parties. This fact was vaguely recognized in the common law doctrine of intrinsic fraud, that is, fraud which can be presumed from the grossly unfair nature of the terms of the contract. See the oft-quoted statement of Lord Hardwicke in Earl of Chesterfield v. Janssen, 28 Eng. Rep. 82, 100 (1751):

"... (Fraud) may be apparent from the intrinsic nature and subject of the bargain itself; such as no man in his senses and not under delusion would make...."

And *cf.* Hume v. United States, [...], 132 U.S. at 413, 10 S.Ct. at 137 [1889], where the Court characterized the English cases as "cases in which one party took advantage of the other's ignorance of arithmetic to impose upon him, and the fraud was apparent from the face of the contracts."

opportunity to understand the terms of the contract, or were the important terms hidden in a maze of fine print and minimized by deceptive sales practices? Ordinarily, one who signs an agreement without full knowledge of its terms might be held to assume the risk that he has entered a one-sided bargain. But when a party of little bargaining power, and hence little real choice, signs a commercially unreasonable contract with little or no knowledge of its terms, it is hardly likely that his consent, or even an objective manifestation of his consent, was ever given to all the terms. In such a case the usual rule that the terms of the agreement are not to be questioned[9] should be abandoned and the court should consider whether the terms of the contract are so unfair that enforcement should be withheld.[10]

In determining reasonableness or fairness, the primary concern must be with the terms of the contract considered in light of the circumstances existing when the contract was made. The test is not simple, nor can it be mechanically applied. The terms are to be considered "in the light of the general commercial background and the commercial needs of the particular trade or case."[11] Corbin suggests the test as being whether the terms are "so extreme as to appear unconscionable according to the mores and business practices of the time and place." 1 Corbin, [*Contracts* § 128 (1963)]. We think this formulation correctly states the test to be applied in those cases where no meaningful choice was exercised upon entering the contract.

Because the trial court and the appellate court did not feel that enforcement could be refused, no findings were made on the possible unconscionability of the contracts in these cases. Since the record is not sufficient for our deciding the issue as a matter of law, the cases must be remanded to the trial court for further proceedings.

So ordered.

DANAHER, CIRCUIT JUDGE (dissenting): The District of Columbia Court of Appeals obviously was as unhappy about the situation here presented as any of us can possibly be. Its opinion in the *Williams* case, quoted in the majority text, concludes: "We think Congress should consider corrective legislation to protect the public from such exploitive contracts as were utilized in the case at bar."

My view is thus summed up by an able court which made no finding that there had actually been sharp practice. Rather the appellant seems to have known precisely where she stood.

---

9. This rule has never been without exception. In cases involving merely the transfer of unequal amounts of the same commodity, the courts have held the bargain unenforceable for the reason that "in such a case, it is clear, that the law cannot indulge in the presumption of equivalence between the consideration and the promise." 1 Williston, *Contracts* § 115 (3d ed. 1957).

10. See the general discussion of "Boiler–Plate Agreements" in Llewellyn, *The Common Law Tradition* 362–371 (1960).

11. Comment, Uniform Commercial Code § 2–307 [*sic*] [UCC § 2–302].

There are many aspects of public policy here involved. What is a luxury to some may seem an outright necessity to others. Is public oversight to be required of the expenditures of relief funds? A washing machine, *e.g.*, in the hands of a relief client might become a fruitful source of income. Many relief clients may well need credit, and certain business establishments will take long chances on the sale of items, expecting their pricing policies will afford a degree of protection commensurate with the risk. Perhaps a remedy when necessary will be found within the provisions of the "Loan Shark" law, D.C.Code §§ 26–601 *et seq.* (1961).

I mention such matters only to emphasize the desirability of a cautious approach to any such problem, particularly since the law for so long has allowed parties such great latitude in making their own contracts. I dare say there must annually be thousands upon thousands of installment credit transactions in this jurisdiction, and one can only speculate as to the effect the decision in these cases will have. I join the District of Columbia Court of Appeals in its disposition of the issues.

IN RE REALNETWORKS, INC., PRIVACY LITIGATION

United States District Court, N.D. Illinois, Eastern Division, 2000.
2000 WL 631341.

KOCORAS, J. Before the Court is Intervenor David Keel's additional arguments in support of Plaintiffs' opposition to arbitration. For the reasons set forth below, the Court rejects Intervenor's additional arguments.

BACKGROUND

Plaintiffs Michael Lieschke, Robert Jackson, and Todd Simon (collectively, the "Plaintiffs"), both on behalf of a class of Illinois plaintiffs and individually, brought suit against Defendant RealNetworks, Inc. ("RealNetworks") under federal and common law. Plaintiffs allege trespass to property and privacy, claiming that RealNetworks' software products secretly allowed RealNetworks to access and intercept users' electronic communications and stored information without their knowledge or consent. Previously, this Court considered and granted RealNetworks' motion to stay this matter and enforce arbitration, finding that the End User License Agreement (the "License Agreement") required arbitration of this dispute. *See* Lieschke v. RealNetworks, Inc., No. 99C 7274, 99 C 7380, 2000 WL 198424 (N.D.Ill. Feb. 11, 2000). Subsequently, this Court allowed Intervenor David Keel (the "Intervenor") to file his additional arguments in support of Plaintiffs' opposition to arbitration in order to raise certain arguments not presented to the Court when it decided the arbitration issue. It is these arguments that the Court presently addresses.

RealNetworks offers free basic versions of two products, RealPlayer and RealJukebox, for users to download from RealNetworks' site on the World–Wide Web. These products allow users to see and hear audio and video available on the Internet and to download, record, and play music.

Before a user can install either of these software packages, they must accept the terms of RealNetworks' License Agreement, which appear on the user's screen. Paragraph 10 of the Agreement includes the following clause:

> This License Agreement shall be governed by the laws of the State of Washington, without regard to conflicts of law provisions, and you hereby consent to the exclusive jurisdiction of the state and federal courts sitting in the State of Washington. Any and all unresolved disputes arising under this License Agreement shall be submitted to arbitration in the State of Washington.

Defendant cites this clause as binding authority for its assertions that arbitration is required. ... Intervenor argues that the arbitration provision is unenforceable because it is unconscionable.

DISCUSSION

Although national policy encourages arbitration of disputes, submission to arbitration is consensual, not coercive. *See* Mastrobuono v. Shearson Lehman Hutton, Inc., 514 U.S. 52, 57, 62, 115 S.Ct. 1212, 1216, 1218, 131 L.Ed.2d 76 (1995). Thus, a court cannot force a party to arbitrate unless that party has entered into a contractual agreement to do so. ... Ambiguities, however, are resolved in favor of arbitration. ...

III.   Unconscionability

... Intervenor claims that the arbitration agreement is unenforceable because it is both procedurally and substantively unconscionable. Procedural unconscionability involves impropriety during the process of forming a contract, whereas substantive unconscionability pertains to those cases where a clause or term in a contract is allegedly one-sided or overly harsh.

Intervenor argues that the License Agreement is procedurally unconscionable because it failed to provide fair notice of its contents and did not provide a reasonable opportunity to understand its terms before it was enforced. Both of these assertions are incorrect. Intervenor claims that the arbitration provision does not provide fair notice because it is "buried" in the License Agreement. Although burying important terms in a "maze of fine print" may contribute to a contract being found unconscionable, the arbitration provision in the License Agreement is not buried. ... The License Agreement sets out the arbitration provision in the same size font as the rest of the agreement. Moreover, it is not buried in the middle of the entire agreement or located in a footnote or appendix, but rather comprises the attention-getting final provision of the agreement. Although RealNetworks could have titled the heading containing the arbitration clause, the choice of law provision, and the forum selection clause in a more descriptive manner than "Miscellaneous," RealNetworks' titling it such does not necessarily bury the provision. While RealNetworks did not set off the arbitration provision and purposely draw attention to it, neither did RealNetworks bury the provision in a sea of words. Although

burying an arbitration clause could contribute to a finding of unconscionability, the Court is unaware of, and Intervenor has not pointed to, any
Washington state caselaw that provides that an arbitration clause is
unconscionable if the contract does not draw attention to it.

Moreover, Intervenor claims that the user is not given a reasonable
opportunity to understand the arbitration provision because the License
Agreement comes in a small pop-up window, which is visually difficult to
read, and because it cannot be printed. The Court has already discussed at
length the capability of printing the License Agreement, and again rejects
Intervenor's contention that the License Agreement cannot be printed.
The Court also finds that the size of the pop-up window, although smaller
than the desktop, does not make the License Agreement visually difficult
to read. The Court finds disingenuous Intervenor's assertion that the
License Agreement appears "in very fine print, requiring the user to
position himself just inches from the monitor in order to read it." The font
size of the License Agreement is no smaller, and possibly larger, than the
font size of all the words appearing on the computer's own display. If
Intervenor needs to plaster his face against the screen to read the License
Agreement, he must then have to do the same to read anything on his
computer, in which case, doing so does not seem like an inordinate
hardship or an adjustment out of the ordinary for him. In addition, the
user has all day to review the License Agreement on the screen. The pop-
up window containing the License Agreement does not disappear after a
certain time period; so, the user can scroll through it and examine it to his
heart's content.

Because the arbitration agreement is not buried in fine print and
because a user is given ample opportunity to understand the arbitration
provision, the Court does not find that the arbitration agreement is
procedurally unconscionable.

In addition, Intervenor asserts that the arbitration provision is substantively unconscionable because it chooses a geographically distant
forum, it fails to provide for classwide arbitration, and the costs of
arbitration are prohibitive.

The Court rejects Intervenor's claim that choosing Washington state
as the arbitration forum renders the arbitration agreement substantively
unconscionable. The designation of any state as a forum is bound to be
distant to some potential litigants of a corporation that has a nationwide
reach. Intervenor would have the Court essentially preclude arbitration
agreements from having any forum selection clause in order to prevent
the designation of a distant forum to any of these litigants. This Court is
not willing to do so. Arbitration provisions containing forum selection
clauses have previously been upheld. Moreover, some courts have even
found that the forum non conveniens doctrine is inapplicable in the
context of arbitrations covered under the FAA. Thus, that Washington is a
distant arbitration forum for some does not render the arbitration clause
substantively unconscionable.

Intervenor also claims that because litigants cannot pursue classwide arbitration without an arbitration provision providing for it, RealNetworks is effectively preventing potential litigants from seeking classwide arbitration by not expressly providing for classwide arbitration. Further, Intervenor reasons that because consumers in cases such as this have relatively small claims, these consumers' rights to bring a case would essentially be vitiated because the costs of the litigation would be so prohibitive. This Court previously rejected this argument in its prior decision. The Seventh Circuit, along with other courts in this district, have considered this issue and upheld arbitration agreements that do not provide for class action and have even upheld arbitration agreements that expressly prohibit class actions. Thus, the Court will not find the License Agreement substantively unconscionable because it does not provide for class arbitration.

Further, the Court rejects Intervenor's argument that allegedly prohibitive arbitration costs render the License Agreement unconscionable. The Seventh Circuit has found that the costs of arbitration do not prevent the enforcement of a valid arbitration agreement. As such, the potential arbitration costs do not render the arbitration clause substantively unconscionable.

CONCLUSION

For the reasons set forth above, the Court rejects Intervenor's additional arguments in support of Plaintiffs' opposition to arbitration.

CHAPTER 8

CONDITIONS, PERFORMANCE AND BREACH

■ ■ ■

SECTION 1. THE NATURE AND EFFECT OF EXPRESS CONDITIONS, THE TIME CLASSIFICATION OF CONDITIONS

(Calamari & Perillo on Contracts §§ 11.1—11.8)

AUDETTE v. L'UNION ST. JOSEPH

Supreme Judicial Court of Massachusetts, 1901.
178 Mass. 113, 59 N.E. 668.

Action by Malvina Audette, administratrix of the estate of Louis Audette, deceased, against L'Union St. Joseph. From a judgment in favor of defendant, plaintiff appeals. Affirmed.

A by-law of the defendant association provided that no sick member should receive any benefits before producing a sworn certificate of a physician. The physician who attended plaintiff's intestate in his last sickness refused to give a sworn certificate because of conscientious scruples against making an oath. ["Conscientious scruples against making an oath," is a standard phrase to indicate a religious belief that an oath is offensive to the Deity. Generally, procedural statutes and the U.S. Constitution allow an "affirmation" to substitute for an oath. Ed.]

LORING, J. This case comes within the rule that where one engages for the act of a stranger he must procure the act to be done, and the refusal of the stranger, without the interference of the other party, is no excuse. That rule has been applied in this commonwealth to the obligation of a person, insured under a fire insurance policy, to furnish to the fire insurance company a certificate, under the hand and seal of a magistrate, notary public, or commissioner of deeds, stating that he has examined the circumstances attending the loss, knows the character and circumstances of the assured, and believes that the assured has, without fraud, sustained loss on the property insured to the amount certified. Johnson v. Insurance

Co., 112 Mass. 49. In that case it was held that the plaintiff was not excused from producing such certificate by showing that he applied to two magistrates for such a certificate in vain, and used his best efforts to procure it, accompanied by proof of the facts which were to be certified to.
. . .

This action, therefore, was prematurely brought; but the plaintiff, on producing a sworn certificate, unless there is some objection to it not now disclosed, can bring a new writ, and recover the sick benefits now sued for. Judgment for the defendant affirmed.

INMAN v. CLYDE HALL DRILLING CO.

Supreme Court of Alaska, 1962.
369 P.2d 498.

DIMOND, JUSTICE. This case involves a claim for damages arising out of an employment contract. The main issue is whether a provision in the contract, making written notice of a claim a condition precedent to recovery, is contrary to public policy.

Inman worked for the Clyde Hall Drilling Company as a derrickman under a written contract of employment signed by both parties on November 16, 1959. His employment terminated on March 24, 1960. On April 5, 1960, he commenced this action against the Company claiming that the latter fired him without justification, that this amounted to a breach of contract, and that he was entitled to certain damages for the breach. In its answer the Company denied that it had breached the contract, and asserted that Inman had been paid in full the wages that were owing him and was entitled to no damages. Later the Company moved for summary judgment on the ground that Inman's failure to give written notice of his claim, as required by the contract, was a bar to his action based on the contract.[1] The motion was granted, and judgment was entered in favor of the Company. This appeal followed.

A fulfillment of the thirty-day notice requirement is expressly made a "condition precedent to any recovery." Inman argues that this provision is void as against public policy. In considering this first question we start with the basic tenet that competent parties are free to make contracts and that they should be bound by their agreements. In the absence of a constitutional provision or statute which makes certain contracts illegal or unenforceable, we believe it is the function of the judiciary to allow men to manage their own affairs in their own way. As a matter of judicial policy

---

1. The portion of the contract with which we are concerned reads: "You agree that you will, within thirty (30) days after any claim (other than a claim for compensation insurance) that arises out of or in connection with the employment provided for herein, give written notice to the Company for such claim, setting forth in detail the facts relating thereto and the basis for such claim; and that you will not institute any suit or action against the Company in any court or tribunal in any jurisdiction based on any such claim prior to six (6) months after the filing of the written notice of claim hereinabove provided for, or later than one (1) year after such filing. Any action or suit on any such claim shall not include any item or matter not specifically mentioned in the proof of claim above provided. It is agreed that in any such action or suit, proof by you of your compliance with the provisions of this paragraph shall be a condition precedent to any recovery."

the court should maintain and enforce contracts, rather than enable parties to escape from the obligations they have chosen to incur.

We recognize that "freedom of contract" is a qualified and not an absolute right, and cannot be applied on a strict, doctrinal basis. An established principle is that a court will not permit itself to be used as an instrument of inequity and injustice. As Justice Frankfurter stated in his dissenting opinion in United States v. Bethlehem Steel Corp., "The fundamental principle of law that the courts will not enforce a bargain where one party has unconscionably taken advantage of the necessities and distress of the other has found expression in an almost infinite variety of cases." [315 U.S. 289, 327–28, 62 S.Ct. 581, 600 (1942).] In determining whether certain contractual provisions should be enforced, the court must look realistically at the relative bargaining positions of the parties in the framework of contemporary business practices and commercial life. If we find those positions are such that one party has unscrupulously taken advantage of the economic necessities of the other, then in the interest of justice—as a matter of public policy—we would refuse to enforce the transaction. But the grounds for judicial interference must be clear. Whether the court should refuse to recognize and uphold that which the parties have agreed upon is a question of fact upon which evidence is required.

The facts in this case do not persuade us that the contractual provision in question is unfair or unreasonable. Its purpose is not disclosed. The requirement that written notice be given within thirty days after a claim arises may have been designed to preclude stale claims; and the further requirement that no action be commenced within six months thereafter may have been intended to afford the Company timely opportunity to rectify the basis for a just claim. But whatever the objective was, we cannot find in the contract anything to suggest it was designed from an unfair motive to bilk employees out of wages or other compensation justly due them.

There was nothing to suggest that Inman did not have the knowledge, capacity or opportunity to read the agreement and understand it; that the terms of the contract were imposed upon him without any real freedom of choice on his part; that there was any substantial inequality in bargaining positions between Inman and the Company. Not only did he attach a copy of the contract to his complaint, which negatives any thought that he really wasn't aware of its provisions, but he also admitted in a deposition that at the time he signed the contract he had read it, had discussed it with a Company representative, and was familiar with its terms. And he showed specific knowledge of the thirty-day notice requirement when, in response to a question as to whether written notice had been given prior to filing suit, he testified:

> A. Well, now, I filed—I started my claim within 30 days, didn't I, from the time I hit here. I thought that would be a notice that I started suing them when I first came to town.

Q. You thought that the filing of the suit would be the notice?

A. That is right.

Under these circumstances we do not find that such a limitation on Inman's right of action is offensive to justice. We would not be justified in refusing to enforce the contract and thus permit one of the parties to escape his obligations. It is conceivable, of course, that a thirty-day notice of claim requirement could be used to the disadvantage of a workman by an unscrupulous employer. If this danger is great, the legislature may act to make such a provision unenforceable.[11] But we may not speculate on what in the future may be a matter of public policy in this state. It is our function to act only where an existent public policy is clearly revealed from the facts and we find that it has been violated. That is not the case here.

Inman's claim arose on March 24, 1960. His complaint was served on the Company on April 14. He argues that since the complaint set forth in detail the basis of his claim and was served within thirty days, he had substantially complied with the contractual requirement.

Service of the complaint probably gave the Company actual knowledge of the claim. But that does not serve as an excuse for not giving the kind of written notice called for by the contract. Inman agreed that no suit would be instituted "prior to six (6) months *after the filing of the written notice of claim.*" (emphasis added) If this means what it says (and we have no reason to believe it does not), it is clear that the commencement of an action and service of the complaint was not an effective substitute for the kind of notice called for by the agreement. To hold otherwise would be to simply ignore an explicit provision of the contract and say that it had no meaning. We are not justified in doing that.

The contract provides that compliance with its requirement as to giving written notice of a claim prior to bringing suit "shall be a condition precedent to any recovery." Inman argues that this is not a true condition precedent—merely being labelled as such by the Company—and that non-compliance with the requirement was an affirmative defense which the Company was required to set forth in its answer under Civ.R. 8(c). He contends that because the answer was silent on this point, the defense was waived under Civ.R. 12(h).

The failure to give advance notice of a claim where notice is required would ordinarily be a defense to be set forth in the answer. But here the parties agreed that such notice should be a condition precedent to any recovery. This meant that the Company was not required to plead lack of notice as an affirmative defense, but instead, that Inman was required to plead performance of the condition or that performance had been waived or excused. The Company may not be charged under Civ.R. 12(h) with

---

11. In Oklahoma the constitution (art. XXIII, § 9) provides: "Any provision of any contract or agreement, express or implied, stipulating for notice or demand other than such as may be provided by law, as a condition precedent to establish any claim, demand, or liability, shall be null and void." *See* Brakebill v. Chicago, R.I. & P. Ry., 37 Okl. 140, 131 P. 540 (1913).

having waived a defense which it was not obliged to present in its answer.
. . .

Inman's last point is that the trial court erred in entering a final judgment. He argues that the failure to give written notice was merely a matter in abatement of his action until the condition could be performed, and that the most the court ought to have done was to dismiss the action without prejudice.

This argument is unsound. At the time judgment was entered Inman could no longer perform the condition precedent to recovery by giving written notice of his claim within thirty days after the claim arose, because this time limitation had expired. In these circumstances his right to seek redress from the court was barred and not merely abated. Final judgment in the Company's favor was proper.

The judgment is affirmed.

———

FEDERAL RULES OF CIVIL PROCEDURE

Rule 9. Pleading Special Matters

(c) Conditions Precedent. In pleading the performance or occurrence of conditions precedent, it is sufficient to aver generally that all conditions precedent have been performed or have occurred. A denial of performance or occurrence shall be made specifically and with particularity.

PROBLEMS

1. A term in a loan agreement (known as an "acceleration clause") allows Lender, in case of default by Borrower, to declare all future payments by Borrower immediately due and payable. The clause further states:

> Prior to acceleration, Lender shall mail a notice to Borrower specifying (1) the breach, (2) the action required to cure such breach, (3) a date, no less than 30 days from which the notice is mailed, within which Borrower must cure its breach, and (4) that failure to cure such breach may result in acceleration of all amounts due Lender. If the breach is not cured on or before the date specified in the notice, Lender may, at Lender's option, declare all of Borrower's obligations immediately due and payable and without further demand recover such sums from Borrower.

On March 22, Lender mailed Borrower the following notice (correctly stating the amount of arrears and the amount due from Borrower in case of acceleration): "This is your thirty-day notice to cure. The arrearage on your loan is $57,865. If you do not pay this amount within 30 days, we are entitled to bring an action against you for your total obligation of $450,700." Borrower received the notice on March 26 but ignored the notice and made no payments to Lender. On May 1, Lender sued Borrower to collect $450,700. Will Lender prevail?

2.   Husband and wife were lost at sea when the Lusitania was sunk. The husband had a policy on his life which provided: "Five Thousand Dollars . . . to his wife, if living; if not, then to the insured's executors, administrators or assigns." Should the money be paid to the administrator of the wife or husband?

3.   A casualty insurance policy provides that no action on the policy can be brought prior to giving proof of loss within 60 days of the loss and no action can be brought after twelve months from the loss. What kind of conditions are present?

4.   D issued a fire insurance policy to P that provided that no liability shall exist under this policy if the building is vacant or unoccupied at the time of loss. The building was destroyed by fire and there was conflicting evidence as to whether the building was vacant. Who has the burden of proof on this issue?

5.   Plaintiff is an advertising salesperson. He had been engaged by Defendant publisher to sell advertising in Defendant's magazine. The contract contained a provision to the effect that Plaintiff would be paid a specified commission when and if the advertisers paid the magazine. After the contract terminated, Plaintiff sued, claiming unpaid commissions. Who has the burden of proof on the question of whether Defendant had been paid by the advertisers?

SECTION 2.   DISTINGUISHING EXPRESS CONDITIONS FROM OTHER PROVISIONS

(Calamari & Perillo on Contracts §§ 11.9—11.15)

(a) DOES THE CONTRACT CREATE AN EXPRESS CONDITION, A PROMISE, OR BOTH?

NEW YORK BRONZE POWDER CO. v. BENJAMIN ACQUISITION CORP.

Court of Appeals of Maryland, 1998.
351 Md. 8, 716 A.2d 230.

MARVIN H. SMITH, JUDGE (retired), Specially Assigned. This case presents the problem of whether a provision in a contract is a condition or a promise or both. The Court of Special Appeals in an unreported opinion reversed a trial court judgment and construed as a condition precedent a provision in a non-negotiable note/contract requiring surrender of the note in order to receive payment.

The facts relevant to this decision may be briefly stated.

New York Bronze Powder Company, Inc. (New York Bronze) entered into an agreement dated March 15, 1990, with Benjamin Acquisition

Corporation (Benjamin) under which Benjamin agreed to purchase from New York Bronze the assets of a business then known as Benjamin F. Rich Company (Rich) for $4.5 million, together with the assumption of certain of Rich's liabilities. Closing was to take place on April 30, 1990. Shortly prior to the closing, Benjamin expressed its concerns to New York Bronze over the valuation of certain assets. The matter was resolved by an April 30, 1990 modification of the purchase agreement (Amendment No. 1). Under Amendment No. 1 $350,000 of the $4.5 million purchase price was deferred, and Benjamin executed a non-negotiable note to New York Bronze for $350,000. Under Section 3 of Amendment No. 1 Benjamin undertook, at its expense, to have prepared a balance sheet of Rich accompanied by the opinion of a specifically named accounting firm, and Benjamin promised to use its best efforts to cause that audited balance sheet to be delivered to New York Bronze no later than June 14, 1990. To the extent that the audited balance sheet reflected a net worth of Rich that was less than $4.5 million, Benjamin was entitled under Section 3 of the note to a dollar for dollar credit against the $350,000 deferred purchase price. . . .

As matters unfolded following the April 30, 1990 closing under the modified asset purchase agreement, the accounting firm specified in Amendment No. 1 never opined on the audited balance sheet, and apparently never completed its audit.

Benjamin never made or tendered any cash payment on the note. In October 1993 New York Bronze sued Benjamin in the Circuit Court for Montgomery County alleging non-payment of the note and breach of the modified asset purchase agreement. After a bench trial the court entered judgment for $350,000 in favor of New York Bronze.

Benjamin appealed to the Court of Special Appeals, raising three issues, but that court found it necessary to address only one. That issue is whether the portion of Section 4.2 of the note, italicized below, should be construed as a condition precedent to payment. That section provides:

> 4.2 *Payments.* Payments of any portion of the principal of this Note shall be made by check drawn on a United States commercial bank and shall be mailed by registered mail, return receipt requested, on or prior to the date on which such payment is due, to the Noteholder at the address set forth in the Purchase Agreement. If the date on which any payment hereunder is due is not a Business Day, then such payment shall be due on the next succeeding Business Day. *The Noteholder shall be required to surrender this Note for cancellation upon the maturity or prepayment in full of this Note in order to receive payment.*

(Emphasis added.) Section 4.4 of the note provides that it "SHALL BE GOVERNED BY AND CONSTRUED IN ACCORDANCE WITH THE LAWS OF THE STATE OF NEW YORK."

The Court of Special Appeals held that, under New York law, the italicized language created a condition, the non-occurrence of which extinguished Benjamin's obligation to pay the $350,000 or any part thereof. New York Bronze then petitioned this Court for the writ of certiorari, which was granted.

The factual foundation for Benjamin's position that the "condition" was not fulfilled lies in the testimony of New York Bronze's chief financial officer. When New York Bronze attempted to introduce *not* the note but *a copy* of the note, the following colloquy took place:

> Q. (Counsel for New York Bronze): Can you identify Exhibit No. 3?
>
> A. This would be the Benjamin Acquisition subordinated promissory note (due) July 30, 1991 for $350,000.
>
> (The document referred to was marked for identification as Plaintiff's Exhibit 3.)
>
> . . . .
>
> Q. Was anything paid on that note?
>
> A. No, nothing has been received.
>
> Q. Is that a true and accurate copy of the original?
>
> A. It appears to be, yes.
>
> (Counsel for New York Bronze): Your Honor, I would move Exhibit No. 3 into evidence(.)
>
> The Court: Any objection?
>
> (Counsel for Benjamin): Yes, Your Honor. *I have a bit of a problem with this exhibit to the extent Plaintiff is suing on a note and exhibiting the copy as opposed to the original.* It causes me a great deal of concern.
>
> The Court: Okay. Can you establish foundation as to the location of the original?
>
> . . . .
>
> Q. (Counsel for New York Bronze): Do you have the original note?
>
> A. No, I don't.
>
> Q. Have you sold the original note?
>
> A. No, I have not.
>
> Q. Has it been encumbered by anyone? Have you encumbered the original note?
>
> A. I just want to say where the original note is.
>
> Q. Where is it?
>
> A. Because I am not sure about the word encumbered. Perpetual Savings Bank was the lender at the time. They had an interest in all the assets. They kept the original documents.

Q.   Is that a true and accurate copy of the original note?

A.   Yes.

(Counsel for New York Bronze): I would move No. 3 into evidence.

The Court: Any further objection?

(Counsel for Benjamin): Yes, Your Honor. That still raises a question. *Now they are suing us on a note they are not even holding.*

The Court: Well, I will receive this over objection. I think a foundation has been laid.

(Emphasis added.) . . .

The Court of Special Appeals held that New York Bronze was not entitled to the principal amount of the note, or any part thereof, because it had not surrendered the original note to Benjamin. In reaching that result, the Court of Special Appeals reasoned:

> New York and Maryland law are congruent on the point that words in a contract (or note) are to be given their ordinary meaning. [citations] The New York courts have defined a condition precedent as "an act or event, other than a lapse of time, which, unless the condition is excused, must occur before a duty to perform a promise in the agreement arises." Oppenheimer & Co. v. Oppenheim, Appel, Dixon & Co., (86 N.Y.2d 685, 636 N.Y.S.2d 734) 660 N.E.2d 415, 418 (N.Y. 1995).[2]

The language in § 4.2 of the note clearly fits that definition. The noteholder is required to surrender the note for cancellation "in order to receive payment." Unquestionably, that requirement does qualify the duty to pay. *See* Gilpin v. Savage, 94 N.E. 656 (N.Y.1911) (requirement of presentment of negotiable instrument construed as condition precedent).

The dominant element in this case is that the note is non-negotiable.[4] The form of the note was an exhibit to Amendment No. 1 to the asset purchase agreement, and the note's provisions concerning set off imple-

---

2.   This squares with Maryland law. This Court has defined a condition precedent as " 'a fact, other than mere lapse of time, which, unless excused, must exist or occur before a duty of immediate performance of a promise arises.' " Chirichella v. Erwin, 270 Md. 178, 182, 310 A.2d 555, 557 (1973). While "no particular form of words is necessary in order to create an express condition, such words and phrases as 'if' and 'provided that,' are commonly used to indicate that performance has expressly been made conditional, as have the words 'when,' 'after,' 'as soon as,' or 'subject to.' " *Id.* (citations omitted). The determination of whether a provision in a contract constitutes a condition precedent is a question of "construction dependent on the intent of the parties to be gathered from the words they have employed and, in case of ambiguity, after resort to the other permissible aids to interpretation." *Id.*

4.   Benjamin does not contend that the note was a negotiable instrument. It did not contain "an unconditional promise or order to pay a sum certain in money," N.Y.U.C.C. § 3–104(1)(b) (McKinney 1991), and it was not "payable to order or to bearer." *Id.* § 3–104(1)(d). In addition, the note was introduced by a legend stating that it "may not be transferred except in compliance with, or pursuant to an exemption from, applicable securities laws." Section 4.1 of the note repeats the same warning and adds the provision that "(a)ny transferee of this Note shall take this Note subject to the terms hereof, including, without limitation, the provisions relating to subordination and set off."

ment the provisions of Amendment No. 1 concerning the audit. The asset purchase agreement, as amended, is one integrated contract that includes the note. Under these circumstances the controlling issue is whether the last sentence of Section 4.2 of the note is to be construed as a promise on the part of New York Bronze to surrender the note for cancellation, for an unsubstantial breach of which Benjamin would not be excused from performance, or whether the last sentence is a condition precedent to enforcement of Benjamin's promise to pay.

The most recent decision of the Court of Appeals of New York dealing with conditions in contracts is Oppenheimer & Co., Inc. v. Oppenheim, Appel, Dixon & Co., 86 N.Y.2d 685, 636 N.Y.S.2d 734, 660 N.E.2d 415 (1995). In that case there was an agreement concerning a proposed sublease. The sublessee had furnished the sublessor plans for construction of a telephone communications linkage system on the premises, and the sublessor obligated itself to obtain the underlying landlord's written consent to that work and to deliver that written consent by a specified date. On the specified date the sublessor telephoned the sublessee, advising that the underlying landlord had consented. The sublessee refused to sign the proposed sublease. The issue before the Court of Appeals of New York was whether the requirement for the sublessor to obtain written consent was a covenant, in which event non-performance would be subject to the doctrine of substantial performance, or whether that doctrine had no application because the provision was a condition. *Id.* at 735, 636 N.Y.S.2d 734, 660 N.E.2d at 416.

The agreement in *Oppenheimer* stated that if the sublessee "had not received the prime landlord's written consent by the agreed date, both the agreement and the sublease were to be deemed 'null and void and of no further force and effect,' and neither party was to have 'any rights against nor obligations to the other.' " *Id.* at 736, 636 N.Y.S.2d 734, 660 N.E.2d at 417. Another provision of the agreement stated that "the parties 'agree not to execute and exchange the Sublease unless and until ... the conditions set forth in (the paragraph requiring, *inter alia*, written consent) are timely satisfied.' " *Id.* The court held that this language created a condition. *Id.* at 737, 636 N.Y.S.2d 734, 660 N.E.2d at 418.

The court in *Oppenheimer* gave guidance for interpreting whether a provision is a condition:

> In determining whether a particular agreement makes an event a condition courts will interpret doubtful language as embodying a promise or constructive condition rather than an express condition. This interpretive preference is especially strong when a finding of express condition would increase the risk of forfeiture by the obligee (*see Restatement (Second) of Contracts* § 227(1)).

Id. ...

In addition to illustrating language that undoubtedly creates a condition, *Oppenheimer* evidences that the Court of Appeals of New York will look to *Restatement (Second) of Contracts* § 227 (1981) (*Restatement*) for the preferred interpretation of language argued to create a condition, as well as to *Restatement* § 229, dealing with excusing the non-occurrence of a condition. Here, the applicable section of the *Restatement* is § 227(2). In the language of that subsection, the duty to be performed is Benjamin's duty to pay the note, so that Benjamin is the "obligor;" New York Bronze is the "obligee;" and the asserted condition is the surrender of the note. Benjamin's position necessarily is that, as of the time of contract formation, surrender of the note was an event within the control of New York Bronze.

Where the above recited factors are present, the preferred interpretation is set forth in *Restatement* § 227(2), which reads:

> Unless the contract is of a type under which only one party generally undertakes duties, when it is doubtful whether
>
> (a) a duty is imposed on an obligee that an event occur, or
>
> (b) the event is made a condition of the obligor's duty, or
>
> (c) the event is made a condition of the obligor's duty and a duty is imposed on the obligee that the event occur,
>
> the first interpretation is preferred if the event is within the obligee's control.

Comment d states the rationale for the preferred interpretation as follows:

> The rule in Subsection (2) states a preference for an interpretation that merely imposes a duty on the obligee to do the act and does not make the doing of the act a condition of the obligor's duty. The preferred interpretation avoids the harsh results that might otherwise result from the non-occurrence of a condition and still gives adequate protection to the obligor under the rules ... relating to performances to be exchanged under an exchange of promises. Under those rules ... the obligee's failure to perform his duty has, if it is material, the effect of the non-occurrence of a condition of the obligor's duty. Unless the agreement makes it clear that the event is required as a condition, it is fairer to apply these more flexible rules. The obligor will, in any case, have a remedy for breach.

Turning to the interpretation of the last sentence of Section 4.2 of the note we conclude, for the reasons hereinafter set forth, that it is "doubtful" that the parties intended to create a condition. Benjamin's interpretation rests entirely on the language "in order to receive payment." Neither in the context of the contract as a whole, nor within the terms themselves, is the creation of a condition so clear that it overcomes the preference for interpretation of the language as a covenant.

The introductory paragraph of the non-negotiable note contains the promise to pay $350,000 and expresses that that promise is "(s)ubject to Sections 2 and 3 below." The former deals with subordination and the latter is the agreement concerning set offs. Had the parties intended the promise to be subject to a condition found in Section 4.2, careful drafting would have included Section 4.2 in the introduction of the note.

Section 4.2 of the note specifies how and when payments "shall be made . . . and shall be mailed." This is the language of covenants. No one could seriously maintain that, if Benjamin, in some immaterial fashion, did not comply with the provisions describing the payment checks and their mailing, then a payment received by New York Bronze could be kept by it without crediting the payment against the obligation. The principal clause of the last sentence in Section 4.2 ("The Noteholder shall be required to surrender this Note for cancellation. . . .") similarly is the language of covenant. Thus, under Benjamin's position, the language, "in order to receive payment," must produce a substantially different legal result than do the other provisions of Section 4.2.

Under the New York cases, it would seem that more explicit language than that used is required in order to achieve that result. For example, the interpretation would be much more clear if the critical clause of the last sentence of Section 4.2 read: "and upon failure to surrender this Note (Benjamin's) obligation to pay any outstanding balance will terminate," or "be extinguished." Instead, the note uses the language, "in order to receive payment." The primary meaning of the verb "to receive" is "to take possession or delivery of," as of a gift or of a letter. *Webster's Third New International Dictionary* 1984 (1976). In the context of the last sentence of Section 4.2, "receive" carries a passive connotation as to the role of New York Bronze while the active role would be that of Benjamin in tendering payment in full of any outstanding balance. Interpreting Section 4.2 as promises to exchange performances is a far cry from interpreting it to provide that the failure to surrender the note causes New York Bronze to lose all rights to take an active role and enforce collection on the note through legal proceedings.

The obvious purpose of the last sentence of Section 4.2 is to protect Benjamin from the risk that the note will fall into the hands of a third party who will in some way force Benjamin to pay twice. If the critical language is interpreted as part of a covenant by New York Bronze, then Benjamin theoretically had a number of options to remedy the breach. Benjamin could take the position that the breach was substantial, thus excusing Benjamin from performance, but that result is not the situation here, as we explain below. Benjamin could demand and possibly obtain from New York Bronze proof satisfactory to Benjamin that Benjamin would not be required to pay twice. Benjamin could claim as damages for the breach the cost of a bond protecting it against double payment. Although the note is non-interest bearing, Benjamin could have utilized the breach by New York Bronze to oppose a claim for the discretionary allowance of interest on any unpaid and overdue balance on the note for the period from maturity until judgment. Further, if after having paid New York Bronze in full a third party claimed against Benjamin on the note, Benjamin could obtain damages from New York Bronze measured by the cost of defending the claim of the third party and demonstrating that payment had been made in full.

Whatever the effect of the critical language might be in an agreement involving a negotiable note, Benjamin's risk of being required to pay twice is *de minimis* in the instant matter because the note is non-negotiable. If we assume that Benjamin paid the full $350,000 without a surrender of the note, an assignee of New York Bronze could not be a holder in due course. That assignee would take the note subject to the defense of payment by Benjamin to New York Bronze.

Under these circumstances it is unlikely that the parties intended to create a condition entitling Benjamin to keep up to $200,000 of assets without paying the agreed consideration. Thus, we apply the preferred construction and hold that the last sentence of Section 4.2 of the note creates a covenant or contractual duty on the part of New York Bronze to surrender the note. . . .

Judgment reversed. . . .

(b) TIME OR EXPRESS CONDITION?

THOS. J. DYER CO. v. BISHOP INTERNATIONAL ENGINEERING CO.

United States Court of Appeals, Sixth Circuit, 1962.
303 F.2d 655.

SHACKELFORD MILLER, JR., CHIEF JUDGE. Appellee, The Thos. J. Dyer Company, a subcontractor [Plumbing Subcontractor] on the project hereinafter referred to, brought this action against the appellant, Bishop International Engineering Company, hereinafter referred to as Engineering Company, the general contractor, to recover the sum of $134,684.53 for materials and labor furnished by it in the construction of the project. The appellant, General Insurance Company of America, was also made a defendant as surety on the "Owner's Protective Bond," executed by the Engineering Company as principal.

The following facts were stipulated by the parties. The Plumbing Subcontractor is an Ohio corporation engaged in the plumbing contracting business. The Engineering Company is a partnership engaged in the general contracting business. On or about August 19, 1958, the Engineering Company entered into a written contract with The Kentucky Jockey Club, Inc., hereinafter referred to as the Jockey Club, by the terms of which it agreed to provide labor and materials required in connection with the construction of a portion of a Horse Racing Plant, known as Latonia Race Track, upon premises belonging to the Jockey Club, situated in Boone County, Kentucky. That portion of the construction project covered by the contract was described as "Phase One."

On or about April 27, 1959, the Plumbing Subcontractor entered into a written subcontract with the Engineering Company, by the provisions of which it agreed to provide materials for and to install certain plumbing and utilities required in connection with the completion of the construction work to be performed by the Engineering Company, pursuant to its contract with the Jockey Club, for which it was to receive the sum of $115,000.00. Paragraph 3 of this subcontract reads as follows:

> 3. The total price to be paid to Subcontractor shall be _____ Dollars ($115,000.00) lawful money of the United States, no part of which shall be due until five (5) days after Owner shall have paid Contractor therefor, provided however, that not more than _____ per cent (90%) thereof shall be due until thirty-five (35) days after the entire work to be performed and completed under said contract shall have been completed to the satisfaction of Owners, and provided further that Contractor may retain sufficient moneys to fully pay and discharge any and all liens, stop-notices, attachments, garnishments and executions. Nothing herein is to be construed as preventing Contractor from paying to the Subcontractor all or any part of said price at any time hereafter as an advance or otherwise.

The Engineering Company has provided all of the labor and material and has done all things necessary for the completion of the work required of it under the contract of August 19, 1958, and has received payment of the sum of $2,236,908.95, specified by the contract as the consideration to be paid to it for the work to be performed by it thereunder.

From time to time following the execution of the contract of August 19, 1958, the Engineering Company was called upon by the Jockey Club to provide labor, services and materials for the completion of various items of construction relating to the above mentioned Horse Racing Plant which had not been included within Phase One of the construction program of the Jockey Club. The Engineering Company has received compensation for certain portions of such additional labor, services and materials provided by it at the request of the Jockey Club but has not yet received payment for all of it. . . .

The Plumbing Subcontractor has provided all the labor and materials and has done all things necessary for the completion of the work required of it under the subcontract, change orders, proposals and acceptances. The Plumbing Subcontractor completed its work as required on or before August 1, 1959, and the completed project was accepted by the owners on or about August 28, 1959.

The Engineering Company has not been paid by the Jockey Club for any work performed or material supplied by the Plumbing Subcontractor, other than that required pursuant to the terms of the original contract, dated August 19, 1958, between the Engineering Company and the Jockey Club.

The Engineering Company has paid to the Plumbing Subcontractor for work performed and materials provided under the subcontract, changes orders, proposals and acceptances the sum of $119,133.06. After the payment of $119,133.06 there remained a balance due from the Engineering Company to the Plumbing Subcontractor of $108,519.11.

Under date of August 19, 1958, the appellant General Insurance Company of America executed a bond to the Jockey Club in the face amount of $2,086,908.75, upon which the Engineering Company was the principal.

On December 4, 1959, the Jockey Club filed in the United States District Court for the Western District of Kentucky, Louisville Division, a proceeding for its reorganization under Chapter X of the Federal Bankruptcy Act. That proceeding is still pending.

The Engineering Company in its defense to the action contends that by the provisions of paragraph 3 of its subcontract with the Plumbing Subcontractor no payment was due thereunder to the Plumbing Subcontractor until five days after the Jockey Club, owner of the construction project to which the contract related, had made payment to the Engineering Company; that the Jockey Club has paid to it on account of the work performed and the materials furnished by the Plumbing Subcontractor certain payments, all of which have been paid by the Engineering Company to the Plumbing Subcontractor; and that because it has not received any further payment from the Jockey Club, now being reorganized in bankruptcy, it has no obligation to make further payment to the Plumbing Subcontractor.

Following the filing of the stipulation of facts, the District Judge made findings of fact and conclusions of law, sustained the Plumbing Subcontractor's motion for summary judgment, and entered judgment for the Plumbing Subcontractor in the principal amount of $108,519.11, together with $9,224.12 as interest due to the date of the judgment. . . .

The parties devote considerable time to the question of whether paragraph 3 in the Plumbing Subcontractor's subcontract is an enforceable provision of the contract, [the Engineering Company] contending that it is enforceable and the Plumbing Subcontractor contending that it is not. We think this argument misconceives the real issue in the case. It appears to be settled law that contract provisions making certain obligations conditional or contingent upon the happening of a certain event are valid and enforceable. . . . But the question remains whether the contract provision relied upon creates such a conditional or contingent obligation. This presents a question of construction or interpretation of the contract provision, not a question of its validity. Lewis v. Tipton, 10 Ohio St. 88.

In construing the contract sued on in this case, the first question is whether paragraph 3 of the subcontract of April 27, 1959, is applicable not only to the original subcontract but also to the several supplemental contracts between the parties for work additional to that covered by the original subcontract.

The Plumbing Subcontractor argues in support of the judgment that paragraph 3 in the subcontract of April 27, 1959, was applicable only to the labor and material covered by that instrument, and the subsequent agreements for additional work by it, which work was not contemplated in the original general contract, or in the initial subcontract, constitute separate contracts which do not contain the provisions of paragraph 3. It contends that the defense relied upon under paragraph 3 of the initial subcontract is not applicable to the work performed under the supplemental contracts. This contention appears to be in accord with the general rule. Canister Co. v. Wood & Selick, 73 F.2d 312, 314, C.A.3rd. The subsequent letter proposals and acceptances do not expressly state that they are subject to the provisions of the initial subcontract and each one contains the elements necessary to constitute a separate, independent contract. However, the fundamental question is one of intention to be determined from the language of the parties, the subject matter of the agreement and in the light of all the surrounding circumstances. ...

We think it is clear that the two change orders of May 25, 1959, and June 9, 1959, are to be considered as part of the original subcontract, to which they specifically refer. ...

Accordingly, we come to the crucial issue in the case, namely, whether, as contended by the Engineering Company, paragraph 3 of the subcontract is to be construed as a conditional promise to pay, enforceable only when and if the condition precedent has taken place which in the present case has not occurred, or, as contended by the Plumbing Subcontractor, it is to be construed as an unconditional promise to pay with the time of payment being postponed until the happening of a certain event, or for a reasonable period of time if it develops that such event does not take place.

Numerous decisions from various courts are cited by the parties in support of their respective contentions. We think that these cases state the basic rule and are examples of its application under the facts of the particular case being considered. For example, in Kentucky, where the contract herein involved was to be performed, the Court of Appeals of Kentucky held in Fox v. Buckingham, *supra*, 228 Ky. 176, 180–181, 14 S.W.2d 421, that the promise to pay was a conditional one, enforceable only when the condition precedent has taken place. In Mock v. Trustees of First Baptist Church of Newport, 252 Ky. 243, 67 S.W.2d 9, the same Court had before it the case of an architect who had been employed to prepare plans and specifications for a Sunday school building, the construction of which was indefinitely suspended because of unexpected construction costs and the church's financial limitations. In a suit by the architect for the unpaid balance of his fee the Trustees of the church contended that he had agreed to wait for the unpaid balance until such time as the church in its judgment and discretion was financially able and deemed it advisable to erect and complete the building. The Court held that such a promise to pay was not conditional upon the completion of the building, but should be construed to mean that payment was to be made within a reasonable time. ... The Court of Appeals of Kentucky in making its ruling . . . quoted with approval from section 2100 of *Page on Contracts* as follows:

> The time of performance is sometimes made to depend upon the doing of some specified act other than that which the parties to the contract agree to do or it is made to depend upon the happening of some event which the parties to the contract do not covenant to cause to happen. The tendency of the courts is to hold that unless the contract shows clearly that such an action is an express condition, the provision with reference to such act is inserted in order to fix the time of performance, but not to make the doing of such act or the happening of such event a condition precedent. If this is the intention of the parties, the fact that such act is not performed or that such event does not happen, does not discharge the contract, and the act which the parties agree to do upon the performance of such act or upon the happening of such event, is to be performed in at least a reasonable time. This principle has been applied to a promise to pay when the maker has finished a church then building; or to pay when a certain dispute is settled; or "as soon as the crop can be sold or the money raised from any other source."

As pointed out in that statement of the basic rule, it is the intention of the parties which is the controlling factor in each particular case.

It is, of course, basic in the construction business, for the general contractor on a construction project of any magnitude to expect to be paid in full by the owner for the labor and material he puts into the project. He would not remain long in business unless such was his intention and such intention was accomplished. That is a fundamental concept of doing business with another. The solvency of the owner is a credit risk necessarily incurred by the general contractor, but various legal and contractual provisions, such as mechanics' liens and installment payments, are used to reduce this to a minimum. These evidence the intention of the parties that the contractor be paid even though the owner may ultimately become insolvent. This expectation and intention of being paid is even more pronounced in the case of a subcontractor whose contract is with the general contractor, not with the owner. In addition to his mechanic's lien, he is primarily interested in the solvency of the general contractor with whom he has contracted. He looks to him for payment. Normally and legally, the insolvency of the owner will not defeat the claim of the subcontractor against the general contractor. Accordingly, in order to transfer this normal credit risk incurred by the general contractor from the general contractor to the subcontractor, the contract between the general contractor and subcontractor should contain an express condition clearly showing that to be the intention of the parties. Section 2100, *Page on Contracts, supra*.

In the case before us we see no reason why the usual credit risk of the owner's insolvency assumed by the general contractor should be transferred from the general contractor to the subcontractor. It seems clear to us under the facts of this case that it was the intention of the parties that the subcontractor would be paid by the general contractor for the labor and materials put into the project. We believe that to be the normal construction of the relationship between the parties. If such was not the intention of the parties it could have been so expressed in unequivocal terms dealing with the possible insolvency of the owner. North American Graphite Corp. v. Allan, 87 U.S.App.D.C. 154, 184 F.2d 387, 390. Paragraph 3 of the subcontract does not refer to the possible insolvency of the owner. On the other hand, it deals with the amount, time and method of payment, which are essential provisions in every construction contract, without regard to possible insolvency. In our opinion, paragraph 3 of the subcontract is a reasonable provision designed to postpone payment for a reasonable period of time after the work was completed, during which the general contractor would be afforded the opportunity of procuring from the owner the funds necessary to pay the subcontractor. Stewart v. Herron, 77 Ohio St. 130, 149, 82 N.E. 956. To construe it as requiring the subcontractor to wait to be paid for an indefinite period of time until the general contractor has been paid by the owner, which may never occur, is to give to it an unreasonable construction which the parties did not intend at the time the subcontract was entered into. . . .

The judgment is affirmed.

J.J. SHANE, INC. v. AETNA CAS. & SURETY CO.

District Court of Appeal of Florida, Third District, 1998.
723 So.2d 302.

GREEN, JUDGE. On this appeal, the plaintiff/subcontractor appeals from an adverse final judgment and order taxing attorney's fees and costs entered pursuant to a jury verdict in favor of the general contractor. We reverse and remand with instructions that this case be dismissed without prejudice as being prematurely filed.

Appellant, J.J. Shane, Inc. ("Shane") was a subcontractor to the general contractor, appellee Recchi America, Inc. ("Recchi") during the construction of the Omni extension of the "People Mover" in downtown Miami. The construction project is owned by Metropolitan Dade County. Shane instituted this breach of contract action when Recchi failed to make complete payment for Shane's work on this project. The center of this dispute involves the interpretation of the following payment provision of the written subcontract between the parties.

Article XIII Method of Payment

a) Subcontractor is relying upon the financial responsibility of Owner in performing the Work. It is understood by Subcontractor that payment for the work is to be made from funds received from Owner by Contractor in respect to the Work.

Recchi maintains that under this provision, its obligation to pay Shane is clearly conditioned upon its receipt of payment from the county/owner. Since it is undisputed herein that Recchi has not been paid for the project by the county/owner and indeed is itself currently embroiled in litigation for such payment, Recchi maintains that its contractual obligation to pay Shane has not yet arisen. Shane, on the other hand, asserts that this payment provision is ambiguous and, as such, must be construed to require Recchi's payment within a reasonable period of time.

In most subcontract agreements, payment by the owner to the contractor ordinarily is not intended to be a condition precedent to the contractor's duty to pay the subcontractor "because small subcontractors, who must have payment for their work in order to remain in business, will not ordinarily assume the risk of the owner's failure to pay the general contractor." Peacock Constr. Co., Inc. v. Modern Air Conditioning, Inc., 353 So.2d 840, 842 (Fla.1977). However, the *Peacock* court recognized that subcontract agreements such as the one before us, may contain valid payment provisions which shift the risk of payment failure by the owner from the general contractor to the subcontractor. *Id.* "But in order to make such a shift the contract must unambiguously express that intention." Peacock, 353 So.2d at 842–43.

Here, we find the subject payment provision to plainly and unambiguously make payment by the county/owner a condition precedent to payment by the general contractor to the subcontractor herein, rather than simply fixing a reasonable time for payment as contended by the subcontractor. Thus, where the owner's non-payment to the general contractor is undisputed, this cause for payment by the subcontractor was prematurely filed. Accordingly, we reverse the final judgment and the order awarding fees and costs with directions that this case be dismissed without prejudice.

Editor's note: If the contractor/subcontractor contract is interpreted to create a "pay if paid" provision (payment by owner to contractor is an express condition precedent to the contractor's duty to pay the subcontractor), some jurisdictions would declare such a condition void. *See, e.g.,* Wm. R. Clarke Corporation v. Safeco Ins. Co. of America, 15 Cal.4th 882, 938 P.2d 372, 64 Cal.Rptr.2d 578. (1997) (a pay if paid provision "is void because it violates the public policy that underlies the anti-waiver provisions of the mechanic's lien laws. The Legislature's carefully articulated anti-waiver scheme would amount to little if parties to construction contracts could circumvent it by means of pay if paid provisions having effects indistinguishable from waivers prohibited [by statute].").

(c) CONDITION TO FORMATION OR CONDITION TO PERFORMANCE?

THOMPSON v. LITHIA CHRYSLER JEEP DODGE OF GREAT FALLS

Supreme Court of Montana, 2008.
343 Mont. 392, 185 P.3d 332

JUSTICE JIM RICE delivered the Opinion of the Court. Corey and Kimber Thompson (Thompsons) appeal from the order of the District Court for the Eighth Judicial District, Cascade County, granting the Defendants' motions to compel arbitration of Plaintiffs' claims related to a 2005 transaction for a truck. We reverse and remand.

We restate the issues on appeal as follows:

1. Where a contract containing an arbitration clause is challenged on the basis of the failure of a condition precedent to contract formation, who is the appropriate adjudicator, an arbitrator or the court?

2. Was the approval of financing upon terms stated in the contract documents a condition precedent to the formation of a contract between the parties?

FACTUAL AND PROCEDURAL BACKGROUND

On January 31, 2005, the Thompsons went to the Lithia Chrysler Jeep Dodge of Great Falls (an assumed business name of Lithia of Great Falls, Inc., hereinafter "Lithia") automobile dealership with the intention of purchasing a new vehicle. The Thompsons identified a 2005 Dodge Ram 1500 (Dodge truck) they wished to purchase, which had a sales price of $39,224. The Thompsons made a cash down payment of $2,000 on the Dodge truck, traded in their 2000 GMC Sierra 2500 (GMC truck), which had a trade-in value of $23,612 (offset by a $22,100 loan pay-off for a net trade-in allowance of $1,512), and offered to finance the remainder.

The Thompsons signed a Retail Installment Contract (Contract) with Lithia. The Contract listed the transaction for the Dodge truck as having an annual percentage rate of 3.9 percent. The reverse side of the Contract contained a number of terms and conditions, including a series of arbitration provisions. One of these stated:

> Any claim or dispute, whether in contract, tort or otherwise (including any dispute over the interpretation, scope, or validity of the contract, the arbitration clause or the arbitrability of any issue), between us or Creditor's employees, agents, successors or assigns, which arise out of or relate to a credit application, this contract, or any resulting transaction or relationship (including any such relationship with third parties who do not sign this contract) shall, at the election of either of us (or the election of any such third party), be resolved by a neutral, binding arbitration and not by a court action.

. . .

The Thompsons also signed a Vehicle Buyer's Order (Order), which likewise listed the annual percentage rate at 3.9 percent and contained a number of terms and conditions. The front of the Order contained a "Notice to Purchaser" which stated:

> If this transaction is to be a retail installment sale, then this order is not a binding contract to the dealer and dealer shall not be obligated to sell until approval of the terms hereof is given by a bank or finance company willing to purchase a retail installment contract between the parties hereto based on such terms. If this approval is obtained, however, this order is a binding contract. If the purchaser is obtaining his own financing, this order is a binding contract as it is written. If a purchaser has received a copy of a retail installment contract as a part of this transaction, it shall not be binding to the dealer until accepted by the bank or finance company to which it will be assigned.

The Order likewise addressed arbitration, stating that "any controversy or claim arising out of or relating to this order, or breach thereof, shall be settled by arbitration. . . ."

The Thompsons were permitted to take the Dodge truck home, and they operated it for a little over a week. The Thompsons allege that, on February 8, 2005, Lithia's Finance Manager, Jeffery Crocker, contacted them and told them that they would need to sign new finance papers with a higher annual percentage rate of 4.9 percent.[5] The Thompsons contend that they refused to accept a higher rate and that Crocker informed them that they would have to return the Dodge truck if they failed to sign. The Thompsons allege that they brought the Dodge truck back to Lithia's dealership that same day and attempted to recover the GMC truck they had offered in trade, but Lithia informed them that it had already been sold and that Lithia refused to return the Thompsons' $2,000 cash down payment. The Thompsons maintain that Lithia refused to accept the Dodge truck at this point, but they left the truck with its keys at the dealership.

After returning the Dodge truck, the Thompsons claim that they contacted Daimler Chrysler Services North America (now Daimler Chrysler Financial Services Americas, d/b/a Chrysler Financial) (hereinafter "DCFS") several times to verify that the Contract and Order were not enforced. They claim that DCFS informed them that there was no record of a loan. Later, Lithia submitted financing papers to DCFS, which accepted the loan. On January 9, 2006, counsel for the Thompsons received a letter from Lithia's counsel stating that although the contract signed by the Thompsons contained a provision "allowing the dealership the right to rescind the contract" in the event the dealership could not sell

---

5. Many of the Thompsons' assertions are contested by the Defendants. Because the District Court granted Defendants' motion to stay the proceedings, the parties did not conduct any discovery and the District Court did not enter any findings of fact.

the loan for the quoted rate, Lithia decided, rather than rescind the transaction, to execute a "rate buy down concession." According to the letter, the "rate buy down concession" occurred when "the dealership paid money towards the loan on (Thompsons') behalf so that the interest rate reflected on the original contract could be maintained."

The Thompsons filed suit against the above-named Defendants on March 1, 2006, bringing six causes of action: (1) Fraud; (2) Conversion; (3) Damage of Chattle (*sic*) with Malace (*sic*); (4) Negligence; (5) Violation of the Montana Consumer Protection Act; and (6) Punitive Damages.

[Defendants filed motions to stay the proceedings and compel arbitration as well as motions seeking protective orders to preclude the Thompsons from conducting any discovery while the court considered Defendants' motions to stay the proceedings. Ed.]

The District Court entered an order on December 15, 2006, granting the Defendants' motions to compel arbitration and to stay the proceedings. In reaching its decision, the District Court relied on the United States Supreme Court's holding in Buckeye Check Cashing, Inc. v. Cardegna, 546 U.S. 440, 126 S.Ct. 1204, 163 L.Ed.2d 1038 (2006), that "a challenge to the validity of the contract as a whole, and not specifically to the arbitration clause, must go to the arbitrator," Buckeye, 546 U.S. at 449, 126 S.Ct. at 1210. . . . The District Court concluded that because the Thompsons were challenging the contract as a whole, and not just the arbitration clause, *Buckeye* . . . required that the matter be heard by the arbitrator. This appeal followed.

STANDARD OF REVIEW

We review a district court's order granting a motion to compel arbitration *de novo*. [citation] We review a district court's conclusions of law to see if they are correct. [citation]

DISCUSSION

Issue One. Where a contract containing an arbitration clause is challenged on the basis of the failure of a condition precedent to contract formation, who is the appropriate adjudicator, an arbitrator or the court?

The Federal Arbitration Act (FAA), 9 U.S.C. §§ 1–16, governs contracts "involving commerce" that contain arbitration clauses. . . .

In *Buckeye,* the Supreme Court examined the FAA in the context of a challenge to a contract containing an arbitration clause, and outlined three key principles of federal arbitration law. First, "an arbitration provision is severable from the remainder of the contract." Buckeye, 546 U.S. at 445, 126 S.Ct. at 1209. Second, and most relevant to this appeal, "unless the challenge is to the arbitration clause itself, the issue of the contract's validity is considered by the arbitrator in the first instance." Buckeye, 546 U.S. at 445–46, 126 S.Ct. at 1209. Finally, the Supreme Court reaffirmed that "this arbitration law applies in state as well as federal courts." Buckeye, 546 U.S. at 446, 126 S.Ct. at 1209. The Supreme

Court concluded that because the respondent challenged the validity of the contract as a whole, and not the arbitration clause specifically, the challenge had to go to the arbitrator. Buckeye, 546 U.S. at 449, 126 S.Ct. at 1210. . . .

The Thompsons . . . maintain that their situation is distinguishable on the ground that they are challenging the *existence* of a contract containing an arbitration clause, rather than the *validity* of such a contract (as was the case in . . . *Buckeye* . . .). They argue that . . . if the contract does not exist, then there is no agreement to arbitrate. They maintain that the contract, and arbitration clause therein, never came into existence due to the failure of a condition precedent—namely, approval of the Order and Contract by a bank or finance company at the interest rate of 3.9 percent. Since Lithia allegedly requested that the Thompsons either sign new papers at a higher rate or return the truck, which the Thompsons assert they did prior to approval of financing, the Thompsons claim that the condition precedent was not met and no contract was formed. The Thompsons argue, consequently, there was no arbitration clause and no obligation to engage in arbitration. The Defendants reply that the distinction between a challenge to the existence of a contract and a challenge to the validity of a contract is one without a difference, and argue that the Thompsons must submit the matter to the arbitrator pursuant to *Buckeye*. . . .

The Ninth Circuit recently considered a challenge to the existence of a contract containing an arbitration clause and concluded that the challenge was a matter for the court to consider, distinguishing it from *Buckeye*. In Sanford v. Memberworks, Inc., 483 F.3d 956 (9th Cir.2007), the plaintiff argued that she never agreed to a "membership agreement" containing an arbitration clause and thus, a basic requirement for formation of a contract had not been met. Analyzing the case in light of *Buckeye*, the Ninth Circuit stated, "[i]ssues regarding the validity or enforcement of a putative contract mandating arbitration should be referred to an arbitrator, but *challenges to the existence of a contract as a whole* must be determined by the court prior to ordering arbitration." Sanford, 483 F.3d at 962 (emphasis added). . . .

The Ninth Circuit highlighted the fact that the Supreme Court, in a *Buckeye* footnote, had recognized the distinction between the validity of a contract and the question of whether a contract had been formed. Sanford, 483 F.3d at 962 n. 8. . . . The fact that the Supreme Court distinguished between contracts that are void and contracts that never existed in the first place supports the Thompsons' contention that there is a difference between challenging the validity of a contract as a whole (as void *ab initio*, for example) and challenging the existence of a contract. . . .

We agree with the above-cited authority. When a party challenges a contract containing an arbitration clause on the ground the parties never entered a contract, the court, not arbitration, is the appropriate forum to determine whether a contract existed, prior to compelling arbitration. If formation of a contract never occurred, then the parties never agreed to arbitrate and it would be inappropriate to submit the matter to arbitration. This is a narrow exception to the rule established in *Buckeye*. . . .

Having determined that the court is the proper body to hear a challenge to the existence of a contract containing an arbitration provision, we must now examine whether failure of a condition precedent is such a contract formation issue. When deciding whether an agreement to arbitrate has been reached by the parties, courts look to state law principles of contract formation. . . . Accordingly, we examine Montana law regarding conditions precedent and contract formation. . . .

It is important to distinguish between a condition precedent to the formation of a contract and a condition precedent to performance of a contract obligation. "In the law of contracts, conditions may relate to the existence of contracts or to the duty of immediate performance under them. Thus, there may be conditions to the formation of a contract, or conditions to performance of a contract." Samuel Williston & Richard A. Lord, *A Treatise on the Law of Contracts* vol. 13, § 38:4, 375 (4th ed., West 2000). [I]f a condition precedent to formation is not fulfilled, then there is no agreement and the contract is not binding. This is distinguished from a condition precedent to performance of a contract obligation, which assumes the contract was formed.

A challenge to a contract containing an arbitration clause on the ground of a failure of a condition precedent to formation goes directly to whether the parties formed a contract and, on the basis of the above-discussed authorities, the matter is appropriate for the court to hear, instead of an arbitrator. We thus agree with the Thompsons that the District Court erred in granting the motion to compel arbitration at this juncture. The question of whether a contract was formed by the parties must first be determined by the court.

Issue Two. Was the approval of financing upon terms stated in the contract documents a condition precedent to the formation of a contract between the parties?

The Thompsons argue that the plain language of the Contract and Order makes clear that there was no binding contract until the Contract and Order were accepted by the bank or finance company, *i.e.*, that approval of 3.9 percent financing of their purchase was a condition precedent to formation of the contract. The Order states:

> If this transaction is to be a retail installment sale, then this order is not a binding contract to the dealer and dealer shall not be obligated to sell until approval of the terms hereof is given by a bank or finance company willing to purchase a retail installment contract between the parties hereto based on such terms. If this approval is obtained, however, this order is a binding contract. If the purchaser is obtaining his own financing, this order is a binding contract as it is written. If a purchaser has received a copy of a retail installment contract as a part

of this transaction, it shall not be binding to the dealer until accepted by the bank or finance company to which it will be assigned.

. . . The above-quoted language from the contract documents appears clear and explicit on its face and unambiguous, serving to demonstrate that the contract was dependent on approval of financing for the Thompsons upon the terms stated within the contract. However, DCFS points to the language in the Vehicle Order stating that neither the Contract nor the Order are binding *to the dealer* unless financing is obtained, and contends that the condition precedent only applies to the dealer, not the Thompsons. DCFS argues that "(n)othing in the sale documents indicate that the financing acceptance clause was a 'condition precedent' for *the Thompsons'* performance, and nothing in the sale documents permit the Thompsons to repudiate the contract when the sale terms have not changed." (Emphasis added.)

However, though the express terms of the contract speak only of the dealer not being bound if financing is not approved, a review of the totality of the contract language clearly demonstrates the same is true for the Thompsons, even though not expressly stated. The Contract first states that the Thompsons agreed to buy the Dodge truck "on a credit price basis ('Total Sale Price')." The "Total Sale Price," defined by the Contract as "(t)he total price of your purchase on credit, including your down payment," was listed as $44,351.20. The contract explained that this amount included the total amount of payments ($38,539.20), which was calculated based on the amount financed ($34,899.00) at a 3.9 percent "annual percentage rate," which was explained as "(t)he cost of your credit as a yearly rate." The Contract listed the total finance charge as $3,640.20, or "(t)he dollar amount the credit will cost you." Thus, the total sales price agreed to by the Thompsons was based upon financing at the rate of 3.9 percent, and the corresponding finance charge they agreed to was likewise premised upon a 3.9 percent rate. A change in rate would thus change the finance charge and the total sales price for the vehicle, unless other terms were re-negotiated or adjusted. Although some of these financial figures were designated by the Contract as "Estimates," they were nonetheless calculated on the basis of the 3.9 annual percentage rate, which was not designated as an estimate.

Regarding a change in terms, paragraph 9 of the Contract states that "(a)n [sic] change in this contract must be in writing and signed by all the parties. . . ." Paragraph 2 of the Vehicle Order provides that if the manufacturer changes the price to the dealer, the dealer may change the cash delivered price to the purchaser; however, if the cash delivered price is increased by the dealer, "Purchaser may, if dissatisfied therewith, cancel this Order. . . ."

A review of the contract documents convinces us that the Thompsons agreed to purchase the Dodge for a specific price which was premised upon 3.9 percent financing, and that no contract would have been formed unless financing under those terms was approved. To hold otherwise would potentially obligate the Thompsons to purchase the Dodge at whatever interest rate could be obtained. Just as the contract was not binding on the dealer unless financing was approved at the stated terms, it was likewise not binding on the Thompsons without such approval. Therefore, this was a condition precedent to the contract's formation.

The Thompsons further maintain that this condition precedent was not satisfied based on their assertions that Lithia requested that they sign new contract documents at a higher interest rate or return the truck, and that they refused the higher rate. DCFS contends that the financing was accepted on the terms in the Order and Contract and also maintains that there is no document showing rejection of the terms by DCFS. On this point, the Thompsons assert that such documents exist showing a financial institution rejected the 3.9 percent interest rate but that they have not been allowed to pursue discovery on the matter. Further, the Thompsons point to the January 9, 2006 letter from Lithia's counsel indicating that Lithia performed a "rate buy down concession" to keep the Thompsons' original interest rate.

It is clear that there are questions of disputed fact which warrant further inquiry into whether the condition precedent was satisfied and the contract formed. These questions cannot be answered without further fact finding by the District Court.

The District Court erred by granting the Defendants' motion to compel arbitration and stay the proceedings. Therefore we remand the case to the District Court for further proceedings consistent herewith. Discovery will need to be conducted so that the factual issues related to whether the financing condition was satisfied may be determined.

Reversed and remanded. . . .

PROBLEMS

6. Plaintiff alleges that defendant agreed to sell him a lot and to construct a residence and that "it was understood" that the marsh on which the lot fronted would be cleaned out by a named third party and that, when the marsh had been cleaned out and turned into a lake, the defendant would install a sand beach. The plaintiff promised to pay $350,000 when the house was completed. Plaintiff did pay on completion. Later plaintiff sues, alleging that defendant failed to transform the marsh into a lake and to install the sand beach; consequently the house was worth less than it would have been worth if it was located on a beachfront. Is a cause of action stated?

7. S entered into a contract with B to build a yarn-spinning mill for B. The contract provided the standards that had to be met before performance would be deemed completed. The work was not accepted because the machinery supplied by S lacked the capacity to produce the quantity and quality of yarn described in the contract. The contract was ambiguous on the issue of whether S promised to meet these standards. B asserts a claim for damages for breach of contract. S contends that B is entitled only to withhold the unpaid portion of the contract price. Who is right?

8. Vendee entered into a written agreement with Vendor for the purchase and sale of a specific house on specified terms and conditions. The agreement stated: "This contract is contingent upon buyer being able to obtain mortgage loan in the amount of $50,000." (Further terms and conditions of the prospective loan were detailed.) Vendor seeks a declaratory judgment that the alleged contract is void as the purchaser's promise is illusory. The purchaser, he argues, can effectively defeat the "contract" by failing to seek out mortgage financing. What result?

9. In a sale of a steamboat, there is the following clause: "And it is understood and agreed that this sale is upon this express condition that said steamboat or vessel is not within 10 years from the first day of 1867 to be run upon any routes of travel of the State of California or the Columbia River or its tributaries." Plaintiff seller brings an action for damages for breach of contract alleging that defendant violated the aforesaid terms of the contract. What result?

SECTION 3.   CONSTRUCTIVE CONDITIONS

(Calamari & Perillo on Contracts §§ 11.16—11.19 and 11.21)

STEWART v. NEWBURY

Court of Appeals of New York, 1917.
220 N.Y. 379, 115 N.E. 984.

CRANE, J. The defendants are partners in the pipe fitting business under the name of Newbury Manufacturing Company. The plaintiff is a contractor and builder residing at Tuxedo, N.Y.

The parties had the following correspondence about the erection for the defendants of a concrete mill building at Monroe, N.Y.:

Alexander Stewart,
Contractor and Builder,
Tuxedo, N.Y., July 18, 1911.

Newbury Mfg. Company, Monroe, N.Y.

Gentlemen: With reference to the proposed work on the new foundry building I had hoped to be able to get up and see you this afternoon, but find that impossible and am, in consequence, sending you these prices, which I trust you will find satisfactory.

I will agree to do all excavation work required at sixty-five ($.65) cents per cubic yard.

I will put in the concrete work, furnishing labor and forms only, at two and 05–100 ($2.05) dollars per cubic yard.

I will furnish labor to put in reenforcing at four ($4.00) dollars per ton.

I will furnish labor only to set all window and door frames, window sash and doors, including the setting of hardware for one hundred twelve ($112) dollars. As alternative I would be willing to do any or all of the above work for cost plus 10 per cent., furnishing you with first class mechanics and giving the work considerable of my personal time.

Hoping to hear favorably from you in this regard, I am,

Respectfully yours,
[Signed] Alexander Stewart

The Newbury Mfg. Co.,
Steam Fittings, Grey Iron Castings,
Skylight Opening Apparatus,
Monroe, N.Y.

Telephone Connection. Monroe, N.Y., July 22, 1911.

Alexander Stewart, Tuxedo Park, N.Y.

Dear Sir: Confirming the telephone conversation of this morning we accept your bid of July the 18th to do the concrete work on our new building. We trust that you will be able to get at this the early part of next week.

Yours truly,
The Newbury Mfg. Co.,
H.A. Newbury

Nothing was said in writing about the time or manner of payment. The plaintiff, however, claims that after sending his letter, and before receiving that of the defendant, he had a telephone communication with Mr. Newbury and said: "I will expect my payments in the usual manner," and Newbury said, "All right, we have got the money to pay for the building." This conversation over the telephone was denied by the defendants. The custom, the plaintiff testified, was to pay 85 per cent. every 30 days or at the end of each month, 15 per cent. being retained till the work was completed.

In July the plaintiff commenced work and continued until September 29th, at which time he had progressed with the construction as far as the first floor. He then sent a bill for the work done up to that date for $896.35. The defendants refused to pay the bill and work was discontinued. The plaintiff claims that the defendants refused to permit him to perform the rest of his contract, they insisting that the work already done was not in accordance with the specifications. The defendants claimed upon the trial that the plaintiff voluntarily abandoned the work after their refusal to pay his bill.

On October 5, 1911, the defendants wrote the plaintiff a letter containing the following:

Notwithstanding you promised to let us know on Monday whether you would complete the job or throw up the contract, you have not up to this time advised us of your intention. ... Under the circumstances, we are compelled to accept your action as being an abandonment of your contract and of every effort upon your part to complete your work on our building. As you know, the bill which you sent us and which we declined to pay is not correct, either in items or amount, nor is there anything due you under our contract as we understand it until you have completed your work on our building.

To this letter the plaintiff replied the following day. In it he makes no reference to the telephone communication agreeing, as he testified, to make "the usual payments," but does say this:

There is nothing in our agreement which says that I shall wait until the job is completed before any payment is due, nor can this be reasonably implied. ... As to having given you positive date as to when I should let you know what I proposed doing, I did not do so; on the contrary, I told you that I would not tell you positively what I would do until I had visited the job, and I promised that I would do this at my earliest convenience and up to the present time I have been unable to get up there.

The defendant Herbert Newbury testified that the plaintiff "ran away and left the whole thing." And the defendant F.A. Newbury testified that he was told by Mr. Stewart's man that Stewart was going to abandon the job; that he thereupon telephoned Mr. Stewart, who replied that he would let him know about it the next day, but did not.

In this action, which is brought to recover the amount of the bill presented, as the agreed price and $95.68 damages for breach of contract, the plaintiff had a verdict for the amount stated in the bill, but not for the other damages claimed, and the judgment entered thereon has been affirmed by the Appellate Division.

The appeal to us is upon exceptions to the judge's charge. The court charged the jury as follows:

Plaintiff says that he was excused from completely performing the contract by the defendants' unreasonable failure to pay him for the work he had done during the months of August and September. ... Was it understood that the payments were to be made monthly? If it was not so understood, the defendants' only obligation was to make payments at reasonable periods, in view of the character of the work, the amount of work being done, and the value of it. In other words, if there was no agreement between the parties respecting the payments, the defendants' obligation was to make payments at reasonable times. ... But whether there was such an agreement or not, you may consider whether it was reasonable or unreasonable for him to exact a payment at that time and in that amount.

The court further said, in reply to a request to charge:

I will say in that connection, if there was no agreement respecting the time of payment, and if there was no custom that was understood by both parties, and with respect to which they made the contract, then the plaintiff was entitled to payments at reasonable times.

The defendants' counsel thereupon made the following request, which was refused:

> I ask your honor to instruct the jury that, if the circumstances existed as your honor stated in your last instruction, then the plaintiff was not entitled to any payment until the contract was completed.

The jury was plainly told that if there were no agreement as to payments, yet the plaintiff would be entitled to part payment at reasonable times as the work progressed, and if such payments were refused he could abandon the work and recover the amount due for the work performed.

This is not the law. Counsel for the plaintiff omits to call our attention to any authority sustaining such a proposition and our search reveals none. In fact, the law is very well settled to the contrary. This was an entire contract. Ming v. Corbin, 142 N.Y. 334, 340, 341, 37 N.E. 105. Where a contract is made to perform work and no agreement is made as to payment, the work must be substantially performed before payment can be demanded. . . .

The judgment should be reversed, and a new trial ordered, costs to abide the event.

MONROE STREET PROPERTIES, INC. v. CARPENTER

United States Court of Appeals, Ninth Circuit, 1969.
407 F.2d 379.

HUFSTEDLER, CIRCUIT JUDGE. Appellant, Monroe Street Properties, Inc. ("Monroe"), appeals from a judgment in favor of the defendant Carpenter entered after Carpenter's motion for a summary judgment was granted. Carpenter is a party in his capacity as a trustee for Western Equities, Inc. ("Western"). Federal jurisdiction is based upon diversity of citizenship.

Monroe's action is for claimed breach of a written contract between Monroe and Western in which Western agreed to buy from Monroe ten insured first mortgages and notes having a face value of $1,250,000 in exchange for $1,000,000 worth of Western's common stock. The District Court granted summary judgment on the ground that the uncontroverted facts showed that Monroe neither performed nor tendered performance on its side and, therefore, Western was not in breach of contract. Monroe contends that there was a genuine issue of material fact within the meaning of Rule 56 of the Federal Rules of Civil Procedure: Could Monroe have performed its agreement by delivering clear insured title to the first mortgages during the life of the contract? We reject Monroe's contention and affirm the judgment.

The following facts are undisputed. On March 27, 1962, Western submitted its written offer to Monroe to buy the ten first mortgages and notes. Monroe promptly accepted the offer. Western's offer was expressly subject to "verification by Union Title Company that the ten first mortgages . . . are valid first mortgages." The offer further provided that Monroe would secure a policy of title insurance at its expense, would take the Western stock "as investment stock without plans for redistribution," and would execute voting proxies for the stock in favor of the Executive Committee of Western for three years. Western agreed to have the stock listed on the American Stock Exchange and to seek with due diligence registration of the stock with the Securities and Exchange Commission.

Pursuant to the contract the parties opened an escrow with Union Title Company on March 30, 1962. The escrow agreement provided that the terms and conditions of the agreement were to be complied with "on or before the date upon which (Western) stock has been listed on the American Stock Exchange, and delivered to Union Title Company." The Western stock was listed on the American Stock Exchange sometime before June 29, 1962, although the precise date of the listing is not clearly stated in the affidavits filed in connection with the motion for summary judgment. Monroe never deposited into escrow ten valid first mortgages or the policy of title, and Western never deposited its stock. Monroe did deposit the mortgage instruments in the escrow, but a preliminary title report received by Western on May 7, 1962, revealed that the properties subject to the ten mortgages were also subject to heavy prior encumbrances. After Monroe deposited those instruments in escrow, Monroe sent a demand to Western to deposit the stock. Western did not comply with the demand. Nothing further was done by either of the parties to perform the agreement and Monroe brought this action in October 1966.

According to the facts presented by Monroe in its own affidavits, which are uncontradicted in this respect by Western's affidavits, the only means by which Monroe could have delivered clear title to the first mortgages and could have obtained the policy of title insurance was to hypothecate Western stock to raise the money to pay off the prior encumbrances. Monroe had no ability or means to perform its part of the agreement unless Western deposited its stock in escrow before Monroe performed.

The District Court correctly decided that Monroe never made an adequate tender of its own performance. Monroe's duty to deposit the insured first mortgages and Western's duty to deposit its stock were concurrent conditions. (Wilhorn Builders, Inc. v. Cortaro Management Co. (1957), 82 Ariz. 48, 308 P.2d 251.) Neither party could place the other in breach for failure to perform without a tender of its own performance. "Tender" as used in this connection means " 'a readiness and willingness to perform in case of the *concurrent* performance by the other party, with present ability to do so, and notice to the other party of such readiness.' " (Emphasis added. 6 Williston, *Contracts* (3d ed. 1962) § 833, p. 105.) Monroe's offer to perform its concurrent condition upon condition that

Western perform first was not an adequate tender and could not be relied upon by Monroe to place Western in breach of contract.[1]

The judgment is affirmed.

JACOB & YOUNGS, INC. v. KENT

Court of Appeals of New York, 1921.
230 N.Y. 239, 129 N.E. 889.

CARDOZO, J. The plaintiff built a country residence for the defendant at a cost of upwards of $77,000, and now sues to recover a balance of $3,483.46, remaining unpaid. The work of construction ceased in June, 1914, and the defendant then began to occupy the dwelling. There was no complaint of defective performance until March, 1915. One of the specifications for the plumbing work provides that—

> All wrought-iron pipe must be well galvanized, lap welded pipe of the grade known as "standard pipe" of Reading manufacture.

The defendant learned in March, 1915, that some of the pipe, instead of being made in Reading, was the product of other factories. The plaintiff was accordingly directed by the architect to do the work anew. The plumbing was then encased within the walls except in a few places where it had to be exposed. Obedience to the order meant more than the substitution of other pipe. It meant the demolition at great expense of substantial parts of the completed structure. The plaintiff left the work untouched, and asked for a certificate that the final payment was due. Refusal of the certificate was followed by this suit.

The evidence sustains a finding that the omission of the prescribed brand of pipe was neither fraudulent nor willful. It was the result of the oversight and inattention of the plaintiff's subcontractor. Reading pipe is distinguished from Cohoes pipe and other brands only by the name of the manufacturer stamped upon it at intervals of between six and seven feet. Even the defendant's architect, though he inspected the pipe upon arrival, failed to notice the discrepancy. The plaintiff tried to show that the brands installed, though made by other manufacturers, were the same in quality, in appearance, in market value, and in cost as the brand stated in the contract—that they were, indeed, the same thing, though manufactured in another place. The evidence was excluded, and a verdict directed for the defendant. The Appellate Division reversed, and granted a new trial.

We think the evidence, if admitted, would have supplied some basis for the inference that the defect was insignificant in its relation to the project. The courts never say that one who makes a contract fills the measure of his duty by less than full performance. They do say, however, that an omission, both trivial and innocent, will sometimes be atoned for by allowance of the resulting damage, and will not always be the breach of

---

1. The cases cited by Monroe do not assist it. The cases support the principle that a vendor's failure to have title to property, which is the subject of the sale, before the vendor's performance is due, is not a breach of contract by the vendor. [citations] Monroe's problem is not to avoid a charge based on breach attributed to it, but to establish a breach by Western.

a condition to be followed by a forfeiture. Spence v. Ham, 163 N.Y. 220, 57 N.E. 412, 51 L.R.A 238. The distinction is akin to that between dependent and independent promises, or between promises and conditions. *Anson on Contracts* (Corbin's Ed.) § 367; 2 *Williston on Contracts*, § 842. Some promises are so plainly independent that they can never by fair construction be conditions of one another. Rosenthal Paper Co. v. Nat. Folding Box & Paper Co., 226 N.Y. 313, 123 N.E. 766. Others are so plainly dependent that they must always be conditions. Others, though dependent and thus conditions when there is departure in point of substance, will be viewed as independent and collateral when the departure is insignificant. 2 *Williston on Contracts*, §§ 841, 842; Eastern Forge Co. v. Corbin, 182 Mass. 590, 592, 66 N.E. 419. Considerations partly of justice and partly of presumable intention are to tell us whether this or that promise shall be placed in one class or in another. The simple and the uniform will call for different remedies from the multifarious and the intricate. The margin of departure within the range of normal expectation upon a sale of common chattels will vary from the margin to be expected upon a contract for the construction of a mansion or a "skyscraper." There will be harshness sometimes and oppression in the implication of a condition when the thing upon which labor has been expended is incapable of surrender because united to the land, and equity and reason in the implication of a like condition when the subject-matter, if defective, is in shape to be returned. From the conclusion that promises may not be treated as dependent to the extent of their uttermost minutiae without a sacrifice of justice, the progress is a short one to the conclusion that they may not be so treated without a perversion of intention. Intention not otherwise revealed may be presumed to hold in contemplation the reasonable and probable. If something else is in view, it must not be left to implication. There will be no assumption of a purpose to visit venial faults with oppressive retribution.

Those who think more of symmetry and logic in the development of legal rules than of practical adaptation to the attainment of a just result will be troubled by a classification where the lines of division are so wavering and blurred. Something, doubtless, may be said on the score of consistency and certainty in favor of a stricter standard. The courts have balanced such considerations against those of equity and fairness, and found the latter to be the weightier. The decisions in this state commit us to the liberal view, which is making its way, nowadays, in jurisdictions slow to welcome it. Dakin & Co. v. Lee, 1916, 1 K.B. 566, 579. Where the line is to be drawn between the important and the trivial cannot be settled by a formula. "In the nature of the case precise boundaries are impossible." 2 *Williston on Contracts*, § 841. The same omission may take on one aspect or another according to its setting. Substitution of equivalents may not have the same significance in fields of art on the one side and in those of mere utility on the other. Nowhere will change be tolerated, however, if it is so dominant or pervasive as in any real or substantial measure to frustrate the purpose of the contract. Crouch v. Gutman, 134 N.Y. 45, 51, 31 N.E. 271, 30 Am.St.Rep. 608. There is no general license to install whatever, in the builder's judgment, may be regarded as "just as good." Easthampton L. & C. Co., Ltd. v. Worthington, 186 N.Y. 407, 412, 79 N.E. 323. The question is one of degree, to be answered, if there is doubt, by the triers of the facts (*Crouch v. Gutmann, supra*), and, if the inferences are certain, by the judges of the law (*Easthampton L. & C. Co., Ltd. v. Worthington, supra*). We must weigh the purpose to be served, the desire to be gratified, the excuse for deviation from the letter, the cruelty of enforced adherence. Then only can we tell whether literal fulfillment is to be implied by law as a condition. This is not to say that the parties are not free by apt and certain words to effectuate a purpose that performance of every term shall be a condition of recovery. That question is not here. This is merely to say that the law will be slow to impute the purpose, in the silence of the parties, where the significance of the default is grievously out of proportion to the oppression of the forfeiture. The willful transgressor must accept the penalty of his transgression. Schultze v. Goodstein, 180 N.Y. 248, 251, 73 N.E. 21. For him there is no occasion to mitigate the rigor of implied conditions. The transgressor whose default is unintentional and trivial may hope for mercy if he will offer atonement for his wrong. *Spence v. Ham, supra.*

In the circumstances of this case, we think the measure of the allowance is not the cost of replacement, which would be great, but the difference in value, which would be either nominal or nothing. Some of the exposed sections might perhaps have been replaced at moderate expense. The defendant did not limit his demand to them, but treated the plumbing as a unit to be corrected from cellar to roof. In point of fact, the plaintiff never reached the stage at which evidence of the extent of the allowance became necessary. The trial court had excluded evidence that the defect was unsubstantial, and in view of that ruling there was no occasion for the plaintiff to go farther with an offer of proof. We think, however, that the offer, if it had been made, would not of necessity have been defective because directed to difference in value. It is true that in most cases the cost of replacement is the measure. *Spence v. Ham, supra.* The owner is entitled to the money which will permit him to complete, unless the cost of completion is grossly and unfairly out of proportion to the good to be attained. When that is true, the measure is the difference in value. Specifications call, let us say, for a foundation built of granite quarried in Vermont. On the completion of the building, the owner learns that through the blunder of a subcontractor part of the foundation has been built of granite of the same quality quarried in New Hampshire. The measure of allowance is not the cost of reconstruction. "There may be omissions of that which could not afterwards be supplied exactly as called for by the contract without taking down the building to its foundations, and at the same time the omission may not affect the value of the building for use or otherwise, except so slightly as to be hardly appreciable." Handy v. Bliss, 204 Mass. 513, 519, 90 N.E. 864, 134 Am.St.Rep. 673. The rule that gives a remedy in cases of substantial performance with compensation for defects of trivial or inappreciable importance has been developed by the courts as an instrument of justice. The measure of the allowance must be shaped to the same end.

The order should be affirmed, and judgment absolute directed in favor of the plaintiff upon the stipulation, with costs in all courts.

McLAUGHLIN, J. I dissent. The plaintiff did not perform its contract. Its failure to do so was either intentional or due to gross neglect which, under the uncontradicted facts, amounted to the same thing, nor did it make any proof of the cost of compliance, where compliance was possible. ...

I am of the opinion the trial court was right in directing a verdict for the defendant. The plaintiff agreed that all the pipe used should be of the Reading Manufacturing Company. Only about two-fifths of it, so far as appears, was of that kind. If more were used, then the burden of proving that fact was upon the plaintiff, which it could easily have done, since it knew where the pipe was obtained. The question of substantial performance of a contract of the character of the one under consideration depends in no small degree upon the good faith of the contractor. If the plaintiff had intended to, and had, complied with the terms of the contract except as to minor omissions, due to inadvertence, then he might be allowed to recover the contract price, less the amount necessary to fully compensate the defendant for damages caused by such omissions. Woodward v. Fuller, 80 N.Y. 312; Nolan v. Whitney, 88 N.Y. 648. But that is not this case. It installed between 2,000 and 2,500 feet of pipe, of which only 1,000 feet at most complied with the contract. No explanation was given why pipe called for by the contract was not used, nor that any effort made to show what it would cost to remove the pipe of other manufacturers and install that of the Reading Manufacturing Company. The defendant had a right to contract for what he wanted. He had a right before making payment to get what the contract called for. It is no answer to this suggestion to say that the pipe put in was just as good as that made by the Reading Manufacturing Company, or that the difference in value between such pipe and the pipe made by the Reading Manufacturing Company would be either "nominal or nothing." Defendant contracted for pipe made by the Reading Manufacturing Company. What his reason was for requiring this kind of pipe is of no importance. He wanted that and was entitled to it. It may have been a mere whim on his part, but even so, he had a right to this kind of pipe, regardless of whether some other kind, according to the opinion of the contractor or experts, would have been "just as good, better, or done just as well." He agreed to pay only upon condition that the pipe installed were made by that company and he ought not to be compelled to pay unless that condition be performed. The rule, therefore, of substantial performance, with damages for unsubstantial omissions, has no application. ...

HISCOCK, CH. J., HOGAN and CRANE, JJ., concur with CARDOZO, J.; POUND and ANDREWS, JJ. concur with McLAUGHLIN, J.

Order affirmed, etc.

JACOB & YOUNGS, INC. v. KENT

Court of Appeals of New York, 1921.
230 N.Y. 656, 130 N.E. 933.

On motion for reargument. Motion denied.

PER CURIAM. The court did not overlook the specification which provides that defective work shall be replaced. The promise to replace, like the promise to install, is to be viewed, not as a condition, but as independent and collateral, when the defect is trivial and innocent. The law does not nullify the covenant, but restricts the remedy to damages.

VRT, INC. v. DUTTON–LAINSON

Supreme Court of Nebraska, 1995.
247 Neb. 845, 530 N.W.2d 619.

CAPORALE, JUSTICE. The plaintiff-appellee seller, VRT, Inc., formerly known as Sanitas, Inc., sought a judgment declaring its right to past and future royalties under a provision within a purchase and sale contract. VRT alleged that the defendant-appellant buyer, Dutton–Lainson Company, breached its contract with VRT by failing to pay VRT royalties contemplated under the royalty provision. The district court ruled that Dutton–Lainson was obligated to pay both past-due and future royalties as provided in the contract. ... For the reasons hereinafter set forth, we now reverse the judgment of the district court and remand the cause for dismissal. ...

Sanitas was formed to manufacture, market, and distribute James Vanderheiden's invention, which improved devices used in hospitals and nursing homes to lift and move patients, hereinafter referred to as the patient care equipment.

After retaining an attorney to file a patent application on the patient care equipment, Sanitas sought out a manufacturer. Having been told by Sanitas that a patent application on the patient care equipment had been filed and having been assured by its own patent attorney that there was good reason to expect that a patent would issue, Dutton–Lainson and Sanitas executed a contract whereunder Sanitas sold and Dutton–Lainson purchased those Sanitas assets which related to the patient care equipment. ...

The contract further requires Sanitas to deliver to Dutton–Lainson at the closing "(s)pecific assignments to the assets described ... above as shall be reasonably required by Dutton–Lainson."

At the closing, Sanitas delivered to Dutton–Lainson a document labeled "BILL OF SALE AND ASSIGNMENT," assigning to Dutton–

Lainson all of its "current inventions, blueprints, drawings, plans, specifications, procedures and confidential information; all vendor and sales information including customer lists and other marketing information; and the name Sanitas, Inc. and any other related or similar trade name relating to the production and marketing of Sanitas, Inc.'s Patient Care Equipment." Sanitas also delivered documents purporting to assign to Dutton–Lainson the patent application and Sanitas' interest in the invention disclosed therein. Sanitas thereafter changed its name to VRT, Inc. Although the contract refers to patents and applications for patents, there was but one application and it referred to the patent being sought. There was no other patent. Dutton–Lainson produced the patient care equipment and sold it with some modifications to the invention; part of the invention was not being used at all because the design was unstable.

It turns out that Sanitas' attorney had not filed the patent application when he represented that he had and did not file it until after the parties executed the contract. It was stipulated that because of the late filing, a patent could not issue. As a result, VRT filed an action for professional negligence against its attorney, claiming that the attorney had been negligent in failing to file the patent application, in concealing his failure, and in providing false information. VRT further claimed that as a result of those actions, it was forced to incur substantial legal fees to enforce the royalty contract against Dutton–Lainson and sought recovery from its attorney for the loss of royalties beyond the 10th year. In addition, VRT claimed its future royalty payments would be reduced because Dutton–Lainson would not have the exclusive right to manufacture and market the patient care equipment. VRT and its attorney ultimately settled the action.

To successfully bring an action on a contract, a plaintiff must first establish that the plaintiff substantially performed the plaintiff's obligations under the contract. To establish substantial performance under a contract, any deviations from the contract must be relatively minor and unimportant. Lange Indus. v. Hallam Grain Co., 244 Neb. 465, 507 N.W.2d 465 (1993). If there is substantial performance, a contract action may be maintained but without prejudice to any showing of damage on the part of the defendant for failure to receive full and complete performance. Church of the Holy Spirit v. Bevco, Inc., 215 Neb. 299, 338 N.W.2d 601 (1983). . . .

The relationship between attorney and client is one of agency. Spier v. Thomas, 131 Neb. 579, 269 N.W. 61 (1936). Therefore, the general agency rules of law apply to the relation of attorney-client.

Consequently, the omissions and commissions of an attorney are to be regarded as the acts of the client whom the attorney represents, and the attorney's neglect is equivalent to the neglect of the client. In re Marriage of Castor, 249 Mont. 495, 817 P.2d 665 (1991). Moreover, a principal holding out an agent as having authority to represent the principal and thereby asserting or impliedly admitting that the agent is worthy of trust and confidence is bound by all the agent's acts within the apparent scope of the employment. Hence, the principal may be held responsible for the fraudulent acts of the agent. . . .

The contract reveals that the very essence of the transaction was to enable Dutton–Lainson to manufacture, market, and distribute the improvements which were the subject of the patent application. While Dutton–Lainson took the risk that, for reasons beyond the control of the parties, a patent might not issue, Dutton–Lainson did not bargain for the certainty that a patent would not issue because, contrary to the representation made to it, no application had been filed.

Thus, VRT's failure to deliver and assign a filed application was not a relatively minor and unimportant deviation from VRT's obligation. As a consequence, VRT's misrepresentation with regard to the application means there was no honest endeavor in good faith on its part to perform its part of the contract. It therefore necessarily follows that there was no substantial performance on its part and that it is precluded from maintaining this action against Dutton–Lainson. . . .

Reversed and remanded.

WALKER & CO. v. HARRISON

Supreme Court of Michigan, 1957.
347 Mich. 630, 81 N.W.2d 352.

SMITH, JUSTICE. This is a suit on a written contract. The defendants are in the dry-cleaning business. Walker & Company, plaintiff, sells, rents, and services advertising signs and billboards. These parties entered into an agreement pertaining to a sign. The agreement is in writing and is termed a "rental agreement." It specifies in part that:

> The lessor agrees to construct and install, at its own cost, one 18' 9" high x 8' 8" wide pylon type d.f. neon sign with electric clock and flashing lamps. . . . The lessor agrees to and does hereby lease or rent unto the said lessee the said SIGN for the term, use and rental and under the conditions, hereinafter set out, and the lessee agrees to pay said rental. . . .
>
> (a) The term of this lease shall be 36 months. . . .
>
> (b) The rental to be paid by lessee shall be $148.50 per month for each and every calendar month during the term of this lease; . . . .
>
> (d) Maintenance. Lessor at its expense agrees to maintain and service the sign together with such equipment as supplied and installed by the lessor to operate in conjunction with said sign under the terms of this lease; this service is to include cleaning and repainting of sign in original color scheme as often as deemed necessary by lessor to keep sign in first class advertising condition and make all necessary repairs to sign and equipment installed by lessor. . . . "

At the "expiration of this agreement," it was also provided, "title to this sign reverts to lessee." This clause is in addition to the printed form of agreement and was apparently added as a result of defendants' concern over title, they having expressed a desire "to buy for cash" and the salesman, at one time, having "quoted a cash price."

The sign was completed and installed in the latter part of July, 1953. The first billing of the monthly payment of $148.50 was made August 1, 1953, with payment thereof by defendants on September 3, 1953. This first payment was also the last. Shortly after the sign was installed, someone hit it with a tomato. Rust, also, was visible on the chrome, complained defendants, and in its corners were "little spider cobwebs." In addition, there were "some children's sayings written down in here." Defendant Herbert Harrison called Walker for the maintenance he believed himself entitled to under subparagraph (d) above. It was not forthcoming. He called again and again. "I was getting, you might say, sorer and sorer. . . . Occasionally, when I started calling up, I would walk around where the tomato was and get mad again. Then I would call up on the phone again." Finally, on October 8, 1953, plaintiff not having responded to his repeated calls, he telegraphed Walker that:

> You Have Continually Voided Our Rental Contract By Not Maintaining Signs As Agreed As We No Longer Have A Contract With You Do Not Expect Any Further Remuneration.

Walker's reply was in the form of a letter. After first pointing out that "your telegram does not make any specific allegations as to what the failure of maintenance comprises," and stating that "We certainly would appreciate your furnishing us with such information," the letter makes reference to a prior collateral controversy between the parties, "wondering if this refusal on our part prompted your attempt to void our rental contract," and concludes as follows:

> We would like to call your attention to paragraph G in our rental contract, which covers procedures in the event of a Breach of Agreement. In the event that you carry out your threat to make no future monthly payments in accordance with the agreement, it is our intention to enforce the conditions outlined under paragraph G[1] through

---

1. "(g) Breach of Agreement. Lessee shall be deemed to have breached this agreement by default in payment of any installment of the rental herein provided for; abandonment of the sign or vacating premises where the sign is located; termination or transfer of lessee's interest in the premises by insolvency, appointment of a receiver for lessee's business; filing of a voluntary or involuntary petition in bankruptcy with respect to lessee or the violation of any of the other terms or conditions hereof. In the event of such default, the lessor may, upon notice to the lessee, which notice shall conclusively be deemed sufficient if mailed or delivered to the premises where the sign was or is located, take possession of the sign and declare the balance of the rental herein provided for to be forthwith due and payable, and lessee hereby agrees to pay such balance upon any such contingencies. Lessor may terminate this lease and without notice, remove and repossess said sign and recover from the lessee such amounts as may be unpaid for the remaining unexpired term of this agreement. Time is of the essence of this lease with respect to the payment of rentals herein provided for. Should lessee after lessor has declared the balance of rentals due and payable, pay the full amount of rental herein provided, he shall then be entitled to the use of the sign, under all the terms and provisions hereof, for the balance of the term of this lease. No waiver by either party hereto of the nonperformance of any term, condition or obligation hereof shall be a waiver of any subsequent breach of, or failure to perform the same, or any other term, condition or obligation hereof. It is understood and agreed that the sign is especially constructed for the lessee and for use at the premises now occupied by the lessee for the term herein provided;

the proper legal channels. We call to your attention that your monthly rental payments are due in advance at our office not later than the 10th day of each current month. You are now approximately 30 days in arrears on your September payment. Unless we receive both the September and October payments by October 25th, this entire matter will be placed in the hands of our attorney for collection in accordance with paragraph G which stipulates that the entire amount is forthwith due and payable.

No additional payments were made and Walker sued in assumpsit for the entire balance due under the contract, $5,197.50, invoking paragraph (g) of the agreement. Defendants filed answer and claim of recoupment, asserting that plaintiff's failure to perform certain maintenance services constituted a prior material breach of the agreement, thus justifying their repudiation of the contract and grounding their claim for damages. The case was tried to the court without a jury and resulted in a judgment for the plaintiff. The case is before us on a general appeal.

Defendants urge upon us again and again, in various forms, the proposition that Walker's failure to service the sign, in response to repeated requests, constituted a material breach of the contract and justified repudiation by them. Their legal proposition is undoubtedly correct. Repudiation is one of the weapons available to an injured party in event the other contractor has committed a material breach. But the injured party's determination that there has been a material breach, justifying his own repudiation, is fraught with peril, for should such determination, as viewed by a later court in the calm of its contemplation, be unwarranted, the repudiator himself will have been guilty of material breach and himself have become the aggressor, not an innocent victim.

What is our criterion for determining whether or not a breach of contract is so fatal to the undertaking of the parties that it is to be classed as "material"? There is no single touchstone. Many factors are involved. They are well stated in section 275 of Restatement of the Law of Contracts in the following terms:

> In determining the materiality of a failure fully to perform a promise the following circumstances are influential:
>
> (a) The extent to which the injured party will obtain the substantial benefit which he could have reasonably anticipated;
>
> (b) The extent to which the injured party may be adequately compensated in damages for lack of complete performance;
>
> (c) The extent to which the party failing to perform has already partly performed or made preparations for performance;
>
> (d) The greater or less hardship on the party failing to perform in terminating the contract;

---

that it is of no value unless so used and that it is a material consideration to the lessor in entering into this agreement that the lessee shall continue to use the sign for the period of time provided herein and for the payment of the full rental for such term."

(e) The wilful, negligent or innocent behavior of the party failing to perform;

(f) The greater or less uncertainty that the party failing to perform will perform the remainder of the contract.

We will not set forth in detail the testimony offered concerning the need for servicing. Granting that Walker's delay (about a week after defendant Herbert Harrison sent his telegram of repudiation Walker sent out a crew and took care of things) in rendering the service requested was irritating, we are constrained to agree with the trial court that it was not of such materiality as to justify repudiation of the contract, and we are particularly mindful of the lack of preponderant evidence contrary to his determination. Jones v. Eastern Michigan Motorbuses, 287 Mich. 619, 283 N.W. 710. The trial court, on this phase of the case, held as follows:

> Now Mr. Harrison phoned in, so he testified, a number of times. He isn't sure of the dates but he sets the first call at about the 7th of August and he complained then of the tomato and of some rust and some cobwebs. The tomato, according to the testimony, was up on the clock; that would be outside of his reach, without a stepladder or something. The cobwebs are within easy reach of Mr. Harrison and so would the rust be. I think that Mr. Bueche's argument that these were not materially a breach would clearly be true as to the cobwebs and I really can't believe in the face of all the testimony that there was a great deal of rust seven days after the installation of this sign. And that really brings it down to the tomato. And of course, when a tomato has been splashed all over your clock, you don't like it. But he says he kept calling their attention to it, although the rain probably washed some of the tomato off. But the stain remained, and they didn't come. I really can't find that that was such a material breach of the contract as to justify rescission. I really don't think so.

Nor, we conclude, do we. There was no valid ground for defendants' repudiation and their failure thereafter to comply with the terms of the contract was itself a material breach, entitling Walker, upon this record, to judgment. . . .

Affirmed. Costs to appellee.

K & G CONSTR. CO. v. HARRIS

Court of Appeals of Maryland, 1960.
223 Md. 305, 164 A.2d 451.

PRESCOTT, JUDGE. Feeling aggrieved by the action of the trial judge of the Circuit Court for Prince George's County, sitting without a jury, in finding a judgment against it in favor of a subcontractor, the appellant, the general contractor on a construction project, appealed.

The principal question presented is: Does a contractor, damaged by a subcontractor's failure to perform a portion of his work in a workmanlike manner, have a right, under the circumstances of this case, to withhold, in partial satisfaction of said damages, an installment payment, which, under the terms of the contract, was due the subcontractor, unless the negligent performance of his work excused its payment?

The appeal is presented on a case stated in accordance with Maryland Rule 826g.

The statement, in relevant part, is as follows:

... K & G Construction Company, Inc. (hereinafter called Contractor), plaintiff and counter-defendant in the Circuit Court and appellant herein, was owner and general contractor of a housing subdivision project being constructed (herein called Project). Harris and Brooks (hereinafter called Subcontractor), defendants and counter-plaintiffs in the Circuit Court and appellees herein, entered into a contract with Contractor to do excavating and earth-moving work on the Project. Pertinent parts of the contract are set forth below: ...

Section 4. (b) Progress payments will be made each month during the performance of the work. Subcontractor will submit to Contractor, by the 25th of each month, a requisition for work performed during the preceding month. Contractor will pay these requisitions, less a retainer equal to ten per cent (10%), by the 10th of the months in which such requisitions are received.[2]

(c) No payments will be made under this contract until the insurance requirements of Sec. 9 hereof have been complied with. ...

Section 8. ... All work shall be performed in a workmanlike manner, and in accordance with the best practices.

Section 9. Subcontractor agrees to carry, during the progress of the work, ... liability insurance against ... property damage, in such amounts and with such companies as may be satisfactory to Contractor and shall provide Contractor with certificates showing the same to be in force.

While in the course of his employment by the Subcontractor on the Project, a bulldozer operator drove his machine too close to Contractor's house while grading the yard, causing the immediate collapse of a wall and other damage to the house. The resulting damage to Contractor's house was $3,400.00. Subcontractor had complied with the insurance provision (Sec. 9) of the aforesaid contract. Subcontractor reported said damages to their liability insurance carrier. The Subcontractor and its insurance carrier refused to repair damage or compensate Contractor for damage to the house, claiming that there was no liability on the part of the Subcontractor. ...

Subcontractor performed work under the contract during July, 1958, for which it submitted a requisition by the 25th of July, as required by the contract, for work done prior to the 25th of July payable under the terms of the contract by Contractor on or before

---

2. This section is not a model for clarity.

August 10, 1958. Contractor was current as to payments due under all preceding monthly requisitions from Subcontractor. The aforesaid bulldozer accident damaging Contractor's house occurred on August 9, 1958. Contractor refused to pay Subcontractor's requisition due on August 10, 1958, because the bulldozer damage to Contractor's house had not been repaired or paid for. Subcontractor continued to work on the project until the 12th of September, 1958, at which time they discontinued working on the project because of Contractor's refusal to pay the said work requisition and notified Contractor by registered letters of their position and willingness to return to the job, but only upon payment. At that time, September 12, 1958, the value of the work completed by Subcontractor on the project for which they had not been paid was $1,484.50. . . .

Contractor filed suit against the Subcontractor in two counts: (1), for the aforesaid bulldozer damage to Contractor's house, alleging negligence of the Subcontractor's bulldozer operator, and (2) for the $450.00 costs above the contract price in having another excavating subcontractor complete the uncompleted work in the contract. Subcontractor filed a counter-claim for recovery of work of the value of $1,484.50 for which they had not received payment and for loss of anticipated profits on uncompleted portion of work in the amount of $1,340.00. By agreement of the parties, the first count of Contractor's claim, *i.e.*, for aforesaid bulldozer damage to Contractor's house, was submitted to jury who found in favor of Contractor in the amount of $3,400.00. Following the finding by the jury, the second count of the Contractor's claim and the counter-claims of the Subcontractor, by agreement of the parties, were submitted to the Court for determination, without jury. All of the facts recited herein above were stipulated to by the parties to the Court. Circuit Court Judge Fletcher found for counter-plaintiff Subcontractor in the amount of $2,824.50 from which Contractor has entered this appeal.

The $3,400 judgment has been paid.

It is immediately apparent that our decision turns upon the respective rights and liabilities of the parties under that portion of their contract whereby the subcontractor agreed to do the excavating and earth-moving work in "a workmanlike manner, and in accordance with the best practices," with time being of the essence of the contract, and the contractor agreed to make progress payments therefor on the 10th day of the months following the performance of the work by the subcontractor. The subcontractor contends, of course, that when the contractor failed to make the payment due on August 10, 1958, he breached his contract and thereby released him (the subcontractor) from any further obligation to perform. The contractor, on the other hand, argues that the failure of the subcontractor to perform his work in a workmanlike manner constituted a material breach of the contract, which justified his refusal to make the August 10 payment; and, as there was no breach on his part, the subcontractor had no right to cease performance on September 12, and his refusal to continue work on the project constituted another breach, which rendered him liable to the contractor for damages. The vital question, more tersely stated, remains: Did the contractor have a right, under the circumstances, to refuse to make the progress payment due on August 10, 1958?

The answer involves interesting and important principles of contract law. Promises and counter-promises made by the respective parties to a contract have certain relations to one another, which determine many of the rights and liabilities of the parties. Broadly speaking, they are (1) independent of each other, or (2) mutually dependent, one upon the other. They are independent of each other if the parties intend that *performance* by each of them is in no way conditioned upon *performance* by the other. 5 Page, *The Law of Contracts*, ¶ 2971. In other words, the parties exchange promises for promises, not the *performance* of promises for the *performance* of promises. 3 Williston, *Contracts* (Rev.Ed.), ¶ 813, n. 6. A failure to perform an independent promise does not excuse non-performance on the part of the adversary party, but each is required to perform his promise, and, if one does not perform, he is liable to the adversary party for such non-performance. (Of course, if litigation ensues questions of set-off or recoupment frequently arise.) Promises are mutually dependent if the parties intend *performance* by one to be conditioned upon *performance* by the other, and, if they be mutually dependent, they may be (a) precedent, *i.e.*, a promise that is to be performed before a corresponding promise on the part of the adversary party is to be performed, (b) subsequent, *i.e.*, a corresponding promise that is not to be performed until the other party to the contract has performed a precedent covenant, or (c) concurrent, *i.e.*, promises that are to be performed at the same time by each of the parties, who are respectively bound to perform each. *Page, op.cit.*, ¶¶ 2941, 2951, 2961. . . .

In the early days, it was settled law, that covenants and mutual promises in a contract were *prima facie* independent and that they were to be so construed in the absence of language in the contract clearly showing that they were intended to be dependent. *Williston, op.cit.*, ¶ 816; *Page, op.cit.*, ¶¶ 2944, 2945. In the case of Kingston v. Preston, 2 Doug. 689, decided in 1774, Lord Mansfield, contrary to three centuries of opposing precedents, changed the rule, and decided that performance of one covenant might be dependent on prior performance of another, although the contract contained no express condition to that effect. *Page op.cit.* ¶ 2946; *Williston op.cit.* ¶ 817. The modern rule, which seems to be of almost universal application, is that there is a presumption that mutual promises in a contract are dependent and are to be so regarded, whenever possible. *Page, op.cit.*, ¶ 2946; *Restatement, Contracts*, ¶ 266. *Cf. Williston, op.cit.*, ¶ 812. . . .

Considering the presumption that promises and counter-promises are dependent and the statement of the case, we have no hesitation in holding that the promise and counter-promise under consideration here were mutually dependent, that is to say, the parties intended performance by one to be conditioned on performance by the other; and the subcontractor's promise was, by the explicit wording of the contract, precedent to the promise of payment, monthly, by the contractor. . . .

We hold that when the subcontractor's employee negligently damaged the contractor's wall, this constituted a breach of the subcontractor's promise to perform his work in a "workmanlike manner, and in accordance with the best practices." And there can be little doubt that the breach was material: the damage to the wall amounted to more than double the payment due on August 10. Speed v. Bailey, 153 Md. 655, 661, 662, 139 A. 534. 3A Corbin, *Contracts*, § 708, says: "The failure of a contractor's (in our case, the subcontractor's) performance to constitute 'substantial' performance may justify the owner (in our case, the contractor) in refusing to make a progress payment. . . . . . . If the refusal to pay an installment is justified on the owner's (contractor's) part, the contractor (subcontractor) is not justified in abandoning work by reason of that refusal. His abandonment of the work will itself be a wrongful repudiation that goes to the essence, even if the defects in performance did not." *See also Restatement, Contracts*, § 274 [citations] *and compare Williston, op.cit.*, §§ 805, 841 and 842. Professor Corbin, in § 954, states further: "The unexcused failure of a contractor to render a promised performance when it is due is always a breach of contract. . . . Such failure may be of such great importance as to constitute what has been called herein a 'total' breach. . . . For a failure of performance constituting such a 'total' breach, an action for remedies that are appropriate thereto is at once maintainable. Yet the injured party is not required to bring such action. He has the option of treating the non-performance as a 'partial' breach only. . . ." In permitting the subcontractor to proceed with work on the project after August 9, the contractor, obviously, treated the breach by the subcontractor as a partial one. As the promises were mutually dependent and the subcontractor had made a material breach in his performance, this justified the contractor in refusing to make the August 10 payment; hence, as the contractor was not in default, the subcontractor again breached the contract when he, on September 12, discontinued work on the project, which rendered him liable (by the express terms of the contract) to the contractor for his increased cost in having the excavating done—a stipulated amount of $450.

. . . [The subcontractor] also contend[s] that the contractor had no right to refuse the August 10 payment, because the subcontractor had furnished the insurance against property damage, as called for in the contract. There is little, or no, merit in this suggestion. The subcontractor and his insurance company denied liability. The furnishing of the insurance by him did not constitute a license to perform his work in a careless, negligent, or unworkmanlike manner; and its acceptance by the contractor did not preclude his assertion of a claim for unworkmanlike performance directly against the subcontractor.

Judgment against the [contractor] reversed; and judgment entered in favor of the [contractor] against the [subcontractor] for $450, the [subcontractor] to pay the costs.

PROBLEMS

10. (a) B, buyer, and S, seller, entered into a contract for the purchase and sale of four planes. The first plane was to be delivered at S's place of business on June 1 and the others on July 10, subject to no delays by the manufacturer. No delay in fact occurred and S had the planes ready on the dates fixed in the contract. No further action was taken by either party until an action was begun by B against S on October 8. What result?

(b) Plaintiff, a court reporter, contracted with defendant to provide a transcript of the civil trial to which it was a party. Defendant paid $8,125 as a down payment, representing half of the estimated total cost. The contract provided that "the total cost of the transcript is based on $3.00 per page and will be due when the last volume is delivered." (A volume is generally the transcript of one day's proceedings.) All but the last two volumes were delivered. Plaintiff sent defendant a final bill and wrote stating that these two volumes would be delivered upon receipt of the balance due." Defendant did not reply. After repeated unanswered demands for payment, Plaintiff sues. What result?

11. Plaintiffs contracted to buy a house from Developer in a tract development that was under construction. They selected, from a map of yet unbuilt houses, a house with a Southeast exposure. In the course of construction, they noticed that the contractor was building the house with a Northwest exposure. Instead of facing the trade winds, those winds were blocked. Plaintiffs protested, but Developer directed the contractor to ignore their protests. (a) Are they entitled to refuse to proceed with the purchase? (b) Assuming they take possession and sue Developer, are they be entitled to damages measured by the cost of reconstruction? (c) Should their damages be decreased by the amount their house increased in value since they took possession?

12. On Sept. 26 defendant made a contract with plaintiff for the erection of 19 houses on property owned by defendant. This contract provided that all buildings should be finished by April 1 of the following year and that the contract price should be paid "by the owner to the contractor in installments as follows: 70 per cent of the above amount to be paid on estimated amount of work done as buildings progress." In timely fashion, plaintiff presented an estimate of work already done and requested payment of 70% according to the contract. Defendant failed to pay without any justification. Plaintiff suspended work immediately and three months later declared the contract at an end. Was plaintiff justified in his conduct?

13. Plaintiff, a contractor, agreed to do certain construction work for defendant for the sum of $800,000. It was stipulated that estimates of the work completed should be furnished on the first of each month and that 85% of the sum found due should be paid on the 20th of the month. In August plaintiff submitted a statement showing $50,000 to be due. Defendant said

that $40,000 was due and submitted his check. Plaintiff abandoned the contract six days later. Defendant made an offer to pay at once any amount which could be shown to be due. Plaintiff refused to submit its calculation for inspection and verification; instead, it brought this action. What result?

14. Plaintiff agreed to sell and defendant agreed to buy certain realty on or before May 1. On May 1, plaintiff was not ready and able to perform. Plaintiff was ready on May 2 and so informed defendant but defendant said that it was "too late." What are the rights of the parties?

15. The parties entered into a real estate contract that set a closing date of December 15. On the following January 8, P sent a letter to V stating that there had been a delay in obtaining mortgage financing and requested that closing be set on or about February 1. V sent a letter to P notifying P that the new closing date would be January 17. V also advised P that the failure to close on that date would result in default. P did not object to the contents of the letter. On January 17 P appeared at the place set for closing, stated that V's unilateral scheduling of the closing date was ridiculous and demanded a new closing date of January 31. V refused. When V did not appear on January 31, P commenced an action for specific performance. What result?

SECTION 4. CONSTRUCTIVE CONDITIONS UNDER THE UCC

(Calamari & Perillo on Contracts § 11.20)

BARTUS v. RICCARDI

City Court, City of Utica, 1967.
55 Misc.2d 3, 284 N.Y.S.2d 222.

HAROLD H. HYMES, JUDGE. The plaintiff is a franchised representative of Acousticon, a manufacturer of hearing aids. On January 15, 1966, the defendant signed a contract to purchase a Model A–660 Acousticon hearing aid from the plaintiff. The defendant specified Model A–660 because he had been tested at a hearing aid clinic and had been informed that the best hearing aid for his condition was this Acousticon model. An ear mold was fitted to the defendant and the plaintiff ordered Model A–660 from Acousticon.

On February 2, 1966, in response to a call from the plaintiff the defendant went to the plaintiff's office for his hearing aid. At that time he was informed that Model A–660 had been modified and improved, and that it was now called Model A–665. This newer model had been delivered by Acousticon for the defendant's use. The defendant denies that he understood this was a different model number. The hearing aid was fitted to the defendant. The defendant complained about the noise, but was assured by the plaintiff that he would get used to it.

The defendant tried out the new hearing aid for the next few days for a total use of 15 hours. He went back to the hearing clinic, where he was informed that the hearing aid was not the model that he had been advised to buy. On February 8, 1966, he returned to the plaintiff's office complaining that the hearing aid gave him a headache, and that it was not the model he had ordered. He returned the hearing aid to the plaintiff, for which he received a receipt. At that time the plaintiff offered to get Model A–660 for the defendant. The defendant neither consented to nor refused the offer. No mention was made by either party about canceling the contract, and the receipt given by the plaintiff contained no notation or indication that the plaintiff considered the contract canceled or rescinded.

The plaintiff immediately informed Acousticon of the defendant's complaint. By letter dated February 14, 1966, Acousticon writing directly to the defendant, informed him that Model A–665 was an improved version of Model A–660, and that they would either replace the model that had been delivered to him or would obtain Model A–660 for him. He was asked to advise the plaintiff immediately of his decision so that they could effect a prompt exchange. After receiving this letter the defendant decided that he did not want any hearing aid from the plaintiff, and he refused to accept the tender of a replacement, whether it be Model A–665 or A–660.

The plaintiff is suing for the balance due on the contract. Although he had made a down payment of $80.00, the defendant made no claim for repayment of his down payment until the case was ready to go to trial. The plaintiff objected to the counterclaim as being untimely. There is nothing in the pleadings to show that such a claim had been previously made by the defendant and, therefore, the court will not consider any counterclaim in this matter.

The question before the court is whether or not the plaintiff, having delivered a model which admittedly is not in exact conformity with the contract, can nevertheless recover in view of his subsequent tender of the model that did meet the terms of the contract.

The defendant contends that since there was an improper delivery of goods, the buyer has the right to reject the same under Sections 2–601 and 2–602(2)(c) of the Uniform Commercial Code. He further contends that even if the defendant had accepted delivery he may, under Section 2–608(1)(b) of the U.C.C., revoke his acceptance of the goods because "his acceptance was reasonably induced ... by the seller's assurances." He also relies on Section 2–711, claiming that he may recover not only the down payment but also consequential damages.

The defendant, however, has neglected to take into account Section 2–508 of the Uniform Commercial Code which has added a new dimension to the concept of strict performance. This section permits a seller to cure a non-conforming delivery under certain circumstances. Sub-paragraph (1) of this section enacts into statutory law what had been New York case law. This permits a seller to cure a non-conforming delivery *before the expiration of the contract time* by notifying the buyer of his intention to so cure and by making a delivery within the contract period. This has long been the accepted rule in New York. (Lowinson v. Newman, 201 App.Div. 266, 194 N.Y.S. 253).

However, the U.C.C. in sub-paragraph (2) of Section 2–508 goes further and extends *beyond the contract time* the right of the seller to cure a defective performance. Under this provision, even where the contract period has expired and the buyer has rejected a non-conforming tender or has revoked an acceptance, the seller may "substitute a conforming tender" if he had "reasonable grounds to believe" that the nonconforming tender would be accepted, and "if he seasonably notifies the buyer" of his intention "to substitute a conforming tender."

This in effect extends the contract period beyond the date set forth in the contract itself unless the buyer requires strict performance by including such a clause in the contract.

> The section (2–508(2) U.C.C.) rejects the time-honored and perhaps time-worn notion that the proper way to assure effective results in commercial transactions is to require strict performance. Under the Code a buyer who insists upon such strict performance must rely on a special term in his agreement or the fact that the seller knows as a commercial matter that strict performance is required.

(48 Cornell Law Quarterly 13; 29 Albany Law Review 260).

This section seeks to avoid injustice to the seller by reason of a surprise rejection by the buyer. (Official Comment, McKinney's Cons.Laws of N.Y., Book 62½, Uniform Commercial Code, Section 2–508).

An additional burden, therefore, is placed upon the buyer by this section. "As a result a buyer may learn that even though he rejected or revoked his acceptance within the terms of Sections 2–601 and 2–711, he still may have to allow the seller additional time to meet the terms of the contract by substituting delivery of conforming goods." (*Bender's U.C.C. Service–Sales and Bulk Transfers*—Vol. 3, Section 14–02(1)(a)(ii)).

Has the plaintiff in this case complied with the conditions of Section 2–508?

The model delivered to the defendant was a newer and improved version of the model than was actually ordered. Of course, the defendant is entitled to receive the model that he ordered even though it may be an older type. But under the circumstances the plaintiff had reasonable grounds to believe that the newer model would be accepted by the defendant.

The plaintiff acted within a reasonable time to notify the defendant of his tender of a conforming model. (Section 1–204 U.C.C.) [Revised UCC § 1–205, ed.]. The defendant had not purchased another hearing aid elsewhere. His position had not been altered by reason of the original non-conforming tender.

The plaintiff made a proper subsequent conforming tender pursuant to Section 2–508(2) of the Uniform Commercial Code.

Judgment is granted to plaintiff.

A.B. PARKER v. BELL FORD, INC.

Supreme Court of Alabama, 1983.
425 So.2d 1101.

EMBRY, JUSTICE. This appeal is from a judgment entered on a directed verdict in behalf of the defendants Bell Ford, Inc. and Ford Motor Company, Inc. We affirm.

Plaintiff A.B. Parker purchased a 1979 Ford F–100 pickup truck from defendant Bell Ford, Inc. of Atmore, Alabama, on 6 August 1979. The purchase price was $6,155.40. The truck was manufactured by defendant Ford Motor Company, Inc., which provided the new truck warranty on the vehicle. Parker made several complaints to Bell Ford of excessive tire wear requiring replacement of the tires on the vehicle after approximately 4,000 miles of use. Bell Ford gave Parker a purchase order to have the vehicle aligned at Combs & Dailey, an alignment shop in Mobile, where repairs were allegedly made on the vehicle. Parker was not informed as to what had been done to the vehicle at the alignment shop. Whatever work was performed, however, did not cure Parker's complaint of excessive tire wear and his second set of tires had to be replaced shortly thereafter.

Parker never returned the vehicle to Bell Ford for repairs and never registered any further complaint with Bell Ford until Parker initiated suit against Bell Ford and the manufacturer, the Ford Motor Company. At an inspection of the vehicle after this suit was filed, it was determined by the service manager of Peach Ford, Inc. of Brewton, Alabama, that the vehicle had a defective wheel housing, causing the tires to wear excessively.

On 1 July 1980 Parker filed his complaint containing four counts: one against Bell Ford for misrepresentation; one against Bell Ford for breach of contract; one against Bell Ford and Ford Motor Company for breach of warranty; and one against Bell Ford and Ford Motor Company for breach of implied warranty of merchantability. The trial court granted Ford Motor Company's motion to dismiss count four involving implied warranty of merchantability whereupon Parker amended his complaint accordingly. Parker originally demanded damages of $20,000; a later amendment increased that demand for damages to $30,000. After trial before a jury, upon motion, the trial court directed a verdict in favor of Bell Ford and Ford Motor Company and entered judgment accordingly.

Parker urges as error the trial court's direction of a verdict denying his claims. Parker contends there was a scintilla of evidence in support of the allegations of his complaint; therefore, the trial court should have allowed the case to go to the jury.

We disagree.

Section 7–2–607(3)(a), Code 1975, [UCC 2–607(3)(a)] describes the buyer's obligation upon learning of a defect in a product he has accepted:

(3) Where a tender has been accepted:

(a) The buyer must within a reasonable time after he discovers or should have discovered any breach notify the seller of breach or be barred from any remedy....

The transaction between Parker and Bell Ford and Ford Motor Company was one that required compliance with § 7–2–607.

This court, on several occasions, has characterized notice, such as required by § 7–2–607, as a condition precedent to recovery. *See* Smith v. Pizitz of Bessemer, Inc., 271 Ala. 101, 122 So.2d 591 (1960). ...

Official notice has been determined to be the degree of notice which at least comports with the notice an ordinary tortfeasor would have of his breach of duty. Page [v. Camper City & Mobile Home Sales, 292 Ala. 562, 297 So.2d 810 (1974)]. The evidence adduced at trial reveals that Parker was not satisfied with the repairs made on behalf of Bell Ford by the alignment shop. Parker admits that at no time did he contact Ford Motor Company about this problem, nor did he return the vehicle to Bell Ford after he took the vehicle from the alignment shop.

> ... Notice of breach serves two distinct purposes. First, express notice opens the way for settlement through negotiation between the parties.... Second, proper notice minimizes the possibility of prejudice to the seller by giving him "ample opportunity to cure the defect, inspect the goods, investigate the claim or do whatever may be necessary to properly defend himself or minimize his damages while the facts are fresh in the minds of the parties."

Standard Alliance Industries, Inc. v. Black Clawson Company, 587 F.2d 813, 826 (6th Cir.1978), quoting in part from Note, *Notice of Breach and the Uniform Commercial Code,* 25 U.Fla.L.Rev. 520, 522 (1973). Bell Ford had no notice that the work performed by Combs & Dailey did not eliminate Parker's tire wear problem. In fact, Bell Ford never heard from Parker again until six months later when it received the summons initiating this lawsuit. This court held in *Pizitz of Bessemer, supra,* that one reason for the notice requirement is to apprise the vendor that a claim will be made against him and give him an opportunity to prepare a defense or notify his supplier. We expand that rationale to also include the requirement of notice in order to enable the seller to make adjustments or replacements, or to suggest opportunities for cure, to the end of minimizing the buyer's loss and reducing the seller's own liability to the buyer. *See* White and Summers, *Uniform Commercial Code,* § 11–9 (1972). ...

The judgment in this case is due to be, and is hereby, affirmed.

EMANUEL LAW OUTLINES, INC. v. MULTI-STATE LEGAL STUDIES, INC.

Southern District of New York, 1995.
899 F.Supp. 1081.

BERNARD NEWMAN, SENIOR JUDGE, by designation: Emanuel Law Outlines, Inc. (hereinafter "ELO"), a publisher of study aids for law students, brings this diversity action against Multi–State Legal Studies, Inc., (hereinafter "Multi–State"), a company that conducts state bar review preparation courses. ELO seeks $60,000 in damages for breach of contract; Multi–State counterclaims for $20,000 in damages, alleging breach of contract by ELO. This matter arises under the court's diversity jurisdiction in conformity with 28 U.S.C. § 1332(a), and the case was tried to the court in a one day bench trial. Pursuant to F.R.C.P. Rule 52(a), the following constitutes the court's findings of fact and conclusions of law.

The Record

ELO offered the following two witnesses: Lazar Emanuel (hereinafter Lazar), General Counsel and Vice President of ELO and Steven Emanuel (hereinafter Steven), President of ELO. Multi–State offered one witness, Robert Feinberg, Multi–State's President. The parties submitted 16 documentary exhibits.

Contentions of the Parties

ELO contends that Multi–State's failure to pay the base fees for the second and third years of a three year installment contract breaches the agreement. According to the relevant terms of the contract, ELO was to provide Multi–State with a criminal procedure outline supplement (hereinafter "supplement") no later than May 1, 1993. Although the supplement was not delivered until June 3, 1993, ELO maintains that it performed its obligation under the contract. ELO argues that: (1) Multi–State orally agreed to change the May 1, 1993 contractual deadline to early June 1993; (2) any alleged breach was cured under the terms of the contract; (3) any alleged breach by ELO caused by failing to meet the May 1, 1993 deadline was not material; (4) the nonconforming delivery did not substantially impair the value of the entire contract; and (5) Multi–State reinstated the contract by accepting the supplement without seasonably notifying ELO of the breach.

Multi–State maintains that the failure of ELO to provide the supplements by May 1, 1993 constituted a breach of the agreement and excused Multi–State's obligations under the contract. Specifically, Multi–State disputes the existence of any modification or waiver of the May 1, 1993 deadline. It is further asserted by Multi–State that it sent ELO two letters, dated April 27, 1993 and May 7, 1993 respectively, informing ELO that the failure to meet the May 1st deadline would be considered a material breach of the contract. When ELO did not provide the supplement by May 1, 1993, Multi–State claims that ELO breached the agreement and excused any further performance by Multi–State. Multi–State also insists that the failure to timely provide the supplement by the agreed-upon date caused damage to Multi–State's business in the amount of $20,000.

Findings of Fact

Since 1978, ELO (a New York corporation) has been a leading publisher and distributor of study aids for law students. Steven is the main editor and writer of the Emanuel Law Outline series. The corporation is a continuation of the business started by Steven during his first year at Harvard Law School. The company enjoys an outstanding reputation among law students across the country. In addition to writing and editing, Steven negotiates transactions for the corporation. Lazar, Steven's father, is ELO's general counsel and administrative officer. An experienced attorney and businessman, Lazar runs the office, finalizes contracts, oversees all printing and production of materials, and supervises the collections of accounts.

Multi–State Legal Studies, Inc. (a California corporation) conducts bar review courses for law school graduates. The company, which employs approximately 15 people, offers courses in 42 states and is run by its president and founder Robert Feinberg, who is admitted to the bar of several states, including New York and California. As president of the company, Feinberg develops course materials, directs promotion and marketing of the company, and is one of Multi–State's principle lecturers around the country.

In August 1992, Feinberg contacted ELO to propose an agreement whereby ELO would provide materials which could be distributed to students enrolled in Multi–State's course. As a result, the parties entered into a three-year contract beginning September 1, 1992 and ending August 31, 1995. Under the contract, ELO was required to supply at least 950 copies of each of two volumes of capsule summaries in nine subjects tested on the California bar exam in each of the three years. Multi–State agreed to pay ELO a fee of $30,000 per year and in addition pay printing and delivery costs.... For all subjects except Constitutional Law and Criminal Procedure, ELO was required to take verbatim text of the Capsule Summaries it had published in the Emanuel Law Outline for the particular subject and cosmetically change them as required by Multi–State. For Constitutional Law, ELO was to prepare, edit, and revise a text outline from the review portion of the Constitutional Law Audio Tapes sold commercially by ELO. The Criminal Procedure Supplement was to be created from scratch by ELO, but be similar in format and detail to the other outlines provided to Multi–State.

Under the first year of the contract, ELO agreed to produce two volumes containing materials for eight of the subjects as well as a Criminal Procedure Supplement. The two volumes were to be delivered to ELO's warehouse no later than October 10, 1992, whereas the supplement, because it required more time for preparation, was to be delivered to the warehouse no later than May 1, 1993. There is no dispute that respecting the two volumes, ELO adequately performed under the contract.

In February 1993, Steven underwent quadruple bypass surgery. As a result of a six week convalescent period, he fell behind in his work on the supplement. Multi–State was informed of the upcoming surgery sometime in January 1993. ELO contends that in accordance with an early April telephone conversation between Steven and Feinberg, Multi–State orally agreed to move back the deadline for the production of the supplement. Specifically, Steven testified that he told Feinberg he had fallen behind in his work due to the operation and while he could still meet the May 1, 1993 deadline, he hoped that the deadline could be "relaxed." Steven also stated that Feinberg told him a delay would be acceptable if the supplement was ready by "early June," and that it "doesn't sound like a big deal." The evidence presented by Multi–State directly conflicts with ELO's claim. Feinberg, in his testimony, flatly denies that he ever agreed to any change in the May 1, 1993 deadline. He emphatically stated that "(i)n 17 years of business, I can never remember one oral waiver that I would have agreed to."

Resolving this factual dispute, the court finds that there was insufficient evidence to establish any change in the May 1st deadline. First, ELO failed to produce written confirmation of any waiver. Considering the experience of both Steven and Lazar, it is likely that if such a change in terms of the contract were made, a confirmatory letter would have been sent by ELO to Multi–State. Moreover, it was demonstrated that ELO relied on the letter of the contract as evidenced by its written demand for payment very soon after the December deadline for the second installment. Accordingly, ELO did not treat changes in the terms of the agreement casually. In sum, no writing from Multi–State was ever produced to corroborate ELO's claim that there was any change in the May 1, 1993 deadline. Therefore, considering the experience of Steven and Lazar, the lack of any writing either sent to Multi–State or even kept in ELO's files, the practice of ELO to closely adhere to the contract terms, and the failure to produce any writing from Multi–State, the court finds the weight of the evidence in favor of Multi–State and concludes that there was no oral modification regarding the May 1, 1993 deadline.

However, another factual dispute arises regarding Multi–State's claim that two letters were sent to ELO regarding the May 1 deadline. The first letter, dated April 27, 1993, purportedly notified ELO that failure to meet the May 1 deadline would be considered a material breach of the agreement. The second letter, dated May 7, 1993, purportedly canceled Multi–State's obligations under the contract based on ELO's failure to meet the May 1 deadline. ELO, on the other hand, insists that it did not receive either letter.

The court concludes that ELO did not receive either letter. As a member of the bar of several states including New York, a lecturer on the law, an experienced businessman, and negotiator of the contract, Feinberg must have been aware that the contract specifically called for *receipt* of notice by the breaching party.[2] Additionally, Feinberg admitted knowledge that ELO would hold him to the specifics of the contract. ELO was, in

---

2. The contract states: "9.(a) Initial Term: Neither party may terminate this Agreement during the Initial Term, except on account of a material breach by the other, which breach shall have gone uncured for 30 days after the breaching party has *received* written notice of breach...." (emphasis added).

Feinberg's words, "sticklers" regarding the agreement. Further, Feinberg testified that these letters, supposedly notifying ELO of a material breach, were sent by ordinary mail, rather than a method which provides proof of receipt. This is significant because receipt of written notice of a claimed breach by the breaching party was a critical factor under the contract. Finally, if these letters were received, common sense dictates that there would be some response from ELO regarding the letters. Not only was Multi–State unable to produce evidence of any written response from ELO, but Feinberg never clearly demonstrated that there was any oral response. Based on the evidence presented, even if the court were to assume the letters were sent, the evidence is insufficient to find that either letter was received by ELO.

When the May 1 deadline passed, Multi–State contacted ELO by phone stating that the materials were needed, to which ELO replied that the supplement was being rushed and that it would be forthcoming. Regarding the materials, a third factual dispute arises. The parties agree that the ELO materials were to be utilized by Multi–State bar review course to help marketability, improve the quality of the materials, and give the Multi–State students additional materials for study purposes. Feinberg further argues that he needed the supplement to help prepare his criminal procedure "early-bird"[3] lecture. ELO responds that the materials were not meant to be used either for lecture preparation or as reference points in any of the lectures.

The court credits the position of ELO and determines that the primary purpose of the outlines was to act as a supplement to Multi–State's materials and not as a research or reference tool for lecturers. Multi–State had its own outlines, and for seventeen years has been conducting reviews specifically for the multi-state portion of the bar examination of which Criminal Procedure is a part. It is difficult to imagine that a lecturer of Feinberg's experience would need to rely on an outline prepared by another company. Indeed, the fact that the lecture was scheduled only 17 days after the contractual due date for the materials to arrive at ELO's warehouse, renders it unlikely that any lecturer would have been able to substantially rely on those materials for preparation. . . .

The supplement did arrive at ELO's warehouse on June 3, 1993. After having the materials shipped by UPS, Multi–State received the materials on June 10, 1993 and distributed them to the students. Multi–State maintains that the late delivery caused substantial damage to its reputation. Stressing that the "key in our business is word of mouth," Multi–State argues that student satisfaction with the course is critical. Although Feinberg testified that there were numerous complaints about the late shipment, no documentary evidence was produced regarding any negative feedback received by Multi–State.[4]

---

3. The "Early Bird Lecture Series" is a short review of each of the multi-state subjects held in mid-May. The regular course schedule began in early June.

4. After the 1993 Bar examination, Multi–State decided not to continue its full service California course. Feinberg stated the reason for this decision was "because we entered into a

On August 19, 1993 under the terms of the contract, ELO wrote Multi–State requesting instructions for printing and delivery of the materials for the second year of the contract. On August 23, 1993 Multi–State sent a fax to ELO stating that ELO's failure to deliver the supplement by the May 1 deadline constituted a material breach of the contract and consequently Multi–State was excused from all future obligations under the contract. This fax constituted the last correspondence between the parties.

Discussion

By the terms of the contract, this case is governed by New York law. Since this action involves a contract for the sale of goods, New York's version of the Uniform Commercial Code is the applicable legal authority. Because the court concludes that there is insufficient evidence of any modification of the May 1, 1993 deadline for the supplement, the failure to print the supplement by that date constitutes a breach of contract. While the failure to meet the deadline constituted a breach, the court credits ELO's contentions that the breach was subsequently cured as provided by the agreement and in any case, the delay was not a material breach. Accordingly, Multi–State was still bound by the contract.

A.

Multi–State did not give ELO adequate notice of the breach as required by the agreement. The contract unequivocally requires that the agreement may not be terminated unless the breaching party *receives* written notice of the breach and such breach is not cured [within] 30 days after the receipt of such notice. New York law states, "[A] person *receives* a notice or notification when (a) it comes to his attention; or (b) it is duly delivered to (his) place of business ..." N.Y.U.C.C. § 1–201(26) (emphasis in the original). In this case, there was inadequate evidence to prove that ELO received either the April 27th or May 7th letter. Accordingly, ELO did not have notice of the breach.

Multi–State's claim that N.Y.U.C.C. § 2–607 does not require notice of a contract breach be received, is inapplicable to this case. While Multi–State accurately states the provision of § 2–607, it ignores the fact that in this case there was a specific provision requiring receipt of written notice of a breach. It is recognized within the Code itself that parties may vary the terms of the statute and determine the standards by which performance of obligation is to be measured under the code, as long as the variations do not disclaim the obligations of good faith, diligence, reasonableness, care and the standards are not manifestly unreasonable. N.Y.U.C.C. § 1–102. It cannot be said that the written receipt of notice requirement is unreasonable. . . .

license agreement with Barpassers, another California course, and ... under the terms of the license agreement, basically we were assigning our rights to certain materials to them and they were assigning their rights to Multi–State question to us. So we made a business decision."

Since no notice of a breach was received by ELO prior to its performance on June 3, this Court finds that ELO cured any breach within the guidelines of the agreement. Hence, Multi–State presents no valid basis to justify non-performance of the contract.

B.

Even if the Court were to agree that there was an uncured breach of contract by ELO, Multi–State's right to be relieved of its obligations requires a demonstration of substantial impairment of the whole contract. Inasmuch as this contract requires the delivery of goods in separate lots to be separately accepted, it is an installment contract as defined by N.Y.U.C.C. § 2–612(1). Under § 2–612(3), Multi–State's right to cancel the entire agreement required a showing of substantial impairment of the whole contract. Whether a breach constitutes "substantial impairment" is a question of fact. *Stinnes Interoil v. Apex Oil Co.*, 604 F.Supp. 978, 981 (1985). . . . Here, there is no evidence to support Multi–States argument that failure to have the supplements ready by May 1, 1993 substantially impaired the entire contract.

Multi–State's only contention with regard to damages is that the company received oral complaints from students enrolled in the course. This claim is tenuous at best, considering that Multi–State offered no proof of any written complaints, nor did it provide any written records of the complaints, and it failed to show that it had to refund any tuition money to students. Moreover, Multi–State's students did in fact receive eight of the nine promised outline [*sic*] on time and subsequently received the supplement more than a month prior to the bar exam. Finally, Multi–State's own actions demonstrate the minor nature of any breach. When ELO shipped the goods in June, Multi–State made no effort to expedite delivery. Because it was responsible for the cost of shipping, it could have utilized any delivery method it desired, including overnight mail. Instead, Multi–State opted for UPS delivery, which is far from the fastest method. Inasmuch as Multi–State's actions do not indicate significant urgency, it would be very difficult for the court to so find.

Nor can it be said that the June delivery of the supplements had any effect on future enrollment in Multi–State's course. After the 1993 course, Multi–State no longer offered the full service California bar review course. It is undisputed that Multi–State's decision was unrelated to the instant action. Since Multi–State no longer offered the full service course, ELO's breach could not have had any damaging effect whatsoever for subsequent years.

The very purpose of the substantial impairment requirement of N.Y.U.C.C. § 2–612(3) is to preclude a party from canceling the contract for trivial defects. Multi–State has failed to demonstrate any substantial or lingering harm incurred from ELO's failure to have the supplement ready by May 1, 1993. Accordingly, Multi–State had no legal justification for not performing on the contract.

Conclusion

With regard to ELO's claim, the court determines that while ELO's delay in delivering the supplement breached the agreement it was cured under the terms of the contract. Moreover, the delay in delivery did not substantially impair the value of the instant contract with Multi–State. Accordingly, Multi–State was not entitled to cancel its performance thereof. Therefore, ELO shall recover the sum of $60,000 plus prejudgment interest at the New York statutory rate accruing from August 23, 1993, which represents the date when Multi–State repudiated the contract. Further, Multi–State's counterclaim is hereby dismissed. Each party shall bear its own expenses.

The Clerk of the Court is directed to enter judgment accordingly.

It is so ordered.

PROBLEMS

16.   Pursuant to a contract, the seller tendered delivery of 10,000 widgets. The buyer, motivated by a desire to reject them so as to take advantage of a reduction of the market price, after careful inspection, found a number of defective widgets and rejected the entire shipment. In a suit by the seller against the buyer, what argument can the seller make?

17.   B contracted to buy from S a system of equipment designed to process and refine fructose. The system was to produce, as an end product, 55% fructose, which is used as a sweetener in many foods. S warranted that the system could produce a certain minimum quantity of 55% fructose per day. Nine months later the system was put into operation. Although the system did produce 55% fructose it was never able to meet the production guarantee. For the following 10 months S unsuccessfully attempted to bring the system into compliance with its production guarantee, after which it left B with a list of suggestions for further remedial efforts. Six months later, after B's further unsuccessful attempts to remedy the system, B notified S that it was revoking its acceptance and demanded a refund of the purchase price.

(a) Was B justified in revoking its acceptance? Was the notice of revocation timely? Did B have to offer to return the equipment?

(b) B continued to use the equipment during the pendency of the trial. What is the effect of B's post-revocation use of the system?

18.   S agreed to sell B a chemical known as "Prussian blue" in stated installments. Payment was to be made on each delivery. B refused to accept the first shipment, claiming it did not meet contract specifications, and also cancelled the contract. S sues for breach of contract. What is the issue to be resolved?

SECTION 5. CONTRACTUAL RECOVERY BY A PARTY IN DEFAULT: DIVISIBILITY, INDE-PENDENT PROMISES, AND SEPARATE CONTRACTS*

(Calamari & Perillo on Contracts §§ 11.23—11.26)

SCAVENGER, INC. v. GT INTERACTIVE SOFTWARE, INC.

New York Supreme Court, Appellate Division, 2000.
273 A.D.2d 60, 708 N.Y.S.2d 405.

[Scavenger, a computer game developer, brought an action against a computer game distributor. The Supreme Court, New York County, Barry Cozier, J., granted developer's motion for partial summary judgment on its cause of action for payments and entered judgment for $2,411,114 against distributor. Distributor appealed.]

MEMORANDUM DECISION. . . . Defendant's contract with plaintiff, containing separate production and payment schedules for each of the four CD–ROM games plaintiff was to deliver to defendant, was a divisible contract (*see*, Christian v. Christian, 42 N.Y.2d 63, 73, 396 N.Y.S.2d 817, 365 N.E.2d 849). Accordingly, plaintiff's right to recover payments guaranteed under the contract for the two CD–ROM games delivered to defendant was not impaired by plaintiff's failure to deliver the two remaining games. . . .

PROBLEMS

19. Plaintiff employee entered into a bilateral contract of employment to commence on April 1 for a one-year term, to be paid "$150 per year, payable monthly, if he wishes." At breakfast on July 8, plaintiff, who had not previously requested his pay, demanded that he be paid what was due him by noon of that day. Defendant, not having ready cash because the job site was distant from defendant's business headquarters, refused the demand and plaintiff quit at noon. What, if anything, may plaintiff recover?

20. Defendant, the owner of a motel, contracted for seven signs to be painted and installed by the plaintiff along the roadside. The signs were designed to lead motorists to the motel. Each sign had an apportioned price. Signs number 1, 2, 3, 6, and 7 were duly installed. Sign number 4 was never installed and sign number 5 was installed at a location other than that provided in the contract. Defendant refused to pay anything. The trial judge, sitting without a jury, found the contract to be severable. Defendant appeals. What result?

---

* Restitutionary recovery in favor of the breaching party is treated in Chapter 10, Section 2(b). Ed.

21. Plaintiff controlled and was the editor of, a small, but successful, specialized publishing corporation. On the same date, he entered into two written agreements with the defendant, a major publisher. Under the first, all the assets of his corporation were sold to the defendant. Under the second, he was to be employed by defendant for a five-year period. The plaintiff was wrongfully discharged under the second contract and has been awarded damages. In the same proceeding, he also seeks to cancel the first contract. What result?

Short Essay Examination Question

Plaintiff, the developer of a tract of land, entered into a contract with the defendant whereby the latter would do specified grading and excavation work for $146,000, and, in addition, paving, storm drain and curb installation at specified unit prices, totaling $30,000. When the grading and excavation work was about 98% completed, the parties had a disagreement about whether certain requested excavation work constituted an "extra" or was within the scope of the contract. As a result, defendant ceased performance. Defendant had received $100,000 in progress payments. The paving and installation work had not yet commenced. Plaintiff retained another contractor to perform the balance of the contract at a greater cost. Plaintiff sues. Defendant counterclaims. The court concludes that defendant breached the contract by ceasing to work and refusing to do the requested work which the court determines was within the scope of the contract. Raise and resolve the legal issues presented by these facts.

SECTION 6.   WRONGFUL PREVENTION, HINDRANCE AND NONCOOPERATION

(Calamari & Perillo on Contracts §§ 11.27, 11.28, 11.38 and 11.39)

CANTRELL–WAIND & ASSOCIATES, INC. v. GUILLAUME MOTORSPORTS, INC.

Court of Appeals of Arkansas, 1998.
62 Ark.App. 66, 968 S.W.2d 72.

BIRD, JUDGE. Cantrell–Waind & Associates, Inc., [Broker] has appealed from a summary judgment entered for appellee Guillaume Motorsports, Inc., [Owner] in its action to recover a real estate brokerage commission. Because we agree with Broker that the circuit judge erred in his interpretation of the applicable law and because genuine issues of material fact remain to be tried, we reverse and remand.

On August 1, 1994, Owner, represented by its president and sole stock-holder Todd Williams, agreed to lease real property in Bentonville to Kenneth Bower and Kay Bower. The lease gave the Bowers an option to purchase and provided for the payment of a commission to Broker, the real estate broker in this transaction, as follows:

In the event of the exercise of this option within the first twenty-four (24) month period, ten per cent (10%) of the monthly rental payments shall apply to the purchase price. Thereafter, this credit shall reduce two per cent (2%) per year until the expiration of the original lease term hereof, to the effect that the credit will be eight per cent (8%) during the third year, six per cent (6%) during the fourth year, and four per cent (4%) during the fifth year. The sales price shall be $295,000.00. GUILLAUME MOTORSPORTS, INC., agrees (to) pay CANTREL–WAIND & ASSOCIATES, INC. [*sic*], a real estate commission of $15,200.00 upon closing of sale of the property under this Option to Purchase, provided the closing occurs within two (2) years from the date of execution of the Lease with Option to Purchase.

The Bowers' attorney, Charles Edward Young, III, notified Williams in writing on April 23, 1996, that the Bowers chose to exercise the option to purchase, and that they anticipated closing at the earliest possible date. Young also sent a copy of this letter to Samuel Reeves, Owner's attorney. Soon after this, Williams approached Mr. Bower and offered to credit him with one-half of the Broker's $15,200 commission if he would agree to delay closing until after August 1, 1996. Mr. Bower declined this offer.

Ruth Ann Whitehead, a loan officer at the Bank of Bentonville, notified Mr. Bower on July 19, 1996, that the loan had been approved and that she awaited notification of a closing date. In his deposition, Young said that he attempted to set a July closing date on behalf of the Bowers but had been told by Ms. Whitehead, Reeves, and a representative of the title company that Williams had told them he would be out of the country in late July and unavailable for closing until after August 1.

Young also said that he had asked Reeves if Williams would utilize a power of attorney for closing before August 1 but Williams refused. Williams did not leave the country and was in Bentonville July 22 through 25. Closing occurred on August 14, 1996, and the commission was not paid.

Broker filed a complaint against Guillaume Motorsports, Inc., on August 12, 1996, for breach of contract. Owner moved for summary judgment on the ground that it was under no obligation to close the transaction before August 1. In support of its motion, Owner filed the affidavits of Ms. Whitehead and Mr. Carroll, who stated that, to their knowledge, a closing date was not scheduled before August 14, 1996.

. . . Williams also filed his affidavit stating that a closing date was not established before August 14, 1996, and that the Bowers had not demanded an earlier closing date. Further, he admitted: "While I did in fact approach Kenneth Bower with a proposal to reduce the purchase price if he would agree to establish a closing date after August 1, 1996, my offer was not accepted and no such agreement was made." He said although it would not have bothered him to put the closing off until after August 1, he did not think it was a "conscious decision" not to be available until after August 1.

In a hearing on the motion for summary judgment, counsel for Owner argued that neither the corporation nor Williams was under any obligation to close prior to August 1. He contended there was no bad faith to be inferred by the deliberate avoidance of a real estate commission that is keyed to a "drop-dead" date. He said the real estate broker agreed to the terms of the contract and was bound by it. Counsel pointed out the two separate terms used in the contract when referring to the option to purchase and the closing. The contract stated that to get the maximum discount in the purchase price the Bowers had to exercise the option before August 1, 1996. However, the clause referring to the commission stated that the transaction had to close by August 1. Counsel stated, "I believe my client had every right to do anything within his power, short of breaching his contract with this buyer, to see that this closing didn't occur earlier than that date so he would not owe the commission."

In response to Owner's motion for summary judgment, Broker argued that Owner (by Williams) had a duty to act in good faith and that, in taking steps to prevent the transaction from closing before August 1, 1996, Owner had not acted in good faith. Broker contended that all contingencies and requirements for the loan had been satisfied by July 19, 1996, and that Mr. and Ms. Bower had attempted to establish a closing date before August 1, but had been deliberately prevented from doing so by Williams's misrepresentations that he would be out of the country and unavailable to close until after August 1. . . .

In his order granting summary judgment, the judge stated that Owner had no obligation to Broker to arrange for a closing date that would have entitled Broker to a commission and said that the real estate commission was "clearly avoidable" by Owner. . . .

The term of the contract providing that a commission would be due Broker only if closing occurred before August 1, 1996, is a condition precedent. . . .

Comment b to section 225 of the *Restatement (Second) of Contracts* (1981) provides that the non-occurrence of a condition of a duty is said to be "excused" when the condition need no longer occur in order for performance of the duty to become due: "It may be excused by prevention or hindrance of its occurrence through a breach of the duty of good faith and fair dealing." The *Restatement (Second) of Contracts* § 205 (1981) states: "Every contract imposes upon each party a duty of good faith and fair dealing in its performance and its enforcement." This legal principle also applies to contracts providing for the payment of commissions to real estate agents. McKay and Co. v. Garland, 17 Ark.App. 1, 701 S.W.2d 392 (1986). Accordingly, we hold that the circuit court erred in failing to recognize that a duty of good faith and fair dealing was included in this contract and, therefore, Owner was obligated to not deliberately avoid closing the transaction before August 1, 1996.

Our above holding requires a determination of whether there is a genuine issue of material fact as to whether Owner's actions prevented or hindered the occurrence of the condition precedent. The burden of sustaining a motion for summary judgment is on the moving party. . . .

In its brief, Broker asserts that it was entitled to summary judgment. We note, however, that Broker did not move for summary judgment. . . . [E]ven if the trial court had applied the correct principle of law, and if Broker had properly moved for summary judgment, we could not agree that summary judgment was warranted. In his deposition, . . . Williams testified that he was ready, willing, and able to close and would have closed the transaction before August 1 if he had been contacted. He also stated that, although he was in Bentonville on July 22 through 25, he was not aware until the afternoon of the 25th that the Bowers wanted to close the transaction as soon as possible. In our opinion, genuine issues of material fact remained for trial. Accordingly, we reverse the circuit judge's entry of summary judgment for Owner and remand this case for trial.

Reversed and remanded. ROBBINS, C.J., and ROAF, J., agree.

LOCKE v. WARNER BROS. INC.

Court of Appeal, Second District, 1997.
57 Cal.App.4th 354, 66 Cal.Rptr.2d 921.

KLEIN, PRESIDING JUSTICE. Plaintiffs and appellants Sondra Locke (Locke) and Caritas Films, a California corporation (Caritas) (sometimes collectively referred to as Locke) appeal a judgment following a grant of summary judgment in favor of defendant and respondent Warner Bros. (Warner).

The essential issue presented is whether triable issues of material fact are present which would preclude summary judgment.

We conclude triable issues are present with respect to whether Warner breached its development deal with Locke by categorically refusing to work with her. . . . The judgment therefore is reversed as to the second and fourth causes of action and otherwise is affirmed.

FACTUAL AND PROCEDURAL BACKGROUND

1. *Locke's dispute with Eastwood.*

In 1975, Locke came to Warner to appear with Clint Eastwood in *The Outlaw Josey Wales.* During the filming of the movie, Locke and Eastwood began a personal and romantic relationship. For the next dozen years, they lived in Eastwood's Los Angeles and Northern California homes. Locke also appeared in a number of Eastwood's films. In 1986, Locke made her directorial debut in *Ratboy.*

In 1988, the relationship deteriorated, and in 1989 Eastwood terminated it. Locke then brought suit against Eastwood, alleging numerous causes of action. That action was resolved by a November 21, 1990 settlement agreement and mutual general release. Under said agreement, Eastwood agreed to pay Locke additional compensation in the sum of

$450,000 "on account of past employment and Locke's contentions" and to convey certain real property to her.

2. *Locke's development deal with Warner.*

According to Locke, Eastwood secured a development deal for Locke with Warner in exchange for Locke's dropping her case against him. Contemporaneously with the Locke/Eastwood settlement agreement, Locke entered into a written agreement with Warner, dated November 27, 1990. It is the Locke/Warner agreement which is the subject of the instant controversy.

The Locke/Warner agreement had two basic components. The first element states Locke would receive $250,000 per year for three years for a "non-exclusive first look deal." It required Locke to submit to Warner any picture she was interested in developing before submitting it to any other studio. Warner then had 30 days either to approve or reject a submission. The second element of the contract was a $750,000 "pay or play" directing deal. The provision is called "pay or play" because it gives the studio a choice: it can either "play" the director by using the director's services, or pay the director his or her fee.

Unbeknownst to Locke at the time, Eastwood had agreed to reimburse Warner for the cost of her contract if she did not succeed in getting projects produced and developed. Early in the second year of the three-year contract, Warner charged $975,000 to an Eastwood film, "Unforgiven."

Warner paid Locke the guaranteed compensation of $1.5 million under the agreement. In accordance with the agreement, Warner also provided Locke with an office on the studio lot and an administrative assistant. However, Warner did not develop any of Locke's proposed projects or hire her to direct any films. Locke contends the development deal was a sham, that Warner never intended to make any films with her, and that Warner's sole motivation in entering into the agreement was to assist Eastwood in settling his litigation with Locke.

3. *Locke's action against Warner.*

On March 10, 1994, Locke filed suit against Warner, alleging four causes of action. ... [The first and third causes of action charged gender discrimination and the fourth alleged fraud. Ed.]

The second cause of action alleged that Warner breached the contract by refusing to consider Locke's proposed projects and thereby deprived her of the benefit of the bargain of the Warner/Locke agreement. ...

4. *Warner's motion for summary judgment and opposition thereto.*

On January 6, 1995, Warner filed a motion for summary judgment. Warner contended it did not breach its contract with Locke because it did consider all the projects she presented, and the studio's decision not to put any of those projects into active development or "hand" Locke a script which it already owned was not a breach of any express or implied contractual duty. Warner asserted the odds are slim a producer can get a project into development and even slimmer a director will be hired to direct a film. During the term of Locke's deal, Warner had similar deals with numerous other producers and directors, who fared no better than Locke. . . .

In opposing summary judgment, Locke contended Warner breached the agreement in that it had no intention of accepting any project regardless of its merits. . . .

Locke's opposition papers cited the deposition testimony of Joseph Terry, who recounted a conversation he had with Bob Brassel, a Warner executive, regarding Locke's projects. Terry had stated to Brassel: " 'Well, Bob, this woman has a deal on the lot. She's a director that you want to work with. You have a deal with her. . . . I've got five here that she's interested in.' And then I would get nothing. . . . I was told (by Brassel), 'Joe, we're not going to work with her,' and then, 'That's Clint's deal.' And that's something I just completely did not understand."

Similarly, the declaration of Mary Wellnitz stated: She worked with Locke to set up projects at Warner, without success. Shortly after she began her association with Locke, Wellnitz submitted a script to Lance Young, who at the time was a senior vice president of production at Warner. After discussing the script, Young told Wellnitz, "Mary, I want you to know that I think Sondra is a wonderful woman and very talented, but, if you think I can go down the hall and tell Bob Daly that I have a movie I want to make with her he would tell me to forget it. They are not going to make a movie with her here."

5. *Trial court's ruling.*

On February 17, 1995, the trial court granted summary judgment in favor of Warner. Thereafter, the trial court signed an extensive order granting summary judgment. The order stated:

> Under the contract, Warner had no obligation either to put into development any of the projects submitted to the studio for its consideration, or to "hand off" to Locke any scripts for her to direct that it previously had acquired from someone else. The implied covenant of good faith and fair dealing cannot be imposed to create a contract different from the one the parties negotiated for themselves. Warner had the option to pass on each project Locke submitted. Warner was not required to have a good faith or "fair" basis for declining to exercise its right to develop her material. Such a requirement would be improper and unworkable. A judge or jury cannot and should not substitute its judgment for a film studio's when the studio is making the creative decision of whether to develop or produce a proposed motion picture. Such highly subjective artistic and business decisions are not proper subjects for judicial review. Moreover, Warner had legitimate commercial and artistic reasons for declining to develop the projects Locke submitted.

. . .

Locke filed a timely notice of appeal from the judgment.

CONTENTIONS

Locke contends: the trial court erred by granting Warner's motion for summary judgment based on its conclusion there were no disputed issues of material fact; the trial court erred in weighing the evidence, resolving doubts against Locke, the non-moving party, and adopting only those inferences favorable to Warner where the evidence supported contrary inferences; and the trial court committed reversible error first by failing to make any findings or evidentiary rulings and then by adopting Warner's defective ruling.

DISCUSSION

1. *Standard of appellate review.* [Omitted. Ed.]

2. *A triable issue exists as to whether Warner breached its contract with Locke by failing to evaluate Locke's proposals on their merits.*

As indicated, the second cause of action alleged Warner breached the contract by "refusing to consider the projects prepared by (Locke) and depriving (Locke) of the benefit of the bargain of the Warner–Locke agreement." In granting summary judgment on this claim, the trial court ruled "(a) judge or jury cannot and should not substitute its own judgment for a film studio's when the studio is making the creative decision of whether to develop or produce a proposed motion picture. Such highly-subjective artistic and business decisions are not proper subjects for judicial review."

The trial court's ruling missed the mark by failing to distinguish between Warner's right to make a subjective creative decision, which is not reviewable for reasonableness, and the requirement the dissatisfaction be bona fide or genuine.

a. *General principles.*

" '(W)here a contract confers on one party a discretionary power affecting the rights of the other, a duty is imposed to exercise that discretion in good faith and in accordance with fair dealing.' " (Perdue v. Crocker National Bank (1985) 38 Cal.3d 913, 923, 216 Cal.Rptr. 345, 702 P.2d 503.) It is settled that in " 'every contract there is an implied covenant that neither party shall do anything which will have the effect of destroying or injuring the right of the other party to receive the fruits of the contract. . . .' " (Kendall [v. Ernest Pestana, Inc. (1985) 40 Cal.3d 488, 500, 220 Cal.Rptr. 818, 709 P.2d 837.)

Therefore, when it is a condition of an obligor's duty that he or she be subjectively satisfied with respect to the obligee's performance, the subjective standard of *honest satisfaction* is applicable. (1 Witkin, *Summary of Cal. Law* (9th ed. 1987) *Contracts,* § 729, p. 659; *Rest.2d, Contracts,* § 228, cmts. a, b.) "Where the contract involves matters of fancy, taste or judgment, the promisor is the sole judge of his satisfaction. If he asserts *in good faith* that he is not satisfied, there can be no inquiry into the reasonableness of his attitude. (Citations.) Traditional examples are employment contracts ... and agreements to paint a portrait, write a literary or scientific article, or produce a play or vaudeville act." (1 Witkin, *Summary of Cal. Law, supra,* § 730, p. 660.) In such cases, "the promisor's determination that he is not satisfied, *when made in good faith*, has been held to be a defense to an action on the contract." (*Mattei v. Hopper* (1958) 51 Cal.2d 119, 123, 330 P.2d 625, italics added.)

Therefore, the trial court erred in deferring entirely to what it characterized as Warner's "creative decision" in the handling of the development deal. If Warner acted in bad faith by categorically rejecting Locke's work and refusing to work with her, irrespective of the merits of her proposals, such conduct is not beyond the reach of the law.

    b. *Locke presented evidence from which a trier of fact reasonably could infer Warner breached the agreement by refusing to consider her proposals in good faith.*

Merely because Warner paid Locke the guaranteed compensation under the agreement does not establish Warner fulfilled its contractual obligation. As pointed out by Locke, the value in the subject development deal was not merely the guaranteed payments under the agreement, but also the opportunity to direct and produce films and earn additional sums, and most importantly, the opportunity to promote and enhance a career.

Unquestionably, Warner was entitled to reject Locke's work based on its subjective judgment, and its creative decision in that regard is not subject to being second-guessed by a court. However, bearing in mind the requirement that subjective dissatisfaction must be an honestly held dissatisfaction, the evidence raises a triable issue as to whether Warner breached its agreement with Locke by not considering her proposals on their merits.

[T]he deposition testimony of Joseph Terry ... [and] ... the declaration of Mary Wellnitz ... [, quoted above, raise] ... a triable issue of material fact as to whether Warner breached its contract with Locke by categorically refusing to work with her, irrespective of the merits of her proposals. While Warner was entitled to reject Locke's proposals based on its subjective dissatisfaction, the evidence calls into question whether Warner had an honest or good faith dissatisfaction with Locke's proposals, or whether it merely went through the motions of purporting to "consider" her projects.

    c. *No merit to Warner's contention Locke seeks to rewrite the instant agreement to limit Warner's discretionary power.*

Warner argues that while the implied covenant of good faith and fair dealing is implied in all contracts, it is limited to assuring compliance with the express terms of the contract and cannot be extended to create obligations not contemplated in the contract. (Racine & Laramie, Ltd. v.

Department of Parks & Recreation (1992) 11 Cal.App.4th 1026, 1032, 14 Cal.Rptr.2d 335.)

This principle is illustrated in Carma Developers (Cal.), Inc. v. Marathon Development California, Inc. (1992) 2 Cal.4th 342, 351–352, 6 Cal. Rptr.2d 467, 826 P.2d 710, wherein the parties entered into a lease agreement which stated that if the tenant procured a potential sublessee and asked the landlord for consent to sublease, the landlord had the right to terminate the lease, enter into negotiations with the prospective sublessee, and appropriate for itself all profits from the new arrangement. *Carma* recognized "(t)he covenant of good faith finds particular application in situations where one party is invested with a discretionary power affecting the rights of another." (*Id.*, at p. 372, 6 Cal.Rptr.2d 467, 826 P.2d 710.) The court expressed the view that "(s)uch power must be exercised in good faith." (*Ibid.*) At the same time, *Carma* upheld the right of the landlord under the express terms of the lease to freely exercise its discretion to terminate the lease in order to claim for itself—and deprive the tenant of—the appreciated rental value of the premises. (*Id.*, at p. 376, 6 Cal.Rptr.2d 467, 826 P.2d 710.)

In this regard, *Carma* stated: "We are aware of no reported case in which a court has held the covenant of good faith may be read to prohibit a party from doing that which is expressly permitted by an agreement. On the contrary, as a general matter, implied terms should never be read to vary express terms. ... This is in accord with the general principle that, in interpreting a contract "an implication ... should not be made when the contrary is indicated in clear and express words." 3 Corbin, *Contracts*, § 564, p. 298 (1960).... *As to acts and conduct authorized by the express provisions of the contract,* no covenant of good faith and fair dealing can be implied which forbids such acts and conduct." (Carma Developers (Cal.), Inc., *supra,* 2 Cal.4th at p. 374, 6 Cal.Rptr.2d 467, 826 P.2d 710, italics added.)

In Third Story Music, Inc. v. Waits (1995) 41 Cal.App.4th 798, 801, 48 Cal.Rptr.2d 747, the issue presented was "whether a promise to market music, or to refrain from doing so, at the election of the promisor is subject to the implied covenant of good faith and fair dealing where substantial consideration has been paid by the promisor."

In that case, Warner Communications obtained from TSM the worldwide right to manufacture, sell, distribute and advertise the musical output of singer/songwriter Tom Waits. (Third Story Music, Inc., *supra,* 41 Cal.App.4th at pp. 800–801, 48 Cal.Rptr.2d 747.) The agreement also specifically stated that Warner Communications "may at our election refrain from any or all of the foregoing." (*Id.*, at p. 801, 48 Cal.Rptr.2d 747.) TSM sued Warner Communications for contract damages based on breach of the implied covenant of good faith and fair dealing, claiming Warner Communications had impeded TSM's receiving the benefit of the agreement. (*Id.*, at p. 802, 48 Cal.Rptr.2d 747.) Warner Communications demurred to the complaint, alleging the clause in the agreement permitting it to " 'at (its) election refrain' from doing anything to profitably exploit the music is controlling and precludes application of any implied covenant." (*Ibid.*) The demurrer was sustained on those grounds. (*Ibid.*)

The reviewing court affirmed, holding the implied covenant was unavailing to the plaintiff. (Third Story Music, Inc., *supra*, 41 Cal.App.4th at pp. 808–809, 48 Cal.Rptr.2d 747.) Because the agreement expressly provided Warner Communications had the right to refrain from marketing the Waits recordings, the implied covenant of good faith and fair dealing did not limit the discretion given to Warner Communications in that regard. (*Ibid.*)

Warner's reliance herein on *Third Story Music, Inc.* is misplaced. The Locke/Warner agreement did not give Warner the express right to refrain from working with Locke. Rather, the agreement gave Warner discretion with respect to developing Locke's projects. The implied covenant of good faith and fair dealing obligated Warner to exercise that discretion honestly and in good faith.

In sum, the Warner/Locke agreement contained an implied covenant of good faith and fair dealing, that neither party would frustrate the other party's right to receive the benefits of the contract. (Comunale [v. Traders & General Ins. Co. (1958) 50 Cal.2d 654, 658, 328 P.2d 198.) Whether Warner violated the implied covenant and breached the contract by categorically refusing to work with Locke is a question for the trier of fact.
. . .

DISPOSITION

The judgment is reversed with respect to the second and fourth causes of action and is otherwise affirmed. Locke to recover costs on appeal.

KITCHING and ALDRICH, JJ., concur.

SWARTZ v. WAR MEMORIAL COMMISSION OF ROCHESTER

N.Y. Supreme Court, Appellate Division, Fourth Department, 1966.
25 A.D.2d 90, 267 N.Y.S.2d 253.

PER CURIAM. Plaintiff's complaint, dismissed by Special Term for lack of merit, alleges, *inter alia*, that by contract with defendant Commission he has the exclusive concession for the sale of food and refreshments in the Rochester War Memorial Building [a sports arena, ed.]; that on November 15, 1965 defendant Commission removed its prohibition against the sale of beer and ale therein and decided that sale thereof be permitted; that plaintiff chose not to sell said beverages; that on November 30, 1965 defendant Commission notified him that unless he made application for a license to sell beer and ale within 30 days he would be removed and would not be permitted to continue as concessionaire in said building. He further alleges that defendants threaten to violate his rights under the contract and he seeks a judgment declaring the rights and legal relations of the parties and decreeing that defendants are precluded by the contract from doing any act which may interfere with his right to continue as sole concessionaire. . . .

The introductory clause of the agreement recites: "It is the mutual desire of the parties hereto to enter into a contract whereby . . . the Concessionaire shall furnish such services as are hereinafter provided. . . ." The contract provides for sale of food, beverages, novelties, souvenirs, tobacco, cigars, candy, and other items. The contract further provides in paragraph 6 as follows:

> The privileges and sales rights granted herein shall not include the right to sell any alcoholic beverages during any period or periods in which such sale or sales are prohibited. However, in the event that such prohibition is removed at any time during the term of this agreement, the exclusive sales rights granted herein shall extend to the sale of such alcoholic beverages and the amount to be paid by the Concessionaire to the Commission on such sales as rental shall be identical to that provided for sales of food and beverages.

The agreement recognizes the need of a license to sell beer and ale and provides that the Commission will cooperate with the Concessionaire in obtaining one. Although paragraph 6 contains no express provision requiring the Concessionaire to apply for a license, the thirteenth paragraph provides:

> Prior to entering into any and all operations contemplated hereunder, the Concessionaire shall obtain and keep in force all necessary local, state and/or federal permits or licenses. . . .

Considering all the provisions of the contract and the inferences naturally derivable therefrom as to the intent and object of the parties in making it and the result which they intended to accomplish by its performance, we conclude that it was plaintiff's duty to attempt to qualify himself to sell beer and ale by applying for a license to do so.

Here the agreement expressed the mutual intent of the parties that plaintiff should perform the services provided for in the contract, one of which was to sell alcoholic beverages whenever the prohibition against such sale had been removed. The intent and object of the parties and the result which they intended to accomplish by its performance are apparent. Both parties would derive income from its performance. The public would be convenienced by being able to purchase the food, beverages, and merchandise specified in the contract. Acceptance by plaintiff of the exclusive sales right given him by the contract was an assumption of its duties. Unless he sold the items specified in the contract neither party would derive income from it. His promise to pay defendant Commission a percentage of the gross receipts resulting from the exclusive agency was a promise to use reasonable efforts to bring profits and revenues into existence (Wood v. Lucy, Lady Duff–Gordon, 222 N.Y. 88, 91, 92, 118 N.E. 214, 215). It was indispensable to defendant Commission that plaintiff having the exclusive right to sell should use all diligence to the end that sales be made of the specified items including beer and ale. (Booth v. Cleveland Rolling Mill Co., 74 N.Y. 15, 25.) The reasonable efforts and diligence required of plaintiff to bring profits and revenues into existence imposed upon him the duty to apply for a license to sell beer and ale. His failure to do so amounted to a default on his part of an obligation of the contract. The default continued unremedied for thirty days after his receipt of written notice of it, and the contract was terminated in accordance with its terms.

The judgment and order should be modified in accordance with this opinion, and as so modified affirmed.

Judgment and order unanimously modified on the law and facts in accordance with the opinion and as modified affirmed, without costs of this appeal to either party.

STOP & SHOP, INC. v. GANEM
Supreme Judicial Court of Massachusetts, 1964.
347 Mass. 697, 200 N.E.2d 248.

WHITTEMORE, JUSTICE. The defendants in this bill for declaratory relief are lessors under a percentage lease. They have appealed from the final decree in the Superior Court that ruled that the lease does not expressly or impliedly require the plaintiff, as lessee, to use the demised premises for any particular purpose or to keep the premises open and there engage in the supermarket business. Except for brief testimony which is reported, the facts were stipulated.

The lease, dated August 24, 1953, demised a lot and building at 154 Merrimack Street, Haverhill, for thirteen years and six months from September 1, 1953, for "the minimum rental" of $22,000 a year and the further rent of 1¼% "of all gross sales" above $1,269,230.60 "made by the Lessee on the leased premises during each twelve month period." But the percentage rent was to be paid only if sales at the demised premises and at premises in Lawrence exceeded $3,000,000 a year. . . .

The lease required that the lessee should pay the amount of the increases in the annual real estate taxes and should receive the amount of the decreases therein, measured on the 1946 figure.

The lease does not state the purposes for which the premises are to be used. Nothing therein in terms requires that the premises be used for any purpose or bars the opening by the lessee of places of business competitive to the lessee's business in the demised premises. The lease does, however, require the lessee to us [sic] suitable cash registers to record all sales, to keep accurate books, to furnish statements of gross sales on demand, and at the end of each yearly period to furnish such a statement certified by a certified public accountant. The testimony showed that when the lease was made the plaintiff was engaged in the supermarket business and that the lessors knew it. The premises prior to August 24, 1953, had been used for the conduct of a market.

The plaintiff had occupied the premises as a supermarket through 1962. It had paid percentage rent in 1956 ($2,288.15) and in 1957 ($377.21) but in no other year, and had paid excess taxes in each year. The plaintiff intended to cease operating a supermarket in the premises shortly after January 1, 1963, but to continue to pay the minimum rent and any excess real estate taxes and otherwise to conform to the lease. The defendant lessors had threatened suit to compel the continued operation of a supermarket or, alternatively, for damages.

The defendant lessors filed a counterclaim which alleged that the plaintiff beginning in 1956 had opened two competing stores in Haverhill, one within one-half mile and the other within about one mile of the demised premises. The prayers of the counterclaim were (1) that the lease be reformed to provide that the plaintiff continuously operate the premises as a supermarket, (2) that the plaintiff be ordered to pay to the defendants as part of the rent of the demised premises $1\frac{1}{4}\%$ of gross sales from all the plaintiff's stores in Haverhill in excess of $1,269,230.60, and (3) for general relief. . . .

Other facts are referred to later in the opinion.

The issue presented by the bill for declaratory relief is whether there is in the lease an implied covenant to continue operations.[2] The counterclaim presents the issue whether the lessee may open competing stores and then discontinue operations. We consider first the issue under the bill.

The controlling principles are well established. An omission to specify an agreement in a written lease is evidence that there was no such understanding. Snider v. Deban, 249 Mass. 59, 65, 144 N.E. 69. Covenants will not be extended by implication unless the implication is clear and undoubted. Smiley v. McLauthlin, 138 Mass. 363, 364–365. Justice, common sense and the probable intention of the parties are guides to construction of a written instrument. Clark v. State St. Trust Co., 270 Mass. 140, 153, 169 N.E. 897. "Since the governing principle . . . is the justifiable assumption by one party of a certain intention on the part of the other, the undertaking of each promisor in a contract must include any promises which a reasonable person in the position of the promisee would be justified in understanding were included." Williston, *Contracts* (Rev. ed.) § 1293, p. 3682.

The plaintiff contends that notwithstanding the interest of the lessors in having the premises operated so as to give it the benefit of possible percentage rent, the absence of an express requirement to operate together with a more than nominal minimum rent exclude the implication of a covenant to continue operations.

---

2. The cessation of operations was threatened several years before the end of the lease. Hence, we need not consider whether an implied covenant to continue operations would be enforceable shortly before the end of the term.

This may state too broad a rule. For even if there is a more than nominal minimum rent, other circumstances such as that the fixed rent is significantly below the fair rental value of the property might justify the conclusion that the parties intended that the lessors have the benefit of the percentage rent throughout the term.

The record does not show the fair rental value of the demised premises. An apparently substantial minimum rent in an apparently complete written lease, in the absence of a showing of disparity between the fixed rent and the fair rental value, gives ground for the inference that fixed rent and the lessee's self-interest in producing sales were the only assurance of rent that the lessor required. Other circumstances may give rise to the same inference. In cases where the minimum rent was not substantial continued operation has been held contemplated.

In Smiley v. McLauthlin, 138 Mass. 363, this court held that where rent under a lease of a brick yard was to be computed on the basis of bricks made with no provision for minimum rent, there was no implied covenant that the lessee would operate the yard. The opinion stressed the extrinsic circumstances attending the making of the lease.

> The premises leased were not a brick yard in operation, equipped for work, but barren, unoccupied land. The parties did not know the amount of clay on the land, nor whether brick could be made on the land at a profit. . . . The lease, applied to the subject matter, furnishes indications that the parties regarded the enterprise as experimental, and that any stipulation binding the lessee to work the yard was purposely omitted.

Id. 138 Mass. at 365. The questions may be asked whether the parties did not intend a contract, and if so whether an implied covenant at least to try to operate the brick yard was the only consideration given by the lessee. *Compare* Wood v. Lucy, Lady Duff–Gordon, 222 N.Y. 88, 118 N.E. 214. As to output and requirement contracts *see* Neofotistos v. Harvard Brewing Co., 341 Mass. 684, 686–687, 171 N.E.2d 865.

The minimum rent in this lease appears to be substantial. The figure of $22,000 is obviously not nominal in a lease that fixes as a base real estate tax figure the 1946 tax of $3,744.90. The total of real estate taxes for 1954 was $5,127.71. This roughly indicates the valuation for tax purposes of the demised premises at about the time the lease was made.

The burden of showing a disparity between fixed rent and fair rental value such as to furnish ground for implying a covenant to operate would be on the lessors.

Had the lessors brought an action for damages for breach of an implied covenant to continue operations they would, of course, have had the burden of showing the covenant. That the lessee initiated the proceeding for declaratory relief does not shift that burden to the lessee. . . .

There is in this record no basis for implying a covenant to continue to operate beyond that time when in the business judgment of the lessee operations at the demised location should cease. The lessors have not shown that "a reasonable person in the position of the . . . (lessors) would be justified in understanding" (Williston, *Contracts* (Rev. ed.) § 1293) that such a covenant was intended and hence implied.

The percentage rent provision of course gave the lessors an interest in the lessee's operations of the demised premises as a retail store. We assume, without deciding, that such interest could be protected against certain acts of the lessee, as for example, discontinuance of operations for spite or to inflict harm. Such issues are outside this record for there is no intimation that the plaintiff has acted or proposes to act in respect of the leased premises otherwise than as its sound business judgment dictates in fairly promoting its retail business in Haverhill.

[Next, considering defendant's counterclaim, the court holds that defendant was not entitled to reformation of the lease. Ed.]

The allegations underlying the prayer that the sales of other stores be included in the computation of percentage rent are, that the "plaintiff has not in good faith operated the demised premises so as to obtain the greatest volume of sales at this location, but has opened wrongfully (two) other stores at nearby locations, selling the same merchandise at lower prices." The effect of the two newly opened stores was, it is alleged, to diminish sales. . . .

The allegation "not in good faith" adds nothing to the facts stated. In context, it says no more than that the plaintiff has acted in violation of implied obligations of the lease. The lessors do not contend otherwise.

The lessee, being free to disregard the effect on the lessors of its business decisions in respect of stopping operations, was free also to open stores elsewhere. We assume, without deciding, that had the lessee opened a competing store in the same location as the demised premises, that is adjacent, or nearly so, there might have been a basis for requiring it to regard the lessors' interest under the percentage rent provisions in its conduct of the two stores. In such a case the lessee's acts would affirm the business advantage of remaining at the very place at which it had committed itself as tenant of the lessors. . . .

[Affirmed. Ed.]

MARKET STREET ASSOCIATES LIMITED PARTNERSHIP v. FREY

United States Court of Appeals, Seventh Circuit, 1991.
941 F.2d 588.

POSNER, CIRCUIT JUDGE. Market Street Associates Limited Partnership and its general partner appeal from a judgment for the defendants, General Electric Pension Trust and its trustees, entered upon cross-motions for summary judgment in a diversity suit that pivots on the doctrine of "good faith" performance of a contract. *Cf.* Robert Summers, *"Good Faith" in General Contract Law and the Sales Provisions of the*

Uniform Commercial Code, 54 *Va.L.Rev.* 195, 232–43 (1968). Wisconsin law applies—common law rather than Uniform Commercial Code, because the contract is for land rather than for goods, UCC § 2–102; Wis.Stat. § 402.102....

We come at last to the contract dispute out of which the case arises. In 1968, J.C. Penney Company, the retail chain, entered into a sale and leaseback arrangement with General Electric Pension Trust in order to finance Penney's growth. Under the arrangement Penney sold properties to the pension trust which the trust then leased back to Penney for a term of 25 years. Paragraph 34 of the lease entitles the lessee to "request Lessor (the pension trust) to finance the costs and expenses of construction of additional Improvements upon the Premises," provided the amount of the costs and expenses is at least $250,000. Upon receiving the request, the pension trust "agrees to give reasonable consideration to providing the financing of such additional Improvements and Lessor and Lessee shall negotiate in good faith concerning the construction of such Improvements and the financing by Lessor of such costs and expenses." Paragraph 34 goes on to provide that, should the negotiations fail, the lessee shall be entitled to repurchase the property at a price roughly equal to the price at which Penney sold it to the pension trust in the first place, plus 6 percent a year for each year since the original purchase. So if the average annual appreciation in the property exceeded 6 percent, a breakdown in negotiations over the financing of improvements would entitle Penney to buy back the property for less than its market value (assuming it had sold the property to the pension trust in the first place at its then market value).

One of these leases was for a shopping center in Milwaukee. In 1987 Penney assigned this lease to Market Street Associates, which the following year received an inquiry from a drugstore chain that wanted to open a store in the shopping center, provided (as is customary) that Market Street Associates built the store for it. Whether Market Street Associates was pessimistic about obtaining financing from the pension trust, still the lessor of the shopping center, or for other reasons, it initially sought financing for the project from other sources. But they were unwilling to lend the necessary funds without a mortgage on the shopping center, which Market Street Associates could not give because it was not the owner but only the lessee. It decided therefore to try to buy the property back from the pension trust. Market Street Associates' general partner, Orenstein, tried to call David Erb of the pension trust, who was responsible for the property in question. Erb did not return his calls, so Orenstein wrote him, expressing an interest in buying the property and asking him to "review your file on this matter and call me so that we can discuss it further." At first, Erb did not reply. Eventually Orenstein did reach Erb, who promised to review the file and get back to him. A few days later an associate of Erb called Orenstein and indicated an interest in selling the property for $3 million, which Orenstein considered much too high.

That was in June of 1988. On July 28, Market Street Associates wrote a letter to the pension trust formally requesting funding for $2 million in improvements to the shopping center. The letter made no reference to paragraph 34 of the lease; indeed, it did not mention the lease. The letter asked Erb to call Orenstein to discuss the matter. Erb, in what was becoming a habit of unresponsiveness, did not call. On August 16, Orenstein sent a second letter—certified mail, return receipt requested—again requesting financing and this time referring to the lease, though not expressly to paragraph 34. The heart of the letter is the following two sentences: "The purpose of this letter is to ask again that you advise us immediately if you are willing to provide the financing pursuant to the lease. If you are willing, we propose to enter into negotiation to amend the ground lease appropriately." The very next day, Market Street Associates received from Erb a letter, dated August 10, turning down the original request for financing on the ground that it did not "meet our current investment criteria": the pension trust was not interested in making loans for less than $7 million. On August 22, Orenstein replied to Erb by letter, noting that his letter of August 10 and Erb's letter of August 16 had evidently crossed in the mails, expressing disappointment at the turndown, and stating that Market Street Associates would seek financing elsewhere. That was the last contact between the parties until September 27, when Orenstein sent Erb a letter stating that Market Street Associates was exercising the option granted it by paragraph 34 to purchase the property upon the terms specified in that paragraph in the event that negotiations over financing broke down.

The pension trust refused to sell, and this suit to compel specific performance followed. Apparently the price computed by the formula in paragraph 34 is only $1 million. The market value must be higher, or Market Street Associates wouldn't be trying to coerce conveyance at the paragraph 34 price; whether it is as high as $3 million, however, the record does not reveal.

The district judge granted summary judgment for the pension trust on two grounds that he believed to be separate although closely related. The first was that, by failing in its correspondence with the pension trust to mention paragraph 34 of the lease, Market Street Associates had prevented the negotiations over financing that are a condition precedent to the lessee's exercise of the purchase option from taking place. Second, this same failure violated the duty of good faith, which the common law of Wisconsin, as of other states, reads into every contract. [citations] In support of both grounds the judge emphasized a statement by Orenstein in his deposition that it had occurred to him that Erb mightn't know about paragraph 34, though this was unlikely (Orenstein testified) because Erb or someone else at the pension trust would probably check the file and discover the paragraph and realize that if the trust refused to negotiate over the request for financing, Market Street Associates, as Penney's assignee, would be entitled to walk off with the property for (perhaps) a song. The judge inferred that Market Street Associates didn't

want financing from the pension trust—that it just wanted an opportunity to buy the property at a bargain price and hoped that the pension trust wouldn't realize the implications of turning down the request for financing. Market Street Associates should, the judge opined, have advised the pension trust that it was requesting financing pursuant to paragraph 34, so that the trust would understand the penalty for refusing to negotiate.
. . .

The pension trust's argument, which the district judge bought, is that either as a matter of simple contract interpretation or under the compulsion of the doctrine of good faith, a provision requiring Market Street Associates to remind the pension trust of paragraph 34 should be read into the lease.

It seems to us that these are one ground rather than two. A court has to have a reason to interpolate a clause into a contract. The only reason that has been suggested here is that it is necessary to prevent Market Street Associates from reaping a reward for what the pension trust believes to have been Market Street's bad faith. So we must consider the meaning of the contract duty of "good faith." The Wisconsin cases are cryptic as to its meaning though emphatic about its existence, so we must cast our net wider. We do so mindful of Learned Hand's warning, that "such words as 'fraud,' 'good faith,' 'whim,' 'caprice,' 'arbitrary action,' and 'legal fraud' . . . obscure the issue." Thompson–Starrett Co. v. La Belle Iron Works, 17 F.2d 536, 541 (2d Cir.1927). Indeed they do. *Summers, supra,* at 207–20; 2 [E. Allan Farnsworth,] *Farnsworth on Contracts* § 7.17a [(1990)], at pp. 328–32. The particular confusion to which the vaguely moralistic overtones of "good faith" give rise is the belief that every contract establishes a fiduciary relationship. A fiduciary is required to treat his principal as if the principal were he, and therefore he may not take advantage of the principal's incapacity, ignorance, inexperience, or even naivete. [citations] If Market Street Associates were the fiduciary of General Electric Pension Trust, then (we may assume) it could not take advantage of Mr. Erb's apparent ignorance of paragraph 34, however exasperating Erb's failure to return Orenstein's phone calls was and however negligent Erb or his associates were in failing to read the lease before turning down Orenstein's request for financing.

But it is unlikely that Wisconsin wishes, in the name of good faith, to make every contract signatory his brother's keeper, especially when the brother is the immense and sophisticated General Electric Pension Trust, whose lofty indifference to small (= < $7 million) transactions is the signifier of its grandeur. In fact the law contemplates that people frequently will take advantage of the ignorance of those with whom they contract, without thereby incurring liability. *Restatement, supra,* § 161, comment d. The duty of honesty, of good faith even expansively conceived, is not a duty of candor. You can make a binding contract to purchase something you know your seller undervalues. Laidlaw v. Organ, 15 U.S. (2 Wheat.) 178, 181 n.2, 4 L.Ed. 214 (1817); 1 *Farnsworth on Contracts, supra,* § 4.11, at pp. 406–10; Anthony T. Kronman, *Mistake, Disclosure,*

Information, and the Law of Contracts, 7 J. Legal Stud. 1 (1978). That of course is a question about formation, not performance, and the particular duty of good faith under examination here relates to the latter rather than to the former. But even after you have signed a contract, you are not obliged to become an altruist toward the other party and relax the terms if he gets into trouble in performing his side of the bargain. Kham & Nate's Shoes No. 2, Inc. v. First Bank, 908 F.2d 1351, 1357 (7th Cir.1990). Otherwise mere difficulty of performance would excuse a contracting party—which it does not. Northern Indiana Public Service Co. v. Carbon County Coal Co., 799 F.2d 265, 276–78 (7th Cir.1986); 2 *Farnsworth on Contracts, supra*, § 7.17a, at p. 330.

But it is one thing to say that you can exploit your superior knowledge of the market—for if you cannot, you will not be able to recoup the investment you made in obtaining that knowledge—or that you are not required to spend money bailing out a contract partner who has gotten into trouble. It is another thing to say that you can take deliberate advantage of an oversight by your contract partner concerning his rights under the contract. Such taking advantage is not the exploitation of superior knowledge or the avoidance of unbargained-for expense; it is sharp dealing. Like theft, it has no social product, and also like theft it induces costly defensive expenditures, in the form of overelaborate disclaimers or investigations into the trustworthiness of a prospective contract partner, just as the prospect of theft induces expenditures on locks. *See generally* Steven J. Burton, *Breach of Contract and the Common Law Duty to Perform in Good Faith*, 94 Harv.L.Rev. 369, 393 (1980).

The form of sharp dealing that we are discussing might or might not be actionable as fraud or deceit. That is a question of tort law and there the rule is that if the information is readily available to both parties the failure of one to disclose it to the other, even if done in the knowledge that the other party is acting on mistaken premises, is not actionable. [citations] All of these cases, however, with the debatable exception of Guyer [v. Cities Service Oil Co., 440 F.Supp. 630 (E.D.Wis.1977)], involve failure to disclose something in the negotiations leading up to the signing of the contract, rather than failure to disclose after the contract has been signed. (*Guyer* involved failure to disclose during the negotiations leading up to a renewal of the contract.) The distinction is important, as we explained in Maksym v. Loesch, 937 F.2d 1237, 1242 (7th Cir.1991). Before the contract is signed, the parties confront each other with a natural wariness. Neither expects the other to be particularly forthcoming, and therefore there is no deception when one is not. Afterwards the situation is different. The parties are now in a cooperative relationship the costs of which will be considerably reduced by a measure of trust. So each lowers his guard a bit, and now silence is more apt to be deceptive.

Moreover, this is a contract case rather than a tort case, and conduct that might not rise to the level of fraud may nonetheless violate the duty of good faith in dealing with one's contractual partners and thereby give rise to a remedy under contract law. *Burton, supra*, at 372 n. 17. This duty is, as it were, halfway between a fiduciary duty (the duty of *utmost* good faith) and the duty merely to refrain from active fraud. Despite its moralistic overtones it is no more the injection of moral principles into contract law than the fiduciary concept itself is. Tymshare, Inc. v. Covell, 727 F.2d 1145, 1152 (D.C.Cir.1984); *Summers, supra,* at 204–07, 265–66. It would be quixotic as well as presumptuous for judges to undertake through contract law to raise the ethical standards of the nation's business people. The concept of the duty of good faith like the concept of fiduciary duty is a stab at approximating the terms the parties would have negotiated had they foreseen the circumstances that have given rise to their dispute. The parties want to minimize the costs of performance. To the extent that a doctrine of good faith designed to do this by reducing defensive expenditures is a reasonable measure to this end, interpolating it into the contract advances the parties' joint goal.

It is true that an essential function of contracts is to allocate risk, and would be defeated if courts treated the materializing of a bargained-over, allocated risk as a misfortune the burden of which is required to be shared between the parties (as it might be within a family, for example) rather than borne entirely by the party to whom the risk had been allocated by mutual agreement. But contracts do not just allocate risk. They also (or some of them) set in motion a cooperative enterprise, which may to some extent place one party at the other's mercy. "The parties to a contract are embarked on a cooperative venture, and a minimum of cooperativeness in the event unforeseen problems arise at the performance stage is required even if not an explicit duty of the contract." AMPAT/Midwest, Inc. v. Illinois Tool Works, Inc., [896 F.2d 1035, 1041 (7th Cir.1990). The office of the doctrine of good faith is to forbid the kinds of opportunistic behavior that a mutually dependent, cooperative relationship might enable in the absence of rule. " 'Good faith' is a compact reference to an implied undertaking not to take opportunistic advantage in a way that could not have been contemplated at the time of drafting, and which therefore was not resolved explicitly by the parties." Kham & Nate's Shoes No. 2, Inc. v. First Bank, *supra,* 908 F.2d at 1357. The contractual duty of good faith is thus not some newfangled bit of welfare-state paternalism or (*pace* Duncan Kennedy, *Form and Substance in Private Law Adjudication,* 89 Harv.L.Rev. 1685, 1721 (1976)) the sediment of an altruistic strain in contract law, and we are therefore not surprised to find the essentials of the modern doctrine well established in nineteenth-century cases. . . . [citations]

The emphasis we are placing on postcontractual versus precontractual conduct helps explain the pattern that is observed when the duty of contractual good faith is considered in all its variety, encompassing not only good faith in the *performance* of a contract but also good faith in its *formation, Summers, supra,* at 220–32, and in its *enforcement.* Harbor Ins. Co. v. Continental Bank Corp., 922 F.2d 357, 363 (7th Cir.1990). The formation or negotiation stage is precontractual, and here the duty is minimized. It is greater not only at the performance but also at the enforcement stage, which is also postcontractual. "A party who hokes up a phony defense to the performance of his contractual duties and then when that defense fails (at some expense to the other party) tries on another defense for size can properly be said to be acting in bad faith." *Id*. At the formation of the contract the parties are dealing in present realities; performance still lies in the future. As performance unfolds, circumstances change, often unforeseeably; the explicit terms of the contract become progressively less apt to the governance of the parties' relationship; and the role of implied conditions—and with it the scope and bite of the good-faith doctrine—grows.

We could of course do without the term "good faith," and maybe even without the doctrine. We could, as just suggested, speak instead of implied conditions necessitated by the unpredictability of the future at the time the contract was made. Farnsworth, *Good Faith Performance and Commercial Reasonableness under the Uniform Commercial Code*, 30 U.Chi. L.Rev. 666, 670 (1963). . . .

But whether we say that a contract shall be deemed to contain such implied conditions as are necessary to make sense of the contract, or that a contract obligates the parties to cooperate in its performance in "good faith" to the extent necessary to carry out the purposes of the contract, comes to much the same thing. They are different ways of formulating the overriding purpose of contract law, which is to give the parties what they would have stipulated for expressly if at the time of making the contract they had had complete knowledge of the future and the costs of negotiating and adding provisions to the contract had been zero.

The two formulations would have different meanings only if "good faith" were thought limited to "honesty in fact," an interpretation perhaps permitted but certainly not compelled by the Uniform Commercial Code, *see Summers, supra*, at 207–20—and anyway this is not a case governed by the UCC. We need not pursue this issue. The dispositive question in the present case is simply whether Market Street Associates tried to trick the pension trust and succeeded in doing so. If it did, this would be the type of opportunistic behavior in an ongoing contractual relationship that would violate the duty of good faith performance however the duty is formulated. There is much common sense in Judge Reynolds' conclusion that Market Street Associates did just that. The situation as he saw it was as follows. Market Street Associates didn't want financing from the pension trust (initially it had looked elsewhere, remember), and when it learned it couldn't get the financing without owning the property, it decided to try to buy the property. But the pension trust set a stiff price, so Orenstein decided to trick the pension trust into selling at the bargain price fixed in paragraph 34 by requesting financing and hoping that the pension trust would turn the request down without noticing the paragraph. His preliminary dealings with the pension trust made this hope a realistic one by revealing a sluggish and hidebound bureaucracy unlikely to have retained in its brontosaurus's memory, or to be able at short notice to retrieve, the details of a small lease made twenty years earlier. So by requesting financing without mentioning the lease Market Street Associates might well precipitate a refusal before the pension trust woke up to paragraph 34. It is true that Orenstein's second letter requested financing "pursuant to the lease." But when the next day he received a reply to his first letter indicating that the pension trust was indeed oblivious to paragraph 34, his response was to send a lulling letter designed to convince the pension trust that the matter was closed and could be forgotten. The stage was set for his thunderbolt: the notification the next month that Market Street Associates was taking up the option in paragraph 34. Only then did the pension trust look up the lease and discover that it had been had.

The only problem with this recital is that it construes the facts as favorably to the pension trust as the record will permit, and that of course is not the right standard for summary judgment. The facts must be construed as favorably to [Market Street Associates] as the record permits. . . . When that is done a different picture emerges. [The court proceeds to interpret the facts favorably to Market Street Associates. Ed.]

On this interpretation of the facts there was no bad faith on the part of Market Street Associates. . . . The fault was the pension trust's incredible inattention, which misled Market Street Associates into believing that the pension trust had no interest in financing the improvements regardless of the purchase option. We do not usually excuse contracting parties from failing to read and understand the contents of their contract; and in the end what this case comes down to—or so at least it can be strongly argued—is that an immensely sophisticated enterprise simply failed to read the contract. On the other hand, such enterprises make mistakes just like the rest of us, and deliberately to take advantage of your contracting partner's mistake during the performance stage (for we are not taking advantage of superior knowledge at the formation stage) is a breach of good faith. To be able to correct your contract partner's mistake at zero cost to yourself, and decide not to do so, is a species of opportunistic behavior that the parties would have expressly forbidden in the contract had they foreseen it. The immensely long term of the lease amplified the possibility of errors but did not license either party to take advantage of them. . . .

The district judge jumped the gun in choosing between these alternative characterizations. The essential issue bearing on Market Street Associates' good faith was Orenstein's state of mind, a type of inquiry that ordinarily cannot be concluded on summary judgment, and could not be here. If Orenstein believed that Erb knew or would surely find out about paragraph 34, it was not dishonest or opportunistic to fail to flag that paragraph, or even to fail to mention the lease, in his correspondence and (rare) conversations with Erb, especially given the uninterest in dealing with Market Street Associates that Erb fairly radiated. To decide what Orenstein believed, a trial is necessary. . . .

Reversed and remanded.

PROBLEMS

22.   The 1919 contract between Charlie Comiskey, owner of the Chicago White Sox, and Eddie Cicotte, his star pitcher, provided for a salary of $6,000 and a $10,000 bonus if Cicotte pitched 30 winning games that season. According to Studs Terkel, noted chronicler of the Chicago scene, "as [Cicotte] neared that mark, Comiskey had him benched for the remainder of the season rather than open his wallet." Had Cicotte sued to collect the bonus, what should have been the result?

23.   Husband (H) and his wife entered into an alimony agreement in connection with an order for divorce, in which H was obligated to pay alimony of $1,200 per week. The agreement stated, "the alimony is non-modifiable unless the husband's income is greater than $600,000 or less than $200,000 in any given year." (Thus, if H's annual income falls below $200,000 the court could reduce his alimony obligations in an equitable manner.) H, who had been earning well over $200,000 annually, remarried, quit his job, moved out-of-state, and joined his new father-in-law's real estate business where he earned about $80,000 a year. He applies to the court to reduce his alimony obligations to his first wife. Should the application be granted?

24.   Plaintiff contracted with the state to erect a building according to state specifications and to lease it to the state. Time was made of the essence in the contract. Plaintiff completed the building two months late. The state cancelled the contract and leased space elsewhere. Plaintiff sues, alleging and proving that the delay was caused by failure of the state to indicate locations for electrical fixtures, outlets and other details as required by the contract. What result?

25.   Plaintiff is the author of several highly successful books on electricity published by defendant under an agreement whereby defendant had an exclusive right to publish the books in return for a 15% royalty for the plaintiff. Defendant undertook to use "best efforts" to promote plaintiff's works. After plaintiff had refused to lower his royalty rate, defendant hired M to write competing books for a 3% royalty. When the books written by M were published, defendant ceased its advertisements for plaintiff's books and encouraged its sales personnel to devote their efforts to the new series of books. Plaintiff sues for damages and to enjoin defendant from marketing the competing books. What result?

SECTION 7. WAIVER, ESTOPPEL, AND ELECTION

(Calamari & Perillo on Contracts §§ 11.29—11.34)

CLARK v. WEST
Court of Appeals of New York, 1908.
193 N.Y. 349, 86 N.E. 1.

. . . On February 12th, 1900, the plaintiff and defendant entered into a written contract under which the former was to write and prepare for publication for the latter a series of law books the compensation for which was provided in the contract. After the plaintiff had completed a three-volume work known as "Clark & Marshall on Corporations," the parties disagreed. The plaintiff . . . brought this action to recover what he claims to be due him, for an accounting and other relief. The defendant demurred to the complaint on the ground that it did not state facts sufficient to constitute a cause of action. The Special Term overruled the demurrer, but upon appeal to the Appellate Division, that decision was reversed and the demurrer sustained. . . .

The appeal is by permission of the Appellate Division and the following questions have been certified to us: 1. Does the complaint herein state facts sufficient to constitute a cause of action? 2. Under the terms of the contract alleged in the complaint, is the plaintiff's total abstinence from the use of intoxicating liquors a condition precedent which can be waived so as to render defendant liable upon the contract notwithstanding plaintiff's use intoxicating liquors? 3. Does the complaint herein allege facts constituting a valid and effective waiver of plaintiff's non-performance of such condition precedent? . . .

Werner, J. The contract before us, stripped of all superfluous verbiage, binds the plaintiff to total abstention from the use of intoxicating liquors during the continuance of the work which he was employed to do. The stipulations relating to the plaintiff's compensation provide that if he does not observe this condition he is to be paid at the rate of $2 per page, and if he does comply therewith he is to receive $6 per page. The plaintiff has written one book under the contract known as "Clark & Marshall on Corporations," which has been accepted, published and copies sold in large numbers by the defendant. The plaintiff admits that while he was at work on this book he did not entirely abstain from the use of intoxicating liquors. He has been paid only $2 per page for the work he has done. He claims that, despite his breach of this condition, he is entitled to the full compensation of $6 per page because the defendant, with full knowledge of plaintiff's non-observance of this stipulation as to total abstinence, has waived the breach thereof and cannot now insist upon strict performance in this regard. This plea of waiver presents the underlying question which determines the answers to the questions certified.

Briefly stated, the defendant's position is that the stipulation as to plaintiff's total abstinence is the consideration for the payment of the difference between $2 and $6 per page and therefore could not be waived except by a new agreement to that effect based upon a good consideration; that the so-called waiver alleged by the plaintiff is not a waiver but a modification of the contract in respect of its consideration. The plaintiff on the other hand argues that the stipulation for his total abstinence was merely a condition precedent intended to work a forfeiture of the additional compensation in case of a breach and that it could be waived without any formal agreement to that effect based upon a new consideration.

The subject-matter of the contract was the writing of books by the plaintiff for the defendant. The duration of the contract was the time necessary to complete them all. The work was to be done to the satisfaction of the defendant, and the plaintiff was not to write any other books except those covered by the contract unless requested so to do by the defendant, in which latter event he was to be paid for that particular work by the year. The compensation for the work specified in the contract was to be $6 per page, unless the plaintiff failed to totally abstain from the use of intoxicating liquors during the continuance of the contract, in which event he was to receive only $2 per page. That is the obvious import of the contract construed in the light of the purpose for which it was made, and in accordance with the ordinary meaning of plain language. It is not a contract to write books in order that the plaintiff shall keep sober, but a contract containing a stipulation that he shall keep sober so that he may write satisfactory books. When we view the contract from this standpoint it will readily be perceived that the particular stipulation is not the consideration for the contract, but simply one of its conditions which fits in with those relating to time and method of delivery of manuscript, revision of proof, citation of cases, assignment of copyrights, keeping track of new cases and citations for new editions, and other details which might be waived by the defendant, if he saw fit to do so. This is made clear, it seems to us, by the provision that, "In consideration of the above promises," the defendant agrees to pay the plaintiff $2 per page on each book prepared by him, and if he "abstains from the use of intoxicating liquor and otherwise fulfills his agreements as hereinbefore set forth, he shall be paid an additional $4 per page in manner hereinbefore stated." The compensation of $2 per page, not to exceed $250 per month, was an advance or partial payment of the whole price of $6 per page, and the payment of the two-thirds which was to be withheld pending the performance of the contract, was simply made contingent upon the plaintiff's total abstention from the use of intoxicants during the life of the contract. . . . It is obvious that the parties thought that the plaintiff's normal work was worth $6 per page. That was the sum to be paid for the work done by the plaintiff and not for total abstinence. If the plaintiff did not keep to the condition as to total abstinence, he was to lose part of that sum. . . . This, we think, is the fair interpretation of the contract, and it follows that the stipulation as to the plaintiff's total abstinence was nothing more nor less than a condition precedent. If that conclusion is well founded there can be no escape from the corollary that this condition could be waived; and if it was waived the defendant is clearly not in a position to insist upon the forfeiture which his waiver was intended to annihilate. The forfeiture must stand or fall with the condition. If the latter was waived, the former is no longer a part of the contract. Defendant still has the right to counterclaim for any damages which he may have sustained in consequence of the plaintiff's breach, but he cannot insist upon strict performance. (Dunn v. Steubing, 120 N. Y. 232.)

This whole discussion is predicated of course upon the theory of an express waiver. We assume that no waiver could be implied from the defendant's mere acceptance of the books and his payment of the sum of $2 per page without objection. It was the defendant's duty to pay that amount in any event after acceptance of the work. The plaintiff must stand upon his allegation of an express waiver and if he fails to establish that he cannot maintain his action.

The theory upon which the defendant's attitude seems to be based is that even if he has represented to the plaintiff that he would not insist upon the condition that the latter should observe total abstinence from intoxicants, he can still refuse to pay the full contract price for his work. The inequity of this position becomes apparent when we consider that this contract was to run for a period of years, during a large portion of which the plaintiff was to be entitled only to the advance payment of $2 per page, the balance being contingent, among other things, upon publication of the books and returns from sales. Upon this theory the defendant might have waived the condition while the first book was in process of production, and yet when the whole work was completed, he would still be in a position to insist upon the forfeiture because there had not been strict performance. Such a situation is possible in a case where the subject of the waiver is the very consideration of a contract (Organ v. Stewart, 60 N. Y. 413, 420), but not where the waiver relates to something that can be waived. In the case at bar, as we have seen, the waiver is not of the consideration or subject-matter, but of an incident to the method of performance. The consideration remains the same. The defendant has had the work he bargained for, and it is alleged that he has waived one of the conditions as to the manner in which it was to have been done. He might have insisted upon literal performance and then he could have stood upon the letter of his contract. If, however, he has waived that incidental condition, he has created a situation to which the doctrine of waiver very precisely applies.

The cases which present the most familiar phases of the doctrine of waiver are those which have arisen out of litigation over insurance policies where the defendants have claimed a forfeiture because of the breach of some condition in the contract, but it is a doctrine of general application which is confined to no particular class of cases. A waiver has been defined to be the intentional relinquishment of a known right. It is voluntary and implies an election to dispense with something of value, or forego some advantage which the party waiving it might at its option have demanded or insisted upon and this definition is supported by many cases in this and other states. In the recent case of Draper v. Oswego Co. Fire R. Assn. (190

N. Y. 12, 16) Chief Judge Cullen, in speaking for the court upon this subject, said:

> While that doctrine and the doctrine of equitable estoppel are often confused in insurance litigation, there is a clear distinction between the two. A waiver is the voluntary abandonment or relinquishment by a party of some right or advantage. As said by my brother Vann in the *Kiernan* case (150 N. Y. 190): 'The law of waiver seems to be a technical doctrine, introduced and applied by the court for the purpose of defeating forfeitures. . . . While the principle may not be easily classified, it is well established that if the words and acts of the insurer reasonably justify the conclusion that with full knowledge of all the facts it intended to abandon or not to insist upon the particular defense afterwards relied upon, a verdict or finding to that effect establishes a waiver, which, if it once exists, can never be revoked.' The doctrine of equitable estoppel, or estoppel *in pais,* is that a party may be precluded by his acts and conduct from asserting a right to the detriment of another party who, entitled to rely on such conduct, has acted upon it. . . . As already said, the doctrine of waiver is to relieve against forfeiture; it requires no consideration for a waiver, nor any prejudice or injury to the other party.

It remains to be determined whether the plaintiff has alleged facts which, if proven, will be sufficient to establish his claim of an express waiver by the defendant of the plaintiff's breach of the condition to observe total abstinence. In the 12th paragraph of the complaint, the plaintiff alleges facts and circumstances which we think, if established, would prove defendant's waiver of plaintiff's performance of that contract stipulation. These facts and circumstances are that long before the plaintiff had completed the manuscript of the first book undertaken under the contract, the defendant had full knowledge of the plaintiff's non-observance of that stipulation, and that with such knowledge he not only accepted the completed manuscript without objection, but

> repeatedly avowed and represented to the plaintiff that he was entitled to and would receive said royalty payments (*i. e.,* the additional $4 per page), and plaintiff believed and relied upon such representations . . . and at all times during the writing of said treatise on corporations, and after as well as before publication thereof as aforesaid, it was mutually understood, agreed and intended by the parties hereto that notwithstanding plaintiff's said use of intoxicating liquors, he was nevertheless entitled to receive and would receive said royalty as the same accrued under said contract.

The demurrer not only admits the truth of these allegations, but also all that can by reasonable and fair intendment be implied therefrom. . . . [W]e think it cannot be doubted that the allegations contained in the 12th paragraph of the complaint, if proved upon the trial, would be sufficient to establish an express waiver by the defendant of the stipulation in regard to plaintiff's total abstinence.

The three questions certified should be answered in the affirmative, the order of the Appellate Division reversed, the interlocutory judgment of the Special Term affirmed, with costs in both courts, and the defendant be permitted to answer the complaint within twenty days upon payment of costs.

CULLEN, CH. J., EDWARD T. BARTLETT, HAIGHT, VANN, HISOCK and CHASE, JJ., concur.

Order reversed, etc.

SCHENECTADY STEEL CO., INC. v. BRUNO TRIMPOLI GENERAL CONST. CO., INC.

N.Y. Supreme Court, Appellate Division, Third Department, 1974.
43 A.D.2d 234, 350 N.Y.S.2d 920.

REYNOLDS, JUSTICE. This is an appeal from a judgment of the Supreme Court in favor of respondent [hereinafter, Contractor], entered April 30, 1973 in Schenectady County, upon a decision of the court at a Trial Term, without a jury.

On May 8, 1968, Contractor entered into a contract with the State of New York to build, by December 31, 1969, a bridge over the Alplaus Creek in Schenectady County. Contractor, first orally on May 10, 1968 and later by writing, contracted with appellant [hereinafter, Steel Supplier] to have the steel supplier furnish the structural steel necessary for said bridge. The signed contract provided that "time is of the essence" and that the "work will be completed in 1968."

Steel Supplier originally had contemplated that it could obtain the 125–foot steel beams involved in one piece from its supplier, but this proved not to be the case and Steel Supplier was required to purchase smaller beams and then splice them together, not an unusual process but one which obviously created the additional problem that all welds would have to pass a radiographic test before final acceptance. In August, 1968 Steel Supplier began its buttwelding but its completed welds could not pass the radiographic tests despite Steel Supplier's conceded repeated efforts. Then weather conditions in December forced Steel Supplier to suspend its efforts until February, 1969, when it was able to rearrange its facilities to move the welding process indoors. During all of this period Contractor was aware of Steel Supplier's difficulties and by January of 1969 began to attempt to bring pressure on Steel Supplier to complete its obligations. Finally, by letters dated January 29, 1969 and February 11, 1969, Contractor insisted that Steel Supplier provide it a schedule as to how Steel Supplier would complete its obligation, threatening to contract elsewhere for the steel and charge Steel Supplier with the additional cost if Steel Supplier failed to do so. Steel Supplier responded by letter dated February 12, 1969 that it would proceed "with all possible speed" but that it could not yet provide an accurate completion date. On March 1, 1969 Contractor's president visited Steel Supplier's shop and apparently was so dissatisfied at what appeared to be the progress, that as of March 5, 1969

Contractor cancelled the contract with Steel Supplier and contracted for the steel elsewhere. Steel Supplier's subsequent letter of March 11, 1969, proposing a definite completion date did not alter Contractor's decision.

Steel Supplier then brought the instant proceeding to recover the reasonable value of the services it had provided, and Contractor counter-claimed asserting damages for Steel Supplier's failure to perform. After a lengthy trial, the trial court dismissed Steel Supplier's complaint and gave judgment for Contractor in the amount of $8,628.08 on its counterclaim. The instant appeal ensued.

The first issue that must be resolved in this appeal is the correctness of the trial court's assumption that the Uniform Commercial Code applied to the instant contract. It was the trial court's position that it did and that Steel Supplier's failure to give adequate assurances following the February 11th letter requesting a completion schedule justified Contractor's cancellation of the contract. Of course, at common law no such duty to provide adequate assurances existed. (2 Anderson, *Uniform Commercial Code*, (2d ed.), § 2–609:3).

In our opinion the Uniform Commercial Code was not applicable here. The Code applies to transactions involving goods, but its provisions, as with its predecessor, the Uniform Sales Act, are not applicable to either "service" or "construction" contracts. [citations] If service predominates and the transfer of title to personal property is an incidental feature of the transaction, the contract does not fall within the ambit of the Code ... (Perlmutter v. Beth Israel Hosp., 308 N.Y. 100, 104–105, 123 N.E.2d 792, 793–794). And the contract in the instant case was a contract for the rendition of services, a work, labor and materials contract, rather than a contract for the sale of goods, the steel beams involved. Upon an examination of the contractual terms, Steel Supplier was obligated to "furnish and erect the structural steel".... Contractor was not contracting simply for the steel beams but in essence for their erection and installation with the transfer of the title to the steel a mere incident of the overall transaction, a mere accessory to the work and labor to be performed.

At common law the pivotal issue is the timeliness of Steel Supplier's performance. As previously noted, the contract required Steel Supplier to complete the work in 1968 and provided that "time is of the essence." Thus, Contractor could properly have cancelled the contract on December 31, 1968 as Steel Supplier had not completed the work by that date (Taylor v. Goelet, 208 N.Y. 253, 259, 101 N.E. 867, 868). However, Contractor did not so elect, and instead permitted the contract to continue. By this action Contractor at that time waived its right to cancel for an untimely performance (Lawson v. Hogan, [93 N.Y. 39, 44]) and effectively converted the contract into one under which performance within a reasonable time was all that was required (Lawson v. Hogan, *supra*), although it retained its right to seek damages for the delay (General Supply & Constr. Co. v. Goelet, [241 N.Y. 28, 148 N.E. 778]). However, even following this waiver Contractor could reimpose time as essential element upon notice to

Steel Supplier calling for performance within a reasonable time (Taylor v. Goelet, *supra*, 208 N.Y. at 258, 101 N.E. at 868) and this we find to have occurred by Contractor's letters of January 29 and February 11. These letters restored timeliness and Steel Supplier's failure to give more than assurances, after all the previous delays, that it would proceed "with all possible speed" as opposed to the requested definite schedule, plus the state of progress viewed by Contractor's president on his March 1 visit, justified Contractor's termination of the contract. Accordingly, we agree with the trial court's dismissal of Steel Supplier's complaint. . . .

[Judgment affirmed with modifications as to damages on Contractor's counterclaim. Ed.]

HERLIHY, P.J., and KANE, J., concur. . . .

GREENBLOTT, JUSTICE (concurring). I concur. I do not disagree with the conclusions arrived at on the basis of common law principles, but I feel that the trial court was correct in applying the Uniform Commercial Code. . . .

COOKE, JUSTICE (concurring in part and dissenting in part). I dissent and vote to reverse. I agree with the majority that the Uniform Commercial Code does not apply to a contract such as the instant one where service predominates and the provision of goods is a mere incident. . . . The instant contract, requiring plaintiff to "Furnish labor, equipment and materials *to install*" and *"erect* structural steel" (emphasis supplied), was clearly a service or construction contract and thus outside the ambit of the Code. Therefore, in determining the rights and remedies of the respective parties, it is necessary to resort to case law.

Time was clearly of the essence in the original contract which expressly so provided and set the work completion date in 1968. However, compliance with that provision was waived by Contractor's failure to cancel the contract upon Steel Suppliers' non-performance within the time limits. (General Supply & Constr. Co. v. Goelet, 241 N.Y. 28, 148 N.E. 778.) Thereupon, the contract was effectively converted into one under which performance within a reasonable time was all that was required (Lawson v. Hogan, [93 N.Y. 39]) although Contractor was free to seek damages attributable to the delay (Mawhinney v. Millbrook Woolen Mills, 234 N.Y. 244, 137 N.E. 318). If performance within a reasonable time was the sole criterion, clearly such time had not expired as of the cancellation date, March 5, 1969. Contractor was aware of the circumstances causing the delay—Steel Supplier's inability to obtain State approval of the splice welds in the steel beams—and could reasonably anticipate further delays attributable thereto. However, even if Contractor's letters of January 29 and February 11, which called upon Steel Supplier to set a completion date, are viewed as reimposing time as an essential element in the contract, nevertheless, Contractor again waived compliance with that provision by failing to cancel the contract after Steel Supplier's refusal, in its letter of February 12, to set a completion date. In fact, work on the project was resumed on February 24 or 25 and the inspection of Steel

Supplier's premises by Contractor's president on March 1, 1969 indicates that at least as of that date, performance in the absence of a completion date was being permitted.

Contractor's cancellation of the contract on March 5, 1969 came about when time was once again not of the essence, and termination, without providing a reasonable time for completion of the contract, was improper (General Supply & Constr. Co. v. Goelet, *supra*, 241 N.Y. at 36, 37, 148 N.E. at 779) though, as mentioned earlier, Contractor was entitled to seek damages for the delay. . . .

I would reverse and remit the matter for an assessment of Steel Supplier's damages. . . .

SCHENECTADY STEEL CO., INC. v. BRUNO TRIMPOLI GENERAL CONST. CO., INC.

New York Court of Appeals, 1974.
34 N.Y.2d 939, 359 N.Y.S.2d 560, 316 N.E.2d 875.

The order of the Appellate Division should be affirmed on the record before us.

We agree with the majority below that once the "time of the essence" provision in the contract was waived by the general contractor, performance by the steel supplier within a reasonable time was all that was required. We would not, however, concur with the majority's reasoning insofar as it is indicated that the "time of the essence" element was reimposed; but upon any view of the evidence the lesser standard of reasonable time was not even complied with and we thus find no cause for disturbing the result appealed from. We would further indicate that on the facts of this case it is immaterial whether article 2 of the Uniform Commercial Code applies. . . .

Order affirmed, with costs.

PROBLEMS

26. On December 15, S promised to sell B a machine for $1,000 with delivery to be made on or before March 1. On January 1, B told S he would be willing to take delivery on April 1.

(a) S delivered the machine on April 1. B rejected it on grounds of lateness. S sues for breach of contract. What result?

(b) On January 3, B changed his mind and insisted on delivery by March 1. Upon S's failure to deliver on March 1, B canceled the contract. S sues B. What result?

27. On September 1, X promised to construct a house for Y on Y's land "to be completed by June 30." The parties agreed that time was of the essence. Nonetheless, on December 1, Y told X that he would not insist on the June 30 deadline. X delayed an order for materials needed in the construction of the house. When X had not substantially completed by June 30, Y cancelled

the contract. If X can show that it would have been ready, willing and able to complete the house sometime in August, should it succeed in an action to collect damages from Y?

28.   Seller contracted to sell a parcel of realty to buyer. At the request of the buyer, the contract provided that "this contract is contingent upon the purchaser obtaining a rezoning for a mobile home court. This contract is to be void if the rezoning is not obtained within 120 days." After 60 days, buyer notified seller that he would buy the property irrespective of a zoning change. The zoning change was not obtained. The seller refused to convey. In an action by the buyer against the seller, what result?

29.   Plaintiff contracted with defendant for the purchase of unimproved realty, payable in monthly installments. For the first three years plaintiff was punctual in making payment. In the next four years payments were made tardily and at sporadic intervals. The defendant made no protest. Towards the end of the fourth year, the defendant rejected a tardy payment and declared the contract at an end pursuant to provisions in the contract making time of each payment of the essence (with a 31–day grace period). The contract also provided: "no waiver of a breach or any term or condition shall be a waiver of any other or subsequent breach of the same or any other term or condition." Plaintiff sues to enforce the contract. What result?

30.   Defendant insured plaintiff under a liability policy. Plaintiff was involved in an accident and failed to give the notice required by the policy. Plaintiff's late notice was received by the defendant, which proceeded for two months to try to settle the claim. It then called upon the plaintiff for further information and for the papers which had been served in the case. Shortly before the trial of the action, the defendant returned the papers and said that it would not defend the action. What result?

31.   D, a contractor, built a structure for P on P's property. After it was completed P formally accepted the building pursuant to its architect's recommendation. Shortly afterwards the roof began to leak. D tried to remedy the situation but failed. There was evidence that the roof could not be repaired. P sues for damages. What result?

32.   Flight Airlines entered into a contract with Aluminum Aircraft to purchase 99 jet planes for a price of a half billion dollars. Delivery of the planes, pursuant to a schedule in the contract, was invariably late. Although Flight occasionally grumbled, it took no action until the last plane was delivered when it brought this action for breach of contract claiming damages of $25,000,000 caused by the delays. Aluminum denies liability because Flight accepted deliveries without indicating it intended to hold Aluminum for breach. What result?

SECTION 8.   RELIEF FROM FORFEITURE

(Calamari & Perillo on Contracts §§ 11.35 and 11.36)

BURGER KING CORP. v. FAMILY DINING, INC.

United States District Court, E.D. Pennsylvania, 1977.
426 F.Supp. 485, *aff'd mem.* 566 F.2d 1168 (3d Cir. 1977).

HANNUM, DISTRICT JUDGE. Presently before the Court is defendant's motion for an involuntary dismissal in accordance with Rule 41(b), Federal Rules of Civil Procedure, advanced at the close of plaintiff's case. The trial is before the Court sitting without a jury.

In bringing the suit plaintiff seeks a determination under the Declaratory Judgment Act, Title 28, United States Code § 2201, that a contract between the parties, by its own terms, is no longer of any force and effect. . . .

FACTS ESTABLISHED IN PLAINTIFF'S CASE

Plaintiff Burger King Corporation (hereinafter "Burger King") is a Florida corporation engaged in franchising the well-known Burger King Restaurants. In 1954, James W. McLamore, founder of Burger King Restaurants, Inc. (the corporate predecessor of Burger King) built the first Burger King Restaurant in Miami, Florida. In 1961 the franchise system was still relatively modest [in] size having only about 60 or 70 restaurants in operation outside of Florida. By 1963, however, Burger King began to experience significant growth and was building and operating, principally through franchisees, 24 restaurants per year. It was also at this time that Burger King's relationship with defendant Family Dining, Inc., (hereinafter "Family Dining") was created.

Family Dining is a Pennsylvania corporation which at the present time operates ten Burger King Restaurants (hereinafter "Restaurant") in Bucks and Montgomery Counties in Pennsylvania. Family Dining was founded and is currently operated by Carl Ferris who had been a close personal friend of McLamore's for a number of years prior to 1963. In fact they had attended Cornell University together in the late 1940's. It would seem that this friendship eventually led to the business relationship between Burger King and Family Dining which was conceived in the "Burger King Territorial Agreement" (hereinafter "Territorial Agreement") entered on May 10, 1963.

In accordance with the Territorial Agreement Burger King agreed that Family Dining would be its sole licensee, and thus have an "exclusive territory," in Bucks and Montgomery Counties provided Family Dining operated each Restaurant pursuant to Burger King license agreements[1] and maintained a specified rate of development. Articles I and II of the Territorial Agreement are pertinent to this dispute. They provide as follows:

---

1.   Each Restaurant is opened pursuant to a separate Burger King license agreement.

I.

For a period of one year, beginning on the date hereof, Company will not operate or license others for the operation of any BURGER KING restaurant within the following described territory hereinafter referred to as "exclusive territory," to-wit:

The counties of Bucks and Montgomery, all in the State of Pennsylvania

as long as licensee operates each BURGER KING restaurant pursuant to BURGER KING restaurant licenses with Company and faithfully performs each of the covenants contained.

This agreement shall remain in effect and Licensee shall retain the exclusive territory for a period of ninety (90) years from the date hereof, provided that at the end of one, two, three, four, five, six, seven, eight, nine and ten years from the date hereof, and continuously thereafter during the next eighty years, Licensee has the following requisite number of BURGER KING restaurants in operation or under active construction, pursuant to Licenses with Company:

One (1) restaurant at the end of one year;

Two (2) restaurants at the end of two years;

Three (3) restaurants at the end of three years;

Four (4) restaurants at the end of four years;

Five (5) restaurants at the end of five years;

Six (6) restaurants at the end of six years;

Seven (7) restaurants at the end of seven years;

Eight (8) restaurants at the end of eight years;

Nine (9) restaurants at the end of nine years;

Ten (10) restaurants at the end of ten years;

and continually maintains not less than ten (10) restaurants during the next eighty (80) years. . . .

II.

If at the end of either one, two, three, four, five, six, seven, eight, nine or ten years from the date hereof, or anytime thereafter during the next eighty (80) years, there are less than the respective requisite number of BURGER KING operations or under active construction in the "exclusive territory" pursuant to licenses by Company, this agreement shall terminate and be of no further force and effect. Thereafter, Company may operate or license others for the operation of BURGER KING Restaurants anywhere within the exclusive territory, so long as such restaurants are not within the "Protected Area," as set forth in any BURGER KING Restaurant License to which the Licensee herein is a party.

The prospect of exclusivity for ninety years was clearly intended to be an inducement to Family Dining to develop the territory as prescribed and it appears that it had exactly this effect as Family Dining was to become one of Burger King's most successful franchisees. While Burger King considered Carl Ferris to be somewhat of a problem at various times and one who was overly meticulous with detail, it was nevertheless through his efforts which included obtaining the necessary financing and assuming significant risks, largely without assistance from Burger King, that enabled both parties to benefit from the arrangement.

On August 16, 1963, [nine months early, ed.] Family Dining opened the First Restaurant.... The second Restaurant was opened on July 2, 1965, [two months late, ed.] ... and the third Restaurant was opened October 19, 1966 [four months late, ed.]....

However, by April, 1968, Family Dining had not opened or begun active construction on a fourth Restaurant which, in accordance with the development rate, should have been accomplished by May 10, 1967, and it was apparent that a fifth Restaurant would not be opened by May 10, 1968, the date scheduled. On May 1, 1968, the parties entered into a Modification of the Territorial Agreement (hereinafter "Modification") whereby Burger King agreed to waive Family Dining's failure to comply with the development rate. There is nothing contained in the record which indicates that Burger King received anything of value in exchange for entering this agreement. However, McLamore testified that if the fourth and fifth Restaurants would be built nearly in compliance with the development rate for the fifth year he would overlook the year or so default in the fourth Restaurant. This attitude seems to be consistent with his overall view toward the development rate with respect to which, he testified, was "designed to insure the company of an orderly process of growth which would also enable the company to produce a profit on the sale of its franchises and through the collection of royalties that the restaurants would themselves produce."

The fourth Restaurant was opened on July 1, 1968, [fourteen months late, ed.] ... and the fifth Restaurant was opened on October 17, 1968, [five months late, ed.]....

On April 18, 1969, Ferris forwarded a letter to McLamore pertaining to certain delays in site approval and relating McLamore's earlier statement that there would be no problem in waiving the development schedule for the sixth Restaurant. The letter expressed Ferris' concern regarding compliance with the development rate. By letter dated April 26, 1969, from Howard Walker of Burger King, Ferris was granted a month extension in the development rate. With respect to this extension McLamore testified that "it never crossed my mind to call a default of this agreement on a technicality."

On October 1, 1969, the sixth Restaurant was opened.... The seventh Restaurant was opened on February 2, 1970, ahead of schedule....

At this point in time Burger King was no longer a modest sized franchise system. It had became a wholly owned subsidiary of the Pillsbury Company and had, in fact, evolved into a complex corporate entity. McLamore was elevated to Chairman of the Board of Burger King and, while he remained the chief executive officer for a time, Arthur A. Rosewall was installed as Burger King's President. Ferris was no longer able to expect the close, one to one relationship with McLamore that had previously obtained in his dealings with the company. It seems clear that as a result Family Dining began to experience difficulties in its day to day operations with Burger King.

One of the problem areas which arose concerned site selection. In a typical situation when a franchisee would seek approval for a building site an application would be submitted to the National Development Committee comprised of various Burger King officials. Based on Ferris' prior showing regarding site selection it could be expected that he would have little difficulty in obtaining their approval. In McLamore's view, Ferris was an exceptionally fine franchisee whose ability to choose real estate locations was exceptional. However, in August, 1970, a ... location selected by Ferris was rejected by the National Development Committee. The reasons offered in support of the decision to reject are not entirely clear and it seems that for the most part it was an exercise of discretion. The only plausible reason, given Ferris' expertise, was that the site was 2.7 miles from another Burger King franchise ... outside Family Dining's exclusive territory. Yet Burger King chose not to exercise its discretion in similar circumstances when it permitted another franchisee to build a Restaurant in Devon, Pennsylvania, approximately 3 miles away from an existing Family Dining Restaurant.

... This was during a time, as Burger King management was well aware, where it was one thing to select a location and quite another to actually develop it. That is, local governing bodies were taking a much stricter view toward allowing this type of development. It was also during this time ... Burger King realized that the Bucks–Montgomery territory was capable of sustaining substantially more Restaurants than originally thought.

Amidst these circumstances, the eighth Restaurant was opened ahead of schedule on October 7, 1970, ... [a]nd in December, 1971, Burger King approved Family Dining's proposed sites for two additional Restaurants in Ambler, Pennsylvania and Levittown, Pennsylvania.

In early 1972, Arthur Rosewell became the chief executive officer of Burger King. At this time it also became apparent that the ninth Restaurant would not be opened or under construction by May 10, 1972. On April 27, 1972, in a telephone conversation with McLamore, Ferris once again expressed his concern to Burger King regarding compliance with the development rate. ... [McLamore] indicated to him that, due to the fact that he was in the process of developing four sites at this time, the company would consider he had met, substantially, the requirements of exclusivity. McLamore testified that at that time he had in mind a further delay of 3 to 6 months.

In April, 1973, Burger King approved Family Dining's proposed site for a Restaurant in Warminster, Pennsylvania. However, as of May 10, 1973, neither the ninth or the tenth Restaurant had been opened or under active construction.

A letter dated May 23, 1973, from Helen D. Donaldson, Franchise Documents Administrator for Burger King, was sent to Ferris. The letter provides as follows:

Dear Mr. Ferris:

During a periodic review of all territorial agreements we note that as of this date your development schedule requiring ten restaurants to be open or under construction by May 10, 1973, has not been met. Our records reflect eight stores open in Bucks and/or Montgomery County, and one site approved but not manned.

Under the terms of your territorial agreement failure to have the required number of stores in operation or under active construction constitutes a default of your agreement.

If there are extenuating circumstances about which this office is not aware, we would appreciate your earliest advice.

It is doubtful that the Donaldson letter was intended to communicate to Ferris that the Territorial Agreement was terminated. The testimony of both Rosewall and Leslie W. Paszat, an executive of Burger King, who worked closely with Rosewall on the Family Dining matter indicates that even Burger King had not settled its position at this time. . . .

It seems that throughout this period Burger King treated the matter as something of a "hot potato" subjecting Ferris to contact with several different Burger King officials. . . . Ultimately Paszat was given responsibility for Family Dining and it appears that he provided Ferris with the first clear indication that Burger King considered the Territorial Agreement terminated in his letter of November 6, 1973. Burger King's corporate structure had become so complex that the question of who, when or where the decision was made could not be answered. The abrupt manner in which Burger King's position was communicated to Family Dining, under the circumstances, was not straightforward.

From November, 1973, until some point early in 1975, the parties attempted to negotiate their differences with no success. The reason for the lack of success is understandable given that Burger King from the outset considered exclusivity a non-negotiable item. . . .

Several months before the instant litigation was begun Family Dining informed Burger King that it intended to open a ninth Restaurant on or about May 15, 1975, on Street Road, Warminster, Pennsylvania. . . .

In May, 1975, Burger King filed a complaint, which was the inception of this lawsuit, seeking to enjoin the use of Burger King trademarks by

Family Dining at the Warminster Restaurant. ... On May 13, 1975, the parties reached an agreement on terms under which the Burger King trademarks could be used at the Warminster Restaurant [and at a tenth Restaurant in Willow Grove, the construction of which had begun on March 28, 1975, ed.]. Pursuant to the agreement Burger King filed an amended complaint seeking the instant declaratory relief. ...

DISCUSSION

Family Dining raises several arguments in support of its motion pursuant to Rule 41(b).[2] One of its principal arguments is that the termination provision should be found inoperative because otherwise it would result in a forfeiture to Family Dining. For reasons which have become evident during the presentation of Burger King's case the Court finds Family Dining's position compelling both on legal and equitable grounds and is thus persuaded that the Territorial Agreement should not be declared terminated. ...

In bringing this suit Burger King maintains that the Territorial Agreement is a divisible contract wherein Family Dining promised to open or have under active construction one new Restaurant in each of the first ten years of the contract in exchange for which Burger King promised to grant one additional year of exclusivity for each new Restaurant. This, to be followed by an additional eighty years of exclusivity provided the first ten Restaurants were built on time. In support Burger King relies on the opening language of Article I of the Territorial Agreement which provides that "(f)or a period of one year, beginning on the date hereof, Company will not operate or license ...".... It is thus argued that since Family Dining clearly failed to perform its promises the Court must, in accordance with the express language of Article II, declare the contract terminated. Burger King further argues that because Family Dining did not earn exclusivity beyond the ninth year, upon termination, it could not be found that Family Dining would forfeit anything in which it had an interest.

Contrary to the analysis offered by Burger King, the Court considers the development rate a condition subsequent, not a promise, which operates to divest Family Dining of exclusivity. Where words in a contract raise no duty in and of themselves but rather modify or limit the promisees' right to enforce the promise such words are considered to be a condition. Whether words constitute a condition or a promise is a matter of the intention of the parties to be ascertained from a reasonable construction of the language used, considered in light of the surrounding circumstances. Feinberg v. Automobile Banking Corporation, 353 F.Supp. 508, 512 (E.D.Pa.1973); Williston, *Contracts*, §§ 665, 666. It seems clear that the true purpose of the Territorial Agreement was to create a long-

---

2. It is apparent that if this case were to proceed to the presentation of Family Dining's evidence, Family Dining would attempt to establish that the 1968 Modification modified the development rate and/or that there was an effective waiver of said rate. The Court reaches no conclusion on these grounds.

term promise of exclusivity to act as an inducement to Family Dining to develop Bucks and Montgomery Counties within a certain time frame. A careful reading of the agreement indicates that it raises no duties, as such, in Family Dining. Both Article I and Article II contain language which refers to ninety years of exclusivity subject to limitation. For instance, Article I provides in part that "(t)his Agreement shall remain in effect and licensee shall retain the exclusive territory for a period of ninety (90) years from the date hereof, provided that at the end of one, two. . . ." Failure to comply with the development rate operates to defeat liability on Burger King's promise of exclusivity. Liability, or at least Family Dining's right to enforce the promise, arose upon entering the contract. The fact that Burger King seeks affirmative relief premised on the development rate and the fact that it calls for a specified performance by Family Dining tend to obscure its true nature. Nevertheless, in the Court's view it is a condition subsequent.

Furthermore, the fact that performance is to occur in installments does not necessarily mean that the contract is divisible. Once again, this is a question of the intention of the parties ascertained, if possible, from a reasonable interpretation of the language used. Continental Supermarket Food Service, Inc. v. Soboski, 210 Pa.Super. 304, 232 A.2d 216, 217 (1967). In view of the fact that there was a single promise of exclusivity to have a ninety year duration, assuming the condition subsequent did not occur by a failure to comply with the development rate, the Court believes, consistent with the views previously expressed herein, that the contract was intended to be entire rather than severable.

The question arises whether Burger King has precluded itself from asserting Family Dining's untimeliness on the basis that Burger King did not demand literal adherence to the development rate throughout most of the first ten years of the contract. Nothing is commoner in contracts than for a promisor to protect himself by making his promise conditional. Ordinarily a party would be entitled to have such an agreement strictly enforced, however, before doing so the Court must consider not only the written contract but also the acts and conduct of the parties in carrying out the agreement. As Judge Kraft, in effect, provided in Dempsey v. Stauffer, 182 F.Supp. 806, 810 (E.D.Pa.1960), after one party by conduct indicates that literal performance will not be required, he cannot without notice and a reasonable time begin demanding literal performance.

In the early going Burger King did not demand that Family Dining perform in exact compliance with the development schedule. It failed to introduce any evidence indicating that a change in attitude had been communicated to Family Dining. At the time of the Donaldson letter Family Dining's non-compliance with the development rate was no worse than it was with respect to the fourth and fifth Restaurants. The letter itself was sent by a documents administrator rather than a Burger King official and it seems to imply that the Territorial Agreement would not be terminated. Assuming that at some point between May and November, or even at the time of the Donaldson letter, Ferris realized literal performance would be required, the circumstances of this type of development are such that Burger King was unreasonable in declaring a termination such a short time after, if not concurrent with, notice that literal performance would be required.

Considerable time was consumed in negotiations between November, 1973, until shortly before suit although it appears that these efforts were an exercise in futility given Burger King's view on exclusivity. Moreover, it could be expected that Burger King would have sued to enjoin any further progress by Family Dining, during this lengthy period, just as it did when Family Dining attempted to get the ninth Restaurant under way. The upshot being that the hiatus in development from November, 1973, until active construction began on the ninth and tenth Restaurants is not fully chargeable to Family Dining.

Based on the foregoing the Court concludes that Burger King is not entitled to have the condition protecting its promise strictly enforced.

Moreover and more important, even though a suit for declaratory relief can be characterized as neither legal nor equitable, United States Fidelity & Guaranty Co. v. Koch, 102 F.2d 288, 290 (3d Cir.1939), giving strict effect to the termination provision involves divesting Family Dining of exclusivity, which, in the Court's view, would amount to a forfeiture. As a result the Court will not ignore considerations of fairness and believes that equitable principles, as well, ought to govern the outcome of this suit. Barraclough v. Atlantic Refining, 230 Pa.Super. 276, 326 A.2d 477 (1974).

The Restatement, Contracts, § 302 provides:

"A condition may be excused without other reason if its requirement

"(a) will involve extreme forfeiture or penalty, and

"(b) its existence or occurrence forms no essential part of the exchange for the promisor's performance."

Taking the latter consideration first, it seems clear that throughout the early duration of the contract Burger King was more concerned with a general development of the territory than it was with exact compliance with the terms of the development rate. Burger King offered no evidence that it ever considered literal performance to be critical. In fact, the evidence indicates quite the contrary. Even though McLamore testified that he never contemplated a delay of the duration which occurred with the ninth and tenth Restaurants, he felt a total delay of approximately 19 months with respect to the fourth and fifth Restaurants was nearly in compliance. On the basis of his prior conduct and his testimony considered in its entirety his comments on this point command little weight.

Clearly Burger King's attitude with respect to the development rate changed. Interestingly enough it was sometime after Burger King realized Bucks and Montgomery Counties could support substantially more than ten Restaurants as had been originally thought. It was also at a time after Rosewall replaced McLamore as chief executive officer.

Burger King maintains that Ferris' conduct indicates that he knew strict compliance with the development rate was required. This is based on the several occasions where Ferris expressed concern over non-compliance. However, during the presentation of Burger King's evidence it was established that Ferris was an individual who was overly meticulous with details which caused him to be, in many respects, ignored by Burger King officials. Given this aspect of his personality and Burger King's attitude toward him very little significance can be attached to Ferris' expressions of concern. In short, the evidence fails to establish that either Burger King or Family Dining considered the development rate critical. If it eventually did become critical it was not until very late in the first ten years and in such a way that, in conscience, it cannot be used to the detriment of Family Dining.

As previously indicated, the Court believes that if the right of exclusivity were to be extinguished by termination it would constitute a forfeiture. In arguing that by termination Family Dining will lose nothing that it earned, Burger King overlooks the risks assumed and the efforts expended by Family Dining, largely without assistance from Burger King, in making the venture successful in the exclusive territory. While it is true that Family Dining realized a return on its investment, certainly part of this return was the prospect of continued exclusivity. Moreover, this is not a situation where Burger King did not receive any benefit from the relationship.

In making the promise of exclusivity Burger King intended to induce Family Dining to develop its Restaurants in the exclusive territory. There is no evidence that the failure to fulfill the time feature of this inducement was the result of any intentional or negligent conduct on the part of Family Dining. And at the present time there are ten Restaurants in operation which was all the inducement was intended to elicit. Assuming all ten were built on time Burger King would have been able to expect some definable level of revenue, a percentage of which it lost due to the delay. Burger King did not, however, attempt to establish the amount of this loss at trial.

In any event if Family Dining were forced to forfeit the right of exclusivity it would lose something of incalculable value based on its investment of time and money developing the area, the significant risks assumed and the fact that there remains some 76 years of exclusivity under the Territorial Agreement. Such a loss would be without any commensurate breach on its part since the injury caused to Burger King by the delay is relatively modest and within definable limits. Thus, a termination of the Territorial Agreement would result in an extreme forfeiture to Family Dining.

In accordance with the foregoing the Court finds that under the law and based upon the facts adduced in Burger King's case, it is not entitled to a declaration that the Territorial Agreement is terminated. Therefore, Family Dining's Rule 41(b) motion for an involuntary dismissal is granted.

R & R OF CONNECTICUT, INC. v. STIEGLER

Appellate Court of Connecticut, 1985.
4 Conn.App. 240, 493 A.2d 293.

HULL, JUDGE. This case involves the narrow issue of whether a tenant's late notice of intention to renew a lease of commercial property should be excused on equitable principles. The plaintiff tenant sought an injunction to prohibit the defendant landlord from terminating the lease. The defendant, in her counterclaim, sought a declaratory judgment that the lease would expire on December 31, 1984, because of the plaintiff's failure to exercise its option to extend the lease. The defendant appeals from the judgment of the trial court, A. Aronson, J., that the option to extend the lease has been properly exercised. We find error.

The plaintiff is a tenant of premises located at 172 Washington Street, Hartford, where it operates a supermarket. On June 13, 1979, the defendant leased the premises to Pedro Ortiz. On January 27, 1981, Ortiz assigned the lease to the plaintiff. The term of the lease was for five years and six months, from June 15, 1979, to December 31, 1984. Paragraph six of the lease gave the tenant an option to renew the lease for an additional five-year period which could only be exercised by sending written notice to the landlord at least twelve months prior to December 31, 1984, the termination date of the lease. Paragraph 28 of the lease contained a right of first refusal giving the tenant the right to purchase the property first if the landlord received an offer to buy it.

On January 26, 1984, the defendant notified the plaintiff, in writing, that the lease would terminate on its expiration date of December 31, 1984, because of the plaintiff's failure to exercise the renewal option. On February 6, 1984, counsel for the plaintiff wrote to the defendant's agent advising him that Attorney Arnold E. Bayer, who died on December 14, 1983, had been the attorney for the plaintiff, and stating: "I believe it was probably his intention to send a letter of the clients' intention to renew under the terms of said lease." The letter said the plaintiff wanted to exercise the option and asked the defendant for a reconsideration of the notice of termination. On March 23, 1983, the defendant had entered into an agreement to sell the premises for $425,000 to McDonald's Corporation for a McDonald's restaurant. The defendant's appraiser testified at trial that the fair market value of the property was only $225,000. The defendant was required to deliver the premises to the purchaser "free and clear of all tenancies and parties in possession." The purchase agreement contained no performance date but was dependent on the purchaser being able to close title when it purchased adjoining premises from another party and secured necessary zoning approval and other governmental permits. The plaintiff, upon notice of this agreement on February 24, 1984, did not exercise its right of first refusal on the property.

The court found the McDonald's offer to be a bona fide offer but that in reality it was an option to purchase under certain conditions of benefit to the optionee. It concluded that the loss to the landlord was speculative. It further found that the plaintiff had invested $40,000 and borrowed $390,000 from the small business administration to equip the supermarket. The removal of the fixtures and freezers and loss of business would cost the plaintiff $50,000. Further, there is no suitable location in the area for the plaintiff to relocate its neighborhood type store.

The court succinctly stated the issue to be whether a tenant can exercise late an option to renew a lease, by claiming that his attorney would have properly exercised the option for the tenant, but for the attorney's untimely death, and that equitable considerations will prevent a forfeiture of the lease. The court concluded that Bayer's death, the large monetary loss to be suffered by the plaintiff, the speculative loss which the landlord might incur, and the customer loss from the neighborhood community justified equitable relief for the plaintiff.

The law in Connecticut on this issue is well settled. In F.B. Fountain Co. v. Stein, 97 Conn. 619, 118 A. 47 (1922), the plaintiff tenant was four days late in meeting a thirty day notice requirement for renewal of its lease, with the defendant landlord. The lease was for five years with a privilege of four five year renewals. The tenant had occupied the premises for twenty years prior to the time when it failed to give timely notice of intent to renew the lease. Both the tenant and its sublessees had erected buildings and made improvements on the site. The Supreme Court found error in the trial court's denial of equitable relief because of the court's exclusion of evidence of the value of good will of the plaintiff's business in this location. In so doing, the court stated the rule as follows: "We think the better rule to be that in cases of wilful or gross negligence in failing to fulfil a condition precedent of a lease, equity will never relieve. But in case of mere neglect in fulfilling a condition precedent of a lease, which does not fall within accident or mistake, equity will relieve when the delay has been slight, the loss to the lessor small, and when not to grant relief would result in such hardship to the tenant as to make it unconscionable to enforce literally the condition precedent of the lease." Id., 626–27, 118 A. 47.

The case of Xanthakey v. Hayes, 107 Conn. 459, 140 A. 808 (1928), strongly reaffirmed the F.B. Fountain Co. doctrine, in upholding the granting of an injunction ordering the landlord to execute a renewal of the lease despite untimely notice. The lease was for ten years with a five year extension on sixty days notice before the termination of the lease. Proper notice would have been on December 31, 1926. The tenants gave notice on January 3, 1927. The first day of neglect of notice was a holiday, the second a Sunday, and on the following day, Monday, notice was given. The trial court found that without the renewal of the lease the tenants would lose about $4000 in improvements together with a substantial loss of good will to their business, that the lack of notice was due to mere forgetfulness, and that the landlord suffered no damages from the three day delay. The court then found that case "peculiarly one for the interposition of equity to prevent the consummation of unconscionable hardship to the plaintiffs." *Id.*, 476, 140 A. 808.

In Galvin v. Simons, 128 Conn. 616, 25 A.2d 64 (1942), the Supreme Court ruled for the tenants who were awarded an injunction ordering the landlord to renew a lease. The lease ran from October 10, 1938, to April 30, 1941, with a right of renewal for one year based on ninety days notice before its expiration. The landlord told the tenants that she would record the lease but she did not do so. The tenants lost their copy of the lease and were under the impression that the right to renew could be exercised within sixty days of the expiration of the lease. The tenants had spent $500 on improvements and it would cost $100 to move. In finding that the trial court did not abuse its discretion in finding the notice sufficient, the Supreme Court noted (1) that there was no hint of loss to the lessor from the tenants' use of the property for another year; (2) that no space was available in Cheshire for the tenants' purposes; and (3) that thirteen days delay was a small percentage of the notice required.

The defendant argues that the rule of *F.B. Fountain Co. v. Stein, supra*, has been limited to three types of cases: (1) *F.B. Fountain Co. v. Stein, supra,* where the forfeiture of the buildings and improvements would unjustly enrich the landlord; (2) *Xanthakey v. Hayes, supra*, where the delay was very slight; and (3) *Galvin v. Simons, supra*, where the landlord misrepresented that she would record the lease. The plaintiff claims that the facts of this case bring it within the rules enunciated in these cases.

The plaintiff claims: (1) that the delay was slight, pointing out that in *F.B. Fountain Co.* the tenant was thirty-seven days late on a thirty day notice and in *Galvin* the notice was thirteen days late on a ninety day renewal period; (2) that the plaintiff's delay was not wilful since the trial court found that the tenant may have been neglectful or forgetful but this was excused because of Bayer's death; and (3) that the plaintiff would suffer severe hardship if the lease were not renewed.

An analysis of the *F.B. Fountain Co.* criteria which must be met before equity will grant relief in cases such as this one reveals error in the court's judgment.

(1) *Whether the failure to give notice was mere neglect or gross or wilful negligence*: "As a general rule a party will not be given relief against a mistake induced by his own culpable negligence. . . . But the rule is not inflexible and in many cases relief may be granted although the mistake was not unmixed with some element of negligence, particularly where the other party has been in no way prejudiced." *F.B. Fountain Co. v. Stein, supra*, 626, quoting 21 *Corpus Juris*, Equity § 64, p. 88. The court, in finding Bayer's death to be justification for equitable intervention, found only that the tenant "may have been forgetful or neglectful" in giving notice.

The court's finding fails to state whether the plaintiff's failure to give notice amounted to wilful or gross negligence which would not allow equitable relief or was merely neglect which would permit such relief under *F.B. Fountain Co.* The plaintiff's attorney's statement that he *believed* it was *probably* Bayer's *intention* to send a renewal letter is completely devoid of any probative value. Sanctioning the acceptance of such "evidence" would open the courtroom door to myriad statements of interested lawyers favorable to their clients and lacking any factual basis.

(2) *Whether or not the delay has been slight*: The court made no specific finding in this regard but its reliance on *F.B. Fountain Co.* in granting relief makes such a finding implicit in the court's judgment. By comparison with *F.B. Fountain Co.* (four days late on a thirty day notice), *Xanthakey* (three days late on a sixty day notice), and *Galvin* (thirteen days late on a sixty day notice, applying a percentage factor) we conclude that the delay was slight.

(3) *Whether the loss to the lessor is small*: The propriety of considering the possible loss to the landlord of a more advantageous use of its property was not challenged in the trial court or in this court. Since such evidence is immaterial to the question involved in this case we do not consider the issue of error in the court's rejection of the evidence concerning the McDonald's agreement as "speculative." It was error for the court to consider the evidence in any event. The application of the *F.B. Fountain Co.* rule requires that the landlord be prejudiced by a change in position during the period between the time when notice was due and the time when it was given. In other words, the delay itself must have caused the loss. "(W)here an option is contained in a lease or other contract involving an estate in land, some courts of equity, especially in recent years, have tended to treat the offer as not automatically lapsing on expiration of the option period, as for instance, in case of renewal of a long term lease, where to do so would involve substantial forfeiture and the lessor has not materially changed his position in reliance on the optionee's failure to exercise his option within the stated time. [citations]" 1 Williston, *Contracts* (3d Ed. Jaeger) § 76, pp. 248–49 n. 4.

We do not reach the ultimate question of possible unconscionability if the plaintiff is not granted a renewal of the lease since a new trial is necessary to make a finding on the missing element of the *F.B. Fountain Co.* criteria, that is, the degree of the plaintiff's negligence in failing to give notice. If the court finds this necessary predicate to relief in the plaintiff's favor it will then be in a position to determine the ultimate equitable question involved.

There is error, the judgment is set aside and the case is remanded for further proceedings in accordance with this opinion.

In this opinion the other Judges concurred.

C & J FERTILIZER, INC. v. ALLIED MUTUAL INS. CO.

Supreme Court of Iowa, 1975.
227 N.W.2d 169.

REYNOLDSON, JUSTICE. This action to recover for burglary loss under two separate insurance policies was tried to the court, resulting in a finding plaintiff had failed to establish a burglary within the policy definitions. Plaintiff appeals from judgment entered for defendant. We reverse and remand.

Trial court made certain findings of fact in support of its conclusion reached. Plaintiff operated a fertilizer plant in Olds, Iowa. At time of loss, plaintiff was insured under policies issued by defendant and titled "BROAD FORM STOREKEEPERS POLICY" and "MERCANTILE BURGLARY AND ROBBERY POLICY." Each policy defined "burglary" as meaning,

> . . . the felonious abstraction of insured property (1) from within the premises by a person making felonious entry therein by actual force and violence, of which force and violence there are visible marks made by tools, explosives, electricity or chemicals upon, or physical damage to, the exterior of the premises at the place of such entry. . . .

On Saturday, April 18, 1970, all exterior doors to the building were locked when plaintiff's employees left the premises at the end of the business day. The following day, Sunday, April 19, 1970, one of plaintiff's employees was at the plant and found all doors locked and secure. On Monday, April 20, 1970, when the employees reported for work, the exterior doors were locked, but the front office door was unlocked.

There were truck tire tread marks visible in the mud in the driveway leading to and from the plexiglas door entrance to the warehouse. It was demonstrated this door could be forced open without leaving visible marks or physical damage.

There were no visible marks on the exterior of the building made by tools, explosives, electricity or chemicals, and there was no physical damage to the exterior of the building to evidence felonious entry into the building by force and violence.

Chemicals had been stored in an interior room of the warehouse. The door to this room, which had been locked, was physically damaged and carried visible marks made by tools. Chemicals had been taken at a net loss to plaintiff in the sum of $9,582. Office and shop equipment valued at $400.30 was also taken from the building.

Trial court held the policy definition of "burglary" was unambiguous, there was nothing in the record "upon which to base a finding that the door to plaintiff's place of business was entered feloniously, by actual force and violence," and, applying the policy language, found for defendant.

Certain other facts in the record were apparently deemed irrelevant by trial court because of its view the applicable law required it to enforce the policy provision. Because we conclude different rules of law apply, we also consider those facts.

The "BROAD FORM STOREKEEPERS POLICY" was issued April 14, 1969; the "MERCANTILE BURGLARY AND ROBBERY POLICY" on April 14, 1970. Those policies are in evidence. Prior policies apparently were first purchased in 1968. The agent, who had power to bind insurance coverage for defendant, was told plaintiff would be handling farm chemicals. After inspecting the building then used by plaintiff for storage he made certain suggestions regarding security. There ensued a conversation in which he pointed out there had to be visible evidence of burglary. There was no testimony by anyone that plaintiff was then or thereafter informed the policy to be delivered would define burglary to require "visible marks made by tools, explosives, electricity or chemicals upon, or physical damage to, the exterior of the premises at the place of . . . entry."

The import of this conversation with defendant's agent when the coverage was sold is best confirmed by the agent's complete and vocally-expressed surprise when defendant denied coverage. From what the agent saw (tire tracks and marks on the interior of the building) and his contacts with the investigating officers ". . . the thought didn't enter my mind that it wasn't covered. . . ." From the trial testimony it was obvious the only understanding was that there should be some hard evidence of a third-party burglary vis-a-vis an "inside job." The latter was in this instance effectively ruled out when the thief was required to break an interior door lock to gain access to the chemicals.

The agent testified the insurance was purchased and "the policy was sent out afterwards." The president of plaintiff corporation, a 37–year–old farmer with a high school education, looked at that portion of the policy setting out coverages, including coverage for burglary loss, the amounts of insurance, and the "location and description." He could not recall reading the fine print defining "burglary" on page three of the policy.

Trial court's "findings" must be examined in light of our applicable rules. Ordinarily in a law action tried to the court its findings of fact having adequate evidentiary support shall not be set aside unless induced by an erroneous view of the law. It follows, the rule does not preclude inquiry into the question whether, conceding the truth of a finding of fact, the trial court applied erroneous rules of law which materially affected the decision. Beneficial Finance Company of Waterloo v. Lamos, 179 N.W.2d 573, 578 (Iowa 1970) and citations.

Extrinsic evidence that throws light on the situation of the parties, the antecedent negotiations, the attendant circumstances and the objects they were thereby striving to attain is necessarily to be regarded as relevant to ascertain the actual significance and proper legal meaning of the agreement. Hamilton v. Wosepka, 261 Iowa 299, 306, 154 N.W.2d 164, 168 (1967); 3 *Corbin on Contracts*, 1971 pocket part § 543AA, pp. 91–95.

The question of *interpretation, i.e.,* the meaning to be given contractual words, is one to be determined by the court unless the interpretation depends on extrinsic evidence or on a choice among reasonable inferences to be drawn from extrinsic evidence. *Construction* of a contract means determination of its legal operation—its effect upon the action of the courts. Porter v. Iowa Power and Light Company, 217 N.W.2d 221, 228 (Iowa 1974); 3 *Corbin on Contracts* § 534, pp. 7–9; 4 *Williston on Contracts* § 602, p. 320. "(C)onstruction (of a contract) is always a matter of law for the court." 3 *Corbin on Contracts* § 554, p. 227. "(C)ourts in construing and applying a standardized contract seek to effectuate the reasonable expectations of the average member of the public who accepts it." *Restatement (Second) of Contracts*, [§ 211, cmt. e*]. . . .

Insofar as trial court was construing the policy—that being a matter of law for the court—we are not bound by its conclusions. Neither are we bound by trial court's rule this case is controlled by the fineprint "definition" of burglary, if that rule was erroneously applied below. *Beneficial Finance Company of Waterloo v. Lamos, supra.*

Trial court did find "(T)here does not appear to have been a discussion of the policy provisions between the parties at the time the policy was secured. . . ." That finding is well supported: there is no evidence plaintiff knew of the definition of burglary contained in the policy until after the event. But both parties agree there was conversation concerning the type of insurance and the property to be insured. While plaintiff's president's testimony is ambivalent as to whether it occurred before or after the predecessor policies were issued, the defendant's agent was clear the conversation occurred before any policies were delivered.

There is nothing about trial court's factual findings which precludes this court from construing said contract to arrive at a proper determination of its legal operation as between these parties, or from considering whether the decision appealed from resulted from the application of an erroneous rule of law. And if the definition of "burglary" in defendant's policy is not enforceable here, then trial court's finding there was no evidence of forcible entry through an outside door is not controlling in the disposition of this case.

Plaintiff's theories of recovery based on "reasonable expectations," implied warranty and unconscionability must be viewed in light of accelerating change in the field of contracts.

I. *Revolution in formation of contractual relationships.*

Many of our principles for resolving conflicts relating to written contracts were formulated at an early time when parties of equal strength negotiated in the historical sequence of offer, acceptance, and reduction to writing. The concept that both parties assented to the resulting document had solid footing in fact.

Only recently has the sweeping change in the inception of the document received widespread recognition:

---

* The court's citations to tentative drafts of the Restatement (Second) of Contracts have been updated throughout the opinion. Ed.

Standard form contracts probably account for more than ninety-nine percent of all contracts now made. Most persons have difficulty remembering the last time they contracted other than by standard form; except for casual oral agreements, they probably never have. But if they are active, they contract by standard form several times a day. Parking lot and theater tickets, package receipts, department store charge slips, and gas station credit card purchase slips are all standard form contracts. . . .

. . . The contracting still imagined by courts and law teachers as typical, in which both parties participate in choosing the language of their entire agreement, is no longer of much more than historical importance.

—W. Slawson, *Standard Form Contracts and Democratic Control of Lawmaking Power*, 84 Harv.L.Rev. 529 (1971).

With respect to those interested in buying insurance, it has been observed that:

His chances of successfully negotiating with the company for any substantial change in the proposed contract are just about zero. The insurance company tenders the insurance upon a "take it or leave it" basis. . . .

. . . Few persons solicited to take policies understand the subject of insurance or the rules of law governing the negotiations, and they have no voice in dictating the terms of what is called the contract. They are clear upon two or three points which the agent promises to protect, and for everything else they must sign ready-made applications and accept ready-made policies carefully concocted to conserve the interests of the company. . . . The subject, therefore, is *sui generis,* and the rules of a legal system devised to govern the formation of ordinary contracts between man and man cannot be mechanically applied to it.

—7 *Williston on Contracts* § 900, pp. 29–30 (3d Ed.1963).

It is generally recognized the insured will not read the detailed, cross-referenced, standardized, mass-produced insurance form, nor understand it if he does. 7 *Williston on Contracts* § 906B, p. 300 ("But where the document thus delivered to him is a contract of insurance the majority rule is that the insured is not bound to know its contents"); 3 *Corbin on Contracts* § 559, pp. 265–66 ("One who applies for an insurance policy . . . may not even read the policy, the number of its terms and the fineness of its print being such as to discourage him"); Note, *Unconscionable Contracts: The Uniform Commercial Code*, 45 Iowa L.Rev. 843, 844 (1960) ("It is probably a safe assertion that most involved standardized form contracts are never read by the party who 'adheres' to them. In such situations, the proponent of the form is free to dictate terms most advantageous to himself").

The concept that persons must obey public laws enacted by their own representatives does not offend a fundamental sense of justice: an inherent element of assent pervades the process. But the inevitable result of enforcing all provisions of the adhesion contract, frequently, as here, delivered subsequent to the transaction and containing provisions never assented to, would be an abdication of judicial responsibility in face of basic unfairness and a recognition that persons' rights shall be controlled by private lawmakers without the consent, express or implied, of those affected. A question is also raised whether a court may constitutionally allow that power to exist in private hands except where appropriate safeguards are present, including a right to meaningful judicial review. *See W. Slawson, supra* at 553. . . .

The mass-produced boiler-plate "contracts," necessitated and spawned by the explosive growth of complex business transactions in a burgeoning population left courts frequently frustrated in attempting to arrive at just results by applying many of the traditional contract-construing stratagems. As long as fifteen years ago Professor Llewellyn, reflecting on this situation in his book, *The Common Law Tradition—Deciding Appeals*, pp. 362–71 wrote,

> What the story shows thus far is first, scholars persistently off-base while judges grope over well-nigh a century in irregular but dogged fashion for escape from a recurring discomfort of imbalance that rests on what is in fact substantial *non* agreement despite perfect semblance of agreement. (pp. 367–368). . . .

> The answer, I suggest, is this: Instead of thinking about "assent" to boiler-plate clauses, we can recognize that so far as concerns the specific, there is no assent at all. What has in fact been assented to, specifically, are the few dickered terms, and the broad type of transaction, and but one thing more. That one thing more is a blanket assent (not a specific assent) to any not unreasonable or indecent terms the seller may have on his form, which do not alter or eviscerate the reasonable meaning of the dickered terms. The fine print which has not been read has no business to cut under the reasonable meaning of those dickered terms which constitute the dominant and only real expression of agreement, but much of it commonly belongs in." (p. 370)

. . .

Plaintiff's claim it should be granted relief under the legal doctrines of reasonable expectations, implied warranty and unconscionability should be viewed against the above backdrop.

II.   *Reasonable expectations.*

This court adopted the doctrine of reasonable expectations in Rodman v. State Farm Mutual Ins. Co., 208 N.W.2d 903, 905–908 (Iowa 1973). The *Rodman* court approved the following articulation of that concept:

> The objectively reasonable expectations of applicants and intended beneficiaries regarding the terms of insurance contracts will be honored even though painstaking study of the policy provisions would have negated those expectations.

—208 N.W.2d at 906.

See Gray v. Zurich Insurance Company, 65 Cal.2d 263, 54 Cal.Rptr. 104, 107–108, 419 P.2d 168, 171–172 (1966); *Restatement (Second) of Contracts* [§ 211, cmts. e and f]; 1 *Corbin on Contracts* § 1, p. 2 ("That portion of the field of law that is classified and described as the law of contracts attempts the realization of reasonable expectations that have been induced by the making of a promise"); 7 *Williston on Contracts* § 900, pp. 33–34 ("Some courts, recognizing that very few insureds even try to read and understand the policy or application, have declared that the insured is justified in assuming that the policy which is delivered to him has been faithfully prepared by the company to provide the protection against the risk which he had asked for. ... Obviously this judicial attitude is a far cry from the old motto '*caveat emptor*.' ").

At comment f to § [211] of *Restatement (Second) of Contracts*, ... we find the following analysis of the reasonable expectations doctrine:

> Although customers typically adhere to standardized agreements and are bound by them without even appearing to know the standard terms in detail, they are not bound to unknown terms which are beyond the range of reasonable expectation. A debtor who delivers a check to his creditor with the amount blank does not authorize the insertion of an infinite figure. Similarly, a party who adheres to the other party's standard terms does not assent to a term if the other party has reason to believe that the adhering party would not have accepted the agreement if he had known that the agreement contained the particular term. Such a belief or assumption may be shown by the prior negotiations or inferred from the circumstances. Reason to believe may be inferred from the fact that the term is bizarre or oppressive, from the fact that it eviscerates the non-standard terms explicitly agreed to, or from the fact that it eliminates the dominant purpose of the transaction. The inference is reinforced if the adhering party never had an opportunity to read the term, or if it is illegible or otherwise hidden from view. This rule is closely related to the policy against unconscionable terms and the rule of interpretation against the draftsman.

Nor can it be asserted the above doctrine does not apply here because plaintiff knew the policy contained the provision now complained of and cannot be heard to say it reasonably expected what it knew was not there. A search of the record discloses no such knowledge.

The evidence does show, as above noted, a "dicker" for burglary insurance coverage on chemicals and equipment. The negotiation was for what was actually expressed in the policies' "Insuring Agreements": the insurer's promise "To pay for loss by burglary or by robbery of a watchman, while the premises are not open for business, of merchandise, furniture, fixtures and equipment within the premises. . . ."

In addition, the conversation included statements from which the plaintiff should have understood defendant's obligation to pay would not arise where the burglary was an "inside job." Thus the following exclusion should have been reasonably anticipated:

Exclusions

> This policy does not apply:
>
> . . .
>
> (b) to loss due to any fraudulent, dishonest or criminal act by any Insured, a partner therein, or an officer, employee, director, trustee or authorized representative thereof. . . .

But there was nothing relating to the negotiations with defendant's agent which would have led plaintiff to reasonably anticipate defendant would bury within the definition of "burglary" another exclusion denying coverage when, no matter how extensive the proof of a third-party buglary, no marks were left on the exterior of the premises. This escape clause, here triggered by the burglar's talent (an investigating law officer, apparently acquainted with the current modus operandi, gained access to the steel building without leaving any marks by leaning on the overhead plexiglas door while simultaneously turning the locked handle), was never read to or by plaintiff's personnel, nor was the substance explained by defendant's agent.

Moreover, the burglary "definition" which crept into this policy comports neither with the concept a layman might have of that crime, nor with a legal interpretation. The most plaintiff might have reasonably anticipated was a policy requirement of visual evidence (abundant here) indicating the burglary was an "outside" not an "inside" job. The exclusion in issue, masking as a definition, makes insurer's obligation to pay turn on the skill of the burglar, not on the event the parties bargained for: a bonafide third party burglary resulting in loss of plaintiff's chemicals and equipment.

. . . [T]he doctrine [of reasonable expectations] demands reversal and judgment for plaintiff.

III. *Implied warranty.*

Plaintiff should also prevail because defendant breached an implied warranty that the policy later delivered would be reasonably fit for its intended purpose: to set out in writing the obligations of the parties (1) without altering or impairing the fair meaning of the protection bargained for when read alone, and (2) in terms that are neither in the particular nor in the net manifestly unreasonable and unfair. *See* K. Llewellyn, *The Common Law Tradition—Deciding Appeals,* p. 371.

More than 75 years ago this court, without statutory support, recognized in contracts for sale of tangible property there was a warranty implied by law that the goods sold "were reasonably fit for the purpose for which they were intended." Alpha Check–Rower Co. v. Bradley, 105 Iowa 537, 547, 75 N.W. 369, 372 (1898). This seminal concept of basic fairness grew by progressive court decisions and statutory enactments into that network of protection which today guards the chattel purchaser from exploitation.

> The final and perhaps most significant characteristic of insurance contracts differentiating them from ordinary, negotiated commercial contract, is the increasing tendency of the public to look upon the insurance policy not as a contract but as a special form of chattel. The typical applicant buys "protection" much as he buys groceries.

—7 *Williston on Contracts* § 900, p. 34.

We would be derelict in our duty to administer justice if we were not to judicially know that modern insurance companies have turned to mass advertising to sell "protection." A person who has been incessantly assured a given company's policies will afford him complete protection is unlikely to be wary enough to search his policy to find a provision nullifying his burglary protection if the burglar breaks open an inside, but not an outside, door.

There is little justification in depriving purchasers of merchandized "protection" of those remedies long available to purchasers of goods:

> Although implied warranties of fitness for intended purpose have traditionally been attached only to sales of tangible products, there is no reason why they should not be attached to "sales of promises" as well. Whether a product is tangible or intangible, its creator ordinarily has reason to know of the purposes for which the buyer intends to use it, and buyers ordinarily rely on the creator's skill or judgment in furnishing it. The reasonable consumer for example depends on an insurance agent and insurance company to sell him a policy that "works" for its intended purpose in much the same way that he depends on a television salesman and television manufacturer. In neither case is he likely to be competent to judge the fitness of the product himself; in both, he must rely on common knowledge and the creator's advertising and promotion.

—W. *Slawson, supra* at 546–47.

See also K. Llewellyn, *The Common Law Tradition—Deciding Appeals,* pp. 370–71.

Effective imposition of an implied warranty would encourage insurers to make known to insurance buyers those provisions which would limit the implied warranty inherent in the situation. These exclusions would then become part of the initial bargaining. Such provisions, mandated by the Uniform Commercial Code to be "conspicuous" in the sale of goods (§ 554.2316, The Code) [UCC § 2–316], should be conspicuously presented by the insurer in the sale of protection. This would be no more difficult than the manner in which they advertise their product's desirable features. *See* Henningsen v. Bloomfield Motors, Inc., 32 N.J. 358, 400, 161 A.2d 69, 93 (1960). From a public policy viewpoint, such a requirement (in order to enforce what is essentially an exclusion) might promote meaningful competition among insurers in eliminating technical policy provisions which drain away bargained-for protection. The ultimate benefit would be a chance for knowledgeable selection by insurance purchasers among various coverages. . . .

Ten years ago this court banished the ancient doctrine of *caveat emptor* as the polestar for business. Syester v. Banta, 257 Iowa 613, 616, 133 N.W.2d 666, 668 (1965). In Mease v. Fox, 200 N.W.2d 791 (Iowa 1972) we joined a scant handful of courts pioneering the concept that implied warranty relief was not the captive of chattel sales law, but was available to resolve long-standing inequities in the law of dwelling leases. It is now time to provide buyers of protection the same safeguards provided for buyers of personalty and lessees of dwellings.

The policy provided by defendant in this instance breached the implied warranty of fitness for its intended purpose. It altered and impaired the fair meaning of the bargain these parties made for plaintiff's insurance protection. This law theory further requires reversal of trial court's decision.

IV. *Unconscionability.*

Plaintiff is also entitled to a reversal because the liability-avoiding provision in the definition of the burglary is, in the circumstances of this case, unconscionable.

We have already noted the policies were not even before the negotiating persons when the protection was purchased. The fair inference to be drawn from the testimony is that the understanding contemplated only visual evidence of bona-fide burglary to eliminate the risk of an "inside job."

The policies in question contain a classic example of that proverbial fine print (six point type as compared with the twenty-four point type appearing on the face of the policies: "BROAD FORM STOREKEEPERS POLICY" and "MERCANTILE BURGLARY AND ROBBERY POLICY") which "becomes visible only after the event." Such print is additionally suspect when, instead of appearing logically in the "exclusions" of the policies, it poses as a part of an esoteric definition of burglary. A similar contract containing a vast volume of printed conditions neither mentioned nor discussed between the parties once elicited the following comment from this court,

> It is enough at this time to say that, if it be a contract it is like the Apostle's conception of the human frame, "fearfully and wonderfully made," and one upon the construction and effect of which a competent and experienced lawyer may spend days of careful study, without exhausting its possibilities.

—New Prague Flouring Mill Co. v. Spears, 194 Iowa 417, 438–39, 189 N.W. 815, 824 (1922).

The situation before us plainly justifies application of the unconscionability doctrine:

Standardized contracts such as insurance policies, drafted by powerful commercial units and put before individuals on the "accept this or get nothing" basis, are carefully scrutinized by the courts for the purpose of avoiding enforcement of "unconscionable" clauses.

—6A *Corbin on Contracts* § 1376, p. 21.

The rule of selective elimination of unconscionable provisions is articulated in . . . *Restatement (Second) of Contracts* [§ 208]:

§ [208]. Unconscionable Contract or Term

If a contract or term thereof is unconscionable at the time the contract is made a court may refuse to enforce the contract, or may enforce the remainder of the contract without the unconscionable term, or may so limit the application of any unconscionable term as to avoid any unconscionable result.

The following statement appears in comment *"a. Scope":*

Particularly in the case of standardized agreements, the rule of this Section permits the court to pass directly on the unconscionability of the contract or clause rather than to avoid unconscionable results by interpretation.

Comment *"d. Weakness in the bargaining process"* incorporates the following observation,

(G)ross inequality of bargaining power, together with terms unreasonably favorable to the stronger party, may confirm indications that the transaction involved elements of deception or compulsion, or may show that the weaker party had no meaningful choice, no real alternative, or did not in fact assent or appear to assent to the unfair terms.

The resources of a court to avoid unconscionable provisions are not exhausted after a determination of inapplicability of the *contra proferentem* rule: "Even in such a case, the court may refuse to enforce an unconscionable provision and may give such remedy as justice requires. . . . A contractor may defeat his own ends by the use of complex printed forms devised with intent to get the most and to give the least." 3 *Corbin on Contracts* § 559, pp. 270–71. *See* Campbell Soup Co. v. Wentz, 172 F.2d 80 (3 Cir.1948); *Henningsen v. Bloomfield Motors, Inc., supra*; § 554.2302, The Code [UCC § 2–302].

The following reference to the *Henningsen* court and to the unconscionability relief in the commercial code (§ 554.2302, The Code) [UCC § 2–302] appears in *Grismore, supra*, § 294, pp. 508–509:

After an extensive discussion of some of the cases, the court took the forthright position that the attempted disclaimer in the instant case was "so inimical to the public good as to compel an adjudication of its invalidity." This court said what it meant instead of interpreting or constructing its way to the just result. This frontier decision may help to guide other courts to add to the development of a doctrine of unconscionability which will gain the necessary certainty by the traditional process of case-by-case adjudication.

Adding to the probability that unconscionability will be the stated basis for refusing to enforce oppressive contracts or provisions in the future is the Uniform Commercial Code provision which permits courts to police contracts on this basis. . . . (T)he section is an express recognition of the basic principle. Though the Code is technically applicable only to contracts for the sale of goods, its influence cannot help but be felt in other types of transactions so that most of our courts can say what they mean in refusing to enforce harsh contracts or provisions. Those who would obstruct the development of the unconscionability concept on grounds of uncertainty, indefiniteness and judicial lawmaking, must be characterized as misunderstanding the dynamic nature of the common law and statutory interpretation.

The Iowa court quoted extensively from *Henningsen* and adopted its sound reasoning in State Farm Mut. Auto. Ins. Co. v. Anderson–Weber, Inc., [252 Iowa 1289, 110 N.W.2d 449 (1961)].

A policy of relying solely on traditional techniques of construction in an effort to avoid the effect of unconscionable provisions ultimately compounds the problem:

> First, since they (such techniques) all rest on the admission that the clauses in question are permissible in purpose and content, they invite the draftsman to recur to the attack. Give him time, and he will make the grade. Second, since they do not face the issue, they fail to accumulate either experience or authority in the needed direction: that of making out for any given type of transaction what the *minimum decencies* are which a court will insist upon as essential to an enforceable bargain of a given type, or as being inherent in a bargain of that type. Third, since they purport to construe, and do not really construe, nor are intended to . . . they seriously embarrass later efforts . . . to get at the true meaning of those wholly legitimate contracts and clauses which call for their meaning to be got at instead of avoided.

—Llewellyn, *Book Review*, 52 Harv.L.Rev. 700, 703 (1939).

See Note, supra, 45 Iowa L.Rev. at 845–46 (1960). In the same vein, *see* 3 *Corbin on Contracts* § 561, p. 279:

> (A) better brand of justice may be delivered by a court that is clearly conscious of its own processes, than by one that states hard-bitten traditional rules and doctrines and then attains an instinctively felt justice by an avoidance of them that is only half-conscious, accompanied by an extended exegesis worthy of a medieval theologian.

It should be observed that even less justice is attained where, as here, trial court simply stopped with the hard-bitten rules.

Commentators suggest a court considering a claim of unconscionability should examine the factors of assent, unfair surprise, notice, disparity of bargaining power and substantive unfairness. W. *Slawson, supra* at 564, and citations, n. 79. We have already touched on those considerations in the factual discussions, above. In addition, it would seem appropriate, in every trial when the unconscionability of a contractual provision is a viable issue, to permit either party the right granted by § 554.2302(2), The Code [UCC § 2–302(2)]:

> When it is claimed or appears to the court that the contract or any clause thereof may be unconscionable the parties shall be afforded a reasonable opportunity to present evidence as to its commercial setting, purpose and effect to aid the court in making the determination.

In the case *sub judice,* plaintiff's evidence demonstrated the definitional provision was unconscionable. Defendant never offered any evidence, let alone evidence which might support a conclusion the provision in issue, considered in its commercial setting, was either a reasonable limitation on the protection it offered or should have been reasonably anticipated by plaintiff.

Trial court's decision must be reversed because the above provision is unconscionable in view of all the circumstances, including the initial negotiations of these parties.

We reverse and remand for judgment in conformance herewith.

Reversed and remanded.

HARRIS and McCORMICK, JJ., concur.

MASON and RAWLINGS, JJ., concur in Divisions I, II and IV and the result.

LeGRAND, J., MOORE, C.J., and REES and UHLENHOPP, JJ., dissent.

LeGRAND, JUSTICE (dissenting). I dissent from the result reached by the majority because it ignores virtually every rule by which we have heretofore adjudicated such cases and affords plaintiff *ex post facto* insurance coverage which it not only did not buy but which it *knew* it did not buy.
. . .

While it may be very well to talk in grand terms about "mass advertising" by insurance companies and "incessant" assurances as to coverage which mislead the "unwary," particularly about "fine-print" provisions, such discussion should somehow be related to the case under review. Our primary duty, after all, is to resolve *this* dispute for *these* litigants under *this* record.

There is total silence in this case concerning any of the practices the majority finds offensive; nor is there any claim plaintiff was beguiled by such conduct into believing it had more protection than it actually did.

The record is even stronger against the majority's fine-print argument, the stereotype accusation which serves as a *coup de grâce* in all insurance cases. Except for larger type on the face sheet and black (but not larger) print to designate divisions and sub-headings, the entire policies are of one size and style of print. To compare the *face* sheet with the body of the policy is like comparing a book's jacket cover with the narrative content; and the use of black type or other means of emphasis to separate one part of an instrument from another is an approved editorial expedient which serves to *assist,* not *hinder,* readability. In fact many of our opinions, including that of the majority in the instant case, resort to that device.

Tested by any objective standard, the size and style of type used cannot be fairly described as "fine print." The majority's description, right or wrong, of the plight of consumers generally should not be the basis for resolving the case now before us.

Like all other appeals, this one should be decided on what the record discloses—a fact which the majority concedes but promptly disregards.

Crucial to a correct determination of this appeal is the disputed provision of each policy defining burglary as "the felonious abstraction of insured property ... by a person making felonious entry ... by actual force and violence, of which force and violence there are visible marks made by tools, explosives, electricity or chemicals upon, or physical damage to, the exterior of the premises at the place of such entry...." The starting point of any consideration of that definition is a determination whether it is ambiguous. Yet the majority does not even mention ambiguity.

The purpose of such a provision, of course, is to omit from coverage "inside jobs" or those resulting from fraud or complicity by the assured. The overwhelming weight of authority upholds such provisions as legitimate in purpose and unambiguous in application. [citations]

Once this indisputable fact is recognized, plaintiff's arguments virtually collapse. We may not—at least we *should* not—by any accepted standard of construction meddle with contracts which clearly and plainly state their meaning simply because we dislike that meaning, even in the case of insurance policies. [citations]

Nor can the doctrine of reasonable expectations be applied here. We adopted that rule in Rodman v. State Farm Mutual Automobile Insurance Company, 208 N.W.2d 903, 906, 907 (Iowa 1973). We refused, however to apply it in that case, where we said:

> The real question here is whether the principle of reasonable expectations should be extended to cases where an ordinary layman would not misunderstand his coverage from a reading of the policy and where there are no circumstances attributable to the insurer which foster coverage expectations. Plaintiff does not contend he misunderstood the policy. He did not read it. He now asserts in retrospect that

if he had read it he would not have understood it. He does not say he was misled by conduct or representations of the insurer. He simply asked trial court to rewrite the policy to cover his loss because if he had purchased his automobile insurance from another company the loss would have been covered, he did not know it was not covered, and if he had known it was not covered he would have purchased a different policy. Trial court declined to do so. We believe trial court correctly refused in these circumstances to extend the principle of reasonable expectations to impose liability.

Yet here the majority would extend the doctrine far beyond the point of refusal in *Rodman*. Here we have affirmative and unequivocal testimony from an officer and director of the plaintiff corporation that he knew the disputed provision was in the policies because "it was just like the insurance policy I have on my farm."

I cannot agree plaintiff may now assert it reasonably expected from these policies something it knew was not there.

These same observations should dispose of plaintiff's claim of implied warranty, a theory incidentally for which there is no case authority at all. The majority apparently seeks to bring insurance contracts within the ambit of the Uniform Commercial Code governing sales of *goods*. I believe the definitional section of the Code itself precludes that notion. *See* § 554.2105, The Code [UCC § 2–105]. This *should* put an end to the majority's argument that buying insurance protection is the same as buying groceries. The complete absence of support from other jurisdictions would also suggest it is indefensible. At least it has done so to some courts. *See* Drabbels v. Skelly Oil Company, 155 Neb. 17, 50 N.W.2d 229, 231 (Neb.1951).

The remaining ground upon which the majority invalidates the policies—unconscionability—has also been disavowed by the great majority of courts which have decided the question, usually in connection with public policy considerations. [citations]

For these several reasons—the principal one being that the findings of the trial court have substantial evidentiary support—I would affirm the judgment. . . .

PROBLEMS

33. C, a carrier, agreed to carry goods for A. The agreement provided that C would not be liable for damage to A's cargo unless "written notice of claim for loss" is given within 15 days after delivery of goods. C was aware that A's cargo was damaged during the voyage. Within 10 days of delivery, A gave written notice of damage and oral notice of claim, and C inspected the goods. A did not give written notice of claim until 26 days after delivery of the goods. Is A barred from recovery against C?

34. A contracts to make repairs on B's house for which B agrees to pay $10,000 on the express condition that repairs are completed by October 1. The

repairs are completed on October 2. Is A entitled to recover the price provided by the agreement?

35.   (a) Tenant purchased a restaurant from a prior tenant and with the landlord's consent assumed the existing lease that had six years to run with an option to renew for 24 additional years by giving notice at least six months prior to expiration of the lease. The restaurant was highly successful and the tenant invested heavily in physical improvements. About 2 months prior to the expiration of the lease, Tenant received a note from the landlord inquiring about Tenant's plans to vacate. Tenant consulted his attorney who drafted and sent a notice of exercise of the option to the landlord, following which Tenant brought an action for specific performance. What result?

(b) Tenant entered into a three-year lease of commercial premises. The lease gave Tenant an option to purchase the property for $200,000 during the first year. The lease provided that the option period could be extended for an additional year by the payment of $10,000 on or before January 1 of the second year. On January 1, Tenant wrote a check in the amount of $10,000 payable to the landlord and placed it in the mail slot of the landlord's door. The landlord deposited the check but Tenant's bank returned the check unpaid with the notation, "Drawn on Uncollected Funds." Tenant then sent a notice of exercise of the option and sued for specific performance. What result?

36.   Plaintiff deposited $30,000 with an escrow agent pursuant to an agreement with the owner of a department store building. The $30,000 was to be applied to a $555,000 purchase price, the balance to be paid on or before October 31. Plaintiff made no commitment to purchase. The agreement provided that if the balance were not paid by October 31, it would be forfeited to the seller and neither party would have any further rights against the other. Plaintiff failed to tender the balance by October 31 and defendant declared the money forfeited. Soon thereafter, plaintiff tendered the balance and now sues for specific performance or damages. What result? Would your analysis be different if plaintiff had made a commitment to purchase?

SECTION 9. CONDITIONS OF SATISFACTION

(Calamari & Perillo on Contracts § 11.37)

WESTERN HILLS, OREGON, LTD. v. PFAU
Supreme Court of Oregon, 1973.
265 Or. 137, 508 P.2d 201.

MCALLISTER, JUSTICE. This is a suit to compel specific performance of an agreement to purchase real property. The plaintiff, the owner of the property, is a limited partnership. Defendants are members of a joint venture, formed for the purpose of purchasing the property from plaintiff and developing it. The trial court found that plaintiff was entitled to specific performance of the agreement, and entered its decree accordingly.

Defendants appeal, contending that they were excused from performing by a failure of a condition contained in the agreement, and that the agreement is too indefinite to permit specific enforcement.

Plaintiff Western Hills owned a tract of approximately 286 acres in Yamhill County which it had listed for sale with a Salem real estate firm. Defendant Pfau, who is also a real estate broker, heard about this listing early in 1970. He contacted the other defendants, and they jointly submitted a proposal to purchase the property. Their original proposal was not accepted, but negotiations with Western Hills took place which culminated, on or about March 6, 1970, in the execution of the written agreement which is the subject of this suit. The agreement consists of a filled-in form entitled "Exchange Agreement" together with several attached documents. Generally, it provides that in exchange for the Yamhill County property, defendants agreed to pay Western Hills $15,000 in cash, to convey to Western Hills four parcels of real property "subject to appraisal and acceptance" by Western Hills, and to pay a balance of $173,600 on terms specified in the agreement. In addition to other terms not material to this appeal, the agreement provides:

> Closing of transaction is subject to ability of purchasers to negotiate with City of McMinnville as to a planned development satisfactory to both first and second parties within 90 days from date. A reasonable extension not to exceed 6 months to be granted if necessary.

Defendants made preliminary proposals for a planned development to the McMinnville Planning Commission, but, although the Commission's reaction to these proposals was favorable, defendants abandoned their attempts to secure approval of a development plan. In September, 1970, defendant Pfau, who represented the other defendants in the transaction, met with some of the partners in Western Hills and notified them that defendants did not wish to go through with the purchase. Western Hills refused to release defendants from the agreement. This suit followed.

Defendants contend that their obligation to purchase the property never became absolute because the condition quoted above was never fulfilled. It appears from the evidence that defendants did not proceed with their application for Planning Commission approval of a planned development because they believed the development would be too expensive, primarily because city sewers would not be available to serve the property for several years. Immediate development would have required the developers to provide a private system of sewage treatment and disposal.

It also appears that at the time they executed the agreement, defendants knew that city sewers would not be available for some time. Defendants' initial offer of purchase included a proposal that the closing of the transaction be subject to satisfactory sewer development. This term was deleted from the final agreement because, according to plaintiff's witnesses, the parties knew that sewers would not be available. Pfau testified that he agreed to the deletion of that term because he was led to believe that the provision for approval of a planned development accomplished the same thing.

The question is whether defendants were excused from performing their agreement to purchase the property because they never secured the city's approval of a "satisfactory" planned development, when the evidence shows that they abandoned their application for an approved planned development because the expense of providing an alternative sewer system made the development financially unattractive. In Anaheim Co. v. Holcombe, 246 Or. 541, 426 P.2d 743 (1967) we considered an earnest money agreement which contained a provision making the purchaser's offer "contingent on obtaining a loan of $25,000." We held that when an agreement contains such a term, it imposes upon the vendee an implied condition that he make a reasonable effort to procure the loan. 246 Or. at 547, 426 P.2d 743. *See, also,* Aldrich v. Forbes, 237 Or. 559, 570, 385 P.2d 618, 391 P.2d 748 (1964). In the present case defendants had a similar duty, arising by implication, to make a reasonable effort to secure the city's approval of a planned development. As related above, defendants abandoned their attempt to secure the approval of the city Planning Commission in spite of that body's favorable reaction to their initial proposals. There was never any indication that defendants' plan was likely to be rejected.

The condition required, however, not only approval of a planned development, but of a development which was "satisfactory" to the parties. When a contract makes a party's duty to perform conditional on his personal satisfaction the courts will give the condition its intended effect. *See, generally,* 3A *Corbin on Contracts,* 78–109, §§ 644–648; 5 *Williston on Contracts* (3d ed. 1961) 189–218, §§ 675A, 675B; *Restatement of Contracts* § 265. Discussing such contracts, this court said in Johnson v. School District No. 12, 210 Or. 585, 590–591, 312 P.2d 591, 593 (1957):

> ... Such contracts are generally grouped into two categories:
>
> (1) Those which involve taste, fancy or personal judgment, the classical example being a commission to paint a portrait. In such cases the promisor is the sole judge of the quality of the work, and his right to reject, if in good faith, is absolute and may not be reviewed by court or jury.
>
> (2) Those which involve utility, fitness or value, which can be measured against a more or less objective standard. In these cases, although there is some conflict, we think the better view is that performance need only be "reasonably satisfactory," and if the promisor refuses the proffered performance, the correctness of his decision and the adequacy of his grounds are subject to review.

The condition with which we are concerned in this case properly belongs in the first of these categories as it requires the exercise of the parties' personal judgment. There is no objective test by which a court or jury could determine whether a particular development plan ought to be "satisfactory" to reasonable men in defendants' position. The condition is similar to that in Mattei v. Hopper, 51 Cal.2d 119, 330 P.2d 625 (1958) in which the purchaser's duty under a land sale contract was "subject to Coldwell Banker & Company obtaining leases satisfactory to the purchaser." In a suit by the purchaser to compel specific performance, the seller contended that because of this provision there was no mutuality of obligation. The court held that there was a valid contract. Discussing the two types of "satisfaction" clauses, the court said:

> . . . However, it would seem that the factors involved in determining whether a lease is satisfactory to the lessor are too numerous and varied to permit the application of a reasonable man standard as envisioned by this line of cases. . . .
>
> This multiplicity of factors which must be considered in evaluating a lease shows that this case more appropriately falls within the second line of authorities dealing with "satisfaction" clauses, being those involving fancy, taste, or judgment. Where the question is one of judgment, the promisor's determination that he is not satisfied, when made in good faith, has been held to be a defense to an action on the contract.

330 P.2d at 627. The condition in the present case is similar to that in *Mattei* in another respect as well. In that case as in this one the question of satisfaction was not concerned with the quality of the other party's performance. The court in *Mattei* held that the general rule was nevertheless applicable:

> . . . Even though the "satisfaction" clauses discussed in the above-cited cases dealt with performances to be received as parts of the agreed exchanges, the fact that the leases here which determined plaintiff's satisfaction were not part of the performance to be rendered is not material. The standard of evaluating plaintiff's satisfaction—good faith—applies with equal vigor to this type of condition. . . .

Id. As in *Mattei* we are concerned in this case with a "satisfaction" clause of the type requiring the exercise of personal judgment as to a matter which was not part of the other party's agreed performance. The test, as indicated, is the promisor's real, not feigned, dissatisfaction. *See* Johnson v. School District, *supra*, 210 Or. at 591, 312 P.2d 591.

It is clear from the authorities, however, that this dissatisfaction must be not only bona fide and in good faith, but also must relate to the specific subject matter of the condition. General dissatisfaction with the bargain will not suffice.

> . . . Where a promise is conditional, expressly or impliedly, on his own satisfaction, he must give fair consideration to the matter. A refusal to examine the . . . performance, or a rejection of it, not in reality based on its unsatisfactory nature but on fictitious grounds or none at all, will amount to prevention of performance of the condition and excuse it.

5 *Williston, op. cit.* 203–204. As Corbin points out, although the promisor is under no duty if, in good faith, he is dissatisfied with a performance to be rendered to his personal satisfaction, nevertheless

> . . . (n)ot infrequently it is possible to prove that the defendant is satisfied in fact, that the work has been done exactly as he specified, and that his dissatisfaction is either with his own specifications or merely with having to pay money that he prefers to use otherwise. . . .

3A *Corbin, op. cit.* 92.

It is inherent in the requirement that dissatisfaction be bona fide and in good faith that the promisor cannot be allowed to base a claim of dissatisfaction on circumstances which were known or anticipated by the parties at the time of contracting.[1] In the present case the evidence is clear that the defendants entered the agreement with full knowledge that city sewer service would not be immediately available and that their development of the property would have to include a sewage disposal system of some kind. The *Brydon* case is in point and its reasoning is persuasive. Although defendants were entitled under the contract to be the judges of their own satisfaction with any development plan that might be approved by the city, they should not be permitted to rely on the "satisfaction" clause in order to reject the contract because of an expense known and contemplated at the time of contracting. We hold, therefore, that defendants were not justified in abandoning their attempts to secure city approval of a development plan simply because of the expense of providing a sewer system which they knew when they entered the contract would have to be provided as a part of the development. Not having performed their duty to use reasonable diligence to obtain city approval of a development plan, defendants may not rely on the nonoccurrence of the condition. *Anaheim Co. v. Holcombe, supra.* . . .

The decree of the trial court is affirmed.

INDOE v. DWYER

Superior Court of New Jersey, Law Division, 1980.
176 N.J.Super. 594, 424 A.2d 456, 15 A.L.R.4th 752.

Gaynor, J. S. C. These cross-motions for summary judgment involve primarily the scope and effect of an attorney approval clause in a contract for the purchase of real estate. A secondary question relates to the binding effect upon a husband of such a contract executed solely by the wife where the only evidence of the husband's interest was a provision in the contract providing that the deed was to be taken in both names. The primary issue

---

1. *See* Baltimore & Ohio R. Co. v. Brydon, 65 Md. 198, 3 A. 306, 9 A. 126 (1886):

> . . . [The coal was] to be satisfactory to the officers who were named. But this term of the contract did not give them a capricious or arbitrary discretion to reject it. . . . Certainly they were not obliged to accept the coal, if they thought it was not fit for the uses contemplated by the contract; *neither on the other hand would they be justified in rejecting it for the reason that it did not possess qualities, which at the time of the contract it was known by the parties that it did not possess.* . . . " 65 Md. At 22, 3A. At 309, 9A. 126. (Emphasis added.) . . .

presented is one of first impression and, in our opinion, must be resolved by an interpretation which permits an unlimited application of the attorney approval provision in the contract.

The facts of the case are not in dispute. In August 1976 plaintiffs listed their home in Bernardsville for sale at a price of $235,000. The property was not sold and it was listed again in 1977 at the same price. In August 1977 defendant Christine Dwyer was shown the house by a realtor in the absence of plaintiffs. She returned the following weekend with her husband, defendant John Dwyer, for a further inspection. No offer was made because defendants determined they were not interested in purchasing the property.

The following February Mrs. Dwyer inquired of the realtor as to whether plaintiffs' home was still available for purchase. Being informed that it was, but that an offer was then being considered, Mrs. Dwyer contacted her husband, who was on a business trip, and obtained his approval to submit a bid for the property. Accordingly, an offer of $225,000 was submitted orally by Mrs. Dwyer to the realtor. Later that day a realtor's printed form of contract for the sale and purchase of real estate was prepared by the realtor and presented to Mrs. Dwyer for signature. Believing the document to be merely a "bid" and that if acceptable to plaintiffs a purchase contract would thereafter be prepared, with the assistance of counsel and which would include terms acceptable to her husband and their attorney, Mrs. Dwyer signed the agreement. That evening the contract was presented to plaintiffs and executed by them.

When a copy of the fully executed document was returned later the same evening to Mrs. Dwyer, she was informed that, contrary to her expectations, plaintiffs did not intend to include the wall-to-wall carpeting in the sale. She thereupon called her attorney who instructed her to deliver a copy of the agreement to him the following morning. Two or three days later Mr. Dwyer returned from his trip and conferred with their attorney concerning the contract. Following this conference defendants' attorney notified plaintiffs and the relator that, as attorney for defendants and in accordance with the provisions of the agreement, he was withholding his approval of the contract, and accordingly defendants would not proceed with the transaction. It was indicated that such disapproval was not based upon the price or financing terms. Pretrial discovery disclosed that such notification was given because the carpeting was not included in the sale and there was no specification in the agreement as to what personal property was indicated; the concern of defendants as to the close proximity of the swimming pool to the kitchen doors; the lack of provisions for potability and septic system tests; the shortness of the time period for satisfaction of the mortgage contingency; the inadequacy of the agreement in that Mr. Dwyer was not a signatory thereto, and other intangible considerations.

As indicated, the form utilized by the realtor was the "Standard Form of Real Estate Contract Adopted by the New Jersey Association of Realtor Boards for Use by New Jersey Realtors." The property was described by reference to the municipal tax map, and the purchase price, deposit and mortgage amount were handwritten insertions. The type of deed to be delivered was specified as "C. vs. Grantor," and the rate of interest on the mortgage to be obtained by the purchaser was stated as "prevailing rate." The agreement contained typed contingency clauses for the obtaining of a $75,000 conventional mortgage within 20 days and a termite inspection within 7 days. No provision was made for the inclusion in the sale of any personal property, except for gas and electric fixtures, etc., if any, as provided by the printed language of the form. The agreement also contained the following typewritten provision, which is being relied upon by defendants in opposing plaintiffs' motion for summary judgment for breach of the contract and in support of their motion for a dismissal of the complaint:

> This contract, except as to price and financing terms (if any), is contingent upon approval by the respective attorneys for purchasers and sellers within three (3) business days of the date hereof. The parties agree that such approval shall be deemed to have been given, and this contingency satisfied or waived, unless an objection or amendment or addition or other express statement witholding (*sic*) approval is made in writing within said three day period and delivered to the realtor or exchanged between the respective attorneys if they are known to each other.

Inasmuch as there does not exist any dispute concerning the material facts relating to the issues presented, it is appropriate that the motions of the parties be determined in a summary proceeding. R. 4:46–2; Judson v. Peoples Bank & Trust Co. of Westfield, 17 N.J. 67, 110 A.2d 24 (1954).

It is plaintiffs' contention that defendants breached the contract by their failure to consummate the purchase in accordance with the agreement and that their attorney's notification of disapproval was not sufficient to excuse them from such performance. They assert that the "attorney approval clause" in the contract does not permit disapproval for unspecified reasons nor for any of the reasons as disclosed by defendants' answers to interrogatories. Plaintiffs argue that it would be unreasonable to conclude otherwise because of the specific language precluding an objection based upon price or financing terms. Additionally, they contend that a reasonable interpretation of the clause would not support a claim that the parties intended *carte blanche* disapproval rights after entering into what purports on its face to be a legally binding contract. Rather, a more logical conclusion is that the intention of the parties was to provide for a disapproval based upon legal deficiencies of the contract, which would be matters within the special expertise of an attorney.

On the other hand, defendants argue that there was no breach of contract as the inclusion of the subject clause in the agreement rendered its efficacy contingent upon the approval of either party's attorney and, so long as there is no showing of bad faith, the contract is not enforceable in the event of a disapproval by the stipulated counselor. Also, defendants suggest that the reasonable expectation of a purchaser and seller of residential property is that such a provision, in a contract presented to them for execution by a real estate broker or salesperson, grants the right to obtain the unfettered approval or disapproval of their attorney.

While a clause providing for approval of the contract, within a specified time, by the attorney for either party, has not been judicially construed or applied, there appears to be varying interpretations ascribed to such a provision by professionals and others who are involved in real estate transactions. Thus, some may interpret it as meaning that the right of approval is restricted to negotiating the inclusion or exclusion of certain standard clauses, or the modification of included provisions, while others consider that the right is unlimited, thereby permitting the attorney to disapprove the contract for any reason. Under the latter interpretation there is no requirement that the disapproval be reasonable or even that the other contracting party be informed of the reasons for such disapproval. The effect of an unlimited right of disapproval is to place the parties in the same position they would have been if they had been able to consult with an attorney before signing the contract. *See* Horn, *Residential Real Estate Law and Practice in New Jersey*, § 1.1.

Although the effect of a general attorney approval clause in a contract for the purchase of real estate has not been judicially passed upon, a somewhat analogous issue has been presented in cases involving contractual provisions requiring that title to the subject property be satisfactory to the purchaser's attorney. Varying conclusions have been reached as to the manner in which the attorney may exercise such contractual right of approval or disapproval. One line of cases holds that any dissatisfaction with the title is to be tested by objective standards, the test being whether the title meets the standard of marketability, or whether the objections are reasonable. Beardslee v. Underhill, 37 N.J.L. 309 (Sup.Ct.1875). A different view is represented by the group of cases which consider that such provisions constitute the attorney as the sole judge of his dissatisfaction, subject only to the limitation that the decision be arrived at in good faith and not be arbitrary or capricious. Janger v. Slayden, 26 S.W. 847 (Tex.Civ.App. 1894).

The objective approach, *i.e.* where the dissatisfaction is tested by the standard of marketability, proceeds on the basis that a clause making the title subject to an attorney's approval is nothing more than an expression of that which is implied in every real estate purchase contract, namely, that the title shall be good and marketable. Accordingly, the purchaser is required to be satisfied with a title which is in fact marketable. Any claim of dissatisfaction must therefore be judged by what the law holds to be a merchantable title, and title cannot be rejected by a simple expression of dissatisfaction based on insufficient legal reason.

Those cases which apply what might be termed the subjective criterion consider that, by providing for an attorney's approval of title, the contracting parties have bargained for something more than a good or marketable title, namely, the attorney's acceptance of the title as satisfactory. It being competent for parties to so stipulate, the attorney's disapproval is conclusive if made in good faith, although in the opinion of others, including the court, the title may be good as a matter of law. Such an interpretation follows the apparent intention of the parties that the attorney be the sole and final arbiter as to the acceptability of the title. To conclude otherwise would deny to the purchaser his right under the contract to the benefit of his attorney's judgment as to the sufficiency of the title. The rationale of this view was expressed in *Sanger v. Slayden, supra,* in the following terms:

> Such a contract is permissible and legal, and, when deliberately executed, should be enforced. It is an express authority to Sanger to disaffirm when he is dissatisfied with the title. To only allow him to disaffirm when his dissatisfaction rests upon some valid and reasonable objection to the title is to practically deny him the exercise of this privilege expressly conferred by the contract, and denies him the right to the exercise of his judgment in the matter, and makes his right depend solely upon what others may think as to the merits of the title he has acquired. It substitutes their judgment for his. Others may be perfectly satisfied with the title, and think that a man of ordinary caution and prudence should be likewise, and that no reasonable ground for dissatisfaction exists. But, on the other hand, Sanger may, with equal good faith, be dissatisfied with the title for reasons that are satisfactory to him, and may think that a man of caution and prudence had grounds for his dissatisfaction. The true rule of construction of contracts of this character, and the one supported, we think, by reason and the weight of authority, is that the vendee may disaffirm the contract if he is dissatisfied, and his reasons or grounds of dissatisfaction may not be determined or inquired into by any one else.

While these rules are not controlling of the present case, it seems that where the contract permits disapproval thereof by either party's attorney as to its sufficiency or acceptability in general, and not only as to the state of the title, there is even more justification for considering that the right granted by such a provision should not be diluted or denied by requiring that the attorney's judgment be measured by some standard, other than good faith, or another's opinion. The purpose of such an attorney approval clause is to provide the purchaser or seller with the opportunity of obtaining legal advice with respect to the transaction, and its value lies in the fact that the contract may be canceled upon receiving such advice. Parties to a real estate transaction are entitled to the benefit of the judgment of a trusted counselor, and an approval contingency is designed to accord this right to those who, for some reason, enter into a purchase and sale agreement before reviewing the matter with their attorney.

Applying these observations to the present case compels the conclusion that the disapproval of the contract by defendants' attorney effectively terminated the contract. The clause in question expressly made the agreement contingent upon the attorney's approval, except as to price and financing terms, and thereby bound the parties to abide the opinion of either party's attorney with respect to the efficacy of the contract, limited only by the requirement that the attorney act in good faith. The disapproval voiced by the defendants' attorney was an exercise of his judgment, and his reasons therefor were not subject to review or contradiction. The contract cannot be rewritten to qualify the clear and express language of the agreement by limiting the applicability of the attorney approval contingency to those circumstances where the reason for disapproval meets some standard or the concurrence of the plaintiffs, or their attorney. Defendants are entitled to the fruits of their bargain. There is no basis for a claim of bad faith or capriciousness on the part of defendants, or their attorney, in the use of this contingency provision, which would render the notice of disapproval ineffective.

We would also note that a contract for the purchase and sale of a residence determines the rights and responsibilities of the parties as to the entire transaction and is of such importance in this respect as to require preparation or, in the least, preliminary review by an attorney. A text writer has described the significance of the contract in the following manner:

> The contract of sale is the key to the real estate transaction. It is the critical document which fixes the fundamental rights and obligations of the parties from the time it is signed through the closing of title and, in many cases, even beyond. (Horn, *Residential Real Estate Law and Practice in New Jersey*, § 1.1).

The complexity of the law of contracts and of real property demand that one qualified by education and experience determine the legal sufficiency of a real estate sale agreement and advise the prospective seller or purchaser as to the rights and obligations arising thereunder. Objective counseling by one's own attorney as to the practicability or desirability of undertaking the sale or purchase is also often necessary to avoid precipitous actions which may prove to be legally, financially or socially disadvantageous.

The conclusion reached herein is in accord with the public policy as expressed by the Legislature by including the right of rescission in recent statutes pertaining to retail installment sales, financing of home repairs and the disposition of land in subdivisions. *See* N.J.S.A. 17:16C–61.5; N.J.S.A. 17:16C–99; N.J.S.A. 45:15–16.12(d).

Our determination that the contract was terminated by operation of the attorney approval contingency provision renders it unnecessary to consider the secondary question concerning the liability of defendant John Dwyer.

Accordingly, plaintiffs' motion for summary judgment for damages is denied and defendants' motion for summary judgment dismissing the complaint is granted.

PROBLEMS

37.   Plaintiff and defendant entered into an agreement which permitted plaintiff to render valet and laundry services at the defendant's hotel for a period of three years. Plaintiff was to pay $325.00 per month for the concession. The agreement also provided: "It is distinctly understood and agreed that the services to be rendered by the second party (plaintiff) shall meet with the approval of the first party (defendant) who shall be the sole judge of the sufficiency and propriety of the services." Before the three-year period was over, defendant discharged plaintiff. Plaintiff sues for breach and defendant counterclaims for breach of contract. Analyze the possible results.

38.   A construction contract required payments to be made only upon submission of the certificate of the architect. The architect refused to issue a certificate because "the owner has instructed me to put on mouldings in accordance with his desires, although I have never seen that kind of moulding which he desires, at the same time he states that nothing else will be accepted by him so there is no alternative and I cannot issue the certificate until this has been done." What result?

39.   In a construction contract, plaintiff promised to do the work in a workmanlike manner and "to the satisfaction of the architect to be testified to by his certificate." Plaintiff obtained such a certificate. Defendant offered proof that the work had not been performed in a workmanlike manner and plaintiff objected. Is this evidence admissible?

SECTION 10. PROSPECTIVE NONPERFORMANCE AND BREACH BY REPUDIATION

(Calamari & Perillo on Contracts §§ 12.1—12.10)

HOCHSTER v. DE LA TOUR
In the Queen's Bench, 1853.
2 Ellis & Bl. 678, 118 Eng.Rep. 922.

[The plaintiff brought this action on May 22, 1852, for breach of a bilateral contract whereby the defendant had promised to employ the plaintiff to accompany him as a courier on the continent of Europe for three months beginning on June 1, 1852, and to pay £10 per month for the service. The plaintiff remained ready and willing to begin service on June 1 as agreed; but the defendant wrongfully discharged him and repudiated the contract on May 11. On receiving notice of his discharge the plaintiff obtained similar employment with Lord Ashburton, but this employment would not begin until July. Ed.]

The defendant's counsel objected that there could be no breach of the contract before the 1st of June. The learned judge was of a contrary opinion, but reserved leave to enter a nonsuit on this objection. The other questions were left to the jury, who found for plaintiff.

Hugh Hill, in the same term, obtained a rule nisi to enter a nonsuit or arrest the judgment. In last Trinity Term.

Hannen showed cause. . . . If one party to an executory contract gave the other notice that he refused to go on with the bargain, in order that the other side might act upon that refusal in such a manner as to incapacitate himself from fulfilling it, and he did so act, the refusal could never be retracted; and, accordingly, in Cort. v. Ambergate & c. R. Co. (17 Q.B. 127) this court after considering the cases, decided that in such a case the plaintiff might recover, though he was no longer in a position to fulfil his contract. That was a contract under seal to manufacture and supply iron chairs. The purchasers discharged the vendors from manufacturing the goods; and it was held that an action might be maintained by the vendors. It is true, however, that in that case the writ was issued after the time when the chairs ought to have been received. In the present case, if the writ had been issued on the 2nd of June, Cort v. Ambergate & c. R. Co. would be expressly in point. The question, therefore, comes to be: Does it make any difference that the writ was issued before the 1st of June? If the dicta of Parke, B., in Phillpotts v. Evans, 5 M. & W. 475, are to be taken as universally applicable it does make a difference; but they cannot be so taken. In a contract to marry at a future day, a marriage of the man before that day is a breach. Short v. Stone, 8 Q.B. 358. The reason of this is, that the marriage is a final refusal to go on with the contract. It is not on the ground that the defendant has rendered it impossible to fulfil the contract; for, as was urged in vain in Short v. Stone, the first wife might be dead before the day came. So also, on a contract to assign a term of years on a day future, a previous assignment to a stranger is a breach. Lovelock v. Franklyn, 8 Q.B. 371. (Lord Campbell, C.J. It probably will not be disputed that an act on the part of the defendant incapacitating himself from going on with the contract would be a breach. But how does the defendant's refusal in May incapacitate him from travelling in June? It was possible that he might do so.) It was; but the plaintiff, who, so long as the engagement subsisted, was bound to keep himself disengaged and make preparations so as to be ready and willing to travel with the defendant on the 1st of June, was informed by the defendant that he would not go on with the contract, in order that the plaintiff might act upon that information; and the plaintiff then was entitled to engage himself to another, as he did. In Planche v. Colburn (8 Bing. 14) the plaintiff had contracted with defendants to write a work for "The Juvenile Library"; and he was held to be entitled to recover on their discontinuing the publication; yet the time for the completion of the contract, that is for the work being published in "The Juvenile Library," had not arrived, for that would not be till a reasonable time after the author had completed the work. Now in that case the author never did complete the work. (Lord Campbell, C.J. It certainly would have been cruelly hard if the author had been obliged, as a condition precedent to redress, to compose a work which he knew could never be published. Crompton, J. When a party announces his intention not to fulfill the contract, the other side may take him at his word and rescind the contract. That word "rescind" implies that both parties have agreed that the contract shall be at an end as if it had never been. But I am inclined to think that the party may also say: "Since you have announced that you will not go on with the contract, I will consent that it shall be at an end from this time; but I will hold you liable for the damage I have sustained; and I will proceed to make that damage as little as possible by making the best use I can of my liberty." This is the principle of those cases in which there has been a discussion as to the measure of damages to which a servant is entitled on a wrongful dismissal. They were all considered in Elderton v. Emmens (6 C.B. 160). Lord Campbell, C.J. The counsel in support of the rule have to answer a very able argument.)

Hugh Hill and Deighton, *contra*. In Cort v. Ambergate & c. R. Co., the writ was taken out after the time for completing the contract. That case is consistent with the defendant's position, which is, that an act incapacitating the defendant, in law, from completing the contract is a breach, because it is implied that the parties to a contract shall keep themselves legally capable of performing it; but that an announcement of an intention to break the contract when the time comes is no more than an offer to rescind. It is evidence, till retracted, of a dispensation with the necessity of readiness and willingness on the other side; and, if not retracted, it is, when the time for performance comes, evidence of a continued refusal; but till then it may be retracted. Such is the doctrine in Phillpotts v. Evans (5 M. & W. 475) and Ripley v. McClure (4 Exch. 345). (Crompton, J. May not the plaintiff, on notice that the defendant will not employ him, look out for other employment, so as to diminish the loss?) If he adopts the defendant's notice, which is in legal effect an offer to rescind, he must adopt it altogether. (Lord Campbell, C.J. So that you say the plaintiff, to preserve any remedy at all, was bound to remain idle. Erle, J. Do you go one step further? Suppose the defendant, after the plaintiff's engagement with Lord Ashburton, had retracted his refusal and required the plaintiff to travel with him on the 1st of June, and the plaintiff had refused to do so, and gone with Lord Ashburton instead? Do you say that the now defendant could in that case have sued the now plaintiff for a breach of contract?) It would be, in such a case, a question of fact for a jury, whether there had not been an exoneration. In Phillpotts v. Evans, it was held that the measure of damages was the market price at the time when the contract ought to be completed. If a refusal before that time is a breach, how could these damages be ascertained? (Coleridge, J. No doubt it was possible, in this case, that, before the 1st of June, the plaintiff might die, in which case the plaintiff would have gained nothing had the contract gone on. Lord Campbell, C.J. All contingencies should be taken into account by the jury in assessing the damages. Crompton, J. That objection would equally apply to the action by a servant for dismissing him before the end of his term, and so disabling him from earning his wages; yet that action may be brought immediately on the dismissal; note to Cutter v. Powell (6 T.R. 320)). It is quite possible that the plaintiff himself might have intended not to go on; no one can tell what intention is. (Lord Campbell, C.J. The intention of the defendant might be proved by showing that he entered in his diary a memorandum to that effect; and certainly, no action would lie for entering such a memorandum. But the question is as to the effect of a communication to the other side, made that he might know that intention and act upon it.)

*Cur.adv.vult.**

LORD CAMPBELL, C.J., now delivered the judgment of the Court.

On this motion in arrest of judgment, the question arises, Whether, if there be an agreement between A and B, whereby B engages to employ A on and from a future day for a given period of time, to travel with him into a foreign country as a courier, and to start with him in that capacity on that day, A being to receive a monthly salary during the continuance of such service, B may, before the day, refuse to perform the agreement and break and renounce it, so as to entitle A before the day to commence an action against B to recover damages for breach of the agreement; A having been ready and willing to perform it, till it was broken and renounced by B. The defendant's counsel very powerfully contended that, if the plaintiff was not contented to dissolve the contract and to abandon all remedy upon it, he was bound to remain ready and willing to perform it till the day when the actual employment as courier in the service of the defendant was to begin; and that there could be no breach of the agreement before that day to give a right of action. But it cannot be laid down as a universal rule that, where by agreement an act is to be done on a future day, no action can be brought for a breach of the agreement till the day for doing the act has arrived. If a man promises to marry a woman on a future day, and before that day marries another woman, he is instantly liable to an action for breach of promise of marriage. Short v. Stone (8 Q.B. 358). If a man contracts to execute a lease on and from a future day for a certain term, and before that day executes a lease to another for the same term, he may be immediately sued for breaking the contract. Ford v. Tiley (6 B. & C. 325). So, if a man contracts to sell and deliver specific goods on a future day, and before the day he sells and delivers them to another, he is immediately liable to an action at the suit of the person with whom he first contracted to sell and deliver them. Bowdell v. Parsons (10 East, 359). One reason alleged in support of such an action is, that the defendant has, before the day, rendered it impossible for him to perform the contract at the day, but this does not necessarily follow; for prior to the day fixed for doing the act, the first wife may have died, a surrender of the lease executed might be obtained, and the defendant might have

_____

* The Latin abbreviation stands for *"curia advisari vult"* (literally, the court wishes to be advised) meaning that the court retires to consider the matter before giving its judgment. Ed.

repurchased the goods so as to be in a situation to sell and deliver them to the plaintiff. Another reason may be that, where there is a contract to do an act on a future day, there is a relation constituted between the parties in the meantime by the contract, and that they impliedly promise that in the meantime neither will do anything to the prejudice of the other inconsistent with that relation. As an example, a man and woman engaged to marry are affianced to one another during the period between the time of the engagement and the celebration of the marriage.

In this very case of traveller and courier, from the day of the hiring till the day when the employment was to begin, they were engaged to each other; and it seems to be a breach of an implied contract if either of them renounces the engagement. This reasoning seems in accordance with the unanimous decision of the Exchequer Chamber in Elderton v. Emmens (6 C.B. 160), which we have followed in subsequent cases in this court. The declaration in the present case, in alleging a breach, states a great deal more than a passing intention on the part of the defendant which he may repent of, and could only be proved by evidence that he had utterly renounced the contract, or done some act which rendered it impossible for him to perform it.

If the plaintiff has no remedy for breach of the contract unless he treats the contract as in force, and acts upon it down to the 1st of June, 1852, it follows that, till then, he must enter into no employment which will interfere with his promise "to start with the defendant on such travels on the day and year," and that he must then be properly equipped in all respects as a courier for a three months' tour on the continent of Europe. But it is surely much more rational, and more for the benefit of both parties, that, after the renunciation of the agreement by the defendant, the plaintiff should be at liberty to consider himself absolved from any future performance of it, retaining his right to sue for any damage he has suffered from the breach of it. Thus, instead of remaining idle and laying out money in preparations which must be useless, he is at liberty to seek service under another employer, which would go in mitigation to the damages to which he would otherwise be entitled for a breach of the contract. It seems strange that the defendant, after renouncing the contract, and absolutely declaring that he will never act under it, should be permitted to object that faith is given to his assertion, and that an opportunity is not left to him of changing his mind. If the plaintiff is barred of any remedy by entering into an engagement inconsistent with starting as a courier with the defendant on the 1st of June, he is prejudiced by putting faith in the defendant's assertion, and it would be more consonant with principle, if the defendant were precluded from saying that he had not broken the contract when he declared that he entirely renounced it.

Suppose that the defendant, at the time of his renunciation, had embarked on a voyage for Australia, so as to render it physically impossible for him to employ the plaintiff as a courier on the continent of Europe in the months of June, July, and August, 1852, according to decided cases, the action might have been brought before the 1st of June; but the renunciation may have been founded on other facts, to be given in evidence, which would equally have rendered the defendant's performance of the contract impossible. The man who wrongfully renounces a contract into which he has deliberately entered cannot justly complain if he is immediately sued for a compensation in damages by the man whom he has injured; and it seems reasonable to allow an option to the injured party, either to sue immediately, or to wait till the time when the act was to be done, still holding it as prospectively binding for the exercise of this option, which may be advantageous to the innocent party, and cannot be prejudicial to the wrongdoer. An argument against the action before the 1st of June is urged from the difficulty of calculating the damages, but this argument is equally strong against an action before the 1st of September, when the three months would expire. In either case, the jury in assessing the damages would be justified in looking to all that had happened, or was likely to happen, to increase or mitigate the loss of the plaintiff down to the day of trial. We do not find any decision contrary to the view we are taking of this case. . . .

Upon the whole, we think that the declaration in this case is sufficient. It gives us great satisfaction to reflect that, the question being on the record, our opinion may be reviewed in a court of error. In the meantime we must give judgment for the plaintiff.

Judgment for plaintiff.

DRAKE v. WICKWIRE

Supreme Court of Alaska, 1990.
795 P.2d 195.

MATTHEWS, CHIEF JUSTICE. This is a malpractice action against an attorney for allegedly inducing his client to break an earnest money sales agreement. The underlying facts are set forth in *Drake v. Hosley*, 713 P.2d 1203 (Alaska 1986). We excerpt them at this point:

On March 5, 1984, Paul Drake signed an exclusive listing agreement with The Charles Hosley Company, Realtors (hereafter "Hosley"). The agreement authorized Hosley to act as Drake's agent until March 30, 1984, to sell some land Drake owned in North Pole, Alaska. The agreement provided for payment of a ten percent commission if, during the period of the listing agreement, 1) Hosley located a buyer "willing and able to purchase at the terms set by the seller," or 2) the seller entered into a "binding sale" during the term set by the seller.

Hosley found a group of three buyers, Robert Goldsmith, Dwayne Hofschulte and David Nystrom (hereafter "buyers"), who were interested in the property. On March 23, 1984, Drake signed a purchase and sale agreement, entitled "earnest money receipt," in which he agreed to sell the land to the buyers at a specified price and terms. The buyers also signed the agreement. It provided that closing would occur "within 10 days of clear title" and "ASAP, 1984." [Time was stated to be "of the essence." Ed.] A typed addendum stated that Drake agreed to pay Hosley a commission of ten percent of the price paid for the property. Both Drake and Hosley signed the addendum.

On April 3, 1984, Hosley received a preliminary commitment for title insurance. The title report listed a judgment in favor of Drake's ex-wife as the sole encumbrance on the title. The next day Hosley called Drake's attorney, Tom Wickwire, to ask about the judgment. Wickwire stated that the judgment would be paid with the cash received at closing.

Two or three days later, attorney Wickwire called Hosley and stated that his client (Drake) wanted the sale closed by April 11. Wickwire explained that he had negotiated a discounted settlement with Drake's ex-wife that required payment by April 11. Wickwire claims that Hosley agreed to close by April 11. Hosley disagrees, and claims he merely stated that he would try to close as quickly as possible.

When Hosley became concerned that the buyers would not be able to close on April 11, he telephoned the attorney for Drake's ex-wife and learned that the April 11 deadline for payment of the judgment had been extended to the end of the month. On April 11, Wickwire called Hosley to set up the closing. Hosley told Wickwire that the buyers could not close that day because they did not have the money and would not have it before May 1. Wickwire indicated that he would advise Drake to call off the sale because the buyers had refused to perform. Wickwire mailed a letter to Hosley, dated April 11, stating that Drake's offer to sell was withdrawn. Hosley received the letter on approximately April 18. On April 12, Drake sold his property through another broker to different buyers. On April 12, Hosley went to Wickwire's office to close the sale and submitted checks from the buyers totalling $33,000 for the down payment. Wickwire refused the checks, stating that another buyer already had purchased the property.

Id. at 1204–05.

In *Drake*, Hosley sued Drake for his real estate commission. The trial court granted summary judgment to Hosley. On appeal we affirmed, holding that Hosley was Drake's agent, not the agent of the buyers and thus would have had no authority to change the deadline for closing from April 12 or 13 to April 11 as Drake contended. . . .

In the present action, Drake alleges that Wickwire was negligent in advising him that he could sell his property to another buyer on April 11. Wickwire moved for summary judgment. Wickwire contended that he believed that there had been an anticipatory breach of the earnest money agreement when Hosley told him the buyer would not have the money until May 1 and that his conduct "did not fall below an acceptable standard of care." He supported this contention with the affidavits of two attorneys. Drake filed a memorandum in opposition to the motion for summary judgment but did not submit testimony or affidavits from attorneys opining that Wickwire had been negligent.

The trial court granted Wickwire's motion in a written decision which adopted a rule requiring expert evidence to establish a breach of an attorney's duty of care, except in non-technical situations where negligence is evident to lay people or where the fault is so clear as to constitute negligence as a matter of law. After adopting this rule the court applied it to the facts of this case, finding that Wickwire's negligence, if any, was not so obvious that it could be determined as a matter of law, nor was the subject matter non-technical so that negligence might be evident to lay people. The court therefore concluded that expert testimony from Drake was required. Since none was presented by Drake, summary judgment was granted. . . .

On appeal, Drake does not take issue with the rule of law adopted by the court. Instead, he argues that this case involves obvious breaches of duty on the part of Wickwire and, in addition, urges us to "find negligence as a matter of law. . . ."

We agree with the rule of law adopted by the Superior Court in this case. . . . However, we are of the view that Wickwire was negligent as a matter of law. In Drake's brief, authored by Wickwire, in the case of *Drake v. Hosley*, the critical conversation between Hosley and Wickwire relating to the alleged anticipatory repudiation is set forth as follows:

(O)n the morning of April 11 (Wickwire) called Hosley to select a specific time and place for closing. But Hosley's response was that his buyers could not close on that day as they did not have the money but would need until May 1 to get it. Wickwire asked Hosley if the problem was just getting the time to get the money out of the bank or did they not have the downpayment. Hosley replied that the buyers in fact had the money but were "resisting the pressure to close."

The law of anticipatory repudiation is set forth in sections 253, 250 and 251 of the *Restatement (Second) of Contracts (1981)* (hereafter *Restatement*). Section 253(1) of the *Restatement* provides:

Where an obligor repudiates a duty before he has committed a breach by non-performance and before he has received all of the agreed exchange for it, his repudiation alone gives rise to a claim for damages for total breach.

The concept of repudiation is explained in § 250 as follows: "A repudiation is (a) a statement by the obligor to the obligee indicating that the obligor will commit a breach that would of itself give the obligee a claim for damages. . . ."

The commentary to this section explains that a statement, in order to qualify as a repudiation, must be reasonably clear:

In order to constitute a repudiation, a party's language must be sufficiently positive to be reasonably interpreted to mean that the party will not or cannot perform. Mere expression of doubt as to his willingness or ability to perform is not enough to constitute a repudiation, although such an expression may given [*sic*] an obligee reasonable grounds to believe that the obligor will commit a serious breach and may ultimately result in a repudiation under the rule stated in § 251. However, language that under a fair reading "amounts to a statement of intention not to perform except on conditions which go beyond the contract" constitutes a repudiation.

Restatement § 250, cmt. b (citation omitted).

In our view, Wickwire did not act reasonably in treating Hosley's statement as a repudiation. As recited by Wickwire, it was ambiguous on its face. Hosley first indicated that the buyers would need until May 1 to get the money. Later, though, Hosley indicated that the buyers had the money but were "resisting the pressure to close." The latter statement itself is ambiguous in that it is unclear whether the buyers were resisting the pressure to close on April 11 as Drake desired, or on April 12 or 13 as the contract required.

If the former meaning was intended, there would have been no anticipatory repudiation because the buyers had no contractual obligation to close on the 11th. If the latter meaning was intended, Wickwire would have had at most reasonable grounds to believe that the buyers would breach the contract. Neither meaning justifies treating the statement as a repudiation. Instead, Wickwire could have sought assurances of performance under the rule stated in § 251 of the Restatement. That rule states:

> (1) Where reasonable grounds arise to believe that the obligor will commit a breach by nonperformance that would of itself give the obligee a claim for damages for total breach ... the obligee may demand adequate assurance of due performance and may, if reasonable, suspend any performance for which he has not already received the agreed exchange until he receives such assurance.

> (2) The obligee may treat as a repudiation the obligor's failure to provide within a reasonable time such assurance of due performance as is adequate in the circumstances of the particular case.

Wickwire's negligence in this case was in advising precipitate conduct in the face of an ambiguous statement which was insufficient to indicate that the buyers would breach the contract.

The judgment is reversed and this case is remanded for further proceedings consistent with this decision.

RABINOWITZ, JUSTICE, dissenting. I dissent from the court's holding that Wickwire was, as a matter of law, guilty of malpractice.

COHEN v. KRANZ

Court of Appeals of New York, 1963.
12 N.Y.2d 242, 238 N.Y.S.2d 928, 189 N.E.2d 473.

BURKE, JUDGE. On September 22, 1959 plaintiff contracted to purchase defendants' one-family house in Nassau County for $40,000. Four thousand dollars was paid on the signing of the contract and the balance due upon delivery of the deed was in the form of $24,500 cash and the assumption of an $11,500 first mortgage. Closing was set for November 15. Plaintiff obtained an adjournment of the closing date to December 15 without any indication that title would be rejected. On November 30, plaintiff's attorney sent defendants' attorney a letter stating: "An investigation has disclosed that the present structure of the premises is not legal and thus title is unmarketable. Unless a check to the order of Lester Cohen, as attorney in fact, for Sarah Cohen is received in five days, we shall be obligated to commence proceedings against your client."

Plaintiff's attorney appeared at the office of defendants' attorney on the adjourned law date and demanded return of the $4,000 deposit, which was refused by the latter. Neither party was then able to perform and neither made any tender. Plaintiff thereafter commenced this action for return of the deposit plus the costs of searching title; defendants counterclaimed for damages for breach of contract.

Trial Term, Nassau County, gave judgment for plaintiff. The court found that the premises were subject to protective covenants filed in the Nassau County Clerk's office and that the insurability clause of the contract was not complied with because a swimming pool on the premises, installed under a permit, lacked a certificate of occupancy from the Oyster Bay Architectural Control Committee. Further, a split rail fence projected beyond the front line of the dwelling. The court also found that plaintiff had notified defendants of the claimed defects prior to the December 15 closing date and that defendants had taken no steps to remedy the defects, nor had it been established that the violations were minor. The court held, therefore, that the defective title excused plaintiff from tender of payment and awarded plaintiff judgment in the amount of her deposit.

The Appellate Division, Second Department, unanimously reversed Trial Term on the law and facts and directed judgment on the counterclaim for $1,500. It is from this judgment that plaintiff appeals.

In reversing Trial Term's findings of fact, the Appellate Division expressly found that plaintiff's letter of November 30 rejecting title and demanding return of the deposit failed to specify the claimed illegality, and that specific objections to title were not raised until January 25, 1960. The letter speaks for itself and the Appellate Division is obviously correct. Plaintiff's arguments directed at the Appellate Division's finding of January 25th as the date when specific objections were first communicated to defendants are unavailing inasmuch as the earliest further communication of objections supported by the evidence took place upon the commencement of this action by plaintiff on December 31st, still more than two weeks after the law date. It was also found, contrary to the trial court, that the objections to title were curable upon proper and timely notice and demand. We think the weight of the evidence supports the Appellate Division here too. The swimming pool was constructed with a permit and lacked only a certificate of occupancy (which was in fact obtained before defendants sold the house to a third person). The fence projection likewise could clearly be found to be a readily curable objection. These were the only two objections that possibly violated the "Declaration of Protective Covenants" recorded in the Nassau County Clerk's office and to which the title insurer excepted.

The Appellate Division also found that defendants had not waived a tender by plaintiff and that plaintiff's rejection of title in advance was a default precluding her from recovery of the deposit. Since it is undisputed that defendants made no tender, the Appellate Division's award of damages for breach of contract necessarily implies that no such tender was required. We agree.

While a vendee can recover his money paid on the contract from a vendor who defaults on law day without a showing of tender or even of willingness and ability to perform where the vendor's title is incurably defective (Greene v. Barrett, Nephews & Co., 238 N.Y. 207, 144 N.E. 503), a tender and demand are required to put the vendor in default where his title could be cleared without difficulty in a reasonable time. (Higgins v. Eagleton, 155 N.Y. 466, 50 N.E. 287). Further, the vendor in such a case is entitled to a reasonable time beyond law day to make his title good (Ballen v. Potter, 251 N.Y. 224, 167 N.E. 424). It is, therefore, clear that plaintiff's advance rejection of title and demand for immediate return of the deposit was unjustified and an anticipatory breach of contract. This position, adhered to throughout, prevented defendants' title defects from ever amounting to a default. Consequently, plaintiff is barred from recovering the deposit from a vendor whose title defects were curable and whose performance was never demanded on law day. (*Higgins v. Eagleton*, *supra*.) Ansorge v. Belfer, 248 N.Y. 145, 150, 161 N.E. 450, 452, is not to the contrary. It merely holds that a vendee may recover his deposit from a clearly defaulting vendor despite his own unjustified refusal to agree to an adjournment of the law date. It does not deny the doctrine that a vendor whose title defects are curable is not automatically in default but, rather, must be put in default by the vendee's tender of performance and demand for a good title deed. The vendor was there put in default by the vendee's tender. The vendor simply never retrieved his default by curing the defects and tendering a good title (as he could have—Harris v. Shorall, 230 N.Y. 343, 130 N.E. 572). True, defendants here never offered to clear their title and perform; but they were never put in default in the first place by a demand for good title. So Ansorge merely holds with respect to curable title defects what *Greene v. Barrett, Nephews & Co., supra*, held with respect to incurable defects—namely, that where the vendor is in default the deposit can be recovered even though the vendee himself is in default or breach, *e.g.*, no showing of performance of conditions precedent or excuse for nonperformance (the *Greene* case); or an unjustified refusal to adjourn the closing date (the *Ansorge* case). The difference is that a vendor with incurable[1] title defects is automatically in default, whereas a

---

1. We use "incurable" to mean not within the vendor's power to remedy within a reasonable time. (*See* Greene v. Barrett, Nephews & Co., *supra*, 238 N.Y. pp. 211–212, 144 N.E. pp. 504–505.)

vendor with curable title defects must be placed in default by a tender and demand, which was not done here.

Defendants obtained an affirmative recovery on their counterclaim for breach of contract based on the loss they sustained when they sold the house to a third person for what the courts below found to be its fair market value. This recovery stands on a different footing from their right to retain the deposit. As Judge Andrews pointed out, in speaking of a vendee, in *Greene v. Barrett, Nephews & Co., supra*, while the vendee's right to recover the deposit from a defaulting vendor can rest solely upon the latter's default, an action for *damages* for breach of contract requires a showing that the plaintiff himself (the vendee in the *Greene* case) has performed all conditions precedent and concurrent, unless excused. In the case of a purchase of real estate, this would be a showing of tender and demand or, if that be unnecessary, an idle gesture, because of the incurable nature of the title defect, then at least a showing at the trial that the plaintiff vendee was in a position to perform had the vendor been willing and able to perform his part. (*Greene v. Barrett, Nephews & Co., supra*; *Restatement, Contracts*, § 306.) Likewise, a vendor such as the defendants here must show a basic ability to perform even if actual tender and demand is unnecessary. However, while it cannot be denied that defendants did not have a title conformable to the contract at law date, an applicable corollary of the above rule excuses even inability to perform conditions precedent or concurrent where such inability is caused by advance notice from the other party that he will not perform his part. (Clarke v. Crandall, 27 Barb. 73; *Restatement, Contracts*, §§ 270, 284, 306). Not only did plaintiff's unjustified attempt to cancel the contract and recover her deposit before the adjourned law date render unnecessary and wasteful any attempt by defendants to cure the minor defects before that date, but the failure to specify the objections rendered it impossible. The finding of the Appellate Division, supported by the weight of the evidence, that the defects were curable, means that defendants were basically able to perform and whatever technical inability existed in this regard on the law date was caused by plaintiff and is excused fully as much as the lack of formal tender.

The judgment should be affirmed, without costs.

PROBLEMS

40.   C entered into a contract with O to build a residence for O. Shortly after C began work, O failed to pay a progress payment when due and refused to make any further payments to C. Does C have the usual election available after a material breach by the other party?

41.   Plaintiff agreed to build a house for defendant. Plaintiff began work on April 29 and continued until Sept. 11 when plaintiff told defendant that he could not continue unless defendant advanced him money to meet his payroll. In response, defendant ordered plaintiff off the job. (a) Was defendant justified in ordering plaintiff off the job? (b) Assuming that defendant was so justified, would defendant also have a counterclaim?

42. On Jan. 11, D contracted with P to purchase four lots of land from P. Closing was to take place in seven months. D was to commence, on or before Feb. 10, the erection of a house on each of the lots and the houses were to be completed in 7 months. P promised to advance $4,000 on each house to D and D promised to return the $4,000 and to pay an additional $11,000 for each lot when the houses were completed. On the same day the contract was entered into, P conveyed the premises to a third party and D refused to commence erection of the buildings. Before the closing date, the third party reconveyed the property to P who then brought this action for breach of contract. What result?

43. Defendant agreed to convey to plaintiff certain property. In turn, plaintiff agreed to convey to defendant certain lots. At the time of the agreement, plaintiff did not have title to the lots in question but his wife had a contract with the owner that would have permitted plaintiff to perform on time. When defendant learned that plaintiff did not have title, he called off the deal. What result?

44. Plaintiff contracted on April 2 to buy from defendant for immediate delivery 100 coin-operated weighing scales, payment by $1,500 cash as a down payment and the balance by three and six month notes. Plaintiff's check for $1,500 was dishonored for insufficient funds and defendant's subsequent credit investigation of plaintiff revealed unsatisfied judgments against him. Consequently, on April 21, defendant wrote saying that it did not feel justified in delivering the machines on credit, but hoped that plaintiff would consent to a purchase for cash. This plaintiff refused. When defendant refused to deliver on credit, plaintiff sued for breach of contract and proved he was a wealthy man with large cash reserves. Defendant counterclaims. What result?

45. Defendant agreed to pay plaintiff a total of $37,500 for certain interests in corporate stock and realty. The agreement required the payment of $5,000 on Jan. 1, 1956, which defendant paid. Defendant, pursuant to the agreement, then gave a series of promissory notes for the balance payable in installments of $5,000. At the same time, plaintiff transferred his interests in the stock and realty to the defendant. Defendant failed to pay the next installment when it was due and notified plaintiff that the balance would not be paid. For how much may plaintiff recover judgment?

46. Defendant purchased and accepted delivery of certain machinery. The contract of sale required it to pay $10,000 within 30 days and the balance in five annual installments and to execute instruments giving the seller a security interest in the machinery. Before the 30 days elapsed and before fulfilling any of its obligations, defendant resold the machinery. Plaintiff immediately brought suit. What result?

CHAPTER 9

IMPOSSIBILITY, IMPRACTICABILITY AND FRUSTRATION

■ ■ ■

(Calamari & Perillo on Contracts §§ 13.1—13.24)

SECTION 1. IMPOSSIBILITY AND IMPRACTICABILITY

PARADINE v. JANE

King's Bench, 1647.
Aleyn, 26, 82 Eng.Rep. 897.

[The case arises during the first part of the English civil war between the Parliamentarians (supporters of the Long Parliament) and the Royalists (supporters of Charles I). Prince Rupert, though a German prince, was a nephew of Charles I (son of his sister Elizabeth Stuart) and, at 23, commander of the Royal cavalry. At the time the opinion was written the King was a prisoner of Parliament and Prince Rupert had been banished from England, hence his label as an "enemy." Ed.]

In debt the plaintiff declares upon a lease for years rendering rent at the four usual feasts; and for rent behind for three years, ending at the Feast of the Annunciation, 21 Car. [1646] brings his action; the defendant pleads, that a certain German prince, by name Prince Rupert, an alien born, enemy to the King and kingdom, had invaded the realm with an hostile army of men; and with the same force did enter upon the defendant's possession, and him expelled, and held out of possession from the 19 of July 18 Car. [1642] till the Feast of the Annunciation, 21 Car. [1646] whereby he could not take the profits; whereupon the plaintiff demurred, and the plea was resolved insufficient. . . .

3. It was resolved, that the matter of the plea was insufficient; for though the whole army had been alien enemies, yet he ought to pay his rent. And this difference was taken, that where the law creates a duty or charge, and the party is disabled to perform it without any default in him, and hath no remedy over, there the law will excuse him. As in the case of waste, if a house be destroyed by tempest, or by enemies, the lessee is

521

excused. Dyer, 33. a. Inst. 53. d. 283. a. 12 H. 4. 6. So of an escape. Co. 4. 84. b. 33 H. 6. 1. So in 9 E. 3. 16. a *supersedeas* was awarded to the justices, that they should not proceed in a *cessavit* upon a *cesser* during the war, but when the party by his own contract creates a duty or charge upon himself, he is bound to make it good, if he may, notwithstanding any accident by inevitable necessity, because he might have provided against it by his contract. And therefore if the lessee covenant to repair a house, though it be burnt by lightning, or thrown down by enemies, yet he ought to repair it. Dyer 33. a. 40 E. 3. 6. h. Now the rent is a duty created by the parties upon the reservation, and had there been a covenant to pay it, there had been no question but the lessee must have made it good, notwithstanding the interruption by enemies, for the law would not protect him beyond his own agreement, no more than in the case of reparations; this reservation then being a covenant in law, and whereupon an action of covenant hath been maintained (as Roll said) it is all one as if there had been an actual covenant. Another reason was added, that as the lessee is to have the advantage of casual profits, so he must run the hazard of casual losses, and not lay the whole burthen of them upon his lessor; and Dyer 56. 6. was cited for this purpose, that though the land be surrounded, or gained by the sea, or made barren by wildfire, yet the lessor shall have his whole rent: and judgment was given for the plaintiff. [Another report of the case gives as an additional reason that the defendant has an action over against the trespassers. Ed.]

TAYLOR v. CALDWELL

King's Bench, 1863.
3 B. & S. 826, 122 Eng.Rep. 309.

BLACKBURN, J. In this case the plaintiffs and defendants had, on the 27th May, 1861, entered into a contract by which the defendants agreed to let the plaintiffs have the use of The Surrey Gardens and Music Hall on four days then to come, *viz.*, the 17th June, 15th July, 5th August and 19th August, for the purpose of giving a series of four grand concerts, and day and night fêtes at the Gardens and Hall on those days respectively; and the plaintiffs agreed to take the Gardens and Hall on those days, and pay 100*l.* for each day.

The parties inaccurately call this a "letting," and the money to be paid a "rent"; but the whole agreement is such as to shew that the defendants were to retain the possession of the Hall and Gardens so that there was to be no demise of them, and that the contract was merely to give the plaintiffs the use of them on those days. Nothing however, in our opinion, depends on this. The agreement then proceeds to set out various stipulations between the parties as to what each was to supply for these concerts and entertainments, and as to the manner in which they should be carried on. The effect of the whole is to shew that the existence of the Music Hall in the Surrey Gardens in a state fit for a concert was essential for the fulfilment of the contract,—such entertainments as the parties contemplated in their agreement could not be given without it.

After the making of the agreement, and before the first day on which a concert was to be given, the Hall was destroyed by fire. This destruction, we must take it on the evidence, was without the fault of either party, and was so complete that in consequence the concerts could not be given as intended. And the question we have to decide is whether, under these circumstances, the loss which the plaintiffs have sustained is to fall upon the defendants. The parties when framing their agreement evidently had not present to their minds the possibility of such a disaster, and have made no express stipulation with reference to it, so that the answer to the question must depend upon the general rules of law applicable to such a contract.

There seems no doubt that where there is a positive contract to do a thing, not in itself unlawful, the contractor must perform it or pay damages for not doing it, although in consequence of unforeseen accidents, the performance of his contract has become unexpectedly burthensome or even impossible. ... But this rule is only applicable when the contract is positive and absolute, and not subject to any condition either express or implied: and there are authorities which, as we think, establish the principle that where, from the nature of the contract, it appears that the parties must from the beginning have known that it could not be fulfilled unless when the time for the fulfilment of the contract arrived some particular specified thing continued to exist, so that, when entering into the contract, they must have contemplated such continuing existence as the foundation of what was to be done; there, in the absence of any express or implied warranty that the thing shall exist, the contract is not to be construed as a positive contract, but as subject to an implied condition that the parties shall be excused in case, before breach, performance becomes impossible from the perishing of the thing without default of the contractor.

There seems little doubt that this implication tends to further the great object of making the legal construction such as to fulfil the intention of those who entered into the contract. For in the course of affairs men in making such contracts in general would, if it were brought to their minds, say that there should be such a condition.

Accordingly, in the Civil law, such an exception is implied in every obligation of the class which they call *obligatio de certo corpore*. ... The examples are of contracts respecting a slave, which was the common illustration of a certain subject used by the Roman lawyers, just as we are apt to take a horse; and no doubt the propriety, one might almost say necessity, of the implied condition is more obvious when the contract relates to a living animal, whether man or brute, than when it relates to some inanimate thing (such as in the present case a theatre) the existence of which is not so obviously precarious as that of the live animal, but the principle is adopted in the Civil law as applicable to every obligation of which the subject is a certain thing. The general subject is treated of by Pothier, who in his *Traité des Obligations*, partie 3, chap. 6, art. 3, § 668 states the result to be that the debtor *corporis certi* is freed from his obligation when the thing has perished, neither by his act, nor his neglect, and before he is in default, unless by some stipulation he has taken on himself the risk of the particular misfortune which has occurred.

Although the Civil law is not of itself authority in an English Court, it affords great assistance in investigating the principles on which the law is grounded. And it seems to us that the common law authorities establish that in such a contract the same condition of the continued existence of the thing is implied by English law.

There is a class of contracts in which a person binds himself to do something which requires to be performed by him in person; and such promises, *e.g.*, promises to marry, or promises to serve for a certain time, are never in practice qualified by an express exception of the death of the party; and therefore in such cases the contract is in terms broken if the promisor dies before fulfilment. Yet it was very early determined that, if the performance is personal, the executors are not liable; Hyde v. The Dean of Windsor (Cro.Eliz. 552, 553). *See* 2 Wms.Exors. 1560, 5th ed., where a very apt illustration is given. "Thus," says the learned author, "if an author undertakes to compose a work, and dies before completing it, his executors are discharged from this contract: for the undertaking is merely personal in its nature, and, by the intervention of the contractor's death, has become impossible to be performed." For this he cites a dictum of Lord Lyndhurst in Marshall v. Broadhurst (1 Tyr. 348, 349), and a case mentioned by Patteson J. in Wentworth v. Cook (10 A. & E. 42, 45–46). In Hall v. Wright (E.B. & E. 746, 749), Crompton J., in his judgment, puts another case. "Where a contract depends upon personal skill, and the act of God renders it impossible, as, for instance, in the case of a painter employed to paint a picture who is struck blind, it may be that the performance might be excused."

It seems that in those cases the only ground on which the parties or their executors, can be excused from the consequences of the breach of the contract is, that from the nature of the contract there is an implied condition of the continued existence of the life of the contractor, and, perhaps in the case of the painter of his eyesight. In the instances just given, the person, the continued existence of whose life is necessary to the fulfilment of the contract, is himself the contractor, but that does not seem in itself to be necessary to the application of the principle; as is illustrated by the following example. In the ordinary form of an apprentice deed the apprentice binds himself in unqualified terms to "serve until the full end and term of seven years to be fully complete and ended," during which term it is covenanted that the apprentice his master "faithfully shall serve," and the father of the apprentice in equally unqualified terms binds himself for the performance by the apprentice of all and every covenant on his part. (*See* the form, 2 *Chitty on Pleading*, 370, 7th ed. by Greening.) It is undeniable that if the apprentice dies within the seven years, the covenant of the father that he shall perform his covenant to serve for seven years is not fulfilled, yet surely it cannot be that an action would lie against the father? Yet the only reason why it would not is that he is excused because of the apprentice's death.

These are instances where the implied condition is of the life of a human being, but there are others in which the same implication is made as to the continued existence of a thing. For example, where a contract of sale is made amounting to a bargain and sale, transferring presently the property in specific chattels, which are to be delivered by the vendor at a future day; there, if the chattels, without the fault of the vendor, perish in the interval, the purchaser must pay the price and the vendor is excused from performing his contract to deliver, which has thus become impossible. . . .

It may, we think, be safely asserted to be now English law, that in all contracts of loan of chattels or bailments if the performance of the promise of the borrower or bailee to return the things lent or bailed, becomes impossible because it has perished, this impossibility (if not arising from the fault of the borrower or bailee from some risk which he has taken upon himself) excuses the borrower or bailee from the performance of his promise to redeliver the chattel. . . .

In none of these cases is the promise in words other than positive, nor is there any express stipulation that the destruction of the person or thing shall excuse the performance; but that excuse is by law implied, because from the nature of the contract it is apparent that the parties contracted on the basis of the continued existence of the particular person or chattel. In the present case, looking at the whole contract, we find that the parties contracted on the basis of the continued existence of the Music Hall at the time when the concerts were to be given; that being essential to their performance.

We think, therefore, that the Music Hall having ceased to exist, without fault of either party, both parties are excused, the plaintiffs from taking the gardens and paying the money, the defendants from performing their promise to give the use of the Hall and Gardens and other things. Consequently the rule must be absolute to enter the verdict for the defendants.

Rule absolute.

CNA INTERNATIONAL REINSURANCE CO., LTD. v. PHOENIX

Florida District Court of Appeals, 1st District, 1996.
678 So.2d 378.

JOANOS, JUDGE. . . . The case arises from the unfortunate death of the young actor, River Phoenix, originally of Gainesville, Florida, apparently due to an overdose of illegal drugs, before completion of two films, "Dark Blood" and "Interview With the Vampire," in which he had contracted to appear. As a result of the death, the "Dark Blood" project was totally abandoned. "Interview With the Vampire" was completed with another actor replacing Phoenix. CNA and American Casualty ... had written entertainment package insurance policies covering various aspects of the two productions. After paying the policy holders, CNA and American Casualty became subrogated to the claims the insureds had against the estate. ...

[Allegations of Phoenix's breach of contract were based upon his "general obligation not to do anything which would deprive the parties to the agreement of its benefits." In addition, it was alleged that "by deliberately taking illegal drugs in quantities in excess of those necessary to kill a human being, Phoenix deprived the parties of his services and breached his obligation." Ed.]

The estate moved to dismiss ..., contending there could be no cause of action for breach of contract because the personal services contracts were rendered impossible to perform due to the death. ... After hearings, the trial court granted the motion[ ] to dismiss with prejudice.

On appeal, CNA and American Casualty contend that the defense of impossibility of performance does not apply in this case because that doctrine requires that the impossibility be fortuitous and unavoidable, and that it occur through no fault of either party. They contend that because the death occurred from an intentional, massive overdose of illegal drugs, that this is not a situation in which neither party was at fault. The trial court very clearly ruled that even if the death was a suicide (there is no indication in the record that it was) or the result of an intentional, self-inflicted act, the doctrine of impossibility of performance applied.

[CNA and American Casualty] have candidly conceded that no case authorities exist in support of their position concerning fault in a case of impossibility due to death. [They] ask this court to find support for their theory in the following language of the *Restatement of Contracts 2d* §§ 261 and 262:

§ 261   Where, after a contract is made, a party's performance is made impracticable without his fault by the occurrence of an event the non-occurrence of which was a basic assumption on which the contract was made, his duty to render that performance is discharged, unless the language or the circumstances indicate the contrary.

§ 262   If the existence of a particular person is necessary for the performance of a duty, his death or such incapacity as makes performance impracticable is an event the nonoccurrence of which was a basic assumption on which the contract was made.

[CNA and American Casualty] contend the *Restatement* dictates that impossibility of performance due to the destruction of one's own health is not the sort of conduct that will excuse performance, citing Handicapped Children's Education Board v. Lukaszewski, 112 Wis.2d 197, 332 N.W.2d 774 (Wis.1983), and that the same reasoning should apply in a case of self-induced death. [They] also suggest a policy basis for the ruling they advocate, arguing that in a society dealing with increasing problems created by illegal drug abuse, such conduct should not excuse the performance of the contract.

At oral argument of this case, it became apparent that any attempt to discern fault in a death case such as this one, or in a similar case, perhaps involving the use of tobacco or alcohol would create another case by case and hard to interpret rule of law. Being mindful that there are already too many of these in existence, we are not persuaded by the facts or the arguments presented to depart from the clear and unambiguous rule that death renders a personal services contract impossible to perform. *See* 17A *Am.Jur.2d "Contracts"* § 688 (1991). In such contracts, "there is an implied condition that death shall dissolve the contract." *Id.* With this implied condition in mind, we believe the parties to the agreements could have provided specifically for the contingency of loss due to the use of illegal drugs, as they provided for other hazardous or life threatening contingencies.[3] We affirm the trial court's ruling that the doctrine of impossibility of performance applies in this case. . . .

CLARK v. WALLACE COUNTY COOPERATIVE EQUITY EXCHANGE

Court of Appeals of Kansas, 1999.
26 Kan.App.2d 463, 986 P.2d 391.

. . .

LEWIS, P.J. Ray C. Clark is a farmer. The Wallace County Cooperative Equity Exchange (Coop) operates, among other things, a grain elevator through which it buys and sells grain. In January 1995, Clark and Coop entered into a written agreement in which Clark agreed to sell Coop 4,000 bushels of corn to be delivered after the crop was harvested. At the time the contract was made, there may have been corn planted somewhere in Kansas, but it would have been far short of maturity. In September 1995, there was a freeze in the area, which severely damaged the corn crop. As a result of this freeze, Clark raised only 2,207.41 bushels of corn, which he delivered to Coop. Clark then maintained he was excused from delivering the remaining 1,392.59 bushels (after an allowed 10% reduction) because of the freeze. Coop insisted he was not excused and held the cost of the shortage out of the grain sale by Clark to Coop. This action was brought by Clark to recover the $1,622.97 that Coop withheld from his grain sale.

First, we note that these are rather common agreements used in the grain business. Anyone involved in this sort of an agreement realizes that one of the big risks is that the farmer may not be able to grow sufficient

---

3. For example, the actor loanout agreement pertaining to "Interview With the Vampire" provided:

From the date two (2) weeks before the scheduled start date of principal photography until the completion of all services required of Employee hereunder, Employee will not ride in any aircraft other than as a passenger on a scheduled flight of a United States or other major international air carrier maintaining regularly published schedules, or engage in any ultrahazardous activity without Producer's written consent in each case.

The entertainment package policies contained exclusions based on similar activities.

grain to deliver the required number of bushels. Clark seeks to be excused from his obligation to deliver because his crop was damaged by the weather. We suspect that if we adopted his reasoning, we would put an end to trading grain in this manner throughout the entire state of Kansas. It would have the effect of taking all the risk away from the farmer and placing the entire risk of loss on the grain elevators and, in fact, creating a potential situation where grain elevators could be bankrupted in the event of a large area crop loss.

Clark first argues that K.S.A. 84–2–613 [UCC § 2–613] excuses his performance. That particular provision of the Uniform Commercial Code (UCC) provides that

> Where the contract requires for its performance *goods identified when the contract is made*, and the goods suffer casualty without fault of either party before the risk of loss passes to the buyer . . .
>
> > (b) if the loss is partial . . . the buyer may . . . accept the goods with due allowance from the contract price for the deterioration or the deficiency in quantity but without further right against the seller. (Emphasis added.)

We conclude this particular statute does not relieve defendant from his obligation under the agreement in question because the goods were not identified at the time the contract was made.

In Milling Co. v. Edwards, 108 Kan. 616, 618, 197 P. 1113 (1921), the Kansas Supreme Court stated that in order to constitute a contract for the sale of a certain commodity under which the performance of delivery is excused by the destruction of the commodity, the contract must specify the land on which the commodity is to be grown.

Since the Edwards decision, the UCC was adopted in Kansas. There are, to the best of our knowledge, no post-UCC cases from Kansas which address this issue. However, we focus on a decision from the state of Washington. In Colley v. Bi–State, Inc., 21 Wash.App. 769, 586 P.2d 908 (1978), Colley failed to deliver the remaining bushels of wheat due under certain contracts with Bi–State, Inc. Colley was short on wheat and did not raise enough wheat to make delivery due to a hot, dry summer. He argued that because of the hot, dry summer, that Washington UCC § 2–613 excused delivery of the remaining wheat. The Washington court held that the contract did not expressly require Colley to grow the wheat himself or to grow it in any particular location, only to deliver 25,000 bushels to the elevator. Under those circumstances, the Washington court concluded that UCC § 2–613 did not excuse the delivery performance of the farmer. The court also indicated that the parties to this type of agreement intend to be bound to it regardless of the success of the seller's crop. *Id*. at 773–74, 586 P.2d 908.

We believe that the Washington decision is soundly reasoned and should be adopted as the law of this state.

Clark argues the trial court should have looked at the parties' intent when the agreement was made. However, at the same time, Clark stipulates that the agreement was complete, unambiguous, and free of uncertainty. Whether a contract's terms are ambiguous is a question of law to be decided by the court. If the contract is found to be unambiguous, the court must interpret the contract solely within its four corners, and extrinsic evidence is inadmissible. U.S. v. Mintz, 935 F.Supp. 1178, 1179 (D.Kan.1996). Insofar as Clark's specific complaint is concerned, there is no evidence in the record on appeal to indicate that Clark ever attempted to submit evidence of trade usage for the parties' intent or that the trial court ever denied the admission of such evidence. . . . We hold that a seller of grain is not excused by K.S.A. 84–2–613 from the delivery performance specified in an agreement of this nature when the grain is not identified by a specific tract of land on which it is to be grown.

Clark next argues that K.S.A. 84–2–615 [UCC § 2–615] provides some relief. Again, we do not agree. K.S.A. 84–2–615 reads as follows:

Except so far as a seller may have assumed a greater obligation and subject to the preceding section on substituted performance:

(a) Delay in delivery or nondelivery in whole or in part by a seller who complies with paragraphs (b) and (c) is not a breach of his duty under a contract for sale *if performance as agreed has been made impracticable by the occurrence of a contingency the nonoccurrence of which was a basic assumption on which the contract was made.* (Emphasis added.)

The first element which must be established to apply the statute quoted above is that performance must be impracticable. We addressed the issue of impracticability in Sunflower Electric Coop., Inc. v. Tomlinson Oil Co., 7 Kan.App.2d 131, 638 P.2d 963 (1981). In that case, we indicated there was a difference between subjective and objective impracticability. This difference can be illustrated by an individual who says "I cannot do it" versus a statement to the effect that "the thing cannot be done." Only objective impracticability may relieve a party of his or her contractual obligation. *Id.* at 139, 638 P.2d 963. In this case, there was no objective impracticability since the corn was not identified to be from specific land. The thing Clark had to do in this case was deliver 4,000 bushels of corn to the elevator. He could have done this. This is shown by the fact that Coop was able to cover the shortage on the instant contract by acquiring corn from another source. The fact is, Clark did not want to deliver the grain, but he had the ability to do so by purchasing grain to replace the grain he did not raise.

The Kansas comments to K.S.A. 84–2–615 state:

A seller . . . will not be excused under this section if (1) the non-occurrence of the contingency was the seller's fault; (2) the seller had reason to know of the impracticability (*i.e.,* the contingency was foreseeable); or (3) the seller assumed the risk of the contingency.

We do not deem it difficult to conclude that farmers in Kansas can foresee late September freezes which will reduce their corn yields. It has happened a number of times. If we were to excuse Clark from his obligation to deliver on the agreement, we would allow a farmer to enter into a forward grain contract on unspecified land, gamble on the extent of his supply, being aware of the fact that he may not raise sufficient grain, and then escape with impunity when his grain crop proves inadequate.

In addition, official UCC comments (5) and (9) to K.S.A. 84–2–615 refer to the concept of identifying the source of supply of the crop to be sold. As we pointed out above, the contract before this court did not identify a particular source of supply or a particular area where the corn was to be grown.

We hold that Clark's performance on the grain sales agreement in question was not excused by the provisions of K.S.A. 84–2–615.

Affirmed.

TRANSATLANTIC FINANCING CORP. v. UNITED STATES

United States Court of Appeals, District of Columbia Circuit, 1966.
363 F.2d 312.

J. SKELLY WRIGHT, CIRCUIT JUDGE. This appeal involves a voyage charter between Transatlantic Financing Corporation, operator of the SS CHRISTOS, and the United States covering carriage of a full cargo of wheat from a United States Gulf port to a safe port in Iran. The District Court dismissed a libel filed by Transatlantic against the United States for costs attributable to the ship's diversion from the normal sea route caused by the closing of the Suez Canal. We affirm.

On July 26, 1956, the Government of Egypt nationalized the Suez Canal Company and took over operation of the Canal. On October 2, 1956, during the international crisis which resulted from the seizure, the voyage charter in suit was executed between representatives of Transatlantic and the United States. The charter indicated the termini of the voyage but not the route. On October 27, 1956, the SS CHRISTOS sailed from Galveston for Bandar Shapur, Iran, on a course which would have taken her through Gibraltar and the Suez Canal. On October 29, 1956, Israel invaded Egypt. On October 31, 1956, Great Britain and France invaded the Suez Canal Zone. On November 2, 1956, the Egyptian Government obstructed the Suez Canal with sunken vessels and closed it to traffic.

On or about November 7, 1956, Beckmann, representing Transatlantic, contacted Potosky, an employee of the United States Department of Agriculture, who appellant concedes was unauthorized to bind the Government, requesting instructions concerning disposition of the cargo and seeking an agreement for payment of additional compensation for a voyage around the Cape of Good Hope. Potosky advised Beckmann that Transatlantic was expected to perform the charter according to its terms, that he did not believe Transatlantic was entitled to additional compensation for a voyage around the Cape, but that Transatlantic was free to file such a claim. Following this discussion, the CHRISTOS changed course for the Cape of Good Hope and eventually arrived in Bandar Shapur on December 30, 1956.

Transatlantic's claim is based on the following train of argument. The charter was a contract for a voyage from a Gulf port to Iran. Admiralty principles and practices, especially stemming from the doctrine of deviation, require us to imply into the contract the term that the voyage was to be performed by the "usual and customary" route. The usual and customary route from Texas to Iran was, at the time of contract, via Suez, so the contract was for a voyage from Texas to Iran via Suez. When Suez was closed this contract became impossible to perform. Consequently, appellant's argument continues, when Transatlantic delivered the cargo by going around the Cape of Good Hope, in compliance with the Government's demand under claim of right, it conferred a benefit upon the United States for which it should be paid in *quantum meruit.*

The doctrine of impossibility of performance has gradually been freed from the earlier fictional and unrealistic strictures of such tests as the "implied term" and the parties' "contemplation." Page, *The Development of the Doctrine of Impossibility of Performance,* 18 Mich.L.Rev. 589, 596 (1920). *See generally* 6 Corbin, *Contracts* §§ 1320–1372 (rev.ed. 1962); 6 Williston, *Contracts* §§ 1931–1979 (rev. ed. 1938). It is now recognized that "A thing is impossible in legal contemplation when it is not practicable; and a thing is impracticable when it can only be done at an excessive and unreasonable cost." Mineral Park [L]and Co. v. Howard, 172 Cal. 289, 293, 156 P. 458, 460, L.R.A. 1916F, 1 (1916). *Accord, Restatement, Contracts* § 454 (1932); Uniform Commercial Code § 2–615, cmt. 3. The doctrine ultimately represents the ever-shifting line, drawn by courts hopefully responsive to commercial practices and mores, at which the community's interest in having contracts enforced according to their terms is outweighed by the commercial senselessness of requiring performance.[1] When the issue is raised, the court is asked to construct a condition of performance based on the changed circumstances, a process which involves at least three reasonably definable steps. First, a contingency—something unexpected—must have occurred. Second, the risk of the unexpected occurrence must not have been allocated either by agreement or by custom. Finally, occurrence of the contingency must have rendered performance commercially impracticable.[3] Unless the court finds these three requirements satisfied, the plea of impossibility must fail.

---

1. While the impossibility issue rarely arises, as it has here, in a suit to recover the cost of an alternative method of performance, *compare Annot.,* 84 A.L.R.2d 12, 19 (1962), there is nothing necessarily inconsistent in claiming commercial impracticability for the method of performance actually adopted; the concept of impracticability assumes performance was physically possible. Moreover, a rule making nonperformance a condition precedent to recovery would unjustifiably encourage disappointment of expectations.

3. *Compare* Uniform Commercial Code § 2–615(a), which provides that, in the absence of an assumption of greater liability, delay or non-delivery by a seller is not a breach if performance as

The first requirement was met here. It seems reasonable, where no route is mentioned in a contract, to assume the parties expected performance by the usual and customary route at the time of contract.[4] Since the usual and customary route from Texas to Iran at the time of contract was through Suez, closure of the Canal made impossible the expected method of performance. But this unexpected development raises rather than resolves the impossibility issue, which turns additionally on whether the risk of the contingency's occurrence had been allocated and, if not, whether performance by alternative routes was rendered impracticable.

Proof that the risk of a contingency's occurrence has been allocated may be expressed in or implied from the agreement. Such proof may also be found in the surrounding circumstances, including custom and usages of the trade. *See* 6 *Corbin, supra,* § 1339, at 394–397; 6 *Williston, supra,* § 1948, at 5457–5458. The contract in this case does not expressly condition performance upon of the Suez route. Nor does it specify "via Suez" or, on the other hand, "via Suez or Cape of Good Hope." Nor are there provisions in the contract from which we may properly imply that the continued availability of Suez was a condition of performance.[8] Nor is there anything in custom or trade usage, or in the surrounding circumstances generally, which would support our constructing a condition of performance. The numerous cases requiring performance around the Cape when Suez was closed, *see e.g.,* Ocean Tramp Tankers Corp. v. V/O Sovfracht (The Eugenia), (1964) 2 Q.B. 226, and cases cited therein, indicate that the Cape route is generally regarded as an alternative means of performance. So the implied expectation that the route would be via Suez is hardly adequate proof of an allocation to the promisee of the risk of closure. In some cases, even an express expectation may not amount to a condition of performance.[9] The doctrine of deviation supports our

agreed is made "impracticable" by the occurrence of a "contingency" the non-occurrence of which was a "basic assumption on which the contract was made." To the extent this limits relief to "unforeseen" circumstances, cmt. 1, *see* the discussion below, and *compare* Uniform Commercial Code § 2–614(1). There may be a point beyond which agreement cannot go, Uniform Commercial Code § 2–615, cmt. 8, presumably the point at which the obligation would be "manifestly unreasonable," § 1–102(3) [Revised § 1–302], in bad faith, § 1–203 [Revised § 1–304], or unconscionable, § 2–302. For an application of these provisions see Judge Friendly's opinion in United States v. Wegematic Corporation, 360 F.2d 674 (2d Cir. 1966).

4. Uniform Commercial Code § 2–614, cmt.1, states: "Under this Article, in the absence of specific agreement, the normal or usual facilities enter into the agreement either through the circumstances, usage of trade or prior course of dealing." So long as this sort of assumption does not necessarily result in construction of a condition of performance, it is idle to argue over whether the usual and customary route is an "implied term." The issue of impracticability must eventually be met. One court refused to imply the Suez route as a contract term, but went on to rule the contract had been "frustrated." Carapanayoti & Co. Ltd. v. E. T. Green Ltd., (1959) 1 Q.B. 131. The holding was later rejected by the House of Lords. Tsakiroglou & Co. Ltd. v. Noblee Thorl G.m.b.H., (1960) 2 Q.B. 348.

8. The charter provides that the vessel is "in every way fitted for the voyage," and the "P. & I. Bunker Deviation Clause" refers to "the contract voyage" and the "direct and/or customary route." Appellant argues that these provisions require implication of a voyage by the direct and customary route. Actually they prove only what we are willing to accept-that the parties expected the usual and customary route would be used. The provisions in no way condition performance upon nonoccurrence of this contingency. . . .

9. Uniform Commercial Code § 2–614(1) provides: "Where without fault of either party . . . the agreed manner of delivery . . . becomes commercially impracticable but a commercially

assumption that parties normally expect performance by the usual and customary route, but it adds nothing beyond this that is probative of an allocation of the risk.[10]

If anything, the circumstances surrounding this contract indicate that the risk of the Canal's closure may be deemed to have been allocated to Transatlantic. We know or may safely assume that the parties were aware, as were most commercial men with interests affected by the Suez situation, *see The Eugenia, supra,* that the Canal might become a dangerous area. No doubt the tension affected freight rates, and it is arguable that the risk of closure became part of the dickered terms. Uniform Commercial Code § 2–615, cmt. 8. We do not deem the risk of closure so allocated, however. Foreseeability or even recognition of a risk does not necessarily prove its allocation.[11] *Compare* Uniform Commercial Code § 2–615, cmt.1; *Restatement, Contracts* § 457 (1932). Parties to a contract are not always able to provide for all the possibilities of which they are aware, sometimes because they cannot agree, often simply because they are too busy. Moreover, that some abnormal risk was contemplated is probative but does not necessarily establish an allocation of the risk of the contingency which actually occurs. In this case, for example, nationalization by Egypt of the Canal Corporation and formation of the Suez Users Group did not necessarily indicate that the Canal would be blocked even if a confrontation resulted.[12] The surrounding circumstances do indicate, however, a

---

reasonable substitute is available, such substitute performance must be tendered and accepted." *Compare* Mr. Justice Holmes' observation: "You can give any conclusion a logical form. You always can imply a condition in a contract. But [why] do you imply it? It is because of some belief as to the practice of the community or of a class, or because of some opinion as to policy...." Holmes, *The Path of the Law*, 10 Harv.L.Rev. 457, 466 (1897).

10. The deviation doctrine, drawn principally from admiralty insurance practice, implies into all relevant commercial instruments naming the termini of voyages the usual and customary route between those points. 1 Arnould, *Marine Insurance and Average* § 376, at 522 (10th ed. 1921). Insurance [is] cancelled when a ship unreasonably "deviates" from this course, for example by extending a voyage or by putting in at an irregular port, and the shipowner forfeits the protection of clauses of exception which might otherwise have protected him from his common law insurer's liability to cargo. *See* Gilmore & Black, *supra* note 8, § 2–6, at 59–60. This practice, properly qualified, *see id.* § 3–41, makes good sense, since insurance rates are computed on the basis of the implied course, and deviations in the course increasing the anticipated risk make the insurer's calculations meaningless. Arnould, *supra*, § 14, at 26. Thus the route, so far as insurance contracts are concerned, is crucial, whether express or implied. But even here, the implied term is not inflexible. Reasonable deviations do not result in loss of insurance, at least so long as established practice is followed. *See* Carriage of Goods by Sea Act § 4(4), 49 Stat. 1210, 46 U.S.C. § 1304(4); and discussion of "held covered" clauses in Gilmore & Black, *supra*, § 3–41, at 161. Some "deviations" are required. *E.g.*, Hirsch Lumber Co. v. Weyerhaeuser Steamship Co., 2 Cir., 233 F.2d 791, *cert. denied*, 352 U.S. 880, 77 S.Ct. 102, 1 L.Ed.2d 80 (1956). The doctrine's only relevance, therefore, is that it provides additional support for the assumption we willingly make that merchants agreeing to a voyage between two points expect that the usual and customary route between those points will be used. The doctrine provides no evidence of an allocation of the risk of the routes unavailability.

11. *See* Note, *The Fetish of Impossibility in the Law of Contracts*, 53 Colum.L.Rev. 94, 98 n. 23 (1953), suggesting that foreseeability is properly used "as a factor probative of assumption of the risk of impossibility."

12. Sources cited in the briefs indicate formation of the Suez Canal Users Association on October 1, 1956, was viewed in some quarters as an implied threat of force. *See N.Y. Times*, Oct. 2, 1956, p. 1, col. 1, noting, on the day the charter in this case was executed, that "Britain has declared her freedom to use force as a last resort if peaceful methods fail to achieve a satisfactory settlement." Secretary of State Dulles was able, however, to view the statement as evidence of the

willingness by Transatlantic to assume abnormal risks, and this fact should legitimately cause us to judge the impracticability of performance by an alternative route in stricter terms than we would were the contingency unforeseen.

We turn then to the question whether occurrence of the contingency rendered performance commercially impracticable under the circumstances of this case. The goods shipped were not subject to harm from the longer, less temperate Southern route. The vessel and crew were fit to proceed around the Cape.[13] Transatlantic was no less able than the United States to purchase insurance to cover the contingency's occurrence. If anything, it is more reasonable to expect owner-operators of vessels to insure against the hazards of war. They are in the best position to calculate the cost of performance by alternative routes (and therefore to estimate the amount of insurance required), and are undoubtedly sensitive to international troubles which uniquely affect the demand for and cost of their services. The only factor operating here in appellant's favor is the added expense, allegedly $43,972.00 above and beyond the contract price of $305,842.92, of extending a 10,000 mile voyage by approximately 3,000 miles. While it may be an overstatement to say that increased cost and difficulty of performance never constitute impracticability, to justify relief there must be more of a variation between expected cost and the cost of performing by an available alternative than is present in this case, where the promisor can legitimately be presumed to have accepted some degree of abnormal risk, and where impracticability is urged on the basis of added expense alone.[15]

We conclude, therefore, as have most other courts considering related issues arising out of the Suez closure,[16] that performance of this contract was not rendered legally impossible. Even if we agreed with appellant, its theory of relief seems untenable. When performance of a contract is deemed impossible it is a nullity. In the case of a charter party involving carriage of goods, the carrier may return to an appropriate port and unload its cargo, The Malcolm Baxter, Jr., 277 U.S. 323, 48 S.Ct. 516, 72 L.Ed. 901 (1928), subject of course to required steps to minimize damages.

---

canal users' "dedication to a just and peaceful solution." *The Suez Problem* 369–370 (Department of State Pub. 1956).

13. The issue of impracticability should no doubt be "an objective determination of whether the promise can reasonably be performed rather than a subjective inquiry into the promisor's capability of performing as agreed." Symposium, *The Uniform Commercial Code and Contract Law: Some Selected Problems*, 105 U.Pa.L.Rev. 836, 880, 887 (1957). Dealers should not be excused because of less than normal capabilities. But if both parties are aware of a dealer's limited capabilities, no objective determination would be complete without taking into account this fact.

15. *See* Uniform Commercial Code § 2–615, cmt. 4: "Increased cost alone does not excuse performance unless the rise in cost is due to some unforeseen contingency which alters the essential nature of the performance." *See also* 6 *Corbin, supra,* § 1333; 6 *Williston, supra,* § 1952, at 5468.

16. Appellant [unsuccessfully] seeks to distinguish the English cases supporting our view. . . . These cases certainly are not distinguishable, as appellant suggests, on the ground that they refer to "frustration" rather than to "impossibility." The English regard "frustration" as substantially identical with "impossibility." 6 *Corbin, supra,* § 1322, at 327 n. 9.

If the performance rendered has value, recovery in *quantum meruit* for the entire performance is proper. But here Transatlantic has collected its contract price, and now seeks *quantum meruit* relief for the additional expense of the trip around the Cape. If the contract is a nullity, Transatlantic's theory of relief should have been *quantum meruit* for the entire trip, rather than only for the extra expense. Transatlantic attempts to take its profit on the contract, and then force the Government to absorb the cost of the additional voyage. When impracticability without fault occurs, the law seeks an equitable solution, *see* 6 *Corbin, supra,* § 1321, and *quantum meruit* is one of its potent devices to achieve this end. There is no interest in casting the entire burden of commercial disaster on one party in order to preserve the other's profit. Apparently the contract price in this case was advantageous enough to deter appellant from taking a stance on damages consistent with its theory of liability. In any event, there is no basis for relief.

Affirmed.

EASTERN AIR LINES, INC. v. McDONNELL DOUGLAS CORP.

United States Court of Appeals, Fifth Circuit, 1976.
532 F.2d 957.

[A jury returned a verdict of about $24,500,000, in favor of Eastern Airlines against the defendant for breaches of a series of contracts for the delivery of approximately 100 jet planes. The breaches consisted of late deliveries. The contracts were negotiated in early 1965 at which time the Vietnam War "was having no significant effect on the American economy," and President Johnson was predicting a reduction in the military budget for the coming fiscal year. Between January 1965 and December 31, 1966, American troops deployed in Vietnam rose from 23,000 to 455,000. There was a concommitant escalation of production of military aircraft. Under the Defense Production Act, directives could be issued by government officials to manufacturers to give priority to military production. The evidence showed, however, that such directives were rarely issued. Instead "jawboning" was preferred. This usually consisted of telephone calls to business executives requesting priority on an informal basis. Implicit in such requests was a threat that a formal directive would be issued if the requests were not honored.

The defendant attributes its delays to government "jawboning" which caused it to subordinate civilian to military production. Similar "jawboning" caused the suppliers of component parts, such as landing gears, to make late deliveries. The trial judge ruled that evidence of government "jawboning" techniques was inadmissible. Ed.]

Ainsworth, Circuit Judge. . . .

IV.   The Vietnam War as an Excuse for Delayed Deliveries

. . .

B. The "Excusable Delay" Clause

McDonnell Douglas contends that the trial judge's instructions to the jury undercut the defense available to it under the excusable delay clause found in all of the contracts at issue in this appeal. In relevant part, the provision reads as follows:

> Seller shall not be responsible nor deemed to be in default on account of delays in performance ... due to causes beyond Seller's control and not occasioned by its fault or negligence, including but not being limited to ... any act of government, governmental priorities, allocation regulations or orders affecting materials, equipment, facilities or completed aircraft, ... failure of vendors (due to causes similar to those within the scope of this clause) to perform their contracts ..., provided such cause is beyond Seller's control.

1. Ejusdem Generis and the Applicability of U.C.C. § 2–615

McDonnell's first contention in this regard is that the District Court unduly narrowed the scope of this clause by instructing the jury that an excusable delay must be the result of "one or more of the listed events in the excusable delay clause of the contracts, or ... a similar cause beyond the defendant's control. ..." This instruction, in McDonnell's view, effectively construes the specifically listed excusable causes of delay as restricting the application of the more general phrase which exempts Douglas from liability for delays beyond its control and not due to its negligence. McDonnell feels, therefore, that its affirmative defense was unjustifiably limited to delays caused by events similar to those specifically listed when, in fact, the contracts excused all delays which were not its fault.

The trial judge's construction of the clause, moreover, affords McDonnell Douglas a narrower range of excuses than is available under the modern view of impossibility as it is codified in U.C.C. § 2–615. Simply stated, section 2–615 excuses delay or nondelivery when the agreed upon performance has been rendered "commercially impracticable" by an unforeseen supervening event not within the contemplation of the parties at the time the contract was entered into. Uniform Commercial Code § 2–615 (Cal.Comm.Code § 2615) cmts. 1 & 8; *see Restatement, Contracts* §§ 454, 457 (1932); 6 A. Corbin, *Contracts* §§ 1321, 1339 (1962).

Under section 2–615, the impossibility defense is available to the seller only if he has not "assumed a greater obligation" than that imposed upon him by this provision. During the trial, the court below ruled that section 2–615 was not applicable for this reason. Although the trial judge failed to explain his holding, it must have been based upon his restrictive construction of the excusable delay clause. Presumably, then, the protections of section 2–615 were deemed to have been waived because the contracts were interpreted as limiting McDonnell's impossibility defense to delays caused by events similar to those specifically provided for in the excusable delay clause.

In support of this approach, Eastern argues that the District Court correctly applied *ejusdem generis,* a canon of judicial construction limiting the application of general terms which follow specific ones to matters similar in kind or classification to those specified. This maxim, however, "is only an instrumentality for ascertaining the correct meaning of words when there is uncertainty." Gooch v. United States, 297 U.S. 124, 128, 56 S.Ct. 395, 397, 80 L.Ed. 522, 526 (1936). Obviously, the application of the doctrine in this case would make superfluous the unambiguous words "including but not being limited to" which precede the specifically listed excuses for delay. It is clear, then, that by excusing delays not within McDonnell's control nor due to its negligence, "including but not being limited to" governmental acts, priorities, or orders, the parties intended to excuse all delays coming within the general description regardless of their similarity to the listed excuses. Consequently, there is no basis for the trial judge's conclusion that McDonnell waived the protections of section 2–615 and that its contract excuses are narrower than those available under the doctrine of commercial impracticability.

2.   *The Foreseeability Issue*

McDonnell also challenges the trial judge's jury instruction which limited excusable delivery delays to those resulting from events which were not "reasonably foreseeable" at the time a contract was executed. By writing a foreseeability requirement into the excusable delay clause, the District Court appeared to construe the contracts as constituting nothing more than an application of the Code's commercial impracticability rule to those particular events specified in the contracts.[93]

Although there has been some doubt expressed as to whether the Code permits parties to bargain for exemptions broader than those available under section 2–615, this concern is ill-founded. *See* Hawkland, *The Energy Crisis and Section 2–615 of the Uniform Commercial Code,* 79 Com.L.J. 75 (1974). Comment 8 to this provision plainly indicates that parties may "enlarge upon or supplant" section 2–615. *See* United States v. Wegematic Corp., 2 Cir., 1966, 360 F.2d 674, 677 (Friendly, J.).

There appear to be however, certain strictures imposed upon judicial interpretation of such agreements. Comment 8 provides:

> Generally, express agreements as to exemptions designed to enlarge upon or supplant the provisions of this section are to be read in light of mercantile sense and reason, for this section itself sets up the commercial standard for normal and reasonable interpretation and provides a minimum beyond which agreement may not go.

While this provision could have been drafted in less vague terms, we presume that Comment 8 establishes "mercantile sense and reason" as a

---

93.   The trial court's instructions on this issue were as follows:

In seeking to excuse its delayed performance on the theory that the delays were due to causes beyond its control and not occasioned by its fault or negligence, the defendant has the burden of proving that any excusing event or occurrence upon which it relies was not reasonably foreseeable at the time the contract was entered into.

general standard governing our construction of agreements enlarging upon the protections of section 2–615. As we understand Comment 8, where there is doubt concerning the parties' intention, exemption clauses should not be construed as broadening the excuses available under the Code's impracticability rule. Applying this standard to the excusable delay clause, we cannot, in the absence of evidence to the contrary, hold that McDonnell is exempt from liability for any delay, regardless of its foreseeability, that is due to causes beyond its control. Exculpatory provisions which are phrased merely in general terms have long been construed as excusing only unforeseen events which make performance impracticable. [citations] Courts have often held, therefore, that if a promisor desires to broaden the protections available under the excuse doctrine he should provide for the excusing contingencies with particularity and not in general language.

We realize, of course, that this rule of construction developed in the pre-U.C.C. era when the scope of the impossibility and frustration doctrines was unclear and varied from jurisdiction to jurisdiction. Because of the uncertainty surrounding the law of excuse, parties had good reason to resort to general contract provisions relieving the promisor of liability for breaches caused by events "beyond his control." Although the Uniform Commercial Code has ostensibly eliminated the need for such clauses, lawyers, either through an abundance of caution or by force of habit, continue to write them into contract. *See generally* Squillante & Congalton, *Force Majeure*, 80 Com.L.J. 4, 8–9 (1975). Thus, even though our interpretation would render the general terms of the excusable delay clause merely duplicative of section 2–615, we will adhere to the established rule of construction because it continues to reflect prevailing commercial practices.

We reiterate, however, that we are applying only a canon of contract interpretation which generally reflects commercial standards of reasonableness. We disagree with the suggestion of [Professor Hawkland] that section 2–615 imposes a fixed standard governing the interpretation of exemption clauses. [*Hawkland, supra,* at 79.] The Code establishes no absolute requirement that any agreement purporting to enlarge upon section 2–615 must do so in plain and specific language. Even in the absence of detailed wording, trade usage and the circumstances surrounding a particular agreement may indicate that the parties intended to accord the seller an exemption broader than is available under the U.C.C.[96]

---

96. As Comment 8 indicates, however, there is a point beyond which any such agreement may not go. Professor Hawkland suggests that the "minimum" established by section 2–615 includes the duty of the seller to allocate deliveries among his customers and to notify the buyer of any delivery delay or nondelivery. *Hawkland, supra,* at 79. One student commentator, though, appears to construe Comment 8 as limiting the degree to which a seller's protections under section 2–615 can be narrowed. Note, *UCC § 2–615: Sharp Inflationary Increases in Cost as Excuse from Performance of Contract,* 50 Notre Dame Law. 297, 300–301 (1974). In any event, exemption provisions are limited by those sections of the Code prohibiting agreements which are "manifestly unreasonable"(§ 1–102(3)) [Revised § 1–302], in bad faith (§ 1–203) [Revised § 1–

While we hold that the provision of the excusable delay clause exempting McDonnell from liability for delays beyond its control should be interpreted as incorporating the Code's commercial impracticability doctrine, we disagree with the trial judge's jury instruction on foreseeability insofar as it implies that the events specifically listed in the excusable delay clause in each contract must have been unforeseeable at the time the agreement was executed. The rationale for the doctrine of impracticability is that the circumstance causing the breach has made performance so vitally different from what was anticipated that the contract cannot reasonably be thought to govern. 6 S. Williston, *Contracts* § 1963 at 5511 (rev. ed. 1938). However, because the purpose of a contract is to place the reasonable risk of performance on the promisor, he is presumed, in the absence of evidence to the contrary, to have agreed to bear any loss occasioned by an event which was foreseeable at the time of contracting. Lloyd v. Murphy, 1944, 25 Cal.2d 48, 54, 153 P.2d 47, 50 (Traynor, J.). Underlying this presumption is the view that a promisor can protect himself against foreseeable events by means of an express provision in the agreement.

Therefore, when the promisor has anticipated a particular event by specifically providing for it in a contract, he should be relieved of liability for the occurrence of such event regardless of whether it was foreseeable. *See* Edward Maurer Co. v. Tubeless Tire Co., 6 Cir., 1922, 285 F. 713, 714–15. As Justice Traynor noted for the California Supreme Court under different but nonetheless analogous circumstances,

> the question whether a risk was foreseeable is quite distinct from the question whether it was contemplated by the parties. ... When a risk has been contemplated and voluntarily assumed ... foreseeability is not an issue and the parties will be held to the bargain they made.

Glenn R. Sewell Sheet Metal, Inc. v. Loverde, 1969, 70 Cal.2d 666, 451 P.2d 721, 728 n. 13. In this case, it is clear that Eastern specifically "contemplated and voluntarily assumed" the risk that deliveries would be delayed by governmental acts, priorities, regulations or orders. Moreover, unlike the only case cited to us by Eastern which construes a similar provision, United States v. Brooks–Callaway Co., 318 U.S. 120, 63 S.Ct. 474, 87 L.Ed. 653 (1943), there is no indication from the wording of the excusable delay clause that McDonnell's defenses are to be limited to breaches caused by unforeseeable events. Therefore, we must conclude that the trial judge erred in instructing the jury that the events specifically listed in the excusable delay clause must have been unforeseeable at the time the contracts were entered into for McDonnell to claim exemption from liability.

3. *Informal Demands for Priority as an "Act of Government"*

Turning next to the question of whether the Government's informal priorities policy came within the ambit of the excusable delay clause, we

---

304], or unconscionable (§ 2–302). *See* Transatlantic Financing Corp. v. United States, 1966, 124 U.S.App.D.C. 183, 363 F.2d 312, 315 n. 3.

have seen in Part IV–A of this opinion that McDonnell and its suppliers, in granting priority to the military, were cooperating with the established, publicly announced procurement policy of the Federal Government. Eastern contends, however, that this informal program did not come within the scope of the contract clause specifically excusing "any act of government, governmental priorities, allocations, or orders affecting materials." Asserting that the Defense Production Act authorizes the Government to obtain precedence for certain orders only by means of formal, published regulations, Eastern concludes that any other method is illegal, if not unconstitutional, and therefore cannot be deemed an act of Government. We disagree for the following reasons.

The Defense Production Act, in "a sweeping delegation of power," grants the President broad authority to require that defense-related contracts be given precedence over less essential orders. D.P.A. § 101(a), 50 App.U.S.C. § 2071(a). Congress created no detailed scheme by which this power was to be exercised, providing only that "(t)he President may make such rules, regulations, and orders as he deems necessary or appropriate." D.P.A. § 704, 50 App.U.S.C. § 2154. There is, moreover, nothing in either the legislative history of the D.P.A. or in the wording of the Act itself which gives any indication that the Government may not seek compliance with its priorities policies by informal means. It is reasonable to conclude, therefore, that Congress intended to accord the Executive Branch great flexibility in molding its priorities policies to the frequently unanticipated exigencies of national defense.

This conclusion is reinforced by the fact that the Defense Production Act of 1950 was enacted in the face of established legal authority which had consistently construed previous procurement statutes as authorizing informal and indirect methods of securing compliance with the Government's military priorities policy. It was recognized that, for reasons of practical necessity, urgently needed government orders had to be obtained "by non-mandatory directions based ultimately on the powers of compulsion rather than by the actual exercise of the statutory compulsive powers." Dodd, *Impossibility of Performance of Contracts Due to War–Time Regulations*, 32 Harv.L.Rev. 789, 798 (1919). The military's need for speed and flexibility in directing the flow of necessary materials precluded a ponderous bureaucratic procurement process. Thus, even though the World War I National Defense Act, 39 Stat. 213 (June 3, 1916), specifically provided that either the President or a department head placed priorities orders, several decisions held that literal compliance with this requirement was not necessary. . . .

During World War II, a similarly liberal view was taken of the Government's procurement authority. . . .

There can be little question, then, that the Defense Production Act granted the Government authority to seek compliance with its priorities programs by informal means of persuasion whether written or oral. For this reason, many of the decisions relied on by Eastern are inapposite here.

We note, moreover, that this case precisely fits an established pattern of decisions rejecting the contention that breaches of contract are excused only by formal or technical acts of Government. Whether predicated on a contractual provision or simply on the common law defense of impossibility these decisions indicate in the clearest terms that fundamentally coercive acts of Government, whatever their form, constitute an excuse for breach. Thus, a promisor is not liable merely because the government order causing a breach is technically deficient. Texas Co. v. Hogarth Shipping Corp., 256 U.S. 619, 41 S.Ct. 612, 65 L.Ed. 1123 (1921). Neither is he required to resist a government requisition in order to be excused from performance. The Claveresk, 2 Cir., 1920, 264 F. 276. As the *Claveresk* court observed, "it would be 'a strange law' which required . . . (a promisor) to resist, 'till the hand of power was laid upon him, an order which it was his duty to obey.'" 264 F. at 280–81. The Supreme Court, moreover, has excused breaches caused by a promisor's anticipation of government action. The Kronprinzessin Cecilie, 244 U.S. 12, 37 S.Ct. 490, 61 L.Ed. 960 (1917). Writing for the Court, Mr. Justice Holmes found the impossibility doctrine applicable to a ship which returned to port in expectation of World War I but before its actual declaration:

> (I)t hardly could change . . . (the ship owner's) liability that he prophetically and rightly had anticipated the . . . (war) by twenty-four hours. We are wholly unable to accept the argument that although a shipowner may give up his voyage to avoid capture after war is declared, he never is at liberty to anticipate war.

244 U.S. at 24, 37 S.Ct. at 492, 61 L.Ed. at 966. Thus, the "apprehension of restraint, something much less than actual government compulsion, may suffice to dissolve the obligation of a contract." The Claveresk, *supra*, 264 F. at 282. . . .

Consequently, we will not permit the form of the military priorities policy to disguise what was in substance a governmental act beyond the control of McDonnell Douglas. The excusable delay clause cannot be made to turn on a distinction which for so long has been held to be entirely artificial and unrealistic. As Mr. Justice Holmes stated in a very similar context, "(b)usiness contracts must be construed with business sense, as they naturally would be understood by intelligent men of affairs." The Kronprinzessin Cecilie, *supra*, 244 U.S. at 24, 37 S.Ct. at 492, 61 L.Ed. at 966.

This approach, moreover, is consistent with that required under the Uniform Commercial Code. In Comment 10 to section 615, the draftsmen of Article 2 stated:

> Following its basic policy of using commercial practicability as a test for excuse, this section . . . disregards any technical distinctions between "law," "regulation," "order" and the like. Nor does it make the present action of the seller depend upon the eventual judicial

determination of the legality of the particular governmental action. The seller's good faith belief in the validity of the regulation is the test under this Article and the best evidence of his good faith is the general commercial acceptance of the regulation.

Given McDonnell's unquestioned good faith in complying with the Government's demands for priority and the uncontroverted evidence of the entire aviation industry's acceptance of the policy, we must hold as a matter of law that McDonnell is not liable for any delivery delay proximately resulting from the informal procurement program. . . .

Reversed and remanded for a new trial.

ALBRE MARBLE AND TILE CO., INC.
v. JOHN BOWEN CO., INC.

Supreme Judicial Court of Massachusetts, Suffolk., 1959.
338 Mass. 394, 155 N.E.2d 437.

SPALDING, JUSTICE. . . . The plaintiff . . . seeks damages for the defendant's alleged breach of two subcontracts under which the plaintiff agreed to supply labor and materials to the defendant as general contractor of the Chronic Disease Hospital and Nurses' Home in Boston. [The defendant's defense is that "the performance of the subcontracts became impossible when the defendant's general contract with the Commonwealth was declared invalid by this court in Gifford v. Commissioner of Public Health, 328 Mass. 608, 105 N.E.2d 476."] . . . [T]he plaintiff [also] seeks to recover [based on *quantum meruit*] the value of work and labor furnished by it to the defendant at the defendant's request [to which the defendant asserts several defenses]. . . . [The trial court allowed the defendant's motion for the "immediate entry of judgment in its favor" on all counts, to which the plaintiff excepted and appealed.]

The first question is whether the pleadings and affidavits show that a genuine issue of fact exists as to . . . breach of contract. . . . The facts and circumstances leading to the declaration of the invalidity of the defendant's general contract with the Commonwealth have been recited in prior decisions and need not be recounted here. *See* Gifford v. Commissioner of Public Health, 328 Mass. 608, 105 N.E.2d 476; M. Ahern Co. v. John Bowen Co. Inc., 334 Mass. 36, 133 N.E.2d 484; Boston Plate & Window Glass Co. v. John Bowen Co. Inc., 335 Mass. 697, 141 N.E.2d. [The plaintiff's affidavit asserts on information and belief] that the defendant wilfully submitted a bid that was contrary to law in that the cost of performance bonds for the subcontractors was not included; that the general contract awarded to the defendant was procured by fraud; and that the defendant, with knowledge of the infirmities of the general contract, fraudulently induced the plaintiff to enter into the subcontracts. The plaintiff thus attempted to avoid the defence [*sic*] of impossibility by asserting that the invalidity of the general contract was caused by the wrongful acts of the defendant. [The court finds that plaintiff's affidavit stating facts "on information and belief" without pursuing discovery against defendant fails to comply with statutory requirements for a showing that a genuine issue of material fact exists as to defendant's breach of contract. It therefore affirms the judgment below based upon the defense of impossibility. Ed.]

We turn now to ... [*quantum meruit* claims] by which the plaintiff seeks a recovery for the fair value of work and labor furnished to the defendant prior to the termination of the general contract. The plaintiff seeks recovery ... for "preparation of samples, shop drawings, tests and affidavits" in connection with the tile [and marble] work....

The defendant in its affidavit maintains that the tile and marble work to be furnished by the plaintiff could not have been done until late in the construction process; that no tile or marble was actually installed in the building; and that the expenses incurred by the plaintiff prior to the time the general contract was declared invalid consisted solely of expenditures in preparation for performance. Relying on the decision in Young v. Chicopee, 186 Mass. 518, 72 N.E. 63, the defendant maintains that where a building contract has been rendered impossible of performance a plaintiff may not recover for expenses incurred in preparation for performance, but may recover only for the labor and materials "wrought into" the structure. Therefore, the defendant says, the plaintiff should take nothing here.

The plaintiff places its reliance upon a clause appearing in both contracts which provides in part: "It is agreed you (the plaintiff) will furnish and submit all necessary or required samples, shop drawings, tests, affidavits, etc., for approval, all as ordered or specified...." The plaintiff in effect concedes that no labor or materials were actually wrought into the structure, but argues that the contract provision quoted above placed its preparatory efforts under the supervision of the defendant, and that this circumstance removes this case from the ambit of those decisions which apply the "wrought-in" principle. ...

The problem of allocating losses where a building contract has been rendered impossible of performance by a supervening act not chargeable to either party is a vexed one. In situations where the part performance of one party measurably exceeds that of the other the tendency has been to allow recovery for the fair value of work done in the actual performance of the contract and to deny recovery for expenditures made in reliance upon the contract or in preparing to perform. This principle has sometimes been expressed in terms of "benefit" or "lack of benefit." In other words, recovery may be had only for those expenditures which, but for the supervening act, would have enured to the benefit of the defendant as contemplated by the contract. The "wrought-in" principle applied in building contract cases is merely a variant of this principle. It has long been recognized that this theory is unworkable if the concept of benefit is applied literally. In M. Ahern Co. v. John Bowen Co. Inc., 334 Mass. 36, 41, 133 N.E.2d 484, 487, we quoted with approval the statement of Professor Williston that "It is enough that the defendant has actually received in part performance of the contract something for which when completed he had agreed to pay a price." *Williston on Contracts* (Rev. ed.) § 1976.

Although the matter of denial of reliance expenditures in impossibility situations seems to have been discussed but little in judicial opinions, it has, however, been the subject of critical comment by scholars. *See* Fuller and Perdue, *The Reliance Interest in Contract Damages*, 46 Yale L.J. 52, 373, 379–383. In England the recent frustrated contracts legislation provides that the court may grant recovery for expenditures in reliance on the contract or in preparation to perform it where it appears *"just to do so having regard to all the circumstances of the case"* (emphasis supplied). 6 & 7 George VI, c. 40.

We are of opinion that the plaintiff here may recover for those expenditures made pursuant to the specific request of the defendant as set forth in the contract clause quoted above. A combination of factors peculiar to this case justifies such a holding without laying down the broader principle that in every case recovery may be had for payments made or obligations reasonably incurred in preparation for performance of a contract where further performance is rendered impossible without fault by either party.

The factors which determine the holding here are these: First, this is not a case of mere impossibility by reason of a supervening act. The opinion of this court in M. Ahern Co. v. John Bowen Co. Inc., 334 Mass. 36, 133 N.E.2d 484, points out that the defendant's involvement in creating the impossibility was greater than that of its subcontractors. The facts regarding the defendant's conduct are set forth in that opinion and need not be restated. Although the defendant's conduct was not so culpable as to render it liable for breach of contract (Boston Plate & Window Glass Co. v. John Bowen Co. Inc., 335 Mass. 697, 141 N.E.2d 715), nevertheless, it was a contributing factor to a loss sustained by the plaintiff which as between the plaintiff and the defendant the latter ought to bear to the extent herein permitted.

We attach significance to the clause in the contract, which was prepared by the defendant, specifically requesting the plaintiff to submit samples, shop drawings, tests, affidavits, etc., to the defendant. This is not a case in which all efforts in preparation for performance were solely within the discretion and control of the subcontractor. . . .

Moreover, the acts requested here by their very nature could not be "wrought into" the structure. In Angus v. Scully, 176 Mass. 357, 57 N.E. 674, 49 A.L.R. 562, recovery for the value of services rendered by house movers was allowed although the house was destroyed midway in the moving. . . .

We hold that the damages to be assessed are limited solely to the fair value of those acts done in conformity with the specific request of the defendant as contained in the contract. Expenses incurred prior to the execution of the contract, such as those arising out of preparing the plaintiff's bid, are not to be considered.

. . . [T]he case is remanded to the Superior Court for further proceedings in conformity with this opinion. . . .

So ordered.

PROBLEMS

1. Farmer S entered into a written agreement to sell to B 40,000 bushels of soybeans from the crop S expected to plant in about a month on her local farm "BarBean." When a drought destroyed S's crop so that she was unable to fulfill her contract, B sued her for damages. Is S liable for breach under the UCC? (See UCC § 2–501(1) for the timing of identification of goods to the contract for sale.)

2. D contracted to build a building for P on a certain piece of land according to plans prepared by D, annexed to, and made part of, the written contract. Twice in succession the building collapsed after it had been raised to the third floor due to presence of quicksand in the subsoil. D then refused to rebuild and P sued for damages. What result?

3. Plaintiff contracted to repair a wooden bridge over the Connecticut River and had completed a goodly portion of the repairs when a fire totally destroyed the bridge as well as a large amount of lumber plaintiff had stored near the bridge for use in repairing it. Plaintiff sues. For what, if anything, may plaintiff recover?

4. Kelley, a mining engineer, was hired by Thompson to supervise the prospecting of coal on a large tract of land. It was agreed that he would be paid $125 per month. In addition, if the prospecting were successful and certain other conditions were met, Thompson agreed to form and manage a corporation to operate a coal mine at the site and to give Kelley a one-eighth interest in the corporation. Kelley located a rich vein of coal and the other conditions occurred. Thompson died before forming a corporation and his representative refused to carry out the promise to form a corporation and to give Kelley a one-eighth interest in it. Kelley sues. What result?

5. In consideration of a right of way given by plaintiff to defendant, a railroad, the defendant agreed to give to the plaintiff annual passes during plaintiff's life. After about 10 years the Federal Government enacted a law that made it illegal for the defendant to issue any further annual passes. What are the rights of the parties?

6. Plaintiff contracted with the defendant for the sale and purchase of certain silk. By the terms of the agreement shipment was to be made by freight before March 4. Shipment was not made until March 12 because of an embargo placed by the Railroad Administration on shipments of silk by rail. What result?

7. D contracted to deliver to P fixed quantities of pulpwood over a fixed period of time from a particular tract at $5.50 per cord. Before any deliveries were called for under the contract all of the pulpwood on the tract was fortuitously destroyed by fire except the trees on top of a high mountain

which could be cut and delivered only at an expense of $20 per cord. D refused to deliver this pulpwood. P sues for damages for failure to deliver pursuant to the terms of the contract. What result? Would the result be different if some of the pulpwood could and should have been delivered prior to the fire?

8.   Gasco contracted to deliver to plaintiff all plaintiff's requirements of propane for a five year term up to a total maximum amount. Gasco has numerous other customers, but is not bound by contract to any of the other customers. During the energy crisis of 1973, there was a shortfall of propane available to Gasco. The circumstances were such that the shortfall was due to "a contingency the non-occurrence of which was a basic assumption on which the contract was made." Gasco has notified plaintiff that it would limit deliveries to a stated percentage of plaintiff's actual requirements. Plaintiff sues, contending truthfully that Gasco has adequate supplies to supply plaintiff's requirements. Plaintiff argues that the shortfall should be visited solely upon Gasco's non-contract customers. What result?

9.   When a buyer is rightfully told by the seller that because of impracticability she will be shipped only 75% of the quantity of goods she has contracted to buy, must the buyer accept?

SECTION 2.   FRUSTRATION

KRELL v. HENRY

Court of Appeal, 1903.
[1903] 2 K.B. 740.

The plaintiff, Paul Krell, sued the defendant, C.S. Henry, for 50*l*, being the balance of a sum of 75*l*, for which the defendant had agreed to hire a flat at 56A, Pall Mall on the days of June 26 and 27, for the purpose of viewing the processions to be held in connection with the coronation of His Majesty [Edward VII]. The defendant denied his liability, and counter-claimed for the return of the sum of 25*l*, which had been paid as a deposit, on the ground that, the processions not having taken place owing to the serious illness of the King, there had been a total failure of consideration for the contract entered into by him.

The facts, which were not disputed, were as follows. The plaintiff on leaving the country in March, 1902, left instructions with his solicitor to let his suite of chambers at 56A, Pall Mall on such terms and for such period (not exceeding six months) as he thought proper. On June 17, 1902, the defendant noticed an announcement in the windows of the plaintiff's flat to the effect that windows to view the coronation processions were to be let. The defendant interviewed the housekeeper on the subject, when it was pointed out to him what a good view of the processions could be obtained from the premises, and he eventually agreed with the housekeeper to take the suite for the two days in question for a sum of 75*l*.

On June 20 the defendant wrote the following letter to the plaintiff's solicitor:—

> I am in receipt of yours of the 18th instant, inclosing form of agreement for the suite of chambers on the third floor at 56A, Pall Mall, which I have agreed to take for the two days, the 26th and 27th instant, for the sum of 75*l*. For reasons given you I cannot enter into the agreement, but as arranged over the telephone I inclose herewith cheque for 25*l* as deposit, and will thank you to confirm to me that I shall have the entire use of these rooms during the days (not the nights) of the 26th and 27th instant. You may rely that every care will be taken of the premises and their contents. On the 24th inst. I will pay the balance, *viz.*, 50*l*, to complete the 75*l* agreed upon.

On the same day the defendant received the following reply from the plaintiff's solicitor:—

> I am in receipt of your letter of to-day's date inclosing cheque for 25*l* deposit on your agreeing to take Mr. Krell's chambers on the third floor at 56A, Pall Mall for the two days, the 26th and 27th June, and I confirm the agreement that you are to have the entire use of these rooms during the days (but not the nights), the balance, 50*l*, to be paid to me on Tuesday next the 24th instant.

The processions not having taken place on the days originally appointed, namely, June 26 and 27, the defendant declined to pay the balance of 50*l* alleged to be due from him under the contract in writing of June 20 constituted by the above two letters. Hence the present action.

Darling J., on August 11, 1902, held, upon the authority of *Taylor* v. *Caldwell* and *The Moorcock*, that there was an implied condition in the contract that the procession should take place, and gave judgment for the defendant on the claim and counter-claim.

The plaintiff appealed. . . .

VAUGHAN WILLIAMS L.J. read the following written judgment:—The real question in this case is the extent of the application in English law of the principle of the Roman law which has been adopted and acted on in many English decisions, and notably in the case of *Taylor* v. *Caldwell*. That case at least makes it clear that

> where, from the nature of the contract, it appears that the parties must from the beginning have known that it could not be fulfilled unless, when the time for the fulfilment of the contract arrived, some particular specified thing continued to exist, so that when entering into the contract they must have contemplated such continued existence as the foundation of what was to be done; there, in the absence of any express or implied warranty that the thing shall exist, the contract is not to be considered a positive contract, but as subject to an implied condition that the parties shall be excused in case, before breach, performance becomes impossible from the perishing of the thing without default of the contractor.

Thus far it is clear that the principle of the Roman law has been introduced into the English law. The doubt in the present case arises as to how far this principle extends. . . .

I do not think that the principle of the civil law as introduced into the English law is limited to cases in which the event causing the impossibility of performance is the destruction or nonexistence of some thing which is the subject-matter of the contract or of some condition or state of things expressly specified as a condition of it. I think that you first have to ascertain, not necessarily from the terms of the contract, but, if required, from necessary inferences, drawn from surrounding circumstances recognised by both contracting parties, what is the substance of the contract, and then to ask the question whether that substantial contract needs for its foundation the assumption of the existence of a particular state of things. If it does, this will limit the operation of the general words, and in such case, if the contract becomes impossible of performance by reason of the nonexistence of the state of things assumed by both contracting parties as the foundation of the contract, there will be no breach of the contract thus limited.

Now what are the facts of the present case? The contract is contained in two letters of June 20 which passed between the defendant and the plaintiff's agent, Mr. Cecil Bisgood. These letters do not mention the coronation, but speak merely of the taking of Mr. Krell's chambers, or, rather, of the use of them, in the daytime of June 26 and 27, for the sum of 75*l*, 25*l* then paid, balance 50*l* to be paid on the 24th. But the affidavits, which by agreement between the parties are to be taken as stating the facts of the case, shew that the plaintiff exhibited on his premises, third floor, 56A, Pall Mall, an announcement to the effect that windows to view the Royal coronation procession were to be let, and that the defendant was induced by that announcement to apply to the housekeeper on the premises, who said that the owner was willing to let the suite of rooms for the purpose of seeing the Royal procession for both days, but not nights, of June 26 and 27. In my judgment the use of the rooms was let and taken for the purpose of seeing the Royal procession. It was not a demise of the rooms, or even an agreement to let and take the rooms. It is a licence to use rooms for a particular purpose and none other. And in my judgment the taking place of those processions on the days proclaimed along the proclaimed route, which passed 56A, Pall Mall, was regarded by both contracting parties as the foundation of the contract; and I think that it cannot reasonably be supposed to have been in the contemplation of the contracting parties, when the contract was made, that the coronation would not be held on the proclaimed days, or the processions not take place on those days along the proclaimed route; and I think that the words imposing on the defendant the obligation to accept and pay for the use of the rooms for the named days, although general and unconditional, were not used with reference to the possibility of the particular contingency which afterwards occurred.

It was suggested in the course of the argument that if the occurrence, on the proclaimed days, of the coronation and the procession in this case were the foundation of the contract, and if the general words are thereby limited or qualified, so that in the event of the non-occurrence of the coronation and procession along the proclaimed route they would discharge both parties from further performance of the contract, it would follow that if a cabman was engaged to take some one to Epsom on Derby Day at a suitable enhanced price for such a journey, say 10*l*, both parties to the contract would be discharged in the contingency of the race at Epsom for some reason becoming impossible; but I do not think this follows, for I do not think that in the cab case the happening of the race would be the foundation of the contract. No doubt the purpose of the engager would be to go to see the Derby, and the price would be proportionately high; but the cab had no special qualifications for the purpose which led to the selection of the cab for this particular occasion. Any other cab would have done as well. Moreover, I think that, under the cab contract, the hirer, even if the race went off, could have said, "Drive me to Epsom; I will pay you the agreed sum; you have nothing to do with the purpose for which I hired the cab," and that if the cabman refused he would have been guilty of a breach of contract, there being nothing to qualify his promise to drive the hirer to Epsom on a particular day.

Whereas in the case of the coronation, there is not merely the purpose of the hirer to see the coronation procession, but it is the coronation procession and the relative position of the rooms which is the basis of the contract as much for the lessor as the hirer; and I think that if the King, before the coronation day and after the contract, had died, the hirer could not have insisted on having the rooms on the days named. It could not in the cab case be reasonably said that seeing the Derby race was the foundation of the contract, as it was of the licence in this case. Whereas in the present case, where the rooms were offered and taken, by reason of their peculiar suitability from the position of the rooms for a view of the coronation procession, surely the view of the coronation procession was the foundation of the contract, which is a very different thing from the purpose of the man who engaged the cab—namely, to see the race—being held to be the foundation of the contract. Each case must be judged by its own circumstances. In each case one must ask oneself, first, what, having regard to all the circumstances, was the foundation of the contract? Secondly, was the performance of the contract prevented? Thirdly, was the event which prevented the performance of the contract of such a character that it cannot reasonably be said to have been in the contemplation of the parties at the date of the contract? If all these questions are answered in the affirmative (as I think they should be in this case). I think both parties are discharged from further performance of the contract. I think that the coronation procession was the foundation of this contract, and that the non-happening of it prevented the performance of the contract; and, secondly, I think that the non-happening of the procession, to use the words of Sir James Hannen in *Baily* v. *De Crespigny*, was an event of such a character that it cannot reasonably be supposed to have been in the contemplation of the contracting parties when the contract was made, and that they are not to be held bound by general words which, though large enough to include, were not used with reference to the possibility of the particular contingency which afterwards happened.

The test seems to be whether the event which causes the impossibility was or might have been anticipated and guarded against. It seems difficult to say, in a case where both parties anticipate the happening of an event, which anticipation is the foundation of the contract, that either party must be taken to have anticipated, and ought to have guarded against, the event which prevented the performance of the contract. . . .

I myself am clearly of opinion that in this case, where we have to ask ourselves whether the object of the contract was frustrated by the nonhappening of the coronation and its procession on the days proclaimed, parol evidence is admissible to shew that the subject of the contract was rooms to view the coronation procession, and was so to the knowledge of both parties. When once this is established, I see no difficulty whatever in the case. It is not essential to the application of the principle of *Taylor* v. *Caldwell* that the direct subject of the contract should perish or fail to be in existence at the date of performance of the contract. It is sufficient if a state of things or condition expressed in the contract and essential to its performance perishes or fails to be in existence at that time. In the present case the condition which fails and prevents the achievement of that which was, in the contemplation of both parties, the foundation of the contract, is not expressly mentioned either as a condition of the contract or the purpose of it; but I think for the reasons which I have given that the principle of *Taylor* v. *Caldwell* ought to be applied. This disposes of the plaintiff's claim for 50*l* unpaid balance of the price agreed to be paid for the use of the rooms. The defendant at one time set up a cross-claim for the return of the 25*l* he paid at the date of the contract. As that claim is now withdrawn it is unnecessary to say anything about it. . . .

WESTERN PROPERTIES v. SOUTHERN UTAH AVIATION, INC.

Court of Appeals of Utah, 1989.
776 P.2d 656.

DEAN E. CONDER, JUDGE. The trial court granted partial summary judgment in this case, awarding plaintiff Western Properties rent accrued to June 27, 1986, from which the defendants appeal. Western Properties appeals from the final judgment dismissing its claims for additional rent and for breach of a lease covenant regarding construction of a building. We affirm both the partial summary judgment and the final judgment.

Western Properties leased from Cedar City certain vacant land at the Cedar City Airport. Western Properties in turn subleased part of the land to the defendants for a 15–year term beginning March 6, 1985, with a covenant that the defendants "shall construct on the premises a maintenance building," which, upon termination of the sublease, was to have become property of Western Properties. In July of 1985, Cedar City approved the sublease in an addendum to it.

The defendants thereafter applied to Cedar City for site plan approval for the maintenance building, but as of the time of trial had not obtained such approval from Cedar City. Cedar City had also not approved a master plan for the airport as a whole. The defendants defaulted in payment of rent and abandoned the subleased land on June 27, 1986, without ever constructing a maintenance building on the land.

Western Properties sued for unpaid rent and the value of the maintenance building that it was to have received following the 15–year term of the sublease. The trial court granted partial summary judgment and awarded rent accrued to the date of abandonment, but reserved issues of further damages. Later, following trial, the trial court dismissed Western Properties' claims for further rent and for the residual income value of the maintenance building, and from that dismissal Western Properties appeals. The defendants have cross-appealed from the earlier summary judgment, arguing that a factual question concerning the intention of an individual defendant to be bound by the sublease precluded summary judgment. [The court concluded that the individual defendant was bound by the sublease through his signature "regardless of whether he read or understood the full import of what he signed." Ed.] . . .

Impossibility and Frustration

The trial court based its post-trial judgment on grounds of impossibility. Under the contractual defense of impossibility, an obligation is deemed discharged if an unforeseen event occurs after formation of the contract and without fault of the obligated party, which event makes performance of the obligation impossible or highly impracticable. The rationale for this rule is founded on principles of assent and basic equity. Parties are ordinarily thought to have made certain assumptions in visualizing their agreement, and those assumptions comprise part of the basis and extent of their assent. The impossibility defense serves to prevent enforcement where those assumptions, and hence, the parties' assent, prove to be faulty.

In this case, the parties appear to have tacitly assumed that the City would cooperate in the development of the leased land. The lease makes no provision for the prospect that the City would not approve the development. In the absence of any contractual allocation of the risk of the City's non-cooperation, the failure of the City to approve development of the land is an eventuality sufficiently unforeseen[5] for application of the impossibility defense.

---

5. We recognize that the City's failure to approve seems, from our present perspective, to be rather easy to foresee. However, the critical fact is not whether the event *could* have been foreseen, but rather, whether the parties *actually did* foresee it and provide accordingly in their contract. A dictum in one Utah case on impossibility employs the word "unforeseeable" in

The other facts required for application of the impossibility defense appear to have been sufficiently established at trial. The district court found that the defendants "could not build the maintenance building without city approval and the city did not ever give its approval." There appears to be no factual basis for implicating the defendants in the failure of the City to approve, and the defendants seem to have made every effort that could reasonably be required in order to induce the City to give its approval. In the absence of facts which could indicate fault or a lack of diligence on the part of the defendants, we rely on the trial court's findings in concluding that performance of the defendants' obligations was indeed impossible through no fault of their own. We therefore treat the obligation to construct the maintenance building as discharged from the time when performance of their obligations became impossible.

Construction of the promised building was impossible, but occupancy of the land pursuant to the lease was not necessarily precluded by the inability to construct the building. The land was, however, wholly undeveloped and uncultivated. Without a way of productively using the land, the purpose of the leasehold was effectively frustrated. Frustration of purpose differs from the defense of impossibility only in that performance of the promise, rather than being impossible or impracticable, is instead pointless. There was no point in leasing this land once its development became impossible. The covenant to pay rent is therefore also discharged, effective as of June 27, 1986.

The judgment is affirmed. . . .

PROBLEM

10.   Mr. & Mrs. Hester, now deceased, pledged $25,000 to Cotter College, "in consideration of our interest in Christian education." The pledge was to be used to endow a scholarship for two students to be selected by the President of Cotter College and the Head of the Sacred Literature Department. Before the pledge was paid, the College ran into financial difficulties. To stay afloat, it ended all educational programs except for its Department of Agriculture. The executor of the Mr. Hester's estate resists payment. Does the estate have a good defense?

Short Essay Question Covering Chapters 8 & 9 of This Casebook

In the 1970's a new professional football league, The World Football League, now defunct, was formed. Greenwood, a professional football player with the Pittsburgh Steelers, was offered a position by the Birmingham Americans, a newly formed team in that league. The offer was made in early 1974. The offer was to a three-year contract, for services to commence at the beginning of the 1975 season when Greenwood would have fully performed his obligations to the Steelers and would be a free agent. He accepted the offer

describing the event causing impossibility, Holmgren v. Utah–Idaho Sugar Co., 582 P.2d at 861 (Utah 1978); however, the better and more widely accepted rule looks not to whether the parties could or should have foreseen the event, but rather whether, as a fact of assent, they did foresee it. *Restatement (Second) of Contracts* § 261 & cmt. b (1981).

and a detailed written contract was subscribed by both parties. By the terms of the contract, the Americans were to pay Greenwood $350,000. On the signing of the contract he was to receive and did receive $50,000. The balance was to be "1975–$90,000; 1976–$100,000; 1977–$110,000."

Despite a good 1974 playing season, the Birmingham Americans came to be in a precarious financial position. The players were not paid for the last five games of the season and the team was in arrears in paying withholding taxes to the IRS. After the last game, the team's uniforms were seized by the sporting goods dealer who had not received payment for them and the telephone company disconnected service because of nonpayment. Greenwood's lawyer attempted to contact the corporate managers of the Birmingham team, without success. The World Football League canceled the Birmingham franchise. Thereupon Greenwood signed a contract with the Pittsburgh Steelers for the three-year period covered by his contract with the Birmingham team. The Birmingham Americans went out of the football business. They have brought the instant action against Greenwood, seeking restitution of the $50,000 and damages. Discuss the issues that will be argued before the court and their probable resolution.

CHAPTER 10

ENFORCEMENT REMEDIES

■ ■ ■

SECTION 1. DAMAGES

(a) GENERAL PRINCIPLES AND LIMITATIONS ON RECOVERY

(Calamari & Perillo on Contracts §§ 14.1—14.2, 14.4—14.17)

HAWKINS v. McGEE

Supreme Court of New Hampshire, 1929.
146 A. 641, 84 N.H. 114.

See p. 16 *supra;* see also *Restatement (Second) of Contracts* § 344. Purposes of Remedies, *supra* p. 22.

PROTECTORS INSURANCE SERVICE, INC. v. UNITED STATES FIDELITY & GUARANTY COMPANY

United States Court of Appeals, Tenth Circuit, 1998.
132 F.3d 612.

WESLEY E. BROWN, DISTRICT JUDGE. The defendants (hereinafter "USF & G") appeal a jury verdict in plaintiff's favor totaling $844,650.00. The jury found that USF & G breached a contract with plaintiff and that, as a result, plaintiff lost future profits in the amount of $809,650.00 and received $35,000.00 less than fair market value upon the sale of its business. On appeal, USF & G concedes liability for breaching the contract, but argues that the lost profits award should be vacated because it represents an impermissible double recovery. ... The parties agree that the law of Colorado governs this contract dispute.

SUMMARY OF FACTS

The plaintiff, a Colorado corporation, was an insurance agency formed in 1979. The sole owner of plaintiff's corporate stock was Earl Colglazier.

Plaintiff was an agent of USF & G and had a written contract authorizing it to solicit and submit applications for USF & G insurance. If the applications were accepted, plaintiff would be paid a commission by USF & G. Although plaintiff was an independent agency, it had contracts with only two insurance carriers; thus, over 80% of the insurance it sold from 1979 to 1992 was USF & G business. Insofar as termination of the agency agreement between plaintiff and USF & G was concerned, the contract stated that the parties "agree to make a good faith effort to provide for rehabilitation and thereby avoid termination of this Agreement."

In March of 1992, USF & G notified Colglazier that because of profitability concerns it was establishing a formal rehabilitation program for plaintiff. The program set a goal of achieving certain "earned loss ratios" (which measure the agent's profitability to the insurance company) in plaintiff's commercial and personal lines of insurance in 1992. In October of 1992, USF & G notified Colglazier that it was going to terminate its personal lines contract with plaintiff in 180 days if the goals of the rehabilitation program were not met by the end of 1992. The letter stated that after May 1, 1993, USF & G would not accept any new personal lines business and would nonrenew the current business. In response, Colglazier wrote USF & G and asserted that his personal and commercial accounts were intertwined and that terminating the personal lines, although only 20% of his sales, would effectively put him out of business. Faced with this situation, Colglazier decided to sell all of plaintiff's assets, including the rights, title and interest on its insurance policies, to Centennial Agency, Inc., on January 1, 1993. The purchase agreement called for plaintiff to receive cash payments of slightly over $148,000.00.

Plaintiff later brought this suit alleging that USF & G breached the contract by not making a good faith effort at rehabilitation to avoid termination of the agreement. For our purposes it suffices to say that the jury could reasonably find from the evidence that USF & G breached the agreement by improperly measuring plaintiff's loss ratios, by unfairly changing the goals and criteria of the rehabilitation program, and/or by certain other arbitrary actions.

With respect to damages, plaintiff presented the testimony of John Putnam, an expert in valuation of insurance agencies. Putnam testified that plaintiff's business was sold at a "distressed" price because of the circumstances under which it was sold, including time pressure to make a sale and USF & G's stated intention of terminating the agency's personal lines insurance. Putnam testified that the agency would have been worth approximately $175,000 had it not been sold under distress. Putnam arrived at this value by using three different methods: a multiple of revenues, a price/earnings ratio, and a capitalization of earnings. In addition to this evidence, Earl Colglazier testified that he would have continued to operate the agency for at least ten more years had USF & G not given him the termination notice. Plaintiff also presented rather confusing evidence with respect to its net profits in the years before the sale. According to Colglazier's testimony, Protectors Insurance Service was operated in conjunction with a company called Protectors Management Service, which conducted "all of the office insurance activities, salary, payroll, paying everybody on behalf of Protectors Insurance Service." The returns of Protectors Insurance Service showed reported net income in the years before the sale ranging from a low of about $36,000 to a high of about $84,000, with an average of about $59,000. Plaintiff argues that the returns of the two companies show that plaintiff made under $2,0000.00 [*sic*] in 1991 and lost over $17,000.00 in 1992.

The district court instructed the jury with respect to damages as follows:

To the extent that actual damages have been proved by the evidence you shall award as actual damages:

1. The amount of net income and earnings the Plaintiff ... would have earned if the Defendants had not breached the contract; and

2. The amount which is the difference between the price the Plaintiff ... received for the sale of the agency's business and the reasonable sale value of the agency's business if the Defendants had not breached the contract. ...

USF & G objected to this instruction, arguing that it permitted plaintiff to obtain a double recovery because the reasonable sale value of the agency was based on the agency's ability to earn future profits and, thus, plaintiff would be compensated twice if it received lost profits on top of the sale price. The district court rejected this, finding that the two items were distinct because the sale value in 1992 was a "snapshot in time" that did not include lost future profits. As indicated previously, the jury returned a special verdict finding $809,650 in lost profits and a $35,000 difference between the actual sale price of the agency and its reasonable sale value.

Discussion

USF & G first argues that the district court's damage instruction was erroneous because it permitted the plaintiff to obtain a double recovery. We agree. In a breach of contract action, the objective is to place the injured party in the same position it would have been in but for the breach. McDonald's Corp. v. Brentwood Center, 942 P.2d 1308, 1310 (Colo.App.1997). A double or duplicative recovery for a single injury, however, is invalid. Westric Battery Co. v. Standard Elec. Co., 482 F.2d 1307, 1317 (10th Cir.1973). Plaintiff contends there was no double recovery here because "(t)he record is devoid of any factual basis for believing that the damages for the decreased sales price are based upon or included future lost profits." This assertion is contradicted both by the record and by common sense. The testimony of plaintiff's expert, John Putnam, shows that his determination of the reasonable sale value of the agency was based largely—if not entirely—upon the agency's ability to generate future profits. His testimony makes clear that the value of an agency to a buyer is determined from its potential to generate a future income stream.

Putnam conceded that all of the methods he used to determine value took into account the agency's ability to generate future profits. When asked what the reasonable sale price of the agency's business would have been but for the distress factors brought about by the defendant, Putnam replied:

> Well, at the time that it was sold, you know, based upon income, because to a large degree this is what we all—and I am talking about commission revenue, what kind of income is coming into the agency, what kind of expenses they had. In my opinion the agency was worth approximately $175,000 at the time that it was sold had it not been sold under duress or distress.

. . . Numerous jurisdictions hold to the view that "when the loss of business is alleged to be caused by the wrongful acts of another, damages are measured by one of two alternative methods: (1) the going concern value; or (2) lost future profits." Malley–Duff & Assoc. v. Crown Life Ins. Co., 734 F.2d 133, 148 (3rd Cir.1984). The "going concern value" is the price a willing buyer would pay and a willing seller would accept in a free marketplace for the business in question. Malley–Duff, 734 F.2d at 148. It measures damages by awarding the difference between the going concern value and the price actually received by the plaintiff upon sale of the business. This is clearly the measure of damages that was presented by plaintiff's expert in the instant case and it properly supports the consequent award of $35,000 by the jury. The award of lost profit damages in addition to this amount, however, was an improper double recovery.

Plaintiff contends that Atlas Building Products Co. v. Diamond Block & Gravel Co., 269 F.2d 950 (10th Cir.1959) supports the view that an injured plaintiff can recover lost profits as well as a "diminution in value" of the business. *Atlas* is distinguishable because the plaintiff in that case continued to operate the business despite the injury. Such a plaintiff might not be made whole by receiving lost profits because the business may be left with assets (*e.g.*, intangible assets such as goodwill) that have less value than before the injury. Such a loss would be realized by the owner upon a subsequent sale of the business. But where the business is sold as a going concern and the owner is awarded the fair market value of the business without the injury, the owner has been made whole because that value takes into account the prospect of future profits as well as the unreduced value of all the business' assets. . . .

In sum, we conclude that the judgment must be vacated in part because it awards plaintiff an impermissible double recovery.

Not surprisingly, the parties disagree as to what effect a double recovery has upon disposition of the appeal. Plaintiff argues that only the $35,000 award for diminished sale value should be vacated and that the lost profits award should stand, while USF & G argues just the opposite. Although, as indicated above, the "going concern" and "lost profit" measures are generally considered alternative remedies, in this case we conclude that the award of lost profits must be vacated. [H]ere we have "clear proof in the record of the value of plaintiff's business as a going concern, and that value must necessarily take into consideration its future profit-earning potential." Albrecht [v. The Herald Co., 452 F.2d 124, 129 (8th Cir. 1971)]. In fact, plaintiff's expert in this case testified solely to the going concern value and did not make an estimate of lost future profits. Lost future profits may be used as a method of calculating damage where no other reliable method of valuing the business is available, *see id.*, but that was not the case here. Plaintiff has been made whole by receiving the fair market value of the business; he "is not entitled to sell the (business), receive full compensation therefor, and still receive the profits the (business) might have made over his reasonable work-life expectancy." *Id.* Moreover, we note that the lost profits award in this case would still be duplicative even if the $35,000 were vacated because the former fails to take into account the additional sum received by plaintiff (over $148,000) for the sale of the business. Thus, the award of lost profits cannot stand.

Under the circumstances, we conclude that the proper course is to vacate the portion of the judgment awarding $809,650 in lost profit damages. The alternative award of $35,000 for diminution in market value is appropriate and is affirmed. The case is remanded to the district court for entry of judgment in accordance with this opinion.

HADLEY v. BAXENDALE

Court of Exchequer, 1854.
9 Ex. 341, 156 Eng.Rep. 145.

At the trial before Crompton, J., at the last Gloucester Assizes, it appeared that the plaintiffs carried on an extensive business as millers at Gloucester; and that, on the 11th of May, their mill was stopped by a breakage of the crank shaft by which the mill was worked. The steam-engine was manufactured by Messrs. Joyce & Co., the engineers, at Greenwich, and it became necessary to send the shaft as a pattern for a new one to Greenwich. The fracture was discovered on the 12th, and on the 13th the plaintiffs sent one of their servants to the office of the defendants, who are the well-known carriers trading under the name of Pickford & Co., for the purpose of having the shaft carried to Greenwich. The plaintiffs' servant told the clerk that the mill was stopped, and that the shaft must be sent immediately; and in answer to the inquiry when the shaft would be taken, the answer was, that if it was sent up by twelve o'clock any day, it would be delivered at Greenwich on the following day. On the following day the shaft was taken by the defendants, before noon, for the purpose of being conveyed to Greenwich, and the sum of 2£. 4s. was paid for its carriage for the whole distance; at the same time the defendants' clerk was told that a special entry, if required, should be made to hasten its delivery. The delivery of the shaft at Greenwich was delayed by some neglect; and the consequence was, that the plaintiffs did not receive the new shaft for several days after they would otherwise have done, and the working of their mill was thereby delayed, and they thereby lost the profits they would otherwise have received.

On the part of the defendants, it was objected that these damages were too remote, and that the defendants were not liable with respect to them. The learned Judge left the case generally to the jury, who found a verdict with £25. damages beyond the amount paid into Court.

Whateley, in last Michaelmas Term, obtained a *rule nisi* for a new trial, on the ground of misdirection. . . .

ALDERSON, B. We think that there ought to be a new trial in this case; but, in so doing, we deem it to be expedient and necessary to state explicitly the rule which the Judge, at the next trial, ought, in our opinion, to direct the jury to be governed by when they estimate the damages.

It is, indeed, of the last importance that we should do this; for, if the jury are left without any definite rule to guide them, it will, in such cases as these, manifestly lead to the greatest injustice. The Courts have done this on several occasions; and, in Blake v. Midland Railway Company (18 Q.B. 93), the Court granted a new trial on this very ground, that the rule had not been definitely laid down to the jury by the learned Judge at *Nisi Prius*.

"There are certain established rules," this Court says, in Alder v. Keighley (15 M. & W. 117), "according to which the jury ought to find." And the Court, in that case, adds: "and here there is a clear rule, that the amount which would have been received if the contract had been kept, is the measure of damages if the contract is broken."

Now we think the proper rule in such a case as the present is this: Where two parties have made a contract which one of them has broken, the damages which the other party ought to receive in respect of such breach of contract should be such as may fairly and reasonably be considered either arising naturally, *i.e.*, according to the usual course of things, from such breach of contract itself, or such as may reasonably be supposed to have been in the contemplation of both parties, at the time they made the contract, as the probable result of the breach of it. Now, if the special circumstances under which the contract was actually made were communicated by the plaintiffs to the defendants, and thus known to both parties, the damages resulting from the breach of such a contract, which they would reasonably contemplate, would be the amount of injury which would ordinarily follow from a breach of contract under these special circumstances so known and communicated. But, on the other hand, if these special circumstances were wholly unknown to the party breaking the contract, he, at the most, could only be supposed to have had in his contemplation the amount of injury which would arise generally, and in the great multitude of cases not affected by any special circumstances, from such a breach of contract. For, had the special circumstances been known, the parties might have specially provided for the breach of contract by special terms as to the damages in that case; and of this advantage it would be very unjust to deprive them. Now the above principles are those by which we think the jury ought to be guided in estimating the damages arising out of any breach of contract. It is said, that other cases such as breaches of contract in the non-payment of money, or in the not making a good title to land, are to be treated as exceptions from this, and as governed by a conventional rule. But as, in such cases, both parties must be supposed to be cognisant of that well-known rule, these cases may, we think, be more properly classed under the rule above enunciated as to cases under known special circumstances, because there both parties may reasonably be presumed to contemplate the estimation of the amount of damages according to the conventional rule.

Now, in the present case, if we are to apply the principles above laid down, we find that the only circumstances here communicated by the plaintiffs to the defendants at the time the contract was made, were, that the article to be carried was the broken shaft of a mill, and that the plaintiffs were the millers of that mill. But how do these circumstances shew reasonably that the profits of the mill must be stopped by an unreasonable delay in the delivery of the broken shaft by the carrier to the third person? Suppose the plaintiffs had another shaft in their possession put up or putting up at the time, and that they only wished to send back the broken shaft to the engineer who made it; it is clear that this would be quite consistent with the above circumstances, and yet the unreasonable delay in the delivery would have no effect upon the intermediate profits of the mill. Or, again, suppose that, at the time of the delivery to the carrier, the machinery of the mill had been in other respects defective, then, also, the same results would follow. Here it is true that the shaft was actually sent back to serve as a model for a new one, and that the want of a new one was the only cause of the stoppage of the mill, and that the loss of profits really arose from not sending down the new shaft in proper time, and that this arose from the delay in delivering the broken one to serve as a model. But it is obvious that, in the great multitude of cases of millers sending off broken shafts to third persons by a carrier under ordinary circumstances, such consequences would not, in all probability, have occurred; and these special circumstances were here never communicated by the plaintiffs to the defendants. It follows, therefore, that the loss of profits here cannot reasonably be considered such a consequence of the breach of contract as could have been fairly and reasonably contemplated by both the parties when they made this contract. For such loss would neither have flowed naturally from the breach of this contract in the great multitude of such cases occurring under ordinary circumstances, nor were the special circumstances, which, perhaps, would have made it a reasonable and natural consequence of such breach of contract, communicated to or known by the defendants. The Judge ought, therefore, to have told the jury, that, upon the facts then before them, they ought not to take the loss of profits into consideration at all in estimating the damages. There must therefore be a new trial in this case.

Rule absolute.

Note: A noted text on damages states that the *Hadley* decision "diminishes the risk of business enterprise, and the result harmonized

well with the free trade economic philosophy of the Victorian era...."
McCormick on Damages p. 567 (1935). *Compare*, Walter E. Houghton, *The Victorian Frame of Mind*, 1830–1870 p.61 (1957): "The major worry [of the business class] was 'failure.' In a period when hectic booms alternated with financial panics and there was no such thing as limited liability, the business magnate and the public investor were haunted by specters of bankruptcy and the debtor's jail. So great was the physical and mental strain that many men, it was said, were forced 'to break off (or to break down) in mid-career, shattered, paralyzed, reduced to premature action or senility.' "

MADER v. STEPHENSON

Supreme Court of Wyoming, 1976.
552 P.2d 1114.

PER CURIAM. Plaintiffs-appellants were awarded a judgment against defendant-appellee in the sum of $1000 with interest from October 11, 1973, the date of the contract, in the sum of $143.86, for a total of $1143.86.

We shall take appellants' words to describe the scope of their appeal: "From this judgment the Plaintiffs have appealed the second finding which denied damages." ... In their brief they assert and argue the right to recover certain general items of damage, being $500 as the amount of the fee paid to their attorney for prosecuting this action, and also a claim for $212, being for air transportation to return from Kentucky for the trial, and a $500 estimate of the costs for the time spent in travel, for telephone calls, and various expenses in what they style the "pursuit of justice"....

Absent statutory authority, or contractual agreement, attorney fees are not recoverable by a party [citations]; nor are travel expenses in connection with the suit recoverable. [citations] There is no statutory provision for recovery of travel expenses or time for preparation of a lawsuit. Any recovery for costs is purely statutory [citation]. ...

Affirmed.

ROCKINGHAM COUNTY v. LUTEN BRIDGE CO.

United States Court of Appeal, Fourth Circuit, 1929.
35 F.2d 301, 66 A.L.R. 735.

PARKER, CIRCUIT JUDGE. This was an action at law instituted in the court below by the Luten Bridge Company, as plaintiff, to recover of Rockingham county, North Carolina, an amount alleged to be due under a contract for the construction of a bridge, but [the county] contends that notice of cancellation was given the bridge company before the erection of the bridge was commenced, and that it is liable only for the damages which the company would have sustained, if it had abandoned construction at that time. ...

On January 7, 1924, the board of commissioners of Rockingham county voted [3 to 2 in a highly contested vote, ed.] to award to plaintiff a contract for the construction of the bridge in controversy. . . .

[After a change of county commissioners, at] a regularly advertised called meeting [of the board of commissioners], held on February 21st, a resolution was unanimously adopted declaring that the contract for the building of the bridge was not legal and valid, and directing the clerk of the board to notify plaintiff that it refused to recognize same as a valid contract, and that plaintiff should proceed no further thereunder. This resolution also rescinded action of the board theretofore taken looking to the construction of a hard-surfaced road, in which the bridge was to be a mere connecting link. The clerk duly sent a certified copy of this resolution to plaintiff. . . . [N]otwithstanding the repudiation of the contract by the county, the bridge company continued with the work of construction. . . .

As the county now admits the execution and validity of the contract, and the breach on its part, the ultimate question in the case is one as to the measure of plaintiff's recovery. . . . [W]e do not think that, after the county had given notice, while the contract was still executory, that it did not desire the bridge built and would not pay for it, plaintiff could proceed to build it and recover the contract price. It is true that the county had no right to rescind the contract, and the notice given plaintiff amounted to a breach on its part; but, after plaintiff had received notice of the breach, it was its duty to do nothing to increase the damages flowing therefrom. If A enters into a binding contract to build a house for B, B, of course, has no right to rescind the contract without A's consent. But if, before the house is built, he decides that he does not want it, and notifies A to that effect, A has no right to proceed with the building and thus pile up damages. His remedy is to treat the contract as broken when he receives the notice, and sue for the recovery of such damages, as he may have sustained from the breach, including any profit which he would have realized upon performance, as well as any other losses which may have resulted to him. In the case at bar, the county decided not to build the road of which the bridge was to be a part, and did not build it. The bridge, built in the midst of the forest, is of no value to the county because of this change of circumstances. When, therefore, the county gave notice to the plaintiff that it would not proceed with the project, plaintiff should have desisted from further work. It had no right thus to pile up damages by proceeding with the erection of a useless bridge.

The contrary view was expressed by Lord Cockburn in Frost v. Knight, L.R. 7 Ex. 111, but, as pointed out by Prof. Williston (*Williston on Contracts*, vol. 3, p. 2347), it is not in harmony with the decisions in this country. The American rule and the reasons supporting it are well stated by Prof. Williston as follows:

> There is a line of cases running back to 1845 which holds that, after an absolute repudiation or refusal to perform by one party to a

contract, the other party cannot continue to perform and recover damages based on full performance. This rule is only a particular application of the general rule of damages that a plaintiff cannot hold a defendant liable for damages which need not have been incurred; or, as it is often stated, the plaintiff must, so far as he can without loss to himself, mitigate the damages caused by the defendant's wrongful act. The application of this rule to the matter in question is obvious. If a man engages to have work done, and afterwards repudiates his contract before the work has been begun or when it has been only partially done, it is inflicting damage on the defendant without benefit to the plaintiff to allow the latter to insist on proceeding with the contract. The work may be useless to the defendant, and yet he would be forced to pay the full contract price. On the other hand, the plaintiff is interested only in the profit he will make out of the contract. If he receives this it is equally advantageous for him to use his time otherwise.

The leading case on the subject in this country is the New York case of Clark v. Marsiglia, 1 Denio (N.Y.) 317, 43 Am.Dec. 670. In that case defendant had employed plaintiff to paint certain pictures for him, but countermanded the order before the work was finished. Plaintiff, however, went on and completed the work and sued for the contract price. In reversing a judgment for plaintiff, the court said:

> The plaintiff was allowed to recover as though there had been no countermand of the order; and in this the court erred. The defendant, by requiring the plaintiff to stop work upon the paintings, violated his contract, and thereby incurred a liability to pay such damages as the plaintiff should sustain. Such damages would include a recompense for the labor done and materials used, and such further sum in damages as might, upon legal principles, be assessed for the breach of the contract; but the plaintiff had no right, by obstinately persisting in the work, to make the penalty upon the defendant greater than it would otherwise have been.

And the rule as established by the great weight of authority in America is summed up in the following statement in 6 R.C.L. 1029, which is quoted with approval by the Supreme Court of North Carolina in the recent case of Novelty Advertising Co. v. Farmers' Mut. Tobacco Warehouse Co., 186 N.C. 197, 119 S.E. 196, 198:

> While a contract is executory a party has the power to stop performance on the other side by an explicit direction to that effect, subjecting himself to such damages as will compensate the other party for being stopped in the performance on his part at that stage in the execution of the contract. The party thus forbidden cannot afterwards go on and thereby increase the damages, and then recover such damages from the other party. The legal right of either party to violate, abandon, or renounce his contract, on the usual terms of compensation to the other for the damages which the law recognizes

and allows, subject to the jurisdiction of equity to decree specific performance in proper cases, is universally recognized and acted upon.

This is in accord with the earlier North Carolina decision of Heiser v. Mears, 120 N.C. 443, 27 S.E. 117, in which it was held that, where a buyer countermands his order for goods to be manufactured for him under an executory contract, before the work is completed, it is notice to the seller that he elects to rescind his contract and submit to the legal measure of damages, and that in such case the seller cannot complete the goods and recover the contract price.

. . . [T]here was error in directing a verdict for plaintiff for the full amount of its claim. The measure of plaintiff's damage, upon its appearing that notice was duly given not to build the bridge, is an amount sufficient to compensate plaintiff for labor and materials expended and expense incurred in the part performance of the contract, prior to its repudiation, plus the profit which would have been realized if it had been carried out in accordance with its terms.

. . . The judgment below will accordingly be reversed, and the case remanded for a new trial.

Reversed.

GRUBER v. S–M NEWS CO.

United States District Court, S.D. New York, 1954.
126 F.Supp. 442.

MURPHY, DISTRICT JUDGE. Plaintiffs, invoking jurisdiction of this court on the basis of diverse citizenship, seek damages for breach of contract. Plaintiffs allege in the first count of their complaint (the other two have been withdrawn), that a contract between them and defendant was made about September 10, 1945 at their principal place of business in New York. Under this agreement, plaintiffs allege that they promised to manufacture in conformity with samples approved by defendant, 90,000 sets of twelve Christmas greeting cards for the impending Christmas season; to pack every set in a box of design approved by defendant and be ready for shipment to a list of wholesalers to be furnished by defendant not later than the second week in October; to give defendant exclusive sale and distribution rights to these sets. According to plaintiffs' complaint, in consideration of their promises, defendant bound itself to exercise reasonable diligence to sell all of the sets and use its resources for scientific sales promotion, national advertising, newsstand outlets and sales organization. Defendant further agreed, plaintiffs claim, to pay eighty-four cents for each set f.o.b. its wholesalers' respective places of business where, according to defendant's regular checkup, the cards had been sold at retail. Credit was to be allowed for all sets returned to plaintiffs unsold. It is further alleged that plaintiffs manufactured and packed the sets in accordance with the agreement, notified the defendant to this effect on October 2, 1945, and that defendant then refused its promised performance. Damages for $101,800 are demanded.

. . . It is clear that distribution of samples in September to four out of over 700 wholesalers and jobbers who in turn supply over 90,000 outlets, is not an exercise of "reasonable diligence" to sell, in the face of a binding agreement requiring production by plaintiffs of 90,000 sets by the second week in October. Accordingly, the defense of performance by defendant is far from complete, and defendant must assume liability for breach of this contract. . . .

For breach of a contract of exclusive distribution and return, plaintiffs should be entitled to damages measured by the difference between what they actually obtained for their cards and what they would have obtained had defendant exercised its promised reasonable diligence. On this, plaintiffs have the burden of proof to the extent of a reasonably certain and definite factual basis of computation. Under the evidence, such basis in this case is too speculative for an award in a sum certain. The past experience of the defendant in distribution of a high proportion of jig-saw puzzles, maps and cleaning fluids is hardly a basis for prophecy with respect to Christmas cards. And a single retailer's opinion that he would have disposed of 50 boxes of the cards is a precarious foundation for generalization with respect to 90,000 such boxes. Accordingly, plaintiffs have not sustained their burden of proof with respect to their expectation under the breached agreement.

However, alternative to damages for loss of their expectation, plaintiffs have demanded at the close of trial at least their out-of-pocket expenses. The basis for these damages is not plaintiffs' expectation of profits but rather their expenditures made in "essential reliance" upon defendant's promise. Defendant, for its part, insists that there can be no recovery upon this theory of essential reliance because there would have been a loss to plaintiffs had defendant fully performed its promise of distribution.

The few cases in point in New York are apparently not entirely in accord with respect to the relationship between anticipated loss in event of full performance by the defendant, on one hand, and a plaintiff's recovery of his out-of-pocket expenses in reliance on defendant's unperformed promise, on the other. There are situations where there is no such relationship, and a plaintiff may recover his expenditures in reliance upon defendant's promise without regard to profit if that promise had been fully performed by defendant, as in actions for restitution and ones based upon fraud. The *Restatement* has suggested that if full performance by defendant would have resulted in loss to a plaintiff, then this loss must be deducted from plaintiff's expenditures. . . . "(O)n those occasions in which the performance would not have covered the promisee's outlay, such a result (*i.e.*, recovery of expenses by the promisee) imposes the risk of the promisee's contract upon the promisor. We cannot agree that the promisor's default in performance should under this guise make him an insurer of the promisee's venture. . . ."[8]

---

8. L. Albert & Son v. Armstrong Rubber Co., 2 Cir., 178 F.2d 182, 189. *See also* Fuller, *Reliance Interest in Contract Damages*, 46 Yale L.J. 52, 75–80 (1936).

We accept as the rule that plaintiff's recovery for their out-of-pocket expenses must be diminished by any loss that would result from defendant's full performance. We are not persuaded that defendant has established the probability of such loss. True, plaintiffs were able to obtain merely six cents per box on a sale of 40,000 boxes in 1949, rather than the promised eighty-four cents for sale in 1945 under their agreement with defendant. But the Christmas cards had a novelty appeal, designed as they were to exploit a dozen different nations at the time of the newly-formed United Nations in 1945. The glamour of the caricatures may well have been clouded by the worsening world situation that gathered in the succeeding years.

The burden of proving loss in event of performance properly rests on the defendant who by its wrong has made the question relevant to the rights of the plaintiffs. We do not find that defendant has sustained this burden.

Only the amount of plaintiffs' expenditures reasonably made in performance of the contract or in necessary preparation therefor, may be recovered. This does not include, as plaintiffs have requested, the cost of making the plates from which the cards were printed since these had already been fabricated prior to making the contract with defendant. The amount of plaintiffs' expenditures for labor and material reasonably made in essential reliance on defendant's promise was $19,934.44. From this sum must be deducted the *net* amount realized by plaintiffs from sale of 40,000 sets at six cents a set which was $2,080. Accordingly plaintiffs are entitled to $17,854.44 in damages.

Judgment accordingly.

ANGLIA TELEVISION LTD. v. REED

House of Lords.
[1971] 3 All E.R. 690.

LORD DENNING [Master of the Rolls]. Anglia Television Ltd., the plaintiffs, were minded in 1968 to make a film of a play for television entitled "The Man of the Wood." It portrayed an American married to an English woman. The American has an adventure in an English wood. The film was to last for 90 minutes. Anglia Television made many arrangements in advance. They arranged for a place where the play was to be filmed. They employed a director, a designer and a stage manager, and so forth. They involved themselves in much expense. All this was done before they got the leading man. They required a strong actor capable of holding the play together. He was to be on the scene the whole time. Anglia Television eventually found the man. He was Mr. Robert Reed, an American who has a very high reputation as an actor. He was very suitable for this part. By telephone conversation on 30th August 1968 it was agreed by Mr. Reed through his agent that he would come to England and be available between 9th September and 11th October 1968 to rehearse and play in this film. He was to get a performance fee of £1,050, living expenses of £100 a week, his first class fares to and from the United States, and so forth. It was all subject to the permit of the Ministry of Labour for him to come here. That was duly given on 2nd September 1968. So the contract was concluded. But unfortunately there was some muddle with the bookings. It appears that Mr. Reed's agent had already booked him in America for some other play. So on 3rd September 1968 the agent said that Mr. Reed would not come to England to perform in this play. He repudiated his contract. Anglia Television tried hard to find a substitute but could not do so. So on 11th September they accepted his repudiation. They abandoned the proposed film. They gave notice to the people whom they had engaged and so forth.

Anglia Television then sued Mr. Reed for damages. He did not dispute his liability, but a question arose as to the damages. Anglia Television do not claim their profit. They cannot say what their profit would have been on this contract if Mr. Reed had come here and performed it. So, instead of claim for loss of profits, they claim for the wasted expenditure. They had incurred the director's fees, the designer's fees, the stage manager's and assistant manager's fees, and so on. It comes in all to £2,750. Anglia Television say that all that money was wasted because Mr. Reed did not perform his contract.

Mr. Reed's advisers take a point of law. They submit that Anglia Television cannot recover for expenditure incurred *before* the contract was concluded with Mr. Reed. They can only recover the expenditure *after* the contract was concluded. They say that the expenditure *after* the contract was only £854.65, and that is all that Anglia Television can recover. The master rejected that contention; he held that Anglia Television could recover the whole £2,750; and now Mr. Reed appeals to this court. [Counsel] for Mr. Reed has referred us to the recent [unreported] case of Perestrello & Companhia Limitada v. United Paint Co. Ltd., ... in which Thesiger J. quoted the words of Tindal C.J. in Hodges v. Earl of Litchfield (1985) 1 Bing. N.C. 492, 498: "The expenses preliminary to the contract ought not to be allowed. The party enters into them for his own benefit at a time when it is uncertain whether there will be any contract or not." Thesiger J. applied those words, saying: "In my judgment pre-contract expenditure, though thrown away, is not recoverable."

I cannot accept the proposition as stated. ... If he has not suffered any loss of profits—or if he cannot prove what his profits would have been—he can claim in the alternative the expenditure which has been thrown away, that is, wasted, by reason of the breach. ...

If the plaintiff claims the wasted expenditure, he is not limited to the expenditure incurred *after* the contract was concluded. He can claim also the expenditure incurred *before* the contract, provided that it was such as would reasonably be in the contemplation of the parties as likely to be wasted if the contract was broken. Applying that principle here, it is plain that, when Mr. Reed entered into this contract, he must have known perfectly well that much expenditure had already been incurred on director's fees and the like. He must have contemplated—or, at any rate, it is reasonably to be imputed to him—that if he broke his contract, all that expenditure would be wasted, whether or not it was incurred before or after the contract. He must pay damages for all the expenditures so wasted and thrown away. . . .

I think the master was quite right and this appeal should be dismissed.

PROBLEMS

1. D, a shipping company, contracted to consign a package to P. D was aware that the package contained motion picture films for exhibition. P operated a motion picture theater and the films were to be exhibited during Christmas week when attendance is predictably high, but D was unaware that P was the operator of a theater or of the seasonal nature of theater attendance. As a result of D's delay in shipment, P was forced to close its theater during Christmas week. P sues for the profits it would have made during this period. What result?

2. D contracted with P, a building contractor, to have a house constructed on D's lot. D repudiated after P had just begun to perform. In mitigation, D offers evidence that immediately after the repudiation P entered into another more profitable building contract in the same vicinity. Is this evidence relevant?

3. P provides recorded music to restaurants and other public places. P contracted to provide music to D's place of business for a three year term. After seventeen months, D moved his place of business and repudiated the contract. T, the new tenant in the premises formerly occupied by D, has subscribed to P's services at a higher price than D had contracted to pay. P sues D for damages. D denies that P has suffered any economic injury. What result?

4. (a) P, an author, contracted with D, a publisher, to publish P's manuscript on modern drama within 18 months. D was to pay P a percentage of the retail price of each book sold. Because of a change in its publishing policy D refused to publish the book. P brought suit and the lower court granted $10,000 damages measured by the cost of publication because the value of the lost royalties is speculative. On appeal, what result?

(b) Landlord promised Tenant occupancy of certain retail space for a six-month term, beginning October 1, in exchange for Tenant's promise of $10,000. In September, Tenant ordered and paid for a perishable inventory of $50,000. Landlord totally breached his promise and Tenant was unable to find comparable space for rent. The goods Tenant bought were sold at a distress sale for $9,000. Tenant seeks $41,000 in damages. Will Tenant succeed?

(b) SALE OF GOODS AND REALTY

(Calamari & Perillo on Contracts §§ 14.20—14.27, 14.30)

HESSLER v. CRYSTAL LAKE CHRYSLER–PLYMOUTH, INC.

Appellate Court of Illinois, Second District, 2003.
338 Ill.App.3d 1010, 273 Ill.Dec. 96, 788 N.E.2d 405.

JUSTICE CALLUM delivered the opinion of the court: Plaintiff, Donald R. Hessler, sued defendant, Crystal Lake Chrysler–Plymouth, Inc., for breach of contract. Following a bench trial, the court entered judgment for plaintiff and awarded him $29,853 in damages. Defendant appeals, arguing that the trial court erred in . . . calculating the damages award. We affirm.

I. BACKGROUND

In February 1997, Chrysler Corporation introduced a new promotional vehicle called the Plymouth Prowler. However, the company did not reveal whether it would manufacture any of the vehicles. Plaintiff became aware of the vehicle and of its uncertain production, and, on February 4, 1997, contacted several dealerships to inquire about purchasing a Prowler. On February 5, 1997, plaintiff met with Gary Rosenberg, co-owner of defendant-dealership and signed a "Retail Order for a Motor Vehicle" (hereinafter Agreement). The Agreement, which was filled out primarily by Rosenberg [and initialed by him], stated that the order was for a 1997, V6, two-door, purple Plymouth Prowler. Moreover, it read:

> Customer to pay $5,000 over list price by manufacturer. Money refundable if can not (deliver) by 12/30/97. Dealer to keep car 2 weeks.

. . . The order also noted that plaintiff had deposited $5,000 by check. The Agreement contained a box labeled "TO BE DELIVERED ON OR ABOUT." Inside the box was written "ASAP" . . . [written by] a salesperson . . . in the process of "finishing up" the transaction. Rosenberg did not instruct the person to do so, but he routinely delegates to defendant's employees the processing of customer checks and the dispensing of receipts. Rosenberg stated that the term "ASAP" is used in his business "in lieu of a stock number. Just line it up in order. As soon as you can get it done, do it." He also testified that "(i)n the literary form" it means as soon as possible. . . .

Rosenberg testified that plaintiff was the first person to place an order for a Prowler. Further, Rosenberg was "pretty sure" that plaintiff's order was the first order on which he received a deposit. . . . They agreed that the information they had received was that the manufacturer's list price would be $39,000. . . .

On May 23, 1997, Salvatore Palandri entered into a contract with defendant to purchase a 1997 Plymouth Prowler. His contract reflects a purchase price of "50,000 + tax + lic + doc" and a $10,000 deposit. It further states that Palandri would receive the "first one delivered to (the) dealership." Palandri testified that he wrote a check for his deposit on the same day that he entered into the contract. Palandri stated that his initial discussions with Rosenberg about the Prowler, however, occurred about one to three months before the contract date. . . .

Plaintiff . . . testified that he attended a Chrysler customer appreciation event at Great America on September 19 and spoke to a company representative about the Prowler. Two days later, the representative sent him a fax that contained a tentative list of dealers who were to receive Prowlers. Defendant's name was on the list. . . . Plaintiff testified that he called Rosenberg on September 22 to notify him that his dealership was on a list of dealers due to receive Prowlers. Rosenberg informed plaintiff that he would not sell plaintiff a car because plaintiff had gone behind Rosenberg's back and that contacting Chrysler would cause Rosenberg problems. Rosenberg also stated that plaintiff was not the first person with whom he contracted to sell a Prowler. . . . Rosenberg testified that he had a conversation at this time with plaintiff about the Great America show and that he told plaintiff that he was "pretty sure," given the dealership's sales, that it would receive at least one car. When plaintiff requested confirmation that it would be his car, Rosenberg told him that the car was already "committed."

Beginning on September 23, 1997, plaintiff contacted 38 Chrysler–Plymouth dealerships to inquire about purchasing a 1997 Prowler, but did not obtain one. Plaintiff had "serious doubts" about whether Rosenberg would deliver to him a Prowler.

On October 24, 1997, plaintiff attended a Prowler coming-out party at the Hard Rock Café and saw a purple Prowler in the parking lot with a sign in its window that had defendant's name written on it. On October 25, plaintiff went to defendant's showroom and saw a Prowler parked there. He found Rosenberg and informed him that he was there to pick up his car. Rosenberg stated that he was not going to sell plaintiff the car and that he did not want to do business with him. Later that day, plaintiff purchased a Prowler from another dealer for $77,706.

On October 27, 1997, defendant sold the only Prowler it received in that year to Palandri for a total sale price of $54,859, including his $10,000 deposit.

In November 1997, plaintiff directed his attorney to send defendant a demand letter to purchase a Prowler. Plaintiff testified that he was prepared to purchase a vehicle from defendant even though he had already purchased one elsewhere. Plaintiff continued to research prices for Prowlers and, by January 1998, had not seen a price lower than the $77,706 he had paid for his vehicle. On January 7, 1998, plaintiff received his $5,000 deposit back from defendant.

On April 23, 1998, plaintiff sued defendant for breach of contract. Defendant moved to dismiss plaintiff's complaint, and the motion was granted. Plaintiff appealed, and this court reversed and remanded the cause for an evidentiary hearing to determine the meaning of the contract. [citation] This court found the contract ambiguous and further found that plaintiff could prove a set of facts to show that defendant breached the contract.

Following a bench trial, the court entered judgment for plaintiff and awarded him $29,853 in damages. It concluded that defendant [repudiated and] breached the Agreement and that plaintiff properly covered by purchasing a replacement vehicle for $29,853 more than the contract price. Further, the court found that the term "ASAP" ... means "if and when a car is delivered" and "as soon as something can be done(,) do it." ... It concluded that delivery of a Prowler was to be as soon as possible ... [and] found plaintiff "ready, willing, and able to perform the contract." The court found that the price plaintiff paid for the car at another dealership was the best price he could receive for a Prowler after Rosenberg's refusal to sell to him a car.

II. ANALYSIS

... This transaction involves the sale of goods and thus is governed by the Uniform Commercial Code–Sales (UCC) (810 ILCS 5/2–101 et seq. (West 2000)). [In Parts A and B, the court analyzes issues of formation, parol evidence rule and interpretation under the UCC, affirming the trial court's conclusions. The central issue is whether the notation "ASAP" in the written Agreement bound defendant to sell plaintiff its first Prowler. The "ASAP" term is held to be part of the Agreement, which the court finds completely integrated, but ambiguous pursuant to a prior finding that binds the court in this proceeding under the law of the case doctrine. Addressing the issue of interpretation de novo, the court notes that the UCC parol evidence rule (UCC § 2–202) does not bar admission of extrinsic evidence to interpret a term and that Illinois UCC law does not require a finding of ambiguity as a condition to interpretation of a term in an integrated writing. Ed.]

... All of the foregoing evidence confirmed that the commonly recognized meaning of the term ["ASAP"] was that which was intended in the contract. ... We therefore conclude that the trial court did not err in interpreting the term "ASAP."

C. Judgment for Plaintiff

... [W]here the testimony is conflicting in a bench trial, the court's findings will not be disturbed unless they are against the manifest weight of the evidence. Neibert v. Schwenn Agri–Production Corp., 219 Ill.App.3d 188, 190–91, 161 Ill.Dec. 841, 579 N.E.2d 389 (1991).

1. Repudiation

... Comment 1 to section 2–610 provides, in relevant part: "(A)nticipatory repudiation centers upon an overt communication of intention or an action which renders performance impossible or demonstrates a clear determination not to continue with performance." ... We conclude that the trial court did not err in finding that defendant's foregoing actions reasonably indicated to plaintiff that defendant would not deliver to him a

Prowler under the Agreement. As we determined above, defendant contracted to deliver a Prowler to plaintiff as soon as possible. It was not against the manifest weight of the evidence for the trial court to find that defendant repudiated the Agreement when it repeatedly informed plaintiff that it would not deliver to him the first Prowler it received. . . .

Defendant next asserts that plaintiff's testimony that he would have purchased a second Prowler indicates an intent to perform under the contract. Thus, there cannot be a repudiation where both parties' actions indicated an intent to perform. We disagree. As we discussed above, defendant's actions indicated to plaintiff that defendant would *not* perform under the Agreement. With respect to plaintiff's actions, section 2–610(b) of the UCC provides that an aggrieved party may "resort to any remedy for breach" of the contract "even though he has notified the repudiating party that he would await the latter's performance." One such remedy is to cover. [UCC 2–711(1)(a)] (buyer may effect cover, upon seller's repudiation, whether or not buyer cancels the contract). The statute is clear that a buyer's willingness to proceed with performance under a contract does not excuse a repudiation. Thus defendant's argument fails. . . . The UCC does not require a party to request assurances as a condition precedent to recovery.

For the foregoing reasons, we conclude that the trial court's finding of repudiation was not against the manifest weight of the evidence.

2. Breach of Contract

[The court finds that defendant's obligation was not limited to locking in a price, but required it to sell its first Prowler to plaintiff. Ed.] The trial court's finding that defendant breached the Agreement when it sold the first Prowler it received in 1997 to Palandri was . . . not against the manifest weight of the evidence.

3. Calculation of Damages

Defendant next asserts that the trial court erred in calculating the damages award. Defendant argues that, assuming a breach, the proper measure of damages for repudiation of the Agreement is set forth in section 2–713 of the UCC: the difference between market price at the time the plaintiff learned of the breach and the contract price. Thus, damages should have been awarded in the amount of $5,000, which equals the difference between Palandri's purchase price and the Agreement's price. [Citations to the Illinois statutes are omitted.]

Section 2–711 of the UCC provides, in relevant part:

§ 2–711. Buyer's Remedies in General; Buyer's Security Interest in Rejected Goods.

(1) Where the seller fails to make delivery or repudiates or the buyer rightfully rejects or justifiably revokes acceptance then with respect to any goods involved, and with respect to the whole if the breach goes to the whole contract (Section 2–612), the buyer may cancel and

whether or not he has done so may in addition to recovering so much of the price as has been paid

> (a) "cover" and have damages under the next section as to all the goods affected whether or not they have been identified to the contract; or

> (b) recover damages for non-delivery as provided in this Article (Section 2–713). (Emphasis added.)

Section 2–712 of the UCC provides, in relevant part:

> § 2–712. "Cover"; Buyer's Procurement of Substitute Goods.

> (1) After a breach within the preceding section the buyer may "cover" by making in good faith and without unreasonable delay any reasonable purchase of or contract to purchase goods in substitution for those due from the seller.

> (2) The buyer may recover from the seller as damages the difference between the cost of cover and the contract price together with any incidental or consequential damages as hereinafter defined (Section 2–715), but less expenses saved in consequence of the seller's breach.

Section 2–713 of the UCC provides:

> § 2–713. Buyer's Damages for Non–Delivery or Repudiation.

> (1) Subject to the provisions of this Article with respect to proof of market price (Section 2–723), the measure of damages for non-delivery or repudiation by the seller is the difference between the market price at the time when the buyer learned of the breach and the contract price together with any incidental and consequential damages provided in this Article (Section 2–715), but less expenses saved in consequence of the seller's breach.

> (2) Market price is to be determined as of the place for tender or, in cases of rejection after arrival or revocation of acceptance as of the place of arrival.

Comment 5 to section 2–713 of the UCC provides: "5. *The present section provides a remedy which is completely alternative to cover under the preceding section and applies only when and to the extent that the buyer has not covered.*" (Emphasis added.)

We reject defendant's argument that section 2–713 provides the correct formula to calculate damages in the case of a repudiation and where the aggrieved party has covered. As noted in comment 5 to that section, section 2–713 applies in cases where the aggrieved party has not effected cover. Rather, in situations where the party has effected cover, section 2–712(2) provides the appropriate measure of damages: the difference between the cost of cover and the contract price.

The trial court utilized this formula to calculate the damages award, and we do not quarrel with its calculation.

4. Appropriateness of Plaintiff's Cover

Defendant's final argument is that the trial court erred in calculating the damages award because plaintiff effected an inappropriate cover. Defendant contends that plaintiff did not recontact the 38 dealers he had called in September 1997 to inquire if they would sell him a Prowler. Instead, on the same day that Rosenberg refused to sell him a car, plaintiff visited another dealership and purchased a Prowler for about $40,000 over the list price. Comment 2 to section 2–712 of the UCC provides, in relevant part: "The test of proper cover is whether at the time and place the buyer acted in good faith and in a reasonable manner, and it is immaterial that hindsight may later prove that the method of cover used was not the cheapest and most effective."

Plaintiff testified that he called Rosenberg on September 22 to inform him that defendant was on a tentative list to receive a Prowler and that Rosenberg responded that he would not sell to plaintiff a car and that plaintiff was not the first person with whom he had contracted. Rosenberg testified that he informed plaintiff on this date that the Prowler was "already committed." The trial court also heard plaintiff's testimony that, following his September 22 conversation with Rosenberg, he had "serious doubts" that defendant would sell to him a Prowler and he contacted about 38 dealerships to inquire about purchasing a vehicle, but was unable to obtain a car. Following Rosenberg's refusal to sell a car to plaintiff on October 25, plaintiff visited another dealership on that day and purchased a Prowler for about $30,000 over what he would have paid defendant for the same car. The trial court concluded that the price plaintiff ultimately paid for a Prowler was the "best price" he could receive after defendant refused to sell a car to him. We agree. The trial court heard testimony from both parties about the Prowler's limited supply. It also heard plaintiff's testimony about his efforts to obtain a car one month before his purchase date. We conclude that the court's determination that plaintiff effected a proper cover was not against the manifest weight of the evidence.

For the foregoing reasons, the judgment of the circuit court of McHenry County is affirmed.

Affirmed.

NATIONAL CONTROLS, INC. v. COMMODORE BUSINESS MACHINES, INC.

Court of Appeal, First District, Division 3, California, 1985.
163 Cal.App.3d 688, 209 Cal.Rptr. 636.

SCOTT, ASSOCIATE JUSTICE. Respondent National Controls, Inc. (NCI) brought an action for breach of contract against appellant Commodore Business Machines, Inc. (Commodore). After a court trial, judgment was entered awarding NCI over $280,000 in damages, and Commodore has appealed.

I

NCI manufactures electronic weighing and measuring devices. Among its products is the model 3221 electronic microprocessor technology load cell scale (the 3221), which is designed to interface with a cash register for use at check-out stands. NCI sells the 3221 to cash register manufacturers, also termed original equipment manufacturers, or O.E.M.s. NCI does not maintain an inventory stock of the scales, but builds them to specific order by an O.E.M. The 3221 is a standard unit, which is modified by NCI to meet the specifications of each O.E.M. with respect to cash register compatability, paint, and logo.

In November 1980, Commodore had initial discussions with NCI about the possibility of Commodore becoming an O.E.M. customer. By telephone, Commodore purchased one 3221, which was sent by NCI to Commodore's Texas facility, along with NCI's standard specifications for the 3221 and its standard price schedule. In December 1980, Commodore ordered and paid for four more scales. Again, the orders were made by telephone. NCI did not receive a purchase order from Commodore; instead, Commodore merely gave NCI a Commodore purchase order number over the phone; that number was written on the sales order prepared by NCI and sent to Commodore.

In March 1981, Terry Rogers of Commodore ordered an additional 30 scales. The order was placed by telephone, and once again Commodore did not send NCI a purchase order. Instead, Rogers gave Wiggins of NCI a purchase order number by telephone; that number was entered by Wiggins on NCI's sales order.

On March 31, 1981, in a phone conversation with Wiggins, Rogers placed a firm order for 900 scales: 50 to be delivered in May, 150 in June, 300 in July, and 400 in August. Wiggins and Rogers agreed on quantity, price, and delivery schedule. As in the previous transactions, Rogers gave Wiggins a purchase order number over the telephone, Wiggins then prepared an NCI sales order, entered on it the Commodore purchase order number, and mailed a copy of that sales order to Commodore. NCI also sent a copy of its sales order to its Florida manufacturing facility, which began manufacture of the units. ...

Delivery was made to Commodore of the first 200 units, and 300 units were ready to ship in June of 1981. As of that date, the remaining 400 units of the order were nearly complete. However, Commodore accepted only the first 50 scales, and did not accept or pay for the remaining 850 units. Thereafter, all of the 850 units were resold to National Semiconductor, an existing O.E.M. customer. NCI's vice president and general manager in charge of its Florida manufacturing facility testified that in 1980 and 1981, the plant had the production capacity to more than double its output of 3221's.

Among its findings and conclusions, the trial court concluded that the terms of the parties' contract were those established during their telephone discussions prior to and on March 31, 1981, and in the November

1980 letter from NCI to Commodore enclosing a price schedule, as well as "the terms" of NCI's prior sales orders. ... The court also found that NCI was a "lost volume seller" who was entitled to recover the loss of profit it would have made on the sale of the 850 units to Commodore, notwithstanding its subsequent resale of those units to another customer.

[Section II of the opinion which discusses the terms of the contract is omitted. Ed.]

III

Commodore also contends that the trial court erred when it relied on [Uniform Commercial Code] section 2–708, subdivision (2), to award NCI damages by way of lost profits. In a related argument, Commodore contends that if lost profits were the proper measure of damages, it was entitled under the plain language of section 2–708 to credit for the proceeds of NCI's resale of the contract goods to National Semiconductor.

Damages caused by a buyer's breach or repudiation of a sales contract are usually measured by the difference between the resale price of the goods and the contract price, as provided by Uniform Commercial Code section 2–706. When it is not appropriate to use this difference to measure the seller's loss (as when the goods have not been resold in a commercially reasonable manner), the seller's measure of damages is the difference between the market and the contract prices as provided in Uniform Commercial Code section 2–708, subdivision (1). Ordinarily, this measure will result in recovery equal to the value of the seller's bargain. However, under certain circumstances this formula is also not an adequate means to ascertain that value, and the seller may recover his loss of expected profits on the contract under subdivision (2) of Uniform Commercial Code section 2–708. (3 Hawkland, *Uniform Commercial Code Series* (1982–1984) §§ 2–708–2–708:04.)

Section 2–708 provides:

(1) Subject to subdivision (2) and to the provisions of this division with respect to proof of market price (Section 2–723), the measure of damages for nonacceptance or repudiation by the buyer is the difference between the market price at the time and place for tender and the unpaid contract price together with any incidental damages provided in this division (Section 2–710), but less expenses saved in consequence of the buyer's breach.

(2) If the measure of damages provided in subdivision (1) is inadequate to put the seller in as good a position as performance would have done then the measure of damages is the profit (including reasonable overhead) which the seller would have made from full performance by the buyer, together with any incidental damages provided in this division (Section 2–710), due allowance for costs reasonably incurred and due credit for payments or proceeds of resale.

When buyers have repudiated a fixed price contract to purchase goods, several courts elsewhere have construed subdivision (2) of Uniform

Commercial Code section 2–708 or its state counterpart to permit the award of lost profits under the contract to the seller who establishes that he is a "lost volume seller," *i.e.*, one who proves that even though he resold the contract goods, that sale to the third party would have been made regardless of the buyer's breach. (Neri v. Retail Marine Corporation (1972) 30 N.Y.2d 393, 334 N.Y.S.2d 165, 168, 285 N.E.2d 311, 314). The lost volume seller must establish that had the breaching buyer performed, the seller would have realized profits from two sales. (*See* Goetz & Scott, *Measuring Sellers' Damages: The Lost–Profits Puzzle* (1979) 31 Stan. L.Rev. 323, 326.)

In Neri v. Retail Marine Corporation, *supra*, 285 N.E.2d 311, seller contracted to sell a new boat, which it ordered and received from its supplier. The buyer then repudiated the contract. Later, seller sold the boat to another buyer, for the same price. The court relied on Uniform Commercial Code section 2–708, subdivision (2), to award the seller its lost profits under the contract, reasoning that the record established that market damages would be inadequate to put the seller in as good a position as performance would have done. The court drew an analogy to an auto dealer with an inexhaustible supply of cars. A breach of an agreement to buy a car at a standard price would cost that dealer a sale even though he was able to resell the car at the same price. In other words, had the breaching buyer performed, seller would have made two sales instead of one. (*Id.*, at pp. 312–315.)

While the seller in *Neri* was a retailer, the lost volume seller rule is also applicable to manufacturers. (Nederlandse, etc. v. Grand Pre–Stressed Corp., [(E.D.N.Y.1979) 466 F.Supp. 846, *affd.* (2nd Cir.) 614 F.2d 1289].) In *Nederlandse*, seller, a manufacturer of steel strand, brought an action against buyer for breach of an agreement to purchase approximately 1,180 metric tons of strand. Defendant had accepted only about 221 tons, and repudiated the remaining 958 tons, of which 317 tons had been already produced by seller. Seller resold the 317 tons to various third party purchasers. The court held that seller was entitled to lost profits under Uniform Commercial Code section 2–708, subdivision (2), and that no set-off would be allowed for profits earned through the sales to third parties. The evidence established that seller had sufficient production capacity to supply not only the 1,180 tons required by the contract, but also the 317 tons sold to third parties. The fact that seller was a manufacturer rather than a retailer, and that he produced only to order rather than maintaining an inventory, was of no significance in determining the applicability of Uniform Commercial Code section 2–708.

Commodore accurately points out that the lost volume seller rule has been criticized by some commentators as overly simplistic. (Goetz & Scott, *supra*, 31 Stan.L.Rev. 323, 330–354.) Nevertheless, those courts considering the question have held that Uniform Commercial Code section 2–708 does allow lost profits to a "lost volume seller" and that criticism has not resulted in any revision of the section.

Commodore also contends that if NCI was entitled to lost profits under the contract, Commodore should have received credit for the proceeds of the resale. The literal language of section 2–708, subdivision (2), does provide some support for that contention:

> If the measure of damages provided in subdivision (1) is inadequate to put the seller in as good a position as performance would have done then the measure of damages is the profit (including reasonable overhead) which the seller would have made from full performance by the buyer, *together with . . . due credit for payments or proceeds of resale.*

(Emphasis added.) However, courts elsewhere have uniformly held that the underscored language does not apply to a lost volume seller.

As the court in Snyder v. Herbert Greenbaum & Assoc., Inc., *supra*, 380 A.2d 618, 625 explained,

> Logically, lost volume status, which entitles the seller to the § 2–708(2) formula rather than the formula found in § 2–708(1), is inconsistent with a credit for the proceeds of resale. The whole concept of lost volume status is that the sale of the goods to the resale purchaser could have been made with other goods had there been no breach. In essence, the original sale and the second sale are independent events, becoming related only after breach, as the original sale goods are applied to the second sale. To require a credit for the proceeds of resale is to deny the essential element that entitles the lost volume seller to § 2–708(2) in the first place—the mutual independence of the contract and the resale.

> Practically, if the "due credit" clause is applied to the lost volume seller, his measure of damages is no different from his recovery under § 2–708(1). Under § 2–708(1) he recovers the contract/market differential and the profit he makes on resale. If the "due credit" provision is applied, the seller recovers only the profit he makes on resale plus the difference between the resale price and the contract price, an almost identical measure to § 2–708(1). If the "due credit" clause is applied to the lost volume seller, the damage measure of "lost profits" is rendered nugatory, and he is not put in as good a position as if there had been performance.

In this case, the evidence was undisputed that in 1980 and 1981, NCI's manufacturing plant was operating at approximately 40 percent capacity. The production of the 900 units did not tax that capacity, and the plant could have more than doubled its output of 3221's and still have stayed within its capacity. That evidence was sufficient to support the court's findings that NCI had the capacity to supply both Commodore and National Semiconductor, and that had there been no breach by Commodore, NCI would have had the benefit of both the original contract and the resale contract. Accordingly, the trial court correctly determined that NCI was a lost volume seller, that the usual "contract price minus market price" rule set forth in subdivision (1) of section 2–708 was inadequate to put NCI in as good a position as performance would have done, and that NCI was therefore entitled to its lost profits on the contract with Commodore, without any set-off for profits on the resale to National Semiconductor.

Judgment is affirmed.

WHITE, P.J., and BARRY-DEAL, J., concur.

LUCAS, J., is of the opinion the petition should be granted.

HORTON v. O'ROURKE

District Court of Appeal of Florida, Second District, 1975.
321 So.2d 612.

McNULTY, CHIEF JUDGE. Appellant Howard P. Horton, individually and as owner of H & H Construction Company, appeals from a final judgment awarding compensatory damages for breach of four land sale contracts due to an unmarketable title. We reverse.

The operative facts are simply stated. Between March 3, 1972 and May 3, 1972, the four appellee families executed written contracts with H & H Construction Company to purchase homes being constructed on land owned by appellee Overlord Investments, Inc. Upon completion of the homes in the summer of 1972, the families took possession without closing, under rental agreements ranging from $90 to $135 per month. Closing was conditioned upon clearance of all outstanding title defects.

Upon taking possession, the purchasers-lessees received a notice of the existence of a Federal Tax Lien encumbering the property in excess of $94,000. After receiving several assurances that the lien would soon be removed, they made improvements and continued the rental agreement for 22 months. But on March 15, 1974, appellant notified the purchasers in writing that clearance of the defect was impossible. Appellant offered either to return the earnest money deposits or enter into new rental agreements at a higher rate.

Thereafter, on April 15, 1974, appellee Overlord Investments, Inc., record title holder of the land, brought suit to oust each purchaser. After answering, the purchasers-appellees filed individual suits for specific performance against both Overlord Investments and appellant, alleging a principal-agent relationship, which resulted in this appeal.

Following a non-jury trial on the four consolidated cases, a final judgment was rendered denying specific performance, exonerating Overlord from any obligation to purchasers-appellees and awarding the purchasers pecuniary damages against appellant. In arriving at the amount of such damages, the court applied the standard measure of contract damages whereby a purchaser ordinarily receives the benefit of his bargain, measured by the court in this case by the difference between the value of the land when it should have been conveyed less the contract price as yet unpaid.

In the one meritorious point on appeal, appellant contends that application of this standard measure of damages giving purchasers *in a land sale contract* the benefit of their bargain is error in the absence of a showing of bad faith. We agree. In Florida and many other jurisdictions,[2] the courts follow the English rule announced in *Flureau v. Thornhill*[3] whereby in the absence of bad faith the damages recoverable for breach by the vendor of an executory contract to convey title to real estate are the purchase money paid by the purchaser together with interest and expenses of investigating title. Lest there be unjust enrichment, under the facts in this case, we would add to that here the cost of improvements made by purchasers in contemplation of the conveyance, with the express or implied approval of the vendor, which inure to the benefit of the vendor.

Appellees' reliance on *A. J. Richey Corp. v. Garvey*[4] as authority to the contrary is misplaced in that, in that case, there was clearly a lack of good faith. Here, there is no suggestion of bad faith on appellant's part. Indeed, the record reveals that he dealt above board, made every effort and went to considerable expense to clear the title defect and to consummate ultimately the contract to convey. . . .

Accordingly, the judgment appealed from should be, and it is hereby, reversed; and the cause is remanded for further proceedings not inconsistent herewith. . . .

PROBLEMS

5. Seller and Buyer entered into a contract whereby Buyer would purchase all its requirements of a certain type of valves from Seller. The contract had no duration term. The parties operated under the contract for several years at which point Buyer repudiated. In Seller's lawsuit against Buyer, how should Seller's damages be calculated?

6. B bought a Ford truck from an authorized dealer in Mobile, Alabama. He received a written warranty whereby the Ford Motor Company promised that within the warranty period certain repairs would be made by the dealer. It also provided: "If the owner is traveling . . . any authorized Ford dealer will perform the repairs." Because of a defect in manufacture the truck broke down in Orlando, Florida, within the warranty period. The dealer in Orlando refused to make the necessary repairs and Ford Motor Company officials on the scene wrongfully refused to recognize the warranty. B has had the repairs done elsewhere and was deprived of the use of the truck for four months. He seeks to recover the value of the loss of use of the truck. His evidence showed that if the truck had been operative he could have used the truck in his business or leased the truck with a driver to others for $22.50 per hour. What is B entitled to?

---

2.   77 Am.Jur.2d *Vendor and Purchaser* § 522 (1975); 5 A. Corbin *Contracts* § 1097 (1964).

3.   2 W.Bl. 1078 (1776).

4.   (1938), 132 Fla. 602, 182 So. 216.

7. S contracted with B whereby S would manufacture a specially designed stud driving machine for $11,750. Production was about one half completed when B repudiated the contract. S ceased manufacture. The half completed machine had a salvage value of about $1,500. (a) What is the proper measure of damages? (b) Do you have sufficient information to calculate damages?

8. Seller contracted to sell 1,875 hundredweight (cwt) of beans for $16 a cwt, to be delivered at harvest time. Seller repudiated the contract at a time when the price for forward contracts for beans was still $16. Because of a drought, at harvest time the price of beans had risen to $36 a cwt. What measure of damages should be applied to Buyer's claim?

(c) EMPLOYMENT AND SERVICE CONTRACTS

(Calamari & Perillo on Contracts §§ 14.18—14.19)

PARKER v. TWENTIETH CENTURY–FOX FILM CORP.

Supreme Court of California, In Bank, 1970.
3 Cal.3d 176, 474 P.2d 689, 89 Cal.Rptr. 737.

BURKE, JUSTICE. Defendant Twentieth Century–Fox Film Corporation appeals from a summary judgment granting to plaintiff the recovery of agreed compensation under a written contract for her services as an actress in a motion picture. As will appear, we have concluded that the trial court correctly ruled in plaintiff's favor and that the judgment should be affirmed.

Plaintiff [Shirley MacLaine] is well known as an actress, and in the contract between plaintiff and defendant is sometimes referred to as the "Artist." Under the contract, dated August 6, 1965, plaintiff was to play the female lead in defendant's contemplated production of a motion picture entitled "Bloomer Girl." The contract provided that defendant would pay plaintiff a minimum "guaranteed compensation" of 53,571.42 per week for 14 weeks commencing May 23, 1966, for a total of $750,000. Prior to May 1966 defendant decided not to produce the picture and by a letter dated April 4, 1966, it notified plaintiff of that decision and that it would not "comply with our obligations to you under" the written contract.

By the same letter and with the professed purpose "to avoid any damage to you," defendant instead offered to employ plaintiff as the leading actress in another film tentatively entitled "Big Country, Big Man" (hereinafter, "Big Country"). The compensation offered was identical, as were 31 of the 34 numbered provisions or articles of the original contract.[1] Unlike "Bloomer Girl," however, which was to have been a

---

1. Among the identical provisions was the following found in the last paragraph of Article 2 of the original contract: "We (defendant) shall not be obligated to utilize your (plaintiff's) services in

musical production, "Big Country" was a dramatic "western type" movie. "Bloomer Girl" was to have been filmed in California; "Big Country" was to be produced in Australia. Also, certain terms in the proffered contract varied from those of the original.[2] Plaintiff was given one week within which to accept; she did not and the offer lapsed. Plaintiff then commenced this action seeking recovery of the agreed guaranteed compensation.

The complaint sets forth two causes of action. The first is for money due under the contract; the second, based upon the same allegations as the first, is for damages resulting from defendant's breach of contract. Defendant in its answer admits the existence and validity of the contract, that plaintiff complied with all the conditions, covenants and promises and stood ready to complete the performance, and that defendant breached and "anticipatorily repudiated" the contract. It denies, however, that any money is due to plaintiff either under the contract or as a result of its breach, and pleads as an affirmative defense to both causes of action plaintiff's allegedly deliberate failure to mitigate damages, asserting that she unreasonably refused to accept its offer of the leading role in "Big Country."

Plaintiff moved for summary judgment . . ., the motion was granted, and summary judgment for $750,000 plus interest was entered in plaintiff's favor. This appeal by defendant followed. . . .

The general rule is that the measure of recovery by a wrongfully discharged employee is the amount of salary agreed upon for the period of service, less the amount which the employer affirmatively proves the employee has earned or with reasonable effort might have earned from other employment. (W. F. Boardman Co. v. Petch (1921) 186 Cal. 476, 484, 199 P. 1047.) However, before projected earnings from other employment

---

or in connection with the Photoplay hereunder, our sole obligation, subject to the terms and conditions of this Agreement, being to pay you the guaranteed compensation herein provided for."

2. Article 29 of the original contract specified that plaintiff approved the director already chosen for "Bloomer Girl" and that in case he failed to act as director plaintiff was to have approval rights of any substitute director. Article 31 provided that plaintiff was to have the right of approval of the "Bloomer Girl" dance director, and Article 32 gave her the right of approval of the screenplay. Defendant's letter of April 4 to plaintiff, which contained both defendant's notice of breach of the "Bloomer Girl" contract and offer of the lead in "Big Country," eliminated or impaired each of those rights. It read in part as follows: "The terms and conditions of our offer of employment are identical to those set forth in the 'BLOOMER GIRL' Agreement, Articles 1 through 34 and Exhibit A to the Agreement, except as follows: 1. Article 31 of said Agreement will not be included in any contract of employment regarding 'BIG COUNTRY, BIG MAN' as it is not a musical and it thus will not need a dance director. 2. In the 'BLOOMER GIRL' agreement, in Articles 29 and 32, you were given certain director and screenplay approvals and you had preapproved certain matters. Since there simply is insufficient time to negotiate with you regarding your choice of director and regarding the screenplay and since you already expressed an interest in performing the role in 'BIG COUNTRY, BIG MAN,' we must exclude from our offer of employment in 'BIG COUNTRY, BIG MAN' any approval rights as are contained in said Articles 29 and 32; however, we shall consult with you respecting the director to be selected to direct the photoplay and will further consult with you with respect to the screenplay and any revisions or changes therein, provided, however, that if we fail to agree . . . the decision of . . . (defendant) with respect to the selection of a director and to revisions and changes in the said screenplay shall be binding upon the parties to said agreement."

opportunities not sought or accepted by the discharged employee can be applied in mitigation, the employer must show that the other employment was comparable, or substantially similar, to that of which the employee has been deprived; the employee's rejection of or failure to seek other available employment of a different or inferior kind may not be resorted to in order to mitigate damages. (Gonzales v. Internat. Assn. of Machinists (1963) 213 Cal.App.2d 817, 822–824, 29 Cal.Rptr. 190.)

In the present case defendant has raised no issue of *reasonableness of efforts* by plaintiff to obtain other employment; the sole issue is whether plaintiff's refusal of defendant's substitute offer of "Big Country" may be used in mitigation. Nor, if the "Big Country" offer was of employment different or inferior when compared with the original "Bloomer Girl" employment, is there an issue as to whether or not plaintiff acted reasonably in refusing the substitute offer. Despite defendant's arguments to the contrary, no case cited or which our research has discovered holds or suggests that reasonableness is an element of a wrongfully discharged employee's option to reject, or fail to seek, different or inferior employment lest the possible earnings therefrom be charged against him in mitigation of damages.[5]

Applying the foregoing rules to the record in the present case, with all intendments in favor of the party opposing the summary judgment motion—here, defendant—it is clear that the trial court correctly ruled that plaintiff's failure to accept defendant's tendered substitute employment could not be applied in mitigation of damages because the offer of the "Big Country" lead was of employment both different and inferior, and that no factual dispute was presented on that issue. The mere circumstance that "Bloomer Girl" was to be a musical review calling upon plaintiff's talents as a dancer as well as an actress, and was to be produced in the City of Los Angeles, whereas "Big Country" was a straight dramatic role in a "Western Type" story taking place in an opal mine in Australia, demonstrates the difference in kind between the two employments; the female lead as a dramatic actress in a western style motion picture can by no stretch of imagination be considered the equivalent of or substantially similar to the lead in a song-and-dance production.

Additionally, the substitute "Big Country" offer proposed to eliminate or impair the director and screenplay approvals accorded to plaintiff under the original "Bloomer Girl" contract (see fn. 2, *ante*), and thus constituted an offer of inferior employment. No expertise or judicial notice is required in order to hold that the deprivation or infringement of an employee's rights held under an original employment contract converts the available "other employment" relied upon by the employer to mitigate damages, into inferior employment which the employee need not seek or accept.

---

5. Instead, in each case the reasonableness referred to was that of the *efforts* of the employee to obtain other employment that was not different or inferior; his right to reject the latter was declared as an unqualified rule of law. . . .

Statements found in affidavits submitted by defendant in opposition to plaintiff's summary judgment motion, to the effect that the "Big Country" offer was not of employment different from or inferior to that under the "Bloomer Girl" contract, merely repeat the allegations of defendant's answer to the complaint in this action, constitute only conclusionary assertions with respect to undisputed facts, and do not give rise to a triable factual issue so as to defeat the motion for summary judgment.

In view of the determination that defendant failed to present any facts showing the existence of a factual issue with respect to its sole defense—plaintiff's rejection of its substitute employment offer in mitigation of damages—we need not consider plaintiff's further contention that for various reasons, including the provisions of the original contract set forth in fn. 1, *ante*, plaintiff was excused from attempting to mitigate damages.

The judgment is affirmed.

SULLIVAN, ACTING CHIEF JUSTICE (dissenting). The basic question in this case is whether or not plaintiff acted reasonably in rejecting defendant's offer of alternate employment. The answer depends upon whether that offer (starring in "Big Country, Big Man") was an offer of work that was substantially similar to her former employment (starring in "Bloomer Girl") or of work that was of a different or inferior kind. To my mind this is a factual issue which the trial court should not have determined on a motion for summary judgment. The majority have not only repeated this error but have compounded it by applying the rules governing mitigation of damages in the employer-employee context in a misleading fashion. Accordingly, I respectfully dissent.

The familiar rule requiring a plaintiff in a tort or contract action to mitigate damages embodies notions of fairness and socially responsible behavior which are fundamental to our jurisprudence. Most broadly stated, it precludes the recovery of damages which, through the exercise of due diligence, could have been avoided. Thus, in essence, it is a rule requiring reasonable conduct in commercial affairs. This general principle governs the obligations of an employee after his employer has wrongfully repudiated or terminated the employment contract. Rather than permitting the employee simply to remain idle during the balance of the contract period, the law requires him to make a reasonable effort to secure other employment.[1] He is not obliged, however, to seek or accept any and all types of work which may be available. Only work which is in the same field and which is of the same quality need be accepted.[2]

---

1. The issue is generally discussed in terms of a duty on the part of the employee to minimize loss. The practice is long-established and there is little reason to change despite Judge Cardozo's observation of its subtle inaccuracy. "The servant is free to accept employment or reject it according to his uncensored pleasure. What is meant by the supposed duty is merely this: That if he unreasonably reject, he will not be heard to say that the loss of wages from then on shall be deemed the jural consequence of the earlier discharge. He has broken the chain of causation, and loss resulting to him thereafter is suffered through his own act." (McClelland v. Climax Hosiery Mills (1930) 252 N.Y. 347, 359, 169 N.E. 605, 609, concurring opinion.)

2. This qualification of the rule seems to reflect the simple and humane attitude that it is too severe to demand of a person that he attempt to find and perform work for which he has no

Over the years the courts have employed various phrases to define the type of employment which the employee, upon his wrongful discharge, is under an obligation to accept. Thus in California alone it has been held that he must accept employment which is "substantially similar"; "comparable employment"; employment "in the same general line of the first employment"; "equivalent to his prior position"; "employment in a similar capacity"; employment which is "not . . . of a different or inferior kind. . . ." [citations]

For reasons which are unexplained, the majority cite several of these cases yet select from among the various judicial formulations which contain one particular phrase, "Not of a different or inferior kind," with which to analyze this case. I have discovered no historical or theoretical reason to adopt this phrase, which is simply a negative restatement of the affirmative standards set out in the above cases, as the exclusive standard. Indeed, its emergence is an example of the dubious phenomenon of the law responding not to rational judicial choice or changing social conditions, but to unrecognized changes in the language of opinions or legal treatises. However, the phrase is a serviceable one and my concern is not with its use as the standard but rather with what I consider its distortion.

The relevant language excuses acceptance only of employment which is of a *different kind*. [citations] It has never been the law that the mere existence of *differences between two jobs* in the same field is sufficient, as a matter of law, to excuse an employee wrongfully discharged from one from accepting the other in order to mitigate damages. Such an approach would effectively eliminate any obligation of an employee to attempt to minimize damage arising from a wrongful discharge. The only alternative job offer an employee would be required to accept would be an offer of his former job by his former employer.

Although the majority appear to hold that there was a difference "in kind" between the employment offered plaintiff in "Bloomer Girl" and that offered in "Big Country," an examination of the opinion makes crystal clear that the majority merely point out differences between the two *films* (an obvious circumstance) and then apodically [*sic*] assert that these constitute a difference in the *kind of employment*. The entire rationale of the majority boils down to this: that the "*mere circumstances*" that "Bloomer Girl" was to be a musical review while "Big Country" was a straight drama "demonstrates the difference in kind" since a female lead in a western is not "the equivalent of or substantially similar to" a lead in a musical. This is merely attempting to prove the proposition by repeating it. It shows that the vehicles for the display of the star's talents are different but it does not prove that her employment as a star in such vehicles is of necessity different *in kind* and either inferior or superior.

---

training or experience. Many of the older cases hold that one need not accept work in an inferior rank or position nor work which is more menial or arduous. This suggests that the rule may have had its origin in the bourgeois fear of resubmergence in lower economic classes.

I believe that the approach taken by the majority (a superficial listing of differences with no attempt to assess their significance) may subvert a valuable legal doctrine.[5] The inquiry in cases such as this should not be whether differences between the two jobs exist (there will always be differences) but whether the differences which are present are substantial enough to constitute differences in the *kind* of employment or, alternatively, whether they render the substitute work employment of an *inferior kind*.

It seems to me that *this* inquiry involves, in the instant case at least, factual determinations which are improper on a motion for summary judgment. Resolving whether or not one job is substantially similar to another or whether, on the other hand, it is of a different or inferior kind, will often (as here) require a critical appraisal of the similarities and differences between them in light of the importance of these differences to the employee. This necessitates a weighing of the evidence, and it is precisely this undertaking which is forbidden on summary judgment. [citation]

This is not to say that summary judgment would never be available in an action by an employee in which the employer raises the defense of failure to mitigate damages. No case has come to my attention, however, in which summary judgment has been granted on the issue of whether an employee was obliged to accept available alternate employment. Nevertheless, there may well be cases in which the substitute employment is so manifestly of a dissimilar or inferior sort, the declarations of the plaintiff so complete and those of the defendant so conclusionary and inadequate that no factual issues exist for which a trial is required. This, however, is not such a case.

It is not intuitively obvious, to me at least, that the leading female role in a dramatic motion picture is a radically different endeavor from the leading female role in a musical comedy film. Nor is it plain to me that the rather qualified rights of director and screenplay approval contained in the first contract are highly significant matters either in the entertainment industry in general or to this plaintiff in particular. Certainly, none of the declarations introduced by plaintiff in support of her motion shed any light on these issues. Nor do they attempt to explain why she declined the offer of starring in "Big Country, Big Man." Nevertheless, the trial court granted the motion, declaring that these approval rights were "critical" and that their elimination altered "the essential nature of the employment."

The plaintiff's declarations were of no assistance to the trial court in its effort to justify reaching this conclusion on summary judgment. In-

---

5. The values of the doctrine of mitigation of damages in this context are that it minimizes the unnecessary personal and social (*e.g.*, nonproductive use of labor, litigation) costs of contractual failure. If a wrongfully discharged employee can, through his own action and without suffering financial or psychological loss in the process, reduce the damages accruing from the breach of contract, the most sensible policy is to require him to do so. I fear the majority opinion will encourage precisely opposite conduct.

stead, it was forced to rely on judicial notice of the definitions of "motion picture," "screenplay" and "director" [citation] and then on judicial notice of practices in the film industry which were purportedly of "common knowledge." [citation] This use of judicial notice was error. ...

I cannot accept the proposition that an offer which eliminates *any* contract right, regardless of its significance, is, as a matter of law, an offer of employment of an inferior kind. Such an absolute rule seems no more sensible than the majority's earlier suggestion that the mere existence of differences between two jobs is sufficient to render them employment of different kinds. Application of such *per se* rules will severely undermine the principle of mitigation of damages in the employer-employee context.

I remain convinced that the relevant question in such cases is whether or not a particular contract provision is so significant that its omission create [*sic*] employment of an inferior kind. This question is, of course, intimately bound up in what I consider the ultimate issue: whether or not the employee acted reasonably. This will generally involve a factual inquiry to ascertain the importance of the particular contract term and a process of weighing the absence of that term against the countervailing advantages of the alternate employment. In the typical case, this will mean that summary judgment must be withheld.

In the instant case, there was nothing properly before the trial court by which the importance of the approval rights could be ascertained, much less evaluated. Thus, in order to grant the motion for summary judgment, the trial court misused judicial notice. In upholding the summary judgment, the majority here rely upon *per se* rules which distort the process of determining whether or not an employee is obliged to accept particular employment in mitigation of damages.

I believe that the judgment should be reversed so that the issue of whether or not the offer of the lead role in "Big Country, Big Man" was of employment comparable to that of the lead role in "Bloomer Girl" may be determined at trial.

Rehearing denied; SULLIVAN, J., dissenting.

IN RE WORLDCOM, INC.

United States Bankruptcy Court, Southern District of New York, 2007.
361 B.R. 675.

ARTHUR J. GONZALEZ, BANKRUPTCY JUDGE.

INTRODUCTION

Before the Court are cross-motions for summary judgment separately brought by Michael Jordan ("Jordan") and WorldCom, Inc. ("Debtors" or "MCI").

BACKGROUND

On or about July 10, 1995, Jordan and the Debtors entered into an endorsement agreement (the "Agreement"). At that time, Jordan was considered to be one of the most popular athletes in the world. The Agreement granted MCI a ten-year license to use Jordan's name, likeness, "other attributes," and personal services to advertise and promote MCI's telecommunications products and services beginning in September 1995 and ending in August 2005. The Agreement did not prevent Jordan from endorsing most other products or services, although he could not endorse the same products or services that MCI produced. In addition to a \$5 million signing bonus, the Agreement provided an annual base compensation of \$2 million for Jordan. The Agreement provided that Jordan would be treated as an independent contractor and that MCI would not withhold any amount from Jordan's compensation for tax purposes. The Agreement provided that Jordan was to make himself available for four days, not to exceed four hours per day, during each contract year to produce television commercials and print advertising and for promotional appearances. The parties agreed that the advertising and promotional materials would be submitted to Jordan for his approval, which could not be unreasonably withheld, fourteen days prior to their release to the general public. From 1995 to 2000, Jordan appeared in several television commercials and a large number of print ads for MCI.

On July 1, 2002, MCI commenced a case under chapter 11 of title 11 of the United States Code (the "Bankruptcy Code") in the Bankruptcy Court for the Southern District of New York. On January 16, 2003, Jordan filed Claim No. 11414 in the amount of \$2 million plus contingent and unliquidated amounts allegedly due under the Agreement. On July 18, 2003, the Debtors rejected the Agreement as of that date, pursuant to § 365(a) of the Bankruptcy Code. Following that rejection of the Agreement, Jordan filed Claim No. 36077 (the "Claim") in the amount of \$8 million—seeking \$2 million for each of the payments that were due in June of 2002, 2003, 2004, and 2005. MCI does not object to the Claim to the extent Jordan seeks \$4 million for the 2002 and 2003 payments under the Agreement. As of the rejection in July 2003, two years remained under the Agreement.

The Parties' Contentions

MCI asserts [as one of two bases, the other being omitted here, ed.] for disallowance of the Claim ... that Jordan had an obligation to mitigate his damages and failed to do so. MCI argues that ... [it is entitled] to summary judgment with respect to its objection to the Claim, and assert[s] that ... the Claim should be reduced to \$4 million. MCI argues that it is under no obligation to pay Jordan for contract years 2004 and 2005.

Jordan argues for summary judgment allowing the Claim in full and overruling and dismissing MCI's objections to the Claim. ... Regarding MCI's mitigation argument, Jordan argues that the objection should be overruled and dismissed for three independent reasons (1) Jordan was a "lost volume seller" and thus mitigation does not apply, (2) there is no evidence that Jordan could have entered into a "substantially similar" endorsement agreement, and (3) Jordan acted reasonably when he decided not to pursue other endorsements after MCI's rejection of the Agreement.

Discussion

... C. Mitigation

The doctrine of avoidable consequences, which has also been referred to as the duty to mitigate damages, "bars recovery for losses suffered by a non-breaching party that could have been avoided by reasonable effort and without risk of substantial loss or injury." Edward M. Crough, Inc. v. Dep't of Gen. Servs. of D.C., 572 A.2d 457, 466 (D.C.1990). The burden of proving that the damages could have been avoided or mitigated rests with the party that committed the breach. *See* ... Norris v. Green, 656 A.2d 282, 287 (D.C.1995) ("The failure to mitigate damages is an affirmative defense and the (breaching party) has the burden of showing the absence of reasonable efforts to mitigate"). The efforts to avoid or mitigate the damages do not have to be successful, as long as they are reasonable.

Jordan argues that as a "lost volume seller" he was under no obligation to mitigate damages. ... MCI counters that Jordan is not a lost volume seller and that MCI has shown that Jordan failed to take reasonable steps to mitigate damages.

1. Whether Jordan Was a "Lost Volume Seller"

Jordan argues that MCI's mitigation defense does not apply here because Jordan is akin to a "lost volume seller." Jordan points to testimony demonstrating that he could have entered into additional endorsement contracts even if MCI had not rejected the Agreement. Thus, he argues, any additional endorsement contracts would not have been substitutes for the Agreement and would not have mitigated the damages for which MCI is liable.

"A lost volume seller is one who has the capacity to perform the contract that was breached in addition to other potential contracts due to unlimited resources or production capacity." Precision Pine & Timber, Inc. v. United States, 72 Fed.Cl. 460, 490 (Fed.Cl.2006). A lost volume seller does not minimize its damages by entering into another contract because it would have had the benefit of both contracts even if the first were not breached. The lost volume seller has two expectations, the profit from the breached contract and the profit from one or more other contracts that it could have performed at the same time as the breached contract. "The philosophical heart of the lost volume theory is that the seller would have generated a second sale irrespective of the buyer's breach" and that "(i)t follows that the lost volume seller cannot possibly mitigate damages." D. Matthews, *Should the Doctrine of Lost Volume Seller Be Retained? A Response to Professor Breen*, 51 U. Miami L.Rev. 1195, 1214 (July 1997).

The lost volume seller theory is recognized in the *Restatement (2d) of Contracts*, §§ 347, 350 (1981).[8] The lost volume seller theory applies to contracts for services as well as goods. *See Restatement (2d)*, § 347, ill. 16; *see also* ... Gianetti v. Norwalk Hosp., 64 Conn.App. 218, 779 A.2d 847, 853 (2001) (applying theory to provider of medical services), *aff'd in part, rev'd in part*, 266 Conn. 544, 833 A.2d 891 (2003).

This case offers a twist on the typical lost volume seller situation. In what the Court regards as the typical situation, the non-breaching seller has a near-inexhaustible supply of inventory. In the typical situation, when a buyer breaches an agreement to buy a good or service from the seller, the item is returned to inventory and the lost volume seller continues in its efforts to sell its goods or services. However, the transactions that occur following the breach are not necessarily the result of the breach but fundamentally the result of the seller continuing efforts to market its goods and services. It is this continuous effort coupled with a virtually limitless supply that warrants the lost volume exception to mitigation. As stated above, the transactions that may occur after the breach would in the context of the lost volume seller have occurred independent of the breach. Here, Jordan lacked a nearly limitless supply and had no intention of continuing to market his services as a product endorser.[10]

Although not addressed by a D.C. court, the majority of cases hold that Jordan bears the burden of proving that he is a lost volume seller. [citations] To claim lost volume seller status, Jordan must establish that he would have had the benefit of both the original and subsequent contracts if MCI had not rejected the Agreement. Although there is no definitive set of elements that the non-breaching party must show, many cases seem to follow the language from the *Restatement (2d)*, Section 347, that the non-breaching party must show that it "could and would have entered into" a subsequent agreement. *See* ... Green Tree [Fin. Corp. v. ALLTEL Info. Servs., Inc., No. Civ. 02–627 JRTFLN], 2002 WL 31163072, at *9 [D.Minn. Sept. 26, 2002] ("(t)o recover lost profits under this theory,

---

8. Comment f to § 347 states in part[:]

"Lost volume." Whether a subsequent transaction is a substitute for the broken contract sometimes raises difficult questions of fact. If the injured party could and would have entered into the subsequent contract, even if the contract had not been broken, and could have had the benefit of both, he can be said to have "lost volume" and the subsequent transaction is not a substitute for the broken contract. The injured party's damages are then based on the net profit that he has lost as a result of the broken contract.

Comment d to § 350 states[:]

"Lost volume." The mere fact that an injured party can make arrangements for the disposition of the goods or services that he was to supply under the contract does not necessarily mean that by doing so he will avoid loss. If he would have entered into both transactions but for the breach, he has "lost volume" as a result of the breach. *See* Comment f to § 347. In that case the second transaction is not a "substitute" for the first one. *See* Illustrations 9 and 10.

10. On one hand, the "lost volume seller" exception does not appear to be available to a product endorser because of the understandable concern over dilution through overexposure. However, if an endorser has not approached what would be his or her endorsement limit, prior to dilution, it would seem that the continuous effort then to obtain more endorsements would be akin to the traditional lost volume seller, and the defense then available. As will be discussed herein, Jordan's situation is not indicative of a lost volume seller under any analysis.

a non-breaching party must prove three things: (1) that the seller of services had the capability to perform both contracts simultaneously; (2) that the second contract would have been profitable; and (3) that the seller of service would have entered into the second contract if the first contract had not been terminated").

In his arguments, Jordan focuses primarily on his *capacity* to enter subsequent agreements, arguing that the loss of MCI's sixteen-hour annual time commitment hardly affected his ability to perform additional endorsement services. On this prong alone, Jordan likely would be considered a lost volume seller of endorsement services because he had sufficient time to do multiple endorsements. Although he does not have the "infinite capacity" that some cases discuss, a services provider does not need unlimited capacity but must have the requisite capacity and intent to perform under multiple contracts at the same time. *See* Gianetti, 266 Conn. at 561–62, 833 A.2d 891 (plastic surgeon could be considered a lost volume seller if it were determined that he had the capacity and intent to simultaneously work out of three or four hospitals profitably).

Contrary to Jordan's analysis, courts do not focus solely on the seller's capacity. The seller claiming lost volume status must also demonstrate that it *would have* entered into subsequent transactions. Jordan has not shown he could and would have entered into a subsequent agreement. Rather, the evidence shows that Jordan did not have the "subjective intent" to take on additional endorsements. The testimony from Jordan's representatives establishes that although Jordan's popularity enabled him to obtain additional product endorsements in 2003, Jordan desired to scale back his level of endorsements. Jordan's financial and business advisor, Curtis Polk, testified that at the time the Agreement was rejected, Jordan's desire was "not to expand his spokesperson or pitchman efforts with new relationships." Polk testified that had Jordan wanted to do additional endorsements after the 2003 rejection, he could have obtained additional deals. Jordan's agent, David Falk, testified that "there might have been twenty more companies that in theory might have wanted to sign him" but that Jordan and his representatives wanted to avoid diluting his image. Jordan's Memorandum for Summary Judgment stated that at the time the Agreement was rejected, Jordan had implemented a strategy of not accepting new endorsements because of a belief that new deals would jeopardize his ability to achieve his primary goal of National Basketball Association ("NBA") franchise ownership. . . .

One of the classic examples of the lost volume seller is found in Neri v. Retail Marine Corp., 30 N.Y.2d 393, 399–400, 334 N.Y.S.2d 165, 169–70, 285 N.E.2d 311 (N.Y.1972)[:]

> (I)f a private party agrees to sell his automobile to a buyer for $2,000, a breach by the buyer would cause the seller no loss (except incidental damages, *i.e.*, expense of a new sale) if the seller was able to sell the automobile to another buyer for $2,000. But the situation is different with dealers having an unlimited supply or standard-priced goods.

Thus, if an automobile dealer agrees to sell a car to a buyer at the standard price of $2,000, a breach by the buyer injures the dealer, even though he is able to sell the automobile to another for $2,000. If the dealer has an inexhaustible supply of cars, the resale to replace the breaching buyer costs the dealer a sale, because, had the breaching buyer performed, the dealer would have made two sales instead of one. The buyer's breach, in such a case, depletes the dealer's sales to the extent of one, and the measure of damages should be the dealer's profit on one sale.

This example would surely have a different result if the car dealership was winding down its business and had agreed to sell one of its last cars to a buyer. If that buyer subsequently breached the contract and did not purchase the car, the dealership could hardly be expected to recover lost profits damages if the dealer put the car back onto a deserted car lot, made no attempts to sell it, and kept the dealership shuttered to new customers. Those modifications are analogous to Jordan's situation, with his stated desire to withdraw his services from the endorsement marketplace, and the lost volume seller theory accordingly does not apply to his circumstances.

Jordan states that it is a "red herring" to speculate under the lost volume analysis on what he *would* have done because that

> ignores the central point of the lost volume principle: if Jordan had … accepted a substantially similar endorsement opportunity—exactly what (MCI) argues he was required to do to mitigate damages—the damages for which (MCI) is liable would not have been reduced by one penny because the lost volume principle would allow Jordan to retain the benefits of both the (MCI) Agreement and the hypothetical additional endorsement.

Jordan overlooks an important point about the lost volume seller theory—that the "original sale and the second sale are independent events," Snyder [v. Herbert Greenbaum & Assocs., 38 Md.App. 144, 380 A.2d 618, 625 (1977)], because the lost volume seller's intent to enter into new contracts is the same before and after a purchaser's breach. The lost volume seller's desire to sell more units of goods or services is virtually unaffected by the loss of a single sale or agreement.

Next, even if Jordan had mitigated damages by entering one subsequent endorsement agreement, this, without more, does not mean that Jordan was a lost volume seller. The lost volume seller has the intent and capacity to sell multiple units despite the breach of a contract for one transaction.

Finally, if Jordan had entered into a subsequent agreement or agreements, and if he had showed both the capacity and the intent to make subsequent sales, that might have had the effect of helping him to establish his status as a lost volume seller, which generally would relieve him of the duty to mitigate. This would not be a novel situation but it ignores the fact that he did not do so. *See, e.g.,* … Chicago Title Ins.

Corp. v. Magnuson, No. 2:03–CV–368, 2005 WL 2373430, at *23 (S.D.Ohio Sept. 26, 2005) (when there is no evidence in the record that plaintiff "turned away or would have turned away business during the relevant period" and the "only evidence on the issue supports that the (plaintiff) could and would have completed such transactions," the consequent instructions to the jury that the plaintiff was a lost volume seller and therefore had no duty to mitigate its damages were not erroneous).

Because the evidence establishes, among other things, that Jordan would not have entered into subsequent agreements, Jordan has not established that he is a lost volume seller. This theory thus does not relieve Jordan from the duty to mitigate damages.

2. *Whether Jordan Made Reasonable Efforts to Mitigate*

Jordan argues at length that MCI must show that Jordan could have entered a "substantially similar" endorsement contract in order to mitigate damages. However, this is not the law of the mitigation of damages or the avoidable consequences theory. This language stems from federal employment cases concerning back pay and mitigation, which this case, while similar in many respects, is not. *See, e.g.*, Ford Motor Co. v. E.E.O.C., 458 U.S. 219, 231–32, 102 S.Ct. 3057, 3065–66, 73 L.Ed.2d 721 (1982) (the duty to mitigate damages, "rooted in an ancient principle of law, requires the claimant to use reasonable diligence in finding other suitable employment. Although the . . . claimant need not go into another line of work, accept a demotion, or take a demeaning position, he forfeits his right to back pay if he refuses a job substantially equivalent to the one he was denied").

Several of the justifications for the "substantially similar or equivalent" standard of employment law, aside from the general remedial policy of making the non-breaching party whole for losses caused by the breaching party, show why there is less concern here regarding a "substantially equivalent" opportunity as Jordan was not an employee of MCI. For one, the standard exists in part to ensure the employee's future advancement by mandating that the employee's promotional opportunities and status should be virtually identical to the prior position. Since Jordan was never an employee of MCI, this is not relevant. Second, to require acceptance of inferior employment can mean "that one who has been discriminated against would be obliged, in order to mitigate damages, to submit to the very discrimination of which he complains." *See* Williams v. Albemarle City Bd. of Ed., 508 F.2d 1242, 1244 (4th Cir.1974). This, obviously, has no application here. Finally, the employee's duty to make reasonable efforts in finding substantially equivalent employment is "based both on the doctrine of mitigation of damages and on the policy of promoting production and employment." *See* N.L.R.B. v. Miami Coca–Cola Bottling Co., 360 F.2d 569, 575 (5th Cir.1966). . . .

More accurately, MCI must show the absence of reasonable efforts by Jordan to avoid consequences or minimize his damages. *See* . . . Joseph M. Perillo, *Calamari & Perillo on Contracts*, § 14.15, at 584 (5th Ed.2003)

("The doctrine of avoidable consequences merely requires reasonable efforts to mitigate damages"). . . . MCI carries its burden by showing that Jordan has not taken affirmative steps to mitigate damages. Jordan admits in his brief that at the time of the rejection of the Agreement, "Jordan had already implemented a business strategy of not accepting new endorsements." . . . Based on the foregoing, and drawing all permissible factual inferences in favor of Jordan, the Court determines that MCI has established that Jordan did not take affirmative steps to mitigate damages. . . .

3. Whether Jordan's Beliefs that Another Endorsement Would Dilute His Impact as an Endorser or Harm His Reputation Were Reasonable Justifications for not Mitigating Damages

Jordan cites the risk that entering another endorsement contract could dilute his impact as an endorser or damage his reputation or business interests. . . . MCI convincingly responds that adding an agreement to replace a lost one is merely maintaining the status quo, not a dilution of Jordan's impact by addition. . . . While the Court recognizes that Jordan's image is the true commodity here and its market value could be diluted from overexposure, MCI has shown that Jordan's image was not at risk of dilution by replacing the MCI endorsement agreement with another one. . . .

Under the risk to reputation theory Jordan cites, an injured party is not allowed to recover from a wrongdoer those damages that the injured party "could have avoided without undue risk, burden or humiliation." See Restatement (2d), § 350(1). Jordan's "harm to reputation" argument is flawed because the envisioned harm to Jordan's reputation does not rise to the level of harm found in the cited case law. The cases cited by Jordan illustrate the harm to reputation that will excuse a party's duty to mitigate. In Eastman Kodak Co. v. Westway Motor Freight, Inc., 949 F.2d 317 (10th Cir.1991), Kodak shipped a load of sensitized photographic material on a truck operated by the defendant. Most of the material was destroyed in transit because of the defendant's mishandling. The Tenth Circuit held that Kodak was not required to sell the damaged merchandise to mitigate damages, stating that the record revealed that Kodak's reputation, which it spent considerable resources in developing, "could be harmed if it was required to sell damaged merchandise in order to mitigate damages." Id. at 320. . . .

4. Whether Focusing on NBA Ownership Was a Reasonable Decision

. . . [Cited] cases demonstrate that a court will not sharply second-guess the decisions made by a non-breaching party when it attempts to mitigate the damages caused by the breaching party. The cases differ from Jordan's situation because his decision to focus on NBA team ownership was independent of MCI's rejection and was not contemplated as one that would lessen the harm of that rejection. Such a decision was unrelated to the duty to mitigate damages resulting from a rejected agreement as a product endorser. In short, the argument that Jordan acted reasonably by focusing solely on his efforts to become an NBA team owner is a red herring. It may have been reasonable for Jordan to focus on becoming an NBA team owner in the scope of Jordan's overall future desires but that does not mean it can support a determination that he was relieved of his obligation to mitigate damages in response to MCI's rejection of the Agreement. . . .

CONCLUSION

. . . The Court finds [as a matter of law, ed.] that Jordan failed to mitigate damages but a further evidentiary hearing is necessary to determine what Jordan could have received had he made reasonable efforts to mitigate, a determination that consequently will affect the Claim.

The Debtors are to settle an order consistent with this opinion.

PROBLEMS

9. Jack was a highly skilled production manager in the ladies' ready-to-wear industry. He entered into a three-year contract with defendant to work in this capacity in Dallas, a city in which positions of this type were rare. Soon after the performance of the contract began, Jack was fired without cause. He spent over $1300 in advertising and travel costs in an unsuccessful attempt to find a comparable position. He ultimately took a temporary and less skilled job at a lesser salary for a period of time that was less than the unexpired contract term. Under the principle of mitigation of damages how should his expenses and his temporary job earnings be treated?

10. Employee entered into a contract for 16 years employment with Employer at $100,000 per year. Since the employment was predicated on Employee's great expertise in managing a process on which Employer owned a patent, there was no similar employment available to Employee elsewhere. At the end of one year Employer wrongfully terminated Employee's employment. Upon finding that Employee could not mitigate damages, the trial court entered judgment for Employee for $1,500,000. Was the court's judgment mathematically sound?

11. P was hired as a radio "talk show" host for one year on station WMCA at a salary of $50,000 per year. In mid year she was discharged without cause. The balance of her salary for the year was tendered. She refused the tender and sued for $500,000 claiming damages for "lost publicity." What result?

12. Defendant, a highly skilled hairdresser, entered into a bilateral contract with plaintiff to work for plaintiff for one year at $750 per week. Defendant quit without cause to take another hairdressing job at $1000 per week. Are damages sufficiently shown by the facts stated?

(d) CONSTRUCTION CONTRACTS

(Calamari & Perillo on Contracts §§ 14.28—14.29)

JACOB & YOUNGS v. KENT
Court of Appeals of New York, 1921.
230 N.Y. 239, 129 N.E. 889, 23 A.L.R. 1429.

See p. 411 *supra*.

PEEVYHOUSE v. GARLAND COAL & MINING COMPANY
Supreme Court of Oklahoma, 1962.
382 P.2d 109.

JACKSON, JUSTICE. In the trial court, plaintiffs Willie and Lucille Peevyhouse sued the defendant, Garland Coal and Mining Company, for damages for breach of contract. Judgment was for plaintiffs in an amount considerably less than was sued for. Plaintiffs appeal and defendant cross-appeals.

In the briefs on appeal, the parties present their argument and contentions under several propositions; however, they all stem from the basic question of whether the trial court properly instructed the jury on the measure of damages.

Briefly stated, the facts are as follows: plaintiffs owned a farm containing coal deposits, and in November, 1954, leased the premises to defendant for a period of five years for coal mining purposes. A "stripmining" operation was contemplated in which the coal would be taken from pits on the surface of the ground, instead of from underground mine shafts. In addition to the usual covenants found in a coal mining lease, defendant specifically agreed to perform certain restorative and remedial work at the end of the lease period. It is unnecessary to set out the details of the work to be done, other than to say that it would involve the moving of many thousands of cubic yards of dirt, at a cost estimated by expert witnesses at about $29,000.00. However, plaintiffs sued for only $25,000.00.

During the trial, it was stipulated that all covenants and agreements in the lease contract had been fully carried out by both parties, except the remedial work mentioned above; defendant conceded that this work had not been done.

Plaintiffs introduced expert testimony as to the amount and nature of the work to be done, and its estimated cost. Over plaintiffs' objections, defendant thereafter introduced expert testimony as to the "diminution in value" of plaintiffs' farm resulting from the failure of defendant to render performance as agreed in the contract—that is, the difference between the present value of the farm, and what its value would have been if defendant had done what it agreed to do.

At the conclusion of the trial, the court instructed the jury that it must return a verdict for plaintiffs, and left the amount of damages for jury determination. On the measure of damages, the court instructed the jury that it might consider the cost of performance of the work defendant agreed to do, "together with all of the evidence offered on behalf of either party." It thus appears that the jury was at liberty to consider the "diminution in value" of plaintiffs' farm as well as the cost of "repair work" in determining the amount of damages.

It returned a verdict for plaintiffs for $5000.00—only a fraction of the "cost of performance," *but more than the total value of the farm even after the remedial work is done.*

On appeal, the issue is sharply drawn. Plaintiffs contend that the true measure of damages in this case is what it will cost plaintiffs to obtain performance of the work that was not done because of defendant's default. Defendant argues that the measure of damages is the cost of performance "limited, however, to the total difference in the market value before and after the work was performed."

It appears that this precise question has not heretofore been presented to this court. In Ardizonne v. Archer, 72 Okl. 70, 178 P. 263, this court held that the measure of damages for breach of a contract to drill an oil well was the reasonable cost of drilling the well, but here a slightly different factual situation exists. The drilling of an oil well will yield valuable geological information, even if no oil or gas is found, and of course if the well is a producer, the value of the premises increases. In the case before us, it is argued by defendant with some force that the performance of the remedial work defendant agreed to do will add at the most only a few hundred dollars to the value of plaintiffs' farm, and that the damages should be limited to that amount because that is all plaintiffs have lost.

Plaintiffs rely on Groves v. John Wunder Co., 205 Minn. 163, 286 N.W. 235, 123 A.L.R. 502. In that case, the Minnesota court, in a substantially similar situation, adopted the "cost of performance" rule as-opposed to the "value" rule. The result was to authorize a jury to give plaintiff damages in the amount of $60,000, where the real estate concerned would have been worth only $12,160, even if the work contracted for had been done.

It may be observed that Groves v. John Wunder Co., *supra*, is the only case which has come to our attention in which the cost of performance rule has been followed under circumstances where the cost of performance greatly exceeded the diminution in value resulting from the breach of contract. Incidentally, it appears that this case was decided by a plurality rather than a majority of the members of the court.

Defendant relies principally upon Sandy Valley & E. R. Co. v. Hughes, 175 Ky. 320, 194 S.W. 344; Bigham v. Wabash–Pittsburg Terminal Ry. Co., 223 Pa. 106, 72 A. 318; and Sweeney v. Lewis Const. Co., 66 Wash. 490, 119 P. 1108. These were all cases in which, under similar circumstances, the appellate courts followed the "value" rule instead of the "cost of performance" rule. Plaintiff points out that in the earliest of these cases

(Bigham) the court cites as authority on the measure of damages an earlier Pennsylvania *tort* case, and that the other two cases follow the first, with no explanation as to why a measure of damages ordinarily followed in cases sounding in tort should be used in contract cases. Nevertheless, it is of some significance that three out of four appellate courts have followed the diminution in value rule under circumstances where, as here, the cost of performance greatly exceeds the diminution in value.

The explanation may be found in the fact that the situations presented are artificial ones. It is highly unlikely that the ordinary property owner would agree to pay $29,000 (or its equivalent) for the construction of "improvements" upon his property that would increase its value only about ($300) three hundred dollars. The result is that we are called upon to apply principles of law theoretically based upon reason and reality to a situation which is basically unreasonable and unrealistic.

In Groves v. John Wunder Co., *supra*, in arriving at its conclusions, the Minnesota court apparently considered the contract involved to be analogous to a building and construction contract, and cited authority for the proposition that the cost of performance or completion of the building as contracted is ordinarily the measure of damages in actions for damages for the breach of such a contract.

In an annotation following the Minnesota case beginning at 123 A.L.R. 515, the annotator places the three cases relied on by defendant (*Sandy Valley, Bigham and Sweeney*) under the classification of cases involving "grading and excavation contracts."

We do not think either analogy is strictly applicable to the case now before us. The primary purpose of the lease contract between plaintiffs and defendant was neither "building and construction" nor "grading and excavation." It was merely to accomplish the economical recovery and marketing of coal from the premises, to the profit of all parties. The special provisions of the lease contract pertaining to remedial work were incidental to the main object involved.

Even in the case of contracts that are unquestionably building and construction contracts, the authorities are not in agreement as to the factors to be considered in determining whether the cost of performance rule or the value rule should be applied. The American Law Institute's *Restatement of the Law, Contracts*, Volume 1, Sections 346(1)(a)(i) and (ii) submits the proposition that the cost of performance is the proper measure of damages "if this is possible and does not involve *unreasonable economic waste*"; and that the diminution in value caused by the breach is the proper measure "if construction and completion in accordance with the contract would involve *unreasonable economic waste*." (Emphasis supplied.) In an explanatory comment immediately following the text, the *Restatement* makes it clear that the "economic waste" referred to consists of the destruction of a substantially completed building or other structure. Of course no such destruction is involved in the case now before us.

On the other hand, in McCormick, *Damages*, Section 168, it is said with regard to building and construction contracts that "... in cases where the defect is one that can be repaired or cured without undue expense" the cost of performance is the proper measure of damages, but where "... the defect in material or construction is one that cannot be remedied without *an expenditure for reconstruction disproportionate to the end to be attained*" (emphasis supplied) the value rule should be followed. The same idea was expressed in Jacob & Youngs, Inc. v. Kent, 230 N.Y. 239, 129 N.E. 889, 23 A.L.R. 1429, as follows:

> The owner is entitled to the money which will permit him to complete, unless the cost of completion is grossly and unfairly out of proportion to the good to be attained. When that is true, the measure is the difference in value.

It thus appears that the prime consideration in the Restatement was "economic waste"; and that the prime consideration in McCormick, *Damages*, and in Jacob & Youngs, Inc. v. Kent, *supra*, was the relationship between the expense involved and the "end to be attained"—in other words, the "relative economic benefit."

In view of the unrealistic fact situation in the instant case, and certain Oklahoma statutes to be hereinafter noted, we are of the opinion that the "relative economic benefit" is a proper consideration here. This is in accord with the recent case of Mann v. Clowser, 190 Va. 887, 59 S.E.2d 78, where, in applying the cost rule, the Virginia court specifically noted that "... the defects are remediable from a practical standpoint and the costs *are not grossly disproportionate to the results to be obtained*" (emphasis supplied). 23 O.S.1961 §§ 96 and 97 provide as follows:

> § 96. ... Notwithstanding the provisions of this chapter, no person can recover a greater amount in damages for the breach of an obligation, than he would have gained by the full performance thereof on both sides....

> § 97. ... Damages must, in all cases, be reasonable, and where an obligation of any kind appears to create a right to unconscionable and grossly oppressive damages, contrary to substantial justice no more than reasonable damages can be recovered.

Although it is true that the above sections of the statute are applied most often in tort cases, they are by their own terms, and the decisions of this court, also applicable in actions for damages for breach of contract. It would seem that they are peculiarly applicable here where, under the "cost of performance" rule, plaintiffs might recover an amount about nine times the total value of their farm. Such would seem to be "unconscionable and grossly oppressive damages, contrary to substantial justice" within the meaning of the statute. Also, it can hardly be denied that if plaintiffs here are permitted to recover under the "cost of performance" rule, they will receive a greater benefit from the breach than could be gained from full performance, contrary to the provisions of Sec. 96.

An analogy may be drawn between the cited sections, and the provisions of 15 O.S.1961 §§ 214 and 215. These sections tend to render void any provisions of a contract which attempt to fix the amount of stipulated damages to be paid in case of a breach, except where it is impracticable or extremely difficult to determine the actual damages. This results in spite of the agreement of the parties, and the obvious and well known rationale is that insofar as they exceed the actual damages suffered, the stipulated damages amount to a penalty or forfeiture which the law does not favor.

23 O.S.1961 §§ 96 and 97 have the same effect in the case now before us. *In spite of the agreement of the parties*, these sections limit the damages recoverable to a reasonable amount not "contrary to substantial justice"; they prevent plaintiffs from recovering a "greater amount in damages for the breach of an obligation" than they would have "gained by the full performance thereof."

We therefore hold that where, in a coal mining lease, lessee agrees to perform certain remedial work on the premises concerned at the end of the lease period, and thereafter the contract is fully performed by both parties except that the remedial work is not done, the measure of damages in an action by lessor against lessee for damages for breach of contract is ordinarily the reasonable cost of performance of the work; however, where the contract provision breached was merely incidental to the main purpose in view, and where the economic benefit which would result to lessor by full performance of the work is grossly disproportionate to the cost of performance, the damages which lessor may recover are limited to the diminution in value resulting to the premises because of the non-performance.

We believe the above holding is in conformity with the intention of the Legislature as expressed in the statutes mentioned, and in harmony with the better-reasoned cases from the other jurisdictions where analogous fact situations have been considered. It should be noted that the rule as stated does not interfere with the property owner's right to "do what he will with his own" Chamberlain v. Parker, 45 N.Y. 569, or his right, if he chooses, to contract for "improvements" which will actually have the effect of reducing his property's value. Where such result is in fact contemplated by the parties, and is a main or principal purpose of those contracting, it would seem that the measure of damages for breach would ordinarily be the cost of performance.

The above holding disposes of all of the arguments raised by the parties on appeal. Under the most liberal view of the evidence herein, the diminution in value resulting to the premises because of non-performance of the remedial work was $300.00. After a careful search of the record, we have found no evidence of a higher figure, and plaintiffs do not argue in their briefs that a greater diminution in value was sustained. It thus appears that the judgment was clearly excessive, and that the amount for which judgment should have been rendered is definitely and satisfactorily shown by the record. We are asked by each party to modify the judgment in accordance with the respective theories advanced, and it is conceded that we have authority to do so. [citations]

We are of the opinion that the judgment of the trial court for plaintiffs should be, and it is hereby, modified and reduced to the sum of $300.00, and as so modified it is affirmed.

WELCH, DAVISON, HALLEY, and JOHNSON, JJ., concur.

WILLIAMS, C. J., BLACKBIRD, V. C. J., and IRWIN and BERRY, JJ., dissent.

IRWIN, JUSTICE (dissenting). By the specific provisions in the coal mining lease under consideration, the defendant agreed as follows: . . .

> 7b Lessee agrees to make fills in the pits dug on said premises on the property line in such manner that fences can be placed thereon and access had to opposite sides of the pits.

> [7]c Lessee agrees to smooth off the top of the spoil banks on the above premises.

> 7d Lessee agrees to leave the creek crossing the above premises in such a condition that it will not interfere with the crossings to be made in pits as set out in 7b.

> . . .

> 7f Lessee further agrees to leave no shale or dirt on the high wall of said pits. . . .

Following the expiration of the lease, plaintiffs made demand upon defendant that it carry out the provisions of the contract and to perform those covenants contained therein.

Defendant admits that it failed to perform its obligations that it agreed and contracted to perform under the lease contract and there is nothing in the record which indicates that defendant could not perform its obligations. Therefore, in my opinion defendant's breach of the contract was wilful and not in good faith.

Although the contract speaks for itself, there were several negotiations between the plaintiffs and defendant before the contract was executed. Defendant admitted in the trial of the action, that plaintiffs insisted that the above provisions be included in the contract and that they would not agree to the coal mining lease unless the above provisions were included.

In consideration for the lease contract, plaintiffs were to receive a certain amount as royalty for the coal produced and marketed and in addition thereto their land was to be restored as provided in the contract.

Defendant received as consideration for the contract, its proportionate share of the coal produced and marketed and in addition thereto, the *right to use* plaintiffs' land in the furtherance of its mining operations.

The cost for performing the contract in question could have been reasonably approximated when the contract was negotiated and executed and there are no conditions now existing which could not have been reasonably anticipated by the parties. Therefore, defendant had knowledge, when it prevailed upon the plaintiffs to execute the lease, that the cost of performance might be disproportionate to the value or benefits received by plaintiff for the performance.

Defendant has received its benefits under the contract and now urges, in substance, that plaintiffs' measure of damages for its failure to perform should be the economic value of performance to the plaintiffs and not the cost of performance.

If a peculiar set of facts should exist where the above rule should be applied as the proper measure of damages, (and in my judgment those facts do not exist in the instant case) before such rule should be applied, consideration should be given to the benefits received or contracted for by the party who asserts the application of the rule.

Defendant did not have the right to mine plaintiffs' coal or to use plaintiffs' property for its mining operations without the consent of plaintiffs. Defendant had knowledge of the benefits that it would receive under the contract and the approximate cost of performing the contract. With this knowledge, it must be presumed that defendant thought that it would be to its economic advantage to enter into the contract with plaintiffs and that it would reap benefits from the contract, or it would have not entered into the contract.

Therefore, if the value of the performance of a contract should be considered in determining the measure of damages for breach of a contract, the value of the benefits received under the contract by a party who breaches a contract should also be considered. However, in my judgment, to give consideration to either in the instant action, completely rescinds and holds for naught the solemnity of the contract before us and makes an entirely new contract for the parties.

In Goble v. Bell Oil & Gas Co., 97 Okl. 261, 223 P. 371, we held:

> Even though the contract contains harsh and burdensome terms which the court does not in all respects approve, it is the province of the parties in relation to lawful subject matter to fix their rights and obligations, and the court will give the contract effect according to its expressed provisions, unless it be shown by competent evidence proof that the written agreement as executed is the result of fraud, mistake, or accident.

In Cities Service Oil Co. v. Geolograph Co. Inc., 208 Okl. 179, 254 P.2d 775, we said: "While we do not agree that the contract as presently written is an onerous one, we think the short answer is that the folly or wisdom of a contract is not for the court to pass on." In Great Western Oil & Gas Company v. Mitchell, Okl., 326 P.2d 794, we held: "The law will not make a better contract for parties than they themselves have seen fit to enter into, or alter it for the benefit of one party and to the detriment of the others; the judicial function of a court of law is to enforce a contract as it is written."

I am mindful of Title 23 O.S.1961 § 96, which provides that no person can recover a greater amount in damages for the breach of an obligation than he could have gained by the full performance thereof on both sides, except in cases not applicable herein. However, in my judgment, the above statutory provision is not applicable here. In my judgment, we should follow the case of Groves v. John Wunder Company, 205 Minn. 163, 286 N.W. 235, 123 A.L.R. 502, which defendant agrees "that the fact situation is apparently similar to the one in the case at bar," and where the Supreme Court of Minnesota held:

> The owner's or employer's damages for such a breach (*i.e.* breach hypothesized in 2d syllabus) are to be measured, not in respect to the value of the land to be improved, but by the reasonable cost of doing that which the contractor promised to do and which he left undone.

The hypothesized breach referred to states that where the contractor's breach of a contract is wilful, that is, in bad faith, he is not entitled to any benefit of the equitable doctrine of substantial performance.

In the instant action defendant has made no attempt to even substantially perform. The contract in question is not immoral, is not tainted with fraud, and was not entered into through mistake or accident and is not contrary to public policy. It is clear and unambiguous and the parties understood the terms thereof, and the approximate cost of fulfilling the obligations could have been approximately ascertained. There are no conditions existing now which could not have been reasonably anticipated when the contract was negotiated and executed. The defendant could have performed the contract if it desired. It has accepted and reaped the benefits of its contract and now urges that plaintiffs' benefits under the contract be denied. If plaintiffs' benefits are denied, such benefits would inure to the direct benefit of the defendant.

Therefore, in my opinion, the plaintiffs were entitled to specific performance of the contract and since defendant has failed to perform, the proper measure of damages should be the cost of performance. Any other measure of damage would be holding for naught the express provisions of the contract; would be taking from the plaintiffs the benefits of the contract and placing those benefits in defendant which has failed to perform its obligations; would be granting benefits to defendant without a resulting obligation; and would be completely rescinding the solemn obligation of the contract for the benefit of the defendant to the detriment of the plaintiffs by making an entirely new contract for the parties.

I therefore respectfully dissent to the opinion promulgated by a majority of my associates.

[A supplemental opinion on rehearing is omitted.]

PROBLEMS

13. D contracted to build on D's land and to convey to P a suburban house with a garage and driveway. Rather than excavate a rock formation, D

built the driveway with a 22½% grade, which is so steep the driveway cannot be used safely and conveniently. A 12% grade is considered the permissible maximum. The evidence showed that the cost of redoing the driveway and lowering the garage would be $20,000. The full purchase price was $68,000. D offered evidence to show that the property's value, despite the existence of the defect, exceeded the purchase price. The trial judge excluded this evidence and entered judgment on the jury's verdict for $20,000. Should the judgment be affirmed?

14. L, a municipality, owned a waterfront pier which it leased to T for a ten-year term at $200,000 per year. T agreed to keep the pier in good and sufficient repair at T's expense. At the expiration of the leasehold L discovered that T had failed to maintain the pier in good repair and that costs of repair would be about $200,000. Soon thereafter L demolished the pier for replacement by a containership terminal. In an action by L for damages, T argues that L suffered no damages as the pier had been scheduled for demolition and was, in fact, demolished. What result?

15. P, a potato farmer in Idaho, contracted with D whereby D would construct a potato cellar for frost-free protection of stored potatoes. The agreed completion date was September 1st. Construction, however, was not completed until October 28. As a result of the delay a large part of P's crop was destroyed by frost. It is predictable that killing frost will arrive in Idaho prior to October 28. Is D liable for the loss?

(e) PUNITIVE DAMAGES, PENALTIES, EFFICIENT BREACH, AGREED DAMAGES AND LIMITATIONS OF LIABILITY

(Calamari & Perillo on Contracts §§ 14.3, 14.31—14.36)

PATTON v. MID–CONTINENT SYSTEMS, INC.

United States Court of Appeals, Seventh Circuit, 1988.
841 F.2d 742.

POSNER, CIRCUIT JUDGE. [The plaintiffs operated truck stops on I–94 in Indiana and Michigan. The defendant entered into a franchise agreement with them, giving them an exclusive territory, within which no other truck stops would be franchised to accept defendant's credit cards in payment of fuel and related items. The jury found that defendant had breached its contracts with plaintiffs by franchising other truck stops, starting with a franchise to Truck–O–Mat, within the plaintiffs' exclusive territorial area. The jury awarded compensatory damages to the plaintiffs and in addition awarded them $2,250,000 in punitive damages, reduced by the district judge to $100,000. The case involved a number of issues, including the choice of Indiana law by acquiescence. After determining that the award of compensatory damages was excessive, the court turned to the question of punitive damages. Ed.] . . .

Indiana allows punitive damages to be awarded in suits for breach of contract if, "mingled" with the breach, are "elements of fraud, malice, gross negligence or oppression." Travelers Indemnity Co. v. Armstrong, [442 N.E.2d 349, 359 (Ind.1982)]. In trying to give concrete meaning to these terms (especially "oppression"), it is important to bear in mind certain fundamentals of contractual liability. First, liability for breach of contract is, *prima facie*, strict liability. That is, if the promisor fails to perform as agreed, he has broken his contract even though the failure may have been beyond his power to prevent and therefore in no way blameworthy. The reason is that contracts often contain an insurance component. The promisor promises in effect either to perform or to compensate the promisee for the cost of nonperformance; and one who voluntarily assumes a risk will not be relieved of the consequences if the risk materializes.

Even if the breach is deliberate, it is not necessarily blameworthy. The promisor may simply have discovered that his performance is worth more to someone else. If so, efficiency is promoted by allowing him to break his promise, provided he makes good the promisee's actual losses. If he is forced to pay more than that, an efficient breach may be deterred, and the law doesn't want to bring about such a result. *See* J. Yanan & Associates, Inc. v. Integrity Ins. Co., 771 F.2d 1025, 1034 (7th Cir.1985). Suppose that by franchising Truck–O–Mat in the plaintiffs' territory, Mid–Continent increased its own profits by $150,000 and inflicted damages of $75,000 on the plaintiffs. That would be an efficient breach. But if Mid–Continent had known that it would have to pay in addition to compensatory damages $100,000 in punitive damages, the breach would not have been worthwhile to it and efficiency would have suffered because the difference between Mid–Continent's profits of $150,000 and the plaintiffs' losses of $75,000 would (certainly after the plaintiffs were compensated) represent a net social gain.

Not all breaches of contract are involuntary or otherwise efficient. Some are opportunistic; the promisor wants the benefit of the bargain without bearing the agreed-upon cost, and exploits the inadequacies of purely compensatory remedies (the major inadequacies being that pre-and post-judgment interest rates are frequently below market levels when the risk of nonpayment is taken into account and that the winning party cannot recover his attorney's fees). This seems the common element in most of the Indiana cases that have allowed punitive damages to be awarded in breach of contract cases; see the discussion of cases in Travelers Indemnity Co. v. Armstrong, *supra*, 442 N.E.2d at 359. Granted, this is not how the legal test is phrased; in particular the category of "gross negligence" seems unrelated to opportunistic breach. We may have captured the core of the Indiana rule but missed the periphery. But whatever the exact dimensions of the rule, the facts of the present case are pretty clearly outside it.

There is no evidence that the action of Mid–Continent in franchising Truck–O–Mat in the plaintiffs' exclusive territory was opportunistic or even deliberate. So far as can be discerned from the record it was an honest mistake resulting from the ambiguous description of the territory in the franchise agreement with the plaintiffs. However, Mid–Continent's failure to correct the violation year after year after the plaintiffs had called its attention to it—even after it acknowledged the violation—converted an innocent breach into a deliberate one; but no clear and convincing evidence enables the breach to be characterized as malicious, fraudulent, oppressive, or even grossly negligent. As we saw in discussing the issue of compensatory damages, the breach did little, perhaps no, damage to either plaintiff, and it is therefore quite possible that it was an efficient breach in the sense that it increased Mid–Continent's profits by more than it caused anyone losses. If so, the refusal to rectify the breach, while deliberate, would not justify an award of punitive damages. Mid–Continent's unfulfilled promises to rectify the breach could be viewed as a form of deceit designed to prevent the plaintiffs from resorting to legal remedies, but this is just the kind of conjecture that seems excluded by the requirement of proving entitlement to punitive damages by clear and convincing evidence. . . .

The award of punitive damages must be vacated. The finding of breach of contract is affirmed and the case remanded for a new trial limited to compensatory damages.

DANIEL FRIEDMANN, THE EFFICIENT BREACH FALLACY

18 J. Legal Studies 1 (1989).

The only universal consequence of a legally binding promise is that the law makes the promisor pay damages if the promised event does not come to pass. In every case it leaves him free from interference until the time for fulfillment has gone by, and therefore free to break his contract if he chooses.[1]

So wrote Oliver Wendell Holmes in his seminal discussion of contract remedies in *The Common Law*. That position, while widely discussed, is not acceptable as a normative (nor, as will be shown, as a positive) account of the question of contract remedies. Stated in a phrase, the weakness of Holmes's approach lies in its conclusion that the remedy provides a perfect substitute for the right, when in truth the purpose of the remedy is to vindicate that right, not replace it. Holmes's analysis mistakenly converts the remedy into a kind of indulgence that the wrongdoer is unilaterally always entitled to purchase. As with any unifying ideal, Holmes's proposition is difficult to confine to the contract cases to which it was originally applied. Why not generalize the proposition so that every person has an "option" to transgress another's rights and to violate the law, so long as he is willing to suffer the consequences? The legal system

---

1. O.W. Holmes, Jr., *The Path of the Law*, in *Collected Legal Papers* 167, 175 (1920); and O.W. Holmes, Jr., *The Common Law*, 300–301 (1881).

could thus be viewed only as establishing a set of prices, some high and some low, which then act as the only constraints to induce lawful conduct.

The modern theory of "efficient breach" is a variation and systematic extension of Holmes's outlook on contractual remedy. It assumes that role because of the dominance that it gives to the expectation measure of damages in cases of contract breach: the promisor is allowed to breach at will so long as he leaves the promisee as well off after breach as he would have been had the promise been performed, while any additional gain is retained by the contract breakers. . . .

I. Entitlement and Economic Efficiency

Proponents of the efficient breach theory have embraced Holmes's approach and endowed it with economic apparel and terminology. In their view, if the promisor's profits from the breach exceed the loss of the promisee, the breach is to be permitted or even encouraged on the ground that it leads to maximization of resources.[2] Under this theory of efficient breach, the promisor is given the option not to perform his contract as long as he is prepared to pay plaintiff his expectation damages, that is, a sum necessary to make the plaintiff indifferent between the performance of the contract and the damages so paid. The theory of efficient breach is that the defendant will exercise this option only if the gains from breach are greater than the moneys so paid over. The pristine form of the theory implies that the plaintiff is left as well off from the breach as before, while the defendant is made better off. If so, the program of expectations damages, if faithfully implemented, satisfies not only the Kaldor–Hicks standard of hypothetical compensation but the more restrictive Pareto standards of efficiency as well: not only is there a net social gain for the contracting parties, but no one is left worse off after breach than before. Consequently, under either view of efficiency the optimal level of damages is that which compensates the plaintiff only for this loss, and no more.

Originally, this theory was religiously preached and was hardly capable of suffering any qualification. Its modern version, as formulated in the latest (1986) edition of Posner's *Economic Analysis of Law,* evidences a certain retreat from this extreme position. A distinction is drawn between "opportunistic breach" and other breaches of contract. Breaches in the latter category still enjoy respectability and, if considered efficient, are lauded. Opportunistic breaches have lost the patronage of the efficient breach theory and are harshly denounced. The distinction is unsatisfactory[6] and in fact undermines much of the efficient breach theory. Indeed,

---

2. Richard A. Posner, *Economic Analysis of Law* 107 (3d ed. 1986).

6. Opportunism means taking advantage of the promisee's vulnerability. Posner regards the vulnerability mainly as created by the sequential character of performance under the contract. Hence, if *A* pays in advance for goods or services to be supplied by *B* in the future, A is vulnerable until *B* performs. . . . However, the sequence in which the performances are to be made is only one relevant factor. Thus, suppose A paid part of the price in advance while *B* has not yet performed. Although *A* has already partly performed, *B* may be more vulnerable if his need to receive the remaining part of *A's* payment is greater than A's need for *B's* promised performance.

Posner states that the opportunistic contract breaker should be made to "hand over all his profits from the breach to the promisee." Recovery of these gains is diametrically opposed to the efficient breach theory, the essence of which is that the promisor should be allowed or even encouraged to commit a breach whenever his gains exceed the promisee's loss. The theory clearly assumes that the promisor should be allowed to keep his gain, for otherwise he would lose interest in committing the breach that is supposedly so desirable. It is not explained why opportunistic breaches should be discouraged even if they are efficient. Is it because they are morally reprehensible? Is morality more important than efficiency? Or is it because they undermine the institution of contract in general?

A. Contracts Relating to Existing Property

The essence of the theory is "efficiency." The "right" to break a contract is not predicated on the nature of the contractual right, its relative "weakness," or its status as merely *in personam*, as opposed to the hardier rights *in rem*. Rather it is on the ground that the breach is supposed to lead to a better use of resources. The theory, therefore, is, in principle, equally applicable to property rights, where it leads to the adoption of a theory of "efficient theft" or "efficient conversion." ...

The real issue in both the conversion and the breach situation is who should benefit from C's willingness to pay a high price for the goods owned by B (the conversion example) or promised to him (the breach example). In principle, there should be in both situations only one transaction; in my view it should be between C and B (the owner or the promisee). If A promised to sell a piece of property to B for $10,000 and C is willing to have it for $18,000, he should negotiate its purchase from B. A is simply not entitled to sell to C something he has promised to return or transfer to B, the promisee. Similarly, with a bailment, C must negotiate with B (the owner) and not with the bailee. Hence, the question of additional transaction costs does not arise. ...

Moreover, the efficient breach rule is inefficient on its own terms. Neither it nor the analogous efficient conversion rule has the desired effect of minimizing either the number of transactions or, more decisively, the total amount of transaction costs. In fact these rules may often lead to an increase in total transaction costs. In the above contract example, the breach is likely to require two transactions instead of one. If A performs his contract with B, there will be only one additional transaction, that between B and C. If, however, A is "allowed" to break his contract with B, there will be two transactions: one between A and C over the sale of the property promised to B, and the other a dispute between A and B regarding the measure of damages. The implied assumption in Posner's analysis is that the payment of damages by A to B entails no transaction costs. This, however, is totally unrealistic. The payment of damages is hardly ever a standard transaction of the type the parties are routinely

---

In fact, vulnerability is a matter of degree. The greater the need for other party's performance and the more difficult it is to obtain a substitute, the greater the vulnerability.

engaged in. It is likely to follow protracted negotiations, or even litigation, over difficult questions of fact and law. . . .

The relaxation of contract remedies also has deleterious effects on the willingness of parties to enter into mutually beneficial contracts in the first place. If the legal system imposes severe limitations on specific performance (irrespective of whether they are based on the right to break the contract theory or its modern "efficient breach" (offshoot), it undermines the parties' faith in getting what they bargained for, and the consequence is inefficiency and a waste of resources.[15] If a party in need of contracting with another cannot rely on the contract to guarantee performance, then he may turn to another more costly and less efficient means (for example, becoming a self-supplier or vertically integrating with his supplier) to gain greater assurance that he will get what he seeks. . . .

WASSENAAR v. PANOS

Supreme Court of Wisconsin, 1983.
111 Wis.2d 518, 331 N.W.2d 357, 40 A.L.R.4th 266.

ABRAHAMSON, JUSTICE. . . . The circuit court entered a judgment in favor of an employee, Donald Wassenaar, against his former employer, Theanne Panos, d/b/a The Towne Hotel, enforcing the stipulated damages clause in the employment contract and confirming a $24,640 jury award. The circuit court interpreted the stipulated damage clause in the contract as providing that in the event of wrongful discharge the employee was to be paid a sum equal to his salary for the unexpired term of the contract. The court of appeals reversed, holding the stipulated damages clause unenforceable as a penalty and remanding the cause to the circuit court for a new trial on the issue of damages only. . . .

The employer terminated Wassenaar's employment as of March 31, 1978, 21 months prior to the contract's expiration date. Wassenaar was unemployed from April 1, 1978, until June 14, 1978, when he obtained employment in a Milwaukee area hotel where he remained employed at least until the time of trial in May, 1981. . . .

After a trial . . . the jury found that the employer terminated the employment without just cause. The circuit court, over the employee's objection, submitted to the jury the question of what sum of money would compensate the employee for his losses resulting from the breach of the employment agreement. The jury answered $24,640, which is the sum the employee had calculated as his damages on the basis of the stipulated damages clause of the contract, that is, his salary for 21 months, the unexpired term of the contract.

On review, the court of appeals characterized the question of whether a stipulated damages clause should be held void as a penalty because it

---

15. *See also* Alan Schwartz, *The Case for Specific Performance*, 89 Yale L.J. 271 (1979), who points out that the availability of specific performance would not generate greater transaction costs than the damages remedy . . . and that it would actually produce certain efficiency gains. . . .

fixes unreasonably large damages as a question of law to be determined independently by the reviewing court. It then scrutinized the stipulated damages clause and decided that the clause was void as a penalty. The court of appeals reached that conclusion reasoning that the amount of damages for breach of an employment contract could easily be measured and proved at trial and that the contractual formula fixing damages at full salary without considering how long the employee would need to find a new job or the probable earnings from substitute employment was unreasonable on its face. In its analysis, the court of appeals did not consider any facts other than the actual contract language and the black-letter law relating to the measure of damages for breach of employment contracts.

We agree with the court of appeals that the validity of a stipulated damages clause is a question of law for the trial judge rather than a mixed question of fact and law for the jury. The validity of a stipulated damages clause is a matter of public policy, and as in other contract cases the question of contractual validity as a matter of public policy is an issue the trial judge initially decides. But we disagree with the court of appeals that the label of "question of law" automatically relieves the trial court from its duty to consider evidence or gives the appellate court free rein in reviewing the trial court's decision.

Even though the trial court's conclusion regarding the validity of the stipulated damages clause is a legal conclusion—a policy judgment—that legal conclusion will frequently be derived from a resolution of disputed facts or inferences. The trial judge, not the jury, determines these facts and inferences. In deciding whether a stipulated damages clause is valid, then, the trial judge should inquire into all relevant circumstances, including such matters as the existence and extent of the anticipated and actual injury to the nonbreaching party.

The trial court's decision that a clause is or is not valid involves determinations of fact and law and will be reviewed as such. ... [O]rdinarily the appellate court need not defer to the trial court's determination of a question of law. ... Nevertheless, because the trial court's legal conclusion, that is, whether the clause is reasonable, is so intertwined with the factual findings supporting that conclusion, the appellate court should give weight to the trial court's decision, although the trial court's decision is not controlling. ...

Because the employer sought to set aside the bargained-for contractual provision stipulating damages, it had the burden of proving facts which would justify the trial court's concluding that the clause should not be enforced. ...

We turn now to the test that the trial court (and the appellate court) should apply in deciding whether a stipulated damages clause is valid. The overall single test of validity is whether the clause is reasonable under the totality of circumstances. *See* sec. 356(1), *Restatement (Second) of Contracts* (1979), and [UCC § 2–718(1)].

The reasonableness test is a compromise the courts have struck between two competing viewpoints toward stipulated damages clauses, one favoring enforcement of stipulated damages clauses and the other disfavoring such clauses.

Enforcement of stipulated damages clauses is urged because the clauses serve several purposes. The clauses allow the parties to control their exposure to risk by setting the payment for breach in advance. They avoid the uncertainty, delay, and expense of using the judicial process to determine actual damages. They allow the parties to fashion a remedy consistent with economic efficiency in a competitive market, and they enable the parties to correct what the parties perceive to be inadequate judicial remedies by agreeing upon a formula which may include damage elements too uncertain or remote to be recovered under rules of damages applied by the courts. In addition to these policies specifically relating to stipulated damages clauses, considerations of judicial economy and freedom of contract favor enforcement of stipulated damages clauses.

A competing set of policies disfavors stipulated damages clauses, and thus courts have not been willing to enforce stipulated damages clauses blindly without carefully scrutinizing them. Public law, not private law, ordinarily defines the remedies of the parties. Stipulated damages are an exception to this rule. Stipulated damages allow private parties to perform the judicial function of providing the remedy in breach of contract cases, namely, compensation of the nonbreaching party, and courts must ensure that the private remedy does not stray too far from the legal principle of allowing compensatory damages. Stipulated damages substantially in excess of injury may justify an inference of unfairness in bargaining or an objectionable *in terrorem* agreement to deter a party from breaching the contract, to secure performance, and to punish the breaching party if the deterrent is ineffective.

The reasonableness test strikes a balance between the two competing sets of policies by ensuring that the court respects the parties' bargain but prevents abuse. *See* Macneil, *Power of Contract and Agreed Remedies*, 47 Cornell L.Q. 495 (1962). Over time, the cases and commentators have established several factors to help determine whether a particular clause is reasonable:(1) Did the parties intend to provide for damages or for a penalty? (2) Is the injury caused by the breach one that is difficult or incapable of accurate estimation at the time of contract? and (3) Are the stipulated damages a reasonable forecast of the harm caused by the breach?

Recent discussions of the test of reasonableness have generally discarded the first factor, subjective intent of the parties, because subjective intent has little bearing on whether the clause is objectively reasonable. The label the parties apply to the clause, which might indicate their intent, has some evidentiary value, but it is not conclusive. Seeman v. Biemann, 108 Wis. 365, 374, 84 N.W. 490 (1900). The second factor, sometimes referred to as the "difficulty of ascertainment" test, is generally viewed as helpful in assessing the reasonableness of the clause. The greater the difficulty of estimating or proving damages, the more likely the stipulated damages will appear reasonable. ... The third factor concerns whether the stipulated damages provision is a reasonable forecast of compensatory damages. Courts test the reasonableness of the parties' forecast, as they test the "difficulty of ascertainment" by looking at the stipulated damages clause from the perspective of both the time of contracting and the time of the breach (or trial).

The second and third factors are intertwined, and both use a combined prospective-retrospective approach. Although courts have frequently said that the reasonableness of the stipulated damages clause must be judged as of the time of contract formation (the prospective approach) and that the amount or existence of actual loss at the time of breach or trial is irrelevant, except as evidence helpful in determining what was reasonable at the time of contracting (the retrospective approach), the cases demonstrate that the facts available at trial significantly affect the courts' determination of the reasonableness of the stipulated damages clause. ...

With the reasonableness test and the policies underlying the test in mind, we now consider the circuit court's conclusion that the stipulated damages clause is reasonable. The employer argues that the stipulated damages clause is void as a penalty because the harm to the employee was capable of estimation at the formation of the contract and was relatively easy to prove at trial. The employer further contends that calculating damages based on the entire wage for the unexpired term of the employment contract does not reasonably forecast the loss caused by the breach because such a calculation gives the employee a windfall recovery. ...

When the parties to an employment contract estimate the harm which might result from the employer's breach, they do not know when a breach might occur, whether the employee will find a comparable job, and if he or she does, where the job will be or what hardship the employee will suffer. Nevertheless, the standard measure of damages provides, as the court of appeals noted in its opinion, a simple formula which is generally fairly easy to apply. According to black-letter law, when an employee is wrongfully discharged, damages are the salary the employee would have received during the unexpired term of the contract plus the expenses of securing other employment reduced by the income which he or she has earned, will earn, or could with reasonable diligence earn, during the unexpired term. These damages are usually easily ascertainable at the time of trial.

The standard calculation of damages after breach, however, may not reflect the actual harm suffered because of the breach. In addition to the damages reflected in the black-letter formulation, an employee may suffer consequential damages, including permanent injury to professional reputation, loss of career development opportunities, and emotional stress. When calculating damages for wrongful discharge courts strictly apply the rules of foreseeability, mitigation, and certainty and rarely award consequential damages. Damages for injury to the employee's reputation, for example, are generally considered too remote and not in the parties' contemplation. Thus, actual harm suffered and damages that would be awarded in a legal action for breach of contract may not be the same. Nevertheless, in providing for stipulated damages, the parties to the contract could anticipate the types of damages not usually awarded by law. The usual arguments against allowing recovery for consequential damages—that they are not foreseeable and that no dollar value can be set by a court—fail when the parties foresee the possibility of such harm and agree on an estimated amount. . . .

In examining the instant stipulated damages clause and the record, we conclude that the parties' estimate at the time of contract formation of anticipated damages was reasonable when consequential damages are taken into account. Consequential damages may be difficult to ascertain at the time of contracting or breach and are difficult to prove at trial. The contract formula of full salary for the period after breach seems to be a simple and fair way of calculating all damages. . . .

In this case we find it difficult to uphold the employer's position that the employee suffered no harm, because there is evidence in the record that the employee did suffer harm in being unemployed for approximately two and a half months after his discharge. At the end of this time, the employee obtained employment at another hotel, but there is no evidence that the jobs he held were comparable in terms of salary, opportunity for advancement, etc., to the job he held as manager of the Towne Hotel. There is no evidence that the employee's total compensation from the new job was equal to or exceeded the salary under the breached contract, and the record does not reveal whether the employee suffered consequential damages. All we know is that the employee appears to have suffered some harm. This case is therefore distinguishable from Fields Foundation, Ltd. v. Christensen, 103 Wis.2d 465, 476, 309 N.W.2d 125 (Ct.App.1981), upon which the employer relies, where the court held the stipulated damages clause unenforceable when the record established that the non-breaching party suffered no harm.

Since the record in this case can be read to show that the employee suffered some harm, the question remains whether the stipulated damages are so much greater than the loss suffered by the employee that the stipulated damages constitute a penalty.

The employer has repeatedly asserted that this clause is a penalty because it does not take into account the amount the employee earned during the unexpired term of the contract. The employer argues that allowing the employee to recover the stipulated damages in this case gives the employee a windfall because he receives both the agreed upon salary and the ability to sell his services to another employer during the unexpired term of the contract: the employee will receive 21 months salary from the defendant employer and 18 months salary from the new employer. Ordinarily the circuit court would, in this type of stipulated damages case, use evidence of the employee's actual or potential earnings in assessing the overall reasonableness of the clause, since subsequent earnings would be relevant to the issue of the employee's actual loss resulting from the breach. In this case, as we discuss further below, there is no evidence in the record showing the employee's subsequent earnings, so there is no evidence supporting the employer's position that the employee would get a windfall from enforcement of the stipulated damages clause.

. . . In short, the employer did not meet his burden of proof on the unreasonableness of the stipulated damages clause. Since we conclude that the record shows that the employee suffered some actual injury and that the record does not show that actual damages are disproportionate to the stipulated damages, we affirm the circuit court's ruling that the stipulated damages provision is reasonable and enforceable.

This court asked the parties to brief what it characterized as a sub-issue, namely, the employee's duty to mitigate damages. In breach of contract cases not involving liquidated damages clauses, this court has consistently held that a discharged employee has a duty to use ordinary care and reasonable efforts to seek other comparable employment and that in calculating damages the employer should be credited to the extent that the employee obtains work and earns wages or might have done so. . . .

We hold that once a stipulated damages clause is found reasonable, the liquidated damages should not be reduced at trial by an amount the employee did earn or could have earned. [citation] Recalculating liquidated damages to credit the breaching party with the amount the employee earned or could have earned is antithetical to the policies favoring liquidated damages clauses. . . .

[T]he judgment of the circuit court should be affirmed.

KVASSAY v. MURRAY

Court of Appeals of Kansas, 1991.
15 Kan.App.2d 426, 808 P.2d 896.

RICHARD B. WALKER, DISTRICT JUDGE, Assigned: Plaintiff Michael Kvassay, d/b/a Kvassay Exotic Food, appeals the trial court's finding that a liquidated damages clause was unenforceable and from the court's finding that damages for lost profits were not recoverable. Kvassay contends these damages occurred when Great American Foods, Inc., (Great American) breached a contract for the purchase of baklava. . . . [The court affirmed a holding that Great American was the alter ego of the Murrays, the defendants in this case. Ed.]

On February 22, 1984, Kvassay, who had been an independent insurance adjuster, contracted to sell 24,000 cases of baklava to Great American at $19.00 per case. Under the contract, the sales were to occur over a one-year period and Great American was to be Kvassay's only customer. The contract included a clause which provided: "If Buyer refuses to accept or repudiates delivery of the goods sold to him, under this Agreement, Seller shall be entitled to damages, at the rate of $5.00 per case, for each case remaining to be delivered under this Contract."

Problems arose early in this contractual relationship with checks issued by Great American being dishonored for insufficient funds. Frequently one of the Murrays issued a personal check for the amount due. After producing approximately 3,000 cases, Kvassay stopped producing the baklava because the Murrays refused to purchase any more of the product. . . .

In April 1985, Kvassay filed suit for damages arising from the collapse of his baklava baking business. . . . The court conducted bench hearings on the validity of the liquidated damages clause . . . [and] ruled that liquidated damages could not be recovered. . . .

Kvassay first attacks the trial court's ruling that the amount of liquidated damages sought by him was unreasonable and therefore the liquidated damages clause was unenforceable. Kvassay claimed $105,000 in losses under the liquidated damages clause of the contract, representing $5 per case for the approximately 21,000 cases of baklava which he was not able to deliver. The trial court determined that Kvassay's use of expected profits to formulate liquidated damages was improper because the business enterprise lacked duration, permanency, and recognition. The court then compared Kvassay's previous yearly income (about $20,000) with the claim for liquidated damages ($105,000) and found "the disparity becomes so great as to make the clause unenforceable."

Since the contract involved the sale of goods between merchants, the Uniform Commercial Code governs. *See* K.S.A. 84–2–102. "The Code does not change the pre-Code rule that the question of the propriety of liquidated damages is a question of law for the court." 4 Anderson, *Uniform Commercial Code* § 2–718:6, p. 572 (3d ed. 1983). Thus, this court's scope of review of the trial court's ruling is unlimited. Hutchinson Nat'l Bank & Tr. Co. v. Brown, 12 Kan.App.2d 673, 674, 753 P.2d 1299, *rev. denied* 243 Kan. 778 (1988).

Liquidated damages clauses in sales contracts are governed by K.S.A. 84–2–718, which reads in part:

(1) Damages for breach by either party may be liquidated in the agreement but only at an amount which is reasonable in the light of the anticipated or actual harm caused by the breach, the difficulties of proof of loss, and the inconvenience or nonfeasibility of otherwise obtaining an adequate remedy. A term fixing unreasonably large liquidated damages is void as a penalty.

To date, the appellate courts have not interpreted this section of the UCC in light of facts similar to those presented in this case. In ruling on this issue, the trial court relied on rules governing liquidated damages as expressed in U.S.D. No. 315 v. DeWerff, 6 Kan.App.2d 77, 626 P.2d 1206 (1981). *DeWerff*, however, involved a teacher's breach of an employment contract and was not governed by the UCC. Thus, the rules expressed in that case should be given no effect if they differ from the rules expressed in 84–2–718.

In *DeWerff*, this court held a "stipulation for damages upon a future breach of contract is valid as a liquidated damages clause if the set amount is determined to be reasonable and the amount of damages is difficult to ascertain." 6 Kan.App.2d at 78, 626 P.2d 1206. This is clearly a two-step test: Damages must be reasonable and they must be difficult to ascertain. Under the UCC, however, reasonableness is the only test. K.S.A. 84–2–718. K.S.A. 84–2–718 provides three criteria by which to measure reasonableness of liquidated damages clauses: (1) anticipated or actual harm caused by breach; (2) difficulty of proving loss; and (3) difficulty of obtaining an adequate remedy.

In its ruling, the trial court found the liquidated damages clause was unreasonable in light of Kvassay's income before he entered into the manufacturing contract with Great American. There is no basis in 84–2–718 for contrasting income under a previous unrelated employment arrangement with liquidated damages sought under a manufacturing contract. Indeed, the traditional goal of the law in cases where a buyer breaches a manufacturing contract is to place the seller " 'in the same position he would have occupied if the vendee had performed his contract' " Outcault Adv. Co. v. Citizens Nat'l Bank, 118 Kan. 328, 330–31, 234 P. 988 (1925). Thus, liquidated damages under the contract in this case must be measured against the anticipated or actual loss under the baklava contract as required by 84–2–718. The trial court erred in using Kvassay's previous income as a yardstick. Was the trial court correct when it invalidated the liquidated damages clause, notwithstanding the use of an incorrect test? If so, we must uphold the decision even though the trial court relied on a wrong ground or assigned an erroneous reason for its decision. Sutter Bros. Constr. Co. v. City of Leavenworth, 238 Kan. 85, 93, 708 P.2d 190 (1985). To answer this question, we must look closer at the first criteria for reasonableness under 84–2–718, anticipated or actual harm done by the breach.

Kvassay produced evidence of anticipated damages at the bench trial showing that, before the contract was signed between Kvassay and Great American, Kvassay's accountant had calculated the baklava production costs. The resulting figure showed that, if each case sold for $19, Kvassay would earn a net profit of $3.55 per case after paying himself for time and labor. If he did not pay himself, the projected profit was $4.29 per case. Nevertheless, the parties set the liquidated damages figure at $5 per case. In comparing the anticipated damages of $3.55 per case in lost net profit with the liquidated damages of $5 per case, it is evident that Kvassay would collect $1.45 per case or about 41 percent over projected profits if Great American breached the contract. If the $4.29 profit figure is used, a $5 liquidated damages award would allow Kvassay to collect 71 cents per case or about 16½ percent over projected profits if Great American breached the contract.

An examination of these pre-contract comparisons alone might well lead to the conclusion that the $5 liquidated damages clause is unreasonable because enforcing it would result in a windfall for Kvassay and serve as a penalty for Great American. A term fixing unreasonably large liquidated damages is void as a penalty under 84–2–718.

A better measure of the validity of the liquidated damages clause in this case would be obtained if the actual lost profits caused by the breach were compared to the $5 per case amount set by the clause. However, no attempt was made by Kvassay during the bench trial to prove actual profits or actual costs of production. Thus, the trial court could not compare the $5 liquidated damages clause in the contract with the actual profits lost by the breach. It was not until the jury trial that Kvassay attempted to prove his actual profits lost as part of his damages. Given the trial court's ruling that lost profits were not recoverable and could not be presented to the jury, it is questionable whether the court would have permitted evidence concerning lost profits at the bench trial.

The trial court utilized an impermissible factor to issue its ruling on the liquidated damages clause and the correct statutory factors were not directly addressed. We reverse the trial court on this issue and remand for further consideration of the reasonableness of the liquidated damages clause in light of the three criteria set out in 84–2–718. . . .

WEDNER v. FIDELITY SECURITY SYSTEMS, INC.

Superior Court of Pennsylvania, 1973.
228 Pa.Super. 67, 307 A.2d 429.

WATKINS, JUDGE, in support of affirmance. This is an appeal from the judgment of the Court of Common Pleas of Allegheny County entered after a non-jury trial on a burglar alarm system contract, in the amount of $312.00 in favor of Charles Wedner, doing business as Wedner Furs, the appellant, and against Fidelity Security Systems, Inc., the appellee.

This action involved a contract for a burglar alarm system. There was a burglary involving the loss of $46,180.00 in furs. It was first tried by Judge Silvestri without a jury and a nonsuit resulted. The nonsuit was removed and a new trial granted. It was then tried by Judge McLean without a jury and although he found the contract had been negligently breached, the appellant was only entitled to liquidated damages in the amount of $312.00 by the terms of the contract. Exceptions were filed and the Court *En Banc* by a majority vote dismissed the exceptions. This appeal followed.

The appellant suffered a loss of $46,180.00 due to the appellee's wrongful failure to perform under a burglary protection service contract, but because of a contract provision he was allowed recovery of only $312.00. The contract provided that the appellee, FEPS, was not to be liable for any loss or damages to the goods of the appellant and then continued:

> If there shall, notwithstanding the above provisions, at any time arise any liability on the part of FEPS by virtue of this agreement, whether due to the negligence of FEPS or otherwise, such liability is and shall be limited to a sum equal in amount to the yearly service charge hereunder, which sum shall be paid and received by the Subscriber as liquidated damages.

The appellant contends that this is an unreasonable forecast of the probable damages resulting from a breach of the contract.

The court below treated the matter as one of liquidated damages and said:

> In his decision the trial judge pointed out, and the parties agree, that there is a well settled general principle that courts will not give effect to a provision in a contract which is a penalty, but will give effect to a provision in a contract which is deemed a liquidated damages provision. The trial judge further noted that deciding which is which can be difficult. In the absence of any Pennsylvania cases making the determination in the context of a contract for burglary alarm protection, the trial judge determined that the instant provision was one for liquidated damages, rather than a penalty....

However, although he ably supported his judgment on the theory of liquidated damages, he did not have to decide the matter on the premise alone.

Much reliance is placed upon the *Restatement of Contracts* § 339, but the appellant disregards Comment [g], which provides:

> An agreement limiting the amount of damages recoverable for breach is not an agreement to pay either liquidated damages or a penalty. Except in the case of certain public service contracts, the contracting parties can by agreement limit their liability in damages to a specified amount, either at the time of making their principal contract, or subsequently thereto. Such a contract does not purport to make an estimate of the harm caused by a breach; nor is its purpose to operate *in terrorem* to induce performance.

It can hardly be contended that the words "liability is and shall be limited" to the yearly service charge of $312 are anything but a limitation of liability and not really a liquidated damage clause. Surely, if the loss to the customer was $150, the expressed mutual assent was that recovery should be $150 and not $312.

The fact that the words "liquidated damages" were used in the contract has little bearing on the nature of the provision. It is well settled that in determining whether a particular clause calls for liquidated damages or for a penalty, the name given to the clause by the parties "is but of slight weight, and the controlling elements are the intention of the parties and the special circumstances of the case." Laughlin v. Baltalden, Inc., 191 Pa.Super. 611, 617, 159 A.2d 26, 29 (1960). The same principle applies here. Nor can it be argued that the use of these words automatically creates an ambiguity to be resolved against the appellee as the drafter of the instrument. The meaning of the words is clear—the fixed limit of liability was $312. We are, therefore, not dealing with a liquidated damage problem.

The real question is whether any reason exists why the limitation on liability should not be given effect. There is no doubt as to its legality as between ordinary business men. "The *validity* of a contractual provision which exculpates a person from liability for his own acts of negligence is well settled if the contract is between persons relating entirely to their own private affairs." Dilks v. Flohr Chevrolet, 411 Pa. 425, 433, 192 A.2d 682, 687 (1963). . . .

In accord is the *Restatement of Contracts* §§ 574, 575. It is also the rule with respect to the sale of goods under the Uniform Commercial Code, 12A P.S. § 2–719(3), which provides:

> Consequential damages may be limited or excluded unless the limitation or exclusion is unconscionable. Limitation of consequential damages for injury to the person in the case of consumer goods is *prima facie* unconscionable but limitation of damages where the loss is commercial is not.

The common law exception as to public utilities, Turek v. Pennsylvania R.R. Co., 361 Pa. 512, 64 A.2d 779 (1949), has been expanded to some extent by Thomas v. First Nat. Bank of Scranton, 376 Pa. 181, 185–186, 101 A.2d 910, 912 (1954), where the court concluded:

> Banks, like common carriers, utility companies, etc., perform an important public service. The United States Government and the Commonwealth respectively stipulate how banks under their respective jurisdictions shall be incorporated and organized. All banks are examined and supervised by government or state officers with extreme particularity. The United States insures deposits in banks up to a stipulated amount. If a person desires to deposit money in a bank, necessarily, he is relegated to a governmental or state regulated banking institution. The situation of a depositor is quite analogous to that of a passenger on a public carrier who is required to accept such means of transportation and to purchase a ticket in the nature of a contract. This Court has consistently decided that it is against public policy to permit a common carrier to limit its liability for its own negligence: (Citations).

In this case, however, we have a private arrangement between two firms without the attendant state regulation that exists with banks and public utilities. The appellant had a choice as to how to protect his property, and whether or not he should obtain insurance. Although protection against burglary is becoming increasingly important, we believe that it has not yet reached the level of necessity comparable to that of banking and other public services.

Nor do we consider this a case of an unconscionable provision, assuming that unconscionability is applicable by adoption of the prevailing rule with respect to the sale of goods. Even under the foregoing reference to the Uniform Commercial Code the limitation of liability under the facts of the case is *prima facie* conscionable. Furthermore, there is this significant fact pointed out in the opinion of the trial judge: "In our case both plaintiff and defendant are experienced, established business persons. Additionally, plaintiff had for some 20 years prior to the instant contract had a similar type protection service with similar type clause, with a competitor of defendant."

Thus in this respect the case is comparable to K & C, Inc. v. Westinghouse Elec. Corp., 437 Pa. 303, 308, 263 A.2d 390, 393 (1970), where the court concluded that "it is clear that the exclusion was not unconscionable here, where the buyer was hardly the sheep keeping company with wolves that it would have us believe."

I would affirm the judgment of the court below.

CERCONE, JUDGE, in support of reversal. The facts in this case as found by the trial judge who sat as the fact-finder are as follows:

Plaintiff, who was in the retail fur business, entered into a contract with defendant Security Systems whereby defendant was to provide plaintiff's store with electronic burglar alarm protection. While this contract was in full force and effect, and had been for several years, a burglary occurred, setting off devices at defendant's headquarters. Plaintiff brought suit in trespass against defendant for losses ensuing from the said burglary, plaintiff alleging negligence, willfulness, and wantonness of the defendant in failing to carry out its duties towards plaintiff's establishment. After trial, the trial judge found, as stated in his opinion, "defendant negligently failed to carry out those duties and render those services which its contract required of it upon the receipt of such alarm, with the result that the burglars were able to get away with merchandise of the value of $38,862.00. The loss of merchandise put plaintiff out of business until he could replenish his stock of goods, to the further loss of $7,318." The trial judge entered an award for the plaintiff, but limited that award to the amount of $312 (plus interest from the date of loss). This award was based on the trial judge's conclusion that this was the sum of the "liquidated damages" provided for in the contract. The provision so relied upon by the trial judge reads as follows: "If there shall, notwithstanding the above provisions, at any time arise any liability on the part of FEPS by virtue of this agreement, whether due to the negligence of FEPS or otherwise, such liability is and shall be limited to a sum equal in amount to the yearly service charge hereunder, which sum shall be paid and received by the Subscriber as liquidated damages."

The plaintiff took exceptions to the findings and conclusions of the trial judge, which exceptions were dismissed by the court *en banc* with one judge dissenting. This appeal by plaintiff followed.

Neither the court below nor any of the parties to this action at any time prior to oral argument before this court regarded the provision in question as other than what the parties expressed it to be, to wit: a "liquidated damages" clause. The affirming opinion, however, views the language differently than did the lower court and the parties and refers to it as a "limitation of liability" clause. It apparently views a "limitation of liability" clause as more binding than a "liquidated damages" clause under the circumstances. I cannot agree. If the parties can escape their contractual provisions for liquidated damages because the amount stated is unreasonably disproportionate (either higher or lower) to the actual damages involved, there is no logical reason why the same test of reasonableness should not apply to a contractual limitation of liability. I would hold therefore, that a contractual *limitation*, as well as a contractual *liquidation* of damages, is not binding where unreasonable and bearing no relation to the loss that would result from defendant's failure to fulfill the terms of its contract. The limitation in this case "to a sum equal in amount to the yearly service charge hereunder" was clearly unreasonable and arbitrary, bearing no relationship whatever to the damages flowing from defendant's breach. In my opinion this provision, whether viewed as one of liquidated damages or as a limitation of damages, should not be enforced.

Section 2–718 of the Uniform Commercial Code of Sales, which by its expressed title "Liquidation *or Limitation of Damages*" necessarily refers to limitation as well as liquidation of damages, provides: "(1) Damages for breach by either party may be liquidated in the agreement but only at an amount which is reasonable in the light of the anticipated or actual harm caused by the breach, the difficulties of proof of loss, and the inconvenience or nonfeasibility of otherwise obtaining an adequate remedy. A term fixing unreasonably large liquidated damages is void as a penalty." The Uniform Commercial Code comment to that subsection 1 is: "A term fixing unreasonably large liquidated damages is expressly made void as a penalty. *An unreasonably small amount would be subject to similar criticism and might be stricken under the section on unconscionable contracts or clauses.*" (emphasis added)

Section 2–719 of the Code is entitled "Contractual Modification or *Limitation of Remedy*" and subsection 1 of that section states that "subject to the provisions . . . of the preceding section on liquidation *and limitation of damages*, (a) the agreement . . . may limit or alter the measure of damages recoverable under this Article. . . ." The official comment to that section is:

1. Under this section parties are left free to shape their remedies to their particular requirements and *reasonable* agreements *limiting* or modifying remedies are to be given effect.

However, it is of the very essence of a sales contract that at least minimum adequate remedies be available. If the parties intend to conclude a contract for sale within this Article they must accept the legal consequence that there be at least a fair quantum of remedy for breach of the obligations or duties outlined in the contract. *Thus any clause purporting to modify or limit the remedial provisions of this Article in an unconscionable manner is subject to deletion* and in that event the remedies made available by this Article are applicable as if the stricken clause had never existed. Similarly, under subsection (2), where an apparently fair and reasonable clause because of circumstances fails in its purpose or operates to deprive either party of the substantial value of the bargain, it must give way to the general remedy provisions of this Article. (emphasis added)

The clause here in question (whether viewed as a liquidated damages clause or a limitation of damages clause) unreasonably limits plaintiff's recovery to a return of the service charge and deprives plaintiff of the bargain of his contract. As construed in the affirming opinion, the clause in effect works a rescission of the contract, completely freeing defendant from proper performance of its terms and requiring only a return of the service charge when defendant has failed to properly perform thereunder. The contract thus becomes, in effect, an illusory one with defendant not being bound to perform and plaintiff not being entitled to performance by defendant. By limiting plaintiff's remedy upon defendant's breach to a return of the service charge, the defendant is permitted to effectuate a cancellation of its duties to perform under the contract, leaving plaintiff without the bargained-for performance and without any reasonable compensation for defendant's failure to perform as contracted.

It is my opinion, therefore, that the clause in question is unreasonable and unconscionable and should not be enforced.

I therefore respectfully, but vigorously, dissent from the affirming opinion in this case.

PROBLEMS

16. P sold to D the timber on his land to be severed by D. Payment was based on the amount of timber cut. It was further agreed that the land would be clear-cut and in the event D left any merchantable trees standing D would pay P $1 per tree. D left 1339 such trees standing. D resists payment of P's claim for $1339 by asserting that since the breach the market value of the remaining trees has markedly increased. What result?

17. A contract for the purchase and sale of lumber contained this provision: "If the Buyer breaches this contract and the enforcement thereof, or any provision thereof, or the collection of any monies due thereunder is turned over to an attorney, the Buyer herein agrees to pay, in addition to all of Seller's expenses, a reasonable counsel fee; and in the event the matter turned over is the collection of monies, such reasonable counsel fee is hereby agreed to be Thirty (30%) per cent. The guarantor shall also be liable for such counsel fee and expenses." Is the provision valid?

18. Schlitz Brewing Company entered into merger negotiations with Heilman Brewing Company looking towards the takeover of Schlitz by Heil-

man. In order to retain key executives in its employ during the merger talks, it entered into "golden parachute" contracts with them, promising that, in the event of their termination or their resignation because of a substantial reduction in their duties, their salaries would be paid in full until the end of the contract terms. K, a member of Schlitz's legal staff, entered into such a contract. The merger talks were unsuccessful but subsequent negotiations resulted in Schlitz's takeover by Stroh's. K's duties were reduced. She resigned and immediately obtained other employment at her then current salary. She claims $44,000, the balance that would be payable during the remaining twelve months of the contract with Schlitz. In the light of her other employment, is she entitled to recover this sum?

19. In the motion picture, "Roustabout," the character played by Elvis Presley enters into an eleven-week contract at a salary of $350 a week, but is informed at the time of contracting that his written and signed contract provides that if he quits before the end of the eleven-week period, he must pay back one-half of all the payments he has received. When he quits after three weeks he is threatened with a lawsuit for one-half of the $1050 he has been paid. In the film, he hands over $50, saying that this is a payment on account. Assuming the employer sues for the balance, what would be the result?

20. B contracted with S whereby S agreed to sell steel to B for use in a project to build a dredge for the United States. S was aware that B's contract with the United States contained provisions requiring the payment of liquidated damages in the event of delay. At the time of contracting steel was readily available on the market. S breached by delivering late. At the time of the breach, because of supervening wartime shortages, steel was not generally available on the market. B seeks to hold S liable for damages measured by the amount it was required to pay the United States in damages. What result?

SECTION 2. RESTITUTION

(a) TO AN AGGRIEVED PARTY

(Calamari & Perillo on Contracts §§ 15.1—15.7)

UNITED STATES v. ALGERNON BLAIR, INC.

United States Court of Appeals, Fourth Circuit, 1973.
479 F.2d 638.

CRAVEN, CIRCUIT JUDGE: May a subcontractor, who justifiably ceases work under a contract because of the prime contractor's breach, recover in *quantum meruit* the value of labor and equipment already furnished pursuant to the contract irrespective of whether he would have been entitled to recover in a suit on the contract? We think so, and, for reasons to be stated, the decision of the district court will be reversed.

The subcontractor, Coastal Steel Erectors, Inc., brought this action under the provisions of the Miller Act, 40 U.S.C.A. § 270a *et seq.*, in the name of the United States against Algernon Blair, Inc., and its surety, United States Fidelity and Guaranty Company. Blair had entered a contract with the United States for the construction of a naval hospital in Charleston County, South Carolina. Blair had then contracted with Coastal to perform certain steel erection and supply certain equipment in conjunction with Blair's contract with the United States. Coastal commenced performance of its obligations, supplying its own cranes for handling and placing steel. Blair refused to pay for crane rental, maintaining that it was not obligated to do so under the subcontract. Because of Blair's failure to make payments for crane rental, and after completion of approximately 28 percent of the subcontract, Coastal terminated its performance. Blair then proceeded to complete the job with a new subcontractor. Coastal brought this action to recover for labor and equipment furnished.

The district court found that the subcontract required Blair to pay for crane use and that Blair's refusal to do so was such a material breach as to justify Coastal's terminating performance. This finding is not questioned on appeal. The court then found that under the contract the amount due Coastal, less what had already been paid, totaled approximately $37,000. Additionally, the court found Coastal would have lost more than $37,000 if it had completed performance. Holding that any amount due Coastal must be reduced by any loss it would have incurred by complete performance of the contract, the court denied recovery to Coastal. While the district court correctly stated the " 'normal' rule of contract damages,"[1] we think Coastal is entitled to recover in *quantum meruit*.

In United States for Use of Susi Contracting Co. v. Zara Contracting Co., 146 F.2d 606 (2d Cir. 1944), a Miller Act action, the court was faced with a situation similar to that involved here—the prime contractor had unjustifiably breached a subcontract after partial performance by the subcontractor. The court stated:

> For it is an accepted principle of contract law, often applied in the case of construction contracts, that the promisee upon breach has the option to forego any suit on the contract and claim only the reasonable value of his performance.

146 F.2d at 610. The Tenth Circuit has also stated that the right to seek recovery under *quantum meruit* in a Miller Act case is clear. *Quantum meruit* recovery is not limited to an action against the prime contractor but may also be brought against the Miller Act surety, as in this case. Further, that the complaint is not clear in regard to the theory of a plaintiff's recovery does not preclude recovery under *quantum meruit*. Narragansett Improvement Co. v. United States, 290 F.2d 577 (1st Cir. 1961). A plaintiff may join a claim for *quantum meruit* with a claim for damages from breach of contract.

---

1. Fuller & Perdue, *The Reliance Interest in Contract Damages*, 46 Yale L.J. 52 (1936); *Restatement of Contracts* § 333 (1932).

In the present case, Coastal has, at its own expense, provided Blair with labor and the use of equipment. Blair, who breached the subcontract, has retained these benefits without having fully paid for them. On these facts, Coastal is entitled to restitution in *quantum meruit.*

The "restitution interest," involving a combination of unjust impoverishment with unjust gain, presents the strongest case for relief. If, following Aristotle, we regard the purpose of justice as the maintenance of an equilibrium of goods among members of society, the restitution interest presents twice as strong a claim to judicial intervention as the reliance interest, since if A not only causes B to lose one unit but appropriates that unit to himself, the resulting discrepancy between A and B is not one unit but two. Fuller & Perdue, *The Reliance Interest in Contract Damages*, 46 Yale L.J. 52, 56 (1936).[6]

The impact of *quantum meruit* is to allow a promisee to recover the value of services he gave to the defendant irrespective of whether he would have lost money on the contract and been unable to recover in a suit on the contract. Scaduto v. Orlando, 381 F.2d 587, 595 (2d Cir. 1967). The measure of recovery for *quantum meruit* is the reasonable value of the performance, *Restatement of Contracts* § 347 (1932); and recovery is undiminished by any loss which would have been incurred by complete performance. 12 *Williston on Contracts* § 1485, at 312 (3d ed. 1970). While the contract price may be evidence of reasonable value of the services, it does not measure the value of the performance or limit recovery.[7] Rather, the standard for measuring the reasonable value of the services rendered is the amount for which such services could have been purchased from one in the plaintiff's position at the time and place the services were rendered.

Since the district court has not yet accurately determined the reasonable value of the labor and equipment use furnished by Coastal to Blair, the case must be remanded for those findings. When the amount has been determined, judgment will be entered in favor of Coastal, less payments already made under the contract. Accordingly, for the reasons stated above, the decision of the district court is reversed and remanded with instructions.

OLIVER v. CAMPBELL

Supreme Court of California, In Bank, 1954.
43 Cal.2d 298, 273 P.2d 15.

CARTER, J. Plaintiff appeals from a judgment for defendant, administratrix of the estate of Roy Campbell, deceased, in an action for attorney's fees.

---

6. This case also comes within the requirements of the *Restatements* for recovery in *quantum meruit. Restatement of Restitution* § 107 (1937); *Restatement of Contracts* §§ 347–357 (1932).

7. ... It should be noted, however, that in suits for restitution there are many cases permitting the plaintiff to recover the value of benefits conferred on the defendant, even though this value exceeds that of the return performance promised by the defendant. In these cases it is no doubt felt that the defendant's breach should work a forfeiture of his right to retain the benefits of an advantageous bargain. *Fuller & Perdue, supra* at 77.

Plaintiff's cause of action was stated in a common count alleging that Roy Campbell became indebted to him in the sum of $10,000, the reasonable value of services rendered as attorney for Campbell; that no part had been paid except $450. Campbell died after the services were rendered by plaintiff. Plaintiff filed a claim against his estate for the fees which defendant rejected. Defendant in her answer denied the allegations made and as a "further" defense alleged that plaintiff and Campbell entered into an "express written contract" employing plaintiff as attorney for a stated fee of $750, and all work alleged to have been performed by plaintiff was performed under that contract.

According to the findings of the trial court the claim against the estate was founded on the alleged reasonable value of legal services rendered by plaintiff for Campbell in an action for separate maintenance by defendant, Campbell's wife, against Campbell and in which the latter cross-complained for a divorce. Plaintiff was not counsel when the pleadings in that action were filed. He came into the case on December 16, 1949, before trial of the action. He and Campbell entered into a written contract on that date for plaintiff's representation of Campbell in the action, the contract stating that plaintiff agrees to represent Campbell in the separate maintenance and divorce action which has been set for trial in the superior court for a "total fee" of $750 plus court costs and other incidentals in the sum of $100 making a total of $850. The fees were to be paid after trial. Plaintiff represented Campbell at the trial consuming 29 days and lasting until May, 1950. (Defendant's complaint for separate maintenance was changed to one for divorce.) After the trial ended the court indicated its intention to give Mrs. Campbell a divorce. But while her proposed findings were under consideration by plaintiff and the court, defendant Campbell substituted himself instead of plaintiff and thereby the representation by plaintiff of Campbell was "terminated." The findings in the divorce action were filed in May, 1951. Plaintiff's services were furnished pursuant to the contract. The reasonable value of the services was $5,000. Campbell paid $450 to plaintiff and the $100 costs.

The court concluded that plaintiff should take nothing because neither his claim against the estate nor his action was on the contract but were in *quantum meruit* and no recovery could be had for the reasonable value of the services because the compensation for those services was covered by the express contract.

According to plaintiff's undisputed testimony Campbell told him after defendant had offered proposed findings in the divorce action that he was dissatisfied with plaintiff as his counsel and would discharge him and asked him if he would sign a substitution of attorneys under which Campbell would represent himself. Plaintiff replied that he recognized Campbell had a right to discharge him but that he was prepared to carry the case to conclusion; that he expected to be paid the reasonable value of his services which would be as much as defendant's counsel in the divorce action received, $9,000, to which Campbell replied he was not going to pay "a cent more." (At that time Campbell had paid $450.) Thereupon the substitution (dated January 25, 1951) was signed and Campbell took plaintiff's file in the divorce case with him.

It seems that the contract of employment contemplated that plaintiff was to continue his services and representation at least until and including final judgment in the divorce action. *See* Neblett v. Getty, 20 Cal. App.2d 65, 66 P.2d 473. It might thus appear that plaintiff was discharged before he had fully completed his services under the contract and the discharge prevented him from completing his performance. (That question is later discussed.)

One alleged rule of law applied by the trial court and that urged by defendant is that where there is a contract of employment for a definite term which fixes the compensation, there cannot be any recovery for the reasonable value of the services even though the employer discharges the employee—repudiates the contract before the end of the term; that the only remedy of the employee is an action on the contract for the fixed compensation or damages for the breach of the contract. The trial court accepted that theory and rendered judgment for defendant because plaintiff did not state a cause of action on the contract nor for damages for its breach; it was for the reasonable value of the services performed before plaintiff's discharge. Accordingly there is no express finding on whether the discharge was wrongful or whether there was a rescission of the contract by plaintiff because of Campbell's breach of it, or whether plaintiff had substantially performed at the time of this discharge.

The rule applied is not in accord with the general contract law, the law applicable to employment contracts or employment of an attorney by a client. The general rule is stated: "... that one who has been injured by a breach of contract has an election to pursue any of three remedies, to wit: 'He may treat the contract as rescinded and may recover upon a *quantum meruit* so far as he has performed; or he may keep the contract alive, for the benefit of both parties, being at all times ready and able to perform; or, third, he may treat the repudiation as putting an end to the contract for all purposes of performance, and sue for the profits he would have realized if he had not been prevented from performing.' " Alder v. Drudis, 30 Cal.2d 372, 381, 182 P.2d 195; *see Rest. Contracts*, § 347. It is the same in agency or contract for services cases. ...

It should further be noted that under the only evidence on the subject, above mentioned, plaintiff in effect promptly notified Campbell of the rescission of the contract when he advised him that he would execute the substitution of attorneys when he was discharged by Campbell but told Campbell he would hold him for the reasonable value of the services. On the issue of the necessity of restoration or offer to restore the part payment for the services which Campbell had made, the rule applies that such restoration is not necessary where plaintiff would be entitled to it in any event. ... It is clear that plaintiff was entitled to receive the $450 paid to him either under the contract or for the reasonable value of his services.

The question remains, however, of the application of the foregoing rules to the instant case. Plaintiff had performed practically all of the services he was employed to perform when he was discharged. The trial was at an end. The court had indicated its intention to give judgment against Campbell and all that remained was the signing of findings and judgment. The full sum called for in the contract was payable because the trial had ended. Under these circumstances it would appear that in effect, plaintiff had completed the performance of his services and the rule would apply that:

> The remedy of restitution in money is not available to one who has fully performed his part of a contract, if the only part of the agreed exchange for such performance that has not been rendered by the defendant is a sum of money constituting a liquidated debt; but full performance does not make restitution unavailable if any part of the consideration due from the defendant in return is something other than a liquidated debt.

Rest. Contracts, § 350; Locke v. Duchesnay, 84 Cal.App. 448, 258 P. 418; *Williston on Contracts* (rev.ed.), § 1459; *Corbin on Contracts*, § 1110; Civ. Code, § 3302.) In such cases he recovers the full contract price and no more. As we have seen, as far as pleading is concerned, however, the action may be stated as a common count other than a declaration on the special contract. Here plaintiff alleged an indebtedness on defendant's part for services performed by plaintiff of a reasonable value of $10,000 of which only $450 had been paid. While it may have been more appropriate for him to have alleged that the price of such services was the contract figure, any deficiency of the pleading is eliminated by defendant's answer setting forth that factor. Plaintiff's action can thus be said to be common count *indebitatus assumpsit*, and there being no dispute as to the amount called for in the contract, the services having been in effect fully performed, the court should have rendered judgment for the balance due on the contract which is conceded to be $300.

The judgment is therefore reversed and the trial court is directed to render judgment in favor of plaintiff for the sum of $300. ...

SCHAUER, J. I dissent. I agree with a great deal of the discussion in the majority opinion, and even to a larger extent with the authorities therein cited, relative to the rules of law which should govern this case but I think this court misapplies the very rules it cites.

Specifically, I think this court errs when it says "there being no dispute as to the amount called for in the contract, the services having been in effect fully performed, the court should have rendered judgment for the balance due on the contract which is conceded to be $300." The foregoing statement is neither supported factually by the record nor legally by the authorities cited. [The dissent stated its agreement with the opinion of Justice Vallee in the District Court of Appeal which it quotes, ed.:]

I am of the opinion that the judgment should be reversed with directions to the superior court to render judgment for plaintiff for $5,000. The court found that the reasonable value of the services performed by plaintiff is $5,000. Plaintiff was the only witness who testified concerning his discharge by Dr. Campbell. The opinion of this court fails to state all of the testimony of plaintiff with respect to his discharge. I set it forth *in toto* in the margin. I think no reasonable conclusion can be drawn from the evidence other than that the discharge amounts to a clear repudiation and abrogation of the contract in its entirety, in which case plaintiff is entitled to recover the reasonable value of the service performed. *The contract plaintiff made with Dr. Campbell did not limit his services to the trial of the case.* (Italics added.) Under the contract he agreed to represent the doctor until final judgment, and he told the doctor that he "*thought the case would be reversed on appeal.*" (Italics added.) ...

PROBLEMS

21. P, an architect, was retained by D to design a 56–unit motel and draw up the final working plans. P's fee was to be 4% of the construction costs. P drew up the preliminary plans. D decided not to build the motel because a survey revealed D's land was insufficient in size to accommodate a 56–unit motel with sufficient parking facilities. This constituted a breach by D as D knew the size of the plot while P did not. P sues for the reasonable value of the architectural services performed. D defends, claiming that P's services were of no value to D. What result?

22. P bought a horse known as Cur–Non for breeding purposes for $3,500. Cur–Non was warranted by D to be a stallion. In fact it was a gelding. After the purchase, P incurred expenses for medical care of Cur–Non relating to an old fracture. Expenses were also incurred in routine care and feeding of the horse. Upon discovering that Cur–Non was a gelding, P offered to return the horse, demanding return of the purchase price, veterinary fees and maintenance costs. D refused the demand. (a) In an action by P against D, what result? (b) Suppose P could show that if Cur–Non had in fact been a stallion its market value would be $5000. How would this fact affect your answer to (a)?

(b) TO A PARTY IN DEFAULT

(Calamari & Perillo on Contracts § 11.22)

MARTIN v. SCHOENBERGER
Supreme Court of Pennsylvania, 1845.
8 W. & c. S. 367.

. . . To permit a man to recover for part performance of an entire contract, or to permit him to recover on his agreement where he has failed to perform, would tend to demoralize the whole country. If the law were so, a man would just perform as much of his contract as would suit his convenience or cupidity; all faith and fair dealing would be at an end, and all confidence between man and man would be destroyed. . . .

LANCELLOTTI v. THOMAS
Superior Court of Pennsylvania, 1985.
341 Pa.Super. 1, 491 A.2d 117.

SPAETH, PRESIDENT JUDGE. This appeal raises the question of whether a defaulting purchaser of a business who has also entered into a related lease for the property can recover any part of his payments made prior to default. The common law rule precluded a breaching buyer from recovering these payments. Today, we reject this rule, which created a forfeiture of the breaching buyer's payments and unjustly enriched the nonbreaching seller, and adopt § 374 of the *Restatement (Second) Contracts* (1979), which permits limited restitution. This case is remanded for further proceedings so that the trial court may apply the *Restatement* rule.

–1–

On July 25, 1973, the parties entered into an agreement in which appellant agreed to purchase appellees' luncheonette business and to rent from appellees the premises on which the business was located. Appellant agreed to buy the name of the business, the goodwill, and equipment; the inventory and real estate were not included in the agreement for the sale of the business. Appellees agreed to sell the business for the following consideration: $25,000 payable on signing of the agreement; appellant's promise that only he would own and operate the business; and appellant's promise to build an addition to the existing building, which would measure 16 feet by 16 feet, cost at least $15,000, and be 75 percent complete by May 1, 1973.[1]

It was also agreed that appellees would lease appellant the property on which the business was operated for a period of five years, with appellant having the option of an additional five-year term. The rent was $8,000 per year for a term from September 1, 1973, to August 31, 1978. A separate lease providing for this rental was executed by the parties on the same date that the agreement was executed. This lease specified that the

---

1. The parties agree that this date was incorrect, and that the date the parties intended was May 1, 1974.

agreement to build the existing building was a condition of the lease. In exchange for appellant's promise to build the addition, there was to be no rental charge for the property until August 31, 1973. Further, if the addition was not constructed as agreed, the lease would terminate automatically. An addendum, executed by the parties on August 14, 1973, modified this agreement, providing that "if the addition to the building as described in the Agreement is not constructed in accordance with the Agreement, the Buyer shall owe the Sellers $6,665 as rental for the property...." for the period from July 25, 1973, to the end of that summer season. The addendum also provided that all the equipment would revert to appellees upon the appellant's default in regard to the addition.

Appellant paid appellees the $25,000 as agreed, and began to operate the business. However, at the end of the 1973 season, problems arose regarding the construction of the addition. Appellant claims that the building permit necessary to construct the addition was denied. Appellees claim that they obtained the building permit and presented it to appellant, who refused to begin construction. Additionally appellees claim that appellant agreed to reimburse them if they built the addition. At a cost of approximately $11,000, appellees did build a 20 feet by 40 feet addition. In the spring of 1974 appellees discovered that appellant was no longer interested in operating the business. There is no evidence in the record that appellant paid any rent from September 1, 1973, as the first rental payment was not due until May 15, 1974. Appellees resumed possession of the business and, upon opening the business for the 1974 summer season, found some of their equipment missing.

Appellant's complaint in assumpsit demanded that appellees return the $25,000 plus interest. . . .

–2–

At one time the common law rule prohibiting a defaulting party on a contract from recovering was the majority rule. J. Calamari and J. Perillo, *The Law of Contracts* § 11–26, at 427 (2d ed.1977). However, a line of cases, apparently beginning with Britton v. Turner, 6 N.H. 481 (1834), departed from the common law rule. The merit of the common law rule was its recognition that the party who breaches should not be allowed "to have advantage from his own wrong." Corbin, *The Right of a Defaulting Vendee to the Restitution of Instalments Paid*, 40 Yale L.J. 1013, 1014 (1931). As Professor Perillo states, allowing recovery "invites contract-breaking and rewards morally unworthy conduct." *Restitution in the Second "Restatement of Contracts,"* 81 Colum.L.Rev. 37, 50 (1981). Its weakness, however, was its failure to recognize that the nonbreaching party should not obtain a windfall from the breach. The party who breaches after almost completely performing should not be more severely penalized than the party who breaches by not acting at all or after only beginning to act. Under the common law rule the injured party retains more benefit the more completely the breaching party has performed prior to the default. Thus it has been said that "to allow the injured party to retain the benefit of the part performance . . ., without making restitution of any part of such value, is the enforcement of a penalty or forfeiture against the contract-breaker." *Corbin, supra,* at 1013.

Critics of the common law rule have been arguing for its demise for over fifty years. *See Corbin, supra. See also Calamari and Perillo, supra,* at § 11–26; 5A *Corbin on Contracts* §§ 1122–1135 (1964); 12 S. Williston, *A Treatise on the Law of Contracts* §§ 1473–78 (3d ed. 1970). In response to this criticism an alternative rule has been adopted in the *Restatement of Contracts* [generally permitting a restitutionary recovery for the defaulting plaintiff if] "the plaintiff's breach or non-performance is not wilful and deliberate. . . ."

In 1979, this rule was liberalized. *Restatement (Second) of Contracts* § 374 (1979) provides:

§ 374. Restitution in Favor of Party in Breach

(1) Subject to the rule stated in Subsection (2), if a party justifiably refuses to perform on the ground that his remaining duties of performance have been discharged by the other party's breach, the party in breach is entitled to restitution for any benefit that he has conferred by way of part performance or reliance in excess of the loss that he has caused by his own breach.

(2) To the extent that, under the manifested assent of the parties, a party's performance is to be retained in the case of breach, that party is not entitled to restitution if the value of the performance as liquidated damages is reasonable in the light of the anticipated or actual loss caused by the breach and the difficulties of proof of loss.

Thus the first *Restatement's* exclusion of the willful defaulting purchaser from recovery was deleted, apparently in part due to the influence of the Uniform Commercial Code's permitting recovery by a buyer who willfully defaults.[2] *Id.,* Reporter's Note at 218. Professor Perillo suggests that the injured party has adequate protection without the common law rule.[3]

---

2. In Pennsylvania, 13 Pa.C.S. § 2718, provides:

§ 2718. Liquidation or limitation of damages; deposits

(a) Liquidated damages in agreement.—Damages for breach by either party may be liquidated in the agreement but only at an amount which is reasonable in the light of the anticipated or actual harm caused by the breach, the difficulties of proof of loss, and the inconvenience or nonfeasibility of otherwise obtaining an adequate remedy. A term fixing unreasonably large liquidated damages is void as a penalty.

(b) Right of buyer to restitution.—Where the seller justifiably withholds delivery of goods because of the breach of the buyer, the buyer is entitled to restitution of any amount by which the sum of his payments exceeds:

(1) the amount to which the seller is entitled by virtue of terms liquidating the damages of the seller in accordance with subsection (a); or

(2) in the absence of such terms, 20% of the value of the total performance for which the buyer is obligated under the contract or $500 whichever is smaller.

. . .

3. He identifies four types of protection:

Choosing "the just path," he therefore rejects the common law rule, explaining this choice by saying that times have changed. "What appears to be just to one generation may be viewed differently by another." *Perillo, supra,* at 50. *See also* 12 S. *Williston, supra,* § 1473, at 222 ("The mores of the time and place will often determine which policy will be followed.").

Many jurisdictions have rejected the common law rule and permit recovery by the defaulting party. . . . This development has been called the modern trend. *See* Quillen v. Kelley, 216 Md. 396, 140 A.2d 517 (1958). *See also* 12 S. *Williston, supra,* § 1473, at 222 (cases permitting recovery are now the weight of the authority); 5A *Corbin on Contracts, supra,* § 1122, at 3 (common law rule is broad statement not supported by the actual decisions). *But see* 1 G. Palmer, *The Law of Restitution* 568 (1978) (no valid generalization may be made regarding when a defaulting vendee can recover). It may be that the growing number of jurisdictions permitting recovery have been influenced by the widespread adoption of the Uniform Commercial Code § 2–718. *See, e.g.,* Maxey v. Glindmeyer, 379 So.2d 297 (Miss.1980) (allowing recovery of excess of seller's actual damages in land sale contract by following the logic of the state statute equivalent to § 2–718 of the Uniform Commercial Code). Indeed, the common law rule is no longer intact even with respect to land sales contracts. *See* 1 G. Palmer, *supra,* at 596 n. 15 (citing cases).

In Pennsylvania, the common law rule has been applied to contracts for the sale of real property. Kaufman Hotel & Restaurant Co. v. Thomas, 411 Pa. 87, 190 A.2d 434 (1963); Luria v. Robbins, 223 Pa.Super. 456, 302 A.2d 361 (1973). In such cases, however, the seller has several remedies against a breaching buyer, including, in appropriate cases, an action for specific performance or for the purchase price. *See* Trachtenburg v. Sibarco Stations, Inc., 477 Pa. 517, 384 A.2d 1209 (1978). *See also* 5A *Corbin on Contracts, supra,* § 1145. As long as the seller remains ready, able, and willing to perform a contract for the sale of real property, the breaching buyer has no right to restitution of payments made prior to default. *See* 5A *Corbin on Contracts, supra,* at § 1130.

The common law rule has also been applied in Pennsylvania to contracts for the sale of goods. Atlantic City Tire and Rubber Corp. v. Southwark Foundry & Machine Co., 289 Pa. 569, 137 A. 807 (1927). However, Pennsylvania has since adopted the Uniform Commercial Code, which, as to contracts for the sale of goods, has modified the common law rule by 13 Pa.C.S. § 2718(b), which permits a breaching party to recover restitution. *See* note 2, *supra.*

First, the defaulting party's right to recovery is subject to the aggrieved party's right to offset his damages. Second, the measure of benefit is limited to the actual enrichment and cannot exceed a ratable portion of the contract price. Third, restitution is denied to the extent that the criteria for a valid liquidated damages clause are present. Fourth, restitution is denied if the aggrieved party seeks and is entitled to specific performance. *Perillo, supra,* at 50 (footnotes omitted).

The viability of the common law rule permitting forfeiture has also been undermined in other areas of Pennsylvania law. In Estate of Cahen, 483 Pa. 157, 168 n. 10, 394 A.2d 958, 964 n. 10 (1978), the Supreme Court held that assuming that a breaching fiduciary could recover in unjust enrichment, the basis would be *Restatement of Contracts* § 357 (1932), which allows recovery by a breaching party to the extent that the benefits exceed the losses sustained by the other party.

–3–

In regard to the present case, § 374 of the *Restatement (Second) of Contracts* represents a more enlightened approach than the common law rule. "Rules of contract law are not rules of punishment; the contract breaker is not an outlaw." Perillo, *supra,* at 50. The party who committed a breach should be entitled to recover "any benefit . . . in excess of the loss that he has caused by his own breach." *Restatement (Second) of Contracts* § 374(1).

This conclusion leads to the further conclusion that we should remand this case to the trial court. The trial court rested its decision on the common law rule. . . . Thus it never considered whether appellant is entitled to restitution, *Restatement (Second) of Contracts* § 374(1), nor, if appellant is not entitled to restitution, whether retention of the $25,000 was "reasonable in the light of the anticipated or actual loss caused by the breach and the difficulties of proof of loss," *id.,* § 374(2).

Remanded for further proceedings consistent with this opinion. Jurisdiction relinquished.

TAMILIA, JUDGE, dissenting: I strongly dissent. In the first instance, the majority does not and cannot cite *any* Pennsylvania authority adopting the rule cited in § 374 of the *Second Restatement of Contracts.* Although the ostensible basis for remand is the trial court's reliance on outmoded law, the majority relies on law so new as to be virtually unknown in this jurisdiction. The law in Pennsylvania has been and continues to be that where a binding contract exists, and there is no allegation that the contract itself is void or voidable, a breaching party is not entitled to recovery. Luria v. Robbins, 223 Pa.Super. 456, 302 A.2d 361 (1973). While our Supreme Court may yet abrogate the forfeiture principle in this Commonwealth, it has not yet seen fit to do so, and we may not usurp its prerogatives, particularly when the result would be unjust. . . .

PROBLEMS

23. Buyer agreed to purchase a specified quantity of vegetable oil for $1,000,000, making a down payment of $217,000. Buyer defaulted and Seller justifiedly withheld delivery of the oil. In this action Buyer seeks to recover its down payment. Seller counter-claims, alleging it has been damaged because of the drop in value of oil. What, if anything, may Buyer recover?

24. Plaintiff, a consulting engineer, took a part-time job with the defendant in its research and development department. In return for plaintiff's

promise to work a minimum of fifteen hours a week for a year, plaintiff was promised $40,000 payable at the end of the year. After six months, plaintiff quit to take jobs elsewhere on more favorable terms. Plaintiff seeks to recover the reasonable value of her services. What result?

SECTION 3. SPECIFIC PERFORMANCE

(a) SUBSTANTIVE BASIS

(Calamari & Perillo on Contracts §§ 16.1—16.6)

CENTEX HOMES CORP. v. BOAG

Superior Court of New Jersey, 1974.
128 N.J.Super. 385, 320 A.2d 194.

GELMAN, J. S. C., Temporarily Assigned. Plaintiff Centex Homes Corporation (Centex) is engaged in the development and construction of a luxury high-rise condominium project in the Boroughs of Cliffside Park and Fort Lee. The project when completed will consist of six 31–story buildings containing in excess of 3600 condominium apartment units, together with recreational buildings and facilities, parking garages and other common elements associated with this form of residential development. As sponsor of the project Centex offers the condominium apartment units for sale to the public and has filed an offering plan covering such sales with the appropriate regulatory agencies of the States of New Jersey and New York.

On September 13, 1972 defendants Mr. & Mrs. Eugene Boag executed a contract for the purchase of apartment unit No. 2019 in the building under construction and known as "Winston Towers 200." The contract purchase price was $73,700, and prior to signing the contract defendants had given Centex a deposit in the amount of $525. At or shortly after signing the contract defendants delivered to Centex a check in the amount of $6,870 which, together with the deposit, represented approximately 10% of the total purchase [price] of the apartment unit. Shortly thereafter Boag was notified by his employer that he was to be transferred to the Chicago, Illinois, area. Under date of September 27, 1972 he advised Centex that he "would be unable to complete the purchase" agreement and stopped payment on the $6,870 check. Centex deposited the check for collection approximately two weeks after receiving notice from defendant, but the check was not honored by defendants' bank. On August 8, 1973 Centex instituted this action in Chancery Division for specific performance of the purchase agreement or, in the alternative, for liquidated damages in the amount of $6,870. The matter is presently before this court on the motion of Centex for summary judgment.

Both parties acknowledge, and our research has confirmed, that no court in this State or in the United States has determined in any reported decision whether the equitable remedy of specific performance will lie for the enforcement of a contract for the sale of a condominium apartment. The closest decision on point is Silverman v. Alcoa Plaza Associates, 37 A.D.2d 166, 323 N.Y.S.2d 39 (App.Div.1971), which involved a default by a contract-purchaser of shares of stock and a proprietary lease in a cooperative apartment building. The seller, who was also the sponsor of the project, retained the deposit and sold the stock and the lease to a third party for the same purchase price. The original purchaser thereafter brought suit to recover his deposit, and on appeal the court held that the sale of shares of stock in a cooperative apartment building, even though associated with a proprietary lease, was a sale of personalty and not of an interest in real estate.* Hence, the seller was not entitled to retain the contract deposit as liquidated damages.[1]

As distinguished from a cooperative plan of ownership such as involved in *Silverman*, under a condominium housing scheme each condominium apartment unit constitutes a separate parcel of real property which may be dealt with in the same manner as any real estate. Upon closing of title the apartment unit owner receives a recordable deed which confers upon him the same rights and subjects him to the same obligations as in the case of traditional forms of real estate ownership, the only difference being that the condominium owner receives in addition an undivided interest in the common elements associated with the building and assigned to each unit. *See* the Condominium Act, N.J.S.A. 46:8B–1 *et seq.*; *Note*, 77 Harv.L.Rev. 777 (1964).

Centex urges that since the subject matter of the contract is the transfer of a fee interest in real estate, the remedy of specific performance is available to enforce the agreement under principles of equity which are well-settled in this state.

The principle underlying the specific performance remedy is equity's jurisdiction to grant relief where the damage remedy at law is inadequate. The text writers generally agree that at the time this branch of equity jurisdiction was evolving in England, the presumed uniqueness of land as well as its importance to the social order of that era led to the conclusion that damages at law could never be adequate to compensate for the breach of a contract to transfer an interest in land. Hence specific performance became a fixed remedy in this class of transactions. *See* 11 *Williston on Contracts* (3d ed. 1968) § 1418A; 5A *Corbin on Contracts* § 1143 (1964). The judicial attitude has remained substantially unchanged....

While the inadequacy of the damage remedy suffices to explain the origin of the vendee's right to obtain specific performance in equity, it does not provide a rationale for the availability of the remedy at the instance of the vendor of real estate. Except upon a showing of unusual

---

* [The court applied UCC § 2–718 in permitting the defaulting purchaser to obtain restitution of the downpayment. Ed.]

1. Under New York law, if the contract was deemed to be for the sale of realty, the seller could retain the deposit in lieu of damages.

circumstances or a change in the vendor's position, such as where the vendee has entered into possession, the vendor's damages are usually measurable, his remedy at law is adequate and there is no jurisdictional basis for equitable relief. *But see Restatement, Contracts* § 360, cmt. c.[2] The early English precedents suggest that the availability of the remedy in a suit by a vendor was an outgrowth of the equitable concept of mutuality, *i.e.*, that equity would not specifically enforce an agreement unless the remedy was available to both parties. . . .

No other *rationale* has been offered by our decisions subsequent to Hopper [v. Hopper, 16 N.J.Eq. 147 (Ch.1863)], and specific performance has been routinely granted to vendors without further discussion of the underlying jurisdictional issue.

Our present Supreme Court has squarely held, however, that mutuality of remedy is not an appropriate basis for granting or denying specific performance. Fleischer v. James Drug Stores, 1 N.J. 138, 62 A.2d 383 (1948); *see also, Restatement, Contracts* § 372; 11 Williston, *Contracts* (3d ed. 1968), § 1433. The test is whether the obligations of the contract are mutual and not whether each is entitled to precisely the same remedy in the event of a breach. . . .

The disappearance of the mutuality of remedy doctrine from our law dictates the conclusion that specific performance relief should no longer be automatically available to a vendor of real estate, but should be confined to those special instances where a vendor will otherwise suffer an economic injury for which his damage remedy at law will not be adequate, or where other equitable considerations require that the relief be granted. *Cf.* Dover Shopping Center, Inc. v. Cushman's Sons, Inc., 63 N.J.Super. 384, 394, 164 A.2d 785 (App.Div.1960). As Chancellor Vroom noted in King v. Morford, 1 N.J.Eq. 274, 281–282 (Ch.Div.1831), whether a contract should be specifically enforced is always a matter resting in the sound discretion of the court and

> . . . considerable caution should be used in decreeing the specific performance of agreements, and . . . the court is bound to see that it really does the complete justice which it aims at, and which is the ground of its jurisdiction.

Here the subject matter of the real estate transaction—a condominium apartment unit—has no unique quality but is one of hundreds of virtually identical units being offered by a developer for sale to the public. The units are sold by means of sample, in this case model apartments, in

---

2. The *Restatement's* reasoning, as expressed in § 360, comment c amounts to the inconsistent propositions that (1) because the vendor may not have sustained any damage which is actionable at law, specific performance should be granted, and (2) he would otherwise sustain damage equal to the loss of interest on the proceeds of the sale. Yet loss of interest is readily measurable and can be recovered in an action at law, and to the extent that the vendor has sustained no economic injury, there is no compelling reason for equity to grant to him the otherwise extraordinary remedy of specific performance. At the end of the comment, the author suggests that the vendor is entitled to specific performance because that remedy should be mutual, a concept which is substantially rejected as a decisional basis in §§ 372 and 373 of the *Restatement*.

much the same manner as items of personal property are sold in the market place. The sales prices for the units are fixed in accordance with schedule filed by Centex as part of its offering plan, and the only variance as between apartments having the same floor plan (of which six plans are available) is the floor level or the building location within the project. In actuality, the condominium apartment units, regardless of their realty label, share the same characteristics as personal property.

From the foregoing one must conclude that the damages sustained by a condominium sponsor resulting from the breach of the sales agreement are readily measurable and the damage remedy at law is wholly adequate. No compelling reasons have been shown by Centex for the granting of specific performance relief and its complaint is therefore dismissed as to the first count.

Centex also seeks money damages pursuant to a liquidated damage clause in its contract with the defendants. It is sufficient to note only that under the language of that clause (which was authored by Centex) liquidated damages are limited to such moneys as were paid by defendant at the time the default occurred. Since the default here consisted of the defendant's stopping payment of his check for the balance of the down-payment, Centex's liquidated damages are limited to the retention of the "moneys paid" prior to that date, or the initial $525 deposit. Accordingly, the second count of the complaint for damage relief will also be dismissed.

LACLEDE GAS CO. v. AMOCO OIL CO.

United States Court of Appeals, Eighth Circuit, 1975.
522 F.2d 33.

ROSS, CIRCUIT JUDGE. The Laclede Gas Company (Laclede), a Missouri corporation, brought this diversity action alleging breach of contract against the Amoco Oil Company (Amoco), a Delaware corporation. It sought relief in the form of a mandatory injunction prohibiting the continuing breach or, in the alternative, damages. The district court held a bench trial on the issues of whether there was a valid, binding contract between the parties and whether, if there was such a contract, Amoco should be enjoined from breaching it. It then ruled that the "contract is invalid due to lack of mutuality" and denied the prayer for injunctive relief. The court made no decision regarding the requested damages. This appeal followed, and we reverse the district court's judgment.

I.

... As a practical matter, ... Laclede is bound to buy all the propane it distributes from Amoco in any subdivision to which the supplemental agreement applies and for which the distribution system has been established. When analyzed in this manner, it can be seen that the contract herein is simply a so-called "requirements contract." Such contracts are routinely enforced by the courts where, as here, the needs of the purchaser are reasonably foreseeable and the time of performance is reasonably limited. [citations]

We conclude that there is mutuality of consideration within the terms of the agreement and hold that there is a valid, binding contract between the parties as to each of the developments for which supplemental letter agreements have been signed.

II.

Since he found that there was no binding contract, the district judge did not have to deal with the question of whether or not to grant the injunction prayed for by Laclede. He simply denied this relief because there was no contract.

Generally the determination of whether or not to order specific performance of a contract lies within the sound discretion of the trial court. Landau v. St. Louis Public Service Co., 364 Mo. 1134, 273 S.W.2d 255, 259 (1954). However, this discretion is, in fact, quite limited; and it is said that when certain equitable rules have been met and the contract is fair and plain "specific performance goes as a matter of right." Miller v. Coffeen, 365 Mo. 204, 280 S.W.2d 100, 102 (1955), *quoting*, Berberet v. Myers, 240 Mo. 58, 77, 144 S.W. 824, 830 (1912). (Emphasis omitted.)

With this in mind we have carefully reviewed the very complete record on appeal and conclude that the trial court should grant the injunctive relief prayed. We are satisfied that this case falls within that category in which specific performance should be ordered as a matter of right. *See* Miller v. Coffeen, *supra*, 280 S.W.2d at 102.

Amoco contends that four of the requirements for specific performance have not been met. Its claims are: (1) there is no mutuality of remedy in the contract; (2) the remedy of specific performance would be difficult for the court to administer without constant and long-continued supervision; (3) the contract is indefinite and uncertain; and (4) the remedy at law available to Laclede is adequate. The first three contentions have little or no merit and do not detain us for long.

There is simply no requirement in the law that both parties be mutually entitled to the remedy of specific performance in order that one of them be given that remedy by the court. [citations]

While a court may refuse to grant specific performance where such a decree would require constant and long-continued court supervision, this is merely a discretionary rule of decision which is frequently ignored when the public interest is involved.

Here the public interest in providing propane to the retail customers is manifest, while any supervision required will be far from onerous.

Section 370 of the *Restatement of Contracts* (1932) provides:

Specific enforcement will not be decreed unless the terms of the contract are so expressed that the court can determine with reasonable certainty what is the duty of each party and the conditions under which performance is due.

We believe these criteria have been satisfied here. As discussed in part I of this opinion, as to all developments for which a supplemental agreement has been signed, Amoco is to supply all the propane which is reasonably foreseeably required, while Laclede is to purchase the required propane from Amoco and pay the contract price therefor. The parties have disagreed over what is meant by "Wood River Area Posted Price" in the agreement, but the district court can and should determine with reasonable certainty what the parties intended by this term and should mold its decree, if necessary accordingly. Likewise, the fact that the agreement does not have a definite time of duration is not fatal since the evidence established that the last subdivision should be converted to natural gas in 10 to 15 years. This sets a reasonable time limit on performance and the district court can and should mold the final decree to reflect this testimony.

It is axiomatic that specific performance will not be ordered when the party claiming breach of contract has an adequate remedy at law. [citations] This is especially true when the contract involves personal property as distinguished from real estate.

However, in Missouri, as elsewhere, specific performance may be ordered even though personalty is involved in the "proper circumstances." Mo.Rev.Stat. § 400.2–716(1); *Restatement of Contracts, supra,* § 361. And a remedy at law adequate to defeat the grant of specific performance "must be as certain, prompt, complete, and efficient to attain the ends of justice as a decree of specific performance." [citations]

... [T]he evidence indicates that at the present time propane is readily available on the open market. However, this analysis ignores the fact that the contract involved in this lawsuit is for a long-term supply of propane to these subdivisions. ... Additionally, there was uncontradicted expert testimony that Laclede probably could not find another supplier of propane willing to enter into a long-term contract such as the Amoco agreement, given the uncertain future of worldwide energy supplies. And, even if Laclede could obtain supplies of propane for the affected developments through its present contracts or newly negotiated ones, it would still face considerable expense and trouble which cannot be estimated in advance in making arrangements for its distribution to the subdivisions.

Specific performance is the proper remedy in this situation, and it should be granted by the district court.

[Reversed and remanded] for the fashioning of appropriate injunctive relief in the form of a decree of specific performance....

ALAN SCHWARTZ, THE CASE FOR SPECIFIC PERFORMANCE
89 Yale L.J. 271 (1979).

The purpose of contract remedies is to place a disappointed promisee in as good a position as he would have enjoyed had his promisor performed. Contract law has two methods of achieving this "compensation goal": requiring the breaching party to pay damages, either to enable the promisee to purchase a substitute performance, or to replace the net gains that the promised performance would have generated; or requiring the breaching party to render the promised performance. Although the damages remedy is always available to a disappointed promisee under current law, the remedy of specific performance is available only at the discretion of the court. Moreover, courts seldom enforce contract clauses that explicitly provide for specific performance in the event of breach. . . .

It is useful to begin by examining the paradigm case for granting specific performance under current law, the case of unique goods. When a promisor breaches and the promisee can make a transaction that substitutes for the performance the promisor failed to render, the promisee will be fully compensated if he receives the additional amount necessary to purchase the substitute plus the costs of making a second transaction. In some cases, however, such as those involving works of art, courts cannot identify which transactions the promisee would regard as substitutes because that information often is in the exclusive possession of the promisee. Moreover, it is difficult for a court to assess the accuracy of a promisee's claim. For example, if the promisor breaches a contract to sell a rare emerald, the promisee may claim that only the Hope Diamond would give him equal satisfaction, and thus may sue for the price difference between the emerald and the diamond. It would be difficult for a court to know whether this claim is true. If the court seeks to award money damages, it has three choices: granting the price differential, which may overcompensate the promisee; granting the dollar value of the promisee's forgone satisfaction as estimated by the court, which may overcompensate or undercompensate; or granting restitution of any sums paid, which undercompensates the promisee. The promisee is fully compensated without risk of overcompensation or undercompensation if the remedy of specific performance is available to him and its use encouraged by the doctrine that damages must be foreseeable and certain.

If specific performance is the appropriate remedy there are three reasons why it should be routinely available. The first reason is that in many cases damages actually are undercompensatory. Although promisees are entitled to incidental damages, such damages are difficult to monetize. They consist primarily of the costs of finding and making a second deal, which generally involve the expenditure of time rather than cash; attaching a dollar value to such opportunity costs is quite difficult. Breach can also cause frustration and anger, especially in a consumer context, but these costs also are not recoverable.

Substitution damages, the court's estimate of the amount the promisee needs to purchase an adequate substitute, also may be inaccurate in many cases less dramatic than the emerald hypothetical discussed above. This is largely because of product differentiation and early obsolescence. As product differentiation becomes more common, the supply of products that will substitute precisely for the promisor's performance is reduced. For example, even during the period when there is an abundant supply of new Datsuns for sale, two-door, two-tone Datsuns with mag wheels, stereo, and air conditioning may be scarce in some local markets. Moreover, early obsolescence gives the promisee a short time in which to make a substitute purchase. If the promisor breaches late in a model year, for example, it may be difficult for the promisee to buy the exact model he wanted. For these reasons, a damage award meant to enable a promisee to purchase "another car" could be undercompensatory.

In addition, problems of prediction often make it difficult to put a promisee in the position where he would have been had his promisor performed. If a breach by a contractor would significantly delay or prevent completion of a construction project and the project differs in important respects from other projects—for example, a department store in a different location than previous stores—courts may be reluctant to award "speculative" lost profits attributable to the breach.

Second, promisees have economic incentives to sue for damages when damages are likely to be fully compensatory. A breaching promisor is reluctant to perform and may be hostile. This makes specific performance an unattractive remedy in cases in which the promisor's performance is complex, because the promisor is more likely to render a defective performance when that performance is coerced, and the defectiveness of complex performances is sometimes difficult to establish in court. Further, when the promisor's performance must be rendered over time, as in construction or requirements contracts, it is costly for the promisee to monitor a reluctant promisor's conduct. If the damage remedy is compensatory, the promisee would prefer it to incurring these monitoring costs. Finally, given the time necessary to resolve lawsuits, promisees would commonly prefer to make substitute transactions promptly and sue later for damages rather than hold their affairs in suspension while awaiting equitable relief. The very fact that a promisee requests specific performance thus implies that damages are an inadequate remedy.[24]

The third reason why courts should permit promisees to elect routinely the remedy of specific performance is that promisees possess better information than courts as to both the adequacy of damages and the difficulties of coercing performance. Promisees know better than courts whether the damages a court is likely to award would be adequate because promisees are more familiar with the costs that breach imposes on them.

---

24. Noneconomic motives could sometimes impel a promisee to seek specific performance; the German experience, however, provides some confirmation of this point. Although specific performance is much more widely available in Germany than in the United States, promisees there seek the damage remedy "in a high percentage of cases." [citations]

In addition, promisees generally know more about their promisors than do courts; thus they are in a better position to predict whether specific performance decrees would induce their promisors to render satisfactory performances.

In sum, restrictions on the availability of specific performance cannot be justified on the basis that damage awards are usually compensatory. On the contrary, the compensation goal implies that specific performance should be routinely available. This is because damage awards actually are under compensatory in more cases than is commonly supposed; the fact of a specific performance request is itself good evidence that damages would be inadequate; and courts should delegate to promisees the decision of which remedy best satisfies the compensation goal. Further, expanding the availability of specific performance would not result in greater exploitation of promisors. Promisees would seldom abuse the power to determine when specific performance should be awarded because of the strong incentives that promisees face to seek damages when these would be even approximately compensatory.

PROBLEMS

25. Seller entered into a contract with Buyer for the sale of a large quantity of lipsticks and containers of nail polish at cut-rate prices. Seller repudiated the contract. Buyer brought an action for specific performance. What will be the outcome?

26. P, a social club, entered into a contract with D whereby D would lend to P $125,000, to be secured by a mortgage. The funds were to be used to build a new clubhouse which was to be mortgaged to D. P then sold its existing clubhouse, purchased land and entered into construction contracts for building the new clubhouse. D refused to honor the agreement and P sues for specific performance. What result?

27. M, an unwed pregnant woman, entered into a contract with F, the putative father of the expected child. F contracted to pay M $10 per week until the child's eighteenth birthday. After eleven years F ceased making payments. M seeks a decree for specific performance. What result? Consider the material in § 12.9 of the *Calamari & Perillo* hornbook in addition to the assigned readings to arrive at your conclusion.

(b) COVENANTS NOT TO COMPETE

(Calamari & Perillo on Contracts §§ 16.19—16.22)

KARPINSKI v. INGRASCI

Court of Appeals of New York, 1971.
28 N.Y.2d 45, 320 N.Y.S.2d 1, 268 N.E.2d 751.

FULD, CHIEF JUDGE. This appeal requires us to determine whether a covenant by a professional man not to compete with his employer is enforceable and, if it is, to what extent.

The plaintiff, Dr. Karpinski, an oral surgeon, had been carrying on his practice alone in Auburn—in Cayuga County—for many years. In 1953, he decided to expand and, since nearly all of an oral surgeon's business stems from referrals, he embarked upon a plan to "cultivate connections" among dentists in the four nearby Counties of Tompkins, Seneca, Cortland and Ontario. The plan was successful, and by 1962 twenty per cent of his practice consisted of treating patients referred to him by dentists located in those counties. In that year, after a number of those dentists had told him that some of their patients found it difficult to travel from their homes to Auburn, the plaintiff decided to open a second office in centrally-located Ithaca. He began looking for an assistant and, in the course of his search, met the defendant, Dr. Ingrasci, who was just completing his training in oral surgery at the Buffalo General Hospital and was desirous of entering private practice. Dr. Ingrasci manifested an interest in becoming associated with Dr. Karpinski and, after a number of discussions, they reached an understanding; the defendant was to live in Ithaca, a locale with which he had no prior familiarity, and there work as an employee of the plaintiff.

A contract, reflecting the agreement, was signed by the defendant in June, 1962. It was for three years and, shortly after its execution, the defendant started working in the office which the plaintiff rented and fully equipped at his own expense. The provision of the contract with which we are concerned is a covenant by the defendant not to compete with the plaintiff. More particularly, it recited that the defendant

> promises and convenants that while this agreement is in effect and forever thereafter, he will never practice dentistry and/or Oral Surgery in Cayuga, Cortland, Seneca, Tompkins or Ontario counties except: (a) In association with the (plaintiff) or (b) If the (plaintiff) terminates the agreement and employs another oral surgeon.

In addition, the defendant agreed, "in consideration of the ... terms of employment, and of the experience gained while working with" the plaintiff, to execute a $40,000 promissory note to the plaintiff, to become payable if the defendant left the plaintiff and practiced "dentistry and/or Oral Surgery" in the five enumerated counties.[1]

---

1. Either party was privileged to terminate the agreement on 60 days' notice within the three-year period and, if the plaintiff were to do so, the contract recited, the defendant was released from the restrictive covenant and the note.

When the contract expired, the two men engaged in extended discussions as to the nature of their continued association—as employer and employee or as partners. Unable to reach an accord, the defendant, in February, 1968, left the plaintiff's employ and opened his own office for the practice of oral surgery in Ithaca a week later. The dentists in the area thereupon began referring their patients to the defendant rather than to the plaintiff, and in two months the latter's practice from the Ithaca area dwindled to almost nothing and he closed the office in that city. In point of fact, the record discloses that about 90% of the defendant's present practice comes from referrals from dentists in the counties specified in the restrictive covenant, the very same dentists who had been referring patients to the plaintiff's Ithaca office when the defendant was working there.[2]

The plaintiff, alleging a breach of the restrictive covenant, seeks not only an injunction to enforce it but also a judgment of $40,000 on the note. The Supreme Court, after a nonjury trial, decided in favor of the plaintiff and granted him both an injunction and damages as requested. On appeal, however, the Appellate Division reversed the resulting judgment and dismissed the complaint; it was that court's view that the covenant was void and unenforceable on the ground that its restriction against the practice of both dentistry *and* oral surgery was impermissibly broad.

There can be no doubt that the defendant violated the terms of the covenant when he opened his own office in Ithaca. But the mere fact of breach does not, in and of itself, resolve the case. Since there are "powerful considerations of public policy which militate against sanctioning the loss of a man's livelihood," the courts will subject a covenant by an employee not to compete with his former employer to an "overriding limitation of 'reasonableness.' " ...

Each case must, of course, depend, to a great extent, upon its own facts. It may well be that, in some instances, a restriction not to conduct a profession or a business in two counties or even in one, may exceed permissible limits. But, in the case before us, having in mind the character and size of the counties involved, the area restriction imposed is manifestly reasonable. The five small rural counties which it encompasses comprise the very area from which the plaintiff obtained his patients and in which the defendant would be in direct competition with him. Thus, the covenant's coverage coincides precisely with "the territory over which the practice extends," and this is proper and permissible. [citations] In brief, the plaintiff made no attempt to extend his influence beyond the area from which he drew his patients, the defendant being perfectly free to practice as he chooses outside the five specified counties.

Nor may the covenant be declared invalid because it is unlimited as to time, forever restricting the defendant from competing with the plaintiff.

---

2. There are two other oral surgeons, in addition to the plaintiff and the defendant, serving the Ithaca area.

It is settled that such a covenant will not be stricken merely because it "contains no time limit or is expressly made unlimited as to time." [citations] ... In the present case, the defendant opened an office in Ithaca, in competition with the plaintiff, just one week after his employment had come to an end. Under the circumstances presented, we thoroughly agree with the trial judge that it is clear that nearly all of the defendant's practice was, and would be, directly attributable to his association with his former employer.

This brings us to the most troublesome part of the restriction imposed upon the defendant. By the terms of the contract, he agreed not to practice "dentistry and/or Oral Surgery" in competition with the plaintiff. Since the plaintiff practices only "oral surgery," and it was for the practice of that limited type of "dentistry" that he had employed the defendant, the Appellate Division concluded that the plaintiff went beyond permissible limits when he obtained from the defendant the covenant that he would not engage in any "dentistry" whatsoever. The restriction, *as formulated*, is, as the Appellate Division concluded, too broad; it is not reasonable for a man to be excluded from a profession for which he has been trained when he does not compete with his former employer by practicing it.

The plaintiff seeks to justify the breadth of the covenant by urging that, if it had restricted only the defendant's practice of oral surgery and permitted him to practice "dentistry"—that is, to hold himself out as a dentist generally—the defendant would have been permitted, under the Education Law (§ 6601, subd. 3), to do all the work which an oral surgeon could. We have no sympathy with this argument; the plaintiff was not privileged to prevent the defendant from working in an area of dentistry in which he would not be in competition with him. The plaintiff would have all the protection he needs if the restriction were to be limited to the practice of oral surgery, and this poses the question as to the court's power to "sever" the impermissible from the valid and uphold the covenant to the extent that it is reasonable.

Although we have found no decision in New York directly in point, cases in this court support the existence of such a power. [citations] Moreover, a number of out-of-state decisions, and they are supported by authoritative texts and commentators, explicitly recognize the court's power of severance and divisibility in order to sustain the covenant insofar as it is reasonable. As Professor Blake put it (73 Harv.L.Rev., at pp. 674–675), "If in balancing the equities the court decides that his (the employee's) activity would fit within the scope of a reasonable prohibition, it is apt to make use of the tool of severance, paring an unreasonable restraint down to appropriate size and enforcing it." In short, to cull from the Washington Supreme Court's opinion in Wood v. May, 73 Wash.2d 307, 314, 438 P.2d 587, 591, "We find it just and equitable to protect appellant (employer) by injunction to the extent necessary to accomplish the basic purpose of the contract insofar as such contract is reasonable." Accordingly, since his practice is solely as an oral surgeon, the plaintiff gains all the injunctive protection to which he is entitled if effect be given only to that part of the covenant which prohibits the defendant from practicing oral surgery.

The question arises, however, whether injunctive relief is precluded by the fact that the defendant's promissory note for $40,000 was to become payable if he breached the agreement not to compete. We believe not. The mere inclusion in a covenant of a liquidated damages provision does not automatically bar the grant of an injunction. [citations] As this court wrote in the Diamond Match Co. case (106 N.Y. [473], at 486, 13 N.E. [419], at p. 424.), "It is a question of intention, to be deduced from the whole instrument and the circumstances; and if it appear that the performance of the covenant was intended, and not merely the payment of damages in case of a breach, the covenant will be enforced." The covenant under consideration in this case may not reasonably be read to render "the liquidated damages provision . . . the sole remedy." (Rubinstein v. Rubinstein, 23 N.Y.2d 293, 298, 296 N.Y.S.2d 354, 358, 244 N.E.2d 49, 51. . . .) On the other hand, it would be grossly unfair to grant the plaintiff, in addition to an injunction, the full amount of damages ($40,-000) which the parties apparently contemplated for a total breach of the covenant, since the injunction will halt any further violation. The proper approach is that taken in Wirth [& Hamid Fair Booking v. Wirth, 265 N.Y. 214, 192 N.E. 297]. The court, there faced with a similar situation, granted the injunction sought and, instead of awarding the amount of liquidated damages specified, remitted the matter for determination of the actual damages suffered during the period of the breach.

The hardship necessarily imposed on the defendant must be borne by him in view of the plaintiff's rightful interest in protecting the valuable practice of oral surgery which he built up over the course of many years. The defendant is, of course, privileged to practice "dentistry" generally in Ithaca or continue to practice "oral surgery" anywhere in the United States outside of the five small rural counties enumerated. The covenant, part of a contract carefully negotiated with no indication of fraud or overbearing on either side, must be enforced, insofar as it reasonably and validly may, according to its terms. In sum, then, the plaintiff is entitled to an injunction barring the defendant from practicing oral surgery in the five specified counties and to damages actually suffered by him in the period during which the defendant conducted such a practice in Ithaca after leaving the plaintiff's employ.

The order appealed from should be reversed, with costs, and the case remitted to Supreme Court, Cayuga County, for further proceedings in accordance with this opinion. . . .

HOWARD SCHULTZ & ASSOCIATES v. BRONIEC

Supreme Court of Georgia, 1977.
239 Ga. 181, 236 S.E.2d 265.

HILL, JUSTICE. This case involves a covenant not to compete and a covenant against disclosure of confidential information. In Rita Personnel Services v. Kot, 229 Ga. 314, 191 S.E.2d 79 (1972), this court was called upon to adopt or reject the "blue-pencil theory of severability" as to a covenant not to compete. In deciding that issue, the court was called upon to decide whether covenants not to compete should or should not be favored, and it was decided that they should not be favored. Thus the "blue-pencil" case, as *Rita Personnel* is known here, is somewhat of a landmark in this area of Georgia law and as such may even represent a turning point. In this case we are asked to overrule *Rita Personnel* if the restriction on competition is found to be overly broad.

At the outset it is necessary to determine whether the contract under consideration here is to be treated for these covenant purposes as an employment agreement in view of the fact that it expressly declares that it creates only the relationship of independent contractor and not that of master and servant. *Rita Personnel, supra*, involved a franchise agreement which was treated as an employment agreement. We find that the agreement here under review is to be treated similarly. Having made this determination, the parties can be identified by use of the traditional labels of "employer" and "employee."

An employer sought an injunction to enforce a covenant not to compete contained in an employment agreement and to restrain the former employee from divulging confidential and privileged information received by him during his employment. After hearing evidence and argument the trial court dismissed the complaint. The employer appeals.

On November 20, 1972, Frank D. Broniec (employee) entered into an agreement with Edward C. Aubitz by which the employee was to audit the accounts of clients of Aubitz and his principal, Howard Schultz and Associates, Inc., to determine if the clients had overpaid accounts payable because they were unaware of the availability of special discounts or allowances. The agreement contained a restrictive covenant whereby employee

> will not, for a period of two years after the termination of this agreement, for any reason thereafter, engage, directly or indirectly, as principal, agent, employer, employee, or in any capacity whatsoever, in any business, activity, auditing practice, or any other related activities, in competition with the principal (Howard Schultz & Associates) or associate's (Aubitz) business within any area or areas from time to time constituting the principal's or associate's area of activity in the conduct of their respective businesses, as of the date of said termination. . . .

The agreement also contained a paragraph concerned with confidential and privileged information which stated that employee

> shall receive information and knowledge with reference to clients, customers, and other sources of income of the principal and the associate, and with reference to auditing techniques, forms, standards, and other practices of the principal and the associate in performing the services in which the principal and the associate are engaged, and that all of said knowledge and information is confidential and privileged, and . . . (employee) agrees to keep said information confidential and not reveal the same to any party. . . .

. . .

1.   By both constitutional and legislative provision, Georgia prohibits contracts or agreements in general restraint of trade. Const. 1976, Art. III, Sec. VIII, Par. VIII, Code Ann. § 2–1409; Code Ann. § 20–504. Georgia courts have consistently held that the prohibition does not impose an absolute bar against every kind of restrictive agreement. A covenant not to compete ancillary to an employment contract is enforceable only where it is strictly limited in time and territorial effect and is otherwise reasonable considering the business interest of the employer sought to be protected and the effect on the employee. [citations]

Insofar as territorial restrictions are concerned, some of them relate to the territory in which the employee was employed; others relate to the territory in which the employer does business. The former generally will be enforced. [citations] The latter generally are unenforceable absent a showing by the employer of the legitimate business interests sought to be protected. [citations] It appears that the justification for this difference in treatment is that a court will accept as *prima facie* valid a covenant related to the territory where the employee was employed as a legitimate protection of the employer's investment in customer relations and good will. Thus a court will enforce an agreement prohibiting an employee from pirating his former employer's customers served by the employee, during the employment, at the employer's direct or indirect expense. Conversely, a court will not accept as *prima facie* valid a covenant related to the territory where the employer does business where the only justification is that the employer wants to avoid competition by the employee in that area.

In the case before us the employee was prohibited from engaging in competition within "any area or areas from time to time constituting the principal's or associate's area of activity in the conduct of their respective businesses, as of the date of said termination." This area would be, as to the employer's territory, not to mention the principal's territory, Alabama, Georgia, Florida, North Carolina, South Carolina and Tennessee. The employer has not justified this territorial restriction. It therefore stands as a bald attempt by the employer to prevent competition by the employee and is unenforceable.

2. This covenant not to compete must fall for two more reasons. This court has held on several occasions that a covenant wherein the employee agreed not to accept employment with a competitor "in any capacity" imposes a greater limitation upon the employee than is necessary for the protection of the employer and therefore is unenforceable. [citations]

A covenant not to compete is also unreasonable where the nature of the business activities in which the employee is forbidden to engage is not specified with particularity. [citations] These indefinite business activities generally are identified by reference to the employer's business; *e.g.*, the employee agrees not to engage in or be employed by any "business similar to employer's business."

The restrictive covenant here prohibits the employee from engaging "in any capacity whatsoever, in any business, activity, auditing practice, or in any other related activities, in competition with the principal or associate's business." We find that the covenant is unreasonable because the employee is prohibited from working in any capacity for a competitor. The covenant also fails to specify with any particularity the nature and kind of business which is or will be competitive with the employer; *i.e.*, the covenant fails to specify with particularity the activity which the employee is prohibited from performing.

3. The employer urges us to overrule Rita Personnel Services v. Kot, 229 Ga. 314, 191 S.E.2d 79, *supra*, and adopt the "blue-pencil theory" of severability. In *Rita Personnel* this court considered the severance theory and declined to apply it. The court has consistently followed *Rita Personnel*. [citations]

The employer argues that the *Restatement of Contracts*, § 518, approves the blue-pencil theory. However, Draft No. 12 of *Restatement of the Law, Second, Contracts*, § 326, pp. 95–96 (March 1, 1977) [now § 184], approved by the American Law Institute, rejects the blue-pencil theory as contrary to the weight of recent authority. *Rita Personnel* is cited with approval. . . .

According to the contract before us the employee agreed that for a period of two years he would not engage, directly or indirectly, as principal, agent, employer, employee, or in any capacity whatsoever, in any business activity, auditing practice, or any other related activity, in competition with the employer in Alabama, Georgia, Florida, North Carolina, South Carolina and Tennessee, or in competition with employer's principal wherever it may operate. The employer requests us to restrict the territory, to strike the offensive words "in any capacity" and to add words of our choosing to specify the activity forbidden to the employee.

It is these very requests which are the reason for rejecting severability of employee covenants not to compete. Employers covenant for more than is necessary, hope their employees will thereby be deterred from competing, and rely on the courts to rewrite the agreements so as to make them enforceable if their employees do compete. When courts adopt severability of covenants not to compete, employee competition will be deterred even more than it is at present by these overly broad covenants against competition. We choose to reaffirm Rita Personnel Services v. Kot, *supra*.

4. We next must consider whether the trial court erred in not issuing an injunction with reference to the employee's covenant against disclosure of confidential information. In Durham v. Stand–By Labor, Inc., *supra*, we made it clear that a nondisclosure covenant in an employment agreement could be enforced independently from a claim under a covenant not to compete such as has been discussed above. *See also* Aladdin v. Krasnoff, [214 Ga. 519, 105 S.E.2d 730 (1958)].

Also, at the outset, it is important to note that here the employer does not have a "trade secret" such as can be protected by law absent a contract provision. [citations] "A trade secret, within the rules pertaining to the rights which can be protected by injunction, is a plan, process, tool, mechanism, or compound, known only to its owner and those of his employees to whom it must be confided in order to apply it to the uses intended." [citations] . . .

Judgment affirmed. . . .

PROBLEMS

28. A law partnership agreement provided that upon termination of the partnership the clients of the partnership were to be allocated to individual members of the firm. It further provided: "[A]ll partners shall be restricted from doing business with a client designated as that of another partner for a period of 5 years." The Model Rules of Professional Conduct of the A.B.A., Rule 5.6 provides: "A lawyer shall not participate in offering or making: (a) a partnership, shareholders, operating, employment, or other similar type of agreement that restricts the right of a lawyer to practice after termination of the relationship, except an agreement concerning benefits upon retirement; or (b) an agreement in which a restriction on the lawyer's right to practice is part of the settlement of a client controversy." Adopted in 1983, the Model Rules are reflected in the ethics rules of most states. Rule 5.6 is based upon the earlier A.B.A. Code of Professional Responsibility.

(a) Upon termination of the partnership, is the quoted clause of the partnership agreement enforceable?

(b) Suppose, instead, the parties were physicians. Would the result be the same?

29. P, a large nation-wide firm that specialized in advising businesses on how to minimize their unemployment compensation costs, hired D in 1962. D's employment contract provided that after a voluntary termination of D's employment D would refrain for three years from entering any competing business in 7 named counties, one of which was the place of his employment. D rose to the position of vice-president in charge of operations and was thoroughly conversant with all aspects of the operation, but had little involvement with sales. P's services were sold to major companies listed in industrial directories. After eleven years, D resigned and set up a competing business in

the same community. P seeks an injunction: (1) prohibiting D from operating a competing business for three years within the designated area and (2) permanently enjoining D from soliciting P's customers. What analysis and result in (a) New York, (b) in Georgia?

CHAPTER 11

THIRD PARTY BENEFICIARIES

■ ■ ■

SECTION 1. INTENDED, INCIDENTAL, CREDITOR AND DONEE BENEFICIARIES

(Calamari & Perillo on Contracts §§ 17.1—17.9)

LAWRENCE v. FOX

Court of Appeals of New York, 1859.
20 N.Y. 268.

Appeal from the Superior Court of the city of Buffalo. On the trial before Mr. Justice Masten, it appeared by the evidence of a bystander, that one Holly, in November, 1857, at the request of the defendant, loaned and advanced to him $300, stating at the time that he owed that sum to the plaintiff for money borrowed of him, and had agreed to pay it to him the then next day; that the defendant in consideration thereof, at the time of receiving the money, promised to pay it to the plaintiff the then next day. Upon this state of facts the defendant moved for a nonsuit, upon three several grounds, *viz.*: That there was no proof tending to show that Holly was indebted to the plaintiff; that the agreement by the defendant with Holly to pay the plaintiff was void for want of consideration, and that there was no privity between the plaintiff and defendant. The court overruled the motion, and the counsel for the defendant excepted. The cause was then submitted to the jury, and they found a verdict for the plaintiff for the amount of the loan and interest, $344.66, upon which judgment was entered; from which the defendant appealed to the Superior Court, at general term, where the judgment was affirmed, and the defendant appealed to this court. The cause was submitted on printed arguments.

H. GRAY, J. The first objection raised on the trial amounts to this: That the evidence of the person present, who heard the declarations of Holly giving directions as to the payment of the money he was then advancing to the defendant, was mere hearsay and therefore not competent. Had the plaintiff sued Holly for this sum of money no objection to the competency of this evidence would have been thought of; and if the defendant had performed his promise by paying the sum loaned to him to the plaintiff, and Holly had afterwards sued him for its recovery, and this evidence had been offered by the defendant, it would doubtless have been received without an objection from any source. All the defendant had the right to demand in this case was evidence which, as between Holly and the plaintiff, was competent to establish the relation between them of debtor and creditor. For that purpose the evidence was clearly competent; it covered the whole ground and warranted the verdict of the jury.

But it is claimed that notwithstanding this promise was established by competent evidence, it was void for the want of consideration. It is now more than a quarter of a century since it was settled by the Supreme Court of this State—in an able and pains-taking opinion by the late Chief Justice Savage, in which the authorities were fully examined and carefully analysed—that a promise in all material respects like the one under consideration was valid; and the judgment of that court was unanimously affirmed by the Court for the Correction of Errors. (Farley v. Cleaveland,* 4 Cow., 432; *same case in error,* 9 *id.*, 639.) In that case one Moon owed Farley and sold to Cleaveland a quantity of hay, in consideration of which Cleaveland promised to pay Moon's debt to Farley; and the decision in favor of Farley's right to recover was placed upon the ground that the hay received by Cleaveland from Moon was a valid consideration for Cleaveland's promise to pay Farley, and that the subsisting liability of Moon to pay Farley was no objection to the recovery. The fact that the money advanced by Holly to the defendant was a loan to him for a day, and that it thereby became the property of the defendant, seemed to impress the defendant's counsel with the idea that because the defendant's promise was not a trust fund placed by the plaintiff in the defendant's hands, out of which he was to realize money as from the sale of a chattel or the collection of a debt, the promise although made for the benefit of the plaintiff could not enure to his benefit. The hay which Cleaveland [received from]** Moon was not to be paid to Farley, but the debt incurred by Cleaveland for the purchase of the hay, like the debt incurred by the defendant for money borrowed, was what was to be paid. That case has been often referred to by the courts of this State, and has never been doubted as sound authority for the principle upheld by it. (Barker v. Bucklin, 2 Denio, 45; Hudson Canal Company v. The Westchester Bank, 4 *id.*, 97.) It puts to rest the objection that the defendant's promise was void for want of consideration.

The report of [*Farley*] shows that the promise was not only made to Moon but to the plaintiff Farley. In this case the promise was made to Holly and not expressly to the plaintiff; and this difference between the

---

* [Spelled "Cleaveland" throughout this published opinion, but "Cleveland" in the published reports of *Farley v. Cleveland*. Ed.]

** [Original erroneously states, "delivered to." Ed.]

two cases presents the question, raised by the defendant's objection as to the want of privity between the plaintiff and defendant. [The court then discusses New York cases beginning in 1806 holding "[t]hat where one person makes a promise to another for the benefit of a third person, that third person may maintain an action upon it," Schemerhorn v. Vanderheyden (1 Johns. 139, 140), and that when a promise is made to a debtor to pay the creditor the law implies a promise to the creditor. Ed.] But it is urged that because the defendant was not in any sense a trustee of the property of Holly for the benefit of the plaintiff, the law will not imply a promise. I agree that many of the cases where a promise was implied were cases of trusts, created for the benefit of the promiser. The case of Felton v. Dickinson (10 Mass., 189, 190), and others that might be cited, are of that class; but concede them all to have been cases of trusts, and it proves nothing against the application of the rule to this case. The duty of the trustee to pay the *cestuis que trust,* according to the terms of the trust, implies his promise to the latter to do so. In this case the defendant, upon ample consideration received from Holly, promised Holly to pay his debt to the plaintiff; the consideration received and the promise to Holly made it as plainly his duty to pay the plaintiff as if the money had been remitted to him for that purpose, and as well implied a promise to do so as if he had been made a trustee of property to be converted into cash with which to pay. The fact that a breach of the duty imposed in the one case may be visited, and justly, with more serious consequences than in the other, by no means disproves the payment to be a duty in both. The principle illustrated by the example so frequently quoted (which concisely states the case in hand) "that a promise made to one for the benefit of another, he for whose benefit it is made may bring an action for its breach," has been applied to trust cases, not because it was exclusively applicable to those cases, but because it was a principle of law, and as such applicable to those cases.

It was also insisted that Holly could have discharged the defendant from his promise, though it was intended by both parties for the benefit of the plaintiff, and therefore the plaintiff was not entitled to maintain this suit for the recovery of a demand over which he had no control. ... Suppose the defendant had given his note in which, for value received of Holly, he had promised to pay the plaintiff and the plaintiff had accepted the promise, retaining Holly's liability. Very clearly Holly could not have discharged that promise, be the right to release the defendant as it may. No one can doubt that he owes the sum of money demanded of him, or that in accordance with his promise it was his duty to have paid it to the plaintiff; nor can it be doubted that whatever may be the diversity of opinion elsewhere, the adjudications in this State, from a very early period, approved by experience, have established the defendant's liability; if, therefore, it could be shown that a more strict and technically accurate application of the rules applied, would lead to a different result (which I by no means concede), the effort should not be made in the face of manifest justice.

The judgment should be affirmed.

JOHNSON, CH. J., DENIO, SELDEN, ALLEN and STRONG, JS., concurred. JOHNSON, CH. J., and DENIO, J., were of opinion that the promise was to be regarded as made to the plaintiff through the medium of his agent, whose action he could ratify when it came to his knowledge, though taken without his being privy thereto.

COMSTOCK, J. (Dissenting.) The plaintiff had nothing to do with the promise on which he brought this action. It was not made to him, nor did the consideration proceed from him. If he can maintain the suit, it is because an anomaly has found its way into the law on this subject. In general, there must be privity of contract. The party who sues upon a promise must be the promisee, or he must have some legal interest in the undertaking. In this case, it is plain that Holly, who loaned the money to the defendant, and to whom the promise in question was made, could at any time have claimed that it should be performed to himself personally. He had lent the money to the defendant, and at the same time directed the latter to pay the sum to the plaintiff. This direction he could countermand, and if he had done so, manifestly the defendant's promise to pay according to the direction would have ceased to exist. The plaintiff would receive a benefit by a complete execution of the arrangement, but the arrangement itself was between other parties, and was under their exclusive control. If the defendant had paid the money to Holly, his debt would have been discharged thereby. So Holly might have released the demand or assigned it to another person, or the parties might have annulled the promise now in question, and designated some other creditor of Holly as the party to whom the money should be paid. It has never been claimed, that in a case thus situated, the right of a third person to sue upon the promise rested on any sound principle of law. We are to inquire whether the rule has been so established by positive authority. . . .

The cases in which some trust was involved are also frequently referred to as authority for the doctrine now in question, but they do not sustain it. If A delivers money or property to B, which the latter accepts upon a trust for the benefit of C, the latter can enforce the trust by an appropriate action for that purpose. (Berly v. Taylor, 5 Hill, 577.) If the trust be of money, I think the beneficiary may assent to it and bring the action for money had and received to his use. If it be of something else than money, the trustee must account for it according to the terms of the trust, and upon principles of equity. There is some authority even for saying that an express promise founded on the possession of a trust fund may be enforced by an action at law in the name of the beneficiary, although it was made to the creator of the trust. . . . But further than this we cannot go without violating plain rules of law. In the case before us there was nothing in the nature of a trust or agency. The defendant borrowed the money of Holly and received it as his own. The plaintiff had no right in the fund, legal or equitable. The promise to repay the money created an obligation in favor of the lender to whom it was made and not in favor of any one else. . . .

GROVER, J., also dissented.

Judgment affirmed.

SEAVER v. RANSOM

Court of Appeals of New York, 1918.
224 N.Y. 233, 120 N.E. 639.

POUND, J. Judge Beman and his wife were advanced in years. Mrs. Beman was about to die. She had a small estate consisting of a house and lot in Malone and little else. Judge Beman drew his wife's will according to her instructions. It gave $1,000 to plaintiff, $500 to one sister, plaintiff's mother, and $100 each to another sister and her son, the use of the house to her husband for life, remainder to the American Society for the Prevention of Cruelty to Animals. She named her husband as residuary legatee and executor. Plaintiff was her niece, thirty-four years old, in ill health, sometimes a member of the Beman household. When the will was read to Mrs. Beman she said that it was not as she wanted it; she wanted to leave the house to plaintiff. She had no other objection to the will, but her strength was waning and although the judge offered to write another will for her, she said she was afraid she would not hold out long enough to enable her to sign it. So the judge said if she would sign the will he would leave plaintiff enough in his will to make up the difference. He avouched the promise by his uplifted hand with all solemnity and his wife then executed the will. When he came to die it was found that his will made no provision for the plaintiff.

This action was brought and plaintiff recovered judgment in the trial court on the theory that Beman had obtained property from his wife and induced her to execute the will in the form prepared by him by his promise to give plaintiff $6,000, the value of the house, and that thereby equity impressed his property with a trust in favor of plaintiff. Where a legatee promises the testator that he will use property given him by the will for a particular purpose, a trust arises. [citations] Beman received nothing under his wife's will but the use of the house in Malone for life. Equity compels the application of property thus obtained to the purpose of the testator, but equity cannot so impress a trust except on property obtained by the promise. Beman was bound by his promise, but no property was bound by it; no trust in plaintiff's favor can be spelled out.

An action on the contract for damages or to make the executors trustees for performance stands on different ground. (Farmers' Loan & Trust Co. v. Mortimer, 219 N.Y. 290, 294, 295.) The Appellate Division properly passed to the consideration of the question whether the judgment could stand upon the promise made to the wife, upon a valid consideration, for the sole benefit of plaintiff. The judgment of the trial court was affirmed by a return to the general doctrine laid down in the great case of Lawrence v. Fox (20 N.Y. 268) which has since been limited as herein indicated.

Contracts for the benefit of third persons have been the prolific source of judicial and academic discussion. (Williston, *Contracts for the Benefit of a Third Person*, 15 Harvard Law Review, 767; Corbin, *Contracts for the Benefit of Third Persons*, 27 Yale Law Review, 1008.) The general rule, both in law and equity (Phalen v. U. S. Trust Co., 186 N.Y. 178, 186), was that privity between a plaintiff and a defendant is necessary to the maintenance of an action on the contract. The consideration must be furnished by the party to whom the promise was made. The contract cannot be enforced against the third party and, therefore, it cannot be enforced by him. On the other hand, the right of the beneficiary to sue on a contract made expressly for his benefit has been fully recognized in many American jurisdictions, either by judicial decision or by legislation, and is said to be "the prevailing rule in this country." (Hendrick v. Lindsay, 93 U.S. 143.) It has been said that "the establishment of this doctrine has been gradual, and is a victory of practical utility over theory, of equity over technical subtlety." (*Brantly on Contracts* (2d Ed.) p. 253.) The reasons for this view are that it is just and practical to permit the person for whose benefit the contract is made to enforce it against one whose duty it is to pay. Other jurisdictions still adhere to the present English rule [citations] that a contract cannot be enforced by or against a person who is not a party. [citations]

In New York the right of the beneficiary to sue on contracts made for his benefit is not clearly or simply defined. It is at present confined, *first,* to cases where there is a pecuniary obligation running from the promisee to the beneficiary.... (Farley v. Cleveland, 4 Cow. 432; *Lawrence v. Fox, supra,* Vrooman v. Turner, 69 N.Y. 280.) *Secondly,* to cases where the contract is made for the benefit of the wife (Buchanan v. Tilden, 158 N.Y. 109), affianced wife (De Cicco v. Schweizer, 221 N.Y. 431), or child (Todd v. Weber, 95 N.Y. 181) of a party to the contract. The close relationship cases go back to the early King's Bench case (1677), long since repudiated in England, of Dutton v. Poole (2 Lev. 210; s. c., 1 Ventris, 318, 332). (Schemerhorn v. Vanderheyden, 1 Johns. 139.) The natural and moral duty of the husband or parent to provide for the future of wife or child sustains the action on the contract made for their benefit. . . .

The right of the third party is also upheld in, *thirdly,* the public contract cases [citations] where the municipality seeks to protect its inhabitants by covenants for their benefit and, *fourthly,* the cases where, at the request of a party to the contract, the promise runs directly to the beneficiary although he does not furnish the consideration. [citations] It may be safely said that a general rule sustaining recovery at the suit of the third party would include but few classes of cases not included in these groups, either categorically or in principle.

The desire of the childless aunt to make provision for a beloved and favorite niece differs imperceptibly in law or in equity from the moral duty of the parent to make testamentary provision for a child. The contract was made for the plaintiff's benefit. She alone is substantially damaged by its breach. The representatives of the wife's estate have no interest in enforcing it specifically. It is said in *Buchanan v. Tilden* [*supra*] that the common law imposes moral and legal obligations upon the husband and the parent not measured by the necessaries of life. It was, however, the love and affection or the moral sense of the husband and the parent that imposed such obligations in the cases cited rather than any common-law duty of husband and parent to wife and child. If plaintiff had been a child of Mrs. Beman, legal obligation would have required no testamentary provision for her, yet the child could have enforced a covenant in her favor identical with the covenant of Judge Beman in this case. *(De Cicco v. Schweizer, supra.)* The constraining power of conscience is not regulated by the degree of relationship alone. The dependent or faithful niece may have a stronger claim than the affluent or unworthy son. No sensible theory of moral obligation denies arbitrarily to the former what would be conceded to the latter. We might consistently either refuse or allow the claim of both, but I cannot reconcile a decision in favor of the wife in *Buchanan v. Tilden* based on the moral obligations arising out of near relationship with a decision against the niece here on the ground that the relationship is too remote for equity's ken. . . .

Kellogg, P.J., writing for the court below well said: "The doctrine of *Lawrence v. Fox* is progressive, not retrograde. The course of the late decisions is to enlarge, not to limit the effect of that case." The court in that leading case attempted to adopt the general doctrine that any third person, for whose direct benefit a contract was intended, could sue on it. . . . [B]ut *Vrooman v. Turner (supra)* confined its application to the facts on which it was decided. "In every case in which an action has been sustained," says Allen, J., "there has been a debt or duty owing by the promisee to the party claiming to sue upon the promise." (69 N.Y. 285.) . . .

[O]n principle, a sound conclusion may be reached. If Mrs. Beman had left her husband the house on condition that he pay the plaintiff $6,000 and he had accepted the devise, he would have become personally liable to pay the legacy and plaintiff could have recovered in an action at law against him, whatever the value of the house. [citations] That would be because the testatrix had in substance bequeathed the promise to plaintiff and not because close relationship or moral obligation sustained the contract. The distinction between an implied promise to a testator for the benefit of a third party to pay a legacy and an unqualified promise on a valuable consideration to make provision for the third party by will is discernible but not obvious. The tendency of American authority is to sustain the gift in all such cases and to permit the donee-beneficiary to recover on the contract. [citation] The equities are with the plaintiff and they may be enforced in this action, whether it be regarded as an action for damages or an action for specific performance to convert the defendants into trustees for plaintiff's benefit under the agreement. . . .

Judgment affirmed. [Three of the seven judges dissented without opinion. Ed.]

H.R. MOCH CO. v. RENSSELAER WATER CO.

Court of Appeals of New York, 1928.
247 N.Y. 160, 159 N.E. 896.

CARDOZO, CH. J. The defendant, a water works company under the laws of this State, made a contract with the city of Rensselaer for the supply of water during a term of years. Water was to be furnished to the city for sewer flushing and street sprinkling; for service to schools and public buildings; and for service at fire hydrants, the latter service at the rate of $42.50 a year for each hydrant. Water was to be furnished to private takers within the city at their homes and factories and other industries at reasonable rates, not exceeding a stated schedule. While this contract was in force, a building caught fire. The flames, spreading to the plaintiff's warehouse near by, destroyed it and its contents. The defendant according to the complaint was promptly notified of the fire, "but omitted and neglected after such notice, to supply or furnish sufficient or adequate quantity of water, with adequate pressure to stay, suppress or extinguish the fire before it reached the warehouse of the plaintiff, although the pressure and supply which the defendant was equipped to supply and furnish, and had agreed by said contract to supply and furnish, was adequate and sufficient to prevent the spread of the fire to and the destruction of the plaintiff's warehouse and its contents." By reason of the failure of the defendant to "fulfill the provisions of the contract between it and the city of Rensselaer," the plaintiff is said to have suffered damage, for which judgment is demanded. A motion, in the nature of a demurrer, to dismiss the complaint, was denied at Special Term. The Appellate Division reversed by a divided court.

Liability in the plaintiff's argument is placed on one or other of three grounds. The complaint, we are told, is to be viewed as stating: (1) A cause of action for breach of contract within Lawrence v. Fox (20 N.Y. 268); (2) a cause of action for a common-law tort, within MacPherson v. Buick Motor Company (217 N.Y. 382); or (3) a cause of action for the breach of a statutory duty. These several grounds of liability will be considered in succession.

(1) We think the action is not maintainable as one for breach of contract.

No legal duty rests upon a city to supply its inhabitants with protection against fire (Springfield Fire Ins. Co. v. Village of Keeseville, 148 N.Y. 46). That being so, a member of the public may not maintain an action under *Lawrence v. Fox* against one contracting with the city to furnish water at the hydrants, unless an intention appears that the promisor is to be answerable to individual members of the public as well as to the city for any loss ensuing from the failure to fulfill the promise. No such intention is discernible here. On the contrary, the contract is significantly divided into two branches: one a promise to the city for the benefit of the city in its corporate capacity, in which branch is included the service at the hydrants; and the other a promise to the city for the benefit of private takers, in which branch is included the service at their homes and factories. In a broad sense it is true that every city contract, not improvident or wasteful, is for the benefit of the public. More than this, however, must be shown to give a right of action to a member of the public not formally a party. The benefit, as it is sometimes said, must be one that is not merely incidental and secondary. It must be primary and immediate in such a sense and to such a degree as to bespeak the assumption of a duty to make reparation directly to the individual members of the public if the benefit is lost. The field of obligation would be expanded beyond reasonable limits if less than this were to be demanded as a condition of liability. A promisor undertakes to supply fuel for heating a public building. He is not liable for breach of contract to a visitor who finds the building without fuel, and thus contracts a cold. The list of illustrations can be indefinitely extended. The carrier of the mails under contract with the government is not answerable to the merchant who has lost the benefit of a bargain through negligent delay. The householder is without a remedy against manufacturers of hose and engines, though prompt performance of their contracts would have stayed the ravages of fire. "The law does not spread its protection so far" (Robins Dry Dock & Repair Co. v. Flint, 275 U.S. 303).

So with the case at hand. By the vast preponderance of authority, a contract between a city and a water company to furnish water at the city hydrants has in view a benefit to the public that is incidental rather than immediate, an assumption of duty to the city and not to its inhabitants. Such is the ruling of the Supreme Court of the United States (German Alliance Ins. Co. v. Home Water Supply Co., 226 U.S. 220). Such has been the ruling in this state [citations] though the question is still open in this court. Such with few exceptions has been the ruling in other jurisdictions [citations]. The diligence of counsel has brought together decisions to that effect from twenty-six States. ... Only a few States have held otherwise (Page, *Contracts*, § 2401). An intention to assume an obligation of indefinite extension to every member of the public is seen to be the more improbable when we recall the crushing burden that the obligation would impose. The consequences invited would bear no reasonable proportion to those attached by law to defaults not greatly different. A wrongdoer who by negligence sets fire to a building is liable in damages to the owner where the fire has its origin, but not to other owners who are injured when it spreads. The rule in our State is settled to that effect, whether wisely or unwisely [citations]. If the plaintiff is to prevail, one who negligently omits to supply sufficient pressure to extinguish a fire started by another, assumes an obligation to pay the ensuing damage, though the whole city is laid low. A promisor will not be deemed to have had in mind the assumption of a risk so overwhelming for any trivial reward.

The cases that have applied the rule of *Lawrence v. Fox* to contracts made by a city for the benefit of the public are not at war with this conclusion. Through them all there runs as a unifying principle the presence of an intention to compensate the individual members of the public in the event of a default. For example, in Pond v. New Rochelle Water Co. (183 N.Y. 330) the contract with the city fixed a schedule of rates to be supplied not to public buildings but to private takers at their homes. In Matter of International Railway Co. v. Rann (224 N.Y. 83, 85) the contract was by street railroads to carry passengers for a stated fare. In Smyth v. City of N.Y. (203 N.Y. 106) and Rigney v. N.Y.C. & H.R.R.R. Co. (217 N.Y. 31) covenants were made by contractors upon public works, not merely to indemnify the city, but to assume its liabilities. These and like cases come within the third group stated in the comprehensive opinion in Seaver v. Ransom (224 N.Y.233, 238). The municipality was contracting in behalf of its inhabitants by covenants intended to be enforced by any of them severally as occasion should arise.

(2) We think the action is not maintainable as one for a common law tort. . . .

(3) We think the action is not maintainable as one for the breach of a statutory duty. . . .

The judgment should be affirmed with costs. . . .

WESTERN WATERPROOFING CO. v. SPRINGFIELD HOUSING AUTHORITY

United States District Court, C.D. Illinois, 1987.
669 F.Supp. 901.

MILLS, DISTRICT JUDGE: As far as the Court and the parties can discern, this case presents a novel issue under Illinois law.

The ultimate issue: Whether a third party beneficiary contract action may be asserted by an unpaid subcontractor against a public entity where such entity has failed to procure from a general contractor a payment bond as required by the Illinois Bond Act.

The case is before this Court on cross motions for summary judgment. Under Count III of their complaint, Plaintiff Western Waterproofing Company, Inc., prays for judgment in the amount of $129,000. Under Count VI of their complaint, Mid–Continental Restoration Company, Inc., prays for judgment in the amount of $22,456. Defendant Springfield Housing Authority prays for judgment dismissing Counts III and VI of Plaintiffs' complaint. . . .

The pertinent facts of this suit are undisputed. Plaintiffs were subcontractors for a federally funded construction project of the Defendant, Springfield Housing Authority (SHA). In January 1985, the SHA entered into an agreement with Bildoc, Inc. (Bildoc), for the waterproofing and weatherization of five hi-rise apartment buildings. The general contractor, Bildoc, then entered into contracts with various subcontractors which included Plaintiffs Western Waterproofing Company, Inc. (Western) and Mid–Continental Restoration Company, Inc. (Mid–Continental). Both Plaintiffs contributed labor and materials toward the completion of the project. Both were to receive payment 63 days from completion of the project. Work was completed and final payment, less retainage in the amount of $12,481.16, was made to Bildoc on December 13, 1985.

Western was to be paid $129,000 under its agreement with Bildoc. Mid–Continental was to be paid $22,456 under its agreement with Bildoc. Neither Plaintiff has received any payments for work performed.

Plaintiffs filed their complaint on May 2, 1986. They secured a default judgment against Defendant Bildoc based on Counts I and IV of the complaint in a judgment order entered July 11, 1986. The Plaintiffs have been unable to collect on this judgment. Plaintiffs then resumed proceedings in this case in February 1987 against the SHA. Plaintiffs confessed SHA's motion to strike Counts II and V of the complaint. Thus, Counts III and VI of the complaint, which allege that the Plaintiffs are third party beneficiaries of SHA's contract with Bildoc, remain unlitigated and are the subject of the cross motions for summary judgment.

I.

The basis of the Plaintiffs' claim as a third party beneficiary of the contract between SHA and Bildoc stems from the following provision in the general contract:

Performance and Payment Bond

A performance bond in the amount of total amount of contract for cost of installation of windows will be furnished to the authority as a separate cost item and will be added to the contract price. After the first shipment of windows and payment thereof by SHA, the Contractor shall provide SHA with a Waiver of Lien against all materials on site.

The SHA failed to procure from Bildoc either a performance bond or a payment bond. Both parties agree that had a payment bond been secured the Plaintiffs, as subcontractors, would have collected monies due them under such bond. The parties further agree that subcontractors have no rights under a performance bond. Thus, the initial bone of contention is, what exactly was required under the contract. If only a performance bond was required, as stated in the body of the provision, then Western and Mid–Continental as subcontractors have no claim. If, however, a payment bond was also required as stated in the heading of the provision, then Plaintiffs have stated a colorable claim.

The nature of the bonds involved is as follows. Generally, as a condition of the construction contract between an owner (SHA) and a general contractor (Bildoc), the owner requires the contractor to obtain a surety bond. "There are two kinds of surety bonds, performance bonds and payment bonds. A performance bond simply insures that the contractor will perform the work as contracted. . . . A payment bond, on the other hand, requires that the contractor pay all subcontractors and materialmen before the owner will make final payment." Taylor Woodrow Blitman

Const. Corp. v. Southfield Gardens Co., 534 F.Supp. 340, 344 (D.Mass. 1982); *see also* J. Calamari & J. Perillo, *The Law of Contracts* 621 (2d ed. 1977). Thus, although the two bonds can be combined into a single bond, they serve separate and distinct purposes. *J. Calamari & J. Perillo, supra.*

It is the SHA's contention that although the above quoted "section is entitled Performance and Payment Bond, it requires only a Performance Bond. There is nothing that requires Bildoc to supply a Payment Bond under the contract." The Court disagrees with this interpretation for two reasons. First, under 29 Ill.Rev.Stat. ¶ 15 (1985), An Act in Relation to Bonds of Contractors Entering into Contracts for Public Construction (Bond Act),

> all officials, boards, commissions or agents of this State, or of any political subdivision thereof in making contracts for public work of any kind to be performed for the State, or a political subdivision thereof *shall require* every contractor for such work to furnish, supply and deliver a bond to the State, or to the political subdivision thereof entering into such contract, as the case may be, with good and sufficient sureties. The amount of such bond shall be fixed by such officials, boards, commissions, commissioners or agents, and such bond, among other conditions, shall be conditioned for the completion of the contract, for the payment of material used in such work and for all labor performed in such work, *whether by subcontractor or otherwise.*

Id. (emphasis added). The Act contains mandatory language directing the requirement of a payment bond to protect materialmen and subcontractors. Fodge v. Board of Educ. of the Village of Oak Park, Dist. 97, 309 Ill.App. 109, 124, 32 N.E.2d 650 (1941).

Under Illinois law, "statutory provisions applicable to a contract . . . are deemed to form a part of that contract and must be construed in connection therewith." DC Electronics, Inc. v. Employers Modern Life Co., 90 Ill.App.3d 342, 348, 45 Ill.Dec. 690, 413 N.E.2d 23 (1st Dist.1980). . . . Similarly, this same rule should apply to the Bond Act where a contract for public work is involved as it has been held that "paragraphs 15 and 16 (of Chapter 29) are remedial and were intended to protect subcontractors and materialmen for whom no right of mechanic's lien exists against a public work." Board of Educ., *ex rel.* Palumbo v. Pacific Nat'l Fire Ins. Co., 19 Ill.App.2d 290, 299, 153 N.E.2d 498 (1st Dist.1958). Thus, because the mechanic's lien was inapplicable under this public works contract, and because the Bond Act was established to achieve the same remedial goal as the mechanic's lien in a public works situation, it follows that the Bond Act should be read into the public works contract between SHA and Bildoc, requiring the procurement of a payment bond as required by the Bond Act.

The second reason a payment bond and not simply a performance bond is held to be required under the contract is that ambiguous contractual language is to be construed against the drafter of the language.

Duldulao v. St. Mary of Nazareth Hosp. Center, 115 Ill.2d 482, 106 Ill.Dec. 8, 505 N.E.2d 314 (1987). The contract was apparently drawn by the SHA and would therefore be construed against it. Under this rule, again, a payment bond would be required under the contract. Additionally, it should be noted that, the contract language notwithstanding, the Executive Director of SHA stated in his deposition that: "It is our policy there should be a performance and payment bond. So—I am not sure how to phrase this. Our directors just didn't follow their responsibilities and duties here in regard to that (getting a performance and payment bond from Bildoc)."

II.

Having established that a payment and performance bond was necessary under the contract, the Court must now decide whether Plaintiffs are third party beneficiaries under the contract and are, therefore, able to assert the bond provision. The Court determines that they are.

There is no question that had a payment bond been procured Plaintiffs would have been third party beneficiaries under it. The question arises here, however, whether Plaintiffs are third party beneficiaries under the contract provision to procure a bond where none has been procured. The answer in Illinois appears to be that they are.

The general rule with respect to third party beneficiary actions in Illinois is well settled. If the contract is entered into for a direct benefit of a third person, not party to the contract, such third person may sue for breach thereof. The test is whether the benefit to the third person is direct or incidental. If direct, he may sue on the contract; if incidental, there is no right of recovery. Carson Pirie Scott & Co. v. Parrett, 346 Ill. 252, 257, 178 N.E. 498 (1931).

... The *Avco* court [Avco Delta Corp. Canada Ltd. v. United States, 484 F.2d 692 (7th Cir.1973)] determined that the subcontractors were third party beneficiaries under a provision in a construction contract providing for retainage by the owner until the general contractor provided to the owner an affidavit stating that all the general contractor's bills were paid. It is only logical, then, that a subcontractor would also be a third party beneficiary of a contract provision to procure a payment bond since a payment bond is, by definition, for the protection of subcontractors. *See* Ill.Rev.Stat. ch. 29, ¶ 15 (1985). In fact, the Seventh Circuit stated in *Avco:*

> A materialman may be a third party beneficiary of a promise by a general contractor to obtain a surety bond for the prompt payment of all laborers and materialmen, and, in the context of a government contract, an unpaid materialman of a subcontractor was allowed to sue the general contractor who had failed to provide such a bond as he had covenanted in the construction contract.

Avco, 484 F.2d at 702 (*citing* Strong v. American Fence Constr. Co., 245 N.Y. 48, 156 N.E. 92, 94 (1927) (opinion by Cardozo, C.J.)). Thus, this

Court holds that Plaintiffs are third party beneficiaries under the SHA–Bildoc contract. . . .

Ergo, for the reasons given above, the Court allows Plaintiffs' motion for summary judgment. . . . Conversely, [SHA's] motion for summary judgment is denied.

LUCAS v. HAMM

Supreme Court of California, In Bank, 1961.
56 Cal.2d 583, 15 Cal.Rptr. 821, 364 P.2d 685.

GIBSON, CHIEF JUSTICE. Plaintiffs, who are some of the beneficiaries under the will of Eugene H. Emmick, deceased, brought this action for damages against defendant L.S. Hamm, an attorney at law who had been engaged by the testator to prepare the will. They have appealed from a judgment of dismissal entered after an order sustaining a general demurrer to the second amended complaint without leave to amend.

The allegations of the first and second causes of action are summarized as follows: Defendant agreed with the testator, for a consideration, to prepare a will and codicils thereto for him by which plaintiffs were to be designated as beneficiaries of a trust provided for by paragraph Eighth of the will and were to receive 15% of the residue as specified in that paragraph. Defendant, in violation of instructions and in breach of his contract, negligently prepared testamentary instruments containing phraseology that was invalid by virtue of section 715.2 and former sections 715.1 and 716 of the Civil Code relating to restraints on alienation and the rule against perpetuities. . . . After the death of the testator the instruments were admitted to probate. Subsequently defendant, as draftsman of the instruments and as counsel of record for the executors, advised plaintiffs in writing that the residual trust provision was invalid and that plaintiffs would be deprived of the entire amount to which they would have been entitled if the provision had been valid unless they made a settlement with the blood relatives of the testator under which plaintiffs would receive a lesser amount than that provided for them by the testator. As the direct and proximate result of the negligence of defendant and his breach of contract in preparing the testamentary instruments and the written advice referred to above, plaintiffs were compelled to enter into a settlement under which they received a share of the estate amounting to $75,000 less than the sum which they would have received pursuant to testamentary instruments drafted in accordance with the directions of the testator. . . .

It was held in Buckley v. Gray, 110 Cal. 339, 42 P. 900, 31 L.R.A. 862, that an attorney who made a mistake in drafting a will was not liable for negligence or breach of contract to a person named in the will who was deprived of benefits as a result of the error. The court stated that an attorney is liable to his client alone with respect to actions based on negligence in the conduct of his professional duties, and it was reasoned that there could be no recovery for mere negligence where there was no privity by contract or otherwise between the defendant and the person injured. 110 Cal. at pages 342–343, 42 P. 900. The court further concluded that there could be no recovery on the theory of a contract for the benefit of a third person, because the contract with the attorney was not expressly for the plaintiff's benefit and the testatrix only remotely intended the plaintiff to be benefited as a result of the contract. 110 Cal. at pages 346–347, 42 P. 900. For the reasons hereinafter stated the case is overruled. . . .

Neither do we agree with the holding in *Buckley* that beneficiaries damaged by an error in the drafting of a will cannot recover from the draftsman on the theory that they are third-party beneficiaries of the contract between him and the testator. Obviously the main purpose of a contract for the drafting of a will is to accomplish the future transfer of the estate of the testator to the beneficiaries named in the will, and therefore it seems improper to hold, as was done in *Buckley*, that the testator intended only "remotely" to benefit those persons. It is true that under a contract for the benefit of a third person performance is usually to be rendered directly to the beneficiary, but this is not necessarily the case. *(See Rest., Contracts,* § 133, cmt. d; 2 *Williston on Contracts* (3rd ed. 1959) 829.) For example, where a life insurance policy lapsed because a bank failed to perform its agreement to pay the premiums out of the insured's bank account, it was held that after the insured's death the beneficiaries could recover against the bank as third-party beneficiaries. [citation] Persons who had agreed to procure liability insurance for the protection of the promisees but did not do so were also held liable to injured persons who would have been covered by the insurance, the courts stating that all persons who might be injured were third-party beneficiaries of the contracts to procure insurance. [citations] Since, in a situation like those presented here and in the *Buckley* case, the main purpose of the testator in making his agreement with the attorney is to benefit the persons named in his will and this intent can be effectuated, in the event of a breach by the attorney, only by giving the beneficiaries a right of action, we should recognize, as a matter of policy, that they are entitled to recover as third-party beneficiaries. *See* 2 *Williston on Contracts* (3rd ed. 1959) pp. 843–844; 4 *Corbin on Contracts* (1951) pp. 8, 20.

Section 1559 of the Civil Code, which provides for enforcement by a third person of a contract made "expressly" for his benefit, does not preclude this result. The effect of the section is to exclude enforcement by persons who are only incidentally or remotely benefited. [citations] As we have seen, a contract for the drafting of a will unmistakably shows the intent of the testator to benefit the persons to be named in the will, and the attorney must necessarily understand this.

Defendant relies on language in Smith v. Anglo–California Trust Co., 205 Cal. 496, 502, 271 P. 898, and Fruitvale Canning Co. v. Cotton, 115 Cal.App.2d 622, 625, 252 P.2d 953, that to permit a third person to bring an action on a contract there must be "an intent clearly manifested by the promisor" to secure some benefit to the third person. This language, which was not necessary to the decision in either of the cases, is unfortunate. Insofar as intent to benefit a third person is important in determining his right to bring an action under a contract, it is sufficient that the promisor must have understood that the promisee had such intent. (*Cf. Rest., Contracts*, § 133, subds. 1(a) and 1(b); 4 *Corbin on Contracts* (1951) pp. 16–18; 2 *Williston on Contracts* (3rd ed. 1959) pp. 836–839.) No specific manifestation by the promisor of an intent to benefit the third person is required. The language relied on by defendant is disapproved to the extent that it is inconsistent with these views.

We conclude that intended beneficiaries of a will who lose their testamentary rights because of failure of the attorney who drew the will to properly fulfill his obligations under his contract with the testator may recover as third-party beneficiaries.

However, an attorney is not liable either to his client or to a beneficiary under a will for errors of the kind alleged in the first and second causes of action.

The general rule with respect to the liability of an attorney for failure to properly perform his duties to his client is that the attorney, by accepting employment to give legal advice or to render other legal services, impliedly agrees to use such skill, prudence, and diligence as lawyers of ordinary skill and capacity commonly possess and exercise in the performance of the tasks which they undertake. [citations] The attorney is not liable for every mistake he may make in his practice; he is not, in the absence of an express agreement, an insurer of the soundness of his opinions or of the validity of an instrument that he is engaged to draft; and he is not liable for being in error as to a question of law on which reasonable doubt may be entertained by well-informed lawyers. These principles are equally applicable whether the plaintiff's claim is based on tort or breach of contract.

The complaint, as we have seen, alleges that defendant drafted the will in such a manner that the trust was invalid because it violated the rules relating to perpetuities and restraints on alienation. These closely akin subjects have long perplexed the courts and the bar. Professor Gray, a leading authority in the field, stated:

> There is something in the subject which seems to facilitate error. Perhaps it is because the mode of reasoning is unlike that with which lawyers are most familiar. ... A long list might be formed of the demonstrable blunders with regard to its questions made by eminent men, blunders which they themselves have been sometimes the first to acknowledge; and there are few lawyers of any practice in drawing wills and settlements who have not at some time either fallen into the net which the Rule spreads for the unwary, or at least shuddered to think how narrowly they have escaped it.

Gray, *The Rule Against Perpetuities* (4th ed. 1942) p. xi; *see also* Leach, *Perpetuities Legislation* (1954) 67 Harv.L.Rev. 1349 (describing the rule as a "technicality-ridden legal nightmare" and a "dangerous instrumentality in the hands of most members of the bar''). Of the California law on perpetuities and restraints it has been said that few, if any, areas of the law have been fraught with more confusion or concealed more traps for the unwary draftsman; that members of the bar, probate courts, and title insurance companies make errors in these matters; that the code provisions adopted in 1872 created a situation worse than if the matter had been left to the common law, and that the legislation adopted in 1951 (under which the will involved here was drawn), despite the best of intentions, added further complexities. (*See* 38 Cal.Jur.2d 443; Coil, *Perpetuities and Restraints; A Needed Reform* (1955) 30 State Bar J. 87, 88–90.)

In view of the state of the law relating to perpetuities and restraints on alienation and the nature of the error, if any, assertedly made by defendant in preparing the instrument, it would not be proper to hold that defendant failed to use such skill, prudence, and diligence as lawyers of ordinary skill and capacity commonly exercise. . . .

The judgment is affirmed. . . .

PROBLEMS

1.   A Corp. was indebted to a number of creditors. A asked B for a loan with which to pay its debts. B made a loan commitment but failed to make the loan. Are the creditors of A third party beneficiaries of the arrangement between A and B?

2.   A hired P as an employee contingent on passing a drug test administered by D, a drug testing company hired by A to perform drug testing services and report the results to A. Two urinalyses of P tested positive for opiates. P claimed the results must have been based on her daily consumption of a poppy seed muffin, but D advised A that the positive results were too high to be attributable to that source. As a result, P lost her job. P brought suit against D claiming the tests were improperly administered. Does P have a cause of action for breach of contract against D?

3.   D contracted with the City of Duluth to do certain work, including blasting, in connection with the construction of a sewer. The contract provided that the D would "be liable for any damages done to the work or other structure or public or private property and injuries sustained by persons" in the operation. P's property, located some 100 yards outside the City's boundaries, was damaged by blasting. May P recover in a contract action against D?

4.   The New York State Thruway Authority entered into an agreement with defendant under which defendant was granted the exclusive franchise for automobile servicing along the Thruway. Plaintiff's car became disabled due to a flat tire. Despite many calls for assistance, the defendant did not respond. After three hours, plaintiff, a middle aged accountant who was unaccustomed to physical exertion, attempted to change the tire and died of a heart attack.

The contract between the defendant and the Authority expressly provided that defendant "agrees that it will have sufficient roadside automotive services vehicles, equipment and personnel to provide roadside automotive services to disabled vehicles within a maximum of thirty (30) minutes from the time a call is assigned to service vehicle." Is plaintiff an intended beneficiary?

5. PepsiCo entered into agreements with numerous franchisees. Each contract provides the franchisee with an exclusive territory in which to bottle and distribute Pepsi–Cola and forbids the franchisee from distributing Pepsi–Cola into the territory of any other franchisee. Plaintiff has the franchise for described areas in Kansas and Missouri. Defendant has a neighboring franchise. Plaintiff alleges that Defendant has repeatedly made large sales to buyers in Plaintiff's territory in breach of Defendant's contract with PepsiCo. Has Plaintiff stated a cause of action?

6. Customer Co. entered into a contract to purchase Mfg. Co.'s entire output for the next two years. Soon afterwards, a union local entered into a two-year contract with Mfg. Co. providing that the union would not call a strike for the two-year term of the union contract. A strike was called by the union in violation of this promise. Does Customer Co. have a cause of action against the union if the strike caused Mfg. Co.'s output to decrease drastically?

7. Landlord contracted with Macy's to construct a large shopping center on Landlord's land and Macy's agreed to lease 60% of the shopping center. Landlord then contracts with Contractor to construct the center. Contractor defaults. Does Macy's have a cause of action versus Contractor? Versus Landlord?

8. In a case such as *Lucas v. Hamm*, does the plaintiff have a cause of action in tort as well as in contract?

9. In 1989, Apex Cars, Ltd., a sports car dealer, entered into a contract with Distributor, making Apex a dealer in Maserati cars. Manufacturer, an Italian corporation, was not a party to the contract but was designated as a third party beneficiary so that it could monitor and sue for any misuse of the Maserati trademark. In 1990, Manufacturer ceased to make cars for the U.S. market as its cars failed to meet U.S. emission standards. Apex continued to hold itself out as a Maserati dealer and it was furnished with spare parts. After a ten-year gap, Manufacturer resumed making cars for the U.S. market, set up a new dealership network excluding Apex, and told Apex to cease holding itself out as a Maserati dealer. Distributor no longer exists and Apex brings an action against Manufacturer for breach of the 1989 contract. Manufacturer defends on the ground that it is not in privity with Apex. What result?

SECTION 2. DEFENSES, VESTING AND RELATIVE RIGHTS OF THE PARTIES

(Calamari & Perillo on Contracts §§ 17.10—17.14)

ERICKSON v. GRANDE RONDE LUMBER CO.
Supreme Court of Oregon, 1939.
162 Or. 556, 94 P.2d 139.

ROSSMAN, JUSTICE. [Defendants petition for rehearing of the case reported at 92 P.2d 170, holding both defendants liable to plaintiff Erickson. In connection with a purchase of the assets of Grand Ronde, Stoddard Company had become liable upon assuming its debts, including that owed to plaintiff for accounting services. Ed.] . . .

From the offer made by the Stoddard Company to and accepted by the Grande Ronde Company which culminated in the sale by the Grande Ronde of all of its assets to the Stoddard Company, we quote:

> The Stoddard Lumber Company does hereby offer to purchase all of your property and assets of every nature and description for thirty-six hundred (3600) shares of the capital stock of this company.

> It is understood that in addition to the stock to be delivered to you that we are to assume all of the indebtedness of the Grande Ronde Lumber Company except liability for income tax incurred or accrued prior to January 1st, 1929. . . .

. . . [Defendants] argue that after the Stoddard Company had agreed to pay the Grande Ronde Company's debts, the plaintiff, as a creditor of the Grande Ronde Company, was not entitled to judgment against both of these companies. They insist that he was entitled to a remedy against only one of them, and that it was incumbent upon him to make an election. The defendants argue: "It may even be that so far as the commencement of the action was concerned that he had a right to pursue his remedy against both, but manifestly when the time came for the case to be decided he was not entitled to judgment against both." They argue that since he took judgment against the Grande Ronde Company he made his election and, therefore, cannot have relief against the Stoddard Company. In support of these contentions, the defendants cite Wood v. Moriarty, 15 R.I. 518, 9 A. 427 [and] Bohanan v. Pope, 42 Me. 93.

. . . [These] decisions . . . support the [defendants'] position, but both of them regarded the new promise as the consummation of a novation; and, of course, a novation is the substitution of a new right for an existing obligation. *Williston on Contracts*, Rev.Ed., § 393, referring to these two decisions, among others, states: "Courts which hold that the original contract is in effect an offer of novation to the creditor naturally hold that if the creditor accepts the promisor as his debtor he releases the original debtor, and on the other hand, if he elects to sue the original debtor he thereby rejects the proffered novation and cannot afterwards sue the new promisor." From § 353 of the same treatise, we quote: "A few states, however, have erroneously resorted to an implied novation theory for enforcement of the creditor beneficiary type of third party contract." Among the decisions which he states "have erroneously resorted to an implied novation theory" he cites the *Bohanan* and *Wood* decisions. In § 393, after the language quoted above, Williston continues:

> The weight of authority, however, in the jurisdictions which allow a creditor beneficiary a direct right against the promisor supports the conclusion that the creditor has rights against both the promisor and the promisee, not merely a choice of rights; being entitled, of course, to but a single satisfaction. And in some states he is allowed to join both as defendants in the same action. He ought to be compelled to do so.

From *Restatement of the Law, Contracts*, § 141, we quote:

> (1) A creditor beneficiary who has an enforceable claim against the promisee can get judgment against either the promisee or the promisor or against each of them on their respective duties to him. Satisfaction in while or in part of either of these duties, or of judgments thereon, satisfies to that extent the other duty or judgment.

The principle embraced in the *Restatement* represents the law of this state. From the carefully prepared annotations to § 141, subd. 1, of the *Restatement of the Law of Contracts* prepared by Professor Charles G. Howard (12 Oregon Law Review 283), we quote: "Oregon cases are in accord with this section and hold uniformly that there can be but one satisfaction, though both promisor and promisee are liable. [citations]" ... We conclude that the plaintiff was entitled to maintain this action against the promisor (the Stoddard Company) as well as against his original debtor (the Grande Ronde Company). He was entitled to judgment against both; however, to only one complete satisfaction.

[Defendants also argue that they may not both be sued in the same action because they are principal and surety.] In Feldman v. McGuire, [34 Or. 309, 55 P. 872, 873 (1899)] ... Mr. Chief Justice Wolverton, in disposing of a [similar] contention ..., stated:

> ... [T]he contract is not one of suretyship, but an original undertaking between the debtor and the promisor, based upon a sufficient consideration, which operates to the benefit of the creditor. The party promising has for his object some benefit or advantage accruing to himself, and on that consideration makes the promise; and this, it is said, distinguishes the transaction as an original undertaking. Furthermore, the promise is not to the creditor, but to the debtor, and is to pay such debtor the amount due him, or the consideration agreed upon, by paying or answering for it to his creditor; and the law implies the contract between the promisor and the creditor because it is incidentally for his benefit, and therefore gives him the right of action.

We are satisfied that this contention is without merit.

... The petition for a rehearing is denied. ...

DETROIT BANK AND TRUST CO. v. CHICAGO
FLAME HARDENING CO.

United States District Court, N.D. Indiana, 1982.
541 F.Supp. 1278.

LEE, DISTRICT JUDGE. . . .

FINDINGS OF FACT

. . . In 1956, Chicago Flame Hardening Company (Chicago Flame), was founded in East Chicago, Indiana by Marvin R. Scott, a Michigan domiciliary, and Gainor D. Scott and John R. Keeler, Indiana domiciliaries. . . .

Marvin R. Scott, although continuing to reside in Michigan, visited the new firm periodically and acted as its President while utilizing his expertise in the flame hardening industry to establish the East Chicago, Indiana operation as an investment and a means of livelihood for his brother, Gainor D. Scott, and brother-in-law, John R. Keeler.

On July 29, 1964, Marvin R. Scott, Gainor D. Scott and John R. Keeler, the owners of the entire issue of Chicago Flame's capital stock, unanimously agreed by corporate resolution that upon the death of these specifically named shareholders (M.R. Scott, G.D. Scott and J.D.[sic] Keeler), the corporation would pay to his wife, if then living, commencing with the date of her husband's death, a graduated monthly stipend over a fifteen (15) year period totaling $150,300 to terminate in the event of her death if prior to the expiration of the payment period.[3] The signatories to this 1964 resolution did not expressly reserve the right to alter and/or amend. . . .

Within a reasonable time following the adoption of this resolution Marvin R. Scott's wife, Roxanne, became aware that this document's beneficial terms were potentially available to her in the future. She then "forgot the whole thing."

The provisions of the 1964 widow's resolution were initially implemented on July 12, 1967 when Marjorie Scott Keeler signed the requisite

---

3. That resolution which specifically avoided naming the current wives of the signatories provides in pertinent part:

> That immediately following the death of each stockholder, his wife, if then living, will be asked to sign a statement agreeing to make herself available at all reasonable times to said corporation as a consultant for same and further agreeing to make available to said corporation any and all knowledge as to the business thereof as revealed to her by her husband during his lifetime including any and all technical know-how, and further agreeing that she will not for a 15 year period following the death of her husband compete with said corporation in any way, directly or indirectly, nor knowingly permit her husband's name, knowledge or reputation to be used in competition with the corporation during said period, in exchange for which undertakings, it is agreed that she shall, commencing with the date of her husband's death be paid a monthly salary by the corporation of $1,250 for the first five year period after her husband's death, a monthly salary of $835 for the second five year period following her husband's death, and a monthly salary of $420 for the third five year period following her husband's death, it being understood and agreed, however, that the aforesaid salary arrangement will take effect only in case said deceased stockholder is survived by his wife and that same will forthwith terminate in the event of her death at anytime prior to the expiration of the aforesaid 15 year period.

statement agreeing to abide by the resolution's consideration requirements, following the July 8, 1967 death of her husband, John R. Keeler. Marjorie Scott Keeler thereinafter continually received a monthly stipend pursuant to the express terms of this agreement, except for an eighteen (18) month period during 1971 and 1972 when she voluntarily consented to a postponement in recognition of Chicago Flame's deteriorating financial posture.

Marvin R. Scott's wife, Roxanne, was fully and continuously aware that Marjorie Scott Keeler (her sister-in-law) was receiving the benefits provided by the 1964 resolution for surviving spouses of the original signatories.

On February 15, 1971 Marvin R. Scott participated in and approved the adoption of a second corporate resolution along with the other owners of the entire issue of Chicago Flame's capital stock, Gainor D. Scott and Marjorie Scott Keeler. This subsequent agreement was executed to rescind the right of Marvin R. Scott's surviving spouse to receive graduated monthly payments as formerly provided in the 1964 resolution. Marvin R. Scott's motivation for entering into this second resolution was to sustain the future financial integrity of Chicago Flame.

Following a lengthy period of convalescence, Marvin R. Scott died on October 31, 1971 leaving plaintiff's current ward, Roxanne Scott, as his surviving spouse.

Although there remains conflicting testimony, it is the determination of the Court that, while Mrs. Roxanne Scott may not have actually seen the February 15, 1971 rescission document prior to the instigation of this suit, she became aware of her husband's relinquishment of the widow's benefits during the interim following his death and the filing of this suit. . . .

APPLICATION OF LAW

Plaintiff initiated this litigation on September 19, 1977 by way of a complaint which seeks to enforce the terms of the 1964 widow's resolution for the benefit of its ward, Mrs. Roxanne Scott. Plaintiff asserts its contentions on the basis of (1) the failure to expressly reserve the right to rescind, (2) a presumption of acceptance for a donee beneficiary, (3) Roxanne Scott's medical condition precluding the earlier assertion of her rights as a means of acceptance, and (4) that this agreement vested a right in its ward which could not be denied by the 1971 rescission. . . .

The old *Restatement* rule provided that the promisor and promisee could make no change in the promise made to a donee beneficiary unless such a power is reserved.[9] *Restatement of Contracts* § 142 at 168 (1932). Nor could a change be made by the promisor and promisee in their

---

9. This position promulgated by the initial *Restatement* was not followed by the vast majority of states even at the time of its adoption. The express reservation requirement was thereafter abandoned in tentative drafts and the final adopted version of the *Restatement (Second)*; *see* 2 Williston, *Contracts* §§ 396–97 (3d Ed.1959).

promise to a creditor beneficiary if he has changed his position in reliance on that promise. *Id.; see* Page, *The Power of Contracting Parties to Alter a Contract for Rendering Performance to a Third Person,* 12 Wis.L.Rev. 141, 149–50 (1937). Evolutionary changes in the law, however, have transformed the aforementioned position of the original *Restatement.* The *Second Restatement of Contracts* as adopted and promulgated, eliminates this distinction between a donee and creditor beneficiary and recognizes that modification on the part of the promisor and promisee is ineffective only if the agreement so provides, unless the third party beneficiary has changed his position in reliance on the promise or has accepted, adopted or acted upon it. *Restatement (Second) of Contracts* § [311] (1979). . . .

Indiana specifically reaffirmed its adoption of this majority view as later expressed in the *Second Restatement.* . . .

In the case of contracts entered into for the benefit of a third party,[11] Indiana follows the rule found in most jurisdictions. That is, the parties to a third party beneficiary contract may rescind, vary or abrogate the contract as they see fit, without the approval of the third party, at any time before the contract is accepted, adopted or acted upon by a third party beneficiary. [*In Re* Estate of] Fanning, [263 Ind.414,] 333 N.E.2d [80,] 84. A rescission prior to the required change in position by a third party deprives that third party of any rights under or because of the contract. *Id.*

In this case the 1964 agreement was adopted as a corporate resolution by Chicago Flame Hardening, Inc. All of the officers and shareholders of the corporation approving the initial agreement. On February 15, 1971 the officers and shareholders mutually agreed to rescind the July 29, 1964 resolution. Recognizing the majority view followed by Indiana, the rescission of the prior agreement is valid without a specific reservation of the power to rescind so long as the third-party beneficiary, Mrs. Roxanne Scott, had not accepted, adopted or acted upon the original widow's resolution. Therefore, an express reservation of the right to rescind is not required to abrogate the third party beneficiary agreement.

Plaintiff next contends that since Mrs. Roxanne Scott had knowledge of the original 1964 resolution, her acceptance of this beneficial agreement must be presumed. In support of this position plaintiff offers three vintage cases which recognize a presumption of acceptance.

These cases are clearly distinguishable from the present cause. The primary and controlling distinction is that while acceptance was presumed in cases cited by plaintiff, the intended beneficiaries were infants at the time of the transaction. A presumption is necessary in such instances to

---

11. As neither the general common law nor related statutes from other jurisdictions distinguish between various types of beneficiaries, between release and rescission, between unilateral and bilateral, or between partially executed and wholly executory contracts, this Court will not. *See* 2 Williston, *Contracts,* §§ 396–398 (3d Ed.1959); *see also* Holbrook v. Pitt, 643 F.2d 1261, 1271 (7th Cir.1981) (while addressing federal common law the three classes of beneficiaries (donee, creditor, and incidental) were disdained in favor of the *Second Restatement's* two divisions (intended and incidental) which permitted review of intent without further distinction.)

protect the interests of minor beneficiaries. Mrs. Scott, however, was an adult at the time of the 1964 widow's resolution, completely able to assert her own rights, and as such is not afforded the same protection. Moreover, the same authority submitted by plaintiff in support of a presumption of acceptance provides *a fortiori* a strong argument for the opposite proposition—a lack of such protection for a competent adult through negative implication. . . .

Plaintiff's next focus theorizes that "but for" Roxanne Scott's declining health, she would have instituted this litigation at an earlier date. Plaintiff attempts thereby to utilize its ward's acknowledged mental and physical difficulties as a vehicle to excuse not only the failure to sue before rescission, but also to demonstrate why prompt commencement of this action to preserve her benefits was prevented. The net effect of this proposition is to attempt to transform this 1977 litigation into a belated substitute for acceptance prior to rescission.

Although the Court recognizes that the filing of a suit by a third party beneficiary may be considered as acceptance by that individual, *Zimmerman v. Zehender*, 164 Ind. 466, 73 N.E. 920 (1905), the Court may not consider Mrs. Scott's health as dispositive of the issue before it. Perhaps equity might demand some presumption of acceptance had Mrs. Scott been totally incapacitated prior to rescission; however, plaintiff's own evidence makes it clear that the February 15, 1971 rescission took place before Mrs. Scott's inhibiting physical and mental decline occurred and the appointment of guardians to represent her interests. . . .

The analysis above establishes that acceptance may not be presumed by this Court and that this contract for the benefit of a third party is enforceable only if the third party beneficiary has accepted, adopted or acted upon it prior to rescission. Because prior decisions fail to provide an adequate definition, the Court must examine the somewhat nebulous term "acceptance" in an effort to identify if some form of assent took place on the part of Mrs. Roxanne Scott if it is to conclude that the 1971 rescission was ineffective and that her derivative rights were preserved.

Acceptance may be an overt act, or the adoption of a benefit which is a question of intent and thereby also a factual determination. *See Corbin, supra,* §§ 782–793; Jones, *Legal Protection of Third Party Beneficiaries: On Opening Courthouse Doors,* 46 Cinn.L.Rev. 313 (1977). Nevertheless, even in instances such as this where plaintiff has provided no specific evidence of an overt act or of a change in position, it must still be remembered that "the power of promisor and promisee to vary the promisor's duty to an intended beneficiary is terminated when the beneficiary manifests assent to the promise in a manner invited by the promisor or promisee." *Restatement (Second) on Contracts, supra,* § 311 at cmt. (h). This rule utilizes an analogy to the law of offer and acceptance by recognizing that a third party beneficiary may well rely in ways difficult or impossible to prove. *Id.*

Fortunately for this Court, the narrow question currently before it does not present this circumstance characterized by an impossibility of proof. The converse is true as the Court's determination of the factual question regarding Roxanne Scott's intent to accept the benefits afforded by the 1964 resolution was answered in the negative by her own sworn testimony. While facing cross-examination, Mrs. Scott was specifically asked whether she made any long range plans or depended upon the 1964 widow's resolution. Her answer was, "No, I forgot the whole thing." In addition to this testimonial controversion, the Court also failed to discern any other corroborative evidence which might sustain plaintiff's claim of acceptance or change in position in reliance on that resolution. *See generally* Note, *The Requirements of Promissory Estoppel as Applied to Third Party Beneficiaries,* 30 U. Pitt. L. Rev. 174 (1968). Furthermore, the Court's position regarding the failure to establish adoptive intent is not gleaned from this single negatory response, but is supported by a detailed review of the entire record. It is therefore the conclusion of the Court that Roxanne Scott failed to accept, adopt or act upon the 1964 resolution prior to the 1971 rescission. Consequently, the Court must hold that Mrs. Scott's failure to act or rely upon the original agreement extinguished any benefits which might have accrued to her from the 1964 agreement. ...

It is hereby ordered that Judgment be entered for the defendant, Chicago Flame Hardening Company, Inc., consistent with this Memorandum Decision and the findings and conclusions herein.

ROUSE v. UNITED STATES

United States Court of Appeals, District of Columbia Circuit, 1954.
215 F.2d 872, 94 U.S.App.D.C. 386.

EDGERTON, CIRCUIT JUDGE. Bessie Winston gave Associated Contractors, Inc., her promissory note for $1,008.37, payable in monthly installments of $28.01, for a heating plant in her house. The Federal Housing Administration guaranteed the note and the payee endorsed it for value to the lending bank, the Union Trust Company.

Winston sold the house to Rouse. In the contract of sale Rouse agreed to assume debts secured by deeds of trust and also "to assume payment of $850 for heating plant payable $28 per Mo." Nothing was said about the note.

Winston defaulted on her note. The United States paid the bank, took an assignment of the note, demanded payment from Rouse, and sued him for $850 and interest.

Rouse alleged as defenses (1) that Winston fraudulently misrepresented the condition of the heating plant and (2) that Associated Contractors did not install it satisfactorily. The District Court struck these defenses and granted summary judgment for the plaintiff. The defendant Rouse appeals.

Rouse ... is not liable to the United States at all unless his contract with Winston makes him so. The contract says the parties to it are not "bound by any terms, conditions, statements, warranties or representations, oral or written" not contained in it. But this means only that the written contract contains the entire agreement. It does not mean that fraud cannot be set up as a defense to a suit on the contract.[1] Rouse's promise to "assume payment of $850 for heating plant" made him liable to Associated Contractors, Inc., only if and so far as it made him liable to Winston; one who promises to make a payment to the promisee's creditor can assert against the creditor any defense that the promisor could assert against the promisee. Accordingly Rouse, if he had been sued by the corporation, would have been entitled to show fraud on the part of Winston. He is equally entitled to do so in this suit by an assignee of the corporation's claim. It follows that the court erred in striking the first defense. We do not consider whether Winston's alleged fraud, if shown, would be a complete or only a partial defense to this suit, since that question has not arisen and may not arise.

We think the court was right in striking the second defense.

If the promisor's agreement is to be interpreted as a promise to discharge whatever liability the promisee is under, the promisor must certainly be allowed to show that the promisee was under no enforceable liability. . . . On the other hand, if the promise means that the promisor agrees to pay a sum of money to A, to whom the promisee says he is indebted, it is immaterial whether the promisee is actually indebted to that amount or at all. . . . Where the promise is to pay a specific debt . . . this interpretation will generally be the true one.[3]

The judgment is reversed and the cause remanded with instructions to reinstate the first defense.

Reversed and remanded.

PROBLEMS

10. M, mortgagee, brings an action under the standard mortgagee clause of a fire insurance policy which provides that the coverage of the mortgagee "shall not be invalidated by any act or neglect of the mortgagor or owner." Defendant, insurer, seeks to set up as a defense to the action the fact that the owner who had procured the insurance was guilty of a breach of warranty. May the defense be raised?

11. Employer promised Employee to pay certain sums to Employee's minor son if Employee died before the son reached the age of 21. Later, Employer and Employee modified the agreement so that payments were to be made to Employee's wife rather than his son. What are the rights of the parties?

12. Defendant promised Plaintiff that if Plaintiff would organize a freight-forwarding corporation and work in the business, Defendant would

---

1. 3 Williston, *Contracts* § 811A (Rev.Ed.1936).

3. 2 *id.* § 399.

lend the corporation $60,000 for working capital. Although Plaintiff organized such a corporation, and caused it to engage in the freight-forwarding business, Defendant failed to provide the promised working capital. As a result the business failed and Plaintiff lost his initial investment and also lost his job. Plaintiff sues. Defendant claims that only the corporation would have a cause of action on these allegations. What result?

CHAPTER 12

ASSIGNMENT AND DELEGATION

■ ■ ■

SECTION 1. THE NATURE AND EFFECT OF AN ASSIGNMENT

(Calamari & Perillo on Contracts §§ 18.1—18.9, 18.17—18.18, 18.23)

HERZOG v. IRACE

Supreme Judicial Court of Maine, 1991.
594 A.2d 1106.

BRODY, JUSTICE. Anthony Irace and Donald Lowry appeal from an order entered by the Superior Court (Cumberland County, *Cole, J.*) affirming a District Court (Portland, *Goranites, J.*) judgment in favor of Dr. John P. Herzog in an action for breach of an assignment to Dr. Herzog of personal injury settlement proceeds[1] collected by Irace and Lowry, both attorneys, on behalf of their client, Gary G. Jones. On appeal, Irace and Lowry contend that the District Court erred in finding that the assignment was valid and enforceable against them. They also argue that enforcement of the assignment interferes with their ethical obligations toward their client. Finding no error, we affirm.

The facts of this case are not disputed. Gary Jones was injured in a motorcycle accident and retained Irace and Lowry to represent him in a personal injury action. Soon thereafter, Jones dislocated his shoulder, twice, in incidents unrelated to the motorcycle accident. Dr. Herzog examined Jones's shoulder and concluded that he needed surgery. At the time, however, Jones was unable to pay for the surgery and in consideration for the performance of the surgery by the doctor, he signed a letter dated June 14, 1988, written on Dr. Herzog's letterhead stating:

I, Gary Jones, request that payment be made directly from settlement of a claim currently pending for an unrelated incident, to John

---

1. This case involves the assignment of proceeds from a personal injury action, not an assignment of the cause of action itself.

680

Herzog, D.O., for treatment of a shoulder injury which occurred at a different time.

Dr. Herzog notified Irace and Lowry that Jones had signed an "assignment of benefits" from the motorcycle personal injury action to cover the cost of surgery on his shoulder and was informed by an employee of Irace and Lowry that the assignment was sufficient to allow the firm to pay Dr. Herzog's bills at the conclusion of the case. Dr. Herzog performed the surgery and continued to treat Jones for approximately one year.

In May, 1989, Jones received a $20,000 settlement in the motorcycle personal injury action. He instructed Irace and Lowry not to disburse any funds to Dr. Herzog indicating that he would make the payments himself. Irace and Lowry informed Dr. Herzog that Jones had revoked his permission to have the bill paid by them directly and indicated that they would follow Jones's directions. Irace and Lowry issued a check to Jones for $10,027 and disbursed the remaining funds to Jones's other creditors. Jones did send a check to Dr. Herzog but the check was returned by the bank for insufficient funds and Dr. Herzog was never paid.

Dr. Herzog filed a complaint in District Court against Irace and Lowry seeking to enforce the June 14, 1988 "assignment of benefits." The matter was tried before the court on the basis of a joint stipulation of facts. The court entered a judgment in favor of Dr. Herzog finding that the June 14, 1988 letter constituted a valid assignment of the settlement proceeds enforceable against Irace and Lowry. Following an unsuccessful appeal to the Superior Court, Irace and Lowry appealed to this court. Because the Superior Court acted as an intermediate appellate court, we review the District Court's decision directly. . . .

Validity of Assignment

An assignment is an act or manifestation by the owner of a right (the assignor) indicating his intent to transfer that right to another person (the assignee). *See* Shiro v. Drew, 174 F.Supp. 495, 497 (D.Me.1959). For an assignment to be valid and enforceable against the assignor's [debtor] (the obligor), the assignor must make clear his intent to relinquish the right to the assignee and must not retain any control over the right assigned or any power of revocation. *Id.* The assignment takes effect through the actions of the assignor and assignee and the obligor need not accept the assignment to render it valid. Palmer v. Palmer, 112 Me. 149, 153, 91 A. 281, 282 (1914). Once the obligor has notice of the assignment, the fund is "from that time forward impressed with a trust; it is . . . impounded in the (obligor's) hands, and must be held by him not for the original creditor, the assignor, but for the substituted creditor, the assignee." *Id.* at 152, 91 A. 281. After receiving notice of the assignment, the obligor cannot lawfully pay the amount assigned either to the assignor or to his other creditors and if the obligor does make such a payment, he does so at his peril because the assignee may enforce his rights against the obligor directly. *Id.* at 153, 91 A. 281.

... In Maine, the transfer of a future right to *proceeds* from pending litigation has been recognized as a valid and enforceable equitable assignment. McLellan v. Walker, 26 Me. 114, 117–18 (1846). An equitable assignment need not transfer the entire future right but rather may be a partial assignment of that right. Palmer, 112 Me. at 152, 91 A. 281. We reaffirm these well established principles.

... Irace and Lowry contend that Jones's June 14, 1988 letter is invalid and unenforceable as an assignment because it fails to manifest Jones's intent to permanently relinquish all control over the assigned funds and does nothing more than request payment from a specific fund. We disagree. The June 14, 1988 letter gives no indication that Jones attempted to retain any control over the funds he assigned to Dr. Herzog. Taken in context, the use of the word "request" did not give the court reason to question Jones's intent to complete the assignment and, although no specific amount was stated, the parties do not dispute that the services provided by Dr. Herzog and the amounts that he charged for those services were reasonable and necessary to the treatment of the shoulder injury referred to in the June 14 letter. Irace and Lowry had adequate funds to satisfy all of Jones's creditors, including Dr. Herzog, with funds left over for disbursement to Jones himself. ... Given that Irace and Lowry do not dispute that they had ample notice of the assignment, the court's finding on the validity of the assignment is fully supported by the evidence and will not be disturbed on appeal.

Ethical Obligations

Next, Irace and Lowry contend that the assignment, if enforceable against them, would interfere with their ethical obligation to honor their client's instruction in disbursing funds. Again, we disagree.

... The [Maine] Bar Rules ... require that an attorney "promptly pay or deliver to the client, as requested by the client, the funds, securities, or other properties in the possession of the lawyer which the client is entitled to receive." M.Bar R. 3.6(f)(2)(iv). The rules say nothing, however, about a client's power to assign his right to proceeds from a pending lawsuit to third parties. Because the client has the power to assign his right to funds held by his attorney, McLellan v. Walker, 26 Me. at 117–18, it follows that a valid assignment must be honored by the attorney in disbursing the funds on the client's behalf. The assignment does not create a conflict under Rule 3.6(f)(2)(iv) because the client is not entitled to receive funds once he has assigned them to a third party. ... Irace and Lowry were under no ethical obligation, and the record gives no indication that they were under a contractual obligation, to honor their client's instruction to disregard a valid assignment. The District Court correctly concluded that the assignment is valid and enforceable against Irace and Lowry.

The entry is: Judgment affirmed. ...

PROBLEMS

1. Mr. Cobb owned a wholesale meat business. Although he had accounts receivable which were payable weekly or, in some cases, monthly, he was short of cash. He entered into a written agreement with Mrs. Baxter in which he stated that he had "sold" certain described accounts to Mrs. Baxter at a specified discount. Does the writing amount to an assignment?

2. C had some money which was being held for him by the Continental Escrow Company. When C hired A, an attorney, C told A that, "If I get this money, I will pay you from this fund." Does this amount to an assignment?

3. D owes C $1,000. C writes to D, "Please pay the balance due me to A." Does this amount to an assignment?

SECTION 2. ARE THE RIGHTS ASSIGNABLE AND PERFORMANCES DELEGABLE?

(a) GENERAL PRINCIPLES

*(Calamari & Perillo on Contracts §§ 18.10—
18.15, 18.28—18.29, 18.31—18.32)*

MACKE CO. v. PIZZA OF GAITHERSBURG, INC.

Court of Appeals of Maryland, 1970.
259 Md. 479, 270 A.2d 645.

SINGLEY, JUDGE. The appellees and defendants below, Pizza of Gaithersburg, Inc.; Pizzeria, Inc.; The Pizza Pie Corp., Inc. and Pizza Oven, Inc., four corporations under the common ownership of Sidney Ansell, Thomas S. Sherwood and Eugene Early and the same individuals as partners or proprietors (the Pizza Shops) operated at six locations in Montgomery and Prince George's Counties. The appellees had arranged to have installed in each of their locations cold drink vending machines owned by Virginia Coffee Service, Inc., and on 30 December 1966, this arrangement was formalized at five of the locations, by contracts for terms of one year, automatically renewable for a like term in the absence of 30 days' written notice. A similar contract for the sixth location, operated by Pizza of Gaithersburg, Inc., was entered into on 25 July 1967.

On 30 December 1967, Virginia's assets were purchased by The Macke Company (Macke) and the six contracts were assigned to Macke by Virginia. In January, 1968, the Pizza Shops attempted to terminate the five contracts having the December anniversary date, and in February, the contract which had the July anniversary date.

Macke brought suit in the Circuit Court for Montgomery County against each of the Pizza Shops for damages for breach of contract. From judgments for the defendants, Macke has appealed.

The lower court based the result which it reached on two grounds: first, that the Pizza Shops, when they contracted with Virginia, relied on its skill, judgment and reputation, which made impossible a delegation of Virginia's duties to Macke. . . .

In the absence of a contrary provision—and there was none here—rights and duties under an executory bilateral contract may be assigned and delegated, subject to the exception that duties under a contract to provide personal services may never be delegated, nor rights be assigned under a contract where *delectus personae* was an ingredient of the bargain. 4 *Corbin on Contracts* § 865 (1951) at 434. Crane Ice Cream Co. v. Terminal Freezing & Heating Co., 147 Md. 588, 128 A. 280 (1925) held that the right of an individual to purchase ice under a contract which by its terms reflected a knowledge of the individual's needs and reliance on his credit and responsibility could not be assigned to the corporation which purchased his business. In Eastern Advertising Co. v. McGaw & Co., 89 Md. 72, 42 A. 923 (1899), our predecessors held that an advertising agency could not delegate its duties under a contract which had been entered into by an advertiser who had relied on the agency's skill, judgment and taste. . . .

We cannot regard the agreements as contracts for personal services. They were either a license or concession granted Virginia by the appellees, or a lease of a portion of the appellees' premises, with Virginia agreeing to pay a percentage of gross sales as a license or concession fee or as rent and were assignable by Virginia unless they imposed on Virginia duties of a personal or unique character which could not be delegated [citation].

The appellees earnestly argue that they had dealt with Macke before and had chosen Virginia because they preferred the way it conducted its business. Specifically, they say that service was more personalized, since the president of Virginia kept the machines in working order, that commissions were paid in cash, and that Virginia permitted them to keep keys to the machines so that minor adjustments could be made when needed. Even if we assume all this to be true, the agreements with Virginia were silent as to the details of the working arrangements and contained only a provision requiring Virginia to "install . . . the above listed equipment and . . . maintain the equipment in good operating order and stocked with merchandise." We think the Supreme Court of California put the problem of personal service in proper focus a century ago when it upheld the assignment of a contract to grade a San Francisco street:

> All painters do not paint portraits like Sir Joshua Reynolds, nor landscapes like Claude Lorraine, nor do all writers write dramas like Shakespeare or fiction like Dickens. Rare genius and extraordinary skill are not transferable, and contracts for their employment are therefore personal, and cannot be assigned. But rare genius and extraordinary skill are not indispensable to the workmanlike digging down of a sand hill or the filling up of a depression to a given level, or

the construction of brick sewers with manholes and covers, and contracts for such work are not personal, and may be assigned.

Taylor v. Palmer, 31 Cal. 240 at 247–248 (1866). Moreover, the difference between the service the Pizza Shops happened to be getting from Virginia and what they expected to get from Macke did not mount up to such a material change in the performance of obligations under the agreements as would justify the appellees' refusal to recognize the assignment, Crane Ice Cream Co. v. Terminal Freezing & Heating Co., *supra*, 147 Md. 588, 128 A. 280.

In support of the proposition that the agreements were for personal services, and not assignable, the Pizza Shops rely on three Supreme Court cases, Burck v. Taylor, 152 U.S. 634, 14 S.Ct. 696, 38 L.Ed. 578 (1894); Delaware County Comm'rs v. Diebold Safe & Lock Co., 133 U.S. 473, 10 S.Ct. 399, 33 L.Ed. 674 (1890); and Arkansas Valley Smelting Co. v. Belden Mining Co., 127 U.S. 379, 8 S.Ct. 1308, 32 L.Ed. 246 (1888), all of which were cited with approval by our predecessors in Tarr v. Veasey, 125 Md. 199, 207, 93 A. 428 (1915). We find none of these cases persuasive. *Burck* held that the contractor for the state capitol in Texas, who was prohibited by the terms of his contract from assigning it without the state's consent, could not make a valid assignment of his right to receive three-fourths of the proceeds. In *Delaware County,* Diebold Safe and Lock, which was a subcontractor in the construction of a county jail, was barred from recovering from the county commissioners for its work on the theory that there had been a partial assignment of the construction contract by the prime contractor, which had never been assented to by the commissioners. This result must be limited to the facts: *i.e.*, to the subcontractor's right to recover under the assignment, and not to the contractor's right to delegate. *Arkansas Valley,* which held invalid an attempt to assign a contract for the purchase of ore, is clearly distinguishable because of a contract provision which stipulated that payment for the ore was to be made after delivery, based on an assay to be made by the individual purchaser named in the contract. The court concluded that this was a confidence imposed in the individual purchaser's credit and responsibility and that his rights under the contract could not be transferred to another. *Tarr v. Veasey* involved a situation where duties were delegated to one person and rights assigned to another and our predecessors held the rights not to be assignable, because of the parties' intention that duties and rights were interdependent.

We find more apposite two cases which were not cited by the parties. In The British Waggon Co. & The Parkgate Waggon Co. v. Lea & Co., 5 Q.B.D. 149 (1880), Parkgate Waggon Company, a lessor of railway cars, who had agreed to keep the cars "in good and substantial repair and working order," made an assignment of the contract to British Waggon Company. When British Waggon Company sued for rent, the lessee contended that the assignment had terminated the lease. The court held that the lessee remained bound under the lease, because there was no provision making performance of the lessor's duty to keep in repair a duty personal to it or its employees.

Except for the fact that the result has been roundly criticized, *see Corbin, supra*, at 448–49, the Pizza Shops might have found some solace in the facts found in Boston Ice Co. v. Potter, 123 Mass. 28 (1877). There, Potter, who had dealt with the Boston Ice Company, and found its service unsatisfactory, transferred his business to Citizens' Ice Company. Later, Citizens' sold out to Boston, unbeknown to Potter, and Potter was served by Boston for a full year. When Boston attempted to collect its ice bill, the Massachusetts court sustained Potter's demurrer on the ground that there was no privity of contract, since Potter had a right to choose with whom he would deal and could not have another supplier thrust upon him. Modern authorities do not support this result, and hold that, absent provision to the contrary, a duty may be delegated, as distinguished from a right which can be assigned, and that the promisee cannot rescind, if the quality of the performance remains materially the same.

Restatement, Contracts § 160(3) (1932) reads, in part:

Performance or offer of performance by a person delegated has the same legal effect as performance or offer of performance by the person named in the contract, unless,

(a) performance by the person delegated varies or would vary materially from performance by the person named in the contract as the one to perform, and there has been no ... assent to the delegation....

In cases involving the sale of goods, the *Restatement* rule respecting delegation of duties has been amplified by Uniform Commercial Code § 2–210(5), Maryland Code (1957, 1964 Repl.Vol.) Art. 95B § 2–210(5), which permits a promisee to demand assurances from the party to whom duties have been delegated.

As we see it, the delegation of duty by Virginia to Macke was entirely permissible under the terms of the agreements. In so holding, we do not put ourselves at odds with Eastern Advertising Co. v. McGaw, *supra*, 89 Md. 72, 42 A. 923, for in that case, the agreement with the agency contained a provision that "the advertising cards were to be 'subject to the approval of Eastern Advertising Company as to style and contents,'" at 82, 42 A. at 923, which the court found to import that reliance was being placed on the agency's skill, judgment and taste, at 88, 42 A. 923. ...

[Reversed and remanded.]

SALLY BEAUTY CO. v. NEXXUS PRODUCTS CO.

United States Court of Appeals, Seventh Circuit, 1986.
801 F.2d 1001.

CUDAHY, CIRCUIT JUDGE. Nexxus Products Company entered into a contract with Best Barber & Beauty Supply Company, Inc., under which Best would be the exclusive distributor of Nexxus hair care products to barbers and hair stylists throughout most of Texas. When Best was acquired by and merged into Sally Beauty Company, Inc., Nexxus cancelled the agreement. Sally Beauty is a wholly-owned subsidiary of Alberto–Culver Company, a major manufacturer of hair care products and a competitor of Nexxus'. Sally Beauty claims that Nexxus breached the contract by cancelling; Nexxus asserts by way of defense that the contract was not assignable or, in the alternative, not assignable to Sally Beauty. The district court granted Nexxus' motion for summary judgment, ruling that the contract was one for personal services and therefore not assignable. We affirm on a different theory—that this contract could not be assigned to the wholly-owned subsidiary of a direct competitor under section 2–210 of the Uniform Commercial Code.

I.

Only the basic facts are undisputed and they are as follows. Prior to its merger with Sally Beauty, Best was a Texas corporation in the business of distributing beauty and hair care products to retail stores, barber shops and beauty salons throughout Texas. Between March and July 1979, Mark Reichek, Best's president, negotiated with Stephen Redding, Nexxus' vice-president, over a possible distribution agreement between Best and Nexxus. Nexxus, founded in 1979, is a California corporation that formulates and markets hair care products. Nexxus does not market its products to retail stores, preferring to sell them to independent distributors for resale to barbers and beauticians. On August 2, 1979, Nexxus executed a distributorship agreement with Best, in the form of a July 24, 1979 letter from Reichek, for Best, to Redding, for Nexxus. . . .

In July 1981 Sally Beauty acquired Best in a stock purchase transaction and Best was merged into Sally Beauty, which succeeded to Best's rights and interests in all of Best's contracts. Sally Beauty, a Delaware corporation with its principal place of business in Texas, is a wholly-owned subsidiary of Alberto–Culver. Sally Beauty, like Best, is a distributor of hair care and beauty products to retail stores and hair styling salons. Alberto–Culver is a major manufacturer of hair care products and, thus, is a direct competitor of Nexxus in the hair care market.

Shortly after the merger, Redding met with Michael Renzulli, president of Sally Beauty, to discuss the Nexxus distribution agreement. After the meeting, Redding wrote Renzulli a letter stating that Nexxus would not allow Sally Beauty, a wholly-owned subsidiary of a direct competitor, to distribute Nexxus products:

> As we discussed in New Orleans, we have great reservations about allowing our NEXXUS Products to be distributed by a company which is, in essence, a direct competitor. We appreciate your argument of autonomy for your business, but the fact remains that you are totally owned by Alberto–Culver.

> Since we see no way of justifying this conflict, we cannot allow our products to be distributed by Sally Beauty Company.

. . .

II.

Sally Beauty's breach of contract claim alleges that by acquiring Best, Sally Beauty succeeded to all of Best's rights and obligations under the distribution agreement. It further alleges that Nexxus breached the agreement by failing to give Sally Beauty 120 days notice prior to terminating the agreement and by terminating it on other than an anniversary date of its formation. Nexxus, in its motion for summary judgment, argued that the distribution agreement it entered into with Best was a contract for personal services, based upon a relationship of personal trust and confidence between Reichek and the Redding family. As such, the contract could not be assigned to Sally without Nexxus' consent.

In opposing this motion Sally Beauty argued that the contract was freely assignable because (1) it was between two corporations, not two individuals and (2) the character of the performance would not be altered by the substitution of Sally Beauty for Best. It also argued that "the Distribution Agreement is nothing more than a simple, non-exclusive contract for the distribution of goods, the successful performance of which is in no way dependent upon any particular personality, individual skill or confidential relationship."

In ruling on this motion, the district court framed the issue before it as "whether the contract at issue here between Best and Nexxus was of a personal nature such that it was not assignable without Nexxus' consent."
. . .

We cannot affirm this summary judgment on the grounds relied on by the district court. . . . Although it might be "reasonable to conclude" that Best and Nexxus had based their agreement on a "relationship of personal trust and confidence," and that Reicheck's participation was considered essential to Best's performance, this is a finding of fact. Since the parties submitted conflicting affidavits on this question, the court erred in relying on Nexxus' view as representing undisputed fact in ruling on this summary judgment motion.

We may affirm this summary judgment, however, on a different ground if it finds support in the record. . . . We agree with Sally that the provisions of the UCC govern this contract and for that reason hold that the assignment of the contract by Best to Sally Beauty was barred by the UCC rules on delegation of performance, UCC § 2–210(1), Tex.Bus. & Com.Code Ann. § 2–210(a) (Vernon 1968)*.

III.

The UCC codifies the law of contracts applicable to "transactions in goods." UCC § 2–102. Texas applies the "dominant factor" test to determine whether the UCC applies to a given contract or transaction: was the essence of or dominant factor in the formation of the contract the provision of goods or services? [citations] No Texas case addresses whether

---

* Subsequent citations to the Texas UCC are omitted. Ed.

a distribution agreement is a contract for the sale of goods, but the rule in the majority of jurisdictions is that distributorships (both exclusive and non-exclusive) are to be treated as sale of goods contracts under the UCC. [citations] . . .

IV.

The fact that this contract is considered a contract for the sale of goods and not for the provision of a service does not, as Sally Beauty suggests, mean that it is freely assignable in all circumstances. The delegation of performance under a sales contract (whether in conjunction with an assignment of rights, as here, or not) is governed by UCC section 2–210(1). The UCC recognizes that in many cases an obligor will find it convenient or even necessary to relieve himself of the duty of performance under a contract, *see* Official Comment 1, UCC § 2–210 ("(T)his section recognizes both delegation of performance and assignability as normal and permissible incidents of a contract for the sale of goods."). The Code therefore sanctions delegation except where the delegated performance would be unsatisfactory to the obligee: "A party may perform his duty through a delegate unless otherwise agreed to [*sic*] or unless the other party has a substantial interest in having his original promisor perform or control the acts required by the contract." UCC § 2–210(1). Consideration is given to balancing the policies of free alienability of commercial contracts and protecting the obligee from having to accept a bargain he did not contract for.

We are concerned here with the delegation of Best's duty of performance under the distribution agreement, as Nexxus terminated the agreement because it did not wish to accept Sally Beauty's substituted performance. Only one Texas case [McKinnie v. Milford, 597 S.W.2d 953 (Tex.Civ. App. 1980, writ ref'd, n.r.e.)] has construed section 2–210 in the context of a party's delegation of performance under an executory contract. . . . In *McKinnie*, the Texas court recognized and applied the UCC rule that bars delegation of duties if there is some reason why the non-assigning party would find performance by a delegate a substantially different thing than what he had bargained for.

In the exclusive distribution agreement before us, Nexxus had contracted for Best's "best efforts" in promoting the sale of Nexxus products in Texas. UCC § 2–306(2). . . . This implied promise on Best's part was the consideration for Nexxus' promise to refrain from supplying any other distributors within Best's exclusive area. It was this contractual undertaking which Nexxus refused to see performed by Sally.

In ruling on Nexxus' motion for summary judgment, the district court noted: "Unlike Best, Sally Beauty is a subsidiary of one of Nexxus' direct competitors. This is a significant distinction and in the court's view, it raises serious questions regarding Sally Beauty's ability to perform the distribution agreement in the same manner as Best." In Berliner Foods Corp. v. Pillsbury Co., 633 F.Supp. 557 (D.Md.1986), the court stated the same reservation more strongly on similar facts. Berliner was an exclusive distributor of Haagen–Dazs ice cream when it was sold to Breyer's, a manufacturer of a competing ice cream line. Pillsbury Co., manufacturer of Haagen–Dazs, terminated the distributorship and Berliner sued. The court noted, while weighing the factors for and against a preliminary injunction, that "it defies common sense to require a manufacturer to leave the distribution of its products to a distributor under the control of a competitor or potential competitor. *Id.* at 559–60.[7] We agree with these assessments and hold that Sally Beauty's position as a wholly-owned subsidiary of Alberto–Culver is sufficient to bar the delegation of Best's duties under the agreement.

We do not believe that our holding will work the mischief with our national economy that the appellants predict. We hold merely that the duty of performance under an exclusive distributorship may not be delegated to a competitor in the market place—or the wholly-owned subsidiary of a competitor—without the obligee's consent. We believe that such a rule is consonant with the policies behind section 2–210, which is concerned with preserving the bargain the obligee has struck. Nexxus should not be required to accept the "best efforts" of Sally Beauty when those efforts are subject to the control of Alberto–Culver. It is entirely reasonable that Nexxus should conclude that this performance would be a different thing than what it had bargained for. At oral argument, Sally Beauty argued that the case should go to trial to allow it to demonstrate that it could and would perform the contract as impartially as Best. It stressed that Sally Beauty is a "multi-line" distributor, which means that it distributes many brands and is not just a conduit for Alberto–Culver products. But we do not think that this creates a material question of fact in this case. When performance of personal services is delegated, the trier merely determines that it is a personal services contract. If so, the duty is *per se* nondelegable. There is no inquiry into whether the delegate is as skilled or worthy of trust and confidence as the original obligor: the delegate was not bargained for and the obligee need not consent to the substitution.[9] And so here: it is undisputed that Sally Beauty is wholly owned by Alberto–Culver, which means that Sally Beauty's "impartial" sales policy is at least acquiesced in by Alberto–Culver—but could change whenever Alberto–Culver's needs changed. Sally Beauty may be totally sincere in its belief that it can operate "impartially" as a distributor, but who can guarantee the outcome when there is a clear choice between the demands of the

---

7. The effort by the dissent to distinguish *Berliner* merely because the court there apparently assumed in passing that distributorship agreements were a species of personal service contracts must fail. The *Berliner* court emphasizes that the sale of a distributorship to a competitor of the supplier is by itself a wholly sufficient reason to terminate the distributorship.

9. Of course, the obligee makes such an assessment of the prospective delegate. If it thinks the delegated performance will be as satisfactory, it is of course free to consent to the delegation. Thus, the dissent is mistaken in its suggestion that we find it improper—a "conflict of interest"— for one competitor to distribute another competitor's products. Rather, we believe only that it is commercially reasonable that the supplier in those circumstances have consented to such a state of affairs. To borrow the dissent's example, Isuzu allows General Motors to distribute its cars because it considers this arrangement attractive.

Nor is distrust of one's competitors a trait unique to lawyers (as opposed to ordinary businessmen), as the dissent may be understood to suggest.

parent-manufacturer, Alberto–Culver, and the competing needs of Nexxus? The risk of an unfavorable outcome is not one which the law can force Nexxus to take. Nexxus has a substantial interest in not seeing this contract performed by Sally Beauty, which is sufficient to bar the delegation under section 2–210. Because Nexxus should not be forced to accept performance of the distributorship agreement by Sally, we hold that the contract was not assignable without Nexxus' consent.

The judgment of the district court is affirmed.

POSNER, CIRCUIT JUDGE, dissenting. My brethren have decided, with no better foundation than judicial intuition about what businessmen consider reasonable, that the Uniform Commercial Code gives a supplier an absolute right to cancel an exclusive-dealing contract if the dealer is acquired, directly or indirectly, by a competitor of the supplier. I interpret the Code differently.

Nexxus makes products for the hair and sells them through distributors to hair salons and barbershops. It gave a contract to Best, cancellable on any anniversary of the contract with 120 days' notice, to be its exclusive distributor in Texas. Two years later Best was acquired by and merged into Sally Beauty, a distributor of beauty supplies and wholly owned subsidiary of Alberto–Culver. Alberto–Culver makes "hair care" products, too, though they mostly are cheaper than Nexxus's, and are sold to the public primarily through grocery stores and drugstores. My brethren conclude that because there is at least a loose competitive relationship between Nexxus and Alberto–Culver, Sally Beauty cannot—as a matter of law, cannot, for there has been no trial on the issue—provide its "best efforts" in the distribution of Nexxus products. Since a commitment to provide best efforts is read into every exclusive-dealing contract by section 2–306(2) of the Uniform Commercial Code, the contract has been broken and Nexxus can repudiate it. Alternatively, Nexxus had "a substantial interest in having his original promisor perform or control the acts required by the contract," and therefore the delegation of the promisor's (Best's) duties to Sally Beauty was improper under section 2–210(1).

... My brethren cite only one case in support of their conclusion: A district court case from Maryland, Berliner Foods Corp. v. Pillsbury Co., 633 F.Supp. 557 (D.Md. 1986), which, since it treated the contract at issue there as one for personal services, *id.* at 559 (a characterization my brethren properly reject for the contract between Nexxus and Best), is not helpful. ... By rejecting that characterization here, my brethren have sawn off the only limb on which they might have sat comfortably. ...

My brethren find this a simple case—as simple (it seems) as if a lawyer had undertaken to represent the party opposing his client. But notions of conflict of interest are not the same in law and in business, and judges can go astray by assuming that the legal-services industry is the pattern for the entire economy. The lawyerization of America has not reached that point. Sally Beauty, though a wholly owned subsidiary of Alberto–Culver, distributes "hair care" supplies made by many different companies, which so far as appears compete with Alberto–Culver as vigorously as Nexxus does. Steel companies both make fabricated steel and sell raw steel to competing fabricators. General Motors sells cars manufactured by a competitor, Isuzu. What in law would be considered a fatal conflict of interest is in business a commonplace and legitimate practice. The lawyer is a fiduciary of his client; Best was not a fiduciary of Nexxus.

. . .

How likely is it that the acquisition of Best could hurt Nexxus? Not very. Suppose Alberto–Culver had ordered Sally Beauty to go slow in pushing Nexxus products, in the hope that sales of Alberto–Culver "hair care" products would rise. Even if they did, since the market is competitive Alberto–Culver would not reap monopoly profits. Moreover, what guarantee has Alberto–Culver that consumers would be diverted from Nexxus to it, rather than to products closer in price and quality to Nexxus products? In any event, any trivial gain in profits to Alberto–Culver would be offset by the loss of goodwill to Sally Beauty; and a cost to Sally Beauty is a cost to Alberto–Culver, its parent. Remember that Sally Beauty carries beauty supplies made by other competitors of Alberto–Culver; Best alone [also?] carries "hair care" products manufactured by Revlon, Clairol, Bristol–Myers, and L'Oreal, as well as Alberto–Culver. Will these powerful competitors continue to distribute their products through Sally Beauty if Sally Beauty displays favoritism for Alberto–Culver products? Would not such a display be a commercial disaster for Sally Beauty, and hence for its parent, Alberto–Culver? Is it really credible that Alberto–Culver would sacrifice Sally Beauty in a vain effort to monopolize the "hair care" market, in violation of section 2 of the Sherman Act? Is not the ratio of the profits that Alberto–Culver obtains from Sally Beauty to the profits it obtains from the manufacture of "hair care" products at least a relevant consideration?

Another relevant consideration is that the contract between Nexxus and Best was for a short term. Could Alberto–Culver destroy Nexxus by failing to push its products with maximum vigor in Texas for a year? In the unlikely event that it could and did, it would be liable in damages to Nexxus for breach of the implied best-efforts term of the distribution contract. Finally, it is obvious that Sally Beauty does not have a bottleneck position in the distribution of "hair care" products, such that by refusing to promote Nexxus products vigorously it could stifle the distribution of those products in Texas; for Nexxus has found alternative distribution that it prefers—otherwise it wouldn't have repudiated the contract with Best when Best was acquired by Sally Beauty.

Not all businessmen are consistent and successful profit maximizers, so the probability that Alberto–Culver would instruct Sally Beauty to cease to push Nexxus products vigorously in Texas cannot be reckoned at zero. On this record, however, it is slight. And there is no principle of law that if something happens that trivially reduces the probability that a dealer will use his best efforts, the supplier can cancel the contract. Suppose there had been no merger, but the only child of Best's president had gone to work for Alberto–Culver as a chemist. Could Nexxus have canceled the contract, fearing that Best (perhaps unconsciously) would favor Alberto–Culver products over Nexxus products? That would be an absurd ground for cancellation, and so is Nexxus's actual ground. At most, so far as the record shows, Nexxus may have had grounds for "insecurity" regarding the performance by Sally Beauty of its obligation to use its best efforts to promote Nexxus products, but if so its remedy was not to cancel the contract but to demand assurances of due performance. *See* UCC § 2–609; Official Comment 5 to § 2–306. No such demand was made. An anticipatory repudiation by conduct requires conduct that makes the repudiating party unable to perform. Farnsworth, *Contracts* 636 (1982). The merger did not do this. At least there is no evidence it did. The judgment should be reversed and the case remanded for a trial on whether the merger so altered the conditions of performance that Nexxus is entitled to declare the contract broken.

PROBLEMS

4.   S and B entered into a contract for the purchase and sale of a piece of real property. B was to pay one half of the purchase price in cash and the other half by giving a bond and mortgage. Before closing, B assigned her rights and delegated performance of her duties to A. When A tendered cash and his own bond, S refused. (a) What result? (b) What result if A had tendered a bond of B?

5.   A client retains a lawyer for a certain task. Unknown to the client, the lawyer delegates performance of the duties and assigns the right to payment of the fee to a second lawyer. The second lawyer, without the client's knowledge, performs, and the performance is successful. To whom, if anyone, does the client owe a fee?

6.   Penny had a bad back. She consulted Dr. Doolittle who recommended surgery. Penny consented in writing to having Dr. Doolittle operate. When Penny was anesthetized, Dr. Doolittle left the room and Dr. Domuch operated. The surgery was not successful. What recourse does Penny have?

7.   Peterson was the anchorman on channel 9 in Washington, D.C. under a contract that had several years to go when the owners of channel 9 sold it to the plaintiff. Prior to the sale, Peterson had a close personal relationship with his managers and was able to discuss programming options as an equal. When the station was sold, Peterson declared that the contract had been breached by the sale and commenced working for a competitive channel. The new owners of channel 9 sued to enjoin Peterson from working for the competition. What result?

8.   S offers to sell a specific car to B for $10,000. B assigns the offer to C who tenders $10,000 to S. Is S bound to take the money?

9.   S offers to sell a certain car to B if B drives the car in the Indianapolis 500 and wins, and if B pays $52,000 thereafter, and if B gives $100 to keep the offer open until after the race. B gives S $100. May B now assign the rights and delegate the performance of the conditions to C?

(b) CONTRACTUAL PROHIBITIONS AGAINST ASSIGNMENT

(Calamari & Perillo on Contracts § 18.16)

IN RE KAUFMAN

Supreme Court of Oklahoma, 2001.
37 P.3d 845.

KAUGER, J.: We are asked to answer two questions [by the United States Bankruptcy Court for the Western District of Oklahoma]: 1) whether anti-assignment provisions restricting the power of an annuitant to sell, mortgage, encumber, or anticipate future payments, by assignment or otherwise, are valid; and 2) whether a purchase agreement between an annuitant/assignor and third-party/assignee for future annuity payments in exchange for a lump-sum payment is enforceable if the annuitant is restricted by an anti-assignment provision from selling, mortgaging, encumbering, or anticipating future payments by assignment or otherwise?
. . .

FACTS

In April of 1996, the debtor, John A. Kaufman (Kaufman/debtor/annuitant/assignor), settled a wrongful death claim with Love's Country Stores, Inc. and United States Fidelity & Guaranty Company (USF & G/insurer). In association with his claim, Kaufman signed a Settlement Agreement and Release (settlement agreement) providing that it would be construed and interpreted in accordance with Oklahoma law. The settlement agreement provides for a lump-sum payment and for periodic monthly payments of $2,008.75 measured by Kaufman's life with a twenty-year payment guarantee.[3] The settlement agreement specifically provides that Kaufman has no "power to sell, mortgage, encumber, or anticipate the future payments by assignment or otherwise."

As contemplated by the settlement agreement, the insurer entered into a qualified agreement with SAFECO Assigned Benefits Company (SAFECO) under which SAFECO assumed the responsibility of making Kaufman's periodic payments. Pursuant to the settlement agreement, SAFECO purchased . . . an annuity[7] to ensure Kaufman's monthly payments.[8]

---

3. In essence, the Settlement Agreement and Release is a structured settlement. A structured settlement agreement releases the defendant/obligor from liability in consideration for the agreement to make periodic payments to the claimant over time. . . .

7. An annuity contract is the exact inverse of a life insurance contract. In return for a lump sum, the insurance company typically promises the annuitant periodic payments that will continue until the death of the annuitant. The lump sum is determined by the life expectancy of the annuitant, and the insurance company gambles that the annuitant will die prior to actuarial predictions. Variable Annuity Life Ins. Co. v. Clarke, 998 F.2d 1295, 1301 (5th Cir.1993) (*Rev'd on other grounds*, 513 U.S. 251, 115 S.Ct. 810, 130 L.Ed.2d 740 (1995)).

8. . . . [L]ike the settlement agreement, the qualified assignment and annuity contract contain language restricting Kaufman's right to sell, use as collateral or assign the annuity benefits. . . .

After seeing a television commercial involving purchases of structured settlements aired by J.G. Wentworth S.S.C., Limited Partnership (Wentworth/creditor/assignee),[9] Kaufman called and requested the paperwork necessary to complete the sale. Via a purchase agreement executed on June 9, 1999, Kaufman sold his right to receive sixty monthly annuity payments of $2,008.75 with a total value of $120,525.00 to Wentworth for a lump sum payment of $80,507.26. The purchase agreement provided that Wentworth was entitled to receive payments beginning in July of 1999 and running through June of 2004. The creditor has received no payments since May of 2000.

Kaufman used the monies received under the purchase agreement to start a trenching business. When the business failed, the debtor filed a voluntary Chapter 13 bankruptcy petition on September 22, 2000. In the bankruptcy petition, the debtor listed the purchase agreement with the creditor as an unsecured claim and proposed that the annuity payments be utilized to fund the Chapter 13 plan. On November 27, 2001, Wentworth filed a motion for relief from the automatic stay requesting permission to seize the contracted-for annuity payments. It is this action and Kaufman's assertion that the purchase agreement is invalid due to the anti-assignment language in the settlement agreement which prompted the bankruptcy court to certify questions to this Court. . . .

I.

WHERE THE ANTI–ASSIGNMENT PROVISION IS CLEAR AND UNAMBIGUOUS IN ITS LIMITATION OF THE POWER OF THE ANNUITANT TO SELL, MORTGAGE, ENCUMBER, OR ANTICIPATE FUTURE PAYMENTS, BY ASSIGNMENT OR OTHERWISE, THE RESTRICTION ON ALIENABILITY IS VALID.

Kaufman asserts that the clear language of the anti-assignment provision of the structured settlement requires that the provision be enforced. Because the contractual language does not specifically provide that any attempted assignment will be void, Wentworth argues that the anti-assignment provision is invalid.[13]

---

9. Wentworth is a factoring company—an entity which purchases future payments for a lump sum. L. Andrada, *Structured Settlements: The Assignability Problem*, 9 S. Cal.Inter. L.J. 465 (2000). Wentworth's business is the purchasing of the rights to receive payments coming from royalties, structured settlements, and lotteries. *In re* Berghman, 235 B.R. 683, 688 (Bkrtcy. M.D.Fla.1999).

13. [Wentworth argues that UCC Article 9 supports the invalidity of the anti-assignment provision.] The assertion is unconvincing. . . .

Wentworth also relies on two provisions of the *Restatement (Second) of Contracts* in support of its position. Section 317(2) provides:

A contractual right can be assigned unless

(a) the substitution of a right of the assignee [for] the right of the assignor would materially change the duty of the obligor, or materially increase the burden or risk imposed on him by his contract, or materially impair his chance of obtaining return performance, or materially reduce its value to him, or

An assignment is the expressed intent of one party to pass rights owned to another. It realigns the parties to a contract. Valid assignments pass the assignor's title, leaving no interest to be reached by a creditor. In Oklahoma, contractual rights are presumed to be assignable. Nevertheless, parties may expressly provide otherwise. The issue here is whether the language utilized in the settlement agreement—stripping Kaufman of the "power to sell, mortgage, encumber, or anticipate the future payments by assignment or otherwise"—is sufficient to support a determination that the annuity payments are inalienable. We determine that it is.

Absent clear, unambiguous language, the majority of courts generally will not honor attempts to restrict the right to assign freely. Some jurisdictions require language providing that an assignment will be void or invalid before anti-assignment provisions are upheld. These courts treat anti-assignment provisions as personal covenants which will not invalidate an otherwise proper transfer determining that unless the contractual provision eliminates both the power and the right to assign, an assignment may give rise to damages for breach but will not render the assignment ineffective.

However, a number of courts have enforced anti-assignment provisions similar to the one at issue here which explicitly deprive the assignor of the assignment *power*. Others are less insistent on the use of any particular phraseology and simply uphold anti-assignment provisions if the prohibitive language utilized is clear and unambiguous while some jurisdictions enforce such provisions as a general matter. Decisions upholding anti-assignment provisions containing language limiting the power of assignment are characterized as being within the modern legal approach to the assignability of contracts.

The courts addressing the precise issue of whether an anti-assignment provision in a structured settlement agreement prohibiting the alienation of future payments made under an annuity policy is enforceable have reached differing results. No clear majority has emerged. Rather, the decisions are divided almost evenly.

(b) the assignment is forbidden by statute or is otherwise inoperative on grounds of public policy, or

(c) assignment is validly precluded by contract.

Restatement (Second) of Contracts § 322 provides in pertinent part:

... (2) [A] contract term prohibiting assignment of rights under the contract, unless a different intention is manifested,

(a) does not forbid assignment of a right to damages for breach of the whole contract or a right arising out of the assignor's due performance of his entire obligation;

(b) gives the obligor a right to damages for breach of the terms forbidding assignment but does not render the assignment ineffective;

(c) is for the benefit of the obligor, and does not prevent the assignee from acquiring rights against the assignor or the obligor from discharging his duty as if there were no such prohibition....

Our determination that the contract language clearly and unambiguously precludes assignment places the clause squarely within the exceptions allowing enforcement of anti-assignment provisions outlined in subsection (c) of § 317 (assignment precluded by contractual language) and § 322 (allowing for the expression of a different intent).

The jurisdictions striking anti-assignment provisions have done so: on the basis that no harm comes to the party obligated to perform by the mere assignment of contractual payments; due to a lack of specific language binding the tort victim to assignment restrictions; or because the anti-assignment provisions circumscribe the right, but not the power, to assign. The courts enforcing anti-assignment provisions in the structured settlement context have grounded their decisions on: the premise that such provisions, included for the benefit of the insurer, could not be waived by the annuitant; policy arguments supporting enforcement of the provisions in relation to structured settlements; or the clear language of the provision taking it out of the general rule of assignability.

In Oklahoma, the cardinal rule in contract interpretation is to determine and give effect to the intent of the parties. In considering whether contractual rights may be alienated, we look to the parties' intent manifested by the agreement's language. Here, the settlement agreement specifically provides that Kaufman has no "power to sell, mortgage, encumber, or anticipate the future payments by assignment or otherwise." The anti-assignability clause is a condition of the contract for which the parties bargained. The language is clear and definite in its intent to prohibit Kaufman from alienating—by assignment or otherwise—the annuity payments. We determine that where the anti-assignment provision is clear and unambiguous in its limitation of the power of the annuitant to sell, mortgage, encumber, or anticipate future payments, by assignment or otherwise, the restriction on alienability is valid. Oklahoma's tenets of contract construction, as well as decisions from other jurisdictions upholding anti-assignment provisions limiting the assignor's "power" to alienate contractual rights along with the general policy considerations favoring steady income, long-term security and tax-favorable treatment underlying structured settlements support our determination.

II.

ALTHOUGH AN ANTI–ASSIGNMENT PROVISION IS VALID, WELL SETTLED PRINCIPLES OF OKLAHOMA LAW PREVENT AN ASSIGNOR FROM ENFORCING THE CLAUSE AGAINST ITS ASSIGNEE.

Kaufman argues that a finding that the anti-assignment provision is valid requires that the purchase agreement with Wentworth be declared void and unenforceable. Wentworth asserts that notwithstanding the anti-assignment provision in the settlement agreement, a debtor/assignor may not rely on principles of nonassignability to defeat the contract as against its creditor/assignee. We agree.

Kaufman seeks to void the purchase agreement on general public policy grounds intended to protect tort victims. [The court declines to do so. Ed.] . . .

If we were inclined to accept the argument for avoidance of the contract on public policy grounds, we would be hard pressed to ignore a principle characterized as well settled in Oklahoma jurisprudence as early as 1939. The following language appears in Harris v. Tipton, 1939 OK 256, ¶ 17, 185 Okla. 146, 90 P.2d 932:

> An assignor is not permitted to raise (nonassignability) as against the assignee, and it is right and just that he should not be permitted to do so, for a more perfect illustration of the necessity for the doctrine of estoppel could hardly be stated. The rule that an assignor cannot as against his assignee allege nonassignability is well settled.

Harris involved an attempt by an assignor to void alienation of what he believed, at the time, to be an unenforceable tort claim to his former partner/assignee. When the partner/assignee was able to recover on the tort claim against the state, the assignor sought to recover what he believed to be his portion of the recovery.

In Oklahoma, an assignor cannot maintain the inequitable position of asserting, as against its assignee, nonassignability. Based on this well-settled legal principle, we determine that an assignor of a contract containing a valid anti-assignment provision may not invoke the clause as against its assignee.

CONCLUSION

Policy supporting free alienability is not so absolute as to override contract provisions clearly prohibiting assignment. To hold otherwise would require us to ignore validly executed, and freely made, anti-assignment provisions in contravention of well settled principles of Oklahoma's contract law allowing parties to include such provisions in their negotiations. This we will not do. Rather, we maintain a healthy respect for the power of independent persons to bargain for, or away, contractual provisions and maintain our position that it is not this Court's province to remake contracts to suit the changing whims of contracting parties. Although we recognize the rights of contracting parties to negotiate for valid anti-assignment provisions, we also note that well settled principles of Oklahoma law prohibit an assignor, as against an assignee, to allege nonassignability.

The bankruptcy court certified the questions as unanswered in Oklahoma law. Nevertheless, we note that the responses supplied are grounded in well settled principles of contract construction and our jurisprudence relating to the relationship between an assignor and an assignee.

QUESTIONS ANSWERED.

The questions are answered as follows:

1) Where the anti-assignment provision is clear and unambiguous in its limitation of the power of the annuitant to sell, mortgage, encumber, or anticipate future payments, by assignment or otherwise, the restriction on alienability is valid.

2) Although an anti-assignment provision is valid, well settled principles of Oklahoma law prevent an assignor from enforcing the clause against its assignee.

. . .

PROBLEM

10. A lease of commercial space in a shopping center provided that Landlord would pay Tenant a $15,000 construction allowance after Tenant had completed certain improvements to the leased premises. The lease provided: "Tenant agrees not to assign this lease in whole or in part. Any such assignment shall be void and shall, at Landlord's option, constitute an event of default." Alice advanced Tenant $8,000 to pay for improvements in exchange for Tenant's assignment to Alice of the right to receive the first $8,000 of the construction allowance. Alice notified Landlord, but when the improvements were completed Landlord paid the entire allowance to Tenant. Alice sues Landlord for $8,000. What result?

(c) IMPROPER ASSIGNMENT OR DELEGATION— EFFECT OF WAIVER

(Calamari & Perillo on Contracts §§ 18.14 and 18.29)

SEALE v. BATES

Supreme Court of Colorado, 1961.
145 Colo. 430, 359 P.2d 356.

DOYLE, JUSTICE. Plaintiffs in error will be referred to by name or as they were designated in the trial court where they were plaintiffs in an action against John Bates, individually, the Bates Dance Studio, Inc. and the Dance Studio of Denver, Inc. The Seales sought to recover $2,040 which had been paid to the Bates Dance Studio to defray the cost of 300 hours of dance instruction. The plaintiff Hanscome sought to recover $4,131.34 which he had paid to the Bates Dance Studio for 612 hours of dance instruction. From their complaints it would appear that the contracts which the plaintiffs entered into with the Bates Dance Studio had been assigned to the Dance Studio of Denver, doing business as Dale Dance Studio. It is alleged that the defendants refused to carry out their obligations and duties under the said contracts.

The Seales started taking dance lessons at the Dale Dance Studios in June of 1956. They signed up for a series of lessons costing in excess of $200, but in a short time they became dissatisfied with the arrangement and had the contract cancelled upon the basis that they would be allowed to take the balance of their lessons at the Bates Studio. After completion of this first series they entered into a new contract with the Bates Dance Studio whereby they undertook to take a total of 600 one-half hour lessons. These lessons were interrupted due to illness in the family and upon the Seales' resuming classes they were told that the remainder of the lessons would be given at the Dale Studio. They then went to the Dale Studio to discuss the situation and were there advised by one of the former Bates employees, who was then working for Dale, that the latter had assumed the obligations of the Bates contracts.* The Seales were told that the "students and the instructors, the entire organization was transferred to the Dale Studios; that we would have the same instructors, the same instruction, a continuation of what we had had at Bates." They proceeded to take lessons at Dale, but after some 30 one-half hours of instruction they became dissatisfied with the conditions. This dissatisfaction arose from the fact that the room was much smaller and more crowded and the music from another room interfered with the lessons. Each of the Seales did not have his or her own instructor, Mr. Seale being required to take his lessons from a male instructor; there were difficulties in getting appointments and on some occasions when appointments were made an instructor would not be available. Mr. and Mrs. Seale complained to the management of the Dale Studio, but the conditions did not improve. After two or three lessons at Dale, Mr. Seale had demanded that he have a former instructor, Miss Valie, and though he was assured that he could and although he made repeated requests, Miss Valie was never available to him. As a result of this dissatisfaction, Mr. and Mrs. Seale stopped taking lessons in May of 1957. The following August they complained to Mr. John Bates of the Bates Studio and demanded that he refund their money or make proper arrangements for completing their contract. Bates informed them that his school was then closed and that there was no money to reimburse them. Later, in August of 1957, Mr. Bates attended a meeting of 13 or 14 of his former pupils for the purpose of discussing the problems which had arisen as a result of the assignment of the contracts. He then assured the persons in attendance that he would speak to the manager of the Dale Studio and he did so. At the trial, in answer to a question as to why he continued to take lessons at the Dale Studios, Seale explained "I kept hoping that somebody would get the thing arranged to where we could continue as had been promised."

The grievances of the plaintiff Hanscome are similar to those of the Seales. . . .

The cause was tried to the court and at the close of plaintiffs' testimony, which included cross-examination of Bates, the court dismissed the plaintiffs' claims and entered informal findings and conclusions, giving these reasons:

The complaint against Bates was dismissed on the ground that the Bates Dance Studio, Inc., a corporation, was the contracting party. The

---

* The text of the opinion describes "the contract of assignment" as follows, ed.:

It requires Dale to complete all pending contracts. Under the terms of this agreement Dale acquired all outstanding accounts and was entitled to collect amounts as the same became due. As to those contracts which had been fully paid, Dale agreed to perform them. Thus it was, under the terms of this agreement, that Bates was allowed to retain the monies paid by the plaintiffs and Dale was required to fulfill the terms of these agreements in consideration of other benefits provided in the contracts.

basis for dispositions as to the Bates and Dale Studios was the assent of the plaintiffs to the assumption by Dale of the obligations under the contracts; that this acceptance of Dale was apparent from the plaintiffs' conduct. The court further found that neither Dale nor Bates had defaulted; that the contract did not require that a certain instructor be furnished or that instruction be given at appointed times. It was also pointed out that there was no evidence of refusal on the part of the defendants to give the number of lessons guaranteed by the contract. The court rejected plaintiffs' theory that the plaintiffs consented to the assignment on any kind of conditional basis and that essentially dissatisfaction did not arise from the assignment but rather arose in connection with the terms of performance. . . .

A further stipulation of the form contract signed by both the plaintiffs is relevant. It provides:

> I fully understand that *this agreement cannot be cancelled,* that my failure to take the lessons contracted for shall not relieve me of my obligations hereunder; and that any delay on your part in proceeding against me after any default by me shall not be deemed a waiver of any of your rights. This agreement expresses our entire understanding and agreement, and neither you nor I shall be bound by any statements, representations or understandings not stated and set forth herein

. . . The argument of plaintiffs that this was a personal service contract and therefore non-assignable without their consent is valid. [citation] This assignment did not result in release of the assignor. 4 Corbin, *Contracts,* 476 (1951). 1 *Restatement, Contracts,* § 160(4) (1932). This, however, does not furnish a reason for holding that plaintiffs are now entitled to recover. On the contrary, there *is* evidence to support the trial court's finding and conclusion that the plaintiffs accepted the assignment as such; they did not elect to rescind when it was brought to their attention that the contracts had been assigned to Dale Dance Studio. The undisputed evidence shows that they accepted the assignment and proceeded to take lessons from the Dale Dance Studio. This conduct is inconsistent with plaintiffs' present theory that they at all times objected to the assignment. Had they refused to receive instruction from Dale and had they taken the position that their contract was with Bates and no other, there would be substance to their present contention that this violation justified the rescission.

We turn now to the question of whether the matters of complaint appearing in the evidence were sufficiently substantial to justify rescission. It is to be noted that none of these matters are specifically treated in the contract. In other words, there are no stipulations relative to the size of the ballroom or the number of people participating, or that the instruction will always be given by one of the opposite sex. While we sympathize with Mr. Seale's preference for Miss Valie over Mr. Ritchie, we do not consider this a breach of a promise implicit in the contract.

Apparently Mr. Ritchie was assigned to Mr. and Mrs. Seale. It is probable that Mrs. Seale preferred to be taught by Mr. Ritchie. It thus appears to us that the proper remedy for this problem is an express stipulation in the contract requiring a partner of the opposite sex.

We are called upon to determine whether from the nature of this instruction contract we must imply stipulations of the kind which plaintiffs say existed and were violated. Considered in this context, we conclude that the plaintiffs cannot succeed. *First,* the warranties which the plaintiffs would have us read into the contracts do not arise by necessary implication. *Secondly,* these breaches cannot be regarded as sufficiently substantial to justify the remedy of rescission. *Thirdly,* there is a failure of proof with respect to the essential element set forth in the complaint, namely, a refusal on the part of the Dale Dance Studio to furnish lessons. All of the evidence supports the finding that Dale was willing to continue the lessons.

The above factors and considerations must be weighed in the light of the express stipulation in the contract that it is non-cancellable and that the monies cannot be returned. Its presence in the contract is entitled to some weight against the contentions of plaintiffs that implied provisions of the contract have been violated. In the light of such a stipulation, the plaintiffs cannot raise the inconsequential variations in the course of instruction as a ground for rescission. Stipulations of the contract will not be implied unless the surrounding circumstances require it. . . .

The case of Barngrover v. Maack, 46 Mo.App. 407, further illustrates the workings of the applicable principle. There the proprietor of a school undertook in his prospectus to teach specific branches of study by thus advertising. It was held that he had undertaken to teach in the listed areas and it was also held that there was an inability to speak English and thus be able to communicate with the students. It was concluded that there was sufficient evidence to justify submission of the case to the jury. *See also* Kentucky Military Institute v. Cohen, 131 Ark. 121, 198 S.W. 874, L.R.A. 1918B, 709. There it was held that mistreatment of a student justified his withdrawal from the school. Restitution plus incidental damages were there held to be recoverable. Here again the case illustrates that breach of an implied stipulation must involve an important or substantial part of the performance. *Cf.* Timmerman v. Stanley, 123 Ga. 850, 51 S.E. 760, 1 L.R.A., N.S., 379, wherein the school abandoned the contract and ceased the teaching after payment had been made.

It follows that the only substantial breach of the contract apparent from a careful reading of the record here is the assignment to the Dale Dance Studio. Had plaintiffs refused to accept this, there would have been a remedy by rescission or perhaps in breach of contract and they could have recovered at least the unused portion of the consideration. Accordingly the trial court's finding and conclusion that the plaintiffs waived any rights which may have arisen from the assignment must be upheld. Plaintiffs' conduct in accepting the transfer to Dale was in effect a waiver of this breach, and the evidence does not undisputedly show that the consent thereto was in any way conditional. . . .

The judgment is affirmed. . . .

SECTION 3. OTHER PROBLEMS RELATING TO ASSIGNMENT AND DELEGATION

(Calamari & Perillo on Contracts §§ 18.24—18.27, 18.30)

WESTERN OIL SALES CORP. v. BLISS & WETHERBEE

Commission of Appeals of Texas, 1927.
299 S.W. 637.

HARVEY, P.J. On March 7, 1923, McCamey, Sheerin & Dumas, a partnership, who will be designated herein as the sellers, held certain tracts of land under oil leases, from which they were producing oil. On that day they made and entered into the following contract of sale with Western Oil Sales Corporation, the plaintiff in error, to wit:

Agreement made and entered into on this 7th day of March, A.D.1923, by and between J.E. McCamey, J.J. Sheerin, and H.O. Dumas a partnership, as party of the first part, and the Western Oil Sales Corporation, a corporation, as party of the second part, witnesseth:

That the party of the first part, in consideration of the premises and agreements hereinafter contained, and by the party of the second part to be done, kept, paid, performed, and carried out, hereby sells and agrees to deliver to said party of the second part, in tanks, at its wells, all of the crude oil produced from said wells located in what is known as the Pioneer oil field at Pioneer, Eastland county, Tex., and on four leases known as the Armstrong lease consisting of 20 acres more or less; the Armstrong lease consisting of 60 acres more or less; the Moore lease consisting of 30 acres more or less; the Moore lease consisting of 10 acres more or less.

The party of the first part agrees to sell and deliver the oil from the above-described leases to the party of the second part for a period of six months from the date the party of the second part connects up and begins running the oil, subject to the terms and conditions of a certain division order, a copy of which is hereto attached. It is agreed that in case of any conflict of terms between the said division order and this contract, the terms of this contract shall govern.

In consideration whereof, party of the second part hereby agrees to lay its gathering lines to and connect same with the tanks of the party of the first part and to run oil therefrom, and to pay therefor the posted market price of the Prairie Pipe Line Company for crude oil on the date said oil is run by the party of the second part, plus 25 cents per barrel premium.

This agreement shall extend to and be binding on the parties hereto, their heirs, executors, administrators, successors, and assigns.

In witness whereof, the parties hereto have hereunto set their hands and seals on the day and year hereinabove written.

By mutual consent of the contracting parties, no division order was attached to the contract, as mentioned therein, and the contract was put in operation without such division order. The terms of the contract were carried out by the parties for about three months, when the plaintiff in error, who will be designated herein as the Western Corporation, assigned the foregoing instrument to the American Oil Company; the latter company assuming all obligations of the Western Corporation under the instrument, and acquiring all its rights thereunder. Thereupon the Western Corporation notified the sellers of such assignment, demanding that they look to the American Oil Company for their pay for all future deliveries of oil under the contract of sale, and disclaiming and renouncing all liability on the part of said corporation for any future deliveries of oil under the contract. The American Oil Company, claiming to have succeeded to all the obligations of the Western Corporation under the contract of sale, as well as to the rights of the corporation thereunder, made demand of the sellers that the latter continue to make deliveries of oil to said oil company under the sale contract; the said oil company being solvent at the time. This demand was refused by the sellers, except upon condition that the Western Corporation should recognize its liability under the contract, which the said corporation refused to do, but reiterated its renunciation of liability thereunder. This attitude of the Western Corporation was maintained by it on the asserted ground, which is urged here also, that because the contract of sale, by its terms, ran to the assigns of the contracting parties, the assignment that had been made to the American Oil Company had effect to transfer to that company the obligations of the Western Corporation under the contract of sale and to relieve the corporation of those obligations. The sellers treated the contract of sale in question as terminated. On July 13, 1923, they conveyed their leaseholds to the defendants in error, Bliss & Wetherbee, and assigned to them all their rights and claims against the Western Corporation growing out of the contract of sale in question. The defendants in error thereafter brought this suit against the Western Corporation for damages resulting from its alleged breach of said contract of sale in repudiating its liability under the contract, as stated above. The trial court found as a fact that the sellers and their assignees, the defendants in error, exercised due diligence in minimizing their damage resulting from said breach, and rendered judgment for the defendants in error for $4,420.25 damages. The Court of Civil Appeals affirmed that judgment.

The contract of sale, at the time it was made, was wholly executory, and was constituted of the promise of the sellers, on the one hand, to the effect that they or their assigns would sell and deliver to the Western Corporation, or its assigns, the oil produced from the leaseholds named, as it was produced during the six months' period named in the contract, and, on the other hand, of the promise of that corporation to the effect that it or its assigns would pay for the oil thus delivered, as stipulated in the contract. These obligations of the respective parties were interdependent, and there is no provision in the contract for the release of either promisor by the substitution of the promise of another. The provision declaring that the agreement should extend to and be binding on the assigns of the parties is not to be construed as authorizing such a release.

The mere fact that a contract is invested, by consent of the parties or otherwise, with the quality of assignability, does not signify that either party may, by assigning the contract, release himself from liability under it. When a contract is assignable, a party may assign the benefits of his contract to another, and delegate to his assignee the performance of his obligations under the contract; but he remains liable for the proper performance of those obligations, unless the other party to the contract consents for the assignment to have the effect of releasing him. 5 *C.J.* § 45, p. 878, and authorities there cited.

The Western Corporation was not released from its contract by the assignment to the American Oil Company. The unexecuted portion of the contract remained constituted, as it was in the beginning, of the mutual promises of the contracting parties. When, therefore, the corporation repudiated all liability for future deliveries of oil, it committed an anticipatory breach, and the sellers thereupon became entitled to terminate the contract. [citations]

The contract having been thus terminated, the sellers' obligation to make future deliveries of oil under it was released; and the sellers were under no obligation which required them to substitute the promise of the American Oil Company for that of the Western Corporation which had been repudiated. Nor was it the duty of the sellers, in order to minimize their damage, to waive the breach and continue to deliver oil to the oil company under the contract. Nor is the evidence such as to establish, as a matter of law, that the sellers, or the defendants in error, failed to exercise ordinary prudence and diligence to mitigate the damage flowing from said breach.

We recommend that the judgment of the Court of Civil Appeals affirming the judgment of the trial court be affirmed.

[Affirmed.]

PROBLEMS

11. O, the owner of a mare, leased her to L with a guarantee of restitution if she proved barren. Soon thereafter O transferred ownership in the mare and assigned the lease to D in partial satisfaction of a debt owed by O to D. When L was notified of the transaction L wrote to D, informing D that

the mare was barren, offering to return her, and requesting a refund of the rental payments. D refused and L brought suit against D. What result?

12.   X Corp. leased 125 air conditioning units from P. The lease was for a period of five years at a stipulated monthly rental. The lease contained an acceleration clause. There was also a realty mortgage on X's property which required the presence of 125 air conditioning units. The lease was recorded. X failed to make payments in June and July, and P invoked the acceleration clause. In July, X sold the property to the defendant. P notified defendant that it was owed $29,000. Defendant replied that it had not assumed any contractual obligation to P and agreed that P could remove the air conditioners. However, when the mortgagee of the realty learned of this, it informed defendant that the mortgage would be foreclosed if the units were removed and not replaced by similar units. Defendant then refused to allow P to remove the units. Is defendant contractually obligated to P?

13.   D Inc. (D) obtained approval for a subdivision on the Oregon coast. It contracted to sell the lots to purchasers who agreed to pay the price in installments prior to receipt of their deeds (what in many jurisdictions are known as contracts for deed). Each of the contracts contained a promise by D to install a water supply system for use of the purchasers. D assigned some of these contracts to X, Y and Z, giving them a deed to the parcels to which the contracts related. The balance of the contracts were assigned to K, who agreed to assume D's obligation to install the water supply system that would service each of the lots in the subdivision. K failed to provide the water system and has been declared bankrupt. Because of the lack of water the contract purchasers have ceased to pay X, Y, and Z and the lots are practically worthless. X, Y, and Z would like to make a claim against D. Under what theory should they proceed?

SECTION 4.   DEFENSES, COUNTERCLAIMS AND LATENT EQUITIES

(Calamari & Perillo on Contracts §§ 18.17—18.22)

ASSOCIATES LOAN CO. v. WALKER

Supreme Court of New Mexico, 1966.
76 N.M. 520 416 P.2d 529.

SPIESS, JUDGE, Court of Appeals. The appellant, Associates Loan Company, brought suit against appellees, Earl Walker and his wife, Billie Walker, upon a written contract executed by them and involving the sale of a mechanical water softener. Appellant will be referred to as Associates, and appellees as Walkers.

Walkers were the owners of and operated a dairy farm in Roosevelt County. One, Daniel R. Partin, was engaged in the business of selling mechanical water softeners under the trade name of Lindsay Soft Water

Company of Portales. On or about May 1, 1962, Partin solicited Walkers to purchase a water softener to be used by Walkers to improve the drinking water for their dairy herd. Partin represented to Walkers that through use of the device their milk production would be increased and the water softener could be paid for through such increased production.

Walkers were interested in purchasing the device if it, in fact, would increase their milk production. It was accordingly orally agreed that Partin would install a water softener at the Walker farm upon a trial basis. If, through use of the device, milk production was actually increased then Walkers would buy it. If the condition did not happen and the device did not serve to increase production as represented by Partin, the Walkers would not be obligated to buy the device and Partin would remove it from the farm.

At the time of, or subsequent to the making of the oral agreement, and at Partin's request, Walkers executed an instrument entitled "All Goods Retail Installment Contract," being the contract upon which suit was brought. The contract states that Walkers purchased the water softener for a stated sum to which was added a finance charge. The total amount was to be paid in monthly installments commencing June 6, 1962.

The contract, in addition to containing usual remedies in the event of default, provided that title to the device would remain in the seller until the price was fully paid. Partin orally agreed that the contract would not be assigned or transferred. After Partin had obtained the execution of the instrument by Walkers he caused it to be assigned to Associates. The device was installed on the Walker farm and after trial it was determined by Walkers and Partin that it had not and would not increase milk production.

Walkers made no payments upon the contract which had been assigned to Associates. A number of payments, however, were made to Associates by Partin and by a Stirman Rivers, who acquired the Partin business and assumed payment of the particular contract held by Associates, which was treated by both Partin and Rivers as Partin's obligation. The water softener was ultimately removed by Rivers from the Walker farm. . . .

The defense, in substance, is that Partin and Walkers agreed that there would be no sale and the contract would not be effective unless after trial the water softener served to increase Walkers' milk production. This agreement was made orally at the time, or prior to the signing of the written contract. Walkers contend that the oral agreement created a condition precedent to the written contract becoming a valid obligation.

It is further asserted that since the condition failed the contract did not come into existence.

The trial court found the issues in favor of Walkers and entered judgment against Associates from which it has appealed. . . .

The fundamental rule of law ... is that an assignee of a chose in action acquires by virtue of his assignment nothing more than the assignor had and all equities and defense which could have been raised by the debtor against the assignor are available to the debtor against the assignee.

This rule is so well recognized and settled that it needs no authoritative support. In our opinion, ... if the contract in Partin's hands was subject to a condition precedent under which it was not to become effective until the happening of a contingency, upon assignment the assignee took the contract subject to the same condition. The trial court correctly held that the defense raised by Walkers was available against the assignee, Associates. ...

We find no error in the judgment of the district court. It is, accordingly affirmed. It is so ordered.

CHAPTER 13

THE STATUTE OF FRAUDS

■ ■ ■

SECTION 1. THE ONE YEAR PROVISION

*(Calamari & Perillo on Contracts §§ 19.1,
19.35, 19.17—19.22, 19.36, 19.25)*

C.R. KLEWIN, INC. v. FLAGSHIP PROPERTIES, INC.
Supreme Court of Connecticut, 1991.
220 Conn. 569, 600 A.2d 772.

PETERS, CHIEF JUSTICE. The sole question before us in this certified appeal is whether the provision of the statute of frauds, General Statutes § 52–550(a)(5), requiring a writing for an "agreement that is not to be performed within one year from the making thereof," renders unenforceable an oral contract that fails to specify explicitly the time for performance when performance of that contract within one year of its making is exceedingly unlikely. This case comes to this court upon our grant of an application for certification from the United States Court of Appeals for the Second Circuit. . . .

The Second Circuit has provided us with the following facts. The plaintiff, C.R. Klewin, Inc. (Klewin), is a Connecticut based corporation that provides general construction contracting and construction management services. The defendants, Flagship Properties and DKM Properties (collectively Flagship), are engaged in the business of real estate development; although located outside Connecticut, they do business together in Connecticut under the trade name Conn–Tech.

Flagship became the developer of a major project (ConnTech Project) in Mansfield, near the University of Connecticut's main campus. The master plan for the project included the construction of twenty industrial buildings, a 280 room hotel and convention center, and housing for 592 graduate students and professors. The estimated total cost of the project was $120 million.

In March, 1986, Flagship representatives held a dinner meeting with Klewin representatives. Flagship was considering whether to engage Klewin to serve as construction manager on the ConnTech Project. During the discussions, Klewin advised that its fee would be 4 percent of the cost of construction plus 4 percent for its overhead and profit. This fee structure was, however, subject to change depending on when different phases of the project were to be constructed. The meeting ended with Flagship's representative shaking hands with Klewin's agent and saying, "You've got the job. We've got a deal." No other specific terms or conditions were conclusively established at trial. The parties publicized the fact that an agreement had been reached and held a press conference, which was videotaped. Additionally, they ceremoniously signed, without filling in any of the blanks, an American Institute of Architects Standard Form of Agreement between Owner and Construction Manager.

Construction began May 4, 1987, on the first phase of the ConnTech Project, called Celeron Square. The parties entered into a written agreement regarding the construction of this one part of the project. Construction was fully completed by the middle of October, 1987. By that time, because Flagship had become dissatisfied with Klewin's work, it began negotiating with other contractors for the job as construction manager on the next stage of the ConnTech Project. In March, 1988, Flagship contracted with another contractor to perform the sitework for Celeron Square II, the next phase of the project.

After having been replaced as construction manager, Klewin filed suit in the United States District Court for the District of Connecticut, claiming (1) breach of an oral contract to perform as construction manager on all phases of the project; (2) *quantum meruit* recovery for services performed in anticipation of future stages of the project; and (3) detrimental reliance on Flagship's promise to pay for preconstruction services. Flagship moved for summary judgment, claiming, *inter alia*, that enforcement of the alleged oral contract was barred by the statute of frauds. The district court granted summary judgment, reasoning that (1) "the contract was not of an indefinite duration or open-ended" because full performance would take place when all phases of the ConnTech Project were completed, and (2) the contract "as a matter of law" could not possibly have been performed within one year. In drawing this second conclusion, the court focused on the sheer scope of the project and Klewin's own admission that the entire project was intended to be constructed in three to ten years.

Klewin appealed to the United States Court of Appeals for the Second Circuit. The Court of Appeals held that "the issues presented involve substantial legal questions for which there is no clear precedent under the decisions of the Connecticut Supreme Court"; and certified to this court the following questions:[3]

---

3. These certified questions do not involve the question, which these facts raise, of whether the alleged oral contract was too vague to be enforceable.

A. Whether under the Connecticut Statute of Frauds, Conn. Gen.Stat. § 52–550(a)(5), an oral contract that fails to specify explicitly the time for performance is a contract of "indefinite duration," as that term has been used in the applicable Connecticut precedent, and therefore outside of the Statute's proscriptions?

B. Whether an oral contract is unenforceable when the method of performance called for by the contract contemplates performance to be completed over a period of time that exceeds one year, yet the contract itself does not explicitly negate the possibility of performance within one year?

We answer "yes" to the first question, and "no" to the second.

I

The Connecticut statute of frauds has its origins in a 1677 English statute entitled "An Act for the [P]revention of Fraud and Perjuries." *See* 6 W. Holdsworth, *A History of English Law* (1927) pp. 379–84. The statute appears to have been enacted in response to developments in the common law arising out of the advent of the writ of assumpsit, which changed the general rule precluding enforcement of oral promises in the King's courts. Thereafter, perjury and the subornation of perjury became a widespread and serious problem. Furthermore, because juries at that time decided cases on their own personal knowledge of the facts, rather than on the evidence introduced at trial, a requirement, in specified transactions, of "some memorandum or note . . . in writing, and signed by the party to be charged" placed a limitation on the uncontrolled discretion of the jury. *See* 2 A. Corbin, *Contracts* (1950) § 275, pp. 2–3; 6 *W. Holdsworth, supra,* pp. 387–89; An Act for Prevention of Fraud and Perjuries, 29 Car. 2, c. 3, § 4 (1677), quoted in J. Perillo, *The Statute of Frauds in the Light of the Functions and Dysfunctions of Form,* 43 Fordham L.Rev. 39, 39 n. 2 (1974). Although the British Parliament repealed most provisions of the statute, including the one-year provision, in 1954; *see* The Law Reform (Enforcement of Contracts) Act, 2 & 3 Eliz. 2, c. 34 (1954); the statute nonetheless remains the law virtually everywhere in the United States.[5]

Modern scholarly commentary has found much to criticize about the continued viability of the statute of frauds. The statute has been found wanting because it serves none of its purported functions very well; *see* J. Perillo, *supra;* and because it permits or compels economically wasteful behavior; *see* M. Braunstein, *Remedy, Reason, and the Statute of Frauds: A Critical Economic Analysis,* 1989 Utah L.Rev. 383. It is, however, the one-year provision that is at issue in this case that has caused the greatest puzzlement among commentators. As Professor Farnsworth observes, "of all the provisions of the statute, it is the most difficult to rationalize."

If the one-year provision is based on the tendency of memory to fail and of evidence to go stale with the passage of time, it is ill-

---

5. "The one-year provision has been omitted in North Carolina and Pennsylvania." 2 E. Farnsworth, *Contracts* (2d Ed.1990) § 6.4, p. 110 n. 5.

contrived because the one-year period does not run from the making of the contract to the proof of the making, but from the making of the contract to the completion of performance. If an oral contract that cannot be performed within a year is broken the day after its making, the provision applies though the terms of the contract are fresh in the minds of the parties. But if an oral contract that can be performed within a year is broken and suit is not brought until nearly six years (the usual statute of limitations for contract actions) after the breach, the provision does not apply, even though the terms of the contract are no longer fresh in the minds of the parties.

If the one-year provision is an attempt to separate significant contracts of long duration, for which writings should be required, from less significant contracts of short duration, for which writings are unnecessary, it is equally ill-contrived because the one-year period does not run from the commencement of performance to the completion of performance, but from the making of the contract to the completion of performance. If an oral contract to work for one day, 13 months from now, is broken, the provision applies, even though the duration of performance is only one day. But if an oral contract to work for a year beginning today is broken, the provision does not apply, even though the duration of performance is a full year.

2 E. Farnsworth, *Contracts* (2d Ed.1990) § 6.4, pp. 110–11; *see also* 1 *Restatement (Second), Contracts* (1979) § 130, cmt. a; J. Calamari & J. Perillo, *Contracts* (3d Ed.1987) § 19–18, p. 807.

Historians have had difficulty accounting for the original inclusion of the one-year provision. Some years after its enactment, one English judge stated that "the design of the statute was, not to trust to the memory of witnesses for a longer time than one year." Smith v. Westall, 1 Ld.Raym. 316, 317, 91 Eng.Rep. 1106, 1107 (1697). That explanation is, however, unpersuasive, since, as Farnsworth notes, the language of the statute is ill suited to this purpose. One eminent historian suggested that because such contracts are continuing contracts, it might be very difficult to give evidence of their formation, inasmuch as the rules of evidence of that time prohibited testimony by the parties to an action or any person who had an interest in the litigation. 6 *W. Holdsworth, supra,* 392. That argument, however, proves too much, since it would apply equally to all oral contracts regardless of the duration of their performance. The most extensive recent study of the history of English contract law offers plausible explanations for all of the other provisions, but acknowledges that this one is "curious." A. Simpson, *A History of the Common Law of Contract* (1975) p. 612. More recently, it has been suggested that the provision "may have been intended to prevent oral perjury in actions of assumpsit against customers who had forgotten the details of their purchases." P. Hamburger, *The Conveyancing Purposes of the Statute of Frauds*, 27 Am.J.Leg.Hist. 354, 376 n. 85 (1983).

In any case, the one-year provision no longer seems to serve any purpose very well, and today its only remaining effect is arbitrarily to forestall the adjudication of possibly meritorious claims. For this reason, the courts have for many years looked on the provision with disfavor, and have sought constructions that limited its application. *See, e.g.*, Landes Construction Co. v. Royal Bank of Canada, 833 F.2d 1365, 1370 (9th Cir.1987) (noting policy of California courts "of restricting the application of the statute to those situations precisely covered by its language"); Cunningham v. Healthco, Inc., 824 F.2d 1448, 1455 (5th Cir.1987) (one-year provision does not apply if the [contract] "conceivably" can be performed within one year); Hodge v. Evans Financial Corporation, 823 F.2d 559, 561 (D.C.Cir.1987) (statute of frauds "has long been construed narrowly and literally"); Goldstick v. ICM Realty, [788 F.2d 456, 464 (7th Cir.1986)] ("Courts tend to take the concept of 'capable of full performance' quite literally ... because they find the one-year limitation irksome.")

II

Our case law in Connecticut, like that in other jurisdictions, has taken a narrow view of the one-year provision of the statute of frauds now codified as § 52–550(a)(5). In Russell v. Slade, 12 Conn. 455, 460 (1838), this court held that "it has been repeatedly adjudged, that unless it appear *from the agreement itself*, that it is *not* to be performed within a year, the statute does not apply. ... The statute of frauds plainly means an agreement not to be performed within the space of a year, and *expressly* and *specifically* so agreed. A *contingency* is not within it; nor any case that *depends upon contingency*. It does *not* extend to cases where the thing only *may* be performed within the year." (Emphases in original; citation and internal quotation marks omitted.) ...

More recently, in Finley v. Aetna Life & Casualty Co., 202 Conn. 190, 197, 520 A.2d 208 (1987), we stated that " '(u)nder the prevailing interpretation, the enforceability of a contract under the one-year provision does not turn on the actual course of subsequent events, nor on the expectations of the parties as to the probabilities. Contracts of uncertain duration are simply excluded; the provision covers *only* those contracts whose performance *cannot possibly* be completed within a year.' (Emphasis added.) 1 *Restatement (Second), Contracts, supra.*"

In light of this unbroken line of authority, the legislature's decision repeatedly to reenact the provision in language virtually identical to that of the 1677 statute suggests legislative approval of the restrictive interpretation that this court has given to the one-year provision. "(T)he action of the General Assembly in re-enacting the statute, including the clause in question ... is presumed to have been done in the light of those decisions." Turner v. Scanlon, 146 Conn. 149, 156, 148 A.2d 334 (1959).

III

Bearing this history in mind, we turn to the questions certified to us by the federal court. Our case law makes no distinction, with respect to exclusion from the statute of frauds, between contracts of uncertain or indefinite duration and contracts that contain no express terms defining the time for performance. The two certified questions therefore raise only one substantive issue. That issue can be framed as follows: in the exclusion from the statute of frauds of all contracts except those "whose performance cannot possibly be completed within a year"; (emphasis omitted) Finley v. Aetna Life & Casualty Co., *supra*, 202 Conn. at 197, 520 A.2d 208; what meaning should be attributed to the word "possibly"? One construction of "possibly" would encompass only contracts whose completion within a year would be inconsistent with the express terms of the contract. An alternate construction would include as well contracts such as the one involved in this case, in which, while no time period is expressly specified, it is (as the district court found) realistically impossible for performance to be completed within a year. We now hold that the former and not the latter is the correct interpretation. "The critical test . . . is whether 'by its terms' the agreement is not to be performed within a year," so that the statute will not apply where "the alleged agreement contain(s) (no) provision which directly or indirectly regulated the time for performance." Freedman v. Chemical Construction Corporation, 43 N.Y.2d 260, 265, 372 N.E.2d 12, 401 N.Y.S.2d 176 (1977). "It is the law of this state, as it is elsewhere, that a contract is not within this clause of the statute unless *its terms are so drawn that* it cannot by any possibility be performed fully within one year." (Emphasis added.) Burkle v. Superflow Mfg. Co., 137 Conn. [488] at 492, 78 A.2d 698 [1951].

Flagship contends, to the contrary, that the possibility to which this court referred in *Burkle* must be a reasonable possibility rather than a theoretical possibility. It is true that in *Burkle* this court rejected the argument that "since all the members of a partnership (that was a party to the contract) may possibly die within a year, the contract is not within the statute." We noted that "(n)o case has come to our attention where the rule that the possibility of death within a year removes a contract from the statute has been extended to apply to the possibility of the death of more than one individual." *Id.*, at 494, 78 A.2d 698. In *Burkle*, however, we merely refused to extend further yet another of the rules by which the effect of the provision has been limited. *Burkle* did not purport to change the well-established rule of narrow construction of the underlying one-year provision.

Most other jurisdictions follow a similar rule requiring an express contractual provision specifying that performance will extend for more than one year. Only "(a) few jurisdictions, contrary to the great weight of authority . . . hold that the intention of the parties may put their oral agreement within the operation of the Statute." 3 S. Williston, *Contracts* (3d Ed. W. Jaeger 1960) § 495, pp. 584–85. In "the leading case on this section of the Statute"; *id.*, p. 578; the Supreme Court of the United States undertook an extensive survey of the case law up to that time and concluded that (i)t . . . appears to have been the settled construction of this clause of the statute in England, before the Declaration of Independence, that an oral agreement which, according to the intention of the parties, *as shown by the terms of the contract*, might be fully performed within a year from the time it was made, was not within the statute, although the time of its performance was uncertain, and might probably extend, and be expected by the parties to extend, and did in fact extend, beyond the year. The several States of the Union, in reenacting this provision of the statute of frauds in its original words, must be taken to have adopted the known and settled construction which it had received by judicial decisions in England.

(Emphasis added.) Warner v. Texas & Pacific R. Co., 164 U.S. 418, 422–23, 17 S.Ct. 147, 149–50, 41 L.Ed. 495 (1896). The agreement at issue was one in which a lumbermill agreed to provide grading and ties and the railway agreed to construct rails and a switch and maintain the switch as long as the lumbermill needed it for shipping purposes. Although the land adjoining the lumbermill contained enough lumber to run a mill for thirty years, and the lumbermill used the switch for thirteen years, the court held that the contract was not within the statute.

The parties may well have expected that the contract would continue in force for more than one year; it may have been very improbable that it would not do so; and it did in fact continue in force for a much longer time. But they made no stipulation which in terms, or by reasonable inference, required that result. The question is not what the probable, or expected, or actual performance of the contract was; but whether the contract, *according to the reasonable interpretation of its terms*, required that it should not be performed within the year.

(Emphasis added.) *Id.*, at 434, 17 S.Ct. at 153–54.

Because the one-year provision "is an anachronism in modern life . . . we are not disposed to expand its destructive force." Farmer v. Arabian American Oil Co., 277 F.2d 46, 51 (2d Cir.1960). When a contract contains no express terms about the time for performance, no sound reason of policy commends judicial pursuit of a collateral inquiry into whether, at the time of the making of the contract, it was realistically possible that performance of the contract would be completed within a year. Such a collateral inquiry would not only expand the "destructive force" of the statute by extending it to contracts not plainly within its terms, but would also inevitably waste judicial resources on the resolution of an issue that has nothing to do with the merits of the case or the attainment of a just outcome. *See* 2 *A. Corbin, supra*, § 275, p. 14 (the statute "has been in part the cause of an immense amount of litigation as to whether a promise is within the statute or can by any remote possibility be taken out of it. This latter fact is fully evidenced by the space necessary to be devoted to the subject in this volume and by the vast number of cases to be cited").

We therefore hold that an oral contract that does not say, in express terms, that performance is to have a specific duration beyond one year is, as a matter of law, the functional equivalent of a contract of indefinite duration for the purposes of the statute of frauds. Like a contract of indefinite duration, such a contract is enforceable because it is outside the proscriptive force of the statute regardless of how long completion of performance will actually take.

The first certified question is answered "yes." The second certified question is answered "no." No costs will be taxed in this court to either party.

In this opinion the other Justices concurred.

J. M. PERILLO, THE STATUTE OF FRAUDS IN THE LIGHT OF THE FUNCTIONS AND DYSFUNCTIONS OF FORM

43 Fordham L. Rev. 39, 77 (1974).

No one knows why agreements not performable within a year were selected to be within the Statute. Usually, it is speculated that the selection of this class was motivated by a policy akin to that of the statute of limitations, *i.e.,* if the interval between the making of the promise and its proof in court is overly long, the difficulties of proof make desirable a more cogent type of evidence than testimony. If this is indeed the rationale the statute serves it poorly. [A footnote to this part of the article says, "It seems quite likely, however, that, as in the case of the other subdivisions, the draftsmen had in mind a transaction type: employment and similar relationships such as apprenticeships and fiduciary retainers. The common law rule was that a general hiring was presumed to be for a one-year term. 1 W. Blackstone *Commentaries* *425. But long-term apprenticeships, clerkships, etc. were commonplace."]

EHRLICH v. DIGGS

United States District Court, E.D.N.Y., 2001.
169 F.Supp.2d 124.

DEARIE, DISTRICT JUDGE. Plaintiff David M. Ehrlich, a manager of musical groups, seeks a portion of defendant Robert Diggs's earnings arising from his activities as a member [of] the Gravediggaz, a rap music group, and as a solo artist. Defendant moves to dismiss and, in the alternative, for summary judgment. The critical issues raised concern the enforceability of an oral management contract between plaintiff and the Gravediggaz. The resolution of this question, and the appropriateness of dismissal or of summary judgment, depends on the choice of law to be applied.

BACKGROUND

Plaintiff David Ehrlich is a manager of musical groups and an attorney. He conducts business under the name DME Management, and he formerly worked under the name DuKane Management. Plaintiff is a resident of California and is admitted to practice law in New York. Defendant Robert Diggs is a popular rap artist, professionally known as RZA and Prince Rakim. He is a resident of New York. Although defendant maintains an affiliation with his original musical group, known as the Gravediggaz, he has gone on to an extremely successful career as a solo recording artist, producer and member of another rap group, the Wu Tang Clan.

On July 1, 1993, plaintiff and the Gravediggaz entered into a written contract under which the Gravediggaz retained plaintiff as their exclusive representative in negotiating a record contract with a major record label (the "Shopping/Finders Agreement"). On July 2, 1993, allegedly as a result of plaintiff's efforts, the Gravediggaz entered into a written contract with Gee Street Records (the "Gravediggaz/Gee Street Contract"). This contract contains a provision giving Gee Street an option for the recording services of defendant as a solo artist.

In August 1993, plaintiff was hired as the manager of the Gravediggaz pursuant to an oral agreement (the "Management Agreement"). The Management Agreement was never reduced to writing. Plaintiff claims that he was to receive fifteen percent of the gross earnings of the Gravediggaz and each of its members for "all entertainment-related employment, engagements or agreements commenced or entered into" while he served as manager of the group. In addition, the Management Agreement was terminable by either plaintiff or the group at any time. The enforceability of this oral contract is the primary focus of this dispute. Plaintiff contends that the duties of a manager, including the duty to advise and counsel each member of a group individually, are universally known in the music recording industry and that these understandings were shared by all parties, including defendant, at the time the oral Management Agreement was made. Moreover, according to plaintiff, it is standard industry practice that the manager of a musical group is entitled to commissions on entertainment-related work by each member of the group, whether performed individually or performed as a group member.

On December 20, 1996, defendant entered into a written contract with Gee Street as a solo recording artist (the "Gee Street/Diggs Contract"). Defendant argues that this contract is independent of the earlier relationship between plaintiff and defendant. Plaintiff counters that the option given to Gee Street for defendant's individual recording services at ¶ 22 of the Gravediggaz/Gee Street Contract was largely the result of discussions between plaintiff and defendant regarding the possibility of defendant working solo and was negotiated by plaintiff at defendant's specific request. Because defendant ultimately contracted with Gee Street to record as an individual, the 1993 Gravediggaz/Gee Street Contract and the 1996 Gee Street/Diggs Contract are, according to plaintiff, "inextricably linked."

The complaint asserts five claims based on the written and oral contracts between the parties relating to periods in which defendant was a member of the Gravediggaz as well as subsequent periods in which defendant was a solo artist and member of the Wu Tang Clan. In the first claim, plaintiff seeks commissions based on defendant's earnings from individual work, both as a recording artist and as a producer. In the second claim, he seeks a portion of the "ancillary sums" earned by defendant as a result of defendant's work as a member of the Gravediggaz. Plaintiff seeks a percentage of earnings from defendant's production of two Gravediggaz albums and direction of a Gravediggaz music video in the third claim. In the fourth claim, plaintiff seeks an accounting of all sums of money received by defendant and seeks commissions due on such sums as a result of his efforts. Finally, in the fifth claim, plaintiff seeks damages for substantial cost overruns and depressed album sales suffered as a result of defendant's late or canceled appearances for Gravediggaz tours, concerts, events, recording and video sessions.

. . . [D]efendant contends that the claims must be dismissed because enforcement of the Management Agreement is barred by the statute of frauds.

Notwithstanding defendant's detailed arguments that plaintiff's claims based on the Shopping/Finders Agreement must be dismissed, the gravamen of the complaint is that defendant breached the oral Management Agreement. Accordingly, this Court will not address the defendant's contentions with respect to the Shopping/Finders Agreement. The remaining issues are whether the enforcement of the Management Agreement is barred by the statute of frauds and whether the agreement is too indefinite to be enforced. For the reasons set forth below, this Court finds that enforcement is not barred and the agreement is not void for indefiniteness. Accordingly, defendant's motion is denied.

DISCUSSION

The California and New York Statutes of Frauds

Defendant contends that New York law applies and that New York's Statute of Frauds bars enforcement of the oral Management Agreement. Plaintiff counters that California law should apply and that under the California Statute of Frauds, the Management Agreement is enforceable. To resolve the issue, this Court must apply New York's choice of law rules. . . .

The relevant New York and California provisions are nearly facially identical. New York's Statute of Frauds provides:

> (e)very agreement, promise or undertaking is void, unless it or some note or memorandum thereof be in writing, and subscribed by the party to be charged therewith, or by his lawful agent, if such agreement, promise or undertaking: 1. By its terms is not to be performed within one year from the making thereof. . . .

N.Y.Gen.Oblig.Law § 5–701(a)(1). Similarly, California's statute provides:

(t)he following contracts are invalid, unless they, or some note or memorandum thereof, are in writing and subscribed by the party to be charged or by the party's agent: (1) An agreement that by its terms is not to be performed within a year from the making thereof.

Cal.Civ.Code § 1624(a)(1). However, as set forth more fully below, the statutes have been interpreted differently. California's statute has been interpreted literally and narrowly. Rosenthal v. Fonda, 862 F.2d 1398, 1401 (9th Cir.1988). Court's [*sic*] have held that employment contracts that are terminable at the will of either party fall outside the bar. *Id.* In contrast, the New York Statute of Frauds has been interpreted to bar enforcement of an employment contract requiring commission payments unless after the plaintiff has performed, "the defendant can unilaterally terminate the contract, discharging all promises made to the plaintiff including the promise to make commission payments." *Id.*

California Law

An oral contract is unenforceable under California law only if it expressly precludes performance within one year or by its terms cannot possibly be performed within one year. [citations] This has been interpreted to exempt contracts that are terminable within one year by either party from the Statute of Frauds. As set forth in Plumlee [v. Poag]:

> (a)lthough the majority of jurisdictions have held that a party's option to put an end to a contract within a year does not take it out of the operation of the statute of frauds, on the grounds that to be discharged from liability under a contract is not to "perform" it, the California rule is to the contrary: A contract . . . may be taken out of (the statute of frauds's) operation by the fact that a party (or at least a defendant) may rightfully terminate it within a year.

150 Cal.App.3d [541] at 550, 198 Cal.Rptr. 66 [(Cal.Ct.App.1984)]. Because contracts that may be terminated at will by either party can, by their terms, be "performed" within one year, they are enforceable. White Lighting [Co. v. Wolfson], 68 Cal.2d [336] at 344, 66 Cal.Rptr. 697, 438 P.2d 345 [(Cal.1968)]; *see also* Jenkins v. Family Health Program, 214 Cal.App.3d 440, 445–46, 262 Cal.Rptr. 798 (Cal.Dist.Ct.App.1989) (if plaintiff employee can terminate at will and defendant employer can terminate for cause, the contract is enforceable). Moreover, employment contracts providing for payment upon termination of the employment relationship or payment of a bonus ascertainable only after one year are not barred. White Lighting, 68 Cal.2d at 344, 66 Cal.Rptr. 697, 438 P.2d 345.

Thus, under California law, the oral Management Agreement, as alleged, is not barred by the Statute of Frauds. Rosenthal v. Fonda, 862 F.2d 1398 (9th Cir.1988), supports this conclusion in dicta. In *Rosenthal*, plaintiff alleged that defendant actress Jane Fonda entered into an oral contract with him for a variety of services in exchange for a percentage of income derived from projects initiated during his tenure. Although the court ultimately applied New York law, it concluded that because the oral contract was terminable at the will of either party, the contract would fall outside California's Statute of Frauds as a contract capable of being performed within one year. Rosenthal, 862 F.2d at 1401.

New York

New York courts have interpreted the Statute of Frauds somewhat differently. The key issue in determining the applicability of New York's Statute of Frauds is whether the defendant can unilaterally terminate the contract, discharging all promises made. North Shore Bottling Co. v. C. Schmidt & Sons, Inc., 22 N.Y.2d 171, 176–77, 239 N.E.2d 189, 292 N.Y.S.2d 86 (N.Y.1968). Contracts involving performance which is dependent on the will of a third party, and not solely upon the will of the parties to the contract, fall within the Statute of Frauds. [citations] Commission sales arrangements that extend beyond an employee's termination, therefore, are barred. *See, e.g,* Zupan v. Blumberg, 2 N.Y.2d 547, 141 N.E.2d 819, 161 N.Y.S.2d 428 (N.Y.1957) (agreement for 25% commission on any account brought so long as account was active barred).

As alleged by plaintiff, defendant does not have a unilateral right to terminate the Management Agreement. Defendant is obligated to turn over fifteen percent of his gross earnings "for all entertainment-related employment, engagements or agreements commenced or entered into while (plaintiff) served as manager of the (Gravediggaz)." The earnings in which plaintiff has an interest may continue indefinitely, as recordings and other musical works sold to third parties will generate earnings far into the future. Thus, defendant has an ongoing obligation to pay plaintiff that he cannot terminate. This open-ended interest is squarely within the Statute of Frauds under New York law. *See, e.g.,* Grossberg v. Double H. Licensing Corp., 86 A.D.2d 565, 446 N.Y.S.2d 296 (1982) (agreement to produce a record in exchange for a royalty on all records sold barred; "defendants' liability endured so long as a single record ... was sold anywhere in the world"); Kantor v. Watson, 167 A.D.2d 297, 298, 562 N.Y.S.2d 39 (N.Y.App.Div.1990) (agreement to develop, produce and market screenplay based on defendant's childhood barred; "payments to plaintiff contemplated under the alleged agreement clearly could not be accomplished within one year, as plaintiff was to share any compensation received from exploitation of defendant's screenplay").[4]

[Applying New York's choice of law rule (the "center of gravity" or "grouping of contacts" test generally applicable in contracts cases), the court determined that California substantive law governed. It then held the contract to be sufficiently definite for enforcement. Ed.]'

4. Cron v. Hargro Fabrics, Inc., 91 N.Y.2d 362, 694 N.E.2d 56, 670 N.Y.S.2d 973 (N.Y.1998), enforcing an alleged oral agreement to pay a bonus consisting of a percentage of a company's annual pretax profits, calculable after the close of the year, does not alter treatment of continuing commission arrangements like the one at issue. The ruling represents only a "slight modification of the language in previous case law concerning the necessity of full payment by all parties within a year to satisfy the Statute of Frauds." *Id.* at 370, 670 N.Y.S.2d 973, 694 N.E.2d 56.

Conclusion

For the reasons set forth above, the Court concludes that California law applies to this contract dispute and that the oral Management Agreement is not barred by the California Statute of Frauds. Further, the Court concludes that the oral contract as alleged is sufficiently definite to be enforced. Accordingly, defendant's motion to dismiss and, in the alternative, for summary judgement is denied. ... In addition, the Court denies defendant's motion to dismiss plaintiff's fifth claim seeking damages as a result of defendant's late or canceled appearances.

PROBLEMS

1. Plaintiff and defendant entered into an oral contract for services for one year to be rendered by plaintiff. The term of service was to commence as soon as plaintiff could amicably sever her employment with her present employer. Is the contract within the Statute of Frauds?

2. On November 20 plaintiff and defendant entered into an oral agreement whereby plaintiff would be employed as defendant's advertising manager. The employment term was to be one year, commencing the following January 1st. Plaintiff commenced working for defendant, on January 1st as agreed, and on January 2nd plaintiff and defendant had a conversation in which the terms and conditions of employment, including the period of employment, were again discussed and agreed to. On June 15, plaintiff's employment was terminated. Plaintiff sues and defendant raises the defense of the Statute of Frauds. What result?

3. P entered Georgetown Law School as a first year student. D, an old friend of the family, hired P to be a part-time resident manager of an apartment complex controlled by D. P was promised a rent-free apartment plus a salary. The agreement, which was oral, provided that the position was to continue "until P completed his law studies at Georgetown or was obliged to discontinue these studies." Five weeks after the agreement was made, P was dismissed from his job at the apartment complex. When P sued for breach, D raised the defense of the Statute of Frauds. What result?

4. Which, if any, of the following contracts is within the Statute of Frauds?

(a) A agrees to work for B for two years.

(b) A agrees to work for B for A's lifetime, not exceeding two years.

(c) A agrees to work for B for two years if A lives that long.

(d) A agrees to work for B for two years but if A dies the contract shall be terminated.

5. Defendant, a grocer, sold his stock of groceries and his good will to the plaintiff and orally agreed that he would not re-enter the grocery business in the City of Chicopee for five years. Plaintiff sues for breach of this oral promise. Defendant raises the defense of the Statute of Frauds. What result?

SECTION 2. THE MEMORANDUM

(Calamari & Perillo on Contracts §§ 19.26—19.33)

CRABTREE v. ELIZABETH ARDEN SALES CORP.

Court of Appeals of New York, 1953.
305 N.Y. 48, 110 N.E.2d 551.

FULD, JUDGE. In September of 1947, Nate Crabtree entered into preliminary negotiations with Elizabeth Arden Sales Corporation, manufacturers and sellers of cosmetics, looking toward his employment as sales manager. Interviewed on September 26th, by Robert P. Johns, executive vice-president and general manager of the corporation, who had apprised him of the possible opening, Crabtree requested a three-year contract at $25,000 a year. Explaining that he would be giving up a secure well-paying job to take a position in an entirely new field of endeavor—which he believed would take him some years to master—he insisted upon an agreement for a definite term. And he repeated his desire for a contract for three years to Miss Elizabeth Arden, the corporation's president. When Miss Arden finally indicated that she was prepared to offer a two-year contract, based on an annual salary of $20,000 for the first six months, $25,000 for the second six months and $30,000 for the second year plus expenses of $5,000 a year for each of those years, Crabtree replied that that offer was "interesting." Miss Arden thereupon had her personal secretary make this memorandum on a telephone order blank that happened to be at hand:

> EMPLOYMENT AGREEMENT WITH
> NATE CRABTREE   Date Sept. 26–1947
> At 681—5th Ave   6: PM
>   . . .
> Begin   20000.
> 6 months   25000.
> 6   "   30000.
>   5000.—per year
>   Expense money
>   [2 years to make good]
>   Arrangement with Mr. Crabtree
>   By Miss Arden
>   Present Miss Arden
>   Mr. John [*sic*]
>   Mr. Crabtree
>   Miss OLeary

A few days later, Crabtree phoned Mr. Johns and telegraphed Miss Arden; he accepted the "invitation to join the Arden organization," and Miss Arden wired back her "welcome." When he reported for work a "pay-roll change" card was made up and initialed by Mr. Johns, and then forwarded to the payroll department. Reciting that it was prepared on September 30, 1947, and was to be effective as of October 22d, it specified the names of the parties, Crabtree's "Job Classification" and, in addition, contained the notation that "This employee is to be paid as follows":

First six months of employment	$20,000.	per annum
Next six months of employment	25,000.	" "
After one year of employment	30,000.	" "

Approved by RPJ [initialed]

After six months of employment, Crabtree received the scheduled increase from $20,000 to $25,000, but the further specified increase at the end of the year was not paid. Both Mr. Johns and the comptroller of the corporation, Mr. Carstens, told Crabtree that they would attempt to straighten out the matter with Miss Arden, and, with that in mind, the comptroller prepared another "pay-roll change" card, to which his signature is appended, noting that there was to be a "Salary increase" from $25,000 to $30,000 a year, "per contractual arrangements with Miss Arden." The latter, however, refused to approve the increase and, after further fruitless discussion, plaintiff left defendant's employ and commenced this action for breach of contract.

At the ensuing trial, defendant denied the existence of any agreement to employ plaintiff for two years, and further contended that, even if one had been made, the statute of frauds barred its enforcement. The trial court found against defendant on both issues and awarded plaintiff damages of about $14,000, and the Appellate Division, two justices dissenting, affirmed. Since the contract relied upon was not to be performed within a year, the primary question for decision is whether there was a memorandum of its terms, subscribed by defendant, to satisfy the statute of frauds, Personal Property Law, § 31 [now McKinney's N.Y.Gen'l Obl.L. § 5–701(a)(1), ed.].

Each of the two payroll cards—the one initialed by defendant's general manager, the other signed by its comptroller—unquestionably constitutes a memorandum under the statute. That they were not prepared or signed with the intention of evidencing the contract, or that they came into existence subsequent to its execution, is of no consequence, *see* Marks v. Cowdin, 226 N.Y. 138, 145, 123 N.E. 139, 141; *see, also, Restatement, Contracts*, §§ 209, 210, 214; it is enough to meet the statute's demands, that they were signed with intent to authenticate the information contained therein and that such information does evidence the terms of the contract. *See* ... 2 *Corbin on Contracts* (1951), pp. 732–733, 763–764; 2 *Williston on Contracts* (Rev. ed., 1936), pp. 1682–1683. Those two writings contain all of the essential terms of the contract—the parties to it, the position that plaintiff was to assume, the salary that he was to receive—except that relating to the duration of plaintiff's employment. Accordingly, we must consider whether that item, the length of the contract, may be supplied by reference to the earlier unsigned office memorandum, and, if so, whether its notation, "2 years to make good," sufficiently designates a period of employment.

The statute of frauds does not require the "memorandum . . . to be in one document. It may be pieced together out of separate writings, connected with one another either expressly or by the internal evidence of subject-matter and occasion." Marks v. Cowdin, *supra*, 226 N.Y. 138, 145, 123 N.E. 139, 141, *see also*, 2 *Williston*, p. 1671; *Restatement, Contracts*, § 208, subd. [a]. Where each of the separate writings has been subscribed by the party to be charged, little if any difficulty is encountered. *See, e.g.*, Marks v. Cowdin, *supra*, 226 N.Y. 138, 144–145, 123 N.E. 139, 141. Where, however, some writings have been signed, and others have not—as in the case before us—there is basic disagreement as to what constitutes a sufficient connection permitting the unsigned papers to be considered as part of the statutory memorandum. The courts of some jurisdictions insist that there be a reference, of varying degrees of specificity, in the signed writing to that unsigned, and, if there is no such reference, they refuse to permit consideration of the latter in determining whether the memorandum satisfies the statute. That conclusion is based upon a construction of the statute which requires that the connection between the writings and defendant's acknowledgment of the one not subscribed, appear from examination of the papers alone, without the aid of parol evidence. The other position—which has gained increasing support over the years—is that a sufficient connection between the papers is established simply by a reference in them to the same subject matter or transaction. The statute is not pressed "to the extreme of a literal and rigid logic," Marks v. Cowdin, *supra*, 226 N.Y. 138, 144, 123 N.E. 139, 141, and oral testimony is admitted to show the connection between the documents and to establish the acquiescence, of the party to be charged, to the contents of the one unsigned.

The view last expressed impresses us as the more sound, and, indeed—although several of our cases appear to have gone the other way—this court has on a number of occasions approved the rule, and we now definitively adopt it, permitting the signed and unsigned writings to be read together, provided that they clearly refer to the same subject matter or transaction.

The language of the statute—"Every agreement . . . is void, unless . . . some note or memorandum thereof be in writing, and subscribed by the party to be charged," Personal Property Law, § 31 [now McKinney's N.Y.Gen'l Obl.L. § 5–701(a)(1), ed.]—does not impose the requirement that the signed acknowledgment of the contract must appear from the writings alone, unaided by oral testimony. The danger of fraud and perjury, generally attendant upon the admission of parol evidence, is at a minimum in a case such as this. None of the terms of the contract are supplied by parol. All of them must be set out in the various writings presented to the court, and at least one writing, the one establishing a contractual relationship between the parties, must bear the signature of the party to be charged, while the unsigned document must on its face refer to the same transaction as that set forth in the one that was signed. Parol evidence—to portray the circumstances surrounding the making of the memorandum—serves only to connect the separate documents and to show that there was assent, by the party to be charged, to the contents of the one unsigned. If that testimony does not convincingly connect the papers, or does not show assent to the unsigned paper, it is within the province of the judge to conclude, as a matter of law, that the statute has not been satisfied. True, the possibility still remains that, by fraud or perjury, an agreement never in fact made may occasionally be enforced under the subject matter or transaction test. It is better to run that risk, though, than to deny enforcement to all agreements, merely because the signed document made no specific mention of the unsigned writing. As the United States Supreme Court declared, in sanctioning the admission of parol evidence to establish the connection between the signed and unsigned writings[:]

> There may be cases in which it would be a violation of reason and common sense to ignore a reference which derives its significance from such (parol) proof. If there is ground for any doubt in the matter, the general rule should be enforced. But where there is no ground for doubt, its enforcement would aid, instead of discouraging, fraud.

Beckwith v. Talbot, 95 U.S. 289, 292, 24 L.Ed. 496.

Turning to the writings in the case before us—the unsigned office memo, the payroll change form initialed by the general manager Johns, and the paper signed by the comptroller Carstens—it is apparent, and most patently, that all three refer on their face to the same transaction. The parties, the position to be filled by plaintiff, the salary to be paid him, are all identically set forth; it is hardly possible that such detailed information could refer to another or a different agreement. Even more, the card signed by Carstens notes that it was prepared for the purpose of a "Salary increase per contractual arrangements with Miss Arden." That certainly constitutes a reference of sorts to a more comprehensive "arrangement," and parol is permissible to furnish the explanation.

The corroborative evidence of defendant's assent to the contents of the unsigned office memorandum is also convincing. Prepared by defendant's agent, Miss Arden's personal secretary, there is little likelihood that that paper was fraudulently manufactured or that defendant had not assented to its contents. Furthermore, the evidence as to the conduct of the parties at the time it was prepared persuasively demonstrates defendant's assent to its terms. Under such circumstances, the courts below were fully justified in finding that the three papers constituted the "memorandum" of their agreement within the meaning of the statute.

Nor can there be any doubt that the memorandum contains all of the essential terms of the contract. Only one term, the length of the employment, is in dispute. The September 26th office memorandum contains the notation, "2 years to make good." What purpose, other than to denote the length of the contract term, such a notation could have, is hard to imagine. Without it, the employment would be at will, *see* Martin v. New York Life Ins. Co., 148 N.Y. 117, 121, 42 N.E. 416, 417, and its inclusion may not be treated as meaningless or purposeless. Quite obviously, as the courts below decided, the phrase signifies that the parties agreed to a term, a certain and definite term, of two years, after which, if plaintiff did not "make good," he would be subject to discharge. And examination of other parts of the memorandum supports that construction. Throughout the writings, a scale of wages, increasing plaintiff's salary periodically, is set out; that type of arrangement is hardly consistent with the hypothesis that the employment was meant to be at will. The most that may be argued from defendant's standpoint is that "2 years to make good," is a cryptic and ambiguous statement. But, in such a case, parol evidence is admissible to explain its meaning. Having in mind the relations of the parties, the course of the negotiations and plaintiff's insistence upon security of employment, the purpose of the phrase—or so the trier of the facts was warranted in finding—was to grant plaintiff the tenure he desired.

The judgment should be affirmed, with costs. . . .

PROBLEMS

6.   Plaintiff and defendant railroad reached an oral contract whereby for a five–year term plaintiff would have the exclusive concession for advertising on defendant's rights of way, stations and cars. A written memorandum of the agreement was drawn up by defendant's staff, approved by its president and signed by the vice-president in charge. One hour after he signed it, the vice-president was called by the president who told him that she had changed her mind. The vice-president struck off his signature and placed the memorandum in the company's files. Defendant refuses to honor the agreement and plaintiff sues. What result?

7.   Defendant wrote to plaintiff offering a franchise for a two-year term on given terms. Plaintiff accepted orally. In an action by plaintiff for breach, the defendant pleads the Statute of Frauds. What result?

8.   The president of defendant XYZ company dictated a memorandum of an oral contract within the Statute of Frauds to his secretary in plaintiff's presence. The memorandum on plain white paper started out as follows: "XYZ undertakes to perform the following services"; the services were duly listed. After dictating the memorandum he left the premises, stating he had to rush to catch a plane and directing his secretary to give plaintiff a copy of the memorandum once it was typed. The secretary followed this direction. In a suit for breach of the contract, defendant pleads the Statute of Frauds, arguing that the memorandum is unsigned. What result?

9.   A and B entered into a contract within the one year provision of the Statute of Frauds. A writing was signed by both parties. Neither party noticed that the typist had mistakenly typed $40,000, where $90,000 was intended. How does this error affect the rights of the parties?

10. Assume the same facts as in the prior problem. However, assume that $40,000 was typed instead of $90,000 to confuse any unauthorized third persons who might read the document. What are the rights of the parties?

SECTION 3.   EFFECT OF PART OR FULL PERFORMANCE, RESCISSION AND MODIFICATION AND THE ONE YEAR PROVISION

(Calamari & Perillo on Contracts §§ 19.23—19.24, 19.37—19.48)

McINTOSH v. MURPHY
Supreme Court of Hawai'i, 1970.
52 Haw. 29, 469 P.2d 177.

LEVINSON, JUSTICE. This case involves an oral employment contract which allegedly violates the provision of the Statute of Frauds requiring "any agreement that is not to be performed within one year from the making thereof" to be in writing in order to be enforceable. HRS § 656–1(5). In this action the plaintiff-employee Dick McIntosh seeks to recover damages from his employer, George Murphy and Murphy Motors, Ltd., for the breach of an alleged one-year oral employment contract.

While the facts are in sharp conflict, it appears that defendant George Murphy was in southern California during March, 1964 interviewing prospective management personnel for his Chevrolet–Oldsmobile dealerships in Hawai'i. He interviewed the plaintiff twice during that time. The position of sales manager for one of the dealerships was fully discussed but no contract was entered into. In April, 1964 the plaintiff received a call from the general manager of Murphy Motors informing him of possible employment within thirty days if he was still available. The plaintiff indicated his continued interest and informed the manager that he would be available. Later in April, the plaintiff sent Murphy a telegram to the effect that he would arrive in Honolulu on Sunday, April 26, 1964. Murphy then telephoned McIntosh on Saturday, April 25, 1964 to notify him that the job of assistant sales manager was open and work would begin on the following Monday, April 27, 1964. At that time McIntosh expressed surprise at the change in job title from sales manager to assistant sales manager but reconfirmed the fact that he was arriving in Honolulu the next day, Sunday. McIntosh arrived on Sunday, April 26, 1964 and began work on the following day, Monday, April 27, 1964.

As a consequence of his decision to work for Murphy, McIntosh moved some of his belongings from the mainland to Hawai'i, sold other possessions, leased an apartment in Honolulu and obviously forwent any other employment opportunities. In short, the plaintiff did all those things which were incidental to changing one's residence permanently from Los Angeles to Honolulu, a distance of approximately 2200 miles. McIntosh continued working for Murphy until July 16, 1964, approximately two and one-half months, at which time he was discharged on the grounds that he was unable to close deals with prospective customers and could not train the salesmen.

At the conclusion of the trial, the defense moved for a directed verdict arguing that the oral employment agreement was in violation of the Statute of Frauds, there being no written memorandum or note thereof. The trial court ruled that as a matter of law the contract did not come within the Statute, reasoning that Murphy bargained for acceptance by the actual commencement of performance by McIntosh, so that McIntosh was not bound by a contract until he came to work on Monday, April 27, 1964. Therefore, assuming that the contract was for a year's employment, it was performable within a year exactly to the day and no writing was required for it to be enforceable. Alternatively, the court ruled that if the agreement was made final by the telephone call between the parties on Saturday, April 25, 1964, then that part of the weekend which remained would not be counted in calculating the year, thus taking the contract out of the Statute of Frauds. With commendable candor the trial judge gave as the motivating force for the decision his desire to avoid a mechanical and unjust application of the Statute.[1]

The case went to the jury ... [which] returned a verdict for the plaintiff in the sum of $12,103.40. The defendants appeal to this court on four principal grounds, three of which we find to be without merit. The remaining ground of appeal is whether the plaintiff can maintain an action on the alleged oral employment contract in light of the prohibition of the Statute of Frauds making unenforceable an oral contract that is not to be performed within one year.

I. TIME OF ACCEPTANCE OF THE EMPLOYMENT AGREEMENT

The defendants contend that the trial court erred in refusing to give an instruction to the jury that if the employment agreement was made more than one day before the plaintiff began performance, there could be no recovery by the plaintiff. The reason given was that a contract not to be performed within one year from its making is unenforceable if not in writing.

The defendants are correct in their argument that the time of acceptance of an offer is a question of fact for the jury to decide. But the trial court alternatively decided that even if the offer was accepted on the Saturday prior to the commencement of performance, the intervening Sunday and part of Saturday would not be counted in computing the year for the purposes of the Statute of Frauds. The judge stated that Sunday was a non-working day and only a fraction of Saturday was left which he

---

1. THE COURT: You make the law look ridiculous, because one day is Sunday and the man does not work on Sunday; the other day is Saturday; he is up in Fresno. He can't work down there. And he is down here Sunday night and shows up for work on Monday. To me that is a contract within a year. I don't want to make the law look ridiculous, Mr. Clause, because it is one day later, one day too much, and that one day is a Sunday, and a non-working day.

would not count. In any event, there is no need to discuss the relative merits of either ruling since we base our decision in this case on the doctrine of equitable estoppel which was properly briefed and argued by both parties before this court, although not presented to the trial court.

II. ENFORCEMENT BY VIRTUE OF ACTION IN RELIANCE ON THE ORAL CONTRACT

In determining whether a rule of law can be fashioned and applied to a situation where an oral contract admittedly violates a strict interpretation of the Statute of Frauds, it is necessary to review the Statute itself together with its historical and modern functions. . . .

The first English Statute was enacted almost 300 years ago to prevent "many fraudulent practices, which are commonly endeavored to be upheld by perjury and subornation of perjury." 29 Car. 2, c. 3 (1677). Certainly, there were compelling reasons in those days for such a law. At the time of enactment in England, the jury system was quite unreliable, rules of evidence were few, and the complaining party was disqualified as a witness so he could neither testify on direct-examination nor, more importantly, be cross-examined. Summers, *The Doctrine of Estoppel and the Statute of Frauds*, 79 U.Pa.L.Rev. 440, 441 (1931). The aforementioned structural and evidentiary limitations on our system of justice no longer exist.

Retention of the Statute today has nevertheless been justified on at least three grounds: (1) the Statute still serves an evidentiary function thereby lessening the danger of perjured testimony (the original rationale); (2) the requirement of a writing has a cautionary effect which causes reflection by the parties on the importance of the agreement; and (3) the writing is an easy way to distinguish enforceable contracts from those which are not, thus channelling certain transactions into written form.

In spite of whatever utility the Statute of Frauds may still have, its applicability has been drastically limited by judicial construction over the years in order to mitigate the harshness of a mechanical application.[3] Furthermore, learned writers continue to disparage the Statute regarding it as "a statute for promoting fraud" and a "legal anachronism."[4]

Another method of judicial circumvention of the Statute of Frauds has grown out of the exercise of the equity powers of the courts. Such judicially imposed limitations or exceptions involved the traditional dis-

---

3. Thus a promise to pay the debt of another has been construed to encompass only promises made to a creditor which do not benefit the promisor (*Restatement of Contracts* § 184 (1932); 3 Williston, *Contracts* § 452 (Jaeger ed. 1960)); a promise in consideration of marriage has been interpreted to exclude mutual promises to marry (*Restatement, supra* § 192; 3 *Williston, supra* § 485); a promise not to be performed within one year means a promise not performable within one year (*Restatement, supra* § 198; 3 *Williston, supra*, § 495); a promise not to be performed within one year may be removed from the Statute of Frauds if one party has fully performed (*Restatement, supra* § 198; 3 *Williston, supra* § 504); and the Statute will not be applied where all promises involved are fully performed (*Restatement, supra* § 219; 3 *Williston, supra* § 528).

4. Burdick, *A Statute for Promoting Fraud*, 16 Colum.L.Rev. 273 (1916); Willis, *The Statute of Frauds–A Legal Anachronism*, 3 Ind.L.J. 427, 528 (1928).

pensing power of the equity courts to mitigate the "harsh" rule of law. When courts have enforced an oral contract in spite of the Statute, they have utilized the legal labels of "part performance" or "equitable estoppel" in granting relief. Both doctrines are said to be based on the concept of estoppel, which operates to avoid unconscionable injury. 3 *Williston, supra* § 553A at 791; *Summers, supra* at 443–49; Monarco v. Lo Greco, 35 Cal.2d 621, 220 P.2d 737 (1950) (Traynor, J.).

Part performance has long been recognized in Hawai'i as an equitable doctrine justifying the enforcement of an oral agreement for the conveyance of an interest in land where there has been substantial reliance by the party seeking to enforce the contract. [citations] Other courts have enforced oral contracts (including employment contracts) which failed to satisfy the section of the Statute making unenforceable an agreement not to be performed within a year of its making. This has occurred where the conduct of the parties gave rise to an estoppel to assert the Statute. [citations]

It is appropriate for modern courts to cast aside the raiments of conceptualism which cloak the true policies underlying the reasoning behind the many decisions enforcing contracts that violate the Statute of Frauds. There is certainly no need to resort to legal rubrics or meticulous legal formulas when better explanations are available. The policy behind enforcing an oral agreement which violated the Statute of Frauds, as a policy of avoiding unconscionable injury, was well set out by the California Supreme Court. In Monarco v. Lo Greco, 35 Cal.2d 621, 623, 220 P.2d 737, 739 (1950), a case which involved an action to enforce an oral contract for the conveyance of land on the grounds of 20 years performance by the promisee, the court said:

> The doctrine of estoppel to assert the statute of frauds has been consistently applied by the courts of this state to prevent fraud that would result from refusal to enforce oral contracts in certain circumstances. Such fraud may inhere in the unconscionable injury that would result from denying enforcement of the contract after one party has been induced by the other seriously to change his position in reliance on the contract. . . .

In seeking to frame a workable test which is flexible enough to cover diverse factual situations and also provide some reviewable standards, we find very persuasive section 217A [now § 139, ed.] of the *Second Restatement of Contracts*. That section specifically covers those situations where there has been reliance on an oral contract which falls within the Statute of Frauds. Section [139] states:

> (1) A promise which the promisor should reasonably expect to induce action or forbearance on the part of the promisee or a third person and which does induce the action or forbearance is enforceable notwithstanding the Statute of Frauds if injustice can be avoided only by enforcement of the promise. The remedy granted for breach is to be limited as justice requires.

(2) In determining whether injustice can be avoided only by enforcement of the promise, the following circumstances are significant: (a) the availability and adequacy of other remedies, particularly cancellation and restitution; (b) the definite and substantial character of the action or forbearance in relation to the remedy sought; (c) the extent to which the action or forbearance corroborates evidence of the making and terms of the promise, or the making and terms are otherwise established by clear and convincing evidence; (d) the reasonableness of the action or forbearance; (e) the extent to which the action or forbearance was foreseeable by the promisor.

We think that the approach taken in the *Restatement* is the proper method of giving the trial court the necessary latitude to relieve a party of the hardships of the Statute of Frauds. Other courts have used similar approaches in dealing with oral employment contracts upon which an employee had seriously relied. *See* Alaska Airlines, Inc. v. Stephenson, 217 F.2d 295 (9th Cir.1954); Seymour v. Oelrichs, 156 Cal. 782, 106 P. 88 (1909). This is to be preferred over having the trial court bend over backwards to take the contract out of the Statute of Frauds. In the present case the trial court admitted just this inclination and forthrightly followed it.

There is no dispute that the action of the plaintiff in moving 2200 miles from Los Angeles to Hawai'i was foreseeable by the defendant. In fact, it was required to perform his duties. Injustice can only be avoided by the enforcement of the contract and the granting of money damages. No other remedy is adequate. The plaintiff found himself residing in Hawai'i without a job.

It is also clear that a contract of some kind did exist. The plaintiff performed the contract for two and one-half months receiving $3,484.60 for his services. The exact length of the contract, whether terminable at will as urged by the defendant or for a year from the time when the plaintiff started working, was up to the jury to decide.

In sum, the trial court might have found that enforcement of the contract was warranted by virtue of the plaintiff's reliance on the defendant's promise. Naturally, each case turns on its own facts. Certainly there is considerable discretion for a court to implement the true policy behind the Statute of Frauds, which is to prevent fraud or any other type of unconscionable injury. We therefore affirm the judgment of the trial court on the ground that the plaintiff's reliance was such that injustice could only be avoided by enforcement of the contract.

Affirmed.

ABE, JUSTICE (dissenting).

. . . I cannot agree, as intimated by this court, that we should circumvent the Statute of Frauds by the exercise of the equity powers of courts. As to statutory law, the sole function of the judiciary is to interpret the statute and the judiciary should not usurp legislative power and enter into the legislative field. [citations] Thus, if the Statute of Frauds is too harsh as intimated by this court, and it brings about undue hardship, it is for the legislature to amend or repeal the statute and not for this court to legislate.

PROBLEMS

11. C loaned D $4,000 two years ago, payable last month at a specified interest rate. The oral loan agreement had no prepayment provision. D has repudiated the agreement and C has sued. D has interposed the defense of the Statute of Frauds. Can C recover?

12. A and B entered into an oral contract whereby A agreed to render periodic services to B for a two-year term for the sum of $5,000 payable at the end of the term.

   a) At the end of the two-year period, A brought suit for the reasonable value of the services. What result?

   b) Suppose, instead, that after six months A refused to perform unless the compensation was raised to $7,500. B refused. A discontinued services and brought suit for the reasonable value of the services rendered prior to this disagreement. What result?

   c) Suppose, instead, that after six months A offered to sign a memorandum, asked B to sign a memorandum, and B refused. A discontinued services and sued for the reasonable value of A's services. What result?

13. Plaintiff entered into a written contract for two years' employment as a physician with the defendant clinic. After six weeks the parties orally agreed that the agreement would be rescinded immediately. Plaintiff soon thereafter, and before any change of position by defendant, changed her mind, tendered her services which were refused, and brought suit to enforce the written contract. What result?

14. Assume the same facts as in the previous problem except that the oral conversation resulted in an agreement that the employment term would be extended an additional 6 months. What result?

SECTION 4. STATUTE OF FRAUDS AND SALES OF GOODS

(Calamari & Perillo on Contracts §§ 19.16, 19.34)

AZEVEDO v. MINISTER
Supreme Court of Nevada, 1970.
86 Nev. 576, 471 P.2d 661.

MOWBRAY, JUSTICE. This case centers about the enforceability of an oral agreement to purchase 1500 tons of hay. The principal issue presented for our determination is whether the periodic accountings prepared by the seller and sent to the buyer covering the sale of the hay constituted confirming memoranda within the provisions of NRS 104.2201(2) [§ 2–201(2)] of the Uniform Commercial Code and, if so, whether the seller sent them within a reasonable time as required by that statute so that the oral agreement is not barred by the statute of frauds. The district judge ruled that the mandates of NRS 104.2201(2) had been satisfied, and he upheld the validity of the agreement. We agree, and we affirm the judgment of the lower court.

1.　THE FACTS

Appellant J.L. Azevedo is a rancher who buys and sells hay. . . . Respondent Bolton F. Minister operates the Minister Ranch near Yerington, Nevada, where he raises and sells large quantities of hay.

In early November 1967, Azevedo approached Minister for the purpose of buying hay. Terms were discussed. Several days later an agreement was reached by telephone. Both parties acknowledge that Azevedo agreed to purchase hay from Minister at a price of $26.50 per ton for the first and second cuttings and $28 per ton for the third cutting and that the parties opened an escrow account in a Yerington Bank in Minister's favor, where Azevedo agreed to deposit sufficient funds to cover the cost of the hay as he hauled it from the Minister Ranch. The parties are in dispute as to the total quantity of hay Azevedo agreed to purchase. Minister claims Azevedo contracted to purchase 1,500 tons. Azevedo maintains that they never had an agreement as to quantity. Soon after this telephone conversation, Azevedo deposited $20,000 in the designated escrow account and began hauling hay from the Minister Ranch. As Azevedo hauled the hay, Minister furnished him with periodic accountings, commencing December 4, which specified the dates the hay was hauled, names of the truckers, bale count, and weight. This arrangement was satisfactory to the parties, and it continued until the latter part of March 1968, when Minister loaded only two of four trucks sent by Azevedo for hay, because the funds on deposit in the escrow account were insufficient to cover all four loads. Azevedo then refused to buy any more hay, and Minister commenced this action in district court.

2.　THE STATUTE OF FRAUDS

The determination of the legal issues presented for our consideration will turn on our interpretation of NRS 104.2201(2) of the Uniform Commercial Code. Since the enactment of the Uniform Commercial Code, sweeping changes have been effectuated in the law of commercial transactions. . . .

As with all codifications, it was impossible for the Uniform Commercial Code to encompass every conceivable factual situation. Realizing this limitation, its drafters couched much of the language of the text and comments in broad generalities, leaving many problems to be answered by future litigation.

The development of the action of *assumpsit* in the fourteenth century gave rise to the enforceability of the oral promise. Although parties to an action could not be witnesses, the alleged promise could be enforced on the strength of oral testimony of others not concerned with the litigation. Because of this practice, a party could readily suborn perjured testimony, resulting in marked injustice to innocent parties who were held legally obligated to promises they had never made. The statute of frauds was enacted to preclude this practice. The passage of the statute did not eliminate the problem, but rather, has precipitated a controversy as to the relative merits of the statute. Those favoring the statute of frauds insist that it prevents fraud by prohibiting the introduction of perjured testimony. They also suggest that it deters hasty action, in that the formality of a writing will prevent a person from obligating himself without a full appreciation of the nature of his acts. Moreover, it is said, since business customs almost entirely conform to the mandates of the statute, an abolition of the statute would seriously disrupt such affairs.

On the other hand, in England the statute of frauds has been repealed. The English base their position upon the reasoning that the assertion of the technical defense of the statute aids a person in breaking a contract and effects immeasurable harm upon those who have meritorious claims. It is further maintained by the advocates of the English position that the rationale for the necessity of the statute has been vitiated, because parties engaged in litigation today may testify as witnesses and readily defend against perjured testimony.[9]

The Uniform Commercial Code, however, has attempted to strike a balance between the two positions by seeking to limit the defense of the statute to only those cases where there is a definite possibility of fraud. It is in the light of this historical background that we turn to consider whether the oral agreement of the parties in this case is barred by the statute of frauds.

There is no question that the Azevedo–Minister agreement was oral and that its enforceability is governed by NRS 104.2201(2), *supra*. The sale of hay is included within the definition of the sale of "goods" as defined by NRS 104.2105(1) [UCC § 2–105(1)] and NRS 104.2107(2) [UCC § 2–107(2)], which when read together provide that the sale of "growing crops," when they are to be "severed by the buyer or by the seller," constitutes the sale of goods within the definition of that expression in the Uniform Commercial Code. The parties agree that they are "merchants" within the meaning of that term as defined in the Code.

It is also true that the statute of frauds is no defense to that portion of the contract that has been performed under the provisions of NRS

---

9. L. Vold, *Sales* § 14, at 88 (2d ed. 1959). Advocates of The Sales Act have advanced the argument that the technical safeguard of a writing is more important in the United States than in England because in this country a litigant has a basic right to demand trial by jury. In England such a right is within the discretion of the court; thus, in most instances the court and not the jury will make the ultimate determination as to the existence of the contract. 68 Harv.L.Rev. 383, 384 (1954).

104.2201(3)(c) [UCC § 2–201(3)(c)], which makes enforceable an oral contract "(w)ith respect to goods ... which have been received and accepted."

The legal issues are, therefore, (1) whether Minister's accountings constituted confirming memoranda within the standards of NRS 104.2201(2) and, if so, (2) whether Minister sent them within a reasonable time as required by the statute.

3. THE CONFIRMING MEMORANDA

(a) The Accounting of January 21, 1968

In addition to the data set forth in the periodic accountings covering the dates on which hay was hauled, the names of the truckers, and the bale counts and weights, Minister added the following statement in his January 21 accounting to Azevedo:

> From your original deposit of $20,000.00 there is now a balance of $1819.76. *At this time there remains (sic) approximately 16,600 bales of hay yet to be hauled on your purchase,* about 9200 of which are first crop, 7400 of which are second crop.

> We would appreciate hearing when you plan to haul the *balance of the hay.* Also please make a deposit to cover the hay, sufficient in amount to pay for the hay you will be currently hauling. At this time you have only about *$2.25 deposit per ton on the remaining balance of the hay,* and we cannot permit a lower deposit per ton and still consider the hay as being sold. (Emphasis added.)

Azevedo did not challenge or reply to Minister's accountancy of January 21. Rather, he deposited an additional $3,000 in the escrow account and continued hauling hay.

(b) The Accounting of February 22, 1968

In the regular accounting of February 22, Minister added the following:

> "Balance of deposit on approximately 14000 bales remaining to be hauled—$1635.26."

Azevedo did not challenge or reply to the February 22 accounting.

It is these two accountings that the district judge found constituted confirming memoranda within the meaning of NRS 104.2201(2). There is little authority articulating the meaning of a confirming memorandum as used in the Code. The official Comment, Uniform Laws Annotated, Uniform Commercial Code § 2–201 (1968), states at 90, 91:

> Only three definite and invariable requirements as to the (confirming) memorandum are made by this subsection. First, it must evidence a contract for the sale of goods; second, it must be "signed," a word which includes any authentication which identifies the party to be charged; and third, it must specify a quantity.

The parties concede that the memoranda were "signed" within the meaning of the statute, but appellant Azevedo urges that neither memorandum confirms the existence of an oral contract.

While § 2–201(2) of the Code is entirely new in the commercial law field, its only effect is to eliminate the defense of the statute of frauds. The party alleging the contract still has the burden of proving that an oral contract was entered into *before* the written confirmation. The purpose of the subsection of the Code is to rectify an abuse that had developed in the law of commerce. The custom arose among business people of confirming oral contracts by sending a letter of confirmation. This letter was binding as a memorandum on the sender, but not on the recipient, because he had not signed it.[12] The abuse was that the recipient, not being bound, could perform or not, according to his whim and the market, whereas the seller had to perform.[13] Obviously, under these circumstances, sending any confirming memorandum was a dangerous practice. Subsection (2) of Section 2–201 of the Code cures the abuse by holding a recipient bound unless he communicates his objection within 10 days.

Appellant urges that the January and February accountings do not meet the standards of the subsection because neither memorandum makes reference to any oral agreement between the parties. A fair reading of the memoranda shows otherwise. The January memorandum states that, "At this time there remains (*sic*) approximately 16,600 bales of hay yet to be hauled on your purchase," and, further, that, "We (Minister) would appreciate hearing when you plan to haul the balance of the hay." Although neither the January nor the February memorandum refers to the previous November agreement by telephone, the language clearly demonstrates that the referred-to agreement between the parties was not an *in futuro* arrangement, but a pre-existing agreement between Azevedo and Minister. As the court said in Harry Rubin & Sons, Inc. v. Consolidated Pipe Co., 396 Pa. 506, 153 A.2d 472, 476 (1959), in ruling on a case involving subsection (2) of section 2–201: "Under the statute of frauds as revised in the Code[,] 'All that is required is that the writing afford a basis for believing that the offered oral evidence rests on a real transaction.' " (Footnote omitted.)

The district judge found that it did so in the instant case, and the record supports his finding.

4. THE "REASONABLE TIME" FACTOR

Subsection 2 of NRS 104.2201 provides that the confirming memorandum must be sent within a reasonable time after the oral contract is made. Appellant argues that the delay of 10 weeks (November 9 to January 21) as a matter of law is an unreasonable time. We do not agree. What is reasonable must be decided by the trier of the facts under all the

---

12. As indicated in the instant case, Minister, who signed the memorandum, could be held to deliver to Azevedo the balance of the hay on the terms indicated.

13. The record reflects the price of hay was lower in March than in the previous November, when the parties had agreed on a tonnage price.

circumstances of the case under consideration. Subsection 2 of NRS 104.1204 [former UCC § 1–204; Rev. § 1–205(a)] provides: "What is a reasonable time for taking any action depends on the nature, purpose and circumstances of such action."

In this case, the parties commenced performance of their oral agreement almost immediately after it was made in early November. Azevedo deposited $20,000 in the designated escrow account and began hauling hay. Minister commenced sending his periodic accounting reports to Azevedo on December 14. It is true that the accounting containing the confirming memorandum was not sent until January 21. It was at that time that Azevedo's deposit of $20,000 was nearing depletion. Minister so advised Azevedo in the January memorandum. Azevedo responded by making an additional deposit. He did not object to the memorandum, and he continued to haul the hay until the latter part of March. Under "the nature, purpose and circumstances" of the case, we agree with the district judge that the delay was not unreasonable.

The judgment is affirmed. . . .

COHN v. FISHER

Superior Court of New Jersey, Law Div., 1972.
118 N.J.Super. 286, 287 A.2d 222.

ROSENBERG, J.C.C. (temporarily assigned). Plaintiff Albert L. Cohn moves for summary judgment against defendant Donal L. Fisher. The controversy concerns an alleged breach of contract for the sale of Cohn's boat by Fisher.

On Sunday, May 19, 1968, Fisher inquired of Cohn's advertisement in the New York Times for the sale of his 30–foot auxiliary sloop. Upon learning the location of the sailboat, Fisher proceeded to the boatyard and inspected the sloop. Fisher then phoned Cohn and submitted an offer of $4,650, which Cohn accepted. Both agreed to meet the next day at Cohn's office in Paterson. At the meeting on Monday, May 20, Fisher gave Cohn a check for $2,325 and affixed on same: "Deposit on aux. sloop, D'Arc Wind, full amount $4,650." Both parties agreed to meet on Saturday, May 25, when Fisher would pay the remaining half of the purchase price and Cohn would presumably transfer title.

A few days later Fisher informed Cohn that he would not close the deal on the weekend because a survey of the boat could not be conducted that soon. Cohn notified Fisher that he would hold him to his agreement to pay the full purchase price by Saturday. At this point relations between the parties broke down. Fisher stopped payment on the check he had given as a deposit and failed to close the deal on Saturday.

Cohn then re-advertised the boat and sold it for the highest offer of $3,000. In his suit for breach of contract Cohn is seeking damages of $1,679.50 representing the difference between the contract price with

Fisher and the final sales price together with the costs incurred in reselling the boat. . . .

As to the element of formality of memorialization, N.J.S.A. 12A:2–201 requires that a contract for the sale of goods for the price of $500 or more, to be enforceable, must comply with the statute of frauds. . . .

[I]n the present case, there are three alternatives by which the contract could be held enforceable:

    (1) under N.J.S.A. 12A:2–201(1) the check may constitute a sufficient written memorandum;

    (2) under N.J.S.A. 12A:2–201(3)(b) defendant's testimony in depositions and his answers to demands for admission may constitute an admission of the contract or

    (3) under N.J.S.A. 12A:2–201(3)(c) payment and acceptance of the check may constitute partial performance.

The above issues, arising under the Uniform Commercial Code adopted by this State on January 1, 1963, are novel to the courts of New Jersey. For such reason this court will determine the enforceability of the contract under each of the alternatives. Ample authority for resolving the issues is found in the notes provided by the framers of the Code and in the decisions of our sister states.

With regard to the question of whether the check satisfies the statute of frauds as a written memorandum, N.J.S.A. 12A:2–201(1) requires (1) a writing indicating a contract for sale, (2) signed by the party to be charged, and (3) the quantity term must be expressly stated. The back of the check in question bore the legend "deposit on aux. sloop, D'Arc Wind, full amount $4,650." Thus the check seems to *prima facie* satisfy the requirements in that: it is a writing which indicates a contract for sale by stating the subject matter of the sale (aux. sloop, D'Arc Wind), the price ($4,650), part of the purchase terms—50% down (deposit of $2,325), and by inferentially identifying the seller (Albert Cohn, payee) and the purchaser (Donal Fisher, drawer); it is signed by the party against whom enforcement is sought (Donal Fisher); and it expressly states the quantity term (the D'Arc Wind). Thus the check, although not a sales contract, would comply with the requirements of the statute of frauds under N.J.S.A. 12A:2–201(1).

Such a result, however, would be in conflict with the case law of New Jersey. As noted in the New Jersey Study Comment to § 12A:2–201, par. 3, under both the Uniform Sales Act and the Uniform Commercial Code a sales contract not in writing is not unenforceable if there is a memorandum of the agreement in writing signed by the party to be charged or his authorized agent. Although the Uniform Sales Act was silent as to the required terms for a satisfactory memorandum, the courts of New Jersey had restrictively interpreted "memorandum" to mean a writing containing the *full terms of the contract. See* Bauer v. Victory Catering Co., 101 N.J.L. 364, 370, 128 A. 262 (E. & A. 1925). N.J.S.A. 12A:2–201(1), in stating, with the exception of the quantity term, that "A writing is not insufficient because it omits or incorrectly states a term agreed upon ...," clearly changes the law in New Jersey as to the requirements of the memorandum exception to the statute of frauds. As evidenced by the Uniform Commercial Code Comment to § 12A:2–201, par. 1, such a change was clearly intended:

> The required writing need not contain all the material terms of the contract and such material terms as are stated need not be precisely stated. All that is required is that the writing afford a basis for believing that the offered oral evidence rests on a real transaction. ... The price, time and place of payment or delivery, the general quality of the goods, or any particular warranties may all be omitted. ...

> Only three definite and invariable requirements as to the memorandum are made by this subsection. First, it must evidence a contract for the sale of goods; second, it must be " 'signed," a word which includes any authentication which identifies the party to be charged; and third, it must specify a quantity.

In holding that the check in the present litigation sufficiently satisfies the requirements of N.J.S.A. 12A:2–201(1) to constitute a memorandum of the agreement, this court is not without judicial authority. In Herzog v. Tidaback, 67 N.J.Super. 14, 169 A.2d 726 (Ch.Div.1961), the court took a half step in such a direction. There the court held that where a purchaser of real estate gave the seller's agent a check which bore the notation that it was a deposit on specific premises in accordance with a listing agreement, and where the seller's agent accepted, endorsed and cashed said check, the notation together with the endorsement of seller's authorized agent would be sufficient to satisfy the requirements of the statute of frauds. Thus, in order for a check to satisfy the memorandum exception, Herzog required that an outside agreement be incorporated by reference. But this distinction is due to the fact that the sale in Herzog involved real estate rather than goods, as in the present case. This distinction between a contract for the sale of land which requires that a check refer to a written agreement, and a contract for the sale of goods which does not require incorporation by reference on a check, has been clearly drawn. See 20 A.L.R. 363; 153 A.L.R. 1112. The decisions under the Uniform Commercial Code involving a contract for the sale of goods are to the effect that a check alone is sufficient to constitute a writing in compliance with the statute of frauds.

Accordingly, this court concludes that by the adoption of the Uniform Commercial Code in New Jersey, the case law concerning the sufficiency of memorandum has been changed. It therefore appears to the satisfaction of this court that the check in the case at bar satisfies the requirements of N.J.S.A. 12A:2–201(1) and thereby renders the contract enforceable under the statute of frauds.

Had the check not satisfied the requirements of N.J.S.A. 12A:2–201(1), the check, together with defendant's admission of a contract in his depositions and demands for admission, may satisfy N.J.S.A. 12A:2–201(3)(b). This subsection states, in effect, that where the requirements of 12A:2–201(1) have not been satisfied, an otherwise valid contract will be held enforceable if the party charged admits that a contract was made. Such a contract would be enforceable only with respect to the quantity of goods admitted.

The New Jersey Study Comment to § 12A:2–201, par. 7, points out that "The cases from other states are in disagreement on the question of giving effect to admissions in court for purposes of satisfying the statute of frauds." The theory behind the dissension under § 2–201(3)(b) seems to be that ". . . the defendant should be privileged not to make the admission if it has the legal effect of depriving him of the defense of the Statute of Frauds." Hawkland, *Sales and Bulk Sales*, 31 (1958).

This court is of the opinion that if a party admits an oral contract, he should be held bound to his bargain. The statute of frauds was not designed to protect a party who made an oral contract, but rather to aid a party who did not make a contract, though one is claimed to have been made orally with him. This court would therefore hold that the check, together with defendant's admission of an oral contract, would constitute an enforceable contract under N.J.S.A. 12A:2–201(3)(b).

Finally, under N.J.S.A. 12A:2–201(3)(c) the check may constitute partial performance of the contract in that payment for goods was made and accepted, and, as such, the contract would be held enforceable under the statute of frauds. N.J.S.A. 12A:2–201(3)(c) provides that although the requirements of N.J.S.A. 12A:2–201(1) have not been met, an otherwise valid contract will be held enforceable with respect to goods (1) for which payment has been made and accepted, or (2) which have been received and accepted.

As noted in the New Jersey Study Comment to § 2–201, par. 8, this subsection partially changes New Jersey case law which held that either part payment or the actual receipt and acceptance of part of the goods satisfies the statute of frauds for the entire contract. Under the Code oral contracts would be held enforceable only to the extent that goods have been paid for or received. Thus, part payment or receipt and acceptance of part of the goods would satisfy the statute of frauds, not for the entire contract, but only for the *quantity* of goods which have been received and accepted or for which payment has been made and accepted.

In the present case, since the quantity term has been clearly indicated by the check itself, namely "aux. sloop, D'Arc Wind," the check, by representing that payment had been made and accepted, would constitute partial performance and the contract would be held enforceable under N.J.S.A. 12A:2–201(3)(c). That such a decision results in upholding the entire contract is due solely to the fact that the entire contract concerned only the sale of one boat. . . .

In sum, the case at bar has fully complied with the statute of frauds in that under each of the alternative subsections—N.J.S.A. 12A:2–201(1), (3)(b), and (3)(c)—the enforceability of the contract is upheld. . . .

POTTER v. HATTER FARMS, INC.

Court of Appeals of Oregon, 1982.
56 Or.App. 254, 641 P.2d 628.

GILLETTE, PRESIDING JUDGE. In this oral contract action, defendant appeals from a jury verdict in favor of plaintiffs (Potters). Defendant argues that: there was no substantial evidence that a contract existed between it and Potters; even if an oral agreement was reached, it was unenforceable because it violated the Uniform Commercial Code (UCC) Statute of Frauds; and plaintiffs were not entitled to raise promissory estoppel as a bar to their Statute of Frauds defense. We affirm.

Plaintiffs operate a turkey hatchery in Oregon. The hatchery processes turkey eggs through incubation to hatching, at which time new turkey "poults" are sold to growers. Defendant is a turkey grower in Oklahoma; it raises turkeys and sells them to food processing companies.

. . . Plaintiff Charles Potter testified that Gil Kent, production manager of Hatter Farms, first contacted him by phone in November or December, 1978, and stated an interest in purchasing some poults from the Potters' company. The men then met in January, 1979, at the Tulsa, Oklahoma, airport. At that time, according to Potter, he and Kent entered into an oral contract. Potter testified that he agreed to sell and Kent agreed that Hatter Farms would buy 192,000 poults for eighty cents per poult, plus charges for egg dipping, inspections and toe clipping. . . . [Later they agreed "to find transportation that was as quick and inexpensive as possible" (because poults are not fed or watered in transit) but failed to settle the details. After a June 1979 meeting to assess defendant's continued need for the poults, plaintiff turned down other offers to buy them.]

In August, 1979, Gil Kent informed Potter that defendant would be unable to use the poults. This action followed. . . . [The court finds the evidence sufficient to support the jury's finding of an oral contract between the parties despite failure to agree on the exact transportation. It holds that the open transportation term withstands the test of UCC § 2–204(3).] The fact that the transportation term was left open is not fatal to the agreement, because Potter testified that the agreement was not conditioned upon finding ideal transportation. The cost of the poults shipped by the available transportation [*i.e.*, by air to Chicago, then trucking to Oklahoma] was, according to the evidence, high but not unreasonable [during the off-season].

Defendant next argues that the trial court erred by not granting defendant's motions for summary judgment, for directed verdict and for judgment n.o.v., because the alleged oral contract was unenforceable in that it violated the UCC Statute of Frauds. ORS 72.2010. Plaintiffs respond that the defendant was barred on the basis of promissory estoppel from raising the Statute of Frauds as a defense.

Traditionally, a promissory estoppel claim has been used to supply the element of consideration where to refuse to enforce an otherwise valid promise would work an injustice on a party who relied to his detriment on the promise. Calamari & Perillo, *The Law of Contracts,* §§ 99–105 (1970). In Stevens v. Good Samaritan Hosp., 264 Or. 200, 504 P.2d 749 (1972), however, the Oregon Supreme Court held that promissory estoppel could be used to defeat the application of Oregon's general Statute of Frauds.

The issue in the present case is whether promissory estoppel should be allowed as an exception to the UCC Statute of Frauds. ORS 72.2010 [UCC § 2–201]. . . .

Estoppel is introduced into the Code through [former UCC § 1–103, Rev. UCC § 1–103(b)] which states:

> *Unless displaced by the particular provisions of the Uniform Commercial Code,* the principles of law and equity, including the law merchant and the law relative to capacity to contract, principal and agent, *estoppel,* fraud, misrepresentation, duress, coercion, mistake, bankruptcy, or other validating or invalidating cause shall supplement its provisions. (Emphasis supplied.)

Our examination of those two provisions leads us to the conclusion that promissory estoppel should be allowed to defeat reliance upon the UCC Statute of Frauds. The central issue is whether promissory estoppel is specifically displaced by [UCC 2–201]. Because it is not mentioned in the statute, the only arguable means of displacement is the legislature's silence. We do not believe that silence constitutes displacement of estoppel from the Statute of Frauds. In light of [former UCC § 1–103, Rev. UCC § 1–103(b)], we hold that if the legislature did not want estoppel to apply to application of the Statute of Frauds, it would have stated that intent expressly. Our conclusion is also influenced by [former UCC § 1–203, Rev. UCC § 1–304], which states:

> Every contract or duty within the Uniform Commercial Code imposes an obligation of good faith in its performance or enforcement.

Allowing promissory estoppel as an exception to the Statute of Frauds is consistent with the obligation of good faith. Exclusion of promissory estoppel, on the other hand, would allow a party to enter into an oral contract, induce the other party to rely to its detriment and yet completely escape liability under the contract. We do not believe the legislature intended such a result. *See* J. White and R. Summers, *Uniform Commercial Code,* § 2–6 at 69–70 (2d ed. 1980).

Defendant argues that allowing promissory estoppel to defeat the Statute of Frauds would render the statute meaningless. It is true that any exception to such a writing requirement increases the possibility of fraud through perjury. Despite that fact, the Supreme Court has created exceptions to the general Statute of Frauds for both promissory estoppel and for part performance, and the Code's Statute of Frauds contains some express exceptions. *See* [UCC § 2–201(3)]. Neither the Oregon court nor the legislature apparently believed that creating exceptions to the statute render it a nullity. As the court made clear in *Stevens v. Good Samaritan Hosp., supra,* a promissory estoppel exception essentially enhances the Statute of Frauds by preventing its use as an instrument of fraud. Neither do we believe that a promissory estoppel exception eliminates the incentive for merchants to memorialize their agreements in writing. Those who would comply with the statute to avoid unenforcibility of their agreements would likewise comply to avoid the uncertainty and difficulty of having to prove the elements of promissory estoppel at trial.

To avoid a Statute of Frauds defense through promissory estoppel, it is necessary to prove 1) actual reliance on a promise, 2) a definite and substantial change of position occasioned by the promise and 3) foreseeability to the promisor, as a reasonable person, that the promise would induce conduct of the kind that occurred. Schafer *et al.* v. Fraser *et ux.,* 206 Or. 446, 472, 290 P.2d 190 (1955). The difficulty of meeting that burden of proof should both encourage merchants to put agreements into writing and decrease the likelihood of a proponent of a contract being able to prove its existence through perjury.

It has been suggested that allowing a reliance exception to the statute would make it possible for one party unilaterally to create an enforceable contract simply by relying substantially on discussions that did not, in fact, result in any actual agreement. It is highly unlikely, however, that any merchant would rely to his significant detriment on a nonexistent agreement in hope that he could convince a trier of fact that an agreement was actually reached and that the elements of promissory estoppel were satisfied.

Defendant also argues that the promissory estoppel exception would hamper the consistency and predictability which the Code was designed to bring to commercial transactions. As the Code provisions cited above concerning the application of good faith and estoppel suggest, the legislature did not intend to provide predictability and consistency at the expense of equitable principles. The Code's Statute of Frauds provides a means of assuring certainty in dealings between merchants. The promissory estoppel exception assures that, when merchants do not avail themselves of the protections provided by the Statute of Frauds, the requirement of good faith is not abrogated. We are convinced that such a balance between predictability and good faith is consistent with the legislature's intent.

Finally, we must decide whether there was substantial evidence to satisfy the requirements of promissory estoppel. As we pointed out above, Potter's testimony provides substantial evidence that a promise was made. Potter's testimony that he turned down offers to sell the poults to buyers in California in reliance on defendant's promise satisfies the actual reliance and substantial change of position requirements. His testimony that he reached an agreement with Gil Kent in January, 1979, that in June of that year he told defendant of the offers he had from other buyers and that Hatter Farms did not indicate to him that it was no longer interested in the poults satisfies the reasonable foreseeability requirement.

There was substantial evidence of the existence of an oral contract between plaintiff and defendant. Although the contract would otherwise be unenforceable for violating the Statute of Frauds, there was substantial evidence here of promissory estoppel barring defendants' assertion of that defense.

Affirmed.

COSTCO WHOLESALE CORP. v. WORLD WIDE LICENSING CORP.

Court of Appeals of Washington, Division 1, 1995.
78 Wash.App. 637, 898 P.2d 347.

WEBSTER, JUDGE. This case involves modifications allegedly made to a contract for the sale of jewelry. Costco Wholesale Corporation contends that the price it agreed to pay Worldwide Licensing Corporation was modified when Worldwide's agent agreed, in writing, to rebate part of the purchase price. Worldwide alleges Costco orally modified the contract by promising to buy more jewelry. Each party contends that the modification alleged by the other is barred by the statute of frauds, which requires certain contracts to be written. We hold that the contract's initial satisfaction of the statute passes through to the modification, but that the contract as modified can only be enforced up to the quantity stated. Thus, the statute of frauds bars the oral promise to purchase additional jewelry, but not the rebate claim. Although the rebate claim is not barred, Costco must still prove that there was a modification. Because there is an issue of material fact about the extent of the agent's apparent authority to agree to the rebate, we reverse the summary judgment in favor of Costco and remand for trial.

FACTS

Worldwide Licensing Corporation[1] sells jewelry to wholesale buyers. Worldwide's sales are negotiated by independent sales representatives known as brokers. When Worldwide decided to pursue Costco as a potential buyer, it contacted Loren Coleman, an independent sales representative. Ed Dose, a Worldwide division president, flew to Seattle to meet Coleman. Coleman and Dose met with Megghan Harruff, a Costco division manager. At the meeting, Coleman presented Worldwide's merchandise, including its packaging. Costco agreed to purchase 5 pallets of 416 boxes each, for a total of $74,880.00, and paid by check. After Harruff described the purchase as "test marketing," and expressed the opinion that the merchandise would quickly sell out, the parties discussed the possibility of subsequent orders. Dose told Harruff that re-ordering would take 8 weeks.

---

1.   The pleading caption misspells appellant's name; the proper name is Worldwide.

Outside of the meeting and Harruff's hearing, Coleman urged Dose to produce more than the five pallet loads ordered. Although the jewelry was a specialty item not easily marketed, Dose reluctantly agreed to manufacture three additional pallets.

In Costco's opinion, the jewelry it received was poorly packaged, and not the quality it expected. Subsequently, Costco did not sell the jewelry as quickly as it had hoped. Coleman told Worldwide about Costco's displeasure. Although Worldwide believed in the quality of its product, it was concerned about selling Costco the already manufactured three pallet loads of jewelry. Dose told Coleman to "approach Costco with an $8 per box adjustment in price *providing they agreed to purchase the remaining 3 pallets at the adjusted price*." According to Dose, Coleman "indicated" that Costco "had agreed to the additional order." Coleman's declaration, on the other hand, asserts that Dose authorized an $8 per unit rebate, but it says nothing about the alleged additional order, or any instruction to make the rebate contingent on a promise to buy the other three pallets. Costco agreed to the rebate amount, and sent a rebate form to Coleman. Coleman signed it and faxed a copy to Worldwide. Worldwide entered the rebate in its accounting system, pending Dose's approval. When Costco did not order the three additional pallets, Worldwide refused to pay the rebate. When Worldwide paid Coleman's sales commission, however, it was based on the rebated sales price.

Costco sued Worldwide, seeking $16,640 (2,080 boxes at $8 per box). Worldwide denied the rebate agreement and alleged the statute of frauds as an affirmative defense. The trial court entered summary judgment in favor of Costco.

DISCUSSION

. . . The only cause of action alleged is breach of a promise to rebate $16,640. Worldwide asserts three alternative defenses. First, Worldwide contends the rebate modification is unenforceable because it does not satisfy the Uniform Commercial Code's statute of frauds.[2] Second, Worldwide contends the modification was an exchange of promises in which Worldwide promised to rebate, and Costco promised to purchase three additional pallets of jewelry. Because Costco did not perform, it is not entitled to enforce the rebate. Third, Worldwide contends that if Coleman agreed to the rebate without securing Costco's promise to purchase additional jewelry, Coleman exceeded his authority and the modification is not binding on Worldwide.

---

2. RCW 62A.2–201(1) [U.C.C. § 2–201(1)] provides:

Except as otherwise provided in this section a contract for the sale of goods for the price of five hundred dollars or more is not enforceable by way of action or defense unless there is some writing sufficient to indicate that a contract for sale has been made between the parties and signed by the party against whom enforcement is sought or by his authorized agent or broker. A writing is not insufficient because it omits or incorrectly states a term agreed upon but the contract is not enforceable under this paragraph beyond the quantity of goods shown in such writing.

I. Statute of Frauds

This case addresses the interplay between the statute of frauds and contract modifications under the U.C.C. The statute of frauds denies enforcement of a contract for the sale of goods worth more than $500 when no writing evidences the agreement. RCW 62A.2–201. When a contract is modified, U.C.C. § 2–209(3) requires the statute of frauds to be satisfied if "the contract as modified" falls within the provisions of the statute of frauds.[3] The Costco/Worldwide contract, as modified, involved a sale of goods for more than $500 and is within the statute of frauds. Therefore, the only issue is whether the statute has been satisfied.

The original contract satisfied the statute of frauds. The plain language of U.C.C. § 2–209(3) only requires a satisfaction of the statute if the "contract as modified" is within the statute; it does *not* require a satisfaction for the modification itself. We hold that the original satisfaction of the statute passes through to the contract as modified.[4] Thus, a modification to a contract which initially satisfied the statute does not require a new memorandum.[5] This interpretation respects plain statutory language and the common commercial practice of oral modifications.[6]

Assuming the contract in this case was modified to include the rebate (a price modification) and the additional purchase (a quantity modification), the pass-through power of the original contract's satisfaction infuses the contract as modified with the characteristic of enforceability. The rebate, which modified the price, did not require an additional writing to satisfy the statute of frauds. *But,* under the statute of frauds, a contract can only be enforced up to the quantity shown in the writing. RCW 62A.2–201(1), (3), Alaska Independent Fishermen's Marketing Ass'n. v. New England Fish Co., 15 Wash.App. 154, 157, 548 P.2d 348 (1976). Without a writing showing the three additional pallet load order, the quantity modification is not enforceable by way of action or defense, despite the pass-through nature of the original satisfaction of the statute. II E.A.

---

3. RCW 62A.2–209(3) [U.C.C. § 2–209(3)] provides: "The requirements of the statute of frauds section of this Article (RCW 62A.2–201) must be satisfied if the contract as modified is within its provisions." Although the contract, as modified, includes some terms from the original contract, and some terms from the modification, "the new contract is viewed as a whole" when applying the statute. *Restatement (Second) of Contracts* § 149, cmt. a (1979). The following examples help clarify when a "contract as modified" is within the statute. A sales contract originally for a $400 television, but modified to include a second $400 television is, as modified, within the statute of frauds because the price now exceeds $500. A contract for a $1,000 stereo later modified to exclude all components except a $200 tuner is, as modified, outside of the statute because the price is less than the $500 threshold.

4. 2 A. Corbin, *Contracts* § 304 (1950); U.C.C. § 2–209, cmt. 3; Eisler, *Modification of Sales Contracts Under the Uniform Commercial Code: Section 2–209 Reconsidered*, 57 Tenn.L.Rev. 401, 430 (1990).

5. We disagree with decisions that require every modification to be in writing. [citations] "There is not a scintilla of support in the drafting history of § 2–209(3) for the notion that § 2–209(3) was designed to require a formalistic validation for unsupported modifications and to incorporate the requirements of § 2–201 for all modifications." Murray, *The Modification Mystery: Section 2–209 of the Uniform Commercial Code*, 32 Vill.L.Rev. 1, 15 (1987); *see also* J. White & R. Summers, *Uniform Commercial Code* § 1–6 (3d ed.1988).

6. RCW 62A.2–209(3), 62A.1–102(2)(a)–(b); Hillman, *A Study of Uniform Commercial Code Methodology: Contract Modification Under Article Two*, 59 N.C.L.Rev. 335, 360 (1981).

Farnsworth, *Contracts* §§ 6.7 n. 44, 6.2 n. 22–24 (1990); RCW 62A.2–201(1); *see also* RCW 62A.2–201(3)(b); and U.C.C. § 2–209, cmt. 3 (an authenticated "memo is limited in its effect to the quantity of goods set forth in it"). Therefore, Worldwide cannot avoid summary judgment on the rebate claim by arguing that Costco breached an oral promise to purchase more jewelry.

In summary, we hold that the contract, as modified to include a rebate, has satisfied the statute of frauds, but the alleged promise to purchase additional jewelry is barred. The court's summary judgment order was proper insofar as its effect was to strike Worldwide's affirmative defense.

The absence of a statute of frauds defense does not, however, prove or disprove the *existence* or *terms* of a contract, nor does absence of the defense alter the plaintiff's burden, which is to prove the contract, the defendant's breach, and damages. U.C.C. § 2–201, cmt. 3, Perdue Farms, Inc. v. Motts, Inc. of Miss., 459 F.Supp. 7, 16 (N.D.Miss.1978). Because enforcement of any promise to purchase additional jewelry is barred by the statute of frauds, the record contains no dispute over the terms of the modification. On this record, if there was a modification, it was a rebate for $16,640 in favor of Costco. There still remains, however, an issue over the *existence* of the modification. We therefore turn to Worldwide's alternative contention, that the rebate modification does not bind Worldwide because Coleman exceeded his authority as agent.

II. Agency

... The record in this case establishes an agency in which Worldwide was a principal and Coleman was its agent. Taking the facts most favorably to Worldwide, Coleman was a special agent because he represented Worldwide only in this specific transaction. Coleman could bind Worldwide only if he had actual or apparent authority. Drawing all inferences in favor of Worldwide, Coleman did not have actual authority because Dose authorized him only to grant a rebate in exchange for Costco's promise to buy three additional pallets of jewelry. As regards apparent authority, the evidence is inconclusive. ... This record cannot sustain a finding, as a matter of law, that Coleman had apparent authority to rebate part of the purchase price.

Using Costco's alleged promise to create an issue of material fact may seem to conflict with the court's holding on the statute of frauds. But the statute of frauds merely proscribes judicial enforcement, by way of action or defense, of the alleged promise. RCW 62A.2–201(1). In this context, Worldwide is not alleging Costco's promise in an effort to procure *enforcement*. It is seeking instead to establish the lack of *any* valid modification. Worldwide can utilize the three pallet load evidence to prove that no valid modification existed, without offending the statute of frauds proscription on enforcement.

In conclusion, there is an issue of material fact concerning the existence of the modification because Worldwide is only bound if Coleman had actual or apparent authority. Therefore, summary judgment was inappropriate. We strike Worldwide's statute of frauds defense, reverse the trial court's grant of summary judgment, and remand for proceedings consistent with this opinion. Reversed and remanded. ...

PROBLEMS

15. X, a salesman for S, visited B, a physician, at his office and attempted to sell him a sailboat for $12,500. B asked for a week or two to think it over. X falsely reported to S that an oral agreement was reached and S sent B a written confirmation of the alleged sale. B, in annoyance, ripped up and threw the paper into the wastebasket. A month later, S tendered delivery of the boat, B refused to accept it and S sues. May B successfully raise the UCC statute of frauds?

16. S & B entered into an oral contract for the purchase and sale of 500,000 bushels of oats at a price of $2.10/bu. ($1,050,000) to be delivered over a 16 month period. S sent B a written confirmation of the oral contract bearing "#6077." After several months B wrote S, stating: "We have no further need for oats, consequently we will accept no further deliveries under contract #6077." S brought suit and B pleads the UCC and the one year provisions of the Statute of Frauds. What result?

17. Seller wrote out and signed a short note memorializing her agreement to sell to her friend Maurice three hundred tall white 4″ diameter candles at a stated price of $10 each for his daughter's wedding. Two weeks before the wedding, Maurice called Seller to ask for a guarantee that the candles were "dripless." Seller made the requested promise over the telephone. If the candles turn out to be the drippy sort, will the oral warranty be enforceable?

SECTION 5. THE SURETYSHIP STATUTE OF FRAUDS

(Calamari & Perillo on Contracts §§ 19.2—19.12)

LAWRENCE v. ANDERSON
Supreme Court of Vermont, 1936.
108 Vt. 176, 184 A. 689.

POWERS, CHIEF JUSTICE. Answering an emergency call from an unknown source, the plaintiff, a licensed physician, administered to John Anderson, who had suffered severe injuries in an automobile accident somewhere on the "Williston Road" outside of the city of Burlington. This was on October 1, 1933. When the plaintiff arrived at the scene of the accident, he found there the defendant, a daughter of the injured man;

and when he had introduced himself to her, she directed him, as he testified, to "do everything you can under the sun to see this man is taken care of." Thereupon, the plaintiff called an ambulance, in which Anderson was taken to a hospital where the plaintiff treated him until the next morning, when he was discharged by the defendant after she had conferred with her father about it. The patient died from the effects of the injuries a few days later. The plaintiff made his charges for his services to Mr. Anderson, and sent bills to his estate. He engaged a Burlington lawyer to proceed against the estate, for the collection of his charges, and some effort in that direction was made, but nothing came of it. About a year after the accident, the plaintiff began sending bills to Anderson's widow, but nothing came from that. Finally, about a year and half after the accident, this suit was brought. It was returnable to the Chittenden municipal court, and there tried to a jury. At the close of the plaintiff's evidence, on motion therefor, a verdict was ordered for the defendant. The plaintiff excepted.

It is apparent that the facts above stated, standing alone, did not make a case for the jury; and if nothing more had been shown, the judgment would have to be affirmed. For it fully appears that the defendant's relations with her father were such that she was not liable for the plaintiff's services unless she became so by reason of what she said or did. The rule is fully established that one who merely calls a physician to render services to another is not liable therefor in the absence of an express agreement, unless he is legally bound to furnish such service, [or unless]* it is a fair inference from the evidence that it was the intention of both parties that he should pay for it. The services here sued for were not, so far as the above recited facts show, beneficial, in a legal sense, to the defendant, and she would not be liable therefor. Smith v. Watson, 14 Vt. 332, 337.

But in addition to what has been recited, one Charles Brown, who was at the scene of the accident when the plaintiff arrived there, testified that in his presence the defendant said to the plaintiff, "I want my father taken care of, and give him the best care you can give him, and what the charges are . . . I will pay for it."

Ordinarily, this statement might make an entirely different case for the plaintiff. It shows that the defendant not only requested the services, but also that she made a direct promise to pay the plaintiff. Such a promise is not collateral or secondary, but primary and original. . . . To such a contract the statute of frauds (P.L. 1675) does not apply, for the simple reason that it is not a promise to pay the debt of another, but is a promise to pay the debt of the promisor—one that he makes his own by force of his engagement.

---

* The opinion inexplicably reads "as it is a fair inference," implying a result opposite to what is otherwise indicated here and in the case relied upon, *Smith v. Watson*, which says, "*unless* it was the intention of both the parties that he should be so liable." [emphasis added]

But before we can apply this rule to the case in hand, we must consider the effect of the plaintiff's conduct.

When the defendant made the promise that Brown testified to, the plaintiff was at liberty to accept it and to rely upon it. But he was not obliged to do so. He could, if he chose, treat Anderson on his own credit. But he could not hold both Anderson and the defendant. If he gave the credit to Anderson, he could not hold the defendant, though she had tendered an engagement direct, in form. The plaintiff could not turn the defendant's sole obligation into a joint obligation without her concurrence. If he gave any credit to Anderson, he elected to accept the defendant's engagement as collateral to that of Anderson. Of course it is only where the promise sued on is primary and direct that this question we are now discussing arises. 27 *C.J.* p. 42. But in such cases, the extension of any credit to the third party involved requires a written promise on the part of the promisor. Blodgett v. Town of Lowell, 33 Vt. 174, 175, 176.

As we have seen, it appears here that the plaintiff made his original charges against Anderson. Such a fact is not always conclusive evidence of the person who is to be regarded as the original debtor. It is subject to explanation, to be sure, Greene [*sic*] v. Burton and Sowles, 59 Vt. 423, 425, 10 A. 575, but to rebut the inference arising from the fact that the charges were so made, the proof must be of a strong character. Hardman v. Bradley, 85 Ill. 162. As we said in Enos v. Owens Slate Co., 104 Vt. 329, 333, 160 A. 185, the quality of a defendant's promise may usually be found by ascertaining whether the third person continues to be liable after the defendant's oral promise is made. In that case, it did not appear that the original charges for the services rendered by the plaintiff were made against the third person; and the plaintiff explained why he attempted to collect his pay from such person. Here no explanation is made or attempted. No reason is given why these charges were made against Anderson. So it must be taken that it was because the plaintiff considered him responsible therefor. Lomax v. McKinney, 61 Ind. 374. Having given credit to Anderson, the plaintiff cannot collect from the defendant. There being no error in the ruling on the motion for a verdict, there is no occasion to consider the other exceptions argued.

Judgment affirmed.

YARBRO v. NEIL B. McGINNIS EQUIPMENT CO.

Supreme Court of Arizona, In Banc, 1966.
101 Ariz. 378, 420 P.2d 163.

BERNSTEIN, VICE CHIEF JUSTICE. This case is before us on an appeal from a judgment of the Superior Court of Maricopa County. The appellee, McGinnis Equipment Co., brought suit to recover payments due it pursuant to a conditional sales contract for the sale of one used Allis–Chalmers Model HD–5G tractor. The contract was negotiated in August of 1957 and called for twenty-three monthly installments of $574.00 each. The buyer, Russell, failed to make the first monthly payment, and on his suggestion a

McGinnis company representative met with the appellant, Yarbro, to ask if he would help with the payments. As a result of this meeting Yarbro agreed to, and did, pay the September installment.

In the months that followed there was a continued failure on the part of Russell to make any of the monthly installment payments. During the late months of 1957 and the early months of 1958, there were numerous discussions between McGinnis Co., Russell and Yarbro relative to these monthly payments and at various times during this period, the defendant orally agreed to make some of the payments for Russell. Late in December of 1957, Yarbro gave the McGinnis Co. a check to cover one of the delinquent payments but the check was returned due to insufficient funds. In March of 1958, Yarbro agreed to bring the account of Russell current and allocated $2,378.00 of a check for this purpose. This check, however, was also returned by the bank for lack of sufficient funds.

In May, 1958 when McGinnis Co. indicated that the tractor soon would have to be repossessed, Yarbro again assured the company that it would be paid as soon as two pending real estate escrows were closed. This promised payment was not made. A similar promise was made by Yarbro in July on the strength of proceeds that were to be forthcoming from an oat crop in New Mexico but again no payment was made. An ultimatum was issued by the McGinnis Co. at the end of July, 1958 and finally steps to repossess were taken in August of 1958.

Persons at the Yarbro ranch prevented the repossession, leading to further negotiations which also provided unfruitful. The tractor was finally repossessed in January of 1959. Subsequently, the McGinnis Co. brought an action to recover the payments due under the conditional sales contract, naming Russell and Yarbro as defendants. A default judgment was entered against Russell and the only question before this court now concerns the liability of the defendant, Yarbro. The trial court found Yarbro liable for the entire balance under the conditional sales contract ($8,751.95).

The errors assigned by the defendant on this appeal are threefold. First, he contends that his promises to pay the debts of Russell, being oral, are unenforceable by reason of the Statute of Frauds. § 44–101, subsec. 2. Second, he contends that there was insufficient consideration to support the promise assuming it was otherwise enforceable. Third, he contends that if the Statute of Frauds were held to be inapplicable to this case, the judgment rendered by the trial court was excessive. The third assignment of error is based on defendant's arguments that he only promised to pay four, rather than all, of the unpaid monthly installments. We will consider these contentions separately. . . .

Although the promises made by Yarbro clearly were of the type covered in the [suretyship Statute of Frauds], the plaintiff contends that the leading object or primary purpose exception recognized by this court in the case of Steward v. Sirrine, 34 Ariz. 49, 267 P. 598, is applicable. Simply stated, this rule provides that where the leading object of a person promising to pay the debt of another is actually to protect his own interest, such promise if supported by sufficient consideration, is valid, even though it be oral. This rule has been adopted by a great number of states although the rationale has often been stated in varying terms. This exception to the Statute of Frauds no matter how stated, is based upon the underlying fact that the Statute does not apply to promises related to debts created at the instance, and for the benefit, of the promisor, (*i.e.* "original" promises) but only to those by which the debt of one party is sought to be charged upon and collected from another (*i.e.* "collateral" promises). Although a third party is the primary debtor, situations may arise where the promisor has a personal, immediate and pecuniary interest in the transaction, and is therefore himself a party to be benefitted by the performance of the promisee. In such cases the reason which underlies and which prompted the above statutory provision fails, and the courts will give effect to the promise. Schumm, by Whyner v. Berg, 37 Cal.2d 174, 231 P.2d 39, 21 A.L.R.2d 1051; *Restatement of Contracts*, § 184.

Recognizing the leading object rule as a well reasoned exception, the question remains whether the facts presently before this court make the exception applicable. There are no easy, mathematical guidelines to such a determination. To ascertain the character of the promise in question and the intention of the parties as to the nature of the liability created, regard must be had to the form of expression, the situation of the parties, and to all the circumstances of each particular case. [citations] The assumption behind the exception is that it is possible for a court to infer from the circumstances of any given case whether the "leading object" of the promisor was to become a surety for another or whether it was to secure a pecuniary advantage to himself and so, in effect, to answer for his own debt. The leading object may be inferred from that which he expected to get as the exchange for his promise. Thus, it is neither "consideration" alone (for there must be consideration to make any promise enforceable, including one of guaranty) nor "benefit" alone (for in most every guaranty situation at least some benefit will flow to the promisor-guarantor) that makes an oral promise to pay the debt of another enforceable. Rather, there must be consideration and benefit *and* that benefit must be the primary object of making the promise as distinguished from a benefit which is merely incidental, indirect, or remote. It is when the leading and main object of the promisor is *not* to become surety or guarantor of another, even though that may be the effect, but is to serve some purpose or interest of his own, that the oral promise becomes enforceable. *Schumm, by Whyner v. Berg, supra.*

The facts in the present case show that before the McGinnis Co. ever began its dealings with Russell, Yarbro had sought to purchase the tractor in question for himself, but that no sale had resulted because the financing institution with which the McGinnis Equipment Co. financed such deals would not accept Yarbro's credit. It was at this point that Yarbro said that he thought he could get Russell to buy the tractor. Further evidence of Yarbro's interest in the tractor comes from the fact that after its purchase he had borrowed it on a series of occasions. When repairs were needed shortly after Yarbro had made the first installment payment, the McGinnis Co. repairman found the machine on Yarbro's land. He admits that a number of times he used the tractor for jobs around his ranch, and witnesses stated at the trial that Yarbro had asked on several occasions that the McGinnis Co. not repossess the tractor because he needed it. These requests were usually in conjunction with a promise to pay what was owing on the tractor.

We have often stated that this court will not disturb the findings and judgment of the trial court when supported by substantial evidence and that all the evidence and inferences therefrom must be viewed in a manner strongest in favor of the appellees. [citations] We find that there was substantial evidence to support the trial court's conclusion that the main and leading object of Yarbro in making his promises to McGinnis Co. was not to become Russell's guarantor but rather was to serve interests of his own.

Yarbro further contends that if the oral character of the promise does not prevent its enforcement, then a failure of consideration does. We, of course, recognize that a promise must be supported by consideration or some substitute in order to be legally enforceable, but find this requirement to be fulfilled in the present instance. In Cavanagh v. Kelly, 80 Ariz. 361, 297 P.2d 1102, we held that a benefit to a promisor or a loss or detriment to the promisee is good consideration to legally support a promise. In the present case, the McGinnis Co. had a legal right to repossess the subject of its conditional sales contract, but the evidence shows that it forbore from doing so because Yarbro promised that he would pay the delinquent installment payments. This forbearance was not only a legal detriment to the McGinnis Co., but as previously noted, was a substantial benefit to Yarbro. Forbearance by a creditor to seize his debtor's property or enforce a lien against it, has often been held to be sufficient consideration to support an oral promise of guaranty when such forbearance enables the promisor to obtain an advantage or benefit. [citations]

Thus, when the main purpose of the promisor is not to answer for the debt of another, but to obtain a substantial benefit to himself, which he actually secures as the consideration for his promise, then not only is the promise valid though oral, it is supported by good and sufficient consideration.

The defendant also contends that assuming his promise was not within the contemplation of the Statute of Frauds, the eventual judgment rendered against him was excessive. With this contention, we agree.

The trial court granted judgment in the amount of $8,751.95 which represents the entire unpaid balance of the contract purchase price reduced by the $5,000 received by the plaintiff at an auction sale of the repossessed machine. To hold Yarbro liable for the complete contract price, the evidence must indicate that his promises to pay went not only to delinquent payments but also to the remainder of the payments under the contract. The evidence, however, does not show this.

It is clear from the testimony of the creditor's agents that each time they visited Yarbro and Russell, only past due payments were requested. It is also clear from their testimony that there were no promises by Yarbro to assume future installment payments. The only evidence regarding a promise to pay in the future appears in Yarbro's own testimony on direct examination, and is as follows:

Q.   What was said by you concerning the ... Russell obligation?

A.   I told them that ... if they would give me time I would pay for this tractor and take it over.

The creditors failed to make any such arrangements, and under such circumstances the above statement cannot be considered to rise to the dignity necessary to obligate the defendant to pay future installment payments. When one assumes a portion of the debt of another it does not necessarily follow that he has assumed his entire debt.

The record indicates that the last time that Yarbro was contacted prior to repossession was shortly after the July, 1958 installment came due. At this time, claiming anticipated crop proceeds for assurance, he promised to make all past due payments on the equipment. No later promises were made. Accordingly, we find Yarbro liable for the monthly installments from October, 1957 through July, 1958 only. The trial court judgment is reduced correspondingly.

Judgment affirmed as modified.

PROBLEMS

18.   D says to C, "Deliver these goods to TP and I will see that you are paid." C delivers the goods to TP but manifests an intent not to treat TP as her debtor, relying solely on the credit of D. Is D's promise enforceable?

19.   TP owes C $1,000. D says to C, release TP and I will pay. C releases TP. Is D's promise enforceable?

20.   TP owes C $1,000. TP and D enter into an oral contract by the terms of which D, for a consideration, agrees to assume the obligation. Is D's promise enforceable?

21.   TP owes C $1,000. For a consideration, D orally promises C to become a surety. Is D's promise enforceable?

22.   TP owes C $1,000. C is about to levy an attachment on TP's factory. D, who is an unsecured creditor of TP, orally promises that if C forbears D will pay TP's debt if TP does not. Is D's promise enforceable?

23.   TP is indebted to C and as a result C has a lien upon TP's property. D orally promises to pay the debt if TP does not, provided that C discharges the lien of the mortgage. C discharges the lien of the mortgage. Is D's promise enforceable?

24. A, for a consideration, orally promises B that, in the event B's car is damaged in a collision, A will reimburse B for the loss. C and B have a collision for which C is responsible. Is A's promise enforceable?

25. A, for a consideration, orally promises B that in the event that C, B's employee, steals money from B, A will reimburse B. Is A's promise enforceable?

SECTION 6. STATUTE OF FRAUDS AND MARRIAGE

(Calamari & Perillo on Contracts § 19.13)

DIENST v. DIENST
Supreme Court of Michigan, 1913.
175 Mich. 724, 141 N.W. 591.

McALVAY, J. Complainant filed her bill of complaint against defendant, praying for divorce on the ground of extreme cruelty. Defendant appeared and filed an answer to said bill of complaint, coupled with a cross-bill, wherein he set up a verbal antenuptial contract, by which it is claimed that she agreed to make provision for him after the marriage by executing a will of all her property in his favor in case he survived her. The relief prayed for in said cross-bill is that complainant produce and file such will, which is claimed to have been made soon after the marriage, and that it be declared binding as a settlement of the property rights of the parties; that in case the will has been destroyed by her she be required to make and execute a duplicate thereof; that in case she refuses so to do within the period of five days after decree, the decree stand in the place and stead of said will and be final; that the rights and interest of defendant in said property be declared fixed, binding, and vested; that complainant be enjoined from disposing of any of her property except in accordance with the agreement claimed, and for general relief. He does not pray for a decree of divorce. Issue was joined by a replication to the answer.

A general demurrer was interposed by complainant to the cross-bill of defendant on the ground of want of equity for several reasons, the chief of which was that the claimed antenuptial contract was within the statute of frauds. This provision of the statute reads:

> Every agreement, promise or undertaking, made upon consideration of marriage, except the mutual promises to marry, shall be void unless such agreement, contract or promise, or some note or memorandum thereof, be in writing signed by the party to be charged therewith.

Section 9515, subd. 3, C.L.1897. . . .

A very brief statement of the circumstances which brought about the marriage between these parties will be made. It appears that in November, 1908, a correspondence between them was begun, the initial letter having been written by complainant. Both were subscribers to the publication of a marriage brokerage called *The Correspondent*, in which complainant discovered an attractive description of defendant. Complainant was of the age of 62 years and defendant 66 years. Both had been previously married, and each had been widowed by death. She was possessed of an estate, real and personal, in her own right, of between sixty and seventy thousand dollars. Defendant was penniless. A lurid correspondence, thus begun between the parties, of which we are furnished only that of complainant, appears as exhibits to his cross-bill (he modestly withholding his contributions to the same), and within a few months culminated in their engagement, which was speedily followed by a marriage, growing out of which this litigation, to sever the marital relations between them, naturally followed.

Counsel for defendant apparently appreciates and admits that if the agreement sought to be enforced was made and entered into upon consideration of marriage, not having been reduced to writing, it is void under the statute of frauds. However, he contends that the agreement relied upon by him was "not made upon consideration of marriage"; that the agreement was that if defendant would give up his home and employment and abandon prospective political preferment, come to Kalamazoo, marry, and reside with complainant and not return to Kansas, she would not only support him, but would make a will, as already stated. It appears, however, that the only agreement which defendant charges in his cross-bill was entered into by complainant, and which he avers he relied upon, is the agreement set forth in . . . his cross-bill . . . to the effect that she *"then and there, as a further consideration for the consummation of such engagement of marriage promised and agreed* that she would, immediately after their said marriage, make such provision that the said defendant would come into possession and ownership of all of her said property upon her death." That this was the inducement appears from his averment as follows: "And that thereupon immediately thereafter, relying upon such representations, promises, and agreements on the part of the said plaintiff, and in consideration thereof, he gave up and abandoned his employment, position, and prospects, . . . which he then and there had, and immediately proposed marriage to the said complainant," which proposal complainant immediately accepted. It is clear to us that this claimed agreement and undertaking between these parties was made upon consideration of marriage, and was within the prohibition of the statute of frauds. It was therefore void and not enforceable.

The other questions discussed in the briefs of the parties do not require consideration.

The order and decree of the circuit court in sustaining the demurrer of complainant is affirmed, and the cross-bill is dismissed, with costs of both courts to complainant. The cause will be remanded, and will proceed in due course.

PROBLEMS

26. A and B, an engaged couple, orally agree that after their marriage they will live in A's house. In exchange B agrees to pay $70,000 to A. Is the agreement within the Statute of Frauds?

27. A and B were engaged to be married. C, who is A's mother, orally promised A and B a new Jaguar automobile as a wedding gift. She subsequently repudiated. Is her promise enforceable?

SECTION 7. STATUTE OF FRAUDS AND REAL PROPERTY

(Calamari & Perillo on Contracts §§ 19.14—19.15)

SHAUGHNESSY v. EIDSMO

Supreme Court of Minnesota, 1946.
222 Minn. 141, 23 N.W.2d 362, 166 A.L.R. 435.

MATSON, JUSTICE. In an action for specific performance, defendant Bernt Eidsmo appeals from an order denying his motion for a new trial.

Plaintiffs, husband and wife, on April 5, 1943, by oral agreement, leased from the defendant Bernt Eidsmo a dwelling house and lot . . . for a term of one year from May 1, 1943, at a rental of $47.50 per month, and, in consideration for the making of said lease and as a part thereof, defendant agreed to give, and gave, plaintiffs an option to purchase said property at the expiration of the lease term at a price between $4,750 and $5,000 on a contract for deed, subject to the proviso that plaintiffs should be allowed as a credit on the purchase price the total rent paid for the lease term with the balance of the purchase price to be paid in monthly installments of $32.50, inclusive of unpaid taxes and five percent interest per annum on the unpaid balance. Defendant also agreed to sell plaintiffs a stove for $119.50, payable in installments of $4 per month without interest. Plaintiffs entered into possession May 1, 1943, and continued in possession throughout the one-year lease term ending April 30, 1944, and paid during said term a total rental of $570 and a total of $48 on the purchase price of the stove. At and before the expiration of said lease term, plaintiffs notified defendant that they wished to exercise their option of purchase according to the terms thereof, and on several occasions they demanded of defendant that he deliver a contract for deed as agreed. On each of these occasions, defendant told plaintiffs that he did not have time to have a contract drawn, but that his word was good and they should not worry. Plaintiffs fully performed their part of the option agreement and have at all times been ready, willing, and able to execute a contract for deed. Since the expiration of the lease term, plaintiffs have continued in possession, and from May 1, 1944, to May 1, 1945, have paid an additional $570 on the purchase of said property and a further sum on the purchase of the stove. When the option and lease agreement were made, the premises were subject to a $4,200 mortgage of which no mention was made to the plaintiffs and in regard to which no agreement was made that plaintiffs should assume said mortgage or take the property subject to the same. . . .

The trial court decreed that plaintiffs have a vendees' interest in the property and that they were entitled to a contract for deed from defendant specifying a purchase price of $5,000, subject to a credit on said price for the gross sum of all rents and purchase money paid, with a proviso that the balance of the price should be paid in monthly installments of $32.50 each, inclusive of taxes and interest at five percent per annum. . . .

The instant . . . plaintiffs exercised their option by notifying defendant of their election to buy the premises a new contract, an oral contract for the purchase and sale of land, came into being. It was clearly within the statute of frauds (§ 513.04 (§ 8459)), unless taken therefrom by part performance, § 513.06 (§ 8461). According to *Restatement, Contracts*, § 197, the applicable rule is as follows:

> Where, acting under an oral contract for the transfer of an interest in land, the purchaser with the assent of the vendor . . .
>
> (b) takes possession thereof or retains a possession thereof existing at the time of the bargain, and also pays a portion or all of the purchase price,
>
> the purchaser or the vendor may specifically enforce the contract.

In other words, the acts of taking possession and of making part payment, when they are performed under or in reliance upon the oral contract as to be unequivocally referable to the vendor-vendee relationship and not referable to any other relation between the parties, are sufficient to remove the contract from the statute of frauds. The doctrine of part performance, exemplified by the above rule, was followed by this court in Wentworth v. Wentworth, 2 Minn. 277, 2 Gil. 238, 72 Am.Dec. 97; Gill v. Newell, 13 Minn. 462, 13 Gil. 430; and Bresnahan v. Bresnahan, 71 Minn. 1, 73 N.W. 515. In Brown v. Hoag, 35 Minn. 373, 375, 29 N.W. 135, 137, however, the court expressly rejected the unequivocal reference theory upon which the earlier cases were based and adopted the fraud theory under which the plaintiff must show that his acts or part performance in reliance upon the contract so altered his position that he would incur an unjust and irreparable injury in the event the defendant were permitted to rely on the statute of frauds. This latter decision, though apparently overlooked in *Bresnahan v. Bresnahan, supra,* has been followed in subsequent cases. We now adopt the *Restatement* principle to the effect that the taking of possession, coupled with the making of part payment, in reliance upon and with unequivocal reference to the vendor-vendee relationship, *without proof of irreparable injury through fraud,* is sufficient to avoid the statute. *Brown v. Hoag, supra,* and subsequent decisions based thereon, in so far as they require proof of irreparable injury or great hardship in addition to part performance, are expressly overruled. In other jurisdictions, as well as our own, in losing sight of historical antecedents considerable confusion has resulted in determining the basis for the removal of cases from purview of the statute of frauds.

> The origin of the doctrine of the part performance as applied to permit the specific performance of an oral contract for the sale of real estate may be traced to a rule of equity which, antedating the English statute of frauds, required as a prerequisite of the enforcement of parol contracts concerning land that the plaintiff show that the contract had been partly performed, *or* that he had so altered his position in reliance on the agreement that a refusal to enforce it would amount to a fraud upon him.

(Italics supplied.) 49 Am.Jur., *Statute of Frauds*, § 420. Dean Pound, *The Progress of the Law*, in 33 Harv.L.Rev. 929, 937, with clarity explains the basis for the confusion that has arisen in so many American jurisdictions:

> ... It is important to insist that the taking of cases out of the statute is a historical anomaly, only to be understood by reference to seventeenth-century and eighteenth-century legal institutions and modes of thought in equity and that, like all historical anomalies of the sort, it defies logically satisfactory analytical treatment.

> What is the actual situation? We say that for the purposes of courts of equity, cases are taken out of the purview of the statute in either of two ways: by fraud *or* by part performance. Recently there has been a tendency to run the two together, largely under the influence of Pomeroy's doctrine of 'equitable fraud.' But they had an independent origin and have developed along independent lines. Hence they call first for independent consideration. (Italics supplied.)

and *Id.*, at pp. 939, 940:

> Before a decade had passed after its (statute of frauds) enactment, the Court of Chancery began to take cases out of the operation of the statute where purchaser had been put in possession under the contract. Sugden (*Vendor and Purchaser* (14 ed.) 152, note p) long ago called attention to some old cases which indicate that this was the result of ideas as to livery of seisin. *Putting the purchaser in possession was taken to be the substance of a common-law conveyance.* The rule thus derived became established in England and in a majority of American jurisdictions. But its original basis was soon overlooked and attempts to rationalize the subject led writers and courts to turn to the idea of "fraud" in order to make a reasoned doctrine of "part performance" on the basis of the old cases where the chancellor had dispensed with the statute. Different developments of this idea gave rise to many varieties of doctrine. Thus we get to-day cases taken out by possession alone; cases taken out by possession coupled with something else, arbitrarily prescribed by judicial decision or by statute; cases taken out by possession when joined to circumstances of

great hardship upon purchaser; cases of part performance other than by taking possession, where there are acts solely referable to a contract as to the very land or showing a change in the character of the preexisting possession, and cases where it is not possible to take possession but relief is given on a theory of fraud or of irreparable injury to purchaser, without more. (Italics supplied.) . . .

Samuel Williston, under whose direction *Restatement, Contracts*, § 197, was drafted, in *Commentaries on Contracts, Restatement No. 4*, pp. 14, 15, dated February 23, 1928, states:

. . . Courts of equity early adopted the doctrine that such acts as the taking of possession, making of improvements, and the like by the purchaser with consent of the vendor make the contract enforceable though there is no written memorandum. This doctrine has been rested upon two main reasons: (1) that the rule of the Statute of Frauds is an evidential rule and that any acts clearly and solely referable to the existence of the contract satisfy in equity the purpose of the Statute; (2) that equity should relieve against the operation of the Statute in cases where it would be unconscionable for the vendor to rely upon it in defense.

These two main reasons given by Williston correspond to Dean Pound's analysis that "cases are taken out of the purview of the statute in either of two ways: by fraud *or* by part performance." (Italics supplied.) Obviously, the evidential purpose of the statute is fully satisfied by adequate part performance without proof of irreparable injury.

Whether the acts of part performance are unequivocally referable to the vendor-vendee relationship under the oral contract is (in this case) a question of fact for the trier of fact.

In the instant case, the two essential elements of possession and part payment are present. Defendant contends, however, that possession is not unequivocally referable to the vendor-vendee relationship, but is equally referable to the relation of landlord and tenant. The entire record, however, is pregnant with indications of a dominant intent of the parties from the inception of their transaction that a purchase-and-sale relation should be established upon the expiration of the lease term. The purchase of the stove also indicated an understanding that plaintiffs were to occupy the premises permanently. After plaintiffs exercised their option and an oral contract of purchase and sale then came into being, defendant's conduct and statements were consistent only with a mutual understanding that plaintiffs' possession of the premises was no longer that of a tenant but that of a vendee with unequivocal reference to the oral contract. When plaintiffs, on several occasions, requested the preparation of a contract for deed, defendant, instead of rejecting the vendor-vendee relationship, affirmed it by stating "that he did not have time to have a contract drawn; that his word was good; that plaintiff Mark Shaughnessy was not to worry about getting his contract." In fact, defendant finally presented to plaintiffs a written memorandum to be used as a basis for drawing a contract for deed. The conduct of the parties indicated no misunderstanding as to the nature of their transaction and the relation that each bore to the other. There was a dispute as to the amount of the purchase price and the terms of payment, but as to these matters the findings of the court are sustained by the evidence. Similar considerations support the findings that the payments made by plaintiffs were solely referable to the oral contract of purchase and sale.

The order denying a new trial is affirmed. . . .

PROBLEMS

28. S orally retained X, a licensed real estate broker, to procure a buyer who would pay $10,000 cash for Blackacre. S promised X a commission of 6%. X produced B who purchased Blackacre for $10,000. In an action by X against S for the commission, S pleads the Statute of Frauds. What result?

29. S made a written offer to sell Blackacre to B. B accepted orally. B breached the contract. When sued by S, B sets up the defense of the Statute of Frauds. What result?

30. S made an oral offer to sell Blackacre to B for $10,000. B accepted and paid the $10,000 to S. S now refuses to convey. In an action by B, S raises the defense of the Statute of Frauds. What result?

31. S orally agreed to transfer Blackacre to B. B agreed to pay the purchase price in one year. Pursuant to further terms of the agreement, S conveyed the property to B. At the end of the year B has not paid. Is the Statute of Frauds a defense to S's action for the price?

CHAPTER 14

DISCHARGE OF CONTRACTS

■ ■ ■

(Calamari & Perillo on Contracts §§ 21.1—21.15)

GOLDBARD v. EMPIRE STATE MUTUAL LIFE INS. CO.

Supreme Court of New York, Appellate Division, 1958.
5 A.D.2d 230, 171 N.Y.S.2d 194.

BREITEL, J. Plaintiff appeals from a determination of the Appellate Term modifying a judgment rendered in his favor against defendant after trial without a jury in the Municipal Court. The Appellate Term modification, one Justice dissenting, reduced plaintiff's recovery from $2,800 to $800. That court granted leave for plaintiff to appeal to this court.

Plaintiff is the insured under an accident and health insurance policy providing monthly indemnity; defendant is the insurer. . . .

The issue which divided the Appellate Term is whether plaintiff insured settled and compromised his claims against defendant insurer prior to suit, with finality, and, as a consequence, is limited in recovery to the settlement figure of $800. The trial court found that insured was not so limited, but a majority of the Appellate Term disagreed.

It is concluded that the settlement negotiations between insured and insurer did not constitute either a substituted agreement or an enforceable executory accord; and, that therefore, insured is not prevented from pursuing his original claim. . . .

Insured is a barber by trade. Before his illness he ran his own one-man shop. In December, 1951 insurer issued its annually renewable policy to insured, who maintained his payments of premiums as required by the policy. In 1955 insured filed claims based upon a fungus hand infection from which he was suffering and which he asserted totally disabled him from engaging in his occupation. If true, he was entitled to monthly indemnity at fixed amounts under the policy. There then ensued a sequence of events in which some payments, vouchered as final, were offered by insurer, which insured refused to accept, believing they were less than that to which he was entitled. Insurer had misgivings concerning the nature of insured's illness and the extent of its disabling character.

The parties remained in genuine dispute. In the early fall of 1955 insured made complaint to the State Insurance Department, and this triggered the occurrence upon which the main issue on this appeal is based.

While the disputants were before the department representative, insurer offered to settle the claims for $800, conditioned on a surrender of the policy, with consequent termination of its renewability. Insured, concededly, refused. He was willing to accept the $800, but not to surrender the renewable policy. However, later that day insured telephoned the department representative and asked him to advise insurer that he would accept the $800, without requiring that the policy be renewed. The department representative relayed the call. Insurer thereupon wrote insured a letter asking him to call at the office with his policy for surrender and advising, in effect, that he would then be paid the $800 upon signing a release. Insured ignored the letter, and in due time started this action.

Insurer contends that on the facts related there was a "settlement and compromise" which limits insured's right of recovery. Insured, on the other hand, contends that there was no more involved than a new offer by insurer, not accepted by insured, or, at best, an executory accord which is unenforceable for lack of a writing as required by section 33–a of the Personal Property Law.*

There is no magic to the words "settlement" or "compromise" in deciding whether a disputed claim has been discharged with such finality that no action may be brought upon it, but only upon the later agreement. As a matter of fact, the words are used interchangeably to describe either a subsequent agreement which discharges an earlier agreement, that is, a substituted or superseding agreement (Morehouse v. Second Nat. Bank, 98 N.Y. 503), or an executory accord which does not (Larscy v. Hogan & Sons, 239 N.Y. 298). Consequently, one does not advance the solution of any problem in this area by attaching either label, or presuming to conclude the discussion by making an initial determination that a negotiation has or has not achieved a "settlement" or a "compromise." (6 Corbin, *Contracts*, § 1268.)

The question always is whether the subsequent agreement, whatever it may be, and in whatever form it may be, is as a matter of intention, expressed or implied, a superseder of, or substitution for, the old agreement or dispute; or whether it is merely an agreement to accept performance, *in futuro,* as future satisfaction of the old agreement or dispute. The literature on the subject is voluminous. *Restatement, Contracts*, §§ 417–419; 6 Williston, *Contracts*, Rev. ed., § 1838, *et seq., but esp.,* §§ 1841, 1846, 1847; 6 Corbin, *Contracts, supra,* § 1268, *et seq.,* esp. § 1293, at pp. 148–149; 1937 Report N.Y.Law Rev.Comm., p. 210 *et seq.*There is, then, no simple rule to be applied, as a matter of law, to determine in all given situations whether the subsequent agreement extinguishes the old.

---

* [Now § 15–501 of McKinney's N.Y.Gen'l Obl.L. *See Calamari & Perillo on Contracts* § 21.4. Ed.]

Nevertheless, there are principles which occasionally assist in the determination of the question of intention where settlement negotiations have consummated in an agreement. The *Restatement* has described these as giving rise to presumptions. (*See Restatement, Contracts*, § 419, cmt. a.) The New York Law Revision Commission takes the same view (1937 Report, p. 213). This court recently followed a similar analysis (Blair & Co. v. Otto V., 5 A.D.2d 276).

There has arisen, however, a certain class of cases which have given color to the view that some settlements are, as a matter of law, superseding or substituted agreements discharging the old obligations, without involving the determination of intention. Nothing said, or held, in those cases, however, warrants such a conclusion. In each there were circumstances pointed to, at least impliedly, as grounding the findings of intention to supersede the old agreement with the new. The persistent principle to be applied is that of determination of the intention of the parties, as objectively manifested (Reilly v. Barrett, 220 N.Y. 170, 115 N.E. 453).

Sometimes, of course, the matter of intention may be determined from documents exclusively, in which event the conclusion may be drawn, as a matter of law, by the court (*e.g.*, Moers v. Moers, 229 N.Y. 294, 301, 128 N.E. 202, 204.). At other times, the determination of intention will depend upon conversation, surrounding circumstances, or extrinsic proof, in addition to documentation, if any exist, in which event the issue is one of fact, for the trier of the facts, be it court or jury (*e.g.*, Katz v. Bernstein, 236 App.Div. 456; 6 Corbin, *Contracts, supra* § 1293, pp. 148–149).

The complex of facts—conversations, circumstances and documents, if there be any—presents the basis for making inferences. Both experience and logic suggest that some recurring factors are more indicative of intention than others. These have given rise to what have been earlier described as presumptions. So it is that the courts hasten to find an intention to have a substituted or superseding agreement discharging the old where the settlement has resulted in formalized papers with unequivocal language (as in *Blair & Co. v. Otto V., supra*), or in formalized or deliberate proceedings in court during the pendency of an action. These, of course, are not the only relevant recurring factors, or the only bases for presumptions; nor would it be true to suggest that the search for evidentiary inferences has not been influenced by various policy considerations.

When, however, it is concluded that the settlement negotiations have resulted in no more than in [*sic*] an agreement to accept a future performance, albeit by a promise presently made, in future satisfaction of the old obligations—in this State especially—another principle of law intervenes. In New York, an executory accord not fully performed was, prior to the enactment of section 33–a of the Personal Property Law, unenforceable. It was not even available as a defense. This was the rule at common law. 1937 Report of N.Y.Law Rev.Comm., pp. 211–217; *Restatement, Contracts*, § 417, N.Y. Annotations. Since the enactment of section 33–a an executory accord may be enforced, provided it is in writing and signed by the party to be held. If it remain unperformed, the promisee may elect to sue on the accord or the original obligation.

On this analysis, one does not reach the requirements for a writing provided in section 33–a, unless one has first found that the subsequent agreement is not one that supersedes or substitutes for the old one, and, therefore, extinguishes it. Such a subsequent agreement need not be in writing, unless, of course, a writing is required by some independent statute, such as a Statute of Frauds. But, if it is determined that the intention of the parties, expressed by their conduct or words, is that the subsequent agreement was designed to do no more than result in agreement that a future performance, albeit of a promise presently made, would be accepted as future satisfaction of the old obligations, then section 33–a comes into play and the subsequent agreement is unenforceable unless it is in writing and signed.

Applying these principles to the facts in this case, the question is whether there was a substituted agreement, an executory accord, or no contract at all.

In the first place, we have a series of distinctly informal conversations with bargaining give and take. At no time are the bargainers, and the intermediary, agreeing on one occasion and in one place as to what the settlement should be. Instead, there was a triangular operation, the purportedly final terms of which were never expressed in the presence of all. Secondly, at no point do the conversations and communications converge on the precise terms, time or place for consummation. These were the facts that impelled the trial court to find no contract at all.

Thirdly, and crucially, there is nothing in the record which would support an inference that insured ever intended, let alone agreed, to accept only a promise of $800 to be paid in the future (as distinguished from an actual payment here and now) as a present discharge and satisfaction of the insurer's obligations.

Taking the three enumerated elements outlined above, they do not suggest the finality, the deliberateness, or the occasional formalization with which one associates substituted agreements and the specific intention to discharge pre-existing obligations. They do not attain the considered resolution of the entire dispute between the parties that moved the court in Moers v. Moers, *supra*, 229 N.Y. 294, 128 N.E. 202, or in Langlois v. Langlois, [5 A.D.2d 75, 169 N.Y.S.2d 170] to find a superseding agreement. Indeed, they fall far short of the circumstances which the court held insufficient to infer a superseding agreement in cases like Atterbury v. Walsh Paper Corp., 261 App.Div. 529, *affd.*, 286 N.Y. 578.

Generally, it is assumed that one does not surrender an existing obligation for a promise to perform in the future (*Moers v. Moers*, *supra*, p. 300; *see* 6 Williston, *Contracts* [Rev. ed.], § 1847, where it was said: "[I]t is not a probable inference that a creditor intends merely an exchange of his present cause of action for another. It is generally more reasonable to suppose that he bound himself to surrender his old rights only when the new contract of accord was performed"; 6 Corbin, *Contracts*, §§ 1268, 1271, 1293). The *Restatement* would seem to have taken a somewhat more advanced position (*Restatement, Contracts*, § 419[2]), but it is explicitly stated to be merely a guide for interpretation in case of doubt. So treated it is akin to a canon of construction, rather than a presumption that a court is bound to follow in the absence of proof to the contrary. Considering the inchoate and staccato negotiations that ensued in this case, culminating in a relayed telephone call, there is no warrant for inferring the making of a superseding agreement which thereby discharged insured's claims and his renewable policy.

Assuming then, although the trial court found to the contrary, that there was a contract, the factors present in this case, whether subsumed under some rule of interpretation or examined on an *ad hoc* basis, suggest that if any settlement was reached it was not a superseding or substituted agreement but at best only an executory accord. (Actually there is still another possibility applicable to this case, but it is not one urged here: the conversations which took place may have never achieved the finality of concluding a settlement. All negotiations in which parties verbally, and especially, if orally, concur on a settlement are not necessarily intended, *instanter*, to be binding. Just as often, in quite informal settings, the parties do no more than agree to agree, and consummation awaits some degree of implementation. This, of course, is also merely a matter of intention.)

And, of course, on the principles earlier discussed, if all that resulted from the telephone conversations and the letter written by insurer was an executory accord, it was not cognizable under New York law for lack of a writing as required by section 33–a of the Personal Property Law.

Accordingly, the determination of the Appellate Term modifying the judgment rendered in favor of plaintiff against defendant in the Municipal Court by reducing the recovery from $2,800 to $800 should be modified, on the law and on the facts, to reinstate the judgment of the Municipal Court, except as modified, in accordance with the concession of plaintiff, by reduction to the sum of $2,600, together with costs and disbursements of this appeal to plaintiff-appellant. . . .

FIRST AMERICAN COMMERCE CO. v. WASHINGTON MUTUAL SAVINGS BANK

Supreme Court of Utah, 1987.
743 P.2d 1193.

DURHAM, JUSTICE: In this interlocutory appeal, First American Commerce (Borrower) seeks relief from a summary judgment entered against

---

2. "Where a contract is made for the satisfaction of a pre-existing contractual duty, or duty to make compensation, the interpretation is assumed in case of doubt, if the pre-existing duty is an undisputed duty either to make compensation or to pay a liquidated sum of money, that only performance of the subsequent contract shall discharge the pre-existing duty; but if the pre-existing duty is of another kind, that the subsequent contract shall immediately discharge the pre-existing duty, and be substituted for it." For applications of this rule in New York, *see Restatement*, N.Y. Annotations, to this section. (*See also*, 6 Corbin, *Contracts*, § 1271.)

it dismissing all but its claim for fraud against First Security Realty Services (Lender). . . .

The facts as asserted by Borrower are that Borrower received a loan from Lender, securing repayment with a deed of trust and an assignment of rents on a commercial building owned by Borrower. Under the loan documents, Lender's written approval was required on new leases and a percentage of the loan was withheld in a "hold-back" fund pending the completion of certain tenant improvements. On the day the loan documents were signed, Lender assigned the loan to Washington Mutual Savings Bank (Assignee). The assignment was made with the knowledge and consent of Borrower. Borrower desired to lease space in the building and contacted both Lender and Assignee, neither of which would give written consent. Borrower lost the opportunity to lease the space. Upon completion of the tenant improvements, Borrower made a written request that Lender release the held-back funds. Lender refused to release the funds on the theory that its duty to do so had been delegated to Assignee. Borrower sued Lender and Assignee.

Lender obtained summary judgment on the theory that when it assigned the loan documents to Assignee, it ceased to have any responsibility to Borrower, including the duty to release the held-back funds. Borrower argues that although Lender assigned its right to receive payments, it remained obligated to perform its duties under the loan agreement. In the absence of a novation agreement between Lender and Borrower whereby Assignee's performance would be substituted for that of Lender, Lender remained responsible for its duties under the loan. We believe that Borrower is correct.

A review of basic contract law vocabulary is helpful to a resolution of the issue. An assignment is the transfer of rights; a delegation is the transfer of duties. J. Calamari & J. Perillo, *Contracts* § 18–24 (2d ed. 1977). The term "assignment" is often used imprecisely by courts. We agree with the Second Circuit Court of Appeals that "lawyers seem prone to use the word 'assignment' inartfully, frequently intending to encompass within the term the distinct (concept) of delegation. . . ." Contemporary Mission, Inc. v. Famous Music Corp., 557 F.2d 918, 924 (2d Cir.1977) (*quoting* J. Calamari & J. Perillo, *Contracts* § 254 (1970)). Regardless of the terminology they use, courts agree that a party who delegates his duties under a contract to a third person is not relieved of his responsibilities, but rather remains ultimately responsible to the party with whom he contracted for guaranteeing the successful execution of the contractual duties.

Lender contends that ordinary contract law principles do not apply to bank loans and that the language of the loan documents contemplated a novation rather than an assignment. Lender's argument is that while the usual rules of contract law should apply when a party delegates a duty to provide goods or services, a bank that delegates duties under a loan agreement should have no further liability. . . . An examination of the policy underlying the general rule demonstrates the weakness of Lender's position. The usual rule requiring that a delegating party remain liable is designed to protect the expectations of the party receiving the performance. The delegating party should not be able to foist upon the other party to the contract a performer whose skills, goods, reliability, or solvency might differ from those of the delegator. *See* Foster v. Cross, 650 P.2d 406, 410–11 (Alaska 1982). That reasoning applies equally to duties under loan documents. Borrower is entitled to look to Lender's reasonableness and policies respecting the approval of leases and to Lender's solvency to guarantee the release of the remainder of the loan funds.

Lender insists that whether a novation occurred is a matter of law, not of fact. Lender asserts that the language of the loan documents clearly describes a novation. We disagree with Lender on both assertions. Whether an agreement is a novation is a matter of intent. The essential element of a novation is the discharge of one of the parties to a contract and the acceptance of a new performer by the other party as a substitute for the first original party. *See* Kennedy v. Griffith, 98 Utah 183, 187, 95 P.2d 752 (1939). A novation must be intended by the parties to the original contract.

> (T)he burden of proof as to a novation by the transaction in question rests upon the party who asserts it; ... an intention to effect a novation will not be presumed; ... in the absence of evidence indicating a contrary intention, it will be presumed, *prima facie*, that the new obligation was accepted merely as additional or collateral security, or conditionally, subject to the payment thereof; and that the intention to effect a novation must be clearly shown.

D.A. Taylor Co. v. Paulson, 552 P.2d 1274, 1275 (Utah 1976).

Borrower filed an affidavit from one of its general partners stating that Borrower at all times intended to look to Lender for the held-back funds and intended to acknowledge only the assignment of money due in repayment of the loan when it acknowledged the assignment. While it is possible that a document could by its unambiguous terms provide for a novation, the documents in this case do not. Lender argues that the duties under the contract belong to the "Beneficiary," who is defined as "the holder of the note, whether or not named herein," and that by calling Assignee the holder of the note, the contract relieved Lender of its obligations. That interpretation ignores another clause in the loan documents which defines the beneficiary by name as Lender and a provision stating that the agreements bind the parties to the documents *and* their heirs and assigns, not the parties *or* their assigns, as a novation would. Further, if the parties had intended to draft a novation agreement, we think that Lender's counsel would have called the arrangement a novation or at least provided clear language consistent with the intent to substitute Assignee for Lender.

We reverse the grant of summary judgment and remand the matter to the trial court in order to determine the intent of the parties and the other factual issues. . . .

PROBLEMS

1. A and B enter into a binding contract by the terms of which A agrees to work for B for a period of one year and B agrees to pay $500 to A each week. The parties mutually agree to rescind their duties under the contract before performance begins. Is their rescission effective?

2. In problem 1, if A works for a week and then the parties mutually rescind, should A be paid for the week's work?

3. In problem 1, would an agreement to mutually rescind be effective if A has completely performed?

4. A agreed to furnish specifications for a unique machine and B agreed to furnish machine design drawings. Both parties failed to cooperate and to act in good faith in trying to create such a machine. What are the rights of the parties?

5. P commenced an action against defendant, an auto dealer, for restitution of financing charges that exceeded the maximum allowed by state law, plus a penalty. P's total claim was about $6,000. After settlement discussions, P signed a release of this claim that recited a consideration of "$5 and other consideration." P subsequently pursued the claim. The dealer pleaded an affirmative defense based on the release. P testifies that the "other consideration" was supposed to be title to a described used Thunderbird automobile which was never delivered. P's testimony was credited by the trial court. What effect does the failure to deliver the Thunderbird have upon the release?

6. D is indebted to C and they enter into an agreement by the terms of which C presently discharges D's debt in exchange for a promise made by D to deliver a horse. D materially breaches the promise. May C still successfully sue D on the original claim?

7. C has a claim against D in the amount of $1,000. C and D agree that C will take a horse worth $300 in exchange.

(a) D refuses to deliver the horse. What are C's rights?

(b) D tenders the horse and C refuses to take it. What are the rights of the parties? Would the result be different if the horse were worth $2,000?

8. C is a mortgagee and D is a mortgagor. C agrees to take $5,000 less than the face amount of the mortgage loan if D tenders the amount prior to July 1. D makes the tender which C refuses to accept. What are the rights of the parties?

9. D owes C $1,000. T agreed with D to assume this debt for a consideration. Is there a novation? Would the result be different if C promised to release D from liability in exchange for T's promise?

CHAPTER 15

BARGAINS THAT ARE ILLEGAL OR AGAINST PUBLIC POLICY

■ ■ ■

SECTION 1. SOME VARIETIES OF PUBLIC POLICIES

(Calamari & Perillo on Contracts § 22.1)

T.F. v. B.L.

Supreme Judicial Court of Massachusetts, Hampshire, 2004.
442 Mass. 522, 813 N.E.2d 1244.

COWIN, J. The plaintiff, T.F., and the defendant, B.L., are two women who lived together from 1996 to 2000. During this time, the plaintiff became pregnant through artificial insemination, and in July, 2000, after the couple had separated, she gave birth to a child. In January, 2001, the plaintiff filed a complaint in the Probate and Family Court Department. Based on theories of promissory estoppel and breach of an oral contract, she requested that the defendant be ordered to pay child support under the child support guidelines. The judge found that there was an agreement "to create a child," which the defendant had breached. However, the judge did not issue an order of support. Instead, she reported the matter to the Appeals Court . . . , for a determination whether "parenthood by contract is the law of Massachusetts." If this question were answered in the affirmative, she opined, "then (the defendant) is a parent." We granted the plaintiff's application for direct appellate review. We conclude that while the plaintiff has established the existence of an implied agreement, "parenthood by contract" is not the law of Massachusetts and the agreement is unenforceable as against public policy. Therefore, this defendant has no obligation of child support and the Probate and Family Court cannot create such an obligation pursuant to its equity jurisdiction.

Background. . . . The plaintiff and defendant met in 1995, and began living together in the fall of 1996. On May 30, 1999, the couple held a "commitment ceremony." Subsequently, they pooled their money and nominated each other as beneficiaries of their respective life insurance policies and retirement plans. The plaintiff had long wanted to have a child, and communicated her feelings to the defendant.... [But the defendant resisted] until one day in June or July of 1999, when she telephoned the plaintiff at work and told her that she had changed her mind. ... [At that time the couple discussed] such topics as whether they would rather have a boy or a girl, the defendant's reasons for her change of heart, whether the defendant's brother would be a suitable sperm donor, baptism and schooling, and the division of labor between the couple, should they have a child. ... [B]oth parties attended appointments with a ... doctor at a facility specializing in reproduction and fertility procedures (clinic). ... After rejecting other options such as adoption or a foster child, the parties decided to proceed with the plaintiff's artificial insemination. [Both parties signed the clinic's consent form in the space labeled "Recipient."] ... The parties worked together to select an anonymous donor. The couple used joint funds for insemination and prenatal care expenses. The defendant's actions during this period were at least in part an effort to preserve her relationship with the plaintiff, which she believed would have suffered had she attempted to prevent the plaintiff from having a child.

... In December, 1999, the plaintiff became pregnant as the result of the second insemination.The parties' relationship deteriorated in the following months, and the defendant moved out of their apartment in May, 2000. Prior to leaving, the defendant expressed her regrets about being a "separated parent," said she desired to adopt the child, and "promised financial support and promised to talk later about the details since she wanted to just focus on the break-up of the relationship at that time." On July 1, 2000, the plaintiff went into premature labor and gave birth to a boy.

... The defendant visited the mother and child in the hospital several times, participated in selecting his name, and promised to provide support and to change her work hours to help raise him. During one of these visits, the defendant gave the plaintiff $800. On July 26, 2000, the defendant sent pictures of herself with the child, via the Internet, to friends.... In October, 2000, the parties argued for over an hour about support for the child, who, as the result of his premature birth, required a great deal of medical attention. The plaintiff had been parenting the child and working full time, and wanted financial assistance from the defendant. The defendant "acknowledged that she was not paying child support because she was angry at (the plaintiff)." Later that month, the defendant sent a letter to the plaintiff, declaring that she desired no further contact with the plaintiff or the child.

The judge found that there was no written agreement between the parties regarding having a child together, that the defendant is not biologically related to the child, and that she has never lived with him. The judge found further that the defendant's name does not appear on the birth certificate, that she did not adopt the child, and that she has made no financial contributions for the benefit of the child, except the payment of $800 to the plaintiff shortly after the baby was born.

Analyzing the facts, the judge concluded that there was no evidence of an explicit oral promise by the defendant, except to "explore the possibility of having a child." However, the judge concluded that this promise, because of the defendant's subsequent behavior and failure to "stop or slow down" the plaintiff's pregnancy, "grew naturally and actively into the creation of a child," and thus the creation of a binding contract between the parties. The defendant breached this contract, the judge continued, by refusing to perform the obligations of parenthood (*i.e.*, to provide child support).

Analysis. The plaintiff's argument for imposing a child support obligation on the defendant is essentially two pronged. First, she claims that the defendant entered into an enforceable implied contract with her to coparent a child, or at least that she impliedly promised to support the child, and is now estopped from denying that support. The defendant's refusal to pay child support, the argument goes, is therefore a breach of contract. Second, the plaintiff asserts that an order of child support in the present situation would be consistent with oft-expressed legislative policies as manifested in related statutes, and that the "broad and flexible" equity powers of the Probate and Family Court can and should be invoked to implement said polices. We discuss these arguments in turn.

A. *"Parenthood by contract."* The plaintiff does not contend that there was any express written agreement between the parties, but rather that the defendant's initial statement, in the summer of 1999, that she wished to discuss having a child, followed by her course of conduct, reflect an implied contract to create a child. In the absence of an express agreement, an implied contract may be inferred from (1) the conduct of the parties and (2) the relationship of the parties. An implied contract requires proof that there was a benefit to the defendant, that the plaintiff expected the defendant to pay for that benefit, and that the defendant expected, or a reasonable person should have expected, that he or she would have to pay for that benefit. LiDonni, Inc. v. Hart, [355 Mass. 580, 583], 246 N.E.2d 446 [1969]. When the defendant was, or should have been, aware of the plaintiff's expectations in this regard, the defendant's failure to object can create a contract. The defendant's subjective intent is irrelevant when she knows or has reason to know that her objective actions manifest the existence of an agreement. *See Restatement (Second) of Contracts* § 19 (1981).

In this case, the evidence warranted the judge's finding that there was an agreement by the defendant to undertake the responsibilities of a parent in consideration of the plaintiff's conceiving and bearing a child. Although the defendant claims that the plaintiff should not have relied on her passive silence, the judge reasonably concluded that the circumstances and relations of the parties, as stated in her findings, told a different story. . . . [T]he defendant not only did not object, but actively participated in medical decisions and procedures, and in discussions about the child's future and the finances related to the conception and raising of the child. . . . A finding of an implied contract based on these facts, while not compelled, was certainly permissible.

The conclusion does not end our analysis; the question remains whether the court can enforce this contract. Contracts between unmarried cohabitants regarding property, finance, and other matters are normally enforceable. *See* Wilcox v. Trautz, 427 Mass. 326, 332, 693 N.E.2d 141 (1998). Such contracts may concern the welfare and support of children, provided they do not contravene the best interests of the child.[6] *Id.* at 334 n. 7, 693 N.E.2d 141. Contracts between unmarried same-sex couples concerning the welfare and support of a child stand on the same footing as any other agreement between unmarried cohabitants. *See* [E.N.O. v. L.M.M., 429 Mass. 824,] 831 n. 9, 711 N.E.2d 886 [(1999)]. However, when a contract violates or conflicts with public policy, we treat it as void and will not enforce it. A.Z. v. B.Z., 431 Mass. 150, 160, 725 N.E.2d 1051 (2000), and cases cited. *Contrast* Green v. Richmond, 369 Mass. 47, 49–52, 337 N.E.2d 691 (1975). This is such a contract.

In A.Z. v. B.Z., *supra* at 159–160, 725 N.E.2d 1051, we refused to enforce an agreement that compelled a party "to become a parent against his or her will." In that case, the plaintiff successfully prevented his estranged wife from using his own sperm (which had been frozen and stored by an in vitro fertilization clinic) to create a child. *Id.* at 150–153, 725 N.E.2d 1051. "(F)orced procreation," we concluded, "is not an area amenable to judicial enforcement." *Id.* at 160, 725 N.E.2d 1051. The present case is factually distinguishable in that the defendant's contribution to the conception and birth of the child arose from contractual intent rather than from her genetic material. However, important concerns underlying that decision also apply here.

We determine public policy by looking "to the expressions of the Legislature and to those of this court." *Id.* at 160–161, 725 N.E.2d 1051, *citing* Capazzoli v. Holzwasser, 397 Mass. 158, 160, 490 N.E.2d 420 (1986). In the *A.Z.* case we noted that, by statute, a contract to enter into a marital relationship is not enforceable. *Id.* at 161, 725 N.E.2d 1051, *citing* G.L. c. 207, § 47A. We also discussed earlier cases that had "indicated a reluctance to enforce prior agreements that bind individuals to future family relationships." *Id.*, *citing* R.R. v. M.H., 426 Mass. 501, 510, 689 N.E.2d 790 (1998) (agreement by which surrogate mother agreed to give up child at birth was unenforceable unless agreement contained, *inter alia*, "reasonable" waiting period consistent with waiting period in adoption surrender); Capazzoli v. Holzwasser, *supra* at 160–161, 490 N.E.2d

---

6. We disagree with the dissent's assertion that "parenthood by contract" would weaken the "best interests" standard. Where a person's obligation to support a child is established, a court uses the "best interests" standard to measure whether and how that obligation is being fulfilled. However, this standard is irrelevant unless and until the person in question has a legal relationship to the child. Here, where there is no legal relationship (other than an unenforceable contract), the "best interests" standard does not come into play.

420 (contract requiring individual to abandon marriage unenforceable). We concluded that in order to protect the "freedom of personal choice in matters of marriage and family life," A.Z. v. B.Z., *supra* at 162, 725 N.E.2d 1051, *quoting* Moore v. East Cleveland, 431 U.S. 494, 499, 97 S.Ct. 1932, 52 L.Ed.2d 531 (1977), "prior agreements to enter into familial relationships (marriage or parenthood) should not be enforced against individuals who subsequently reconsider their decisions." A.Z. v. B.Z., *supra*.

The principles expressed by this court in *A.Z. v. B.Z., supra,* are applicable, and of like force, in the present case. The decision to become, or not to become, a parent is a personal right of "such delicate and intimate character that direct enforcement ... by any process of the court should never be attempted." *Id., quoting* Kenyon v. Chicopee, 320 Mass. 528, 534, 70 N.E.2d 241 (1946). "Parenthood by contract" is not the law in Massachusetts, and to the extent the plaintiff and the defendant entered into an agreement, express or implied, to coparent a child, that agreement is unenforceable.[8, 9]

The dissent acknowledges that the agreement to create a child was unenforceable, but insists that this agreement "includes" an enforceable promise to pay child support. Our authority to enforce the lawful portion of an otherwise illegal contract depends on whether that portion is severable from the larger agreement. [citation] In the present case, the appropriate inquiry is whether there was a specific identifiable agreement to support the child contained within the implied contract to create and parent the child, and, if so, whether that agreement is severable from the implied contract. The Probate and Family Court judge suggested that an agreement to become a parent inherently involves four promises: (1) that the "parties will continue to love the child," (2) "support each other," (3) "provide child care," and (4) "provide financial support for the child." Nothing in the record gives substance or meaning to any specific promise to provide child support separate and apart from the implied agreement to create a child; support was, as the judge stated, one of the inherent consequences of parenthood. ... [N]othing in the record shows a distinct consideration in return for child support apart from the core, unenforceable promise to coparent. Therefore, any implied promise that the defendant made respecting child support is inextricably linked to her unenforceable promise to coparent the child, and is similarly unenforceable.[10]

---

8. Concluding, as we do, that there was an implied contract to create a child but that it was unenforceable, we need not address the plaintiff's promissory estoppel argument. The same public policy considerations apply to this alternative theory of recovery.

9. In light of our conclusion that a contract to become a parent is unenforceable as against public policy, we do not consider the defendant's contention that such agreements must be in writing. Although our past cases evince a preference for written contracts between unmarried cohabitants, *see, e.g., Wilcox v. Trautz,* 427 Mass. 326, 330, 693 N.E.2d 141 (1998), we have never announced such a requirement, and we decline to do so here.

10. The dissent's conclusion that "parenthood by contract" is not the law, yet that a separate support obligation may nevertheless be imposed on a nonparent, is conspicuously silent on the possible ramifications of such a conclusion. Given the unprecedented nature of imposing a long-lasting support obligation independent of parenthood, we have no recognized legal principles for determining the defendant's status. For example, although the defendant voluntarily ceased

B. *Equity power of the Probate and Family Court.* The plaintiff and the dissenting Justices do not rely exclusively on contract theory, but also invoke the equity powers of the Probate and Family Court, arguing, as the dissent puts it, that "(t)he existence of an agreement to support on the part of the defendant, buttressed by society's interests (as expressed through our statutes and our case law) and the best interests of the child standard, requires relief here." ... This argument, however informed by genuinely good intentions, misapprehends the extent and purpose of the Probate and Family Court's equity powers. The equity powers conferred by the Legislature on the Probate and Family Court are intended to enable that court to provide remedies to enforce existing obligations; they are not intended to empower the court to create new obligations.

The duty to support a minor child is statutory. L.W.K. v. E.R.C., 432 Mass. 438, 443, 735 N.E.2d 359 (2000).[11] A parent's duty to support his child financially has existed by statute in some form since as early as 1692. [citations] Over time, the Legislature has created a comprehensive statutory scheme governing child support, imposing that duty on a person who acknowledges paternity or is adjudicated the father. [citation] The dissent highlights statutory language that "dependent children shall be maintained, as completely as possible, from the resources of their parents," but ignores that the Legislature has reserved this duty for *parents.*

The Legislature has identified those persons who are liable as parents to support their children. *See, e.g.,* G.L. c. 209C, § 1 (person who is adjudicated father of child born out of wedlock); G.L. c. 210, § 6 (person who adopts child). In addition, G.L. c. 46, § 4B, provides that, if the spouse of a woman who undergoes artificial insemination consents to the procedure, that spouse is considered the legitimate parent of a resulting child, and is thus obligated to pay child support. But the Legislature has not addressed the situation, present in this case, where a nonmarital cohabitant consents to such a procedure. This absence of legislative action is not a nod in our direction.

Here, the defendant is not a parent of the child under any statutory provision. She has not become a *"de facto"* parent by virtue of a long-term relationship with the child.[12] Apart from the unenforceable contractual

---

visitation, would she have visitation rights, or some right to resume contact with the child, that she could seek to enforce? While presumably not having a right to custody, would she have any say in some aspects of the child's care, or at least in those aspects that would profoundly affect her own financial obligations (*e.g.*, the decision to send the child to private as opposed to public school)? What if the plaintiff marries and her spouse wants to adopt the child? With an adoptive second parent to provide support, would there still be a basis for continuing the defendant's obligation? What if the plaintiff dies, or becomes incapable of caring for the child? Would the defendant then have the obligation (or the right) of full custody? Given the novel and unprecedented status the defendant would have under the dissent's theory, the Probate and Family Court would be called on to supervise the relationship between the parties and the child for many years to come, and none of them would fully comprehend their rights and obligations until each such right and obligation gave rise to a disagreement and was later defined by way of litigation.

11. At common law, a father having sufficient financial ability was bound to support those of his children who lived with him. Creeley v. Creeley, 258 Mass. 460, 155 N.E. 424 (1927).

12. To date, we have not considered whether a *"de facto"* parent has an obligation to support a child, and we express no opinion on that issue. We merely point out that the defendant had no relationship with the child and would not qualify as a *"de facto"* parent.

obligation found by the Probate and Family Court judge, the defendant is legally a stranger to the child. Because the defendant is not a parent under any of the statutory provisions enacted to establish parenthood, she has no duty to support the child financially, and she may not be ordered to pay child support.

Because nonparents have no duty to pay child support absent a statutory duty, equity does not provide a remedy in this case. "It is a maxim that equity follows the law as declared by a statute." Rossi Bros. v. Commissioner of Banks, 283 Mass. 114, 119, 186 N.E. 234 (1933). 2 J.N. Pomeroy, *Equity Jurisprudence* § 425 (5th ed.1941). Similarly, we cannot infer that a void in the comprehensive statutory scheme that imposes an obligation of child support on parents authorizes us to fill that void by legislating an outcome that suits us.[13] Equity is not an all-purpose judicial tool by which the "right thing to do" can be fashioned into a legal obligation possessing the legitimacy of legislative enactment.

Similarly, the "best interests of the child" is not a free-floating concept that empowers probate judges to impose legal obligations on people who have no legal obligations to begin with. The Legislature has specifically defined when the "best interests of the child" standard is to be applied and has tailored the factors to be considered, depending on the nature of the proceeding. . . .

In response to the Probate and Family Court judge's report of the matter, we conclude that "parenthood by contract" is not the law in Massachusetts. This case is remanded to the Probate and Family Court for further proceedings consistent with this opinion.

So ordered.

GREANEY, J. (concurring in part and dissenting in part, with whom MARSHALL, C.J., and IRELAND, J., join). An obligation to support a child can be created by express or implied agreement (as the court recognizes because the proposition is indisputable) or by conduct showing that the party to be charged has affirmatively committed to the obligation (equally indisputable). Based on the strong findings of the judge in the Probate and Family Court, there is an enforceable obligation to pay support here.

a.   I agree that parenthood by contract is not the law in Massachusetts, for the reason, if no other, that parenthood is a status conferred by law and not one that can be conferred by a private agreement to which the child is not (and cannot be) a party. Both the Legislature and this court have stated many times, and in many contexts, that the Probate and

---

13.   The dissent cites to the American Law Institute's *Principles of the Law of Family Dissolution: Analysis and Recommendations* § 3.03(1) (2000), which recommend imposing parental obligations by agreement even where the person may not be a parent under State law. While § 3.03(1) would provide some definition limiting the types of persons who could potentially be subject to an order of support, the articulation of the factors to be considered concludes with the open-ended invitation to base a support order on "any other facts that may relate to the equity of imposing a parental support duty on the person." *Principles of the Law of Family Dissolution Analysis and Recommendations*, *supra* at § 3.03(2)(d), at 415. Given the elusive nature of this definition, and the magnitude of the obligations being imposed, the task is better left to the Legislature and not to individual judges.

Family Court has full authority to review any agreement within its purview that implicates a child's best interests. Parenthood by contract could oust, or at least weaken, the established power of the court to protect the child's best interests.

b. The inquiry, however, does not end here. The judge ... made careful findings and concluded that: "The decision to create this child was even more conscious and deliberate than the decision that is made by some couples who are both biological parents and conceive a child by direct sexual intercourse. That was the agreement: to create a child. First the parties explored the ways to accomplish that agreement and then they went forward together to accomplish it." The defendant cannot be held to be a parent by contract, but her agreement with the plaintiff includes a promise to support the child that she and the plaintiff agreed to create (by way of artificial insemination) and to parent together. That promise to support is well established by the judge's findings and should not be facilely cast aside as the court does. ... [P]romises were made to parent (that are unenforceable) and to support (that are enforceable). A person cannot participate, in the way the defendant did, in bringing a child into the world, and then walk away from a support obligation.

The plaintiff ultimately seeks an order of child support. The Legislature has long recognized the importance of child support for all children. It has expressed, in unmistakable terms, that "dependent children shall be maintained, as completely as possible, from the resources of their parents" and not by the taxpayers, and that support determinations should be made in "the best interests of the child." G.L. c. 119A, § 1. G.L. c. 209C, § 9(c). With respect to children born out of wedlock, the Legislature has declared that "(c)hildren born to parents who are not married to each other shall be entitled to the same rights and protections of the law as all other children." G.L. c. 209C, § 1. ... In G.L. c. 46, § 4B, the Legislature made clear that the parentage of children born as a result of artificial insemination does not depend on biology but may be determined on the basis of consent. We have stated that "(r)epeatedly, forcefully, and unequivocally, the Legislature has expressed its will that all children be 'entitled to the same rights and protections of the law' regardless of the accidents of their birth." Woodward v. Commissioner of Social Sec., [435 Mass. 536, 546], 760 N.E.2d 257. The Legislature has yet to contemplate the situation here.

[The dissent addresses the equity jurisdiction of the Probate and Family Court, concluding that it has broad authority extending to specific enforcement of agreements, whether supported by consideration or estoppel principles analogous to promissory estoppel. It finds that "[t]he prerequisites for a successful claim based on a theory of promissory estoppel are met in this case" and that the the Probate and Family Court may address "child-related issues that have not been foreseen by statute."]

The existence of an agreement to support on the part of the defendant, buttressed by society's interests (as expressed through our statutes and our case law) and the best interests of the child standard, requires relief here.[3] A.R. v. C.R., 411 Mass. 570, 575–576, 583 N.E.2d 840 (1992). This conclusion finds support in decisions of courts in other jurisdictions involving facts of a similar nature.

The conclusion is also in accord with those principles of the American Law Institute's (ALI) *Principles of the Law of Family Dissolution*, which, insofar as this case is concerned, recommend imposing a parental support obligation on a "person who may be not the child's parent under [S]tate law, but whose prior course of affirmative conduct equitably estops that person from denying a parental support obligation to the child." ALI *Principles of the Law of Family Dissolution: Analysis and Recommendations* § 3.03 & comment c (2002).[4] Section 3.03(1)(c) allows imposition of an order of support when a child is conceived "pursuant to an agreement between the person (to be charged) and the child's parent that they would share responsibility for raising the child and each would be a parent to the child." [. . .] In the case of same-sex couples that "wish to have children together (by way of) a sperm donation or a surrogate mother," a support obligation may be imposed on a party "who is not a parent but who has made a (§ 3.03(1)(c)) agreement with the child's parent."[5] . . .

In summary: even though we do not recognize parenthood by contract, an agreement between the parties has been proved, which includes a promise of support, and the Probate and Family Court, acting under G.L.

---

3. My analysis would be no different were the defendant an unmarried male partner who purposefully put himself in the position of a parent, by taking affirmative steps that resulted in the birth of a child whom he considered, for a time, to be his son, but subsequently attempted to disavow all of his parental responsibilities when his relationship with the child's mother deteriorated. This case is not about establishing parental rights of same-sex couples. It is about the defendant's taking financial responsibility for a child whom she had promised, by words and deeds, to support. When two adults decide together to create a child by way of artificial insemination, and agree together to assume financial responsibility for that child, and their decision and subsequent conduct leads to the birth of a child, that child is no less entitled to the financial support of both adults than had the adults been married, or had the child been conceived through sexual intercourse and thus was biologically linked to both adults.

4. Section 3.03(1) of the American Law Institute's (ALI) *Principles of the Law of Family Dissolution: Analysis and Recommendations* (2002) provides that a support obligation may arise when: "(a) there was an explicit or implicit agreement or undertaking by the person to assume a parental support obligation to the child; (b) the child was born during the marriage or cohabitation of the person and the child's parent; or (c) the child was conceived pursuant to an agreement between the person and the child's parent that they would share responsibility for raising the child and each would be a parent to the child."

In determining whether a support obligation is justified, § 3.03(2) of the ALI Principles directs that a judge should consider: "(a) whether the person and the child act toward each other as parent and child and, if so, the duration and strength of that behavior; (b) whether the parental undertaking of the person supplanted the child's opportunity to develop a relationship with an absent parent and to look to that parent for support; (c) whether the child otherwise has two parents who owe the child a duty of support and are able and available to provide support; and (d) any other facts that may relate to the equity of imposing a parental support duty on the person."

5. . . . The proviso in § 7.04(1), cited by the defendant, that "[a]n agreement is not enforceable if it is not set forth in a writing signed by both parties," is not determinative in this case. . . . The entire text of chapter 7, as well as its accompanying comments and illustrations, demonstrates that § 7.04 contemplates premarital, marital, and separation agreements, and not agreements purporting to assume responsibility for parenting a child.

c. 215, § 6, has jurisdiction to hear the case and specifically to enforce that promise.[6] That the defendant may regret her words and conduct, and view the remedy as harsh, is of no consequence. Equity does not relieve from difficult agreements simply because they are regretted. The child may have been abandoned by the defendant, but he should not be abandoned by the court. [An appendix of facts is omitted from the dissent.]

TROUTMAN v. SOUTHERN RAILWAY CO.
United States Court of Appeals, Fifth Circuit, 1971.
441 F.2d 586.

WISDOM, CIRCUIT JUDGE. Robert B. Troutman, Jr., a member of the State Bar of Georgia, brought this diversity action against the Southern Railway Company seeking to recover the sum of $200,000 as the reasonable value of legal services rendered to Southern in two separate matters—the Central of Georgia case and the grain rate case—during the years 1962 and 1963. On Southern's motion for summary judgment, the district court ruled that Troutman's claim with respect to the Central of Georgia matter was barred by the Georgia four-year statute of limitations. Troutman took no appeal from that ruling, and the Central of Georgia matter has dropped out of the case. A jury awarded Troutman the sum of $175,000 as the reasonable value of his services in the grain rate case. We affirm.

I

In 1963 the Interstate Commerce Commission issued an order directing Southern to increase certain rates on grain shipments from the Midwest to the Southeast by approximately 16 percent. The order created a difficult situation for Southern: if allowed to stand, the order, according to Southern, would result in its losing a $13,000,000 investment in "Big John" railroad cars plus a "tremendous" loss of revenue in the future. Sim S. Wilbanks, a vice president and assistant to the president of Southern, turned for help to Troutman, who had only recently come to Southern's aid in the Central of Georgia case. Troutman, an Atlanta attorney, had no experience in I.C.C. matters, but he was known to Wilbanks as a personal friend and political ally of President John F. Kennedy. Wilbanks told Troutman that Southern was filing suit in a federal district court in Ohio to enjoin the order of the I.C.C. He asked Troutman to persuade the President and the Department of Justice, then headed by the President's brother, Robert F. Kennedy, to "ditch" the I.C.C. and enter the case on the side of Southern. What Wilbanks actually

6. The court's concerns over what rights, if any, the defendant, if ordered to pay child support, might seek in the future with respect to the child address issues that are beyond the scope of this opinion. A relationship of financial support between the defendant and the child arguably could entitle the defendant to concomitant rights and responsibilities which, if asserted, would be considered by a judge in the Probate and Family Court under general principles of family law and the best interests of the child. Speculation as to such matters, however, is not a proper basis on which to deny the relief sought here. The same types of concerns have been raised, and dealt with, in other cases presenting novel or difficult family law issues.

told Troutman, what he engaged Troutman to do, and what Troutman eventually did are of course the crucial issues in this case, and we shall deal with them later in this opinion. Troutman's efforts were successful: the Department of Justice filed an answer in the Ohio lawsuit opposing the I.C.C. and supporting Southern's position. As a result of the Ohio litigation (in which Troutman played no further part), the I.C.C. order was struck down. In return for Troutman's services (in connection with the Central of Georgia case as well as the grain rate case), Southern agreed to look into the joint development of air rights that Troutman owned on property in downtown Atlanta adjacent to property owned by Southern. Efforts to work out the joint development of the air rights continued for several years. When it became apparent, however, that Southern would not join in the development of the air rights, Troutman demanded compensation for his services in the grain rate case in "the usual manner"—*i.e.*, by the payment of money. When Southern refused to pay, Troutman filed suit.

Southern defended the action on three grounds: (1) that Troutman's claim was barred by the Georgia four-year statute of limitations; (2) that Troutman's activities on behalf of Southern were not legal services and were gratuitously rendered; and (3) that because of the nature of the services rendered, it would be contrary to public policy to enforce a claim for compensation. On these grounds Southern moved for the entry of summary judgment in its favor. The district court denied the Motion and a jury returned a verdict for Troutman in the amount of $175,000. The court denied Southern's motion for judgment notwithstanding the verdict or for a new trial, and Southern appealed.

II

Southern's first contention is that the district court erred in refusing to grant Southern's motion for judgment notwithstanding the verdict because the evidence conclusively establishes that the contract upon which Troutman sued was "to exert his personal and political influence upon the President of the United States." Southern argues that such a contract is in violation of public policy and unenforceable; therefore, the court erred as a matter of law in failing to render judgment for Southern. We cannot agree.

It is of course true that a contract to influence a public official in the exercise of his duties is illegal and unenforceable when that contract contemplates the use of personal or political influence rather than an appeal to the judgment of the official on the merits of the case. Nevertheless, all citizens possess the right to petition the government for redress of their grievances. United States Constitution, Amendment I. To that end, one may employ an agent or attorney to use his influence to gain access to a public official. Moreover, once having obtained an audience, the attorney may fairly present to the official the merits of his client's case and urge the official's support for that position. *E.g.*, Hall v. Anderson, 1943, 18 Wash.2d 625, 140 P.2d 266, 148 A.L.R. 760. As the district court well stated in its opinion overruling Southern's motion for summary judgment, it is "only the elements of 'personal influence' and 'sinister means' (that) will void the contract and deny it enforcement." Troutman v. Southern Ry. Co., N.D.Ga.1968, 296 F.Supp. 963, 972. Moreover, the illegal or sinister nature of a contract for professional services will not be presumed; the burden of proving the illegality of the contract is clearly upon the party asserting it. Steele v. Drummond, 1927, 275 U.S. 199, 48 S.Ct. 53, 72 L.Ed. 238.

It necessarily follows then that the decision whether to enforce a claim for compensation for these kinds of legal services will depend largely upon the facts of each case. Whether the parties in fact entered into a contract calling for the improper exercise of personal influence upon a public official is therefore a question for the jury, guided of course by proper instructions. [citations] In this case the jury concluded that Troutman had agreed with Southern to use his influence merely to gain access to the President and present to him the merits of Southern's case; therefore, the contract was valid and enforceable. On appeal from the order of the district court denying Southern's motion for judgment notwithstanding the verdict, it is our task to examine the record to see whether substantial evidence supports the jury's conclusion.

Troutman himself testified that Wilbanks asked him to go to the President and persuade him "to listen to the case and to see if (the I.C.C.'s order) was not truly against the national interest of this country." He testified that Wilbanks did not ask him to use personal or political influence to get the President to do something for that reason alone. Because he was convinced of the merit of Southern's position, Troutman went to Washington and talked with the President, the President's Special Deputy Counsel Myer Feldman, Assistant Attorney General William H. Orrick, Jr., and officials in the Department of Agriculture.

Feldman testified by deposition that upon being advised of the grain rate problem the President asked him to look into it and "to report back to him on the merits of the case." He said that Troutman supplied him with material helpful to an understanding of the issues and that their conversations dealt with what was in the best interest of the nation, the South, and the farm community. After carefully studying the matter, Feldman reported to the President that he thought that the I.C.C.'s order would adversely affect the economy of the South and therefore was not in the national interest. Finally, Feldman testified that Troutman did not make any request of the President that Feldman considered in any way improper; he did not consider it improper to bring the grain rate case to the attention of the President.

Orrick testified, also by deposition, that he and his staff studied the legal questions and that the decision of the Department of Justice to file an answer in the Ohio court contrary to the position of the I.C.C. was based entirely on the merits of the case, unaffected by any outside influence. He also stated that it was not unusual for an attorney to call upon him for the purpose of presenting to him, as an Assistant Attorney General, the contentions, both legal and economic, of the attorney's client; and such activities come within the general scope of the performance of legal services for the client.

From this evidence we conclude that a jury could reasonably find that Troutman was employed to use his influence, such as it was, merely to obtain an audience with the President and there to present to him the merits of Southern's position. Such an employment contract is not in violation of public policy and is therefore enforceable. It follows then that the district court did not err in refusing to grant Southern's motion for judgment notwithstanding the verdict. . . .

Therefore, the judgment of the district court is affirmed. . . .

PROBLEMS

1. P, a woman, and D, a man, lived together while unmarried. During their relationship they had acquired a truck, a car, and two motorcycles. P paid substantially all of the purchase prices of the vehicles, but they were registered in D's name to save on insurance premiums. At the breakup of their relationship P seeks to obtain title and possession of the vehicles. What result?

2. Defendant operated a "dating service" which was a front for the providing of prostitutes. Idaho law made it a crime to knowingly receive "without consideration" the earnings of a woman engaged in prostitution. The customers paid fifty dollars for each act of prostitution. Of this sum, the defendant received twenty-five dollars plus one-half of any tips received. The defendant appeals from a conviction, arguing that his services—advertising, maintaining files, providing a telephone and a place of business—constituted consideration. What result?

There is nothing in the text or case readings to assist you in the proper resolution of problems 3 and 4. Assume there is no case on point. It is up to you to determine public policy.

3. "Plaintiff was a Democrat, publishing a Democratic newspaper of independent proclivities. The defendant was a Republican, seeking a nomination to Congress from a Republican convention." The parties agreed that for a fee the plaintiff's "services as editor would be at the command of the defendant for the campaign" and that he "was to do all he could to influence the choice of delegates and secure the defendant's nomination." Assuming the agreement was made and the services performed, should Plaintiff be able to recover judgment for his fee?

4. Plaintiff's wife was a compulsive gambler. She was indebted to the defendant, a legal card club, because some checks she had cashed bounced for insufficient funds. Plaintiff agreed to pay her debt provided the defendant would deny his wife access to the club in the future. Defendant agreed and plaintiff paid. The defendant nevertheless permitted plaintiff's wife to patronize the club where she lost about $30,000. Much of this money was made available to her by the defendant's cashing of her checks. Plaintiff sues for

breach. Defendant argues that denial of access to the wife would violate a statute that provides "all persons are free and equal, and no matter what their sex, race, color, religion, ancestry, or national origin are entitled to the full and equal accommodations, advantages, facilities, privileges, or services in all business establishments." Is the agreement illegal and therefore void?

SECTION 2.　EFFECT OF ILLEGALITY

(Calamari & Perillo on Contracts §§ 22.2—22.9)

NORTHERN INDIANA PUBLIC SERVICE CO. v. CARBON COUNTY COAL CO.

United States Court of Appeals, Seventh Circuit, 1986.
799 F.2d 265.

[NIPSCO, an electrical utility, agreed to purchase 1.5 million tons of coal every year for 20 years from Carbon County Coal at $24 per ton subject to various provisions for escalation. Time has shown that this was an onerous agreement for NIPSCO. It now seeks a declaratory judgment to the effect that it need not honor the agreement for various reasons, including that the agreement violated § 2(c) of the Federal Mineral Land Leasing Act of 1920 because of Carbon County Coal's affiliation with a railroad. Carbon County Coal counterclaimed for breach of contract. The district court entered a judgment for damages on behalf of the seller.]

POSNER, CIRCUIT JUDGE. . . . Section 2(c) of the Mineral Lands Leasing Act of 1920 provides in pertinent part that "no company or corporation operating a common-carrier railroad shall be given or hold a permit or lease under the provisions of this chapter [relating to federal lands] for any coal deposits except for its own use for railroad purposes. . . ." Oddly in this litigious age, no reported decision has interpreted section 2(c) in the 66 years since its enactment. NIPSCO contends that if the statute is not to be made a dead letter, it must be read to forbid a railroad's affiliate to hold a mineral lease or permit on federal lands. Roughly 15 percent of Carbon County's projected output for the contract with NIPSCO was to come from federal lands that Carbon County had a permit to mine, and Carbon County is a partnership of two firms (each with a half interest in the partnership), Dravo Coal Company and Rocky Mountain Energy Company, the latter a wholly owned subsidiary of the Union Pacific Corporation, whose principal subsidiary is the Union Pacific Railroad Company. . . .

Since this is not a case where the contract itself is illegal—as it would be if it were a contract in restraint of trade and therefore a violation of section 1 of the Sherman Act, or a contract to commit a bank robbery and therefore a criminal conspiracy—it is not governed by Kaiser Steel Corp. v. Mullins, 455 U.S. 72, 77–83, 102 S.Ct. 851, 856–59, 70 L.Ed.2d 833

(1982). Kaiser agreed to make extra contributions to a union welfare fund if Kaiser failed to adhere to an allegedly illegal boycott; the Court sustained the defense of illegality to a suit to enforce the agreement. The extra contributions were in effect a penalty for abandoning the boycott; the underlying agreement that the penalty was designed to enforce was thus an agreement to participate in the boycott. In contrast, the contract in this case is not "intrinsically illegal," Trustees of the Operative Plasterers' and Cement Masons' Local Union Officers & Employees Pension Fund v. Journeyman Plasterers' Protective & Benevolent Soc'y, Local Union No. 5, 794 F.2d 1217, 1220 (7th Cir.1986); and the defense of illegality does not come into play just because a party to a lawful contract (here a contract to supply coal to an electric utility) commits unlawful acts to carry out his part of the bargain.

Second, supposing that the contract does violate section 2(c) of the Mineral Lands Leasing Act, this does not necessarily make it unenforceable. This issue, too, is one of federal rather than state law, though we have no reason to think Indiana law would require a different resolution of it; federal and state law on the contract defense of illegality—the latter well described in Farnsworth, *Contracts* §§ 5.5, 5.6 (1982)—seem quite similar. When the statute is federal, federal law determines not only whether the statute was violated but also, if so, and assuming the statute itself is silent on the matter, the effect of the violation on the enforceability of the contract. Kelly v. Kosuga, 358 U.S. 516, 519, 79 S.Ct. 429, 431, 3 L.Ed.2d 475 (1959).

But when we ask what is the federal rule on illegality as a contract defense, we find, alas, that the course of decision has not run completely true. Compare, for example, the hard line taken in government-contract cases such as United States v. Mississippi Valley Generating Co., 364 U.S. 520, 563–66, 81 S.Ct. 294, 316–17, 5 L.Ed.2d 268 (1961), where the defense seems almost automatic, with the very soft line taken in antitrust cases such as *Kelly v. Kosuga, supra*. The best generalization possible is that the defense of illegality, being in character if not origins an equitable and remedial doctrine, is not automatic but requires (as NIPSCO's counsel acknowledged at argument) a comparison of the pros and cons of enforcement.

There are, after all, statutory remedies (*e.g.*, cancellation of the lease or permit, *see* 30 U.S.C. § 188(b)) for violations of section 2(c); the question is whether there should be an additional, a judge-made, remedy. To decide whether there should be, we must consider the reciprocal dangers of overdeterrence and underdeterrence. Applied too strictly, the doctrine that makes the unenforceability of a contract an additional remedy for the violation of a statute can produce a disproportionately severe sanction; and the overdeterrence of illegality is as great a danger to freedom and prosperity as underdeterrence. The benefits of enforcing the tainted contract—benefits that lie in creating stability in contract relations and preserving reasonable expectations—must be compared with the costs in forgoing the additional deterrence of behavior forbidden by statute that is brought about by refusing to let the violator enforce the contract.

The balance in this case favors enforcement. This makes it irrelevant whether the district judge improperly instructed the jury that in order to uphold the defense of illegality, it must find both that Carbon County was an alter ego of the railroad and that NIPSCO had been injured by the violation of section 2(c), or even whether the contract itself could be viewed as illegal under any interpretation of the statute. . . . In any event the violation of section 2(c) (if any) was trivial given the attenuated linkage between the Union Pacific Railroad and Carbon County, and so far as appears completely harmless. No competitor of Union Pacific in the railroad business, and no competitor of Rocky Mountain Energy Company in the coal business who might be dependent on Union Pacific to transport his coal—no competitor of any member of the Union Pacific "family," however broadly defined—has complained that Carbon County is violating section 2(c). Nor has the Department of the Interior or the Department of Justice. Nor has any customer of any of the entities involved (however peripherally) in this lawsuit. Only NIPSCO complains.

Section 2(c) is an anachronism—a regulatory statute on which the sun set long ago. It could serve as Exhibit A to Dean Calabresi's proposal that courts be empowered to invalidate obsolete statutes without having to declare them unconstitutional. *See* Calabresi, *A Common Law for the Age of Statutes* (1982). We do not believe that we have the power to declare a constitutional statute invalid merely because we, or for that matter everybody, think the statute has become obsolete. But the question in this case is not whether section 2(c) is enforceable but whether an alleged violation of the statute makes a contract unenforceable, and the obsolescence of the statute may be relevant to that determination.

NIPSCO does not argue that Carbon County's alleged violation of the statute hurt NIPSCO or that invalidating this contract under section 2(c) would help anyone, anywhere, at any time. The only consequence, other than to the parties to this suit, would be to throw a cloud of uncertainty over hundreds, perhaps thousands, of contracts for the supply of coal by firms affiliated with railroads, and to inject uncertainty into the contracting process generally. Persons negotiating contracts would have to worry about whether their contract might someday be found to have violated some old, little-known, and newly reinterpreted statute. Lawyers would benefit from the need to do more legal research before signing a contract, but no one else would. We conclude that the Mineral Lands Leasing Act is not a defense to the enforcement of this contract. . . .

COCHRAN v. DELLFAVA

City Court, City of Rochester, Monroe County, Small Claims Branch, 1987.
136 Misc.2d 38, 517 N.Y.S.2d 854.

JOHN R. SCHWARTZ, JUDGE. The issue here is whether the plaintiff can recover from the defendant the Two Thousand Two Hundred Dollars ($2,200.00) she gave to him to play in the so-called "airplane game."

The game consists of a total of fifteen players or investors. Each player must initially pay Two Thousand Two Hundred Dollars ($2,200.00) to enter the airplane game. There is an out-going pilot, two co-pilots, four flight attendants, and eight passengers. The pilot, co-pilots and flight attendants are already on the plane and they attempt to sell tickets to eight new passengers. As each of these eight passengers boards the airplane, he [she] pays $2,200.00 for his [her] ticket to the flight attendant, who in turn passes the money onto the co-pilot, who in turn gives it to the out-going pilot. When the eight passenger tickets are sold, the out-going pilot collects a total of Seventeen Thousand Two Hundred Dollars ($17,200.00) for his or her original $2,200.00 investment. After all eight passenger tickets are sold, the out-going pilot leaves the game and the plane is split off into two new airplanes. Each co-pilot becomes an out-going pilot of his or her own plane; the four flight attendants split off and each becomes a co-pilot of one of the new planes. The passengers split off and become flight attendants of the new planes. The members of the new airplane then try to solicit eight new passengers and the game goes on as explained.

Clearly this is a "chain distribution scheme" as defined in General Business Law 359–fff(2):

> ... a chain distribution scheme is a sales device whereby a person, upon condition that he make an investment, is granted a license or right to solicit or recruit for profit or economic gain one or more additional persons who are also granted such license or right upon condition of making an investment and may further perpetuate the chain of persons who are granted such license or right upon such condition....

It is illegal and prohibited for any person to promote, offer or grant participation in a chain distribution scheme, General Business Law 359–fff(1), and anyone who does shall be guilty of an unclassified misdemeanor. General Business Law 359–g(2).

FACTS

On January 13, 1987, the plaintiff went to a meeting called by the defendant whereby she was persuaded by the defendant to join the so-called "airplane game." She alleged that he was the pilot but the facts revealed he was only the co-pilot, and therefore, he had not started to make a profit yet. The plaintiff stated that she knew it was illegal to play in the game but she was assured by the defendant that "if they got caught, he would take all responsibility." After the meeting, she gave Two Thousand Two Hundred Dollars ($2,200.00) to her friend, another participant, who gave it to the defendant, who gave it to the pilot. At the next meeting, the plaintiff found out that she had become a flight attendant on a plane she did not wish to be on and asked the defendant for her money back. He told her that he did not have her money because he gave it to the pilot. He suggested that she call the pilot. The pilot refused to give the plaintiff her money back. The plane crashed and the plaintiff never recovered her initial investment or made a profit. She brings this action against the defendant for the return of her money.

LAW

The issue here is, does the plaintiff have a cause of action to recover her money in a civil court?

It is illegal and criminal "to promote, offer or grant participation in" the so-called "airplane game." (*See* General Business Law 359–fff(1) and 359–g(2).) "It is settled law in this State (and probably of every other state) that a party to an illegal contract cannot ask a court of law to help him (her) carry out his (her) illegal object, nor can such a person plead or prove in any court a case in which he (she), as a basis for his (her) claim, must show forth his (her) illegal purpose. (Reiner v. North Amer. Newspaper Alliance, 259 N.Y. 250, 181 N.E. 561). For no court should be required to serve as a paymaster of the wages of crime, or referee between thieves. Therefore, the law 'will not extend its aid to either of the parties' or 'listen to their complaints against each other, but will leave them where their own acts have left them.' " (Stone v. Freeman, 298 N.Y. 268, 271, 82 N.E.2d 571, *quoting* Schermerhorn v. Talman, 14 N.Y. 93, 141).

However, there are exceptions to this general principal [*sic*] of law. Courts have allowed recovery by a plaintiff to an illegal contract provided the plaintiff's conduct was *malum prohibitum* and not *malum in se*. Here, the plaintiff's conduct was only *malum prohibitum* (conduct prohibited by statute) as opposed to *malum in se* (conduct prohibited by the nature of the act). To fall under the exception to the general principal of law, not only must the plaintiff establish that the agreement was only *malum prohibitum,* but she must also establish that she entered the agreement under duress or undue influence and that the defendant's conduct was more culpable. Courts have permitted recovery to a widow who became involved in an illegal marriage brokerage contract (Duval v. Wellman, 124 N.Y. 156) and to a Russian Jewish family who illegally loaned money to another Russian Jewish family so that family could emigrate from a communist country (Birger v. Tuner, 104 Misc.2d 63, 427 N.Y.S.2d 904). A court has also mandated the return of a plaintiff's money based on an illegal agreement for the proprietary operation by plaintiff of defendant's restaurant, including plaintiff's use of defendant's liquor license, which was against public policy. (Smith v. Pope, 72 A.D.2d 913, 422 N.Y.S.2d 192).

In each of the cases, the courts held that the parties were not *in pari delicto*. The plaintiff either acted under duress, undue influence, or out of good will.

Therefore, plaintiff's standing to bring this lawsuit stands or falls on whether she violated General Business Law Section 359–fff(1). Did she, by contributing her Two Thousand Two Hundred Dollars ($2,200.00) to the airplane game in the first instance, "promote" the game as declared illegal in the statute?

This Court finds, as a matter of law, that by entering the so-called "airplane game" as a passenger, one is in fact "promoting" the game in violation of the General Business Law (*e.g.* encouraging the pilot to make an illegal profit; encouraging others to enter the game by example; and eventually hoping to make an illegal profit). Therefore, plaintiff's cause of action must fail as a matter of law. It matters not whether the defendant was the more culpable party, whether the defendant was a pilot, as plaintiff testified, and did actually recover a profit or whether he took money because he never made out-going pilot as defendant testified.

The plaintiff by entering the game had larceny in her heart. If the plane did not crash she would have made a substantial illegal profit. If this Court permitted her to recover, in effect this Court would become a referee amongst thieves. The law will not extend its aid to the parties to such an agreement. Therefore, the complaint is dismissed.

MAIZITIS v. TUV AMERICA, INC.

United States District Court, N.D. Ohio, Eastern Division, 2007.
(Not Reported in Fed. Supp.2d).
2007 WL 582391 (N.D.Ohio).

KATHLEEN MCDONALD O'MALLEY, UNITED STATES DISTRICT JUDGE. This matter arises on Defendant TUV America, Inc.'s Motion for Summary Judgment. ... For the reasons articulated below, TUV America, Inc.'s Motion for Summary Judgment is granted.

I. BACKGROUND

The allegations of Maizitis's complaint are minimal. Paragraph six, which appears to be the basis for Maizitis's claim, states that TUV: "compell(ed) Maizitis to enter into and be bound by a contract that did not conform to the laws of the State of Ohio ... (and as a result) Maizitis has sustained severe and substantial injuries." Maizitis's claim, therefore, seems to be based upon the novel contention that he is entitled to damages as a result of entering into, and performing, a contract that was unenforceable as violative of Ohio public policy.

The uncontested, relevant facts are as follows. On March 27, 2000, Maizitis accepted a promotion to the position of service unit manager with TUV America. The position came with a $10,000 salary increase.[1] Prior to beginning work in his new position, Maizitis [read and] signed a new Employment Agreement. Paragraph 3 of the Agreement is a non-solicitation clause*.... Maizitis worked as a service unit manager from April 17,

---

1. Maizitis specifically disavows the argument that the consideration supporting the Agreement was inadequate. (... "Maizitis does not contend that the contract was void or voidable due to a want of consideration.")

* The clause provides:

   3. Non–Solicitation. You agree that during the period of your employment with the Company, and for a period of two (2) years following your termination of employment with the Company for whatever reason, you shall not, directly or through another person or entity:

2000 through May 22, 2002, when his position was eliminated and his employment was terminated. TUV never began any action, formal or informal, to enforce any of the terms of Maizitis's employment agreement. The non-solicitation clause expired on May 22, 2004. Maizitis filed his Complaint in this matter on February 16, 2005.

II. DISCUSSION.

Maizitis's argument is threefold: (1) the Agreement is governed by Ohio, not Massachusetts, law; (2) the non-solicitation clause was void as against (Ohio's) public policy; and (3) he is entitled to damages for entering into the Agreement. The Court, however, finds that each of these arguments fail [*sic*] to address the pivotal issue in this case: whether Maizitis has a cognizable claim under either Massachusetts or Ohio contract law. . . .

A. Standard of Review [omitted].

B. Law and Analysis.

The most challenging aspect of this case is deciphering the basis for Maizitis's claim(s)—a challenge the Court has faced since the initial filing of the complaint. . . . [He] has not stated a claim for breach of contract. Simply put, he has not alleged a *breach* of the Agreement by TUV. As discussed above, Maizitis received a raise, a promotion, and continued to work for TUV for two years after signing the Agreement. Nothing in the complaint, the briefs, or the record provides *any* indication that TUV failed to comply with any provision of the Agreement.

Upon closer examination, Maizitis's argument is not that TUV failed to perform its portion of the Agreement, but that TUV compelled him "to enter into and be bound by a contract that did not conform to the laws of the State of Ohio." In the alternative, Maizitis seems to claim: "that his mistaken belief that his restrictive employment agreement was valid led him to leave his job with (another employer)." Assuming, *arguendo*, that the non-solicitation clause is void as against public policy, these statements neither describe a breach of contract, nor, as discussed below, provide a basis for any other cause of action relating to the Agreement.[3]

(a) solicit, encourage, or otherwise aid any employee of the Company to leave the employ of the Company for the purpose of becoming associated with any business with which you intend to be, or are then associated;

(b) retain, hire, engage, solicit or induce any supplier of any product or service or vendor (whether as a wholesaler, distributor, agent, commission agent, employee or otherwise) of the Company to terminate, reduce or refrain from renewing or extending his, her, or its contractual or other relationship with the Company; or

(c) solicit, induce, contact or persuade any Customer (as defined below) [footnote omitted] of the Company to terminate, reduce or refrain from renewing or extending its contractual or other relationship with the Company in regard to the purchase of products or services marketed and sold by the Company, or to become a customer of or enter into any contractual or other relationship with you or any other individual, person or entity in regard to the purchase of products or services manufacture[d], marketed or sold by the Company.

3. Maizitis has stated no basis for his claim other than the existence of the allegedly void non-solicitation clause. In other words, if the non-solicitation clause is valid, Maizitis has no basis for

1.   Maizitis Has Not Supported a Claim For Relief Under the Agreement.

At the outset, the Court observes that neither party has addressed whether, under Massachusetts or Ohio law,[4] a remedy even exists when two parties (both of the age of majority) enter into, and completely perform, a contract that violates public policy. The Court's own research has not uncovered any case providing a remedy under these circumstances. Indeed, Ohio cases addressing actions brought under a void contract have stated that: "no damages can be recovered for breach of a contract that is violative of public policy." Westco Group, Inc. v. City Mattress, No. 12619, 1985 WL 144712, at *5 (Ohio App.2d Dist. Aug. 15, 1991). Similarly, Massachusetts law bars actions arising under a contract that is void as against public policy whether those actions sound in tort or contract, or seek an equitable or legal remedy. Citizens for Citizens, Inc. v. Lambert, No. CIV.A.B99–00305, 2000 WL 744569, at *6–7 (Mass.Super. May 23, 2000). In Massachusetts,

> (a) contract which is void *ab initio*, or void from the beginning, may not be enforced. No contractual duty exists, *no breach of contract is possible, and no judgment for money damages can be obtained under the contract. Judicial or equitable doctrines cannot breathe life into such a contract.*

Massachusetts Mun. Wholesale Elec. Co. v. Town of Danvers, 577 N.E.2d 283, 292–93 (Mass.1991) (emphasis added); *see also* Eisenstein v. David G. Conlin, P.C., 827 N.E.2d 686, 692 (Mass.2005) (stating that contracts void as against public policy are not enforceable on an alternative theory of promissory estoppel) (*citing* T.F. v. B.L., 813 N.E.2d 1244, n. 8 (Mass. 2004)).

As discussed above, the prohibition on actions for breach of a void contract is clear. Thus, if it were true, as Maizitis claims, that the contract is void or unenforceable, then it is clear that *neither* party could pursue an action for its breach. Even if some ambiguity remained, however, Maizitis still would not have a cause of action because he is not alleging a breach of the Agreement; he is asking the Court to grant relief for the *non-breach* of that allegedly void contract. In other words, Maizitis believes that the Court should provide him a remedy under the circumstances because he (arguably) *could or should* have breached his Agreement with TUV (or sought to have it declared unenforceable) but failed to do so. The Court has not found, nor has Maizitis presented, any caselaw supporting the contention that one party is entitled to receive *additional*[5] compensation for performing obligations under a contract because he could have invali-

---

his claims. Because the non-solicitation clause which provides the basis for his complaint has expired, moreover, any potential action for declaratory or injunctive relief would be moot. Indeed, Maizitis appears to recognize this fact by seeking only monetary damages.

4.   The parties dispute whether Massachusetts or Ohio law governs the contract. The issue, however, is irrelevant because the principles at issue here are so fundamental to contract law that the states' laws do not meaningfully conflict.

5.   As noted above, Maizitis was already compensated once, at the time the Agreement was executed, and he does not argue that the consideration was insufficient or inadequate.

dated that agreement. In sum, Maizitis has failed to allege or support a recognizable claim under either Massachusetts or Ohio contract law. The Court, therefore, declines to further entertain what he describes as "an action under the contract."

2.　Maizitis Has Disavowed Any Claims in Equity or Tort.

Ordinarily, the Court might try to scour Maizitis's complaint in an attempt to discover whether its bare allegations were designed to assert an action sounding in tort or equity (perhaps breach of fiduciary duty, unjust enrichment, or fraud). Maizitis, however, has repeatedly-and unequivocally-disavowed any tort or equity-based claims. . . .

. . . Maizitis does not address how he was "compelled" to enter into the Agreement with TUV, and the Court cannot permit the case to proceed on the bald assertion alone that Maizitis felt "compelled" to sign the Agreement. Tangwall v. Jablonski, 111 Fed.Appx. 365, 368 (6th Cir.2004). Nor has Maizitis provided any facts or argument that would support the contention that TUV owed him a fiduciary duty, interfered with his ability to contract, or defrauded him.

. . . After examining the briefs and considering the uncontested facts, the Court finds that Maizitis has failed to make a showing sufficient to establish the existence of elements essential to his claims.

III.　CONCLUSION.

For the reasons discussed above, TUV's Motion for Summary Judgment is granted. This case is hereby dismissed in its entirety. . . .

PROBLEMS

5.　Plaintiff, mother, is suing her son for specific performance of a contract to convey. She wished to buy a house. She was informed that it would be difficult for her to obtain mortgage financing and was advised that a male family member would more likely be able to obtain such financing. Her son (the defendant) agreed to apply for mortgage financing, take title in his name and then convey to her. He successfully applied for a GI mortgage (a government guaranteed loan at reduced interest available only to veterans). Plaintiff paid the down payment and closing costs. Defendant now refuses to convey and points out that his agreement with his mother is expressly illegal under the Servicemen's Readjustment Act. She points out that she was unaware of the kind of financing he had applied for. What result?

6.　A sold milk to B in excess of 3,000 pounds in one month. The agreed price was $11,000. Both were milk dealers. In an action for the price B set up as an affirmative defense the fact that A was not licensed as required by State law. The relevant statute provided in part that it shall be unlawful for an unlicensed milk dealer to sell milk to another dealer. It also provided: "The commissioner may by official order exempt from the license requirements provided by this article, milk dealers who purchase or handle milk in total quantity not exceeding three thousand pounds in any month, and/or milk dealers selling milk in any quantity in markets of one thousand population or less." The primary requirement for obtaining a license was proof of financial soundness. Violation of the statute is a misdemeanor which is punishable by imprisonment or fine. What result?

7.   At all relevant times the sale of Irish Sweepstakes lottery tickets was illegal in Michigan. Plaintiff and defendant were nonetheless jointly engaged in the business of selling these illegal tickets in Michigan. As compensation, they received two free tickets for every twenty they sold. They agreed that they would split the proceeds of any winning ticket that either of them possessed. A ticket entered in defendant's name won $500,000. Upon her refusal to share the winnings with plaintiff, the latter brought this action to claim 50% of the winnings. Defendant raises the defense of illegality. Will the defense be successful?

8.   S turned over $10,000 to her agent, A, which A was to use in bribing purchasing agents to facilitate the sale of S's goods. A has used $5,000 for this purpose. S demanded that the remaining $5,000 be returned and A refused. S sues A. What result? Would the result be different if S had demanded the return of the money before any part of the $10,000 was used?

9.   A statute forbade the construction of a class of buildings in Boston with a roof having a pitch of more than 20 degrees. Defendant's architect designed a hotel within this class having a roof pitch of 30 degrees. Plaintiff contractor agreed to erect the building in accordance with the architect's plan and in conformity with all applicable statutes. When the time came to construct the roof, plaintiff learned that construction would violate the statute and attempted to negotiate for the revision of the plans. Defendant adamantly insisted that the plans be followed. Plaintiff refused, abandoned the job, and sues for the reasonable value of the work done. What result?

10.   In December 1966 the Maryland Court of Appeals reaffirmed its traditional common law rule that contracts made on Sunday are illegal and unenforceable. In the opinion so holding it invited the legislature to change the Sunday law. On Sunday, March 19, 1967, the parties entered into a signed agreement for the sale of real property, postdating it to March 20. The purchaser made a down payment of $3,500. On April 14, 1967 the governor signed into law a bill enacted by the legislature permitting Sunday contracts. On June 20, 1967, the purchasers brought a bill in equity for rescission of the contract of sale and restitution of its down payment. What arguments are likely to be made by the parties?

APPENDIX A

UNIFORM COMMERCIAL CODE

■ ■ ■

The standard version of Articles 1 and 2 of the UCC is reproduced here as appears in Commercial and Debtor–Creditor Law: Selected Statutes 2010 Edition, compiled by Douglas G. Baird, Theodore Eisenberg and Thomas H. Jackson (Foundation Press 2010) and reprinted here with permission. It includes Revised Article 1 (2001). Former Article 1 is reproduced in Appendix B.

ARTICLE 1

GENERAL PROVISIONS

PART 1

GENERAL PROVISIONS

§ 1–101. Short Titles.

(a) This [Act] may be cited as the Uniform Commercial Code.

(b) This article may be cited as Uniform Commercial Code—General Provisions.

§ 1–102. Scope of Article.

This article applies to a transaction to the extent that it is governed by another article of [the Uniform Commercial Code].

§ 1–103. Construction of [Uniform Commercial Code] to Promote its Purposes and Policies; Applicability of Supplemental Principles of Law.

(a) [The Uniform Commercial Code] must be liberally construed and applied to promote its underlying purposes and policies, which are:

(1) to simplify, clarify, and modernize the law governing commercial transactions;

(2) to permit the continued expansion of commercial practices through custom, usage, and agreement of the parties; and

(3) to make uniform the law among the various jurisdictions.

(b) Unless displaced by the particular provisions of [the Uniform Commercial Code], the principles of law and equity, including the law merchant and the law relative to capacity to contract, principal and agent, estoppel, fraud, misrepresentation, duress, coercion, mistake, bankruptcy, and other validating or invalidating cause supplement its provisions.

§ 1–104. Construction Against Implied Repeal.

[The Uniform Commercial Code] being a general act intended as a unified coverage of its subject matter, no part of it shall be deemed to be impliedly repealed by subsequent legislation if such construction can reasonably be avoided.

§ 1–105. Severability.

If any provision or clause of [the Uniform Commercial Code] or its application to any person or circumstance is held invalid, the invalidity does not affect other provisions or applications of [the Uniform Commercial Code] which can be given effect without the invalid provision or application, and to this end the provisions of [the Uniform Commercial Code] are severable.

§ 1–106.   Use of Singular and Plural; Gender.

In [the Uniform Commercial Code], unless the statutory context otherwise requires:

(1) words in the singular number include the plural, and those in the plural include the singular; and

(2) words of any gender also refer to any other gender.

§ 1–107.   Section Captions.

Section captions are part of [the Uniform Commercial Code].

§ 1–108.   Relation to Electronic Signatures in Global and National Commerce Act.

This [Act] modifies, limits, and supersedes the federal Electronic Signatures in Global and National Commerce Act, (15 U.S.C. Section 7001, et seq.) but does not modify, limit, or supersede Section 101(c) of that act (15 U.S.C. Section 7001(c)) or authorize electronic delivery of any of the notices described in Section 103(b) of that act (15 U.S.C. Section 103(b)).

PART 2

GENERAL DEFINITIONS AND PRINCIPLES OF INTERPRETATION

§ 1–201.   General Definitions.

(a) Unless the context otherwise requires, words or phrases defined in this section, or in the additional definitions contained in other articles of [the Uniform Commercial Code] that apply to particular articles or parts thereof, have the meanings stated.

(b) Subject to definitions contained in other articles of [the Uniform Commercial Code] that apply to particular articles or parts thereof:

(1) "Action", in the sense of a judicial proceeding, includes recoupment, counterclaim, set-off, suit in equity, and any other proceeding in which rights are determined.

(2) "Aggrieved party" means a party entitled to pursue a remedy.

(3) "Agreement", as distinguished from "contract", means the bargain of the parties in fact, as found in their language or inferred from other circumstances, including course of performance, course of dealing, or usage of trade as provided in Section 1–303.

(4) "Bank" means a person engaged in the business of banking and includes a savings bank, savings and loan association, credit union, and trust company.

(5) "Bearer" means a person in control of a negotiable electronic document of title or a person in possession of a negotiable instrument, a negotiable tangible document of title, or a certificated security that is payable to bearer or indorsed in blank.

(6) "Bill of lading" means a document of title evidencing the receipt of goods for shipment issued by a person engaged in the business of directly or indirectly transporting or forwarding goods. The term does not include a warehouse receipt.

(7) "Branch" includes a separately incorporated foreign branch of a bank.

(8) "Burden of establishing" a fact means the burden of persuading the trier of fact that the existence of the fact is more probable than its nonexistence.

(9) "Buyer in ordinary course of business" means a person that buys goods in good faith, without knowledge that the sale violates the rights of another person in the goods, and in the ordinary course from a person, other than a pawnbroker, in the business of selling goods of that kind. A person buys goods in the ordinary course if the sale to the person comports with the usual or customary practices in the kind of business in which the seller is engaged or with the seller's own usual or customary practices. A person that sells oil, gas, or other minerals at the wellhead or minehead is a person in the business of selling goods of that kind. A buyer in ordinary course of business may buy for cash, by exchange of other property, or on secured or unsecured credit, and may acquire goods or documents of title under a preexisting contract for sale. Only a buyer that takes possession of the goods or has a right to recover the goods from the seller under Article 2 may be a buyer in ordinary course of business. "Buyer in ordinary course of business" does not include a person that acquires goods in a transfer in bulk or as security for or in total or partial satisfaction of a money debt.

(10) "Conspicuous", with reference to a term, means so written, displayed, or presented that a reasonable person against which it is to operate ought to have noticed it. Whether a term is "conspicuous" or not is a decision for the court. Conspicuous terms include the following:

(A) a heading in capitals equal to or greater in size than the surrounding text, or in contrasting type, font, or color to the surrounding text of the same or lesser size; and

(B) language in the body of a record or display in larger type than the surrounding text, or in contrasting type, font, or color to the surrounding text of the same size, or set off from surrounding text of the same size by symbols or other marks that call attention to the language.

(11) "Consumer" means an individual who enters into a transaction primarily for personal, family, or household purposes

(12) "Contract", as distinguished from "agreement", means the total legal obligation that results from the parties' agreement as determined by [the Uniform Commercial Code] as supplemented by any other applicable laws.

(13) "Creditor" includes a general creditor, a secured creditor, a lien creditor, and any representative of creditors, including an assignee for the benefit of creditors, a trustee in bankruptcy, a receiver in equity, and an executor or administrator of an insolvent debtor's or assignor's estate.

(14) "Defendant" includes a person in the position of defendant in a counterclaim, cross-claim, or third-party claim.

(15) "Delivery", with respect to an electronic document of title means voluntary transfer of control and with respect to an instrument, a tangible document of title, or chattel paper, means voluntary transfer of possession.

(16) "Document of title" means a record (i) that in the regular course of business or financing is treated as adequately evidencing that the person in possession or control of the record is entitled to receive, control, hold, and dispose of the record and the goods the record covers and (ii) that purports to be issued by or addressed to a bailee and to cover goods in the bailee's possession which are either identified or are fungible portions of an identified mass. The term includes a bill of lading, transport document, dock warrant, dock receipt, warehouse receipt, and order for delivery of goods. An electronic document of title is evidenced by a record consisting of information stored in an electronic medium. A tangible document of title is evidenced by a record consisting of information that is inscribed on a tangible medium.

(17) "Fault" means a default, breach, or wrongful act or omission.

(18) "Fungible goods" means:

    (A) goods of which any unit, by nature or usage of trade, is the equivalent of any other like unit; or

    (B) goods that by agreement are treated as equivalent.

(19) "Genuine" means free of forgery or counterfeiting.

(20) "Good faith," except as otherwise provided in Article 5, means honesty in fact and the observance of reasonable commercial standards of fair dealing.

(21) "Holder" means:

    (A) the person in possession of a negotiable instrument that is payable either to bearer or to an identified person that is the person in possession;

(B) the person in possession of a negotiable tangible document of title if the goods are deliverable either to bearer or to the order of the person in possession; or

(C) a person in control of a negotiable electronic document of title.

(22) "Insolvency proceeding" includes an assignment for the benefit of creditors or other proceeding intended to liquidate or rehabilitate the estate of the person involved.

(23) "Insolvent" means:

(A) having generally ceased to pay debts in the ordinary course of business other than as a result of bona fide dispute;

(B) being unable to pay debts as they become due; or

(C) being insolvent within the meaning of federal bankruptcy law.

(24) "Money" means a medium of exchange currently authorized or adopted by a domestic or foreign government. The term includes a monetary unit of account established by an intergovernmental organization or by agreement between two or more countries.

(25) "Organization" means a person other than an individual.

(26) "Party", as distinguished from "third party", means a person that has engaged in a transaction or made an agreement subject to [the Uniform Commercial Code].

(27) "Person" means an individual, corporation, business trust, estate, trust, partnership, limited liability company, association, joint venture, government, governmental subdivision, agency, or instrumentality, public corporation, or any other legal or commercial entity.

(28) "Present value" means the amount as of a date certain of one or more sums payable in the future, discounted to the date certain by use of either an interest rate specified by the parties if that rate is not manifestly unreasonable at the time the transaction is entered into or, if an interest rate is not so specified, a commercially reasonable rate that takes into account the facts and circumstances at the time the transaction is entered into.

(29) "Purchase" means taking by sale, lease, discount, negotiation, mortgage, pledge, lien, security interest, issue or reissue, gift, or any other voluntary transaction creating an interest in property.

(30) "Purchaser" means a person that takes by purchase.

(31) "Record" means information that is inscribed on a tangible medium or that is stored in an electronic or other medium and is retrievable in perceivable form.

(32) "Remedy" means any remedial right to which an aggrieved party is entitled with or without resort to a tribunal.

(33) "Representative" means a person empowered to act for another, including an agent, an officer of a corporation or association, and a trustee, executor, or administrator of an estate.

(34) "Right" includes remedy.

(35) "Security interest" means an interest in personal property or fixtures which secures payment or performance of an obligation. "Security interest" includes any interest of a consignor and a buyer of accounts, chattel paper, a payment intangible, or a promissory note in a transaction that is subject to Article 9. "Security interest" does not include the special property interest of a buyer of goods on identification of those goods to a contract for sale under Section 2–401, but a buyer may also acquire a "security interest" by complying with Article 9. Except as otherwise provided in Section 2–505, the right of a seller or lessor of goods under Article 2 or 2A to retain or acquire possession of the goods is not a "security interest", but a seller or lessor may also acquire a "security interest" by complying with Article 9. The retention or reservation of title by a seller of goods notwithstanding shipment or delivery to the buyer under Section 2–401 is limited in effect to a reservation of a "security interest." Whether a transaction in the form of a lease creates a "security interest" is determined pursuant to Section 1–203.

(36) "Send" in connection with a writing, record, or notice means:

   (A) to deposit in the mail or deliver for transmission by any other usual means of communication with postage or cost of transmission provided for and properly addressed and, in the case of an instrument, to an address specified thereon or otherwise agreed, or if there be none to any address reasonable under the circumstances; or

   (B) in any other way to cause to be received any record or notice within the time it would have arrived if properly sent.

(37) "Signed" includes using any symbol executed or adopted with present intention to adopt or accept a writing.

(38) "State" means a State of the United States, the District of Columbia, Puerto Rico, the United States Virgin Islands, or any territory or insular possession subject to the jurisdiction of the United States.

(39) "Surety" includes a guarantor or other secondary obligor.

(40) "Term" means a portion of an agreement that relates to a particular matter.

(41) "Unauthorized signature" means a signature made without actual, implied, or apparent authority. The term includes a forgery.

(42) "Warehouse receipt" means a document of title issued by a person engaged in the business of storing goods for hire.

(43) "Writing" includes printing, typewriting, or any other intentional reduction to tangible form. "Written" has a corresponding meaning.

§ 1–202. Notice; Knowledge.

(a) Subject to subsection (f), a person has "notice" of a fact if the person:

(1) has actual knowledge of it;

(2) has received a notice or notification of it; or

(3) from all the facts and circumstances known to the person at the time in question, has reason to know that it exists.

(b) "Knowledge" means actual knowledge. "Knows" has a corresponding meaning.

(c) "Discover", "learn", or words of similar import refer to knowledge rather than to reason to know.

(d) A person "notifies" or "gives" a notice or notification to another person by taking such steps as may be reasonably required to inform the other person in ordinary course, whether or not the other person actually comes to know of it.

(e) Subject to subsection (f), a person "receives" a notice or notification when:

(1) it comes to that person's attention; or

(2) it is duly delivered in a form reasonable under the circumstances at the place of business through which the contract was made or at another location held out by that person as the place for receipt of such communications.

(f) Notice, knowledge, or a notice or notification received by an organization is effective for a particular transaction from the time it is brought to the attention of the individual conducting that transaction and, in any event, from the time it would have been brought to the individual's attention if the organization had exercised due diligence. An organization exercises due diligence if it maintains reasonable routines for communicating significant information to the person conducting the transaction and there is reasonable compliance with the routines. Due diligence does not require an individual acting for the organization to communicate information unless the communication is part of the individual's regular duties or the individual has reason to know of the transaction and that the transaction would be materially affected by the information.

§ 1–203. Lease Distinguished From Security Interest.

(a) Whether a transaction in the form of a lease creates a lease or security interest is determined by the facts of each case.

(b) A transaction in the form of a lease creates a security interest if the consideration that the lessee is to pay the lessor for the right to possession and use of the goods is an obligation for the term of the lease and is not subject to termination by the lessee, and:

(1) the original term of the lease is equal to or greater than the remaining economic life of the goods;

(2) the lessee is bound to renew the lease for the remaining economic life of the goods or is bound to become the owner of the goods;

(3) the lessee has an option to renew the lease for the remaining economic life of the goods for no additional consideration or for nominal additional consideration upon compliance with the lease agreement; or

(4) the lessee has an option to become the owner of the goods for no additional consideration or for nominal additional consideration upon compliance with the lease agreement.

(c) A transaction in the form of a lease does not create a security interest merely because:

(1) the present value of the consideration the lessee is obligated to pay the lessor for the right to possession and use of the goods is substantially equal to or is greater than the fair market value of the goods at the time the lease is entered into;

(2) the lessee assumes risk of loss of the goods;

(3) the lessee agrees to pay, with respect to the goods, taxes, insurance, filing, recording, or registration fees, or service or maintenance costs;

(4) the lessee has an option to renew the lease or to become the owner of the goods;

(5) the lessee has an option to renew the lease for a fixed rent that is equal to or greater than the reasonably predictable fair market rent for the use of the goods for the term of the renewal at the time the option is to be performed; or

(6) the lessee has an option to become the owner of the goods for a fixed price that is equal to or greater than the reasonably predictable fair market value of the goods at the time the option is to be performed.

(d) Additional consideration is nominal if it is less than the lessee's reasonably predictable cost of performing under the lease agreement if the option is not exercised. Additional consideration is not nominal if:

(1) when the option to renew the lease is granted to the lessee, the rent is stated to be the fair market rent for the use of the goods for the term of the renewal determined at the time the option is to be performed; or

(2) when the option to become the owner of the goods is granted to the lessee, the price is stated to be the fair market value of the goods determined at the time the option is to be performed.

(e) The "remaining economic life of the goods" and "reasonably predictable" fair market rent, fair market value, or cost of performing under the lease agreement must be determined with reference to the facts and circumstances at the time the transaction is entered into.

Subsections (d) and (e) provide definitions and rules of construction.

§ 1–204. Value.

Except as otherwise provided in Articles 3, 4, [and] 5, [and 6], a person gives value for rights if the person acquires them:

(1) in return for a binding commitment to extend credit or for the extension of immediately available credit, whether or not drawn upon and whether or not a charge-back is provided for in the event of difficulties in collection;

(2) as security for, or in total or partial satisfaction of, a preexisting claim;

(3) by accepting delivery under a preexisting contract for purchase; or

(4) in return for any consideration sufficient to support a simple contract.

§ 1–205. Reasonable Time; Seasonableness.

(a) Whether a time for taking an action required by [the Uniform Commercial Code] is reasonable depends on the nature, purpose, and circumstances of the action.

(b) An action is taken seasonably if it is taken at or within the time agreed or, if no time is agreed, at or within a reasonable time.

§ 1–206. Presumptions.

Whenever [the Uniform Commercial Code] creates a "presumption" with respect to a fact, or provides that a fact is "presumed," the trier of fact must find the existence of the fact unless and until evidence is introduced that supports a finding of its nonexistence.

Legislative Note: Former Section 1–206, a Statute of Frauds for sales of "kinds of personal property not otherwise covered," has been deleted. The other articles of the Uniform Commercial Code make individual determinations as to requirements for memorializing transactions within their scope, so that the primary effect of former Section 1–206 was to impose a writing requirement on sales transactions not otherwise governed by the UCC. Deletion of former Section 1–206 does not constitute a recommendation to legislatures as to whether such sales transactions should be covered by a Statute of Frauds; rather, it reflects a determination that there is no need for uniform commercial law to resolve that issue.

PART 3

TERRITORIAL APPLICABILITY AND GENERAL RULES

§ 1–301. Territorial Applicability; Parties' Power to Choose Applicable Law.

(a) Except as otherwise provided in this section, when a transaction bears a reasonable relation to this state and also to another state or nation the parties may agree that the law either of this state or of such other state or nation shall govern their rights and duties.

(b) In the absence of an agreement effective under subsection (a), and except as provided in subsection (c), [the Uniform Commercial Code] applies to transactions bearing an appropriate relation to this state.

(c) If one of the following provisions of [the Uniform Commercial Code] specifies the applicable law, that provision governs and a contrary agreement is effective only to the extent permitted by the law so specified:

(1) Section 2–402;

(2) Sections 2A–105 and 2A–106;

(3) Section 4–102;

(4) Section 4A–507;

(5) Section 5–116;

[(6) Section 6–103;]*

(7) Section 8–110;

(8) Sections 9–301 through 9–307.

§ 1–302. Variation By Agreement.

(a) Except as otherwise provided in subsection (b) or elsewhere in [the Uniform Commercial Code], the effect of provisions of [the Uniform Commercial Code] may be varied by agreement.

(b) The obligations of good faith, diligence, reasonableness, and care prescribed by [the Uniform Commercial Code] may not be disclaimed by agreement. The parties, by agreement, may determine the standards by which the performance of those obligations is to be measured if those standards are not manifestly unreasonable. Whenever [the Uniform Commercial Code] requires an action to be taken within a reasonable time, a time that is not manifestly unreasonable may be fixed by agreement.

(c) The presence in certain provisions of [the Uniform Commercial Code] of the phrase "unless otherwise agreed", or words of similar import, does not imply that the effect of other provisions may not be varied by agreement under this section.

§ 1–303. Course of Performance, Course of Dealing, and Usage of Trade.

(a) A "course of performance" is a sequence of conduct between the parties to a particular transaction that exists if:

(1) the agreement of the parties with respect to the transaction involves repeated occasions for performance by a party; and

(2) the other party, with knowledge of the nature of the performance and opportunity for objection to it, accepts the performance or acquiesces in it without objection.

---

* Conforming deletion with the repeal of Article 6 (eds.)

(b) A "course of dealing" is a sequence of conduct concerning previous transactions between the parties to a particular transaction that is fairly to be regarded as establishing a common basis of understanding for interpreting their expressions and other conduct.

(c) A "usage of trade" is any practice or method of dealing having such regularity of observance in a place, vocation, or trade as to justify an expectation that it will be observed with respect to the transaction in question. The existence and scope of such a usage must be proved as facts. If it is established that such a usage is embodied in a trade code or similar record, the interpretation of the record is a question of law.

(d) A course of performance or course of dealing between the parties or usage of trade in the vocation or trade in which they are engaged or of which they are or should be aware is relevant in ascertaining the meaning of the parties' agreement, may give particular meaning to specific terms of the agreement, and may supplement or qualify the terms of the agreement. A usage of trade applicable in the place in which part of the performance under the agreement is to occur may be so utilized as to that part of the performance.

(e) Except as otherwise provided in subsection (f), the express terms of an agreement and any applicable course of performance, course of dealing, or usage of trade must be construed whenever reasonable as consistent with each other. If such a construction is unreasonable:

(1) express terms prevail over course of performance, course of dealing, and usage of trade;

(2) course of performance prevails over course of dealing and usage of trade; and

(3) course of dealing prevails over usage of trade.

(f) Subject to Section 2–209, a course of performance is relevant to show a waiver or modification of any term inconsistent with the course of performance.

(g) Evidence of a relevant usage of trade offered by one party is not admissible unless that party has given the other party notice that the court finds sufficient to prevent unfair surprise to the other party.

§ 1–304. Obligation of Good Faith.

Every contract or duty within [the Uniform Commercial Code] imposes an obligation of good faith in its performance and enforcement.

§ 1–305. Remedies to be Liberally Administered.

(a) The remedies provided by [the Uniform Commercial Code] must be liberally administered to the end that the aggrieved party may be put in as good a position as if the other party had fully performed but neither consequential or special damages nor penal damages may be had except as specifically provided in [the Uniform Commercial Code] or by other rule of law.

(b) Any right or obligation declared by [the Uniform Commercial Code] is enforceable by action unless the provision declaring it specifies a different and limited effect.

§ 1–306. Waiver or Renunciation of Claim or Right After Breach.

A claim or right arising out of an alleged breach may be discharged in whole or in part without consideration by agreement of the aggrieved party in an authenticated record.

§ 1–307. Prima Facie Evidence By Third–Party Documents.

A document in due form purporting to be a bill of lading, policy or certificate of insurance, official weigher's or inspector's certificate, consular invoice, or any other document authorized or required by the contract to be issued by a third party is prima facie evidence of its own authenticity and genuineness and of the facts stated in the document by the third party.

§ 1–308. Performance or Acceptance Under Reservation of Rights.

(a) A party that with explicit reservation of rights performs or promises performance or assents to performance in a manner demanded or offered by the other party does not thereby prejudice the rights reserved. Such words as "without prejudice," "under protest," or the like are sufficient.

(b) Subsection (a) does not apply to an accord and satisfaction.

§ 1–309. Option to Accelerate at Will.

A term providing that one party or that party's successor in interest may accelerate payment or performance or require collateral or additional collateral "at will" or when the party "deems itself insecure," or words of similar import, means that the party has power to do so only if that party in good faith believes that the prospect of payment or performance is impaired. The burden of establishing lack of good faith is on the party against which the power has been exercised.

§ 1–310. Subordinated Obligations.

An obligation may be issued as subordinated to performance of another obligation of the person obligated, or a creditor may subordinate its right to performance of an obligation by agreement with either the person obligated or another creditor of the person obligated. Subordination does not create a security interest as against either the common debtor or a subordinated creditor.

ARTICLE 2

SALES

---

* Revised Article 1 repeals § 2–208.

PART 1

SHORT TITLE, GENERAL CONSTRUCTION AND SUBJECT MATTER

§ 2–101. Short Title.

This Article shall be known and may be cited as Uniform Commercial Code—Sales.

§ 2–102. Scope; Certain Security and Other Transactions Excluded From This Article.

Unless the context otherwise requires, this Article applies to transactions in goods; it does not apply to any transaction which although in the form of an unconditional contract to sell or present sale is intended to operate only as a security transaction nor does this Article impair or repeal any statute regulating sales to consumers, farmers or other specified classes of buyers.

§ 2–103. Definitions and Index of Definitions.

(1) In this Article unless the context otherwise requires

(a) "Buyer" means a person who buys or contracts to buy goods.

(b) ["Good faith" in the case of a merchant means honesty in fact and the observance of reasonable commercial standards of fair dealing in the trade.]*

(c) "Receipt" of goods means taking physical possession of them.

(d) "Seller" means a person who sells or contracts to sell goods.

(2) Other definitions applying to this Article or to specified Parts thereof, and the sections in which they appear are:

"Acceptance". Section 2–606.

"Banker's credit". Section 2–325.

"Between merchants". Section 2–104.

"Cancellation". Section 2–106(4).

"Commercial unit". Section 2–105.

"Confirmed credit". Section 2–325.

"Conforming to contract". Section 2–106.

"Contract for sale". Section 2–106.

"Cover". Section 2–712.

"Entrusting". Section 2–403.

"Financing agency". Section 2–104.

"Future goods". Section 2–105.

"Goods". Section 2–105.

"Identification". Section 2–501.

"Installment contract". Section 2–612.

"Letter of Credit". Section 2–325.

"Lot". Section 2–105.

"Merchant". Section 2–104.

"Overseas". Section 2–323.

"Person in position of seller". Section 2–707.

"Present sale". Section 2–106.

"Sale". Section 2–106.

"Sale on approval". Section 2–326.

"Sale or return". Section 2–326.

"Termination". Section 2–106.

(3) The following definitions in other Articles apply to this Article:

"Check". Section 3–104.

---

* Revised Article 1 deletes this language because it incorporates this definition of "good faith" into Article 1 and makes it universally applicable.

"Consignee". Section 7–102.

"Consignor". Section 7–102.

"Consumer goods". Section 9–102.

"Control". Section 7–106.

"Dishonor". Section 3–502.

"Draft". Section 3–104.

(4) In addition Article 1 contains general definitions and principles of construction and interpretation applicable throughout this Article.

§ 2–104. Definitions: "Merchant"; "Between Merchants"; "Financing Agency".

(1) "Merchant" means a person who deals in goods of the kind or otherwise by his occupation holds himself out as having knowledge or skill peculiar to the practices or goods involved in the transaction or to whom such knowledge or skill may be attributed by his employment of an agent or broker or other intermediary who by his occupation holds himself out as having such knowledge or skill.

(2) "Financing agency" means a bank, finance company or other person who in the ordinary course of business makes advances against goods or documents of title or who by arrangement with either the seller or the buyer intervenes in ordinary course to make or collect payment due or claimed under the contract for sale, as by purchasing or paying the seller's draft or making advances against it or by merely taking it for collection whether or not documents of title accompany or are associated with the draft. "Financing agency" includes also a bank or other person who similarly intervenes between persons who are in the position of seller and buyer in respect to the goods (Section 2–707).

(3) "Between merchants" means in any transaction with respect to which both parties are chargeable with the knowledge or skill of merchants.

§ 2–105. Definitions: Transferability; "Goods"; "Future" Goods; "Lot"; "Commercial Unit".

(1) "Goods" means all things (including specially manufactured goods) which are movable at the time of identification to the contract for sale other than the money in which the price is to be paid, investment securities (Article 8) and things in action. "Goods" also includes the unborn young of animals and growing crops and other identified things attached to realty as described in the section on goods to be severed from realty (Section 2–107).

(2) Goods must be both existing and identified before any interest in them can pass. Goods which are not both existing and identified are "future" goods. A purported present sale of future goods or of any interest therein operates as a contract to sell.

(3) There may be a sale of a part interest in existing identified goods.

(4) An undivided share in an identified bulk of fungible goods is sufficiently identified to be sold although the quantity of the bulk is not determined. Any agreed proportion of such a bulk or any quantity thereof agreed upon by number, weight or other measure may to the extent of the seller's interest in the bulk be sold to the buyer who then becomes an owner in common.

(5) "Lot" means a parcel or a single article which is the subject matter of a separate sale or delivery, whether or not it is sufficient to perform the contract.

(6) "Commercial unit" means such a unit of goods as by commercial usage is a single whole for purposes of sale and division of which materially impairs its character or value on the market or in use. A commercial unit may be a single article (as a machine) or a set of articles (as a suite of furniture or an assortment of sizes) or a quantity (as a bale, gross, or carload) or any other unit treated in use or in the relevant market as a single whole.

§ 2–106. Definitions: "Contract"; "Agreement"; "Contract for Sale"; "Sale"; "Present Sale"; "Conforming" to Contract; "Termination"; "Cancellation".

(1) In this Article unless the context otherwise requires "contract" and "agreement" are limited to those relating to the present or future sale of goods. "Contract for sale" includes both a present sale of goods and a contract to sell goods at a future time. A "sale" consists in the passing of title from the seller to the buyer for a price (Section 2–401). A "present sale" means a sale which is accomplished by the making of the contract.

(2) Goods or conduct including any part of a performance are "conforming" or conform to the contract when they are in accordance with the obligations under the contract.

(3) "Termination" occurs when either party pursuant to a power created by agreement or law puts an end to the contract otherwise than for its breach. On "termination" all obligations which are still executory on both sides are discharged but any right based on prior breach or performance survives.

(4) "Cancellation" occurs when either party puts an end to the contract for breach by the other and its effect is the same as that of "termination" except that the cancelling party also retains any remedy for breach of the whole contract or any unperformed balance.

§ 2–107. Goods to Be Severed From Realty: Recording.

(1) A contract for the sale of minerals or the like (including oil and gas) or a structure or its materials to be removed from realty is a contract for the sale of goods within this Article if they are to be severed by the seller but until severance a purported present sale thereof which is not

effective as a transfer of an interest in land is effective only as a contract to sell.

(2) A contract for the sale apart from the land of growing crops or other things attached to realty and capable of severance without material harm thereto but not described in subsection (1) or of timber to be cut is a contract for the sale of goods within this Article whether the subject matter is to be severed by the buyer or by the seller even though it forms part of the realty at the time of contracting, and the parties can by identification effect a present sale before severance.

(3) The provisions of this section are subject to any third party rights provided by the law relating to realty records, and the contract for sale may be executed and recorded as a document transferring an interest in land and shall then constitute notice to third parties of the buyer's rights under the contract for sale.

PART 2

FORM, FORMATION AND READJUSTMENT OF CONTRACT

§ 2–201. Formal Requirements; Statute of Frauds.

(1) Except as otherwise provided in this section a contract for the sale of goods for the price of $500 or more is not enforceable by way of action or defense unless there is some writing sufficient to indicate that a contract for sale has been made between the parties and signed by the party against whom enforcement is sought or by his authorized agent or broker. A writing is not insufficient because it omits or incorrectly states a term agreed upon but the contract is not enforceable under this paragraph beyond the quantity of goods shown in such writing.

(2) Between merchants if within a reasonable time a writing in confirmation of the contract and sufficient against the sender is received and the party receiving it has reason to know its contents, it satisfies the requirements of subsection (1) against such party unless written notice of objection to its contents is given within 10 days after it is received.

(3) A contract which does not satisfy the requirements of subsection (1) but which is valid in other respects is enforceable

    (a) if the goods are to be specially manufactured for the buyer and are not suitable for sale to others in the ordinary course of the seller's business and the seller, before notice of repudiation is received and under circumstances which reasonably indicate that the goods are for the buyer, has made either a substantial beginning of their manufacture or commitments for their procurement; or

    (b) if the party against whom enforcement is sought admits in his pleading, testimony or otherwise in court that a contract for sale was made, but the contract is not enforceable under this provision beyond the quantity of goods admitted; or

(c) with respect to goods for which payment has been made and accepted or which have been received and accepted (Sec. 2–606).

§ 2–202. Final Written Expression: Parol or Extrinsic Evidence.

Terms with respect to which the confirmatory memoranda of the parties agree or which are otherwise set forth in a writing intended by the parties as a final expression of their agreement with respect to such terms as are included therein may not be contradicted by evidence of any prior agreement or of a contemporaneous oral agreement but may be explained or supplemented

(a) [by course of dealing or usage of trade (Section 1–205) or by course of performance (Section 2–208);]* and

(b) by evidence of consistent additional terms unless the court finds the writing to have been intended also as a complete and exclusive statement of the terms of the agreement.

§ 2–203. Seals Inoperative.

The affixing of a seal to a writing evidencing a contract for sale or an offer to buy or sell goods does not constitute the writing a sealed instrument and the law with respect to sealed instruments does not apply to such a contract or offer.

§ 2–204. Formation in General.

(1) A contract for sale of goods may be made in any manner sufficient to show agreement, including conduct by both parties which recognizes the existence of such a contract.

(2) An agreement sufficient to constitute a contract for sale may be found even though the moment of its making is undetermined.

(3) Even though one or more terms are left open a contract for sale does not fail for indefiniteness if the parties have intended to make a contract and there is a reasonably certain basis for giving an appropriate remedy.

§ 2–205. Firm Offers.

An offer by a merchant to buy or sell goods in a signed writing which by its terms gives assurance that it will be held open is not revocable, for lack of consideration, during the time stated or if no time is stated for a reasonable time, but in no event may such period of irrevocability exceed three months; but any such term of assurance on a form supplied by the offeree must be separately signed by the offeror.

§ 2–206. Offer and Acceptance in Formation of Contract.

(1) Unless otherwise unambiguously indicated by the language or circumstances

---

* Revised Article 1 changes this language to " by course of performance, course of dealing, or usage of trade (Section 1–303);".

(a) an offer to make a contract shall be construed as inviting acceptance in any manner and by any medium reasonable in the circumstances;

(b) an order or other offer to buy goods for prompt or current shipment shall be construed as inviting acceptance either by a prompt promise to ship or by the prompt or current shipment of conforming or non-conforming goods, but such a shipment of non-conforming goods does not constitute an acceptance if the seller seasonably notifies the buyer that the shipment is offered only as an accommodation to the buyer.

(2) Where the beginning of a requested performance is a reasonable mode of acceptance an offeror who is not notified of acceptance within a reasonable time may treat the offer as having lapsed before acceptance.

§ 2–207. Additional Terms in Acceptance or Confirmation.

(1) A definite and seasonable expression of acceptance or a written confirmation which is sent within a reasonable time operates as an acceptance even though it states terms additional to or different from those offered or agreed upon, unless acceptance is expressly made conditional on assent to the additional or different terms.

(2) The additional terms are to be construed as proposals for addition to the contract. Between merchants such terms become part of the contract unless:

(a) the offer expressly limits acceptance to the terms of the offer;

(b) they materially alter it; or

(c) notification of objection to them has already been given or is given within a reasonable time after notice of them is received.

(3) Conduct by both parties which recognizes the existence of a contract is sufficient to establish a contract for sale although the writings of the parties do not otherwise establish a contract. In such case the terms of the particular contract consist of those terms on which the writings of the parties agree, together with any supplementary terms incorporated under any other provisions of this Act.

[§ 2–208. Course of performance or Practical Construction.

(1) Where the contract for sale involves repeated occasions for performance by either party with knowledge of the nature of the performance and opportunity for objection to it by the other, any course of performance accepted or acquiesced in without objection shall be relevant to determine the meaning of the agreement.

(2) The express terms of the agreement and any such course of performance, as well as any course of dealing and usage of trade, shall be construed whenever reasonable as consistent with each other; but when such construction is unreasonable, express terms shall control course of

performance and course of performance shall control both course of dealing and usage of trade (Section 1–205).

(3) Subject to the provisions of the next section on modification and waiver, such course of performance shall be relevant to show a waiver or modification of any term inconsistent with such course of performance.]*

§ 2–209. Modification, Rescission and Waiver.

(1) An agreement modifying a contract within this Article needs no consideration to be binding.

(2) A signed agreement which excludes modification or rescission except by a signed writing cannot be otherwise modified or rescinded, but except as between merchants such a requirement on a form supplied by the merchant must be separately signed by the other party.

(3) The requirements of the statute of frauds section of this Article (Section 2–201) must be satisfied if the contract as modified is within its provisions.

(4) Although an attempt at modification or rescission does not satisfy the requirements of subsection (2) or (3) it can operate as a waiver.

(5) A party who has made a waiver affecting an executory portion of the contract may retract the waiver by reasonable notification received by the other party that strict performance will be required of any term waived, unless the retraction would be unjust in view of a material change of position in reliance on the waiver.

§ 2–210. Delegation of Performance; Assignment of Rights.

(1) A party may perform his duty through a delegate unless otherwise agreed or unless the other party has a substantial interest in having his original promisor perform or control the acts required by the contract. No delegation of performance relieves the party delegating of any duty to perform or any liability for breach.

(2) Except as otherwise provided in Section 9–406, unless otherwise agreed, all rights of either seller or buyer can be assigned except where the assignment would materially change the duty of the other party, or increase materially the burden or risk imposed on him by his contract, or impair materially his chance of obtaining return performance. A right to damages for breach of the whole contract or a right arising out of the assignor's due performance of his entire obligation can be assigned despite agreement otherwise.

(3) The creation, attachment, perfection, or enforcement of a security interest in the seller's interest under a contract is not a transfer that materially changes the duty of or increases materially the burden or risk imposed on the buyer or impairs materially the buyer's chance of obtaining return performance within the purview of subsection (2) unless, and then only to the extent that, enforcement actually results in a delegation

---

* Revised Article 1 repeals § 2–208 as these ideas are contained in § 1–303.

of material performance of the seller. Even in that event, the creation, attachment, perfection, and enforcement of the security interest remain effective, but (i) the seller is liable to the buyer for damages caused by the delegation to the extent that the damages could not reasonably be prevented by the buyer, and (ii) a court having jurisdiction may grant other appropriate relief, including cancellation of the contract for sale or an injunction against enforcement of the security interest or consummation of the enforcement.

(4) Unless the circumstances indicate the contrary a prohibition of assignment of "the contract" is to be construed as barring only the delegation to the assignee of the assignor's performance.

(5) An assignment of "the contract" or of "all my rights under the contract" or an assignment in similar general terms is an assignment of rights and unless the language or the circumstances (as in an assignment for security) indicate the contrary, it is a delegation of performance of the duties of the assignor and its acceptance by the assignee constitutes a promise by him to perform those duties. This promise is enforceable by either the assignor or the other party to the original contract.

(6) The other party may treat any assignment which delegates performance as creating reasonable grounds for insecurity and may without prejudice to his rights against the assignor demand assurances from the assignee (Section 2–609).

As amended in 1999.

PART 3

GENERAL OBLIGATION AND CONSTRUCTION OF CONTRACT

§ 2–301. General Obligations of Parties.

The obligation of the seller is to transfer and deliver and that of the buyer is to accept and pay in accordance with the contract.

§ 2–302. Unconscionable Contract or Clause.

(1) If the court as a matter of law finds the contract or any clause of the contract to have been unconscionable at the time it was made the court may refuse to enforce the contract, or it may enforce the remainder of the contract without the unconscionable clause, or it may so limit the application of any unconscionable clause as to avoid any unconscionable result.

(2) When it is claimed or appears to the court that the contract or any clause thereof may be unconscionable the parties shall be afforded a reasonable opportunity to present evidence as to its commercial setting, purpose and effect to aid the court in making the determination.

§ 2–303. Allocation or Division of Risks.

Where this Article allocates a risk or a burden as between the parties "unless otherwise agreed", the agreement may not only shift the allocation but may also divide the risk or burden.

§ 2–304. Price Payable in Money, Goods, Realty, or Otherwise.

(1) The price can be made payable in money or otherwise. If it is payable in whole or in part in goods each party is a seller of the goods which he is to transfer.

(2) Even though all or part of the price is payable in an interest in realty the transfer of the goods and the seller's obligations with reference to them are subject to this Article, but not the transfer of the interest in realty or the transferor's obligations in connection therewith.

§ 2–305. Open Price Term.

(1) The parties if they so intend can conclude a contract for sale even though the price is not settled. In such a case the price is a reasonable price at the time for delivery if

(a) nothing is said as to price; or

(b) the price is left to be agreed by the parties and they fail to agree; or

(c) the price is to be fixed in terms of some agreed market or other standard as set or recorded by a third person or agency and it is not so set or recorded.

(2) A price to be fixed by the seller or by the buyer means a price for him to fix in good faith.

(3) When a price left to be fixed otherwise than by agreement of the parties fails to be fixed through fault of one party the other may at his option treat the contract as cancelled or himself fix a reasonable price.

(4) Where, however, the parties intend not to be bound unless the price be fixed or agreed and it is not fixed or agreed there is no contract. In such a case the buyer must return any goods already received or if unable so to do must pay their reasonable value at the time of delivery and the seller must return any portion of the price paid on account.

§ 2–306. Output, Requirements and Exclusive Dealings.

(1) A term which measures the quantity by the output of the seller or the requirements of the buyer means such actual output or requirements as may occur in good faith, except that no quantity unreasonably disproportionate to any stated estimate or in the absence of a stated estimate to any normal or otherwise comparable prior output or requirements may be tendered or demanded.

(2) A lawful agreement by either the seller or the buyer for exclusive dealing in the kind of goods concerned imposes unless otherwise agreed an obligation by the seller to use best efforts to supply the goods and by the buyer to use best efforts to promote their sale.

§ 2–307. Delivery in Single Lot or Several Lots.

Unless otherwise agreed all goods called for by a contract for sale must be tendered in a single delivery and payment is due only on such tender but where the circumstances give either party the right to make or demand delivery in lots the price if it can be apportioned may be demanded for each lot.

§ 2–308. Absence of Specified Place for Delivery.

Unless otherwise agreed

(a) the place for delivery of goods is the seller's place of business or if he has none his residence; but

(b) in a contract for sale of identified goods which to the knowledge of the parties at the time of contracting are in some other place, that place is the place for their delivery; and

(c) documents of title may be delivered through customary banking channels.

§ 2–309. Absence of Specific Time Provisions; Notice of Termination.

(1) The time for shipment or delivery or any other action under a contract if not provided in this Article or agreed upon shall be a reasonable time.

(2) Where the contract provides for successive performances but is indefinite in duration it is valid for a reasonable time but unless otherwise agreed may be terminated at any time by either party.

(3) Termination of a contract by one party except on the happening of an agreed event requires that reasonable notification be received by the other party and an agreement dispensing with notification is invalid if its operation would be unconscionable.

§ 2–310. Open Time for Payment or Running of Credit; Authority to Ship Under Reservation.

Unless otherwise agreed

(a) payment is due at the time and place at which the buyer is to receive the goods even though the place of shipment is the place of delivery; and

(b) if the seller is authorized to send the goods he may ship them under reservation, and may tender the documents of title, but the buyer may inspect the goods after their arrival before payment is due unless such inspection is inconsistent with the terms of the contract (Section 2–513); and

(c) if delivery is authorized and made by way of documents of title other than by subsection (b) then payment is due regardless of where the goods are to be received (i) at the time and place at which the buyer is to receive delivery of the tangible documents or (ii) at the time the buyer is to receive delivery of the electronic documents and at the seller's place of business or if none, the seller's residence; and

(d) where the seller is required or authorized to ship the goods on credit the credit period runs from the time of shipment but post-dating the invoice or delaying its dispatch will correspondingly delay the starting of the credit period.

§ 2–311.   Options and Cooperation Respecting Performance.

(1) An agreement for sale which is otherwise sufficiently definite (subsection (3) of Section 2–204) to be a contract is not made invalid by the fact that it leaves particulars of performance to be specified by one of the parties. Any such specification must be made in good faith and within limits set by commercial reasonableness.

(2) Unless otherwise agreed specifications relating to assortment of the goods are at the buyer's option and except as otherwise provided in subsections (1)(c) and (3) of Section 2–319 specifications or arrangements relating to shipment are at the seller's option.

(3) Where such specification would materially affect the other party's performance but is not seasonably made or where one party's cooperation is necessary to the agreed performance of the other but is not seasonably forthcoming, the other party in addition to all other remedies

(a) is excused for any resulting delay in his own performance; and

(b) may also either proceed to perform in any reasonable manner or after the time for a material part of his own performance treat the failure to specify or to cooperate as a breach by failure to deliver or accept the goods.

§ 2–312.   Warranty of Title and Against Infringement; Buyer's Obligation Against Infringement.

(1) Subject to subsection (2) there is in a contract for sale a warranty by the seller that

(a) the title conveyed shall be good, and its transfer rightful; and

(b) the goods shall be delivered free from any security interest or other lien or encumbrance of which the buyer at the time of contracting has no knowledge.

(2) A warranty under subsection (1) will be excluded or modified only by specific language or by circumstances which give the buyer reason to know that the person selling does not claim title in himself or that he is purporting to sell only such right or title as he or a third person may have.

(3) Unless otherwise agreed a seller who is a merchant regularly dealing in goods of the kind warrants that the goods shall be delivered free of the rightful claim of any third person by way of infringement or the like but a buyer who furnishes specifications to the seller must hold the seller harmless against any such claim which arises out of compliance with the specifications.

§ 2–313. Express Warranties by Affirmation, Promise, Description, Sample.

(1) Express warranties by the seller are created as follows:

(a) Any affirmation of fact or promise made by the seller to the buyer which relates to the goods and becomes part of the basis of the bargain creates an express warranty that the goods shall conform to the affirmation or promise.

(b) Any description of the goods which is made part of the basis of the bargain creates an express warranty that the goods shall conform to the description.

(c) Any sample or model which is made part of the basis of the bargain creates an express warranty that the whole of the goods shall conform to the sample or model.

(2) It is not necessary to the creation of an express warranty that the seller use formal words such as "warrant" or "guarantee" or that he have a specific intention to make a warranty, but an affirmation merely of the value of the goods or a statement purporting to be merely the seller's opinion or commendation of the goods does not create a warranty.

§ 2–314. Implied Warranty: Merchantability; Usage of Trade.

(1) Unless excluded or modified (Section 2–316), a warranty that the goods shall be merchantable is implied in a contract for their sale if the seller is a merchant with respect to goods of that kind. Under this section the serving for value of food or drink to be consumed either on the premises or elsewhere is a sale.

(2) Goods to be merchantable must be at least such as

(a) pass without objection in the trade under the contract description; and

(b) in the case of fungible goods, are of fair average quality within the description; and

(c) are fit for the ordinary purposes for which such goods are used; and

(d) run, within the variations permitted by the agreement, of even kind, quality and quantity within each unit and among all units involved; and

(e) are adequately contained, packaged, and labeled as the agreement may require; and

(f) conform to the promise or affirmations of fact made on the container or label if any.

(3) Unless excluded or modified (Section 2–316) other implied warranties may arise from course of dealing or usage of trade.

§ 2–315. Implied Warranty: Fitness for Particular Purpose.

Where the seller at the time of contracting has reason to know any particular purpose for which the goods are required and that the buyer is relying on the seller's skill or judgment to select or furnish suitable goods, there is unless excluded or modified under the next section an implied warranty that the goods shall be fit for such purpose.

§ 2–316. Exclusion or Modification of Warranties.

(1) Words or conduct relevant to the creation of an express warranty and words or conduct tending to negate or limit warranty shall be construed wherever reasonable as consistent with each other; but subject to the provisions of this Article on parol or extrinsic evidence (Section 2–202) negation or limitation is inoperative to the extent that such construction is unreasonable.

(2) Subject to subsection (3), to exclude or modify the implied warranty of merchantability or any part of it the language must mention merchantability and in case of a writing must be conspicuous, and to exclude or modify any implied warranty of fitness the exclusion must be by a writing and conspicuous. Language to exclude all implied warranties of fitness is sufficient if it states, for example, that "There are no warranties which extend beyond the description on the face hereof."

(3) Notwithstanding subsection (2)

(a) unless the circumstances indicate otherwise, all implied warranties are excluded by expressions like "as is", "with all faults" or other language which in common understanding calls the buyer's attention to the exclusion of warranties and makes plain that there is no implied warranty; and

(b) when the buyer before entering into the contract has examined the goods or the sample or model as fully as he desired or has refused to examine the goods there is no implied warranty with regard to defects which an examination ought in the circumstances to have revealed to him; and

(c) an implied warranty can also be excluded or modified by course of dealing or course of performance or usage of trade.

(4) Remedies for breach of warranty can be limited in accordance with the provisions of this Article on liquidation or limitation of damages and on contractual modification of remedy (Sections 2–718 and 2–719).

§ 2–317. Cumulation and Conflict of Warranties Express or Implied.

Warranties whether express or implied shall be construed as consistent with each other and as cumulative, but if such construction is unreasonable the intention of the parties shall determine which warranty is dominant. In ascertaining that intention the following rules apply:

(a) Exact or technical specifications displace an inconsistent sample or model or general language of description.

(b) A sample from an existing bulk displaces inconsistent general language of description.

(c) Express warranties displace inconsistent implied warranties other than an implied warranty of fitness for a particular purpose.

§ 2–318. Third Party Beneficiaries of Warranties Express or Implied.

Note: *If this Act is introduced in the Congress of the United States this section should be omitted. (States to select one alternative.)*

Alternative A

A seller's warranty whether express or implied extends to any natural person who is in the family or household of his buyer or who is a guest in his home if it is reasonable to expect that such person may use, consume or be affected by the goods and who is injured in person by breach of the warranty. A seller may not exclude or limit the operation of this section.

Alternative B

A seller's warranty whether express or implied extends to any natural person who may reasonably be expected to use, consume or be affected by the goods and who is injured in person by breach of the warranty. A seller may not exclude or limit the operation of this section.

Alternative C

A seller's warranty whether express or implied extends to any person who may reasonably be expected to use, consume or be affected by the goods and who is injured by breach of the warranty. A seller may not exclude or limit the operation of this section with respect to injury to the person of an individual to whom the warranty extends.

§ 2–319. F.O.B. and F.A.S. Terms.

(1) Unless otherwise agreed the term F.O.B. (which means "free on board") at a named place, even though used only in connection with the stated price, is a delivery term under which

(a) when the term is F.O.B. the place of shipment, the seller must at that place ship the goods in the manner provided in this Article (Section 2–504) and bear the expense and risk of putting them into the possession of the carrier; or

(b) when the term is F.O.B. the place of destination, the seller must at his own expense and risk transport the goods to that place and there tender delivery of them in the manner provided in this Article (Section 2–503);

(c) when under either (a) or (b) the term is also F.O.B. vessel, car or other vehicle, the seller must in addition at his own expense and risk load the goods on board. If the term is F.O.B. vessel the buyer must name the vessel and in an appropriate case the seller must comply with the provisions of this Article on the form of bill of lading (Section 2–323).

(2) Unless otherwise agreed the term F.A.S. vessel (which means "free alongside") at a named port, even though used only in connection with the stated price, is a delivery term under which the seller must

(a) at his own expense and risk deliver the goods alongside the vessel in the manner usual in that port or on a dock designated and provided by the buyer; and

(b) obtain and tender a receipt for the goods in exchange for which the carrier is under a duty to issue a bill of lading.

(3) Unless otherwise agreed in any case falling within subsection (1)(a) or (c) or subsection (2) the buyer must seasonably give any needed instructions for making delivery, including when the term is F.A.S. or F.O.B. the loading berth of the vessel and in an appropriate case its name and sailing date. The seller may treat the failure of needed instructions as a failure of cooperation under this Article (Section 2–311). He may also at his option move the goods in any reasonable manner preparatory to delivery or shipment.

(4) Under the term F.O.B. vessel or F.A.S. unless otherwise agreed the buyer must make payment against tender of the required documents and the seller may not tender nor the buyer demand delivery of the goods in substitution for the documents.

§ 2–320.   C.I.F. and C. & F. Terms.

(1) The term C.I.F. means that the price includes in a lump sum the cost of the goods and the insurance and freight to the named destination. The term C. & F. or C.F. means that the price so includes cost and freight to the named destination.

(2) Unless otherwise agreed and even though used only in connection with the stated price and destination, the term C.I.F. destination or its equivalent requires the seller at his own expense and risk to

(a) put the goods into the possession of a carrier at the port for shipment and obtain a negotiable bill or bills of lading covering the entire transportation to the named destination; and

(b) load the goods and obtain a receipt from the carrier (which may be contained in the bill of lading) showing that the freight has been paid or provided for; and

(c) obtain a policy or certificate of insurance, including any war risk insurance, of a kind and on terms then current at the port of shipment in the usual amount, in the currency of the contract, shown to cover the same goods covered by the bill of lading and providing for payment of loss to the order of the buyer or for the account of whom it may concern; but the seller may add to the price the amount of the premium for any such war risk insurance; and

(d) prepare an invoice of the goods and procure any other documents required to effect shipment or to comply with the contract; and

(e) forward and tender with commercial promptness all the documents in due form and with any indorsement necessary to perfect the buyer's rights.

(3) Unless otherwise agreed the term C. & F. or its equivalent has the same effect and imposes upon the seller the same obligations and risks as a C.I.F. term except the obligation as to insurance.

(4) Under the term C.I.F. or C. & F. unless otherwise agreed the buyer must make payment against tender of the required documents and the seller may not tender nor the buyer demand delivery of the goods in substitution for the documents.

§ 2–321. C.I.F. or C. & F.: "Net Landed Weights"; "Payment on Arrival"; Warranty of Condition on Arrival.

Under a contract containing a term C.I.F. or C. & F.

(1) Where the price is based on or is to be adjusted according to "net landed weights", "delivered weights", "out turn" quantity or quality or the like, unless otherwise agreed the seller must reasonably estimate the price. The payment due on tender of the documents called for by the contract is the amount so estimated, but after final adjustment of the price a settlement must be made with commercial promptness.

(2) An agreement described in subsection (1) or any warranty of quality or condition of the goods on arrival places upon the seller the risk of ordinary deterioration, shrinkage and the like in transportation but has no effect on the place or time of identification to the contract for sale or delivery or on the passing of the risk of loss.

(3) Unless otherwise agreed where the contract provides for payment on or after arrival of the goods the seller must before payment allow such preliminary inspection as is feasible; but if the goods are lost delivery of the documents and payment are due when the goods should have arrived.

§ 2–322. Delivery "Ex-Ship".

(1) Unless otherwise agreed a term for delivery of goods "ex-ship" (which means from the carrying vessel) or in equivalent language is not restricted to a particular ship and requires delivery from a ship which has reached a place at the named port of destination where goods of the kind are usually discharged.

(2) Under such a term unless otherwise agreed

(a) the seller must discharge all liens arising out of the carriage and furnish the buyer with a direction which puts the carrier under a duty to deliver the goods; and

(b) the risk of loss does not pass to the buyer until the goods leave the ship's tackle or are otherwise properly unloaded.

§ 2–323. Form of Bill of Lading Required in Overseas Shipment; "Overseas".

(1) Where the contract contemplates overseas shipment and contains a term C.I.F. or C. & F. or F.O.B. vessel, the seller unless otherwise agreed must obtain a negotiable bill of lading stating that the goods have been loaded in board or, in the case of a term C.I.F. or C. & F., received for shipment.

(2) Where in a case within subsection (1) a tangible bill of lading has been issued in a set of parts, unless otherwise agreed if the documents are not to be sent from abroad the buyer may demand tender of the full set; otherwise only one part of the bill of lading need be tendered. Even if the agreement expressly requires a full set

(a) due tender of a single part is acceptable within the provisions of this Article on cure of improper delivery (subsection (1) of Section 2–508); and

(b) even though the full set is demanded, if the documents are sent from abroad the person tendering an incomplete set may nevertheless require payment upon furnishing an indemnity which the buyer in good faith deems adequate.

(3) A shipment by water or by air or a contract contemplating such shipment is "overseas" insofar as by usage of trade or agreement it is subject to the commercial, financing or shipping practices characteristic of international deep water commerce.

§ 2–324. "No Arrival, No Sale" Term.

Under a term "no arrival, no sale" or terms of like meaning, unless otherwise agreed,

(a) the seller must properly ship conforming goods and if they arrive by any means he must tender them on arrival but he assumes no obligation that the goods will arrive unless he has caused the non-arrival; and

(b) where without fault of the seller the goods are in part lost or have so deteriorated as no longer to conform to the contract or arrive after the contract time, the buyer may proceed as if there had been casualty to identified goods (Section 2–613).

§ 2–325. "Letter of Credit" Term; "Confirmed Credit".

(1) Failure of the buyer seasonably to furnish an agreed letter of credit is a breach of the contract for sale.

(2) The delivery to seller of a proper letter of credit suspends the buyer's obligation to pay. If the letter of credit is dishonored, the seller may on seasonable notification to the buyer require payment directly from him.

(3) Unless otherwise agreed the term "letter of credit" or "banker's credit" in a contract for sale means an irrevocable credit issued by a financing agency of good repute and, where the shipment is overseas, of good international repute. The term "confirmed credit" means that the credit must also carry the direct obligation of such an agency which does business in the seller's financial market.

§ 2–326. Sale on Approval and Sale or Return; Rights of Creditors.

(1) Unless otherwise agreed, if delivered goods may be returned by the buyer even though they conform to the contract, the transaction is

    (a) a "sale on approval" if the goods are delivered primarily for use, and

    (b) a "sale or return" if the goods are delivered primarily for resale.

(2) Goods held on approval are not subject to the claims of the buyer's creditors until acceptance; goods held on sale or return are subject to such claims while in the buyer's possession.

(3) Any "or return" term of a contract for sale is to be treated as a separate contract for sale within the statute of frauds section of this Article (Section 2–201) and as contradicting the sale aspect of the contract within the provisions of this Article on parol or extrinsic evidence (Section 2–202).

§ 2–327. Special Incidents of Sale on Approval and Sale or Return.

(1) Under a sale on approval unless otherwise agreed

    (a) although the goods are identified to the contract the risk of loss and the title do not pass to the buyer until acceptance; and

    (b) use of the goods consistent with the purpose of trial is not acceptance but failure seasonably to notify the seller of election to return the goods is acceptance, and if the goods conform to the contract acceptance of any part is acceptance of the whole; and

    (c) after due notification of election to return, the return is at the seller's risk and expense but a merchant buyer must follow any reasonable instructions.

(2) Under a sale or return unless otherwise agreed

    (a) the option to return extends to the whole or any commercial unit of the goods while in substantially their original condition, but must be exercised seasonably; and

    (b) the return is at the buyer's risk and expense.

§ 2–328. Sale by Auction.

(1) In a sale by auction if goods are put up in lots each lot is the subject of a separate sale.

(2) A sale by auction is complete when the auctioneer so announces by the fall of the hammer or in other customary manner. Where a bid is made while the hammer is falling in acceptance of a prior bid the auctioneer may in his discretion reopen the bidding or declare the goods sold under the bid on which the hammer was falling.

(3) Such a sale is with reserve unless the goods are in explicit terms put up without reserve. In an auction with reserve the auctioneer may withdraw the goods at any time until he announces completion of the sale. In an auction without reserve, after the auctioneer calls for bids on an article or lot, that article or lot cannot be withdrawn unless no bid is made within a reasonable time. In either case a bidder may retract his bid until the auctioneer's announcement of completion of the sale, but a bidder's retraction does not revive any previous bid.

(4) If the auctioneer knowingly receives a bid on the seller's behalf or the seller makes or procures such a bid, and notice has not been given that liberty for such bidding is reserved, the buyer may at his option avoid the sale or take the goods at the price of the last good faith bid prior to the completion of the sale. This subsection shall not apply to any bid at a forced sale.

PART 4

TITLE, CREDITORS AND GOOD FAITH PURCHASERS

§ 2–401. Passing of Title; Reservation for Security; Limited Application of This Section.

Each provision of this Article with regard to the rights, obligations and remedies of the seller, the buyer, purchasers or other third parties applies irrespective of title to the goods except where the provision refers to such title. Insofar as situations are not covered by the other provisions of this Article and matters concerning title become material the following rules apply:

(1) Title to goods cannot pass under a contract for sale prior to their identification to the contract (Section 2–501), and unless otherwise explicitly agreed the buyer acquires by their identification a special property as limited by this Act. Any retention or reservation by the seller of the title (property) in goods shipped or delivered to the buyer is limited in effect to a reservation of a security interest. Subject to these provisions and to the provisions of the Article on Secured Transactions (Article 9), title to goods passes from the seller to the buyer in any manner and on any conditions explicitly agreed on by the parties.

(2) Unless otherwise explicitly agreed title passes to the buyer at the time and place at which the seller completes his performance with reference to the physical delivery of the goods, despite any reservation of a security interest and even though a document of title is to be delivered at a different time or place; and in particular and despite any reservation of a security interest by the bill of lading

(a) if the contract requires or authorizes the seller to send the goods to the buyer but does not require him to deliver them at destination, title passes to the buyer at the time and place of shipment; but

(b) if the contract requires delivery at destination, title passes on tender there.

(3) Unless otherwise explicitly agreed where delivery is to be made without moving the goods,

(a) if the seller is to deliver a tangible document of title, title passes at the time when and the place where he delivers such documents and if the seller is to deliver an electronic document of title, title passes when the seller delivers the document; or

(b) if the goods are at the time of contracting already identified and no documents are to be delivered, title passes at the time and place of contracting.

(4) A rejection or other refusal by the buyer to receive or retain the goods, whether or not justified, or a justified revocation of acceptance revests title to the goods in the seller. Such revesting occurs by operation of law and is not a "sale".

§ 2–402. Rights of Seller's Creditors Against Sold Goods.

(1) Except as provided in subsections (2) and (3), rights of unsecured creditors of the seller with respect to goods which have been identified to a contract for sale are subject to the buyer's rights to recover the goods under this Article (Sections 2–502 and 2–716).

(2) A creditor of the seller may treat a sale or an identification of goods to a contract for sale as void if as against him a retention of possession by the seller is fraudulent under any rule of law of the state where the goods are situated, except that retention of possession in good faith and current course of trade by a merchant-seller for a commercially reasonable time after a sale or identification is not fraudulent.

(3) Nothing in this Article shall be deemed to impair the rights of creditors of the seller

(a) under the provisions of the Article on Secured Transactions (Article 9); or

(b) where identification to the contract or delivery is made not in current course of trade but in satisfaction of or as security for a pre-existing claim for money, security or the like and is made under circumstances which under any rule of law of the state where the goods are situated would apart from this Article constitute the transaction a fraudulent transfer or voidable preference.

§ 2–403. Power to Transfer; Good Faith Purchase of Goods; "Entrusting".

(1) A purchaser of goods acquires all title which his transferor had or had power to transfer except that a purchaser of a limited interest

acquires rights only to the extent of the interest purchased. A person with voidable title has power to transfer a good title to a good faith purchaser for value. When goods have been delivered under a transaction of purchase the purchaser has such power even though

    (a) the transferor was deceived as to the identity of the purchaser, or

    (b) the delivery was in exchange for a check which is later dishonored, or

    (c) it was agreed that the transaction was to be a "cash sale", or

    (d) the delivery was procured through fraud punishable as larcenous under the criminal law.

(2) Any entrusting of possession of goods to a merchant who deals in goods of that kind gives him power to transfer all rights of the entruster to a buyer in ordinary course of business.

(3) "Entrusting" includes any delivery and any acquiescence in retention of possession regardless of any condition expressed between the parties to the delivery or acquiescence and regardless of whether the procurement of the entrusting or the possessor's disposition of the goods have been such as to be larcenous under the criminal law.

(4) The rights of other purchasers of goods and of lien creditors are governed by the Articles on Secured Transactions (Article 9)[, Bulk Sales (Article 6)]* and Documents of Title (Article 7).

PART 5

PERFORMANCE

§ 2–501. Insurable Interest in Goods; Manner of Identification of Goods.

(1) The buyer obtains a special property and an insurable interest in goods by identification of existing goods as goods to which the contract refers even though the goods so identified are non-conforming and he has an option to return or reject them. Such identification can be made at any time and in any manner explicitly agreed to by the parties. In the absence of explicit agreement identification occurs

    (a) when the contract is made if it is for the sale of goods already existing and identified;

    (b) if the contract is for the sale of future goods other than those described in paragraph (c), when goods are shipped, marked or otherwise designated by the seller as goods to which the contract refers;

    (c) when the crops are planted or otherwise become growing crops or the young are conceived if the contract is for the sale of unborn young to be born within twelve months after contracting or for the

---

* Conforming deletion with the repeal of Article 6 (eds.).

sale of crops to be harvested within twelve months or the next normal harvest season after contracting whichever is longer.

(2) The seller retains an insurable interest in goods so long as title to or any security interest in the goods remains in him and where the identification is by the seller alone he may until default or insolvency or notification to the buyer that the identification is final substitute other goods for those identified.

(3) Nothing in this section impairs any insurable interest recognized under any other statute or rule of law.

§ 2–502. Buyer's Right to Goods on Seller's Insolvency.

(1) Subject to subsections (2) and (3) and even though the goods have not been shipped a buyer who has paid a part or all of the price of goods in which he has a special property under the provisions of the immediately preceding section may on making and keeping good a tender of any unpaid portion of their price recover them from the seller if:

(a) in the case of goods bought for personal, family, or household purposes, the seller repudiates or fails to deliver as required by the contract; or

(b) in all cases, the seller becomes insolvent within ten days after receipt of the first installment on their price.

(2) The buyer's right to recover the goods under subsection (1)(a) vests upon acquisition of a special property, even if the seller had not then repudiated or failed to deliver.

(3) If the identification creating his special property has been made by the buyer he acquires the right to recover the goods only if they conform to the contract for sale.

§ 2–503. Manner of Seller's Tender of Delivery.

(1) Tender of delivery requires that the seller put and hold conforming goods at the buyer's disposition and give the buyer any notification reasonably necessary to enable him to take delivery. The manner, time and place for tender are determined by the agreement and this Article, and in particular

(a) tender must be at a reasonable hour, and if it is of goods they must be kept available for the period reasonably necessary to enable the buyer to take possession; but

(b) unless otherwise agreed the buyer must furnish facilities reasonably suited to the receipt of the goods.

(2) Where the case is within the next section respecting shipment tender requires that the seller comply with its provisions.

(3) Where the seller is required to deliver at a particular destination tender requires that he comply with subsection (1) and also in any

appropriate case tender documents as described in subsections (4) and (5) of this section.

(4) Where goods are in the possession of a bailee and are to be delivered without being moved

(a) tender requires that the seller either tender a negotiable document of title covering such goods or procure acknowledgment by the bailee of the buyer's right to possession of the goods; but

(b) tender to the buyer of a non-negotiable document of title or of a record directing the bailee to deliver is sufficient tender unless the buyer seasonably objects, and except as otherwise provided in Article 9 receipt by the bailee of notification of the buyer's rights fixes those rights as against the bailee and all third persons; but risk of loss of the goods and of any failure by the bailee to honor the non-negotiable document of title or to obey the direction remains on the seller until the buyer has had a reasonable time to present the document or direction, and a refusal by the bailee to honor the document or to obey the direction defeats the tender.

(5) Where the contract requires the seller to deliver documents

(a) he must tender all such documents in correct form, except as provided in this Article with respect to bills of lading in a set (subsection (2) of Section 2–323); and

(b) tender through customary banking channels is sufficient and dishonor of a draft accompanying or associated with the documents constitutes non-acceptance or rejection.

§ 2–504. Shipment by Seller.

Where the seller is required or authorized to send the goods to the buyer and the contract does not require him to deliver them at a particular destination, then unless otherwise agreed he must

(a) put the goods in the possession of such a carrier and make such a contract for their transportation as may be reasonable having regard to the nature of the goods and other circumstances of the case; and

(b) obtain and promptly deliver or tender in due form any document necessary to enable the buyer to obtain possession of the goods or otherwise required by the agreement or by usage of trade; and

(c) promptly notify the buyer of the shipment.

Failure to notify the buyer under paragraph (c) or to make a proper contract under paragraph (a) is a ground for rejection only if material delay or loss ensues.

§ 2–505. Seller's Shipment Under Reservation.

(1) Where the seller has identified goods to the contract by or before shipment:

(a) his procurement of a negotiable bill of lading to his own order or otherwise reserves in him a security interest in the goods. His procurement of the bill to the order of a financing agency or of the buyer indicates in addition only the seller's expectation of transferring that interest to the person named.

(b) a non-negotiable bill of lading to himself or his nominee reserves possession of the goods as security but except in a case of conditional delivery (subsection (2) of Section 2–507) a non-negotiable bill of lading naming the buyer as consignee reserves no security interest even though the seller retains possession or control of the bill of lading.

(2) When shipment by the seller with reservation of a security interest is in violation of the contract for sale it constitutes an improper contract for transportation within the preceding section but impairs neither the rights given to the buyer by shipment and identification of the goods to the contract nor the seller's powers as a holder of a negotiable document of title.

§ 2–506. Rights of Financing Agency.

(1) A financing agency by paying or purchasing for value a draft which relates to a shipment of goods acquires to the extent of the payment or purchase and in addition to its own rights under the draft and any document of title securing it any rights of the shipper in the goods including the right to stop delivery and the shipper's right to have the draft honored by the buyer.

(2) The right to reimbursement of a financing agency which has in good faith honored or purchased the draft under commitment to or authority from the buyer is not impaired by subsequent discovery of defects with reference to any relevant document which was apparently regular.

§ 2–507. Effect of Seller's Tender; Delivery on Condition.

(1) Tender of delivery is a condition to the buyer's duty to accept the goods and, unless otherwise agreed, to his duty to pay for them. Tender entitles the seller to acceptance of the goods and to payment according to the contract.

(2) Where payment is due and demanded on the delivery to the buyer of goods or documents of title, his right as against the seller to retain or dispose of them is conditional upon his making the payment due.

§ 2–508. Cure by Seller of Improper Tender or Delivery; Replacement.

(1) Where any tender or delivery by the seller is rejected because nonconforming and the time for performance has not yet expired, the seller may seasonably notify the buyer of his intention to cure and may then within the contract time make a conforming delivery.

(2) Where the buyer rejects a non-conforming tender which the seller had reasonable grounds to believe would be acceptable with or without money allowance the seller may if he seasonably notifies the buyer have a further reasonable time to substitute a conforming tender.

§ 2–509. Risk of Loss in the Absence of Breach.

(1) Where the contract requires or authorizes the seller to ship the goods by carrier

(a) if it does not require him to deliver them at a particular destination, the risk of loss passes to the buyer when the goods are duly delivered to the carrier even though the shipment is under reservation (Section 2–505); but

(b) if it does require him to deliver them at a particular destination and the goods are there duly tendered while in the possession of the carrier, the risk of loss passes to the buyer when the goods are there duly so tendered as to enable the buyer to take delivery.

(2) Where the goods are held by a bailee to be delivered without being moved, the risk of loss passes to the buyer

(a) on his receipt of possession or control of a negotiable document of title covering the goods; or

(b) on acknowledgment by the bailee of the buyer's right to possession of the goods; or

(c) after his receipt of possession or control of a non-negotiable document of title or other written direction to deliver in a record, as provided in subsection (4)(b) of Section 2–503.

(3) In any case not within subsection (1) or (2), the risk of loss passes to the buyer on his receipt of the goods if the seller is a merchant; otherwise the risk passes to the buyer on tender of delivery.

(4) The provisions of this section are subject to contrary agreement of the parties and to the provisions of this Article on sale on approval (Section 2–327) and on effect of breach on risk of loss (Section 2–510).

§ 2–510. Effect of Breach on Risk of Loss.

(1) Where a tender or delivery of goods so fails to conform to the contract as to give a right of rejection the risk of their loss remains on the seller until cure or acceptance.

(2) Where the buyer rightfully revokes acceptance he may to the extent of any deficiency in his effective insurance coverage treat the risk of loss as having rested on the seller from the beginning.

(3) Where the buyer as to conforming goods already identified to the contract for sale repudiates or is otherwise in breach before risk of their loss has passed to him, the seller may to the extent of any deficiency in his effective insurance coverage treat the risk of loss as resting on the buyer for a commercially reasonable time.

§ 2–511.   Tender of Payment by Buyer; Payment by Check.

(1) Unless otherwise agreed tender of payment is a condition to the seller's duty to tender and complete any delivery.

(2) Tender of payment is sufficient when made by any means or in any manner current in the ordinary course of business unless the seller demands payment in legal tender and gives any extension of time reasonably necessary to procure it.

(3) Subject to the provisions of this Act on the effect of an instrument on an obligation (Section 3–310), payment by check is conditional and is defeated as between the parties by dishonor of the check on due presentment.

§ 2–512.   Payment by Buyer Before Inspection.

(1) Where the contract requires payment before inspection non-conformity of the goods does not excuse the buyer from so making payment unless

(a) the non-conformity appears without inspection; or

(b) despite tender of the required documents the circumstances would justify injunction against honor under this Act (Section 5–109(b)).

(2) Payment pursuant to subsection (1) does not constitute an acceptance of goods or impair the buyer's right to inspect or any of his remedies.

§ 2–513.   Buyer's Right to Inspection of Goods.

(1) Unless otherwise agreed and subject to subsection (3), where goods are tendered or delivered or identified to the contract for sale, the buyer has a right before payment or acceptance to inspect them at any reasonable place and time and in any reasonable manner. When the seller is required or authorized to send the goods to the buyer, the inspection may be after their arrival.

(2) Expenses of inspection must be borne by the buyer but may be recovered from the seller if the goods do not conform and are rejected.

(3) Unless otherwise agreed and subject to the provisions of this Article on C.I.F. contracts (subsection (3) of Section 2–321), the buyer is not entitled to inspect the goods before payment of the price when the contract provides

(a) for delivery "C.O.D." or on other like terms; or

(b) for payment against documents of title, except where such payment is due only after the goods are to become available for inspection.

(4) A place or method of inspection fixed by the parties is presumed to be exclusive but unless otherwise expressly agreed it does not postpone identification or shift the place for delivery or for passing the risk of loss. If compliance becomes impossible, inspection shall be as provided in this

section unless the place or method fixed was clearly intended as an indispensable condition failure of which avoids the contract.

§ 2–514. When Documents Deliverable on Acceptance; When on Payment.

Unless otherwise agreed documents against which a draft is drawn are to be delivered to the drawee on acceptance of the draft if it is payable more than three days after presentment; otherwise, only on payment.

§ 2–515. Preserving Evidence of Goods in Dispute.

In furtherance of the adjustment of any claim or dispute

    (a) either party on reasonable notification to the other and for the purpose of ascertaining the facts and preserving evidence has the right to inspect, test and sample the goods including such of them as may be in the possession or control of the other; and

    (b) the parties may agree to a third party inspection or survey to determine the conformity or condition of the goods and may agree that the findings shall be binding upon them in any subsequent litigation or adjustment.

PART 6

BREACH, REPUDIATION AND EXCUSE

§ 2–601. Buyer's Rights on Improper Delivery.

Subject to the provisions of this Article on breach in installment contracts (Section 2–612) and unless otherwise agreed under the sections on contractual limitations of remedy (Sections 2–718 and 2–719), if the goods or the tender of delivery fail in any respect to conform to the contract, the buyer may

    (a) reject the whole; or

    (b) accept the whole; or

    (c) accept any commercial unit or units and reject the rest.

§ 2–602. Manner and Effect of Rightful Rejection.

(1) Rejection of goods must be within a reasonable time after their delivery or tender. It is ineffective unless the buyer seasonably notifies the seller.

(2) Subject to the provisions of the two following sections on rejected goods (Sections 2–603 and 2–604),

    (a) after rejection any exercise of ownership by the buyer with respect to any commercial unit is wrongful as against the seller; and

    (b) if the buyer has before rejection taken physical possession of goods in which he does not have a security interest under the provisions of this Article (subsection (3) of Section 2–711), he is under a duty after rejection to hold them with reasonable care at the seller's disposition for a time sufficient to permit the seller to remove them; but

(c) the buyer has no further obligations with regard to goods rightfully rejected.

(3) The seller's rights with respect to goods wrongfully rejected are governed by the provisions of this Article on Seller's remedies in general (Section 2–703).

§ 2–603. Merchant Buyer's Duties as to Rightfully Rejected Goods.

(1) Subject to any security interest in the buyer (subsection (3) of Section 2–711), when the seller has no agent or place of business at the market of rejection a merchant buyer is under a duty after rejection of goods in his possession or control to follow any reasonable instructions received from the seller with respect to the goods and in the absence of such instructions to make reasonable efforts to sell them for the seller's account if they are perishable or threaten to decline in value speedily. Instructions are not reasonable if on demand indemnity for expenses is not forthcoming.

(2) When the buyer sells goods under subsection (1), he is entitled to reimbursement from the seller or out of the proceeds for reasonable expenses of caring for and selling them, and if the expenses include no selling commission then to such commission as is usual in the trade or if there is none to a reasonable sum not exceeding ten per cent on the gross proceeds.

(3) In complying with this section the buyer is held only to good faith and good faith conduct hereunder is neither acceptance nor conversion nor the basis of an action for damages.

§ 2–604. Buyer's Options as to Salvage of Rightfully Rejected Goods.

Subject to the provisions of the immediately preceding section on perishables if the seller gives no instructions within a reasonable time after notification of rejection the buyer may store the rejected goods for the seller's account or reship them to him or resell them for the seller's account with reimbursement as provided in the preceding section. Such action is not acceptance or conversion.

§ 2–605. Waiver of Buyer's Objections by Failure to Particularize.

(1) The buyer's failure to state in connection with rejection a particular defect which is ascertainable by reasonable inspection precludes him from relying on the unstated defect to justify rejection or to establish breach

(a) where the seller could have cured it if stated seasonably; or

(b) between merchants when the seller has after rejection made a request in writing for a full and final written statement of all defects on which the buyer proposes to rely.

(2) Payment against documents made without reservation of rights precludes recovery of the payment for defects apparent in the documents.

§ 2–606.   What Constitutes Acceptance of Goods.

(1) Acceptance of goods occurs when the buyer

(a) after a reasonable opportunity to inspect the goods signifies to the seller that the goods are conforming or that he will take or retain them in spite of their non-conformity; or

(b) fails to make an effective rejection (subsection (1) of Section 2–602), but such acceptance does not occur until the buyer has had a reasonable opportunity to inspect them; or

(c) does any act inconsistent with the seller's ownership; but if such act is wrongful as against the seller it is an acceptance only if ratified by him.

(2) Acceptance of a part of any commercial unit is acceptance of that entire unit.

§ 2–607.   Effect of Acceptance; Notice of Breach; Burden of Establishing Breach After Acceptance; Notice of Claim or Litigation to Person Answerable Over.

(1) The buyer must pay at the contract rate for any goods accepted.

(2) Acceptance of goods by the buyer precludes rejection of the goods accepted and if made with knowledge of a non-conformity cannot be revoked because of it unless the acceptance was on the reasonable assumption that the non-conformity would be seasonably cured but acceptance does not of itself impair any other remedy provided by this Article for non-conformity.

(3) Where a tender has been accepted

(a) the buyer must within a reasonable time after he discovers or should have discovered any breach notify the seller of breach or be barred from any remedy; and

(b) if the claim is one for infringement or the like (subsection (3) of Section 2–312) and the buyer is sued as a result of such a breach he must so notify the seller within a reasonable time after he receives notice of the litigation or be barred from any remedy over for liability established by the litigation.

(4) The burden is on the buyer to establish any breach with respect to the goods accepted.

(5) Where the buyer is sued for breach of a warranty or other obligation for which his seller is answerable over

(a) he may give his seller written notice of the litigation. If the notice states that the seller may come in and defend and that if the seller does not do so he will be bound in any action against him by his buyer by any determination of fact common to the two litigations, then unless the seller after seasonable receipt of the notice does come in and defend he is so bound.

(b) if the claim is one for infringement or the like (subsection (3) of Section 2–312) the original seller may demand in writing that his buyer turn over to him control of the litigation including settlement or else be barred from any remedy over and if he also agrees to bear all expense and to satisfy any adverse judgment, then unless the buyer after seasonable receipt of the demand does turn over control the buyer is so barred.

(6) The provisions of subsections (3), (4) and (5) apply to any obligation of a buyer to hold the seller harmless against infringement or the like (subsection (3) of Section 2–312).

§ 2–608. Revocation of Acceptance in Whole or in Part.

(1) The buyer may revoke his acceptance of a lot or commercial unit whose non-conformity substantially impairs its value to him if he has accepted it

(a) on the reasonable assumption that its non-conformity would be cured and it has not been seasonably cured; or

(b) without discovery of such non-conformity if his acceptance was reasonably induced either by the difficulty of discovery before acceptance or by the seller's assurances.

(2) Revocation of acceptance must occur within a reasonable time after the buyer discovers or should have discovered the ground for it and before any substantial change in condition of the goods which is not caused by their own defects. It is not effective until the buyer notifies the seller of it.

(3) A buyer who so revokes has the same rights and duties with regard to the goods involved as if he had rejected them.

§ 2–609. Right to Adequate Assurance of Performance.

(1) A contract for sale imposes an obligation on each party that the other's expectation of receiving due performance will not be impaired. When reasonable grounds for insecurity arise with respect to the performance of either party the other may in writing demand adequate assurance of due performance and until he receives such assurance may if commercially reasonable suspend any performance for which he has not already received the agreed return.

(2) Between merchants the reasonableness of grounds for insecurity and the adequacy of any assurance offered shall be determined according to commercial standards.

(3) Acceptance of any improper delivery or payment does not prejudice the aggrieved party's right to demand adequate assurance of future performance.

(4) After receipt of a justified demand failure to provide within a reasonable time not exceeding thirty days such assurance of due performance as is adequate under the circumstances of the particular case is a repudiation of the contract.

§ 2–610. Anticipatory Repudiation.

When either party repudiates the contract with respect to a performance not yet due the loss of which will substantially impair the value of the contract to the other, the aggrieved party may

    (a) for a commercially reasonable time await performance by the repudiating party; or

    (b) resort to any remedy for breach (Section 2–703 or Section 2–711), even though he has notified the repudiating party that he would await the latter's performance and has urged retraction; and

    (c) in either case suspend his own performance or proceed in accordance with the provisions of this Article on the seller's right to identify goods to the contract notwithstanding breach or to salvage unfinished goods (Section 2–704).

§ 2–611. Retraction of Anticipatory Repudiation.

(1) Until the repudiating party's next performance is due he can retract his repudiation unless the aggrieved party has since the repudiation cancelled or materially changed his position or otherwise indicated that he considers the repudiation final.

(2) Retraction may be by any method which clearly indicates to the aggrieved party that the repudiating party intends to perform, but must include any assurance justifiably demanded under the provisions of this Article (Section 2–609).

(3) Retraction reinstates the repudiating party's rights under the contract with due excuse and allowance to the aggrieved party for any delay occasioned by the repudiation.

§ 2–612. "Installment Contract"; Breach.

(1) An "installment contract" is one which requires or authorizes the delivery of goods in separate lots to be separately accepted, even though the contract contains a clause "each delivery is a separate contract" or its equivalent.

(2) The buyer may reject any installment which is non-conforming if the non-conformity substantially impairs the value of that installment and cannot be cured or if the non-conformity is a defect in the required documents; but if the non-conformity does not fall within subsection (3) and the seller gives adequate assurance of its cure the buyer must accept that installment.

(3) Whenever non-conformity or default with respect to one or more installments substantially impairs the value of the whole contract there is a breach of the whole. But the aggrieved party reinstates the contract if he accepts a non-conforming installment without seasonably notifying of cancellation or if he brings an action with respect only to past installments or demands performance as to future installments.

§ 2–613. Casualty to Identified Goods.

Where the contract requires for its performance goods identified when the contract is made, and the goods suffer casualty without fault of either party before the risk of loss passes to the buyer, or in a proper case under a "no arrival, no sale" term (Section 2–324) then

(a) if the loss is total the contract is avoided; and

(b) if the loss is partial or the goods have so deteriorated as no longer to conform to the contract the buyer may nevertheless demand inspection and at his option either treat the contract as avoided or accept the goods with due allowance from the contract price for the deterioration or the deficiency in quantity but without further right against the seller.

§ 2–614. Substituted Performance.

(1) Where without fault of either party the agreed berthing, loading, or unloading facilities fail or an agreed type of carrier becomes unavailable or the agreed manner of delivery otherwise becomes commercially impracticable but a commercially reasonable substitute is available, such substitute performance must be tendered and accepted.

(2) If the agreed means or manner of payment fails because of domestic or foreign governmental regulation, the seller may withhold or stop delivery unless the buyer provides a means or manner of payment which is commercially a substantial equivalent. If delivery has already been taken, payment by the means or in the manner provided by the regulation discharges the buyer's obligation unless the regulation is discriminatory, oppressive or predatory.

§ 2–615. Excuse by Failure of Presupposed Conditions.

Except so far as a seller may have assumed a greater obligation and subject to the preceding section on substituted performance:

(a) Delay in delivery or non-delivery in whole or in part by a seller who complies with paragraphs (b) and (c) is not a breach of his duty under a contract for sale if performance as agreed has been made impracticable by the occurrence of a contingency the non-occurrence of which was a basic assumption on which the contract was made or by compliance in good faith with any applicable foreign or domestic governmental regulation or order whether or not it later proves to be invalid.

(b) Where the causes mentioned in paragraph (a) affect only a part of the seller's capacity to perform, he must allocate production and deliveries among his customers but may at his option include regular customers not then under contract as well as his own requirements for further manufacture. He may so allocate in any manner which is fair and reasonable.

(c) The seller must notify the buyer seasonably that there will be delay or non-delivery and, when allocation is required under paragraph (b), of the estimated quota thus made available for the buyer.

§ 2–616. Procedure on Notice Claiming Excuse.

(1) Where the buyer receives notification of a material or indefinite delay or an allocation justified under the preceding section he may by written notification to the seller as to any delivery concerned, and where the prospective deficiency substantially impairs the value of the whole contract under the provisions of this Article relating to breach of installment contracts (Section 2–612), then also as to the whole,

(a) terminate and thereby discharge any unexecuted portion of the contract; or

(b) modify the contract by agreeing to take his available quota in substitution.

(2) If after receipt of such notification from the seller the buyer fails so to modify the contract within a reasonable time not exceeding thirty days the contract lapses with respect to any deliveries affected.

(3) The provisions of this section may not be negated by agreement except in so far as the seller has assumed a greater obligation under the preceding section.

PART 7

REMEDIES

§ 2–701. Remedies for Breach of Collateral Contracts Not Impaired.

Remedies for breach of any obligation or promise collateral or ancillary to a contract for sale are not impaired by the provisions of this Article.

§ 2–702. Seller's Remedies on Discovery of Buyer's Insolvency.

(1) Where the seller discovers the buyer to be insolvent he may refuse delivery except for cash including payment for all goods theretofore delivered under the contract, and stop delivery under this Article (Section 2–705).

(2) Where the seller discovers that the buyer has received goods on credit while insolvent he may reclaim the goods upon demand made within ten days after the receipt, but if misrepresentation of solvency has

been made to the particular seller in writing within three months before delivery the ten day limitation does not apply. Except as provided in this subsection the seller may not base a right to reclaim goods on the buyer's fraudulent or innocent misrepresentation of solvency or of intent to pay.

(3) The seller's right to reclaim under subsection (2) is subject to the rights of a buyer in ordinary course or other good faith purchaser under this Article (Section 2–403). Successful reclamation of goods excludes all other remedies with respect to them.

§ 2–703. Seller's Remedies in General.

Where the buyer wrongfully rejects or revokes acceptance of goods or fails to make a payment due on or before delivery or repudiates with respect to a part or the whole, then with respect to any goods directly affected and, if the breach is of the whole contract (Section 2–612), then also with respect to the whole undelivered balance, the aggrieved seller may

(a) withhold delivery of such goods;

(b) stop delivery by any bailee as hereafter provided (Section 2–705);

(c) proceed under the next section respecting goods still unidentified to the contract;

(d) resell and recover damages as hereafter provided (Section 2–706);

(e) recover damages for non-acceptance (Section 2–708) or in a proper case the price (Section 2–709);

(f) cancel.

§ 2–704. Seller's Right to Identify Goods to the Contract Notwithstanding Breach or to Salvage Unfinished Goods.

(1) An aggrieved seller under the preceding section may

(a) identify to the contract conforming goods not already identified if at the time he learned of the breach they are in his possession or control;

(b) treat as the subject of resale goods which have demonstrably been intended for the particular contract even though those goods are unfinished.

(2) Where the goods are unfinished an aggrieved seller may in the exercise of reasonable commercial judgment for the purposes of avoiding loss and of effective realization either complete the manufacture and wholly identify the goods to the contract or cease manufacture and resell for scrap or salvage value or proceed in any other reasonable manner.

§ 2–705. Seller's Stoppage of Delivery in Transit or Otherwise.

(1) The seller may stop delivery of goods in the possession of a carrier or other bailee when he discovers the buyer to be insolvent (Section 2–702) and may stop delivery of carload, truckload, planeload or larger

shipments of express or freight when the buyer repudiates or fails to make a payment due before delivery or if for any other reason the seller has a right to withhold or reclaim the goods.

(2) As against such buyer the seller may stop delivery until

(a) receipt of the goods by the buyer; or

(b) acknowledgment to the buyer by any bailee of the goods except a carrier that the bailee holds the goods for the buyer; or

(c) such acknowledgment to the buyer by a carrier by reshipment or as a warehouse; or

(d) negotiation to the buyer of any negotiable document of title covering the goods.

(3)(a) To stop delivery the seller must so notify as to enable the bailee by reasonable diligence to prevent delivery of the goods.

(b) After such notification the bailee must hold and deliver the goods according to the directions of the seller but the seller is liable to the bailee for any ensuing charges or damages.

(c) If a negotiable document of title has been issued for goods the bailee is not obliged to obey a notification to stop until surrender of possession or control of the document.

(d) A carrier who has issued a non-negotiable bill of lading is not obliged to obey a notification to stop received from a person other than the consignor.

§ 2–706. Seller's Resale Including Contract for Resale.

(1) Under the conditions stated in Section 2–703 on seller's remedies, the seller may resell the goods concerned or the undelivered balance thereof. Where the resale is made in good faith and in a commercially reasonable manner the seller may recover the difference between the resale price and the contract price together with any incidental damages allowed under the provisions of this Article (Section 2–710), but less expenses saved in consequence of the buyer's breach.

(2) Except as otherwise provided in subsection (3) or unless otherwise agreed resale may be at public or private sale including sale by way of one or more contracts to sell or of identification to an existing contract of the seller. Sale may be as a unit or in parcels and at any time and place and on any terms but every aspect of the sale including the method, manner, time, place and terms must be commercially reasonable. The resale must be reasonably identified as referring to the broken contract, but it is not necessary that the goods be in existence or that any or all of them have been identified to the contract before the breach.

(3) Where the resale is at private sale the seller must give the buyer reasonable notification of his intention to resell.

(4) Where the resale is at public sale

(a) only identified goods can be sold except where there is a recognized market for a public sale of futures in goods of the kind; and

(b) it must be made at a usual place or market for public sale if one is reasonably available and except in the case of goods which are perishable or threaten to decline in value speedily the seller must give the buyer reasonable notice of the time and place of the resale; and

(c) if the goods are not to be within the view of those attending the sale the notification of sale must state the place where the goods are located and provide for their reasonable inspection by prospective bidders; and

(d) the seller may buy.

(5) A purchaser who buys in good faith at a resale takes the goods free of any rights of the original buyer even though the seller fails to comply with one or more of the requirements of this section.

(6) The seller is not accountable to the buyer for any profit made on any resale. A person in the position of a seller (Section 2–707) or a buyer who has rightfully rejected or justifiably revoked acceptance must account for any excess over the amount of his security interest, as hereinafter defined (subsection (3) of Section 2–711).

§ 2–707. "Person in the Position of a Seller".

(1) A "person in the position of a seller" includes as against a principal an agent who has paid or become responsible for the price of goods on behalf of his principal or anyone who otherwise holds a security interest or other right in goods similar to that of a seller.

(2) A person in the position of a seller may as provided in this Article withhold or stop delivery (Section 2–705) and resell (Section 2–706) and recover incidental damages (Section 2–710).

§ 2–708. Seller's Damages for Non-acceptance or Repudiation.

(1) Subject to subsection (2) and to the provisions of this Article with respect to proof of market price (Section 2–723), the measure of damages for non-acceptance or repudiation by the buyer is the difference between the market price at the time and place for tender and the unpaid contract price together with any incidental damages provided in this Article (Section 2–710), but less expenses saved in consequence of the buyer's breach.

(2) If the measure of damages provided in subsection (1) is inadequate to put the seller in as good a position as performance would have done then the measure of damages is the profit (including reasonable overhead) which the seller would have made from full performance by the buyer, together with any incidental damages provided in this Article (Section 2–710), due allowance for costs reasonably incurred and due credit for payments or proceeds of resale.

§ 2–709. Action for the Price.

(1) When the buyer fails to pay the price as it becomes due the seller may recover, together with any incidental damages under the next section, the price

   (a) of goods accepted or of conforming goods lost or damaged within a commercially reasonable time after risk of their loss has passed to the buyer; and

   (b) of goods identified to the contract if the seller is unable after reasonable effort to resell them at a reasonable price or the circumstances reasonably indicate that such effort will be unavailing.

(2) Where the seller sues for the price he must hold for the buyer any goods which have been identified to the contract and are still in his control except that if resale becomes possible he may resell them at any time prior to the collection of the judgment. The net proceeds of any such resale must be credited to the buyer and payment of the judgment entitles him to any goods not resold.

(3) After the buyer has wrongfully rejected or revoked acceptance of the goods or has failed to make a payment due or has repudiated (Section 2–610), a seller who is held not entitled to the price under this section shall nevertheless be awarded damages for non-acceptance under the preceding section.

§ 2–710. Seller's Incidental Damages.

Incidental damages to an aggrieved seller include any commercially reasonable charges, expenses or commissions incurred in stopping delivery, in the transportation, care and custody of goods after the buyer's breach, in connection with return or resale of the goods or otherwise resulting from the breach.

§ 2–711. Buyer's Remedies in General; Buyer's Security Interest in Rejected Goods.

(1) Where the seller fails to make delivery or repudiates or the buyer rightfully rejects or justifiably revokes acceptance then with respect to any goods involved, and with respect to the whole if the breach goes to the whole contract (Section 2–612), the buyer may cancel and whether or not he has done so may in addition to recovering so much of the price as has been paid

   (a) "cover" and have damages under the next section as to all the goods affected whether or not they have been identified to the contract; or

   (b) recover damages for non-delivery as provided in this Article (Section 2–713).

(2) Where the seller fails to deliver or repudiates the buyer may also

(a) if the goods have been identified recover them as provided in this Article (Section 2–502); or

(b) in a proper case obtain specific performance or replevy the goods as provided in this Article (Section 2–716).

(3) On rightful rejection or justifiable revocation of acceptance a buyer has a security interest in goods in his possession or control for any payments made on their price and any expenses reasonably incurred in their inspection, receipt, transportation, care and custody and may hold such goods and resell them in like manner as an aggrieved seller (Section 2–706).

§ 2–712. "Cover"; Buyer's Procurement of Substitute Goods.

(1) After a breach within the preceding section the buyer may "cover" by making in good faith and without unreasonable delay any reasonable purchase of or contract to purchase goods in substitution for those due from the seller.

(2) The buyer may recover from the seller as damages the difference between the cost of cover and the contract price together with any incidental or consequential damages as hereinafter defined (Section 2–715), but less expenses saved in consequence of the seller's breach.

(3) Failure of the buyer to effect cover within this section does not bar him from any other remedy.

§ 2–713. Buyer's Damages for Non-delivery or Repudiation.

(1) Subject to the provisions of this Article with respect to proof of market price (Section 2–723), the measure of damages for non-delivery or repudiation by the seller is the difference between the market price at the time when the buyer learned of the breach and the contract price together with any incidental and consequential damages provided in this Article (Section 2–715), but less expenses saved in consequence of the seller's breach.

(2) Market price is to be determined as of the place for tender or, in cases of rejection after arrival or revocation of acceptance, as of the place of arrival.

§ 2–714. Buyer's Damages for Breach in Regard to Accepted Goods.

(1) Where the buyer has accepted goods and given notification (subsection (3) of Section 2–607) he may recover as damages for any nonconformity of tender the loss resulting in the ordinary course of events from the seller's breach as determined in any manner which is reasonable.

(2) The measure of damages for breach of warranty is the difference at the time and place of acceptance between the value of the goods accepted and the value they would have had if they had been as warrant-

ed, unless special circumstances show proximate damages of a different amount.

(3) In a proper case any incidental and consequential damages under the next section may also be recovered.

§ 2–715.   Buyer's Incidental and Consequential Damages.

(1) Incidental damages resulting from the seller's breach include expenses reasonably incurred in inspection, receipt, transportation and care and custody of goods rightfully rejected, any commercially reasonable charges, expenses or commissions in connection with effecting cover and any other reasonable expense incident to the delay or other breach.

(2) Consequential damages resulting from the seller's breach include

(a) any loss resulting from general or particular requirements and needs of which the seller at the time of contracting had reason to know and which could not reasonably be prevented by cover or otherwise; and

(b) injury to person or property proximately resulting from any breach of warranty.

§ 2–716.   Buyer's Right to Specific Performance or Replevin.

(1) Specific performance may be decreed where the goods are unique or in other proper circumstances.

(2) The decree for specific performance may include such terms and conditions as to payment of the price, damages, or other relief as the court may deem just.

(3) The buyer has a right of replevin for goods identified to the contract if after reasonable effort he is unable to effect cover for such goods or the circumstances reasonably indicate that such effort will be unavailing or if the goods have been shipped under reservation and satisfaction of the security interest in them has been made or tendered. In the case of goods bought for personal, family, or household purposes, the buyer's right of replevin vests upon acquisition of a special property, even if the seller had not then repudiated or failed to deliver.

§ 2–717.   Deduction of Damages From the Price.

The buyer on notifying the seller of his intention to do so may deduct all or any part of the damages resulting from any breach of the contract from any part of the price still due under the same contract.

§ 2–718.   Liquidation or Limitation of Damages; Deposits.

(1) Damages for breach by either party may be liquidated in the agreement but only at an amount which is reasonable in the light of the anticipated or actual harm caused by the breach, the difficulties of proof of loss, and the inconvenience or nonfeasibility of otherwise obtaining an adequate remedy. A term fixing unreasonably large liquidated damages is void as a penalty.

(2) Where the seller justifiably withholds delivery of goods because of the buyer's breach, the buyer is entitled to restitution of any amount by which the sum of his payments exceeds

    (a) the amount to which the seller is entitled by virtue of terms liquidating the seller's damages in accordance with subsection (1), or

    (b) in the absence of such terms, twenty per cent of the value of the total performance for which the buyer is obligated under the contract or $500, whichever is smaller.

(3) The buyer's right to restitution under subsection (2) is subject to offset to the extent that the seller establishes

    (a) a right to recover damages under the provisions of this Article other than subsection (1), and

    (b) the amount or value of any benefits received by the buyer directly or indirectly by reason of the contract.

(4) Where a seller has received payment in goods their reasonable value or the proceeds of their resale shall be treated as payments for the purposes of subsection (2); but if the seller has notice of the buyer's breach before reselling goods received in part performance, his resale is subject to the conditions laid down in this Article on resale by an aggrieved seller (Section 2–706).

§ 2–719. Contractual Modification or Limitation of Remedy.

(1) Subject to the provisions of subsections (2) and (3) of this section and of the preceding section on liquidation and limitation of damages,

    (a) the agreement may provide for remedies in addition to or in substitution for those provided in this Article and may limit or alter the measure of damages recoverable under this Article, as by limiting the buyer's remedies to return of the goods and repayment of the price or to repair and replacement of non-conforming goods or parts; and

    (b) resort to a remedy as provided is optional unless the remedy is expressly agreed to be exclusive, in which case it is the sole remedy.

(2) Where circumstances cause an exclusive or limited remedy to fail of its essential purpose, remedy may be had as provided in this Act.

(3) Consequential damages may be limited or excluded unless the limitation or exclusion is unconscionable. Limitation of consequential damages for injury to the person in the case of consumer goods is prima facie unconscionable but limitation of damages where the loss is commercial is not.

§ 2–720. Effect of "Cancellation" or "Rescission" on Claims for Antecedent Breach.

Unless the contrary intention clearly appears, expressions of "cancellation" or "rescission" of the contract or the like shall not be construed as a renunciation or discharge of any claim in damages for an antecedent breach.

§ 2–721. Remedies for Fraud.

Remedies for material misrepresentation or fraud include all remedies available under this Article for non-fraudulent breach. Neither rescission or a claim for rescission of the contract for sale nor rejection or return of the goods shall bar or be deemed inconsistent with a claim for damages or other remedy.

§ 2–722. Who Can Sue Third Parties for Injury to Goods.

Where a third party so deals with goods which have been identified to a contract for sale as to cause actionable injury to a party to that contract

(a) a right of action against the third party is in either party to the contract for sale who has title to or a security interest or a special property or an insurable interest in the goods; and if the goods have been destroyed or converted a right of action is also in the party who either bore the risk of loss under the contract for sale or has since the injury assumed that risk as against the other;

(b) if at the time of the injury the party plaintiff did not bear the risk of loss as against the other party to the contract for sale and there is no arrangement between them for disposition of the recovery, his suit or settlement is, subject to his own interest, as a fiduciary for the other party to the contract;

(c) either party may with the consent of the other sue for the benefit of whom it may concern.

§ 2–723. Proof of Market Price: Time and Place.

(1) If an action based on anticipatory repudiation comes to trial before the time for performance with respect to some or all of the goods, any damages based on market price (Section 2–708 or Section 2–713) shall be determined according to the price of such goods prevailing at the time when the aggrieved party learned of the repudiation.

(2) If evidence of a price prevailing at the times or places described in this Article is not readily available the price prevailing within any reasonable time before or after the time described or at any other place which in commercial judgment or under usage of trade would serve as a reasonable substitute for the one described may be used, making any proper allowance for the cost of transporting the goods to or from such other place.

(3) Evidence of a relevant price prevailing at a time or place other than the one described in this Article offered by one party is not admissible unless and until he has given the other party such notice as the court finds sufficient to prevent unfair surprise.

§ 2–724. Admissibility of Market Quotations.

Whenever the prevailing price or value of any goods regularly bought and sold in any established commodity market is in issue, reports in official publications or trade journals or in newspapers or periodicals of general circulation published as the reports of such market shall be admissible in evidence. The circumstances of the preparation of such a report may be shown to affect its weight but not its admissibility.

§ 2–725. Statute of Limitations in Contracts for Sale.

(1) An action for breach of any contract for sale must be commenced within four years after the cause of action has accrued. By the original agreement the parties may reduce the period of limitation to not less than one year but may not extend it.

(2) A cause of action accrues when the breach occurs, regardless of the aggrieved party's lack of knowledge of the breach. A breach of warranty occurs when tender of delivery is made, except that where a warranty explicitly extends to future performance of the goods and discovery of the breach must await the time of such performance the cause of action accrues when the breach is or should have been discovered.

(3) Where an action commenced within the time limited by subsection (1) is so terminated as to leave available a remedy by another action for the same breach such other action may be commenced after the expiration of the time limited and within six months after the termination of the first action unless the termination resulted from voluntary discontinuance or from dismissal for failure or neglect to prosecute.

(4) This section does not alter the law on tolling of the statute of limitations nor does it apply to causes of action which have accrued before this Act becomes effective.

APPENDIX B

UCC ARTICLE 1

■ ■ ■

UNIFORM COMMERCIAL CODE
FORMER ARTICLE 1 (PRE–REVISION)
GENERAL PROVISIONS

PART 1. SHORT TITLE, CONSTRUCTION, APPLICATION
AND SUBJECT MATTER OF THE ACT

PART 1

SHORT TITLE, CONSTRUCTION, APPLICATION AND SUBJECT MATTER OF THE ACT

§ 1–101. Short Title.

This Act shall be known and may be cited as Uniform Commercial Code.

§ 1–102. Purposes; Rules of Construction; Variation by Agreement.

(1) This Act shall be liberally construed and applied to promote its underlying purposes and policies.

(2) Underlying purposes and policies of this Act are

(a) to simplify, clarify and modernize the law governing commercial transactions;

(b) to permit the continued expansion of commercial practices through custom, usage and agreement of the parties;

(c) to make uniform the law among the various jurisdictions.

(3) The effect of provisions of this Act may be varied by agreement, except as otherwise provided in this Act and except that the obligations of good faith, diligence, reasonableness and care prescribed by this Act may not be disclaimed by agreement but the parties may by agreement determine the standards by which the performance of such obligations is to be measured if such standards are not manifestly unreasonable.

(4) The presence in certain provisions of this Act of the words "unless otherwise agreed" or words of similar import does not imply that the effect of other provisions may not be varied by agreement under subsection (3).

(5) In this Act unless the context otherwise requires

(a) words in the singular number include the plural, and in the plural include the singular;

(b) words of the masculine gender include the feminine and the neuter, and when the sense so indicates words of the neuter gender may refer to any gender.

§ 1–103. Supplementary General Principles of Law Applicable.

Unless displaced by the particular provisions of this Act, the principles of law and equity, including the law merchant and the law relative to capacity to contract, principal and agent, estoppel, fraud, misrepresentation, duress, coercion, mistake, bankruptcy, or other validating or invalidating cause shall supplement its provisions.

§ 1–104. Construction Against Implicit Repeal.

This Act being a general act intended as a unified coverage of its subject matter, no part of it shall be deemed to be impliedly repealed by subsequent legislation if such construction can reasonably be avoided.

§ 1–105. Territorial Application of the Act; Parties' Power to Choose Applicable Law.

(1) Except as provided hereafter in this section, when a transaction bears a reasonable relation to this state and also to another state or nation the parties may agree that the law either of this state or of such other state or nation shall govern their rights and duties. Failing such agreement this Act applies to transactions bearing an appropriate relation to this state.

(2) Where one of the following provisions of this Act specifies the applicable law, that provision governs and a contrary agreement is effective only to the extent permitted by the law (including the conflict of laws rules) so specified:

Rights of creditors against sold goods. Section 2–402.

Applicability of the Article on Leases. Sections 2A–105 and 2A–106.

Applicability of the Article on Bank Deposits and Collections. Section 4–102.

Bulk transfers subject to the Article on Bulk Transfers. Section 6–102.

Applicability of the Article on Investment Securities. Section 8–106.

Perfection provisions of the Article on Secured Transactions. Section 9–103.

§ 1–106. Remedies to Be Liberally Administered.

(1) The remedies provided by this Act shall be liberally administered to the end that the aggrieved party may be put in as good a position as if the other party had fully performed but neither consequential or special nor penal damages may be had except as specifically provided in this Act or by other rule of law.

(2) Any right or obligation declared by this Act is enforceable by action unless the provision declaring it specifies a different and limited effect.

§ 1–107. Waiver or Renunciation of Claim or Right After Breach.

Any claim or right arising out of an alleged breach can be discharged in whole or in part without consideration by a written waiver or renunciation signed and delivered by the aggrieved party.

§ 1–108. Severability.

If any provision or clause of this Act or application thereof to any person or circumstances is held invalid, such invalidity shall not affect other provisions or applications of the Act which can be given effect without the invalid provision or application, and to this end the provisions of this Act are declared to be severable.

§ 1–109. Section Captions.

Section captions are parts of this Act.

PART 2

GENERAL DEFINITIONS AND PRINCIPLES OF INTERPRETATION

§ 1–201. General Definitions.

Subject to additional definitions contained in the subsequent Articles of this Act which are applicable to specific Articles or Parts thereof, and unless the context otherwise requires, in this Act:

(1) "Action" in the sense of a judicial proceeding includes recoupment, counterclaim, set-off, suit in equity and any other proceedings in which rights are determined.

(2) "Aggrieved party" means a party entitled to resort to a remedy.

(3) "Agreement" means the bargain of the parties in fact as found in their language or by implication from other circumstances including course of dealing or usage of trade or course of performance as provided in this Act (Sections 1–205 and 2–208). Whether an agreement has legal consequences is determined by the provisions of this Act, if applicable; otherwise by the law of contracts (Section 1–103). (Compare "Contract".)

(4) "Bank" means any person engaged in the business of banking.

(5) "Bearer" means the person in possession of an instrument, document of title, or certificated security payable to bearer or indorsed in blank.

(6) "Bill of lading" means a document evidencing the receipt of goods for shipment issued by a person engaged in the business of transporting or forwarding goods, and includes an airbill. "Airbill" means a document serving for air transportation as a bill of lading does for marine or rail transportation, and includes an air consignment note or air waybill.

(7) "Branch" includes a separately incorporated foreign branch of a bank.

(8) "Burden of establishing" a fact means the burden of persuading the triers of fact that the existence of the fact is more probable than its non-existence.

(9) "Buyer in ordinary course of business" means a person who in good faith and without knowledge that the sale to him is in violation of the ownership rights or security interest of a third party in the goods buys in ordinary course from a person in the business of selling goods of that kind but does not include a pawnbroker. All persons who sell minerals or

the like (including oil and gas) at wellhead or minehead shall be deemed to be persons in the business of selling goods of that kind. "Buying" may be for cash or by exchange of other property or on secured or unsecured credit and includes receiving goods or documents of title under a pre-existing contract for sale but does not include a transfer in bulk or as security for or in total or partial satisfaction of a money debt.

(10) "Conspicuous": A term or clause is conspicuous when it is so written that a reasonable person against whom it is to operate ought to have noticed it. A printed heading in capitals (as: Non-Negotiable Bill of Lading) is conspicuous. Language in the body of a form is "conspicuous" if it is in larger or other contrasting type or color. But in a telegram any stated term is "conspicuous". Whether a term or clause is "conspicuous" or not is for decision by the court.

(11) "Contract" means the total legal obligation which results from the parties' agreement as affected by this Act and any other applicable rules of law. (Compare "Agreement".)

(12) "Creditor" includes a general creditor, a secured creditor, a lien creditor and any representative of creditors, including an assignee for the benefit of creditors, a trustee in bankruptcy, a receiver in equity and an executor or administrator of an insolvent debtor's or assignor's estate.

(13) "Defendant" includes a person in the position of defendant in a cross-action or counterclaim.

(14) "Delivery" with respect to instruments, documents of title, chattel paper, or certificated securities means voluntary transfer of possession.

(15) "Document of title" includes bill of lading, dock warrant, dock receipt, warehouse receipt or order for the delivery of goods, and also any other document which in the regular course of business or financing is treated as adequately evidencing that the person in possession of it is entitled to receive, hold and dispose of the document and the goods it covers. To be a document of title a document must purport to be issued by or addressed to a bailee and purport to cover goods in the bailee's possession which are either identified or are fungible portions of an identified mass.

(16) "Fault" means wrongful act, omission or breach.

(17) "Fungible" with respect to goods or securities means goods or securities of which any unit is, by nature or usage of trade, the equivalent of any other like unit. Goods which are not fungible shall be deemed fungible for the purposes of this Act to the extent that under a particular agreement or document unlike units are treated as equivalents.

(18) "Genuine" means free of forgery or counterfeiting.

(19) "Good faith" means honesty in fact in the conduct or transaction concerned.

(20) "Holder" means a person who is in possession of a document of title or an instrument or a certificated investment security drawn, issued, or indorsed to him or his order or to bearer or in blank.

(21) To "honor" is to pay or to accept and pay, or where a credit so engages to purchase or discount a draft complying with the terms of the credit.

(22) "Insolvency proceedings" includes any assignment for the benefit of creditors or other proceedings intended to liquidate or rehabilitate the estate of the person involved.

(23) A person is "insolvent" who either has ceased to pay his debts in the ordinary course of business or cannot pay his debts as they become due or is insolvent within the meaning of the federal bankruptcy law.

(24) "Money" means a medium of exchange authorized or adopted by a domestic or foreign government as a part of its currency.

(25) A person has "notice" of a fact when

(a) he has actual knowledge of it; or

(b) he has received a notice or notification of it; or

(c) from all the facts and circumstances known to him at the time in question he has reason to know that it exists.

A person "knows" or has "knowledge" of a fact when he has actual knowledge of it. "Discover" or "learn" or a word or phrase of similar import refers to knowledge rather than to reason to know. The time and circumstances under which a notice or notification may cease to be effective are not determined by this Act.

(26) A person "notifies" or "gives" a notice or notification to another by taking such steps as may be reasonably required to inform the other in ordinary course whether or not such other actually comes to know of it. A person "receives" a notice or notification when

(a) it comes to his attention; or

(b) it is duly delivered at the place of business through which the contract was made or at any other place held out by him as the place for receipt of such communications.

(27) Notice, knowledge or a notice or notification received by an organization is effective for a particular transaction from the time when it is brought to the attention of the individual conducting that transaction, and in any event from the time when it would have been brought to his attention if the organization had exercised due diligence. An organization exercises due diligence if it maintains reasonable routines for communicating significant information to the person conducting the transaction and there is reasonable compliance with the routines. Due diligence does not require an individual acting for the organization to communicate information unless such communication is part of his regular duties or unless he has reason to know of the transaction and that the transaction would be materially affected by the information.

(28) "Organization" includes a corporation, government or governmental subdivision or agency, business trust, estate, trust, partnership or association, two or more persons having a joint or common interest, or any other legal or commercial entity.

(29) "Party", as distinct from "third party", means a person who has engaged in a transaction or made an agreement within this Act.

(30) "Person" includes an individual or an organization (See Section 1–102).

(31) "Presumption" or "presumed" means that the trier of fact must find the existence of the fact presumed unless and until evidence is introduced which would support a finding of its non-existence.

(32) "Purchase" includes taking by sale, discount, negotiation, mortgage, pledge, lien, issue or re-issue, gift or any other voluntary transaction creating an interest in property.

(33) "Purchaser" means a person who takes by purchase.

(34) "Remedy" means any remedial right to which an aggrieved party is entitled with or without resort to a tribunal.

(35) "Representative" includes an agent, an officer of a corporation or association, and a trustee, executor or administrator of an estate, or any other person empowered to act for another.

(36) "Rights" includes remedies.

(37) "Security interest" means an interest in personal property or fixtures which secures payment or performance of an obligation. The retention or reservation of title by a seller of goods notwithstanding shipment or delivery to the buyer (Section 2–401) is limited in effect to a reservation of a "security interest". The term also includes any interest of a buyer of accounts or chattel paper which is subject to Article 9. The special property interest of a buyer of goods on identification of those goods to a contract for sale under Section 2–401 is not a "security interest", but a buyer may also acquire a "security interest" by complying with Article 9. Unless a consignment is intended as security, reservation of title thereunder is not a "security interest", but a consignment in any event is subject to the provisions on consignment sales (Section 2–326).

Whether a transaction creates a lease or security interest is determined by the facts of each case; however, a transaction creates a security interest if the consideration the lessee is to pay the lessor for the right to possession and use of the goods is an obligation for the term of the lease not subject to termination by the lessee, and

(a) the original term of the lease is equal to or greater than the remaining economic life of the goods,

(b) the lessee is bound to renew the lease for the remaining economic life of the goods or is bound to become the owner of the goods,

(c) the lessee has an option to renew the lease for the remaining economic life of the goods for no additional consideration or nominal additional consideration upon compliance with the lease agreement, or

(d) the lessee has an option to become the owner of the goods for no additional consideration or nominal additional consideration upon compliance with the lease agreement.

A transaction does not create a security interest merely because it provides that

(a) the present value of the consideration the lessee is obligated to pay the lessor for the right to possession and use of the goods is substantially equal to or is greater than the fair market value of the goods at the time the lease is entered into,

(b) the lessee assumes risk of loss of the goods, or agrees to pay taxes, insurance, filing, recording, or registration fees, or service or maintenance costs with respect to the goods,

(c) the lessee has an option to renew the lease or to become the owner of the goods,

(d) the lessee has an option to renew the lease for a fixed rent that is equal to or greater than the reasonably predictable fair market rent for the use of the goods for the term of the renewal at the time the option is to be performed, or

(e) the lessee has an option to become the owner of the goods for a fixed price that is equal to or greater than the reasonably predictable fair market value of the goods at the time the option is to be performed.

For purposes of this subsection (37):

(x) Additional consideration is not nominal if (I) when the option to renew the lease is granted to the lessee the rent is stated to be the fair market rent for the use of the goods for the term of the renewal determined at the time the option is to be performed, or (ii) when the option to become the owner of the goods is granted to the lessee the price is stated to be the fair market value of the goods determined at the time the option is to be performed. Additional consideration is nominal if it is less than the lessee's reasonably predictable cost of performing under the lease agreement if the option is not exercised;

(y) "Reasonably predictable" and "remaining economic life of the goods" are to be determined with reference to the facts and circumstances at the time the transaction is entered into; and

(z) "Present value" means the amount as of a date certain of one or more sums payable in the future, discounted to the date certain. The discount is determined by the interest rate specified by the parties if the rate is not manifestly unreasonable at the time the transaction is entered into; otherwise, the discount is determined by a commercially reasonable rate that takes into account the facts and circumstances of each case at the time the transaction was entered into.

(38) "Send" in connection with any writing or notice means to deposit in the mail or deliver for transmission by any other usual means of communication with postage or cost of transmission provided for and properly addressed and in the case of an instrument to an address specified thereon or otherwise agreed, or if there be none to any address reasonable under the circumstances. The receipt of any writing or notice within the time at which it would have arrived if properly sent has the effect of a proper sending.

(39) "Signed" includes any symbol executed or adopted by a party with present intention to authenticate a writing.

(40) "Surety" includes guarantor.

(41) "Telegram" includes a message transmitted by radio, teletype, cable, any mechanical method of transmission, or the like.

(42) "Term" means that portion of an agreement which relates to a particular matter.

(43) "Unauthorized" signature or indorsement means one made without actual, implied or apparent authority and includes a forgery.

(44) "Value". Except as otherwise provided with respect to negotiable instruments and bank collections (Sections 3–303, 4–208 and 4–209) a person gives "value" for rights if he acquires them

(a) in return for a binding commitment to extend credit or for the extension of immediately available credit whether or not drawn upon and whether or not a charge-back is provided for in the event of difficulties in collection; or

(b) as security for or in total or partial satisfaction of a pre-existing claim; or

(c) by accepting delivery pursuant to a pre-existing contract for purchase; or

(d) generally, in return for any consideration sufficient to support a simple contract.

(45) "Warehouse receipt" means a receipt issued by a person engaged in the business of storing goods for hire.

(46) "Written" or "writing" includes printing, typewriting or any other intentional reduction to tangible form.

§ 1–202.   Prima Facie Evidence by Third Party Documents.

A document in due form purporting to be a bill of lading, policy or certificate of insurance, official weigher's or inspector's certificate, consular invoice, or any other document authorized or required by the contract to be issued by a third party shall be prima facie evidence of its own authenticity and genuineness and of the facts stated in the document by the third party.

§ 1–203. Obligation of Good Faith.

Every contract or duty within this Act imposes an obligation of good faith in its performance or enforcement.

§ 1–204. Time; Reasonable Time; "Seasonably".

(1) Whenever this Act requires any action to be taken within a reasonable time, any time which is not manifestly unreasonable may be fixed by agreement.

(2) What is a reasonable time for taking any action depends on the nature, purpose and circumstances of such action.

(3) An action is taken "seasonably" when it is taken at or within the time agreed or if no time is agreed at or within a reasonable time.

§ 1–205. Course of Dealing and Usage of Trade.

(1) A course of dealing is a sequence of previous conduct between the parties to a particular transaction which is fairly to be regarded as establishing a common basis of understanding for interpreting their expressions and other conduct.

(2) A usage of trade is any practice or method of dealing having such regularity of observance in a place, vocation or trade as to justify an expectation that it will be observed with respect to the transaction in question. The existence and scope of such a usage are to be proved as facts. If it is established that such a usage is embodied in a written trade code or similar writing the interpretation of the writing is for the court.

(3) A course of dealing between parties and any usage of trade in the vocation or trade in which they are engaged or of which they are or should be aware give particular meaning to and supplement or qualify terms of an agreement.

(4) The express terms of an agreement and an applicable course of dealing or usage of trade shall be construed wherever reasonable as consistent with each other; but when such construction is unreasonable express terms control both course of dealing and usage of trade and course of dealing controls usage of trade.

(5) An applicable usage of trade in the place where any part of performance is to occur shall be used in interpreting the agreement as to that part of the performance.

(6) Evidence of a relevant usage of trade offered by one party is not admissible unless and until he has given the other party such notice as the court finds sufficient to prevent unfair surprise to the latter.

§ 1–206. Statute of Frauds for Kinds of Personal Property Not Otherwise Covered.

(1) Except in the cases described in subsection (2) of this section a contract for the sale of personal property is not enforceable by way of action or defense beyond five thousand dollars in amount or value of

remedy unless there is some writing which indicates that a contract for sale has been made between the parties at a defined or stated price, reasonably identifies the subject matter, and is signed by the party against whom enforcement is sought or by his authorized agent.

(2) Subsection (1) of this section does not apply to contracts for the sale of goods (Section 2–201) nor of securities (Section 8–319) nor to security agreements (Section 9–203).

§ 1–207. Performance or Acceptance Under Reservation of Rights.

(1) A party who with explicit reservation of rights performs or promises performance or assents to performance in a manner demanded or offered by the other party does not thereby prejudice the rights reserved. Such words as "without prejudice", "under protest" or the like are sufficient.

(2) Subsection (1) does not apply to an accord and satisfaction.

§ 1–208. Option to Accelerate at Will.

A term providing that one party or his successor in interest may accelerate payment or performance or require collateral or additional collateral "at will" or "when he deems himself insecure" or in words of similar import shall be construed to mean that he shall have power to do so only if he in good faith believes that the prospect of payment or performance is impaired. The burden of establishing lack of good faith is on the party against whom the power has been exercised.

§ 1–209. Subordinated Obligations.

An obligation may be issued as subordinated to payment of another obligation of the person obligated, or a creditor may subordinate his right to payment of an obligation by agreement with either the person obligated or another creditor of the person obligated. Such a subordination does not create a security interest as against either the common debtor or a subordinated creditor. This section shall be construed as declaring the law as it existed prior to the enactment of this section and not as modifying it. Added 1966.

Note: *This new section is proposed as an optional provision to make it clear that a subordination agreement does not create a security interest unless so intended.*

APPENDIX C

MODEL ANSWERS TO SELECT EXAMINATION PROBLEMS

■ ■ ■

THE PLUMBER AND HIS SUPPLIERS (CHAPTER 4, p. 266)

1. A catalog is not an offer to sell. It is an invitation to potential buyers to place offers.

2. B's letter is an inquiry. It is a request for an offer since it asks for a promise from S.

3. S's reply is an offer to a requirements contract.

4. (a) B's reply as a common law proposition is a counter-offer that results in a rejection when received. (b) One could argue that the brand name provision and the rush provision are implied. However, the provision with respect to special situations is not.

5. Under the UCC, which governs as we are dealing with the sale of goods, the first question about B's reply is:

(a) Was there a definite and seasonable expression of acceptance? On the one hand, the language is definite: "I agree with what you insist on." However, there is authority for the proposition that if a reasonable commercial person would conclude a deal has *not* closed (or there is a disparity in the dickered terms), the expression of acceptance, taken as a whole, cannot be a definite expression of acceptance. Thus, we are uncertain about how a court would rule on the point.

(b) Assuming the court finds a definite expression of acceptance, it must then determine whether it was expressly made conditional on assent to the additional or different terms. There is no language of express condition present here.

(c) Assuming a contract is formed by the writings, what happens to B's terms? Are B's terms additional or different? B's reply embraces the central term of requirements and raises points not dealt with in the offer, so B's terms are probably additional.

(d) Assuming B's terms are additional, since the parties are both merchants, the terms become part of the contract automatically unless they are material alterations, or notification of objection is given. [There is no language in the offer expressly limiting acceptance to the terms of the offer.] There has been no prior or subsequent objection by S (but the reasonable time for notice would only begin when notice of the additional terms is *received*). Are the terms material alterations? This is generally a question of fact. While the provisions with respect to brand names and rush orders are probably immaterial, we have no idea of the scale of B's requirements in relation to Jones' inventory.

(e) If S's terms are deemed to be "different" there are three views, the most popular of which is the "knock out rule." However, applying that rule to these facts would eliminate both parties' quantity terms and result in a void contract. This result would more properly be achieved by concluding that S's communication was not a definite expression of acceptance at all. (See part 5(a) above.)

6. Assuming an acceptance, the above analysis is based on the assumption that the mailbox rule applies to the case. The UCC has no general rule on the mailbox question, so the common law governs.

7. If a contract was made and the "special situation" was not part of the contract, B's purchase from Jones was a breach of B's contract with S. If it was material, S could cancel the contract and demand the 10% increase; if immaterial, S's demand was a breach of the contract. [See Chapter 8.]

B and C

8. C gave B a price quote. It was not an offer because there was no quantity term. Even if it was, say, an implicit offer to a requirements contract, B never expressed assent. Could it be an offer to a series of contracts (I will sell you whatever you may order from time to time)? If so, B's first order would be an acceptance (creating a bilateral contract for that quantity alone) but C's revocation would be effective as to the future.

9. Assuming no offer by C, is C liable on promissory estoppel grounds? C made a promise on which B relied. Did C have reason to foresee B's reliance? Probably some reliance was foreseeable, but was the extent of B's reliance (3 contracts) foreseeable?

B and Jones

10. The original sale by Jones to B appears to be valid. There is (a) a possible unconscionability (or duress) argument but distress sales at greatly reduced prices are commonplace. B did not apply the coercion, the State did. A detailed examination of all the circumstances is required. [See Chapter 7.] (b) Did Jones lack capacity ("I wasn't thinking straight")? Again a detailed factual exploration would be needed. [See Chapter 6.]

11. The letter from jail was an offer which invited acceptance by performance. (a) Under the orthodox view of the matter, a promise made in reply is ineffective. (b) Since what is involved is arguably the renegotiation of a sales contract, the UCC arguably applies and it allows acceptance to be in any reasonable manner unless the offer is unequivocal on the

manner of acceptance. B's promise in response is reasonable. Even if the UCC does not apply on the theory that the sales contract is fully executed, the modern common law view agrees with the UCC.

12.   Was there consideration for B's promise to pay $10,000 to Jones? (a) Jones has given up his right to "pester." This can be taken to mean he is surrendering the claim stated by him in his letter. Under the first Restatement view, this is consideration only if the claim is both objectively doubtful and asserted in good faith; under the Restatement (Second) either one is sufficient. (b) At any rate, since we are dealing with a contract for the sale of goods, is consideration necessary? UCC 2–209 dispenses with the need for consideration for modifications. But inasmuch as the sales contract is fully executed, can we characterize B's promise (assuming Jones' assent is assumed) as a modification? If not, B's promise is not binding.

FLOOD AND THE WELL (CHAPTER 5, p. 300)

1.   The option is clearly irrevocable. The promise to pay the monthly rental of $1,000 for 10 years is consideration for both the lease and the option. One consideration will support many promises. Consequently, it is not material whether the recited $1 was nominal or even sham.

2.   Was the promise with respect to water too vague and indefinite and even illusory? No. It is an output arrangement. It requires Lessor to exercise good faith in the management of the water supply.

3.   Was there consideration for Lessor's promise to pay one-half the cost of the well? (Obviously, Lessor's promise is consideration because Lessor had no duty to supply additional water.) Lessee's promise is consideration because (a) Lessee's paying half the cost of drilling a well on Lessor's land is not a preexisting duty. Moreover (b), we do not know the nature of the dispute. If Lessee had a good faith (and/or reasonable) belief that Lessor was not fulfilling Lessor's obligation under the lease, or that Lessor had fraudulently misrepresented the water supply, surrender of that claim is consideration. (Essentially the each-pay-half agreement is a settlement of a good faith dispute.) Furthermore, (c), there was a signed writing. In some states, e.g., N.Y. and Michigan, no consideration is needed if a lease is modified in writing. In addition (d), if this arrangement could be characterized as a sale of water to Lessee, under the UCC no consideration is needed for a modification.

4.   (a) Under the orthodox view, there is no consideration for Lessor's & Lessee's promise to pay Flood more than the contract price. (b) However, under the view of the second Restatement, because the promise is made to compensate for unanticipated circumstances, a modification without consideration is permitted. (c) We are not told whether the modification is in writing. If it is, in some jurisdictions a modification is binding without consideration when it is made in a signed writing.

5.   [This thought was not on the grading chart, but a number of students mentioned it.] There are no facts to indicate that either the

modification of the lease or of the well-drilling contract was made under duress. There is nothing to indicate that the promisors had no reasonable alternative or that their free wills were overcome.

6.   Assuming the modification was valid, is Flood's claim for the balance discharged by an accord and satisfaction? There is: (a) mutual assent to discharge the claim, and (b) consideration if Lessor and Lessee asserted a good faith (and/or reasonable) claim that they were not bound by the modification agreement. (c) Moreover, in a number of states a claim can be discharged by a signed writing without consideration. There is such a writing here signed by Flood.

7.   (a) Is Lessor's testimony as to the modification of the option barred by the parol evidence rule? It is subsequent to the lease, consequently it is not barred by the lease. (b) It is contemporaneous with the modification agreement and is therefore conceivably barred for that reason. Without further information about the modification agreement; *e.g.*, was it in writing, was the writing complete, etc., it is not possible to rule on the question.

8.   The Statute of Frauds bars proof of oral agreements with respect to leases of land for over a year. Assuming that the modification agreement was not made in the last year of the ten year lease, the statute applies. If the evidence of the oral agreement is not barred by the parol evidence rule, the oral agreement may be introduced into evidence to show that the written modification of the lease did not satisfy the Statute of Frauds and therefore the modification was unenforceable and the original lease is still binding on the parties. [This paragraph is here for completeness, but we realize that the Statute of Frauds has not yet been covered in this casebook.]

INDEX

References are to Pages

867

GOOD FAITH—Cont'd
Duty to read and, 460
Estoppel theory and, 742
Fact and law questions, 70
Fiduciary duties compared, 458
Merchant rules, UCC, 206
Modifications of contracts
    Justifiable modifications, 210
    UCC, 208
Negotiate, agreement to as implying good faith
    obligation, 67
Negotiation of open terms, 9
Performance in good faith, duty of, 453
Policy considerations, 459
Requirements contracts
    Increases and decreases in requirements,
      223
    UCC, 223
Satisfaction, 500
Satisfaction conditions, good faith determina-
    tion as to, 216, 218
UCC
    Definition, 298
    Merchant rules, 206
    Modifications of contracts, 208
    Requirements contracts, 223

GOODS
    See also Sales of Goods, this index; Uniform
      Commercial Code, this index
Growing crops as, 734
Movable materials used to construct immov-
    able fixtures, 59
Tangible goods, licensed software as, 169
UCC applicability to mixed sales of services
    and goods, 57

GRATUITIES
    See also Gifts, this index
Presumptive, 96

GROSS NEGLIGENCE
Punitive damages, 605

HINDRANCE OF PERFORMANCE
Brokerage contract, 439

HYBRID CONTRACTS
UCC applicability, 57

ILLEGAL CONTRACTS
    Generally, 770 et seq.
    See also Public Policy, this index
Chain distribution schemes, 785
Duress, participation under, 787
Effect of illegality, 783
Equity principles, 784
In pari delicto factors, 787
Intrinsic illegality, 784
Malum prohibitum and malum in se conduct
    distinguished, 787
Offer, effect of supervening illegality, 128
Requirements contracts, 783
Supervening illegality, effect on offer, 128
Trivial law violations, 785
Undue influence, participation under, 787

**IMPLIED COVENANT OF GOOD FAITH
AND FAIR DEALING**
At-will employment doctrine vs, 41, 50
Cooperation, 445
Limits of, 444
Policy considerations, 459
Satisfaction provisions, 446

IMPLIED TERMS
    See also Indefiniteness, this index
Duration of a contract, 40

IMPLIED–IN–FACT CONTRACTS
At-will employment doctrine, implied-in-fact
    promise of employment vs, 44
At-will employment doctrine vs, 48
Conduct evidencing, 96
Evidence of, 96
Fact and law questions, 49, 53
Intent to contract, 772
Parenthood, 772
Promises implied by conduct, 94
Services, acceptance as implying a promise to
    pay, 96

IMPLIED–IN–LAW CONTRACTS
At-will employment doctrine, implied-in-law
    contract terms vs, 50
Promissory estoppel, 248

**IMPOSSIBILITY AND IMPRACTICA-
BILITY**
    Generally, 521 et seq.
    See also Frustration, this index
Assumption of risk, 529
Construction contracts, 542
Crop sales contract, 527
Death of promisor, 525
Distinctions of terms, 531
Employment contracts, 524, 525
Excusable delay provisions, 536
Foreseeability, 537
Fortuitous impossibility, 526
Frustration distinguished, 534, 548, 551
Implied conditions, 524
Impracticability, subjective and objective, 529,
    534
Leases, 521, 522
Objective and subjective impracticability, 529,
    534
Personal promises, death of promisor, 524
Quantum meruit recovery, 543
Sales of goods, 535
Subjective and objective impracticability, 529,
    534
Terms distinguished, 531
UCC
    Generally, 528, 534
    Excusable delay provisions, 536
Unavoidable impossibility, 526
Vessel charter, 530
War, 535
War creating, 530
Weather vagaries, 527

UNIFORM COMMERCIAL CODE (UCC)
—Cont'd
Offer and acceptance
Open terms, 741
Shipment, acceptance of offer to sell by, 159
Offer to sell, acceptance by acceptance of delivered goods
Generally, 100
Consumer protection laws, 101
Open terms
Generally, 62
Merchants, 741
Payment terms, 63
Parol evidence rule, 276
Payment terms left open, 63
Performance and breach
Acceptance of goods, 426
Assurances of performance, 427, 693
Strict performance, 426
Post acceptance discovery of defects, 429
Real property sales, applicability to, 31
Reasonable commercial standards, modifications of contracts, 209
Rejection or revocation of acceptance, 428
Remedies, limitation of, 621
Repudiation damages, 572
Requirements contracts, good faith, 223
Restitution, defaulting party claims, 633
Sale or return, 277
Service contracts, 467
Services and goods, UCC applicability to mixed sales of, 57
Shipment, acceptance of offer to sell by, 159
Software licenses, UCC applicability, 170
Statute of frauds
Completed sales under barred contracts, 734
Memorandum requirement, 733
Merchants rules, 741
Modifications of contracts, 744
Substantial impairment of whole contract, material breach resulting in, 436
Tangible goods, licensed software as, 169
Terms in the box, master of the offer rule, 159
Transmission of acceptance, mistake in, 122
Unconscionability, 374, 493
Warranty limitations, battle of the forms, 138

UNIFORM COMPUTER INFORMATION TRANSACTIONS ACT (UCITA)
Generally, 157

UNIFORM LAND SALES PRACTICES ACT
Misrepresentation, 337

UNIFORM RESIDENTIAL LANDLORD AND TENANT ACT
Misrepresentation, 337

UNILATERAL CONTRACTS
Generally, 90
See also Offer and Acceptance, this index
Complete performance, 110
Definition, 104

UNILATERAL CONTRACTS—Cont'd
Offers, unilateral
Revocation, part vs complete performance, 110
Rewards, 90
Part performance, 110, 256
Part vs complete performance, 110
Performance, acceptance by, 107
Performance inducing vs promise inducing offers, 91
Presumptions, 110
Revocation of unilateral offer
Generally, 103
Part vs complete performance, 110
Rewards, 90

UNJUST ENRICHMENT
Damages, 259

USAGE
See Custom and Usage, this index

VAGUENESS
Generally, 54
See also Indefiniteness, this index

VESSEL CHARTERS
Impossibility and impracticability, 530

VOID CONTRACTS
See also Avoidance of Contracts, this index
Avoidable and void contracts distinguished, 317
Illegal Contracts, this index
Public policy, 790
Void ab initio, 402

WAIVER
See also Election, this index
Acceptance of condition waiver, 113
Assignments, improper, waivers of defects, 699
Condition waivers
Generally, 462
Acceptance of, 113
Time of the essence, 466, 467
Course of performance distinguished, 294
Definition, 464
Delegations, improper, waivers of defects, 699
Elections, waivers as, 464, 467
Equitable estoppel distinguished, 465
Evidence, 433
Forfeitures, 464
Modifications of contracts distinguished, 463
Tender, 518
Time of the essence conditions, 466, 467

WAR
Impossibility and impracticability caused by, 530, 535

WARRANTIES
Basis of the bargain test, express warranty, 348
Battle of the forms, 138
Bill of sale descriptions, 345
Breach damages, 18, 349
Certificate of authenticity as express warranty, 348

†